COOKED Alive!

LIFE SAVORING WHOLE FOOD RECIPES
TO END PROCESSED FOOD DEPENDENCE

Nancy Johnson Wirsing

Cooked Alive!

Copyright © 2018 Nancy Johnson Wirsing

All rights reserved. No portion of this publication may be reproduced, stored in a retrieval system, or transmitted by any means—electronic, mechanical, photocopying, recording, or any other—except for brief quotations in printed reviews, without the prior written permission of the publisher.

Editors: Jeanna Fox, Mary Catharine Jaranelli
Cover Design: 3-Sixty Marketing
Interior Design: Catherine Williams/chapter-one-book-production.co.uk

Indigo River Publishing
3 West Garden Street Ste. 352
Pensacola, FL 32502
www.indigoriverpublishing.com

Ordering information:

Quanity sales: Special discounts are available on quantity purchases by corporations, associations and others. For details, contact the publisher at the address above.
Orders by U.S. trade bookstores and wholesalers: Please contact the publisher at the address above.

Printed in the United States of America

Publisher's Cataloging-in-Publication Data is available upon request.

Library of Congress Control Number: 2018938885

ISBN: 978-1-948080-20-0

First Edition

With Indigo River Publishing, you can always expect great books, strong voices, and meaningful messages.
Most importantly, you'll always find … words worth reading.

TABLE OF CONTENTS

PREFACE   1

Introduction: Escaping Processed Food Dependence   5
    The Strangle-Hold of Processed Foods   6
    Breaking Free with Fresh Vegetables and Fruits   16
        Conserving the Vitality of Vegetables and Fruits   27
    Maximizing Recipe Usability   29

PART I

Conserving the Nutritional Quality and Flavoring of *Individual* Vegetables and Fruits   31

    Overview
        Conservation Strategy   31
        General Part I Cooking Tools   34
        Quantity Abbreviations Key for Part I Recipes   35
    General Part I References
        Reference #1: Selecting Top Quality Fresh Whole Vegetables and Fruits   36
        Reference #2: Key Home Storage Guidelines for Conserving Vegetable and
            Fruit Quality   53

Chapter One: Stir-Fried and Stir-Fry/Steamed Vegetable Recipes   65

    Introduction
        Stir-Frying and Stir-Fry/Steaming Description   65
        Organization of Recipes   66
        Stir-Frying and Stir-Fry/Steaming Preparation Notes   67
        Nutritional Term Guide   71
    Recipes
        General Vegetables – Stir-Fried or Stir-Fry/Steamed (#1–22)
            1. Asparagus   75
            2. Beet   78
            3. Bok Choy   80

4. Broccoli	82
5. Brussels Sprouts	86
6. Cabbage	88
7. Carrot	91
8. Cauliflower	94
9. Celery	97
10. Corn	100
11. Eggplant	102
12. Kohlrabi	105
13. Okra	107
14. Parsnip	109
15. Peas, Green	111
16. Peas, Sugar Snap and Snow	114
17. Potato	116
18. Potato, Sweet	120
19. Rutabaga	123
20. Summer Squash (Yellow and Zucchini)	126
21. Winter Squash	129
22. Turnip	133

Dark Green Leafy Vegetables – Stir-Fried or Stir-Fry/Steamed (#23–30)

23. Beet Greens	135
24. Chard	138
25. Collards	141
26. Kale	145
27. Mustard Greens	148
28. Spinach (Pre-Washed)	152
29. Spinach (Un-Washed/Bunched)	154
30. Turnip Greens	157

Seasoning Vegetables – Stir-Fried (#31–37)

31. Garlic	160
32. Ginger Root	163
33. Mushroom	165
34. Onion	168
35. Pepper, Bell	174
36. Pepper, Chili	177
37. Tomato	179

Reference

Reference #3: Summarizing Stir-Frying and Stir-Fry/Steaming Techniques — 182

Chapter Two: Dry Roasted Vegetable Recipes — 187

Introduction

Dry Roasting Description — 187
Dry Roasting Procedure for Cut Soft-Fleshed Vegetables and for Sliced or Diced Firm-Fleshed Vegetables — 188
Dry Roasting Procedure for Whole or Halved Firm-Fleshed Vegetables — 189

Recipes (#38–53)

	38. Roasted Asparagus Spears	191
	39. Roasted Whole Beets	191
	40. Roasted Brussels Sprouts, Halved	191
	41. Roasted Cauliflower Florets	192
	42. Roasted Eggplant, Cubed	192
	43. Roasted Mushrooms, Sliced	193
	44. Roasted Onion, Sliced	193
	45. Roasted Bell Pepper, Sliced	193
	46. Baked Potato, Whole	194
	47. Baked Sweet Potato, Whole	194
	48. Roasted Potato, Oven Fries	195
	49. Roasted Rutabaga, Oven Fries	195
	50. Roasted Summer Squash, Yellow or Zucchini, Sliced or Cubed	196
	51. Baked Winter Squash, Halved	196
	52. Roasted Winter Squash, Cubed	197
	53. Roasted Turnip, Oven Fries or Diced	198

Chapter Three: Boiled Whole Vegetable Recipes — 199

Introduction

Boiling Whole Description — 199
Chapter Three Recipe Organization — 200
Boiling Whole Covered in Water Procedure — 201
Stir-Frying in Water Procedure — 202

Recipes (#54–73)

	54. Boiled Whole Artichoke	204
	55. Boiled Whole Asparagus	205
	56. Stir-Fried in Water Whole Asparagus	205
	57. Boiled Whole Butter Beans	205
	58. Boiled Whole Green or Yellow Wax Beans	206
	59. Boiled Whole Beets	207
	60. Boiled Whole Broccoli or Cauliflower Florets	207
	61. Boiled Whole Brussels Sprouts	208
	62. Boiled Whole Carrots	208
	63. Boiled Whole Chard	208
	64. Boiled Whole Collards	209
	65. Stir-Fried in Water Whole Kernel Corn	209
	66. Boiled Whole Edamame Pods	210
	67. Boiled Whole Kale	210
	68. Boiled Whole Okra	211
	69. Stir-Fried in Water Whole Okra	211
	70. Boiled Whole Sugar Snap or Snow Peas	211
	71. Stir-Fried in Water Whole Green, Sugar Snap, or Snow Peas	211
	72. Boiled Whole Potato	212
	73. Boiled Whole Summer Squash	212

Chapter Four: Raw Fruit Pure and Simple — 213

Introduction
- *Raw Fruit Recipe Description* — 213
- *Raw Fruit Preparation Notes* — 214

Recipes
- *Fruits (#74–101)*
  - 74. Apple — 216
  - 75. Apricot — 219
  - 76. Avocado — 220
  - 77. Banana — 223
  - 78. Blueberries — 225
  - 79. Blackberries — 227
  - 80. Cantaloupe — 228
  - 81. Cherries, Bing and Dark Sweet — 231
  - 82. Grapefruit — 232
  - 83. Grapes, Red and Green Seedless — 235
  - 84. Guava — 238
  - 85. Honeydew Melon — 239
  - 86. Kiwi — 241
  - 87. Mango — 243
  - 88. Nectarine — 245
  - 89. Orange — 248
  - 90. Orange, Clementine and Mandarin — 251
  - 91. Papaya — 253
  - 92. Peach — 255
  - 93. Pear — 258
  - 94. Pineapple — 260
  - 95. Plum — 263
  - 96. Pomegranate Seed — 265
  - 97. Raspberries — 267
  - 98. Strawberries — 269
  - 99. Tangerine — 271
  - 100. Grape Tomato — 273
  - 101. Watermelon — 276
- *Raw Fruit Snacks (#102–110)*
  - 102. Creamy Apricot Dip — 279
  - 103. Peanut or Almond Butter Spread — 281
  - 104. Lettuce Fruit Cups — 283
  - 105. Apple and Warmed Brie — 284
  - 106. Raw Fruit Pita Pizza — 285
  - 107. Fruit and Havarti Cheese Kebabs — 288
  - 108. Grape Tomato and Mozzarella Kebabs — 289
  - 109. Orange and Yogurt Snack — 290
  - 110. Berries and Yogurt Snack — 291

Chapter Five: Raw or Barely Cooked Vegetable Recipes — 294

Introduction
- *Raw and Barely Cooked Vegetable Description* — 294
- *Basic Serving Raw Procedure* — 295
- *Basic Parboiling Procedure* — 296

Recipes
- *Raw (#111–128)*
  - 111. Asparagus — 298
  - 112. Beans, Green and Yellow Wax — 298
  - 113. Bok Choy — 299
  - 114. Broccoli — 299
  - 115. Cabbage — 300
  - 116. Carrot — 300
  - 117. Cauliflower — 301
  - 118. Celery — 301
  - 119. Cucumber — 301
  - 120. Fennel Bulb — 303
  - 121. Kohlrabi — 304
  - 122. Mushroom — 304
  - 123. Peas, Green — 305
  - 124. Peas, Sugar Snap and Snow — 305
  - 125. Pepper, Bell — 306
  - 126. Radish, Regular and Daikon — 306
  - 127. Summer Squash, Yellow and Zucchini — 307
  - 128. Turnip — 308
- *Parboiled (#129–134)*
  - 129. Parboiled Asparagus — 308
  - 130. Parboiled Beans, Green and Yellow Wax — 309
  - 131. Parboiled Broccoli Florets — 309
  - 132. Parboiled Cauliflower Florets — 309
  - 133. Parboiled Peas, Sugar Snap and Snow — 310
  - 134. Parboiled Summer Squash — 310
- *Vegetable Snacks (#135–136)*
  - 135. Herbed Onion and Garlic Dip — 311
  - 136. Raw Vegetable Pita Pizza — 313

PART II

Resurrecting Everyday Dishes

Overview
- *Description of the Approach Used for Resurrecting Traditional Recipes* — 317
- *General Part II Cooking Tools* — 320

General Part II References — 322
- *Reference #4: Selecting Top Quality Whole Food Ingredients for Use in Part II Recipes* — 324

Reference #5: Selecting High Quality Processed Ingredients for Use in Part II Recipes   338
Reference #6: Maximizing the Attractiveness of Whole Food Ingredients Commonly Used in Part II Recipes   350
Reference #7: Juice-Protective Techniques for Preparing Animal Protein   361

Chapter Six: Salads   364

Introduction
- *Salad Recipe Description*   364
- *Salad Recipe Preparation Notes*   364

Recipes

Fruit-Centered Salads (#137–143)
- 137. Nectarine, Grape, Cauliflower, and Greens Salad   367
- 138. Mandarin Orange, Grape, Pomegranate, and Greens Salad   370
- 139. Berry, Cantaloupe, Pineapple, and Greens Salad   373
- 140. Apple, Orange, Apricot, and Spinach Salad   376
- 141. Spiced Lentil, Pineapple, and Greens Salad   378
- 142. Spiced Chicken, Fruit, and Greens Supreme Salad   381
- 143. Mandarin Orange and Red Leaf Lettuce Salad, Traditional 4-Serving Salad   385

Vegetable-Centered Salads (#144–150)
- 144. Greek Salad   388
- 145. Everyday Vegetable Salad   389
- 146. Guest Vegetable Salad   392
- 147. Three Bean Vegetable Salad   395
- 148. Corn and Black Bean Vegetable Salad   399
- 149. Tabbouleh, Traditional 4-Serving Salad   402
- 150. Broccoli, Sugar Snap Pea, and Grape Salad, Traditional 4-Serving Salad   405

Dish Accompaniments (#151–152)
- 151. Boiled Eggs   409
- 152. Hummus   410

Reference
- *Reference #8: Clinching Salad Flavor – Expanded Preparation Support*   412

Chapter Seven: Stir-Fried Dish Recipes   421

Introduction
- *Stir-Fried Dish Description*   421
- *Stir-Fried Dish Preparation Notes*   422

Recipes

Traditional Main Dish – Vegetables with Beefsteak, Chicken, or Egg (#153–159)
- 153. Broccoli, Carrot, and Beefsteak Stir Fry, Master Recipe   426
- 154. Cabbage, Kale, and Beefsteak Stir Fry   429
- 155. Sweet Potato, Broccoli, Pineapple, and Beefsteak Stir Fry   434
- 156. Zucchini, Chard, Corn, and Beefsteak Stir Fry, Herb and Tomato Flavoring   438
- 157. Brussels Sprouts, Kale, Pineapple, and Chicken Stir Fry   443
- 158. Red Potato, Pepper, and Egg Stir Fry   448
- 159. Sweet Potato, Sugar Snap Pea, and Egg Stir Fry   452

Traditional Vegetarian or Vegan Main Dish – Vegetables with Legumes (#160–163)
    160. Broccoli, Pineapple, and Black Bean Stir Fry, Master Recipe — 456
    161. Sweet Potato, Kale, Corn, and Kidney Bean Stir Fry — 460
    162. Cauliflower, Brussels Sprouts, and Garbanzo Bean Stir Fry, Herb and Tomato Flavoring — 464
    163. Okra, Eggplant, Corn, Spinach, and Lentil Stir Fry, Herb and Tomato Flavoring — 469

Traditional Pilaf – Vegetables with Whole Grains or Wild Rice (#164–165)
    164. Vegetables and Whole Cracked Wheat Pilaf, 4 Servings — 473
    165. Guest Vegetable and Wild Rice Pilaf, 4 Servings — 478

Whole Grain and Legume Dish Ingredients (#166–168)
    166. Brown Rice — 484
    167. Wild Rice, Hulled Barley, Wheat Berries, or Quinoa — 486
    168. Lentils — 488

Chapter Eight: Soups and Stews — 490

Introduction
  Soup and Stew Description — 490
  Soup and Stew Preparation Notes — 491

Recipes
  Chunky Vegetable Soup – Milk Sauce Base (#169–172)
    169. Broccoli, Pepper, and Potato Soup — 497
    170. Corn, Pepper, and Potato Soup — 501
    171. Kale and Sweet Potato Soup — 505
    172. Butternut Squash Soup — 509

  Stew – Tomato Sauce Base (#173–177)
    173. Chili Con Carne — 513
    174. Extravagantly Vegetable Chili — 518
    175. Old Fashioned Beef Stew — 523
    176. Lentil Stew — 528
    177. Minestrone Stew — 534

  Stew – Herbed Broth Base (#178)
    178. Old Fashioned Chicken Stew — 539

  Stew – Broth and Milk Sauce Base (#179)
    179. Curried Split Pea and Chicken Stew — 544

Bread Accompaniments:
  100% Whole Wheat Muffins (#180–184)
    180. Blueberry Banana Muffins — 550
    181. Banana Cranberry Muffins — 553
    182. Pineapple Carrot Muffins — 556
    183. Sweet Potato Pineapple Muffins — 559
    184. Zucchini Applesauce Muffins — 562

  100% Whole Corn Bread (#185)
    185. 100% Whole Corn Bread — 565

  100% Whole Rye Bread (#186)
    186. 100% Whole Rye Bread — 567

References
- *Reference #9: Clinching Soup and Stew Flavor – Expanded Preparation Support* — 572
- *Reference #10: Preparing Fresh Chicken Broth* — 578

Chapter Nine: Curries — 581

Introduction
- *Curry Recipe Description* — 581
- *Curry Preparation Notes* — 582

Recipes (#187–191)
- 187. Chicken Curry — 586
- 188. Meatball Curry — 590
- 189. Egg Curry — 594
- 190. Eggplant Curry — 599
- 191. Vegetable Curry — 604

Curry Accompaniments (#192–197)
- 192. Spiced Yogurt (Raita) — 610
- 193. Spiced Lentils (Dhal) — 611
- 194. Pineapple Chutney — 612
- 195. Apple Chutney — 613
- 196. Mango Chutney — 615
- 197. 100% Whole Wheat Flat Bread Rounds (Chapatis) — 617

Reference
- *Reference #11: Clinching Curry Flavor – Expanded Preparation Support* — 620

Chapter Ten: Quiche — 627

Introduction
- *Quiche Description* — 627
- *Quiche Preparation Notes* — 628

Recipes (#198-200)
- 198. Broccoli Quiche — 631
- 199. Asparagus and Green Onion Quiche — 635
- 200. Cabbage and Red Pepper Quiche — 639

Chapter Eleven: Fruit Desserts — 644

Introduction
- *Fruit Dessert Description* — 644
- *Fruit Dessert Preparation Notes* — 645

Recipes (#201–209)
- 201. Fruit Cup Dessert — 646
- 202. Raspberry Sauce and Ice Cream Dessert — 649
- 203. Peaches and Cream Dessert — 651
- 204. Berry, Mandarin Orange, and Yogurt Dessert — 652
- 205. Baked Apples — 654
- 206. Fruit Gelatin with Whipped Cream Dessert — 656

207. Mini Cheesecake Dessert	660
208. Individual Cherry Trifle Dessert	662
209. Fruit Topped Vanilla Pudding Dessert	666

Chapter Twelve: 100% Whole Wheat Pizza — 670

Introduction
- *Pizza Recipe Description* — 670
- *Pizza Preparation Notes* — 670

Recipes
- *Pizza Crust (#210)*
  - 210. 100% Whole Wheat Pizza Crust, 4-6 Servings — 672
- *Assembled Pizza (#211–213)*
  - 211. Basic Roasted Pepper and Cheese Pizza — 675
  - 212. Roasted Pepper, Zucchini, Eggplant, and Ground Beef Pizza — 678
  - 213. Roasted Vegetable, Spinach, and Pineapple Pizza — 683

Reference
- *Reference #12: Clinching Pizza Attractiveness – Expanded Preparation Support* — 687

Chapter Thirteen: 100% Whole Wheat Pancakes — 693

Introduction
- *Pancake Recipe Description* — 693
- *Pancake Preparation Notes* — 693

Recipes
- *100% Whole Wheat Pancakes (#214–218)*
  - 214. Basic 100% Whole Wheat Pancakes, 2 Servings — 695
  - 215. Blueberry and Nectarine Pancakes — 699
  - 216. Zucchini Pancakes — 702
  - 217. Applesauce Pancakes — 705
  - 218. Winter Squash Pancakes — 708
- *Fruit Sauce Toppings (#219–224)*
  - 219. Blueberry Sauce — 711
  - 220. Raspberry Sauce — 713
  - 221. Cherry Sauce, Dark Sweet or Red Tart — 715
  - 222. Peach Sauce — 717
  - 223. Strawberry Rhubarb Sauce — 719
  - 224. Applesauce — 721

Reference
- *Reference #13: Clinching Pancake Attractiveness and Quality – Expanded Preparation Support* — 723

Index — 731

About the Author — 754

Reference Listing

Reference #1. Selecting Top Quality Fresh Whole Vegetables and Fruits	36
Reference #2. Key Home Storage Guidelines for Conserving Vegetable and Fruit Quality	53
Reference #3. Summarizing Stir-Frying and Stir-Fry/Steaming Techniques	182
Reference #4. Selecting Top Quality Whole Food Ingredients for Use in Part II Recipes	324
Reference #5. Selecting High Quality Processed Ingredients for Use in Part II Recipes	338
Reference #6. Maximizing the Attractiveness of Whole Food Ingredients Commonly Used in Part II Recipes	350
Reference #7. *Juice-Protective* Techniques for Preparing Animal Protein	361
Reference #8. Clinching Salad Flavor – Expanded Preparation Support	412
Reference #9. Clinching Soup and Stew Flavor – Expanded Preparation Support	572
Reference #10. Preparing Fresh Chicken Broth	578
Reference #11. Clinching Curry Flavor – Expanded Preparation Support	620
Reference #12. Clinching Pizza Attractiveness – Expanded Preparation Support	687
Reference #13. Clinching Pancake Attractiveness and Quality – Expanded Preparation Support	723

PREFACE

Dear reader, I think it necessary to begin this prefatory note with a disclaimer. No matter how it sounds, this book is definitely not about cruel cannibalism or, indeed, about cooking alive any creature at all. I shamelessly chose this title – *Cooked Alive!* – to draw attention to something of great importance: the need to safeguard our health by adopting an approach to cooking that preserves the freshness, nutritional value, and natural goodness of food – in short its *aliveness*. The fact of the matter is that too many of us have been eating nutrition-stripped and salt/sugar/fat/chemical-padded "dead foods" for far too long, with awful consequences to our health. I offer this book to help make the change to truly wholesome eating habits. So please forgive the title!

Having made this initial confession, I have another. This is not a cookbook to help you avoid spending much time in the kitchen. Its recipes are not chosen to help busy life-stressed people prepare fast and easy meals. Such recipes can't help but shortchange the aliveness of food. Neither is it this cookbook's objective to aid you in dazzling dinner guests with currently fashionable foreign and celebrity-inspired exotic recipes. Cookbooks with this purpose, some of them excellent in quality, already exist in great abundance. Least of all is this a cookbook that relegates cooking to a lowly position in the hierarchy of household activities. On the contrary, it ranks cooking of *nutritious whole foods* at or near the top.

As I strive to make clear in the Introduction, this is a unique cookbook. For one thing, it gives pride of place in its recipes to vegetables and fruits – to those too often lowly-regarded foods that hordes of both governmental and private food authorities have been exhorting us for years to eat in much greater quantity. While this is neither an exclusively vegetarian or vegan cookbook, it shares with these schools of cooking a lofty esteem for vegetables. It starts from the premise that vegetables, along with an amazing variety of fruits and nuts, have formed the core of humankind's diet from its earliest beginnings and that these foods now play, inescapably, a central role in the maintenance of human health and well-being. It is thus a cookbook centrally aimed at *resurrecting* basic and long-established food selection, food storage, food preparation, and food eating practices that have largely been lost in modern society.

This cookbook is also unique in the attention paid to the *conversion* process – to the learning of an array of cooking techniques needed for making a smooth and effective transition from dead to alive food preparation. Learning any new set of skills and how to use the tools associated with them is often bound to be something of a nuisance, and this is as true of cooking skills as of any other. To enable even novice cooks to experience routinely successful whole food cooking, this cookbook supplies methodical, detailed, clearly worded step-by-step guidance. It leaves as little to chance as possible. Its goal is to make conversion to whole foods cooking, if not completely pleasurable, at least reliable and fully satisfying.

A third and immensely important unique property of this cookbook is its commitment to helping cooks break free of the bondage inflicted by processed food dependence. To accomplish this, it arms cooks not only with technical cooking skills but also, and very importantly, with the knowledge needed to understand the costs to human health of processed food dependence. This cookbook has a social mission, so to speak, of *liberation* from an entrenched conventional approach to cooking that has had nothing less than a devastating impact on human well-being.

This cookbook has been many years in the making. Every recipe has been tested and tested again to ensure the best possible meal outcomes. But the recipes themselves could never have been designed had I not demanded of myself a rigorous program of self-education about foods, about the body's food requirements, about the nutritional deficiencies in modern diets, and about the processed food industry. Of simply enormous importance to my self-education were the many food and nutrition authorities I consulted. Their own impressive commitment to healthful eating unquestionably inspired mine, and to them I owe a heartfelt debt of thanks. There is not space to thank them all by name, but I do wish to make explicit mention of a few.

The first is Adelle Davis (*Let's Cook It Right*, 1970), a visionary nutritionist whose thinking about human food requirements was decades ahead of her time (1904-1974). Her recognition of the critical importance of unprocessed foods in general and of vegetables in particular (of the need to "cook them right") shook me out of acquiescence to processed foods and propelled me into a lifetime of whole food cooking. To her my debt is immense.

Today's giant healthy eating advocate is Michael Pollan. In all of his major works, but particularly in *In Defense of Food: An Eater's Manifesto* (2008), he has led the way in prompting a near revolution in how people think about food. Writing with special eloquence and clarity, no one has done more to popularize the crucial importance of naturally whole foods – what he calls "real" foods – to human health. He has been an important mentor to countless people, including me.

Also of great importance in my self-education was a book by Michael Moss (*Salt Sugar Fat*, 2013). Its author's amazingly dogged empiricism, meticulous detail, and fearless exposure of "how the food giants hooked us" helped open my eyes to the profoundness of the sins committed against consumers each and every day by the processed food industry. Another book absolutely bulging with invaluable facts is Jo Robinson's *Eating on the Wild Side: The Missing Link to Optimum Health* (2013). Admirably informing her readers about important modern developments in the science of food plant chemistry, she educates them about the importance to human health of the phytonutrient content of vegetables and fruits, truly "the missing link to optimum health." I am deeply indebted to her. For many of the same reasons, I would like to express appreciation to George Mateljan, author of *The World's Healthiest Foods*, 2nd edition (2015). He profiles the phytonutrient content of each of the vegetables and fruits he includes in his selection of healthiest foods. Profiling overall nutritional content as well, he presents informative and up-to-date summaries of both the already known and projected human health-promoting benefits of these vegetables and fruits.

No one has done more to help me understand the importance of omega-3 essential fatty acids to human health than Susan Allport in her *The Queen of Fats: Why Omega-3s Were Removed from the Western Diet and What We Can Do to Replace Them* (2008). As the parent of omega-3 fatty acids, alpha linolenic acid (ALA) is thoroughly basic to vegetables. Found in the leaves and other green parts of plants, Allport informs us, it is the most abundant fat on earth. Her insights about the omega-3 fatty acids are crucially important parts of my food knowledge. On the subject of fats, of equal importance is the extraordinary danger of industrially processed pure vegetable oils to human health. This danger is forcefully brought to our attention in *Deep Nutrition: Why Your Genes Need Traditional Food* (2016) by Catherine Shanahan, M.D. with Luke Shanahan. In Chapter Seven ("Good Fats and Bad") and Chapter Eight ("Brain Killer"), Shanahan convincingly and unforgettably traces and spells out the direct causal link between unnatural industrial pure vegetable oil and innumerable deadly human health problems, including the hardening of arteries (or atherosclerosis), brain disorders such as Alzheimer's and autism, and tragic birth defects.

Christopher Vasey's book (*The Acid-Alkaline Diet for Optimum Health*, 2nd Edition, 2006) was equally eye opening. From it I learned valuable lessons about the importance of pH balance in human health and the key role played by vegetables and fruits in maintaining this balance. Paul Robert's *The End of Food* (2009), clearly among the best instructive overviews of the modern global food system, contributed immeasurably to my evolving perspective on the world's food problems. Judith Schwartz (*Cows Save the Planet and Other Improbable Ways of Restoring Soil to Heal the Earth*, 2013) similarly expanded my perspective regarding soil's pivotal role in maintaining the health of planet Earth. In this outstanding primer about soil, Schwartz enlightened me about the crucial difference between soil and dirt – the former filled with life and varied minerals while the latter is stripped of trace minerals and microbial life forms (microorganisms and mycorrhizal fungi in particular) and, thus, of the capacity to yield food of nutritional value for humans. Hers is a treasure trove of data about the link between industrial agriculture and the degradation of soil into dirt.

I also wish to express my special thanks to Julie Guthman, author of *Weighing In: Obesity, Food Justice, and the Limits of Capitalism* (2011). Her book stands out as an invaluable resource to me because of the penetrating insights into processed food dependence it provides. Analyzing America's contemporary hyper-capitalistic food system, Guthman lays bare the political and economic values that underlie the successful merger of American government and corporate business and that go far to explain how processed food dependence both came into being and remains firmly entrenched in American society. These values are the no-holds-barred pro-business values that celebrate the market as the optimal allocator of public goods and services. Closely examining obesity, Guthman exposes the far-reaching extent to which largely unconsciously held attitudes, or "healthism" as she labels them, are acting as blinders that obscure the causal link between processed food, particularly its chemical component, and modern obesity, thereby effectively letting processed food producers and their big pharma business allies off the hook and allowing them to shamelessly exploit the obese. Examining alternative food movements, Guthman points out that while the organic food movement is unquestionably very important, it is *only* an alternative food movement. It operates alongside rather than as a challenge to corporate-sponsored processed food dependence. And this does not work. In accepting and being essentially satisfied with this bifurcated food system – one healthy food system for some consumers, those who might also be described as the cultural elite, and another devitalized and chemically-tainted food system for the masses of consumers – the organic food movement ignores industry's role and the government's responsibility for regulating that industry at considerable peril to the organic food movement itself. On the one hand, organic food consumers cannot protect themselves from toxic air and polluted water. These consumers also need to be deeply concerned about the deadly biological effects of environmental toxins and food additives. Furthermore, organic food consumers become complicit in accepting Far Right values being perpetrated by corporate businesses, such as the idea that it is okay that a large portion of consumers cannot afford healthy food and that health, regardless of the role industry plays in causing health breakdown and obesity, is a matter of personal, not public, responsibility. No, Guthman convincingly and admirably argues, alternative market systems cannot work alone. Moving into a more just food system – overcoming processed food dependence for society as a whole – requires that we consider the full range of social and ecological issues that arise from the production and consumption of food. Processed food dependence is a *political* problem that requires a *political* solution.

I am extremely grateful to Dan Vega, co-founder of Indigo River Publishing, for his confidence in the worthiness of this cookbook project from the start and for his steadfast enthusiastic support throughout the months of its final preparation. For their dogged and talented contributions to this project, I want to express warm thanks also to the entire team at Indigo River Publishing, especially Production Manager Bobby Dunaway, Editors Jeanna Fox and Mary Catharine Jaranelli, and Interior Designer Catherine Williams. Finally, I wish here to thank my dear husband Robert, who has been my steadfast supporter and helper of inestimable value over the many, many years it has taken for my work to evolve into *Cooked Alive!* Ever patiently and carefully editing recipes and chapters and then re-editing them yet another time, he has been my indispensable angel in both developing and completing this life-long project.

ONE LAST THOUGHT. I began my adventure in whole food cooking long ago. I do not exaggerate when I say that this adventure has been something of an obsession in my life – in most ways a magnificent obsession I think. You, dear reader, may already be well advanced in the art and science of whole food cooking, in which case you can now head straight for a recipe. The recipes in this book have been designed to be free-standing with the step-by-step guidance in each of them that is required to ensure cooking success. If, however, you are just now launching yourself on your own adventure-filled journey in whole food cooking, I would urge you to start by reading the Introduction to this book, and as you begin to engage with the recipes, to also read the few introductory pages of the chapter containing your chosen recipe. In them is some highly important and useful guidance. I believe you will also find it helpful, as your whole food cooking proceeds, to consult the many references (thirteen of them in all) that are scattered throughout the book. They, too, include valuable information and practical suggestions to ease your path to successful whole food cooking.

Having said this, I want now to wish you all success on this cooking adventure. Happy whole food cooking!

INTRODUCTION

Escaping Processed Food Dependence

COOKED ALIVE! IS a cookbook about learning to love vegetables and fruits, about learning to value, enjoy, and use them to secure your health. It gives substance to the admonition made over and over by food authorities to "eat more vegetables and fruits." It does this by providing recipes that lift these foods, and especially vegetables, from the inferior outsider role they now largely play in everyday eating into "top gun" dish ingredient form. *Cooked Alive!*'s Part I recipes (focused on *individual* vegetables and fruits) accomplish this transformation through use of simple conservation-driven preparation techniques. Capturing the vast – but now overwhelmingly and wantonly wasted – nutritional and flavoring capacity of vegetables and fruits, these techniques convert vegetables and fruits into super nutritious food with powerful flavoring capacity. Built into common everyday dishes (the business of Part II recipes), conserved vegetables and fruits themselves, along with the nutritionally enhancing ingredient changes they make possible, serve to magnify the nutritional quality – and the health-building capacity – of dishes, and they do this while maintaining traditional dish appearance and attractiveness. Part II recipes, as a result, yield dishes with dramatically expanded nutritional quality that are readily accepted by cooks and food consumers alike.

Cooked Alive! is a breakthrough cookbook in that its recipes give cooks effective tools for opening the door to routine and rewarding everyday use of vegetables and fruits. Having effective tools in hand, however, is not enough to accomplish this opening. They alone do not prepare cooks to overcome two giant roadblocks standing in the way. The first of these roadblocks is an obstacle of stupendous proportions – processed food dependence. This paralyzing dependence is the fundamental reason for the devaluing and abandonment of vegetables and fruits that characterizes modern eating. The second roadblock – a void in knowledge about vegetables and fruits – is not in any way as daunting as processed food dependence. Happily, it is fairly easily solved. But filling this void with the information needed simply cannot fit into recipes.

Cooked Alive! is thus more than a cookbook. Along with providing attractive, workable, and genuinely healthful recipes that can be used without reference to the rest of the book, *Cooked Alive!* is also a guidebook. It arms cooks with the information needed to break free of the bondage inflicted by processed food dependence. This includes technical information they require to fully appreciate vegetables and fruits. Thus armed, cooks are motivated to take advantage of the recipes *Cooked Alive!* supplies them. This all-important information-sharing is scattered throughout *Cooked Alive!*, tucked into introductory sections and in references attached to chapters. It begins right here with an explanation of the problem of processed food dependence.

The Stranglehold of Processed Food Dependence

Most modern Americans (and countless of their consumer counterparts in other parts of the world) share a grave problem – daily and life-long dependence on effectively dead, devitalized, chemically tainted, and sometimes outright toxic processed food. Commercially pre-flavored, pre-cooked, pre-packaged, and ready-to-serve food products have crept inexorably into their everyday eating routines. The typical American or westernized consumer has grown almost wholly dependent on food that has been fundamentally altered by historically unprecedented levels of processing. Less readily visible processing commonly begins in the pre-harvesting phase of food production, for instance with the substitution of unnatural for natural food in the production of plants and animals, genetic alteration of seeds, and chemical spraying. Post-harvesting processing of food relentlessly strips away the nutritional content, which provides utterly essential materials needed by the human body for maintaining health. In its place are added copious amounts of fat, sugar, and salt as well as chemical additives for marketing and profit-making purposes. Dependence of consumers on these overhauled and essentially lifeless foods has brought about a nearly complete break in their regular consumption of genuine, nourishing food – vegetables and fruits in particular – and, accordingly, is having a devastating impact on their health.

This is no simple problem. Processed foods are deeply entrenched and have a stranglehold on modern consumers for a variety of reasons. They provide convenience matched to modern, fast-paced life styles; they are scientifically crafted to exploit humans' inborn and commercially priceless craving for sugar, fat, and salt; they are massively advertised and marketed in just about every corner of the world; they dominate mealtime menus in virtually every conceivable eating place (homes, schools, hospitals, restaurants); they are featured in television cook shows and show up wherever people are taught about eating (in cookbooks and cooking magazines, for instance); and they are cheap to boot. In short, people have gotten used to and have accepted commercial alteration of foods. Drawn unsuspectingly into the *business* of food sales, consumers have become obsessed with paying the lowest possible price for food products. With their eyes glued to bargains, consumers have lost sight of the importance of food quality. All too often they fail to ask the bigger question: What good are bargains that barter away their health?[1] Processed foods, as a consequence, play an absolutely central role in the everyday eating habits of the typical modern and westernized consumer and in their (bad) health habits as well.

Warnings about the deleterious effects of processed food dependence on human health began showing up in the 1980s when high blood pressure and obesity frequencies began to skyrocket. A public survey conducted at that time found that one in four Americans had high blood pressure.[2] A follow-up study in 1991 found that more than three-quarters of the salt consumption that was giving consumers high blood pressure – which was as much as ten and even twenty times the amount required by the body[3] – came from processed foods.[4] A study in 1987 had already established that sugary soda was likely a heavy contributor to obesity.[5]

---

1 Susan Allport, *The Queen of Fats: Why Omega-3s Were Removed From the Western Diet and What We Can Do to Replace Them* (Berkeley: University of California Press, 2007), 136. Allport reports that in 2007, the year this book was published, the US was spending fifteen percent of its total economy, an average of $5,440 for each person, on health care.
2 Michael Moss, *Salt Sugar Fat: How the Food Giants Hooked Us* (New York: Random House, 2013), 267.
3 Ibid., 267-268. Moss explains how this amount is far more than the human body can handle: "In large amounts, sodium pulls fluids from the body's tissues and into the blood, which raises the blood volume and compels the heart to pump more forcefully. The result: high blood pressure."
4 Ibid., 270.
5 Ibid., 20.

INTRODUCTION

Almost thirty years later, processed food dependence is still the norm, with the health consequences having become even worse. Obesity has reached epidemic proportions in the United States and is spreading throughout the world.[6] The list of health consequences directly associated with the high and/or processed form of the fat, sugar, and salt content of processed foods is ever expanding, moving beyond high blood pressure, obesity, clogged arteries,[7] and cardiovascular disease to include such debilitating or deadly illnesses as diabetes, autism, dementia, Alzheimer's, chronic inflammation, inflammatory bowel disorders (such as Crohn's disease and ulcerative colitis), osteoporosis, and cancer.

No sign of effective governmental or institutional action to counter processed food dependence is appearing. The reasons are complex. Meanwhile, powerful forces deepen the dependence, as a review of these forces shows.

- **The corporate food marketing industry, which is basically concerned with the conversion of agricultural crops into marketable consumer goods, has not yet undertaken any significant reform of its processed food products, and it shows no sign of interest in doing so.**

Michael Moss, the Pulitzer Prize-winning investigative reporter, explores why in his highly informative 2013 book, *Salt Sugar Fat: How the Food Giants Hooked Us*. His judgments rest on visits to the laboratories of food corporations and extensive interviewing of both the food scientists in charge of these laboratories and the corporation executives directing them. He shows us that food corporations engineer food products with one goal in mind – to create the biggest craving they can, which, in turn, provides the greatest profit. They hire talented scientists from top universities and invest hundreds of millions of dollars to make processed food as enticing as possible. According to Moss, "the industry's pursuit of allure is extremely sophisticated, and it leaves nothing to chance."[8] Food industry scientists have probed deep into the human brain to learn how to use sugar, salt, and fat to expand the consumer appeal of their products.[9] The payoff of this probing has been great. Industry scientists have determined the felicitously named "bliss point"[10] of sugar consumption – the precise amount of sugar needed to achieve maximum allure at minimum cost. They have also determined that fat does not have a bliss point at all – that it is an essentially invisible ingredient that enhances flavor and mouth feel and thus can be included in food products in virtually any amount. Fat doesn't set off the body's natural alarm systems that help regulate body weight by telling us when we've had enough to eat.[11] Finding that the desire for salt, sugar, and fat is largely innate and a product of humans' evolutionary history, food scientists have located the receptors within humans that identify and reward ingestion of foods with these tempting tastes,[12] and corporate executives have gone after these receptors with

---

6   Ibid., 22. Obesity has spread to China, where people who weigh too much now outnumber those who weigh too little. Mexico's obesity rate has tripled in the past three decades. Half of all adults in Qatar are designated obese by the government.

7   Ibid., 214. In 2013 around 32 million Americans were taking drugs to reduce high cholesterol levels. Since the publication of Moss's book, new research, as reported by Anahad O'Connor in "Study doubts link between fatty diet and heart disease," *International New York Times* (March 18, 2015): 8, de-links the connection between consumption of saturated fat and plaque build-up in arteries and explains that trans fat (partially hydrogenated oil), sugary foods, and an excess of refined carbohydrates are the actual causes of the buildup of artery-narrowing plaque.

8   Ibid., xxvii.

9   Ibid., 148-151.

10 Ibid., 10.

11 Ibid., 154. Moss explains how processed food researchers discovered that "… fat is about feel, or texture, and that it is an enormously powerful force in processed food that often flies under our radar, drawing us in without the blaring horns that a dose of sugar or salt will set off in the mouth."

12 Ibid., 275.

a vengeance, shamelessly pushing these "evolutionary buttons" to expand sales and profits.[13] Moss shows that the food industry has also created a desire for salt where none existed before.[14]

Corporate food businesses, Moss explains, are themselves "inexorably hooked on salt."[15] They depend on it for far more than flavor. It is a magical ingredient that serves as a great fixer, making products look better and last longer, covering up unpleasant flavors, and holding ingredients together.[16] In effect, food corporations are stuck. They cannot alter the salt content – nor that of sugar or fat – without fundamentally undermining the consumer appeal of their products, and that, obviously, would heavily impact product sales and profits. At the same time, the food corporations are engaged in fierce competition with other producers who are waiting to take their place in the market. Food corporations, understandably, are loath to give in. Instead, they push ahead – with salt, sugar, and fat in tow – looking for new marketing opportunities around the world. Alongside marketing success stories, Moss charts the failed stories of corporate CEOs who lost their jobs for trying to reduce the fat, sugar, or salt content of processed products.

- **Giant food marketing corporations have no inherent interest in the nutritional quality of products.**

Operating now in a globalized profit-driven economic system, food corporations observe a *business model* of food preparation, one that mimics the ethos, methods, and procedures of the factory. Rather than giving primary consideration to food as intricately connected to human health and vitality – and hence that it should be produced and prepared in a manner that maximizes its health-promoting capacity – this business or factory model is based on the idea that *food can be, and should be, prepared like any other commodity*. In other words, efficiency, cost reduction, and profit-generation should serve as the guiding priorities. In this profit-oriented model, nutritional considerations get sidelined. Cost considerations rule, relentlessly and forcefully pushing the food industry to search constantly for less expensive ingredients to reduce costs.

Downgrading or outright dismissal of nutritional value frees commercial food processing corporations to manipulate food virtually at will. Nutritional value is brought back into play mainly as an image-bolstering gimmick for increasing sales. Unfortunately, for this purpose it is a very effective tool. Moss reports, for example, that Kool-Aid managers add just a splash of real fruit juice to their product. "It was barely half a teaspoon of juice, a mere 5 percent of the total formula, but the Kool-Aid managers already knew that even a hint of fruit was worth a zillion times its weight in marketing gold."[17] Tang managers, he observes, supplemented their product with vitamin C to take advantage of the marketing power of adding nutritional ingredients. Capri Sun, says Moss, acquired a healthy image by being labeled a "natural fruit drink" when the basis of this claim is an ingredient called "juice concentrate," which in fact is a highly refined product that is basically pure sugar.[18]

Countless other food companies similarly use nutrition as an image-boosting gimmick to increase sales of nutritionally stripped products.[19] Even natural food stores are affected. Stores are flooded with

---

13   Michael Pollan, *In Defense of Food: An Eater's Manifesto* (New York: Penguin, 2009): 150; Moss, 278.
14   Moss, *Salt Sugar Fat*, 279-280.
15   Ibid., 292. Moss states that "[w]ithout salt, processed food companies cease to exist."
16   Ibid., 281. Moss states, "Manufacturers view salt as perhaps the most magical of the three pillars of processed foods, for all the things it can do beyond exciting the taste buds."
17   Ibid., 127.
18   Ibid., 134.
19   The feature article "Hijacked: How the Food Industry Converts Diet Advice into Profits," (3-7), in the October 2014 issue of the *Nutrition Action Health Letter* of the Center for Science in the Public Interest identifies many such products.

INTRODUCTION

highly processed, nutritionally stripped food products that carry a certified organic label. The organic label does indicate an important kind of quality; it verifies a food (and all food ingredients contained in a mixed food product) has been produced in a high quality manner (that pesticides, for example, have not been used; natural, not artificial, fertilizer has been used). An organic label, however, is irrelevant as a quality standard concerning physical processing that occurs once a food is harvested. The nutritional stripping that occurs *after* harvesting is in fact completely inconsistent with and contrary to quality production.

This terrific push to downplay genuine nutritional value has totally corrupted the whole notion of nutritional value, which has become much too narrowly defined. It has become okay to remove enormous nutritional content from foods as long as particular "most important" nutrients remain. Provided additives are identified, it has become okay for food processors to add them to products with a vengeance.

- **Walmart, the largest discount retailer in the world, is no exception to the rule that giant food marketing corporations have no inherent interest in the nutritional quality of food products they produce.**

Though Walmart is a big seller of organic food, which is high quality naturally produced food, Walmart remains first and foremost a money-making business. That Walmart announced in June 2014 a promise to sell organic goods cheaply is an important clue about its business status. Like other corporate businesses, Walmart is compelled to produce and sell food as cheaply as possible. Walmart must make money and please its shareholders as first priorities. As it does with its other suppliers, Walmart will squeeze its organic produce suppliers to reduce production costs.[20] The impact of such squeezing will almost inevitably negatively affect both the size of organic producers serving Walmart and the nutritional quality of their products. Large size businesses will best be able to reduce costs through greater production; organic businesses in general will be forced to use less and/or lower quality natural fertilizer for growing organic products. Producers can make these cost-cutting adjustments because United States Department of Agriculture (USDA) organic guidelines do not specify an exact amount or quality of natural fertilizer that must be used. If producers do this, however, the quality of their organic produce is reduced and undermined because natural fertilizer underlies organic food quality.

- **Agribusinesses have no inherent interest in the nutritional quality of foods they produce.**

These businesses, like giant food marketing corporations, observe a business model of food production. Efficiency, cost reduction, expanded production, and profit-generation serve as the guiding priorities, and in applying these principles, it is agribusinesses that begin the food processing process. They select seed varieties on the basis of such factors as disease resistance and productivity rather than nutritional value, which does not visibly enhance profit. Agribusinesses apply artificial rather than natural fertilizer to soil, thereby adding only three minerals as opposed to a wide variety of trace minerals added by natural fertilizer. This chemical reduction of soil composition results in the production of foods with simplified chemical composition, meaning foods with less nutritional content and diversity. Furthermore, agribusinesses heavily rely on the use of pesticides to secure

---

20   Wenonah Hauter, "Walmart Squeezes Organics," *The Progressive* (June 2014): 18-20.

successful food production. This form of processing routinely taints food products, with many fruits and vegetables retaining traces of numerous different kinds of pesticides. Agribusinesses do not have to inform customers of the pesticide content nor do they have to prove the safety of the individual pesticides and certainly not of combinations of pesticides, effectively leaving consumers to serve as guinea pigs until overwhelming evidence against a particular pesticide forces action, as is the case with the herbicide Roundup.[21] This federal government policy has the effect of leaving consumers dangerously exposed to chemicals for extended periods of time.[22]

- **Institutionally, governments are fundamentally ill-disposed to force food corporations to give high priority to nutritional quality.**

Not to leave any stone unturned in their quest for maximizing marketing potential, the food corporations have infiltrated and thus exert massive influence upon government agencies that set and regulate food standards. This insider influence has come to be an especially common practice in the United States. For example, in 2010, seven of the thirteen members on the governing board of The Center for Nutrition Policy and Promotion, the tiny arm[23] of the U.S. Department of Agriculture (USDA) that updates nutritional guidelines for Americans every five years, were nominated by the Grocery Manufacturers' Association.[24] Especially indicative of food corporation lobbying power in the United States is the fact that while there is nearly universal agreement that sugar consumption is directly related to obesity, the federal government was not able to set any recommended sugar consumption limits until 2015.[25] Equally revealing is the fact that while a respected research scientist proved that trans fat (an artificial fat found in margarine and in all manner of processed food

---

21 Mark Bittman, "Stop Making Us Guinea Pigs," *International New York Times* (March 26, 2015): 7. Mr. Bittman points out that in mid-March of 2015, the respected International Agency for Research on Cancer declared that glyphosate, the active ingredient in the widely used herbicide Roundup is a probable cause of cancer (non-Hodgkin's lymphoma) in humans. This was the extraordinary action required, and this authoritative action has opened the door to effective action against Roundup, the main herbicide product containing glyphosate. Following this decision, the state of California declared glyphosate to be carcinogenic and is requiring products containing glyphosate to carry a cancer warning. Monsanto, the agribusiness producer of Roundup, sued California to prevent such action but lost. Monsanto then appealed the case but in early 2017, lost this appeal. Now other action in support of public health can follow.

22 Roundup has been widely used since the 1970s, which means that it has taken at least 45 years for authoritative information about the dangers of glyphosate (the primary chemical in the herbicide Roundup) to human health to be able to effectively challenge the safety of Roundup. During this time farmers, farm workers, domesticated animals, wild animals, and people living on farms and in rural communities were regularly exposed. With the advent of genetically engineered Roundup Ready seeds in the mid-1990s, which enabled crops grown from the seeds to be able to withstand direct spraying with Roundup, use of Roundup dramatically increased. Glyphosate exposure, as a result, expanded to include the general public as well. Because of the many ways that glyphosate disrupts crucial biological processes of humans, animals, and bacteria (including the beneficial bacteria inhabiting human and animal guts and the soil), exposure to glyphosate goes well beyond causing non-Hodgkin's lymphoma cancer and is being increasingly connected to bone, colon, kidney, liver, pancreatic, and thyroid cancer as well. A rapidly growing body of peer-reviewed scientific research by independent researchers (such as Dr. Stephanie Seneff, a respected MIT scholar) links glyphosate to a wide variety of deadly health problems affecting increasing numbers of the American population, including autism, birth defects, gluten intolerance, Alzheimer's, dementia, diabetes, obesity, inflamed bowel disorders, liver and kidney disease, impaired immune function, reproductive problems (including reduced fertility and miscarriage), and behavioral problems (such as attention deficit/hyperactivity disorder). This growing body of independent glyphosate research shows that harm to human health could begin at much lower levels of exposure than the allowable safe levels currently set on the basis of corporate agribusiness sponsored research. That glyphosate binds (chelates) vital minerals in the soil – such as manganese, zinc, and boron – and prevents plants from absorbing them has implications for the nutritional value of foods treated with glyphosate.

23 Moss, *Salt Sugar Fat*, 214. The Center for Nutritional Policy and Promotion's share of the USDA annual budget is only $6.5 million, which is a mere drop in a bucket (0.0045 percent) in comparison to the overall USDA annual outlay of $146 billion.

24 Ibid., 220. United States Department of Agriculture records show that these members represented such corporations as Kraft, Kellogg, Nestle, and PepsiCo. Moss describes (220-221) the intense lobbying effort of these and every other representative of major manufacturers of processed foods – more than 300 companies in all – to affect the 2010 guidelines set forth in Nutritional Policy and Promotion decisions.

25 Ibid., 22.

products sold in grocery stores) was deadly to humans and presented this information to Congress in 1988, she was flatly ignored. Agribusinesses successfully conducted a massive disinformation campaign to keep the products on grocery store shelves. Our government only acted against trans fat several decades later when European countries outlawed use of it.[26]

That the U.S. federal government itself is a big player in industrial food production additionally complicates our society's processed food dependence problem. It is an especially active partner in the beef and dairy industries. As far back as 1985, the USDA began promoting dairy and beef industry products. Today it maintains a tax-financed institution called the U.S. Meat Animal Research Center that is specifically devoted to helping producers of beef, pork, and lamb increase productivity at the lowest possible cost and, hence, to make a higher profit.[27] It also energetically encourages Americans to eat more cheese. Apparently, USDA advocacy of cheese has been an impressive commercial success; cheese consumption has risen steadily, according to the USDA's own records.[28] In this advocacy the USDA is fully complicit with the food industries' deceptive tactic of hiding (adding it in out-of-sight manner) a significant amount of fat-laden cheese in a wide variety of products to make these products more taste-tempting – in effect cloaking the high calorie content of excessive cheese consumption to enhance sales.[29] Another serious problem with the USDA's alliance with the mainstream industrial producers of cheese and beef is that the USDA effectively hands them monopoly control of the cheese and beef market while placing smaller scale producers of much healthier varieties of cheese and beef products – notably organic and grass-fed – at a serious competitive disadvantage. As usual, unwary consumers are big time losers in the bargain.

- **Rather than fighting the processed foods system, the American health services industry has adapted to it.**

Indeed, the health services industry is an active player in the system. It is no agent for change. Rather, it is a disease-care system that reacts to and manages, instead of prevents, disease.[30] The health services industry has invested heavily in specialized training and equipment to treat the illnesses arising from processed food dependence. It profits heavily from processed food consumption.

The attention of the fund-raising arms of the medical profession – such as the American Cancer Society, American Heart Association, and American Diabetic Association – like the medical profession itself, remains rigidly focused not on foods but on individual chemical components of foods[31] and, in particular, on the burgeoning and potentially highly profitable field of bio-genetics. Little, if any, of the donations these organizations collect goes to nutritional research. Heavily reliant on funding by corporate sponsors, these groups also do not promote products or actions at odds with

---

26 Catherine Shanahan, M.D., with Luke Shanahan, *Deep Nutrition: Why Your Genes Need Traditional Food* (New York: Flatiron Books, 2016): 134.

27 Moss, "Animal Welfare at Risk in Experiments for Meat Industry," *The New York Times* (January 19, 2015).

28 Moss, Salt Sugar Fat, 176. "Where Americans, on the average, were eating 11 pounds of cheese a year in 1970, they were up to 18 pounds in 1980, 25 pounds by 1990, 30 pounds in 2000, and 33 pounds by 2007, when the rates dipped in the recession before resuming their surge."

29 Ibid., 180-181. Research shows consumers eat more fat when it is included in hidden form. This is not an insignificant problem considering that the calorie load of saturated fat contained in cheese is more than twice that of either sugar or protein.

30 T. Colin Campbell, *Whole: Rethinking the Science of Nutrition* (Dallas, Texas: BenBella Books, Inc., 2013): 140; Pollan, *In Defense of Food*, 135.

31 Pollan, *In Defense of Food*, 27-36, and Campbell, *Whole*, 45-175. Each explains the underlying ideology that supports our society's health institutions' exclusive focus on particular nutritional components as keys to health cures and why maximum conservation of the natural wholeness of foods is not valued as a means for maintaining human health. Pollan labels this ideology Nutritionism; Campbell labels it reductionism. Both agree that this ideology is a dogma that focuses attention on identifying key nutrients – magic bullets – contained in foods that can be used to treat human health afflictions and diseases.

their sponsors' interests. And even when these groups do seek to call attention to nutritional issues, their efforts wilt in the face of opposition from processed food, medical, and big pharma companies contributing to their support. The American Heart Association did step forward in 2009 and issued a recommended limit for sugar. Noting that people were getting on average 22 teaspoons of added sugar a day, the association recommended a dramatic cutback: 5 teaspoons per day for moderately active women and 9 teaspoons per day for sedentary, middle-aged men.[32] When representatives from every corner of the food industry flooded a summit meeting held by the American Heart Association in 2010 to discuss the recommendation and complained bitterly of it, the recommendation collapsed after failing to receive sufficient support.

- **Independent scientifically researched studies regularly confirm the damage inflicted by commercially processed foods on human health, but they routinely get marginalized.**

When studies linking health to a nutritious diet do emerge, the food corporations quickly and deftly diffuse the criticism and confuse consumers. They orchestrate their own studies that discredit the research and/or hire paid consultants to undertake media campaigns to bewilder the public. Corporate sponsored studies, misuse of supposedly unbiased and authoritative academics, and media attacks blur the connection between good health and nutritionally nourishing foods, between poor health and processed foods, and between genetically modified products and corporate profit and control of food.

For example, evidence recently surfaced showing that the food industry has enlisted academics to support laws favorable to genetically modified products in the U.S. Congress.[33] When a 2007 report by an international group of twenty-one scientists linked red meat, and especially processed red meat, consumption with colon cancer,[34] the organized meat industry immediately acted to undercut the report. It set up its own "Cancer Team,"[35] which hired a consulting firm that went to work on shaping public opinion by reshaping the media's coverage of red meat consumption. In the end the meat industry effectively undermined the study before the news had hardly reached the public.

Food processors and agribusiness food producers mainly block research about the impact of processed and industrially produced food outright, and there is simply very little independent research conducted. Serious scientific research is overwhelmingly dependent on corporations for research grants, and corporations naturally place self-interested limits on the type of research conducted. Corporations themselves conduct their own research, much of which, as has been noted, is intended to deliberately confuse the public. They are known to bury their own research that does not support their products. An important example is the recent (2017) uncovering of a 1960's sugar industry study that linked a high-sugar diet to high cholesterol build up in arteries and cancer in rats.

---

32 Moss, *Salt Sugar Fat*, 23-24.
33 Eric Lipton, "Food Industry Enlisted Academics in G.M.O. Lobbying War, Emails Show," *The New York Times* (September 5, 2015). Evidence gained from emails shows how some academics are given special grants for undisclosed amounts (though evidence shows one academic has received at least $880,000) and that some have moved to being active political lobbyists promoting genetically modified foods and other products (such as seeds and herbicides) and in resisting state efforts to mandate G.M.O. labeling. One academic, Dr. Kevin Folta, the chairman of the horticultural sciences department at the University of Florida, is reportedly actively involved in devising the biotech industry strategy to get Congress to make it illegal for states to mandate G.M.O. labeling.
34 Ibid., 229-230. On the basis of a decade of studies, the scientists concluded the risk of cancer from processed meat to be especially high. The scientists stated "they could find no level of consumption at which processed meats were safe. Every 1.7 ounces of processed meats consumed per day increased the risk of colorectal cancer by 21 percent."
35 Moss, *Salt Sugar Fat*, 229-230.

- **Federal government nutritional recommendations have not been consistent, which has caused widespread nutritional confusion among consumers about what constitutes healthy eating.**

It turns out that many early dietary recommendations were heavily and rather arrogantly based on logical conclusions rather than on hard scientific evidence.[36] New thoroughly researched and published studies, as a result, have often contradicted the recommendations. This has clearly been the case with saturated fat. A new study de-linking consumption of saturated fat and heart disease is an important case in point. A team of international scientists has recently (2014) concluded that there is no evidence that eating saturated fat – the type found in meat, eggs, butter, and cheese – increased heart attacks and other cardiac events.[37] This study fundamentally contradicts guidelines set forth by both the federal government and the American Health Association that have remained rigidly in place since the mid-1980s. Close review of the scientific discoveries about fat, and especially new research about the role of the omega-3 and omega-6 essential fatty acids in heart health, which was already well underway when the war against saturated fat began, show that a severe disconnect between this independent research and governmental dietary recommendations existed already in the 1980s.[38]

- **Standard food preparation practices mimic the nutrition-, flavor-, and texture-stripping practices used by processed food companies.**

Directed by recipes, whether from standard or nutritionally-oriented non-vegetarian and vegetarian cooking magazines and cookbooks,[39] home cooks commonly prepare vegetables and fruits in destructive and wasteful ways that squander valuable nutritional content, color, and flavor and that undermine texture. Home cooks, for example, commonly:

1. **discard edible plant parts.** Cooks often remove skin and sometimes a significant amount of pulp during peeling. For most vegetables and fruits, the skin and tissue right below it contain the greatest concentration of nutrients.[40] Skin is also a valuable source of insoluble fiber. Cooks commonly discard tough parts of vegetables – such as stems and veins of greens, broccoli stalk and floret stems, asparagus bottoms, and celery strings – though these parts are excellent sources of insoluble fiber, such as of cellulose, which is a fiber that encourages the growth of beneficial intestinal bacteria. Cooks also almost routinely discard the green tops of leeks and green onions, which are rich sources of fructan fibers that encourage the growth of valuable beneficial intestinal bacteria. The

---

36   Pollan, "Bad Science," *In Defense of Food*, 61-81. Pollan emphasizes that dietary recommendations have been blinded by prevailing nutritional ideology.
Susan Allport, *The Queen of Fats: Why Omega-3s Were Removed From the Western Diet and What We Can Do to Replace Them* (Berkeley: University of California Press, 2007): 55. Allport quotes a member of the National Institute of Cancer speaking to the U.S. Senate's Committee on Nutrition and Human Needs in 1976 who arrogantly states "nutrition science has developed essentially all the basic knowledge that is necessary" to determine what people should be eating in order to reduce their risk of diet-related cancers and heart disease. She reports that this was the prevailing opinion at the time.
37   Anahad O'Connor, "Study Doubts Link Between Fatty Diet and Heart Disease," *International New York Times* (March 18, 2014): 8.
38   Allport, *The Queen of Fats*, 1-95.
39   An example of such a magazine is *Eating Well*. An example of a nutritionally-oriented cookbook is *Moosewood Restaurant Cooks for a Crowd: Recipes with a Vegetarian Emphasis for 24 or More* (New York: John Wiley & Sons, Inc., 1996), which is but one of a series of popular cookbooks. An upscale cookbook is by Kim Rizk, *Hay Day Country Market Cookbook* (New York, Workman Publishing Co., Inc, 1998). Recipes in this magazine and in these cookbooks commonly cook cut vegetables in water, lump vegetables for cooking, and puree vegetables.
40   Jo Robinson, *Eating on the Wild Side: The Missing Link to Optimum Health* (New York: Little, Brown and Company, 2013): 116.

pith of oranges is commonly ignored, and sometimes the membrane of orange segments is removed and discarded.
2. **char skin.**
3. **caramelize onions.** The cooking involved in caramelizing breaks down the fructan fibers contained by onions. Unlike the fructan fiber content of raw and minimally cooked onion, the shortened fibers of caramelized onion cannot survive the passage through the human digestive system into the intestine and serve as prebiotics, food for the bacteria living in and caring for the intestine.
4. **cook cut vegetables in water, which is then discarded.** Water soluble nutritional components, which include many micronutrients and phytonutrients in addition to soluble fiber, contained in the vegetables dissolve into the water and are lost completely if the water is not used. Soluble flavor and coloring components also dissolve into the cooking water and are irretrievably lost.
5. **lump vegetables together for cooking.** Because vegetables have different cooking times, lumping inevitably results in the overcooking of at least some of the vegetables. Overcooking breaks down cell structure, which allows natural juice and its soluble cargo to spill from the vegetables and to mix with destructive plant acids also released from plant cells.
6. **lump vegetables with long-cooking ingredients.** Many vegetables, for example, are typically cooked with meat, grain, and/or legumes in stews, which inexorably results in overcooking and, as a result, loss of individual vegetable flavor, texture, and color.
7. **extract and drain juice.** Salt is sometimes sprinkled over cut pulp (such as eggplant pulp and cucumbers) to draw out juice, which is then discarded. **Cooked spinach is sometimes squeezed dry.** Vegetables are often marinated in a liquid or pickled, which deliberately draws out natural juice and exchanges flavored liquid in its place.
8. **puree pulp.** Pureeing effectively destroys the insoluble fiber content of pulp. It also results in complete loss of distinctive natural vegetable and fruit flavor and in complete exposure of plant pulp to air, which is destructive of particular nutrients.
9. **discard pulp removed during juicing of fruits and vegetables.**

Nutritional waste,[41] in turn, can leave vegetables and fruits as nutritionally dead as highly refined foods. Flavor, texture, and color loss leaves vegetables limp, colorless, and bland and, as a result, dependent on salt- and fat-based flavoring – such as butter, cheese, cream, canned soup, salted white bread crumbs, and bacon – for successful serving. Limp vegetables also invite pureeing. Preparation

---

[41] This wasteful approach has not always been so dominant. Adelle Davis was a widely popular writer who championed vegetable and fruit conservation in the 1960s and 1970s. It was her book *Let's Cook It Right* that inspired this author into a lifetime of conservation cooking. Why the situation with respect to nutritional conservation is so dismal reflects the domination and power of industrial food producing and food processing corporations, which customarily devalue conservation because of profit-driven motives. This domination directly affects our society's rigid focus on a particular way of maintaining human health, which is perfectly suited to food processing. Michael Pollan (*In Defense of Food*, notably Chapters Two and Three) and T. Colin Campbell (*Whole: Rethinking the Science of Nutrition*, Chapters 4-12) explain the underlying ideological reason why maximum conservation of the natural wholeness of foods (i.e., conservation of all naturally occurring nutritional components) is not valued as a means for maintaining human health. Both agree that this ideology (labeled as Nutritionism by Pollan; labeled as reductionism by Campbell) acts as a dogma that focuses attention on identifying key nutrients – "magic bullets" – contained in foods that can be used to treat human health afflictions and diseases. Labeling the value of vegetables and fruits in terms of isolated "important" individual nutrients happens to suit food processors and nutritional supplement producers perfectly. Processors are free to discard all but those "most important" nutrients labeled and still claim their products to be nutritious; food supplement makers can focus on individual "most important" nutrients and not worry about approximating natural nutritional wholeness, which gives them maximum flexibility in keeping nutrient combinations profit focused.

that strips flavor, color, and texture from vegetables destines them to play only an uninteresting, low status, and a low value role in everyday eating.

- **Urbanization disconnects humans from food production.**

Direct links between fresh vegetables and fruits and farmers producing them are removed. The relationship between consumers and food becomes impersonal. Consumers, as a result, do not act as a check on processing, effectively giving industrial producers and processors a free hand.

In this heavily business-dominated and urban setting, processed food dependence is not effectively challenged,[42] and typical consumers remain effectively stranded and left on their own to cope with the devastating health consequences and medical expenses stemming from processed food dependence. Coping isn't easy. Witness that the food supplement business is booming (Americans spend an estimated $32 billion on supplements per year)[43] and that food supplements are being marketed for every imaginable ailment, and at a hefty price, which are indications that many people are turning to food supplements in an effort to stem the rising tide of health problems they face. In relying on these food supplement products, however, consumers are highly vulnerable because of the very loosely regulated nature of these products. There is no impartial authoritative agency to verify the claims made about the contents of these products, leaving the door wide open to unscrupulous profit-seeking marketers, not to mention harmful health consequences.[44] Indeed the business is plagued with charges of adulteration and mislabeling.[45] Even if products are reliably pure and from reputable merchants, food supplements are man-made, for-profit products that are not equivalent to

---

42 To be sure, processed food dependence is challenged. Michael Pollan stands out as a top and highly respected outspoken critic. He powerfully articulates his challenge in his book *In Defense of Food: An Eater's Manifesto*. The recent decision (April 26, 2015) by Chipotle Mexican Grill, a major restaurant chain, to stop serving genetically altered food is of special significance. This is the first major restaurant to make this decision. As reported by Stephani Strom in "Chipotle to Stop Serving Genetically Altered Food," *The New York Times* (April 26, 2015), Steve Ells, the founder and co-chief executive of Chipotle, announced, "Just because food is served fast doesn't mean it has to be made with cheap materials, highly processed with preservatives and stabilizers and fillers and artificial colors and flavors." The spectacular growth of certified organic foods is clearly a critical response by consumers to industrially produced processed foods. In her persuasive book *Weighing In: Obesity, Social Justice, and the Limits of Capitalism* (Berkeley: University of California Press, 2011), Julie Guthman shows, however, that while the organic foods movement has been "wildly successful" in bringing people into its fold (139), the organic foods movement has developed as an alternative food system that co-exists alongside the processed food system rather than being a serious challenge to it. The organic food movement focuses on the enormously worthy and important task of providing healthy and less toxic alternative foods to consumers. The cost and lower accessibility of organic food, however, keeps it out of the reach of many consumers. The movement turns a blind eye to the fact that essentially unregulated agribusinesses and other corporate producers of processed food have the rest of the nation's consumers in their profit-driven grip, feeding them processed food, which in Guthman's words, is "cheap, standardized, and nutritionally vacuous food" and that exposes them to appreciable amounts of toxic chemicals that cause devastating illnesses and bodily changes, including making them and their children obese.

43 Anahad O'Connor, "Spike in Harm to Liver is Tied to Dietary Aids," *The New York Times* (December 21, 2013): 2. About half of Americans use dietary supplements, and most of them take more than one product at a time.

44 Ibid., 2. "The Federal Drug Administration estimates that 70 percent of dietary supplement companies are not following basic quality control standards that would help prevent adulteration of their products." The article writer informs us that "[b]ecause the supplement industry operates on the honor system, studies show, the market has been flooded with products that are adulterated, mislabeled or packaged in dosages that have not been studied for safety."
Roni Caryn Rabin, "Thyroid Supplements Offer an Extra Punch," *International New York Times* (January 22, 2014): 13. Rabin repeats the message to consumers to use supplements very cautiously because of how loosely they are regulated. In this article, researchers who tested ten popular thyroid-boosting products sold online found that nine contained a potentially dangerous thyroid hormone.

45 Anahad O'Connor, "US retailer to toughen quality tests for diet pills," (*The New York Times*, March 31, 2015): 13. The New York State attorney general's office, for example, accused GNC, the U.S.'s largest specialty retailer of dietary supplements (it has more than 6,500 stores and has an annual revenue of $2.6 billion), of selling herbal supplements that were fraudulent or contaminated with unlisted ingredients that could pose health risks to consumers. The New York State attorney general's office successfully forced GNC to institute sweeping new testing procedures and to submit to making semiannual reports that verify compliance with the testing.

real food[46] and, accordingly, cannot begin to fill the staggering real food gap being left by processed food dependence. Nor do supplements address the problem of the chemical poisoning being faced by consumers as a result of processed food dependence. At best, food supplements serve as expensive Band-Aids.

So, what is the health conscious individual to do?

There is a clear, compelling, and fully workable solution. *Individual consumers must learn to love vegetables and fruits.* They are absolutely essential foods right under our noses. Learning to cook and incorporate them into everyday eating provides a simple and effective means for individuals – any interested individuals whatsoever – to take control of their health. There is nothing theoretical about the nutritional value of these foods. This nutritional value is solidly grounded in hard science-based research that fills innumerable textbooks on nutrition.[47] This research verifies vegetables and fruits to be sources of nutritional components essentially linked to human health needs, an intimate interconnection that has developed over thousands of years. Over and over, studies confirm that a diet rich in vegetables and fruits reduces the risk of dying from practically all Western (and now world) diseases.[48]

Squarely focused on helping cooks prepare vegetables and fruits in a manner that effectively captures the attractiveness, tastiness, and amazing health-promoting capacity of these foods, *Cooked Alive!* is exactly the cookbook to assist cooks in successfully bringing fresh vegetables and fruits into their daily diet.

Breaking Free with Fresh Whole Vegetables and Fruits

Fresh whole vegetables and fruits in general have flavoring and nutritional characteristics that make them essential foods in everyday eating.

With respect to flavoring characteristics, fresh vegetables and fruits naturally contain distinctive flavoring and color components and have attractively juicy texture as well. When these features are retained during the preparation process, prepared vegetables and fruits are independently tasty and attractive with minimal use of outside flavoring (fat, sugar, and salt). Very importantly, they can be used as main flavoring ingredients in dishes, effectively eliminating – or dramatically reducing – use of commercially prepared fat-, sugar-, salt-, and/or artificial chemically-based flavoring.

As for nutritional characteristics, vegetables and fruits carry four types of nutritional components – micronutrients, phytonutrients, fiber, and omega-3 essential fatty acids (alpha linolenic acid, or ALA) – that are essential to human health. Vegetables and fruits serve as primary sources of these nutritional components, which the human body cannot itself produce. While human tampering (as through selective breeding) has reduced the content of these components in many vegetables and fruits and while nutritional content naturally varies – and sometimes varies considerably – among

---

46   Campbell, *Whole*, 163. Campbell describes supplements as "factory-formed fragments of former food". Campbell (150-163) illustrates how "just like prescription drugs, the active agents [of supplements] function imperfectly, incompletely, and unpredictably when divorced from the whole plant food from which they're derived or synthesized."

47   Walter C. Willet, M.D., with Patrick J. Skerrett, "Eat Plenty of Fruits and Vegetables," *Eat, Drink, and Be Healthy: The Harvard Medical School Guide to Healthy Eating* (New York: Free Press, 2001), 132-145. This book is a notable example of a textbook giving this advice.

48   Pollan, *In Defense of Food*, 164; Willet, *Eat, Drink, and Be Healthy*, 136-144.

different varieties of vegetables and fruits as well as within individual vegetable and fruit families, vegetables and fruits in general remain good sources of each of these nutritional components. A review of each of these nutritional components underscores the crucial importance of each to human health and highlights the dreadful consequences to health of abandoning vegetables and fruits in everyday eating, whether outright by not including them, by relying on commercially processed forms, or by using destructive or wasteful preparation practices.

Micronutrients

It is no surprise that the complicated human body has equally complicated nutritional needs for carrying out its essential biological functions.[49] Micronutrients, in the form of vitamins and minerals, are chemical components that enable the human body to meet these nutritional needs. Filling countless textbooks, scientists have charted and linked these nutritional actors to the normal functioning of all human cells,[50] organs, and bodily processes. Supplying micronutrients in amounts and combinations exactly matched to human bodily needs, vegetables and fruits are perfect sources of the micronutrients that maintain human health. Very importantly, vegetables and fruits are the primary sources of the micronutrients required by humans, an intimate relationship established over the thousands of years of human development.

An example of the important link between micronutrients supplied by vegetables and fruits and human health is that micronutrients play important balancing roles.

- Both vegetables and fruits are a rich source of **potassium**. One of the important functions of potassium is to play a balancing role with respect to sodium intake. When potassium is plentiful, it protects humans from developing hypertension (or high blood pressure).[51] The severe potassium/salt imbalance that occurs in a processed food dependent diet – a diet that dramatically increases sodium intake while severely reducing vegetable and fruit intake – helps explain the astonishing prominence of high blood pressure in many modern societies.
- Vegetables in particular serve as good sources of **alkaline minerals** (such as calcium, potassium, and magnesium). Alkaline minerals play a crucial role in enabling the human body to maintain a state of acid-alkaline (pH) balance, which is absolutely essential for overall good human health.[52] The human body constantly needs alkaline minerals to be able to neutralize acids that humans consume in their diet or that they produce during the process of digesting foods.[53] This neutralization is utterly essential. If the body does not get an adequate supply of minerals through diet, it takes the minerals from its own bones and tissues, causing demineralization. With extensive demineralization, bones become brittle and break easily, a condition called osteoporosis. The body also stores

---

49 Pollan, *In Defense of Food*, 47. Pollan states that the human body needs from 50 to 100 different chemical compounds and elements to perform its innumerable functions and remain healthy.
50 George Mateljan, *The World's Healthiest Foods*, 2nd edition (Seattle: George Mateljan Foundation, 2015): 39. Mateljan presents a chart that describes the role of micronutrients in cellular energy production. The micronutrients essential to this process include vitamins B1, B2, B3, B5, B6, and C and the minerals iron, magnesium, and sulfur.
51 Jane E. Brody, "Sodium-Saturated Diet Is a Threat for All," *The New York Times* (December 27, 2011).
52 "The Consequences of Acid-Alkaline Imbalance," *The Acid Alkaline Food Guide: A Quick Reference to Foods & Their Effect on pH Levels*. (Garden City Park, NW: Square One Publishers, 2006): 21-40.
53 Christopher Vasey, *The Acid-Alkaline Diet for Optimum Health*, 2nd edition. (Rochester, Vermont: Healing Arts Press, 2006): 17. Brown and Trivieri, *The Acid Alkaline Food Guide*, 19.

excess acid (acid that cannot be neutralized or eliminated by the kidneys) in bodily tissues.[54] Acid tucked into tissues, in turn, is caustic and can and will degrade tissues. The significance of the contribution by vegetables (and some fruits like banana) of alkaline minerals is clear in light of the fact that most other foods and drinks regularly consumed by humans – including meat, poultry, fish, grains, and legumes; coffee, tea (black especially but also green and some herb teas), alcoholic beverages, and sugary sodas – are acid-forming when consumed. The alkaline mineral content of vegetables makes them one of the few truly alkalizing foods that can provide a counterbalance to acidic and acid-forming foods.[55] If individuals neglect vegetables while eating large amounts of acidic and acid-forming foods, a serious health situation inevitably occurs. Their bodies necessarily take minerals from their own tissues and bones to neutralize the acid. Excess acid stored in their bodily tissues is bound to eventually cause problems.

Another important example of how micronutrients supplied by vegetables and fruits are intricately tied to human health is that they are essential to the human body's utilization of macronutrients (fats, carbohydrates, and protein). Providing needed micronutrients in the amounts and combinations required, vegetables and fruits are central actors in human processing of fats, proteins, and carbohydrates. The conversion of fats, carbohydrates (particularly grain and legume carbohydrate), and protein into energy is a complicated, multi-step process in which a multitude of micronutrients play an important role. The process easily breaks down if needed micronutrients are not available, which occurs when they have not been provided by food consumed. This is easily possible when food consumed is nutrient-stripped refined carbohydrate and fat and/or is especially possible when consumption of refined macronutrients is high. A breakdown in processing, in turn, undermines the nutritional value of a consumed macronutrient. Carbohydrate and fat, for example, are not converted into energy. Incompletely processed macronutrients can also play destructive roles. For example, they remain in an acid state,[56] which adds to the body's acid-neutralizing tasks and, hence, to the need for alkaline minerals, without which acid-neutralizing easily results in the demineralization of bones and tissues and/or the storage of caustic acid in bodily tissues.

Phytonutrients

Phytonutrients are nutritional components that have only recently been directly linked to human health. The development of sophisticated technology has made the study of phytonutrients and the accurate determination of their human health value possible. Phytonutrients (pronounced "fight-o-nutrients" — phyto means plant) are chemical components made by plants to defend themselves from predators (such as attacking insects and birds, browsing animals, molds, fungi, and viruses) as well as from destructive oxygen, UV rays of the sun, and bad weather. While scientific research has so far thoroughly investigated only a small number of the tens of thousands of types of phytonutrients that exist, it has already decisively established and constantly reinforces the stupendous fact that *phytonutrients play the same health protective roles for humans as they do for plants.* When phytonutrients are

---

54 Vasey, *The Acid-Alkaline Diet for Optimum Health*, 10. Acids come in strong and weak form. Weak acids are volatile and can be eliminated through the lungs in the form of vapors and gases. Only the liver and kidneys can neutralize strong acids, such as the acids produced during the digestion of animal protein. Because the kidneys can only eliminate a small amount of strong acid per day, the body necessarily stores extra acid within tissues.
55 Vasey, *The Acid-Alkaline Diet*, 106.
56 Ibid., 54-55.

consumed, they become part of a human's own defense system. Phytonutrients, for example,

- serve as antioxidants. They neutralize highly destructive free radicals produced during bodily processes and ingested from foods that constantly assault and damage human cells and tissues, which is a cause of cancer and dementia.[57]
- detoxify dangerous toxins, including carcinogens. They get into the membrane of cells and the bloodstream and provide protection from the onslaught of such dangerous substances as synthetic chemicals, toxins, automobile and factory emissions, bacteria, pesticides, viruses, fungi, yeast, and food additives.
- serve as anti-inflammatory agents, both controlling and healing inflammation to prevent the development of chronic inflammation, which is linked to many human health problems, including heart disease, cancer, arthritis, and diabetes.
- protect skin from ultraviolet sun rays and radiation.

Phytonutrients with extra potent antioxidant capacity are called **anthocyanins**. Contained in concentrated amounts in the coloring of such vegetables as red, purple, reddish-brown, and dark salad greens and in the coloring of such fruits as blueberries and strawberries, these powerful antioxidants protect human cells from damage caused by free radicals, which leads to the onset of degenerative diseases. Research is steadily identifying the varied human health-protective tasks that anthocyanins perform, such as[58]:

- block inflammation.
- lower blood pressure, LDL (bad) cholesterol, and blood sugar.
- fight cancer.
- slow age-related memory loss.

Though natural genetic mutations and human selection of particular varieties have significantly and sometimes stunningly reduced the phytonutrient content of many popular vegetable and fruit varieties in comparison to that of their wild relatives,[59] vegetables and fruits in general retain significant phytonutrient content, with some varieties still retaining exceptional content. Organically produced produce generally has greater phytonutrient content than industrially grown produce.[60]

When humans neglect vegetables and fruits or prepare them in ways that waste the phytonutrient content, they miss out on the protective armor provided by phytonutrients. They leave themselves naked to the onslaught of free radicals, which is constant and devastating, and to a host of other destructive forces. This is because the human body never developed these protections itself and traditionally depended on getting these protections through plant consumption.

---

57 Willett, *Eat, Drink and Be Healthy*, 176-181. Willett provides an informative discussion about the role of antioxidants in protecting human cells and tissues. Shanahan, Deep Nutrition, 140-142. Shanahan presents a clear and easy to remember description of free radical destruction, also called oxidative stress.
58 Robinson, *Eating on the Wild Side*, 25.
59 Ibid., 3-17. Robinson provides a brief overview of how human selection of food plants and industrial farming have transformed the phytonutrient content of foods.
60 Pollan, *In Defense of Food*, 119-120; Mateljan, *The World's Healthiest Foods*, 2nd edition, 465. Pollan notes that without the protection of chemical pesticides, organically produced vegetables and fruits must be more reliant on phytonutrients. Accordingly, in comparison to industrially produced produce, certified organic produce generally develops more phytonutrients. Mateljan points out a specific phytonutrient difference. He notes that certified organic vegetables and fruits contain significantly higher content of flavonoids than counterpart industrially grown vegetables and fruits.

Fiber

Vegetables and fruits in general contain two main kinds of dietary fiber: **soluble** and **insoluble**. Both forms of fiber are edible parts of plants that cannot be digested (dissolved and broken down for absorption) by humans, including the skin, membranes, and woody/fibrous parts, such as stems and roots. All vegetables and fruits contain both forms in varying degrees, with one form predominating in some and with some having high quantities of both. Both soluble and insoluble fibers, in turn, come in a variety of sub-types.[61] A third category of dietary fiber has recently been added, one called resistant starch.

Science has long established that both insoluble and soluble forms of fiber play crucial roles in maintaining human intestinal health, but recent research using modern technology has brought about an explosion in knowledge about fiber and, as a result, in human understanding of the complexity of the roles that fiber plays in human health.[62]

Soluble Fiber

Examples of fruits and vegetables with significant soluble fiber content are prunes and plums, avocados, berries, ripe bananas, asparagus, the skin of apples and pears, broccoli, carrots, Jerusalem artichokes, garlic, sweet potatoes, and onions.

Soluble fiber dissolves in water. It attracts and holds water and forms itself into a **viscous gel** during digestion. This gel slows both the emptying of the stomach and the transit of food through the intestinal tract, and this slowing serves important bodily functions. Slowing, for example, delays the absorption of glucose by the blood, which helps stabilize blood sugar levels. The gel also shields carbohydrates from destructive enzymes. Some viscous gels bind to bile acids in the small intestine, which has the effect of reducing body cholesterol.

When the viscous gel passes into the large intestine, it is **prebiotic**. It serves as the necessary food of the massive colonies of bacteria living in the digestive tract, also called the gastrointestinal micro-flora. Modern research is confirming that this gut bacteria, which constitutes a world in itself (it is composed of as many as 10,000 individual species of bacteria,[63] with different colonies occupying different parts of the large intestine and with different colonies feeding upon specific kinds of fiber) plays a bigger and a far more amazing role in human health than previously appreciated or even imagined. A form of stewardship exists between the beneficial bacteria and the human

---

61 Examples of insoluble fibers are cellulose, hemicellulose, lignin, plant waxes, and resistant starch. Parts of produce that have rich cellulose content are broccoli stalks, the fibrous tops of leeks, carrot peels, and celery fibers. Examples of soluble fiber compounds are beta-glucans, pectins, natural gums, fructans (inulin and oligofructose fibers together), oligosaccharides, and resistant dextrins.

62 Of particular interest is the connection of intestinal health to brain health and function. Three informative articles about fiber are as follows:
Gretel H. Schueller, "The World Within," *Eating Well* (July/August 2014): 82-88. This interesting article updates known information about the human gut microbiome. In particular she introduces readers to the fascinating work in progress of scientific researcher Jeff Leach, a human microbe field researcher. The illustrations by Tremendousness are excellent as well.
Michael Specter, "Germs Are Us: Bacteria Make Us Sick. Do They Also Keep Us Alive?" *The New Yorker* (October 22, 2012). Specter provides an eye-opening, illuminating, and fascinating look at the role of microorganisms in human health. Specter states: "… the human body turns out to be a vast, highly mutable ecosystem – each of us seems more like a farm than like an individual assembled from a rulebook of genetic instructions."
Shaun Dreisbach, "You Need This," *Eating Well* (March/April 2016): 100-106.

63 Specter, "Germs Are Us: Bacteria Make Us Sick. Do They Also Keep Us Alive?" Specter informs us that microorganisms occupy other body parts as well as the human gut and that the total population forms a three-pound mass, which is the weight of the human brain.

body. The beneficial bacteria live off the indigestible soluble fiber provided by the human diet while playing the invaluable role of fending off bad varieties of bacteria that can undermine intestinal health.

Beneficial gut bacteria provide an abundance of other services as well. A particularly important (perhaps most important) human health-promoting role played by gut bacteria is fermenting soluble fiber, which they do in the process of metabolizing it. This fermentation produces a variety of valuable by-products that benefit human health and are even critical to the health of the colon. In particular, fermentation produces short-chain fatty acids (SCFA), and these SCFAs are involved in numerous significant physiological processes that promote human health. Research shows, for example, that SCFAs are involved in such critically important biological processes as:

- stabilizing blood glucose.
- suppressing cholesterol synthesis by the liver, which reduces blood levels of harmful cholesterol and triglycerides.
- enhancing mineral absorption (calcium and magnesium).
- manufacturing of vitamins (vitamin K and some B vitamins, such as folate).
- strengthening the immune system.
- protecting the colon wall from inflammation, thereby preventing inflammatory bowel disorders (such as Crohn's disease and ulcerative colitis) and reducing the risk of colon cancer.
- producing hormones that control appetite (and, hence, that relate to obesity) and anxiety.

A very interesting point about SCFAs is that different kinds of soluble fiber produce different kinds of SCPA, and each particular SCPA provides distinctive health benefits. Accordingly, the greater variety of rich soluble fiber-containing vegetables and fruits eaten, the greater variety of health benefits received. Conversely, to ignore these vegetables is to miss out on significant health-building opportunities.

Several crucial overall points about soluble fiber cannot be overstated.

- Neglecting to include the vegetables and fruits providing soluble fiber in an everyday diet, whether outright by avoiding vegetables and fruits or through use of fiber-wasting food preparation practices, is to miss out on a wide variety of enormously significant protections that gut bacteria provide and to leave one's intestine defenseless against bad bacteria except through use of antibiotics.
- If over time the good bacteria themselves do not get enough fiber to eat, they also eventually begin to eat the cells lining the colon, which leads to inflammation and, in turn, to deadly health problems.
- Vegetables and fruits contain different combinations of soluble fiber, with different plant parts containing different varieties of fiber and different types of fiber performing somewhat different functions. For example, broccoli is typically listed as a good source of soluble fiber, but it is only a modest source of the soluble fiber called fructan fibers, which serve as prebiotics, food for feeding intestinal flora. The white portion of leeks is an excellent source of soluble fructan fibers but not the green top, which is a source of the insoluble fiber cellulose.

- Preparation affects soluble fiber. Soluble fiber can be washed from cut vegetables and fruits, and cooking can break soluble fiber down, which reduces the chances the fiber will make it through the stomach and into the large intestine where it can be fermented by microbes and converted into human health supportive form.

Insoluble Fiber

Examples of vegetables and fruits with significant insoluble fiber content include green beans, cauliflower, zucchini, celery, avocados, and the skins of potatoes, kiwifruit, grapes, and tomatoes.

Insoluble fibers do not dissolve in water. Certain insoluble fibers are metabolically inert. They are bulking fibers that have the valuable capacity to absorb and retain lots of water. In absorbing water, the fibers increase the bulk and softness of stools and, as a result, ease and speed the passage of food through the intestinal tract. In easing human defecation, insoluble fiber enables humans to avoid constipation and other intestinal problems like hemorrhoids and diverticulitis. In speeding the transit of food through the colon, bulky insoluble fiber also keeps soluble fiber and the masses of bacteria feeding on it evenly spread throughout the colon. This means fermentation will take place all along the length of the colon. Without insoluble fiber, most of the fermentation would take place in the top part of the colon so that the colon cells there would get most of the protective benefits provided by fermentation, which include protection from such serious colon problems as Crohn's disease and even cancer.

Some insoluble fibers are prebiotic. Though typically insoluble fiber compounds have partial or low fermentability in comparison to soluble fiber, some insoluble fibers also serve as food for bacteria in the colon. Bacteria ferment this fiber into gases and healthful compounds, including the short-chained fatty acids (SCFAs), which perform a wide variety of human-health promoting services.

Soluble and insoluble fiber share some human health-promoting characteristics. In addition to some of both being fermentable, both serve to maintain the intestinal acid-alkaline pH balance. They also both increase food volume – adding bulk and weight to meals – without increasing caloric content. In giving early signals of satiety and prolonging the feeling of satiety, fiber supports appetite control and aids in weight maintenance.

The same crucial points about the human health value of soluble fiber apply to insoluble fiber. If people neglect insoluble fiber, throwing away skins and preferring to drink no-pulp juice and to eat smooth-textured pureed foods that do not contain ingredients that they need to chew, they are sabotaging the smooth functioning of important bodily processes and bringing on health problems that range from terrifically irritating to deadly.

Resistant Starch Dietary Fiber

Resistant starch fiber is a form of starch (or carbohydrate) that "resists" being broken down, digested, and absorbed. It passes unchanged into the large intestine where it provides the same benefits as both soluble and insoluble fiber. One notable function is that it helps people feel full for a longer period after eating. It is found in such foods as seeds, unprocessed whole grains, legumes, potatoes, green vegetables, nuts, and fruits (such as bananas).

Omega-3 Essential Fatty Acids

Alpha linolenic acid (ALA) is primarily found in the leaves and other green parts of plants. It is, as a result, the most abundant form of fat on earth.[64] An integral part of plants' complex photosynthetic machinery, this fat enables plants to convert sunlight into sugars, the essential basis of plant life.[65] ALA is the parent form of other omega-3 essential fatty acids, all of which belong to the broader group of polyunsaturated fats that are distinguished from other types of fats by having special connections called "double bonds". The particular position of the double bonds contained in omega-3 essential fatty acids is unique and not found in other fats. While scientific research generally established the importance of omega-3 essential fatty acids to normal human growth in the 1930s, awareness of the specific health benefits of this form of fat only began expanding in the 1980s. Most health benefits identified so far have been linked to the more complicated offspring forms of ALA, the EPA form (eicosapentaenoic acid) and DHA form (docosahexaenoic acid). However, the ALA form is of compelling importance because the human body by itself cannot make either the DHA or EPA form. It must obtain them from food. The human body can, however, create both forms from ALA through consumption of a variety of vegetables and fruits.

Both the EPA and DHA forms of omega-3 essential fatty acids are involved in many extremely important bodily systems and, accordingly, are associated with decreased risk of many chronic health conditions.

- **The DHA form of omega-3 essential fatty acids enables humans to perform tasks requiring particularly speedy action.** Such tasks are those required in the functioning of the human brain, eyes, heart, and sperm.[66] DHA, accordingly, is intricately connected with humans' thinking capacity. It is found in concentrated amounts in the human brain, where it makes up 15-20 percent of the fat content of the brain and functions to enable nerve cells to send their rapid signals. The brain is highly sensitive to changes in DHA content, and any drop in this amount results in neurological problems.[67] These problems include neurodegenerative diseases (like Parkinson's disease), cognitive problems (like reasoning ability in children), and other brain problems (like dementia) and mental health problems, such as depression and postpartum depression, attention deficit disorder, and bipolar disorder.[68] DHA is intricately connected with the proper functioning of the human nervous system, allowing nerves everywhere to send their rapid signals. DHA is found in smaller amounts in cell membranes throughout the human body, where it acts like oil added to an engine,[69] enhancing flexibility and allowing cell reactions to take place faster.[70] DHA is connected with metabolism, acting to speed metabolism.[71] In being connected with metabolism, DHA deficiency plays a role in metabolic disorders, such as diabetes and obesity.[72]

---

64 Learning this, the author now understands how her horses become so fat eating lush grass in their pasture.
65 Allport, *The Queen of Fats*, 4.
66 Allport, *The Queen of Fats*, 12-13.
67 Pollan, *In Defense of Food*, 124.
68 Allport, *The Queen of Fats*, 114.
69 Ibid., 6.
70 Ibid., 126. Allport reports comments about DHA given to her by Burton Litman, a DHA researcher of the National Institute of Health. He describes how DHA makes cell membranes "leaky" and fluid, characteristics which enable the proteins, enzymes, and receptors that are embedded in the cells of membrane to move around freely and do the things they need to do.
71 Ibid., 8 and 151.
72 Ibid., "The Speed of Life," 120-137.

- **The EPA form of omega-3 essential fatty acids is intimately connected with cell communication in humans.** Cells release fatty acids from their membranes as a means of sending messages to other cells in order to affect each other's behavior,[73] and whether the message sender is either EPA-related or omega-6 fatty acids-related dramatically affects the message sent. Fatty acids, for example, direct the functioning of the human inflammatory system. This system depends on a substance called **prostaglandins**, and these prostaglandins can be made from either EPA or omega-6 fatty acids depending on which form successfully competes to get into cell membranes. EPA-associated prostaglandins send messages that have moderating, calming, and slowing effect on cell inflammatory responses while omega-6 fatty acids-associated prostaglandin messages, in contrast, are strongly pro-inflammatory. EPA-associated prostaglandins, as a result, play an important balancing role. When EPA-associated prostaglandins are able to play this balancing role (for example, when the human body is able to create adequate EPA from ALA or when a human does not over-consume omega-6 fatty acids, which crowds out omega-3 fats), they lower inflammation and the risk of getting inflammation-related diseases, such as rheumatoid arthritis, Alzheimer's, lupus, heart disease, stroke, and asthma.[74] When EPA-associated prostaglandins play a balancing role, they provide the same inflammation-calming effect as the commonly taken anti-inflammatory drugs aspirin, ibuprofen, and acetaminophen, but EPA-associated prostaglandins provide this calming without the costs and negative effects of these drugs.[75]
- **DHA and EPA together are closely connected to coronary health.** One of their most important health functions is that they reduce the risk of heart attack and stroke. DHA deficiency is directly related to heart problems, being intricately involved in such potentially fatal problems as irregular heartbeat (arrhythmia) and the build-up of brittle plaque in arteries.[76] EPA serves to reduce platelet stickiness. When EPA-associated prostaglandins are present in cells, blood vessels can use them as an anti-aggregating agent for avoiding the formation of blood clots. Omega-6 fatty acids-associated prostaglandins, in comparison, have an aggregating effect on platelet formation.[77]

A wide variety of vegetables and fruits are good sources of omega-3 essential fatty acids, ALA form.

- Examples of *very good* sources include Brussels sprouts, cauliflower, winter squash, and avocado.
- Examples of *good* sources are green leafy vegetables (such as spinach, Swiss chard, turnip greens, collard greens, and kale), leek, raspberry, strawberry, and Jerusalem artichoke.

While these vegetables and fruits do not contribute omega-3 essential fatty acids, ALA form, in amounts comparable to foods like flax seeds, the amounts they contribute are nutritionally relevant because these vegetables and fruits come perfectly packaged for assisting the human body in first

---

73 Ibid., 6.
74 Pollan, *In Defense of Food*, 128-129.
75 Allport, *The Queen of Fats*, 100.
76 Ibid., 115.
77 Ibid., 64.

absorbing the omega-3 ALA content and then in converting it into the two other essential fatty acid forms. These vegetables and fruits, for example,

- contain the micronutrients known to be needed by the body for using ALA, including vitamin E, the minerals magnesium and zinc, and the vitamins B3, B6, and vitamin C.
- are rich sources of phytonutrients. ALA form of omega-3 essential fatty acids is highly vulnerable to oxidation, and the phytonutrient contents of these vegetables and fruits are antioxidants that protect the omega-3 essential fatty acids from oxidation and the destructive free radicals released by oxidation both before (during photosynthesis) and after they are eaten by humans.
- can be eaten raw. All omega-3 essential fatty acids-containing fruits and many vegetables, including immature greens, can be included in salads and snacks. Eating these foods raw results in maximum conservation of ALA omega-3 essential fatty acids because of the extreme sensitivity of this fat to heat.

The importance of vegetables and fruits as a source of omega-3 essential fatty acids has increased because of the loss of other important sources in the everyday diet of modern consumers, especially, but not only, Americans. Before industrial food production assumed prominence in agriculture in the mid-20th century, cattle, dairy cows, and poultry used for making food products ate leaves as part of their regular diet. As a result, the food products derived from them were good sources of omega-3 essential fatty acids (ALA)[78] and maintained a good omega-6 to omega-3 ratio (one that had more omega-3 than omega-6 fatty acids), which enhances the human body's ability to convert ALA into DHA and EPA. As certified organic dairy cows must spend at least four months per year in a pasture eating grass, certified organic milk and products made from certified organic milk remain good sources of omega-3 essential fatty acids.[79] With the industrialization of meat, dairy, poultry, and egg production, however, the food fed to animals and poultry was switched from grass to grain, and to corn in particular, which has a very unbalanced omega-6 to omega-3 fatty acid imbalance (46:1). As a result, today most meat, dairy, and poultry products consumed by Americans contribute mainly omega-6 essential fatty acids, reducing sources of omega-3 essential fatty acids in everyday diets and dramatically unbalancing the naturally established ratio.

Other significant food developments have effectively cancelled out and made irrelevant the omega-3 essential fatty acid content obtained through consumption of vegetables and fruits. These developments have worked together to promote the inclusion of omega-6 essential fatty acids in the American diet at the expense of omega-3 essential fatty acids.

- Industrial agribusinesses began to produce massive amounts of corn, sunflowers, cotton, peanuts, and soybeans, which dropped the price of these crops.
- Technology was developed that enabled food processors to squeeze every drop of oil from the seeds of these crops.
- Food processors began using this technology to convert oil-containing crops into massive amounts of inexpensive highly refined omega-6 fatty acids-rich oil for use in processed food products as well as for consumers to use in home cooking. Because omega-3 fatty acids are unstable and vulnerable to rancidity, all omega-3 fatty acids were (and are)

---

78 Pollan, *In Defense of Food*, 126.
79 Tom Philpott, "Organic Milk Proves Higher in Healthy Fats: And It's All About the Grass," *Mother Jones* (December 13, 2013).

removed in order to expand the storage life of oil.[80] A significant amount of the oil was also converted into partially hydrogenated oil for use in such products as margarine, and this processing effectively destroys omega-3 fatty acids content while increasing the content of omega-6 fatty acids.
- Plant biologists began selecting for low alpha linolenic varieties of soybeans with the goal of improving stability and cutting down on hydrogenation costs.[81] Most soybean oil, as a result, joined other oils with high omega-6 fatty acid content.
- Governmental dietary guidelines began to advise consumers to use this "pure" omega-6 fatty acids-rich vegetable oil and partially hydrogenated oil as healthy alternatives to saturated fat, which as a dietary source of cholesterol was declared to be the cause of heart disease.[82]

These developments resulted in a dramatic alteration of the traditional ratio of omega-6 to omega-3 fatty acids consumed in the everyday diet of American consumers, and this alteration has far-reaching negative effect on human health. Today all pure vegetable oils except for canola oil (and reliably only certified organic canola oil) have highly unbalanced omega-6 to omega-3 ratios. For example, cottonseed oil, commonly used in commercially prepared salad dressings has a stunning 259:1 ratio! Safflower oil scarcely contains any omega-3 fatty acids at all, which gives it a 115:1 ratio.[83] While most other oils do not have such lopsided ratios in favor of omega-6 fatty acids, and the ratio is typically 10:1,[84] the change is significantly different from the natural ratio, which had traditionally been one slightly favoring omega-3 fatty acids. The effect of this unbalancing is highly destructive of omega-3 fatty acids. Because omega-6 fatty acids and omega-3 fatty acids are competitive, with the acids competing for enzymes and space in membranes of cells, omega-6 fatty acids win out and completely crowd out and effectively eliminate omega-3 fatty acids.[85] As long as people's tissues are filled with omega-6 fatty acids, omega-3 fatty acids content is effectively voided or reduced to very low levels, no matter how many omega-3 rich foods, such as greens, one eats and also no matter the amount of fish or fish capsules one consumes.[86] This situation means that conservation of omega-3 essential fatty acids requires a different strategy from that used to conserve other nutritional components of vegetables and fruits. Applying conservation preparation techniques and expanding use of omega-3 fatty acids-rich vegetables and fruits is clearly not enough. People must also dramatically reduce consumption of omega-6 essential fatty acids. Because excessive consumption of saturated fat also results in the crowding out of omega-3 fatty acids in membranes, saturated fat content must be moderated as well.

---

80   Allport, *The Queen of Fats*, 107. Allport reports the statement made to her by a Frito-Lay official: "Processed foods and alpha linolenic acid [omega-3 fatty acids, ALA form] are incompatible…it is ten times less stable than linoleic acid [omega-6 fatty acids], so it cannot be used in processed foods."
81   Allport, *The Queen of Fats*, 110. Now biologists are selecting for low linolenic acid rapeseed used to make canola oil. While canola oil naturally has a beneficial omega 6 to omega-3 ratio, these changes reduce omega-3 content.
82   Ibid., 55. In the 1980's the prevailing advice given to Americans by health authorities was that the most effective way to prevent the buildup of brittle plaque in arteries was to reduce their intake of saturated fat, which contains dietary cholesterol. This advice stood until 2015 when it was effectively challenged by a group of international scientists. In the intervening decades this advice effectively caused massive numbers of American consumers and restaurants to switch from saturated fat to omega-6 fatty acids-rich pure vegetable oil for use in cooking.
83   Ibid., 117.
84   Pollan, *In Defense of Food*, 127.
85   Allport, *The Queen of Fats*, 82. Allport points out that in a natural ratio, omega-3 typically wins. She effectively pictures the changed competitive situation when omega-6s fill body cells: "Picture 115 women and 1 man all trying to get through the same small door. Though bigger and can push through the crowd, he doesn't stand much of a chance."
86   Ibid., 113.

Conserving the Vitality of Vegetables and Fruits

In *Cooked Alive!*, basic Part I recipes for preparing vegetables and fruits routinely apply simple conservation techniques from the beginning to the end of the preparation process, covering the selection, storage, preparation, and serving of vegetables and fruits. These conservation techniques – *juice-protective* preparation techniques that maximize retention of juice within the protective cell structure of vegetables and fruits – retain the vitality, or aliveness, of vegetables and fruits, converting them into super actors with the capacity to transform the modern everyday diet into healthful form. With the application of *juice-protective* techniques, Part I *Cooked Alive!* recipes reliably yield prepared vegetables and fruits with three distinctive characteristics. These three characteristics and the link of each to a transformed diet are as follows:

> **First, *juice-protected* vegetables and fruits are genuinely attractive and tasty.** Individual prepared vegetables and fruits retain naturally sweet and distinctive flavor, retain natural vivid coloring, are juicy, and have an attractive texture. Family and friends readily accept and consume them. Cooks can easily expand use of vegetables and fruits in everyday eating.

> **Second, *juice-protected* vegetables and fruits are independently attractive and tasty.** Retaining natural flavoring, vivid coloration, and attractive juiciness, individual *juice-protected* vegetables and fruits can in fact serve as side dishes and snacks that stand on their own with minimal use of outside flavoring. These dishes add negligible amounts of salt, sugar, and fat to a meal.

> **Third, *juice-protected* vegetables and fruits are reliably nutritious.** *Juice-protective* techniques maximize over-all conservation of nutritional content.

> - In conserving juice, *juice-protective* techniques conserve all water soluble nutritional components carried in juice.
> - In maximizing retention of natural plant structures in order to retain juice within vegetables and fruits, *juice-protective* techniques conserve the insoluble fiber and the fat-soluble phytonutrients and micronutrients contained in pulp and skin.
> - In minimizing cooking to avoid overcooking, which breaks down cell structures and releases juice, *juice-protective* techniques minimize loss of heat-sensitive nutrients and phytonutrients.
> - In using extra virgin olive oil, which has a relatively balanced omega-3 to omega-6 essential fatty acid ratio, Part I recipes do not waste the natural omega-3 essential fatty acid content of vegetables and fruits. Extra virgin olive oil is also a monounsaturated oil that remains stable during moderate heating.[87]

---

[87] Shanahan, *Deep Nutrition*, 134-143. Pure vegetable oils, in contrast, are not stable during heating. This is because pure vegetable oil (including canola, corn, soy, sunflower, cottonseed, safflower, rice bran, and grapeseed) mostly contains heat-sensitive polyunsaturated fat, which means it easily oxidizes when heated, and this chemical reaction (oxidation) produces free radicals that are highly destructive to the human body. All pure vegetable oils, excluding peanut oil, are highly reactive (vulnerable to oxidation) because they are nutritionally stripped of natural vitamin E and other natural antioxidant content that keeps vegetable oil stable. Heating, as a result, easily distorts and degrades the vegetable oil, leading to the formation of deadly free radicals and turning the oil into toxic compounds including trans fat. When oxidized vegetable oil is consumed, its free radical activity and vulnerability to free radical activity becomes dangerous to normal omega-3 fatty acids contained in the body, but the free radicals can also damage almost any part of the human body, including the human brain. See "Brain Killer" (163-206) for a concise and terrifying description of how oxidized vegetable oil demolishes the human brain.

With the application of *juice-protective* preparation techniques, Part I recipes yield prepared vegetables and fruits that retain as close to full nutritional potency as is possible right up to the moment they are eaten. They are nutritional goldmines with enormous health-promoting capacity.

The utility of *juice-protected* vegetables and fruits, however, extends far beyond using them as side dishes and snacks. Mixing them directly into main dishes serves as a way to multiply the nutritional contribution they can make to everyday eating. Indeed such mixing has an explosive effect. Transferring all of the distinctive characteristics of *juice-protected* vegetables and fruits into a dish, mixing dramatically upgrades the nutritional quality of a dish. On the one hand, *juice-protected* vegetables and fruits boost the diversity and richness of the nutritional components contained in a dish, ensuring important human nutritional needs are met. For example, needed micronutrients are available for the efficient processing of macronutrients contained in a dish; multiple varieties of phytonutrients are available to bolster protection from free radicals, inflammation, and toxins; varied fiber is provided to ensure beneficial intestinal flora flourishes and plays innumerable health-supporting roles. Of equal importance, *juice-protected* vegetables and fruits serve as invaluable flavoring ingredients in the dish. When using *juice-protected* vegetables and fruits as flavoring, cooks can successfully make important nutritionally enhancing ingredient changes in a dish and, very importantly, do so without basically altering the traditional nature of the dish and, hence, its consumer acceptability. Serving as a pleasantly moist, tasty, and juicy flavoring base in dishes, *juice-protected* vegetables and fruits, for example,

- can successfully substitute for and essentially replace commercially processed flavoring ingredients commonly used in dishes, such as commercially prepared salad dressing, processed meats (such as bacon and pepperoni), processed cheese, and canned soups. Cooks making this substitution take a giant step in eliminating fat-, sugar-, salt-, and chemically-laden commercially prepared flavoring products from their diet.
- support the substitution of whole for nutritionally stripped refined grain ingredients, such as brown for white rice and whole for white flour, which are dish ingredient changes that enhance both the nutritional diversity and energy-sustaining capacity of a dish.
- support the substitution of lean for fatty or processed meat and the reduction of the meat content of a dish, steps that enable cooks to take advantage of high quality grass-fed meat and to secure the healthfulness of meat as a dish ingredient.
- welcome the addition of small amounts of such nutrient dense whole foods as raw nuts, legumes, and dried fruits, which serve to enhance the nutritional diversity and health-promoting capacity of a dish.

In its Part II recipes, *Cooked Alive!* takes full advantage of the nutritional boosting and flavoring capacity of *juice-protected* vegetables and fruits by mixing them directly into a variety of popular traditional recipes. This mixing transforms these recipes into a form that yields dishes that are genuinely nutritious, attractive, and tasty all at the same time. Because this mixing also essentially preserves the traditional character and appearance of dishes, Part II recipes, it is important to note, also retain full (and perhaps greater) consumer acceptability despite the enormous nutritional upgrading provided. Family and friends will readily accept and enjoy them. Cooks can feel great satisfaction in preparing Part II recipes.

That *Cooked Alive!* focuses on traditional dishes is because of the mainstream character of these dishes. They are "any person" dishes, popular with the vast majority of the American public as well as having wide global consumer appeal and, hence, are helpful to the greatest number of consumers. It is important to note, however, that Part II recipes illustrate *Cooked Alive!*'s central point that transforming vegetable and fruit use provides the underlying key for consumers to resurrect the nutritional quality of their everyday eating and to take control of their health. Accordingly, transforming vegetable and fruit use provides the key to resurrecting the nutritional quality of dishes in general. Part I recipes, which focus on the preparation of *individual* vegetables and fruits, are fully relevant to and helpful for cooks of any diet whatsoever, be it traditional vegetarian, vegan, paleo, or another form of preferred eating. Part II recipes serve as models for effectively building *juice-protected* vegetables and fruits into dishes and for harnessing the vast nutritional boosting and human health protection they can provide.

In sum, Part II recipes that make *juice-protected* vegetables and fruits "top gun" ingredients give cooks and consumers nutritional security and nutritional peace of mind. There is no confusion whatsoever about the nutritional quality of the dishes. Cooks and consumers alike can feel liberated from the fear of fat. Cooks who prepare Part II recipes can be fully confident that their dishes will without a doubt contribute directly to their own health and vitality and to the health and vitality of those who dine with them.

One final crucial point that *Cooked Alive!* would like to make clear is that though Part I and Part II recipes generally do not direct the selection of certified organic products, instead letting cooks make dish ingredient selections on the basis of economic ability and product availability, *Cooked Alive!* does emphatically support the selection of these naturally produced food products. Reference #1 (Selecting Top Quality Fresh Whole Vegetables and Fruits) and Reference #4 (Selecting Top Quality Whole Food Ingredients for Use in Part II Recipes) spell out the nutritional and environmental significance of selecting certified organic and locally produced products. While making *juice-protected* vegetables and fruits central food ingredients in everyday eating is by itself an effective means of dramatically transforming the health-building and health-maintaining capacity of one's diet, the widespread tainting with pesticides and the general chemical manipulation of industrially produced produce is rapidly deepening the danger of industrially produced food to human health and intensifying the wisdom of maximizing the selection of certified organic and locally produced produce as far as is possible.[88] The more cooks make this extra investment in their health, the more securely these cooks remove themselves and their loved ones from the "sitting duck" health category – that vast group of humans who are awaiting being hit by debilitating or deadly health problems that inevitably arise from processed food dependence.

Maximizing Recipe Usability

While conservation of the natural flavor, color, and attractive texture of vegetables and fruits is the primary strategy that Cooked Alive! uses for achieving the serving success of its recipes, its recipes have a variety of other features that make them reliable and user friendly and, hence, realistically within the reach of cooks in general, including both the busiest and least experienced cooks.

- **Recipes are tried and true.** Recipes are products of a lifetime investment in whole food cooking, one based on extensive cooking practice and deliberate experimentation.

---

88   Timothy Egan, "Poisons are Us," *The New York Times* (April 14, 2017). Egan informs readers of the weakening of federal government public health protections regarding industrial agriculture's use of toxic chemical pesticides on fresh fruits and vegetables and of the perils to human health of this action. Egan notes, for example, that the government is removing a ban on the use of the chemical compound chlorpyrifos, which has been found to be harmful to the brain and nervous system of children.

- **Recipes primarily use two quick and simple cooking methods – skillet stir-frying and skillet stir-fry/steaming – for cooking vegetables.** These are simple cooking methods that can be used with almost 100% of vegetables. They are comfortable cooking methods that for most vegetables reliably yield attractive cooking results within minutes.
- **Part II chapters largely rely on master recipes.** In this system, one reliably attractive flavoring base serves a number of recipes (sometimes many). Recipes within a master recipe group use one flavoring base with a variety of different vegetables, which provides cooks the opportunity to successfully experiment with a variety of vegetables. Recipes within a master recipe group also vary protein ingredients, which can be beef, chicken, eggs, and/or legumes. Cooks, as a result, have the opportunity to vary protein according to taste and food preference. In learning one flavoring base, cooks gain a variety of reliably attractive recipes.
- **Recipe steps are fully detailed to maximize preparation ease and success.** Cooks easily and confidently walk through each step of the preparation process. At the same time, every Part II chapter includes additional preparation details to aid cooks in achieving serving success. Each chapter introduction, for example, includes a "Preparation Notes" section that summarizes or draws attention to key preparation points. Most chapters include a "clinching flavor" reference, which makes suggestions for maximizing the flavor of individual dish ingredients.
- **Most recipes yield 2-3 servings.** Recipes, as a result, accommodate the now common single and two-person family. At the same time recipes easily expand to 4-6 serving size.
- **Recipes use reliably attractive whole food ingredients**. As with vegetables and fruits, recipes prepare other whole foods – such as brown and wild rice, whole wheat flour, lentils, fresh beefsteak and poultry, and eggs – using techniques that are carefully matched to the particular whole characteristics of these foods. This matching predictably yields attractive cooking results, which is a basic key to the successful integration of whole food ingredients into Part II dishes. *Cooked Alive!* goes beyond adapting preparation techniques to whole food characteristics in individual recipes. It also includes two references specifically focused on enhancing whole food attractiveness. Reference #6 (Maximizing the Attractiveness of Whole Food Ingredients Commonly Used in Part II Recipes) contributes a host of helpful suggestions for enhancing the acceptability of a variety of whole food ingredients. Reference #7 (*Juice-Protective* Techniques for Preparing Animal Protein) summarizes *juice-protective* techniques for preparing animal protein.
- **Recipes use many convenient commercially prepared ingredients**. While recipes almost totally exclude pre-flavored and mixed ingredient commercially prepared products, *Cooked Alive!* Part II recipes regularly use a variety of unflavored or flavored only with salt single ingredient commercially prepared products, especially in its sauce recipes. Because significant quality differences exist among alternative single ingredient processed product selections, *Cooked Alive!* includes Reference #5 (Selecting High Quality Processed Ingredients for Use in Part II Recipes) to assist cooks in selecting higher quality ingredients.

PART I

Conserving the Nutritional Quality and Flavoring of *Individual* Vegetables and Fruits

Conservation Strategy Overview

Part I Recipes Routinely Apply *Juice-Protective* Techniques for Preparing Fruits and Vegetables.

PART I RECIPES conserve the vitality of individual vegetables and fruits through application of preparation techniques that protect plant juice. Providing attractive moistening and carrying an invaluable cargo composed of soluble components (including nutritional, flavoring, and coloring components), juice is central to vegetable and fruit nutritional quality, flavor, color, and texture. Juice is, however, highly vulnerable during preparation. Juice easily spills **within** plants where it comes in contact with plant acids that can irrevocably alter flavoring and coloring. Juice also easily spills **from** vegetables and fruits where it comes in contact with other destructive substances including air, light, and liquid, or is discarded. Juice, as a result, requires deliberate protection. Part I recipes provide this protection through use of distinctive *juice-protective* techniques that prevent or minimize spilling of juice during the entire preparation process.

Juice-protective preparation techniques prevent, or minimize, juice spilling or evaporation during preparation in three ways.

First, *juice-protective* preparation techniques maximize retention of natural plant structures. These structures (the skin, pulp, and cell membrane) hold plant juice safely within plants.[89] In addition to retaining skin and minimizing the cutting of pulp, Part I recipes use a variety of simple heating techniques to maximize the keeping of vegetable and fruit cell structure intact. For example, recipes direct cooks to:

---

[89] These *juice-protective* preparation techniques are a modified version of those set forth by Adelle Davis, a very widely respected nutritionist during the l960's and 1970's, in "Serve Your Salads First" (255-279) and "Keep the Flavor and Nutritive Value in Your Vegetables" (308-387) of her *Let's Cook It Right* cookbook (New York, a Signet Book from New American Library, 1970).

- individually cook vegetables and fruits in order to cook them exactly according to the time that cooks them just to tenderness and **before** cell structure breaks down and releases juice content. Recipes never lump vegetables together for cooking unless they have exactly the same cooking times. Lumping of vegetables with different cooking times inevitably results in the overcooking of some vegetables, which results in the breakdown of cell structure and allows juices to spill.
- immediately remove vegetables and fruits from heat (from both the burner and hot skillet) once they are cooked to tenderness to avoid over-cooking.
- quickly re-heat vegetables and fruits just prior to serving to avoid over-cooking. They are added as last ingredients to already hot dishes.

Second, *juice-protective* preparation techniques prevent direct contact between cut pulp and liquid. Because liquid instantly begins to leach juice from cut pulp, Part I recipes direct cooks to:

- dry vegetables and fruits thoroughly before cutting.
- not do any trimming whatsoever to vegetables that will be boiled whole.
- apply a protective oil coating to cut pulp that will come into contact with liquid during cooking.
- set cooked vegetables and fruits aside in a manner that keeps them dry until being assembled for serving, such as placing them in a colander, which allows any spilled juice to drain from them.

Third, *juice-protective* preparation techniques prevent or minimize contact between cut vegetable or fruit pulp and air. Air is destructive of juice in two ways. First, it evaporates juice, dehydrating fruits and vegetables without thick skins. Second, air stimulates plant enzymes in raw pulp. Activated enzymes bring about chemical reactions that are destructive of flavoring (as in the case of onions and garlic) and some nutritional components contained in juice (such as vitamin C content, destruction of which is indicated by browning of cut pulp).

Part I Chapters Present Recipes for *Juice-Protective* Cooking and Serving Raw Methods of Preparing Fruits and Vegetables.

Chapters One, Two, and Three present recipes that use *juice-protective* methods of cooking vegetables. These chapters are:

- **Chapter One: Stir-Fried and Stir-Fry/Steamed Vegetable Recipes.** Stir-frying applies to fastest cooking vegetables. Stir-fry/steaming applies to longer-cooking vegetables. Both methods are comfortable, simple, and fast methods of cooking almost 100% of commonly used vegetables. Chapter One recipes cover preparation steps in detail and includes basic selection, nutritional, and storage information as well.
- **Chapter Two (Dry Roasted Vegetable Recipes)** and **Chapter Three (Boiled Whole Vegetable Recipes)** serve as alternative *juice-protective* methods of cooking. Both are simple cooking methods that yield highly attractive cooked vegetables. Suited to particular vegetables and types of dishes, neither is as versatile as stir-frying and

stir-fry/steaming, which accounts for *Cooked Alive!*'s use of them as alternative cooking methods. Because Chapter One vegetable recipes have already provided basic selection, nutritional, and storage information, Chapter Two and Three recipes are abbreviated to present only basic preparation details needed to apply either a general dry roasting or boiling whole preparation procedure.

Chapters Four and Five present recipes for serving most commonly used fruits and vegetables in raw form, which is the most *juice-protective* preparation method of all. These chapters are:

- **Chapter Four: Raw Fruit Pure and Simple.** These recipes cover most fruits that are commonly served in raw form. Recipes include basic selection, nutritional, and storage information.
- **Chapter Five: Raw or Barely Cooked Vegetable Recipes.** Chapter Five recipes cover most commonly used vegetables. Because Chapter One vegetable recipes have already provided basic selection, nutritional, and storage information for the vegetables included in Chapter Five recipes, Chapter Five recipes are abbreviated to present only basic preparation details.

Part I References Cover the Selection and Storage of Fresh Vegetables and Fruits

For the application of *juice-protective* techniques to result in meaningful conservation of nutritional value and flavoring, cooks must first begin with flavorful and nutrient-rich vegetables and fruits. Accordingly, in addition to *juice-protective* readying, cooking, and serving raw preparation, cooks need to include two other steps in the preparation process: 1) selection of nutritious and flavorful vegetables and fruits and 2) protection of the nutritional quality and flavor of vegetables and fruits during home storage. *Cooked Alive!* attaches the following two references to equip cooks with both necessary information and techniques to use in selecting and storing fresh vegetables and fruits:

- **Reference #1: Selecting Top Quality Fresh Vegetables and Fruits.** Expanding the commonly used definition of whole vegetables and fruits, which narrowly defines wholeness in terms of lifeless physical structure, this reference defines whole vegetables and fruits as those with three equally important characteristics – they are raw, physically intact, and naturally produced. Reference #1 describes each characteristic and its essential tie to nutritional quality.
- **Reference #2: Key Home Storage Guidelines for Conserving Vegetable and Fruit Quality.** This reference equips cooks with specific techniques for effectively preserving the vitality of fresh vegetables and fruits up to the moment they are prepared for serving.

Cooked Alive! draws the attention of readers to an outstanding source of information for locating top quality (most nutritious and tasty) vegetables and fruits. This is the book *Eating on the Wild Side: The Missing Link to Optimum Health* (New York: Little, Brown and Company, 2013) by the author Jo Robinson.

General Cooking Tools for Part I Recipes

A descriptive listing of cooking tools routinely used in Part I recipes is presented below.

- **Brush, scrub.** A scrub brush with firm bristles is necessary for easy and thorough cleaning of vegetables and fruits with rough or bumpy skins.
- **Colander.** An essential tool, a colander should have uniformly spaced holes to provide efficient draining of vegetables and fruits after washing and cooking. Being metal as opposed to plastic enhances efficient drainage and eases cleaning.
- **Cutting board reserved for vegetables and fruits**. A reserved cutting board protects vegetables and fruits being served raw from contamination by raw meat and poultry. It also spares a cook the task of thoroughly washing and drying the board after meat and poultry use. Having nonskid feet or bottom is a helpful cutting board feature. Having a separate cutting board for both vegetables and fruits protects fruit from absorbing onion and garlic flavor.
- **Large cutting board (approx. 16 x 24 in.).** Having an especially large vegetable cutting board immeasurably eases the cutting of bulky green leafy vegetables.
- **Knife, chef's.** Also called a vegetable knife, this is an essential knife for cutting particular vegetables. For example, it easily cuts through long vegetables (such as carrots and celery), large thick vegetables (such as heads of cabbage and cauliflower), firm-fleshed fruits with skin and cores (such as apples and pears), bulb onions with skin, dense root vegetables (such as potatoes, beets, and turnips), and the stems of greens. At the same time, the tapered point and gently rounded blade allows a chef's knife to be used for mincing, dicing, and slicing. The blade of a chef's knife can be from seven to ten inches long. A high quality knife is one made from a continuous piece of metal. This construction provides a firm blade, which is essential for easy, efficient cutting. A knife with a durable blade made from high-carbon stainless steel will both retain sharpness and re-sharpen well. For most comfortable use, the knife should fit one's hand and feel balanced.
- **Knife, paring.** This knife, which typically has a three-inch blade, is very useful for small jobs, such as slicing halved apples and pears, cutting the seeds and pulpy center from pear and apple slices, and cutting fruit from pits. Like a chef's knife, a good paring knife should have a firm, easy-to-sharpen blade.
- **Knife, 5 in. and 7 in. serrated.** The saw-like blade of this type of knife makes it particularly useful for cleanly cutting through juicy and delicate fruits with skins with minimal bruising and juice spilling. A 5 inch serrated knife can serve in place of a paring knife. A 7 inch serrated knife is especially useful for slicing bulky green leafy vegetables. A firm blade is essential for efficient, easy cutting in either size knife. Serrated knives retain sharpness especially well.
- **Knife sharpener.** If this sharpener does not work for both straight and serrated blades, there should be a separate sharpener for each type of blade. For maximum use, the sharpener should be easy to use and stored handy to the food preparation area.
- **Measuring cup set.** This is a set that includes ¼, ⅓, ½, and 1 cup sizes.
- **Measuring spoon set.** This is a set that includes at least ¼ t, ½ t, 1 t, and 1 T spoons. A ⅓ t measure is handy as well. It is useful for the spoons to be attached to a ring to keep them together and easy to find.

- **Vegetable peeler.** When some peeling is necessary, it is important that a peeler remove as little skin as possible. A high quality swivel peeler, such as an "Euro" peeler, with stainless steel blades that can be re-sharpened, is an example of an efficient peeler.
- **Pie plate.** A pie plate is a useful tool for working with small round berries and vegetables. It efficiently collects corn kernels as they are cut from cobs. Any somewhat wide, shallow, and sided container substitutes.
- **Plastic dish scrubber** or **kitchen sponge with both a gentle and rough scrubbing surface.** Both types of scrubbers efficiently clean root vegetables with sturdy and smooth skin, such as beets, carrots, potatoes, and turnips. Both scrubbers also conveniently wrap around narrow foods, such as carrots, for thorough cleaning. The gentle side of a kitchen sponge is a useful tool for performing the "wipe the skillet clean" step in stir-frying and stir-fry/steaming.
- **Plastic wrap.** Wrapping tightly around both even and uneven surfaces, plastic wrap efficiently protects thin-skinned and cut open vegetables from air during storage.
- **Measuring ruler, 12 in. size.** Having a ruler handy is useful and perhaps initially necessary for accurately determining the thickness of slices to be cut and the size of vegetables and fruits (small, medium, or large) called for in recipes.
- **Scissors, kitchen.** Sharp scissors are very useful for performing a variety of cutting tasks, such as snipping tips from green beans and edible pod peas and for snipping fresh herbs and cilantro into serving size pieces.
- **Storage bags, plastic.** Available in both quart and gallon size, plastic bags serve as air-tight containers for storing both cut and whole vegetables and for storing whole fruits with intact skin. Ziploc and zipper bags are easy to open and close. Plastic storage bags have the advantage of being flexible, which allows for a maximum amount of air to be pressed from vegetables before a bag is sealed for storage.
- **Storage containers, glass with air-tight covers.** Glass is ideal for storing cut fruit, which is acidic. Cut fruit can potentially leach chemicals from the plastic during storage.
- **Timer.** An essential cooking tool, a timer should register both seconds and minutes.
- **Towels, terry cloth.** Because the rinsing and drying of both produce and the cook's hands are routine parts of vegetable and fruit preparation, relying on absorptive cotton terry towels rather than paper towels for everyday drying purposes is both an economical and ecologically responsible investment. A convenient terry towel size is 16 x 18 inches.

Quantity Abbreviations Key for Part I Recipes

Tablespoon = T (15 ml)
Teaspoon = t (5 ml)
Cup = c (or 8 oz or ¼ litre)
Quart = qt = 4 cups (or 1 litre)
Ounce = oz
Fluid ounce = fl oz
Pound = lb

1 tablespoon = 3 teaspoons
⅛ cup = 2 tablespoons
¼ c = 4 tablespoons
⅓ c = 5⅓ tablespoons
½ c = 8 tablespoons
1 c = 16 tablespoons

Reference #1

Selecting Top Quality Fresh Whole Vegetables and Fruits

Defining Whole Foods

As COMMONLY USED, the concept of "whole foods" tends to be defined in a way that falls far short of encompassing all that is needed to ensure that the definition implies genuine wholeness and full nutritional quality. Defined narrowly, a whole vegetable or fruit is simply raw and physically intact. It retains all naturally occurring parts in naturally attached form. Structural intactness, however, is only part of the nutritional quality picture. Thus defined, the whole foods label does not serve as a useful guide for selecting the most nutritious vegetables and fruits. Structural intactness casts vegetables and fruits as inert and stable rather than alive foods that are constantly changing and highly perishable. It is precisely their aliveness that makes a variety of other physical indicators vitally relevant in determining the nutritional value of individual vegetables and fruits. Of equal importance in settling what we mean by whole foods is the fact that marketable vegetables and fruits are the end results of an extended production process, and what happens to vegetables and fruits during this lengthy process is directly and immensely relevant to nutritional quality. The extensive tampering that occurs during industrial production of vegetables and fruits – including genetic modification of seeds, use of artificial fertilizer, chemical spraying with pesticides, and other kinds of chemical manipulation – is without a doubt also to be considered processing that affects nutritional quality, but it typically does not get counted as such and instead gets a free pass. This Reference #1, therefore, consciously expands the definition of whole vegetables and fruits to better encompass full nutritional quality and by doing so to better guide cooks in selecting genuinely nutritious vegetables and fruits.

Reference #1 defines top quality whole vegetables and fruits as those having three equally important characteristics: they are **raw**, **physically intact**, and **naturally produced**. It describes in some detail the essential link of each of these characteristics with the nutritional quality of vegetables and fruits. In describing raw and physically intact vegetables and fruits, Reference #1 thus identifies a variety of physical traits as necessary complementary indicators of peak nutritional value, attractiveness, and phytonutrient content. In describing natural production, Reference #1 pointedly links what it labels *natural* production of vegetables and fruits with *unprocessed* condition. It thus compares natural and industrial production in terms of the processing involved – lack of processing in the case of natural production and massive processing in the case of industrial production – to demonstrate the hugely different impact of natural and industrial production on the nutritional quality of vegetables and fruits.

Rawness and Intact Physical Structure as Essential Whole Food Indicators

Both rawness and intact structure directly correlate with full naturally occurring nutritional content and flavor of vegetables and fruits. Rawness indicates aliveness while intact physical structure maintains the freshness of foods. Intact structure indicates effective protection of inner flesh and plant juice – and the nutritional and flavoring components they carry – from contact with destructive air, light, moisture, molds, bacteria, and insects. Raw and intact vegetables and fruits reach the kitchens of home cooks in fully alive and vital form, giving the home cook the opportunity to retain maximum nutritional content and flavor during preparation.

Intact structure has specific physical characteristics.

1. **Skin is intact**. Skin is also the main defense of a vegetable or fruit against light and air, which can both evaporate juice and also activate enzymes that are destructive of juice flavor and nutritional content. To provide this protection, skin:

    - is not peeled.
    - retains flexibility, moistness, and elasticity so that it is tight and supplies effective protection.
    - is not broken open, punctured, or thinned by removal of outer layers of skin during handling for marketing (as is often the case of bulb onions and cabbage), which allows air and contaminating bacteria or mold to enter the plant.
    - does not show any sign of mold.

2. **Leaves, stems, and plant parts are attached.** Removal of leaves, stems (except stems of small berries), and pits makes an entrance through which air and bacteria can enter the inner flesh. Separation of parts initiates natural plant responses that result in loss of nutritional content. Listed below are descriptions of vegetables marketed in freshest and most nutritious form.

    - The leaves of naturally bunched plants (such as looseleaf lettuce and spinach) remain attached to a bottom stem. Removal and separate bagging of leaves undermines both the freshness and phytonutrient content of the vegetable.
    - Bottom leaves of cauliflower fit tightly around bottom cauliflower florets.
    - At least some outer cabbage leaves remain wrapped around a cabbage, and the same goes for individual Brussels sprouts. Brussels sprouts attached to the stalk are a prize.
    - The leafy tops of beets, turnips, parsnips, carrots, and celery remain attached.
    - Kohlrabi retains its stalks and the leafy tops of these stalks.
    - Fennel bulb retains its feathery topped stalks.
    - Cauliflower florets remain attached to the cauliflower head.
    - Broccoli florets remain attached to a broccoli stalk.[90]
    - Green peas remain in shells.
    - Cherries are not pitted and remain attached to stems.
    - Grapes remain attached to stems that are attached to a vine.

3. **Pulp is intact.** It has not been cut into pieces, shredded, pureed, mashed, or otherwise broken open.

---

90 Robinson, *Eating on the Wild Side*. 162. Robinson reports that when broccoli is separated into florets, the vegetable "responds to the injury by doubling its already rapid rate of respiration. It uses up so much of its sugar and antioxidants that little is left for you."

Complementary Physical Indicators of the Nutritional Quality of Vegetables and Fruits

Vegetables and fruits continue to be alive after being harvested, and as alive foods they are constantly changing foods. They contain active enzymes that continually drive both ripening and decay processes, and nutritional status changes with these processes. Stimulated by bruising, enzymes also cause bruised areas on vegetables and fruits to spoil. Selecting top quality vegetables and fruits, as a result, is importantly a matter of selecting unbruised produce at the peak point of the natural growth cycle. Other physical traits – **ripeness, juiciness, color, and flavor** – also identify this peak point. Color and flavor (bitterness) also indicate phytonutrient content. Accordingly, selecting raw and intact vegetables and fruits with these quality-indicating traits serves as a very reliable means of selecting high quality vegetables and fruits.

Each of these quality-indicating physical traits – **ripeness, juiciness, lack of bruising, color, and flavor** – has easily identifiable characteristics.

1. **Ripeness is the point of peak attractiveness and freshness.** Ripeness directly correlates with maximum juiciness, colorfulness, attractive texture, richness of flavor, and nutritional content. An additional important attribute of ripe fruit is that acid content (or acid-forming potential) is also lowest at this point. This means fruit consumed in ripe form places the least acid neutralizing burden on a human body.

    Full ripeness has identifiable physical characteristics. In addition to being juicy, a fully ripe vegetable or fruit:

    - is pleasantly aromatic, especially in the case of fruit. While vegetables are not aromatic, they (and notably onion, garlic, and cabbage family vegetables) should have a neutral scent that is not strong or unpleasant in any way.
    - has brightly colored skin. Any attached leaves are bright green. Smooth skin (such as that of eggplant, cucumber, and sugar snap peas) should have a shiny luster.
    - has fresh, moist-feeling, flexible skin. Skin of zucchini and yellow summer squash should have a "squeaky clean" feel.
    - retains little green coloration on skin. Flecks of green can remain (as in cantaloupe, pineapple, papaya, peach, and nectarine), but there should not be any large, dark green patches, which indicate the produce has not ripened evenly. Such fruit will also not home-ripen evenly, with a portion becoming overripe before the green portion becomes ripe.
    - has flesh that feels firm but gives some indication of slight softening. Exactly what flesh gives this indication varies among fruits and vegetables. The center of soft-fleshed fruit (such as plums and nectarines) typically yields to gentle pressure, but in some fruit varieties (such as pears, cantaloupe, and honeydew melon) it is the stem end that should yield to gentle pressure. Individual raw fruit recipes presented in Chapter Four (Raw Fruit Pure and Simple) include techniques for determining ripeness.
    - is not sprouting. Sprouting in vegetables indicates over-ripeness. Potato eyes should not protrude. Onion bulbs and garlic cloves should not have bright green centers and green shoots breaking out of the tops.
    - does not have green coloration immediately under the skin or that spreads into the flesh, which indicates unnatural ripening. Such green coloration – which commonly

occurs in onions, eggplant, and potatoes – is somewhat toxic for humans and may give the produce an unpleasantly sharp flavor.

Particular fruits can be purchased partially green and then home-ripened. These varieties of fruit – **apple, apricot, avocado, banana, guava, kiwi, mango, nectarine, peach, pear, plum,** and **tomato** – can be kept within a closed paper bag at room temperature and checked regularly until they have ripeness-indicating features before being refrigerated for storage (except for tomato, which should not be refrigerated). Fruits that cannot be home-ripened because they do not ripen after being picked green include **citrus fruits, cherries, grapes, pineapple,** and **pomegranate.**

2. **Juiciness corresponds with full ripeness and maximum freshness.** Juiciness also means a vegetable and fruit has not lost juice due to evaporation caused by exposure to air or over-ripeness. A juicy vegetable or fruit has identifiable physical characteristics. A juicy vegetable or fruit:

   - feels heavy for its size. It should feel solidly plump, not light and hollow.
   - has juicy pulp. When produce is broken open for examination (such as in the case of asparagus, green beans, okra, edible pod peas, and watermelon), the inside flesh should appear moist, shiny, dense, brightly colored, and very juicy.
   - has firm, not limp, leaves.
   - has attached stems (as in the case of cherries and grapes) that are green and flexible, not stiff and dry.
   - has tightly fitting parts. For example,

     - cauliflower and broccoli florets fit tightly together.
     - asparagus tips are tightly closed.
     - leaves of Brussels sprouts fit tightly together.
     - mushroom heads are tightly closed.

3. **Bruising means internal flesh has been damaged.** Bruising stimulates enzyme activity that undermines the flavor, color, and some nutritional content (browning indicates loss of vitamin C) of the affected pulp. While sometimes bruised areas can be cut out of a fruit or vegetable, more often bruised areas indicate that complete internal spoilage has already occurred or that internal spoilage will quickly occur during storage. To avoid selection of bruised produce, select vegetables and fruits that:

   - are uniformly firm without any soft, sunken, or flattened spots.
   - do not have brown areas on the skin.

4. **Colorfulness is a marker of both full ripeness and phytonutrient content.** The coloring of vegetables and fruits communicates important information about the phytonutrient content of vegetables and fruits. Based on what is now known and scientifically established about phytonutrient content, vegetables and fruits with the richest phytonutrient content and greatest human health-supporting capacity have particular characteristics.

- **Most nutritious vegetables and fruits are uniformly colored.** At the same time that uniform coloring corresponds with full ripening, uniform coloring is a clear marker of the phytonutrient content of vegetables and fruits. Uniform color means that plant parts have been uniformly exposed to a common threat, which causes a plant to develop protective phytonutrient armor over all affected parts. Select, for example,

    - red or green looseleaf lettuce. Loosely attached to a root stem, all leaves of loose lettuce grow fully exposed to air, UV rays, and bug predators. All leaves, as a result, develop protective color. In lettuce with tightly wrapped leaves (such as iceberg lettuce) and in lettuce with tightly wrapped inside leaves (such as romaine and Bibb lettuce), only outer, exposed leaves develop color. These lettuces, as a result, are not as good sources of phytonutrients as red and green looseleaf lettuce.
    - dark green leafy vegetables. The leaves of these vegetables (such as kale, chard, collard greens, and spinach) are bunched at an end stem, with leaves being quite equally exposed to the sun.
    - dark green leafy beet and turnip tops.
    - chives. Unlike leeks and scallions, which are part white and green, chive leaves are completely green.
    - red apples that are uniformly red. Apples with mixed red and green color have uneven phytonutrient development. The green areas of these apples indicate lack of full exposure to the sun during growth and, as a result, the apples have a lower phytonutrient content than those with fully red-colored skin, which has been fully exposed to the sun during growth.
    - completely red strawberries. They should not be red on the bottom but white under the hulls.

- **Most nutritious vegetables and fruits are intensely colored.** Deep coloration indicates concentrated phytonutrient content. The deeper the color, the greater the concentration of phytonutrient content and the greater the nutritional value of a vegetable or fruit. For example, select:

    - vegetables with dark orange flesh, such as sweet potatoes and butternut squash and the darkest orange individual sweet potatoes or winter squash of a batch.
    - fruits with dark orange flesh, such as mango, cantaloupe, papaya, mandarin orange, and tangelos, selecting the darkest orange colored individual fruit of a batch.
    - vegetables with edible dark green skin, such as zucchini and cucumber.
    - dark green leafy vegetables, such as spinach, kale, chard, and collards.
    - dark green vegetables, such as broccoli.
    - vegetables with dark green leafy tops, such as beets, turnips, and bok choy.
    - vegetables with dark red flesh, such as red bell peppers and beets.
    - fruits with red flesh, such as raspberries, cherries, and red currants.

It is important to note that it is not a hard and fast rule that only produce with intensely colored flesh has greatest phytonutrient content. Some varieties of white or light-fleshed produce also have high phytonutrient content, including **cauliflower, mushroom, white-fleshed nectarine, white-fleshed peach,** and **artichoke.**

- **Most nutritious vegetables and fruits have particular colors.** Phytonutrient colors are ranked in a hierarchy, and the highest-ranking colors have greatest phytonutrient concentration. Colors ranked highest in the phytonutrient hierarchy are **red, purple,** and **reddish brown.** These colors indicate super concentration of phytonutrients. Ranked just below these colors, dark green indicates somewhat less concentrated phytonutrient content. Vegetables and fruits with highest-ranking color include, for example,

    - dark green lettuce that has red, reddish-brown, or purple coloring, such as red leaf lettuce.
    - red tinted lettuce, such as radicchio.
    - red as opposed to green cabbage.[91]
    - purple as opposed to orange carrots.
    - purple as opposed to red or white potatoes.
    - dark yellow corn rather than white corn.[92]
    - red bell pepper rather than green.
    - red as opposed to green seedless grapes.
    - fruit with dark red color, such as strawberries, watermelon, cranberries, raspberries, currant berries, pomegranate seeds, and pink or red grapefruit.
    - darkest red tomato.
    - blood orange.
    - blue and purple berries, such as blueberries and blackberries.

- **Most nutritious servings of vegetables and fruits include a mixture of different colored vegetables and fruits.** Different phytonutrient families perform different kinds of health protective roles for humans. Because each individual phytonutrient family is also linked with a particular color, selecting a variety of different colored vegetables and fruits is a means of achieving the widest possible health protection that phytonutrients can provide.

The following is an inclusive listing of the different color groups[93]:

- Green vegetables (such as broccoli, cabbage, and kale).
- Orange vegetables (such as carrot, winter squash, and sweet potato) and fruit (such as cantaloupe and mango).
- Orange/yellow fruit (such as citrus fruit, peach, papaya, and nectarine).
- Yellow/green vegetables (such as spinach, collard greens, corn, green peas, and avocado) and fruit (such as honeydew melon).

---

91 Ibid., 167. Robinson states that red cabbage has six times more antioxidant activity than green cabbage.
92 Ibid., 85. Robinson states "Deep yellow varieties [of corn] have up to fifty-eight times more beta-carotene and the related compounds lutein and zeaxanthin than white corn. Lutein and zeaxanthin reduce the risk of two common eye diseases, macular degeneration and cataracts."
93 Jane E. Brody, "The Color of Nutrition: Fruits and Vegetables," *The New York Times*, Science Section, D8 (May 14, 2002).

- Red/purple vegetables (such as red cabbage, red pepper, beet, and eggplant) and fruit (such as blueberries, plum, red and blue grapes, strawberries, and red apple).
- Red vegetables (such as red bell and chili pepper) and fruits (such as tomato, pink grapefruit, and watermelon).
- White/green vegetables (such as garlic, onion except for sweet onion, leek, celery, cauliflower, and asparagus) and fruit (such as pear and green grapes).

5. **Top quality vegetables and fruits are flavorful.**

- Flavor tends to correlate with nutritional quality. This is the case of vegetables like red garnet sweet potato and sugar snap peas and fruits like grape tomato and mandarin orange.
- Flavor correlates with full ripeness, which, in turn, correlates with peak nutritional content in fruits and vegetables. Vegetables and fruits in general contain flavoring components, and these components are most developed in completely ripe form.
- Bitterness of flavor correlates with high phytonutrient content and, hence, high nutritional value. Bitterness indicates a plant retains close ties with its wild ancestors, which typically had significantly more nutritional value than the modern counterpart vegetables and fruits. While bitterness has largely been removed from plants through selective breeding by humans, vegetable and fruit varieties retaining natural bitterness do remain. Arugula, a variety of dark green leafy vegetable, and blackberries are examples of commonly available produce that retain some bitterness.
- Flavor indirectly correlates with nutritional quality in that flavorful vegetables and fruits are minimally reliant on the addition of outside flavoring (which is commonly sugar, salt, and fat) for successful serving.

Natural Production as an Essential Whole Food Indicator

Natural production is agricultural production that does not unnaturally process vegetables and fruits for the sake of convenience and cost reduction. Its methods of production are guided by biologically-based standards that match the natural biological growth processes of vegetables and fruits that have evolved over many centuries. Committing producers to work with naturally evolved plant growth processes and nutritional requirements, these standards anchor production methods and act as an effective block against unnatural tampering with the growing process, such as using genetically modified seeds, chemicals, and artificial fertilizer.

Certified organic production is a form of natural production, and a United States Department of Agriculture (USDA)-certified organic label verifies that a vegetable or fruit has been grown from natural seeds in naturally fertilized soil, essential conditions of natural production. Strictly protecting the production process from tampering, a USDA-certified organic label requires that vegetables and fruits have other characteristics. Certified organic producers must verify that vegetable and fruit produce has:

- been grown without use of artificial pesticides or insecticides.

PART 1

- not been chemically manipulated or manipulated with other synthetic substances for such commercial reasons as extending the market season and making produce easier to ship and store.
- been grown without use of sewage sludge.
- not been irradiated (treated with radiation) to eliminate pests.
- not been grown from genetically engineered seeds.

The focus of natural production methods on maintenance of naturally evolved growth processes directly and reliably links naturally produced vegetables and fruits with human health. Vegetables and fruits provide nutritional components for humans in the amounts and combinations required to maintain health. Maintenance of naturally evolved growth processes correlates with seed, soil, plant, and environmental health as well.

In sharp contrast with natural production, industrial production unleashes unnatural tampering. The dominant method of agriculture used for growing vegetables and fruits in the United States and around the world,[94] modern industrial agriculture is guided by the standard industrial goals of expanded production at the lowest cost, which are goals that yield the greatest profit. Factory production principles – efficiency of operation, large-scale production, production convenience, and mechanization – serve as the means for achieving the goal of expanded production at the lowest cost. In industrial agriculture, vegetables and fruits are treated as commodities to be manipulated according to production needs, and this unleashes unchecked tampering. Disconnected from natural growth processes, industrial production yields vegetables and fruits fundamentally disconnected from human nutritional needs and which also carry toxic chemicals. Diminished regard for natural growth processes disconnects industrial production of vegetables and fruits from environmental health as well, and industrial production has far-reaching negative impacts on soil and the environment surrounding plant production areas.

The following outline summarizes the differing impact of natural and industrial production on seed, soil, human, and environmental health:

1. **Natural production supports seed health while industrial production unnaturally alters seeds and narrows and threatens seed diversity.** In natural production, plants grow from naturally developed seeds. Seeds are either the result of natural spontaneous mutation or of human selection. Seeds, as a result,

    - are highly diverse. There are, as a result, seeds suited to a wide variety of soils and climates.
    - are highly accessible. They are inexpensive; they are not the property of any person or business.
    - do not have traits that are not natural to plants.

    Industrial production, in contrast, both unnaturally alters food seeds and narrows seed diversity. For example:

---

94 Frederic Mousseau, "West's Agri-giants Snap up Ukraine," *Asia Times* (January 28, 2015). This article describes the extent to which American agribusinesses have moved into the newly opened agricultural market in the Ukraine and taken over its entire agricultural production system. This takeover illustrates both world agricultural trends and the aggressiveness of agribusinesses in establishing the industrial production model.

- Seeds are narrowly selected on the basis of production needs, such as disease- and drought-resistance, crop yield capacity, and transportation and storage durability.
- Important general public-supporting long-range goals, such as maintaining seed diversity, have low priority status.
- Genetically modified (GM) seeds are man-engineered in a manner that is not found in nature.[95]
- Because of the extraordinary cost of developing GM seeds, the variety of GM seeds is limited and the cost of seeds is high.
- GM seed-producing businesses are given patents for GM seeds. Agribusinesses and agrichemical businesses that undertake the expensive process of creating GM seeds receive patents for their seeds, which gives them ownership rights and, as a result, monopoly control over GM seeds for several years.[96] During this time they control seed prices and seed use and, in effect, control the entire food system.[97] It is well established that Monsanto, one of the dominant agrichemical corporations, maintains tight control of its monopoly rights, limiting the accessibility of its seeds and suppressing criticism.[98]

2. **Natural production promotes the health of soil and plants while industrial production degrades both soil and plant health.** In natural production, for example,

- soil is naturally fertilized. Natural fertilizer, in turn, maintains healthy soil which, as the natural food of plants, supports plant health. Natural fertilizer adds natural organic matter, such as compost and manure, to soil, which directly supports plant and soil health.

  - organic matter restores nutrients removed during the production of plants, which replenishes soil fertility. Fertile soil increases the nutritional diversity and vitality of plants grown in the soil.

---

[95] Nancy L. Swanson, Andre Leu, Jon Abrahamson, and Bradley Wallet. "Genetically Engineered Crops, Glyphosate and the Deterioration of Health in the United States of America," *Journal of Organic Systems* (September 2, 2014): 7-8. The GMO industry claims that genetic engineering is no different than plant hybridization, which has been practiced by humans for hundreds of years. Genetic engineering, however, transfers genes between separate kingdoms of living things, which definitely does not occur in nature. All living things are classified according to a ranking system, which includes seven ranks. Starting with the highest rank, these ranks include kingdom, phylum or division, class, order, family, genus, and species. In nature, species that belong to different kingdoms such as plants, animals, bacteria and viruses definitely do not inter-breed. This, however, is exactly what is done in genetic engineering. Furthermore, genetic engineering transfers more than one gene between kingdoms. To make the desired trait that is inserted into a seed work, other genes are also included, such as promoter genes and marker genes. "The result is a complex construction of transgenes that come from bacterial, viral, fish, plant and other sources. This is completely different from natural hybridisation."

[96] Roberts, *The End of Food*, 260. Monopoly control of seeds results in the concentration of economic power in a few agrichemical corporations, and this concentration of power is no little matter. Roberts reports that "Monsanto now controls a fifth of the $20 billion global proprietary seed market (and just three companies, Monsanto, DuPont, and Syngenta, account for 44 percent of the market)."

[97] Ibid., 260-61. "Monsanto is creating a giant tollbooth in front of the cotton market and the soybean market and canola market and the corn market." Roberts points out that because seeds are the first link of the food chain and whoever controls the seeds controls the food supply, this narrowing of the control over the food system into fewer and fewer hands should concern everyone.

[98] Ibid., 260. Monsanto sends a letter to all farmers who buy its products to inform them of their contractual agreement to not save seeds, and then it sues those farmers who save the seeds. Monsanto also does not tolerate even indirect criticism. Roberts reports (253) that Monsanto has sued a dairy that marketed its milk as "rBST free," (free of this genetically modified hormone), calling such claims "deceptive" and "misleading."

PART 1

- organic matter feeds and maintains microbacterial life, which, in turn, supports plant health and builds soil.[99] Fungi, for example, have a mutually beneficial symbiotic relationship with plant roots. The fungi provide roots with minerals in a soluble form that the roots can absorb.
- organic matter promotes the water-holding capacity of soil, reducing the amount of water needed during production and increasing the resistance of plants to drought.

- natural fertilizer also increases the pH in the soil (from acidic to neutral).[100]
- plants develop chemical compounds called phytonutrients to defend against predators and other dangerous contact, such as UV sunlight rays.

Industrial production degrades soil and plant quality. In industrial production, for example,

- artificial fertilizer replaces natural fertilizer. Only a few minerals, with heavy emphasis on nitrogen, are routinely returned to the soil, which simplifies the chemistry and nutritional content of plants grown in the soil. High levels of nitrogen also interrupt natural symbiotic relationships between plant roots and mycorrhizal fungi. Fungi no longer provide plants nitrogen for free,[101] increasing the dependence of plants on artificial fertilizer.
- use of artificial fertilizer, which does not return organic material to soil, in combination with the use of pesticides undermines soil's capacity to hold water. The degree of erosion increases as a result. Artificial fertilizer can also increase the salinity of soil, which negatively affects the ability of plants to absorb fertilizer and, as a result, increases the amount of fertilizer needed.
- pesticides destroy soil bacteria and fungi, which interrupts natural biological processes that support plant health, build soil, and hold carbon and water in the ground.[102]

3. **Natural production supports human health while industrial production degrades and even undermines human health.** In natural production,

- natural fertilizer yields complex soil which, in turn, yields vegetables and fruits that contribute a diversity of nutritional components in naturally evolved combinations that match the complicated health-maintaining needs of humans.
- naturally fertilized soil supports colonies of mycorrhizal fungi that transport human health supporting minerals into plant roots, the roots pass the minerals into plants, and humans obtain the minerals when they eat the plants.

---

99 Judith D. Schwartz, *Cows Save the Planet: And Other Improbable Ways of Restoring Soil To Heal the Earth* (White River Junction, Vermont: Chelsea Green Publishing, 2013): 34-35.
100 Courtney White, *Grass, Soil, Hope: A Journey through Carbon Country* (White River Junction, Vermont: Chelsea Green Publishing, 2014): 65.
101 Schwartz, *Cows Save the Planet*, 40.
102 Ibid., 35, 36, and 41.

- the protective capacity of phytonutrients is transferred to humans when humans consume phytonutrient-containing vegetables and fruits.
- plant products do not contain pesticide or other residues from added chemicals, which are unnatural to and potentially toxic for humans.

Industrial production does not support, and even undermines, human health in important known ways. In industrial production, for example,

- giving top priority to the selection of seeds that advance production and cost reduction inevitably results in neglect of the nutritional quality of vegetables and fruits, such as the selection of seeds of plants that enhance the disease resistance of consumers. This is because nutritional quality is not directly linked to profit-making. Jo Robinson, a writer who researches the nutritional quality of vegetables and fruits, makes the following statement:

> "In fact, I've interviewed U.S.D.A. [United States Department of Agriculture] plant breeders who have spent a decade or more developing a new variety of pear or carrot without once measuring its nutritional content."[103]

USDA data confirms that the nutrient content of vegetables and fruits grown using artificial fertilizer has decreased markedly since the 1950s.[104]

- selection of GM seeds perpetuates the selection of seeds that advance increased production and cost reduction and neglect the nutritional quality of vegetables and fruits. This is because chemical-agribusinesses are the cousins of industrial-agribusinesses and apply exactly the same profit- and increased production-driven operating principles.
- plants contain significantly reduced phytonutrient content in comparison with naturally produced plants.[105] To an important extent heavy use of pesticides makes the development of natural protective defenses by plants largely unnecessary.
- vegetables and fruits routinely contain traces of toxic pesticides.[106] Three very important points about this pesticide content are: 1) pesticide content cannot be washed completely away. Scrubbing of potatoes, for example, removes only a small portion of pesticide residue. While peeling can remove a substantial amount, some pesticides are water soluble and are absorbed by plant pulp.[107] Because, in some

---

103 Robinson, *Eating on the Wild Side*, 10-11. Robinson also states, "To this day, the nutritional content of our man-made varieties has been an afterthought. A plant researcher for the United States Department of Agriculture (USDA) can spend years perfecting a new variety of blackberry or apple without ever measuring its phytonutrient content or its effect on blood sugar."
104 Pollan, *In Defense of Food*, 118-121.
105 Ibid., 119-120. Robinson, *Eating on the Wild Side*, 86. In a 2003 survey, Robinson reports, organic corn was found to have 50 percent more phytonutrients than conventionally grown corn. She also reports that an Italian study found that one variety of peaches that was raised organically had significantly more phytonutrients than the same variety grown conventionally (280). Mateljan, *The World's Healthiest Foods*, 355.
106 Robinson, *Eating on the Wild Side*, 264. Samples of conventionally produced strawberries, for example, have been found to contain traces of over 60 different agricultural chemicals.
107 Ibid., 102. Robinson explains, for example, why potatoes routinely make the Environmental Working Group's Dirty Dozen list of the most contaminated foods in the US food supply. "Some of these chemicals are highly soluble and penetrate beneath the skin of the potato. Scrubbing the potatoes removes only 25 percent of these hidden compounds. Peeling gets rid of up to 70 percent, but the rest remains inside the potato –unwelcome ingredients in your baked potatoes and potato salad."

cases, most nutritional content of vegetables and fruits is contained in the skin, removal of skin to reduce exposure to pesticide residues represents substantial nutritional waste. 2) The effects of extensive pesticide use on human health remain largely unknown. This is particularly true with respect to the effect of the mixing of different pesticides on produce. 3) In some cases, respectable independent scientific research contradicts agribusiness-sponsored research and shows commonly used pesticides to be highly toxic for humans and for children in particular.[108] Research shows some commonly used pesticides act as endocrine system disruptors, which are linked to birth defects and miscarriages in humans.[109] A prime example of a commonly used chemical that is being shown to be lethal to humans is glyphosate. Glyphosate is the main active chemical in the herbicide Roundup, which is widely used on industrially produced fruits and vegetables.

- In 2015 the World Health Organization's International Agency for Research on Cancer publicly announced that glyphosate is a "probable human carcinogen."
- In 2016 a court in California ruled that glyphosate causes cancer in humans. Monsanto, the producer of Roundup, appealed the verdict, but in 2017 another court upheld the decision that glyphosate is carcinogenic and that herbicide products containing glyphosate must carry a cancer warning label.
- Glyphosate is known to chelate minerals. It chelates minerals in soil, binding them so that plants cannot absorb them, which undermines the nutritional quality of plants used as human food. It chelates minerals in the human gut, binding them so that the minerals cannot be absorbed for meeting important human health needs.
- Glyphosate is an antibiotic. It is destructive of some beneficial bacteria living in the soil and in the human gut, thereby undermining important soil and human health-supporting roles played by bacteria.

• plants are often chemically treated in other ways to enhance production profits and convenience. For example, immature citrus fruit (orange, grapefruit, and lemon) is routinely force-ripened (or "degreened") by being exposed to ethylene gas, which alters skin color to make the fruit look ripe.[110] Grapes are routinely "gibbed," which means they are sprayed with a plant hormone that increases overall size of the grapes by as much as 75 percent.[111] Potatoes are sprayed with fungicides during growth and are treated with sprout inhibitors while in storage.[112]
• GM (genetically modified) seeds effectively yield new kinds of vegetables and

---

108 *Nutrition Action Health Letter* (October 2012): 5-6. This article reports that there is compelling evidence that low-level exposure to organophosphate insecticides (such as chlorpyrifos) from food and the environment has been contributing to a variety of neurological and developmental problems, such as lost IQ points.
109 Naomi Klein, *This Changes Everything: Capitalism Vs. The Climate* (New York: Simon & Schuster, 2014): 439.
110 Robinson, *Eating on the Wild Side*, 324. Because citrus fruit does not ripen after being picked green, "de-greened" fruit remains unripe and, as a result, more acidic, less sweet, and has fewer phytonutrients than fully ripe fruit.
111 Ibid., 306-307.
112 Ibid., 102.

fruits.¹¹³ They are different from the vegetables and fruits traditionally eaten by humans. They are no longer precisely matched to human nutritional needs, and there is very little genuinely independent research being conducted about either the effect of the unnatural alteration or the nutritionally deficient nature of GM foods on long-term human health. Unfortunately, there is no independent mechanism in the United States available to support such research and to protect the common public interest with regard to GM seeds and food products. GM seed producing corporations are instead essentially allowed to police themselves. The giant agrichemical corporations producing GM seeds attempt to discredit whatever research critical of GM foods does become public.¹¹⁴ These corporations conduct public relations efforts and fund research supportive of GM seeds and products. Patent-protected seed licensing agreements have also been used to severely limit research of GM crops.¹¹⁵

4. **Natural production maintains the health and biodiversity of the environment surrounding vegetable and fruit production areas while industrial production has profound and far-reaching negative impacts on both environmental health and biological diversity.** In natural production, for example,

- natural fertilizer does not pollute and contaminate ground water and the water of ponds and rivers surrounding the production area.
- other forms of life co-exist with growing plant crops. This life includes the bacteria and fungi living in the soil, the bees pollinating plants, insects, and birds that eat insects.

In industrial production, in contrast,

- the nitrogen and phosphorous content of artificial fertilizers negatively impacts the surrounding environment. Nitrogen seeps into ground water, making water unfit for humans. Rain and irrigation water carries these minerals into ponds, where they wipe out the eco-system of ponds, destroying fauna and flora alike and leaving ponds devoid of any form of life. Water contaminated with phosphorous runs into rivers and empties into lakes and the ocean, creating massive aquatic dead zones.¹¹⁶

---

113 Swanson, Leu, Abrahamson, and Wallet, "Genetically Engineered Crops, Glyphosate and the Deterioration of Health in the United States of America," 8. The stance taken by Monsanto, Dow, Bayer, and the other proponents of genetically engineered seeds, and the stance accepted by the U.S. Federal Drug Administration, is that GE food is "substantially equivalent" to non-GE products. But in a comparative study of GE and non-GE ready-to-market soybean products, researchers found significant differences in composition, including differences in the protein, fats and oils, and carbohydrate content. Soybeans grown from Roundup-Ready soybean seeds also contain traces of the herbicide glyphosate. Naturally grown soybeans, in sharp contrast, do not contain such toxic pesticide residue.
114 Roberts, *The End of Food*, 253. Agrichemical corporations discredit critical information in the same way as commercial food processing corporations. When the journal *Nature* published an article by two University of California/Berkeley scientists that was critical of GM crops, several of the "experts" who criticized the article were not from equivalent academic institutions but instead were associates of a public-relations firm hired by Monsanto, an agribusiness giant.
115 Tom Philpott, "Are Genetically Modified Foods Safe to Eat?" *Mother Jones* (September 30, 2011): 2.
116 Erica Goode, "Farmers Put Down the Plow for More Productive Soil," *The New York Times* (March, 10, 2015). Nitrogen and phosphorus pollution in the Upper Mississippi and Ohio River basins, for example, have caused the creation of giant "dead zones" of oxygen-depleted water in the Gulf of Mexico.

Industrial producers and the customers who buy their products do not pay for causing this damage or the cost of correcting it.

- a huge non-renewable energy cost significantly contributes to the carbon emissions problem that is advancing climate change. Artificial fertilizer is produced from petroleum, and the amount of tractor fuel required for the pesticide spraying of crop lands (which involves going over crops many, many times[117]) is stupendous.
- the colossal amount of spraying with pesticides that routinely occurs during the production of plant crops is highly destructive of the environment in at least two important ways. First, extensive use of pesticides leads to the development of super weeds that are resistant to most pesticides. A recent count of superweeds turned up one hundred and ninety-seven varieties.[118] This increase results in the continual development of ever more deadly insecticides and ever more spraying of chemicals.[119] Second, pesticide use is highly destructive of all forms of life in the eco system in and surrounding crop land. As huge swaths of land are sprayed again and again, nearly all biological life is destroyed. Pesticides, for example, are deadly to insects (including important pollinating bees and beloved butterflies) and to birds dependent on insects. Pesticides are also deadly to rodents and the loss of rodents impacts the animals and birds that eat them. Pesticides are selectively destructive of soil bacteria and fungi, giving less beneficial bacteria and fungi destructive of plants an advantage. In massive stretches of American farm land, pesticide use essentially reduces life forms to one plant, which is the crop being produced. In 2013, American farm land industrially planted to corn and soy alone covered about 170 million acres, which means a combined land mass roughly equal to Texas has already been made essentially sterile.[120]
- artificial fertilization and pesticide use combine to significantly increase the amount of water needed for successful production. Without organic substances in soil, soil cannot efficiently hold water, which makes crops dependent on irrigation, which uses staggering amounts of highly valuable water. Like empty soil, the bare ground between crop rows cannot hold water, allowing irrigated water to run off, carrying nitrogen and pesticides into the surrounding land and water sources.
- the use of GM (genetically modified) seeds perpetuates use of artificial fertilizer and pesticides and the environmental destruction this use causes. The gigantic agrichemical corporations producing GM seeds (such as Monsanto, DuPont, and Dow) are first cousins of agribusinesses and commercial food processing corporations. Production is guided and driven by exactly the same production and profit goals that rigidly and overwhelmingly focuses the businesses on economic considerations and makes them essentially indifferent to environmental, food quality, food security, and consumer health concerns.

---

117 Robinson, *Eating on the Wild Side*, 86. The U.S. Department of Agriculture reports in one of its bulletins that "growers in the southern United States spray insecticides as many as 25 to 40 times per season."
118 Kristin Ohlson, *The Soil Will Save Us* (New York: Rodale Inc, 2014): 167.
119 Philpott, "Why I'm Still Skeptical of GMPs," 2. In this article, Mr. Philpott quotes comments made by an agrichemical business official to justify the need for his company's new herbicide product: "an astonishing 86 percent of corn, soybean and cotton growers in the South have herbicide-resistant or hard-to-control weeds on their farms, as do more than 61 percent of farms in the Midwest. Growers need new tools now to address this."
120 Ibid., 5.

As these examples show, the differing impact of natural and industrial production on human, soil, plant, animal, and environmental health is phenomenal. Why then does natural production not join raw intact physical structure as a standard indicator of nutritional quality in vegetable and fruit selection? And how is it that the highly processed condition of industrially produced vegetables and fruits is ignored and gets a free pass in everyday vegetable and fruit selection? **Clearly, it is because of the tenacious grip of processed food dependence in our society.** This de-linking of processing from the nutritional quality of physically intact vegetables and fruits is an indicator of the vast political power of agribusiness and agrichemical corporations in our society. This de-linking secures the economic well-being of these corporate businesses, and they exert sufficient control over government policy to maintain – indeed enforce – the de-linking well into the future.[121]

It is, however, fully within the power of any individual health-conscious home cook to link natural production with nutritional quality. Vegetables and fruits that are raw, physically intact, and naturally produced **are** available. Selection can be somewhat troublesome – naturally produced products can be both more expensive and less widely accessible. However, when home cooks seek out and select, as far as is possible, raw, intact, and naturally produced products, they: 1) vitally support their own health and the health of those for whom they cook, 2) support the continued availability – and the expansion and accessibility – of these products, and 3) take a decisive, indeed giant, step to free themselves from processed food dependence and the massive destruction this dependence is inflicting on food quality and environmental health.

Identifying Top Quality Whole Vegetables and Fruits

Two types of whole vegetable and fruit products that meet the definition of whole food as raw, intact, and unprocessed food – **certified organic and locally produced vegetables and fruits** – are quite commonly available to cooks for use in Part II recipes. In selecting either of these types of produce, evaluation of vegetables and fruits according to the additional physical indicators of peak nutritional quality and attractiveness as set forth earlier in this Reference #1 (ripeness, juiciness, lack of bruising, colorfulness, and flavor) always applies. Relevant additional freshness- and nutrition-enhancing information is included with each type of top quality products to further aid cooks in making the highest quality vegetable and fruit selections.

1. **Raw and fully intact certified organic vegetables and fruits.** Though required verification adds to the cost of certified organic produce, it is crucial to maintenance of natural production standards. Verification protects these standards from dilution, and it also protects vegetables and fruits from tampering. Verification also simplifies selection for consumers. They can be confident that vegetables and fruits selected are in fact naturally produced food selections.

Nutritional-enhancing considerations:

- **Select certified organic vegetables and fruits that have been produced with**

---

[121] Michael Pollan, "Big Food Strikes Back," *The New York Times Magazine* (October 9, 2016): 41-50, 81-83. This article attests to the magnitude of the political power maintained by American Big Food, which collectively includes Big Ag, Big Meat, the supermarket retailers, and fast-food franchises. Pollan describes the decisive victory of Big Food over attempts made by the Barack Obama administration to regulate it.

PART 1

high quality fertilizer. Be willing to pay a higher price for this produce. This information may not be available and likely requires some research and questioning by customers. In some areas of the United States a new category of organic goods called **biodynamics** identifies this high quality organic produce. Selection of such products, whenever it is an option, corrects an important loophole in the certified organic verification process that allows for considerable variation in nutritional quality among organic foods. While a USDA-certified label reliably verifies natural production, which itself basically ensures the nutritional quality of produce, the label does not verify the common nutritional quality of certified organic produce. This is because certified organic standards do not specify an exact amount of fertilizer to be used and instead leaves this amount to the discretion of producers. As a result, there can be and is variable use of natural fertilizer among producers. Because fertilizer use, in turn, directly relates to the nutritional quality of vegetables and fruits, variable use of natural fertilizers results in uneven quality of organic produce. Seeking out and supporting selection of most generously fertilized produce serves as a means of obtaining and of maintaining the availability of highest quality certified organic produce. This is an important contribution because reducing fertilizer quality is a means used by large certified organic producers to squeeze out small producers and, hence, both organic produce quality and variety.

- **Select certified organic vegetables and fruits that have been produced from seeds yielding especially nutritious produce.** Because seeds naturally vary with regard to nutritional quality and nutritional quality tends to correlate with higher price, using lower quality producing seeds is a means for producers to reduce production costs. To an important extent customers can reliably select the most nutritious produce by selecting colorful produce and especially produce with high ranking phytonutrient color. Customers can also do research themselves about the most nutritious selections. An especially valuable source of such information is the book *Eating on the Wild Side* by Jo Robinson.

2. **Select raw and fully intact vegetables and fruits that have been locally grown essentially in accordance with natural production standards.** Sources of locally produced vegetables and fruits include:

    - **farmers' markets.** The production status of products is quite easily determined in the setting of a farmers' market where producers themselves are vendors marketing their foods and, as a result, are available to answer questions. Farmers' markets are likely sources of top quality vegetables and fruits for a variety of reasons.

        - Many small farmers selling their fresh products at farmers' markets across the nation as well as local natural food stores forego obtaining expensive organic certification status but essentially produce food in accordance with USDA organic farming principles.[122]

---

122 Peter Jaret, "Organics: Are They Worth It?" *Eating Well* (August/September, 2006): 32-39.

- Vegetable and fruit products sold at farmers' markets are most likely ripe, in-season products that, as a result, have peak flavor, texture, and nutritional content.
- It is quite common for vegetables and fruits to be marketed in completely intact form at farmers' markets.
- Some vendors may use generous amounts of manure, which they collect from animals and poultry that they also raise, as fertilizer for growing their plant products. These products can be gems in terms of flavor and nutritional quality.
- Some vendors may specialize in particular vegetables and fruits and can, as a result, offer a more varied and distinctive selection than standard stores. They may, for example, offer a variety of garlic, onions, and greens.
- A greater variety of top quality produce may be represented.
- Some vendors may grow especially flavorful genetic varieties of individual kinds of produce. These special varieties – called heirloom varieties – are also generally more expensive than standard varieties. The chance of locating local venders marketing heirloom products is very real in farmers' markets, especially in the case of farmers' markets in urban areas. The chance of large industrial farms raising such produce, in contrast, is slim and even nonexistent as care provided on these farms is necessarily impersonal and because production is largely focused on profit and, hence, most economic production.

- **farm stands that sell seasonal produce.** Seasonal produce is most likely ripe produce.
- **natural food stores.** Store managers are available and can verify the authenticity of naturally produced products. Refrigeration of fragile produce, a key to its top quality form, is most likely provided.
- **natural food sections of regular grocery stores.**
- **local farmers themselves.** Direct contact with the producers makes it possible for customers to personally determine the authenticity of natural production and to have the opportunity to select freshest produce. Listed below are two ways that consumers can directly deal with farmers.

  - Pick vegetables and fruits from U-pick fields.
  - Participate in Community Supported Agriculture (CSA) programs. In these programs local residents subscribe to a farm and receive a weekly box of fresh produce. Natural food stores, farmers' markets, and the Internet are sources of information about the availability of these farm programs.

Nutrition-enhancing considerations:

- There is no standard verification process to assist customers in selecting locally produced foods that have been naturally produced. Naturally produced produce also does not have easily identifiable physical traits to guide customers in selecting produce. Rather the responsibility to determine the authenticity of natural production falls on individual customers. Making the search for such produce is worth the effort for customers, however, because produce in local markets very

likely includes produce that has even higher nutritional quality than the certified organic produce marketed in standard grocery and natural food stores.
- Doing research about particularly nutritious products, such as referring to Jo Robinson's *Eating on the Wild Side*, and asking questions of vendors and natural food store managers is a way to expand selection of most nutritious vegetable and fruit varieties.
- Locally grown produce can be freshest produce. Because cooling and protection from air are crucial to retention of freshness and quality during marketing, look for vendors who provide this care of produce.

Reference #2

Key Home Storage Guidelines for Conserving Vegetable and Fruit Quality

After the selection of top quality vegetables and fruits, the second necessary step in *juice-protective* preparation is maintaining the quality of fresh vegetables and fruits during home storage. Vegetables and fruits are vulnerable to a host of factors that can undermine flavor, color, texture, and nutritional content during home storage. As a result, no matter how flavorful and nutrient rich vegetables and fruits may be at the time of purchase, nutritional quality at preparation time depends on how well vegetables and fruits have been protected from these potentially destructive factors during home storage. Reference #2 presents eight guidelines to aid cooks in applying protective storage techniques.

Storage Guideline #1

Keeping raw vegetables and fruits constantly chilled

Chilling is a key requirement for retaining the quality of fresh vegetables and fruits during home storage. Chilling does not prevent ripening as natural enzymes invisibly and relentlessly advance the ripening process, which inevitably degrades flavor, texture, and nutritional quality (notably antioxidant content).[123] Refrigeration, nevertheless, does effectively slow the ripening process by largely inactivating plant enzymes. This inactivation extends the time produce retains peak flavoring, physical condition, and nutritional value. Listed below are specific techniques for keeping raw produce constantly chilled during home storage.

1. **Immediately refrigerate most vegetables and fruits.** This rule applies to several vegetables and fruits that are commonly not refrigerated. For example, despite standard storage recommendations to the contrary,[124] immediate chilling applies to the following vegetables:

---

123   Robinson, *Eating on the Wild Side*, 311.

- **Onion** and **garlic**. Both vegetables are highly vulnerable to enzyme activity, which causes them to lose sweet natural flavoring quickly during room temperature storage. They also quickly sprout.
- **Banana** and **apple**. Though skins may become brown, refrigeration of ripe bananas significantly extends peak banana flavoring and texture. Apples displayed on the kitchen counter quickly lose crispness and juiciness and, as a result, attractiveness.

There are important exceptions to or necessary modifications of the "refrigerate produce immediately" rule. Listed below are important exceptions.

- **Mature potato (white and red) and sweet potato.** Refrigeration storage is problematic for **mature white** and **red potato**, which can potentially develop unattractive sweetness during long refrigeration. Room temperature storage, however, is also problematic. Potato quickly becomes soft and sprouts, which degrades potato quality (sprouts are even somewhat toxic to humans). While **sweet potato** can develop an unattractive off flavor when refrigerated, they also quickly spoil at room temperature. A fairly satisfactory solution is short refrigeration. Purchase and refrigerate an amount of mature potato and sweet potato that can be used relatively quickly, within a few (2 to 3) weeks. **Immature (or new) white** and **red potato**, however, can be safely refrigerated for a longer period (several weeks).
- **Green (un-ripened) fruit with stones**. This type of fruit – apricots, peaches, nectarines, and plums – is vulnerable to a condition called chilling injury (CI). When this fruit is green, the internal temperature of these fruits must be kept above fifty degrees throughout storage, and if the temperature drops below fifty degrees, the fruit texture and color can be irreparably harmed. Fruit with stones that is purchased green (as is generally the case of commercially produced fruit) must be ripened completely **before** being refrigerated.
- **Tomato.** Tomato should be stored at room temperature because tomato flavor is irreparably harmed by refrigeration.
- **Strawberry.** This fruit retains best flavor when stored at room temperature. Only that portion of a batch of strawberries that will not be quickly used should be immediately refrigerated or dry frozen.
- **Watermelon.** Store watermelon at room temperature until it is cut open, when it should be refrigerated.
- **Lemon and lime.** This fruit can be stored at room temperature for up to a week, but any lemon and lime that will not be used within a week should be immediately refrigerated in partially covered form.
- **Orange and grapefruit.** Like lemon and lime, these fruits can be stored at room temperature for up to a week. Any fruit that will not be used within a week should be immediately refrigerated.

---

124 Standard storage instructions typically direct home cooks to store this produce in a dark and cool area, which usually results in the produce being stored at room temperature because most modern homes do not have a dark and cool area that approximates a root cellar. Providing a dark, well-ventilated, and cool but never freezing temperature, a root cellar does in fact perfectly suit storage of a variety of vegetables (notably onions, garlic, winter squash, potatoes, sweet potatoes, and other root vegetables) and fruits (notably apples and melons).

2. **Quickly chill room temperature leafy lettuce and greens in cold water before refrigerating them.** When leafy lettuce and greens become somewhat warmed on the way home from a market or are freshly picked from a garden, soak the leaves (first separating bunched lettuce leaves and bunched spinach) in very cold water for several minutes (up to 10 minutes) before draining, drying, and refrigerating them.

3. **Remove raw vegetables and fruits from the refrigerator just prior to readying them for cooking or serving raw.**

4. **Immediately re-refrigerate any portion of raw produce that will not be quickly cooked or served raw.** Do not leave extra produce sitting on the kitchen counter.

5. **Immediately refrigerate raw produce not consumed during serving.**

Storage Guideline #2

Regulating contact with air during refrigeration

Air affects fresh raw vegetables and fruits in a variety of ways during refrigeration. While these ways are principally destructive of vegetable and fruit quality, air also plays some necessary or important roles. On the negative side,

- **exposure to air dehydrates produce.** Exposure to air results in the evaporation of too much moisture from almost all fruits and vegetables except for those with the thickest skins. Dehydration very quickly occurs in thin-skinned produce. Dehydration, in turn, causes irreparable harm, leaving vegetables and fruits unattractively limp.
- **oxygen stimulates enzyme activity in plant pulp exposed to air.** In exposed pulp – pulp that has been cut open, has been peeled, or has skin that has been thinned or broken open – the mixing of air and enzymes causes a chemical reaction (oxidation) that is destructive of some nutrients, such as vitamin C. Browning is an indication of this destruction. Resulting chemical reactions can also undermine flavor, as is the case of garlic and onion.
- **oxygen stimulates the respiration rate of vegetables.** Vegetables and fruits continue to respire (take in oxygen and give off carbon dioxide) after being separated from plants during harvesting.[125] For thin-skinned plants with a high respiration rate, exposure to too much air causes the plant to **respire** too quickly, which uses up its stored sugar and phytonutrient reserves and, as a result, quickly undermines flavor and nutritional quality.[126]
- **air carries ethylene gas.** Particular vegetables (notably potatoes and scallions) and fruits (including apples, bananas, and plums) emit ethylene gas, which is harmful to particular vegetables. Exposure to ethylene gas triggers formation of bitter compounds in some produce, such as carrots. Ethylene gas also reduces the storage

---

125 All information that is included about respiration rates of plants comes from *Eating on the Wild Side: The Missing Link to Optimum Health.*
126 Ibid., 31.

life of particular vegetables. For example, it turns some greens yellow, such is the case with kale.
- **air carries moisture.** In the case of particular vegetables, such as onions, garlic, and potatoes, moisture causes sprouting, which is destructive of flavor and nutritional quality. Sprouted eyes of potatoes are even somewhat toxic to humans. Moisture in air can condense on stored plants, which can cause mold to form on the plants and speed spoilage.

On the positive side,

- **oxygen is necessary for plants with a high respiration rate to stay alive.** Sealing these plants off from contact with oxygen, such as storing them in an air-tight container, causes them to die, which completely undermines the attractiveness and nutritional quality of the vegetables or fruits.
- **moist air usefully maintains plant moisture.** Crisper drawers of refrigerators are designed to enhance moist air content.

Seven techniques to manage contact between vegetables and fruits and air during refrigeration are as follows:

1. **Refrigerate produce in naturally whole, intact form.** Complete, intact form provides maximum natural protection from air. Do any trimming and cutting only just prior to readying produce for cooking or serving raw.

2. **Refrigerate almost all intact produce covered in a good quality sealable plastic bag.** With a few exceptions (thick-skinned vegetables and fruits, such as large melons and winter squash; bulb onions and garlic with thick and unbroken skin; and produce that should not be refrigerated at all, such as tomatoes and particular green fruit) refrigerate all produce – big and small produce alike, produce with either a fast or slow respiration rate, and onions and garlic with broken open skin – within in a sealed plastic bag. Covering produce in an air-tight storage bag, and in a few cases in plastic wrap, effectively protects produce with thin and medium-thick skins from evaporation, ethylene gas, and moisture. Plastic bags easily adjust to accommodate vegetables and fruits that have a high respiration rate. Plastic bags are widely marketed.

   - Grocery stores commonly market Ziploc or zipper plastic bags that are easy to open and close and that come in variable sizes to fit different-sized produce.
   - Specialty food and kitchen stores and catalogs marketing kitchen supplies often market more durable and reusable bags. They may also sell specialized bags for larger or irregular shaped produce, such as for bananas.

   Produce is often already marketed in a plastic bag. When a store bag is sealable, home refrigerate the produce in that bag. When a store bag is not resealable, transfer the contents of the bag to a resealable bag once the store bag is opened.

3. **Refrigerate produce with a high respiration rate in a very slightly vented plastic bag.** Refrigerating produce with a high respiration rate in a bag punctured with tiny pin-pricked holes satisfies the need of vegetables and fruits with a high respiration rate for some oxygen while protecting them from contact with too much oxygen, which is equally destructive to them. The tiny holes provide for an exchange of gases, and when a vented bag is stored in the crisper drawer of a refrigerator (the most humid place), a vented bag maintains adequate humidity. This effective storage method, which maximizes retention of the overall quality of vegetables and fruits, is set forth by Jo Robinson in her 2013 book, *Eating on the Wild Side: The Missing Link to Optimum Health*.[127]

   To apply Robinson's vented storage bag method,

   - add dry produce to a sealable plastic storage bag and gently press out as much air as possible without crushing the contents before sealing the bag. If produce comes packaged in a resealable bag, use the market bag but squeeze out as much air as is possible.
   - use a pin or needle point to prick 10-20 evenly spaced holes in a plastic storage bag, 10 pricks for quart-size bags and 20 pricks for gallon-size bags.
   - store the bag in the crisper drawer of a refrigerator.

   To select produce requiring Robinson's vented storage bag method, select

   - **small salad greens.**
   - **leafy green vegetables.** Leafy greens that have a somewhat smooth and flat as opposed to a curly or bumpy texture – such as beet greens, spinach, chard, collards, and some varieties of kale – are especially well suited to the vented bag storage method as leaves can be quite tightly stacked together, which effectively reduces the amount of air stored with the leaves during storage.
   - **other vegetables with a high respiration rate.** Include all variations of high respiration rates, including vegetables with an extremely high respiration rate (such as asparagus, mushroom, parsley, green peas, peas, spinach, and sweet corn), vegetables with a very high respiration rate (including artichoke, bean sprouts, broccoli,[128] Brussels sprouts, endive, green onion, kale, okra, snap beans, and watercress), and vegetables with a high respiration rate (including cauliflower, leek, and leaf lettuce).
   - **fruits with a high respiration rate.** Examples of these fruits include blackberries, cherries, cranberries, grapes, raspberries, and strawberries.
   - **any thin-skinned vegetable or fruit.** As vented bag storage is protective of vegetables and fruits in general, it can be used whenever there is any question about the respiration rate of a vegetable or fruit.

---

127 Ibid., 30-31. Robinson calls the pin-pricked bags "microperforated" bags.
128 Ibid.,162. Robinson reports that refrigerating broccoli using her vented storage method will have more than twice as much antioxidant activity than broccoli stored uncovered or tightly covered in an air-tight bag.

4. **Refrigerate rinsed leaves rolled in paper towels.** This storage method suits particular types of leafy vegetables. It serves as an alternative method of storing these vegetables in vented bags, or it can be used in combination with the vented plastic bag storage method. Leaves rolled in paper towels and refrigerated within a sealed plastic bag from which most air has been removed store very well for an extended period (one or two weeks). During this storage period leaves are on hand and ready to use for quick inclusion in dishes.

    Leaves especially suited to this storage method are those that are bumpy or curly and, as a result, are difficult to pat dry by hand. The paper towels soak up most remaining clinging moisture during storage. These types of leaves include, for example,

    - red and green leaf lettuce, which are bumpy, and as a result, difficult to dry. Leaves are also flexible and won't be crushed during rolling. Though leaves are somewhat crisp, romaine lettuce leaves can be stored rolled in paper towels as well.
    - mature leafy greens that are curly or bumpy, such as some varieties of kale and chard, which makes them difficult to pat dry. Large, smooth greens (such as collards, flat kale, and spinach) can be easily patted dry. A towel soaks up moisture, at least a significant amount of it, left clinging in bumpy and curly leaves.

    To store green leafy vegetables and lettuce wrapped in paper towels,

    - keep leaves refrigerated in store packaging right up to the time they are wrapped in paper towels.
    - rinse and roughly dry leaves. (For rinsing details see Recipe #29 for spinach and individual Chapter One recipes for greens.) After rinsing gently shake excess clinging liquid from the leaves.
    - spread leaves in a single layer over a connected layer of paper towels.
    - top the leaves with another connected layer of towels.
    - roll the paper towels in jelly-roll fashion around the leaves.
    - refrigerate the roll of leaves within a sealed plastic bag, pressing out as much air as possible before sealing the bag.

5. **Refrigerate medium-sized vegetables that have very thin skin and a low respiration rate tightly wrapped in plastic wrap.** This type of vegetable – such as bell pepper, zucchini, yellow summer squash, and cucumber – is highly vulnerable to air, which easily penetrates the skin and evaporates moisture from the plant pulp.

    To individually wrap vegetables in plastic wrap,

    - rinse and thoroughly dry the vegetable.
    - first chill room temperature produce. Refrigerate it uncovered until it becomes thoroughly chilled. This is a very important step in order to avoid having condensation form on the vegetable once it is wrapped.
    - tightly and completely wrap the vegetable with plastic wrap. To ensure an air-tight fit, use a big enough strip of plastic wrap for the ends to overlap. Wrap the ends

around the vegetable or connect the ends with a twist tie.
6. **Refrigerate all *cut* vegetables and fruits tightly covered.** Cutting directly exposes pulp to air. If cut area is not covered during storage, the produce will become unattractively dehydrated and, in the case of some produce, will brown due to enzyme activity. In contrast, protecting exposed cut surfaces from air retains the attractiveness of the produce and avoids its being wasted.

To cover *cut* vegetables and fruits for storage,

- store cut produce in large chunk form to minimize the surface exposed to air.
- leave maximum skin and other natural parts in place on stored cut produce.
- pull plastic wrap tightly over cut vegetable pulp, which is not acidic. To ensure air-tight covering, use a large enough piece of plastic wrap that the plastic completely covers the vegetable with the ends overlapping the covered area. To best ensure an air-tight fit, tie the ends together using a twist tie.
- store fruit cut side up within an air-tight container, preferably a glass container because fruit is acidic and cut fruit pulp can potentially leach chemicals from a plastic container. Do not cover cut fruit pulp with plastic wrap. Storage containers with lids that are designed to force out air are especially desirable. A quick and simple way to store fruit is to store it cut side up in a small bowl that is tall enough for the bowl to be covered with plastic wrap without the plastic touching the fruit.

To store *cut* produce with special storage needs,

- refrigerate **cut bulb onions** halved or quartered lengthwise. Halve or quarter an onion lengthwise without removing the skin or ends. Because bulb (and especially sweet) onions have high moisture content, immediately cover the exposed pulp, pulling plastic wrap tightly over the exposed cut pulp.
- Refrigerate **cut bell pepper** halved or sliced lengthwise. Rinse and dry the pepper before cutting; leave the ends and membrane on in any portion of pepper to be stored. Immediately pull plastic wrap tightly over cut pepper pulp of pepper to be stored.
- Refrigerate **cut cucumber** halved crosswise. Rinse and dry the cucumber before cutting; leave the end and peel on the cucumber half to be stored.
- Refrigerate **cut tomato** halved lengthwise. Very lightly coat the cut pulp of the half to be stored with oil. Because tomato is a fruit and easily spills juice, place it cut-side-up in an air-tight glass storage container. It can also be placed in a covered plastic container when placed cut-side-up.
- Refrigerate **cut produce that is vulnerable to browning** (such as apple, avocado, banana, and eggplant) with exposed cut pulp first dipped in a citrus wash (a 1 T orange or lemon juice and 1 T water mixture). Lightly pat the cut surface dry and store the produce cut-side-up in an air-tight plastic bag, gently pressing out as much air as possible before sealing the bag. For extra protection, lightly coat the cut surface with oil before storing. Cut produce can also be stored cut-side-up in a glass or plastic container with an air-tight lid, especially one designed to force out air.
- Refrigerate **cut apple or pear** halved lengthwise. Do not cut out seeds or the pulpy

center in the portion to be stored.

Storage Guideline #3

Pre-washing and drying of produce before refrigeration

Because moisture hastens spoilage, refrigerating vegetables and fruits unwashed is generally the prudent way to store them as thorough drying is often difficult after rinsing. Pre-washing and drying, nevertheless, is also highly useful as the produce is then on hand in ready-to-use form, which speeds and encourages use of the produce in meals.

To determine which produce to rinse and dry before refrigeration,

- **pre-wash and dry commonly used salad ingredients before storage.** This pre-washing and drying keeps salad ingredients on hand in ready-to-use form, which encourages salad use and the inclusion of a variety of different vegetables in salads. Salad vegetables, along with the recipe number or reference that provides rinsing and drying details, suited to pre-washing and drying include, for example,
    - bunched lettuce, such as green or red looseleaf lettuce, romaine, or bibb lettuce (Reference #8: Clinching Salad Flavor: Expanded Preparation Support, Ingredient #4).
    - cauliflower (Recipe #8).
    - bunched spinach (Recipe #29).
    - green onions/scallions (Recipe #34).
- **pre-wash and dry green leafy vegetables before storage.** With these readying steps completed, greens are on hand for quick and simple stir-frying or stir-fry/steaming. The result of stir-frying or stir-frying steaming, in turn, is reliably tasty cooked greens, which encourages use of these extra nutritious vegetables. Stir-frying and stir-fry/steaming also reliably retain maximum nutritional value. Chapter One recipes for individual greens include rinsing and drying details.
- **re-rinse and dry commercially packaged ready-to-serve small salad greens and baby spinach leaves that are wet when purchased.** Salad greens are originally packaged dry and are not supposed to be wet. Wetness means that somewhere along the way to the grocery shelf the packaged greens were allowed to become warm and then were re-chilled, which caused condensation to cover the leaves. Wetness, in turn, will cause the leaves to spoil well before the "sell by" date on the package. To dry the lettuce/greens, open the package, re-rinse the leaves in very cold water, spin them dry (or dry them in another way), and re-package them within a pin-pricked plastic bag (as described in Storage Guideline #2 above, Technique #3).

To dry wet produce,

- **wrap difficult to dry produce within paper towels during storage.** The towel will soak up moisture remaining after drying. For example, store cauliflower, cabbage, Brussels sprouts, grapes attached to a vine, and bumpy or curly leaves wrapped in

paper towels.
- **roll berries and grape and cherry tomatoes in paper towels or a terry towel for drying.** Line a pie plate with a double thickness of paper towels, pour rinsed berries over the paper towels, wrap the towels around the berries, and gently move the berries around within the towels.
- **pre-wash only a small amount of grapes at a time.** As wet grapes are very susceptible to mold, wash only an amount that will be quickly used. A small amount of grapes is also more easily dried efficiently.
- **invest in a supply of absorbent terry towels.** Terry towels provide quick and effective drying. Investing in terry towels also helps avoid overuse of paper towels, which are both expensive (only good quality towels hold together enough to provide useful wrapping) and environmentally unfriendly.

Storage Guideline #4

Protecting produce from condensation during refrigeration

Condensation will quickly form on any room temperature produce that is refrigerated tightly covered. As has been noted, moisture hastens spoilage, especially in the case of thin-skinned produce. Listed below are specific techniques for avoiding – or minimizing – condensation of moisture on produce during home storage.

1. **Initially refrigerate room temperature produce uncovered.** Vegetables and fruits can be room temperature for a variety of reasons. A vegetable or fruit, for example, can become un-chilled between the time it is purchased at a market and when it reaches a home kitchen. Some produce will always be room temperature when it reaches a kitchen, such as vegetables picked from a vegetable garden, fruit picked from a fruit tree, and home-ripened fruit. To avoid having condensation form on the surface of a vegetable during storage, it is important to thoroughly chill a room temperature vegetable uncovered before tightly covering it for storage.

2. **Regularly check produce refrigerated in air-tight plastic bags for condensation.** If moisture has collected, remove the produce, wipe off moisture on the produce and bag sides, wrap the produce with paper towels, return it to the bag, and add pin pricks to provide for ventilation. For produce with a low respiration rate, experiment with leaving the bag slightly open to allow for modest air circulation.

Storage Guideline #5

Protecting produce from bruising during storage

Bruising stimulates enzyme activity, which is destructive of the flavor and nutritional content of a bruised area. While refrigeration slows enzyme activity in bruised areas, it does not stop it, and in some produce, spoilage spreads to the entire food. Careful handling of fragile produce (such as lettuce, bananas, and thin-skinned fruit such as pears, peaches, and nectarines) to avoid bruising is, therefore, important. Casual handling of produce during refrigeration easily results in considerable wasting of produce. Listed below are two specific techniques for avoiding bruising of produce during refrigeration.

1. **Carefully place fragile produce in a refrigerator.** Do not allow fragile produce to be placed under produce that is heavy and especially that is heavy with sharp edges (such as pineapple or winter squash with stems).

2. **Avoid overcrowding in a refrigerator.** Constantly keep in mind the fact that all produce is perishable and some are highly perishable. A cook's aim, therefore, should be to purchase only what he/she can reasonably expect to use quite quickly.

Storage Guideline #6

Determining length of refrigeration time

The time that vegetables and fruits can be refrigerated without significant flavor and nutritional loss is highly variable. The basic key to successful storage time is proper storage. With proper storage most vegetables and fruits can be satisfactorily refrigerated for at least one week and in some cases, several weeks, though shorter storage time always correlates with best flavor and nutritional conservation. The case of produce with a high respiration rate is different. Storing produce for the least possible time is very important for retaining the most attractive flavor and greatest overall nutritional value.[129]

Storage Guideline #7

Dry freezing of raw ripe fruit

Freezing is a form of processing that is destructive of plant texture (leaving thawed produce limp and soft) and of particular nutrients (notably vitamin C and phytonutrients). Freezing, therefore, should not be a routinely used method for storing fruit. At the same time, new research shows that the negative impact varies among vegetables and fruits. In the case of berries, for example, fast freezing minimizes loss of phytonutrients.[130] Therefore, in particular situations – such as when ripe fruit will spoil before it can be prepared and when in-season produce becomes economically available in amounts that cannot be eaten quickly – quick dry freezing becomes a practical option. While berries with protective skins (such as blueberries and cranberries) are especially good candidates for dry freezing, applying quick freezing techniques maximizes retention of the natural color and flavor of fruits in general. Dry frozen fruit, in turn, is an excellent ingredient for use in pancakes (Recipe

---

129   Ibid.,166. For example, Robinson reports that in just a few days of refrigeration, cabbage loses 30 percent of its sugar. Robinson also notes (160) that new research shows that if cabbage family vegetables are freshly harvested, they are among the most healthful foods of all, but by the end of the total time they are stored – the time they are shipped, warehoused, displayed in the supermarket, and stored in your home refrigerator – they can lose up to 80 percent of their beneficial nutrients.

130   Ibid., 259. Flash frozen fruit freezes so quickly that destructive enzymes do not – or only minimally – affect the nutritional quality. By approximating flash freezing, home cooks themselves can minimize nutritional loss during freezing of fruit.

#215), muffins (Recipe #180), and fruit toppings (Recipes #219 – 223).

To maximize the natural flavor, color, and nutritional value of fruit,

- **dry fruit before freezing.** Drain rinsed berries in a colander, spread them over a double thickness of paper towels (in the case of blueberries and currants, place the paper towels in a pie plate), and wrap the towels around the fruit for drying. Drying keeps fruit pieces from sticking together during freezing.
- **remove stems, pits, and spoiled fruit before freezing.** Pick through the fruit, discarding any stems and spoiled fruit. Carefully remove pits from cherries as pits left in cherries can harm teeth.
- **cut larger fruit into uniformly thin slices for quick freezing.** For example, cut pineapple chunks into ½ in. thick slices, and cut apples and soft-fleshed fruit (such as pears, nectarines, and peaches) into ¼ in. thick lengthwise slices, removing any coarse membrane in the case of pears and apples. Leave strawberries whole.
- **dip cut fruit that easily browns into a citrus wash.** Mix a small amount of orange or fresh lemon juice with an equal amount of water in a small mixing bowl. Toss the cut fruit in the citrus wash, drain the fruit in a colander, spread the fruit over a double layer of paper towels, wrap the towels around the fruit, and gently squeeze the pieces to dry them.
- **evenly spread the fruit in a shallow freezer-safe container with sides.** For example, use a pie plate or rectangular glass baking dish. Spread larger pieces of fruit in a single layer. Spread small berries in a single or double layer.
- **to slow the rate of respiration of the fruit (and, hence, to maximize retention of both flavor and nutritional contents) sprinkle individual cut pieces of fruit with commercial "stay fresh" products.**[131] Berries with skin, such as blueberries and currant berries, can be frozen without such dusting.
- **freeze the fruit until hard.**
- **loosen the frozen fruit from the freezer container.** If the fruit sticks to the bottom, wait a few seconds before trying again. Carefully avoid letting the frozen fruit thaw even slightly.
- **transfer the frozen fruit** into an air-tight plastic freezer bag.
- **press as much air as possible** from the freezer bag before closing it.
- **briefly microwave frozen fruit pieces for quick thawing.** Except for when frozen fruit is added directly to a boiling liquid (as is done in fruit sauce recipes), microwave a single layer of sturdy fruit pieces (such as apples and pineapple) for 20-30 seconds. Microwave berries for 10-15 seconds. Because of the speed involved, microwave thawing is less destructive of nutritional content (in particular vitamin C and phytonutrients) than thawing at room temperature or in a refrigerator.[132] Such pre-thawing is important before adding frozen fruit to pancakes and muffins.
- **quickly use thawed dry frozen fruit.** Nutritional quality and flavor quickly deteriorates.

---

131 Ibid., 248. Robinson's recommendation is that cooks dust pieces of fruit with granulated or powdered sugar, vitamin C powder, or pectin powder, or a combination of all three powders.

132 Ibid., 248. Robinson states that berries thawed in the microwave retain twice as many antioxidants as berries that thaw at room temperature or in the refrigerator. Rapid thawing protects nutrients from enzymes, giving enzymes little time to cause nutritional damage.

Storage Guideline #8

Dry freezing of cooked cut vegetables

While freezing is a form of processing that reduces both nutritional content and texture, dry freezing becomes an option for storing vegetables when cooks have extra vegetables on hand that cannot be quickly consumed. An example of such an occasion is during the in-season of a vegetable, such as a green leafy vegetable, summer squash, and winter squash. Dry freezing of vegetables that are first stir-fried or stir-fry/steamed as directed in Chapter One recipes serves as an effective means of retaining the bright color and flavor of vegetables and of retaining at least a significant amount of some nutritional content. All dry freezing steps that apply to raw fruit as set forth in Storage Guideline #7 (except for dusting with a "stay-fresh" product) apply to dry freezing of cooked vegetables. Salt should not be added to cooked vegetables to be frozen.

CHAPTER ONE

Stir-Fried and Stir-Fry/Steamed Vegetable Recipes

Stir-Frying and Stir-Fry/Steaming Description

STIR-FRYING AND STIR-FRY/STEAMING are highly effective *juice-protective* cooking methods that open the door to simple, satisfying, and nutritious everyday use of vegetables. Easily applied to nearly 100% of vegetables, these cooking methods perfectly match vegetables. Reliably retaining the natural sweet flavor, vivid color, and juiciness of vegetables, these cooking methods lift vegetables into highly attractive form. Conserving maximum amounts of the wide spectrum of nutritional components naturally contained by vegetables, stir-frying and stir-fry/steaming cooking methods yield cooked vegetables that immeasurably contribute to human health. In Chapter One recipes,

- **stir-frying** applies to most fragile vegetables that quickly cook to tenderness. Stir-frying as used in *Cooked Alive!* recipes is adding a small amount of oil to a skillet preheated to medium-high (not high) temperature, mixing uniformly thin pieces of a vegetable into the oil, and constantly flipping the pieces for 30 seconds to one minute, until pieces are fully hot (heated through to the center). Some vegetables require longer heating to become softened. For these vegetables (such as onions and bell peppers) the heating temperature is reduced slightly after brief stir-frying and heating is continued, with occasional stirring, for another 1-2 minutes. Heating for more than 30 seconds is timed. After heating, vegetables are removed from the burner and either immediately served or set aside and kept dry until being quickly re-heated just prior to serving.
- **stir-fry/steaming** applies to more dense or mature vegetables that do not quickly reach tenderness during heating. The vegetable is stir-fried for 1 minute to become very hot, a very small amount of hot water is added to the skillet to create steam, the skillet is tightly covered, the temperature is reduced to low, and the vegetable is steamed for an exactly timed period (a few minutes – almost always no more than 4 minutes), just to tenderness and before cell structure breaks down. Some vegetables, such as potatoes, take a longer time to become very hot. For these vegetables, the heating temperature is reduced to medium after stir-frying and the vegetable is heated for another minute before hot water is added for steaming. Once vegetables are cooked, they are immediately

removed from the hot skillet and either served or set aside away from heat and kept dry until being quickly re-heated just prior to serving.
- **both stir-frying** and **stir-fry/steaming** use extra virgin olive oil as the cooking oil. As minimally processed monounsaturated oil, extra virgin olive oil is high quality oil that withstands moderate heating[133] and that makes a nutritional contribution to dishes. Extra virgin olive oil also enhances the human body's absorption of the valuable fat-soluble phytonutrients and vitamins contained in vegetables.[134] Absorption, in turn, is necessary for fat-soluble nutrients to play human health-supporting roles, an important one being serving as antioxidants.[135]

Chapter One Recipe Organization

Chapter One divides vegetable recipes into three groups. Vegetables in each group are either stir-fried or stir-fried/steamed depending on natural tenderness.

- **General Vegetables (Recipes #1-22).** Covering most commonly used vegetables, this group of recipes yields ready-to-serve vegetables for use as a side dish or in a mixed ingredient dish. Individual recipes include a vegetable profile that provides basic selection, storage, and notable nutritional information. Recipes serve as a preparation and informational reference for vegetable variation suggestions made in Part II dish recipes.
- **Dark Green Leafy Vegetables (Recipes #23-30).** Leafy green vegetables are separately grouped to highlight these highly nutritious vegetables. Stir-fry/steaming reliably and simply yields tasty and colorful cooked greens to bring these outstanding vegetables into easy everyday use, either as a side dish or as a dish ingredient. Individual recipes include a vegetable profile that provides basic selection, storage, and nutritional information. Recipes serve as well as a preparation and informational reference for the leafy vegetable variation suggestions made in Part II dish recipes.
- **Seasoning Vegetables (Recipes #31-37).** These simple and quick cooking vegetables combine with herbs and spices to serve as invaluable flavoring ingredients that minimize the addition of fat-, salt-, or sugar-based outside flavoring to Part II dishes (and in dishes in general). Aiming to assist cooks in taking fullest advantage of these super star flavoring vegetables, recipes detail efficient dicing and mincing technique and provide basic selection and storage information for each vegetable. The onion recipe covers preparation techniques for all varieties of onions, including yellow and red bulb onions, green onions (and similar scallions), shallots, leeks, and chives. Chapter One seasoning vegetable recipes serve as a preparation and informational reference for seasoning vegetable variation suggestions made in Part II dishes.

---

133 Shanahan, *Deep Nutrition*, 131-135. To withstand moderate heating means that extra virgin olive oil is not reactive when it is heated, as is the case of pure vegetable oils. To be reactive means to react with oxygen, which results in the creation of free radicals. Unlike highly processed pure vegetable oil, heating also does not distort extra virgin olive oil and cause it to contain toxic ingredients and trans fat.

134 Robinson, *Eating on the Wild Side*, 37. Research shows that in comparison with other vegetable oils, extra virgin olive oil best enhances absorption of fat-soluble nutritional components. It takes seven times more soybean oil, the oil most commonly used in commercial salad dressing, to get the same absorption results.

135 See the "Nutritional Term Guide" that follows in the Chapter One Introduction for a definition of antioxidants.

PART 1

Stir-Frying and Stir-Fry/Steaming Preparation Notes

Stir-Frying and Stir-Fry/Steaming Preparation Notes provide helpful information that cannot fit into Chapter One recipes. These Notes cover a variety of subjects, including:

- technical details supporting successful recipe preparation (Notes #1-4).
- vegetables that share cooking and nutritional characteristics (Notes #5 and 6).
- selecting and storing vegetables (Note #7).
- cooking tools information (Note #8).

1. **Vary steaming technique when using gas burners.** Chapter One stir-fry/steaming recipes apply to electric burners, which do not quickly adjust to heat setting changes. Because gas burners **do** immediately adjust to heat changes, immediate dropping of the heat to low after one minute of stir-frying can stop the cooking. If the cooking stops, steam will not form, the vegetable will not cook, and the vegetable will be unattractively crisp at the end of the specified steaming time. Described below is the stir-fry/steaming adjustment needed to be made for **gas burners**.

    After one minute of stir-frying, add 1 T hot water as recipes direct but reduce the heat to **medium low**. Cover the skillet and heat the vegetable on medium-low for 30 seconds before reducing the heat to low and setting the timer.

2. An important clue that the skillet temperature is sufficiently hot when adding a vegetable for stir-frying is that **oil immediately and audibly sizzles around the vegetable pieces**. This sizzling should be moderate.

3. An important clue that a vegetable will accurately cook through in the time specified by a recipe is that **water added to a skillet for steaming should immediately sizzle and begin to form steam**.

    - Steaming water should not sizzle wildly as this means that the water will likely evaporate and the vegetable may scorch during steaming. Another 1 T hot water should then be added before reducing the temperature to low, covering the skillet, and setting the timer. Wild sizzling can mean that the skillet being used requires a heavier bottom. It can also mean the medium-high setting of a stove is too high and should be slightly reduced when stir-fry/steaming vegetables.
    - If added water does not sizzle at all, the vegetable is not sufficiently hot and will not, as a result, cook to tenderness in the recipe directed cooking time. In this case, the heating temperature should be increased slightly to bring about sizzling and formation of steam before reducing the heat, covering the skillet, and setting the timer. Failure of steaming water to sizzle immediately likely means the medium-high setting of a stove is too low and needs to be slightly increased for stir-fry/steaming of vegetables.

4. **Chapter One includes a stir-fry and stir-fry/steaming reference to provide cooks with explanatory and trouble-shooting assistance in preparing vegetable recipes.** This

reference (Reference #3: Summarizing Stir-Frying and Stir-Fry/Steaming Techniques) covers all cooking steps, explaining the link of each step to conservation of vegetable attractiveness and nutritional value.

5. **All cabbage family vegetables (also called cruciferous and Brassica vegetables) share common cooking and nutritional characteristics.** Cooks, as a result, can automatically know several important things about the stir-fry/steaming of each of this very large group of vegetables – including bok choy, broccoli, Brussels sprouts, cabbage, cauliflower, kohlrabi, parsnip, rutabaga, and turnip – as well as green leafy vegetables – including collards, kale, mustard greens, and turnip greens. Listed below are important shared characteristics.

   - All cabbage family vegetables have valuable heat-sensitive nutritional content. This content includes vitamin C and phytonutrients of the glucosinolate family. As a result,
     - nonstick skillets are especially useful. They best resist sticking and, as a result, quite reliably protect the vegetables from scorching, which is destructive of heat-sensitive nutritional components.
     - it is important to minimize high temperature heating. Skillet temperature should be accurately gauged before adding vegetables for stir-frying and heat should be quickly reduced after the vegetables are initially heated through at a medium-high heat setting.
     - it is important to minimize overall cooking.
   - All cabbage family vegetables contain sulfur compounds. While these compounds have valuable human-health supporting properties, they can undermine the flavor of cabbage family vegetables. To maintain the sweet natural flavoring of cabbage family vegetables, these compounds must not break down during cooking. This means two important things.
     - It is essential to avoid overcooking, which breaks down cell structure and allows juices to spill from the cell structure. Because sulfur compounds and plant acids that break down sulfur compounds are water soluble, both will be leached into plant juices. Mixed together, plant acids will break down the sulfur compounds.
     - It is essential to coat cut cabbage family vegetables thoroughly with oil in order to hold in juice during cooking. Juice spilling will bring about the mixing of sulfur compounds and plant acids.
   - Cabbage family vegetables include fat-soluble phytonutrients. This characteristic makes stir-fry/steaming especially appropriate for cabbage family preparation. The extra virgin olive oil used in stir-frying enhances the absorption of fat-soluble phytonutrients as they pass through the human digestive system.
   - Most cabbage family vegetables have stems and/or veins. Stems contain valuable nutritional content, notably varied fiber, and should be cooked with the vegetables.

PART 1

Fine chopping of stems, which a chef's knife easily accomplishes, and brief cooking of stems before adding the more tender green leaves successfully softens stems and makes them fully acceptable dish ingredients.

6. **Three kinds of green leafy vegetables – beet greens, chard, and spinach – share common cooking and nutritional characteristics.** This means that cooks can automatically know the following important things about the stir-frying and stir-fry/steaming of these vegetables:

    - Each of these greens has valuable heat-sensitive nutritional content. This content includes vitamin C and phytonutrients of the betalain family. As a result,

        - nonstick skillets are especially useful. They best resist sticking, which quite reliably protects the vegetables from scorching. Scorching is destructive of heat-sensitive nutritional components.
        - it is important to minimize high temperature heating. Skillet temperature should be accurately gauged before adding vegetables for stir-frying, and heat should be quickly reduced once the vegetables are heated until hot at a medium-high heat setting.
        - it is important to minimize all cooking.

    - Stems contain valuable nutritional content, notably varied fiber, and should be cooked with greens. This is easy to do.

        - A chef's knife serves to easily and efficiently chop stems.
        - Thinly chopped stems cook quickly and are completely indiscreet dish ingredients except for adding slight attractive crunchiness.

7. **Cooks can dramatically boost the nutritional value of cooked vegetables through selection of top quality vegetables and retention of top quality form during home storage.** *Cooked Alive!* includes two references to aid cooks in these selecting and storing tasks. Both references, which are identified below, are included in the Part I introduction.

    - Reference #1 (Selecting Top Quality Fresh Whole Vegetables and Fruits). This reference explains the nutritional significance of selecting intact and completely unprocessed (or naturally produced) produce. This is a fresh vegetable that is raw and physically intact; it is not chemically tampered with during either production or marketing. This is either a certified organic or locally grown vegetable.
    - Reference #2 (Key Home Storage Guidelines for Conserving Vegetable and Fruit Quality).

8. **Chapter One recipes require some additional cooking tool information.**

    - The General Cooking Tools list included in the Part I Introduction serves as a descriptive reference for tools commonly used in *all* Part I recipes, but it does not cover tools specific to stir-frying and stir-fry/steaming of vegetables. These cooking tools are listed and described below.

- **Cutting board, large (approx. 16-24 in.): 1 board.** A large cutting board greatly eases the cutting of bulky leafy greens.
- **Kettle, electric tea: 1 kettle.** Heating water for steaming in seconds, an electric tea kettle is an indispensable tool for stir-fry/steaming vegetables.
- **Knife, 7 in. serrated: 1 knife.** This long-handled serrated knife, also called a bread knife, works very well for, and greatly eases, the slicing of piles of leafy greens into small pieces for cooking.
- **Salad spinner: 1 spinner.** This kitchen tool quickly and efficiently dries leafy green vegetables. It works best for drying small and medium size greens.
- **Heavy-bottomed stainless steel skillets with a tight-fitting and opaque lid: at least 1 large (12-14 in.) skillet** and **at least 1 medium (10 in.) skillet**. A **heavy bottom** is a necessary characteristic for both size skillets as it provides even heating and protects vegetables from scorching and burning during steaming. A **tight-fitting and opaque lid** is necessary for efficiently holding in steam during steaming and protecting the B2 (riboflavin) contained in vegetables from destructive light during cooking. A **helper handle** (and especially an insulated handle) is a necessary feature in the case of a large skillet. This handle enables cooks to easily handle the skillet during vegetable preparation, especially while scraping cooked vegetables from the skillet. During this scraping a cook can brace a helper handle against his/her side, which frees one hand for scraping vegetables from the skillet. Another helpful skillet feature is **rounded sides**, which ease stir-frying and removal of ingredients from a skillet. While other heavy-bottomed skillets can be substituted for stainless steel, a cast iron skillet is too heavy to be substituted.
- **Heavy-bottomed nonstick skillets with a tight-fitting and opaque lid: at least 1 medium (10 in) and 1 large (12-14 in) skillet.** Nonstick skillets should have the same features as stainless steel skillets. Green and "eco-friendly" nonstick and ceramic skillets that are made without the chemicals PTFE and PFOLA are both widely and economically marketed and make skillets with a nonstick surface a safe option. With careful attention to heating temperature, however, any other heavy-bottomed nonstick skillet can be substituted.
- **Spatula with a firm handle and a wide and sharp edge: at least 1.** This spatula, called a stir-fry spatula in recipes, should be plastic, plastic coated, or wooden for use on either a nonstick or stainless steel surface. Both a firm handle and sharp edge make for efficient flipping of vegetables during stir-frying.
- **Spatula, rubber or other heat-resistant material: at least 1 but 2 or more spatulas are useful.** This spatula should be firm and pliable to provide efficient scraping of vegetable cooking juice from a skillet after cooking and for including this juice in dishes.

- While each Chapter One recipe lists all cooking tools used, listing them in order of use, some basic working tools are not listed. These tools – including plastic wrap, paper and cloth towels, vegetable scrub brushes and sponges, and at least one multi-purpose cutting board – are routinely used tools that also need to be on hand when preparing Chapter One recipes.

Nutritional Term Guide

While vitamin and mineral content varies among vegetables, vegetables in general are good sources of vitamins and minerals. As a result, recipe nutritional profiles of individual vegetables focus on providing notable or distinctive and more recently learned nutritional information. This includes information about the phytonutrient, fiber, omega-3 essential fatty acid, and pesticide content of vegetables. The following nutritional term guide is included to explain newer and possibly unfamiliar terms used in Chapter One vegetable nutritional profiles. The alphabetically presented terms include: 1) anthocyanin phytonutrients, 2) anti-inflammatory phytonutrients, 3) antioxidants, 4) betalain family of phytonutrients, 5) detoxification phytonutrients, 6) Environmental Working Group, 7) ethylene gas, 8) heat-sensitive fiber, 9) G.I. tract, 10) glycosinolate family of phytonutrients, 11) glycemic index (GI), 12) phytonutrients, 13) respiration rate, and 14) sulfur compounds.

1. **Anthocyanin phytonutrients.** Anthocyanin (an-tho-cy-a-nin) phytonutrients are a group (or class) of plant pigments that have been scientifically demonstrated to have the ability to serve as especially powerful human health-protecting antioxidants. Belonging to a parent class of water soluble molecules called flavonoids, anthocyanins are associated with particular plant pigments, including blue, violet (or purple), and reddish brown. In recognition of the potency of the phytonutrients represented, these colors are the highest-ranking colors in the phytonutrient color hierarchy.

2. **Anti-inflammatory phytonutrients.** Inflammation is the human body's self-protective mechanism to help remove the harmful stimuli that is the cause of the inflammation and to begin healing. Inflammation, however, can itself be harmful. Scientific research is linking chronic and extended inflammation with more and more degenerative diseases, notably heart disease and cancer but also obesity, atherosclerosis, type 2 diabetes, high blood pressure, and several forms of arthritis. This research is making it clear that preventing inflammation is crucial to maintaining good health. Eating vegetables containing phytonutrients with strong anti-inflammatory properties – such as **flavonoid**, **carotenoid**, and **glucosinolate phytonutrients** – in a way that maximizes conservation and absorption of these phytonutrients is an important means of enabling one's body to properly manage and control as well as heal inflammation.

3. **Antioxidants.** Antioxidants are beneficial chemical compounds that protect human bodily parts (such as cell membranes, cholesterol particles, and important compounds like proteins, fatty acids, and DNA) from destructive free radicals, which is called protecting the body from oxidative stress. Antioxidants can also reverse the damage done to bodily parts by free radicals.[136] Natural human oxygen-using processes (such as the burning of fats and carbohydrates to produce energy), exposure to certain substances

---

[136] See footnote 57 for two references that clearly describe free radicals.

in the human environment (such as radiation, cigarette smoke, air and water pollution, irradiation, certain chemicals, and sun rays), and certain foods eaten (such as heated pure vegetable oil) produce free radicals, which are the by-products of oxygen-based reactions (oxidation). Lacking an electron, these free radicals are unstable and disabled molecules. They frantically scavenge bodily components in search of an electron. When they capture an electron from another molecule, this destabilizes the molecule losing the electron, and the newly disabled molecule sets off on its own frantic search for an electron. In capturing an electron from a molecule, in other words, free radicals set off a chain reaction. Thousands of free radical reactions can occur within seconds, and these reactions are highly damaging to bodily parts. The greater the number of hits, the greater the damage. The damage continues until an **antioxidant** comes to the rescue and absorbs the rampaging free radical. When a human body has a deficiency of antioxidants, the damage by free radicals can become cumulative and lead to severe health problems, including cancer, heart disease, arthritis, cataract formation, decline in brain and immune system function, and aging. While the human body itself makes antioxidants, the body has evolved to be biologically dependent on vegetables and fruits to supplement antioxidants. As a result, a deficiency easily occurs when a human does not regularly eat vegetables and fruits, wastes phytonutrient content, and eats large quantities of foods that produce free radicals, such as refined, bleached, and deodorized pure vegetable oils.[137]

Important points about antioxidants are as follows:

- The human body protects itself from free radicals by distributing antioxidants throughout the body. These antioxidants protect human bodily components by neutralizing free radicals. They give up an electron to free radicals and do so without turning into electron-scavenging substances themselves. The greater the number and variety of antioxidants available to bodily components, the greater the protection from free radicals provided.[138]
- Phytonutrients contained by vegetables and fruits are invaluable sources of antioxidants for humans. Plants produce different varieties (or families) of phytonutrients for their own protection from free radicals, and this protection is passed on to humans when they consume vegetables and fruits.
- Other nutrients contained by vegetables and fruits play an important antioxidant role for humans, either directly or in combination with phytonutrients. Vitamins C, E, and A (which the human body makes from beta carotene) and the minerals manganese, zinc, copper, and iron are primary examples.
- Vegetables and fruits provide micronutrients that are essential to the human body's ability to make enzymes, which serve as the body's own natural defense against free radicals.
- Air, light, and heat are destroyers of antioxidants. Industrial processing also destroys or deliberately removes antioxidants, as is the case of pure vegetable oil.

---

137 Shanahan, *Deep Nutrition*, 134-157. In "Good Fats and Bad" (121-162), in the section entitled "The Trouble with Vegetable Oil" (143-153), Shanahan details how pure vegetable oil is highly reactive and produces free radicals when heated. Humans consume free radicals in food cooked in vegetable oil.
138 Robinson, *Eating on the Wild Side*, 160. A common way to measure the antioxidant content of a food is in terms of its ORAC value, which stands for oxygen radical absorbance capacity.

PART 1

4. **Betalain family of phytonutrients.** Betalains are red and yellow pigments that are valuable human health-protecting phytonutrients contained by spinach, chard, and beets (both the greens and root). One of the important human health-supporting functions they are known to perform is serving as antioxidants. Both water soluble and heat-sensitive phytonutrients, betalains are fragile and must be deliberately conserved.

5. **Detoxification phytonutrients.** Some phytonutrients aid the human body's detoxification system for removing/deactivating toxic substances entering the body. For example, glucosinolates, which are phytonutrients contained by all cabbage family vegetables, can be converted to substances that have the ability to improve the human body's detoxification process. Glucosinolates, for example, help increase the liver's ability to produce enzymes that neutralize potentially toxic substances that enter the body, thereby preventing toxin-related damage that can lead to serious health problems, including cancer.

6. **Environmental Working Group.** This is an American nonpartisan, nonprofit environmental research group that charts the pesticide content of common industrially grown vegetables and fruits. Providing a shopper's guide, it makes a yearly ranking of 50 vegetables and fruits according to pesticide content, setting forth a Clean Fifteen group, which includes vegetables and fruits with the least pesticide content, and a Dirty Dozen group, which includes the most contaminated produce.

7. **Ethylene gas.** A variety of ripe fruits (such as apples, bananas, cantaloupe, and plums) and vegetables (such as white potatoes, green onions, and tomatoes) naturally produce ethylene gas and release it during storage. This gas is harmful to particular ethylene-sensitive vegetables and fruits. Ethylene gas, for example, harms the flavor of carrots (turns them bitter), changes the color of leafy greens (and chard in particular) to yellow, and speeds the ripening of sensitive fruits, such as kiwi. Commercial businesses use ethylene gas to force ripen some fruit (such as tomato) and to make citrus fruit look like it is ripe when in fact it is not. This false ripening of citrus fruit is called degreening.

8. **Heat-sensitive fiber.** Heating can damage some plant fiber by shortening the length of its fibers. This shortening negatively affects the capacity of the fiber to benefit human intestinal health. Shortened fibers cannot survive the length of the human intestinal tract and be available for use by beneficial bacteria living in the intestine. Examples of these heat-sensitive fibers are **fructan fiber**, which is a soluble fiber, and **cellulose fiber**, which is an insoluble fiber. When these two forms of fiber reach the intestine, they are valuable prebiotics that support good bacteria living in the human large intestine. They play invaluable human health-protecting roles.

9. **G.I. tract.** Used in discussions of the link between dietary fiber and beneficial microbes inhabiting the human intestinal system, this abbreviation stands for gastrointestinal tract. It refers to both the digestive and intestinal tracts of humans. Human gut also refers to the gastrointestinal tract.

10. **Glucosinolate family of phytonutrients.** Glucosinolates (glu-co-sin-o-lates) are valuable

human health-protecting phytonutrients contained by all cabbage family vegetables. These sulfur-containing phytonutrients have both antioxidant and anti-inflammatory capacity, but they also provide important detoxification support. Glucosinolate phytonutrients, for example, increase the liver's ability to produce enzymes that neutralize potentially toxic substances.[139] Glucosinolates also protect the health of the human digestive system. For example, sulforaphane, a glucosinolate phytonutrient, helps protect the health of the stomach lining. Both water soluble and sensitive to heat, glucosinolates are fragile phytonutrients that require deliberate conservation during food preparation.

11. **Glycemic index (GI)**. Vegetables contain sugar, and when humans eat vegetables, they digest this sugar at differing rates and with differing effects on blood sugar levels. The glycemic index is a scale that ranks vegetables according to how much they raise human blood sugar (glucose) levels when consumed. Low glycemic index vegetables, which are typically fiber rich vegetables that are digested more slowly, release their sugar over a span of a few hours rather than in a short burst, as is the case of high glycemic index vegetables. High glycemic index vegetables tend to be low fiber foods that consist mostly of carbohydrates, such as white potatoes. The glycemic index does not take into consideration the effect of mixing a high glycemic index vegetable with one or more high fiber vegetables or with some protein and some fat. Mixing slows digestion, which is almost always the case of *Cooked Alive!* Part II dishes. Chapter One recipes, as a result, typically do not call attention to the GI of vegetables.

12. **Phytonutrients**. Phytonutrients (pronounced figh-toe nutrients; *phyto* means plant), also called phytochemicals, are plant derived chemicals that protect plants from threats to their health, such as from germs, fungi, bugs, and sun rays. As many as 10,000 different kinds of phytonutrients have so far been identified, and the relatively few phytonutrients contained in vegetables and fruits that have already been thoroughly researched have been proven to provide significant health benefits to humans. This is because the protective benefits of phytonutrients for vegetables and fruits are transferred to humans when they consume vegetables and fruits. Phytonutrients contained by vegetables and fruits are divided into families, and different phytonutrient families are associated with particular colors. Typically different colors are associated with particular kinds of human health protection, with the different protections performed being antioxidant, anti-inflammation, and detoxification. Some phytonutrients, such as the glucosinolate family of phytonutrients, perform all three of these human health-protective functions. Typically the more vibrant the color of a vegetable or fruit, the more concentrated the phytonutrient content of a vegetable or fruit. There are exceptions to this rule, however, with some light-colored vegetables and fruits (such as cauliflower, mushrooms, artichokes, and white-fleshed nectarines and peaches) having concentrated phytonutrient content. There is a color hierarchy, with particular colors (red, purple, and reddish brown) having most potent humanhealth-protective capacity.

13. **Respiration rate**. When vegetables are harvested, they continue to consume oxygen and to produce carbon dioxide. In other words, they continue to breathe. Vegetables

---

[139] Mateljan, *The World's Healthiest Foods*, 2nd edition, 198.

have differing respiration, or breathing, rates, and the faster the respiration rate, the faster both flavorful sugar content and particular nutrients (such as phytonutrients and vitamin C content) are burned and lost. Thus, the higher the respiration rate, the less time a vegetable should be stored before being consumed. Cooks can slow the respiration rate to reduce the loss of vegetable flavor and nutritional value in several ways.[140] Guidelines #2 and #3 of Reference #2 (Key Home Storage Guidelines for Conserving Vegetable and Fruit Quality) identify general storage techniques for slowing the respiration rate of vegetables as well as a specific storage technique. This technique is called the Robinson vented plastic bag storage method.[141]

14. **Sulfur compounds.** These chemical compounds are contained by all cabbage family vegetables (which include bok choy, broccoli, Brussels sprouts, cabbage, cauliflower, kohlrabi, parsnips, rutabaga, and turnips) and cabbage family greens (collards, kale, mustard greens, and turnip greens). If cooking breaks down cell structure, sulfur compounds and plant acids contained in cells mix together. This mixing of sulfur compounds and plant acids breaks down the sulfur compounds, which converts them into negative ingredients. They cause loss of the natural sweet flavor of cabbage family vegetables, cause the release of unpleasant odor during cooking, and can cause digestive discomfort when cabbage family vegetables are eaten by humans. By avoiding the breakdown of cell structure, stir-fry/steaming prevents the breakdown of sulfur compounds, enabling cabbage family vegetables to be reliably tasty, fully acceptable vegetables. Sulfur compounds also play positive human health-supporting roles. By keeping sulfur compounds safely locked within cell structure, stir-frying and stir-fry/steaming conserve the compounds in naturally occurring form for optimum use by human bodies.

General Vegetable Recipes

1. Asparagus
(Stir-Fried/Steamed)
(2 servings)

½ lb chilled uniformly thick asparagus spears (approx. 8 spears asparagus)
1 T extra virgin olive oil

1 T hot water
¼ t salt

Cooking Tools

1 large skillet with a tight-fitting & opaque lid
1 electric tea kettle
1 5 in. serrated knife
dinner plate

1 plastic or plastic-coated stir-fry spatula
1 timer
1 rubber or other heat-resistant spatula
1 colander 1 set measuring spoons   1

---

140 Robinson, *Eating on the Wild Side*, 31.
141 Ibid., 30-31. Robinson uses pinpricks to slightly vent sealed storage bags, which she labels "microperforated" bags.

1. **Gather all cooking tools.**

2. **Heat the skillet at a medium setting.** Begin heating an electric tea kettle to prepare water for steaming.

3. **Prepare the asparagus for stir-fry/steaming.**

    - Rinse the asparagus spears in cool water, shake them to remove clinging water, spread the spears over a layer of paper or cloth towels, add a top layer of towels, roll the towels around the spears, and gently squeeze the spears to dry the pieces completely.
    - Beginning at the thinnest end, bend spears until they naturally snap. Set aside the bottom portion of spears that do not break when bent.
    - Leave the top tips whole but cut the other snapped off portions of the spears crosswise into sections approximately ½ to 1 inch in length.
    - Slice off and discard the bottom tip of each spear. Use a serrated knife to cut the bottom portion of spears that do not break when bent crosswise into thin ⅛ in. thick slices. Keep these slices separate from the rest of the asparagus. Note that larger spears with thicker skins can first be peeled. This skin adds some crunch to the cooked asparagus, but thin slicing largely effectively integrates the skin.

4. **Stir-fry/steam the asparagus.**

    - Increase the skillet heat to medium-high.
    - When a drop of water added to the skillet instantly dances and disappears, add 1 T oil to the skillet, add any bottom spear slices, and cook them for about 30 seconds, stirring often.
    - Add the remaining asparagus and stir-fry it for 1 minute, setting a timer. Stir-frying should at first be vigorous to quickly and thoroughly coat asparagus pieces with oil but can slow to "flip often" pace after one half minute.
    - At the timer, add 1 T hot water, cover the skillet, reduce the heat to low, and steam the asparagus just to tenderness (2 minutes for thin and very fresh, 3 minutes for spears in general), setting a timer.
    - At the timer, remove the skillet from the heat, evenly sprinkle ¼ t salt over the asparagus, and use a rubber spatula to scrape the asparagus and any cooking juice into a serving bowl for immediate serving or into a colander placed over a dinner plate for serving in a mixed ingredient dish.
    - Serve any collected cooking juice with the asparagus.

    VARIATIONS: Add **1 t dried herbs**, such as sweet basil, oregano, marjoram, or dill weed. Evenly sprinkle crushed herb over the asparagus during stir frying.

Asparagus Profile

Asparagus has notable nutritional characteristics.

- Asparagus is one of the richest vegetable sources of phytonutrients marketed in grocery stores. It is an outstanding source of both antioxidant and anti-inflammatory phytonutrients. These phytonutrients include anthocyanins, which are super potent antioxidants. Asparagus also contains a wide variety of antioxidant micronutrients, including vitamins C and E and the minerals zinc, manganese, and selenium. These nutrients combine with phytonutrients to provide exceptional antioxidant protection for humans. Asparagus also contains magnesium, which combines with anti-inflammatory phytonutrients to intensify anti-inflammatory protection.
- Asparagus is a good source of both soluble and insoluble fiber. Its soluble fiber content includes a particularly rich amount of a kind of fibers called fructans, which is a type of prebiotic. This means that fructan fibers feed and encourage good bacteria in the human gut. The thick ends of asparagus are good sources of a kind of insoluble fibers called cellulose. Supportive of beneficial microorganisms in the human gut, cellulose fiber, like fructan fiber, is prebiotic. They are particularly valuable as they are long enough to survive human digestion and reach the big intestine. Gut bacteria ferment these fibers, which converts the fiber into human-health promoting form. Because these fibers are heat sensitive, stir-frying and stir-fry/steaming reliably conserve them in long form.
- The overall mineral content of asparagus classes it as a good alkaline balancing food.
- Industrially produced asparagus is listed in the Environmental Working Group's 2016 Clean Fifteen group of least contaminated with pesticides. However, certified organic and locally produced asparagus provide the other benefits of naturally produced vegetables, notably more potent phytonutrient content and greater nutritional content.

To select most flavorful asparagus,

- select very fresh asparagus. Very fresh asparagus has the sweetest flavor and is also most tender. Fresh asparagus has dark green, shiny, straight, and firm spears with compact tips that are either uniformly green or purplish in color. Inside pulp should be bright green, moist, and juicy. The cut stem end should also be smooth and look moist, not be dry and rough. Both thin and thick stems of very fresh asparagus are tender.
- purchase asparagus from farmers' markets or other local markets, which will be the freshest of all asparagus. To take advantage of the nutritional quality and sweetness of fresh asparagus, it is important to select asparagus that is being chilled during marketing and then to quickly and thoroughly chill it for storage. For example, drop it into ice water for several minutes before drying it thoroughly for storage.

To store asparagus,

- immediately refrigerate it upon purchase to halt loss of phytonutrient content and flavoring, which is rapid because of its high respiration rate. Store it using Robinson's vented sealable plastic bag method (10 uniformly spaced pin pricks for a quart size bag; 20 pin pricks for a gallon bag; bag sealed with as much air squeezed from the bag as possible; stored in the refrigerator's crisper drawer). For very short storage, wrap the asparagus within paper towels and place it within a sealed bag, pressing out as much air as possible before sealing.
- use it quickly, the very day it is purchased if at all possible. While quickly chilled asparagus stores well without obvious spoiling, it's very high respiration rate causes rapid flavor and phytonutrient loss. Asparagus also becomes tougher and more acidic with storage.

2. Beet
(Stir-Fried/Steamed)
(2 servings)

4 medium (approx. 2½ in. diameter) or 8 small (approx. 1½ in. diameter) chilled beets (to yield approx. 2-3 c diced)

1 T extra virgin olive oil
1 T hot water
¼ t salt

Cooking Tools

1 large skillet with a tight-fitting & opaque lid
1 electric tea kettle
1 each chef's & 5 in. serrated knife
1 non-porous cutting board
1 set measuring spoons

1 plastic or plastic-coated stir-fry spatula
1 rubber or other heat-resistant spatula
1 timer
1 colander
1 dinner plate

---

1. **Gather all cooking tools.**

2. **Heat a large skillet on a large burner at a medium setting.** Begin heating an electric tea kettle to prepare water for steaming.

3. **Prepare the beets for cooking.**

    - Scrub and thoroughly dry the beets.
    - Use a chef's knife to cut off the stem end and the bottom tip of each beet and to halve each lengthwise.

- Place the halves cut-side-down on a non-porous cutting board (to avoid staining) and slice each half lengthwise into ¼ in. thick slices.
- Stacking two slices together at a time, cut the beet slices lengthwise into ¼ in. thick strips, and cut the strips crosswise into ¼ in. cubes.

4. **Stir-fry/steam the beets.**

- Increase the skillet heat to a medium-high setting.
- When a drop of water added to the skillet immediately dances and disappears, add 1 T oil to the skillet, add the beets, and stir-fry them for 1 minute, setting a timer. Stir-frying should at first be vigorous to quickly and thoroughly coat beet pieces with oil but can slow to "flip often" pace after one half minute.
- At the timer, reduce the heat to medium (a level where oil gently sizzles around beet pieces) and heat the beets, stirring them occasionally, for 1 minute, setting a timer.
- At the timer, add 1 T hot water, cover the skillet, reduce the heat to low, and steam the beets for 10 minutes, setting a timer.
- At the timer, turn off the heat, uncover the skillet, evenly sprinkle ¼ t salt over the beets, and remove the skillet from the burner.
- For beets to be immediately served as a side dish, use a rubber spatula to scrape the beets and any cooking juice into a serving bowl.
- For beets to be served in a mixed-ingredient dish, scrape the beets into a colander placed over a dinner plate for collecting any steaming juice. Set the beets aside until the dish is assembled, including any steaming juice.

VARIATIONS: Add ½-1 t **dried herb leaves**, such as dill weed and sweet basil, oregano, or marjoram leaves. Crush dried herb leaves between your palms over the beets during stir-frying.

Beet Profile

Beets (also called beet roots) have distinctive nutritional characteristics.

- Beets get red-purple coloring from phytonutrients called **betalains**, which makes them different from almost all other vegetables. Because of this betalain content, beets rank among the healthiest of all commonly eaten vegetables, having more antioxidant properties than all vegetables commonly available in grocery stores except for artichoke, red cabbage, kale, and bell pepper.[142] The valuable betalains are water soluble, highly vulnerable to oxidation, and heat sensitive. By minimizing contact with water, exposure to air, high temperature heating, and cooking time, stir-fry/steaming achieves maximum conservation of betalain phytonutrients.

---

142 Robinson, *Eating on the Wild Side*, 123-124. Beets have nine times more antioxidant activity than the typical tomato and fifty times more antioxidant activity than orange carrots. Robinson describes other nutritional components of beets, such as natural sodium nitrate and boron, which are linked with significant health-building attributes, such as enhancement of physical endurance.

- Beets also contain carotene family phytonutrients, which provide antioxidant protection to humans. These phytonutrients are fat-soluble, and the exra virgin olive oil used in stir-frying/steaming enhances the absorption of these phytonutrients by humans.
- Beets are an outstanding source of soluble fiber.

When selecting beets,

- select small (1½-2 in. diameter) to medium (2½ in. diameter) beets as reliably tender and easy-to-dice beets.
- select beets that are dark red, uniformly firm, and heavy feeling for their size. The skin should be mainly smooth (the skin around the stem end can be somewhat rough) and unblemished.
- select bunched beets (beets with tops attached) as freshest beets. The leafy tops should be firm and bright green without any yellowing.
- select in-season beets. In the United States this is generally from June through October.

To store beets,

- remove and separately store beet greens as directed in Recipe #23, leaving two inches of stem on each beet.
- gently scrub room temperature roots (being careful not to tear open the protective skin), dry the beets, and refrigerate them uncovered in the crisper draw. When they are thoroughly chilled, wrap them within a paper towel and transfer them to a plastic bag, pressing out as much air as possible before sealing the bag.
- use beets within two weeks of storage. As beets have a low respiration rate, they will store without obvious spoilage for two or more months. Because antioxidant value decreases over time, however, using them within two weeks maximizes beet nutritional value.

3. Bok Choy
(Stir-Fried)
(2 servings)

½ lb chilled bok choy (small or medium size; to yield 2-3 c sliced stems & leafy tops)	1 T extra virgin olive oil ¼ t salt

Cooking Tools

1 large nonstick skillet 1 electric tea kettle	1 plastic or plastic-coated stir-fry spatula 1 timer

1 each chef's & 5 in. serrated knife	1 rubber or other heat-resistant spatula
1 cutting board reserved for vegetables & fruits	1 colander
1 set measuring spoons	1 dinner plate

———◆———

1. **Gather all cooking tools.**

2. **Heat a large nonstick skillet on a large burner at a medium setting.** Begin heating an electric tea kettle for preparing water for steaming.

3. **Prepare bok choy for stir-frying.**

    - Rinse and dry the stalks and leafy tops. Use a chef's knife to cut off the very bottom tip of each stalk and to cut the green leafy tops from each stalk.
    - Use the chef's knife to cut each stalk lengthwise into ¼ in. thick strips and to cut the strips crosswise into ¼-in. cubes.
    - Keeping the greens separate from the diced stalks, stack the green leafy tops. While holding the green tops roughly together with one hand, use a serrated knife to cut the leaves first lengthwise and then crosswise into ⅓ in. thick pieces.

4. **Stir-fry the bok choy.**

    - Increase the skillet heat to a medium-high setting.
    - When a drop of water added to the skillet instantly dances and disappears, add 1 T oil, add the diced stalks, heat them (stirring often) for about 30 seconds, add the green tops, and stir-fry the mixture for 1 minute, setting a timer. Stir-frying should at first be vigorous to quickly and thoroughly coat pieces with oil but can slow to "flip often" pace after one half minute.
    - At the timer, remove the skillet from the heat, evenly sprinkle ¼ t salt over the bok choy, and use a rubber spatula to scrape it and any cooking juice into a serving bowl for immediate serving or into a colander placed over a dinner plate for serving the bok choy in a mixed ingredient dish.
    - Serve any collected cooking juice with the bok choy.

    VARIATIONS: Substitute **larger and/or more mature bok choy.** Use stir-fry/steaming and a skillet with a tight-fitting and opaque lid. After the bok choy stir-fries for 1 minute, add 1 T hot water, cover the skillet, reduce the heat to low, and steam the bok choy for 3 minutes, setting a timer, just until the stalks are softened and the leafy tops retain bright green coloration.

———◆———

Bok Choy Profile

A form of Chinese cabbage, bok choy shares the nutritional and cooking characteristics

of other cabbage family vegetable. This means that bok choy, and particularly its green leafy tops, has significant overall nutritional value, contributing to nearly every category of nutritional content. Bok choy, for example,

- contains highly human health-promoting but fragile (water soluble and heat sensitive) phytonutrients called glucosinolates (described in the Chapter One introduction, Nutritional Term Guide, #10) that provide antioxidant, anti-inflammatory, and detoxification protection for humans.
- contains other antioxidant phytonutrients (such as flavonoids and carotenoids) along with a wealth of antioxidant micronutrients (notably vitamin C and the minerals zinc and manganese) that combine with these phytonutrients to expand the antioxidant protection provided humans.
- contains nutrients (notably magnesium, vitamin K, and omega-3 essential fatty acids, alpha linolenic acid form) that combine with glucosinolate phytonutrients to intensify the anti-inflammatory protection provided humans.
- contains sulfur compounds (also described in the Chapter One introduction, Nutritional Term Guide, #14) that are both nutritionally valuable components and potentially dangerous flavor-altering ingredients. These compounds easily undermine the bright green color and flavor of the leafy greens if bok choy is overcooked.
- has stand out content of particular vitamins (vitamins K, folate, and B6), is an excellent or good source of most B vitamins, and is either an excellent or very good source of alkaline minerals in general.

To select bok choy, select products that have heavy-feeling, uniformly firm, and bright white stalks with firm and fresh appearing dark green leaves.

To store bok choy,

- store intact, unwashed heads within a sealed plastic bag. As bok choy has a high respiration rate, wrap the leaves in paper towels and vent the bag using the Robinson vented plastic bag storage method (seal the bag, pressing out as much air as possible; add uniformly placed pin pricks, 10 per quart bag, 20 for gallon bag; refrigerate within the crisper drawer).
- store bok choy for as little time as possible to maximize retention of its sweet flavor and nutritional value.

4. Broccoli
(Stir-Fried/Steamed)
(2 servings)

2 chilled stalks broccoli
1 T extra virgin olive oil

1 T hot water
¼ t salt

Cooking Tools

1 large nonstick skillet with a tight-fitting & opaque lid
1 electric tea kettle
1 5 in. serrated knife
1 set measuring spoons

1 plastic or plastic-coated stir-fry spatula
1 rubber or other heat-resistant spatula
1 timer
1 colander
1 dinner plate

1. **Gather all cooking tools.**

2. **Heat a large nonstick skillet on a large burner at a medium setting.** Begin heating an electric tea kettle for hot water for steaming.

3. **Prepare the broccoli for stir-fry/steaming.**

   - Rinse each broccoli stalk with cool water and shake the stalks to remove clinging water. Drying one stalk at a time, wrap a stalk within paper or cloth towels and firmly squeeze the florets to dry them thoroughly.
   - Turn a broccoli stalk on its side. Rotating around a stalk, use a serrated knife to cut off the florets, cutting the stems off at the stalk. Either set aside the stalk for eating as a raw snack or use a serrated knife to peel it and to cut it crosswise into ¼ in. thick slices for cooking. Note that very thin (⅛ in. thick) slicing makes it possible to include the skin, which becomes scarcely noticeable.
   - Separate and set aside any leaves from the stalks. Halve large leaves.
   - Use the serrated knife to halve each floret lengthwise. Place each floret half cut side down on a cutting board and halve it lengthwise. Cut large floret halves into ¼ in. wide slices.

4. **Stir-fry/steam the broccoli.**

   - Increase the skillet heat to a medium-high setting.
   - When a drop of water added to the skillet instantly dances and disappears, add 1 T oil, add the broccoli florets and any sliced stalk, and stir-fry them for 1 minute, setting a timer. Stir-frying should at first be vigorous to quickly and thoroughly coat pieces with oil but can slow to "flip often" pace after one half minute.
   - At the timer, add 1 T hot water, cover the skillet, reduce the heat to low, and steam the broccoli for 4 minutes, setting a timer.
   - At the timer, remove the skillet from the heat, evenly sprinkle ¼ t salt over the broccoli, and use a rubber spatula to scrape the broccoli and any cooking juice either into a bowl for immediate serving or into a colander placed over a dinner plate for serving in a mixed ingredient dish.
   - Serve any collected juice with the broccoli.

VARIATION: **To ensure the stems of larger florets are tender,** partially remove the stems and cut them into thin pieces for cooking. To make this preparation change, leave only a ½ in. stem on florets, separate any cut-off stems from the florets, group the cut-off stems together, and use a chef's knife to chop these cut-off stems into thin pieces.

Substitute **broccoli raab** (pronounced rob) for broccoli. Leave florets attached to 1½-3 in. long leafy stems and cut remaining stem (except for the bottom 2 inches) crosswise into ½ in. thick slices. Set the bottom stems aside for use in soup stock. Boiling whole perhaps better suits broccoli raab, with individual stems boiled whole for 2 minutes only. Cut the stems into serving size for serving.

Broccoli Profile

Broccoli has celebrated nutritional characteristics.

- As a cruciferous or cabbage family vegetable, broccoli contains rich phytonutrient content, as is indicated by its dark green coloring. This phytonutrient content includes human health-promoting glucosinolates and other antioxidants, including carotenoids, which give broccoli exceptional antioxidant capacity. At the same time broccoli contains antioxidant nutrients, including a stand out amount of the vitamins C, A (in the form of beta carotene), and E and of the mineral manganese. These nutrients add to the antioxidant protection broccoli provides to humans.
- Along with providing super antioxidant protection, glucosinolate phytonutrients provide both anti-inflammatory and detoxification support. Broccoli is also a good source of omega-3 essential fatty acids (alpha-linolenic acid form) and the mineral magnesium, which serve to enhance the anti-inflammatory protection that broccoli provides.
- Broccoli is a super source of the full spectrum of vitamins and minerals, including exceptional folate and vitamin K content.
- Being a good source of both insoluble and soluble fiber, broccoli also promotes the health of the human digestive system.

Broccoli has distinctive cooking characteristics.

- Broccoli's sulfur compound content easily undermines broccoli's natural sweet flavoring and rich green color if broccoli is overcooked.
- The high vitamin C content of broccoli makes it vulnerable to unattractive browning during stir-frying. This browning indicates destruction of vitamin C content, and this browning undermines overall broccoli flavor as well. Browning can occur when the skillet temperature is too high and when broccoli slices are not sufficiently coated with protective oil. Insufficient coating easily occurs when a skillet is not wiped clean and juice from other cooked vegetables remains in the skillet. Such juice prevents oil from forming a protective coating on the exposed flesh of broccoli slices.

To select the most flavorful and nutritious broccoli, select, as far as possible,

- ultra fresh broccoli. Select heavy feeling stalks that have brightly colored and firm florets that fit tightly together and do not have any yellow coloring. Attached leaves should also be brightly colored and firm. The stalk should be firm, and its bottom end should look moist and smooth, not dry and rough. The broccoli should have a mildly sweet or neutral flagrance.
- in-season broccoli, which in the United States is in the colder months of the year.
- locally grown broccoli marketed at farmers' markets and natural food stores. Because broccoli has an extremely high respiration rate, broccoli shipped for long distances loses much of its phytonutrient and antioxidant content and sweet flavor before it reaches markets.[143] Select broccoli from vendors at farmers' markets who keep broccoli chilled during marketing.
- purple broccoli, which has the highest anthocyanin (human disease fighting phytonutrients) content and content of other antioxidant phytonutrients of broccoli varieties.
- certified organic broccoli. Conventionally produced broccoli is given only a middling listing in the Environmental Working Group's 2016 listing that ranks vegetables and fruits by pesticide content, which means its pesticide residue content is quite high. Certified organic broccoli, in contrast, is substantially free of pesticide content and, equally important, has been grown on naturally fertilized soil. Research shows that vegetables produced on naturally fertilized soil have significantly higher phytonutrient content than counterpart industrially produced vegetables. Selection of certified organic broccoli is especially important when it is often included in everyday eating.

To store broccoli,

- immediately refrigerate unwashed broccoli to slow its very high respiration rate, which quickly causes the loss of broccoli's sweetness and high phytonutrient value.
- use the Robinson vented plastic bag storage method (store unwashed broccoli within a sealed gallon-size bag; press out as much air as possible before sealing the bag; add 10 to 20 evenly spaced pin pricks; and refrigerate the broccoli in the crisper drawer). For broccoli to be quickly used, rinse and dry individual stalks, wrap them within paper towels, and store them in a sealed plastic bag from which as much air as possible is removed before sealing. This broccoli is in ready-to-prepare form for quick inclusion in meals.
- use it within 2-3 days of purchase to take fullest advantage of the broccoli's top flavor and nutritional richness.

---

143   Ibid., 160-161. Broccoli can lose up to 80 percent of its beneficial nutrients during shipping, marketing, and home storage.

5. Brussels Sprouts
(Stir-Fried/Steamed)
(2 servings)

½ lb Brussels sprouts, chilled
    (to yield approx. 2-3 c halved sprouts)
1 T extra virgin olive oil

1½ T hot water
¼ t salt

Cooking Tools

1 large nonstick skillet with a tight-fitting & opaque lid
1 electric tea kettle
1 colander
1 pie plate
1 5 in. serrated knife

1 set measuring spoons
1 plastic or plastic-coated stir-fry spatula
1 timer
1 rubber or other heat-resistant spatula
1 dinner plate

---

1. **Gather all cooking tools.**

2. **Heat a large nonstick skillet on a large burner at a medium setting.** Begin heating an electric tea kettle to prepare hot water for steaming.

3. **Prepare the Brussels sprouts for stir-fry/steaming.**

   - Add the sprouts to a colander and quickly rinse them with cold water.
   - Remove and discard any loose and limp outside leaves.
   - Pour the sprouts into a pie plate lined with a double thickness of paper towels and wrap the towels around the sprouts to dry them.
   - Use a serrated knife to cut off protruding stem tips, being careful not to cut off leaves, and to halve each sprout lengthwise.

4. **Stir-fry/steam the sprouts.**

   - Increase the skillet heat to medium-high. Begin heating an electric tea kettle to prepare hot water for steaming.
   - When a drop of water added to the skillet instantly dances and disappears, add 1 T oil, add the Brussels sprouts, and stir-fry them for 1 minute, setting a timer. Stir-frying should at first be vigorous to quickly and thoroughly coat the sprouts with oil but can slow to "flip often" pace after one half minute.
   - At the timer, add 1 T hot water, cover the skillet, reduce the heat to low, and steam the sprouts for 4 minutes, setting a timer.
   - Remove the skillet from the heat, evenly sprinkle ¼ t salt over the sprouts, and use a rubber spatula to scrape them and any cooking juice into a serving bowl for

immediate serving or into a colander placed over a dinner plate for serving the sprouts in a mixed ingredient dish.
- Serve any collected steaming juice with the Brussels sprouts.

VARIATIONS: Quarter rather than halve the sprouts and reduce steaming time to 3 minutes.

Add ½-1 t dried herbs. Add, for example, ½ t dill seeds, cooking the seeds in the oil for 30 seconds before adding the sprouts for stir-frying. Add ½ t dried thyme leaves, ½ t dried dill weed, or ½-1 t each sweet basil and oregano, crushing the leaves between your palms before evenly sprinkling them over the sprouts during stir-frying.

Brussels Sprouts Profile

Brussels sprouts have special nutritional characteristics. This incredible nutritional content, which stir-fry/steaming conserves, includes, for example,

- glucosinolate phytonutrients. Brussels sprouts have the greatest amount of these highly human health-supporting phytonutrients of any cabbage family vegetable. These phytonutrients give Brussels sprouts outstanding antioxidant, anti-inflammatory, and detoxification power. At the same time Brussels sprouts contain rich amounts of antioxidant nutrients that combine with glucosinolate and other antioxidant phytonutrients contained by Brussels sprouts to provide exceptional antioxidant protection for humans. These nutrients include the vitamins C, A (in the form of beta carotene), and E and the mineral manganese. As glucosinolates are sulfur-containing phytonutrients, Brussels sprouts contribute the ingredients needed by the human body to make sulforaphane, which plays a crucial role in protecting the health of the stomach lining.[144]
- stand-out vitamin K, very good omega-3 essential fatty acids (alpha linolenic acid form), and good magnesium content, all nutritional components that enhance the anti-inflammatory protection provided to humans by Brussels sprouts.
- very good folate content. As folate is a heat-sensitive nutrient, diets often have low folate content.
- both soluble and insoluble fiber, which support the health of the human digestive system.

Brussels sprouts have sensitive cooking characteristics.

- Like other cabbage family vegetables, Brussels sprouts contain sulfur compounds, which easily undermine both the flavoring and coloring of Brussels sprouts if the sprouts are overcooked.
- Brussels sprouts become unattractively mushy when overcooked.

---

144 Mateljan, *The World's Healthiest Foods,* 2nd edition, 196. Mateljan presents other updated information about the health-promoting benefits of Brussels sprouts.

To select the most flavorful and nutritious Brussels sprouts,

- select the freshest possible sprouts. Because Brussels sprouts have a high respiration rate, selecting the freshest sprouts is important for retaining natural sweet flavor, maximum tenderness, and phytonutrient content. To identify fresh sprouts, select heavy feeling and uniformly deep green Brussels sprouts with firm, tightly wrapped, small heads. Leaves should not be wilted or have any yellow coloring. The sprouts should not have a strong cabbage odor, which indicates sulfur compounds have already been released from cells.
- select sprouts during their growing season, which in the United States is in the fall and winter. This is when they have peak flavor and tenderness.
- avoid selection of frozen Brussels sprouts, which have significantly reduced antioxidant content.[145]

To store Brussels sprouts,

- quickly refrigerate them after purchase to slow the rapid respiration rate of these vegetables. Treat them as fragile vegetables.
- use the Robinson vented bag storage method (refrigerating them unwashed in the crisper drawer within a sealed bag, squeezing out as much air as possible before sealing the bag, and making uniform pin pricks in the bag – 10 per quart size bag; 20 per gallon size bag).
- use Brussels sprouts within a few days of purchase to take best advantage of the rich phytonutrient content.

6. Cabbage
(Stir-Fried/Steamed)
(2 servings)

½ medium head chilled cabbage (red especially; also green and savoy), halved lengthwise
1 T extra virgin olive oil
1 T hot water
¼ t salt

Cooking Tools

1 large nonstick skillet with a tight-fitting & opaque lid
1 electric tea kettle
1 chef's knife
1 set each measuring cups & spoons

1 plastic or plastic-coated stir-fry spatula
1 timer
1 rubber or other heat-resistant spatula
1 colander
1 dinner plate

---

[145] Robinson, *Eating on the Wild Side*, 165. In comparison to fresh sprouts, frozen sprouts have only 20 percent of antioxidants shown to have cancer-fighting capacity.

PART 1

1. **Gather all cooking tools.**

2. **Heat a large nonstick skillet on a large burner at a medium setting.** Begin heating an electric tea kettle to prepare steaming water.

3. **Prepare the cabbage for stir-fry/steaming.**

    - Remove any limp outer leaves from the cabbage.
    - Place the cabbage half cut side down on a cutting board and halve it lengthwise. Set aside one of the ¼ head wedges to prepare but store the extra ¼ cabbage, tightly wrapping it in plastic wrap and refrigerating it.
    - Place the ¼ cabbage wedge to be prepared cut side down on a cutting board. Use a chef's knife to cut off ½-1 inch of the tip of the wedge, setting this tip aside. For red cabbage, also slice off some of the thick core running through the center of the cabbage, setting this core aside.
    - Use the chef's knife to slice the cabbage wedge lengthwise into ¼ in. thick slices.
    - Cut the slices crosswise into ⅓ in. lengths.
    - Pick through the sliced cabbage to separate very thick pieces. Use the chef's knife to chop any thick pieces and the removed tip into ⅛ in. thick pieces so that all cabbage pieces cook in the same time.

4. **Stir-fry/steam the cabbage.**

    - Increase the skillet heat to medium-high.
    - When a drop of water added to the skillet instantly dances and disappears, add 1 T oil, add the cabbage, including chopped pieces, and stir-fry it for 1 minute, setting a timer. Stir-frying should at first be vigorous to quickly and thoroughly coat cabbage pieces with oil but can slow to "flip often" pace by the end of this minute.
    - At the timer, add 1 T hot water, cover the skillet, reduce the heat to low, and steam green cabbage for 4 minutes and red cabbage for 5½ minutes, setting a timer.
    - At the timer, remove the skillet from the heat, evenly sprinkle ¼ t salt over the cabbage, and use a rubber spatula to scrape the cabbage and any cooking juice into a bowl for immediate serving or into a colander placed over a dinner plate for serving in a mixed ingredient dish.
    - Serve any collected cooking water with the cabbage.

VARIATIONS: Add **½-1 t dried herb leaves.** For example, add dill weed, sweet basil, oregano, marjoram, or mint. Crush dried leaves over the cabbage during stir-frying.

COMMENTS: Rinse and dry a full cabbage head before using a chef's knife to halve it lengthwise for use in Recipe #6.

Cabbage Profile

Cabbage shares the richly endowed nutritional characteristics of other cabbage family vegetables. Cabbage, for example,

- is a rich source of the glucosinolate family of phytonutrients. Giving cabbage significant antioxidant, anti-inflammatory, and detoxification capacity, glucosinolates make cabbage a highly nutritious vegetable. Glucosinolate phytonutrients also contribute to human intestinal health.
- contains a range of antioxidant phytonutrients in addition to glucosinolates. At the same time, cabbage is a good source of antioxidant nutrients, including vitamin C and the mineral manganese, that combine with antioxidant phytonutrients to boost the antioxidant capacity of cabbage.
- is a very good source of both soluble and insoluble fiber, which importantly contributes to the health of the human digestive system. Cabbage fiber, for example, has cholesterol-lowering capacity.[146]
- is a good source of alkaline minerals and an excellent source of vitamin K, which is also linked with healthy bones.

Cabbage has a distinctive nutritional characteristic. Cabbage stands out as a source of the amino acid glutamine, which plays an essential health-supportive role in the human digestive system. Glutamine, for example, nourishes the cells lining the small intestine, which maintains the ability of the cells to absorb nutrients from the intestine.

Cabbage shares the cooking characteristics of other cabbage family vegetables.

- Cabbage contains sulfur compounds that easily undermine cabbage flavor if cabbage is overcooked.
- Cabbage is vulnerable to unattractive browning during stir-frying. This browning indicates destruction of vitamin C content, and this browning undermines overall cabbage flavor as well. Browning can occur when the skillet temperature is too high and when cabbage is not sufficiently coated with oil. Insufficient coating easily occurs if a skillet is insufficiently wiped clean and plant juice remains in the skillet when cabbage is added for stir-frying. Plant juice remaining in a skillet will prevent oil from forming a protective coating on cabbage pieces.

To select the most flavorful and nutritious cabbage,

- select the freshest cabbage, which is by far the sweetest cabbage. Select firm, heavy-feeling, unbroken cabbage that has shiny, squeaky clean-feeling skin, and tight-fitting leaves.
- select in-season cabbage, which is when cabbage has peak flavor and nutritional

---

[146] Mateljan, *The World's Healthiest Foods*, 2nd edition, 206. Cabbage fiber binds to bile acids in the intestines, which stimulates the liver to produce more bile acids. The liver uses cholesterol to make new bile acids, which reduces overall cholesterol content in the body.

value. In the United States in-season for cabbage is the cool time of year, during the fall and winter months.
- select **savoy cabbage**, which has higher antioxidant value than ordinary green cabbage.
- select **red cabbage**, which is significantly more nutritious than green cabbage. The red tint indicates concentrated amounts of antioxidants, including super potent anthocyanins, which makes red cabbage one of the most nutritious vegetables found in most grocery stores.[147]
- select red cabbage with the deepest red-purple color. The deeper the color, the more potent its antioxidant content.
- select certified organic and locally grown cabbage. Though industrially produced cabbage is included among the foods with least pesticide contamination in the Environmental Working Group's 2016 ranking of 50 foods (cabbage is 47th), certified organic and locally grown cabbage is substantially free of pesticides. As naturally grown cabbage, this cabbage has other nutritional benefits, including more potent phytonutrient content and greater overall nutritional content than industrially produced cabbage.

To store cabbage,

- refrigerate a chilled whole head of cabbage unwashed within an air-tight plastic bag to protect it from air, which will dehydrate the cabbage, leaving it limp.
- do not tightly cover an uncut room temperature head of cabbage (such as one from a garden or farmers' market) before refrigerating it. First thoroughly pre-chill a whole cabbage in uncovered form. Once it is chilled, tightly cover and re-refrigerate it for storage. Without this pre-chilling, condensation will form on the cabbage during refrigeration, hastening spoilage.
- always tightly cover a cut open head of cabbage during refrigeration, wrapping it tightly with plastic wrap to protect it from air.
- store cabbage for as short of time as possible. Because cabbage has a low respiration rate, air-tight storage maintains its texture and overall nutritional value for several weeks. Cabbage, nevertheless, loses its sweetness during storage.

7. Carrot
(Stir-Fried/Steamed)
(2 servings)

4 chilled medium carrots (each approx. 8 in. long, 1 in. thick at stem end)
1 T extra virgin olive oil

1 T hot water
¼ t salt

---

147 Robinson, *Eating on the Wild Side*, 167. Red cabbage has six times more antioxidant activity than green cabbage and three times more than savoy cabbage.

Cooking Tools

1 large skillet with a tight-fitting & opaque lid	1 plastic or plastic-coated stir-fry spatula
1 electric tea kettle	1 timer
1 chef's knife	1 rubber or other heat-resistant spatula
1 set measuring spoons	1 colander
	1 dinner plate

---

1. **Gather all cooking tools.**

2. **Heat a large skillet on a large burner at a medium setting.** Begin heating an electric tea kettle to prepare steaming water.

3. **Prepare the carrots for stir-fry/steaming.**

   - Scrub and thoroughly dry the carrots with paper or cloth towels.
   - Use a chef's knife to cut off the ends and to halve each carrot lengthwise.
   - Place the halves cut side down on a cutting board and use the chef's knife to cut them crosswise into ⅛ in. thick slices.

4. **Stir-fry/steam the carrots.**

   - Increase the skillet heat to a medium-high setting.
   - When a drop of water added to the skillet instantly dances and disappears, add 1 T oil, add the carrots, and stir-fry them for 1 minute, setting a timer. Stir-frying should at first be vigorous to quickly and thoroughly coat carrot pieces with oil but can slow to "flip often" pace halfway through the timed minute.
   - At the timer, add 1 T hot water, cover the skillet, reduce the heat to low, and steam the carrot slices for 4 minutes, setting a timer.
   - At the timer, remove the skillet from the heat, evenly sprinkle ¼ t salt over the carrots, and use a rubber spatula to scrape the carrots and any cooking juice into a bowl for immediate serving or into a colander placed over a dinner plate for serving in a mixed ingredient dish.
   - Include any collected steaming liquid when serving the carrots.

VARIATIONS: Substitute **2 large carrots** for medium carrots. Quarter large carrot halves lengthwise before cutting them crosswise into ⅛ in. thick slices.

Add flavoring, for example,

- **½-1 t dried herb leaves**, such as sweet basil, oregano, marjoram, thyme, sage, or dill weed. Crush dried herbs over the carrots during stir-frying.
- **½-1 t curry powder**, sprinkling it over the carrots during stir-frying.

PART 1

Carrot Profile

Carrot has notable nutritional characteristics.

- Though the modern carrot has rather ordinary amounts of phytonutrients in comparison with many other vegetables, carrot nevertheless contains valuable amounts of antioxidant phytonutrients, such as beta carotene and other carotenoids. Carrot also contains antioxidant nutrients, such as vitamin C and the mineral manganese that expand the antioxidant protection provided by phytonutrients. Carrot also contains phytonutrients that provide anti-inflammatory protection for humans.
- Carrot skin is highly edible, and it contributes both soluble and insoluble fiber.
- The overall mineral content of carrot places it among top alkaline balancing vegetables.
- Recent research shows that carrot beta carotene content is relatively stable during extended proper storage.

Carrot has notable flavoring and cooking characteristics.

- Carrot is an outstanding dish ingredient. It adds color, texture, and attractive flavor to all manner of dishes, boosting the attractiveness and acceptability of the dishes.
- Carrot also does not have any special cooking characteristics and, as a result, is among the easiest of all vegetables to cook.

Select the most flavorful carrot. Select, for example,

- fresh carrot. Select carrots that are uniformly firm, not split open, and heavy feeling without any sign of decay.
- carrot with attached bright green and firm tops as the freshest and sweetest carrot.
- either thick or thin carrot. Both can be equally tender.
- in-season carrot. While California carrot is available throughout the year, locally grown carrot is in-season during the summer and fall in other places in the United States.

Select the easiest to prepare carrot. Select, for example,

- carrot with relatively smooth surface without root hairs and bumps. Smooth skinned carrot is far easier to scrub. A dish sponge with one rough side wraps around a smooth carrot and quickly and efficiently scrubs the carrot. Bumpy carrot requires cleaning with a brush.
- Medium size carrot (carrot that is 6-8 inches long and around ½ inches thick at the stem end) as very easy to slice carrot.

To select the most nutritious carrot,

- select deepest orange carrot for greatest phytonutrient (beta carotene) content.
- select purple carrot as the most nutritious carrot. Purple carrot has concentrated anthocyanin content. Purple carrot also contains more beta-carotene than orange carrots, and it contains alpha-carotene, a highly nutritious phytonutrient related to beta-carotene. Purple carrot also tends to be sweeter than orange carrot.
- do not select baby carrot. Baby carrot is processed mature carrot from which the nutrient rich outer portion of the carrot (the skin and tissue immediately under the skin) has been removed and discarded.[148]
- select certified organic and locally grown carrot. Conventionally grown carrot is included in the middle in the Environmental Working Group's 2016 list that ranks fifty vegetables and fruits by pesticide content. In contrast, certified organic carrot, which is commonly marketed at very reasonable cost in natural food sections of standard grocery stores and at natural food stores, has the important advantages of being largely pesticide free and overall produced in accordance with natural production standards, the significance of which is detailed in Reference #1 (Selecting Top Quality Fresh Whole Vegetables and Fruits). Naturally produced carrot, for example, has more potent phytonutrient content than industrially produced carrot.

To store carrot, refrigerate carrot sealed within an air-tight container.

- As carrot has a low respiration rate, it tolerates tight sealing for relatively lengthy storage with minimal loss of nutritional content.
- Sealing protects carrot from air, which quickly dehydrates and unattractively softens carrot.
- Sealing also protects carrot from exposure to ethylene gas, which is given off by particular vegetables and fruits, including apple, cantaloupe, scallion, tomato, plum, and potato. Exposure to ethylene gas makes carrot bitter.

8. Cauliflower
(Stir-Fried/Steamed)
(2 servings)

½ chilled medium head cauliflower (approx. 6 large florets; to yield 2-3 c sliced cauliflower or 2-3 c approximately ½ in. size florets)	1 T extra virgin olive oil 1 T hot water ¼ t salt

---

148 Robinson, *Eating on the Wild Side*, 116. Removal of the carrot skin and the skin next to it results in removal of one-third of its phytonutrients.

PART 1

Cooking Tools

1 large nonstick skillet with a tight-fitting & opaque lid
1 electric tea kettle
1 5 in. serrated knife
1 gallon size sealable plastic bag

1 set measuring spoons
1 plastic or plastic-coated stir-fry spatula
1 rubber or other heat-resistant spatula
1 colander
1 dinner plate

1. **Gather all cooking tools.**

2. **Heat a large nonstick skillet on a large burner at a medium setting.** Begin heating an electric kettle to prepare water for steaming.

3. **Prepare the cauliflower florets for stir-fry/steaming.**

   - Rinse a head of cauliflower with cool water, vigorously shake it to remove clinging water, wrap it within paper towels, and firmly squeeze the cauliflower to dry the florets thoroughly.
   - Turn the head upside down on a cutting board and use a serrated knife to cut off florets, rotating the head as florets are cut, leaving the stems of the florets as long as possible, and cutting florets from only about one half of the head.
   - Immediately wrap the extra cauliflower within a paper towel, place it in a sealable plastic bag, press out as much air as possible before sealing the bag, and re-refrigerate the cauliflower.
   - Break the florets apart, attempting to achieve uniform ½ in. florets.
   - To cut the florets into slices, use a serrated knife to halve each floret lengthwise, place the floret halves cut side down on a cutting board, and cut the halves lengthwise into ¼ in. thick slices.

4. **Stir-fry/steam the cauliflower.**

   - Increase the skillet heat to medium-high.
   - When a drop of water added to the skillet instantly dances and disappears, add 1 T oil, add the cauliflower, and stir-fry it for one minute, setting a timer. Stir-frying should at first be vigorous to quickly and thoroughly coat cauliflower pieces with oil but can slow to a "flip often" pace halfway through the minute.
   - At the timer, add 1 T hot water, cover the skillet, reduce the heat to low, and steam the cauliflower for 4 minutes, setting a timer.
   - At the timer, remove the skillet from the heat, evenly sprinkle ¼ t salt over the cauliflower, and use a rubber spatula to scrape the cauliflower and any cooking juice into a bowl for immediate serving or into a colander placed over a dinner plate for serving the cauliflower in a mixed ingredient dish, such as a stir fry, curry, or tomato sauce-based stew.
   - Serve any collected steaming liquid with the cauliflower.

VARIATIONS: Add flavoring. Add, for example,

- **½-1 t dried herb leaves,** such as thyme, sweet basil, oregano, marjoram, or dill weed. Crush dried herbs over the cauliflower during stir-frying.
- **½-1 t curry powder,** evenly sprinkled over the cauliflower during stir-frying.

Cauliflower Profile

Cauliflower is a highly nutritious vegetable. White cauliflower stands out as an exception to the general rule that deep coloration identifies most phytonutrient rich vegetables.

- As a cabbage family vegetable, cauliflower is a rich source of the glucosinolate family of phytonutrients. This sulfur-containing phytonutrient family gives cauliflower outstanding antioxidant, anti-inflammatory, and detoxification capacity.
- Cauliflower has a variety of other antioxidant phytonutrients. At the same time cauliflower contains antioxidant nutrients, such as vitamin C and manganese, and these nutrients combine with antioxidant phytonutrients to intensify the antioxidant power of cauliflower.
- Cauliflower contains vitamin K, omega-3 fatty acids (alpha linolenic acid form), and magnesium, which combine with phytonutrients to expand the anti-inflammatory capacity of cauliflower.
- Cauliflower contains a stand-out amount of folate, which is a highly perishable B vitamin that is commonly deficient in American diets.
- The overall high mineral content of cauliflower classes it as a top alkaline balancing vegetable.

Cauliflower has particular cooking characteristics.

- Cauliflower is highly absorptive and easily and attractively absorbs spice and herb flavoring.
- Sulfur compound content undermines the sweet natural flavor of cauliflower when cauliflower is overcooked.
- Cauliflower slices are vulnerable to unattractive browning during stir-frying. This browning indicates destruction of vitamin C content, and this browning undermines overall cauliflower flavor. Browning can occur when the skillet temperature is too high and when cauliflower slices are not sufficiently coated with oil. Insufficient coating easily occurs when cauliflower is added to a skillet that has not been sufficiently wiped clean after the cooking of another vegetable. Plant juice remaining in an uncleaned skillet will prevent oil from forming a protective coating on the exposed flesh of cauliflower slices. Florets are not as vulnerable to scorching as sliced cauliflower.

Select the most flavorful and nutritious cauliflower. Select, for example,

- fresh cauliflower. Fresh cauliflower is heavy-feeling and firm. Cauliflower florets

should be compact and tightly closed, have bright white color, and not have any brown spots. Leaves should be bright green, firm, and cling tightly around the bottom of the head.
- in-season cauliflower. In the United States in-season is in the cold months.
- brightly colored orange, green, and purple cauliflower, which have an even greater concentration of antioxidant phytonutrients than white cauliflower. Purple cauliflower has an especially potent phytonutrient content.
- certified organic cauliflower and locally produced cauliflower. Though conventionally produced cauliflower commonly makes the Environmental Working Group's yearly Clean Fifteen list of the vegetables and fruits containing the least pesticide content, certified organic and locally produced cauliflower have the advantages of being largely pesticide free and of being naturally produced, the significance of which is detailed in Reference #1 (Selecting Top Quality Fresh Whole Vegetables and Fruits). The phytonutrient content of naturally produced cauliflower, for example, is more potent than the phytonutrient content of industrially produced cauliflower.

To store cauliflower,

- refrigerate an already chilled whole cauliflower unwashed within its store packing or if purchased uncovered, in a sealable bag, pressing out as much air as possible before sealing it. As cauliflower has a low respiration rate, it stores well (with minimal loss of nutritional content and sweetness) for a week.
- refrigerate room temperature cauliflower, such as one from a U-pick farm or a farmers' market, uncovered until it is thoroughly chilled before wrapping it within a paper towel and transferring it to a sealed bag. If room temperature cauliflower is refrigerated in tightly covered form, condensation will form on the florets, which will hasten spoilage and development of brown spots.

9. Celery
(Stir-Fried/Steamed)
(2 servings)

3-4 chilled organic celery stalks (medium size; stalks that are approx. 10 in. long and 1 in. thick at widest point; to yield 2-3 c sliced)

1 T extra virgin olive oil

Cooking Tools

1 large skillet with a tight-fitting & opaque lid
1 electric tea kettle

1 plastic or plastic-coated stir-fry spatula
1 timer
1 rubber or other heat-resistant spatula

1 chef's knife   1 colander
1 set measuring spoons   1 dinner plate

———◆———

1. **Gather all cooking tools.**

2. **Heat a large skillet on a large burner at a medium setting.**

3. **Prepare the celery for stir-fry/steaming.**

   - Rinse and thoroughly dry the celery stalks with paper towels or a cloth towel.
   - Use a chef's knife to slice off the very tip of the stem end and leafy tops from each stalk.
   - Use the chef's knife to halve each stalk lengthwise and to halve each stalk half lengthwise. Slice the strips crosswise into ¼ in. thick pieces.
   - Collect and save the sliced off ends and leaves for use as broth ingredients, such as in Reference #10 (Preparing Fresh Chicken Broth) or in Recipe #175 (Old Fashioned Beef Stew).

4. **Stir-fry/steam the celery.**

   - Increase the skillet heat to medium-high.
   - When a drop of water added to the skillet instantly dances and disappears, add 1 T oil, add the celery, and stir-fry it for 1 minute, setting a timer. Stir-frying should at first be vigorous to quickly and thoroughly coat celery pieces with oil but can slow to "flip often" pace halfway through the minute.
   - At the timer, cover the skillet, reduce the heat to low, and steam the celery in its own juice for 4 minutes, setting a timer.
   - At the timer, remove the skillet from the heat and use a rubber spatula to scrape the celery and any cooking juice into a bowl for immediate serving or into a colander placed over a dinner plate for serving in a mixed ingredient dish, such as a stir fry or stew.
   - Serve any collected steaming liquid with the celery.

VARIATIONS: Add flavoring. Add, for example,

- **½-1 t dried herb leaves**, such as sweet basil, oregano, thyme, marjoram, sage, Italian seasoning, dill weed, or a mixture of basil and oregano. Crush the dried herbs over the celery during stir-frying.
- **celery leaves.** Unless they are very bitter (as determined by a taste check), use the leaves of organic celery. Remove the leaves from the stems, saving the stems. Group the stems together and use a chef's knife to chop the stems into small pieces. Roughly bunch the leaves together and use a 5 in. serrated knife to cut them into ¼ in. slices. Stir-fry the stems with the sliced celery stalks, mix the leaves into the stir-frying celery

stalks after they have stir-fried for 1 minute, stir-fry the mixture another 30 seconds to heat through the leaves, cover the celery, and steam it as above (for 4 minutes).

Celery Profile

While overall celery has rather ordinary nutritional content in comparison with many other vegetables, celery does make significant nutritional contributions.

- Celery has flavonoid phytonutrients that provide both antioxidant and anti-inflammatory protection to humans. Celery also contains antioxidant nutrients, including vitamin C and the mineral manganese, that combine with the phytonutrients to enhance celery's antioxidant capacity. Its magnesium content combines with phytonutrients to intensify the anti-inflammatory capacity of celery.
- Celery has outstanding folate and vitamin K content.
- Celery has notable fiber content. Celery contributes the insoluble fiber cellulose, which classes celery as prebiotic food that supports the beneficial microbiome contained in the human intestinal tract. Contained in the stringy parts of celery stalks, cellulose fibers are long enough to survive the length of the human digestive system (G.I. tract) and reach the large intestine where they feed and support the growth of good bacteria. Bacteria ferment the cellulose, which converts it into human health supporting form.

Celery has distinctive cooking characteristics. Celery, for example,

- easily absorbs herb and spice flavoring, which enhances the flavoring contribution it can make to dishes.
- is harmed by extended cooking. Long cooking reduces the length of its heat-sensitive cellulose fibers, which undermines its ability to serve as a prebiotic. Shortened fibers cannot make it through the G.I. tract to feed bacteria. Stir-fry/steaming is protective of the cellulose fibers.

To select the most flavorful and nutritious celery,

- select fresh celery. Select celery with uniformly firm and heavy-feeling stalks. Attached leaves should be bright colored, firm, and fresh appearing. Leaves should not have any yellow coloring. When cut open, stalk ends should be uniformly juicy and not reveal a pulpy or hollow center.
- select in-season celery, which is when celery has peak flavor and nutritional value. In the United States locally grown celery is harvested during the summer months.
- select darkest green celery, which has greatest phytonutrient content.
- select certified organic and locally grown celery. Conventionally produced celery is included as the fifth most contaminated vegetable in the Environmental Working Group's 2016 Dirty Dozen list of vegetables and fruits.

To store celery,

- refrigerate unwashed celery within a sealed plastic bag to protect it from dehydration, which undermines celery texture, leaving it limp. Tightly wrapping celery within plastic wrap provides extra protection.
- leave stems and leaves attached to the celery stalks until celery is prepared for cooking.

10. Whole Kernel Sweet Corn
(Stir-Fried)
(2 servings)

3-5 ears yellow sweet corn
   (to yield 2-3 c kernels)

½ T extra virgin olive oil
¼ t salt

Cooking Tools

1 large skillet
1 pie plate
1 chef's knife
1 set measuring spoons

1 plastic or plastic-coated stir-fry spatula
1 timer
1 rubber or other heat-resistant spatula

1. **Gather all cooking tools.**

2. **Heat a large skillet on a large burner at a medium setting.**

3. **Prepare the corn for stir-frying.**

    - Remove the husks and corn silk from the ears. Rubbing the ears with a damp towel efficiently removes corn silk.
    - Stand each ear upright in a pie plate and use a chef's knife to slice off the kernels, cutting close to the cob to include the corn germ.

4. **Stir-fry the corn.**

    - Increase the skillet heat to medium-high and when a drop of water added to the skillet instantly dances and disappears, add ½ T oil to the skillet, add the corn kernels, and stir-fry them for 1 minute, setting a timer. Stir-frying should at first be vigorous to quickly and thoroughly coat the kernels with oil but can slow to "flip often" pace.
    - At the timer, remove the skillet from the heat, evenly sprinkle ¼ t salt over the kernels, and use a rubber spatula to scrape the corn and any cooking liquid in a serving bowl or mixed ingredient dish (such as a stir-fried dish, soup, or stew) for serving.

PART 1

VARIATION: Add ½-1 t dried herb leaves (such as dill weed, sweet basil, oregano, or marjoram) to the corn during stir-frying. Crush the leaves over the corn during stir-frying.

Corn Profile

Corn has notable nutritional characteristics.

- Yellow sweet corn has rich carotenoid phytonutrient content, which provides antioxidant protection for humans. Additionally, sweet corn is a good source of the mineral manganese, which combines with carotenoid phytonutrients to boost the antioxidant protection provided humans by corn.
- Corn contributes valuable fiber, which contributes to human digestive health. Corn fiber can support the growth of friendly bacteria in the large intestine. This bacteria ferments corn fiber, which converts the fiber into short chain fatty acids (SCFAs) that support intestinal and bodily health in a number of ways, including protecting it from cancer.

To select the most flavorful and nutritious ears of corn,

- select fresh corn. Ears of corn should be heavy feeling, have bright green and moist husks, and have fresh and moist appearing silk. Corn kernels should not be either very small or large. The center of kernels should not be sunken. Juice should spurt from cut open kernels.
- select in-season corn. In-season in the United States runs from late summer to early fall. Winter corn from Florida is available from fall to spring.
- locally produced corn, which is the freshest corn.
- ears with deep yellow coloring, which have greatest phytonutrient content. Deep yellow varieties of corn have dramatically more beta carotene and other phytonutrient content than white corn.[149]
- blue corn, which contains super potent anthocyanin antioxidants. Purple sweet corn also has more concentrated phytonutrient content than yellow corn.
- super sweet corn that is certified organic or locally produced. Commercially produced super sweet corn is exceptionally sprayed with chemicals during production.[150] Certified organic super sweet corn is also reliably not genetically modified corn.
- select certified organic and locally produced regular sweet corn. While regular industrially produced sweet corn (corn that is not super sweet) is included in the Environmental Working Group's 2016 Clean Fifteen list as one of the least

---

149 Ibid., 85. Robinson reports that deep yellow corn varieties have up to fifty-eight times more beta-carotene and the related phytonutrient compounds lutein and zeaxanthin than white corn.
150 Ibid., 86. Robinson includes information reported by the U.S. Department of Agriculture's Agricultural Research Service stating that growers in the southern U.S. spray super sweet corn with insecticides as many as twenty-five to forty times per season.

contaminated industrially produced vegetables, certified organic and locally grown regular sweet corn is largely free of pesticide contamination. Certified organic sweet corn is also reliably not a genetically modified food.

To store ears of corn,

- immediately refrigerate the ears within a sealed plastic bag.
- use corn immediately or within a few days to retain the sweetest flavor and greatest nutritional value.

11. Eggplant
(Stir-Fried/Steamed)
(2 servings)

½ lb chilled eggplant (1 small or ½ medium globe eggplant or 2 6 in. long, 1 in. thick Japanese eggplants); enough to yield 2-3 c diced

1 T extra virgin olive oil
1 T water
¼ t salt

Cooking Tools

1 large nonstick skillet with a tight-fitting & opaque lid
1 electric tea kettle
1 chef's knife
1 set each measuring spoons & cups

1 plastic or plastic-coated stir-fry spatula
1 timer
1 rubber or other heat-resistant spatula
1 colander
1 dinner plate

1. **Gather all cooking tools.**

2. **Heat a large nonstick skillet on a large burner at a medium setting.** Begin heating an electric tea kettle to prepare hot water for steaming.

3. **Prepare the eggplant for stir-fry/steaming.**

    - Rinse and dry a whole eggplant with paper towels.
    - Use a chef's knife to slice the ends from the eggplant.
    - Stand the eggplant upright on a flattened end and use the chef's knife to cut the eggplant lengthwise into ¼ in. thick slices.
    - Stacking 2 slices together, cut the slices into ¼ in. thick strips. Holding 2-3 strips together with one hand, cut the strips crosswise into ¼ in. cubes.

4. **Stir-fry/steam the eggplant.**

- Increase the skillet heat to medium-high.
- When a drop of water added to the skillet instantly dances and disappears, add 1 T oil, add the eggplant, and stir-fry it for 1 minute, setting a timer. Stir-frying should at first be vigorous to quickly and thoroughly coat the eggplant pieces with oil but can slow to "flip often" pace midway through the minute.
- At the timer, add 1 T hot water, cover the skillet, reduce the heat to low, and steam the eggplant for 4 minutes (5 minutes for larger, more mature eggplant), setting a timer.
- At the timer, remove the skillet from the heat, evenly sprinkle ¼ t salt over the eggplant, and use a rubber spatula to scrape it and any cooking juice into a bowl for immediate serving or into a colander placed over a dinner plate for serving in a mixed ingredient dish, such as a stir fry, tomato sauce-based stew, or curry dish.
- Serve any collected steaming liquid with the eggplant.

VARIATIONS: Substitute **other varieties of eggplant**. For example, use eggplant fingers or any of the varieties of eggplant that are marketed at natural food stores and farmers' markets.

Add **flavoring**. Add, for example,

- **½-1 t dried herb leaves**, such as sweet basil, oregano, thyme, marjoram, or a mixture of basil and oregano. Crush dried herbs over the eggplant during stir-frying.
- **½-1 t curry powder**, evenly sprinkling it over the eggplant during stir-frying.

Eggplant Profile

Eggplant, also called aubergine, has notable nutritional characteristics.

- Eggplant is a good source of a broad spectrum of nutritional components, including all B-complex vitamins except for B12, alkaline minerals, the fat-soluble vitamins A (in the form of beta-carotene) and K, and omega-3 fatty acids. Eggplant supplies some protein as well.[151]
- Eggplant has outstanding carotenoid phytonutrient content. This fat-soluble phytonutrient content, which is contained in the white flesh and skin (and particularly in purple skin), provides antioxidant protection to the human body. Eggplant skin also contains some flavonoid phytonutrients, including anthocyanins, which are super potent antioxidants. Of particular note, eggplant phytonutrients provide significant antioxidant support to the fats, or lipids, found in brain membranes. By protecting this fat from dangerous free radicals, eggplant phytonutrients protect the health of the human brain.
- Eggplant contains antioxidant nutrients – including vitamins C and E and the minerals manganese, zinc, and selenium – that work with phytonutrients to boost the antioxidant protection provided by eggplant.

---

[151] A good specific source of updated nutritional information about eggplant is George Mateljan's *The World's Healthiest Foods*, 2nd Edition (Seattle, Washington: George Mateljan Foundation, 2015): 278-286.

- Eggplant is a rich source of both soluble and insoluble fiber.

Eggplant has some special cooking characteristics.

- Eggplant flesh is highly absorptive. While it easily absorbs flavorful herb and spice flavoring, which is a positive characteristic, it also easily absorbs oil and can easily absorb excessive oil.
- Flesh quickly browns when exposed to air by cutting. This browning indicates destruction of eggplant's vitamin C content. To minimize this destruction, pre-chill eggplant before cutting and stir-fry it immediately after cutting.
- Eggplant can be bitter. It is important to taste eggplant before cooking and to discard it if it is bitter.
- Stir-fry/steaming is well suited to eggplant. This cooking method maximizes conservation of eggplant's fat soluble phytonutrients and heat- and air-sensitive nutritional content.

Select the most flavorful and nutritious eggplant. Select, for example,

- fresh eggplant. Select eggplant with shiny bright and deep-colored purple skin. The eggplant should be heavy-feeling and have uniformly firm flesh that springs back when gently pressed. The eggplant should not have any soft, sunken, or brown-colored areas, which indicate bruising and damaged flesh underneath. Cut open surface should be almost completely white with few dark specks, which are seeds. The stem and cup at the stem end should be bright green.
- small or medium-sized eggplant. The skin and flesh of both small and medium-size eggplants (medium is approx. 6 in. long and 3 to 4 in. wide for globe eggplants; approx. 6 in. long and 1½ in. thick for Japanese eggplant) tend to be reliably tender.
- in-season eggplant, which is both the freshest and most nutritious eggplant. In the United States in-season is between August and October.
- locally grown eggplant, which is the freshest eggplant.
- certified organic or locally grown eggplant. Though conventionally produced eggplant is included in the Environmental Working Group's 2016 Clean Fifteen list, certified organic and locally grown eggplant has the advantage of being largely pesticide free, which encourages the eating of the nutritious eggplant skin. Certified organic and locally grown eggplant also are naturally produced. One important advantage of naturally produced eggplant is more potent phytonutrient content. Other advantages are detailed in Reference #1 (Selecting Top Quality Fresh Whole Vegetables and Fruits).
- eggplant that does not have green coloration immediately under the skin, which is somewhat toxic to humans.

To store eggplant,

- refrigerate chilled dry eggplant within a sealed plastic bag to protect it from dehydration. Wrapping plastic wrap tightly around the eggplant provides extra protection from air.

- refrigerate room temperature eggplant (such as fresh picked or purchased from a farmers' market) uncovered until it is thoroughly chilled before transferring it to a sealed bag.
- store eggplant for up to a week. Minimally stored eggplant, however, is most likely sweet, not bitter.

12. Kohlrabi
(Stir-Fried/Steamed)
(2 servings)

2 chilled medium (approx. 2½ in.) kohlrabi, with stems & leaves attached if possible
1 T extra virgin olive oil
1 T hot water
¼ t salt

Cooking Tools

1 large nonstick skillet with a tight-fitting & opaque lid
1 electric tea kettle
1 colander
1 each chef's & 5 in. serrated knife

1 set measuring spoons
1 plastic or plastic-coated stir-fry spatula
1 timer
1 rubber or other heat-resistant spatula
1 dinner plate

1. **Gather all cooking tools.**

2. **Heat a large nonstick skillet on a large burner at a medium setting.** Begin heating an electric tea kettle to prepare water for steaming.

3. **Prepare the kohlrabi bulb for stir-fry/steaming.**

    - Slice leafy stems from the bulbs and set them aside.
    - Gently scrub the kohlrabi and thoroughly dry it with a paper or terry towel.
    - Use a chef's knife to slice the ends from the kohlrabi.
    - Stand each kohlrabi on a flattened end and use the chef's knife to cut each lengthwise into ¼ in. thick slices.
    - Stacking two slices together, cut the slices lengthwise into ¼ in. thick strips. Cut the strips crosswise into ¼ in. cubes. Set the cubes aside.

4. **Prepare the kohlrabi stems and leafy tops.**
    - Rinse the leafy tops under cool water and drain them in a colander.
    - Spread the leaves over a layer of paper towels or a terry cloth towel, top the leaves

with another layer of towels, roll the leaves in the towels, and gently squeeze the leaves to dry them.
- Use a chef's knife to cut the stems from the leafy tops. Holding the stems together with one hand, use the chef's knife to chop the stems thinly (into ⅛ in. thick slices). Push the stems aside.
- Stack the leafy tops, facing them in the same direction, and use a serrated knife to cut them first lengthwise and then crosswise into ⅓ in. wide strips.

5. **Stir-fry/steam the kohlrabi.**

    - Increase the skillet heat to medium high.
    - When a drop of water added to the skillet instantly dances and disappears, add 1 T oil, mix the sliced stems into the oil, and cook them, stirring them often, for about 30 seconds.
    - Add the diced kohlrabi and sliced leaves and stir-fry the mixture for 1 minute, setting a timer. Stir-frying should at first be vigorous to quickly and thoroughly coat the kohlrabi pieces with oil but can slow to "flip often" pace midway through the minute.
    - At the timer, add 1 T hot water, cover the skillet, reduce the heat to low, and steam the kohlrabi for 2 minutes, setting a timer.
    - At the timer, remove the skillet from the burner, evenly sprinkle ¼ t salt over the kohlrabi, and use a rubber spatula to scrape it and any cooking juice into a bowl for immediate serving as a side dish or into a colander placed over a dinner plate for serving in a mixed ingredient dish, such as a stir fry, soup, or stew.

VARIATIONS: Substitute larger, more mature for medium kohlrabi. Extend steaming time to 4 minutes.

Add **1 t dried herb leaves**, such as sweet basil, oregano, dill weed, thyme, marjoram, Italian seasoning, or rosemary. Crush dried herbs between your palms over the kohlrabi during stir-frying.

Kohlrabi Profile

Kohlrabi shares the nutritional and cooking characteristics of other cabbage family vegetables. Kohlrabi contains glucosinolate family phytonutrients, which provide antioxidant, anti-inflammatory, and detoxification protection for humans. Kohlrabi contains human health-promoting sulfur compounds that can also undermine kohlrabi flavoring if it is overcooked.

Select the most flavorful and nutritious kohlrabi. Select, for example,

- fresh kohlrabi bulbs that are heavy-feeling and uniformly firm. Fresh kohlrabi most reliably has a sweet, mild, cabbage family flavor.

- kohlrabi with stems and leafy tops attached. Leafy tops should be bright green, firm, and fresh looking. Stems should be firm, not limp.
- in-season kohlrabi, which in the United States is in the fall.
- small or medium kohlrabi bulbs as the most reliably tender kohlrabi. Larger kohlrabi can (but do not necessarily) have a woody texture.
- purple kohlrabi, which contains a greater concentration of phytonutrients than white/greenish tinted kohlrabi.

To store kohlrabi,

- detach stems and separately refrigerate the stems/leafy tops and bulbs, storing them within a sealed plastic storage bag.
- chill leafy tops thoroughly before tightly sealing them within a plastic bag to prevent condensation from forming on the leaves during storage.
- use kohlrabi bulbs within a week or so. As kohlrabi has a low respiration rate, it stores well for even longer. The more quickly it is used, however, the better its flavor and the greater its nutritional contribution.
- use kohlrabi leaves within several days. Leaves are more fragile than the bulbs, both with respect to flavor and nutritional value.

13. Okra
(Stir-Fried/Steamed)
(2 servings)

½ lb chilled okra, either small (approx. 2 in. long) or medium (approx. 3 in. long) size (to yield 2-3 c sliced)

1 T extra virgin olive oil
1 T hot water
¼ t salt

Cooking Tools

1 large nonstick skillet with a tight-fitting & opaque lid
1 electric tea kettle
1 colander
1 each 5 in. serrated & chef's knife

1 set measuring spoons
1 timer
1 plastic or plastic-coated stir-fry spatula
1 rubber or other heat-resistant spatula
1 dinner plate

1. **Gather all cooking tools.**

2. **Heat a large nonstick skillet on a large burner at a medium setting.** Heat an electric tea kettle to prepare hot water for steaming.

3. **Prepare the okra for stir-fry/steaming.**

   - Add the okra to a colander and rinse it with cold water.
   - Sort through the okra and set aside and re-refrigerate large okra.
   - Pour the okra onto a double layer of paper towels and wrap the towels around the okra to dry them.
   - Use a serrated knife to cut off the stem end and tip from each okra, discarding the stems but setting aside the tips.
   - Use the serrated knife to cut each okra pod crosswise into ¼ in. thick slices.
   - Discard any pods that have dry and woody centers.

4. **Stir fry/steam the okra.**

   - Increase the skillet heat to medium-high.
   - When a drop of water added to the skillet instantly dances and disappears, add 1 T oil, add the okra (both pods and tips), and stir-fry it for 1 minute, setting a timer. Stir-frying should at first be vigorous to quickly and thoroughly coat the okra pieces with oil but can slow to "flip often" pace midway through the 1 minute.
   - At the timer, add 1 T hot water, cover the skillet, turn the heat to low, and steam the okra for 2-4 minutes (2 minutes for small okra, 3 minutes for medium okra, and 4 minutes for larger okra), setting a timer.
   - At the timer, remove the skillet from the heat, evenly sprinkle ¼ t salt over the okra, and use a rubber spatula to scrape the okra and any cooking juice into a bowl for immediate serving as a side dish or into a colander placed over a bowl for serving in a mixed ingredient dish, such as a stir fry, curry, or tomato sauce-based stew.
   - Serve any collected steaming liquid with the okra.

VARIATION: Add **½-1 t dried herb leaves**, such as sweet basil, oregano, thyme, or marjoram. Crush dried herb between your palms over the okra during stir-frying.

Okra Profile

Okra has a diverse and rich array of nutritional components.

- Okra is a rich source of antioxidant phytonutrients. Additionally, it is a good source of antioxidant nutrients, including the vitamins C and A (in the form of beta carotene), which work with the phytonutrients to bolster the overall antioxidant capacity of okra.
- Okra is a rich source of both insoluble and soluble fiber, and its soluble fiber is distinctive. This soluble fiber is the source of okra's gooey, or mucilaginous, texture when it is cut and cooked.
- Okra is an exceptionally good source of folate, vitamin K, and alkaline minerals (notably magnesium but also calcium and potassium). It also contributes protein.

Select the most attractive and nutritious okra.

- Select uniformly firm and deep green okra pods. The pods should be soft, flexible, and untainted (no brown areas). Cut open pods should be filled with juicy flesh, not be dry and hollow. The pods should not have a woody texture that resists slicing.
- Select in-season okra, which is also okra with peak flavor and nutritional value. In the United States in-season is from June until November.

To store okra,

- refrigerate unwashed okra within an air-tight plastic bag with as much air removed as possible.
- thoroughly chill room temperature okra before storing it in a tightly closed bag. This pre-chilling keeps condensation from forming on the surface of the okra pods, which hastens spoilage.
- use it within 2-3 days.

14. Parsnip
(Stir-Fried/Steamed)
(2 servings)

4 chilled medium (approx. 1¼ in. diameter at stem end) parsnips
1 T extra virgin olive oil
1 T hot water
¼ t salt

Cooking Tools

1 large nonstick skillet with a tight-fitting & opaque lid
1 electric tea kettle
1 chef's knife
1 set measuring spoons
1 plastic or plastic-coated stir-fry spatula
1 timer
1 rubber or other heat-resistant spatula
1 colander
1 dinner plate

1. **Gather all cooking tools.**

2. **Heat a large nonstick skillet on a large burner at a medium setting.** Heat an electric tea kettle to prepare hot water for steaming.

3. **Prepare the parsnips for stir-fry/steaming.**

- Use a stiff vegetable brush to scrub the parsnips and thoroughly dry them with a paper or terry towel.
- Use a chef's knife to cut off the ends and to halve each parsnip lengthwise.
- Place the halves cut side down on a cutting board, halve each half lengthwise, and cut the strips crosswise into ⅛ in thick slices.

4. **Stir-fry/steam the parsnips.**

   - Increase the skillet heat to medium-high.
   - When a drop of water added to the skillet instantly dances and disappears, add 1 T oil, add the parsnips, and stir-fry them for 1 minute, setting a timer. Stir-frying should at first be vigorous to thoroughly coat parsnip pieces with oil but can slow to "flip often" pace by the end of the minute.
   - At the timer, add 1 T hot water, cover the skillet, reduce the heat to low, and steam the parsnips for 4 minutes, setting a timer.
   - At the timer, remove the skillet from the heat, evenly sprinkle ¼ t salt over the parsnips, and use a rubber spatula to scrape them and any cooking juice into a bowl for immediate serving as a side dish or into a colander placed over a dinner plate for serving in a mixed ingredient dish, such as a stir fry, soup, or stew.
   - Serve any collected cooking juice with the parsnips.

   VARIATIONS: Add **flavoring**. Add, for example,

   - **½-1 t dried herb leaves**, such as sweet basil, oregano, marjoram, thyme, mint, or dill weed. Crush dried herbs between your palms over the parsnips during stir-frying.
   - **½-1 t curry powder**, sprinkling it over the parsnips during stir-frying.

Parsnip Profile

Parsnips share the nutritional and cooking characteristics of cabbage family vegetables in general.

- Parsnips are a rich source of the glucosinolate family of phytonutrients. These phytonutrients provide antioxidant, anti-inflammatory, and detoxification protection for humans. Glucosinolates also support human intestinal health.
- Parsnips contain human health-supporting sulfur compounds that also easily undermine parsnip flavor if parsnips are overcooked.
- Parsnips have distinctively rich soluble fiber content in comparison with other cabbage family vegetables.

To select the most flavorful and nutritious parsnips,

- select fresh parsnips. Select uniformly firm, heavy feeling, and relatively smooth parsnips.

PART 1

- select parsnips with attached leafy tops when available, which should be bright green, firm, and fresh appearing without any yellowing.
- select in-season parsnips, which in the United States is in the summer and fall.

To store parsnips,

- store parsnips unwashed with tops attached within an air-tight plastic bag, pressing out as much air as possible before sealing the bag.
- thoroughly chill room temperature parsnips before storing them in a tightly closed bag.

15. Green Peas
(Stir-Fried)
(2 servings)

1 lb young, small green peas with
    shells (to yield approx. 2 c shelled peas)

½ T extra virgin olive oil
¼ t salt

Cooking Tools

1 large skillet
1 paring knife
1 pie plate
1 set measuring spoons

1 plastic or plastic-coated stir-fry spatula
1 rubber or other heat-resistant spatula
1 colander
1 dinner plate

1. Gather all cooking tools.

2. **Heat a large skillet on a large burner at a medium setting.**

3. **Prepare the peas for stir-frying.**

   - Using a paring knife and cutting from the outside towards the slightly rounded inside of a pea, make a small cut into the protruding stem end of a pea shell.
   - Grasping the stem end between your thumb and a flat side of the knife blade, twist the stem end off and pull the stem and the attached string down the inside curve of a pea shell.
   - Run your thumb down the shell to remove the peas, catching the peas in a pie plate. Set the shells aside (see Comments below).

4. **Stir-fry the peas.**

- Increase the skillet heat to medium-high.
- When a drop of water added to the skillet instantly dances and disappears, add ½ T oil, thoroughly mix in the peas, and stir-fry them for 1 minute, setting a timer. Stir-frying should at first be vigorous but can slow to a "flip often" pace midway through the minute.
- At the timer, remove the skillet from the burner, evenly sprinkle ¼ t over the peas, and use a rubber spatula to scrape the peas and any cooking juice into a bowl for immediate serving as a side dish or into a colander placed over a dinner plate for serving in a mixed ingredient dish, such as a stir fry, curry, stew, or soup.
- Serve any collected juice with the peas.

VARIATIONS: Substitute **larger, more mature peas**. Substitute stir-fry/steaming for stir-frying. Use a skillet with a tight-fitting and opaque lid and heat an electric tea pot to prepare water for steaming. After stir-frying the peas for 1 minute, add ½ T hot water, cover the skillet, reduce the heat to low, and steam the peas for 3 minutes, setting a timer.

COMMENTS: Collect the shells of certified organic and locally grown peas and refrigerate them for use in preparing a broth. Use a chef's knife to chop the shells into relatively small pieces, add the shells, 1½-2 c water, and ¼ t salt to a medium saucepan with a tight-fitting lid, add any other vegetable scraps that are on hand (first also chopping them into small pieces), bring the water to boiling, reduce the heat to a level that maintains gentle boiling, and cook the shells for 45 minutes to 1 hour before draining them in a colander placed over a bowl for collecting the broth. Refrigerate the cooled broth in a closed container. Freeze broth that will not be quickly used. Substitute this broth for an equal amount of canned broth used in dishes, such as curries and stews.

Green Pea Profile

Green peas, which are also called garden peas, have a diverse and rich array of nutritional components. Green peas, for example,

- are a rich source of antioxidant phytonutrients. This content includes flavonoids and both alpha-carotene and beta-carotene carotenoids. Additionally, green peas contain antioxidant nutrients, including vitamin C and the minerals manganese, zinc, and selenium, which combine with phytonutrients to boost the antioxidant capacity of green peas.
- contain phytonutrients that provide anti-inflammatory protection for humans. Peas also contain omega-3 fatty acids (alpha-linolenic acid) and magnesium, which work with anti-inflammatory phytonutrients to boost the anti-inflammatory capacity of peas for humans.
- contribute concentrated amounts of B vitamins (except for B12) and of choline, which is a cardioprotective vitamin.

- are an excellent source of both soluble and insoluble fiber. While peas have greater insoluble fiber, the soluble fiber is distinctive.
- contribute alkaline minerals, including potassium in particular, but also calcium, magnesium, and iron.
- contain small amounts of all amino acids that make up complete protein, which makes it easy to convert peas into a food that contributes some complete protein. This protein content also makes it important to avoid prolonged heating of peas at a medium-high temperature. Prolonged medium-high heating can cause the protein in the pea skin to shrink and toughen, and such toughening can result in the pea skin breaking open. Juice then easily spills or is leached from the pea, which easily results in loss of flavor and nutritional value.

To select the most flavorful and nutritious peas,

- select fresh green peas. Select peas that are slightly bulging, uniformly firm without any wrinkling, heavy feeling, and are shiny bright green in color.
- select in-season peas. In the United States in-season is from spring to the beginning of winter.
- select fresh peas rather than dry frozen peas. In comparison to fresh peas, frozen peas have lost 25 percent of their antioxidants.[152]
- select certified organic dry frozen peas rather than industrially produced frozen peas, which are included in the Environmental Working Group's 2016 listing of foods most contaminated with pesticides. Though industrially produced frozen peas are included among the Clean Fifteen foods (they are ranked #46 out of 50 foods), certified organic frozen green peas are largely free of pesticide residues in comparison.
- select fresh black-eyed peas, which are more nutritious selections than green peas,[153] when they are an option. Prepare them in the same manner as green peas.

To store green peas,

- refrigerate unwashed green peas as quickly as possible to prevent the sugar content from turning to starch.
- refrigerate peas in a sealable plastic bag within the crisper drawer, pressing out as much air as is possible before sealing the bag.
- refrigerate green peas for up to 10 days. Less storage, however, correlates with sweetest flavor.

---

152 Robinson, *Eating on the Wild Side,* 183.
153 Ibid., 183. Fresh black-eyed peas have five times more antioxidant activity than common green peas.

16. Sugar Snap or Snow Peas
(Stir-Fried)
(2 servings)

⅓ lb chilled small sugar snap or snow peas
½ T extra virgin olive oil
¼ t salt

Cooking Tools

1 large skillet
1 colander
1 paring knife
1 pair kitchen scissors
1 set measuring spoons
1 plastic or plastic-coated stir-fry spatula
1 rubber or other heat-resistant spatula
1 dinner plate

---

1. **Gather all cooking tools.**

2. **Heat a large skillet on a large burner at a medium setting.**

3. **Prepare the sugar snap peas for stir-frying.**

    - Add the pods to a colander and rinse them with cold water.
    - Pour the pods onto a double thickness of paper towels or a terry cloth towel. Sort through the pods, pulling out and re-refrigerating large pods.
    - Wrap the towels around the pods to dry them.
    - Remove and discard any strings from the pea pods. Using a paring knife and cutting outside towards the slightly rounded inside of the pod, cut nearly through the protruding stem end of a pea pod, grasp the stem end between your thumb and flat side of the knife blade, and pull the string down the inside curve of a pea pod.
    - Use kitchen scissors to cut off pod tips and to halve the pea pods.

4. **Stir-fry the sugar snap or snow peas.**

    - Increase the skillet heat to medium-high.
    - When a drop of water added to the skillet instantly dances and disappears, add ½ T oil, add the pods, and stir-fry them for 1 minute, setting a timer. Stir-frying should at first be vigorous to thoroughly coat the pods with oil but can slow to "flip often" pace midway through the minute.
    - At the timer, remove the skillet from the burner, evenly sprinkle ¼ t salt over the pods, and use a rubber spatula to scrape them and any cooking juice into a bowl for immediate serving as a side dish or into a colander placed over a dinner plate for serving in a mixed ingredient dish, such as a stir fry.
    - Serve any collected juice with the pea pods.

VARIATIONS: For larger and more mature sugar snap or snow peas, add steaming. Use a skillet with a tight-fitting and opaque lid and heat an electric tea kettle to prepare steaming water. After stir-frying the pods for 1 minute, add ½ T hot water, cover the skillet, reduce the heat to low, and steam the pea pods for 2 minutes, setting a timer, before removing the skillet from the heat and adding salt for serving.

Sugar Snap and Snow Pea Profile

Sugar snap and snow peas share the same rich nutritional characteristics of shelled green peas. Recipe #15 (Green Peas) details these nutritional characteristics. The edible pods of snow and sugar snap peas, however, make for some important nutritional differences between green peas and both sugar snap and snow peas.

- Edible pods enhance the nutritional value of peas. The pods have more fiber and antioxidants than the peas themselves.
- The pods effectively shield the peas during cooking, supporting conservation of nutritional value.
- That the pods of sugar snap and snow peas are edible makes the selection of certified organic and locally produced peas especially important. The pods of industrially produced edible pod peas are directly exposed to chemicals during production. Many of these chemicals are soluble and are absorbed by pea pods. The shells of green peas, in contrast, can be discarded, which reduces the chemical load of industrially produced green peas.

Select the most flavorful and nutritious sugar snap or snow peas.

- Select fresh peas. Select sugar snap peas that have slightly bulging pea pods that are uniformly firm and have deep green color. Select snow pea pods that are uniformly firm and thin, not limp and bulging. Snow peas should also be relatively bright green in color, not pale green. Flesh inside both types of pods should be bright green and juicy, not whitish in color and dry.
- Select in-season peas. In the United States in-season for snow peas is from spring to the beginning of winter, and they can commonly be found in Asian markets. In-season for sugar snap peas is late spring through early summer.
- Avoid imported, conventionally produced snap peas, which can have high pesticide content. They were included in the Environmental Working Group's 2014 Dirty Dozen list of most contaminated produce. They remained listed among the most contaminated foods (#15 of 50 foods) in the 2016 listing.
- Select domestically produced sugar snap and snow peas that are certified organic or locally produced. Domestic industrially produced sugar snap peas are ranked in the middle of the Environmental Working Group's 2016 listing of the fifty most contaminated vegetables and fruits. Certified organic and locally grown sugar snap and snow peas, in contrast, are largely pesticide free. As naturally grown vegetables,

the phytonutrients they contain are also more concentrated and potent than those of industrially produced peas.

To store edible pod peas,

- quickly refrigerate unwashed peas within a sealed plastic bag to preserve the sugar content of the peas.
- use the peas within several days to maximize conservation of the phytonutrient content.

17. Potato
(Stir-Fried/Steamed)
(2 servings)

2 chilled red or Yukon Gold potatoes, medium size (approx. 2½ in. diameter; to yield 2-3 c diced)	1 T extra virgin olive oil 1 T hot water ⅓ t salt

Cooking Tools

1 large, heavy-bottomed nonstick skillet with a tight-fitting & opaque lid	1 each paring & chef's knife
1 electric tea kettle	1 set measuring spoons
1 vegetable scrub brush and/or dish sponge with one rough side	1 plastic or plastic-coated stir-fry spatula
	1 timer
	1 rubber or other heat-resistant spatula

1. **Gather all cooking tools.**

2. **Heat a large skillet on a large burner at a medium setting.** Heat an electric tea kettle to prepare water for steaming.

3. **Prepare the potatoes for stir-fry/steaming.**

   - For dirt-coated potatoes with a bumpy surface, add enough water to cover the potatoes in a kitchen sink or large bowl. Add and soak the potatoes for several minutes before scrubbing each using a dish sponge with one rough side for smooth areas and a vegetable brush for bumpy areas, being careful to avoid rubbing off the skin. For clean-appearing and smooth potatoes, rinse them, gently scrub each using the rough side of a dish sponge, and rinse each again under running water.
   - Thoroughly dry the potatoes with a paper or terry cloth towel.

- Use a paring knife to remove any large eyes from each potato.
- Using a chef's knife, thinly slice the ends off each potato. Standing a potato on a flattened end, cut the potato lengthwise into ¼ in. wide slices. Stacking two slices together, cut the slices into ¼ in. thick strips. Holding several strips together at a time, cut the strips crosswise into ¼ in. cubes.

4. **Stir-fry/steam the potatoes.**

   - Increase the skillet heat to medium high.
   - When a drop of water added to the skillet immediately dances and disappears, add 1 T oil to the skillet, add the potato, and stir-fry the potato for 1 minute, setting a timer. Stir-frying should at first be vigorous to quickly and thoroughly coat potato pieces with oil but can slow to "flip often" pace midway through the minute.
   - At the timer, reduce the heat to medium (the oil should continue to sizzle gently around potato pieces) and heat the potatoes, stirring occasionally for another minute, setting a timer.
   - At the timer, add 1 T hot water, cover the skillet, reduce the heat to a low setting, and steam the potatoes for 10 minutes, setting a timer.
   - At the timer, turn off the heat, uncover the skillet, and evenly sprinkle ⅓ t salt over the potatoes.
   - For potatoes to be served immediately as a side dish, use a rubber spatula to scrape the potatoes and any released juice into a serving bowl. For potatoes to be added to a mixed ingredient dish, such as a soup or stir fry, leave the potatoes in the skillet and set the skillet aside, covered, until assembling the dish for serving.

VARIATIONS: Substitute any tasty variety of potato. While potatoes that have moist flesh work particularly well, medium russet potatoes can work, too. Potato flavor varies enormously, even among products of the same variety of potato.

Add **flavoring**. Add, for example,

- ½-1 t **dried herb leaves**, such as dill weed in particular but also sweet basil, oregano, thyme, marjoram, rosemary, or ½ t each basil and oregano. Crush dried herbs between your palms over the potatoes during stir-frying.
- ½ t **garlic powder**. Evenly sprinkle the powder over the potatoes during stir-frying.

Substitute a **heavy-bottomed stainless steel** or **other heavy-bottomed large skillet** for a nonstick skillet.

COMMENTS: A back-up step to help ensure cooking success (complete softening, which is when potato is most flavorful, without sticking or scorching) is to turn off the skillet heat after 10 minutes of steaming and leave the skillet covered on the burner for another 2 timed minutes before uncovering the skillet to add salt.

Potato Profile

Potato provides outstanding human health-supporting benefits.

- Potato contains antioxidant phytonutrients, such as flavonoids. Additionally, potato is a good source of antioxidant nutrients (including vitamin C and the minerals manganese, selenium, and zinc), which work with phytonutrients to boost the antioxidant capacity of potatoes.
- Potato provides humans a broad range of nutrient support. It is, for example, an excellent source of folate, contributes all other B complex vitamins except for B12, contributes alkaline minerals (including an outstanding amount of potassium), and contains small amounts of all essential amino acids, enabling potatoes to easily be converted into a source of good quality protein.[154]
- The potato skin is an excellent source of both soluble and insoluble fiber, though primarily of insoluble fiber.

Stir-fry/steaming perfectly suits potato.

- Stir-fry/steaming is a practical method of cooking medium and large size potatoes that maximizes both flavor and nutritional conservation. Potato reliably cooks to full softness much more quickly than in alternative boiling whole and roasting whole, other conserving methods of preparing potato.
- Dicing conserves skin, which is the most nutritious part of the potato, contributing both phytonutrients and fiber.
- Dicing makes skin inconspicuous. Scarcely aware of it, consumers readily eat it.
- Stir-fried/steamed potato is tasty with minimal added flavoring. Dried herbs and a small amount of salt suffice.
- Dicing is a way of serving potato that encourages the mixing of potato with fiber-rich vegetables (such as with onion in a soup or stir-fried dish), a serving format that reduces the high glycemic response (quick rise in blood sugar level) typical of potato, as is the case of commonly used russet potatoes.

Select the most flavorful and nutritious potato. Select, for example,

- fresh potato that is uniformly firm, has mainly smooth skin, and is heavy feeling for its size. Avoid potato that has sprouting eyes, green coloration just under the skin (which is somewhat toxic for humans), and shriveled, wrinkled skin.
- in-season potato. In the United States, potatoes are at their best when newly harvested in early fall. These new potatoes cause a lower rise in blood sugar than old potatoes that are fully mature, such as the commonly used russet potatoes, which are stored for at least a short time before being marketed.[155] New potatoes also have thin and easy to eat skins.

---

[154] Mateljan, *The World's Healthiest Foods*, 2nd edition, 370-371. Mateljan presents detailed updated information about the nutritional content and human health-supporting capacity of potatoes.

[155] Robinson, *Eating on the Wild Side*, 104.

- certified organic potato. Industrially produced potato is regularly included in the Environmental Working Group's Dirty Dozen list of vegetables and fruits that are most contaminated with pesticides. Potatoes are sprayed with fungicides and insecticides while growing and with sprout inhibitors during storage. Because many of these pesticides are soluble and are absorbed by potatoes, scrubbing potatoes removes as little as 25 percent.[156] Purchasing certified organic and locally produced potato clears the way for eating the highly nutritious potato peel, which is the most contaminated part of conventionally produced potatoes. Certified organic potato also has the advantage of being naturally produced, the significance of which is detailed in Reference #1 (Selecting Top Quality Fresh Whole Vegetables and Fruits).
- locally grown potatoes. Locally grown potatoes marketed at farmers' markets and natural food stores are freshest and very likely to have been grown in an organic-like (i.e. naturally-produced) manner. In no way are they comparable to commercially grown potatoes with respect to pesticide load. Local markets in urban areas are also more likely to market some especially nutritious potato varieties that have been developed using traditional breeding techniques.
- potato with red, blue, or black skin and deeply colored flesh. Approaching the phytonutrient content of its ancestors, potato with colored skin, and especially with both colored skin and flesh, stand out as especially nutritious potato. The phytonutrient content of these potato varieties acts as antioxidants when consumed by humans. Natural food stores, natural food sections of supermarkets, and farmers' markets are likely sources of colored potato.
- purple potato. Purple potato has the greatest concentration of phytonutrients of potato varieties. The deeper the purple color, the richer the phytonutrient content. Purple potato has antioxidant levels comparable to that of other phytonutrient rich vegetables, such as kale and spinach.

To store potato,

- refrigerate new potatoes (potatoes that are harvested in late summer or early fall and are immediately marketed) loosely wrapped, such as within a net or paper sack, on a refrigerator shelf.
- refrigerate old (fully mature) potatoes either tightly covered in a vegetable crisper drawer (i.e. moisture-controlled section) or loosely covered on a refrigerator shelf.

  - While standard advice recommends that potatoes be stored in a dark, dry, well-ventilated, and cool storage area rather than in a refrigerator, most homes do not have such an area.
  - While prolonged (many weeks long) refrigeration can cause potatoes to develop unattractive sweetness and refrigeration in a crisper drawer can cause them to sprout, refrigeration of covered potatoes in a crisper drawer or loosely covered on a refrigerator shelf reliably retains potato quality for several weeks.
  - Potatoes in general give off ethylene gas that is harmful to particular vegetables and fruits. Storing potatoes either completely covered in a vegetable crisper

---

156 Ibid., 102.

drawer or loosely covered on a refrigerator shelf separated from other produce provides an effective way to protect ethylene gas-sensitive vegetables (notably carrots) and fruits from potatoes.

18. Sweet Potato
(Stir-Fried/Steamed)
(2 servings)

1 large chilled orange-fleshed sweet potato (see Comments below regarding size) or 2 medium sweet potatoes (an amount of potato that yields approx. 3 c diced potato)

1 T extra virgin olive oil
1 T hot water
¼ t salt

Cooking Tools

1 large heavy-bottomed nonstick skillet with a tight-fitting & opaque lid
1 electric tea kettle
1 vegetable brush or dish washing sponge with one rough side

1 chef's knife
1 set measuring spoons
1 plastic or plastic-coated stir-fry spatula
1 timer
1 rubber or other heat-resistant spatula

1. **Gather all cooking tools.**

2. **Heat a large skillet on a large burner at a medium setting.** Heat an electric tea kettle to prepare water for steaming.

3. **Prepare the sweet potato for stir-fry/steaming.**

    - For dirt-coated potato and/or bumpy potato, add enough water to cover the potato in a kitchen sink or large bowl, add the potato, and let it soak 1-2 minutes before scrubbing it using the rough side of a plastic dish scrubber for smooth areas and a vegetable brush for bumpy areas. Avoid rubbing off the skin during scrubbing. Gently scrub relatively clean and smooth potato.
    - Thoroughly dry the potato with paper towels or a terry cloth towel.
    - Use a chef's knife to cut off the potato ends.
    - Standing the potato on a flattened end, use a chef's knife to slice the potato lengthwise into ¼ in. thick slices. Stacking two slices together, cut the potato slices lengthwise into ¼ in. thick strips. Holding 2-3 strips together with one hand, cut the strips crosswise into ¼ in. cubes.

PART 1

4. **Stir-fry/steam the sweet potato.**

- Increase the skillet heat to medium-high.
- When a drop of water added to the skillet instantly dances and disappears, add 1 T oil to the skillet, add the sweet potato, and stir-fry the potato for 1 minute, setting a timer. Stir-frying should at first be vigorous to quickly and thoroughly coat sweet potato pieces with oil but can slow to "flip often" pace midway through the minute.
- At the timer, reduce the heat to medium (oil should continue to sizzle gently around potato pieces) and heat the potato, stirring it occasionally for 1 minute, setting a timer.
- At the timer, add 1 T hot water, cover the skillet, reduce the heat to low, and steam the potato for 10 minutes, setting a timer.
- At the timer, turn off the heat, uncover the potato, evenly sprinkle ¼ t salt over the sweet potato, and mix in the salt.
- For potato to be served immediately as a side dish, use a rubber spatula to scrape the potato and any cooking liquid into a serving bowl. For potato to be added to a mixed ingredient dish (such as a soup, stew, curry, or stir fry), leave the potato in the skillet and set the potato aside, covered, until the dish will be assembled for serving.

VARIATIONS: Add **flavoring**. Add, for example,

- **½-1 t dried herb leaves**, such as rosemary, sweet basil, oregano, mint, or marjoram. Crush the dried herbs between your palms over the potato during stir-frying.
- **½-1 t curry powder**, evenly sprinkled over the potato during stir-frying.

Substitute a **heavy-bottomed stainless steel** or **other heavy-bottomed large skillet** for a nonstick skillet.

COMMENTS: A large sweet potato can be plump (approx. 3 in. thick and 7 in. long) or narrow and long (approx. 2¼ in. thick and 8½ in. long).

A back-up technique that can be used to ensure the potatoes become completely softened is to turn off the heat after steaming and leave the uncovered skillet on the burner for another 2 timed minutes before uncovering the skillet and adding salt.

Sweet Potato Profile

Sweet potato has distinctive nutritional characteristics. Sweet potato, which belongs to the morning glory family,

- has almost two times more antioxidant value than common potatoes. Carotenoids are among the antioxidant phytonutrients contained in sweet potato, and sweet potato contains both alpha-carotene and beta-carotene. Deep orange sweet potato has an outstanding amount of beta carotene. Because this beta carotene is in a form

that humans easily absorb (i.e. it is highly bioavailable), deep orange sweet potato is an exceptionally valuable food for humans.
- is a good source of antioxidant nutrients (including vitamin C and the minerals manganese, selenium, and zinc), which work with carotenoid phytonutrients to boost the antioxidant capacity of sweet potatoes.
- contains phytonutrients that provide both detoxification and anti-inflammatory protection to humans. Additionally, sweet potato contains vitamin E and magnesium, which enhance the anti-inflammatory capacity of sweet potato.
- has nutritious skin. Orange skin contributes phytonutrients. The darker orange the skin, the greater the phytonutrient content. All sweet potato skin is a good source of both insoluble and soluble fiber.
- contributes a broad range of nutritional support for humans. Sweet potato, for example, is a very good source of pantothenic acid and B6 and is a good source of all other B complex vitamins except for B12. Sweet potato is good source of iron and alkaline minerals, particularly of potassium. Sweet potato contains small amounts of all essential amino acids, enabling potato to easily be converted into a source of good quality protein.[157]
- has a lower glycemic index than regular potato. This means eating sweet potato results in less increase in blood sugar than commonly occurs when eating varieties of regular potato.

Stir-fry/steaming suits sweet potato.

- Stir-fry/steaming quickly yields fully soft sweet potato, which encourages regular use of these highly nutritious vegetables.
- Diced sweet potato mixes easily into all manner of dishes, which enables cooks to take maximum advantage of the nutritional contributions sweet potato can make to meals.
- Stir-fry/steamed sweet potato is attractively flavored by dried herbs and salt alone. It does not require butter or brown sugar for successful serving.
- Dicing makes skin inconspicuous. Scarcely (if at all) aware of the skin, those consuming the sweet potato readily consume the nutritious skin.
- Stir-frying sweet potato in extra virgin olive oil enhances the absorption by humans of the valuable fat soluble beta-carotene content of sweet potato.

To select the most flavorful sweet potato,

- select fresh sweet potato. Select heavy-feeling, unbroken, and uniformly firm sweet potatoes that do not have any soft spots, which are distasteful.
- select newly harvested sweet potatoes as the most flavorful potatoes. This means selecting them in the late fall (mid-November) and using them through winter and early spring.
- select sweet potato that has dark orange flesh. This variety of sweet potato, such as

---

[157] Mateljan, *The World's Healthiest Foods*, 2nd edition, 431 and 435-436. Mateljan presents detailed updated nutritional information about sweet potato.

Red Garnet sweet potato, is more flavorful and has softer flesh than sweet potato with dark yellow flesh. Sweet potato with dark orange flesh is sometimes marketed as a yam, but this is technically incorrect labeling as a true yam is an entirely different species that is rarely sold in the United States.

To select the most nutritious sweet potato,

- select sweet potato with either dark orange or deep yellow flesh as sweet potato with the richest phytonutrient (beta-carotene) content. The deeper the orange or yellow color of a sweet potato, the greater its beta-carotene content.
- select sweet potato with purple flesh, which has highest of all antioxidant value. Purple sweet potato contains anthocyanins, which are especially potent antioxidant phytonutrients.
- select certified organic or locally produced sweet potato. The Environmental Working Group regularly includes industrially grown sweet potato in its Clean Fifteen list of vegetables and fruits with least pesticide content, but certified organic and locally grown sweet potato is largely free of pesticide contamination, which clears the way for consumers to use the nutritious skin. Certified organic and locally produced sweet potato also have the other advantages of naturally produced produce, an important one being having more concentrated and potent phytonutrient content than industrially produced produce. Other advantages of natural production are detailed in Reference #1 (Selecting Top Quality Fresh Whole Vegetables and Fruits).

To store sweet potato,

- store sweet potatoes at room temperature when using them within a week to 10 days, storing them in a dark, cool place.
- refrigerate sweet potatoes that will not be used within 10 days loosely covered in the crisper drawer for a short period (one or two weeks) as refrigeration does not suit them. It can give them an unattractive "off" flavor, and sweet potatoes spoil quite quickly. Like common potatoes, they store best uncovered in a dark, dry, cool (fifty to sixty degrees), and well-ventilated area. Unless such a storage area is available, it is best to purchase sweet potatoes in small amounts and refrigerate them for a few weeks only.

19. Rutabaga
(Stir-Fried/Steamed)
(2 servings)

2 medium (approx. 2½ in. diameter) or 1 large (3 in. diameter) rutabaga, chilled (to yield 2-4 c diced)

1 T extra virgin olive oil
1 T hot water
¼ t salt

Cooking Tools

1 large nonstick skillet with a tight-fitting & opaque lid	1 set measuring spoons
	1 plastic or plastic-coated stir-fry spatula
1 electric tea kettle	1 timer
1 vegetable peeler	1 rubber or other heat-resistant spatula
1 chef's knife	

---

1. **Gather all cooking tools.**

2. **Heat a large skillet on a large burner at a medium setting.** Heat an electric kettle to prepare hot water for steaming.

3. **Prepare the rutabaga for stir-fry/steaming.**

    - Thoroughly scrub and dry the rutabaga.
    - Use a peeler to remove the skin if the rutabaga has a wax coating. Otherwise peel off only very thick skin.
    - Use a chef's knife to cut off the ends of the rutabaga. Standing a rutabaga on a flattened end, use the chef's knife to cut it lengthwise into ¼ in. thick slices. Stacking two or more slices together, cut the rutabaga slices lengthwise into ¼ in. thick strips. Cut the strips crosswise into ¼ in. cubes.

4. **Stir-fry/steam the rutabaga.**

    - Increase the skillet heat to medium high.
    - When a drop of water added to the skillet instantly dances and disappears, add 1 T oil to the skillet, add the diced rutabaga, and stir-fry it for 1 minute, setting a timer. Stir-frying should at first be vigorous to quickly and thoroughly coat pieces with oil but can slow to a "flip often" pace midway through the minute.
    - At the timer, reduce the heat to medium (oil should continue to sizzle gently around the pieces) and heat the rutabaga for 1 minute, stirring it occasionally and setting a timer.
    - At the timer, add 1 T hot water, cover the skillet, reduce the heat to low, and steam the rutabaga for 8 minutes (10 minutes for large rutabaga), setting a timer.
    - At the timer, turn off the heat, uncover the skillet, and evenly sprinkle ¼ t salt over the rutabaga.
    - For rutabaga to be served immediately as a side dish, use a rubber spatula to scrape it and any cooking juice into a serving bowl. For rutabaga to be served in a mixed ingredient dish (such as a soup, tomato sauce stew, or stir fry), re-cover the skillet and set it aside until assembling the dish for serving.
    - Collect and serve any cooking juice with the rutabaga.

    VARIATIONS: Substitute **4 small (approx. 2 in. diameter), young rutabagas.** Reduce steaming time to 5 minutes.

Add **½-1 t dried herb leaves**, such as sweet basil, oregano, dill weed, thyme, or marjoram. Crush the dried herbs between your palms over the rutabaga during stir-frying.

Rutabaga Profile

Rutabaga, which is a cross between cabbage and turnip, shares the nutritional and cooking characteristics of other cabbage family vegetables.

- Rutabaga contains rich amounts of the glucosinolate family of phytonutrients, which provide antioxidant, anti-inflammatory, and detoxification protection for humans. Glucosinolates also promote human intestinal health.
- Rutabaga is a good source of a broad spectrum of minerals and vitamins, and these nutrients occur in combinations that further enhance the antioxidant value of the phytonutrients rutabagas are known to contain.
- Rutabaga contains human health-supporting sulfur compounds that also easily undermine the natural sweet flavoring of rutabaga if the rutabaga is overcooked.

Stir-fry/steaming suits rutabaga.

- Stir-fry/steaming is protective of the water soluble and heat-sensitive glycosinolate phytonutrient content.
- Stir-fry/steaming conserves a maximum amount of the nutritional content of rutabaga.
- Stir-fry/steaming keeps sulfur compounds locked within plant cells where they do not damage rutabaga flavor.
- Diced rutabaga mixes easily into all manner of dishes.
- Dicing makes skin inconspicuous. Scarcely (if at all) aware of the skin, those consuming the rutabaga readily consume the nutritious skin.

Select the most flavorful and tender rutabaga. Select, for example,

- fresh rutabaga. Select rutabaga that is uniformly firm, uniformly smooth, and feels heavy for its size.
- small or medium (approx. 2-2½ in. diameter) rutabaga.
- rutabaga with tops attached whenever this is a selection option.
- locally grown rutabaga that is marketed at natural food stores and farmers' markets, which is most reliably fresh rutabaga.
- in-season rutabaga, which is rutabaga that is harvested in the fall.

To store rutabaga,

- refrigerate rutabaga uncovered in the crisper drawer until it is thoroughly chilled and then transfer it to a plastic bag, pushing out as much air as possible before sealing the bag.
- use rutabaga within a few weeks.

20. Yellow and Zucchini Summer Squash
(Stir-Fried/Steamed)
(2 servings)

1 medium (6-8 in. long; 1½-2 in. thick) zucchini or 4 small (approx. 4 in. long; 2-2½ in. bulb diameter) yellow squash, to yield approx. 2-3 c diced squash

1 T extra virgin olive oil
¼ t salt

Cooking Tools

1 large nonstick skillet with a tight-fitting & opaque lid
1 chef's knife
1 set measuring spoons
1 plastic or plastic-coated stir-fry spatula

1 timer
1 rubber or other heat-resistant spatula
1 colander
1 dinner plate

---

1. **Gather all cooking tools.**

2. **Heat a large skillet on a large burner at a medium setting.**

3. **Prepare the summer squash for stir-fry/steaming.**

    - Rinse and thoroughly dry the squash with paper towels or a terry cloth towel.
    - Use a chef's knife to slice off the stem end and bottom tip of zucchini. Slice off the bottom end and entirely remove the long neck of crookneck yellow squash. Set the neck aside. Stand a squash upright on a flattened end and use a chef's knife to cut the squash lengthwise into ¼ in. thick slices, cut the slices lengthwise into ¼ in. wide strips, and cut the strips crosswise into ¼ in. cubes. Slice a removed crookneck yellow squash neck crosswise into ¼ in. thick slices.

4. **Stir-fry/steam the squash.**

    - Increase the skillet heat to medium-high.
    - When a drop of water added to the skillet instantly dances and disappears, add 1 T oil, add the squash, and stir-fry it for 1 minute, setting a timer. Stir-frying should at first be vigorous to quickly and thoroughly coat the squash pieces with oil but can slow to "flip often" pace midway through the minute.
    - At the timer, reduce the heat to low, cover the skillet, and steam the squash in its own juice for 4 minutes, setting a timer.

- At the timer, remove the skillet from the heat and evenly sprinkle ¼ t salt over the squash. For squash to be immediately served as a side dish, use a rubber spatula to scrape the squash and any cooking juice into a serving bowl. For squash to be served in a mixed ingredient dish, scrape the squash into a colander placed over a dinner plate for collecting any spilled juice. Serve any collected steaming juice with the squash.

VARIATIONS: Substitute **1 small (6-8 in. long; 1½-2-in. thick) yellow straightneck or 2 small scallop squashes** for either zucchini or yellow crookneck summer squash.

Add **flavoring**. Add, for example,

- ½-1 t **dried herb leaves**, such as sweet basil, oregano, mint, thyme, or marjoram. Crush dried herbs between your palms over the squash during stir-frying.
- ½-1 t **curry powder**, evenly sprinkled over the stir-frying squash.
- ½-1 t **garlic powder**, evenly sprinkled over squash flavored with either herb or spice flavoring.

COMMENTS: Because summer squash steams in its own juice without any added water, a heavy-bottomed nonstick skillet most reliably works for steaming without scorching.

Summer Squash Profile

Summer squash has an impressive list of notable nutritional characteristics.

- Recent research shows that summer squash, and the skin in particular, has outstanding content of the carotenoid family of phytonutrients. This family includes lutein and zeaxanthin, which serve as key antioxidants that block cellular damage from free radicals when consumed by humans.
- The combination of vitamins and minerals contained by summer squash – notably the vitamin C and manganese content – function like antioxidants and further boost the antioxidant value of the carotenoids. Extra virgin olive oil used in stir-fry/steaming maximizes absorption of the fat-soluble carotenoids.
- The carotenoid content of summer squash provides anti-inflammation protection in addition to antioxidant protection. Summer squash seeds contribute omega-3 fatty acids content (alpha-linolenic acid) and magnesium that combine with carotenoid phytonutrients to enhance the anti-inflammation protection provided humans.
- The overall mineral content of zucchini ranks it among top alkaline balancing vegetables.
- Summer squash is a good source of both insoluble and soluble fiber, but yellow squash contains a distinctive amount of the soluble fiber pectin.
- Summer squash flowers are edible.

- Recent research has shown that summer squash phytonutrient content is quite stable during cooking. While this phytonutrient stability does not apply to boiling and microwave cooking, it does apply to stir fry/steaming.
- Antioxidant stability applies to freezing as well.

To select the most flavorful and tender yellow summer squash,

- select fresh squash, which is bright yellow squash that feels heavy for its size and has shiny skin that feels squeaky clean. Skin should also be relatively smooth, not bumpy. Dark orange-yellow color indicates advanced maturity.
- select small and medium squash as the most reliably tender squash. Much larger squash that is very fresh – as indicated by bright green or yellow skin that is smooth and feels squeaky clean – can also be sweet and tender.

To select the most flavorful and tender zucchini,

- select fresh zucchini. Select bright green squash that feels heavy for its size and has shiny and smooth skin that feels squeaky clean.
- select small and medium squash as the most reliably sweet and tender squash. Much larger squash (even as large as 12 x 2½ in.) that is very fresh (as indicated by bright, shiny, and squeaky clean-feeling skin) can also be attractively tender and tasty. Because larger squash can be bitter, it is important to make a taste check to ensure that large zucchini is not bitter.

To select the most nutritious summer squash,

- select certified organic and locally produced summer squash to clear the way for eating the nutritious summer squash skin. Industrially produced summer squash is regularly included in the middle of the Environmental Working Group's yearly list of vegetables and fruits most contaminated with pesticides. This pesticide content is a significant blemish on the otherwise high quality of summer squash.
- select certified organic and locally produced summer squash to avoid selection of genetically modified squash. Some industrially produced summer squash is genetically modified, and there is no way of knowing for sure except by selecting certified organic produce. Locally produced summer squash is most likely not genetically modified.
- select certified organic and locally grown summer squash to take advantage of the other benefits of naturally produced produce, one of which is more potent phytonutrient content than industrially produced summer squash. Reference #1 (Selecting Top Quality Fresh Whole Vegetables and Fruits) details other benefits of natural production.

21. Winter Squash
(Stir-Fried/Steamed)
(2-3 servings)

1 medium (approx. 7 in. long with a 3½ in. thick bulb end) butternut squash or 1 medium (approx. 4 x 4½ in.) acorn squash, approx. 1½ lb squash; to yield 2-3 c diced squash

1 T extra virgin olive oil
1 T hot water
¼ t salt

Cooking Tools

1 large skillet with a tight-fitting & opaque lid
1 electric tea kettle
1 chef's knife
1 9 in. glass pie plate or small rectangular microwave safe dish
1 large dinner (soup) spoon

1 vegetable peeler
1 set measuring spoons
1 plastic or plastic-coated stir-fry spatula
1 timer
1 rubber or other heat-resistant spatula
1 colander
1 dinner plate

---

1. **Gather all cooking tools.**

2. **Heat a large skillet on a large burner at a low setting.** Heat an electric kettle to prepare hot water for steaming.

3. **Prepare the squash for stir-fry/steaming.**

   - Halve the squash lengthwise. Stand a butternut squash upright on its stem end. If the squash is not stable, slice off a portion of the stem end so that it sits level. Beginning at the top end, use a chef's knife to halve the squash lengthwise. Halve acorn squash in the same way.
   - Working with one half at a time and leaving the seeds and membrane within each half, place a squash half skin side up within a 9 in. glass pie plate dish and heat it on high in a microwave oven for 90 seconds to soften the squash for cutting and peeling.
   - After both halves are softened and are cool enough to handle, use a large dinner spoon to scrape out the seeds and membrane from each half. To prepare the seeds for use as a snack, set them aside and see Comments below for preparation details.
   - Use a chef's knife to cut off the ends of the squash halves and to cut the halves lengthwise into ¼ in. thick slices.
   - Use a vegetable peeler to cut off a thin layer of the skin on each slice.
   - Holding several slices together at a time with one hand, use the chef's knife to cut the slices crosswise into ¼ in. cubes.

4. **Stir-fry/steam the squash.**

- Increase the skillet heat to medium-high.
- When a drop of water added to the skillet instantly dances and disappears, add 1 T oil, add the squash, and stir-fry it for 1 minute, setting a timer. Stir-frying should at first be vigorous to quickly and thoroughly coat squash pieces with oil but can slow to "flip often" pace midway through the minute.
- At the timer, reduce the heat to medium (oil should continue to sizzle gently around pieces) and cook the squash for 1 minute, stirring it occasionally and setting a timer.
- At the timer, add 1 T hot water, cover the skillet, reduce the heat to low, and steam the squash for 10 minutes, setting a timer.
- At the timer, turn off the heat, uncover the skillet, and evenly sprinkle ¼ t salt over the squash.
- For squash to be immediately served as a side dish, use a rubber spatula to scrape the squash and any cooking juice into a serving bowl.
- For squash to be served in a mixed ingredient dish (such as a soup, tomato sauce-based stew, curry, or stir fry), scrape the squash into a colander placed over a dinner plate for collecting any steaming juice and set the squash aside until the dish is assembled for serving.
- Serve any collected cooking juice with the squash.

VARIATIONS: Use a peeler specifically made for peeling winter squash and omit the microwave cooking. Use a chef's knife to slice off the end of each squash half and peel the squash before or after cutting it lengthwise into ¼ in. thick slices. This large and heavy-duty peeler is marketed in kitchen stores and catalogs carrying kitchen tools.

Add **flavoring**. Add, for example,

- **1 t dried herb leaves**, such as sweet basil, oregano, mint, thyme, or marjoram leaves. Crush the herbs between your palms before sprinkling them over the diced squash during stir-frying.
- **½-1 t curry powder**, evenly sprinkled over the diced squash during stir-frying.

COMMENTS: While a chef's knife works for halving a winter squash, a knife with an extra-long (9 in.) and firm blade works even better.

Boil the squash seeds for use as a nutritious snack.

- Rinse the seeds to separate the seeds from the sticky (mucilaginous) membrane.
- Add 1 c water, the seeds, and ⅛ t salt to a small saucepan and bring the water to boiling over high heat.
- Reduce the heat to a level that maintains gentle boiling, cover the pan, and cook the seeds for 15 minutes, setting a timer.
- At the timer, drain the seeds in a colander placed over a bowl for collecting the cooking water, which can be used as a broth in dishes like stew and curry.

- Serve the seeds with a separate container for discarded shells.

Prepare a tasty vegetable broth from the squash skin and membrane for use in curries, soups, and stews.

- Chop the squash skin into relatively small pieces. Add 1½ c water, ¼ t salt, and squash skin and membrane to a small saucepan with a lid. Heat the water to boiling over high heat, reduce the heat to a level that maintains gentle boiling, cover the pan, and cook the squash for 30-60 minutes, setting a timer. Halfway through this cooking time check the broth to ensure that the liquid has not unexpectedly evaporated, restoring water as may be needed.
- At the timer, drain the broth in a colander placed within a large bowl.
- Refrigerate the squash broth within a small glass container. Either use the broth within several days or freeze it for later use.

Winter Squash Profile

Winter squash has a variety of outstanding nutritional characteristics.

- The rich yellow or orange color of winter squash flesh indicates unique and outstanding carotenoid phytonutrient content. Except for pumpkin, current research indicates that no other single food provides more of any one variety of carotenoids or a wider variety of different carotenoid family members. For winter squash in general, the deeper the orange or yellow color of squash flesh, the greater its beta carotene content. The rich and varied carotenoid phytonutrient content gives winter squash outstanding antioxidant and anti-inflammatory capacity. Stir-fry/steaming promotes the absorption of these fat-soluble carotenoids by humans during digestion.
- Winter squash in general contains rich amounts of a wide spectrum of vitamins and minerals, and the particular combination of nutrients contained, notably the vitamin C and manganese content, works to further expand the already exceptionally high antioxidant value of the carotenoid content of winter squash. Squash magnesium content combines with anti-inflammatory phytonutrients to intensify the anti-inflammatory protection provided humans by winter squash.
- Winter squash in general also has high fiber content, which includes the soluble fiber pectin.
- Winter squash seeds contribute omega-3 fatty acids.
- Butternut squash flowers are edible.

To select the most flavorful and nutritious winter squash,

- select fully ripe squash. Ripe squash in general feels heavy for its size and has uniformly deep-colored skin, whether green or orange. Skin (or rind) color should

be somewhat dull, not glossy. The stem should be stout and firmly attached. When tapped, the squash should give a woody sound. For acorn squash, a yellow ground spot (where the squash has lain during growth) is a good indication of ripeness. Pale green and somewhat blotchy or speckled skin on acorn squash, on the other hand, indicate the squash is overripe and likely has dry flesh.
- select fresh squash. The skin should not be wrinkled or have any broken open or soft spots.

  - Select in-season squash as freshest squash, which is squash harvested during September through December.
  - Select locally produced winter squash as freshest squash.

- select certified organic and locally grown winter squash when these options are available.

  - Select certified organic and locally grown winter squash to avoid pesticide content. Because winter squash has the characteristic of efficiently pulling contaminants from soil, industrially grown winter squash has relatively high pesticide content. It is included in the middle of the Environmental Working Group's 2016 list that ranks fifty vegetables and fruits by pesticide content.
  - Select certified organic and locally grown winter squash to take advantage of the other benefits of naturally produced produce. One important benefit is greater and more potent phytonutrient content in comparison to industrially produced produce. Reference #1 (Selecting Top Quality Fresh Whole Vegetables and Fruits) details other benefits of naturally produced produce.

To store winter squash,

- store whole squash in a cool (ideally between 50 and 60 degrees), dry, and well-ventilated area away from light. These conditions ideally suit winter squash, and it stores well for six months or longer under these conditions.
- refrigerate small whole squash (butternut, buttercup, and acorn) on a refrigerator shelf when ideal storage conditions are not available. Because winter squash is prone to decay when ideal storage conditions are not available, refrigerate squash for a short period and use it within several weeks.
- immediately refrigerate cut squash, tightly covered. Spread a very light coating of extra virgin olive oil over the exposed flesh of large chunks of squash before storage. When cut squash flesh will come in contact with the storage container, store it within a glass container.

PART 1

22. Turnip
(Stir-Fried/Steamed)
(2 servings)

2 chilled medium (approx. 2½ in. diameter) turnips (to yield 2-3 c diced turnip)
1 T extra virgin olive oil
1 T hot water
¼ t salt

Cooking Tools

1 large nonstick skillet with a tight-fitting & opaque lid
1 electric tea kettle
1 dish sponge with one rough side
1 chef's knife
1 set measuring spoons
1 plastic or plastic-coated stir-fry spatula
1 timer
1 rubber or other heat-resistant spatula
1 colander
1 dinner plate

---

1. **Gather all cooking tools.**

2. **Heat a large nonstick skillet on a large burner at a medium setting.** Heat an electric tea kettle to prepare water for steaming.

3. **Prepare the turnips for stir-fry/steaming.**

   - Scrub the turnips, being careful not to rub off the skin, and thoroughly dry them using paper towels or a terry cloth towel.
   - Use a chef's knife to slice the stem end and tip from each turnip.
   - Stand each turnip upright on a flattened end and use the chef's knife to cut it lengthwise into ¼ in. thick slices. Stacking two slices together, cut the slices into ¼ in. thick strips. Holding several strips together at a time, cut the strips crosswise into ¼ in. cubes.

4. **Stir-fry/steam the diced turnip.**

   - Increase the skillet heat to a medium-high setting.
   - When a drop of water added to the skillet immediately dances and disappears, add 1 T oil, add the diced turnip, and stir-fry it for 1 minute, setting a timer. Stir-frying should at first be vigorous to quickly and thoroughly mix the turnip into the oil but can slow to "flip often" pace midway through the minute.
   - At the timer, reduce the heat to medium (oil should sizzle gently around the turnip pieces) and heat the turnips for 1 minute, stirring them occasionally and setting a timer.
   - At the timer, add 1 T hot water, cover the skillet, reduce the heat to low, and steam the turnip for 4 minutes, setting a timer.

- At the timer, remove the skillet from the burner and evenly sprinkle ¼ t salt over the turnip. For turnips to be served immediately, use a rubber spatula to scrape the turnips and any cooking juice into a serving bowl. For turnips to be served in a mixed ingredient dish (such as a stir-fried dish, soup, stew, or curry) scrape the turnip into a colander placed over a dinner plate for collecting any steaming juice. Set the turnip aside until assembling the dish for serving.

VARIATIONS: Add **flavoring**. For example, **1 t dried herb leaves**, such as sweet basil, oregano, dill weed, thyme, marjoram, Italian seasoning, or rosemary. Crush dried herbs between your palms over the turnips during stir-frying.

Turnip Profile

Turnip shares the same nutritional and flavoring characteristics of other cabbage family vegetables. Stir-fry/steaming, accordingly, ideally suits turnip.

- Turnip is a rich source of glucosinolate phytonutrients. These phytonutrients provide antioxidant, anti-inflammatory, and detoxification protection for humans. They also promote the intestinal health of humans.
- Turnip with skin is a good source of both soluble and insoluble fiber, and especially of soluble fiber.
- Turnip contains human health-promoting sulfur compounds, which also easily undermine natural sweet turnip flavoring if turnip is overcooked.

To select the most flavorful turnip,

- select fresh turnip that is uniformly firm, has smooth and bright white skin, and is heavy feeling for its size. The turnip should have a slightly sweet odor.
    - Select in-season turnip. In the United States this is turnip harvested from October to March.
    - Select locally produced turnip as the freshest turnip.
- select turnip with attached greens whenever this is a selection option. Turnip greens should be firm and brightly colored without any yellowing.
- select small to medium size (approx. 2½ in. diameter) turnip. Larger and more mature turnip can, but does not necessarily, have a woody texture. Mature turnip can also be bitter. It is important to make a taste test to check for bitterness when preparing large turnip.

To store turnip,

- separately refrigerate the green tops (Recipe #30), storing both tops and roots within

- a sealed plastic bag. When cutting off the green tops, leave 1 inch of stem on the roots during storage.
- refrigerate room temperature turnip, such as those freshly picked from a garden, uncovered in the crisper drawer until it is thoroughly chilled before transferring it to a plastic storage bag. Push out as much air as possible before sealing the bag.
- refrigerate turnip in either unwashed or scrubbed and thoroughly dried form.
- use turnip within a few weeks for sweetest flavor and greatest nutritional value.

Dark Green Leafy Vegetable Recipes

23. Beet Greens
(Stir-Fried/Steamed)
(2 servings)

approx. 1 lb chilled medium (approx. 2½ in. diameter) beets with bright green and fresh looking attached leaves; approx. 4 beets with 6 leaves each, leaves equally divided between larger and smaller leaves; or ½ lb loose mixed leaves

1 T extra virgin olive oil
1 T hot water
¼ t salt

Cooking Tools

1 large nonstick skillet with a tight-fitting & opaque lid
1 electric tea kettle
1 each chef's & 7 in serrated knife
1 colander
1 large (approx. 16 x 24 in.) cutting board

1 set measuring spoons
1 plastic or plastic-coated stir-fry spatula
1 timer
1 rubber or other heat-resistant spatula
1 dinner plate

1. **Gather all cooking tools.**

2. **Heat a large skillet on a large burner at a medium setting.** Heat an electric tea kettle to prepare hot water for steaming.

3. **Prepare the beet greens for stir-fry/steaming.**

    - Use a chef's knife to cut off greens attached to beets, leaving 1 in. stems on the beets and re-refrigerating the beet roots in a sealed bag.

- Add the greens to a sink or large bowl filled with enough cool water to cover them. Wash the leaves individually. Swish each leaf in the water, rub the leaves between your hands, re-swish the leaf in the water, shake clinging water from it, and add it to a colander.
- Dry the leaves. Spread them in a single layer over a strip of paper or cloth towels, and either use a paper or terry cloth towel to pat the leaves dry *or* cover the leaves with another layer of towels, roll the leaves in the towels, and gently squeeze the roll to dry the leaves thoroughly.
- Stack the leaves, forming 2-3 stacks and aligning the stems. Holding the leaves in place with one hand, use a chef's knife to chop off the stems. Set the stems aside.
- Working on a large cutting board and holding the leaves in place with one hand, use a 7 in. serrated knife to cut each stack of leaves into ca ⅓ in. thick pieces, slicing lengthwise and crosswise through the leaves.
- Holding the stems together with one hand, use a chef's knife to chop the stems crosswise into thin (⅛ in. thick) pieces. Keep stems separated from the leaves.

4. **Stir-fry/steam the beet greens**.

- Increase the skillet heat to medium-high.
- When a drop of water added to the skillet instantly dances and disappears, add 1 T oil, mix in the stems, and cook them for about 30 seconds, stirring them occasionally.
- Add the greens and stir-fry them for 1 minute, setting a timer. Stir-frying should be vigorous throughout this minute to quickly and thoroughly coat the greens with oil.
- At the timer, add 1 T hot water, cover the skillet, reduce the heat to low, and steam the greens for 4 minutes, setting a timer.
- At the timer, remove the skillet from the heat and evenly sprinkle ¼ t salt over the greens.
- For greens to be immediately served, use a rubber spatula to scrape the greens and any cooking juice into a serving bowl.
- For greens to be served in a mixed ingredient dish, such as a stir fry or stew, scrape the greens into a colander placed over a dinner plate and set the colander aside until assembling the dish for serving.
- Serve any steaming juice with the greens.

VARIATIONS: Substitute **different size beet greens**. Substitute, for example,

- **pre-washed baby beet greens** for unwashed beet greens. Omit steaming and stir-fry the sliced greens for 1 minute only, just until wilted. While medium beet greens are more flavorful, baby greens are highly convenient to use.
- **mature and larger beet greens** for small and medium beet greens. Evenly cut the greens into slightly thinner (¼ in.) slices.

Add **1 t dried herb leaves**, such as sweet basil, oregano, mint, dill weed, thyme, or marjoram. Crush dried herbs between your palms over greens during stir-frying.

Beet Greens Profile

Beet greens have super nutritional credentials.

- As members of the **chenopod family of vegetables**, beet roots and beet greens have phytonutrients called betalains that provide unique health support for humans. The source of the red-purple coloring of beets, betalains provide humans a wide range of health-protective support, including anti-oxidant, anti-inflammatory, and detoxification support. Stir-fry/steaming conserves maximum content of these water soluble and heat-sensitive phytonutrients.
- Beet greens contain phytonutrients of the carotenoid family, including both alpha-carotene and beta-carotene, which serve as antioxidants. Stir-frying in extra virgin olive oil helps ensure the absorption of fat-soluble carotenoids by humans.
- Beet greens contain antioxidant nutrients, including vitamins C and E and the minerals manganese and zinc, that combine with betalain and carotenoid phytonutrients to intensify the antioxidant protection provided to humans. Beet greens also have excellent magnesium and vitamin E content, which combines with betalain phytonutrients to intensify the anti-inflammatory capacity of beet greens.
- Beet greens are an excellent source of both insoluble and soluble fiber.
- Beet greens are a good source of iron and an outstanding source of alkaline minerals, containing rich potassium content in particular but also a standout amount of both magnesium and calcium as well. Like other chenopod family vegetables, beet greens do contain a relatively high amount of oxalates, which bind with some of the calcium content and prevent its absorption by the body.
- Containing rich amounts of a wide variety of other nutritional components, beet greens provide super whole-body health support. This support reaches to the brain, the blood, the eyes, and most other major human organs.[158]

To select top quality beet greens,

- select fresh greens. Select deep green, firm, and fresh appearing leaves that do not have any yellowing.
- select medium size greens as leaves with the most nutritional value.
- select in-season greens. In the United States in-season is from June to October.
- select locally produced beet greens as the freshest greens. At farmers' markets select greens from vendors who refrigerate greens during marketing.
- select certified organic and locally grown beet greens. These greens will reliably have significantly less pesticide residues than industrially produced beet greens. They will also have the other advantages of naturally produced food, an important one being more potent phytonutrient content than industrially produced greens. Reference #1 (Selecting Top Quality Fresh Whole Vegetables and Fruits) details other advantages of natural production.

---

158 Mateljan, *The World's Healthiest Foods*, 2nd Edition, 141 and 146. Mateljan presents updated details about the enormous human health-promoting capacity of beet greens.

To store beet greens,

- refrigerate already chilled greens unwashed. Treating them as a fragile food, refrigerate them in the crisper (moisture controlled) drawer using the Robinson vented plastic bag method (within a sealed plastic bag that has as much air as possible squeezed from it before sealing; bag vented with uniformly placed pin pricks, 20 pin pricks per gallon bag). The greens will store well for several days (even a week or more), but use them quickly for best flavor and greatest nutritional quality.
- quickly chill room temperature greens (such as those picked fresh or that have become warmed after purchase) before refrigerating them, uncovered. Add the greens to very cold water for several minutes, wash the individual leaves, and dry them as in Step #3 of Recipe #23 above before storing them using the Robinson vented plastic bag method.

24. Chard
(Stir-Fried/Steamed)
(2 servings)

3 large (approx. 6 x 10 in.) chilled chard leaves (Swiss, Rainbow, or other chard variety) or 10 medium (approx. 4 x 6 in.) leaves with attached stems, to yield 3-4 c sliced chard

1 T extra virgin olive oil
1 T hot water
¼ t salt

Cooking Tools

1 colander
1 each paring, chef's, & 7 in. serrated knife
1 large (approx. 16 x 24 in.) cutting board
1 large skillet with a tight-fitting & opaque lid
1 set measuring spoons

1 plastic or plastic-coated stir-fry spatula
1 timer
1 rubber or other heat-resistant spatula
1 dinner plate
1 electric tea kettle

---

1. **Gather all cooking tools.**

2. **Heat a large skillet on a large burner at a medium setting.** Begin heating an electric tea kettle to prepare hot water for steaming.

3. **Prepare the chard for stir-fry/steaming.**

    - Add the leaves to a sink or large bowl filled with enough cold water to cover them completely.

- Wash each leaf individually. Swish it in the water, rub the leaf between your hands to cover both sides, re-swish the leaf in the water, shake off clinging water, and place it in a colander.
- Spread the leaves in a single layer over a strip of paper or terry cloth towels. Add a top layer of towels, roll the leaves in the towels, and gently squeeze the leaves to dry them thoroughly. Unroll the leaves and pat dry any wet spots.
- Use a paring knife to cut out the thick vein running through the center of each leaf, cutting close to each side of the vein and retaining the stem. Slice off the bottom tip of the stem and set the veins with attached stems aside. Form the leaves into two or three stacks, facing leaves in the same way.
- Working with one stack at a time, hold the leaves together with one hand and use a 7 in. serrated knife to slice the leaves into approx. ⅓ in. thick pieces, slicing lengthwise and crosswise through the leaves.
- While holding all the veins/stems together with one hand, use a chef's knife to chop the veins/stems into thin (⅛ in. thick) pieces. Keep the veins/stems separate from the leaves.

4. **Stir-fry/steam the chard.**

- Increase the skillet heat to medium-high.
- When a drop of water added to the skillet instantly dances and disappears, add 1 T oil, add the chopped veins/stems, and cook them for about 30 seconds, stirring occasionally.
- Add the sliced chard and stir-fry it for 1 minute, setting a timer. Stir-frying should be vigorous throughout this minute to quickly and thoroughly cook pieces with oil and to heat all pieces until hot.
- At the timer, add 1 T hot water, cover the skillet, reduce the heat to low, and steam the chard for 4 minutes, setting a timer.
- At the timer, remove the skillet from the heat, evenly sprinkle ¼ t salt over the chard, and either use a rubber spatula to scrape it and any steaming liquid into a serving bowl for immediate serving or into a colander placed over a dinner plate for assembly into a mixed ingredient dish.
- Serve any collected cooking juice with the chard.

VARIATION: Substitute **different size chard leaves**. Substitute, for example,

- **small chard leaves** for medium or large chard leaves. Do not cut out the center veins. Stack the leaves aligning the stems, forming several stacks. Use a chef's knife to chop the stems and set the stems aside. Slice and stir-fry the leaves as above but omit steaming. Small leaves will be tender with one minute of stir-frying, which makes them a highly convenient product selection.
- **very large chard leaves** for medium or large chard leaves. Prepare them in exactly the same way but increase steaming time to 5 minutes. Very large chard leaves may have a more robust flavor than smaller leaves.

Chard Profile

Chard has outstanding nutritional characteristics.

- As a member of the **chenopod family of vegetables**, chard, like beet greens and spinach, contains distinctive phytonutrients called betalains that provide invaluable antioxidant, anti-inflammatory, and detoxification protection for humans. Containing both reddish-purple and yellowish betalain pigments, and with each pigment (nine different pigments have been discovered so far) providing separate health benefits, chard provides even more types of health benefits than beets.
- In most respects, however, chard is very much like beet greens (Recipe #23). Both are nutritional superstars that are sources of an outstanding variety of antioxidant phytonutrients, including carotenoids, which in combination with antioxidant nutrients (including vitamins C, E, and A in the form of beta-carotene and the minerals manganese and zinc) give these greens enormous antioxidant capacity. Like beets, chard phytonutrient content provides anti-inflammatory protection to humans, and particular nutrients (omega-3 fatty acids, vitamin E, and magnesium) combine with these phytonutrients to boost the anti-inflammation protection provided.
- Chard contributes rich amounts of a wide spectrum of nutritional components that provide full system support for humans.[159] While this content includes excellent alkaline mineral content, some of chard's rich calcium content gets bound up by oxalates, which prevents its absorption.
- Stir-fry/steaming effectively conserves the water soluble and heat-sensitive betalain phytonutrients. Stir-frying in extra virgin olive oil enhances the absorption of chard's fat- soluble carotenoid phytonutrients by humans during digestion.

Chard, which is commonly called Swiss chard, is marketed in several varieties.

- White-stemmed chard has especially tender and juicy stems.
- Yellow-stemmed chard and red-stemmed chard have somewhat stronger flavor than Swiss and white-stemmed chard.
- Rainbow chard is a mixture of different varieties of chard.
- Baby Swiss chard is any variety of chard that is harvested in immature form. More tender than more mature chard, it is commonly found in baby green salad mixes. Baby Swiss chard requires minimal slicing and quickly stir-fries in 1 minute, which makes it a highly convenient product selection when it is an option.

To select the most flavorful chard,

- select fresh chard with brilliant dark green, firm, and fresh-appearing leaves. Leaves should not be wilted, bruised, or ragged in appearance. They should not have black spoiled areas, though small spots can be cut out and discarded.
- select in-season chard. In the United States peak season for chard is June through August.

---

159 Mateljan, *The World's Healthiest Foods*, 2nd Edition, 439; 444; 447. Mateljan details updated information about the health-promoting capacity of chard for humans.

- select chard at farmers' markets from vendors that keep chard chilled during marketing.

To store chard,

- quickly refrigerate already chilled greens unwashed. Treating it like a fragile vegetable, use the Robinson vented plastic bag storage method (store the chard in a sealed plastic bag from which as much air as possible has been squeezed; vent the bag by making uniformly spaced pin pricks, 20 per gallon bag; store the bag in the moisture-controlled crisper drawer).
- quickly chill room temperature chard (such as freshly picked chard or chard purchased at a farmers' market). Soak the chard in water for several minutes, dry the chard leaves, loosely wrap them within paper or cloth towels, and thoroughly chill the chard leaves before tightly covering them for storage. In addition to maximizing both chard flavor and nutritional quality, storing chard in this way makes it ready for quick use in meals.
- use chard quickly (within 5 days). Though chard physically stores well (leaves retain bright color and firmness) for a longer period, invisible flavor and nutritional loss quickly begins to occur.
- stir-fry/steam and dry freeze chard (freeze it without any liquid) that cannot be quickly used. Store it vacuum packed (or with maximum air pressed out) within a quart size sealable plastic freezer bag. Quickly thaw frozen chard to maximize retention of its nutritional quality. Either microwave thaw it or add the frozen chard directly to near boiling stew, curry, or soup shortly before serving. Do not allow frozen chard to thaw at room temperature or while refrigerated.

25. Collards
(Stir-Fried/Steamed)
(2 servings)

4 chilled small to medium (approx. 6-8 in. wide; 7-9 in. long) collard leaves (to yield 2-3 c sliced)	1 T extra virgin olive oil 1 T hot water ¼ t salt

Cooking Tools

1 large skillet with a tight-fitting & opaque lid 1 electric tea kettle 1 each paring, chef's, & 7 in. serrated knife 1 large (approx. 16 x 24 in.) cutting board 1 set measuring spoons	1 plastic or plastic-coated stir-fry spatula 1 timer 1 rubber or other heat-resistant spatula 1 colander 1 dinner plate

1. **Gather all cooking tools.**

2. **Heat a large skillet on a large burner at a medium setting.** Heat an electric tea kettle to prepare hot water for steaming.

3. **Prepare the collard greens for stir-fry/steaming.**

    - Rinse each leaf under cool water, shake it to remove clinging water, and place it on a strip of paper or terry cloth towels.
    - Pat the leaf tops dry using a paper or terry cloth towel.
    - Remove the central vein from each leaf. Working on a large cutting board, use a paring knife to cut out the central vein running through the leaf, cutting close to either side of the vein. Cut off the very tip from the attached stem. Set the veins and attached stems aside.
    - Slice the leaves. Stack the leaf halves, facing the leaves in the same direction. While holding the leaves in place with one hand, use a 7 in. serrated knife to cut the leaves in approx. ⅓ in. thick pieces, slicing lengthwise and crosswise through the leaves.
    - Chop the veins/stems. While holding them together with one hand, use a chef's knife to chop the veins/stems crosswise into ⅛ in. thick pieces. Keep the chopped veins/stems separate from the leaves.

4. **Stir-fry/steam the collard greens.**

    - Increase the skillet heat to medium-high.
    - When a drop of water added to the skillet instantly dances and disappears, add 1 T oil, mix the sliced veins/stems into the oil, and cook them, stirring them often for about 30 seconds.
    - Add the collard leaves and stir-fry them for 1 minute, setting a timer. Stir-frying should be vigorous throughout this minute to quickly and thoroughly coat all pieces with oil and to heat all pieces through.
    - At the timer, add 1 T hot water, cover the skillet, reduce the heat to low, and steam the collard greens for 4 minutes, setting a timer.
    - At the timer, remove the skillet from the heat, evenly sprinkle ¼ t salt over the collards, and use a rubber spatula to scrape the collards and any cooking juice into a serving bowl for immediate serving or into a colander placed over a dinner plate for serving the collards and any cooking juice in a mixed ingredient dish, such as a stir fry, stew, soup, curry, or pizza topping.

    VARIATIONS: Substitute **2 larger, more mature collard greens**. Increase the steaming time to 5 minutes.

Collards Profile

Collards are tasty greens that have all of the outstanding nutritional characteristics common to cabbage family vegetables. Collards, for example,

- are a rich source of human health-supporting glucosinolate family of phytonutrients. These phytonutrients provide antioxidant, anti-inflammatory, and detoxification protection to humans. Glucosinolates support the intestinal health of humans.
- are a rich source of antioxidant carotenoid phytonutrients, especially in the form of beta-carotene, which the human body converts to vitamin A. At the same time collards contain
- antioxidant nutrients, including vitamins C and E and the mineral manganese, which combine with the glucosinolate and carotenoid phytonutrients to further enhance the antioxidant capacity of collards.
- are a good source of omega-3 essential fatty acids (alpha-linolenic acid) and magnesium, which combine with glucosinolate phytonutrients to boost the anti-inflammatory capacity of collards.
- are ranked as excellent or good sources of almost every other category of nutritional components, including fat-soluble vitamins K (of which collards are an outstanding source) and A (in the form of beta-carotene), alkaline minerals, B complex vitamins (including exceptional folate content but excluding B12), varied dietary fiber, and protein.[160]

Collards have some distinguishing nutritional characteristics. Collards, for example,

- do not contain oxalic acid, which binds some calcium and prevents its absorption by the human body. As a result, unlike spinach and many other kinds of greens that do contain oxalic acid, collards are a good source of calcium.
- are an outstanding source of both insoluble and soluble fiber, providing more than any other cabbage family vegetable.

Collards share the cooking characteristics of other cabbage family vegetables.

- Collards contain sulfur compounds, which easily undermine collard flavor if collards are overcooked.
- Collards contain human health-promoting substances called isthiocyanates. Deliberately waiting five minutes between cutting and stir-frying helps activate collard enzymes that increase the formation of these substances.
- Stir-fry/steaming achieves maximum conservation of the rich nutritional content of collards. By cooking collards in extra virgin olive oil, stir-fry/steaming enhances human absorption of fat-soluble nutrients and phytonutrients (carotenoids). The minimal and low temperature cooking involved in stir-fry/steaming maximizes conservation of the heat-sensitive glycosinolate phytonutrients and nutrients (such

---

160 Mateljan, *The World's Healthiest Foods*, 2nd Edition: 243, 249-250. Mateljan presents updated information about the enormous human health-supporting capacity of collards.

as folate and B vitamins in general). Stir-fry/steaming effectively keeps sulfur compounds locked within plant cells where they do not undermine collard flavor and remain available to the human body for health-maintaining purposes.

To select the most flavorful and nutritious collards,

- select fresh collards that have deep green leaves that are firm and fresh-looking without any sign of yellowing. Veins running through the leaves should also be firm.
- select young collards with small leaves, which are reliably tasty and tender.
- select in-season collards. Collards are cold season vegetables, and winter months are in-season months when collards have peak flavor and nutritional value.
- select certified organic collards and locally grown collards marketed at farmers' markets and natural food stores. Industrially produced collards made the Environmental Working Group's 2016 Dirty Dozen Plus list of vegetables and fruits most contaminated with pesticides. They were included in this list because of high residues of organophosphate insecticides, which are considered to be highly toxic to the human nervous system. Selecting certified organic and locally produced collards is a means of avoiding this high pesticide content, but these naturally produced products provide other nutritional benefits as well, an important one being more concentrated nutrient and phytonutrient content in comparison to industrially produced collards. Reference #1 (Selecting Top Quality Fresh Whole Vegetables and Fruits) details other natural production benefits.

To store collards,

- immediately refrigerate collards. Treating them like a fragile vegetable, store already chilled collards using the Robinson vented storage method (store the collards in a sealed plastic bag from which as much air as possible has been squeezed; vent the bag by making uniformly spaced pin pricks, 20 per gallon bag; refrigerate the bag in the moisture-controlled crisper drawer).
- refrigerate room temperature or slightly warmed unwashed collards (such as garden picked collards, those purchased at a farmers' market, or collards that have become warm after being purchased) rinsed, dried, and wrapped in paper towels, but only partially covered until they are thoroughly chilled. Once the collards are chilled, immediately transfer the leaves to a plastic storage bag sealed and vented according to the Robinson storage method.
- use collards quickly, within 4-5 days, to maximize retention of sweet flavoring and nutritional content.
- stir-fry/steam and dry freeze collards that cannot be quickly used. For best flavor, color, and nutritional retention, vacuum pack them in serving-size amounts within freezer quality containers. Quickly thaw the collards for serving. Either microwave thaw the frozen collards or drop them directly into a hot stew shortly before serving. Do not slowly thaw the collards at room temperature or in a refrigerator.

26. Kale
(Stir-Fried/Steamed)
(2 servings)

4 chilled medium kale leaves with stems
 (leaves approx. 5-6 in. wide, 6-7 in. long),
 to yield 3-4 c sliced

1 T extra virgin olive oil
1 T hot water
¼ t salt

Cooking Tools

1 large nonstick skillet with a tight-fitting &
 opaque lid
1 electric tea kettle
1 large (approx. 16 x 24 in.) cutting board
1 each paring, 7 in. serrated, & chef's knife
1 set measuring spoons

1 plastic or plastic-coated stir-fry spatula
1 timer
1 rubber or other heat-resistant spatula
1 colander
1 dinner plate

---

1. Gather all cooking tools.

2. **Heat a large skillet on a large burner at a medium setting.** Heat an electric tea kettle to prepare hot water for steaming.

3. **Rinse and dry the kale leaves.**

   - Rinse relatively flat leaves under cool running water and wash curly leaves in a sink or large bowl partly filled with water.
   - Individually wash each leaf. Rub your thumb over the front and back of each leaf or rub a leaf between your hands. Swish curly leaves after this rubbing.
   - Shake clinging water from the leaves, stack them, and when all leaves are rinsed, spread them in a single layer over a strip of paper towels or large terry towel.
   - Pat dry flat leaves. Spread another layer of paper or cloth towels over curly leaves and roll the leaves in the towels. Gently squeeze the towels to maximize water absorption. Unroll the towels.

4. **Prepare the kale leaves for stir-fry/steaming.**

   - Working on a large cutting board, use a paring knife to cut out the thick center vein from each leaf, cutting very close to the vein. Set the veins and attached stems aside.
   - Stack the separated leaf halves, forming two or three stacks and facing the leaves in the same direction. Roughly holding the leaves together with one hand, use a 7 in. serrated knife to cut each stack of leaves in approx. ⅓ in. thick pieces, cutting lengthwise and crosswise through the leaves.

- Slice the tip from each stem end. Group all the veins/stems and, holding them together with one hand, use a chef's knife to chop them crosswise into ⅛ in thick pieces. Keep the stems separate from the leaves.

5. **Stir-fry/steam the kale**.

- Increase the skillet heat to a medium-high setting.
- When a drop of water added to the skillet instantly dances and disappears, add 1 T oil, add the sliced vein/stem slices, and cook them for about 30 seconds, stirring them occasionally.
- Add the kale leaves and stir-fry them for 1 minute, setting a timer. Stir-frying should be vigorous throughout this minute to quickly and thoroughly coat kale pieces with oil and to heat all pieces until hot.
- At the timer, add 1 T hot water, cover the skillet, reduce the heat to low, and steam the kale for 4 minutes, setting a timer.
- At the timer, remove the skillet from the heat, evenly sprinkle ¼ t salt over the kale, and use a rubber spatula to scrape the kale and any cooking juice into a serving bowl for immediate serving as a side dish or into a colander placed over a dinner plate for serving the kale in a mixed ingredient dish, such as a stir fry, soup, stew, curry, or pizza topping.
- Collect and serve any cooking juice with the kale.

VARIATION: Substitute **large kale leaves** for medium leaves. Cook them in exactly the same way except for increasing steaming time to 5 minutes.

Kale Profile

Kale is an especially tasty cabbage family vegetable that stands out as a vegetable with extraordinary nutritional value.[161]

- Kale is an especially rich source of the glucosinolate family of phytonutrients, which provide antioxidant, anti-inflammatory, and detoxification protection for humans. Glucosinolates also promote human intestinal health.
- Kale contains rich amounts of carotenoid phytonutrients, including beta-carotene, that provide additional antioxidant protection to humans.
- Kale contains antioxidant nutrients, including the vitamins C and E and the mineral manganese, that combine with carotenoid and glucosinolate phytonutrients to boost the antioxidant capacity of kale. Kale is a good source of omega-3 essential fatty acids (alpha-linolenic acid), which combines with glucosinolate phytonutrients to bolster the anti-inflammatory capacity of kale.
- Kale contains from excellent to good amounts of nearly every category of nutritional

---

161 Robinson, *Eating on the Wild Side*, 168-169. Robinson describes kale as the "king of crucifers" and as "one of the few vegetables that meets or exceeds the nutritional value of some wild greens."

components, including vitamin K, B complex vitamins except for B12, iron, alkaline minerals, protein, and both soluble and insoluble fiber.[162]
- Stir-fry/steaming effectively conserves maximum amounts of kale's rich nutritional content, including its water soluble and heat-sensitive glucosinolate phytonutrients and micronutrients. Stir-frying in extra virgin olive oil enhances the absorption of kale's fat-soluble carotenoid phytonutrients and vitamins (E and K).

Kale is marketed in several varieties.

- Curly kale is most widely marketed kale. It has broad leaves with frilly edges that are sold in bunches. A thick edible vein runs through the center of each leaf and becomes the leaf stem. Though most commonly sold curly kale has dark green leaves, curly kale is marketed in a variety of colors, including deep blue, Russian red, and black.
- Lacinato or dinosaur kale has a very dark green-blue color and long thin leaves that are imprinted with a reptilian skin-like pattern. It has a slightly sweeter and milder flavor than curly kale. Though small and medium leaves have the sweetest flavor, are more tender, and are most nutritious, large size leaves remain tasty.
- Ornamental kale leaves form into a head much like a head of lettuce. The leaves can be green, white, or purple. In comparison to curly kale, ornamental kale leaves have a milder flavor and the leaf texture is more tender.
- Baby kale is any variety of kale that is harvested while immature. It is often included in salad mixtures of baby greens. Marketed in ready-to-use form and requiring minimal cooking, baby kale is a highly convenient form of kale that can be substituted for medium kale leaves in recipes.

Kale shares the cooking characteristics of other cabbage family vegetables.

- Kale contains sulfur compounds. Sweet natural kale flavor, as a result, is fragile and vulnerable to overcooking.
- Stir-fry/steaming effectively keeps sulfur compounds safely locked within plant cells, where they do not negatively affect kale flavoring and where they remain available to the human body for health-maintaining needs.

To select the most flavorful and nutritious kale,

- select fresh kale as kale with the sweetest flavor and greatest nutritional value. Leaves should have deep green color. They should be uniformly firm but still feel soft and pliable, not stiff. Leaves and edges of leaves should not have any yellowing.
- select in-season kale, which is when kale has peak flavor and nutritional value. In-season is during colder months, from fall to early winter.
- select kale from vendors at farmers' markets who keep leaves chilled during marketing.
- select red-leaved varieties of kale, which have the greatest antioxidant value.

---

[162] Mateljan, *The World's Healthiest Foods*, 2nd Edition, 323; 328-329. Mateljan details up-to-date information about kale's human health-promoting capacity.

- select certified organic or locally produced kale. The Environmental Working Group included kale in its 2016 Dirty Dozen Plus list of vegetables and fruits most contaminated with pesticides. Kale is included in this list because of high residues of organophosphate insecticides, which are considered highly toxic to the human nervous system. Naturally produced certified organic and locally produced kale, in contrast, are relatively free of pesticide content. There are other significant benefits of choosing naturally produced kale over industrially produced kale as well, an important one being more potent phytonutrient content. Reference #1 (Selecting Top Quality Fresh Whole Vegetables and Fruits) details other benefits.

To store kale,

- immediately refrigerate already chilled kale in unwashed form. Treat it like a fragile vegetable. Store it within a sealed plastic bag using the Robinson vented bag method (store the kale in a sealed plastic bag from which as much air as possible has been squeezed; vent the bag by making uniformly spaced pin pricks, 10 per quart bag and 20 per gallon bag; refrigerate the bag in the moisture-controlled crisper drawer).
- quickly chill room temperature kale, such as fresh garden-picked kale and kale purchased from farmers' markets. Soak kale leaves for several minutes in cold water, dry the leaves, wrap them in paper or cloth towels, refrigerate the leaves, and thoroughly chill the leaves before transferring them to a sealed vented bag for refrigerator storage. This kale is in ready-to-cook form for quick use in meals.
- use kale quickly. Though careful storage keeps kale firm and bright green, much invisible change – loss of its rich nutritional content and natural sweet flavoring – quickly begins to occur after it is harvested.
- stir-fry/steam and dry freeze kale that cannot be quickly used. Store it vacuum packed within quart size sealable plastic freezer bags. To maximize retention of nutritional quality, microwave thaw or add the frozen kale to near boiling stew, curry, or soup shortly before serving. Do not slowly thaw kale at room temperature or in a refrigerator.

27. Mustard Greens
(Stir-Fried/Steamed)
(2 servings)

½ lb chilled medium or large mustard greens (to yield 3-4 c sliced greens)

1 T extra virgin olive oil
¼ t salt

Cooking Tools

1 colander
1 large nonstick skillet with a tight-fitting & opaque lid

1 7 in. serrated knife
1 set measuring spoons
1 plastic or plastic-coated stir-fry spatula

PART 1

1 electric tea kettle
1 large (approx. 16 x 24 in.) cutting board
1 each paring & chef's knife

1 timer
1 rubber or other heat-resistant spatula
1 dinner plate

---

1. **Gather all cooking tools.**

2. **Heat a large skillet on a large burner at a medium setting.** Heat an electric kettle to prepare water for steaming.

3. **Rinse and dry the greens.**

   - Fill a kitchen sink or large bowl with enough cool water to cover the greens completely.
   - Individually wash the leaves. Swish each leaf in the water, either rub your thumb over both sides or rub each leaf between your hands, shake off most clinging water, and drain the leaves in a colander.
   - Spread the leaves in a single layer over a strip of paper towels or large terry cloth towel, add a top layer of towels, roll the leaves in the towels, and gently squeeze the leaves to dry them. Unroll the leaves and use a towel to pat dry remaining wet areas.

4. **Prepare the mustard greens for stir-fry/steaming.**

   - Working on a large cutting board, use a paring knife to cut out the vein that runs through the center of each leaf, cutting very close to the vein and setting aside the vein and attached stem. Cut off and discard the very bottom tip of each stem. Group the veins/stems together and holding them together with one hand, use a chef's knife to chop the veins/stems into ⅛ in. thick slices. Keep these pieces separate from the leaves.
   - Stack the leaves, forming 2-3 stacks and facing the leaves in the same direction. Roughly holding the leaves together with one hand, use a 7 in. serrated knife to slice the leaves into approx. ⅓ in. thick pieces, cutting lengthwise and crosswise through the leaves.

5. **Stir-fry/steam the mustard greens.**

   - Increase the skillet heat to medium-high.
   - When a drop of water added to the skillet instantly dances and disappears, add 1 T oil, mix in the stems, and cook them for about 30 seconds, stirring them occasionally.
   - Add the greens and vigorously stir-fry them for 1 full minute, setting a timer.
   - At the timer, add 1 T hot water to the greens, cover the skillet, reduce the heat to low, and steam the greens for 2 minutes, setting a timer.
   - Collect and serve any steaming juice with the greens.

VARIATION: Substitute **young greens** for medium or large leaves. Do not cut out the center vein in each leaf. Cook the greens exactly like larger leaves except omit the steaming.

Let the cut greens sit five minutes before cooking. This step allows enzyme activity to bring about changes that enhance the nutritional content of the greens.

Mustard Greens Profile

Mustard greens are extremely nutritious foods.

- Like all cabbage family vegetables, mustard greens have rich amounts of glucosinolate phytonutrients. Glucosinolates provide antioxidant and anti-inflammatory protection for humans. Helping to activate detoxification enzymes, they provide detoxification protection as well. They also promote human intestinal health. The particular glucosinolates mustard greens provide, however, are somewhat different from those provided by other cabbage family vegetables and, as a result, add another dimension of protection. Stir-frying and stir-fry/steaming conserve maximum amounts of these heat-sensitive and water-soluble phytonutrients.
- Mustard greens contain carotenoid phytonutrients, including outstanding beta-carotene content, which function as antioxidants. In addition, mustard greens have rich content of the antioxidant nutrients, including the vitamins C and E and the mineral manganese, which combine with carotenoids to intensify the antioxidant protection in humans. Stir-frying of mustard greens in extra virgin olive oil enhances the absorption by humans of the fat-soluble carotenoid phytonutrients, vitamins (K and E), and the carotenoid phytonutrients contained by mustard greens.
- Mustard greens have a very high anti-inflammatory value for humans. They have outstanding vitamin K and E content and good magnesium content, which work to enhance the anti-inflammatory protection provided by glucosinolate and other phytonutrients.
- Mustard greens contain either good or outstanding amounts of nearly every category of nutritional components,[163] providing the human body with raw material it requires to efficiently perform a wide variety of bodily processes. Mustard greens, for example, are a very good or good source of B complex vitamins (except for B12), iron, alkaline minerals, and fiber.

Several varieties of mustard greens are marketed.

- Curled mustard greens are most commonly marketed. They have large oval green leaves with curled edges. They have a pungent taste, but pungency is variable

---

163 Mateljan, *The World's Healthiest Foods*, 2nd Edition, 337; 342-343. Mateljan details up-to-date nutritional information about the human health-promoting potential of mustard greens.

depending on the maturity and the particular variety of leaves. Stir-fry/steaming mellows the pungent flavor.
- Red and purple mustard greens have broad and flat oval leaves. Giant Red mustard greens have maroon-colored leaves with green ribs. The leaves of purple mustard greens are green with a purple hue. Both varieties, and especially more mature leaves, have a somewhat peppery mustard flavor.

To select the most flavorful and nutritious mustard greens,

- select fresh greens. Leaves should be fresh looking, firm (not limp or wilted), and uniformly deep green in color (no yellowing).
- select mustard greens from farmers' markets and natural food stores for freshest greens.
- select in-season greens. As winter vegetables, mustard greens are in season in November through March.
- select small and young leaves, which have the distinctive mustard green flavor with only a touch of hotness. The flavor of larger, more mature mustard greens is stronger with a sharper bite.

To store mustard greens,

- immediately refrigerate already chilled mustard greens unwashed. Treating them like a fragile vegetable, store them within a sealed plastic bag using the Robinson vented bag method (store the greens in a sealed plastic bag from which as much air as possible has been squeezed; vent the bag by making uniformly spaced pin pricks, 20 per gallon bag; refrigerate the bag in the moisture-controlled crisper drawer).
- soak room temperature mustard greens (such as garden picked greens, greens purchased from farmers' markets, and greens that have warmed after being purchased) for several minutes in cold water to chill the leaves, drain them a colander, dry them, wrap them in the paper towels, and refrigerate the wrapped leaves. Once the leaves are thoroughly chilled, transfer them to a sealed vented bag for refrigerator storage, pressing out as much air as possible before sealing the bag. These greens are in ready-to-cook form for quick use in meals.
- use mustard greens as quickly as possible to maximize retention of top flavor and nutritional quality.
- stir-fry/steam and dry freeze mustard greens that cannot be used quickly. Store them vacuum packed within quart size sealable plastic freezer bags. To maximize retention of nutritional quality, microwave thaw or directly add the frozen mustard greens to near boiling stew, curry, or soup shortly before serving. Do not slowly thaw frozen mustard greens.

COOKED ALIVE!

28. Spinach
(Pre-Washed)
(Stir-Fried)
(2 servings)

½ lb chilled ready-to-cook spinach leaves, small to medium size (approx. 8-10 c loosely packed leaves)

1 T extra virgin olive oil
¼ t salt

Cooking Tools

1 large skillet
1 large (approx. 16 x 24 in.) cutting board
1 7 in. serrated knife
1 set measuring spoons
1 plastic or plastic-coated stir-fry spatula

1 timer
1 rubber or other heat-resistant spatula
1 colander
1 dinner plate

---

1. **Gather all cooking tools.**

2. **Heat a large skillet on a large burner at a medium setting.**

3. **Prepare the spinach for stir-frying.**

   - Spread the spinach leaves over a cutting board and go through the leaves, removing any that are spoiled.
   - Bunch the leaves together on a large cutting surface. While roughly holding the leaves together with one hand, use a 7 in. serrated knife to slice the spinach into approx. ⅓ in. thick pieces, slicing lengthwise and crosswise through the leaves.

4. **Stir-fry the spinach.**

   - Increase the skillet heat to a medium-high setting.
   - When a drop of water instantly dances and disappears, add 1 T oil, mix in all the spinach, and vigorously stir-fry it for 1 minute, setting a timer (just until all leaves uniformly darken and barely wilt; juice should not spill; the leaves should not flatten).
   - Remove the skillet from the heat, evenly sprinkle ¼ t salt over the spinach, and use a rubber spatula to scrape the spinach and any spilled juice into a serving bowl for immediate serving as a side dish or into a colander placed over a dinner plate for serving in a mixed ingredient dish.
   - Collect and serve any cooking juice with the spinach.

VARIATION: Serve cooked spinach as an attractive dish topping. Preheat a skillet to medium-high, add and quickly re-heat the spinach in stir-fry manner. Alternatively,

PART 1

re-heat the spinach for 30-50 seconds in a microwave oven. Top a dish assembled for serving with the hot spinach.

Substitute **pre-washed baby spinach** for more mature spinach. While not as flavorful as more mature spinach, baby spinach is a highly convenient way to include fresh spinach in meals.

Spinach Profile

A member of the chenopod family of vegetables along with chard and beets, spinach has outstanding nutritional characteristics.

- Spinach is a rich source of phytonutrients that provide antioxidant protection for humans. Spinach, for example, has a variety of carotenoid family phytonutrients, including especially rich beta-carotene content as well as lutein and zeaxanthin, that provide antioxidant protection for humans. Adiitionally, spinach contains rich amounts of antioxidant nutrients, including the vitamins C and E and the minerals manganese and zinc, which combine with carotenoid phytonutrients to boost the overall antioxidant capacity of spinach.
- Carotenoid phytonutrients along with flavonoid phytonutrients also contained by spinach function as anti-inflammatory agents for humans. Spinach also contains a stand-out amount of omega-3 essential fatty acids, vitamin K, and magnesium, which are nutrients that intensify the anti-inflammatory protection provided by the flavonoid phytonutrients.
- Spinach ranges from being a good to excellent source of nearly every category of nutritional components, including B complex vitamins (except for B12), protein, and alkaline minerals, though some of the rich calcium content becomes bound up by oxalates contained in spinach and cannot be absorbed.[164]
- Stir-frying spinach with extra virgin olive oil enhances the absorption by humans of the fat-soluble carotenoid phytonutrients and fat-soluble vitamins E and K contained by spinach.

To select the most flavorful and nutritious spinach,

- select fresh spinach as the tastiest and most nutritious spinach. Fresh spinach has firm leaves with deep green color. Leaves do not have any sign of spoilage (no black spots; no leaves sticking together; no black edges) or bruising (dark green lines).
- select in-season spinach, which is when spinach has peak flavor and nutritional value. A cool season vegetable, in-season for spinach in the United States is from March through May and from September through October.

---

164 Ibid., 414. Mateljan notes that spinach contains a relatively high amount of oxalates and that this content does bind with and prevent some of spinach's high calcium content from being absorbed. However, he determines that research does not seem to support the position that spinach is a poor food choice for increasing calcium intake.

- select baby spinach. In comparison to more mature spinach, baby spinach has a sweeter flavor and contains less oxalates, which block the absorption of some calcium.
- select certified organic and locally produced spinach.

  - Because the Environmental Working Group included spinach in its 2016 Dirty Dozen list of vegetables and fruits most contaminated with pesticides, select certified organic spinach whenever it is an option. In addition to having significantly reduced pesticide residues, these naturally produced have other nutritional advantages in comparison to industrially produced spinach, an important one being more potent phytonutrient value. Reference #1 (Selecting Top Quality Fresh Whole Vegetables and Fruits) details other advantages of naturally produced vegetables.
  - Because the Food and Drug Administration has allowed irradiation of spinach since 2008, and some industrial producers use irradiation without informing customers, select certified organic and locally produced spinach to avoid selection of irradiated spinach. This practice is used to reduce the chance of contamination of raw spinach grown on large farms, but it is processing that reduces the nutritional value of spinach. A certified organic label reliably assures customers that a spinach product has not been irradiated.

To store spinach,

- immediately refrigerate chilled spinach in the package in which it was purchased.
- re-chill spinach that has warmed between purchase and home storage. Remove it from its marketing package, soak it for several minutes in cold water, dry it like un-washed spinach in Recipe #29 (Step #3). wrap the leaves in paper towels, and refrigerate them. When the leaves are thoroughly chilled, store them using the Robinson vented storage bag method (make uniformly spaced pin pricks in a sealable plastic bag, 10 pricks per quart bag and 20 pricks per gallon bag, press out as much air as possible from the bag before sealing it, and refrigerate the bag in the crisper drawer).
- store spinach for a short time, ideally only a few days, to maximize retention of its phytonutrient content.

29. Spinach
(Un-washed/Bunched)
(Stir-Fried)
(2 servings)

½ lb chilled bunched spinach leaves
(to yield 8-10 c loosely packed leaves)

1 T extra virgin olive oil
¼ t salt

PART 1

Cooking Tools

1 large skillet
1 colander
1 large (approx. 16 x 24 in.) cutting board
1 each chef's & 7 in. serrated knife
1 set measuring spoons

1 plastic or plastic-coated stir-fry spatula
1 timer
1 rubber or other heat-resistant spatula
1 colander
1 dinner plate

---

1. **Gather all cooking tools.**

2. **Heat a large skillet on a large burner at a medium setting.**

3. **Rinse and dry the spinach.**

    - Fill a kitchen sink or a very large bowl with enough cool water to cover the leaves completely.
    - Add the spinach to the water and separate the stems from the bottom roots, leaving long stems. Individually wash the leaves. Swish each leaf in the water, either rub both sides with your thumb or rub it between your hands to remove grit, re-swish the leaf in the water, shake off clinging water, and add it to a colander.
    - Spread the leaves in a single layer over a strip of paper towels or terry cloth towel, add a top layer of towels, roll the leaves in the towels, and gently squeeze the rolls to dry the leaves thoroughly. An alternative method for small leaves is to spin the leaves dry in a salad spinner, spinning one third of the leaves at a time.

4. **Slice the spinach.**

    - Unroll the spinach and bunch the leaves together in a pile on a large cutting surface. For large leaves with stems, stack the leaves aligning the stems, and use a chef's knife to chop the stems into ⅛ in. thick slices. Keep the stems separate from the leaves.
    - While roughly holding the leaves together with one hand, use a 7 in. serrated knife to slice the spinach into approx. ⅓ in. pieces, slicing lengthwise and crosswise through the leaves.

5. **Stir-fry the spinach.**

    - Increase the skillet heat to medium-high.
    - When a drop of water added to the skillet instantly dances and disappears, add 1 T oil, add any chopped stems and cook them for about 30 seconds, stirring frequently.
    - Add the sliced spinach and stir-fry it for 1 minute, setting a timer. Stir-frying should be vigorous throughout, stopping stir-frying if the spinach uniformly darkens in color and becomes completely wilted before the minute is up.

- Remove the skillet from the heat, evenly sprinkle ¼ t salt over the spinach, and use a rubber spatula to scrape the spinach and any cooking juice into a serving bowl for immediate serving as a side dish or into a colander placed over a dinner plate for serving the spinach in a mixed ingredient dish.
- Serve any cooking juice with the spinach.

Bunched Spinach Profile

Bunched spinach (spinach leaves with stems attached to roots) is especially flavorful and nutrient rich spinach. Being attached to the roots maximizes retention of spinach freshness and nutritional quality. In other respects bunched spinach shares the same profile as pre-washed spinach (Recipe #28).

To select the most flavorful and nutritious bunched spinach,

- select fresh spinach with fresh-looking leaves as both the tastiest and most nutritious spinach. Leaves should be uniformly deep green, firm (not limp or wilted), and un-bruised (not torn or bent) without any sign of spoilage (leaves should not have black areas; leaves should not be sticking together).
- select mid-size leaves as the most nutritious spinach leaves. Mid-size leaves have more phytonutrients than either baby or larger spinach leaves.[165]
- select in-season spinach, which is when spinach has peak flavor and nutritional quality. As a cool season vegetable, in the United States spinach is in-season from March through May and from September through October.
- select certified organic or locally grown spinach. The Environmental Working Group includes industrially produced spinach in its 2016 Dirty Dozen list of produce that is most contaminated with pesticides. As naturally produced spinach, certified organic spinach and locally grown spinach has significantly less pesticide content than industrially produced spinach. These spinach products are different from industrially produced spinach in other important ways as well. Certified organic and locally produced spinach, for example, have more potent phytonutrient content, and certified organic spinach is also reliably not irradiated while industrially produced spinach might be irradiated. Reference #1 (Selecting Top Quality Fresh Whole Vegetables and Fruits) details other nutritional benefits of naturally produced products.

To store bunched spinach,

- immediately refrigerate unwashed, already chilled but unpackaged spinach. Treating it like a fragile vegetable, store it using the Robinson vented bag method (store the greens in a sealed plastic bag from which as much air as possible has been squeezed; vent the bag by making uniformly spaced pin pricks, 20 per gallon bag; refrigerate the bag in the moisture-controlled crisper drawer).

---

[165] Robinson, *Eating on the Wild Side*, 35.

- quickly chill room temperature spinach, such as freshly picked or spinach that has warmed between purchase and home storage. Add the bunched leaves to enough cold water to cover them completely, let them sit in the cold water for 5 or so minutes, separate the leaves and stems from the roots, dry the leaves as in the recipe above (Step #3), and refrigerate the leaves wrapped in paper or cloth towels. When the leaves are completely chilled, store them using the Robinson vented storage bag method noted above. This spinach is ready for quick use in meals.
- use spinach within a few days of purchase to maximize the retention of phytonutrient content. Though carefully stored spinach remains firm, colorful, and unblemished for several days (and even longer), spinach begins to undergo invisible phytonutrient content loss after harvesting, especially after leaves are detached from roots.

30. Turnip Greens
(Stir-Fried/Steamed)
(2 servings)

1 lb chilled young turnips with greens (to yield approx. 6-8 c loosely packed turnip leaves)

1 T extra virgin olive oil
¼ t salt

Cooking Tools

1 large nonstick skillet with a tight-fitting & opaque lid
1 electric tea kettle
1 colander
1 large (approx. 16 x 24 in.) cutting board
1 each chef's, paring, & 7 in. serrated knife

1 set measuring spoons
1 plastic or plastic-coated stir-fry spatula
1 timer
1 rubber or other heat-resistant spatula
1 dinner plate

1. **Gather all cooking tools.**

2. **Heat a large skillet on a large burner at a medium setting.** Heat an electric kettle to prepare hot water for steaming.

3. **Rinse and dry the turnip greens.**

    - For greens attached to turnips, cut the stems from the turnips, leaving 1 in. stems on the turnips and re-refrigerating the turnip roots.
    - Fill a kitchen sink or large bowl with enough cool water to cover the leaves completely and add the leaves.
    - Individually wash the leaves. Swish each leaf in the water, either rub both of its sides

with your thumb or rub a leaf between your hands, re-swish the leaf in the water, shake most clinging water from it, and add it to a colander.
- Spread the leaves in a single layer over a strip of paper or terry cloth towels, add a top layer of towels, roll the leaves in the towels, and gently squeeze the roll to dry the leaves thoroughly.

4. **Thinly slice the turnip greens.**

    - Unroll and stack the leaves, forming 2-3 stacks and aligning the stems.
    - Use a chef's knife to slice off the stems. Set the stems aside.
    - For larger leaves with thicker center veins, cut out the veins. Use a paring knife to cut the leaves from either side of the vein, cutting closely to the vein. Set the veins and attached stems aside. Stack the leaves, forming several stacks and facing the leaves in the same direction.
    - Holding the leaves of a stack in place with one hand, use a 7 in. serrated knife to slice the leaves into approx. ⅓ in. thick pieces, slicing lengthwise and crosswise through the leaves.
    - Holding the stems or veins with attached stems together with one hand, use the chef's knife to chop them into thin slices.

5. **Stir-fry/steam the turnip greens.**

    - Increase the skillet heat to medium-high.
    - When a drop of water added to the skillet instantly dances and disappears, add 1 T oil, add the chopped stems/veins, and cook them for about 30 seconds, stirring them occasionally.
    - Add the turnip greens and stir-fry them for 1 minute, setting a timer. Stir-frying should be vigorous throughout in order to quickly and completely coat pieces with oil and to heat all pieces until they are hot.
    - At the timer, add 1 T hot water, cover the skillet, reduce the heat to low, and steam the greens for 3 minutes, setting a timer.
    - At the timer, remove the skillet from the heat, evenly sprinkle ¼ t salt over the greens, and use a rubber spatula to scrape the greens and any cooking juice into a serving bowl for immediate serving as a side dish or into a colander placed over a dinner plate for serving in a mixed ingredient dish.
    - Collect and serve any cooking juice with the greens.

Turnip Greens Profile

Turnip greens have exceptional nutritional value.

- As a cabbage family vegetable, turnip greens are a rich source of glucosinolate phytonutrients, which provide antioxidant, anti-inflammatory, and detoxification

support to humans. Turnip greens contain more glucosinolate phytonutrients than most other cabbage family vegetables, including cabbage, kale, cauliflower, and broccoli. Stir-fry/steaming effectively conserves these fragile heat-sensitive and water-soluble phytonutrients.
- Turnip greens are a very good source of many other antioxidant phytonutrients (such as beta-carotene of the carotenoid family) that provide a broad spectrum of antioxidant support. At the same time turnip greens are an excellent source of antioxidant nutrients, including vitamins C and E and the mineral manganese, which work with phytonutrients to intensify the antioxidant protection provided humans by turnip greens.
- Turnip greens are an excellent source of nutrients, including omega-3 fatty acids, vitamin E, and magnesium, that combine with glucosinolate phytonutrients to intensify the anti-inflammatory capacity of turnip greens.
- Stir-frying of turnip greens in extra virgin olive oil enhances the human body's absorption of the fat-soluble carotenoid phytonutrients and the fat-soluble vitamins E and K contained by turnip greens.
- Turnips have outstanding content of some vitamins, including folate and vitamin K, and the minerals calcium and copper. They are good sources of dietary fiber and of nearly every other category of nutritional components,[166] including B-complex vitamins (except for B12), alkaline minerals, and protein.

To select top quality and tastiest turnip greens,

- select small greens that are firm (not limp or wilted) and uniformly deep green (no yellowing). Avoid larger and mature turnip greens, which have an unattractively coarse, gritty texture that is not satisfactorily softened by stir-fry/steaming.
- select in-season turnips. As cool season plants, turnip greens are in peak form from March through May and from September through October.
- select certified organic and locally grown turnip greens. As naturally grown products, these greens reliably contain significantly less pesticide residues, more potent phytonutrient content, and greater overall nutritional content than industrially produced turnip greens.

To store turnip greens,

- immediately refrigerate already chilled greens. Treating them as a fragile vegetable, store them using the Robinson vented plastic storage bag method (add the unwashed dry greens to a sealable gallon size plastic bag, press out as much air as possible before sealing the bag, add 20 uniformly spaced pin pricks, and store the bag in the crisper drawer).
- quickly chill room temperature greens, such as greens that are fresh picked, purchased from a farmers' market, or become warmed between purchase and home storage. Add the turnips to very cold water and allow them to soak for several minutes before

---

[166] Mateljan, *The World's Healthiest Foods*, 2nd Edition, 457; 464. Mateljan details up-to-date information about the human health-promoting capacity of turnip greens.

washing and drying them as in Step #3 in Recipe #30 above. Refrigerate the greens lightly wrapped in towels until thoroughly chilled. Once the leaves are thoroughly chilled, store them using the Robinson vented storage bag method. These greens are in convenient ready-to-cook form for quick inclusion in a dish, such as a stir fry, soup, or stew.

- store turnip greens for a short time, ideally two-three days only, to retain greatest nutritional value.

Seasoning Vegetable Recipes

31. Garlic
(Stir-Fried)
(2 servings)

6-8 medium (¼-½ in. thick) chilled garlic cloves (to yield (1-2 T minced garlic)

1-2 t extra virgin olive oil (1 t per 4 cloves)

Cooking Tools

1 medium skillet
1 each chef's and 5 in. serrated knife
1 plastic or plastic-coated stir-fry spatula

1 timer
1 rubber or other heat-resistant spatula

1. **Gather all cooking tools.**

2. **Heat a medium skillet on a large burner at a medium setting.**

3. **Mince the garlic.** Mincing yields pieces of garlic that are large enough to retain distinctive garlic flavor and small enough to heat through quickly.

    - Pop open each clove to ease peeling. Gently press the flat side of a chef's knife blade down on the side of each clove until it makes an audible popping sound. Use a serrated knife to slice off the ends of the cloves. Peel each clove.
    - Use a serrated knife to cut each clove lengthwise into 3-4 thin slices.
    - Stacking two slices together, cut the slices lengthwise into thin strips. While holding several strips together with one hand and cutting diagonally away from your fingers, cut the strips into uniformly small pieces.

4. **Stir-fry the garlic.**

- Increase the skillet heat slightly above a medium setting.
- When a drop of water added to the skillet instantly sizzles, add oil (1 t per 4 cloves), add the garlic, and stir-fry the garlic for 1 minute, setting a timer. Stir-frying should at first be vigorous to quickly and thoroughly coat pieces with oil but can slow to "flip often" pace midway through the minute.
- At the timer, reduce the heat setting to low and cook the garlic for another 2 minutes, stirring it occasionally and setting a timer.
- At the timer, remove the skillet from the burner and use a rubber spatula to scrape the garlic and any cooking juice into another container.
- Wipe the cutting board used for mincing garlic clean before cutting other vegetables.
- Add the cooked garlic to a heated dish just in time to be heated through before serving. Alternatively, quickly re-heat the garlic just prior to serving and add it as a dish topping.

COMMENTS: Medium cloves are easiest size to mince, but other size garlic cloves can be substituted, especially when using a garlic mincing tool. A garlic mincing tool quickly minces peeled and sliced garlic, which encourages regular use of garlic. Find one or more varieties of such tools at kitchen stores, online, and in catalogs of mail-order businesses that market kitchen tools. Look for tools with stainless steel blades for clean dicing of garlic without bruising.

Garlic Profile

Garlic, an allium family vegetable along with onions and leeks, is a special flavoring ingredient that adds significant nutritional boosting to dishes.

- Garlic adds distinctive flavor without adding fat or salt. For garlic to serve as a flavoring ingredient, however, it is necessary that flavor-altering enzymes be quickly destroyed by fast initial heating. Accordingly, recipes direct that garlic be chilled to deactivate enzymes and then be added to hot oil immediately after mincing to destroy garlic enzymes. This quick destruction of enzymes prevents the conversion of the garlic component alliin into . Without this conversion, garlic flavor is mild, and garlic serves as an attractive flavoring ingredient in dishes.
- Garlic becomes highly nutritious when its alliin content is converted into allicin. While the conversion of garlic's alliin content into allicin undermines garlic's flavoring, giving it a pungent and assertive flavor, this conversion also enormously boosts garlic's nutritional value. When a cut open garlic clove is allowed to be exposed to air, some alliin content chemically reacts with the garlic enzyme called allinase and becomes converted into allicin. Allicin serves as a potent antioxidant for humans, providing special anticancer tumor protection and significant antiviral, antibacterial, and anti-blood clotting protection as well.[167] To obtain the health benefits of allicin,

---

[167] Robinson, *Eating on the Wild Side*, 51-53. Robinson explains how alliin is converted to allicin and discusses some of allicin's known health benefits for humans. Mateljan, *The World's Healthiest Foods*, 2nd Edition, 295; 298; 300. Mateljan profiles the human health-supporting capacity of garlic.

- use room temperature garlic.
- let minced garlic sit exposed to air for 10 minutes before heating.
- combine stir-frying of chilled and room temperature garlic. Stir-fry some garlic for use as flavoring and then stir-fry several room temperature garlic cloves that have been exposed to air, which will contribute allicin to a dish. Alternatively, experiment with adding pressed garlic cloves to stir-frying garlic or directly to a dish. Completely exposing garlic flesh and its alliin content to air, crushing quickly converts alliin into allicin.

- Garlic phytonutrients provide antioxidant, anti-inflammatory, and detoxification protection for humans. Garlic, for example, is a good source of carotenoid and flavonoid phytonutrients, which function as antioxidants. Additionally garlic is a good source of antioxidant nutrients, including vitamin C and the minerals manganese and selenium, which work with flavonoid and carotenoid phytonutrients to boost the antioxidant capacity of garlic to protect humans from oxidative stress caused by free radicals. Supporting heart health, garlic phytonutrients are known to provide human blood vessels protection from inflammation and oxidative stress, causative factors in the build-up of plaque in arteries.
- Garlic, as few as six cloves, is a good source of soluble fibers called fructans. Fructans are a type of prebiotic, which is a kind of food for beneficial microbes living in the human intestinal system. These fibers are long enough to survive the length of the gastrointestinal tract to reach the big intestine where the fibers are fermented by microbes, which converts the fibers into human health supporting form.
- Garlic contains human health-supporting sulfur compounds, some of which are responsible for garlic's pungent odor. Pre-chilling of garlic in combination with brief stir-frying combine to keep the sulfur compounds safely locked within garlic cells where they do not negatively affect garlic flavor.

Garlic is marketed in two forms: softneck and hardneck. Softneck garlic is the most commonly marketed type, and the most widely marketed variety of softneck garlic is called Silverskin garlic. A hollow stem runs through the center and out the top of hardneck garlic, and a single row of bulbs surrounds this stem. While the nutritional credentials of the two kinds of garlic are essentially the same, having a single row of bulbs makes hardneck garlic much easier to separate into cloves. The individual cloves are also easier to peel than those of softneck garlic.

To select top quality garlic,

- select uniformly firm and plump cloves with tightly closed, unbroken skins, which indicate the bulbs have reliably been protected from air. The cloves should not be sprouting, and peeled cloves should not have spoiled brown areas. The garlic should also not have any odor (strong odor indicates the garlic is spoiled).
- select in-season garlic, which is when garlic has peak flavor and nutritional value. In-season for California garlic begins in June and runs through December. In-season for garlic grown in Mexico begins shortly after December.

- select garlic from farmers' markets and from specialty produce and natural food stores, all of which market freshest garlic. These markets also more reliably carry selections of hardneck garlic and garlic with varying degrees of pungency.
- select certified organic and locally grown garlic as garlic with significantly less pesticide content and greater nutritional value than industrially produced garlic.

To store fresh garlic for use as a flavoring ingredient,

- refrigerate whole bulbs uncovered on a refrigerator shelf. The chilling keeps enzymes inactive during storage and mincing for cooking. Storing the garlic on a refrigerator shelf rather than in the crisper drawer protects it from moisture that promotes sprouting. Refrigerated garlic bulbs, as a result, store well for an extended period.
- refrigerate cloves of opened garlic bulbs in a closed container to protect them from dehydration.
- avoid lengthy storage, which increases garlic pungency.

To store garlic to maximize its human health-protective benefits,

- store garlic at room temperature.
- store garlic protected from light and heat in a well-ventilated area. For example, store it in a garlic keeper or within a net in a dark, cool area.
- select freeze-dried garlic as the only processed garlic product that retains its flavor and beneficial health properties.[168]

32. Ginger Root
(Stir-Fried)
(2 servings)

2 ⅛ in. thick slices of fresh ginger root 　　　1 t extra virgin olive oil
　(to yield 1 t minced ginger)

Cooking Tools

1 small skillet　　　　　　　　　　　　　　1 timer
1 5 in. serrated knife　　　　　　　　　　　　1 rubber or other heat-resistant spatula
1 plastic or plastic-coated stir-fry spatula

1. Gather all cooking tools.

2. **Heat a small skillet on a small burner at a medium setting.**

---

168 Robinson, *Eating on the Wild Side*, 56.

3. **Mince the ginger.**

    - Use a serrated knife to cut a 1 in. thick piece of ginger root crosswise into two uniformly thin (⅛ in. thick) slices. Stack the slices.
    - While holding the ginger slices together with one hand and cutting diagonally away from your fingers, use a serrated knife to cut the ginger slices into uniformly ⅛ in. thick strips.
    - Slice the strips crosswise into tiny (¹⁄₁₆ in. wide) pieces.

4. **Stir-fry the ginger.**

    - Increase the skillet heat to medium-high.
    - When a drop of water added to the skillet instantly dances and disappears, add 1 t oil, add the ginger root, and stir-fry it for about 30 seconds.
    - Lower the heat setting to a medium low setting (a setting that keeps oil gently sizzling around ginger pieces) and cook the ginger for another 2 minutes, stirring it occasionally and setting a timer.
    - At the timer remove the skillet from the burner and use a rubber spatula to scrape the ginger and any cooking juice into another container.
    - Add the cooked ginger and any cooking juice to a dish when assembling the dish for serving.

VARIATIONS:

- Substitute coarse shredding for mincing. Shredded ginger has a milder flavor than minced ginger.
- Peel the skin of conventionally grown ginger root. While skin is a source of valuable fiber, the skin of conventionally grown ginger root contains pesticide residues that are not removed with rinsing. Use a sharp vegetable peeler to remove as little skin as possible from slices of ginger root.
- Stir-fry ginger with onion. These ingredients perfectly complement each other.

COMMENTS: Mincing is important for ginger root serving success. Mincing mellows ginger root flavor. It yields mild-flavored ginger pieces while larger pieces are easily too assertive and can undermine dish attractiveness

Ginger Root Profile

Aromatic and pungent, ginger root is an excellent flavoring ingredient. Ginger root is the underground rhizome (somewhat elongated and thickened, tubular stem) of the ginger plant. Use of ginger root as flavoring reduces the need to use salt-, sugar-, and/or fat-based flavoring to secure the serving success of dishes.

Ginger root has notable human health-supportive credentials.

- Ginger root contains phytonutrients called ginerols that have potent anti-inflammatory capacity.
- Ginger roots promotes digestive health. It is known for its ability to soothe the stomach and to relieve nausea.

Ginger root is marketed in two forms: young and mature.

- Young ginger root has a milder flavor than mature ginger. It has smooth, thin, and light tan (somewhat yellowish) colored skin. The skin of young ginger is relatively tender and does not need to be peeled.
- Mature ginger has thicker and more wrinkled skin than young ginger. It also has a more assertive and pungent flavor. Heavy thick skin of mature ginger can be peeled.

To select the most flavorful and nutritious ginger root,

- select fresh ginger root. Select ginger root that is uniformly firm and heavy-feeling for its size. Skin should not be shriveled or have any green mold. When ginger root is cut open, exposed flesh should appear moist.
- select certified organic ginger root, which has the advantage of being largely pesticide-free in comparison to industrially produced ginger root. As naturally produced ginger, certified organic ginger root also has more potent phytonutrient content than industrially produced ginger root. It is also reliably not irradiated while some industrially produced ginger root is.

To store ginger root,

- rinse, thoroughly dry with a paper towel, and refrigerate ginger root either uncovered or wrapped within a paper towel and stored in a partially open container in the crisper (moisture-controlled) drawer. Leave cut open ginger root essentially uncovered as well.
- freeze large pieces of ginger root and coarsely shred ginger directly from the freezer.

33. Mushroom
(Stir-Fried)
(2 servings)

4-6 mushrooms1 T extra virgin olive oil

Cooking Tools

1 medium skillet1 timer
1 5 in. serrated knife1 rubber or other heat-resistant spatula

1 set measuring spoons   1 colander
1 plastic or plastic-coated stir-fry spatula   1 dinner plate

---

1. **Gather all cooking tools.**

2. **Heat a medium skillet on a large burner at a medium setting.**

3. **Prepare the mushrooms.**

    - Wipe the mushrooms clean with a damp paper towel or very quickly rinse them in cool water and immediately dry them with paper towels.
    - Cut each mushroom lengthwise into 4 equal slices.

4. **Stir-fry the mushrooms.**

    - Increase the skillet heat to a medium-high setting.
    - When a drop of water added to the skillet instantly dances and disappears, add 1 T oil, add the mushroom slices, and stir-fry them for 1 minute, setting a timer. This stir-frying should at first be vigorous to quickly and thoroughly coat mushroom slices with oil, but stir-frying can slow to "flip often" pace after pieces are coated. Stir-frying should also end if the mushroom slices become shiny.
    - At the timer or when the mushroom slices become shiny, remove the skillet from the burner and use a rubber spatula to scrape the mushrooms and any cooking juice into a colander placed over a dinner plate for collecting any spilled juice.
    - Add the cooked mushrooms and any collected cooking juice to a mixed ingredient dish or top a dish with the mushrooms when assembling and heating the dish for serving.

Mushroom Profile

Mushroom, which is actually a fungus and not a vegetable, serves as an outstanding flavoring ingredient. Quick and simple to cook, it enhances dish attractiveness without adding sugar, fat, or salt to dishes. Providing pleasing flavoring, mushroom serves to reduce the need to add outside flavoring for dish serving success.[169]

Mushroom makes important nutritional contributions to dishes. The rich nutritional content of mushroom makes it an exception to the general rule that colorful vegetables are most nutritious.

- A distinctive characteristic of mushroom nutritional content is that mushroom is

---

169   The author wishes to apologize to readers for not using mushrooms more commonly in Part II recipes as they deserve. It happens that she has a sensitivity to mushrooms, which has resulted in her neglect of mushrooms.

a very good source of vitamin D, a nutrient not normally contained by vegetables.
- Mushroom is a source of phytonutrients that provides both antioxidant and anti-inflammatory protection to humans. Mushroom, for example, is a concentrated source of the antioxidant phytonutrient ergothioneine. Mushroom also contains nutrients that function as antioxidants – including vitamin C and the minerals manganese, selenium, and zinc – that combine with mushroom phytonutrients to intensify the antioxidant protection provided humans by mushroom.
- Mushroom is a rich source of powerful phytonutrients that support the human immune system.
- Mushroom is a good source of beta-glucans, which are a beneficial kind of fiber. Beta-glucans serve as a bulking agent, giving humans the feeling of being full and satisfied after eating.
- Other standout nutritional components contained by mushroom include a variety of minerals (including copper and selenium, which tend to be hard to get into a diet) and B complex vitamins except for B12, which are essential to the human digestive system's ability to break down proteins, fats, and carbohydrates for use as food.
- All mushroom varieties share the same nutritional profile. Each variety makes essentially the same nutritional contributions for humans, though cremini mushrooms may excel in providing anti-inflammatory protection.

Mushrooms are commonly marketed in a variety of forms.

- White button mushrooms are the most commonly marketed variety of mushrooms. They are cream-colored mushrooms that are harvested when relatively immature. As a result, they are small and mild flavored.
- Cremini mushrooms are a brown-skinned version of button mushrooms. Harvested like white button mushrooms when they are relatively immature, they look very similar to white button mushrooms in size and shape. They are more flavorful than white button mushrooms, having a more pronounced mushroom flavor.
- Portabella mushrooms are large-sized versions of cremini mushrooms. They have a more meaty texture than cremini mushrooms.
- Porcini mushrooms have a long, fleshy stalk. In contrast to white button and cremini mushrooms, this variety of mushroom has a round and convex fleshy cap. It also has vertical tube-like pores rather than gills on the underside of the cap.

To select the most flavorful and nutritious mushrooms,

- select fresh mushrooms. All varieties of mushrooms should be uniformly firm. The mushrooms should not have wrinkled skin or have slimy spots on skin. Button, cremini, and portabella mushrooms should have tightly closed caps. Button mushrooms should be whitish in color and should not be discolored.
- select certified organic mushrooms. While mushrooms are in the bottom half of the Environmental Working Group's 2016 listing of most contaminated vegetables and fruits, which ranks them #35 of 50 foods, select certified organic mushrooms when

they are an option. In addition to being largely free of pesticide contamination, certified organic mushrooms have the other advantages over industrially produced mushrooms. Certified organic mushrooms, for example, are reliably not genetically modified while some industrially produced mushrooms are. Certified organic mushrooms also have more concentrated antioxidant content.

To store mushrooms,

- quickly refrigerate mushrooms unwashed within the container in which they were purchased.
- quickly refrigerate unpackaged mushrooms uncovered until they are thoroughly chilled before wrapping them within paper towels and transferring them to a sealed plastic storage bag vented according to the Robinson storage method (push as much air as possible from a plastic storage bag before sealing it; make uniformly spaced pin pricks in the bag, 10 pricks per quart bag and 20 pricks per gallon bag; refrigerate the bag in the crisper drawer).
- store mushrooms for up to 5 days only to maximize the conservation of the phytonutrients contained in mushrooms.

34. Onion
(Stir-Fried)
(2 servings)

½ chilled medium (2-2½ in. diameter) unpeeled bulb onion, sliced lengthwise (approx. ½ c diced onion)

1 T extra virgin olive oil

Cooking Tools

1 medium skillet
1 chef's knife
1 set measuring spoons
1 plastic or plastic-coated stir-fry spatula

1 timer
1 rubber or other heat-resistant spatula
1 colander
1 dinner plate

1. **Gather all cooking tools.**

2. **Heat a medium skillet on a large burner at a medium setting.**

3. **Dice the onion.** Diced onion pieces are large enough to retain distinctive onion flavor

PART 1

but small enough to cook quickly and evenly. A medium onion is an easy-to-dice size.

- Place the onion half cut side down on a cutting board and use a chef's knife to cut off the ends.
- Peel the onion.
- Again place the half cut side down on a cutting board.
- While holding the onion together with one hand, use a chef's knife to cut the half lengthwise into ¼ in. thick slices. Continuing to hold the slices together, turn the onion sideways and cut the onion crosswise into ¼ in. thick slices to form roughly uniform ¼ in. cubes.
- When approaching the end of the onion while cutting crosswise and holding the onion together becomes difficult, turn the remaining onion end cut side down onto the cutting board and continue cutting the onion crosswise.
- Wipe the cutting board clean. Onion juice left on a cutting board can spoil the flavor of raw fruits and other raw vegetables cut on the board.

4. **Stir-fry the onion.**

- Increase the skillet heat to a medium-high setting.
- When a drop of water added to the skillet instantly dances and disappears, add 1 T oil, add the diced onion, and stir-fry it for about 30 seconds. This stir-frying should be vigorous to quickly and thoroughly coat onion pieces with oil.
- Reduce the heat to medium (a level that keeps oil gently sizzling around pieces) and cook the onion for 2 minutes, stirring it occasionally and setting a timer.
- At the timer, remove the skillet from the heat and use a rubber spatula to scrape the onion and any cooking juice into a colander placed over a dinner plate for collecting any spilled juice.
- Add the onion and any cooking juice to a mixed ingredient dish when assembling the dish for heating and serving.

VARIATIONS: Substitute any other variety of onion for yellow onion. Substitute, for example,

- **½ other unpeeled bulb onion (white, red, or sweet onion)**, halved lengthwise.
- **2-3 green onions (or scallions)**. To prepare green onions:

  - Remove loose outside layers of skin.
  - Rinse the onions with cool water. Shake the onion to remove most clinging water and add the onion to a colander. Use a paper or terry cloth towel to thoroughly dry the white bulb portion and to roughly dry the tops of each green onion.
  - Use a serrated knife to slice off the stem end and to cut off the green tops, leaving at least two inches of green attached to the bulb. Spread the green tops, which contain more concentrated phytonutrient content than the bulb portion, over a strip of paper towels or terry cloth towel. Add a top layer of towels and roll the tops in the towels to dry them.

- Use a serrated knife to cut the white portion of each stalk crosswise into ¼ in. thick slices.
  - Unroll the green tops and while holding them together with one hand, use a chef's knife to chop the green tops crosswise into thin (⅛ in. thick) slices.
  - Stir-fry the green onions exactly like diced yellow bulb onion except for first cooking the green tops for 2 minutes (stir-frying the green tops for 30 seconds, reducing the heat to medium, cooking the greens for 2 minutes, setting a timer, and stirring the green tops occasionally).

- **4 small or 2 medium leeks.** Include the green leaves, which are the most nutritious part of leeks. The greens of small leeks will be more tender than larger leeks. The flavor of leeks is milder than most other onion varieties. Cooked leeks can be dry frozen in serving size amounts to be kept on hand for quick addition to dishes. To prepare and stir-fry leeks:

  - Use a serrated knife to slice off the tiny roots.
  - Use the serrated knife to slice off the tops of the leaves, leaving three inches of dark green remaining in the white area.
  - Fill a sink or large bowl with enough cool water to cover the leek tops.
  - Add the tops to the water, swish them in the water, shake off clinging water, and spread the tops over a strip of paper or terry cloth towels.
  - Use a serrated knife to split the white portion of each leek lengthwise. Place the halves cut side down on a cutting board and split each lengthwise.
  - Separate the leek layers, add the layers to the water used for rinsing the tops, and thoroughly swish the leek layers to remove all grit.
  - Shake the leeks to remove as much clinging water as possible after they are washed and add them to a colander.
  - Spread the rinsed leek layers over the strip of towels holding the tops. Add another layer of towels, roll the leeks in the towels to dry them, and then unroll them.
  - Stacking several white layers, use a serrated knife to cut them lengthwise into ¼ in. thick strips; cut the strips crosswise into ¼ in. thick pieces.
  - Chop the green tops. While holding them together with one hand, use a chef's knife to chop them into very thin (⅛ in. thick) pieces. Keep the green tops separate from the diced white portion.
  - Stir-fry the green tops exactly as yellow bulb onion except for stir-frying the green tops for a full two minutes before adding the white part of the leek. To do so, add the green tops to the oil in the hot skillet, stir-fry the tops for 30 seconds, reduce the heat to medium, and cook the green tops for 2 minutes, setting a timer and stirring the greens occasionally. At the timer, increase the heat to medium-high, add the white portion, and repeat the cooking.

- **6-8 shallot cloves.** To prepare shallot cloves:

  - Use a serrated knife to slice the ends from the shallots.
  - Peel the shallot cloves.

- Standing a clove upright on a flattened end, use a serrated knife to slice each clove lengthwise into ⅛ in. thick slices.
- Stacking 2-3 slices together at a time, cut the slices lengthwise into ⅛ in. thick strips.
- Holding several strips together at a time with one hand, slice the strips crosswise into ⅛ in. cubes.
- Stir-fry the cubes exactly like yellow bulb onion.

Onion Profile

All onion varieties – whether bulb onions, shallots, green onions, scallions, leeks, or chives – are top flavoring ingredients. A member of the allium family of vegetables along with garlic, onion alone, and particularly with the aid of spice and herb flavoring, can secure the attractiveness of any other vegetable while minimally adding to total preparation effort, adding no salt or sugar whatsoever, and contributing only a small amount of fat. The extra virgin olive oil that is added performs the valuable service of enhancing the absorption by humans of the fat-soluble nutrients contained by both onions and other vegetables.

All onion varieties make important nutritional contributions to dishes.

- All onion varieties are a good source of phytonutrients, notably including sulfur and carotenoid phytonutrients, which provide antioxidant protection for humans. While the wild ancestors of onions contained a far greater range and concentration of antioxidant phytonutrients than almost all modern onions, many modern onion varieties, which are noted below, still provide substantial antioxidant phytonutrient content.
- Onions contain flavonoid phytonutrients that provide both antioxidant and anti-inflammatory benefits for humans. The flavonoid phytonutrient quercetin, for example, helps prevent the oxidation of fatty acids, including omega-3 fatty acids, which play a crucial inflammation calming role for humans.[170]
- Onions contain sulfur phytonutrients, such as sulforaphane, which acts as an antioxidant to reduce oxidative stress (a known cause of cancer).
- All onion varieties contain antioxidant micronutrients, including vitamin C and the minerals manganese and copper, which combine with antioxidant phytonutrients to intensify the antioxidant support given humans by onions.
- Onions contain a good supply of most categories of nutritional components, including alkaline minerals, B complex vitamins (notably B6, B1, and folate, though not B12), and both soluble and insoluble fiber.

Sharing common membership in the allium family of vegetables, all onion varieties share common cooking characteristics.

---

[170] Mateljan, *The World's Healthiest Foods*, 2nd Edition, 368.

- All onion varieties contain sulfur compounds, which can undermine the natural sweet flavor of onions. When onion cell structure breaks down – as occurs when onions are overcooked, are bruised, and when room temperature cut onion flesh is exposed to air, which activates enzymes that cause chemical reactions – sulfur compounds break down and alter the natural sweet flavor of onion, emitting an unattractive odor in the process.
- Stir-frying as used in Chapter One recipes reliably maintains the natural sweet flavoring of onions. Stir-frying keeps sulfur compounds safely locked within onion cells where they do not alter the natural sweet flavor of onions and where they remain available for use by the body for health-promoting purposes.

To select the most flavorful and nutritious onion,

- select onions that are in good physical condition. Bulb onions and shallots should be uniformly firm, non-sprouting, have tight-fitting and unbroken skins, and be sweet (or neutral) smelling. Green onions, leeks, and chives should have uniformly firm stalks with tight-fitting skin and have fresh looking green tops. Any onion that is strong smelling, soft, or partially spoiled has undergone irreparable flavor and texture loss and should be discarded.
- select small bulb onions. Small onions have more concentrated phytonutrient content than larger ones and especially very large ones.[171]
- select certified organic bulb onions. The Environmental Working Group regularly lists industrially produced bulb onions among the least contaminated vegetables and fruits (45th of 50), but certified organic bulb onions are largely pesticide free and have the other advantages of naturally produced vegetables, an important one being more potent phytonutrient content. Reference #1 (Selecting Top Quality Fresh Whole Vegetables and Onions) details other important advantages. When bulb onions are used as important flavoring ingredients, as they are in Part II dishes in *Cooked Alive!,* using top quality onions is an important way of enhancing the quality of dishes.
- select certified organic green onions. The Environmental Working Group included industrially produced green onions in the middle of its 2016 listing of most contaminated vegetables and fruits, listing them #29 of 50 foods. Certified organic and locally produced green onions, in contrast, are largely free of pesticide contamination and have the other advantages of naturally produced produce, an important one being more potent phytonutrient content.
- select locally grown onions, which are the freshest onions. Large farmers' markets and specialty and natural food stores also commonly market a variety of onions, including especially nutritious varieties. Locally produced onions are overall naturally produced, which means that in contrast to industrially produced onions, they are largely free of pesticide contamination, are not genetically modified, and have more potent phytonutrient content. Reference #1 (Selecting Top Quality Fresh Whole Vegetables and Fruits) details the advantages of naturally produced vegetables.

---

171 Robinson, *Eating on the Wild Side*, 58.

Select the most nutritious varieties of onion. Select, for example,

- **yellow onion.** While varieties of sweet onion – such as Vidalia, Walla Walla, and Bermuda onion – have a sweeter flavor than yellow onion due to higher sugar content and are juicier as well, yellow onion has dramatically more (as much as eight times more) concentrated phytonutrient content than sweet onion.[172] To take advantage of this rich phytonutrient content, reserve sweet onions for when serving onions raw but use yellow onion for cooking.
- **red onion.** Red onions are sources of anthocyanin phytonutrients, which are super potent antioxidants.
- **shallots.** These onions, which look like big bulbs of garlic, have especially rich phytonutrient content, as much as six times more than the typical onion.[173]
- **leeks.** Leeks also contain especially rich phytonutrient content. They are also a rich source of the soluble fibers called fructan fibers. These fibers are prebiotic, which means they encourage the growth of beneficial microbes in the human gut. They are long enough to survive passage through the human intestinal tract where microbes feed on and ferment them, which converts them to valuable human health-supporting form. Leeks are also good sources of omega-3 essential fatty acids.
- **green onions and scallions,** which are more nutritious than most other onions.[174] While technically not onions – they are a separate species of allium vegetables – they come closest to wild onions in appearance and nutrition. Along with providing a rich flavor similar to regular onions, they provide many times (140 times) more phytonutrients than most onions.[175] The green portions contain the most phytonutrients.
- **chives,** both onion and garlic chives. Chives have especially rich phytonutrient content because they are completely green. Mixing even small amounts of chives with bulb onion, such as yellow onion, enhances the nutritional quality of a dish.

To store onion,

- refrigerate all onions after purchase or harvesting. This direction contradicts standard onion storage information, which directs cooks to store onions in a cool, dark, somewhat humid, and well-ventilated area, such as a basement or unheated garage. Most homes, however, do not have such ideal storing conditions, and short-term chilling effectively maintains onion freshness, keeping them juicy, crisp, and sweet for several weeks. Onions with tight-fitting and unbroken skins refrigerate well for much longer. Chilling also keeps enzymes inactive while onions are cut for stir-frying, which prevents flavor-changing chemical reactions from occurring before the enzymes are inactivated by stir-frying. Without chilling, enzymes are immediately activated when onion pulp comes into contact with air during cutting. This activation causes chemical reactions to occur that lead to loss of natural sweet onion flavor, making onion flavor pungent and assertive.

---

172 Robinson, *Eating on the Wild Side*, 59.
173 Ibid., 64-65. Robinson includes information for gardeners about growing especially nutritious shallots.
174 Ibid., 73.
175 Ibid., 68.

- refrigerate whole bulb onions and shallots loosely covered, such as in a net bag in a crisper (moisture-controlled) drawer or on a refrigerator shelf. Bulb onions and shallots stored on a refrigerator shelf are less likely to sprout.
- refrigerate leeks, green onion, scallions, and chives using the Robinson vented storage bag method to maximize retention of the rich phytonutrient content of these onion varieties, which are very fragile. Refrigerate them within a plastic bag, squeeze out as much air as possible before sealing the bag, vent the bag (20 evenly spaced pin pricks per gallon-size bag), and store the onions in the crisper drawer.
- store a *cut* bulb onion with plastic wrap stretched tightly over the cut surface to protect the onion flesh from contact with air, which dehydrates onion as well as activates destructive onion enzymes and undermines sweet onion flavor during storage.
- store bulb onions and shallots with tight-fitting and unbroken skin for weeks.
- store leeks especially but also green onions, scallions, and chives for a short time only to retain a maximum amount of the fragile phytonutrient content of these varieties of onion.
- stir-fry and dry freeze bulb onions and leeks in serving-size amounts within an air-tight (best of all, vacuum-packed) freezer bag to keep these onions on hand for instant inclusion in dishes.

35. Bell Pepper
(Stir-Fried)
(2 servings)

½ chilled medium bell pepper, halved lengthwise (any color, to yield approx. 1 c diced)

½ T extra virgin olive oil

Cooking Tools

1 medium skillet
1 5 in. serrated knife
1 set measuring spoons
1 plastic or plastic-coated stir-fry spatula

1 timer
1 rubber or other heat-resistant spatula
1 dinner plate

---

1. **Gather all cooking tools.**

2. **Heat a medium skillet on a large burner at a medium setting.**

3. **Uniformly dice the bell pepper.**

    - Use a serrated knife to cut out the stem of the pepper. Discard the stem and hard pulpy core. Remove seeds but leave the white membrane on the lobes of the pepper.

- Use a serrated knife to slice the pepper lengthwise into ¼ in. thick strips.
- While holding several strips together with one hand, cut the strips crosswise into ¼ in. cubes.

4. **Stir-fry the bell pepper.**

- Increase the skillet heat to medium-high.
- When a drop of water added to the skillet instantly dances and disappears, add ½ T oil, add the pepper, and stir-fry the pepper for about 30 seconds. Stir-frying should be vigorous to quickly and thoroughly coat pieces with oil.
- Reduce the heat to medium (oil should gently sizzle around pepper pieces) and cook the pepper for 2 minutes, stirring it occasionally and setting a timer.
- At the timer, use a rubber spatula to scrape the pepper and any cooking juice into a colander placed over a dinner plate.
- Add the pepper and collected cooking juice to a mixed ingredient dish when assembling and heating the dish for serving.

VARIATION: Substitute **2-3 banana peppers** for bell pepper or cook **1 banana pepper** with the bell pepper. Marketed in a variety of colors, banana pepper is sweet and has a distinctively attractive flavor. To prepare a banana pepper, rinse and dry, slice off the stem end, halve lengthwise, cut each pepper half lengthwise into ¼ in. strips, cut the pepper strips crosswise into ¼ in. slices, and cook the pepper exactly like bell pepper.

Bell Pepper Profile

Bell pepper is a super flavoring vegetable. Simple and quick to prepare and cook, bell pepper adds highly attractive color and pleasing flavor to dishes while adding minimal fat and no sugar or salt at all. The small amount of extra virgin olive oil used is high quality fat.

Bell pepper makes outstanding nutritional contributions to dishes.[176]

- Of particular note, bell pepper is an excellent source of carotenoids, containing over 30 different members of this family of phytonutrients, which function as antioxidants for humans. This rich content makes bell pepper one of the very top sources of carotenoids. Additionally, bell pepper is a good source of antioxidant nutrients, including the vitamins C and E and the mineral manganese, which combine with carotenoids to give bell pepper extraordinary antioxidant capacity to protect humans from free radical damage, a known major cause of cancer.
- Bell pepper contains phytonutrients, such as flavonoids, that provide anti-inflammatory benefits for humans.

---

[176] Matlejan, *The World's Healthiest Foods*, 2nd Edition, 158-166. Matlejan details updated information about the nutritional value of bell peppers for humans.

- Bell pepper also contains sulfur compounds. While sulfur compound content is small, bell peppers contain enzymes that play a supportive role in the metabolism of sulfur compounds by humans, thereby making this small sulfur compound content available to play human health-supportive roles.
- Stir-frying conserves maximum bell pepper nutritional content. Avoiding high temperature heating and minimizing heating, stir-frying keeps nutrients safely locked within the bell pepper during cooking. The extra virgin olive oil used in stir-frying enhances absorption of fat soluble carotenoid phytonutrients and fat-soluble vitamin E during human digestion.

To select the most flavorful bell pepper,

- select fresh bell pepper. Select heavy-feeling, vividly-colored bell pepper with glossy skin and thick flesh. The pepper should be uniformly firm. The skin should not be wrinkled or yield to gentle pressure. These physical characteristics describe fully ripe bell pepper, which has peak flavor.
- select red, orange, and yellow bell pepper as especially sweet bell pepper, having almost fruity flavor.
- select in-season bell pepper. In the United States this is pepper marketed during the summer and early fall.

To select the most nutritious bell pepper,

- select fully ripe bell pepper. Fully ripe bell pepper has the greatest vitamin C and phytonutrient (carotenoid) content, which work together to increase the antioxidant capacity of bell pepper.
- select the darkest colored bell pepper, whatever the color, whether green, red, yellow, orange, brown, or black. The darker the color, the greater the phytonutrient content.
- select brown bell pepper as pepper with especially rich carotenoid phytonutrient content.
- select purple and red bell pepper as pepper with most concentrated and varied phytonutrient content. This content includes anthocyanin phytonutrients, which are super potent antioxidants.
- select certified organic and locally produced bell pepper. The Environmental Working Group includes industrially produced bell pepper in its 2016 Dirty Dozen list of vegetables and fruits most contaminated with pesticides, including bell pepper as #10. This high pesticide content warrants selection of certified organic and locally produced bell pepper whenever these products are a selection option, especially when bell pepper is often used, as it is in *Cooked Alive!* recipes. In addition to being essentially free of pesticide contamination, certified organic and locally produced bell pepper has the other advantages of naturally produced foods, an important one being more potent phytonutrient content. Reference #1 (Selecting Top Quality Fresh Whole Vegetables and Fruits) details other advantages of naturally produced foods.

To store bell pepper,

- refrigerate already chilled bell pepper tightly wrapped with plastic wrap to protect it from dehydration, which quickly causes it to become limp. When the bell pepper is also rinsed and dried, the pepper is ready for quick inclusion in dishes.
- refrigerate room temperature bell pepper (such as pepper gathered from a garden, purchased from a farmers' market, or that has warmed between purchase and home storage) unwashed and uncovered until it is thoroughly chilled before tightly covering it for storage. This pre-chilling keeps condensation from forming on the skin during refrigeration, which hastens spoilage.
- store bell peppers for around a week. While they will store well for a longer period, the sooner they are used the greater the nutritional contribution they will make.

36. Chili Pepper
(Stir-Fried)
(2 servings)

1 mild green chili or 2 jalapeño chili peppers (approx. ½ c diced pepper)	1 t extra virgin olive oil

Cooking Tools

1 medium skillet	1 timer
1 5 in. serrated knife	1 rubber or other heat-resistant spatula
1 set measuring spoons	1 colander
1 plastic or plastic-coated stir-fry spatula	1 dinner plate

1. **Gather all cooking tools.**

2. **Heat a medium skillet on a large burner at a medium setting.**

3. **Prepare the chili pepper for stir-frying.**

   - Rinse, dry thoroughly, and use a serrated knife to slice the ends from the chili pepper(s),
   - Halve the pepper(s) lengthwise and scrape out and discard any seeds and membrane.
   - Use a serrated knife to cut the pepper halves lengthwise into ⅛ in. thick strips and cut the strips crosswise into ⅛ in. cubes.
   - Place the chili pepper on plastic wrap and thoroughly rinse your hands, knife, and

cutting board with cold water to protect your lips, nose, and eyes from painful contact with capsaicin, the substance contained by chili peppers that causes painful burning.

4. **Stir-fry the chili pepper.**

- Increase the skillet heat to medium-high.
- When a drop of water added to the skillet instantly dances and disappears, add 1 t oil, add the pepper, and stir-fry it for about 30 seconds. This stir-frying should be vigorous to quickly and thoroughly coat pepper pieces with oil.
- Reduce the heat to medium (a level that maintains gentle sizzling around pieces) and cook the pepper for 2 minutes, stirring it occasionally and setting a timer.
- Use a rubber spatula to scrape the chili and any cooking juice into a container separate from other dish ingredients.
- Add the cooked pepper to a mixed ingredient dish when assembling and heating the dish for serving.

Chili Pepper Profile

Chili peppers serve as distinctive flavoring ingredients with super human health-supporting capacity.

- While capsaicin, chili pepper's heat-producing ingredient, can make chilies fiery hot and unpleasantly so for many humans, it is a potent antioxidant phytonutrient. Capsaicin additionally provides anti-inflammatory protection for humans, and performs a variety of other human health-supportive services as well. For example, capsaicin gives chili peppers anti-bacterial properties within the human digestive system. It also serves to break up mucus congestion in the nose and lungs.
- Chili peppers contain significant amounts of other antioxidants, such as carotenoids, notably beta-carotene. Additionally, chili peppers contain significant amounts of antioxidant nutrients, including the vitamins C and E and the mineral manganese, which combine with phytonutrients to provide outstanding antioxidant protection from injurious free-radical releasing oxidation (a known cause of cancer and dangerous plaque buildup in veins and arteries).
- Chili peppers are good sources of a wide spectrum of nutritional components. They are, for example, very good sources of the vitamins K and B6, the minerals copper and iron, and dietary fiber. They also contribute alkaline minerals, omega-3 essential fatty acids, and most B complex vitamins. The human body needs all of these nutrients to perform health maintaining functions.
- Stir-frying as used in Recipe #36 serves to maximize absorption of the fat soluble vitamins E and K and fat soluble carotenoid phytonutrients contained in chili peppers and to maximize overall conservation of the nutritional content of chili peppers, including heat-sensitive and water soluble B vitamins and water soluble minerals.

To select the most flavorful and nutritious chili pepper,

- select fresh chili pepper. Select uniformly firm, heavy-feeling, and vividly-colored peppers with shiny skin and healthy-appearing stalks.
- select in-season chili pepper, which has peak flavor and nutritional value. In the United States this is during the summer and early fall.
- select green chili (in particular) and jalapeno pepper as quite reliably mildly hot peppers, but any variety of hotter chili pepper can be substituted.
- select certified organic and locally produced chili pepper. The Environmental Working Group includes industrially produced chili pepper as one of the foods most contaminated with pesticides in its 2016 listing, ranking chili pepper 16th most contaminated of 50 foods. In addition to having significantly less pesticide contamination, certified organic and locally produced chili pepper have the other advantages of naturally produced foods, an important one being more potent phytonutrient content. Reference #1 (Selecting Top Quality Fresh Whole Vegetables and Fruits) details other advantages of naturally produced foods.
- select red chili peppers as especially nutritious peppers. Red chilies are sources of anthocyanin phytonutrients, which are super potent antioxidants.

To store chili pepper,

- refrigerate chili pepper wrapped in paper towels within a partially closed plastic bag in the crisper drawer to protect the peppers from dehydration.
- use chili pepper before its skin wrinkles and its texture softens, which can be as long as two weeks or more of storage.

37. Tomato
(Stir-Fried)
(2 servings)

1 medium ripe tomato 2 t extra virgin olive oil

Cooking Tools

1 medium skillet 1 rubber or other heat-resistant spatula
1 5 in. serrated knife 1 colander
1 plastic or plastic-coated stir-fry spatula 1 dinner plate
1 timer

1. Gather all cooking tools.

2. **Heat a medium skillet on a large burner at a medium setting.**

3. **Prepare the tomato for stir-frying.**

    - Rinse and thoroughly dry the tomato.
    - Use a serrated knife to halve the tomato lengthwise, place each half cut side up on a cutting board, make a wedge cut on either side of the pulpy stem end, and lift out and discard the stem end.
    - Place the tomato halves cut side down on a cutting board and use a serrated knife to cut each half lengthwise into ¼ in. thick slices. Cut each slice crosswise into ¼ in. thick cubes.

4. **Stir-fry the tomato.**

    - Increase the skillet heat to medium-high.
    - When a drop of water added to the skillet instantly dances and disappears, add 2 t oil, add the tomato, and stir-fry the tomato for about 30 seconds. This stir-frying should be gentle but constant to quickly and thoroughly coat pieces with oil.
    - Reduce the heat to medium and cook the tomato for 1 minute, stirring pieces occasionally and setting a timer.
    - At the timer, use a rubber spatula to scrape it and any cooking juice into a colander placed over a dinner plate for collecting any spilled juice.
    - Add the tomato and any cooking juice as the last ingredient when assembling a dish for serving, adding it only when other dish ingredients are already hot and heating the dish only long enough to heat through the tomato.

    VARIATIONS: Substitute **6 chilled grape** or **4 cherry tomatoes** for regular tomato. Halve grape tomatoes lengthwise and quarter cherry tomatoes lengthwise.

Tomato Profile

Tomato provides both excellent flavoring and super human health support.

- Adding juiciness and sweet and tangy flavoring, tomato is an attractive ingredient in dishes. By holding maximum juice within the tomato, stir-frying retains tomato flavoring.
- Tomato contains a rich array of antioxidant phytonutrients. Tomato is best known as an outstanding source of the carotenoid lycopene, but tomato contains a variety of other antioxidant phytonutrients as well, such as alpha-carotene and especially beta-carotene. Additionally, tomato contains antioxidant nutrients, including the vitamins C and E and the mineral manganese, which work with carotenoid phytonutrients to intensify the antioxidant protection provided humans. The antioxidant support provided is linked to both the heart and bone health of humans.

- Tomato contains from excellent to good amounts of a wide spectrum of nutritional components. It is, for example, an excellent source of vitamin K and the mineral molybdenum. It is a very good source of the minerals copper and potassium, varied fiber, and several B vitamins, including B6, B3, and folate. Tomato is a good source of several other B complex vitamins (but not B12) and minerals, including zinc and iron.[177]
- By incorporating the tomato skin and avoiding overcooking, stir-frying of tomato maximizes the retention of nutritional content. Cooking in extra virgin olive oil maximizes absorption of the fat-soluble nutrients (vitamins E and K) and fat-soluble carotenoid phytonutrients contained in tomato.

To select the most flavorful and nutritious tomato,

- select fresh tomato. Select uniformly firm, heavy-feeling, and deep-colored tomato. The skin should not be wrinkled. See Recipe #100 (Tomato), a recipe for serving raw tomato, for additional selection information.
- select in-season tomato, which is when tomato has peak flavor and nutritional value. In the United States in-season runs from July through October.
- select certified organic and locally grown tomatoes when they are an option. The Environmental Working Group includes industrially produced tomato in its 2016 Dirty Dozen list of vegetables and fruits most contaminated with pesticides, ranking tomato 9th. Certified organic and locally produced tomatoes, in comparison, are largely free of pesticide contamination, which opens the way for consumers to eat the nutritious tomato skin. Certified organic and locally produced tomatoes also have the other nutritional advantages of naturally produced food, an important one being having more potent phytonutrient content than industrially produced tomato. Reference #1 (Selecting Top Quality Fresh Whole Vegetables and Fruits) details other advantages of naturally produced vegetables.

To store tomato,

- store all varieties of tomato at room temperature protected from direct contact with sunlight.
- do not refrigerate tomato, which undermines its flavor. See Recipe #100 (Tomato), a recipe for serving raw tomato, for explanatory information.
- use tomato before its skin wrinkles and its texture softens, which means storage can be for a week or more.

---

177 Mateljan, *The World's Healthiest Foods*, 2nd Edition, 449 and 454. Mateljan details the amazing nutritional content of tomato.

Reference #3

Summarizing Stir-Frying and Stir-Fry/Steaming Techniques

Juice-protective techniques maximize retention of juice within vegetables and fruits during preparation. Juice retention, as is emphasized throughout *Cooked Alive!*, maximizes nutritional richness, but it also maximizes flavor, color, and attractive texture, which, in turn, maximizes serving success and independence from outside flavoring (salt, sugar, and fat). Juice retention converts vegetables and fruits into super nutritious foods with extraordinarily attractive flavoring capacity.

Chapter One recipes achieve juice retention through use of specific techniques that apply the five following underlying *juice-protective* principles.

- Protect cut plant pulp from direct contact with liquid.
- Cook vegetables and fruits just to the point of tenderness.
- Inactivate or destroy enzymes.
- Strictly limit high and medium-high temperature heating.
- Collect and utilize any juice that does spill during preparation.

Reference #3 summarizes techniques recipes routinely use to apply these *juice-protective* principles. It summarizes techniques applied in each step of the stir-frying and stir-fry/steaming preparation processes used for preparing vegetables in Chapter One recipes, summarizing the steps in the order in which they occur. These four steps are readying, cooking, setting aside between cooking and serving, and combining of vegetables with other dish ingredients for serving.

1. Readying of Vegetables for Stir-Frying and Stir-Fry/Steaming

    - **Thoroughly chill raw vegetables prior to cutting for cooking.** Chilling keeps enzymes inactive when cutting exposes pulp to air. Without chilling, air activates enzymes, which in the case of many vegetables, including all cabbage family vegetables, causes chemical reactions that negatively affect vegetable flavor.
    - **Heat a dry skillet at a medium setting as a first preparation step.** Pre-heating on medium is a useful time-saving technique. Medium temperature will not cause a skillet (including a nonstick one) to overheat while a vegetable is readied for cooking, but the skillet will quickly reach medium-high temperature when cooks are ready to add vegetables for cooking. Pre-heating also helps ensure a skillet **completely** reaches medium-high temperature so that the vegetable immediately begins to cook and cooks to tenderness in the expected cooking time.
    - **Rinse produce with cool, not warm, water for cleaning.** Rinsing with cool water keeps enzymes inactive in enzyme-sensitive vegetables.
    - **Thoroughly dry produce after washing.** Drying is important for ensuring that oil clings to cut vegetable pieces during stir-frying. Pat large produce dry with paper towels or with an absorbent cloth towel, which is a more environmentally friendly way of drying. Spread small produce over paper or cloth towels, wrap the towels

around the pieces, and gently squeeze them for drying. Dry your hands, cutting knife, and working surface before handling produce.

- **Avoid peeling.** In addition to holding in plant juices and protecting pulp from leaching during cooking, skin is a highly nutritious part of vegetables. To take advantage of skin's protective capacity and nutritional content, observe nutritionist Adelle Davis's advice to "[m]ake it a rule to peel vegetables only when the skin is tough, bitter, or too uneven to be thoroughly cleaned".[178] Add to this, "or when a vegetable is coated with wax," or is industrially produced produce listed on the Environmental Working Group's most contaminated with pesticides list, especially its Dirty Dozen list.
- **Use sharp knives for cutting.** Sharp blades cut cleanly, which results in the least possible juice spilling. Sharp knives also greatly ease the cutting of vegetables for stir-frying, which encourages both use of vegetables and stir-frying.
- **Use knives matched to vegetables.** Using knives matched to vegetables eases vegetable preparation and, as a result, supports vegetable use. For example, select a chef's knife for cutting long vegetables (such as carrots, celery, cucumber, and summer squash), large tender vegetables (such as onion, cabbage, and globe eggplant), and vegetables with sturdy, dense flesh (such as potatoes, beets, turnips, and rutabaga) and tough skin (such as winter squash). Use a 5 inch serrated knife for slicing medium and small vegetables (such as garlic), and especially those with skins. Use a 7 inch serrated knife for slicing bulky and/or large green leafy vegetables.
- **Cut vegetables into uniformly thin pieces.** Even-sized pieces will cook in the same amount of time. When pieces are uneven, smaller pieces will cook more quickly than larger ones and will become overcooked before larger size pieces become tender. Thin pieces also cook quickly and, hence, most reliably cook to tenderness before cell structure breaks down and releases juice.
- **Cut vegetables that are vulnerable to air immediately before cooking.** Especially vulnerable vegetables include garlic, onion, and cabbage family vegetables.
- **Mince rather than crush raw garlic.** Garlic in *Cooked Alive!* recipes is used as a flavoring ingredient. To retain its distinctively attractive flavor, garlic is chilled, uniformly minced (as is detailed in Recipe #31), quickly coated with oil after cutting, and quickly heated through. Crushing, in contrast, completely exposes pulp to air, which stimulates enzymes that negatively alter garlic flavor.
- **Dice rather than mince or shred raw onion.** Dicing (cutting into uniformly small pieces as detailed in Recipe #34), in combination with chilling, clean cutting, coating with oil, and quick heating, effectively keeps enzymes inactive during preparation. Onions in general, as a result, reliably retain sweet natural flavoring. Mincing and shredding expose onion pulp to air so completely that chemical reactions that negatively alter onion flavor almost inevitably occur, as is indicated when a cook's eyes water during cutting.
- **Do not marinate or pickle vegetables.** Marinating and pickling result in massive leaching out and wasting of natural juices. Reserve marinated and pickled vegetables for occasional and special occasion use.

---

178 Davis, *Let's Cook It Right*, 310.

- **Do not salt vegetables before cooking.** Because salt draws out juices, salt them after cooking and/or shortly before serving.

2. **Stir-Frying of Vegetables**

    - **Add oil to a clean skillet for stir-frying a vegetable.** Spilled juice from previously cooked ingredients will interfere with oil sticking to vegetable pieces and providing a protective coating. Onions, garlic, and cabbage family vegetables will brown, which undermines flavor and causes loss of vitamin C content. Wipe a skillet with a damp paper towel or kitchen sponge. If more cleaning is necessary, rinse the skillet with hot water to minimize cooling of the skillet.
    - **Cook vegetables individually or only with vegetables with the same cooking time.** Because pulp fragility (and, hence, the time it takes to cook pulp to tenderness) varies from vegetable to vegetable, mixing of vegetables with differing fragility during cooking inevitably results in overcooking and undercooking of some vegetables. Cooking of vegetables and fruits with other dish ingredients also almost certainly results in over-cooking. While this separate and individual cooking of vegetables results in more cooking steps, individual cooking is a 100% effective means of achieving reliably attractive cooking results and, as a result, successful serving.
    - **Add vegetables to a skillet pre-heated to medium-high.** Added to a hot skillet, vegetables immediately begin to cook and reliably cook to tenderness in the recipe-directed cooking time. Enzymes are also immediately destroyed.
    - **Apply observation tests to verify a skillet is fully and accurately pre-heated before adding oil and vegetables for stir-frying.** A drop of water added to a skillet should instantly dance and disappear. Oil added to the skillet should also instantly begin to sizzle moderately (not wildly) around food pieces mixed into it for stir-frying. Observation tests also verify a skillet has not exceeded medium-high temperature. As a result, oil added to a skillet will reliably not smoke, which indicates the oil is being damaged. Vegetables added to the skillet will not immediately scorch.
    - **Do not crowd a skillet.** Overcrowding lowers skillet temperature, which in turn lengthens the time needed to cook vegetable and fruit ingredients to tenderness. Vegetables and especially sturdy ones (such as carrots, potatoes, and apples) will remain undercooked at the end of the recipe-directed cooking time. When cooking is extended to soften a vegetable, particular kinds of vegetables (notably cabbage family vegetables) may overcook. To avoid overcrowding, stir-fry or stir-fry/steam only 2-3 c vegetables at a time in a 12 in. skillet. To prepare a larger amount (4-6 c), either cook two separate batches or use a 14 in. skillet.
    - **Vigorously stir-fry vegetable pieces after adding them to a skillet for stir-frying.** This stir-frying ensures that oil quickly and completely coats cut vegetable pieces and, hence, will effectively hold in juice. It also ensures pieces are uniformly and completely heated through and will steam to tenderness in the recipe directed cooking time.
    - **After stir-frying reduce the heating temperature to medium and heat the vegetable for 1 or 2 minutes, stirring occasionally and setting a timer.** This direction ensures

that tender vegetables (notably onion and bell pepper) reliably reach tenderness without steaming and that sturdier vegetables (notably potatoes) are thoroughly heated through before water is added to steaming.

3. Steaming of Vegetables (For less tender vegetables with dense flesh)

   - **After one minute of stir-frying add a very small amount of measured hot water (1/2 to 1 T only) for steaming.** The aim is to add just enough water to create steam for cooking the vegetable to tenderness. Cold liquid cools the temperature and potentially slows cooking. Too much liquid risks washing away the oil coating on vegetable pieces, which results in leaching out of juices during steaming. A very few very juicy vegetables (notably celery and summer squash) do not require the addition of steaming water and instead steam in their own juice.
   - **Reduce the skillet heat to low after adding steaming water and cover the skillet for steaming.** Immediate reduction in heating temperature is necessary to avoid 1) evaporation of all the steaming water added, which can result in the scorching of vegetables, and 2) to minimize exposure to high temperature. It is important to note that different temperature reductions are needed for electric and gas burners, as is spelled out in the Stir-Frying and Stir-Fry/Steaming Recipe Notes, Note #1, included in Chapter One's introduction.
   - **Set a timer once water is added for steaming and the skillet is covered.** Accurate timing is essential for preventing either over- or under-cooking. Under-cooking is as serious as over-cooking because flavor does not become fully developed and texture does not attractively soften.
   - **Immediately remove cooked vegetables from a hot skillet at the timer's alert.** This important direction avoids overcooking, which instantly undermines cooking success and the application of all *juice-protective* techniques applied up to this point of cooking.
   - **Immediately add cooked vegetables to a colander placed over a dinner plate.** A colander drains any spilling juice away from cooked pieces, and the plate saves any spilled juice. Vegetables can also be placed in a slanted holding container, which allows any spilling juice to drain away from pulp and saves the spilling juice at the same time.
   - **Use a firm rubber or other type of heat-resistant spatula to scrape all cooking juice from a skillet after stir-frying or stir-fry/steaming.** Any cooking juice remaining in a skillet after stir-frying and stir-fry/steaming will contain nutritionally valuable soluble nutrients and soluble fiber.

4. Between Cooking and Assembling Vegetables for Serving

   - **Do not tightly cover hot vegetables after cooking.** In addition to extending cooking time and, thus, causing over-cooking, tight covering will cause steam to condense on pulp surface, which will leach out juice.
   - **Partially cover cooked vegetables with an opaque covering to protect them from light, which is destructive of the B vitamin riboflavin.**

- **Refrigerate cooked vegetables that will not be quickly served,** tightly covering them when they are cooled to protect them from drying air.

5. **Assembling Cooked Vegetables for Serving**

    - **Add vegetables to already preheated dishes to avoid overcooking and to minimize exposure to liquid.** Heat through sauce, grain, legume, and meat/poultry ingredients before adding cooked vegetable ingredients to dishes being assembled for serving.
    - **Serve any collected cooking juice with a cooked vegetable.** Avoid wasting the juice. Use a rubber spatula for efficient scraping. Being a very small amount, cooking juice will be flavorful and will not dilute dish flavor.
    - **Quickly re-heat cooked vegetables after adding them to dishes for serving.** Heat them at a medium-high temperature, stirring frequently, and serve the dish once the vegetable ingredients are hot.
    - **Do not keep extra portions of dishes heated.** Remove un-served portions of dishes from heat, cover and set them aside, and quickly re-heat these extra servings as needed. For example, heat individual servings in a microwave oven. Alternatively, heat a skillet at a low-medium temperature to keep it ready for quick heating of additional servings.

CHAPTER TWO

Dry Roasted Vegetables

Dry Roasting Description

DRY ROASTING IS a simple *juice-protective* cooking method in which vegetables – whole, halved, or cut into even-sized pieces – are roasted without added liquid in an oven at a high temperature until tender. While not a cooking method that is as quick and simple or as widely applicable to vegetables in general as stir-frying and stir-fry/steaming, dry roasting is an attractive cooking method. Its methods are simple. They involve minimal preparation – little cutting and sometimes no cutting at all – and little tending during baking. Dry roasting time for some vegetables is even quite brief, finishing in the time other dishes for a meal are prepared. Dry roasting suits particular vegetables (notably large, firm-fleshed vegetables with thick skins) and particular occasions (especially when an oven is already being heated at a high temperature for one dish) and reliably yields tasty cooking results.

Chapter Two dry roasted vegetable recipes are abbreviated. Each individual Chapter Two dry-roasting vegetable recipe includes only the basic details needed for cooks to apply one of two dry roasting procedures. There is one procedure for **cut soft-fleshed vegetables** and another for **large whole or halved firm-fleshed vegetables**. Because small cutting significantly reduces roasting time, diced and cubed firm vegetables apply the soft-fleshed roasting procedure. Both dry roasting procedures, which are presented below, include a complete listing of all cooking tools needed and detail all preparation steps.

Individual Chapter Two dry roasting recipes include five kinds of information, which are as follows:

- the type of dry roasting procedure to use (soft or firm-fleshed).
- the vegetable amount needed for two servings.
- cutting details, if any.
- vegetable roasting time.
- the recipe number of the Chapter One recipe that serves as a reference. Providing full preparation detail, Chapter One recipes provide background nutritional, selection, and storage information about the vegetable being dry-roasted.

Dry Roasting Procedure for Cut Soft-Fleshed Vegetables
(Asparagus, Brussels Sprouts, Eggplant, Mushroom, Onion, Bell Pepper, Summer Squash)
and
Sliced or Diced Firm-Fleshed Vegetables
(Diced Potato, Potato Fries, Diced Rutabaga, Rutabaga Fries, Diced Turnip, Turnip Fries, and Cubed Winter Squash)

1. **Gather all cooking tools.** These tools include, as follows:

   1 large cutting board.
   1 padded oven glove. A glove is for safely moving the baking dish to and from the very hot oven. Two gloves provide the best protection.
   1 each chef's, 5 in. serrated, and paring knife.
   1 large mixing bowl for mixing cut vegetables with oil and herbs.
   1 large (9 x 13 in.) rectangular baking dish, lightly buttered or nonstick spray coated.
   1 firm rubber (or other heat-resistant) spatula for mixing cut vegetable pieces to coat pieces completely and for efficiently scraping cut roasted vegetables and any cooking juice from the baking dish for serving.
   1 stir-fry spatula for stirring cut vegetables midway during roasting.
   1 set each measuring spoons and cups.
   1 timer.
   1 dinner spoon (for scraping winter squash flesh from skins).
   1 dinner fork (for mashing winter squash and potato).

2. **Gather preparation ingredients.** These include, as follows,

   - extra virgin olive oil for coating cut vegetables (approx. 1 T per 2 serving recipe, which is about 2 c vegetables).
   - dried herb leaves for flavoring vegetables (approx. 1 t per 2 serving recipe, which is about 2 c vegetables).

3. **Preheat the oven to 430 degrees.** Allow around 7 minutes for this pre-heating. This high temperature is important. It quickly deactivates plant enzymes that can destroy vitamin C content and ensures vegetables immediately begin to cook and cook to tenderness in the recipe directed time.

4. **Prepare vegetables for dry roasting.**

   - Wash and thoroughly dry vegetables. Complete drying ensures oil thoroughly coats cut vegetable pieces.
   - Do not peel vegetables except for onions and garlic.
   - Cut vegetables into uniformly sized pieces as specified in the Chapter Two vegetable dry roasting recipe. Cutting vegetables into thick slices or fairly large chunks best retains flavor, but pieces should not be so large that they do not cook to tenderness in the directed cooking time.

- Add the cut vegetables to a large mixing bowl.
- Add extra virgin olive oil: 1 T per 2 servings, which is about 2 c vegetables.
- Thoroughly toss the vegetable pieces into the oil.
- Add dried herb leaves (approx. 1 t per 2 serving vegetable recipe). For example, add sweet basil, oregano, marjoram, Italian spice mix, rosemary, or dill weed. Evenly sprinkle herbs, first crushing them between your palms, over the vegetables. Use a rubber spatula to evenly mix the herbs into the vegetables.
- Evenly spread vegetable pieces in one layer on a baking dish and do not overcrowd the dish. Different vegetables can be mixed together except for sliced mushrooms, which should be added during the second half of roasting.

5. **Roast the vegetables.**

- Center the baking dish on the middle oven rack.
- Roast a vegetable for one half of the specified roasting time, setting a timer.
- At the timer, use oven gloves to remove the baking pan from the oven, use a stir-fry spatula to flip the pieces evenly, return the baking dish to the oven, and roast the vegetable for the same amount of time, again setting a timer.
- At the timer, remove a vegetable from the oven and make a taste check to ensure vegetable pieces are completely softened. Return the baking dish to the oven if the vegetable is not completely soft and re-check the vegetable for tenderness every 5 minutes until it is tender. Vegetables are tastiest when completely softened.
- Add a sprinkling of salt after roasting vegetables other than seasoning vegetables (onion, garlic, bell and chili pepper, and mushrooms).
- Use a rubber spatula to scrape the vegetables and any vegetable juice from the baking dish for serving.

VARIATIONS: Add ½ **yellow onion** to any individually roasted vegetable. Slice the onion lengthwise, cut off the tips, peel the onion, cut it lengthwise into ½ in. slices, and break the slices apart before mixing the onion with a vegetable. Onion is a flavor-enhancing ingredient.

Omit **dried herb leaves**.

Dry Roasting Procedure for Whole or Halved Firm-Fleshed Vegetables
(Beets, Potatoes, Rutabagas, Winter Squash, and Turnips)

1. **Gather all cooking tools.** These tools include, as follows,

    1 large cutting board.
    1 dinner fork for mashing.
    1 each chef's and 5 in. serrated knife.

1 firm-bladed 9 in. slicing knife for halving winter squash.

1 large (9 x 13 in.) rectangular baking dish, lightly buttered or nonstick spray coated. A baking pan can be substituted for any vegetable except for winter squash and sweet potato.

1 padded oven glove (or best of all, two gloves). A glove is for safely moving the baking dish to and from the very hot oven. Two gloves provide best protection.

1 stir-fry spatula. A wide spatula serves to flip halved winter squash.

1 timer. Accurate timing is essential to avoid overcooking.

1 large dinner spoon (or soup spoon) for scraping baked flesh from squash skin.

2. **Gather cooking ingredients.** These ingredients include, as follows:

- softened butter, a small amount for coating the roasting dish and vegetable skin except for winter squash; 1-1½ T for flavoring vegetables for serving after roasting.
- extra virgin olive oil, a small amount for coating all cut vegetable surfaces.

3. **Preheat the oven to 430 degrees for all vegetables except for sweet potato.** Preheat the oven to 400 degrees for sweet potato. Allow at least seven minutes for an oven to reach this temperature. High initial heat ensures vegetables immediately begin to cook and reach tenderness in the recipe directed time. In potatoes and eggplant, high initial heat also quickly deactivates plant enzymes that can destroy vitamin C content. In potatoes this destruction shows up as unattractively brown skin immediately under the skin.

4. **Prepare the vegetables for roasting.**

- Wash and thoroughly dry vegetables. Complete drying ensures oil coats vegetable skin and any exposed cut surface, providing a protective coating.
- Do not peel or trim vegetables to be roasted whole in any way.
- Lightly coat the vegetable skin with butter (except for winter squash); coat the cut surface of halved vegetables with extra virgin olive oil.
- Lightly coat with butter the area of a baking dish where cut vegetable flesh will be placed cut side down.

5. **Roast the vegetables.**

- Roast vegetables at 430 degrees for 15 minutes, setting a timer (roast sweet potato at 400 degrees for 15 minutes).
- At the timer, reduce the oven heat to 400 degrees (375 degrees for sweet potatoes), again setting a timer for the recipe specified roasting time.
- At the timer, check for complete softening. If vegetables do not feel completely soft, continue baking them, re-checking them for readiness every 5 minutes and setting a timer for each extending cooking time.

Roasted Vegetable Recipes
(2-4 servings)

38. Roasted Whole Asparagus Spears
(Soft-Fleshed Procedure)

1. Amount and size of asparagus (Recipe #1): ½ lb; approx. 10 spears; spears left whole and untrimmed when roasted alone; broken into 2-3 in. lengths when roasted with other vegetables.

2. Roasting time: When roasting asparagus with other vegetables, roast for 8 minutes at 430 degrees, stir, and then roast another 8 minutes at 430 degrees. When asparagus is being roasted alone, reduce the total roasting time to 12 minutes, stirring the asparagus after 6 minutes.

39. Whole Roasted Beets
(Firm-Fleshed Procedure)

1. Amount and size of beets (Recipe #2): 2 medium.

2. Roasting time: 15 minutes at 430 degrees; 45 minutes at 400 degrees or until sides feel soft when gently squeezed.

40. Roasted Brussels Sprouts
(Soft-Fleshed Procedure)

1. Amount and size of Brussels sprouts (Recipe #5): ½ lb, approx. 14 medium sprouts.

2. Preparation for roasting: halve the sprouts lengthwise. Being careful not to cut off leaves, use a serrated or chef's knife to slice off the very bottom of the stem end.

3. Roasting time: When roasting Brussels sprouts with other vegetables, roast for 8 minutes at 430 degrees, flip, and then roast another 8 minutes at 430 degrees. When roasting Brussels sprouts alone, roast for 6 minutes at 430 degrees, flip/stir, and then roast another 6 minutes at 430 degrees.

41. Roasted Cauliflower Florets
(Soft-Fleshed Procedure)

1. Amount and size of cauliflower (Recipe #41): approx. ½ head, broken into about 6 large (approx. 1½ in. thick) florets or about 8 medium (approx. 1 in. thick) florets. Leave 1 in. stems on florets.

2. Preparation for roasting:

   - For slices, halve large florets lengthwise; place the halves cut side down on a cutting board and cut each half lengthwise into thick (⅓ in.) slices.
   - For whole florets, use medium (1 in. thick) cauliflower florets.

3. Roasting time: When roasting cauliflower with other vegetables, roast for 8 minutes at 430 degrees, flip, and then roast another 8 minutes at 430 degrees. When roasting cauliflower alone, roast 6 minutes at 430 degrees, flip/stir, and then roast another 6 minutes at 430 degrees.

4. Preparation comments: As cauliflower is highly absorptive, increase oil content to 1½ T oil. Drizzle the oil evenly over the cauliflower before stirring the oil and cauliflower together.

42. Roasted Eggplant
(Soft-Fleshed Procedure)

1. Amount and size of eggplant (Recipe #11): 1 medium globe or 2 Japanese (each approx. 1½ in. thick, 6 or 7 in. long) eggplants.

2. Preparation for roasting:

   - Slice off the ends, stand a globe eggplant upright, and slice eggplant lengthwise into ⅓ in. thick strips; slice the strips crosswise into ⅓ in. cubes.
   - Slice off the ends, stand the eggplant on a flattened end and halve lengthwise, and cut each Japanese eggplant crosswise into ⅓ in. thick slices.

3. Roasting time: When roasting eggplant with other vegetables, roast 8 minutes at 430 degrees, flip, and then roast another 8 minutes at 430 degrees. When roasting eggplant alone, roast 6 minutes at 430 degrees, flip/stir, and then roast another 6 minutes at 430 degrees.

4. Preparation comments: As eggplant is highly absorptive, increase coating oil content to 1½ T oil. Drizzle the oil evenly over the eggplant before stirring in the oil and eggplant together.

PART 1

43. Roasted Mushroom
(Soft-Fleshed Procedure)

1. Amount of mushrooms (Recipe #33): 10 medium mushrooms.

2. Preparation for roasting: Cut each mushroom lengthwise into 3 equal slices.

3. Roasting time: 8 minutes at 430 degrees. When roasting mushrooms with other vegetables, add the mushrooms halfway through roasting. When roasting mushrooms alone, roast the mushrooms for 4 minutes, stir the mushrooms, and roast them another 4 minutes.

4. Preparation Comments: As mushroom is highly absorptive, increase coating oil content to 1½ T oil. Drizzle the oil evenly over the mushroom before stirring in the oil.

44. Roasted Onion
(Soft-Fleshed Procedure)

1. Amount and size of onion (Recipe #34): 1 medium (approx. 2-2½ in. diameter) bulb onion with tight-fitting, unbroken skin.

2. Preparation for roasting: Use a chef's knife to halve the onion lengthwise and cut off the ends of the onion halves. Peel the onion. Place the onion halves cut side down on a cutting board and cut each half lengthwise into ⅓-½ in. thick slices. Break the onion slices apart before adding them to the baking dish and tossing the onions in the oil.

3. Roasting time: When roasting onion with other vegetables, roast 8 minutes at 430 degrees, flip, and then roast another 8 minutes at 430 degrees. When roasting onion alone, roast 6 minutes at 430 degrees, flip/stir and then roast another 6 minutes at 430 degrees.

45. Roasted Bell Pepper
(Soft-Fleshed Procedure)

1. Amount and size of bell pepper (Recipe #35): 1 medium pepper (red, yellow, orange, purple, brown, or a mixture of different colored peppers to equal 1 pepper).

2. Preparation for roasting: Use a serrated knife to halve the pepper lengthwise, to cut out the stem end of the pepper, to cut the pepper lengthwise in uniform ½ in. wide strips, and to cut the strips crosswise into ½ in. cubes.

3. Roasting time: When roasting peppers with other vegetables, roast 8 minutes at 430 degrees, flip, and then roast another 8 minutes at 430 degrees. When roasting peppers alone, roast 6 minutes at 430 degrees, flip/stir, and then roast another 6 minutes at 430 degrees.

46. Whole Roasted (Baked) Potato
(Firm-Fleshed Procedure)

1. Amount and size of potato: 2 chilled medium or 1 large white or red potato; 6-8 small white or red potatoes.

2. Roasting time for potato (Recipe #17): 15 minutes at 430 degrees; approx. 45 more minutes at 400 degrees for medium potato and 60 minutes for large potato, until sides feel soft when gently squeezed.

3. Preparation for serving:

   - To mash roasted potato, make a long lengthwise slit down the center of the potato top, break apart the potato, and use a dinner fork to roughly mash each potato half. Evenly sprinkle ¼ t salt over each potato half, immediately add softened butter (2 t per potato half), and mix in the butter once it melts.
   - To dice potato, halve the potato lengthwise. Place each half cut side down on a cutting board, and slice each potato half lengthwise into ¼ in. thick slices. Holding the slices together with one hand, cut the potato crosswise into ¼ in. thick slices.

47. Whole Roasted (Baked) Sweet Potato
(Firm-Fleshed Procedure)

1. Amount and size of sweet potato (Recipe #18): 2 chilled medium or 1 large sweet potato.

2. Preparation for roasting: lightly coat the scrubbed and dried sweet potato with butter.

3. Roasting time: 15 minutes at 400 degrees; 35-40 minutes at 375 degrees for medium sweet potato; 45-50 minutes for large sweet potato, until sides feel soft when gently squeezed.

4. Preparation for serving:

   - To mash roasted sweet potato, make a lengthwise slit down the center of the potato top, break apart the potato, and use a dinner fork to roughly mash each potato half. Evenly sprinkle ¼ t salt over each potato half, immediately add softened butter (2 t per potato half), and mash in the butter once it melts.
   - To dice sweet potato, halve the potato lengthwise, place each half cut side down on a cutting board, and slice each potato half lengthwise into ¼ in. thick slices. Holding the slices together with one hand, cut the potato crosswise into ¼ in. thick slices.

48. Roasted Potato, Oven Fries
(Soft-Fleshed Procedure)

1. Amount and size of potatoes: 3 chilled medium or 2 large red or white potatoes (Recipe #17) or sweet potatoes (Recipe #18).

2. Preparation for roasting: Use a chef's knife to cut off the ends of each potato. Standing a potato upright on a flattened end, use the chef's knife to cut the potato lengthwise into ¼ in. thick slices. Stacking several slices, cut the slices into ¼ in. thick strips.

3. Roasting time: 10 minutes at 430 degrees, flip/stir, and roast for 10 minutes at 430 degrees, until soft to the center.

49. Roasted Rutabaga, Oven Fries or Diced
(Soft-Fresh Procedure)

1. Amount and size of rutabaga (Recipe #19): 3 chilled medium or 2 large rutabagas.

2. Preparation for roasting:

   - For rutabaga fries, peel a rutabaga with waxed skin or a large rutabaga with thick skin. Use a chef's knife to cut off the ends of each rutabaga. Standing a rutabaga upright on a flattened end, cut the rutabaga lengthwise into ¼ in. thick slices. Cut the slices lengthwise into ¼ in. thick strips.
   - For diced rutabaga, cut ¼ in. thick strips crosswise into ¼ in. cubes.

3. Roasting time:
   - For fries, 10 minutes at 430 degrees, flip/stir, and roast for approx. 10 minutes at 430

degrees, until soft (easily pierced by a sharp knife).
- For diced, 8 minutes at 430 degrees, flip/stir, and roast another 8 minutes at 430 degrees, until soft.

50. Roasted Zucchini or Yellow Summer Squash
(Soft-Fleshed Procedure)

1. Amount and size of summer squash (Recipe #20): 1 medium (8 in. long; 1½ in. thick) zucchini or yellow straightneck squash or 2 small (approx. 4 in. long, excluding the neck) yellow crookneck squash.

2. Preparation for roasting:

   - For slices, use a chef's knife to cut off the ends of the squash (separating and setting aside the neck of crookneck yellow squash) and cut the squash crosswise into ⅓ in. thick strips. Cut the neck of crookneck yellow squash crosswise into ⅓ in. thick slices.
   - For cubes, use a chef's knife to cut off the ends of the squash (separating the neck of crookneck yellow squash), stand the squash upright on a flattened end. Use the chef's knife to slice the squash lengthwise into ⅓ in. thick slices, cut the slices lengthwise into ⅓ in. thick strips, and cut the strips crosswise into ⅓ in. cubes. Cut a crookneck squash neck crosswise into ⅓ in. thick slices.

3. Roasting time:

   - For slices, 8 minutes at 430 degrees, flip/stir, and roast for 10 minutes.
   - For cubed, 6-7 minutes at 430 degrees, flip/stir, and roast for another 6-7 minutes at 430 degrees. When mixed with other vegetables, roast 8 minutes before and after stirring.

51. Roasted (Baked) Winter Squash Halves
(Firm-Fleshed Procedure)

1. Amount and size of winter squash (Recipe #21): 1 medium acorn, butternut, or buttercup squash, halved lengthwise; seeds and membrane left within squash halves; cut flesh of halves coated with oil; halves placed cut side down in the lightly buttered baking dish.

2. Roasting time: 15 minutes at 430 degrees; reduce oven temperature to 400 and roast squash for 25 minutes before checking for readiness. Indications of complete softening are 1) the squash sides feel soft when gently squeezed and 2) the rounded top slightly

caves downward. Overcooking is indicated when juice spills and when flesh in contact with the baking dish is scorched, as indicated by browning.

3. Roasting comments: A stainless steel baking pan can be substituted for a glass baking dish, but do not use a nonstick baking pan, which can be ruined by squash.

4. Serving comments:

- To mash winter squash, use a large dinner spoon to first remove the seeds and membrane. Either leave the flesh in the skin or scrape flesh from the skins of each squash half into a mixing bowl. Use a dinner fork to mash the flesh. Evenly sprinkle ¼ t salt over each half and immediately add softened butter (2 t per half) and use a dinner fork to mix the butter into the squash once it melts. The squash mashed in a bowl can be returned to the skins for serving.
- To dice the firmer flesh of the narrow end of roasted butternut squash, place the squash cut side down on a cutting board and use a serrated knife to cut the squash lengthwise into ¼ in. thick slices. Cutting close to the skin while being careful to avoid including skin, use a serrated or paring knife to slice the squash flesh from the skin. While holding several slices together with one hand, cut the squash crosswise into ¼ in. thick slices.

52. Roasted Winter Squash, Cubed
(Use Soft-Fleshed Procedure)

1. Amount of squash (Recipe #21): ½ medium butternut or buttercup squash.

2. Preparation:

- Halve a squash lengthwise.
- Microwave each squash half skin side up for 1 minute to soften the skin. Once the squash is cool enough to handle, use a serrated knife or vegetable peeler to peel the squash.
- Alternatively, omit the microwave heating, slice off the ends of the squash, and peel the raw squash using a peeler specifically designed for removing winter squash skin.
- Use a chef's knife to cut the peeled squash lengthwise into ⅓ in. wide slices, cut the slices crosswise into ⅓ in. cubes, and add the cubes to a mixing bowl.
- Add 2 T extra virgin olive oil and toss the cubes to thoroughly coat all pieces with oil. Add and mix dried herb leaves, crushed, into the squash.

3. Roasting time: 10 minutes at 430 degrees; stir the squash and roast it another 10 minutes or until the cubes are soft to the center (a pointed knife easily pierces the center).

53. Roasted Turnip, Oven Fries or Diced
(Use Soft-Fleshed Procedure)

1. Amount and size of turnip (Recipe #22): 3 chilled medium turnips.

2. Preparation:

    - For turnip fries, use a chef's knife to cut off the ends of the turnip. Standing a turnip upright on a flattened end, use the chef's knife to cut the turnip halves lengthwise into ¼ in. thick slices and to cut the slices into ¼ in. thick strips.
    - For diced turnip, cut the ¼ in. thick strips crosswise into ¼ in. cubes.

3. Roasting time:

    - For fries, 10 minutes at 430 degrees, flip/stir, and roast for 10 minutes.
    - For diced, 6-7 minutes at 430 degrees, flip/stir, and roast for another 6-7 minutes at 430 degrees. When mixed with other vegetables, roast for 8 minutes at 430 degrees before and after stirring.

CHAPTER THREE

Boiled Whole Vegetables

Boiled Whole in Water Description

BOILING WHOLE IS a simple and convenient *juice-protective* method of cooking vegetables. Completely intact skin effectively protects the vegetable from direct contact with cooking water during cooking, preventing water from penetrating the vegetable and leaching out juice and its valuable soluble content during cooking. When cooking is timed exactly, vegetables, including the nutritious skin, emerge in attractively softened and tasty form. A disadvantage of boiling whole in comparison to stir-frying and stir-fry/steaming is that boiling whole does not combine the vegetables with extra virgin olive oil, which enhances the absorption of the fat-soluble nutrients of vegetables. This disadvantage is easily overcome by mixing cut boiled whole and stir-fried in water vegetables in dishes, as is always done in Chapter Seven stir-fried dishes. A small amount of extra virgin olive oil or butter can also be mixed into whole vegetables once they are cut into serving size pieces.

Chapter Three presents recipes for two types of boiling whole: boiling intact vegetables completely covered with water and stir-frying intact vegetables in a small amount of water.

Boiling intact vegetables completely covered with water suits particular vegetables. This cooking method suits, for example,

- curly greens and greens with small leaves that are difficult and time-consuming to dry after rinsing, as is needed in stir-frying.
- larger, more mature greens in general, such as collard greens. Boiling whole eliminates the need for drying, as is needed in stir-frying.
- large vegetables with sturdy flesh that are somewhat difficult to dice for stir-fry/steaming. The skin of these vegetables, such as potatoes and beets, provides effective protection from water during boiling. Boiling softens the nutritious skin, making it an acceptable part of the vegetable when it is served.
- vegetables that cannot be stir-fried, such as artichoke.

Boiling whole covered in water also suits particular types of dishes, such as dishes that

- serve vegetables in large piece or chunk form. Whereas stir-fried and stir-fried/

steamed vegetables must be sliced thin or diced/minced for quick cooking, boiled whole vegetables can be cut into any size. Chunks can be desirable for some dishes, such as soups and stews.

Stir-frying in water suits very small vegetables with sturdy protective skin. These vegetables – such as green peas, sugar snap and snow peas, and corn kernels – cook very quickly to tenderness without loss of flavor and color. While not quite as tasty as when stir-fried in oil, stir-frying of vegetables in water is just as fast and serves the following useful purposes.

- Stir-frying in water maximizes retention of the color and flavor of dry frozen vegetables. While freezing generally reduces nutritional value, dry frozen vegetables are easy to keep on hand for quick addition to stir-fried dishes, soups, curries, and stews.
- Stir-fried in water, vegetables do not add oil to a dish, which is a plus in any stew or stir-fried dish that contains many vegetables that are stir-fried in oil.

Chapter Three Recipe Organization

Chapter Three boiled whole recipes are abbreviated. Each recipe applies one of two basic boiling whole procedures, either a **boiled whole covered with water** or **stir-fried whole in a small amount of water** procedure. Both procedures, which are presented below, cover all preparation steps and include a complete listing of all cooking tools needed. The Part One introduction listing of cooking tools serves as a descriptive reference for the basic cooking tools used in boiling whole recipes. Tools that are either specific to or of special importance to boiling whole are listed and described below.

- 1 large (12 c) saucepan. This size sauce pan matches medium-sized vegetables. It is sufficiently large enough to hold enough water to completely cover most medium-sized vegetables by several inches.
- 1 Dutch oven, deep and wide soup pot, or deep 14 in. skillet. A Dutch oven holds 8 c (or 2 qt) water, which is more than enough water to cover most large, bulky greens by several inches.
- 1 slotted spoon for removing boiled whole vegetables from boiling water.
- 1 pair of tongs. This tool is useful for removing large greens from boiling water.

Each individual Chapter Three vegetable recipe includes only basic details needed for cooks to apply one of the two boiling whole procedures. These basic details included are as follows:

- The boiling whole procedure to apply. Recipes applying the boiling whole covered with water procedure are titled "boiled whole" and recipes applying the stir-frying in water procedure are titled "stir-fried in water".
- The vegetable amount required for a two- serving portion.
- The cooking time.
- The number of the Chapter One (Stir-Fried and Stir-Fry/Steamed Vegetable Recipes)

PART 1

recipe that serves as a reference for providing background preparation details of vegetables, including selection, cleaning, drying, and cutting for serving details. Chapter One recipes also provide nutritional information about Chapter Three vegetables.
- As **artichoke, lima beans, green and yellow wax beans**, and **edamame** are not included in Chapter One, background information is included in the Chapter Three boiling whole recipes for these vegetables.

Basic Boiled Whole Covered in Water Procedure
(Artichoke, Asparagus, Butter Beans and Baby Lima Beans, Green and Yellow Wax Beans, Beets, Broccoli and Cauliflower, Brussels Sprouts, Carrots, Chard, Collards, Edamame Pods, Kale, Okra, Sugar Snap and Snow Peas, Potatoes, and Summer Squash)

1. **Gather the following cooking tools.**

    1 vegetable scrub brush or 1 dish sponge with one rough surface.
    1 each 5 in. serrated, chef's, and paring knife for cutting cooked vegetables for serving. The paring knife is useful for testing the readiness of longer cooking root vegetables. The knife blade should easily pierce the center of a cooked through vegetable.
    1 large (12 c) sauce pan with an opaque lid.
    1 Dutch oven, a wide and deep soup pot, or deep 14 in. skillet.
    1 large-headed wooden spoon with a long handle. This is a necessary tool for effectively pressing large and bulky greens into boiling water at the start of cooking.
    1 slotted spoon.
    1 pair tongs for preparing large leafy greens.
    1 efficiently draining colander.
    1 timer.
    1 pair kitchen scissors when cooking green beans, snow peas, and sugar snap peas.
    1 melon baller (for artichoke).
    1 vegetable peeler (for artichoke).

2. **Prepare water for boiling.**

    - Select a pot that matches the vegetables to be boiled. For example, a large pot that is both deep and wide is needed for boiling large greens but a large saucepan suits broccoli and cauliflower florets and Brussels sprouts.
    - Add enough water to a pot to cover vegetables being boiled by several inches.
    - Begin heating the water on high heat on a large burner as a first preparation step.
    - Bring the water to full boiling.

3. **Prepare the vegetables.**

    - Rinse vegetables to clean them.
    - Scrub root vegetables thoroughly to remove sticking dirt and dirt in potato eyes,

which encourages eating of the skin after cooking. Be careful to avoid removing or breaking open skin during scrubbing.
- Except for broccoli and cauliflower florets, do not trim vegetables in any way.

4. **Cook the vegetables.**

   - Add the vegetables to fully boiling water without causing the water to stop boiling, adding large vegetables one at a time and small vegetables in small groups.
   - Start a timer immediately once vegetables are added to boiling water.
   - At the timer, immediately use a slotted spoon or tongs to remove the vegetables from the boiling water into a colander and immediately rinse them with cold water to stop the cooking. These steps are essential for avoiding over-cooking. When the boiling water will not be used again, the water and vegetables can be drained into the colander at the end of the cooking time.
   - Set a cooked whole vegetable aside until adding them to a dish being assembled for serving. Refrigerate any vegetables that will not be quickly used or that are extra, covering them once they are cool.

5. **Serve the boiled vegetables.**

   - Cut, but do not peel, the boiled whole vegetables into serving size pieces shortly before serving. Retaining the protective skin for as long as possible protects vegetables from drying air and destructive light. Retaining the skin increases the nutritional value of the vegetable.
   - Sprinkle cut vegetables lightly with salt before serving them or adding them to a mixed ingredient dish.
   - When serving boiled vegetables singly, serve them with butter and extra virgin olive oil, approx. 1 t of either fat per 2-serving amount of vegetable. Butter and extra virgin olive oil adds attractive flavor while enhancing absorption of the valuable fat-soluble phytonutrients and vitamins contained by vegetables.
   - When boiling vegetables whole, boil more than one vegetable to make the best use of the water and energy used.

Basic Stir-Fried in Water Procedure
(Asparagus, Whole Kernel Corn, Okra, and Green, Sugar Snap, and Snow Peas)

1. **Gather the following listed cooking tools.**

   12 in. heavy-bottomed skillet with a tight-fitting and opaque lid.
   1 stir-fry spatula.
   1 rubber (or other heat-resistant) spatula for efficient scraping of a cooked vegetable and any cooking liquid from the skillet.
   1 timer.

1 electric tea kettle. This tool is useful for instantly preparing hot water for steaming of larger or mature vegetables that are not satisfactorily softened after 1 minute of stir-frying in water. A tea kettle with hot water also immediately provides hot water in case water for stir-frying unexpectedly evaporates.

1 set of measuring spoons for exact measurement of stir-frying water content.

1 efficiently draining colander.

1 pair kitchen scissors for trimming some cooked vegetables for serving.

2. **Prepare the vegetable.**

   - Rinse fresh vegetables to clean them, but do not trim them in any way.
   - Break dry frozen vegetables apart while they remain in the freezer packing container but use them unthawed straight from the freezer.

3. **Cook the vegetable.**

   - Bring 2 T water to boiling over high heat in the skillet. This step requires watchfulness as 2 T water can quickly evaporate. Should water evaporate add 2 T more water.
   - Add one kind of vegetable, thoroughly mix the vegetables into the hot water, and when the water again boils, stir-fry the vegetables, turning pieces over and over constantly for 1 minute, setting a timer.
   - Do not add more than 2 c vegetable at a time. For larger batches, cook the vegetable in two batches or use a 14 in. skillet, which easily accommodates 4 c vegetables.
   - Add steaming for larger or mature vegetables. After stir-frying for one minute, add 1 T hot water (only if all cooking water has evaporated), reduce the heat to low, cover the skillet, and steam the vegetable for the recipe specified cooking time, setting a timer.
   - At the timer, immediately remove the skillet from the burner.
   - Lightly and evenly sprinkle the vegetable with salt.
   - Use a rubber spatula to scrape the cooked vegetable and any cooking water into a colander placed over a bowl for collecting and saving any juice. Always serve this collected cooking juice with a cooked vegetable.

4. **Serve the vegetable.**

   - Do not peel the vegetable. Do any trimming and cutting shortly before the vegetable will be served.
   - When a vegetable will not be served in a mixed-ingredient dish that contains some fat, serve the vegetable with a mixture of butter and extra virgin olive oil, approx. 1 t of either fat per 2-serving amount of vegetable. Butter and extra virgin olive oil add attractive flavor. Both fats enhance the absorption by humans of the valuable fat-soluble phytonutrients and nutrients contained by vegetables.

Boiled Whole Recipes for Vegetables
(2 -4 servings)

54. Boiled Whole Artichoke

1. Amount and size of artichoke: 2 top-growing artichokes, approx. ½-¾ lb each.

2. Boiling time: approx. 40 minutes. Add the artichoke to boiling water, return the water to boiling, reduce the heat to a level that maintains gentle boiling, cover the saucepan, and boil the artichoke until the stem end is easily pierced with a sharp knife, beginning to check for readiness after 40 minutes. Drain upside down in a colander.

3. To serve individual bracts:

    - Cool the cooked artichoke. When it is cool enough to handle, use a chef's knife to slice off 1 inch of the top and 1 inch from the bottom of each artichoke.
    - Use kitchen scissors to cut off the thorny tips of the outer bracts (scales or leaves).
    - Use a chef's knife to halve each artichoke lengthwise.
    - Use a melon baller to scoop out the center (or choke) and the first few inner layers of leaves of the artichoke to reach the pale yellow-green heart of each artichoke.
    - Brush the inside of each artichoke half with extra virgin olive oil and lightly sprinkle it with salt.
    - Use a vegetable peeler to remove the fibrous skin from the artichoke stems.
    - Serve the artichokes, 1-2 halves per serving, instructing those being served to pull off the individual bracts and remove the flesh by pulling the leaves through their clenched teeth.
    - Include a fork and knife with each serving for cutting and eating the artichoke stem.
    - Serve a dipping sauce composed of 2 T freshly squeezed lemon juice (approx. ½ lemon) and 2 T extra virgin olive oil, if desired.

4. Artichoke profile:

    - Top-growing artichokes are ones that grow at the top of artichoke plants.
    - An exception to the rule that deep-colored vegetables are most nutritious, light-colored artichoke heart is an extraordinarily nutritious vegetable, containing exceptionally rich antioxidant and fiber content.[179] This fiber content is high in inulin, which is prebiotic. This fiber nourishes the growth of beneficial gut bacteria that keep disease-causing bacteria in check and that perform other human health supporting services.
    - Prepare artichoke quickly after purchasing it as it has a very high respiration rate that results in quick loss of its antioxidant value.

---

179 Robinson, *Eating on the Wild* Side, 196. Artichokes have greater antioxidant value than any other vegetables marketed in supermarkets.

PART 1

55. Boiled Whole Asparagus

1. Amount and size of asparagus (Recipe #1): ½ lb uniform asparagus spears (approx. 8 spears).

2. Boiling time: 2 minutes for thin spears; 3 minutes for thick spears.

56. Whole Asparagus, Stir-Fried in Water

1. Amount and size of asparagus (Recipe #1): ½ lb very fresh and uniformly thin spears.

2. Stir-frying time: 1 minute.

3. Variation: Add 2 minutes of steaming for thicker or more mature asparagus.

57. Boiled Whole Butter Beans and Baby Lima Beans

1. Amount of beans: approx. 2 c fresh shelled beans (approx. 1½ lb beans with shells) or 2 c unthawed frozen shelled beans.

2. Boiling time: approx. 30 minutes of gentle boiling, partially covered, until soft.

3. Nutritional profile:

   - Lima beans are a source of numerous phytonutrients that provide both antioxidant and anti-inflammatory protection to humans.[180]
   - Lima beans are a rich source of protein and of both soluble and insoluble fiber. They are an excellent source of the mineral molybdenum and a very good source of the minerals manganese and copper, which, among other functions, combine with phytonutrients to intensify the antioxidant protection of vegetables. Lima beans are also good sources of folate, potassium, iron, magnesium, and vitamins B6 and B1.

---

180 Mateljan, *The World's Healthiest Foods*, 754 and 770.

- Lima beans offer special digestive health support, particularly to the colon. Lima beans support bacteria that is protective of the lining of the colon.
- Lima beans support blood sugar regulation. The combination of concentrated protein and fiber contained by lima beans slows the movement of food through the human digestive tract, which steadies the breakdown of food and, as a result, the uptake of sugar into blood. Lima beans also contain substances that slow down the breaking down of starch into sugar, which also contributes to blood sugar regulation.[181]

58. Boiled Whole Green and Yellow Wax Beans

1. Amount of beans: ½ lb thin or medium thick (only slightly bulging) beans.

2. Boiling time: 7 minutes.

3. Serving: use kitchen scissors to snip off the tips and halve the beans for serving.

4. Nutritional profile:

    - Green beans are a rich source of antioxidant phytonutrients, including a variety of both flavonoids and carotenoid phytonutrients. They also contain antioxidant nutrients, including the vitamins C and E and the mineral manganese, which combine with phytonutrients to intensify the antioxidant protection provided to humans.
    - The flavonoid and carotenoid phytonutrients contained by green beans also provide anti-inflammatory protection to humans. Additionally, green beans are a good source of magnesium and omega-3 fatty acids (alpha linolenic acid form), which work together with anti-inflammatory phytonutrients to expand the anti-inflammatory protection provided.
    - Green beans contribute from excellent to good amounts of nearly every category of nutritional component. They have excellent vitamin K, which is closely linked with human bone health. Green beans also contain a good amount of alkaline minerals, also linked to bone health. Green beans are a good source of most B complex vitamins, including a very good amount of folate and B2. Beans are also a good source of dietary fiber and protein.

5. Select the freshest and most nutritious green beans.

    - Select purple beans as beans with anthocyanin phytonutrients, which are especially potent antioxidants.
    - Select certified organic and locally produced green beans. The Environmental Working Group lists industrially produced green beans in the middle of its 2016

---

181 Ibid., 754 and 770.

listing of vegetables and fruits most contaminated with pesticides, ranking it #20 out of 50 foods. Certified organic and locally produced, in contrast, are largely free of pesticide content. As naturally produced products, they have other advantages, particularly that they have more potent phytonutrient content and greater overall nutritional value than industrially produced beans.

- In-season for green beans runs from summer through early fall in the United States.

6. Store green beans sealed in a plastic storage bag, pressing out as much air as possible before refrigerating the bag. Thoroughly chill beans uncovered before tightly covering them for storage. Use beans quickly, within 1 week. The shorter the storage time, the greater the phytonutrient content.

7. Serve green beans with butter and/or extra virgin olive oil to enhance absorption of the valuable fat-soluble phytonutrients and nutrients (E and K) contained by beans.

59. Boiled Whole Beets

1. Amount and size of beets (Recipe #2): 4 small or 2 medium beets with 2 in. stems.

2. Boiling time: boil small beets for 20 minutes and medium beets for 30 minutes before testing for readiness. A sharp knife should easily pierce the center. Keep tests to a minimum to avoid loss of juice through puncture slits.

60. Boiled Whole Broccoli or Cauliflower Florets

1. Number of florets and floret preparation:

    - 1 stalk chilled broccoli (Recipe #4). Turn the stalk on its side and use a serrated knife to cut off the florets, leaving the stems as long as possible (cutting them off as close to the stalk as possible) and organize the florets by size. Remove leaves from the stalk and set them handy but separate from the florets.
    - Approx. 6 large cauliflower florets (Recipe #8). Use a serrated knife to cut the florets from ½ small head of cauliflower. Leave as long as possible stems on florets. Break apart the florets to form as uniformly sized florets as possible, keeping florets large (approx. 1-1½ in. diameter).

2. Boiling time: 3 minutes. Add broccoli florets by size, adding largest florets first and adding smaller florets as much as 1 minute after large florets. Add leaves to the broccoli florets during the last minute of boiling.

61. Boiled Whole Brussels Sprouts

1. Number and size of Brussels sprouts (Recipe #5): 14 uniformly small or medium sprouts, loose outer leaves removed but otherwise untrimmed.

2. Boiling time: 2½ minutes for small; 3 minutes for medium. A paring knife should easily pierce the center of a sprout. Accurate timing is crucial for attractive texture.

3. Serving: Use a 5 in. serrated knife to slice off as much of the bottom stem as possible without removing any leaves and to halve the sprouts lengthwise. Evenly sprinkle the florets with ¼ t salt.

62. Boiled Whole Carrots

1. Amount and size of carrots (Recipe #7): 4 medium carrots (approx. 6 in. long, ¾-1in. wide).

2. Boiling time: 5-7 minutes, until a paring knife easily pierces the center of a carrot.

63. Boiled Whole Chard

1. Amount and size of chard (Recipe #24): 3 large chard leaves (8-9 in. long, approx. 6-7 in. wide).

2. Boiling time: 1 minute.

   - Use a deep 14 in. large skillet or a Dutch oven filled with enough water to cover the leaves completely. Trim off the stem ends as may be needed to fit the leaves into the skillet or pot.
   - Add one leaf at a time and use a wooden spoon to push each leaf down into the water as it is added. Begin timing the cooking when all leaves are added.
   - At the timer, use a large spoon or tongs to immediately remove the chard from the boiling water into a colander and rinse the leaves with cold water. When the boiling water will not be used again, drain the water and leaves into a colander at the end of the cooking time.

3. For serving: Cut out the central vein from each leaf and use a chef's knife to chop the veins with attached stems into small pieces. Stack the leaves, facing them in the same direction, and use a 7 in. serrated knife to cut the leaves into ⅓ in. wide slices, cutting both lengthwise and crosswise.

64. Boiled Whole Collards

1. Amount and size of collards (Recipe #25): 3 medium (6-8 in. wide; 7-9 in. long) or 2 larger leaves.

2. Boiling time: 4 minutes.

3. Boiling procedure:

   - Use a deep 14 in. skillet, Dutch oven, or wide soup pot filled with enough water to cover the leaves completely by several inches.
   - Add one leaf at a time and use a wooden spoon to push each leaf down into the water as it is added. Begin timing the cooking when all leaves are added.
   - At the timer, use tongs to remove the collard leaves from the boiling water one at a time, quickly adding each leaf to a colander, and immediately rinsing the leaves with cold water once all leaves are removed from the boiling water. When the boiling water will not be used again, drain the leaves into a colander at the end of the cooking time.

4. For serving: Cut out the central vein from each leaf and use a chef's knife to chop the veins with attached stems. Stack the leaves, facing them in the same direction, and use a 7 in. serrated knife to cut the leaves into ⅓ in. wide slices, cutting both lengthwise and crosswise.

65. Whole Kernel Corn, Stir-fried in Water

1. Amount of corn (Recipe #10): 3 fresh ears (kernels cut from the ears) or 2 c unthawed dry-frozen yellow whole kernel corn.

2. Stir-frying time: 1 minute, timing started once the water returns to boiling after vegetables are added for cooking. Cook the corn just until it is heated through and its color darkens slightly.

66. Boiled Whole Edamame Pods

1. Amount of edamame: 12 oz package dry frozen raw pods, unthawed, or 12 oz fresh pods.

2. Boiling time: 5 minutes.

3. For serving: Remove cooked soybeans from the pods by pulling the pods through your clenched teeth.

4. Nutritional profile:

   - Edamame, like legumes in general, is a highly nutritious food. It is rich in vitamins, minerals, phytonutrients, protein, and both soluble and insoluble fiber. It is also a good source of iron, omega-3 fatty acids, the B vitamin B2 and folate, alkaline minerals (including magnesium, calcium, and potassium), and vitamin K, and it makes a nutritional contribution in every nutritional category except that it does not contribute B12 and vitamin D.
   - Edamame is rich in antioxidant nutrients (including the minerals copper, manganese, zinc, and selenium) that combine with its carotenoid phytonutrient content to intensify the antioxidant protection provided to humans by soybeans.

67. Boiled Whole Kale Leaves

1. Amount and size of kale (Recipe #26): 2 large leaves.

2. Boiling time: 4 minutes.

3. Boiling procedure:

   - Use a deep 14 in. skillet, Dutch oven, or wide soup pot filled with enough water to cover the leaves completely by several inches.
   - Add one leaf at a time to the boiling water and use a wooden spoon to push a leaf down into the water as it is added. Begin the timing when all leaves have been added.
   - At the timer, use tongs to remove the kale leaves from the boiling water, add the leaves to a colander, and immediately rinse the leaves with cold water. When the boiling water will not be used again, drain the water and leaves into a colander at the end of the cooking time.

4. For serving: Cut out the central vein from each leaf and use a chef's knife to chop the veins with attached stems into small pieces. Stack the leaves, facing them in the same direction, and use a 7 in. serrated knife to cut them into ⅓ in. wide slices, cutting both lengthwise and crosswise.

PART 1

68. Boiled Whole Okra

1. Amount and size of okra (Recipe #13): 2 cups same-sized okra.

2. Boiling time: 2 minutes for small, 3 minutes for medium, and 4 minutes for large.

69. Whole Okra, Stir-Fried in Water

1. Amount and size of fresh okra (Recipe #13): 2 cups uniformly small whole okra.

2. Stir-frying time: 1 minute.

3. Variation: Substitute medium or large okra for small and add steaming. After 1 minute of boiling, cover the skillet, reduce the heat to low, and steam the okra, 3 minutes for medium and 4 minutes for large okra.

70. Boiled Whole Sugar Snap and Snow Peas

1. Amount and size of green peas or pea pods (Recipe #16): 2 c uniform-sized small or medium pea pods.

2. Boiling time: 1 minute for small pea pods and 2 minutes for medium pea pods.

71. Green, Sugar Snap, and Snow Peas, Stir-Fried in Water

1. Amount and size of green peas or sugar snap and snow pea pods (Recipe #16): 2 c fresh or dry frozen (unthawed) green peas; 2 c uniform-sized fresh or unthawed dry-frozen sugar snap or snow pea pods.

2. Stir-frying time: 1 minute. Begin constant and timed stir-frying once the stir-frying water resumes boiling after the vegetables have been added.

3. Variation: Substitute uniformly-sized medium or large pods for small pods and add

211

steaming. After the peas boil for 1 minute, cover the skillet, reduce the heat to low, and steam the peas, 2 minutes for medium pods and 3 minutes for large pods, setting a timer.

72. Boiled Whole Potatoes

1. Amount and size of potatoes (Recipe #17 for white and red potatoes; Recipe #18 for sweet potatoes): 6 uniformly small or 2-3 medium red, white, or sweet potatoes.

2. Boiling time: Begin checking for readiness (a sharp paring knife should easily pierce a potato center) after 15 minutes for small potatoes and after 40 minutes for medium potatoes.

73. Boiled Whole Summer Squash

1. Amount and size of squash (Recipe #20): 4 small yellow crookneck squash (approximately 4 in. long and 2 in. wide, excluding the neck, or 2 small zucchini or yellow straightneck squash (each approximately 6 in. long, 1½ in. wide).

2. Boiling time: 2 minutes.

CHAPTER FOUR

Raw Fruit Pure and Simple

Chapter Four Recipe Description

CHAPTER FOUR PRESENTS basic recipes for serving commonly used fruits in raw, unpeeled whole or large chunk form and, for the most part, in completely unflavored form. Fruit eaten in this form contributes maximum content of the full spectrum of naturally occurring nutritional content of fruits. This content is rich and varied. It includes both soluble and heat-sensitive micronutrients and phytonutrients, fat-soluble micronutrients and phytonutrients, both soluble and insoluble fiber, and omega-3 essential fatty acids, which are found in edible seeds of fruits. Fresh fruit juice without skin and pulp, in sharp contrast, loses significant nutritional content, retaining essentially only soluble nutrients and soluble fiber. Juicing also dramatically increases sugar content. While selection of a juice product that is packed in most pulp form retains important nutrient and insoluble fiber content and remixes sugar with moderating fiber, juicing is still processing that is highly destructive of many nutrients and phytonutrients. The phytonutrient content of apple juice, for example, is much lower than in fresh apple.[182] While the pureeing of fruit chunks retains most nutritional content, pureeing is also processing that completely exposes fruit to air and destroys the insoluble fiber content of the fruit pulp. For these reasons, smoothies are not included as a fruit snack option in Chapter Four.

Chapter Four recipes prepare raw fruit for use as snacks in particular but also for use in salads and raw fruit desserts. Recipes serve as a reference for preparing raw fruit variation suggestions made in Chapter Six salad and Chapter Eight fruit dessert recipes. Individual recipes include a brief fruit profile that provides basic nutritional, selection, and storage information about the fruit. Ripe fruit in general is a rich source of varied nutritional content, and this information is assumed except that particular outstanding nutritional content is sometimes noted. The nutritional details included in recipes are instead focused on less widely distributed and updated nutritional information. In particular, information included in fruit profiles covers distinctive enzyme content that affects preparation, phytonutrient content, fiber content, and the alkaline balancing status of individual fruits.[183]

---

182 Mateljan, *The World's Healthiest Foods*, 488.
183 The fruit profiles of Chapter Four recipes primarily draw upon the updated information about the phytonutrient content and other nutritional characteristics of fruits that is provided by the highly informative *Eating on the Wild Side: The Missing Link to Optimum Health*, a recently published book (2013) by Jo Robinson, and *The World's Healthiest Foods*, 2nd edition, by George Mateljan, also a recently published book (2015). An informative article by Gretel H. Schueller, "The Wild World Within," in *Eating Well*, (July/August 2014: 82-88), serves as the source of the information about fructan fibers. *Nutrition Action Health Letter* (December 2014: 6), serves as a main source of top alkaline balancing fruits.

General Chapter Four Notes

Chapter Four Notes provide cooks with helpful information that cannot fit into recipes. The three kinds of information included are:

- reference resources available to cooks for maximizing the nutritional quality of raw fruit recipes (Notes #1-2).
- background information about fruits (Notes #3-5).
- preparation tool information (Note #6).

1. **Cooks substantially boost the nutritional quality of fruit through careful selection and storage of fruit.** *Cooked Alive!* includes two references to aid cooks in the selection and storage of raw fruits.

    - Reference #1 (Selecting Top Quality Fresh Whole Vegetables and Fruits) serves as a basic selection reference. It details indicators of ripeness, a basic key to selecting flavorful and most nutritious fruit. It defines top quality fruit as fruit that is raw, physically intact, and naturally produced. Examples of naturally produced fruit include certified organic and locally produced fruit. Naturally produced fruit has been grown using natural fertilizer in soil; it has not undergone chemical spraying and other forms of chemical tampering during production or marketing.
    - Reference #2 (Key Home Storage Guidelines for Conserving Vegetable and Fruit Quality) serves as a basic storage reference for both refrigerating and dry freezing fruit.

2. **Cooks can dramatically boost the nutritional quality of snacks served with raw fruits through careful selection of ingredients.**

    - Reference #5 (Selecting High Quality Processed Ingredients for Use in Part II Recipes) makes suggestions for selecting ingredients served with raw fruits in Chapter Four's snack recipes (Recipes #102-110). These ingredients include **dairy products (yogurt, cream cheese, and cheese), whole wheat flour, dried fruit**, and **orange juice**.
    - Reference #4 (Selecting Top Quality Whole Food Ingredients for Use in Part II Recipes) makes suggestions for selecting **nuts** used in Chapter Four snack recipes.

3. **All commercially produced citrus fruits – oranges, mandarins and clementines, tangerines, and grapefruit – are commonly degreened.** Degreening means the fruit has been picked while immature and has been treated with ethylene gas to change skin color in order to give the fruit the appearance of ripeness and sweetness. Because citrus fruits do not ripen further after being picked, degreened fruit is both less sweet and less nutritious than fully ripened fruit. To best avoid selection of degreened citrus fruit,

    - avoid selection of citrus fruit from batches that are uniformly orange.
    - avoid selection of early season citrus, which is most likely to be degreened.

- select certified organic oranges. Certified organic rules forbid degreening. Accordingly, deep orange organic citrus fruit is genuinely ripe.
- select fruit grown by small producers, such as those selling citrus fruit at farmers' markets and natural food stores. This fruit likely is not degreened since degreening is an expensive process.

4. **All stone fruits – fruits with one large pit, including apricots, plums, nectarines, and peaches – have the handicap of being highly vulnerable to chilling injury (CI).** Because ripe stone fruit is very fragile, commercially produced stone fruit is generally picked immature, when it is sturdier. Immature stone fruit, however, requires special storage after harvesting. If the internal temperature of these fruits falls below fifty degrees during transport and storage, the texture of the internal (and unseen) flesh can be effectively spoiled or the fruit can simply fail to ripen.[184] To overcome this problem many modern varieties of stone fruits have been bred to improve shipping ability, which has resulted in a reduction in juiciness, texture, and phytonutrient content. Apricots have been particularly affected. There are, however, ways for consumers to avoid selection of fruits that have suffered chilling injury and to make flavorful selections, and individual stone fruit recipes point these techniques out.

5. **The Environmental Working Group, which provides consumers a shopper's guide for assessing the pesticide content of most varieties of industrially produced fruit, is described in the Nutritional Term Guide, Term #6, included in the introduction to Chapter One.**

6. **Important information about the tools used for preparing Chapter Four raw fruit recipes is as follows:**

    - Individual Chapter Four recipes list all needed preparation tools except for some very basic tools that also need to be available. These tools include basic cleaning tools (a scrub sponge with a rough side and scrub brush), drying tools (paper and terry cloth towels), wrapping tools (plastic wrap and sealable plastic storage bags), and a regular, multi-purpose cutting board.
    - The listing of commonly used preparation tools used in Part I recipes that is included in the Part I introduction serves as a descriptive reference for all tools except for those specific to raw fruit recipes.
    - Tools that are specific to raw fruit preparation are a **zesting tool**, which is needed for removing citrus zest (the outer, colored layer of the peel), and a **melon ball cutting tool**.

---

184 Robinson, *Eating on the Wild Side*, 279.

Raw Fruit Recipes

74. Apple
(2 servings)

2 chilled flavorful apples	2 T cold orange or pineapple juice
2 T cold water

Preparation Tools

1 cutting board reserved for fruits	1 small mixing bowl
1 chef's & 1 paring knife

―――――◆―――――

1. **Wash and dry the apples.** Rinse the apples with cold water and thoroughly dry them with paper towels.

2. **Serve the whole apples.** Serve the apples unpeeled and untrimmed with a container for holding the stem and core.

3. **Slice apple for immediate serving.** Serving sliced unpeeled apples is the best way to encourage the eating of apples with skins. The skin of slices is barely noticeable and, hence, acceptable. The eater, as a result, consumes both the nutritious skin and flesh immediately under the skin that is removed by peeling.

    - Use a chef's knife to halve the apples lengthwise and place the halves cut side down on a clean cutting surface. Cut each half lengthwise into 8 slices.
    - Use a paring knife to cut the core and seeds from each slice. Cut out and discard bruised, brown flesh.

4. **Prepare apple slices ahead of serving.**

    - Thoroughly chill the apples.
    - Gather additional preparation tools: measuring spoons, a small mixing bowl, colander, and dinner plate.
    - Combine 1 T water and 2 T orange juice in a medium mixing bowl.
    - Add the apple slices to the citrus rinse as they are cut and quickly and thoroughly swish the apples in the rinse to coat them completely. This coating is important when serving apple slices that will be exposed to air long enough for the apples to reach room temperature. Enzymes become active at room temperature and will cause unattractive browning.
    - Drain the apples in a colander placed over a dinner plate as they are rinsed.
    - Spread the rinsed apples over paper towels and wrap the towels around them to dry them completely.

- Refrigerate the slices, covered, until serving them.
- Collect and save (or drink) any drained citrus rinse.

VARIATION: Substitute **1 T fresh lemon juice** for 1 T water in a citrus rinse for most effective protection from browning. Lemon juice increases the effectiveness of the rinse for a longer period, but it is important to measure the lemon content to ensure it does not sour the apple slices.

Apple Profile

Apple makes notable nutritional contributions.

- Apple is a rich source of antioxidant phytonutrients, including flavonoid and carotenoid phytonutrients. Additionally, apple is a good source of antioxidant nutrients, including vitamins C and E and the mineral manganese, which combine with the phytonutrients to intensify the antioxidant protection provided to humans by apples.
- Apple contains phytonutrients that provide anti-inflammatory protection to humans.
- Apple skin is a rich source of minerals and vitamins, and it contains a significant amount of the phytonutrient content of apples, with the skin containing more of some phytonutrients than the apple flesh.[185] Apple skin contains a concentrated amount of both soluble and insoluble fiber, containing more fiber than the pulp. Its soluble fiber content includes water-soluble pectin.

To select the most flavorful apples,

- select fully ripe and freshest apple picked at the height of the harvesting season, which in the United States is in the fall, between late August and the end of October. Ripeness correlates with maximum sweetness and the least acidity. Green apples, in contrast, place a heavy acid-neutralizing burden on the human body when consumed.
- select locally grown apples during the harvesting season for the freshest of all and most reliably ripest apples.
- choose apples individually as opposed to purchasing them in batches in order to maximize selection of ripe apples.

To maximize the nutritional value of apples,

- select fully ripe apples, which have peak nutritional content.
- select apples with the deepest red skin, which have the greatest phytonutrient content. Apples produce red-pigment in their skin to protect themselves from the

---

[185] Robinson, *Eating on the Wild Side*, 228. An apple skin gives the eater as much as 50 percent more phytonutrients than eating a peeled apple.

sun's ultra-UV rays. Humans get this protection when they eat the red skin.
- choose uniformly deep red apples. Uniformly deep red apples have been evenly exposed to the sun and, as a result, have needed to produce more protective phytonutrients in their skin. There are important exceptions to this rule. Granny Smith apples, for example, while green, have high phytonutrient content.
- select apple varieties with the greatest phytonutrient content, which varies greatly from apple to apple. Apple varieties with extra-high phytonutrient content include **Gala, Granny Smith, Fuji, Red Delicious, Golden Delicious,** and **Ginger Gold.** Other commonly marketed apple varieties with especially rich phytonutrient content include **Cortland** and **Honeycrisp Gold.**[186]
- select certified organic or locally grown apples. Industrially grown apples are regularly ranked as having more pesticide residues than almost any other fruit or vegetable.[187] The Environmental Working Group included industrially produced apples in its 2016 Dirty Dozen, ranking them the second most contaminated fruit or vegetable of fifty foods ranked. Eating organic and locally produced apples makes it possible to eat the skin, which contains the greatest concentration of pesticide content in industrially produced apples. These apples have the other benefits of naturally produced food, an important one being more potent phytonutrients and overall higher nutritional content.

To store apples,

- refrigerate apples to slow ripening. Refrigerated apples store well for many weeks while apples stored at room temperature quite quickly become overripe.
- refrigerate apples tightly covered.

    - Tight covering protects apples from dehydration.
    - Tight covering protects ethylene gas sensitive vegetables and fruits from the ethylene gas given off by apples. Ethylene gas causes carrot flavor to become bitter and changes the color of leafy green vegetables to yellow; it also speeds the ripening of kiwi fruit.

- consume apples relatively quickly. While most refrigerated apples will retain attractive crispness and flavor for several weeks and even longer, invisible nutritional and flavor loss occurs during storage. Freshly picked apples have significantly more nutritional content and flavor than apples stored for a long period.

---

186 Ibid., 217. Robinson presents a chart comparing the phytonutrient content of a variety of modern commonly sold apples with wild ancestors, illustrating the stark contrast between modern apple varieties and their wild ancestors.
187 Ibid., 228. In areas where a fungal disease called apple scab commonly attacks trees, apples are treated with fungicides up to fifteen times a year. Farm workers are exposed to the pesticides and fungicides used.

PART 1

75. Apricot
(2 servings)

4 ripe apricots

Preparation Tool

5 in. serrated knife

1. **Thoroughly rinse and dry the apricots.**

2. **Cut the apricots into chunks for use in a salad or dessert.** Use a serrated knife to halve the apricots lengthwise. Remove the pit, slice the halves lengthwise into ⅓ in. thick strips, and cut the strips crosswise into ⅓ in. cubes.

3. **Serve the apricots halved or whole.** For halves, slice each apricot lengthwise and remove the pit. For serving whole, simply include a container for discarded pits.

Apricot Profile

Apricots stand out as especially nutritious fruits. Less altered from their wild ancestral form than most other fruits, apricots retain rich phytonutrients, including carotenoids (especially beta carotene) and flavonoids. Apricots also contain nutrient antioxidants, including vitamin C, that combine with antioxidant phytonutrients to intensify the antioxidant capacity of apricots.[188] Apricots also contain anti-inflammatory phytonutrients and are a good source of vitamin E, which combines with phytonutrients to boost the anti-inflammatory protection provided humans. The overall high mineral content of apricots makes them among the best alkaline balancing fruits.

To select the most flavorful apricots,

- select ripe apricots that are plump and heavy feeling, tight-skinned, uniformly firm, and have very little pale yellow coloring. The center should yield slightly to gentle pressure. Selecting ripe or nearly ripe apricots helps protect against selecting fruit that has been spoiled by chilling injury.
- select nearly ripe apricots. As apricots continue to ripen after they are harvested, home-ripening successfully ripens immature apricots. After purchasing apricots, carefully examine the apricot and refrigerate only fully ripe apricots. Set aside any immature ones for home-ripening. Place immature apricots within a closed paper bag and store them at room temperature, checking them daily, until they are fully ripe.

---

188 Ibid., 283. They typically have from three to eight times more phytonutrients than peaches or nectarines.

- purchase apricots in midsummer. This is the height of their growing season in the United States, which is when apricots are most likely to be ripe and, hence, most flavorful and nutritious.
- seek out the most flavorful varieties. This is important since many marketed apricot varieties have been selected for transportation durability and other commercial needs rather than for flavor or tenderness due to the vulnerability of apricots to chilling injury. A reliably outstanding apricot selection is **Blenheim apricots**, which are known for their flavor and delicate texture. Farmers' markets, local producers, and natural food stores are sources of these and other flavorful apricot selections.

To select apricots with the greatest phytonutrient content,

- select apricots with the darkest orange flesh. The deeper orange the flesh, the greater the beta-carotene content.
- select red-fleshed apricots as the most nutritious of all apricots.

To store ripe apricots,

- store fully ripe apricots that will be quickly eaten at room temperature for 1-2 days.
- treat apricots as fragile fruit during refrigeration. Refrigerate them covered, using Robinson's vented plastic bag method (with 20 uniformly placed pin-pricked holes; pressing out as much air as possible before sealing the bag and storing the apricots in the crisper drawer).
- thoroughly chill room temperature apricots before covering them tightly to avoid having condensation form on the apricots during storage.
- use apricots quickly, within 3 days, to preserve the nutrients, flavor, and texture.

76. Avocado
(2 servings)

1 chilled ripe avocado
2 T cold orange juice

1 T cold water

Preparation Tools

1 small mixing bowl
1 set measuring spoons
1 5 in. serrated knife

1 small glass storage container with a lid
1 rubber spatula
1 colander

PART 1

1. **Wash and dry the avocado.** Rinse the avocado with cold water and thoroughly dry it with a paper or terry cloth towel.

2. **Prepare a citrus wash.** Combine 2 T cold orange juice and 1 T cold water in a small mixing bowl.

3. **Remove the pit and peel the avocado.**

   - Use a serrated knife to halve the avocado lengthwise, circling all the way around the avocado to cut open the front and back, cutting through to the avocado stone.
   - To separate the flesh of one half from the stone, grab hold of each half with one hand and twist the halves in opposite directions.
   - Refrigerate the avocado half with the stone, first dipping the exposed top flesh into the citrus wash to coat the cut surface. Re-refrigerate this half in a small air-tight glass container.
   - Working with the avocado half without the stone, use the serrated knife to halve the avocado lengthwise. Use your fingers to loosen the edge of the skin at the top of each slice of avocado, grasp the loosened edge with your fingers, and gently pull the skin downward to peel the avocado.

4. **Cut the avocado into serving size pieces.**

   - Cut the half to be served lengthwise into 1/3 in. thick slices. Cut the slices crosswise into ⅓ in. chunks, adding them to the citrus wash and using a rubber spatula to swish the pieces in the wash as they are cut.
   - Drain the pieces in a colander and then evenly spread the pieces over a double thickness of paper towels.
   - Refrigerate the prepared avocado if it will not be served immediately.

VARIATION: Make ingredient substitutions. Substitute, for example,

- **an oil coating** for citrus wash. Begin with 1 t extra virgin olive oil and add touches more as needed. Add the oil to a small mixing bowl, add the cut avocado pieces, and use a rubber spatula to turn the avocado pieces over and over in the oil for thorough coating.
- **1 T fresh lemon juice** for 1 T water in the citrus wash. Lemon juice increases the effectiveness of the rinse for a longer period, but it is important to measure the lemon content to ensure it does not make the pieces sour.

COMMENTS: It is very important to carefully peel the skin from an avocado in order to maximize retention of the dark green flesh that is just beneath the skin. This layer contains the greatest concentration of carotenoid phytonutrients in the avocado.[189]

---

[189] Mateljan, *The World's Healthiest Foods*, 2nd edition, 135. This method is what the California Avocado Commission calls the "pick and peel" method.

Avocado Profile

Avocado has outstanding nutritional characteristics. Avocado, for example,

- has rich and varied carotenoid phytonutrients.[190] Additionally, avocado contains monounsaturated fat called oleic acid, which maximizes human absorption of the valuable fat-soluble phytonutrients that provide antioxidant protection to humans. The oleic acid enhances human absorption of avocado's fat-soluble nutrients, including vitamins E and K, as well. Quite amazingly, when avocado is eaten with other foods that contain fat-soluble phytonutrients and nutrients, avocado's oleic acid content dramatically increases human absorption of the fat-soluble nutrients contained in the foods.[191]
- is a good source of antioxidant nutrients, including vitamins C and E and the mineral manganese, which combine with antioxidant phytonutrients to intensify the antioxidant protection provided to humans by avocado.
- is an outstanding source of soluble fiber and a good source of omega-3 essential fatty acids and B complex vitamins, and of folate and B6 in particular.
- is an overall good source of minerals, and is also slightly alkaline, which distinguishes it from most all other fruits except for banana.

To select the most flavorful avocado,

- select ripe avocado. To identify ripe avocado, select one that is heavy-feeling with a top that feels soft and with a middle that yields slightly when gently pressed (a very soft middle, however, indicates over ripeness). Its pit should be anchored tightly in the flesh. Its upper half should not have dents, which indicates bruising and, as a result, spoiled flesh. The skin of the most commonly available Hass variety of avocado will be nearly black.
- select a nearly ripe avocado. As avocado continues to ripen after it is harvested, home-ripen a green avocado to full ripeness. Place it within a paper bag (including a banana or apple for fast ripening) and check it daily until it is ripe.
- select in-season avocado. In-season for California avocados is during the spring and summer. Florida avocados are in-season in October. In the fall and winter several different varieties of avocado are in-season.

To store a ripe avocado,

- refrigerate a whole ripe avocado uncovered on a refrigerator shelf.
- refrigerate a cut avocado with the pit attached, if possible. Coat the cut pulp with lemon, lime, or orange juice to deactivate enzymes that otherwise will cause browning. Refrigerate the avocado in a small glass storage bowl with an air-tight lid.

---

190 Robinson, *Eating on the Wild Side*, 206. For example, one serving of avocado contributes more antioxidants than a serving of broccoli raab, grapes, red bell pepper or red cabbage.

191 Ibid., 206. The oleic acid fat of avocado added to a salad increases the amount of beta carotene and lutein absorbed from greens by as much as 1500 percent.

- use avocado quickly (within one or two days) to maximize retention of its flavor and nutritional content.

77. Banana
(2 servings)

2 ripe bananas
2 T cold orange or pineapple juice
1 T cold water

Preparation Tools

3 small serving plates
1 set measuring spoons
1 medium mixing bowl
1 paring knife
1 colander
1 dinner plate

1. **Rinse and dry the bananas.** Rinsing removes the risk of transferring chemicals and bacteria on the banana skin into the banana flesh, either by cutting with a knife or during handling of raw banana.

2. **Serve the bananas whole.** Simply provide an extra serving plate for discarding the peel, tips, and strings.

3. **Cut the bananas into slices for serving with a dip or topping.**

   - Pre-chill the bananas before cutting.
   - Prepare a citrus wash. Combine 2 T cold orange or pineapple juice and 1 T cold water in a medium mixing bowl.
   - Just prior to serving, peel the bananas. Use a paring knife to cut partly through the stem end, grasp the banana tip between your thumb and the flat side of the knife, and pull down the skin. Cut out any brown areas, discard any banana with a dark or slimy center (center flesh should look the same as other banana flesh except for a few seeds which show up as dark spots), remove any strings, and cut the bananas crosswise into ½ in. thick slices.
   - Add the slices to, and swish them thoroughly in, the citrus rinse.
   - Drain the banana slices in a colander placed over a dinner plate for collecting any draining citrus rinse. Spread the banana slices over a layer of paper towels for drying. Drink or save any collected citrus wash liquid for another use.

   VARIATION: Add **1 T fresh lemon juice** to enhance the effectiveness of the citrus rinse in preventing browning during serving.

Banana Profile

While the Cavendish banana, which is the favorite and dominantly marketed American variety of banana, has low phytonutrient content in comparison to most other fruits and other varieties of bananas, the Cavendish banana does have several outstanding nutritional characteristics.

- The Cavendish banana, like bananas in general, is a source of a variety of carotenoid phytonutrients, which provide antioxidant protection for humans. Additionally, banana contains antioxidant nutrients, including vitamin C and manganese, which combine with the phytonutrients to intensify the antioxidant protection provided to humans.
- A rich source of potassium in particular but of minerals in general, the Cavendish banana, like other varieties of banana, stands out as an alkaline fruit, which distinguishes bananas from almost all other fruits. This means bananas are not acid forming when consumed by humans. This characteristic makes them an important acid-balancing food for maintaining a natural pH balance in humans and, as a result, for avoiding demineralization.
- The Cavendish banana is a good source of both soluble and insoluble fiber. Its soluble fiber content includes pectins and fructan fibers. The fructan fibers are prebiotic, which means they feed and encourage the growth of good bacteria living in the human large intestine (or gut). Fructan fibers are long enough to survive the length of the intestinal tract and to reach the colon, where they are fermented by bacteria and converted into human health-promoting form.
- The Cavendish banana is also a good source of B complex vitamins, and of vitamin B6 in particular.

To select the most flavorful bananas,

- select ripe and unbruised bananas. A ripe banana is uniformly firm and does not have brown spots, which indicate aging. An unbruised banana should not have any dented areas. The peel should be a mix of green and yellow, with yellow color slightly predominating and with the banana ends and side ridges retaining greenish color. The banana should yield slightly to gentle pressure. A banana with hard flesh is under-ripe and will have a chalky taste and texture if not ripened before being eaten.
- select partially green bananas. Because bananas continue to ripen after being harvested, partially green bananas can be home-ripened to full ripeness and, hence, full flavor. Store them within a closed paper bag at room temperature. Check them daily for ripening and once they are ripe, immediately refrigerate them. Include an apple with the banana to speed ripening.
- select room temperature bananas. Remove bananas from refrigerator storage in time for them to reach room temperature before serving.

PART 1

To select the most nutritious bananas,

- select red bananas, which have phytonutrient-indicating salmon-colored flesh.
- select baby bananas, or Lady Finger bananas, which have phytonutrient-indicating deep yellow-colored flesh.
- select plantains.

To store bananas,

- immediately refrigerate ripe bananas on a refrigerator shelf. Though the skins will darken, refrigeration retains vitamin content and delays over-ripening. Refrigeration retains peak banana flavor for several, even many, days.
- cover bananas once they become chilled in order to protect vegetables and fruits sensitive to ethylene gas that banana releases during storage. This gas speeds the ripening of many fruits, harms the flavor of carrots, and yellows green leafy vegetables. Bananas speed ripening so efficiently that they are usefully stored with immature fruits during home ripening.

78. Blueberries
(2 servings)

½-1 c ripe blueberries

Preparation Tools

1 colander   2 6-oz clear glass bowls
1 pie plate

---

1. **Clean the blueberries.** Add the berries to a colander and rinse them under cool running water, gently tossing the berries to rinse the surface of all berries. Spread the berries in a pie plate lined with a double thickness of paper towels. Sort through them to remove stems and spoiled or broken open berries. Wrap the towels around the berries and gently roll the berries around within the towels to dry them.

2. **Serve the berries.** Divide the berries between 2 small serving bowls that attractively display the blueberries.

Blueberry Profile

Raw blueberries stand out as extraordinarily nutritious fruit.

- While modern plant breeding has reduced nutritional content in comparison to wild blueberry ancestors, blueberries retain significant phytonutrient content.[192]
- Blueberry pigment indicates concentrated anthocyanin content, which consists of phytonutrients that act as especially potent antioxidants when consumed by humans.
- Blueberries contain a variety of carotenoid phytonutrients, which function as antioxidants.
- Blueberries also contain antioxidant nutrients, including vitamins C and E content and the mineral manganese, which combine with antioxidant phytonutrients to intensify the antioxidant protection provided humans by blueberries.
- Blueberries are a good source of both soluble and insoluble fiber and particularly of insoluble fiber. They are a good source of omega-3 essential fatty acids and vitamin K.

Select the most flavorful and nutritious blueberries. Select, for example,

- very fresh ripe berries that are in good physical condition. Berries should be uniformly firm and plump. They should not show any sign of wilting or have any white mold. They should also not have any sign of bruising, as indicated by leaking juice on the package bottom, and should have few, if any, small or partially green unripe berries.
- in-season berries, which are the freshest berries. They are also most likely to be ripe berries, which have the greatest nutritional value. In-season for blueberries in the United States is from May through October.
- berries marketed at farmers' markets and natural food stores, which are likely to be the freshest of all in-season berries. These markets also likely carry a variety of blueberry products, including especially flavorful and nutritious varieties.
- certified organic blueberries. The Environmental Working Group ranked domestic industrially produced blueberries among the most contaminated with pesticides foods on its 2016 list, ranking it #14 of 50 foods. Certified organic blueberries, in contrast, have essentially no (or substantially reduced) pesticide content and have the other benefits of natural production, including more potent phytonutrient content and greater overall nutritional value than industrially produced blueberries.[193]

To store blueberries,

- refrigerate blueberries unwashed within their packing container in the crisper drawer, first removing any spoiled berries. Wash them just prior to eating them to retain the natural waxy coating (called the bloom) of blueberries that conserves

---

[192] Robinson, *Eating on the Wild Side*, 244-456. Blueberries contain both antioxidants and anthocyanins that are being linked with an ever- expanding list of human health-promoting capacities. Blueberry phytonutrient content, for example, shows promise in treating Alzheimer's disease, in reversing age-related mental decline, reducing the risk of cardiovascular disease, and in preventing diabetes.

[193] Mateljan, *The Healthiest Foods in the World*, 2nd Edition, 506. Mateljan reports that a recent study comparing the total antioxidant capacity of organically grown blueberries with non-organically grown blueberries found that the organically grown blueberries had significantly higher total antioxidant capacity.

juiciness and protects them from bacterial attack during storage.
- store berries that are not completely ripe at room temperature within a paper bag to ripen them. Check them every day and immediately refrigerate them once they become ripe.
- store blueberries briefly. Eat them quickly, within 3 days after purchase to maintain top flavor and nutritional quality.
- dry freeze extra blueberries to keep them on hand after the berry season is over. See Reference #2 (Key Home Storage Guidelines for Conserving Vegetable and Fruit Quality), Storage Guideline #7, for dry-freezing details. Research shows that dry freezing with immediate thawing (such as microwave thawing) results in minimal loss of antioxidant, including anthocyanin, phytonutrients.[194]

79. Blackberries
(2 servings)

½-1 c ripe blackberries

Preparation Tools

1 colander   2 6-oz clear glass bowls
1 pie plate

1. **Clean the blackberries.** Add the berries to a colander and rinse them under cool running water, gently tossing the berries to reach all berries. Spread the berries in a pie plate lined with a double thickness of paper towels and sort through them to remove stems and spoiled or broken open berries. Wrap the towels around the berries and very gently roll the berries around within the towels to dry them.

2. **Serve the berries.** Divide the berries between 2 small serving bowls that attractively display the blackberries.

Blackberry Profile

Raw blackberries stand out as special snack, salad, dessert, and pancake topping ingredients. Providing attractive color, distinctive sweet and tart flavoring, and significant nutritional boosting as well, blackberries greatly enhance dish attractiveness. Though expensive, a very few (1-3 berries per serving) raw blackberries provide outstanding flavoring in salads and fruit desserts.

---

194   Ibid., 503.

Blackberries stand out as extraordinarily nutritious fruit. Blackberries contribute essentially the same outstanding antioxidant content as blueberries, but blackberries also contribute super potent anthocyanin phytonutrients, which provide especially valuable antioxidant protection for humans. Dark black color – the highest ranked color in the phytonutrient nutritional hierarchy – indicates this rich anthocyanin content. Blackberries also contribute a stand-out amount of fiber, being one of the top ten food sources of fiber.[195] Loganberries, boysenberries, and marionberries are man-made variations of blackberries that are even more nutritious than blackberries, with marionberries having the highest antioxidant value.

To select the most flavorful blackberries,

- select the freshest berries. Select shiny, bright-colored berries that are uniformly firm and plump. The berries should be in good physical condition without any sign of wilting or white mold. Packages should not have any sign of bruised berries, as indicated by leaking juice on the package bottom.
- select in-season berries, which are the freshest berries with the greatest nutritional value. In the United States in-season is from May through October.
- seek out especially tasty and nutritious blackberry varieties.
- select certified organic and locally produced blackberries whenever they are an option. In addition to having significantly less pesticide residue than counterpart industrially produced blackberries, certified organic and locally produced berries have the other advantages of naturally produced food, an important one being more potent phytonutrient content.

To store blackberries,

- immediately refrigerate unwashed blackberries in their packing container, placing them in the crisper drawer.
- store blackberries for a short time only as they spoil and lose nutritional value quickly.
- dry freeze blackberries to keep them on hand beyond the blackberry season. Reference #2 (Key Home Storage Guideline for Conserving Vegetable and Fruit Quality), Storage Guideline #7, provides nutrient-conserving dry-freezing techniques.

80. Cantaloupe
(2-8 servings)

1 ripe cantaloupe

---

195 Robinson, *Eating on the Wild Side*, 251.

PART 1

Preparation Tools

1 vegetable brush
1 each chef's & 5 in. serrated knife

2 large dinner spoons
2 dessert plates or bowls

1. **Prepare the cantaloupe for cutting.**

   - Thoroughly scrub the cantaloupe with a brush under running water. This washing removes any bacteria and chemical residue on the skin that can be transferred to the melon flesh during cutting and handling. Do not use soap or detergent because cantaloupe is highly porous and will absorb residues.
   - Dry the cantaloupe with paper towels.

2. **Serve cantaloupe halves.** Use a chef's knife to halve a cantaloupe lengthwise. Use a large dinner spoon to scrape out and discard the seeds and membrane from the center of each half. Serve each half on a dessert plate with a large dinner spoon.

3. **Serve cantaloupe slices.** Use a chef's knife to cut each cleaned out cantaloupe half lengthwise into 1 in. thick slices (7-8 slices per half).

4. **Serve cantaloupe chunks.**

   - Working on a clean cutting board and using two or three 1 in. thick slices of cantaloupe, make crosswise slits on each slice, making the slits one inch apart and being very careful to cut to but not through the skin.
   - Using a serrated knife and being careful not to include any green rind, slice the cantaloupe from the rind, holding the cantaloupe slice in place with one hand during the cutting.
   - Add the melon chunks to a small glass container (such as a 6 oz custard bowl or ramekin).
   - Serve the melon with a dessert fork or toothpick.

5. **Serve cantaloupe balls.** Use a **melon ball tool** to cut each melon half into balls, moving from the top of one side to the other side. Serve 6-8 balls per 6 oz glass container (or to taste).

6. **Refrigerate extra cut cantaloupe in a glass container tightly covered.** To retain prime flavor for several days, store cut cantaloupe in a manner that keeps it from contact with its own juice and air. For example, place a small upside down bowl at the bottom of the storage container.

Cantaloupe Profile

Cantaloupe, the technically correct name for which is muskmelon, is a highly nutritious fruit.

- Cantaloupe has rich phytonutrient content and notably varied carotenoid phytonutrients, which provides both antioxidant and anti-inflammatory protection for humans. Additionally, cantaloupe is a good source of antioxidant nutrients, including vitamin C in particular but also the minerals manganese and selenium, which combine with the phytonutrients to intensify the antioxidant protection provided humans. Cantaloupe is also a good source of magnesium, which combines with phytonutrients to expand the anti-inflammatory protection provided to humans.
- Cantaloupe has outstanding carotenoid beta-carotene content, which humans convert into vitamin A.
- Cantaloupe contains a broad spectrum of nutritional content that covers nearly every category of nutritional components. Cantaloupe, for example, is a good source of most B complex vitamins, alkaline minerals (and potassium in particular), vitamin K, and fiber.

To select the most flavorful and nutritious cantaloupe,

- select fully ripe cantaloupe, which is the most flavorful cantaloupe. Ripe cantaloupe also has greatest phytonutrient content and is least acidic. A ripe melon is heavy feeling for its size, which is a good indication of juiciness. Its skin is predominantly pale yellow in color but retains some green color within the netted texture. The melon has a slightly dented stem end that exudes a sweet but slightly musky fragrance and does not have any trace of mold, which indicates age. No stem should remain, which would indicate the melon was likely picked green and will not ripen fully before spoiling. The end opposite the stem end should give slightly when pressed. When cut open, the flesh should be soft and uniformly bright orange in color, not hard and pale, which indicates the melon is still green, or very dark orange in color, which indicates over-ripeness.
- select melon that is in good physical condition. It should not have any soft, sunken areas, which indicate bruising or over-ripeness.
- select a nearly ripe cantaloupe and home ripen it. As cantaloupe continues to ripen after it is harvested, slightly green cantaloupe can be successfully home-ripened. To do so, store the cantaloupe in a closed bag at room temperature, checking it daily, until ripe. Adding an ethylene producing ripe banana speeds ripening.
- select a cantaloupe with dark orange flesh, which indicates high carotenoid content. As skin color does not indicate the color of the inside flesh, selecting a melon that is marketed cut in half is a way to determine color.
- select in-season cantaloupe. California has two harvests, one in June and another in October and November. Farmers markets market newly harvested cantaloupe in mid-August and early fall.
- select certified organic and locally grown cantaloupe. The Environmental Working

Group ranks industrially produced cantaloupe #37 of 50 foods on its 2016 listing of vegetables and fruits most contaminated with pesticides. Certified organic and locally grown cantaloupe, in contrast, are largely free of pesticides and have the other advantages of naturally grown food, important ones being more potent phytonutrient content and greater overall nutritional content. Reference #1 (Selecting Top Quality Fresh Whole Vegetables and Fruits) details the other benefits of naturally produced produce.

To store cantaloupe,

- scrub, dry, and refrigerate a whole cantaloupe on a refrigerator shelf.
- transfer a thoroughly cooled melon to a sealed plastic bag. Covering is necessary because cantaloupe melons give off ethylene gas, which damages the flavor and color of some vegetables and fruits and makes cantaloupe an unpleasantly smelly refrigerator occupant.
- store cantaloupe for a short time, ideally no longer than four days or so, because cantaloupe melons are most flavorful right after harvesting.

81. Bing or Dark Sweet Cherries
(2 servings)

2 c chilled cherries with stems

Preparation Tools

1 colander   2 small bowls or 6 oz ramekins
1 pie plate

---

1. **Wash the cherries.** Add the cherries to a colander and rinse them with cold water. Gently toss the cherries, turning them over and over, to thoroughly rinse all cherries.

2. **Dry the cherries.** Spread the cherries in a pie plate lined with a double thickness of paper towels and sort through them to remove stems and spoiled or broken open cherries. Wrap the towels around the cherries and gently roll the cherries around within the towels to dry them.

3. **Serve the cherries in small individual bowls.** Include a small separate container for holding pits.

Cherry Profile

Bing and other dark sweet cherries stand out as highly nutritious foods. Dark red coloring announces rich phytonutrient content, which includes varied antioxidants, including the super potent anthocyanins. The super sweet and especially tasty but light-colored Rainier cherries are much less nutritious than Bing cherries, having only one fourth the antioxidant value.[196]

To maximize selection of the most flavorful cherries,

- select dark-colored and shiny cherries that are uniformly firm, heavy feeling, and do not have any bruised or broken open areas.
- select cherries with bright green and flexible, not brown and stiff, stems, which are indicators of freshness.
- select in-season cherries, which are the freshest cherries with the best flavor and greatest nutritional content. Bing cherries are in-season from early May to late June.
- select certified organic cherries. The Environmental Working Group includes industrially produced cherries in its 2016 Dirty Dozen list of most contaminated vegetables and fruits, ranking it #7.
- select imported rather than domestically grown cherries since imported varieties have significantly less pesticide content than cherries grown in the US.[197]

To store cherries,

- quickly refrigerate cherries, uncovered and unwashed. Treat cherries to be stored as fragile fruit. Once they are thoroughly cooled, wrap them in paper towels and store them using the Robinson vented bag method (10 evenly spaced pin pricks per quart-size bag; 20 evenly spaced pin pricks per gallon-size bag; press out as much air as possible before sealing the bag; store the bag in the crisper drawer).
- serve only berries that will be eaten immediately, leaving remaining berries refrigerated.
- wash cherries as they are served.
- serve cherries quickly to retain the rich phytonutrient content. Cherries have a high respiration rate and quickly start to lose phytonutrient content (and, as a result, antioxidant value) as soon as they are picked.

82. Grapefruit
(2 servings)

1 grapefruit

---

196 Robinson, *Eating on the Wild Side*, 288-90. Robinson describes some known research findings about the health value of the phytonutrient content of cherries.
197 Ibid., 290.

PART 1

Preparation Tools

1 3-5 in. serrated knife
2 serving bowls
2 grapefruit spoons (pointed spoons with serrated edges)

1 cutting board reserved for fruit
2 dinner plates
2 dessert bowls & small dinner spoons

---

1. **Rinse and dry the grapefruit.**

2. **To serve grapefruit separated into segments,** a simple way of serving that maximizes conservation of grapefruit flesh, juice, and membrane:

   - Remove the grapefruit peel. Slice off the tip of one end to make an opening for beginning hand peeling.
   - Pull apart the grapefruit segments.
   - Use a paring knife to make a small slit in the top of a slice for pushing out any seeds.

3. **To serve grapefruit halves,** which is the easiest if least conserving manner of serving grapefruit:

   - Use a serrated knife to halve the grapefruit crosswise. Place each half in an individual serving bowl.
   - Use the point of a knife to pry seeds gently from the halves.
   - Rotating around a grapefruit half, use a serrated knife to cut the flesh in each segment from the membrane separating segments, cutting close to the membrane.
   - Again rotating around a grapefruit half, use the serrated knife to cut the grapefruit flesh from the grapefruit peel. Cut close to the skin to include as much grapefruit flesh as possible but be careful to not include any bitter grapefruit skin.
   - Serve the grapefruit halves with grapefruit spoons, which very efficiently scrape out flesh. Grapefruit spoons also work to collect juice squeezed from the grapefruit half.

4. **To serve cut grapefruit slices,** a serving method that maximizes conservation of the fiber rich grapefruit membrane:

   - Halve the grapefruit lengthwise.
   - Place each half cut side up on a cutting board. Use a serrated knife to make a wedge cut on either side of the pulpy membrane that runs lengthwise through the center of each grapefruit half and lift out the pulpy center.
   - Use the knife point to pry out exposed seeds gently from the grapefruit.
   - Cut each half lengthwise into 5 or 6 slices, tipping the grapefruit as needed to place the surface to be cut directly on the cutting board.
   - Arrange the slices on a plate, using slices of ½ grapefruit per serving. Serve an additional small plate for collecting skins.

5. **To serve grapefruit chunks**, a serving method that also maximizes conservation of the fiber-rich grapefruit membrane:

    - Cut a grapefruit into slices, as above.
    - Use a serrated knife to make crosswise slits every ½ in. on each grapefruit slice, being very careful to cut just to but not through the skin.
    - Including as much flesh as possible without including any peel, use the serrated knife to slice the flesh from the skin of slices.
    - Add the chunks to a small glass serving bowl (such as a 6 oz custard bowl or ramekin), ½ grapefruit per bowl.
    - Serve the grapefruit with spoons.

Grapefruit Profile

Grapefruit makes notable nutritional contributions.

- Grapefruit has standout phytonutrient content, containing a variety of both carotenoid and flavonoid phytonutrients, both of which provide antioxidant protection to humans.
- Pink and red grapefruit has rich lycopene content, a carotene phytonutrient that has particularly potent antioxidant capacity.
- Grapefruit is an excellent source of vitamin C. Along with numerous other ways of contributing to human health, vitamin C serves as an antioxidant nutrient that combines with phytonutrient antioxidants to intensify the antioxidant protection provided to humans.
- Grapefruit has rich beta-carotene content, which the human body converts into vitamin A.
- Grapefruit makes at least a small contribution in nearly every category of nutritional components. It is, for example, a source of both soluble and insoluble fiber and of soluble fiber in particular. It is a source of most B complex vitamins and alkaline minerals; it is also a good source of potassium.

A distinctive characteristic of grapefruit is that it interacts with particular medicines. It interacts with these medicines (both over-the-counter and prescription) in a way that increases the amount of medicine that enters the bloodstream and, hence, may increase the severity of potential negative side effects linked with the medicine. Medications affected include those for lowering cholesterol, reducing blood pressure, calming anxiety, and reducing the risk of the organ transplant rejection.

Select the most flavorful and nutritious grapefruit. Select, for example,

- fully ripe grapefruit. A grapefruit should be large and feel heavy for its size, which indicates juiciness. The grapefruit should be uniformly firm without any flattened

or caved in area, which indicates bruising. Its skin should be tight (it should spring back when pressed) and smooth, not wrinkled, which indicates dehydration.
- grapefruit that has skin with a reddish blush for red-fleshed grapefruit; select grapefruit that has yellowish skin, not greenish-yellow skin, for white grapefruit.
- in-season grapefruit, which in the United States is mid-December through March. In-season fruit is the ripest fruit and, as a result, the sweetest and most nutritious fruit.
- red and pink-fleshed grapefruit, which is sweeter than white grapefruit. Red-fleshed grapefruit also has significantly higher anthocyanins and richer phytonutrient content than paler-colored grapefruit. The darker the red coloring, the more concentrated the phytonutrient content.
- grapefruit from a batch that does not have uniformly colored skin. Uniform coloring is an indication the grapefruit has been degreened (picked immature and chemically treated to look ripe and sweet but remains unripened) in the case of commercially produced grapefruit.
- certified organic and locally grown grapefruit. The Environmental Working Group ranks grapefruit #38 in its 2016 list of the fifty industrially produced vegetables and fruits most contaminated with pesticides. Certified organic and locally grown grapefruit, in contrast, have significantly reduced pesticide content, and these products have the other advantages of naturally produced fruit, important ones being more potent phytonutrient content and greater overall nutritional content.

To store grapefruit,

- store grapefruit that will be eaten within a week out of sunlight at room temperature.
- refrigerate grapefruit that will be stored for more than a week. Store them uncovered in the crisper drawer or on a refrigerator shelf until they are thoroughly chilled and then transfer them to a sealed plastic bag to protect them from dehydration.
- use grapefruit within 10 days for the greatest nutritional value. Though refrigerated grapefruit stores well for a longer period, grapefruit nutritional quality diminishes with storage.

83. Red or Green Seedless Grapes
(2 servings)

approx. 40 chilled medium red or green seedless grapes (or 20 each)

Preparation Tools

1 colander
1 pie plate

1 serrated knife
2 small serving bowls

1. **Rinse the grapes.** Add the grapes to a colander and rinse them under cold running water. Turn the grapes over several times to rinse all surfaces.

2. **Inspect the grapes.** Pour the grapes into a pie plate lined with a double thickness of paper towels and sort through the grapes, discarding any attached stems and spoiled, soft, or broken open grapes. Replace discarded grapes.

3. **Dry the grapes.** Wrap the towels around the grapes and gently roll the grapes around within the towels to dry them. Use a serrated knife to slice off any brown ends from grapes.

4. **To serve the grapes whole,** divide the grapes between 2 small individual serving bowls.

   VARIATION: Substitute **grapes with seeds**. To remove the seeds, use a serrated knife to halve the grapes lengthwise and use the point of a paring knife to pry seeds gently from grape halves. Serve the grapes with a tooth pick or salad fork. To serve the grapes whole, serve the grapes with a container for holding seeds.

Grape Profile

Grapes have significant nutritional value.

- Grapes supply humans with a rich supply of antioxidant phytonutrients that help protect them from free radical damage, also called oxidative stress. In particular these phytonutrients include a variety of carotenoid phytonutrients. Additionally, grapes contain a wealth of antioxidant nutrients, including vitamins C and E and the mineral manganese, that combine with phytonutrients to intensify the antioxidant protection provided to humans. This protection appears to apply to the brain.
- Grapes also have phytonutrients that provide anti-inflammatory protection to humans.
- The magnesium content of grapes works with these phytonutrients to intensify the anti-inflammatory protection provided.
- Other phytonutrients in grapes have anti-microbial properties that benefit the human intestinal system.
- Grape skin and seeds contain the greatest concentration of phytonutrients contained in grapes, with the seeds of grapes containing omega-3 essential fatty acids. The grape skin is also a good source of insoluble fiber, with the flesh contributing soluble fiber.
- Grapes are a source of nearly every category of nutritional component. This content, for example, includes B complex vitamins (especially good B2 but excluding B12),

very good vitamin K content, good overall alkaline mineral content (especially good potassium), and iron.

Select the most flavorful and nutritious grapes. Select, for example,

- fresh grapes. Grapes should be plump, uniformly firm, unbroken, brightly colored, and attached to bright green and flexible stems. Most grapes should remain attached to a branch when it is gently shaken.
- in-season grapes. For North American varieties of grapes, in-season is September and October. European grape varieties are available throughout most of the year.
- certified organic and locally grown grapes.

    - Industrial producers pick grapes before they are ripe. As grapes do not ripen after they are picked, they remain firm and tart. The flavor of organic grapes ripened on the vine is markedly superior.
    - The Environmental Working Group includes industrially grown grapes in its 2016 Dirty Dozen list of vegetables and fruits most contaminated with pesticides, ranking it 6th most contaminated.
    - In addition to spraying during production, most conventionally grown grapes are also chemically treated after harvesting. They are commonly fumigated twice with sulfur dioxide gas to prevent spoiling and to preserve the appearance of freshness. Because ripe grapes are fragile, industrially produced grapes are typically sprayed with gibberellic acid. This spraying, which is called gibbing, makes grapes longer and sturdier, increasing grape size by as much as 75 percent.[198]

- select red and black grapes. These colored grapes are more nutritious than pale green Thompson seedless grapes, which have far lower phytonutrient (antioxidant) content. Concord grapes have both outstanding flavor and nutritional value.

To store grapes,

- quickly refrigerate grapes unwashed in the vented marketing packaging within which they are purchased as grapes stored at room temperature quickly spoil. Wash grapes as they are used as thorough drying of washed grapes is difficult and clinging moisture hastens spoilage.
- quickly refrigerate unpackaged grapes loosely wrapped within a strip of paper towels within a partially opened plastic bag.
- use grapes within 5 days to retain the best flavor and greatest nutritional value.

---

198 Robinson, *Eating on the Wild Side*, 307.

84. Guava
(2 servings)

2 ripe guavas

Preparation Tools

2 small dinner spoons
2 small serving plates

1 5 in. serrated knife
1 cutting board reserved for fruit

---

1. **Rinse and thoroughly dry the guavas.**

2. **Serve the guava in a variety of ways.**

    - **Serve a guava whole.** Eat it like an apple, eating the skin and seeds, which are edible and nutritious.
    - **Serve a guava halved crosswise and use a spoon to scoop out flesh.**
    - **Cut it into slices.** Use a serrated knife to halve the guava lengthwise, put each half cut side down on a cutting board, and slice each half lengthwise into ⅓ in. wide slices. Divide the slices between two small plates.

Guava Profile

Guava stands out as a highly nutritious fruit.

- More nutritious than most other tropical fruits (including banana, mangoes, papaya, and pineapple), guava has high phytonutrient content, including rich antioxidant phytonutrient content that provides antioxidant protection to humans.
- Guava has significantly greater vitamin C content than orange.[199] In addition to the many other ways vitamin C contributes to human health, it serves as an antioxidant nutrient that combines with antioxidant phytonutrients to intensify the antioxidant protection provided to humans by guava.
- Guava, and notably the skin, has an especially high fiber content.
- Guava seeds are edible and nutritious.

To select the most flavorful and nutritious guava,

- select fresh and fully ripe guava. A guava should be heavy-feeling, aromatic, and have flesh that feels soft when pressed gently. The softer the flesh, the sweeter it is. Skin should be uniformly smooth without any soft spots, dents, or blemishes, which

---

[199] Ibid., 354. One cup of guava has four times more vitamin C than an orange.

indicate bruising and poor flavor. Skin color of white-fleshed guava should be a yellowish-green, not bright green color, which indicates under-ripeness. In white-fleshed guava, a touch of pink in flesh indicates peak ripeness.

- select a green guava and home-ripen it. Store it in a closed paper bag at room temperature, check it daily for ripeness, and immediately refrigerate it once it is ripe. Store it with an ethylene gas-producing ripe banana to speed ripening.
- select red-fleshed guava, which has significantly greater phytonutrient content than white-fleshed guava.

To store guava,

- refrigerate it uncovered in the crisper drawer. Eat it within a week, using very soft guava within two days.

85. Honeydew Melon
(2 servings)
(four 1 in. thick slices per serving)

1 chilled ripe honeydew melon

Preparation Tools

1 each chef's & 5 in. serrated knife
1 large dinner spoon
1 cutting board reserved for fruit

2 small serving bowls
2 dessert forks or toothpicks

1. **Wash and dry the melon.** Thoroughly scrub the melon with a brush under running water and dry it with paper towels. Though the skin is discarded, rinsing at the start of preparation prevents bacteria and chemicals that may be on the skin from being transferred to the melon flesh during cutting and handling.

2. **Cut the melon into serving-size chunks.**

    - Use a chef's knife to halve the melon lengthwise.
    - Use a large dinner spoon to scrape out and discard the seeds and membrane from the center of the half being served. Leave the seeds and membrane in the extra half and re-refrigerate it within a sealed gallon size plastic zippered storage bag, pushing out as much air as possible before sealing.
    - Use the chef's knife to cut the melon half lengthwise into 1 in. thick slices (approx. 8 slices).

- Working on a cutting board reserved for fruit, use a 5 in. serrated knife to make a crosswise slit every ½-¾ inch in each slice, being careful to cut to but not through the peel. Cutting close to the rind to include as much flesh as possible but without including any rind, slice the melon flesh from the rind.
- Evenly divide the chunks between two small bowls (such as 6 oz custard bowls or ramekins) for serving. Serve the chunks with either a dessert fork or toothpick.

3. **To serve melon balls**, use a melon ball tool to cut one melon half into balls. Begin at one end of the half and move crosswise from the top of one side to the other.

4. **To store cut melon,**

- refrigerate the melon in a glass storage container in a manner that keeps the melon dry (not in contact with any spilled juice). For example, place a small upside down bowl in the bottom of the storage container.
- cover the glass storage bowl with either a lid or plastic wrap. The melon will keep for up to two weeks while remaining handy for use as a snack or dessert.

VARIATION: Include a small slice of fresh lime with each serving to be squeezed over the melon.

Honeydew Melon Profile

Honeydew melon is the sweetest of all melons and serves as a special treat.

To select the most flavorful and nutritious honeydew melon,

- select a ripe melon. This is a melon that feels heavy for its size and has cream-colored skin without any green color. The stem end should be fragrant and yield when gently pressed with your thumb, but it should not be soft and mushy, which indicates over-ripeness. The opposite end, the blossom end, should feel slightly soft and spring back when pressed. Skin overall should have some give; it should not be rock hard.
- When cut open, the flesh should be firm and juicy, not hard and dry, which indicates under-ripeness.
- select a slightly green honeydew melon and home-ripen it. Store it within a paper bag at room temperature, check for ripeness daily, and either immediately eat or refrigerate the melon once it is ripe.
- select orange-fleshed varieties, which are honeydew melons crossed with cantaloupe that have high beta-carotene content, which is a phytonutrient that the human body converts into vitamin A. Beta-carotene also provides antioxidant protection to humans.
- select certified organic and locally grown honeydew melon. The Environmental

Working Group includes honeydew melon in its 2016 list of vegetables and fruits most contaminated with pesticides, ranking it #39 out of 50 foods. Certified organic and locally grown honeydew melon, in contrast, are largely free of pesticide content and have the other advantages of naturally produced fruits, particularly that they contain more potent phytonutrients and greater overall nutritional value.

To store ripe whole honeydew melon,

- refrigerate the melon on a refrigerator shelf. Once it is thoroughly chilled, transfer it to a sealed plastic bag, pressing out as much air as possible before sealing the bag.
- use the melon within 4-7 days of purchase.

86. Kiwi
(2 servings)

2 ripe kiwis

Preparation Tools

1 dish sponge with a rough side	1 cutting board
1 5 in. serrated knife	2 small serving bowls
2 small dinner spoons	2 dessert forks or toothpicks

1. **Thoroughly rinse and dry the kiwi.**

2. **Serve kiwi halves.** Use a 5 in. serrated knife to halve each fruit crosswise and serve a small spoon with each half for scooping out the fruit.

3. **Serve kiwi chunks.**

   - Use the rough side of a dish sponge to gently rub off some of the brown fuzz from the kiwifruit skin. As the skin also provides nutritional benefits, it can also be left undisturbed.
   - Use a serrated knife to slice off the very top and bottom of each kiwi and, working on a cutting board, cut each fruit crosswise into ½ in. thick slices.
   - Quarter the slices.
   - Divide the chunks between two small custard bowls or ramekins.
   - Serve each serving of kiwifruit with a dessert fork or toothpick.

Kiwi Profile

Kiwi, also called kiwifruit, has outstanding flavoring capacity for use in dishes.

- Kiwi contributes distinctively attractive emerald green coloring to fruit and vegetable salads and to desserts.
- Kiwi contributes distinctively sweet/tart flavoring to fruit salads and desserts.

Kiwi makes notable nutritional contributions when used alone as a snack or as a dish ingredient.

- Kiwi is an excellent source of a variety of antioxidant phytonutrients, including both carotenoid and flavonoid phytonutrients.
- Compared to other fruits, kiwi has outstanding vitamin C content. In addition to the innumerable other valuable ways vitamin C aids human health, such as in enhancing human absorption of iron, vitamin C serves as an antioxidant nutrient that combines with other antioxidant nutrients contained by kiwi, including vitamin E and manganese, and with phytonutrients to intensify the antioxidant capacity of kiwis to protect humans from oxidative stress (free radical destruction).
- Kiwi is a source of a wide spectrum of nutritional components. Kiwi, for example, is an excellent source of vitamin K, a very good source of fiber, a good source of folate, and its high overall mineral content makes kiwi included among the most alkaline-balancing fruits.
- Kiwi seeds and skin are edible and make significant nutritional contributions. Both, for example, contribute fiber, and the seeds contribute some omega-3 fatty acids (ALA form).

Kiwi has distinctive enzyme content. This enzyme, actinidoin, dissolves and liquefies protein and, accordingly, affects how kiwifruit should be mixed with other ingredients. Because of this enzyme content,

- raw kiwi is unsuitable for use in gelatin fruit salads. Gelatin will not set with raw kiwi added. Brief stir-frying of kiwi chunks in 1-2 T orange juice overcomes this problem.
- cut kiwi should only be mixed with other fruits as a last ingredient shortly before serving. Acting as a food tenderizer, its enzyme content affects fruits when mixed with them for more than a short time, softening them and causing them to become unattractively soggy.
- kiwi should also not be mixed with milk and milk products for any length of time. Two methods – brief stir-frying of kiwi before adding it to a milk-based dish or addition of kiwi to milk-based dishes (such as a pudding topping) very close to serving – can be used to overcome this mixing problem.

To select the most flavorful and nutritious kiwi,

- select fully ripe fruit. This is fruit that is heavy-feeling and is uniformly firm

without soft areas. Flesh should give slightly when gently squeezed between your thumb and forefinger.
- select immature kiwi and home-ripen it. Store it at room temperature within a closed paper bag, check it daily, and either eat it or refrigerate it once it is ripe. Because kiwifruit is very sensitive to ethylene gas and will quickly become over-ripe when exposed to it, only very cautiously include an ethylene gas producing fruit (such as apple or banana) to speed ripening. When kiwi becomes ripe, either serve it or refrigerate it.
- select in-season kiwi. For California kiwi, in-season is from November through May. New Zealand kiwi is in-season from June through October.
- select certified organic kiwi. The Environmental Working Group includes industrially produced kiwi in its 2016 list of vegetables and fruits most contaminated with pesticides, ranking them #41 of 50 foods. Certified organic kiwi, in contrast, is largely free of pesticide content, which clears the way for eating the nutritious skin. Certified organic kiwi has additional advantages of naturally produced food, particularly more potent phytonutrient content and greater overall nutritional value.

To store kiwi,

- do not allow kiwi to sit in direct sunlight, but kiwi that will be used within a few days can be stored at room temperature.
- refrigerate kiwi that will not be used within a day or two. Once the kiwi is completely cool, transfer it to a sealed bag. Do not allow it to become lost in the refrigerator. Tight covering is necessary to protect ripe kiwi from rapid over-ripening should it be exposed to ethylene gas-producing vegetables and fruits during storage.
- use kiwi within 5 days of purchase to retain its flavor and nutritional value.
- dry freeze thickly sliced kiwi to store kiwi that cannot be quickly eaten. Reference #2 (Key Home Storage Guidelines for Conserving Vegetable and Fruit Quality), Storage Guideline #7, presents dry freezing details.

87. Mango
(2 servings; 1 mango per serving)

2 ripe mangoes (any variety)

Preparation Tools

1 5 in. serrated knife
1 swivel peeler
1 cutting board reserved for fruit
2 small serving plates

2 dessert forks
2 small glass bowls
2 small dinner spoons

1. **Thoroughly rinse and dry the mangoes.**

2. **Cut the mangoes into thin strips for serving.**

    - Use a serrated knife to slice off the ends of each mango to reveal the seed (pit or stone).
    - Use a swivel peeler to remove the mango skin.
    - Stand the mango upright on the flattened bottom and slice the fruit lengthwise from each of the flat sides of the seed, closely following the curve of the seed.
    - Turn the mango sideways and slice off the remaining smaller pieces of fruit from the sides, about two strips per side.
    - Place the cut fruit on a cutting board and cut the fruit lengthwise into ½ in. wide by 2-3 in. long strips.
    - Serve the slices on a small plate with dinner forks, one mango per serving.

3. **Cut the mangoes into small cubes.**

    - Slice off a thin slice to flatten one bottom of each mango, stand an unpeeled mango upright on this flattened end, and slice the fruit lengthwise from both flat sides of the seed, closely following the curve of the seed.
    - Placing each slice flesh side up and being careful not to cut through the skin, score the flesh every ½ inch, cutting both lengthwise and crosswise. Push each mango slice inside out so that the scored mango cubes protrude.
    - Cutting close to the skin, slice off the mango cubes.
    - Serve the cubes in a small glass bowl with dessert forks, 1 mango per serving.

4. **Serve mango halves.**

    - Cut crosswise across the middle of an unpeeled mango, cutting to the stone and cutting all around the stone.
    - Holding one half in each hand, twist the mango halves in opposite directions until at least one half separates from the stone.
    - If necessary, use a sharp slicing knife to cut around the pit to remove the remaining half. While holding the mango half, pull out the pit.
    - Serve each half in a small bowl with a small dinner spoon for use as a scoop for eating the mango.

    COMMENTS: In addition to being easy to prepare and tasty snacks, cut mango pieces are ideal salad and dessert ingredients, using ½ mango per salad. Covered and refrigerated, cut mango pieces store well. They can be prepared as long as several hours ahead of serving.

Mango Profile

Mango stands out as an especially tasty and phytonutrient rich fruit. A juicy ripe mango is nearly incomparably delicious. Mango stands out as one of the richest sources of beta-carotene, a member of the carotenoid family of phytonutrients, which the human body converts into vitamin A and which serves as an antioxidant. Mango with dark orange flesh contains the richest beta-carotene content. Mango is a good source of both soluble and insoluble fiber, and especially of soluble fiber.

To select the most flavorful and nutritious mango,

- select a fully ripe mango. A ripe mango should have a pleasant aroma and uniform firmness. Mango flesh should yield to gently applied pressure. Redness, in those varieties having a red blush, is not a good indicator of ripeness. Some varieties are ripe when even solid green.
- select semi-ripe mango and home-ripen it. As mango continues to ripen after it is harvested, a semi-ripe mango can easily be home-ripened to perfection. To do so, store it in a covered paper bag at room temperature, check it daily, and either promptly eat it or refrigerate it once it is ripe. Include an ethylene gas-producing ripe apple or banana to speed ripening.
- select certified organic mango. The Environmental Working Group includes industrially produced mango in its 2016 list of vegetables and fruits that are most contaminated with pesticides, ranking it #43 of 50 foods. Certified organic mango, in contrast, is largely free of pesticide content and has the other advantages of naturally produced fruit, an important one being significantly more potent phytonutrient content. Reference #1 (Selecting Top Quality Fresh Whole Vegetables and Fruits) details other advantages of certified organic fruit in comparison to industrially produced fruit.
- select mangoes marketed at South and Southeast Asian and Hispanic markets, which are likely to carry a larger variety of mangoes than the quite commonly marketed Alphonso (turns dark gold when ripe), Tommy Atkin (large green with red blush), and champagne (large peach size; pale gold in color; less fibrous) mangoes.

To store ripe mango, refrigerate it in the crisper drawer, uncovered, until it is thoroughly chilled and then transfer it to a loosely closed plastic bag.

88. Nectarine
(2 servings)

2 ripe nectarines

Preparation Tools

1 small bowl for collecting pits
1 cutting board reserved for fruit
1 each chef's & 5 in. serrated knife

2 serving bowls
2 dessert forks

1. **Thoroughly rinse and dry the nectarines.**

2. **Serve the fruit whole.** Serve the nectarines untrimmed with a small container for the pit.

3. **Serve the nectarines cut into slices.**

    - Place a nectarine on its side on a cutting board.
    - Use a chef's knife to cut the nectarine lengthwise (end to end) into ¼ in. thick slices, cutting through to the pit and rocking the knife back and forth while cutting from end to end. Rotate around the nectarine until it is sliced completely.
    - If the nectarine is free stone and slices detach easily from the stone, let the slices fall onto a layer of plastic wrap as they are cut.
    - If the nectarine is not free stone and the slices cling to the stone, cut off the slices.
    - Serve the slices, 1 nectarine per serving, as a snack or dessert, serving the slices in two serving bowls with dessert forks.

4. **Cut nectarines into chunks for serving.**

    - Cut the nectarines into slices as above.
    - Cut each slice crosswise into 3 equal pieces.
    - Serve the chunks in two bowls with dessert spoons, 1 nectarine per bowl.
    - Serve the chunks as a snack, dessert, salad ingredient, or pancake topping, ½ nectarine per serving.

    VARIATION: For cut nectarine pieces that will be stored for some time (an hour or more) or served exposed to air for some time, coat the slices with a **citrus wash** to slow browning. Add 2 T cold orange juice and 1 T cold water to a medium bowl, add and swish the cut nectarine pieces in the rinse, drain them in a colander, and spread the pieces over a paper towel to dry them.

Nectarine Profile

Nectarine stands out as an especially attractive fruit selection. Sweet and juicy, nectarine is a delicious snack. Colorful and tender, it lifts the attractiveness of any salad, fruit dessert, and pancake. Nectarine shares this special flavoring status with peach, with which it is identical except for type of skin. Nectarine skin is smooth instead of fuzzy like peach skin.

Nectarine has notable nutritional content.

- Nectarine is a rich source of phytonutrients that provide antioxidant protection for humans.

- Nectarine skin is a good source of both soluble and insoluble fiber. Nectarine skin's soluble fiber content includes valuable fructan fibers. These fibers are long enough to survive passage through the human digestive system and reach the big intestine, where they are fermented by good bacteria into human health-supporting form.
- Nectarine and peach share the identical nutritional profile.

Select the most flavorful and nutritious nectarine. Select, for example,

- fully ripe nectarine, which is both the most flavorful and nutritious nectarine. A ripe nectarine is aromatic fruit with flesh that feels soft overall and gives slightly when gently squeezed.

    - A red blush does not indicate ripeness.
    - Selecting ripe or nearly ripe nectarine is the best way to avoid selection of nectarine damaged by chilling injury (CI) during storage before or during marketing. As a stone fruit (fruit containing one large pit), nectarine is vulnerable to chilling injury, which effectively spoils the flesh or blocks the nectarine from becoming fully ripe.

- nearly ripe nectarine (fruit that already shows some signs of softening). As nectarine continues to ripen after being harvested, it (except for those damaged by chilling injury) can be purchased in nearly ripe form and be home-ripened to fully ripened form. To do so, store the fruit at room temperature within a closed paper bag, check it daily until it is ripe, and either immediately serve it or refrigerate it.
- in-season nectarine, which is when it is most likely to be ripe. In-season for California nectarines is from August through the first half of September. Locally produced nectarines from Florida and Georgia are in-season in June and July.
- locally grown nectarine, which is most likely the freshest and picked ripe nectarine. As it is the industrial practice of picking nectarine early and shipping it for a long distance that makes it vulnerable to chilling injury, locally grown nectarine is also least likely to have chilling injury. Farmers' markets, U-pick farms, and natural food stores that market locally grown produce may very likely also carry a selection of different varieties of nectarine.
- certified organic nectarine. The Environmental Working Group includes industrially produced nectarine in its 2016 Dirty Dozen list, ranking it the 3rd most contaminated with pesticides out of 50 foods. Rinsing removes little of this pesticide content while certified organic nectarine, in contrast, is substantially free of pesticide contamination. Selection of certified organic nectarines clears the way for eating the highly nutritious nectarine skin. Certified organic nectarine also has the other benefits of naturally produced food, an important one being more potent phytonutrient content than counterpart industrially produced nectarine.
- white-fleshed nectarine, which is sweeter and has significantly higher content of the phytonutrient beta-carotene than yellow-fleshed nectarine. Nectarine is an exception to the "select most colorful fruit" rule.
- red-fleshed nectarine. Containing the richest phytonutrient content, red-fleshed nectarine is the most nutritious of all nectarine selections.

To store nectarine,

- refrigerate nectarine loosely covered (within a slightly open plastic bag) in the crisper drawer to protect it from dehydration.
- use nectarine within a week or so of purchase. While nectarine can appear to store well, its flavor and nutritional quality diminishes during storage.

89. Orange
(2 servings)

3 flavorful oranges (any variety of orange, medium size)

Preparation Tools

1 5 in. serrated & 1 paring knife
1 cutting board reserved for fruit
2 dinner plates

2 small glass bowls
2 small dinner spoons

1. **Rinse and dry the oranges.**

2. **Serve orange slices.** This method of serving is the easiest and most reliable way to serve oranges successfully (see comments below).

   - Use a serrated knife to halve the oranges lengthwise and place each half cut side up on a cutting board.
   - Make a wedge cut on either side of the pulpy membrane that runs lengthwise through the center of each orange half and lift out and discard the pulpy center.
   - Use the point of a paring knife to gently pry out any exposed seeds from the orange.
   - Use a serrated knife to cut each half lengthwise into 5 or 6 slices.
   - Arrange the slices on a plate, 1½ orange per serving.
   - Serve with an additional plate for collecting empty skins.

3. **Serve orange chunks.** Though extra preparation is involved, orange chunks make perfect salad and dessert ingredients.

   - Slice the oranges as above.
   - Use a serrated knife to make 3 or 4 equally spaced crosswise slits on each slice, being very careful to cut to but not through the skins.
   - Slice off as much flesh (including pith in the case of navel oranges) as possible without including any peel, adding the chunks to 2 small glass serving bowls (such as a 6 oz custard bowl or ramekin) as they are cut.
   - Serve orange chunks, 1½ orange per serving, with a spoon.

COMMENTS: Serving orange slices is a way of serving oranges that has three important advantages in addition to almost guaranteeing serving success. 1) Slicing oranges uses maximum amount of the nutritious orange flesh[200] and pith when navel oranges are eaten. 2) The technique of removing the pulpy center makes it easy to remove seeds. 3) Easy removal of seeds makes tasty but seedy and typically less expensive oranges, such as temple oranges, as well as seedy oranges that are especially sweet and rich in carotenoid phytonutrients, such as Valencia oranges, easy to use orange choices.

Orange Profile

Orange stands out as a special fruit. Without any adornment whatsoever an orange serves as a delicious and satisfying snack. An orange is also an outstanding salad and dessert ingredient, lifting simple dishes into elegant fare.

Orange is a highly nutritious fruit.

- Orange has rich and varied phytonutrient content, containing more than 170 individual phytonutrients. This content includes a variety of carotenoid phytonutrients and rich content of a human health-promoting flavonoid phytonutrient called hesperidin. All of these phytonutrients work together to provide outstanding antioxidant protection for humans. Additionally, orange is a rich source of vitamin C, which also serves as a powerful antioxidant. It combines with phytonutrients to intensify the antioxidant capacity of orange.
- The overall high mineral content of orange includes it among the most alkaline balancing fruits.
- Orange is a very good source of both insoluble and soluble fiber.

Select the most flavorful orange. Select, for example,

- fully ripe oranges, which are sweetest, most nutritious, and lowest in acid. A ripe orange should be uniformly firm and heavy-feeling for its size, traits that indicate juiciness. An industrially produced orange should not be from a batch of uniformly orange-colored oranges, which likely indicates degreening (chemically treated to look ripe but in fact remaining immature).
- the largest oranges in a batch, which have been on the trees the longest time and, as a result, are more likely to be ripe.[201]
- in-season oranges.

    - In the United States, in-season for commonly marketed oranges is mid-December through March. Oranges picked earlier in the season before they are

---

200 Robinson, *Eating on the Wild Side*, 332. Robinson reports that new research shows that orange flesh (or pulp) contains a number of phytonutrients that have antioxidant, antibacterial, antiviral, anti-inflammatory, and antiallergenic properties.
201 Robinson, *Eating on the Wild Side*, 325.

fully ripe, as is the case of many industrially produced oranges, never do become fully ripe. This is because oranges (like citrus fruit in general) do not ripen further after they are harvested. Consumers, as a result, cannot home-ripen any variety of orange that is picked before it is ripe.
- In-season for the Valencia and blood orange varieties of orange is from March through May.

- oranges grown by small producers, such as producers selling oranges at local markets and natural food stores. This fruit is most likely to be naturally ripe. It is most likely not degreened since degreening is an expensive process.
- oranges that are in good physical condition. They should not have any soft or dented areas, which indicate bruising that undermines flavor. They should have intact protective skin that has not been punctured.
- navel orange, which stands out as an especially nutritious variety of orange.

  - Also called the Washington navel, the navel orange has very high phytonutrient content.
  - The pith (or albedo), the thick layer of spongy white tissue that lines the inside of navel orange skin, has outstanding nutritional value. The pith contains the greatest concentration of phytonutrients (a variety of phytonutrients called flavanones) of a navel orange, and the pith is also rich in fiber (pectin).

- varieties of orange with red-colored flesh, which are the most nutritious of all oranges. Red-colored flesh indicates especially rich content of the phytonutrient lypocene. Select, for example,

  - Cara Cara orange, which has deep rose-colored flesh. Lypocene content gives Cara Cara oranges significantly more antioxidant activity than varieties of orange that do have red flesh.
  - blood orange, which has flesh with color ranging between pinkish orange and deep red. The red color of blood orange indicates high anthocyanin content.

- certified organic and locally grown orange.

  - Certified organic orange is guaranteed not to have been degreened. In addition to avoiding the chemical manipulation involved in degreening, certified organic orange is picked ripe and is, as a result, more flavorful than degreened orange, which never fully ripens or develops full nutritional value.
  - The Environmental Working Group includes industrially produced orange in its 2016 list of the fifty vegetables and fruits most contaminated with pesticides, ranking orange #31. Certified organic and locally produced oranges, in contrast, are largely (or substantially) free of pesticides. Certified organic and locally grown oranges have the other advantages of naturally produced produce, particularly that they contain more potent phytonutrient content and overall greater nutritional value than counterpart industrially produced produce.

- Selection of certified organic and locally grown orange makes it possible to use the orange zest, the outside colored layer of the skin, which adds flavor and phytonutrient content to dishes. The zest of industrially produced orange, in contrast, should be avoided due to the heavy load of pesticide it carries.

To store oranges,

- store oranges that will be eaten within 5 days at room temperature.
- immediately refrigerate oranges that will not be used within 5 days. Refrigerate them uncovered in the crisper drawer until they are thoroughly cooled and then transfer them to a sealed plastic bag to protect them from dehydration.
- convert oranges that cannot be used relatively quickly (a month) into juice, making only an amount of juice that can be immediately consumed and incorporating as much pulp into the juice as possible.

90. Clementine and Mandarin Orange
(2 servings)

4 clementine or mandarin oranges

Preparation Tools

1 5 in. serrated knife
1 serving plate

2 small glass bowls
2 small dinner spoons

1. **Rinse and dry the oranges.**

2. **Serve clementine or mandarin oranges whole and unpeeled.** For easy to peel oranges, simply provide a container for collecting the peeled skin and any seeds. For somewhat difficult to penetrate oranges, use a serrated knife to slice off a bit of the very top or bottom of each orange to create an opening in which to begin peeling.

3. **Serve oranges separated into segments.** This simple method of serving especially suits seedless oranges, such as clementine oranges. For segments with seeds, use a paring knife to make a small slit in the flesh and gently press seeds from the pulp.

4. **Serve sliced oranges.** This method of serving especially suits seedy oranges, such as mandarins. In this method seeds are easy to remove, which encourages use of these especially tasty and nutritious varieties of orange.

- Use a serrated knife to halve the oranges lengthwise and place each half cut side up on a cutting board.
- Make a wedge cut on either side of the pulpy membrane that runs lengthwise through the center of each orange half and lift out the pulpy center.
- Use the point of a paring knife to gently pry out any exposed seeds from the orange.
- Use a serrated knife to cut each half lengthwise into four slices.
- Arrange the slices on a plate, two oranges per serving.
- Serve an additional plate for collecting empty skins.

5. **Serve orange chunks.** Cut oranges into chunks for use in salads and fruit desserts. Because of the small size of clementine and mandarin orange segments, it is important to use a very sharp knife to minimize spilling of juice during cutting.

    - Slice the oranges as above.
    - Use a serrated knife to make one crosswise slit in the middle of each slice, being very careful to cut to but not through the skins.
    - Slice off as much flesh as possible without including any peel, adding the chunks to a small glass serving bowl (such as a 6 oz custard bowl or ramekin) as they are cut.
    - For serving orange chunks in a dessert or salad, cut the fruit immediately before serving when possible. If preparing them somewhat ahead of serving, set the chunks aside in a dry manner, as within a colander, so that they do not sit in juice.

    VARIATION: Substitute other members of the mandarin family of citrus fruit for mandarin or lementine oranges, such as **Satsuma orange, tangerine,** or **tangelo**.

Mandarin and Clementine Orange Profile

Mandarin and clementine oranges stand out as special snacks and salad and fruit dessert ingredients. Simple to peel and delicious without any adornment whatsoever, these fruits are outstanding snacks. The brilliant color (especially in the case of mandarin oranges), tanginess, and juiciness of these oranges combine to lift the attractiveness of any salad or fruit dessert. The only essential difference between these two small-sized varieties of orange is that clementine oranges are seedless while mandarin oranges have seeds.

To select the most flavorful mandarin and clementine oranges,

- select the freshest and ripest produce. Select fruit that is uniformly firm (does not have any soft or flattened areas) and is heavy-feeling for its size, which indicates juiciness. The skin should be taut and brightly colored, not dull, dry, shriveled, or punctured. When opened, individual segments should be plump and very juicy.
- in-season oranges. In the United States this is January through March. In-season oranges are sweetest, least acidic, and most nutritious.

PART 1

To store mandarin and clementine oranges,

- refrigerate them in the crisper drawer in a loosely closed plastic bag.
- use them before they become soft, which can be several weeks.

91. Papaya
(2 servings)

1 ripe papaya (approx. 7 in. long, 1 pound), chilled

Preparation Tools

1 each chef's, paring, & serrated knife 2 small bowls
1 large dinner spoon 2 dessert forks
2 dinner plates

1. **Rinse and dry the papaya.**

2. **Serve papaya halves.**

   - Use a chef's knife to halve the papaya lengthwise.
   - Use a large dinner spoon to scrape out the seeds and membrane from the center of each half.
   - Cut out and discard any dark colored overripe or bruised flesh.
   - Serve the papaya as a snack or dessert, serving each cleaned half on a dinner plate with a large dinner spoon for scooping out the flesh.

3. **Serve papaya chunks.**

   - Halve and clean out the center of each half as above.
   - Slice off the pointed tip of the stem end and the bottom tip of each cleaned half.
   - Use a chef's knife to cut each papaya half lengthwise into ⅓ in. thick slices.
   - Use a serrated knife to make a crosswise slit every ⅓ in. of each slice, being careful to avoid cutting through the skin.
   - Working on a clean cutting board, slice flesh from the slices. Lightly holding one hand flat down on a papaya slice to hold the pieces in place during the cutting and carefully avoiding including any of the inedible skin during cutting, slice the flesh of each papaya slice from the skin.
   - Serve the chunks as a snack or dessert, serving one half papaya per serving in two bowls with dessert forks.

VARIATIONS: Serve the papaya with a small wedge of fresh lime or lemon that can be squeezed over the papaya pieces to taste.

Save, rinse, dry, and use the seeds, which are nutritious, containing the same oil as olive oil and phytonutrients as well. While somewhat bitter, papaya seeds can be added fresh to salads or salad dressings. They can also be dried and ground like pepper. Rinse and dry the seeds by spreading them over paper towels.

Papaya Profile

Papaya is a tasty and nutritious tropical fruit. The variety of papaya that is most commonly marketed in the United States is the spherical-shaped Solo papaya.

- Papaya is a rich source of antioxidant phytonutrients, including carotenoids and flavonoids, as is indicated by the golden color of its flesh. Research indicates that the carotenoid content of papaya may be more easily absorbed by humans than from other sources.
- Papaya is a rich source of vitamin C. Among the many ways vitamin C supports human health, it combines with the phytonutrients to intensify the antioxidant protection provided to humans by papaya.
- Papaya is a rich source of the carotenoid beta-carotene, which serves as a source of vitamin A and provides antioxidant protection for humans. Papaya is also a rich source of the carotenoid lycopene, the valuable human health-promoting phytonutrient commonly associated with tomato.
- Papaya is also a good source of minerals (potassium, calcium, and magnesium) and B-complex vitamins (particularly folate), except for B12.
- Papaya is a good source of fiber and of soluble fiber in particular.

Papaya has two distinguishing characteristics.

- Papaya has a very low glycemic index rating. This means that eating papaya barely causes human blood sugar levels to rise.
- Papaya contains two enzymes, papain and chymopapain, that help digest protein. Because this enzyme content prevents gelatins from setting, papaya should not be included in gelatin salads and desserts.

To select the most flavorful and nutritious papaya,

- select a fully ripe papaya. This is a papaya that is heavy feeling for its size, uniformly firm, and has skin that is largely yellow or orange-yellow with some intermingled green coloration. The skin can have some brown freckles. The rounded end should give slightly when gently pressed, but the stem end should be firm. A ripe papaya should also be aromatic, especially at the stem end.

PART 1

- select papaya that is in good physical condition. It should not have any soft or brown spoiled areas. There should not be mold or mildew growing on the stem end, which indicates age.
- select in-season papaya. Papaya trees produce papaya throughout the year, but there is a slight seasonal peak in early summer and fall.
- select a partially ripe papaya (one that is fifty to seventy-five percent ripe). Because papayas continue to ripen after being harvested, they can be home-ripened to full ripeness within a few days. To home-ripen papaya, store it at room temperature within a closed paper bag, check it daily until it is uniformly bright yellow, and either immediately serve or refrigerate it. A ripe banana can be included to speed ripening.
- select red-fleshed papaya. While papaya in general has rich carotenoid content, red-fleshed papaya has significantly more carotenoids and lycopene.
- select certified organic and locally grown papaya.

    - Certified organic papaya has reliably not been genetically modified.
    - The Environmental Working Group includes papaya in its 2016 list of the 50 vegetables and fruits most contaminated with pesticides, including it as #42. Certified organic and locally grown papaya, in contrast, are substantially free of pesticides and have the other advantages of naturally produced produce, particularly more potent phytonutrient content and greater overall nutritional value than counterpart industrially produced papaya.

- select Maradol papaya, a Mexican and Central American variety of papaya that is reliably not genetically modified.[202]

To store papaya,

- refrigerate papaya uncovered. Once it is thoroughly chilled, place it in a sealed plastic bag to protect it from ethylene gas produced by some other vegetables and fruits, which negatively affects papaya flavor.
- use papaya within several days of purchase.

92. Peach
(2 servings)

2 ripe peaches

Preparation Tools

1 dish sponge with a rough side
1 5 in. serrated knife

2 small glass bowls
2 dessert forks

---

[202] Anthony William, *Medical Medium: Life-Changing Foods* (Carlsbad, California: Hay House, Inc, 2016): 111.

1. **Thoroughly rinse and dry the peaches.** Remove most of the fuzz on the skin by lightly rubbing the skin with the rough side of a dish sponge after rinsing.

2. **Serve peaches whole.** Serve the peaches with a container for the discarded pit.

3. **Serve the peaches sliced as a snack or dessert.**

    - Chill the peaches before cutting.
    - Place a peach on its side and use a serrated knife to cut it lengthwise into ⅓ in. slices, rocking the knife back and forth to cut completely from end to end.
    - Let slices of **free stone** peaches fall into a small glass bowl as they are cut. For peaches firmly attached to the pit, slide a knife blade under the cut slices to cut them free from the stone, cutting under several slices at a time and dropping the slices onto a glass bowl as they are cut.
    - Serve each bowl of sliced peaches with a dessert fork.

4. **Serve peach chunks as a snack or dessert.**

    - Cut ⅓ in. thick slices crosswise into three equal pieces, adding the chunks of each peach to a small glass serving bowl as they are cut.
    - Serve the peaches with dessert forks.

    VARIATION: For peach slices or chunks that will be stored for an hour or more or that will be served exposed to air for some time, coat the slices or chunks with a citrus wash to slow browning. Add 2 T cold orange juice and 1 T cold water to a medium bowl, add and swish the peach slices in the rinse, drain them in a colander, and spread the slices over a paper towel to dry them.

Peach Profile

Peach and nectarine are identical varieties of fruit except for having different skins. A peach has fuzzy skin while nectarine skin is smooth. Peach, like nectarine, stands out as an especially tasty fruit selection. Peach and nectarine share the same rich antioxidant phytonutrient content. As with nectarine, the overall mineral content of peach places it among the most alkaline-balancing fruits. For both peach and nectarine, the skin is one of the most nutritious parts.

To select the most flavorful and nutritious peach,

- select fully ripe peach. Select heavy-feeling, uniformly firm peaches that have flesh that feels soft overall and gives slightly when gently squeezed. In addition to being the best means for selecting flavorful peaches, selecting ripe peaches is the best

way of avoiding selection of peaches damaged by chilling injury. Because peach is a stone fruit (fruit with one large stone), it is highly vulnerable to chilling injury. This damage, which occurs during storage, effectively spoils peach flesh or blocks peaches from becoming fully ripe.
- select in-season peach. The peak season for most states is July. However, peaches can be ready as soon as May and may remain available as late as September.
- select nearly ripe fruit (fruit that shows signs of softening) and home-ripen it. Nearly ripe peaches are also most likely not damaged by chilling injury and can be successfully home ripened. To home-ripen peaches, store them at room temperature within a closed brown paper bag, check them daily until they are ripe, and then either eat them immediately or refrigerate them. Home-ripening provides the opportunity to ripen peaches to perfection, which makes them irresistibly delicious.
- select white-fleshed varieties of peach, which are sweeter and more nutritious than orange-fleshed varieties of peach. Peach is an exception to the "select most colorful fruit" rule as white-fleshed varieties of peach have significantly higher phytonutrient (beta-carotene) content than varieties of peach with yellow flesh.
- select red-fleshed varieties of peach as the most nutritious peach. Red-fleshed (sometimes called blood) peach has significantly higher antioxidant value than white-fleshed peach.
- select certified organic and locally produced peaches.

  - The Environmental Working Group includes industrially produced peaches in its Dirty Dozen list of vegetables and fruits most contaminated with pesticides, ranking them #4 of 50 foods. In selecting certified organic and locally grown peaches, consumers avoid consuming this heavy load of pesticides,[203] and they can safely eat the skin, which is a highly nutritious part of the peach. Certified organic and locally grown peach products also have the other advantages of naturally produced fruit, particularly more potent phytonutrient content and greater overall nutritional value in comparison to counterpart industrially produced peaches.[204]
  - Farmers' markets, U-pick farms, and natural food stores very likely provide a selection of different varieties of peach.

To store peaches,

- refrigerate peaches uncovered until they are thoroughly chilled and then refrigerate them loosely covered in a plastic bag. Alternatively, refrigerate them in a mainly closed plastic bag on a refrigerator shelf.
- eat peaches within a week of purchase for best flavor and texture and for greatest nutritional value.

---

203 Robinson, *Eating on the Wild Side*, 280. Robinson reports that a recent survey of peaches found that some individual peaches had traces of up to sixty-seven different chemicals.
204 Ibid., 280.

93. Pear
(2 servings)

2 chilled ripe pears (any juicy pear, such as Bartlett, Bosc, D'Anjou)

2 T cold orange juice
1 T cold water

Preparation Tools

1 set measuring spoons
1 medium mixing bowl
1 each chef's & paring knife
1 cutting board

1 colander
1 dinner plate
2 small serving plates or bowls
2 dessert forks

---

1. **Rinse and thoroughly dry the pears.**

2. **To serve the pears whole,** serve the pears with a container for holding the stem, seeds, and core.

3. **To serve pear slices,** prepare the pears shortly before serving.

    - Prepare a citrus rinse. Combine 2 T cold orange juice and 1 T cold water in a medium mixing bowl.
    - Use a chef's knife to halve the pears lengthwise.
    - Place the halves cut side down on a clean cutting board and use the chef's knife to cut each half lengthwise into ⅓ in. thick slices.
    - Use a paring knife to cut out the seedy/pulpy area from the slices, add the slices to the juice rinse as they are cut, and swish them in the juice to coat the cut surface completely.
    - Immediately drain the slices in a colander placed over a dinner plate (saving the juice for another use or to drink it), spread the slices over paper towels, and gently wrap the towels around the slices to dry them.
    - Serve the pear slices immediately or cover and refrigerate them.

4. **To serve pear chunks:**

    - Cut ⅓ in. thick slices crosswise into ½ in. thick chunks, adding the chunks to the citrus rinse as they are cut.
    - Swish the chunks in the wash, drain them in a colander placed over a dinner plate, spread them over a double thickness of paper towel, and wrap the towels around the chunks to dry them.
    - Divide the chunks into two small glass bowls, using 1 pear per serving. Serve the pear with dessert forks.

PART 1

VARIATIONS: Add **1 T fresh lemon juice** to the citrus rinse to extend the time the rinse prevents browning. This is a helpful step when using pear slices with a dip, but lemon can also easily sour pear.

Omit the **citrus rinse** when serving pear slices immediately after cutting.

Pear Profile

A fully ripe pear is truly a tasty treat. While the flavor and texture of different pear varieties – such as Bartlett, Red Bartlett, Anjou, Red Anjou, Comice, Bosc, and Asian pears – vary somewhat, ripeness is the key to tastiness for all varieties. A perfectly ripe pear of any variety is a delicious snack, salad and dessert ingredient, and pancake topping.

A fully ripe pear makes a notable nutritious contribution.

- Pear is a rich source of a variety of carotenoid phytonutrients, which provide antioxidant protection for humans. Pear also contains flavonoid phytonutrients that provide anti-inflammatory protection for humans. The pear skin contains a significant amount of the phytonutrients contained by pear, including both antioxidant and anti-inflammatory phytonutrients.
- Pear is a good source of vitamin C, which among its many human health-supporting functions serves as an antioxidant nutrient. It combines with other antioxidant nutrients, such as manganese, and antioxidant phytonutrients to intensify the antioxidant protection provided humans by pear.
- Pear, and particularly the pear skin, is a very good source of both insoluble and soluble fiber and of insoluble fiber in particular. Its soluble fiber content includes valuable fructan fibers. These fibers are long enough to survive passage through the human digestive system to reach the big intestine where they are fermented by good bacteria into human health-supporting form. One health-supporting function they perform is to bind with bile acids in the intestine, which has the effects of reducing the production of cholesterol by the body and of protecting the health of the stomach and intestine.
- The high overall mineral content of pear classes it among most alkaline balancing fruits.
- Pear is a good source of most other categories of nutritional components.

To select the most flavorful and nutritious pears,

- select fully ripe, but not overripe, pears. To determine ripeness, gauge ripeness differently from most other fruits. Because pears ripen from the inside out, it is the **stem end** (not the sides as in most fruits) of a ripe pear that should yield slightly when pressed gently. A uniformly soft pear is already overripe and has unattractively mushy texture.

- select immature pears (even pears that remain quite firm) and oversee the final ripening of them. Home-ripening is the most reliable way to get the tastiest pears. Store them within a closed paper sack at room temperature and check them daily for ripeness. Ripening can take several (even many) days. Adding an ethylene gas-producing ripe banana to the bag can speed ripening.
- select in-season pear. In-season varies somewhat with the different varieties of pear. Bartlett pears start arriving in late summer. Bosc and Comice follow shortly after in the fall and through winter. Anjou is a winter pear. There is a peak selection of pear varieties in October.
- select certified organic and locally grown pears. The Environmental Working Group includes pear in its 2016 list of vegetables and fruits most contaminated with pesticides, ranking it #22 of 50 foods. Certified organic and locally grown pear products, in contrast, have substantially less pesticide contamination and have the other advantages of naturally produced produce, particularly more potent phytonutrient content and overall greater nutritional value than counterpart industrially produced produce. Selecting certified organic and locally grown pear products also makes it safe for consumers to eat the highly nutritious pear skin.

To store pear,

- refrigerate it uncovered in the crisper drawer until it is thoroughly cooled and then transfer it to a sealed plastic bag.
- use ripe pear within 3 days of purchase to reliably prevent it from becoming overripe. Ripening continues during refrigeration, which quite quickly undermines pear texture and flavor.

94. Pineapple
(8 wedges; 1 wedge yields ½ c chunks)

1 ripe pineapple

Preparation Tools

1 each chef's & 5 in. serrated knife
1 cutting board reserved for fruit
2 dinner plates
2 dessert forks
1 colander

1 large dinner plate
2 dessert forks
1 large or medium glass storage bowl with a tight-fitting lid

1. **Twist off and discard the leafy stem top.** Place the pineapple on its side for easiest twisting.

2. **Rinse, scrub with a long-handled dish or vegetable brush, and dry the pineapple.** This scrubbing is important for preventing bacteria on the surface of the skin from being transferred to the pineapple flesh during cutting and handling.

3. **Cut pineapple wedges.**

   - Use a chef's knife to halve the pineapple lengthwise. Place each half cut side down on a clean cutting board, halve each half lengthwise, and halve each half to yield 4 equal wedges per pineapple half. Each wedge is ⅛ of the pineapple.
   - Working with one wedge at a time, slice off both ends from a wedge and place the wedge on a cut side. Cutting lengthwise (from end to end), slice off a ¾ in. wide strip of the wedge tip, enough to remove all hard core. Discard this piece of the pineapple wedge.
   - Stand the wedge on its skin side and while gently pressing one hand down on the top of the wedge to hold the pineapple firmly in place during cutting and being careful not to include skin or coarse pulp during cutting, use a serrated knife to slice the pineapple flesh from the skin.
   - Add the wedges to a dinner plate as they are cut.
   - Serve 1 cut pineapple wedge per plate, letting those being served use their fingers or a dessert fork to eat the pineapple.
   - Refrigerate extra wedges within a large storage bowl with a tight-fitting lid.

4. **Cut pineapple chunks.**

   - Cut two ⅛ pineapple wedges as in step #2 above.
   - Use a serrated knife to make a crosswise slit every ½ in. along each wedge, being careful to cut to but not through the skin.
   - Gently pressing one of your hands flat down on the pineapple wedge to hold the chunks in place during cutting, slice the pineapple flesh from the skin.
   - Add the pineapple chunks to a colander placed over a dinner plate as they are cut.
   - Use chunks from 1 wedge (approx. ½ c) per serving, serving the chunks in a small bowl (such as a 6 oz custard bowl) with dessert forks.

5. **Refrigerate extra cut pineapple in an air-tight glass container.** Place a small upside down bowl in the bottom of the container, one that covers the bowl bottom but that allows spilled juice to run into the bowl bottom and keeps wedges or chunks dry during storage. Tightly cover the bowl with plastic wrap. The pineapple will keep for as long as a week and throughout this time will be handy for use as a snack or dessert.

6. **Dry freeze extra cut pineapple that will not be eaten within a week.** Spread chunks over a freezer proof glass tray that fits within a refrigerator freezer (such as a pie plate or rectangular Pyrex baking dish), place the pineapple in a freezer, freeze the chunks until solid, and quickly transfer them to a good quality gallon size zippered freezer bag. Press out as much air as possible before sealing the bag. When using the pineapple, quickly thaw the chunks to maximize phytonutrient conservation, thawing them by microwave heating for 30 seconds.

VARIATIONS: Use a **pineapple peeler/corer** tool to remove the pineapple from the skin. Kitchen stores carry these tools. Cut the skinned pineapple crosswise into ½ in. thick slices. Cut pineapple slices into ½ in. thick slices.

Pineapple Profile

Pineapple is an exceptional flavoring ingredient. Though pineapple has only modest nutritional content in comparison to other fruit, it contributes invaluable tangy and sweet flavor to salads, stir fries, desserts, muffins, and pancake toppings. Its modest gyclemic response (eating pineapple causes a low rather than high rise in blood sugar content) despite its high sugar content enhances pineapple's usefulness as flavoring.

Pineapple has notable nutritional value.

- Pineapple is a source of beta-carotene, a carotenoid phytonutrient that provides antioxidant protection to the human body. Pineapple is also an excellent source of vitamin C and the mineral manganese, which are antioxidant nutrients that combine with carotenoid phytonutrients to intensify the antioxidant protection provided the human body by pineapple.
- Pineapple is a good source of dietary fiber and of B complex vitamins, and particularly of B1, B6, and folate.
- Pineapple's overall high mineral content places it among most alkaline balancing fruits.

Pineapple has distinctive enzyme content. Raw pineapple contains an enzyme (bromelain) that dissolves and liquefies protein. Raw pineapple, as a result, will keep gelatin from setting. Brief cooking, however, deactivates this enzyme and makes pineapple a safe gelatin ingredient. To briefly cook pineapple, stir-fry diced or thinly sliced pineapple in orange juice (2 T juice per ½-1 c diced pineapple) for 1 minute, adding the pineapple to the boiling juice; time the heating once the juice again boils; stir-fry the pineapple just until it is heated through, and drain the pineapple in a colander placed over a dinner plate for collecting any juice.

To select the most flavorful and nutritious pineapple,

- select a ripe pineapple. Select a pineapple with sides that yield slightly to gentle pressure. Look closely for soft brown spots, which indicate spoiled or over-ripe areas. The pineapple crown leaves should be fresh appearing, have deep green color, and be firmly attached. The stem end should give off a sweet fragrance. The pineapple should be mainly yellow in color but have touches of green intermingled with yellow throughout. The pineapple should also be uniformly colored without any large dark green areas, which indicate uneven ripening. When cut open, the flesh should look moist and juicy, not dry. Flesh should also be uniformly light yellow in color as

PART 1

opposed to being either a whitish color, which indicates un-ripeness, or dark yellow, which indicates over-ripeness. Do not select a nearly ripe pineapple as pineapples do not ripen after harvesting and, as a result, cannot be home-ripened.

- select in-season pineapple, which is when pineapple is most likely to be ripe. In-season is from March through June in the United States.
- select Del Monte Gold Extra Sweet, Hawaii Gold, and Maui Gold, which have higher beta-carotene and vitamin C content than the Cayenne pineapple, which has traditionally dominated the pineapple market.[205] These varieties of pineapples are reliably tasty varieties as well.
- select certified organic pineapple. The Environmental Working Group includes industrially produced pineapple in its 2016 list of vegetables and fruits that are most contaminated with pesticides, ranking it #48 out of 50 foods. Though this is a low ranking, certified organic pineapple, in contrast, is substantially free of pesticide residue and has the other advantages of naturally produced food, particularly more potent phytonutrient content and overall greater nutritional value than industrially grown pineapple.

To store a pineapple,

- leave a ripe pineapple that will quickly be eaten at room temperature, at which it is tastiest.
- refrigerate a whole pineapple to keep it for several days, leaving it uncovered and placing it on a refrigerator shelf.
- use pineapples quickly as they do not store well.
- cut a pineapple into chunks for longer storage. Refrigerate the chunks within a covered glass container that keeps them dry (as in recipe Step #5 above). The pineapple will keep for as long as two weeks and throughout this time will be handy for use as a snack, breakfast dish ingredient, or dessert.
- dry freeze pineapple chunks as directed in Step #6 of the pineapple recipe above.

95. Plum
(2 servings)

4 ripe red or purple plums (ca 2 in. diameter)

Preparation Tools

1 5 in. serrated knife
2 small glass serving plates or bowls

2 dessert forks or toothpicks

---

205 Robinson, *Eating on the Wild Side*, 351.

1. **Thoroughly rinse and dry the plums.** Use a serrated knife to cut out and discard any bruised area.

2. **To serve the plums whole,** serve the plums with a container for holding the pit.

3. **To serve plum slices,**

    - place a plum on its side and use a 5 in. serrated knife to slice the plum lengthwise into ⅓ in. thick slices, cutting to the pit and rocking the knife to follow the curve of the pit. Cut under slices to free them from the pit. Discard the pit.
    - serve the slices in two small bowls or plates, 1 plum per serving.

4. **To serve the plums in chunks,**

    - use a serrated knife to slice all the way around the middle of each plum, cutting to the pit.
    - cut the two plums into ⅓ in. thick slices as above (Recipe Step #3).
    - serve the chunks evenly divided onto 2 small plates or into glass bowls with dessert forks or toothpicks.

Plum Profile

Ripe plum is an outstanding snack and salad and dessert ingredient. A ripe plum is a delicious snack without any adornment. Its attractive color and sweet/tart flavoring heightens the attractiveness of a fruit dessert and salad. Ripe plum serves as an attractive pancake ingredient or topping.

Plum, which is related to peach and nectarine, has notable nutritional content.

- Plum has rich antioxidant phytonutrients, including flavonoid, carotenoid, and phenolic phytonutrients. Plum is also a very good source of antioxidant nutrients, including vitamin C and manganese, which combine with the phytonutrients to intensify the antioxidant protection provided to humans by plum.
- The plum skin contains concentrated amounts of antioxidant phytonutrients, including the super potent anthocyanins. The skin also contributes fiber.
- Plum contains small amounts of most categories of nutritional components. They are a good source of vitamin K and potassium.

Select the most flavorful and nutritious plum. Select, for example,

- fully ripe plum. Ripe plums have both fully developed flavor and nutritional content.

To identify ripe plums, select plums that are heavy feeling, uniformly firm, aromatic, and have smooth and unbroken skin. Plum flesh should yield to gentle pressure. Once rinsed and dried the plum skin should be shiny. Inside flesh should be juicy and uniformly colored without any dark areas, which indicate bruising. In addition to indicating top flavor, ripeness is also an indication that the plums have not suffered chilling injury (CI). As a stone fruit, plum is vulnerable to chilling injury, which effectively spoils the flesh or halts ripening.

- nearly ripe plums for home-ripening. That a plum is nearly ripe is also an indication that it has not suffered chilling injury and that it can be successfully home-ripened. To home-ripen plum, place it within a closed paper bag, store it at room temperature, and check it daily for ripeness.
- in-season fruit. In the United States in-season for plums is May through early October.
- locally produced plums. Plums marketed at farmers' markets and natural food stores are the freshest fruit. As in-season fruit, they are most reliably ripe. Local markets are more likely to market different varieties of plum, of which there are as many as 2,000.
- plum varieties that mature in the summer. In contrast to early maturing plum varieties, summer-maturing plum varieties are sweeter and less acidic.
- plum varieties with deep colored skin and flesh. Varieties of plum with red, purple, blue, or black flesh and particularly skin have greater phytonutrient content than varieties of plum with yellow, rose, or green flesh and/or skin.
- certified organic plums. The Environmental Working Group includes plum in its 2016 list of vegetables and fruits most contaminated with pesticides, ranking it #21 of 50 foods. Certified organic and locally grown plums, in contrast, are substantially free of pesticides and have the other advantages of naturally produced foods, particularly more potent phytonutrient content and greater overall nutritional value than industrially produced plums.

To store plum,

- store plums that will be eaten within a few days at room temperature.
- refrigerate plums that will not be quickly eaten. Refrigerate them uncovered until they are thoroughly chilled and then transfer them to a sealed plastic bag. It is very important that this transfer be made because plums produce ethylene gas during storage and sealing them protects ethylene-sensitive vegetables and fruits from flavor damage.
- avoid refrigerating immature plums. Before refrigerating plums carefully examine them and set aside immature ones for home-ripening.
- refrigerate sealed plums for as long as 10 days or longer.

96. Pomegranate Seeds
(1½-2 c seeds; multiple servings)

1 pomegranate

Preparation Tools

1 5 in. serrated knife
1 small glass storage container
    with an air-tight lid

2 small glass serving bowls (such as
6 oz custard bowls or ramekins)
2 small dinner spoons

---

1. **Rinse and dry the pomegranate.**

2. **Remove the pomegranate seeds.**

   - Being careful to avoid cutting deep into the fruit, use a serrated knife to slice the top end from the pomegranate and to score (cut through) the pomegranate skin lengthwise into quarters. Break the pomegranate apart into quarters.
   - Use your hands to separate the seeds (arils) from the outer skin and white pith, discarding the skin and bitter white pith and dropping the seeds into a bowl as they are separated. This is a somewhat slow process.
   - Transfer the seeds to a small glass storage container with a tight-fitting lid as they are separated.

3. **Serve the seeds (arils) in small bowls with a dinner spoon.** Use ¼ c per serving.

4. **Serve the seeds as a dish ingredient or topping.** Use 2 T per serving.

5. **Store extra seeds tightly covered in a glass storage container.** They will store well for a week, after which time they should be dry frozen.

Pomegranate Profile

Pomegranate seeds are tasty snacks, outstanding flavoring ingredients, and highly nutritious fruit. They contribute lovely color, delicious flavor, and attractive crunch to Chapter Six salads, Chapter Seven stir-fried dishes, Chapter Eleven fruit desserts, and Chapter Thirteen pancakes. They are nutrient-dense fruits that enhance the nutritional quality of snacks and dishes. The bright red color of the pomegranate seeds indicates rich content of potent anthocyanin phytonutrients, which make pomegranate seeds super antioxidants. Pomegranate seeds also have high vitamin C, which further intensifies the antioxidant protection provided to humans by pomegranate, and fiber content. Pomegranate seeds also contribute omega-3 fatty acids (ALA form).

To select flavorful pomegranate seeds,

- select a pomegranate that is heavy feeling and uniformly firm. The skin should be dark or bright red in color, be smooth and unbroken, and feel firm and taut. When opened, the seeds (called arils) inside should be glistening, juicy, and tender.
- select in-season pomegranate. Though they are marketed year-round, pomegranates are in-season in the United States between September and January, which is when they are most flavorful.

To store a whole pomegranate,

- store a pomegranate at room temperature for 5-8 days.
- refrigerate a pomegranate that will not be used within that time uncovered on a refrigerator shelf. Once it is thoroughly chilled, place it within a sealed plastic bag.
- refrigerate a whole pomegranate for as long as several weeks.
- dry freeze extracted seeds that cannot be used within 5-8 days. Reference #2 (Key Home Storage Guidelines for Conserving Vegetable and Fruit Quality), Storage Guideline #7, provides dry freezing details.

97. Raspberries
(1 serving)

16-20 medium red or black raspberries or a mixture of red and black raspberries

1 t sugar

Preparation Tools

1 colander
1 rubber spatula

2 6-oz glass custard bowls or dessert bowls

1. **Gently rinse the raspberries.** To avoid bruising the berries, gently pour them into a colander and rinse them under a slow stream of cool water. Use a rubber spatula to gently flip and turn the berries to rinse all surfaces.

2. **Dry the raspberries.** Spread the berries over a double thickness of paper towels and gently wrap the towels around the raspberries to dry them.

3. **Pick through the berries.** Remove soft, bruised, and moldy berries and place the berries hole down on the paper towels used for drying them as they are inspected.

4. Evenly divide the berries between two glass custard bowls, dessert bowls, or ramekins. Evenly sprinkle ½ t sugar over each bowl.

Raspberry Profile

Raspberries are outstanding flavoring ingredients. They contribute lovely color and pleasingly sweet and tart flavoring to dishes. If expensive, a few berries go a long way in enhancing the attractiveness of a salad, yogurt snack, dessert, or pancakes.

Raspberries have exceptional nutritional characteristics.

- Raspberries contain an astounding diversity and richness of phytonutrients that provide both antioxidant and anti-inflammatory protection to humans. Antioxidant phytonutrients include the super potent anthocyanins. Additionally, raspberries contain rich amounts of antioxidant nutrients, including vitamins C and E and the mineral manganese, that combine with antioxidant phytonutrients to intensify the antioxidant protection provided to humans. Raspberries also contain magnesium and omega-3 fatty acids that combine with anti-inflammatory phytonutrients to expand the anti-inflammatory capacity of raspberries.
- Raspberries are particularly rich sources of soluble fiber. They are better sources of soluble fiber than most other fruits and vegetables.[206] This soluble fiber content includes a group of valuable fibers called fructans. These are prebiotic, which means they feed and encourage the growth of good bacteria living in the human gut. These fibers are long enough to survive the journey through the human digestive system to make it into the large intestine, where they are fermented by bacteria, which transforms the fiber into human health-supporting form. Because cooking breaks down fructan fibers, raw raspberries serve as especially good sources of fructan fibers.
- The many seeds contained in raspberries contribute omega-3 fatty acids (ALA form).
- Raspberries have overall nutritional richness, serving as a good source of most categories of nutritional components. They are, for example, a good source of the vitamins E and K, most B complex vitamins (including folate), alkaline minerals (calcium, magnesium, and potassium), and the minerals iron and zinc.

Select the most flavorful and nutritious raspberries. Select, for example,

- ripe berries, which contain the most powerful antioxidant capacity. Ripe berries are uniformly firm and aromatic berries that hold their shape.
- fresh berries that are in good physical condition. They should not have any sign of mold or bruising as indicated by sunken flesh and leaking juice.
- in-season berries. In-season is from early-July through mid-September in the United States.

---

206 Robinson, *Eating on the Wild Side*, 269.
207 Mateljan, *The World's Healthiest Foods*, 2nd Edition, 587. Mateljan reports that recent research has shown organic raspberries to be significantly higher in total antioxidant capacity than non-organic raspberries.

PART 1

- certified organic and locally grown berries. The Environmental Working Group includes industrially produced raspberries in its 2016 list of vegetables and fruits most contaminated with pesticides, ranking it #23 of 50 foods. Certified organic and locally grown raspberries have the other advantages of naturally produced produce, particularly more potent phytonutrient content and greater nutritional value.[207]
- black raspberries, which are an outstanding source of anthocyanin phytonutrients that serve as super potent antioxidants in protecting humans from free radical cell destruction (also called oxidative stress).

To store raspberries,

- immediately refrigerate them within their store wrapping after purchase on a refrigerator shelf and use them within one or two days.
- dry freeze raspberries that cannot be quickly used. The phytonutrient content of raspberries remains quite stable during freezing. With careful freezing, frozen raspberries, as a result, can be nearly as nutritious as fresh ones. See Reference #2 (Key Home Storage Guidelines for Conserving Vegetable and Fruit Quality), Storage Guideline #7, for basic dry freezing detail.

98. Strawberries
(2 servings)

10 medium strawberries   1 t sugar

Preparation Tools

1 5 in. serrated knife   1 cutting board reserved for fruit
1 colander   2 6-oz custard bowls
1 pie plate

---

1. **Serve strawberries sliced.**

    - Use a serrated knife to slice off the hulls, add the strawberries to a colander, and quickly rinse the strawberries under cool running water.
    - Spread the strawberries in a pie plate lined with a double thickness of paper towels, wrap the towels around the berries, and gently roll them around within the towels to dry them.
    - Examine the strawberries and cut out and discard any bruised and spoiled areas and rough white bottom tips. Pat dry any remaining wet surface.
    - Halve each strawberry lengthwise, place the strawberry halves cut side down onto a

clean cutting board, and use a serrated knife to cut each half lengthwise into 4 equal slices.
- Divide the berries between two small serving bowls.
- Taste the strawberries and, if they are even slightly sour, evenly sprinkle ½ t sugar over the strawberries in each bowl.

2. **Serve strawberries whole with hulls attached.** Carefully rub the hull and the area under the hulls of each strawberry during rinsing. Dry the strawberries exactly as above, giving extra attention to drying under the hulls.

Strawberry Profile

Strawberries have notable nutritional value. While breeding of strawberries for commercial purposes has reduced the nutritional content of modern strawberries, and especially so in comparison to that of wild strawberry ancestors, strawberries retain significant nutritional credentials.

- Strawberries have a rich diversity of phytonutrients that provide both antioxidant and anti-inflammatory protection for humans. The antioxidant phytonutrients include anthocyanin phytonutrients, which are super potent antioxidants. Additionally, strawberries contain an excellent amount of the antioxidant nutrients vitamin C and manganese, which combine with phytonutrients to intensify the antioxidant capacity of strawberries. The magnesium and omega-3 fatty acids contained by strawberries also combine with anti-inflammatory phytonutrients to expand the anti-inflammatory protection provided to humans.
- Strawberries are a very good source of both insoluble and soluble fiber.
- Strawberry seeds contribute omega-3 essential fatty acids (ALA form).
- The high overall mineral content of strawberries places them among the most alkaline balancing fruits.
- Strawberries have overall nutritional richness, serving as a good source of nearly every category of nutritional component.

Select the most flavorful and nutritious strawberries. Select, for example,

- fully ripe strawberries. This is important because strawberries do not ripen further after being harvested. As a result, strawberries that are picked when only three quarters ripe, which is the typical practice of industrial producers, never become full flavored or develop maximum nutritional content. To identify ripe strawberries, select berries that are uniformly firm, have shiny skin, yield to gentle pressure, and are aromatic. They should not have white skin under the hulls.
- fresh and unbruised berries. The strawberries should have attached green and fresh-looking caps (hulls). There should not be any moldy strawberries in a package. There should not be any signs of bruising, such as visible spilled juice and mashed flesh on a package bottom.

- in-season strawberries, which are more likely to be fully field-ripened berries. In-season for California and Florida strawberries is from April through July.
- dark red strawberries. Red coloring indicates rich anthocyanin content, a super potent antioxidant phytonutrient. The darker the red and the more uniformly red, the greater the anthocyanin content of berries.
- locally produced strawberries, which are the freshest possible berries. They also have a greater chance of being grown from flavorful varieties of strawberries than industrially produced strawberries, which are selected on the basis of transportation durability and other commercial needs rather than tastiness.
- certified organic and locally produced strawberries. The Environmental Working Group includes industrially produced strawberries in its 2016 Dirty Dozen group of vegetables and fruits most contaminated with pesticides, ranking them #1, the most contaminated of 50 foods![208] Only a small portion of this chemical content can be washed away. Certified organic and locally produced strawberries, in stark contrast, are relatively free of pesticides. They also have the other advantages of naturally produced foods, particularly more potent phytonutrient content and greater overall nutritional value.

To store strawberries,

- store those strawberries that will be eaten within two or three days on the kitchen counter, washing them as they are eaten.
- immediately refrigerate berries that will not be eaten within two to three days, refrigerating them unwashed within store packaging. Refrigerate unpackaged berries uncovered and unwashed until they are thoroughly chilled and then loosely wrap them in paper towels and transfer them to a loosely closed plastic bag for refrigeration.
- check refrigerated strawberries regularly and remove any spoiled berries before they spoil others.
- serve strawberries within 2 days of purchase to retain flavor and nutritional quality (notably vitamin C and antioxidant phytonutrient content).
- dry freeze strawberries that cannot be quickly used and when plentiful berries are on hand. Freeze the berries whole, first removing hulls, rinsing, and drying the berries. See Reference #2 (Key Home Storage Guidelines for Conserving Vegetable and Fruit Quality), Storage Guideline #7, for dry freezing and quick thawing techniques.

99. Tangerine
(2 servings)

4 tangerines

---

208 Robinson, *Eating on the Wild Side*, 264. This high pesticide rating is partly due to the vulnerability of strawberry plants to fungus. According to Robinson, traces of sixty different agricultural chemicals have been found on industrially raised strawberries.

Preparation Tools

1 each paring & 5 in. serrated knife
1 cutting board reserved for fruit
3 plates

2 small bowls
2 dessert forks

---

1. **Rinse and dry the tangerines.**

2. **Serve the tangerines whole and unpeeled.** Serve the tangerines with a container for holding the peel and seeds.

3. **Serve tangerine segments.**

   - Peel the tangerine and gently separate the tangerine segments. If the tangerine does not easily peel, slice off a bit of one end to make an opening to begin peeling.
   - To remove seeds, use a paring knife to make a tiny slit in one side of a segment and squeeze the segment gently to force seeds out through the slit, using the knife point to pry seeds out as may be needed.

4. **Serve cut tangerine slices.** Slicing works especially well with seedy tangerines. Simplifying seed removal, slicing makes especially tasty and nutritious tangerines easy to use and, hence, competitive orange selections.

   - Use a serrated knife to halve the tangerine lengthwise and place each half cut side up on a clean cutting board.
   - Use the point of a paring knife to pry seeds gently from the halves. Use a serrated knife to cut each half lengthwise into 4 slices, rocking the half slightly while cutting to keep the surface to be cut directly on the cutting board, which minimizes spilling of juice during cutting.
   - Serve the slices on a plate, 2 tangerines per serving. Include an extra plate for skins.

5. **Serve tangerine chunks.** Chunks work well for use of tangerine as a dessert itself and as a salad and dessert ingredient. Given the juiciness of tangerine chunks, they should be added as a last ingredient to salads and mixed ingredient desserts.

   - Use a serrated knife to cut the tangerines into slices as above.
   - Use a serrated knife to make a crosswise slit across the center of each slice, being careful to cut to, but not through, the skin.
   - Including as much flesh as possible without including any peel, cut the flesh from the skin, dropping the chunks into a small glass bowl as they are cut.
   - Use 2 tangerines per serving; serve them with a dessert fork.

PART 1

Tangerine Profile

Tangerine is an outstanding variety of orange. As a member of the mandarin family of citrus fruits, tangerine has brilliant color, tangy flavor, easy to remove peels, and lower acidity than most other varieties of orange. These characteristics make tangerine easily used interchangeably with mandarin and clementine oranges for use as a snack and in salads and desserts. Tangerine also shares the rich phytonutrient content of other Mandarin citrus fruit family members. The source of the reddish flesh of tangerine is the phytonutrient lycopene, which is also the source of tomato coloring.

Tangerine can also be used interchangeably with **tangelo** (sometimes called honeybell), which is a cross between tangerine and grapefruit and which shares the same color (and, hence, rich phytonutrient content) and tanginess of tangerine.

To select the most flavorful tangerine,

- select fully ripe tangerine. A fully ripe tangerine has fully developed flavor and nutritional content. It is uniformly firm, heavy-feeling for its size, and has bright and shiny skin. When opened, individual segments should be plump and very juicy. Because industrially produced tangerine is commonly degreened, avoid selecting tangerine from a batch of uniformly colored tangerine, which is an indication of degreening. Degreened tangerine has been picked green and its color altered to appear ripe. Because tangerine, like other citrus fruit, does not further ripen after being harvested, a degreened tangerine never becomes fully ripe.
- select tangerine picked at the height of its growing season. In the United States in-season is from late October through January. This is when tangerine is most likely to be fully and genuinely ripe.
- select tangerine that is in good physical condition. It should not have any soft or flattened areas, which indicate bruising.
- select certified organic and locally grown tangerine. The Environmental Working Group includes tangerine in its list of vegetables and fruits that are most contaminated with pesticides, ranking it #26 of 50 foods. Because pesticide content does penetrate the inner tangerine, select certified organic and locally grown tangerine, which are substantially free of pesticide content. Certified organic and locally grown tangerine also have the other advantages of naturally produced food, particularly more potent phytonutrient content and greater overall nutritional value.

To store tangerine,

- store tangerines that will be eaten within 5 days at room temperature.
- refrigerate tangerines that will not be used within 5 days. Store them uncovered in the crisper drawer until they are very cold and then loosely cover them, placing them in an unsealed, partially open plastic bag to protect them from dehydration.
- use tangerines before they become soft, but sooner for best flavor.

100. Grape Tomato
(2 servings)

10 grape tomatoes

Preparation Tools

1 5 in. serrated knife   2 small custard bowls

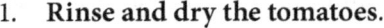

1. **Rinse and dry the tomatoes.**

2. **Serve the tomatoes whole.** Divide the tomatoes between two custard bowls, 5 per bowl.

   VARIATIONS: Substitute any of the following tomatoes:

   - **equally small dark red tomato varieties.**
   - **4 cherry tomatoes**, halved.
   - **any variety of small yellow, purple, and brown tomatoes**, as can be found in farmers' markets and in specialty and natural food stores. Along with all the other rich phytonutrient content of tomato varieties in general, purple and brown colored tomato contain anthocyanin phytonutrients, which have super potent antioxidant capacity.

   COMMENTS: Grape tomato is included with fruits because it, like tomato varieties in general, is botanically classified as a fruit. When cooked, tomato is much more like a vegetable, but when it is used in raw form, tomato tastes (has the sweetness and tanginess) and is used very much like fruit in dishes.

Grape Tomato Profile

Grape tomato is an outstanding snack and flavoring ingredient. Simple to keep and prepare and a variety of tomato that is both reliably flavorful and sturdy enough to hold juice well when cut, grape tomato is an ideal snack food and salad and appetizer ingredient selection.

Grape tomato shares the rich nutritional content of other tomato varieties.

- Grape tomato has particularly rich content of the carotenoid phytonutrient lycopene, which is the source of its red color. The deep red color of the grape tomato indicates its particularly rich lycopene content. The deeper this red color, the greater is the lycopene content of grape tomato. Both the skin and flesh contribute lycopene, which functions as an antioxidant, providing antioxidant protection for humans.
- Grape tomato contains a diverse array of phytonutrients, including other carotenoid

and flavonoid phytonutrients, which expand the total antioxidant protection provided to humans. Additionally, grape tomato is an excellent source of vitamin C and a very good source of both vitamin E and manganese, which are antioxidant nutrients that combine with antioxidant phytonutrients to intensify the antioxidant protection provided to humans by tomato.
- Grape tomato seeds contribute omega-3 essential fatty acids.
- Grape tomato, and particularly the skin, is a very good source of dietary fiber.
- Grape tomato has overall rich nutritional content. It is an excellent source of the nutrients vitamin K and biotin, and it is either a very good or good source of every category of nutritional component, excluding vitamins D and B12 (vegetables and fruits in general lack these two nutrients).

To select the most flavorful and nutritious grape tomato,

- select fully ripe grape tomato, which has the fullest developed flavor and nutritional content. Select deep red tomatoes that are plump, feel heavy for their size, are uniformly firm, have glossy and tight skin, and that give slightly when gently squeezed.
- select partially ripe grape tomato (tomato with some green coloration) and home-ripen it. To home-ripen grape tomato, store grape tomatoes within a closed paper bag at room temperature and check them daily until they become fully ripe. Add a banana to speed ripening.
- select in-season tomato. In the United States in-season runs from July through October.
- select orange and yellow grape tomato. Orange grape tomato also contains the antioxidant phytonutrient lycopene while yellow contains only other carotenoid phytonutrients.
- select certified organic and locally grown tomato. As the Environmental Working Group includes industrially produced cherry tomato in its 2016 list of vegetables and fruits most contaminated with pesticides, ranking it 11th most contaminated of 50 foods, industrially produced grape tomato most likely also carries a heavy pesticide load. Certified organic and locally grown grape tomato, in contrast, reliably contain substantially reduced pesticide content. Customers, as a result, are free to eat the highly nutritious grape tomato skin. Certified organic and locally grown grape tomato have the other advantages of naturally produced produce, particularly more potent phytonutrient content and greater overall nutritional value.

To store grape tomato,

- store grape tomatoes at room temperature out of direct sunshine. Room temperature storage is important for two reasons. First, tomato is most flavorful at room temperature. Second, if the internal temperature of grape tomato, as with tomato varieties in general, falls below fifty-five degrees, it stops producing flavor and aromatic compounds, and its flavor very quickly and steadily fades. It can even become bitter.[209]

---

209 Ibid.,151.

- refrigerate ripe tomatoes on the verge of becoming overripe for a very short period (1-2 days), storing them uncovered on a refrigerator shelf. Use them within 2 days. Allow chilled tomato to reach room temperature before serving.
- use ripe grape tomatoes stored at room temperature within a week to maximize retention of the best flavor and top nutritional value.

101. Watermelon
(2 servings)

1 chilled watermelon, with or without seeds (seeded)

Preparation Tools

1 dish sponge for cleaning
1 each chef's & paring knife
2 large serving plates
2 dinner knives & forks
1 melon ball cutter

1 colander (when cutting balls)
1 dinner plate
2 dessert or salad bowls
2 toothpicks or dessert forks

1. **Prepare the watermelon for cutting.** Rinse and use a dish sponge or paper towel to scrub the entire watermelon and dry the watermelon with paper towels or a terry cloth towel.

2. **Serve watermelon slices with skins**, which is the very simplest way to serve watermelon.

   - Use a chef's knife to halve the watermelon crosswise. Immediately cover the cut open end of one half of the watermelon with plastic wrap and refrigerate it.
   - Beginning at the cut end and cutting crosswise, use a chef's knife to cut two 1½ in. thick slices from the remaining watermelon half.
   - Place each round slice on a large serving plate and halve the slices crosswise. Cover and refrigerate any remaining watermelon.
   - Remove any seeds. Use the point of a paring knife to remove exposed seeds from the slices, attempting to minimize cutting.
   - Serve the slices. Either allow those being served to eat the watermelon by hand or serve the watermelon with knives for cutting the watermelon slices into pieces and with dinner forks for picking up watermelon pieces.

3. **Serve watermelon cubes**, which is perhaps the surest way of successfully serving watermelon.

   - Cut one half watermelon crosswise into two 1½ in. thick slices, as in Step #2 above.
   - Place each slice on a large serving plate, halve each slice, stand each half slice cut side

up, and use a serrated knife to cut the watermelon from the rind, being careful to avoid including any green rind and whitish colored pulp.
- Place the watermelon slices flat on the serving plate and cut each slice into 1½ in. thick strips.
- Remove any seeds from the strips. Use the point of a paring knife to pry out seeds, being careful to minimize cutting and avoid deep or rough gouging.
- Cut the strips crosswise into 1½ in. cubes.
- After cutting the cubes, again remove any visible seeds, leaving seeds deep inside the cubes.
- Serve the cubes in two salad bowls with forks.

4. **Serve melon balls.**

- Halve a seedless melon lengthwise and use a melon ball cutter to cut balls from one half (immediately covering and refrigerating the other half).
- Begin at one end and cut from side to side, adding balls to a colander placed over a dinner plate as balls are cut.
- Serve balls in dessert or salad bowls with dessert forks or toothpicks.

COMMENTS: To minimize juice spilling, cut watermelon as close to serving time as possible. Store *cut* watermelon in a manner that keeps chunks dry. For example, place a small upside down bowl at the bottom of the storage bowl, one that allows juice to escape to the bottom of the bowl.

To take maximum advantage of watermelon's nutritional content when cutting watermelon for serving, be careful to include as much as possible of the flesh just next to the rind, which contains concentrated phytonutrient and nutrient content. Take time to include this flesh on the rounded ends of the watermelon as well.

Watermelon Profile

Watermelon is an outstanding snack and dessert fruit. Absolutely simple to prepare, it is juicy, refreshing, and delicious without any enhancement whatsoever.

Watermelon has notable nutritional content.

- Watermelon is a rich source of a diverse array of carotenoid phytonutrients, including beta-carotene and lycopene, the phytonutrient that gives watermelon flesh its red-pink color. Additionally, watermelon is a good source of antioxidant nutrients, including vitamin C and the minerals manganese and selenium, which combine with the carotenoid phytonutrients to intensify the antioxidant protection provided to humans by watermelon.
- Watermelon phytonutrients, including lycopene, provide both anti-inflammatory

and antioxidant support for humans. Watermelon is a good source of magnesium, which serves to expand the anti-inflammatory protection provided by anti-inflammatory phytonutrients.
- Watermelon is a source of most categories of nutritional components and a good source of many nutrients within these categories, including the alkaline minerals potassium and magnesium and the B complex vitamins B1 and B6.

To select the most flavorful and nutritious watermelon,

- select fully ripe watermelon. Fully ripe watermelon has fully developed flavor and nutritional content, including lycopene content. A ripe watermelon is heavy-feeling with a yellowish (not white or green) underbelly spot (called a ground spot), produces a low pitched and hollow sound when lightly tapped, and is just beginning to lose its bright and shiny color. Flesh of the opened watermelon should be firm and have a juicy appearance. Flesh that is very dark red, smooth, sunken, or broken apart indicates over-ripeness.
- select in-season watermelon, which is when marketed watermelon is most likely to be fully ripe. In the United States summer is in-season for watermelon. In cooler regions in-season is in late summer and early fall.
- select watermelon with dark red flesh. Dark red watermelon is one of the best sources of the phytonutrient lycopene.[210] The darker the red coloring, the greater the lycopene content. Pale watermelon has significantly less lycopene.
- select small "personal" red-fleshed watermelon, which has more lycopene than most larger ones.
- select certified organic and locally grown watermelon. The Environmental Working Group includes industrially produced watermelon in its list of vegetables and fruits most contaminated with pesticides, ranking it #32 out of 50 foods. Both certified organic and locally grown watermelon, in contrast, are substantially free of pesticides and have the other advantages of naturally produced food, particularly more potent phytonutrient content and overall greater nutritional value than counterpart industrially produced watermelon.

To store watermelon,

- leave a whole watermelon at room temperature until cutting, leaving it for up to a week. Storing at room temperature increases the phytonutrient content of the watermelon. During the time that the watermelon is stored at room temperature, lycopene content can increase as much as fifty percent.[211]
- refrigerate a whole watermelon before cutting it for serving if refrigerator space permits. Cut the watermelon once it becomes thoroughly chilled.
- store whole watermelon in a dry, dark, and cool (a temperature between 50-60 degrees F) area whenever such a storage area is available. Under these ideal storage conditions, a whole watermelon will store well for weeks.

---

210 Ibid., 361. Some varieties of dark red watermelon have 40 times more lycopene per ounce than ripe tomatoes.
211 Ibid., 362.

PART 1

- avoid storing an uncut watermelon with an uncovered ethylene gas-producing vegetable (such as potato) or fruit (such as apple, banana, papaya, peach, and pear). Watermelon is sensitive to ethylene gas, which will cause it to ripen very quickly.
- immediately refrigerate unserved *cut* pieces, tightly covered with plastic wrap, to protect the watermelon from drying out. Tightly covered cut watermelon pieces store well for several days but use them quickly for the best flavor.

102. Creamy Apricot Dip
(2 servings)

½ c plain, very fresh mild goat cheese, room temperature
1 T unflavored yogurt or cream
2 T apricot 100% fruit spread
1 organic lemon
4 dried apricot halves

4-6 raw pecan or walnut halves and/or
6-8 raw whole almonds
6 medium organic strawberries
2 chilled organic apples or 1 each chilled apple and pear
2 T cold orange juice and 1 T cold water

Preparation Tools

1 medium mixing bowl
1 set measuring spoons
1 wooden spoon or hand electric mixer
1 citrus zester tool
1 hand citrus juicer
1 each chef's, 5 in. serrated, & 1 paring knife

1 cutting board reserved for fruit
2 6-oz glass bowls (such as custard bowls or ramekins)
1 rubber spatula
1 colander
1 small mixing bowl
2 salad-size serving plates

---

1. Gather together all ingredients and preparation tools.

2. **Combine the cheese, yogurt or cream, and fruit spread.** Crumble the goat cheese and add it to a medium mixing bowl. Add yogurt or cream and use a wooden spoon or electric mixer to stir the ingredients until creamy smooth. Add and mix in the 100% apricot spread.

3. **Prepare the lemon zest and lemon juice.**

   - Rinse and dry the lemon.
   - Use a zester tool to remove ½ t zest. Add the zest to the mixing bowl.
   - Use a citrus juicer to squeeze ½ of the lemon and add 1 T lemon juice to the mixing bowl. Tightly cover and refrigerate remaining juice for another use.
   - Combine the ingredients.

4. **Prepare the dried apricots and nuts.**

    - Use a chef's knife to slice the dried apricots lengthwise into ¼ in. wide strips. Slice the strips crosswise into ¼ in. cubes.
    - Use the chef's knife to coarsely chop the nuts.
    - Mix the apricots and nuts into the cheese mixture.

5. **Transfer the dip to two small bowls.** Use a rubber spatula to scrape the dip into two 6 oz custard bowls or ramekins. Cover each bowl with plastic wrap.

6. **Refrigerate the dip for at least an hour before serving.**

7. **Prepare the dipping fruit while the dip chills.**

    - Use a serrated knife to slice off the hulls of **4 strawberries**. Rinse the strawberries under cool running water, drain the strawberries in a colander, spread the strawberries over a double layer of paper towels, wrap the towels around the berries, and gently roll the strawberries around within the towels to dry them completely. Examine the strawberries and cut out bruised or spoiled spots. Cut each strawberry lengthwise into 4 equal slices.
    - Rinse and thoroughly dry **2 apples** (or 1 apple and 1 pear, preparing the pear exactly like the apple). Use a chef's knife to halve the apples lengthwise and place the halves cut side down on a clean cutting surface. Again using the chef's knife, cut each half lengthwise into 8 slices. Use a paring knife to cut out the core, seeds, and any brown bruised flesh from the slices. Add 2 T cold orange juice and 1 T cold water to a small mixing bowl, add the slices, quickly swish them to coat them completely, immediately drain them in a colander, spread the slices over paper towels, and wrap the towels around the slices to dry them thoroughly. Serve the slices or immediately cover and refrigerate them until serving. Either drink or save the rinsing juice for another use.

8. **Serve each individual bowl of dip on a small plate surrounded by fruit slices.**

    VARIATIONS: Make ingredient or preparation tool substitutions. Substitute, for example,

    - **4 fresh apricots** (Recipe #75), pitted and quartered, or **20 whole cherries, stems attached** (Recipe #81), for strawberries. For cherries include a small container for stems and pits.
    - **1 nectarine** (Recipe #88), **1 peach** (Recipe #92), or **2 plums** (Recipe #95) for either strawberries or apples.
    - **½ c fresh yogurt cheese** for goat cheese. See Comments below for a simple home-prepared recipe that provides the freshest possible and very satisfying cheese.
    - **½ c fromage blanc** for goat cheese. Find this creamy, mild-flavored French-style skim milk cheese in the cheese section of large supermarkets or gourmet food stores. Either sift 1½ T confectioners' sugar over the cheese or spread the sugar over the cheese through a fine sieve.

- **½ c softened cream cheese** or **full fat sheep feta cheese** for goat cheese.
- **2 T frozen fruit concentrate**, thawed, or **1 T honey** for fruit spread.

COMMENTS: Soften very dry apricot halves. Add them to a small mixing bowl, pour 2 T boiling orange juice over them, cover the bowl, and soak the apricots for at least 5 minutes. Drain and collect the soaking liquid. Add 1 t to 1 T of this soaking water to the dip or save it all for another use.

To prepare yogurt cheese,

- Line a colander with a double thickness of cheese cloth and place the colander over a large, deep mixing bowl. The colander should be wide enough for a small plate to sit directly on the yogurt; there should be enough space under the colander for the liquid to drain completely from and not be in contact with the colander.
- Add a 32 oz container of plain yogurt (low or full fat but not non-fat) to the colander, place a small glass plate over the yogurt, and add some kind of weight to the plate. The weight should be heavy enough to press the liquid from the yogurt, such as a 5 pound bag of sugar.
- Set the yogurt aside for at least an hour. Remove the weight, grasp the plate on top of the yogurt, and flip the plate so that the yogurt cheese is on top of the plate. Remove the cheesecloth from the cheese, insert the plate and cheese into a sealable gallon size plastic storage bag, and refrigerate the yogurt cheese.
- Use a rubber spatula to scrape the cheese into a measuring cup when assembling a dip.
- For best flavor, use the yogurt cheese within two days.

103. Peanut or Almond Butter Spread
(approx. ½ c; 2 servings)

⅓ c chunky organic peanut butter or almond butter, chunky or smooth
1-1½ T frozen orange juice concentrate
1-2 T orange juice
1 chilled organic apple, pear, or banana

9 raw walnut halves and either ¼ c raw peanuts or 16 whole raw almonds
2 T cold orange juice
1 T cold water

Preparation Tools

2 small mixing bowls
1 rubber spatula
1 set measuring spoons
1 wooden spoon

1 each 5 in. serrated & paring knife
1 small serving bowl
1 dinner knife
1 dinner plate-size serving platter

1. **Stir the separated oil into the natural peanut or almond butter.** See comments below for stirring details.

2. **Prepare a citrus wash.** Add 2 T cold orange juice and 1 T cold water to a small mixing bowl.

3. **To serve the nut butter as a dip:**

    - Use a rubber spatula to scrape 1/3 c peanut or almond butter into a small mixing bowl.
    - Add 1 T frozen orange juice concentrate.
    - Use a wooden spoon to combine the ingredients, adding touches of more juice as needed to create a creamy, easily spreadable consistency.
    - Use a rubber spatula to scrape the dip into a small serving bowl and add the bowl to the center of a dinner plate size platter.
    - Use a serrated and a paring knife to cut **apple slices** (Recipe #74) or **pear slices** (Recipe #93) or a combination of both apple and pear.
    - Add the slices to and swish them in the citrus rinse to keep them from browning. Spread the slices over paper towels to dry them.
    - Arrange the slices around the dip on the serving platter.

4. **To serve the nut butter as a spread:**

    - Add more orange juice concentrate to the peanut or almond butter, beginning with 1 T and adding no more than 1 t at a time, to achieve a thick spread that will not run.
    - Prepare **1 chilled 6 in. banana**. Trim the banana, removing the bottom tip, bruised area, and strings. Use a serrated knife to halve the banana lengthwise, then cut each half crosswise into 1½ in. lengths (or 4 lengths per half).
    - Add the banana pieces to and swish them in the citrus wash. Spread the banana pieces over paper towels to dry them.
    - Use a dinner knife to spread the nut butter over each banana piece and top each banana piece with **1 walnut half** and either **several peanuts** or **2 whole almonds**.
    - Serve the banana pieces on a dinner plate size serving platter.

    VARIATIONS: Make ingredient substitutions. Substitute, for example,

    - **cashew butter** for peanut or almond butter.
    - **2 T tahini** (either ground toasted or raw sesame seeds) for 2 T nut butter. The ground sesame seeds enhance both the nutritional diversity and flavor of the dip.

    Add **1 T certified organic raisins** or **1 T diced dates**.

    COMMENTS: Natural peanut and almond butter has not been hydrogenated (mixed with hydrogen) to keep the oil and nuts from separating. To stir separated natural butter, begin by dipping a dinner knife into and cutting up and down through the butter.

Repeat this dipping over and over. Switch to stirring as the oil and nuts begin to mix together. Scrape the bottom often to achieve uniform mixing.

104. Lettuce Fruit Cups
(2 servings; 4 leaves per serving)

4 T very fresh goat cheese, room temperature
½ T plain yogurt
½ lemon
8 red seedless grapes

8 very small baby romaine lettuce leaves, approx. 2 in. wide & 3-4 in. long
8 raw pecan or walnut halves

Preparation Tools

1 set measuring spoons
1 small mixing bowl
1 wooden spoon or hand electric mixer
1 hand citrus juicer

1 colander
1 5 in. serrated knife
1 rubber spatula
1 small dinner spoon

---

1. **Gather together all cooking utensils and dish ingredients.**

2. **Prepare the goat cheese spread.** Add the cheese to a small mixing bowl, add 1 T yogurt, and use a wooden spoon or electric mixer to stir the mixture until creamy smooth.

3. **Prepare the lemon juice.** Squeeze ½ lemon and add 1 t juice to the goat cheese mixture. Taste the cheese and add more lemon to taste. Refrigerate remaining juice in a small glass container, tightly covered.

4. **Prepare the grapes.**

    - Add the grapes to a colander, rinse them with cool water, and pour the grapes onto a double layer of paper towels or a terry cloth.
    - Wrap the towels around the grapes to dry them thoroughly.
    - Sort through the grapes to remove spoiled grapes and stems.
    - Use a serrated knife to cut off any brown stem ends and to halve each grape lengthwise.

5. **Prepare the lettuce leaves.**

    - Rinse the leaves under cool water, drain them in a colander, and spread them over a layer of paper towels or a cloth towel. Add a top layer of towels, roll the towels around the leaves, and gently squeeze the towels to dry the leaves.
    - Unroll the leaves and pat dry any remaining wet areas.

6. **Assemble the lettuce for serving.** Use a rubber spatula to scrape 1 small dinner spoonful of the cheese mixture onto each lettuce leaf. Top each pile of cheese with 2 grape halves and either 1 pecan or walnut half.

VARIATIONS: Make ingredient substitutions. Substitute, for example,

- **raw whole almonds** for pecans and walnuts. Use 2 almonds per lettuce cup for a total of 16 almonds.
- **small, firm green-red or green leaf lettuce leaves** or other small crisp lettuce leaves for romaine lettuce leaves.

Add ingredients. Add, for example,

- ½ t **lemon zest** to the cheese. Select an organic lemon and use a lemon zester to remove the zest before halving and juicing the lemon.
- ¼ t **honey** or 1/8 t **sugar** to the cheese mixture.

105. Apple and Warmed Brie
(4 servings)

4 oz wheel Brie cheese	2 T cold orange juice
½ T butter, softened	2 T cold water
¼ c raw whole almonds	2 tasty organic apples, chilled

Preparation Tools

1 small baking dish	1 clean cutting board
1 rubber spatula	1 paring knife
1 small mixing bowl	1 colander
1 set measuring spoons	1 10 in. serving plate
1 chef's knife	1 cheese cutting tool

1. **Preheat the oven to 350 degrees.**

2. **Gather all preparation tools and dish ingredients.**

3. **Prepare the Brie cheese for heating.**

    - Set the Brie in the baking dish.
    - Use a rubber spatula to spread ½ T butter evenly over the top.
    - Use a chef's knife to thinly slice each almond. Evenly sprinkle the almonds over the butter.

4. **Bake the Brie for 12-15 minutes.** The Brie should be softened and heated through.

5. **Prepare the 2 apples while the Brie heats.**

   - Add the 2 T juice and 1 T water to a small mixing bowl.
   - Rinse and thoroughly dry the apples.
   - Use a chef's knife to halve each lengthwise and place the halves cut side down on a clean cutting board. Cut each half lengthwise into 5 slices.
   - Use a paring knife to remove any core, seeds, and brown spots.
   - Quickly swish the slices in the juice wash, drain them in a colander, spread them over a double thickness of paper towels, and wrap the towels around the slices to dry them completely.
   - If the apples will not be served immediately, tightly cover and refrigerate them.

6. **Transfer the Brie to a serving plate.** Arrange the apple slices around the brie. Serve the Brie with a cheese tool for cutting and spreading Brie onto the slices.

   VARIATIONS: Make ingredient substitutions. Substitute, for example,

   - **2 chilled ripe pears** (Recipe #93) or combine **1 apple** and **1 pear** for apple.
   - **4 oz Camembert** for Brie cheese. Omit the baking but allow the Camembert to sit, tightly covered, at room temperature for a few hours before serving. Camembert is a very special cheese. Its flavor develops through a ripening process, with fully ripened cheese having the best flavor. As ripening develops from the outside of the cheese, gauge ripeness by gently pressing your fingers over all of the surface of the cheese to check that it is evenly soft underneath its surface, which indicates ripeness. A hard inner core indicates the cheese is under-ripe.
   - **¼ c sliced almonds** for raw whole almonds. This substitution saves preparation time, but freshly sliced almonds are more flavorful and nutritious.

106. Raw Fruit Pita Pizza
(4 servings; 1 6 in. pizza per serving)

½ c fresh pineapple chunks, approx. ½ in. thick (Recipe #94)
10 red green seedless grapes or 5 each green and red grapes
4 fresh medium organic strawberries
1 t honey
8-10 raw pecan or walnut halves
2 6 in. whole wheat pita bread rounds

½ T plain yogurt
½ T thawed frozen orange juice concentrate
3 oz package cream cheese, softened
1 certified organic or locally produced lemon
1 t sugar
½ c fresh blueberries

Preparation Tools

1 set each measuring cups & spoons
1 5 in. serrated knife
1 colander
1 pie plate
1 cutting board reserved for fruit
1 small mixing bowl

1 wooden spoon or hand electric mixer
1 citrus zester tool
1 hand citrus juicer
1 small dinner spoon
4 dessert plates

---

1. **Gather all preparation tools and ingredients.**

2. **Prepare the fruit.**

    - Use a serrated knife to cut the ½ c **pineapple chunks** lengthwise into ¼ in. thick slices.
    - Rinse the 10 **grapes** under cold water, drain them in a colander, and spread them in a pie plate lined with a double thickness of paper towels or a terry towel. Wrap the towels around the grapes and roll the grapes around within the towels to dry them completely. Go through the grapes to remove spoiled or broken open grapes and stems. Use a serrated knife to slice off any brown stem ends and to halve the grapes lengthwise.
    - Add the 4 **strawberries** to the colander, rinse them, use a serrated knife to cut off the hulls, and rinse them again. Spread the berries over a double thickness of paper towels or a terry towel. Wrap the towels around the berries to dry them. Halve each strawberry lengthwise, place each half cut side down on a cutting board, and slice it lengthwise into 3 equal slices. Spread the strawberries over plastic wrap and evenly sprinkle 1 t sugar over them.
    - Add the ½ c **blueberries** to the colander, rinse them with cold water, spread them in the pie plate lined with a double thickness of paper towels or a terry towel, and pick through them to remove spoiled berries and stems. Wrap the towels around the berries to dry them completely.

3. **Combine the yogurt, frozen orange juice concentrate, and cream cheese.** Add the ½ T yogurt, ½ T frozen orange juice concentrate, and 3 oz cream cheese to a small mixing bowl and use a wooden spoon or electric mixer to combine the ingredients thoroughly.

4. **Prepare the lemon and nuts.** Use a zester tool to make ½ t lemon zest. Juice ½ of the lemon. Add the zest and 1 t lemon juice to the cream cheese mixture. Use a chef's knife to chop the nuts coarsely. Refrigerate unused lemon juice in a small glass container, covered.

5. **Add honey to the cream cheese mixture.** Dip a dinner spoon into a honey container, drizzle the honey over the cream cheese mixture, and stir in the honey. Add 1-2 t more

yogurt as may be needed to achieve a soft, spreadable consistency. Add ½-1 t more lemon juice to taste for enhanced tartness.

6. **Assemble the pita pizzas for serving.**

   - Halve each pita round.
   - Spread ¼ of the cream cheese mixture over the rough side of each pita half.
   - Evenly distribute the fruit over the pita halves, pressing the pieces into the cheese slightly.
   - Evenly distribute the nuts over the rounds.
   - If the pizza will not be served immediately, refrigerate the uncut pizza covered within an air-tight container, such as 2 rectangular baking dishes covered with plastic wrap. Remove the pizzas at least 15 minutes before serving to allow the cream cheese to soften, leaving the pizzas covered during this warming.
   - Use a serrated knife to cut the pizza into wedges for serving.
   - Serve each pita pizza on a dessert plate.

VARIATIONS: Make ingredient substitutions. Substitute, for example,

- **freshly baked 6 in. pizza crusts** for pita bread. Prepare one half pizza dough (Recipe #210). Divide the dough into 4 equal pieces, press the pieces into 6 in. rounds on a buttered pizza stone, and bake the rounds exactly like regular size crust. This bread is superior in quality, flavor, and texture to any commercially prepared pita bread.
- ½ c **fresh pitted sweet cherry halves** (Recipe #81) for strawberry.
- 1 **kiwi** (Recipe #86), sliced, for grapes. Add kiwi slices shortly before serving.
- ½ **nectarine** (Recipe #88) or **peach** (Recipe #92), sliced, for strawberries.
- ¼ c **organic raspberries** (Recipe #97) for strawberries.
- ½ c **mango cubes** (Recipe #87) for strawberries.

Add ingredients. Add, for example,

- ½ c ½ in. **cantaloupe cubes** (Recipe #80).
- ½ c **mango cubes** (Recipe #87).
- 1 **clementine** or **mandarin orange**, separated into sections (Recipe #90).
- ⅓ c **pomegranate seeds** (Recipe #96).

COMMENTS: What is most important about the pita bread used is that it be fresh, moist, tender, and tasty. The bread should be thick enough to hold the fruit, but not too thick. Very thick bread will overwhelm the toppings, making the pizza unattractively dry.

107. Fruit and Havarti Cheese Kebabs
(2 servings; 2 kebabs per serving)

8 moist Turkish or California dried apricot halves
6 seedless green grapes

6 seedless red grapes
approx. 2 x 2 in. chunk of havarti cheese, ½ in. thick, room temperature

Preparation Tools

1 chef's knife
1 pie plate

1 5 in. serrated knife
4 bamboo skewers, 6-8 in. long

---

1. **Prepare the apricots.** Use a chef's knife to cut each apricot into 3 equal slices (to yield 24 slices).

2. **Prepare the grapes.**

   - Rinse the grapes under cool water and spread them over a double thickness of paper towels within a pie plate. Wrap the towels around the grapes and roll the grapes around within the towels to dry them completely. Remove any stems and spoiled grapes.
   - Keeping red and green separate, use a serrated knife to slice off any brown stem ends and to halve the grapes lengthwise, to yield 24 grape halves.

3. **Prepare the cheese.** Use a chef's knife to cut the 2 x 2 x ½ in. chunk of Havarti cheese. Cut the cheese into 4 equal ½ in. thick slices. Cut each slice crosswise into 3 equal pieces, to yield 12 cheese chunks.

4. **Assemble the kebabs.** Thread the cheese and fruit onto each of the four skewers in the following order: red grape, apricot, cheese, green grape, apricot, red grape, apricot, cheese, green grape, apricot, red grape, apricot, cheese, green grape, apricot.

5. **Serve the kebabs.** Serve them immediately or place the kebabs within a large rectangular baking dish, tightly cover the dish with plastic wrap, and refrigerate the kebabs until serving. Remove the kebabs from the refrigerator at least 15 minutes before serving to allow the cheese to reach room temperature. Keep the kebabs covered during warming to protect the cheese from drying air.

   VARIATIONS: Make ingredient substitutions. Substitute, for example,

   - **12 ½-in. fresh mozzarella cheese balls (or halved 1 in. balls)** or **Jarlsberg Swiss, gouda** or **extra sharp cheddar cheese** for havarti cheese chunks.
   - **8 ½-in. cantaloupe cubes or balls (Recipe #80)** or **8 ½-in. honeydew melon cubes or balls (Recipe #85)** for grape halves.

- **8 fresh pitted cherries** (Recipe #81), **½ in. pineapple cubes** (Recipe #94), **½ in. thick plum slices, halved** (Recipe #95), or **½ in. thick nectarine slices, cut into thirds** (Recipe #88) for 8 grape halves.

Add **4 dried prunes**, halved, including one in the center with an apricot in each kebab.

COMMENTS: Soften very dry apricots. Add them to a small mixing bowl, pour 2 T boiling orange juice over them, cover the bowl, and soak the apricots for at least 5 minutes. Drain and collect the soaking liquid for another use.

108. Grape Tomato and Mozzarella Cheese Kebabs
(2 servings; 2 kabobs per serving)

8 grape tomatoes	12 fresh small (½ in.) or 6 1-in. mozzarella balls, room temperature

Preparation Tools

5 in. serrated knife	4 bamboo skewers, 6-8 in. long

1. **Prepare the tomatoes.** Rinse and dry the tomatoes. Use a serrated knife to halve each tomato crosswise to yield 16 halves.

2. **Prepare the mozzarella balls.** Pat the balls dry with a paper towel if necessary. Use a serrated knife to halve 1 in. balls.

3. **Assemble the kebabs.** Thread the cheese and fruit onto the skewers in the following order: tomato, cheese, tomato, cheese, tomato, cheese, and tomato.

4. **Serve the kebabs.** Serve them immediately or place the kebabs within a large rectangular baking dish, tightly cover the dish with plastic wrap, and refrigerate the kebabs until serving. Remove the kebabs from the refrigerator at least 15 minutes before serving to allow the cheese to reach room temperature but keep the kebabs covered to protect them from air until serving.

VARIATION: Substitute **cherry tomato** or any other small tasty variety of tomato for grape tomato.

109. Orange and Yogurt Snack
(2 servings)

1½ medium carrot
1½ c plain yogurt, low or full fat
2 t sugar
1 chilled medium banana (approx. 6 in. long)
2 clementine or mandarin oranges

8 raw pecan or walnut halves
1 T dried tart cherries
1 t honey
2 heaping t certified organic seedless raisins

Preparation Tools

1 5 in. serrated knife
1 vegetable grater
2 individual salad bowls
1 set measuring cups & spoons

1 large dinner spoon
1 cutting board reserved for fruit
1 chef's knife
1 small dinner spoon

---

1. **Gather all preparation tools and ingredients.**

2. **Prepare the carrot.**

    - Scrub and dry the carrot.
    - Use a serrated knife to cut off the end tip of the whole carrot.
    - Coarsely shred the carrot and evenly divide it between two salad bowls.

3. **Divide the yogurt between two serving bowls.** Use a large dinner spoon to stir the yogurt creamy smooth in its marketing container before adding ¾ c yogurt per bowl. Add ½ t sugar to the yogurt in each bowl and use the dinner spoon to roughly mix in the sugar while minimally mixing the yogurt into the carrot.

4. **Prepare the banana.**

    - Rinse, dry, and peel the banana. Use a serrated knife to remove the tip and any bruised area, and remove any strings from the banana.
    - Working on a clean cutting board, use a serrated knife to halve the banana lengthwise and to cut each half crosswise into 8-10 pieces.
    - Add one half of the banana pieces to each bowl of yogurt, piling the banana pieces in the center of the bowl and pressing them slightly under the yogurt surface.

5. **Prepare the clementine or mandarin oranges.**

    - Peel and use a serrated knife to halve the oranges crosswise.
    - Separate the segments of each half and add them to the yogurt in each salad bowl, adding one orange per bowl, first removing any seeds from mandarin orange segments, and piling the oranges in the center of the yogurt.

6. **Prepare the nuts and tart cherries.** Use a chef's knife to chop the nuts coarsely and to halve the cherries.

7. **Assemble the snack for serving.**

   - Dip a dinner spoon into a container of honey and evenly drizzle the honey over the orange chunks in each bowl, approx. ½ spoonful per bowl.
   - Evenly divide the dried cherries, nuts, and raisins between the bowls, adding them as a topping on the orange, and serve the snack.

VARIATIONS: Make ingredient substitutions. Substitute, for example,

- **2 T other favorite nuts**, roughly broken or chopped, for pecans or walnuts.
- **2 tangerines** (Recipe #99) for mandarin or clementine orange.
- **1 small** or **½ large papaya** (Recipe #91), **1 mango** (Recipe #87), **1 nectarine** (Recipe #88), or **1 peach** (Recipe #92) for clementine or mandarin oranges.

COMMENTS: If the dish will not be served immediately, protect the banana from browning. Either swish the banana chunks in 2 T orange juice and blot the chunks dry with a paper towel before adding them to the yogurt. Alternatively, prepare all other individual ingredients – keeping the prepared oranges, yogurt, and banana refrigerated – and combine the ingredients with banana shortly before serving.

Select grass-fed and certified organic yogurt to significantly upgrade the nutritional quality of this snack. To boost yogurt quality another step, select this yogurt in non-homogenized, cream on the top form.

110. Berries and Yogurt Snack
(2 servings)

1½ c plain yogurt, low or full fat
1 t sugar
1 chilled medium (6 in.) banana
5 chilled organic strawberries (medium size)
1 t sugar

½ c fresh organic blueberries
¼ c fresh organic raspberries
1 t honey
8 raw pecan or walnut halves

Preparation Tools

2 individual serving bowls
1 large dinner spoon
1 set each measuring cups & spoons
1 5 in. serrated knife

1 cutting board
1 colander
1 pie plate
1 chef's knife

1. **Gather all preparation tools and dish ingredients.**

2. **Divide the yogurt between two individual serving bowls.**

    - Use a large dinner spoon to stir the yogurt creamy smooth while it remains in its marketing container.
    - Add ¾ c yogurt to each serving bowl.
    - Add ½ t sugar to the yogurt in each bowl and use the dinner spoon to mix in the sugar.

3. **Prepare the fruit.**

    - Rinse and dry the banana.
    - Peel and remove the tips and any strings from the **banana**. Working on a clean cutting board, halve the banana lengthwise, cut each half crosswise into 8-10 pieces, and add one half banana pieces to the yogurt in each bowl, piling them in the center of the bowl and slightly pushing the pieces into the yogurt.
    - Use a serrated knife to slice off the hull of each **strawberry**. Quickly rinse the strawberries under cool running water, drain them in a colander, add the strawberries to a double thickness of paper towels, wrap the towels around the berries, and gently roll the berries in the towels to dry them thoroughly. Pick through the strawberries and cut out bruised/spoiled areas, rough white tips, and white tops. Halve each strawberry lengthwise, place the halves cut side down on a clean cutting board, and cut each half lengthwise into 3 equal slices. Spread the strawberries over plastic wrap and evenly sprinkle 1 t sugar over them.
    - Add the **blueberries** to a colander, thoroughly rinse them with cold water, and pour the blueberries into a pie plate lined with a double thickness of paper towels. Pick through the berries, removing stems and soft or broken open berries. Replace discarded berries. Wrap the towels around the berries and gently roll the berries within the towels to dry them completely. Evenly divide the berries between the salad bowls, piling them in the center over the strawberries.
    - Add the **raspberries** to the colander, thoroughly rinse them with cool water, pour the berries into a pie plate lined with a double thickness of paper towels, and turn the berries open end down for draining. Pick through the berries, removing soft or spoiled berries. Wrap the towels around the berries and very gently roll the berries within the towels to dry them completely. Evenly divide the berries between the salad bowls, piling them in the center over the blueberries.
    - Evenly drizzle approx. ½ t honey over the fruit in each bowl.

4. **Prepare the nuts.** Use a chef's knife to chop the nuts coarsely and evenly divide the nuts over the fruit in each bowl.

5. **Immediately serve the yogurt snack.**

VARIATIONS: Add ingredients. Add, for example,

- **2-3 blackberries** per bowl. Use a serrated knife to halve very large blackberries.
- **dried fruit**, such as **6-8 raisins** and/or **4 tart dried cherries, halved,** per bowl.

Substitute **1 handful raw pistachios**, coarsely chopped, per bowl in place of pecans or walnuts.

COMMENTS: To significantly boost dish quality, select grass-fed and certified organic yogurt.

CHAPTER FIVE

Raw and Barely Cooked Vegetables

Chapter Five Description

CHAPTER FIVE PRESENTS basic recipes for preparing the most commonly used vegetables in raw form and basic recipes for preparing a variety of vegetables in barely cooked form. Serving raw suits vegetables that are essentially tender. The primary advantage of serving raw is preparation simplicity. Because vegetables are not heated, serving raw also conserves heat-sensitive nutritional components, notably vitamin C and B complex vitamins, and folate in particular. Serving vegetables in barely cooked form, in contrast, involves brief boiling, which is called parboiling. The heating involved is somewhat damaging to heat sensitive nutrients, and parboiling also adds a preparation step. Parboiling, however, has some practical benefits. It softens the texture and flavor of vegetables, heightening natural sweetness. Parboiling also both brightens the natural color of vegetables and deactivates enzymes that are otherwise destructive of some nutrients (notably vitamin C) when a vegetable is exposed to air during cutting for serving. At the same time, heating is very brief so that minimal loss of heat sensitive nutrients occurs.

Because Chapter One provides basic nutritional, selection, and storage details for the vegetables used in recipes, Chapter Five raw and parboiled vegetable recipes are abbreviated in the following manner.

- Each individual recipe applies a basic preparation procedure, either one that details raw preparation steps or another that details parboiling preparation steps. These procedures, which are presented below, list all preparation tools used and cover all basic preparation steps.
- Individual Chapter Five raw vegetable recipes regularly include only three kinds of preparation details. These details cover 1) **vegetable amount required for two servings, 2) preparation (cleaning, drying, and cutting) required to serve the vegetable raw as sticks or slices, and 3) the number of the Chapter One reference recipe.**
  - Some recipes also make serving or variation suggestions and/or serving comments.

- Because some vegetables (cucumber, fennel, and radish) are not included in Chapter One, a vegetable profile is included in the raw recipes for these vegetables.

- Individual Chapter Five parboiled vegetable recipes regularly include three kinds of preparation details. These details cover 1) **vegetable amount required for two servings**, 2) **parboiling time**, and 3) **the number of the Chapter One reference recipe**. Some recipes include a variation suggestion.

Chapter Five includes two Vegetable Snack recipes. These full recipes illustrate two ways of serving raw and parboiled vegetables.

Other sections and references of *Cooked Alive!* serve as useful resources for Chapter Five recipe preparation. These resources include:

- The Part One introduction listing of preparation tools, which serves as a descriptive reference for all basic preparation tools used in Chapter Five Recipes.
- Reference #1: Selecting Top Quality Fresh Whole Vegetables and Fruits.
- Reference #2: Key Home Storage Guidelines for Conserving Vegetable and Fruit Quality.

Basic Procedure for Serving Raw Vegetables

1. **Gather all preparation tools.** While the particular tools needed vary depending on the particular vegetable being prepared, recipes generally use similar tools, including:

   - 1 vegetable scrub brush.
   - 1 scrub sponge with 1 rough side.
   - paper or terry cloth towels for drying.
   - 1 swivel vegetable peeler.
   - 1 each paring, 7 in. serrated, and chef's knife.
   - 1 large mixing bowl.
   - 1 set measuring spoons.
   - 2 wooden spoons.
   - 1 pair kitchen scissors.
   - plastic wrap.
   - 1 opaque flat medium-size (such as 8 x 8 in. square) storage dish or plastic container with a tight-fitting and opaque lid.

2. **Gather ingredients.**

   - Intact chilled vegetable(s). Chilling is important for keeping plant enzymes inactive. Active enzymes can be highly destructive of both the flavor and nutritional content of cut raw vegetables.
   - Extra virgin olive oil.

3. **Prepare a vegetable for serving.**

    - Remove a vegetable from the refrigerator shortly before readying.
    - Rinse and dry a vegetable before cutting.
    - Do not peel a vegetable unless it is an industrially produced vegetable.
    - Cut juicy vegetables (such as cucumber) just prior to serving to minimize juice spilling.
    - Very lightly coat cut vegetable flesh with extra virgin olive oil to protect it from contact with air before and during serving. Air stimulates destructive enzyme activity in exposed pulp. While activated enzymes result in the destruction of vitamin C, which shows up as browning, and in the breakdown of cell structure, which shows up as puddles of spilled juice, most nutritional destruction is invisible and on-going as long as vegetable pulp remains exposed to air, especially at room temperature. Coating exposed pulp with oil also prevents air from drying out vegetable pulp, which leaves it unattractively limp.

        - To coat cut vegetable pieces, add cut vegetable pieces to a large bowl and drizzle extra virgin olive oil evenly over them (approx. 1 t oil per 1 c).
        - Use two wooden spoons to toss the vegetable pieces gently and thoroughly.

    - Refrigerate a prepared vegetable that will not be quickly served in a flat and opaque storage container. Store vegetable pieces side by side in a single layer, adding a layer of plastic wrap between layers to prevent direct contact between the cut flesh of individual pieces. An opaque container protects cut vegetable pieces from destructive light. Covering adds double protection of oil-coated vegetable pieces from air.

4. **Serve a prepared raw vegetable.** The vegetable is in ready-to-serve form for use as a snack or for inclusion in a crudités platter, an appetizer dish, or salad.

Basic Parboiling Procedure

1. **Prepare parboiling water.**

    - Add enough water to a pot that is large enough to completely cover the vegetable to be parboiled by several inches. This pot can be a Dutch oven, soup pot, or deep 14 in. skillet.
    - Begin heating the water on high heat as a first preparation step, heating the water on a burner that matches the pot size.
    - Bring the water to full boiling.

2. **Gather other preparation tools.** While the tools needed vary somewhat depending on the particular vegetable being prepared, tools used are generally similar, including,

- **1 slotted spoon.** This spoon makes it possible to remove vegetables quickly from parboiling liquid while saving the boiling water for parboiling other vegetables.
- **1 pair of tongs.** Tongs are useful tools for quickly removing large leafy greens from parboiling water.
- **1 timer.**
- **1 colander.**
- **1 wooden spoon.**
- **paper or terry cloth towels.**
- **1 rubber spatula.** A spatula efficiently scrapes vegetables from a mixing bowl used for coating cut vegetable pieces with oil.

3. **Parboil a vegetable.**

   - Rinse a vegetable to clean it.
   - Except for broccoli and cauliflower florets, leave a vegetable completely intact.
   - Add vegetables to fully boiling water without causing the water to stop boiling, using a wooden spoon to immediately push each vegetable completely into the boiling water as it is added.
   - Start the timer for the recipe-directed parboiling time immediately once all vegetables are added to the boiling water.
   - At the timer, immediately use a slotted spoon or tongs to remove the vegetables from the boiling water into a colander and immediately rinse the vegetables with cold water to stop the cooking. When the boiling water will not be used again, the water and vegetable can be drained together into the colander at the end of the cooking time.
   - Set a parboiled vegetable to be quickly served aside, but refrigerate any vegetable that will not be quickly used, covering it tightly once it has cooled.

4. **Prepare a parboiled vegetable for serving.**

   - Dry parboiled vegetables before cutting them for serving. Spread the vegetables over a double thickness of paper towels or an absorbent cloth towel and either pat the vegetables dry with another towel or add a towel topping and roll the vegetables in the towels.
   - Cut vegetables just prior to serving to minimize juice spilling.

     - Do not peel skin. The skin is nutritious. Maintaining the protective skin coating as long as possible protects cut vegetables from air, which dehydrates them, and from light, which is destructive of some nutrients.
     - Cut juicy parboiled vegetables into pieces that are fairly large but that are still easy to eat. Large pieces are more flavorful than small ones.

   - Protect cut pulp from air and light after parboiling. Keep cut vegetables covered with an opaque lid. Top a storage container covered with plastic wrap with a dark towel.
   - Add any salt to cut parboiled vegetables shortly before serving.

5. **Serve a parboiled vegetable.** The vegetable is in ready-to-serve form for use as a snack or for inclusion in a crudités platter, an appetizer dish, or salad.

Raw Vegetable Recipes
(2 Servings)

111. Asparagus

1. Amount of asparagus (Recipe #1): 8-10 chilled fresh asparagus spears.

2. Preparation for serving raw as sticks:

    - Rinse and thoroughly dry the spears.
    - Gently bend spears until the tips break off. Group tips together as the most attractive parts.
    - Gently bend remaining spears until they break, keeping sticks roughly several inches long.

3. Serving comment: Raw asparagus has greater overall nutritional content than cooked asparagus.

112. Green Snap (or String) and Yellow Wax Beans

1. Amount of green beans: 16-29 fresh thin or medium thick, uniformly firm beans (approx. ¼ lb).

2. Preparation for serving raw as sticks:

    - Rinse the beans and pour them onto a double layer of paper towels or a terry cloth towel.
    - Wrap the towels around the beans, gently squeeze the beans, and move the beans around within the towels to dry them.
    - Use kitchen scissors to snip off the ends and to cut beans into desired length for serving.

3. Green bean profile: See Recipe #58 (Boiled Whole Green or Yellow Wax Beans) for selection and nutritional details.

PART 1

113. Bok Choy

1. Amount of bok choy (Recipe #3): 1-2 bunches baby bok choy (6-8 bright white and firm stalks with bright green and fresh-looking tops).

2. Preparation for serving raw as sticks.

    - Slice off the leafy tops of the stalks. Quickly re-refrigerate the leafy tops, tightly covered, for another use, such as in a stir fry.
    - Quickly rinse the stalks and use paper towels or a terry cloth towel to thoroughly dry each stalk.
    - Slice off the tip of the stem end of each stalk. Halve thick stalks lengthwise and cut the stalks into approx. 2 in. sticks.

    VARIATION: Leave the leafy tops on very small, fresh, and tender bok choy stalks.

114. Broccoli

1. Amount of broccoli (Recipe #4): 1 chilled stalk.

2. Preparation for serving raw as florets or slices:

    - Rinse the broccoli stalk in cool water, wrap the stalk in a double thickness of paper towels or a cloth towel, and firmly squeeze the florets to dry them.
    - Place the stalk on its side and use a serrated knife to slice off the florets, leaving long stems (cutting the stems off at the stalk). Collect and quickly refrigerate any leaves and the stalk for another use.
    - For florets, leave small broccoli florets whole.
    - For slices, slice large florets. Halve large florets lengthwise, place the halves cut side down on a cutting board, and cut the floret halves lengthwise into ¼ in. thick slices.
    - Toss sliced broccoli in a small amount of extra virgin olive oil (2 t). Add the broccoli to a large mixing bowl, drizzle the oil over the broccoli, and use two wooden spoons to toss the broccoli to coat all pieces with oil.

3. Serving comments: The antioxidant content of raw broccoli is much higher than that of cooked broccoli.[212]

---

[212] Robinson, *Eating on the Wild Side*, 163. Fresh broccoli contributes up to twenty times more of the beneficial compound sulforaphane than cooked broccoli.

115. Cabbage

1. Amount of cabbage (Recipe #6): ¼ chilled medium head of fresh green cabbage, particularly certified organic or locally grown cabbage.

2. Preparation for serving raw:

    - Place the ¼ cabbage wedge on a cut side and slice off the very tip of the wedge, saving the tip.
    - Use a chef's knife to cut the cabbage lengthwise into ½ in. thick slices.
    - Cut the slices into 2 in. lengths. Cut the tip into thick slices.
    - Coat the slices with oil. Add the cabbage pieces to a large mixing bowl, drizzle 2 t extra virgin olive oil over the cabbage, and use two wooden spoons to thoroughly toss the pieces with oil.

3. Serving comment: While red/purple cabbage has far greater phytonutrient content than green cabbage, it tends to be less sweet and somewhat tougher. It is, as a result, less suited to being served raw than green cabbage. It is important for cabbage to be very fresh, and very fresh certified organic and locally grown cabbage is most reliably deliciously sweet.

116. Carrot

1. Amount of carrot (Recipe #7): 3 medium or 2 large carrots.

2. Preparation for serving raw as sticks or rounds:

    - Scrub and thoroughly dry the carrots.
    - For sticks, use a chef's knife to cut off the ends, halve each carrot lengthwise, and halve each half lengthwise to form 16 carrot strips. Cut each strip into 2 to 4 sticks.
    - For rounds, use a chef's knife to slice large carrots crosswise into ¼ in. thick rounds.
    - Lightly coat cut carrot with oil. Add the cut carrots to a large mixing bowl, drizzle 2 t extra virgin olive oil over the carrots, and use two wooden spoons to thoroughly toss the carrots to coat all pieces with oil.

3. Serving comment: When refrigerating carrot, refrigerate it tightly covered to protect carrot flavor. Ethylene gas naturally released by particular vegetables like potato and fruits like banana and apple transforms carrot flavor, turning it somewhat bitter.

PART 1

117. Cauliflower

1. Amount of cauliflower (Recipe #8): ½ chilled small head of cauliflower.

2. Preparation for serving raw:

    - Rinse a whole cauliflower in cool water, wrap the head in a double thickness of paper towels or a cloth towel, and firmly squeeze the cauliflower to dry it.
    - Turn the cauliflower upside down and use a chef's knife to cut off one half of the florets, leaving 1-2 in. stems and retaining all internal fleshly parts, which are tender and should be included, except for the tough stem end. Cover and refrigerate the remaining head of cauliflower.
    - For whole florets, break the florets apart as needed to form roughly uniform-sized florets with 1 in. stems.
    - For cauliflower slices, halve large florets lengthwise, place the halved florets cut side down on a cutting board, and cut floret halves lengthwise into ¼ in. thick slices.
    - To coat slices with oil, add the cauliflower slices to a large bowl, drizzle 2 t extra virgin olive oil over the cauliflower slices, and use two wooden spoons to thoroughly toss the slices in the oil.

118. Celery

1. Amount of celery (Recipe #9): 3 certified organic or locally produced medium thick and firm celery stalks.

2. Preparation for serving raw as sticks:

    - Rinse and dry the celery stalks.
    - Use a chef's knife to trim off the very tip of the stem end and the leafy tops of each stalk. Cover and refrigerate the leafy tops for another use.
    - Cut each stalk lengthwise, halve each half lengthwise to form 12 thin strips, and cut the strips crosswise into 2-3 in. sticks. For thin celery stalks, halve the stalks only.
    - Coat the celery sticks with oil. Add the celery to a large mixing bowl, drizzle 2 t extra virgin olive oil over the celery, and use two wooden spoons to thoroughly toss the celery to coat all pieces with oil.

119. Cucumber

1. Amount of cucumber: 1 medium (approx. 6 in. long; 1½ in. thick) Japanese cucumber

301

or other thin variety of cucumber with small seeds and a tender and crisp texture (identified by having the same crisp, hollow feel of a ripe watermelon when tapped), such as pickling size cucumbers.

2. Preparation for serving raw as sticks or slices:

   - Completely peel only commercially grown cucumbers. Partially peel larger and more mature cucumbers, leaving strips of skin.
   - For sticks, use a chef's knife to slice off the tips of the cucumber. Stand the cucumber upright on a flattened end and use the chef's knife to cut the cucumber lengthwise into ⅓ in. thick slices. Stacking 2 slices together, cut the slices lengthwise into ⅓ in. thick strips. Cut the strips crosswise into 2-3 in. long sticks.
   - For rounds, cut the tips from a cucumber and use a chef's knife to slice the cucumber crosswise into ⅓ in. thick rounds.
   - Coat cut cucumber pieces with extra virgin olive oil. Add the cucumber pieces to a large mixing bowl, drizzle 1-2 t oil over the cucumber, and use two wooden spoons to toss the cucumber to thoroughly coat all cut surfaces.

3. Cucumber profile:

   - Cucumber, including the cucumber skin, is a valuable source of antioxidant phytonutrients, including carotenoid and flavonoid phytonutrients. Additionally, cucumber is a good source of antioxidant nutrients, including vitamin C and the mineral manganese, which combine with phytonutrients to intensify the antioxidant capacity of cucumber.
   - Cucumber is also a source of phytonutrients that provide anti-inflammatory protection to humans. The rich magnesium content of cucumber combines with these phytonutrients to expand the anti-inflammatory protection provided to humans.
   - Cucumber also contains a rather distinctive type of human health-supporting phytonutrient called lignans, which are also found in cabbage family vegetables and allium vegetables like onion and garlic.
   - Cucumber contains small amounts and in many cases good amounts (such as in the case of vitamin K and pantothenic acid) of nearly every category of nutritional components.

4. Select the freshest and most nutritious cucumber:

   - Select fresh cucumber. Select cucumber that is uniformly firm, heavy feeling for its size, and brightly colored, not dull. Cucumber skin should be tight, not wrinkled. When lightly tapped, very fresh cucumber makes a hollow-like sound similar to the sound made by a ripe watermelon when tapped. Inside flesh should be juicy without any hollow spaces.
   - Select in-season cucumber, which in the United States is from May through July. In cooler states cucumbers are in-season through August.

PART 1

- Select certified organic and locally grown cucumbers, which are largely free of pesticide content and have other advantages of naturally produced foods, particularly more potent phytonutrient content.
- Quickly refrigerate cucumbers unwashed and store them within the crisper drawer until they are completely chilled before transferring them to a sealed plastic bag, pressing out as much air as possible before sealing the bag.
- Use cucumber within a week of storage. Though cucumber stores well without becoming soft for over a week or more, the potency of its phytonutrient content fades with storage.

120. Fennel Bulb

1. Amount of fennel bulb: 1 large (approx. 1 lb) fennel bulb with fresh appearing feathery tops and uniformly firm stalks.

2. Preparation for serving raw as sticks:

   - Rinse the fennel with cold water, wrap the fennel within a double layer of paper towels or terry cloth towel, and gently squeeze the fennel to dry it. Unwrap the towels.
   - Cut the stalks from the bulb. Use a vegetable peeler to remove any tough strings from the bottoms of stalks surrounding the bulb. Collect the stalks, feathery tops, and any removed strings and refrigerate these parts within a sealed plastic bag for another use, such as for making a broth.
   - Use a chef's knife to slice off the very bottom of the root end of the bulb. Use the chef's knife to halve the fennel bulb lengthwise and to cut out the V-shaped core.
   - Separate the sections of the bulb, dry any wet areas, and slice each section lengthwise into ½ in. thick sticks.

3. Fennel nutritional profile:

   - Fennel is a good source of phytonutrients, including flavonoids and phenolic acids, which provide both antioxidant and anti-inflammatory protection for humans. Additionally, fennel is a source antioxidant nutrients, including a concentrated amount of vitamin C and the mineral manganese, which combine with antioxidant phytonutrients to intensify the antioxidant capacity of fennel. Fennel is also a good source of magnesium, which combines with anti-inflammatory phytonutrients to boost the anti-inflammatory protection provided to humans.
   - Fennel is a very good source of nearly every category of nutritional components, including notable amounts of alkaline minerals, folate, iron, and dietary fiber.

4. Select the freshest and most nutritious fennel:

- Select fresh fennel. Bulbs should be whitish or pale green in color. The bulbs should be uniformly firm and solid. Bottoms of the stalks that surround the bulb should be tightly clustered around the bulb and not split or bruised. Both the stalks and leaves (or fronds) should be green. The leaves should be firm and fresh appearing. The fennel should not have flowering buds, which means the fennel is past peak ripeness.
- Select in-season fennel, which in the United States is in the fall through early spring.
- Quickly refrigerate fennel. Store unwashed fennel in the crisper drawer until it is thoroughly chilled and then wrap it within paper towels and transfer it to a sealed plastic bag, pressing out as much air as possible before sealing the bag.
- Use fennel quickly, within 4 days, to maximize retention of its rich phytonutrient content.

121. Kohlrabi

1. Amount of kohlrabi (Recipe #12): 1 chilled small or medium kohlrabi (2-3 in. diameter).

2. Preparation for serving raw as sticks or rounds:

   - Slice the stems from the kohlrabi bulb, cutting close to the bulb. Collect and save the leafy topped stems for another use. Wrap them within paper towels and quickly refrigerate them within a partially open plastic bag. Once the leaves are chilled, press out as much air as possible and seal the storage bag.
   - Rinse and dry the kohlrabi bulb.
   - For sticks, use a chef's knife to cut off the ends. Stand the kohlrabi upright on a flattened end and use the chef's knife to cut the kohlrabi lengthwise into 4 equal slices. Stacking two slices together, cut the slices lengthwise into ¼ in. thick strips. Cut the strips crosswise into 2-3 in. sticks.
   - For rounds, cut the whole kohlrabi crosswise into ¼ in. thick slices. Halve large rounds.

122. Mushroom

1. Amount of mushrooms (Recipe #33): 5 medium white or crimini mushrooms.

2. Preparation for serving raw:

   - Use a damp paper towel to wipe each mushroom clean.
   - Cut each mushroom lengthwise into 3 or 5 equally thick slices.
   - Either immediately serve the sliced mushrooms or coat them lightly with oil, first

drizzling 2 t extra virgin olive oil over the slices and then thoroughly tossing the slices to evenly coat them with oil.

123. Green Peas

1. Amount of green peas (Recipe #15): 20 fresh green pea pods.

2. Preparation for serving raw:

   - Rinse the pods. Pour them onto a double layer of paper towels or a terry cloth towel, wrap the towels around the pods, and squeeze and move the pods around within the towels to dry them. Unwrap the peas.
   - Serve the whole pea pods. Prepare the pods ahead for easy removal when served. Use a paring knife to cut partially through the stem end, cutting from the outside towards the inner slightly curved side. Instruct those being served to open the pods by grasping the cut end and pulling it down the inside of the pea pod and to use their thumb to scoop out the peas.
   - Serve individual servings of pea pods in small glass bowls.
   - Serve a separate bowl for discarded pods.
   - Collect discarded pea pods for making a broth, as suggested in Recipe #15.

3. Serving raw comment: Eating green peas raw fully conserves their very good vitamin C and folate content.

124. Sugar Snap and Snow Peas

1. Amount of pea pods (Recipe #16): 20 small or medium sugar snap or snow pea pods.

2. Preparation for serving raw:

   - Rinse the pods. Pour them onto a double layer of paper towels or a terry cloth towel, wrap the towels around the pods, and squeeze and move the pods around within the towels to dry them. Unwrap the peas.
   - Before serving, prepare the pods for easy removal of any strings. Use a paring knife to cut partially through the stem end, cutting from the outside towards the inner slightly curved side. Instruct those being served to remove the string by grasping the cut end and pulling it down the inside of the pea pod.
   - Use kitchen scissors to snip off the remaining tip.
   - Serve individual servings of pea pods in small glass bowls.

3. Serving comment: Select certified organic and locally grown sugar snap and snow peas to minimize pesticide content, which is heavy in industrially produced sugar snap and snow peas, both domestic and imported. Certified organic and locally grown sugar snap and snow peas also have the other advantages of naturally produced produce, particularly more potent phytonutrient content and overall greater nutritional value.

125. Bell Pepper

1. Amount of bell pepper (Recipe #35): 1 organic red, green, yellow, purple, or other color bell pepper or ⅓ each of a variety.

2. Preparation for serving raw as sticks:

   - Rinse and thoroughly dry the bell pepper.
   - Use a serrated knife to halve each pepper lengthwise and to cut out the stem end. Remove the seeds but not the white membrane and cut each half lengthwise into ¼ or ⅓ in. thick strips (sticks).
   - For straight sticks, cut off the curved stem end tops of the strips, serving them separately as scoops for a dip or setting them aside (tightly covered and refrigerated) for use in a salad.
   - Coat the sticks with oil. Add the sticks to a large bowl, drizzle 2 t extra virgin olive oil over the sticks, and use two wooden spoons to toss the bell pepper sticks to thoroughly coat cut surface with oil.

3. Serving comments: It is important to select certified organic and locally grown bell pepper because these products are largely free of pesticide content while industrially produced bell pepper is heavily contaminated. Certified organic and locally grown bell pepper also has the other advantages of naturally produced produce, particularly more potent phytonutrient content and overall greater nutritional value.

126. Radish

1. Amount and type of radish: 1 chilled medium daikon radish (no larger than 3 in. diameter) or 8-10 small radishes (1 in. or less diameter, preferably with bright green leafy tops still attached, which indicate freshness).

2. Preparation for serving raw as sticks or rounds:

   - Scrub and thoroughly dry the radish.

- For daikon radish sticks, use a vegetable peeler to remove any tough skin. Use a chef's knife to slice off the ends. Standing the radish upright on a flattened end, use the chef's knife to cut the radish lengthwise into ¼ in. thick slices. Stacking two slices together, cut the slices lengthwise into ¼ in. thick strips. Cut the strips crosswise into 2-3 in. sticks.
- For daikon radish rounds, use a vegetable peeler to remove any tough skin. Use a chef's knife to cut off the radish tips and to cut the radish crosswise into ¼ in. thick slices. Halve large slices.
- For regular American radish, serve the radishes whole with or without tops.

3. Serving comments:

- Daikon radish is a white-fleshed Asian radish that is somewhat sweeter and less peppery than the American radish.
- The smaller and fresher an American radish, the sweeter and milder it is likely to be.
- Radish is a member of the cabbage family of vegetables and shares the rich and varied nutritional content of this family of vegetables.

127. Summer Squash (Yellow and Zucchini)

1. Amount of summer squash (Recipe #20): 2 small squash, yellow crookneck squash (each approx. 4 in. long, excluding the neck, and 2 in. thick) or either zucchini or straightneck yellow squash (each approx. 5 in. long, 1½ in. thick).

2. Preparation for serving raw as rounds or sticks:

- Rinse and thoroughly dry the squash.
- For rounds, use a chef's knife to cut off the ends (and the neck in the case of yellow crookneck squash) and to cut the squash crosswise into ¼ in. thick slices. Collect, cover, and refrigerate the squash neck for another use.
- For sticks, use a chef's knife to cut off the ends (and the neck in the case of yellow crookneck squash), stand squash upright on a flattened end, use a chef's knife to cut the squash lengthwise into ¼ in. thick slices, cut the slices lengthwise into ¼ in. thick strips, and cut the strips crosswise into 2 in. sticks. Halve lengthwise any yellow crookneck necks.
- Coat the cut squash pieces with oil. Add the squash to a large bowl, drizzle 2 t extra virgin olive oil over the squash, and use two wooden spoons to toss the squash to thoroughly coat cut surface with oil.

3. Serving comments: It is important to select certified organic and locally grown summer squash to minimize pesticide content, which clears the way to safely include the nutritious skin. Certified organic and locally grown summer squash also have the

other advantages of naturally produced produce, particularly more potent phytonutrient content and overall greater nutritional value than industrially produced summer squash.

128. Turnip

1. Amount of turnip (Recipe #22): 2 small or 4 medium chilled fresh turnips with smooth skin, preferably bunched turnips with fresh-looking green leafy tops attached.

2. Preparation for serving raw as sticks or rounds:

   - Cut off and save leafy tops for another use. See Recipe #30 for preparation and storage details.
   - Thoroughly scrub and dry the turnip roots.
   - Use a swivel vegetable peeler to remove any rough skin around the stem end.
   - For sticks, use a chef's knife to slice off the turnip ends. Standing each turnip on a flattened end, cut the turnips lengthwise into ¼ in. thick slices. Stacking two slices together, cut the slices into ¼ in. wide strips. Cut the strips crosswise into 2-3 in. sticks.
   - For rounds, use a chef's knife to slice off the turnip ends. Cut each turnip crosswise into ¼ in. slices.

3. Serving comments:

   - As turnips can be bitter, taste the turnip to verify sweetness before serving.
   - As a variation, substitute small, fresh rutabaga (not commercially grown waxed rutabaga) strips, cutting them into sticks exactly like turnips.

Parboiled Vegetable Recipes
(2 Servings)

129. Parboiled Asparagus

1. Amount of asparagus (Recipe #1): 8-10 chilled uniform spears, untrimmed.

2. Parboiling time: 30 seconds for thin spears; 1 minute for medium and large spears.

3. Preparation for serving: Use a serrated knife to cut the whole spears into the desired serving size, leaving tips intact.

PART 1

130. Parboiled Green Snap (or String) and Yellow Wax Beans

1. Amount of green beans: 10 uniformly thin or medium (only slightly bulging) beans.

2. Parboiling time: 1 minute.

3. Preparation for serving: Use kitchen scissors to snip off the tips.

4. Serving Comment: See Recipe #58 (Boiled Whole Green or Yellow Wax Beans) for green bean nutritional profile.

131. Parboiled Broccoli Florets

1. Amount of broccoli (Recipe #4): 1 stalk chilled broccoli, separated into florets with long stems (stems cut off at the stalk). Group the florets into medium and large size and parboil each size separately.

2. Parboiling time: 1 minute for medium florets and 1½ minutes for large florets.

3. Serving preparation:

    - Spread the parboiled florets over paper towels or a cloth towel, wrap the towels around the florets, and gently squeeze the florets to dry them.
    - Serve the florets whole or sliced.
    - To slice florets, use a serrated knife to halve each lengthwise, place the halves cut side down on a cutting board, and cut each half lengthwise into ¼ in. slices.

4. Variation: Substitute 4-6 broccoli raab stalks for florets, parboiling the whole, untrimmed stalks for 1 minute in a large pot before drying and cutting the stalks into serving size pieces.

132. Parboiled Cauliflower Florets

1. Amount of cauliflower (Recipe #8): ½ small chilled head of cauliflower, separated into florets with 2 in. stems (as long as possible). Separate florets into medium and large size; separately parboil large and medium florets.

2. Parboiling time: 1 minute for medium florets and 1½ minutes for large florets.

3. Serving preparation:

   - Spread the parboiled florets over paper towels or a cloth towel, wrap the towels around the florets, and gently squeeze the florets to dry them.
   - Either serve the florets whole or sliced.
   - To slice florets, use a serrated knife to halve each lengthwise, place the halves cut side down on a cutting board, and cut each half lengthwise into ¼ in. slices.

133. Parboiled Sugar Snap and Snow Peas

1. Amount of pea pods (Recipe #16): 20 uniform medium or large pea pods, untrimmed. Separate medium or large florets for parboiling.

2. Parboiling time: 30 seconds for medium pods and 1 minute for large pods.

3. Serving preparation:

   - Rinse the parboiled pods with cool water to stop the cooking.
   - Spread the pods over paper towels or a cloth towel, wrap the towels around the pods, and gently squeeze the pods to dry them.
   - If the pods have strings, see Recipe #123 (Green Peas) above for string-removing details.
   - Use kitchen scissors to snip off the ends for serving.

134. Parboiled Summer Squash

1. Amount of summer squash (Recipe #20): 2 small (approx. 4 in. long, excluding the neck; 2 in. diameter) yellow crookneck squash; 2 small (approx. 5 in. long; 1½ in. diameter) zucchini or yellow straightneck squash

2. Parboiling time: 1 minute.

3. Serving preparation:

   - Rinse and dry the summer squash.
   - For rounds, use a chef's or serrated knife to cut off the ends of squash and the neck of yellow crookneck squash before cutting the squash crosswise into ¼ in. thick rounds for serving.

- For sticks, slice off the ends of the squash and of the neck of yellow crookneck squash. Stand the squash on a flattened end and cut the squash lengthwise into ¼ in. thick slices. Cut the slices into ¼ in. strips and cut the strips into 2 or 3 in. sticks.

135. Herbed Onion and Garlic Dip
(4 servings; approx. 1½ cups)

½ chilled medium bulb onion, sliced lengthwise
4-6 garlic cloves, chilled
1 T extra virgin olive oil
½ t dried dill weed
1½ t apple cider or rice vinegar
1 t sugar or honey
3 oz package cream cheese, softened

1 T plain yogurt (low or full fat)
2 t freshly squeezed lemon juice
¼ t salt
¼ c raw whole pecan halves
2 sprigs fresh dill (opt)
2-serving portion of raw or parboiled vegetable sticks or rounds to use as scoops (Recipes #111-134)

Preparation Tools

1 large nonstick skillet
1 chef's knife
1 plastic or plastic-coated stir-fry spatula
1 timer
1 set measuring spoons

1 medium mixing bowl
1 wooden spoon
1 hand electric mixer
1 rubber spatula
1 pair kitchen scissors

1. **Gather all preparation tools and ingredients.**

2. **Cook the onion and garlic with the dried dill weed.**

    - Heat the skillet at a medium setting. Use a chef's knife to cut off the ends of the onion and garlic cloves. Peel the onion and garlic cloves. Use the chef's knife to dice the onion and to mince the garlic.
    - Increase the skillet heat to medium-high.
    - When a drop of water added to the skillet instantly dances and disappears, add 1 T oil to the skillet, add the onion and garlic, evenly sprinkle the ½ t dill weed (first crushing it between your palms) over the onion and garlic, and stir-fry the mixture for about 30 seconds.
    - Reduce the heat to medium and cook the mixture for 2 minutes, stirring it occasionally to protect the garlic from browning. Set a timer.
    - At the timer, remove the skillet from the heat.

3. **Assemble the dip.**

    - Add 1½ t vinegar, 1 t sugar or honey, 3 oz cream cheese, 1 T yogurt, 2 t lemon juice, and ¼ t salt to a medium mixing bowl.
    - Use a wooden spoon to stir (or beat the mixture with an electric mixer) the ingredients until creamy smooth.
    - Check the flavor and adjust it to taste, adding touches (1-2 t) more lemon juice or vinegar for tartness or sugar/honey for sweetening.
    - Use the wooden spoon to mix in the cooled onion and garlic mixture.
    - Prepare and add the nuts. Use a chef's knife to chop the nuts coarsely. Mix the nuts into the cream cheese mixture.
    - Prepare and mix in the fresh dill (if using). Rinse the dill under cool water, vigorously shake it to remove most clinging water, and spread the dill over a layer of paper towels. Add a paper towel topping and roll the leaves in the towels to dry them. Unroll the towels and use kitchen scissors to snip the leaves from the stems and to snip the leaves into fairly large pieces. Group the stems together and snip them finely. Mix the dill into the dip.
    - Use a rubber spatula to scrape the dip into a serving bowl.
    - Serve the dip at room temperature.

4. **Serve the dip with raw or parboiled vegetable sticks or scoops.** For example, serve with asparagus (Recipe #111 or #129), sugar snap peas (Recipe #124 or #133), broccoli (Recipe #114 or #131), cucumber (Recipe #119), bell pepper (Recipe #125), summer squash (Recipe #127 or #134), grape tomato (Recipe #100), or turnip (Recipe #128). Alternatively, use sticks/scoops made from a combination of these vegetables.

5. **Refrigerate leftover dip, tightly covered, in a glass container.** Use the dip within 4-5 days.

    VARIATIONS: Make ingredient substitutions. Substitute, for example,

    - **½ t dried thyme leaves** for dill weed
    - **1 T snipped fresh thyme** for fresh dill.
    - **¼ c other nut varieties** for pecans. For example, substitute walnut halves or whole almonds. Substitute a combination of nuts.
    - **raw apple cider** for pasteurized vinegar. Raw vinegar is a less processed product than pasteurized vinegar.

    Add flavoring ingredients. Add, for example,

    - **1 T snipped fresh chives.** Rinse and pat dry 2-4 stalks of chives. Holding them together, thinly slice them crosswise and mix them into the assembled dip.
    - **2 raw green onions or 2 T diced fresh shallots,** mixed with 2 t extra virgin olive oil.
    - **1 t paprika** (½ t for hot Hungarian paprika).
    - **½ t prepared horseradish.**

COMMENTS: Select certified organic dried dill weed or dried dill weed marketed by natural food stores or natural food sections of regular grocery stores to reliably avoid selection of irradiated dried dill.

Boost the nutritional quality of this dip by using certified organic cream cheese and best of all, cream cheese that is made from cream produced from dairy cows that are both grass-fed and certified organic.

136. Raw Vegetable Pita Pizza
(4 servings; 1 pizza per serving)

3 oz package cream cheese, softened
1 t honey
1 T plain yogurt
2 t fresh lemon juice
½ t dried dill weed
¼ t garlic powder
¼ c fresh pineapple chunks (Recipe #94), (½ in. thick)
6 small sugar snap pea pods

⅛ each red, green, and yellow bell pepper
1 small Japanese cucumber
1 t extra virgin olive oil
8 grape tomatoes
8 pitted Kalamata olives
¼ c pecan or walnut halves
2 fresh 6 in. whole wheat pita bread rounds

Preparation Tools

1 set measuring spoons
2 medium mixing bowls
1 wooden mixing spoon
1 hand electric mixer (optional)

1 5 in. serrated knife
1 vegetable peeler
1 rubber spatula
plastic wrap

1. **Gather all ingredients and preparation tools.**

2. **Assemble the cream cheese spread.** Add the 3 oz. cream cheese, 1 t honey, 1 T yogurt, 2 t lemon juice, ½ t dried dill weed, and ¼ t garlic powder to a medium mixing bowl and stir the mixture with a wooden spoon or electric mixer until creamy smooth.

3. **Prepare the raw pineapple and vegetable ingredients.**

   - Use a serrated knife to cut the pineapple chunks into ¼ in. thick slices.
   - Rinse, thoroughly dry, remove strings (partially twist off the stem end and pull it down the curved side of the pod), use a serrated knife to cut off the other tip, and halve each sugar snap pea.

- Use a serrated knife to cut out the stem ends of the bell peppers. Remove the seeds but not the white membrane from the bell peppers. Use a serrated knife to cut the bell peppers lengthwise into ¼ in. thick slices and to cut the slices crosswise into thirds.
- Rinse and thoroughly dry the cucumber. Partially peel commercially produced cucumber. Use a serrated knife to cut the cucumber crosswise into ¼ in. thick slices. Add 1 t oil to a medium mixing bowl, add the cucumber, and use a rubber spatula to turn the cucumber slices over repeatedly to coat the pieces.
- Rinse and thoroughly dry the grape tomatoes. Use a serrated knife to halve them lengthwise.

4. **Assemble the pitas for serving.**

    - Gently pry each pita bread apart to separate it into two equal halves.
    - Spread ¼ of the cream cheese mixture over the rough side of each pita half.
    - Evenly distribute the tomato halves, cut side down, and pineapple pieces over the cream cheese mixture on each pita round, pushing the pieces slightly into the cheese.
    - Evenly distribute the sugar snap peas, bell pepper, and cucumber pieces in open spaces on each pita round.
    - Prepare and add the Kalamata olives and nuts to the pita pizzas. Use a serrated knife to quarter the Kalamata olives. Break the nuts into several large pieces. Evenly distribute the olives and nuts over the four pita pizzas.

5. **Cover the pita pizzas with plastic wrap and chill them in the refrigerator.** Remove the pita pizzas from the refrigerator 10-15 minutes ahead of serving to allow the cheese to soften, but keep them protected from air and light until serving. Use a serrated knife to cut the pita pizzas into wedges for serving.

    VARIATIONS: Make ingredient substitutions. Substitute, for example,

    - **freshly baked 6 in. pizza crusts** for pita bread. Prepare one half pizza dough (Recipe #210). Divide the dough into 4 equal pieces, press the pieces into 6 in. rounds on a buttered pizza stone, and bake the rounds exactly like regular size crust.
    - **4 asparagus stalks** (Recipe #111) for sugar snap peas.
    - **3 broccoli florets**, parboiled and sliced (Recipe #131) or **6-8 green beans**, parboiled whole and halved (Recipe #130), for sugar snap peas. Lightly salt both broccoli and green beans before adding them to the pizzas.
    - **¼ c whole almonds** or other favorite raw nuts for pecans or walnuts.

    Add flavoring ingredients. Add, for example,

    - **½-1 t prepared horseradish** to the cream cheese mixture.
    - **1-2 t snipped fresh cilantro**, added as a topping to each assembled pita pizza. Prepare cilantro like fresh dill in Recipe #135, Step #3.

COMMENT: Select organic dried dill weed and garlic powder or products marketed at a natural food store to reliably avoid irradiated dill weed.

Boost the quality of this dish by using certified organic cream cheese. Best of all, select cream cheese made from dairy cattle that are both grass-fed and certified organic.

PART II

Resurrecting Everyday Dishes

Overview

PART II PRESENTS distinctively nutritious and attractive recipes for a variety of traditional everyday dishes – for salads, stir fries, soups and stews, curries, quiche, fruit desserts, pizza, and pancakes. *Cooked Alive!* Part II recipes achieve this distinctive status through the combined use of two different types of conservation techniques: *juice-protective* techniques for preparing individual vegetable and fruit dish ingredients and *juice-protective* methods for serving dishes.

Part II recipes prepare vegetable and fruit ingredients in accordance with the *juice-protective* preparation techniques set forth in Part I recipes to achieve reliably attractive and nutritious cooking results. Part II recipes combine use of these *juice-protective* preparation techniques with use of *juice-protective* serving methods that reliably maintain the attractiveness and high nutritional quality of vegetable and fruit ingredients through serving and up to the moment dishes are eaten. These particular *juice-protective* serving methods are as follows:

- **Dry form serving.** This is completely without liquid serving. Stir-Fried Dish Recipes (Chapter Seven) use "dry form" serving.
- **Effectively dry serving.** Cut vegetable and fruit ingredients are given a protective oil coating before being mixed with a small amount of liquid just prior to serving. Chapter Six salads use "effectively dry" serving.
- **Thick sauce serving.** Recipes serve vegetables and fruits in a thickened sauce made from liquid that is also somewhat protective of vegetable and fruit juice flavor. Soups and Stews (Chapter Eight), Curries (Chapter Nine), Quiche (Chapter Ten), and most desserts (Chapter Eleven) use "thick sauce" serving.
- **Batter serving.** Pancakes (Chapter Thirteen) use "batter" serving. Muffin recipes (Recipes #180-184) and corn bread (Recipe #185) included as accompaniments for soups and stews (Chapter Eight) also use "batter" serving.

Joint application of *juice-protective* preparation techniques and serving methods, in turn, transforms the quality of traditional dishes in two ways. First, joint application significantly boosts the overall nutritional content of vegetables and fruits in traditional recipes and, as a result, overall dish nutritional quality. Second, joint application secures vegetable and fruit flavor, and this is of no less significance for uplifting dish quality. Indeed, securing vegetable and fruit flavor serves as a simple and effective means for fundamentally transforming the overall quality of traditional dishes, and for doing so while maintaining the traditional character of dishes and, hence, dish acceptability.

The securing of vegetable and fruit flavor makes it possible to make two significant ingredient changes in traditional dishes. These changes are 1) expand vegetable and fruit content and 2) improve the nutritional quality of other key dish ingredients.

With respect to expanding the vegetable and fruit content of dishes, flavorful vegetables and fruits are fully acceptable, easy-to-add dish ingredients. Of special importance, this acceptability applies to less familiar and especially nutritious vegetables, such as dark green leafy vegetables.

With respect to improving the nutritional quality of other key dish ingredients, flavorful vegetables and fruits, and especially vegetables and fruits in combination with herb- and spice-flavored seasoning vegetables, provide an attractively flavorful and moist flavoring base that makes it realistically possible to make two kinds of nutritional-enhancing ingredient changes in traditional dishes: 1) substitution of several kinds of more nutritious for less nutritious ingredients and 2) reduction of particular ingredient content of recipes. Taking full advantage of this opportunity, all Part II recipes make these ingredient changes.

With respect to ingredient substitutions, Part II recipes make four kinds of ingredient substitutions.

- First, Part II recipes (those that include grain ingredients, such as stir fries, curries, stews, and some salads) substitute **whole and intact whole grain for refined grain ingredients**. Providing both attractive flavoring and sufficient moistening for the absorptive bran, *juice-protected* vegetables and fruits perform the invaluable service of making nutrient dense, fiber rich, and energy-sustaining intact whole grains acceptable ingredients in dishes.
- Second, Part II recipes (those that include beef) substitute **lean for fatty beef**. A *juice-protected* vegetable/fruit flavoring base makes lean beef a genuine alternative protein selection for use in everyday dishes. Providing attractive moistness and tastiness, herb- or spice-flavored seasoning vegetables in combination with other flavorful vegetable and fruit ingredients serve essentially the same function as fat in a dish. As a result, they successfully compensate for the flavoring loss involved in substituting lean for fatty beef. The substitution of lean for fatty beef in combination with serving beef with nutrient and fiber rich vegetables and fruits, in turn, secures the healthfulness of beef [213] as a dish ingredient.[214]
- Third, Part II recipes (those that include beef) substitute **lean beef for commercially processed and cured animal protein products**. With juicy and flavorful vegetables in combination with spice- or herb-flavored seasoning vegetables serving as attractive

---

[213] Vasey, *The Acid-Alkaline Diet for Optimum Health*, 52-57. Because both meat and saturated fat contained in meat are acidifying ingredients when consumed by humans, a reduction of saturated fat content in combination with serving meat within an alkaline mineral-rich vegetable base importantly reduces the acid neutralizing burden placed on the body.

[214] Fat reduction reduces both saturated fat and overall calorie content. Nutrient and fiber-rich vegetable and fruit flavoring provides the human body with the nutritional raw material it requires to 1) properly manage and use the saturated fat and 2) to balance saturated fat content, keeping it from crowding omega-3 essential fatty acids from human cell membranes.

supplementary flavoring, lean beef successfully substitutes for salt- and fat-laden processed animal protein in Part II dishes. Pizza recipes, for example, substitute herb-flavored lean ground beef for pepperoni; herb- and spice-flavored lean ground beef stands alone without sausage in chili. Removal of cured animal protein products, in turn, significantly reduces the salt and completely removes the hidden chemical additive content contained in processed protein products, which scientific research links to colon cancer.[215]

- Fourth, Part II recipes routinely substitute **un-flavored, single ingredient, commercially-prepared products for flavored commercially-prepared products**.[216] *Juice-protected* vegetables and fruits effectively flavor unflavored single ingredient commercially-prepared products with minimal use of any outside flavoring. Use of flavored commercial products, as a result, is unnecessary. Cooks take a giant step in removing themselves from processed food dependence. Elimination of commercially flavored products results in significant reduction in the fat, sugar, salt, and chemical additive content of traditional dishes. Home cooks take control over the amount of fat, sugar, salt, and chemicals contained in dishes and do so with minimal additional dish preparation time. Equally important, selecting single ingredient, unflavored, commercially-prepared products places cooks in control of the *quality* of individual ingredients contained in products. Profit-making imperatives drive producers to select every ingredient in flavored products with profit-making in mind. As a result, to select a flavored commercially-prepared product is almost inevitably to select a product made from the most processed and least expensive ingredients and, very possibly, ingredients with very high pesticide content as well.[217] In contrast, there is considerable range in the quality of unflavored single ingredient commercially-produced products, and by making higher quality product selections home cooks can significantly improve dish quality.

To make the second kind of nutritionally-enhancing ingredient change (reduction of particular ingredient content) that is made possible with the use of *juice-protected* vegetable and fruit flavoring, Part II recipes routinely reduce **animal protein (meat, poultry, and cheese), legume, and grain content**. This rearranging of ingredient content does not upset dish flavor and attractiveness for two reasons. First, attractive vegetable and fruit flavoring effectively fills in any flavor gaps created by the ingredient reductions. Second, most Part II recipes are mixed ingredient dishes (salads, stir fries, soups and stews, curries, pizza, and quiche) in which protein, grain, and legumes already do not play main ingredient roles. Ingredient reductions are scarcely noticeable and these reductions enhance dish quality in the following ways.

---

215 Moss, *Salt Sugar Fat*, 230. As mentioned earlier, scientists studying processed meat could not find any safe level of processed protein consumption.
216 For example, basic milk mixed with flour and a touch of salt replace canned soup; tomato paste and tomato juice combined with herb-flavored seasoning vegetables replace tomato sauce; extra virgin olive oil and vinegar or fresh lemon juice replace commercially prepared salad dressing; and cream cheese mixed with herbs or spices replaces commercially prepared dips.
217 Such is the case of the highly refined pure cottonseed and soybean oil typically used in commercially prepared salad dressing. In addition to sharing other refined vegetable oil characteristics (they are top heavy with omega-6 fatty acids and become highly acidic during human processing) cottonseed and soybean oil also contain high pesticide content due to heavy chemical spraying of cotton and soybean crops during industrial production. Soybean and cottonseed oil are very likely made from genetically modified soybean as well. Because all antioxidants and vitamin C content are removed during processing, these pure oils are also highly reactive when heated. This means they release free radicals, which are highly destructive of human cells.

- Reductions make room for expanded vegetable content, which enhances the nutritional diversity of dishes and supplies the means for the human body to effectively use the macronutrient ingredients (protein, carbohydrate, and fat) also contained in dishes.
- Reduction of beef further enhances the healthfulness of beef as a dish ingredient. In addition to reducing calorie content, reducing beef content makes the substitution of the highest quality but more expensive grass-fed beef and poultry economically feasible.
- Reduction of legume and grain content eases the burden placed on the human body in digesting these complex carbohydrates and neutralizing the acids produced during the digestion of these foods.

General Cooking Tools for Part II Recipes

Part II recipes use all of the same general tools for preparing vegetables and fruits as listed in the Part I Introduction. Part II recipes, however, use a number of additional general tools because of the expanded ingredient content of recipes. A complete descriptive listing of tools commonly used in Part II recipes follows below. Additional tools that are specific to particular kinds of recipes are listed in the introduction of individual Part II chapters.

- **Bowls, mixing.** Having at least one small (3 cup or 1½ pint), medium (6 cup or 1½ quart), large (10 cup or 2½ quart), and extra large (16 c or 4 quart) bowl on hand covers all recipe preparation needs.
- **Brush, vegetable scrub.** A brush with short, firm bristles is an essential tool for efficiently scrubbing vegetables and fruits with a rough and uneven surface, such as root vegetables and cantaloupe.
- **Brush, general dish brush with a long handle.** This tool is useful for cleaning a vegetable grater, potato masher, whisk, and dinner fork.
- **Colanders, 2.** It is important that a colander has large and evenly spaced holes to drain liquid efficiently.
- **Cutting board reserved for fruits and vegetables.** Because onions and garlic leave lingering flavor, having 1 board each for fruits and vegetables is useful.
- **Cutting board, large.** A large board, such as one approx. 16 x 24 in., greatly eases the slicing of leafy green vegetables.
- **Cutting board reserved for raw meat and poultry.** This board removes the threat of contaminating raw produce used in salads and desserts.
- **Glove, oven.** This glove should be well padded. The more of the arm covered, the more protection provided. Having a glove for each hand is desirable.
- **Grinder, electric.** This is a small grinder, such as a coffee grinder, with a sturdy stainless steel blade and a powerful enough motor (e.g. 180 watts) to grind seeds and hard dried spices.
- **Citrus juicer, hand.** Fresh lemon juice is used in many different types of Part II dishes. One that separates seeds from juice is helpful.
- **Kettle, electric tea.** Providing hot water in seconds, an electric tea kettle is an indispensable tool for stir-fry/steaming vegetables in Part II recipes.
- **Knives.** Having knives matched to different vegetable and fruit ingredients greatly eases preparation. These knives include a **6-7 in. chef's (also called a vegetable) knife**, both a

5 and 7½ in. serrated knife, and a 3 in. paring knife. A 5 in. slicing knife for cutting meat and poultry is also needed. It is important that all knives have high quality blades that do not quickly lose sharpness and that easily re-sharpen. Knives should also have firm blades.
- **Knife sharpener.** This sharpener should sharpen both regular and serrated blades.
- **Measuring cup set.** This set includes ¼ c, ⅓ c, ½ c, and 1 c sizes.
- **Measuring spoon set.** This set includes ¼ t, ½ t, 1 t, and 1 T sizes, but a ⅓ t size is useful as well. It is helpful for spoons to be held together by a large ring of some sort.
- **Paper towels.** Paper towels are indispensable for meeting drying needs. Terry towels are economical and are equally effective for drying purposes.
- **Peeler, vegetable.** This should be a swivel type peeler with sharp blades, such as a stainless steel blade. It should remove only a very thin layer of skin.
- **Peppermill.** Any variety.
- **Pie plate, or other shallow container with sides.** This is a handy tool for drying small round berries and vegetables. It also very useful for catching kernels as they are cut from an ear of corn.
- **Plastic wrap.** Plastic wrap serves as an exceedingly useful covering to protect cut foods from drying air. Its flexibility allows it to fit snugly around irregularly shaped vegetables and to provide an air-tight covering for storage bowls of any size.
- **Ruler, 12 in.** A ruler is useful for determining the size of vegetables and fruits called for in recipes as well as for the size of slices called for in recipes.
- **Saucepans, each with an opaque lid.** Have at least one **medium (2 qt or 8 c) saucepan** and **large (3 qt or 12 c) saucepan** on hand for boiling vegetables whole as well as for cooking legumes and whole grains. A nonstick saucepan works especially well for cooking whole grains.
- **Scissors, kitchen.** Sharp scissors are very useful for performing a variety of small vegetable readying tasks. They are also a useful tool for cutting meat and poultry. The scissors should, as a result, be easy to clean thoroughly.
- **Shredder, vegetable.** Also called a grater, a shredder should have a coarse grating setting as larger shredded pieces are more flavorful than finely shredded pieces. The blades of a stainless steel shredder best remain sharp. A box style shredder with a handle that is free standing is especially easy to use. A scrub brush with a long handle is a very handy cleaning tool, making thorough cleaning easy to accomplish.
- **Skillets, large.** A large skillet is either a 12 in. or 14 in. skillet. Important characteristics of a large skillet to be used for stir-frying and stir-fry/steaming of vegetables, fruits, and animal protein include 1) having a tight-fitting opaque lid, 2) having a heavy bottom, 3) being light enough for easy lifting, 4) having a helper handle to ease the scraping out of ingredients from a skillet (a cook braces the helper handle against his/her side while holding the other handle with one hand, which frees one hand for scraping), and 5) having rounded sides, which eases stir-frying. Having a nonstick surface is an additional essential characteristic of a skillet used for preparing milk-based recipes, including soups, quiche, and some curries. Having a non-reactive surface is an additional essential characteristic of a skillet used for tomato sauce-based stews. Stainless steel, nonstick, and anodized aluminum skillets are examples of skillets with a non-reactive surface.

- **Skillet, medium.** A medium (10 in.) skillet should have all the characteristics of a large skillet except that it does not need to have a helper handle.
- **Spatula, rubber or other heat-resistant.** While a large spatula serves everyday preparation needs, a thin-bladed spatula is helpful for scraping contents from a blender, seed grinder, and thin containers in general. A spatula should be pliable for efficient scraping.
- **Spatula, firm with sharp-edged blade.** Called a stir-fry spatula in recipes, a wide, sharp-edged and firm spatula eases the flipping of ingredients in stir-frying and the flipping of pancakes. To protect both nonstick and stainless steel surfaces, the spatula should be plastic or wood. It can also be metal with a plastic-coated blade.
- **Sponge with one rough side.** A kitchen sponge with one rough side is a very useful tool for cleaning both utensils and smooth vegetables and fruits. The rough side of a kitchen sponge can easily be wrapped around small round vegetables (such as potatoes) and long and thin vegetables (such as carrots) for efficient scrubbing. A flexible plastic scrubbing tool works well, too.
- **Storage containers, glass with air-tight lids.** In various sizes. Glass storage containers are necessary for fruit and tomato-based leftovers. Acid fruit juice and tomato liquid cannot leach chemicals from a glass container into stored food.
- **Storage containers, plastic with air-tight lids.** In various sizes.
- **Storage containers, sealable plastic bags.** In various sizes, including freezer quality plastic bags.
- **Timer.** A timer is essential equipment. It should measure minutes and seconds.
- **Tongs.** Tongs are useful for removing large leafy greens from boiling water when they are being boiled whole.
- **Towels, Terry.** Purchasing absorptive terry towels to use in place of paper towels (at least in part) for drying purposes during preparation and cooking is an economical, as well as ecological, investment.
- **Whisk, small.** This tool is useful for light mixing jobs, such as light beating of eggs and mixing of corn starch into liquid. A long-handled bottle brush is a handy tool for cleaning the whisk quickly and efficiently after use. A dinner fork substitutes for a whisk. If less efficient than a whisk, it is easier to clean.

Part II References

Cooked Alive! recipes focus on use of *juice-protective* preparation techniques and *juice-protective* serving methods for securing the high nutritional quality of vegetable and fruit ingredients in dishes. Because the quality of vegetables and fruits is both highly variable and perishable, cooks also need to give careful attention to two other parts of the preparation process – selection and home storage of vegetables and fruits. Fresh vegetables and fruits must first be nutritious and tasty and this quality and flavor must be maintained during home storage for produce to yield tasty, nutritious dish ingredients. To provide cooks with this important information, which cannot be included in recipes, *Cooked Alive!* has included Reference #1 (Selecting Top Quality Fresh Whole Vegetables and Fruits) and Reference #2 (Key Home Storage Guidelines for Conserving Vegetable and Fruit Quality) in the Part I introduction. These two references serve Part II recipes as well.

The quality of other whole food ingredients in dishes is likewise dependent on the initial quality

PART 2

of the particular whole food ingredient used in a dish. Like vegetables and fruits, other whole foods are both perishable and marketed in variable quality. To assist cooks in selecting reliably high quality whole food products, thereby maximizing the nutritional contribution of a product, this Part II introduction includes two whole food selection references, which are as follows:

- **Reference #4 (Selecting Top Quality Whole Food Ingredients for Use in Part II Recipes).** This reference defines top quality whole foods in the same way that Reference #1 (Selecting Top Quality Fresh Whole Vegetables and Fruits) defines top quality whole vegetables and fruits, which is as food that is raw, physically intact, and naturally produced. This means that plant whole foods are produced using natural fertilizer and without chemical processing during production and marketing, such as certified organic and locally produced products. This means that animal and poultry products are from animals and poultry produced using natural food and in accordance with natural biological processes, such as grass-fed products. Reference #4 identifies specific top quality whole food products that are available to cooks for use in Part II recipes.
- **Reference #5 (Selecting High Quality Processed Ingredients for Use in Part II Recipes).** Though physical processing inevitably reduces the nutritional quality of a food, quality loss is variable depending on the degree of processing. This reference identifies a variety of physically processed food ingredients that, while not completely whole, retain significant nutritional quality.

Cooked Alive! is as equally committed to the attractiveness of its recipes as it is to high nutritional quality. Its primary strategy for achieving dish attractiveness and, hence, serving success, is through giving extra careful attention to the preparation of vegetables and fruits, but it also applies this strategy to the preparation of other dish ingredients. *Cooked Alive!* in particular gives special attention to the preparation of whole food ingredients included in Part II recipes, ingredients that are sometimes somewhat unfamiliar to cooks and that require the use of techniques somewhat different from those used in preparing refined ingredients. To assist cooks in reliably preparing attractive and, hence, fully acceptable whole food ingredients other than vegetables and fruits, *Cooked Alive!* provides the following two references.

- **Reference #6 (Maximizing the Attractiveness of Whole Food Ingredients Commonly Used in Part II Recipes).**
- **Reference #7 (*Juice-Protective* Techniques for Preparing Animal Protein).** *Juice-protective* techniques for preparing animal protein are the same as those for fresh vegetables and fruits and are as simple to apply. They are a basic key to the successful use of lean protein in Part II dishes.

In addition to references focused on securing the attractiveness of whole food ingredients, almost all Part II chapters include a "clinching dish flavor" reference. Aiming to assist cooks in achieving dish serving success, these references make suggestions for securing and enhancing the attractiveness of key flavoring ingredients used in chapter recipes.

Reference #4

Selecting Top Quality Whole Food Ingredients for Use in Part II Recipes

Reference #4 assists cooks in selecting top quality whole food products (other than vegetables and fruits, which are covered in Reference #1) for use in Part II recipes in two ways. First, it expands the standard description of whole foods to more fully encompass nutritional quality and, as a result, to better serve cooks in selecting genuinely nutritious whole food products. Second, it identifies commonly available whole food products that meet this description.

Defining Whole Foods

Reference #4 expands the commonly used description of whole foods. Whole food designation implies nutritional quality, but as noted in Reference #1 in regard to vegetables and fruits, the common meaning of whole foods as structurally intact raw foods only partially encompasses nutritional value. Whole foods do not pop into existence in a grocery store. On the contrary, they go through an extended production process long before being harvested and marketed. The structurally-focused definition of whole foods says nothing about the relevance of the entire production process to the nutritional quality of food. As a result, the enormous tampering with, or processing of, plants, animals, and poultry that routinely occurs during industrial agricultural production – tampering that is every bit as extensive and as destructive of nutritional quality as the processing of foods that occurs in later stages of the commercial processing of foods – gets a free pass. Thus, Reference #4 expands the definition of whole foods to explicitly take account of processing that occurs during the pre-harvesting stage of plant production and the pre-slaughtering stage of animal and poultry production.

Reference #4 defines a whole food as food with three equally important basic characteristics – it is **raw, physically intact,** and **naturally produced**. Reference #4 connects natural production with lack of processing or tampering, which directly correlates with the production of food products that are matched to human nutritional requirements and, hence, are supportive of human health. Reference #4 compares natural production with industrial production, which unleashes unnatural processing of foods (plants, animals, and poultry) during all phases of the production process, to illustrate the far-reaching differential impact of each production method on the nutritional value of produced foods for humans, on the well-being of the plants, animals, and poultry being produced, and on the health of the environment.

Natural Production as an Essential Indicator of Whole Food Quality

Guided by nature-based standards, natural agricultural production methods effectively avoid unnatural processing of plants and animals during production. Matching production methods to unchanging natural biological growth processes that have evolved over hundreds of thousands of years, nature-based standards anchor the production process and act as a block against unnatural tampering. Committing producers to work with naturally evolved growth processes, nature-based standards oblige producers to use natural food and to strictly avoid chemical intervention during production.

Certified organic farming is a prime example of farming that employs natural production methods. Another method is 100% grass-fed pasturing of cattle, dairy cows, and egg-producing hens. Organic farming and grass-fed (or pastured) animal and poultry production are practiced in a variety of ways, but the common thread among organic farmers and grass-fed animal and poultry producers is emphasis on strict non-tampering with natural food and other naturally developed processes. In United States Department of Agriculture-certified organic farming, non-tampering is strictly applied and enforced. A USDA certified organic label means non-tampering has been verified by an independent outside source. This label verifies that a plant product has not been, for example,

- grown with use of sewage sludge.
- irradiated (treated with radiation) to eliminate pests. Irradiation is highly destructive of nutritional value.[218]
- grown with the use of artificial pesticides.
- chemically manipulated or manipulated with any synthetic substance for commercial reasons (such as extending the market season and making produce easier to ship and store).
- grown from genetically engineered seeds.

While natural production acts as a block on unnatural processing, industrial production, in sharp contrast, unleashes unnatural processing. This unleashing relates directly to the primary goal governing industrial production, which is expanded production at the lowest possible cost. Factory methods are adopted to achieve this goal. This means convenience of producers, efficiency of operation, expanded production, mechanization, and profit-making serve as the guiding principles that drive the production process. The effect of the application of these principles is to open the door to unlimited tampering with plants, animals, and poultry. They become commodities and, as objectified commodities, they are manipulated according to expanded production, reduced cost, and profit goals. These are essentially elusive, never fully achievable goals that are also driven by competition from other industrial producers. Additionally, there is no built-in check on unnatural processing. Not directly and visibly contributing to the profitability of food, nutritional quality of products gets low priority status and, accordingly, nutritional standards do not act as a block. Unbridled processing instead proceeds with devastating consequences for plant, human, animal and poultry, and environmental health, as the following comparison between natural and industrial production shows. As this comparison was already considered for vegetables and fruits in Reference #1 (Selecting Top Quality Fresh Whole Vegetables and Fruits), here we deal largely with animals and poultry.

1. **Natural production supports human health while industrial production does not and even undermines human health.** In comparison to industrial production of livestock and poultry, natural production of livestock (including dairy cows) and poultry supports human health in at least three main ways. Natural production 1) yields products that meet important human nutritional requirements, 2) yields products that do not, or only minimally, contain pesticides, and 3) does not routinely use antibiotics and does not, as a result, result in the creation of super bugs that threaten the effectiveness of antibiotics used for treating human bacterial infections.

---

218   Chris Kilham, *The Whole Food Bible* (Rochester, Vermont: Healing Arts Press, 1997): 38-40.

First, food products made from grass-fed cattle, dairy cows, and poultry (and other livestock, such as sheep and hogs) precisely match human nutritional needs in crucial respects. Naturally produced food products contribute healthful amounts of a greater variety of nutritional components.

- Grass-fed animal protein reliably contributes omega-3 essential fatty acids (ALA, alpha linoleic acid), which science has established to be essential to human health. Scientific research shows that protein products from grain-fed livestock, in comparison, contain significantly less omega-3 fatty acids (ALA form).[219] Research likewise verifies eggs from hens given access to grass have significantly more omega-3 essential fatty acids than hens without access[220] and, moreover, that milk from grass-fed dairy cows has greater omega-3 essential fatty acid (ALA) content than milk from industrially raised grain-fed dairy cows. Equally important, protein of grass-fed cattle and poultry contains an omega-3 to omega-6 essential fatty acid ratio that is favorable to human health (one with slightly more omega-3 than omega-6 fatty acids, which prevents omega-6 fatty acids from crowding out omega-3s from human tissue). The ratio in grain-fed cattle, in contrast, is reversed.[221]
- Grass-fed meat has more vitamin E than industrially raised meat.[222]
- Grass-fed meat has greater overall nutritional content than grain-fed beef and poultry. In particular this nutritional content includes beta-carotene (which the body converts to vitamin A and which serves as an antioxidant for humans), but also folate, thiamin, riboflavin, calcium, magnesium, and potassium.[223]
- Protein of grass-fed cattle and the products of grass-fed dairy cows contribute significantly more conjugated linoleic acid (CLA), another fatty acid shown to be intricately connected to optimum human health, than the meat and dairy products of industrially produced cattle.[224]
- Protein of grass-fed cattle and poultry is naturally lean. It contains less saturated fat than protein from animals industrially raised on a grain-fed diet. Of special importance, the saturated fat content of grass-fed beef is different from that of grain-fed beef, having fewer of the types of saturated fat linked with heart disease.[225]
- Unsprayed grass of grass-fed livestock and poultry contains insects, which are a part of the natural diet of poultry. Grass also typically includes a mixture of plants. Plant diversity, like insects, in turn enriches the nutritional diversity of the diet of pastured poultry and livestock, which translates into nutritionally varied food products for humans.

---

219 Lisa Abend, "Save the Planet: Eat More Beef," *Time* (January 25, 2010): 53.
Jo Robinson, *Pasture Perfect* (Vashon, Washington: Vashon Island Press, 2011): 27 and 35.
220 Ben Hewitt, *Eating Well* (March/April, 2010): 72.
Robinson, *Pasture Perfect*, 52.
221 Robinson, *Pasture Perfect*, 28-29 and 40.
222 Ibid., 36. Robinson reports that grass-fed cattle have from three to six times more vitamin E than grain-fed feedlot cattle.
Mateljan, *The World's Healthiest Foods*, 2nd Edition (716 and 720) repeats this nutritional difference between products from grass- and grain-fed cattle.
223 Robinson, *Pasture Perfect*, 37 and 51-52.
224 Ibid., 29. Robinson reports that beef from cattle and the products of dairy cows raised exclusively on grass have two to five times more CLA (conjugated linoleic acid) than similar animals raised on large amounts of grain.
Mateljan, *The World's Healthiest Foods*, 716, repeats this difference in CLA content between grass-fed and grain-fed beef.
225 Robinson, *Pasture Perfect*, 37 and 52.

A second important way that natural production of livestock (including dairy cows) and poultry supports human health is that products of naturally produced livestock and poultry minimally contain pesticides. Products of industrially produced livestock and poultry, in sharp contrast, contain largely unmeasured pesticide content. While grass-fed livestock and poultry are raised in chemically free pastures, industrially produced livestock and poultry are fed chemically dependent grain (corn and soybeans) that is overwhelmingly grown from genetically modified Roundup Ready seeds that allow the grain crops to be heavily sprayed with the herbicide Roundup as they grow in order to control weeds.[226] The grain may be treated with other chemicals as well in order to control particular bugs, as in the case of the corn rootworm. Hay fed to livestock is also commonly grown from Roundup Ready alfalfa seeds, which allows the alfalfa to tolerate spraying with Roundup during growth. Most harvested grain and at least much of the hay fed to livestock, as a result, are heavily laden with pesticide residues, and this pesticide content gets passed on to the livestock and poultry fed the grain/hay and to the food products made from them for human consumption. While, on the whole, little is known about the effects of pesticides, and in particular combinations of pesticides, on human health beyond those facts provided by agribusinesses, independent research is collecting information about the damaging effects on human health, as in the case of glyphosate, the main active chemical in the herbicide Roundup. In 2017 glyphosate was authoritatively determined in an important California court case to be probably carcinogenic for humans. This makes the fact that food products made from industrially produced livestock and poultry contain glyphosate residues of supreme public health significance. Two other known facts about glyphosate intensify the danger it represents to public health. First, glyphosate acts as an antibiotic when consumed by humans and destroys important beneficial bacteria in the human gut. Second, glyphosate has chelating capacity, which means that it binds minerals in the human stomach, keeping them from being absorbed for human health needs.

A third important way that natural production of livestock and poultry supports human health is that naturally raised livestock and poultry are not routinely fed antibiotics. In contrast, industrially raised livestock and poultry are routinely fed antibiotics.[227] Routine administration of antibiotics negatively affects human health both directly and indirectly.

- Food products made from industrially produced livestock and poultry contain antibiotics, which are unnatural substances for humans. While there is little reliably independent research about the specific effects of antibiotic residues on human health, it is known that they are destructive to at least some beneficial human gut bacteria, which play crucial human health promoting roles.
- The mass treatment of animals with antibiotics by concentrated animal feeding operations (CAFOs) – both to control infection and to make them grow faster – leads to

---

226 Philip Lymbery with Isabel Oakeshott, *Farmageddon: The True Cost of Cheap Meat* (London: Bloomsbury, 2014): 271.
227 Melinda Wenner Moyer, "The Looming Threat of Factory-Farm Superbugs," *Scientific American* (December 1, 2016). Moyer reports: "In 2014 pharmaceutical companies sold nearly 21 million pounds of medically important antibiotics for use in food animals, more than three times the amount sold for use in people."

the development of antibiotic-resistant bacteria, or super bugs, which threaten human health in at least three ways.[228]

- First, super bugs cause human illness as they are transferred to workers from animals and animal manure in CAFOs through the air on dust particles and on vapor droplets from open liquid manure holding lagoons and through direct contact with manure. Super bugs also cause human illness beyond the confines of CAFOs as they are transported through the air and polluted water – both from water polluted by overspilling or leaking lagoons and from runoff of lagoon manure used as so-called fertilizer on surrounding fields – to people living on nearby farms and in nearby communities. Super bugs are in CAFO meat, poultry, and egg products marketed to the general public in grocery stores.[229] Hospitalized sick people then bring super bugs to hospitals where super bugs spread to other ill people.[230]
- Secondly, antibiotic resistant super bugs undermine successful treatment of sick persons using standard antibiotics.
- Thirdly, research is showing that super bugs transfer antibiotic resistance to other bacteria, thereby widely spreading antibiotic resistance to bacteria and, as as a result, generally reducing the effectiveness of antibiotics humans depend on for curing bacterial infections.[231]

2. **Natural production supports the health of animals and poultry while industrial production does not.**

   In natural production, for example,

- the primary diet throughout the lives of grass-fed livestock and pastured dairy cows is green grass. A significant part of the diet of certified organic dairy cattle is green grass (it is the main food for 30% of each year, during the primary grass growing season). A significant part of the diet of pastured poultry is also green grass. This natural diet perfectly matches the distinctive digestive systems of cattle and, as a result, naturally produced cattle remain healthy. Green grass provides nutrients needed to maintain the health of poultry as well.

---

[228] Ibid. Moyer informs readers of a landmark 2012 study in which microbiologist Lance Price, now director of the Antibiotics Resistance Action Center at George Washington University's Milken Institute School of Pubic Health, and his colleagues verified the link between factory farm animals and the development of super bugs. This study showed that the deadly MRSA (*Staphylococcus aureus*) bacterium, which is resistant to most antibiotics and which can cause deadly skin, blood, and lung infections, started out in people but jumped into livestock, where it quickly developed antibiotic resistance. Expressing the fear of many researchers, Moyer states: "Stripped of the power of protective drugs, today's pedestrian health nuisances – ear infections, cuts, bronchitis – will become tomorrow's potential death sentences".

[229] Ibid. Moyer reports the results of a 2012 study in which U.S. Federal Drug Administration scientists analyzed raw retail meats sold around the country and found that "84 percent of chicken breasts, 82 percent of ground turkey, 69 percent of ground beef and 44 percent of pork chops were contaminated with intestinal *E.coli*". *E.coli* is an antibiotic resistant microorganism common to CAFOs. These microbes can cause food poisoning if meat or poultry is not cooked completely before it is eaten or if a person handling the raw meat or poultry does not wash his or her hands properly afterward. The FDA study found that more than half of the bacteria in the ground turkey were resistant to at least three classes of antibiotics.

[230] Ibid. Moyer informs readers that MRSA is resistant to several major classes of antibiotics and has become a problem for hospitals.

[231] Ibid. Moyer clearly and forcefully illustrates the vertical and horizontal development of super bugs. Bacteria vertically transfer antibiotic resistance by transferring genes to their offspring. In horizontal development, resistance genes actually "jump" to different strains or species of bacteria, which leads to widespread development of antibiotic resistance and makes drugs ineffective in treating bacterial infections.

- Phytonutrients in grass support the health of naturally produced animals and poultry in the same way as they do humans. The health of industrially produced animals and poultry, in contrast, is dependent on the administration of antibiotics.
- Pastured poultry roam in sunshine and have access to bugs and worms, which as natural parts of the diet of poultry, are directly linked to the health and well-being of poultry.

* the long-term health of naturally raised livestock and poultry matters to their producers. As it takes longer to raise grass-fed livestock and poultry to maturity than it does to raise industrially produced livestock and poultry, maintaining long-term health is important. Natural producers attend to small ailments as they occur.

In industrial production, in contrast to natural production,

* the primary diet of industrially raised livestock (including dairy cows) and poultry is grain, which is not a natural food for livestock and dairy cows and is only a part of the natural diet of poultry. Furthermore, most grain fed to industrially raised animals and poultry is genetically modified grain, which removes it a step further from being a natural food matched to an animal's specific nutritional needs. The guiding industrial production rule – whatever makes animals and poultry grow quickly and gain weight – also leaves their diet open to the addition of filler material. The diets of industrially produced chicken, for example, can and do include such animal by-products like feather meal, chicken litter, dried blood, and ground up meat, poultry, or fish.[232]
* producers, as a rule, ignore the long-range health of animals/poultry. Penned animals and poultry are instead raised as quickly and economically as possible and then deliberately slaughtered before they develop serious health conditions that threaten their monetary value. Health problems that inevitably arise from an unnatural diet and the administration of antibiotics and hormones – such as painful acidosis in the case of cattle (since grain does not match the distinctive digestive system of cattle) and painful udder infections, digestive disorders, and lameness in the case of dairy cows administrated the genetically modified (GM) bovine growth hormone to increase milk production[233] – are essentially ignored and left untreated.
* the relentless push for expanded production and reduced costs sets the stage for abuse, and animals and poultry are in fact raised under highly unnatural, cruel, and exploitative conditions in industrial production businesses. As one writer comments about industrialized poultry production, "Torture a single chicken and you risk arrest. Abuse hundreds of thousands of chickens for their entire lives? That's agribusiness."[234] In 2015, the public got a rare opportunity to confirm the reality of this statement when the chairman of the Perdue Poultry Company publicly claimed that their poultry was "raised cage free" and sometimes "humanely raised." The falseness of these claims so shocked one of the farmers raising Perdue chickens that he opened his four barns

---

232 *Nutrition Action Newsletter* (October, 2012): 7. Certified organic standards specifically forbid use of these ingredients in poultry feed.
233 Lymbery, *Farmageddon: The True Cost of Cheap Meat*, 276.
234 Nicholas Kristof, "Abusing Chickens We Eat," *The New York Times* (December 3, 2014).

to public viewing. This look exposed a barn full of vast numbers of panting chickens jammed tightly together in a space without windows. Bred to have such huge breasts that they often end up too heavy to remain upright, these chickens spend a good part of their lives sitting on their breasts, which means sitting on masses of caustic chicken litter that eats away their skin. The report on these chickens by *The New York Times* states: "Most shocking is that the bellies of nearly all the chickens [of four large barns] have lost their feathers and are raw, angry, red flesh. The entire underside of almost every chicken is a huge, continuous bedsore."[235] Other examples of abusive treatment of poultry include forced molting through starvation, a practice that temporarily increases egg production, and beak cutting that keeps hens from pecking each other.[236]

- the relentless push for expanded production and reduced costs sets the stage for another form of abuse: unregulated experimentation. Such experimentation is routinely carried out with the support of the federal government. The federal government maintains a tax-financed institution called the U.S. Meat Animal Research Center that is specifically devoted to helping producers of beef, pork, and lamb increase productivity at the lowest possible cost and, hence, to make a higher profit.[237] Locked behind a security fence, this institution is housed in a complex of laboratories and pastures that covers over 55 square miles in Nebraska. Because research animals are exempted from protection provided by The Animal Welfare Act of 1966, animal research at the Center is carried on without any outside oversight. A recent investigative report by *The New York Times* describes the high cost paid by the Center's 58,000 animal inmates for this unregulated experimentation, which the Center justifies in terms of the good of humans throughout the world. "We are trying to feed a population that is expanding very rapidly, to nine billion by 2050, and if we are going to feed that population, there are some trade-offs."[238] Unregulated animal research carried out at the U.S. Meat Animal Research Center includes genetic modification research that aims to re-engineer animals to make them produce more and bigger offspring, yield more and leaner meat, and cost less to raise in order to be more profitable.

3. **Natural production supports environmental health while industrial production degrades environmental health.**

In natural production, for example,

- pastures are valued and maintained because retaining grass quality is necessary for raising healthy animals and poultry which, in turn, is necessary for financial success. Maintaining grassy pastures, in turn, supports biodiversity by maintaining the habitats of countless other life forms that coexist with grass-fed livestock and poultry, including small mammals, insects, bees, ground-nesting birds, and soil microbes.
- manure is not a threat to water quality. Because maintaining grass quality requires cattle and poultry be moved frequently, no big build-up of manure and urine occurs in pastures of grass-fed livestock. Manure is dispersed and integrated back into the soil,

---

235 Ibid. This article includes an accessible video that confirms the abused condition of the affected chickens.
236 Kathy Gunst, "A Good Egg," *Eating Well* (March/April, 2016): 93.
237 Michael Moss. "Animal Welfare at Risk in Experiments for Meat Industry," *The New York Times* (January 19, 2015).
238 Ibid. This is a quote by Sherrill E. Echternkamp, a scientist who retired from U.S. Meat Animal Research Center in 2013.

where it serves as an excellent natural fertilizer for nourishing the soil and the microbial universe living in the soil. Nourished soil, in turn, supports grass, which supports a diversity of other life forms.

In industrial production, in contrast to natural production,

- penning of cattle and poultry (in concentrated animal feeding operations or CAFOs) results in a stupendous concentration of untreated manure and urine, which is toxic and becomes a permanent threat to water sources and human health. The cheap untreated manure-holding lagoons constructed to manage this waste are highly vulnerable to both weather conditions (such as cloud bursts that overfill liquid manure-holding lagoons and allow runoff into surrounding ponds and rivers) and leakage (which threatens ground water). When the untreated manure is spread on surrounding fields as so-called fertilizer, toxic ingredients in the manure (including pesticides from grain fed livestock, hard metals also contained in animal/poultry feed, antibiotics, and pathogens) can be carried in rain runoff into surrounding water sources. Contaminated water, in turn, undermines the health of the flora and fauna living in and around the water sources and potentially threatens human health as well. Toxic ingredients contained in the manure are also absorbed into the ground and become a part of food products made from crops grown on the fields.
- massive grain production undermines biodiversity, both with respect to flora and fauna. As expanded production of pesticide-dependent and artificially fertilized grain is carried out to provide food for penned animals, an ever expanding amount of American countryside becomes poisoned and nutritionally depleted and eroded and, as a result, converted into a vast dead zone essentially devoid of all animal and plant life except for the one crop being produced, super weeds, and bugs that become resistant to pesticides.[239] The impact of the poisoning of the environment involved in industrial agriculture reaches far. Research shows that widely used pesticides are harmful to endangered species.[240]
- massive production of grain to feed massive numbers of penned animals results in the relentless conversion of pastures into cropland, which undermines biodiversity. As the demand for grain needed to feed penned cattle grows, the price of grain also increases, which prompts more farmers to plow up their pastures and convert them into higher income earning cropland. As pastures disappear, habitats for countless birds, small mammals, and insects who formerly shared pastures with livestock also vanish.[241]
- penning of livestock results in relentless conversion of hay fields to produce hay used to feed penned livestock. Empty pastures spared conversion into grain crops are continually mowed to provide hay for the penned livestock and poultry, eliminating successful nesting of countless birds.

---

239 Hannah Nordhaus, "Cornboy vs the Billion Dollar Bug," *Scientific American* (March 2017): 66-71. This article portrays the unsuccessful battle and dangers involved in using pesticides to conquer bug pests.
240 Michael Biesecker, "Dow Chemical Tries to Kill Pesticide Study," *The Sioux Falls Argus Leader* (April 21, 2017): 4A. Biesecker informs readers that recent government research shows that three widely used pesticides are harmful to about 1,800 critically endangered species. Dow Chemical is trying to the have the federal government "set aside" the research, contending, as is the common strategy of agri-chemical corporations, that the studies are flawed. As is commonly done by agri-chemical corporations in the face of scientifically established opposition, Dow Chemical has also hired its own scientists to rebut the government studies.
241 The author of *Cooked Alive!*, who lives on farmland, personally attests to the massive conversion of pastures into cropland that is currently occurring. The countryside has been fundamentally transformed; pastures are disappearing.

- the massive use of energy by tractors and mechanized farm machinery required by the production of grain used for feeding penned animals and poultry (which is an enormous percentage of grain produced) means massive emissions release that contributes to global warming and climate change.

These examples illustrate the stupendous differential impact of natural and industrial production on human food quality and on animal, poultry, and environmental health. How is it, then, that production is ignored and completely left out of the standard definition of whole foods? **Clearly, it is because of the tight and deadly grip of processed food dependence in our society.** That production is de-linked from the nutritional quality of intact whole foods is another prime indicator of the vast economic and political power of agribusinesses in America and around world. This de-linking of production from nutritional quality effectively secures the economic well-being of these corporate businesses. Because these giant corporations also exert dominant governmental influence, they will be able to maintain this de-linking well into the future.[242]

Individual health-conscious cooks, however, have the power to affirm the crucial connection between natural production and the nutritional quality of foods. They **can** do the necessary linking themselves and it is imperative that they do. Food products that are both intact and naturally produced are being marketed and they can select these products. Doing so is very likely somewhat troublesome. Such products are typically more expensive and less widely accessible, sometimes considerably less so, than counterpart industrially produced food products. However, for consumers to accept industrially produced food is for them to separate their health from the health of the food chain, which places their health in deadly peril. Selecting naturally produced ingredients **as far as is possible** is a necessary step for them to break free of processed food dependence and to reclaim and secure their health. In doing so consumers 1) connect with genuine human health-building food (and, hence, secure their own health), 2) support the continued availability – and the expansion, accessibility, and reduced cost – of naturally produced products, and 3) disconnect themselves from industrially produced food and the devastating destruction it inflicts on food quality, human health, health of other forms of life, and environmental health.

Identifying Top Quality Whole Food Products

A variety of high quality whole food products are quite widely available for home cooks to use in Part II recipes. These plant and protein (beef, chicken, and egg) products are described below with added freshness and nutrition-enhancing pointers included with each product to further aid cooks in making the most nutritious selections.

1. **Raw and intact certified organic plant products.** Commonly marketed certified organic whole products include, for example,

    - raw intact brown rice without, or with very minimal, bran polishing.
    - other raw intact whole grains, such as hulled barley, wheat berries, and quinoa.
    - intact mature legumes with skin.

---

242 Michael Pollan, "Big Food Strikes Back," *The New York Times Magazine* (October 9, 2016): 40-50, 81-83. This article affirms the aggressiveness of Big Food (a collection of food interests, including Big Ag, Big Meat, the supermarket retailers, and fast-food franchises) in maintaining tight political control of food production and marketing in the United States and of the supportive role being played by the US government in its doing so. Pollan traces Big Food's decisive victory over attempts by the Barack Obama administration to control Big Food through implementation of antitrust laws and new regulatory rules to curb abuses.

PART 2

- raw intact nuts and peanuts, whole or halved, unskinned. As best protected from air and moisture, unshelled raw nuts are the highest quality nut products.
- raw intact seeds, such as sesame, flax, pumpkin, and sunflower seeds, with skin. As the best protected from air and moisture, unshelled raw seeds are the highest quality seed products.

Freshness considerations: The natural oil content of whole grains and nuts makes them highly vulnerable to rancidity, which spoils them and makes them somewhat toxic to humans because they contain free radicals, which are dangerous to human health. To help guard against the selection of rancid whole grain, nut, and seed products,

- learn to identify the odor of rancid products and always check whole grains, nuts, and seeds for rancidity.
- select refrigerated products when possible. Refrigeration keeps rancidity-causing enzymes inactive.
- select products packaged in air-tight containers. Storage in air-tight containers protects products from contact with air, which can stimulate enzymes that bring about rancidity-causing chemical reactions. It is important, nevertheless, to check whole grains, nuts, and seeds packaged in air-tight packages for rancidity.

Nutritional considerations:

- Select certified organic plant products that specify the use of top quality fertilizer. A new category of biodynamic organic produce is being developed to identify the highest quality organic produce. Development of this category is important because the quality of United States Department of Agriculture (USDA) certified organic plant products is now variable as organic standards leave the requirement to use natural fertilizer vague. The decision about the exact amount to use is left up to plant producers, which is a loophole in organic production. Because fertilizer content correlates with soil quality and soil quality, in turn, correlates with the nutritional quality of organic products, variation in fertilizer content opens the door to considerable variation in the nutritional quality of organic products.
- Select a variety of raw nuts. While nuts in general contribute human health-promoting nutritional components (including unprocessed natural oil, a variety of nutrients and phytonutrients, and insoluble fiber), exact nutritional content of nut varieties varies. Mixing nuts takes maximum advantage of the nutritional contribution nuts can provide. Select, for example,
    - almond and Brazil nut as the only alkaline nuts.[243] They, like vegetables, serve as important acid-balancing foods for humans.
    - pecan, almond, and hazelnut as stand-out sources of vitamin E.
    - walnut as an especially rich source of omega-3 essential fatty acids (ALA form). Because of this rich omega-3 content, which is highly vulnerable to heat, it is best to include walnut in non-heated dishes.

---

243 Vasey, *The Acid-Alkaline Diet for Optimum Health*, 76.

- almond and pistachio as good sources of phytonutrients that serve as antioxidants to protect human health.
- almond as an excellent source of fiber.

- Select unbroken nuts. Unbroken nuts are less vulnerable to rancidity.
- Select peanuts with minimum broken peanut content. In addition to being exposed to air (and, hence, rancidity), broken peanuts are particularly susceptible to being contaminated by aflatoxin,[244] a potent carcinogen produced by molds that commonly grow on peanuts (also on field corn and grains, especially in wet areas) and that can cause liver cancer. The threat of aflatoxin contamination is not removed by organic production.

2. **Locally produced raw and intact plant products**. Many small farmers and gardeners selling fresh, raw, intact plant products (such as nuts, whole grains, and legumes, along with vegetables and fruits) at farmers' markets across the nation forego obtaining expensive organic certification status but do essentially produce food in accordance with organic farming principles.[245] Sources of locally produced whole food products include farmers' markets, natural food stores, natural food sections of regular grocery stores, farm stands, and local farmers. Direct contact with food producers, such as at farmers' markets and in Community Supported Agriculture (CSA) programs, in which local residents subscribe to a farm and receive a weekly box of fresh produce, makes it possible for customers to determine the authenticity of natural production.

Freshness considerations:

- Locally grown produce can be very fresh produce. Because cooling and protection from air are crucial to the retention of freshness and quality during marketing, look for and support vendors who cool their produce.

Nutritional considerations:

- The nutritional quality of farmers' market produce is variable. Nutritional quality and flavor, for example, depends on the particular variety of a kind of produce and on the quality of the soil in which it was grown. Physical condition criteria that apply in the selection of grocery store produce apply equally to farmers' market products.

3. **Beef, chunk form, grass-fed**. Chunk form means cut into steak, attached to bone, or roast size. The opposite of chunk form is ground beef, which is completely exposed to air and bacterial contamination. Grass-fed chunk beef products are marketed fresh or frozen in a variety of different ways, including, for example,

- **grass-fed beef, verified to be from completely (or 100%) grass-fed cattle.** Completely grass-fed means the beef is from animals raised on natural grass from birth until

---

244 Chris Kilham, *The Whole Food Bible*, 66.
245 Peter Jaret, "Organics: Are They Worth It?" *Eating Well* (August/September, 2006): 32-39.

being butchered for marketing. It excludes cattle partially grazed in pastures and "finished" in a feed lot on a grain diet before slaughter. Grass-fed beef should be identified with some type of shield that verifies its authenticity, such as a USDA 100% Grass Fed shield[246] or American Grassfed Certification label.

- **beef that is both 100% grass-fed verified and USDA certified organic.** Unlike plant products, a certified organic label does not verify cattle have had a completely grass-based diet. A certified organic label verifies cattle have been fed a 100% organic diet, but this diet can be either unnatural grain *or* natural grass and hay. Because organic status verifies other important protections from processing during production, combining verified grass-fed and organic status expands overall product quality and gives this beef product especially high quality.
- **grass-fed beef verified to be both 100% grass-fed and antibiotic-free.** These products bear a label or shield that verifies antibiotic-free status. Specific products include, for example,

  - American Grassfed Certified shield, which means antibiotics have never been given.
  - USDA Process Verified shield.
  - Global Animal Partnership for Whole Foods Meat label.
  - Animal Welfare Approved label, which means sick animals have been treated with antibiotics, but only under the supervision of a veterinarian.

- **beef of cattle locally raised essentially according to 100% grass-fed principles.** Locally raised grass-fed beef may not have official verification, but direct contact between customers and producers provides the opportunity to verify authenticity. A farmers' market likely requires this verification from vendors. A natural food store will definitely require verification from local beef producers selling products there.

Freshness considerations:

- Freshest beef is the most nutritious beef. Select the most freshly packaged beef products.
- Beef products should be protected from air during marketing. It is best that they are also protected from light.
- Select vacuum-packed frozen products. Frozen products should not have any indication of oxidation (as indicated by change in color) or freezer burn. Products should not be covered with ice.

4. **Eggs from pastured hens.** Pasturing as used here means providing egg-producing hens access to grass and, as a result, to bugs, worms, and sunshine. This access, in turn, directly correlates with the highest nutritional quality. There is, however, no universally accepted definition of pasturing. Both cage-free and free range labels are very loose terms that may or may not include pasturing. A cage-free label may not mean any pasturing at all.

---

246 For a short, very readable, and persuasive argument in defense of pasture- or grass-fed cattle, see: Barry Estabrook, "Feedlots vs Pastures: Two Very Different Ways to Fatten Beef Cattle," *The Atlantic* (December 28, 2011).

Free range typically includes access to outdoors, but this access is completely undefined. Genuine pasturing should include verification that specifies 1) a minimum time that hens are daily allowed to roam in grass and sunshine, 2) a minimum size of the roaming area, and 3) presence of grass.

Pastured egg products are marketed in a variety of ways, including, for example,

- **eggs produced by hens that are verified to be both pastured and certified organic**. A certified organic label alone does not necessarily verify that grass has been part of the diet of egg-producing hens. While an organic label reliably means hens are fed a 100% organic diet, this diet can include both grain and grass or be completely grain-based. Furthermore, while a certified organic label is supposed to mean eggs are from hens that have access to outdoors, recent research shows that many larger producers of organic eggs do not always comply with this requirement.[247] Thus, combining selection of organic and pasture-verified eggs, as a result, best ensures pasturing and top quality eggs.
- **eggs produced by hens verified to be both pastured and antibiotic-free**. This means the hens were not routinely given antibiotics in their feed or water.
- **locally pastured eggs**. It should not be assumed that locally produced eggs are from pastured hens. Consumers need to themselves verify the authenticity of the pasturing of egg-producing hens. Pastured eggs do have an easily identifiable feature to assist customers in locating them: bright orange yolks. Bright orange color indicates that the diet of egg-producing hens has included grass (or green vegetables), very likely insects, and exposure to sunlight. The bright orange color confirms rich phytonutrient content (beta-carotene and lutein), which hens obtain from eating a mixed diet of green grass, a variety of plants, and insects. This diet correlates with eggs containing high content of omega-3 fatty acids.

Freshness considerations:

- The white of a fresh egg is clear and thick; it closely sticks to the yolk.
- Cracked shells expose the internal egg to air, which undermines freshness, as well as to bacterial contamination, such as pathogens like *Salmonella*.
- Though refrigerated eggs technically remain safe for use for four or five weeks after the "sell by" dates marked on one end of cartons, maximum nutritional value correlates with freshly-laid eggs, which means consuming eggs within several days to a week of purchase.

Nutritional considerations:

- A "vegetarian-fed" label on an egg carton means that the eggs come from hens that were fed a vegetarian diet. As chickens are not naturally vegetarians, this diet is unnatural and thus deficient in meeting the nutritional needs of chickens. The nutritional content of eggs from hens fed vegetarian diets is, as a result, not as rich

---

[247] Kathy Gunst, "A Good Egg," *Eating Well* March/April, 2016): 93.

and varied as that of eggs from pastured hens. Eggs from pastured hens, in other words, contain healthful amounts (in terms of both hen and human needs) of a greater variety of nutritional components.
- Supplementing the diet of hens with either flax seed or aquatic algae importantly enhances the nutritional quality of eggs. Supplementation of diets with flax seed boosts the content of omega-3 fatty acid in ALA (alpha-linolenic acid) form. Aquatic algae boosts DHA form omega-3 fatty acid content, which is the kind of omega-3 fatty acids sardines provide.
- Supplementing the diet of hens with a variety of greens and with both grains and legumes boosts the richness and diversity of the nutritional content of eggs.

5. **Raw poultry, whole or chunk form, pastured.** Chunk form means cut into pieces, or even small chunks, as opposed to being ground. As noted above with respect to eggs, pasturing means providing poultry access to grass-filled space. Genuine pasturing should include verification that specifies 1) a minimum time that hens are daily allowed to roam in grass and sunshine, 2) a minimum size of the roaming area, and 3) presence of grass.

Fresh and frozen pastured poultry products are marketed in a variety of ways, including, for example,

- **poultry verified to be pastured.**
- **poultry verified to be both pastured and certified organic.** As with eggs, certified organic status does not necessarily verify poultry has had a natural diet (i.e., one that includes green plants). While a certified USDA organic label does reliably mean that poultry has been fed a 100% organic diet, the diet can be either unnatural grain- or grass-based. A certified organic label also does not verify meaningful pasturing.[248] Therefore, combining verified pasturing with organic status, which verifies poultry are given other important protections, greatly expands product quality.
- **poultry verified to be both pastured and antibiotic-free.**
- **locally produced poultry that has had at least partial authentic pasturing.**

Freshness considerations:

- As maximum nutritional quality correlates with freshness, select the most recently butchered poultry as indicated by the packaging dates on poultry wrapping.
- Select poultry products packaged in air-tight wrapping.
- Best protected from air and light, whole unskinned poultry is the freshest poultry.

Nutritional considerations:

- Pastured poultry, almost by definition, is lean poultry.
- As noted above, supplementing the diet of pastured poultry with either flax seed or aquatic algae adds to the nutritional quality of products made from such poultry.

---

248 *Eating Well* (March/April, 2010): 78. While a certified organic label technically requires that poultry be given living space that meets "free range" criteria, which means the poultry must be given at least minimal space for roaming in sunshine, the exact amount of space or time in sunshine is not defined, which gives producers great latitude in applying the regulations.

Reference #5

Selecting High Quality Processed Ingredients for Use in Part II Recipes

Physical processing of whole foods – such as breaking open, drying, pre-cooking, grinding, and pressing/juicing – is inevitably destructive of nutritional quality in one way or another. The quality of such physically processed products, as a result, is not comparable to that of completely intact whole foods. Product quality, however, is variable depending on a variety of factors, such as the type and degree of physical processing, the protective packaging provided after processing, the storage provided to retain freshness of products during marketing, and the flavoring added. Some products, accordingly, retain significantly more quality than others.

Reference #5 identifies and describes a variety of physically processed products that retain significant quality and that are commonly (or quite commonly) available to cooks for use in Part II recipes. Physically processed products covered include 1) **ground beef**, 2) **dairy products**, 3) **whole wheat flour**, 4) **whole corn flour**, 5) **cracked whole wheat**, 6) **certified organic raisins**, 7) **expeller pressed nut and peanut oil**, 8) **extra virgin olive oil**, 9) **coconut oil**, 10) **canned products with concentrated phytonutrient content**, 11) **dry frozen blueberries**, and 12) **natural soy sauce**. Freshness and nutrition-enhancing considerations are included with each product to assist cooks in making the most nutritious product selections.

1. Grass-Fed Ground Beef

Grass-fed ground beef, fresh or frozen, is a high quality processed food product.

Grinding completely exposes ground beef to air and light, which reduce nutritional quality. Grinding also exposes meat to bacterial contamination. The quality of ground beef, as a result, is not comparable with chunk form beef. The overall negative effect of grinding, however, can be minimized by the handling it receives. Fresh ground beef that is protectively packaged and refrigerated retains high quality, as does frozen ground beef that is quick-frozen, vacuum packed, carefully thawed (not allowed to become warm or exposed to air during thawing), and immediately cooked after thawing.

A variety of grass-fed ground beef products are quite commonly marketed. These products include, for example,

- **ground beef, verified 100% grass-fed.**
- **ground beef, verified 100% grass-fed and certified organic.**
- **ground beef, verified 100% grass-fed and antibiotic-free.** These products will carry the same logos as chunk form grass-fed beef that is verified to be free of antibiotics.
- **ground beef, locally produced essentially in accordance with 100% grass-fed principles.**

Freshness considerations: Freshness directly correlates with top flavor. Select, for example,

- fresh ground beef, which is the most nutritious and flavorful meat. Patronize butcher shops that freshly grind meat for customers whenever such an opportunity exists.
- packaged beef with the most recent "packaged on" date.
- chunk form beef for home grinding.
- ground beef packaged in a way that protects the meat from contact with air and light during marketing. Light is destructive of riboflavin (B2) content.
- vacuum-packed frozen ground beef. Frozen ground beef should not have any sign of oxidation (as indicated by change in color) or freezer burn. It should also not be covered with ice crystals.

2. Grass-Fed and Certified Organic or European Grass-Fed Dairy Products

Dairy products that are both 100% grass-fed and certified organic or are European grass-fed products are examples of high quality processed food products. This is in spite of the fact that dairy products in general – milk, yogurt, cheese, butter, cream cheese, and sour or sweet cream – are very highly processed. Undergoing three distinct kinds of processing – pasteurization, homogenization, and fortification with various nutrients – milk products scarcely qualify as minimally processed products. There are meaningful differences, nevertheless, in the degree and type of processing used that give less processed products higher quality and less acidity[249] than more processed ones. Examples of such less-processed (and higher quality) grass-fed and certified organic dairy products that are at least quite commonly marketed include:

- non-homogenized full fat (also called "cream on the top") milk and yogurt. Homogenization, which is processing in which the fat globules in milk are mechanically reduced to become so tiny that they remain evenly mixed throughout a milk product, is not required by producers but is nearly universal. Certified organic and 100% pastured milk and yogurt products that are also full-fat, non-homogenized, and regular as opposed to ultra-pasteurized are the very highest quality milk products. Specific examples of top quality non-homogenized milk and yogurt products include Organic Valley Full Fat Grassmilk and Organic Valley Plain Whole Milk (Cream on Top) Yogurt.
- grass-fed butter, such as European produced Lurpac and Kerrygold butter.
- grass-fed cheese, such as European produced Kerrygold cheeses.
- grass-fed cheese made from raw milk. Cheese that in addition to being made from the milk of grass-fed and certified organic or European grass-fed dairy cows is also made from raw milk is the very highest quality cheese.

Grass-fed and either certified organic or European grass-fed products that have somewhat reduced nutritional ranking because of greater processing include:

- full fat homogenized milk products (yogurt, cream, cottage cheese, and sweet or sour

---

249 Vasey, *The Acid-Alkaline Diet for Optimum Health*, 82-83.

cream). The processing involved in the removal of fat from fat-reduced and skim milk products results in the stripping out of specific fatty acids, such as CLA (conjugated linoleic acid), from milk. Research shows that these removed fatty acids play an important role in fat storage in the human body and removal is possibly linked with both weight gain (and obesity) and the distribution of weight in humans.[250]

- pasteurized as opposed to ultra-pasteurized milk. Ultra-pasteurization is more destructive of nutritional content. Organic Valley Grassmilk and Organic Valley Plain Whole Milk Yogurt are examples of pasteurized, not ultra-pasteurized, products.
- cheese, reduced fat but not fat-free cheese, whether cheese is made from cows, sheep, or goat milk.
- unsalted butter as opposed to salted butter.

Freshness consideration: To maximize freshness, purchase dairy products with the most distant "sell by" date. This date applies to unopened containers. Milk opened on this date will retain freshness, as indicated by sweetness as opposed to souring, another 1 or 2 weeks.

Nutrition-enhancing consideration: Select milk products packaged in an opaque container. Opaque containers protect milk from light, which is destructive of the riboflavin (B2) content of milk.

3. Whole Wheat Flour

Certified organic hard whole wheat flour, medium ground, packaged in an air-tight and opaque container, is a high quality processed flour product. This flour is sometimes called bread flour.

Freshness consideration: As wheat germ content makes fresh whole wheat flour vulnerable to rancidity, it is important to use techniques that help guard against the selection of rancid flour.

- Learn to identify the distinctive odor and sharp taste of rancid flour. Check unrefrigerated flour for rancidity after opening packaged flour. Check bulk flour before purchasing it.
- Select flour that has been refrigerated during marketing whenever it is an option.
- Select flour packaged in an air-tight package.
- Freshly home grind flour from whole wheat berries followed by immediate refrigeration after the grinding for the freshest possible and highest quality flour. Grind flour from chilled wheat berries as an additional freshness-enhancing step. Home grinders and wheat berries are widely marketed and make this a realistic option for cooks.

Nutrition-enhancing considerations:

---

[250] "Myth: Full-Fat Milk is Unhealthy," *Eating Well* (September/October, 2014): 52.

- Visible pieces of bran identify medium ground flour. Visibility of bran verifies the high quality of the bran content, and this size bran makes a nutritional difference. This size bran can absorb liquid, and absorbability is the basis of its playing a positive role in maintaining human intestinal health. The bits of fiber also feed beneficial bacteria living in the human gut.
- Stone ground flour is heated at a lower temperature during grinding than flour ground with steel blades and, as a result, has a higher nutritional value.
- Hard winter wheat flour has significantly higher protein (gluten) content than flour ground from soft whole wheat berries, such as whole wheat pastry flour and white whole wheat flour. While high gluten content can negatively affect the texture of quick breads, the application of simple gluten-managing preparation techniques reliably yields tender and moist quick breads, as Chapter Thirteen pancake recipes and Chapter Eight muffin recipes (Recipes #180-184) illustrate.
- The importance of selecting certified organic whole wheat flour has increased today given the routine heavy spraying of industrially produced wheat crops with Roundup, a herbicide that contains the chemical glyphosate, which is now classified as a human carcinogen. Independent research is increasingly linking glyphosate with a wide variety of other deadly human health problems.
- Gluten is protein, which is an important macronutrient required for maintaining human health. It should not be automatically avoided because of the widespread gluten intolerance that has recently surfaced in our society. This gluten intolerance is a modern condition that directly relates to our processed food dependent diet, either due to the overwhelming consumption of nutritionally stripped wheat flour, which leaves the human body unable to properly process flour, and/or to the routine chemical tainting of industrially produced flour, which damages human bodily processes. Gluten intolerance is a symptom of an unhealthy body, not an indictment of the protein itself.[251]

4. Whole Corn Flour

Certified organic yellow whole corn flour, medium ground, packaged in an air-tight and opaque container is a high quality processed food product.

Freshness consideration: Corn germ makes whole corn flour highly vulnerable to rancidity. This makes it important to use techniques that help guard against the selection of rancid flour and that maintain freshness during home storage.

- Purchase whole corn packaged in an air-tight container. Check the flour for rancidity upon opening.
- Check bulk marketed whole corn flour for rancidity before purchasing it.
- Purchase corn flour that has been refrigerated whenever this option exists.
- Freshly grind corn flour from corn kernels for the freshest possible flour.

---

251 Shanahan, *Deep Nutrition*, 179.

- Keep corn flour refrigerated.
- Freeze corn flour, tightly covered, that will be stored for some time.

Nutrition-enhancing considerations:

- Visible pieces of bran identify medium corn flour. As in the case of medium ground wheat flour, visibility of bran also verifies the high quality of the bran content. This size bran can absorb liquid, and absorbability is the basis of its playing a positive role in maintaining human intestinal health.
- Yellow color indicates rich phytonutrient content. White corn flour, in comparison, has insignificant phytonutrient content.
- Whole corn flour is alkaline, which contrasts it with other grain flours. Other grain flours are acid-forming foods when consumed by humans. That corn flour is alkaline makes corn bread (Recipe #185) a complementary accompaniment for the tomato sauce-based stews contained in Chapter Eight (Soups and Stews).
- The importance of selecting certified organic corn flour has increased significantly for two reasons. First is the heavy extent to which industrially produced corn is sprayed with the herbicide Roundup. Roundup contains the chemical glyphosate, which has now been authoritatively established to be a human carcinogen. Authoritative independent research also links glyphosate with a wide variety of other deadly human health conditions. Second is the extent to which industrially produced corn is genetically engineered corn.

5. Cracked Whole Wheat

Certified organic whole cracked wheat, medium or coarse cracked, packaged in an air-tight and opaque container is a high quality processed product. Cracking, which significantly reduces the cooking time of wheat berries, converts nutritious wheat berries into practical cooking form with minimal nutritional loss. Chapter Seven Traditional Pilaf Recipe #164 illustrates the use of medium cracked whole wheat. Cracked wheat can substitute for brown rice in Chapter Seven Stir-Fried Dishes. Like brown rice, cracked wheat can be cooked well ahead of serving and has excellent storage capacity. Cooked cracked wheat can be refrigerated for several days, during which time it is on hand for quick use in dishes.

Freshness consideration: Cracking exposes wheat germ to air, which makes cracked grain highly vulnerable to rancidity and reduces flavor. It is important, as a result,

- to always check any cracked wheat product for rancidity.
- to refrigerate or freeze cracked wheat during storage, tightly closed.

Nutrition-enhancing considerations:

- Coarse and medium cracked wheat contribute highly absorptive bran, which is high

quality bran. Though fine cracking reduces cooking time, it also reduces the absorptive capacity of the bran content, reducing the nutritional quality of cracked wheat.
- As pre-cooked products, medium and coarse cracked whole bulgur products have lower nutritional quality than cracked wheat.
- Select certified organic cracked wheat to avoid heavy pesticide content. As a naturally produced product, certified organic grain has other nutritional advantages, particularly greater nutritional value.

6. Raisins

Certified organic raisins are a high quality processed food product. Widely marketed, and at a price quite comparable to industrially produced raisins, organic raisins are very accessible quality products. Being made from ripe grapes, certified organic raisins are reliably more flavorful than industrially produced raisins which, in contrast, are overwhelmingly made from grapes that are harvested before they are ripe. Because grapes do not ripen further after harvesting, early harvested grapes never reach full ripeness, which is when they are most flavorful.

Freshness considerations:

- Protect raisins from air. Store them in an air-tight container.
- Except for keeping a small amount handy for use in dishes, refrigerate raisins to maximize retention of flavor and nutritional quality.

Nutrition-enhancing considerations:

- Certified organic raisins are essentially pesticide and chemical free while industrially produced raisins are heavily tainted with pesticides. Industrially produced grapes are among the most heavily sprayed of all our fruits and vegetables,[252] and grapes dried for making raisins are seriously tainted as well. Industrially produced raisins are also chemically manipulated in another important way. They undergo a process called "gibbing." In this process, they are sprayed with a hormone that increases grape size by as much as seventy-five percent.[253]
- While drying is processing that reduces nutritional quality (in particular vitamin C, but also phytonutrient content), raisins, like dried fruits in general, retain valuable nutritional characteristics. Raisins, for example,

    - retain intact skin and flesh, which makes them a standout source of insoluble fiber.
    - contain concentrated natural sugar packaged within natural fiber. When raisins are eaten, they provide quick energy without causing a spike in blood sugar.
    - are alkaline and serve as acid-balancing ingredients in dishes.

---

252 Robinson, *Eating on the Wild Side*, 310.
253 Ibid., 306-307.

- Raisin varieties have variable nutritional value, and some varieties (such as flame and monukka) are more nutritional than Thompson raisins, which is the main variety of raisins marketed.
- Some other more nutritious dried fruits are interchangeable with raisins, including currants and dried plums (or prunes). These dried fruit varieties are also quite widely available in certified organic form.

7. Expeller Pressed Peanut and Macadamia Nut Oil

Certified organic expeller pressed peanut and macadamia nut oil are high quality processed food products. Both peanut oil and macadamia nut oil are "good fats" because they can handle the heat involved in processing and cooking.[254] While expeller pressed peanut and macadamia nut oil have undergone considerable processing, which includes high temperature heating,[255] expeller pressed peanut and macadamia nut oil tolerate this processing and remain stable when heated during the cooking of food. They do not react with oxygen during heating, and the heating does not change the oil. These oils, as a result, to not produce free radicals or leave toxic substances in foods when heated, as is the case with all pure vegetable oils, including canola oil. Pure polyunsaturated vegetable oils become highly unnatural as a result of the extensive processing they undergo during refining[256] and, as a result, become unstable when heated. They mix with oxygen, which results in a chemical reaction that releases free radicals into food being cooked. Heating also changes the oil, unnaturally distorting it and leaving toxic substances in cooked food that humans consume.[257]

Freshness consideration: Both expeller pressed peanut oil and macadamia nut oil are vulnerable to rancidity, which spoils the oil. It is important, as a result,

- to learn to identify the odor and taste of rancid oil.
- to always check any oil product for rancidity.
- to keep oil refrigerated.
- to keep oil tightly closed to protect it from air, which causes oil to become rancid.

Nutrition-enhancing considerations:

- Select unrefined oil as the highest quality oil. While this oil has rich flavor, which can undermine its acceptability for some consumers, it retains significant naturally-occurring

---

254 Shanahan, *Deep Nutrition*, 132.
255 The processing of refined expeller pressed oil includes degumming (which removes most nutritional content, such as valuable vitamin E and minerals), bleaching (which removes most remaining nutrients, such as carotene, and leaves the oil clear), deodorizing (which involves very high temperature heating), and winterizing (which is a final cleaning process that leaves oil reduced to fatty acids only).
256 Refined pure vegetable oil (including soybean, sunflower, corn, canola, safflower, grape seed, and cottonseed oil) additionally undergoes solvent extraction. Solvent extraction involves mixing a poisonous petrochemical solvent with the broken open oil-containing materials. After the solvent chemically extracts the oil, the solvent is boiled off (supposedly) before the oil material begins the same refining steps as refined expeller pressed oil. This means pure vegetable oil goes through two full rounds of processing, and this processing leaves pure vegetable oil a completely colorless, tasteless, and nutritionally depleted product.
257 Shanahan, *Deep Nutrition*, 122-143.

antioxidants and other natural nutritional components, which makes it a superior quality oil. Its rich flavor serves to reduce its use.

- Expeller pressed peanut oil does not have a relatively balanced omega-3 to omega-6 essential fatty acid content, which is the ratio directly correlated with maintaining the availability of omega-3 essential fatty acids for vital human bodily functions. A high omega-6 to low omega-3 ratio, which is the ratio of peanut oil, results in the crowding out of omega-3 fatty acids. Peanut oil, as a result, should be used relatively sparingly.

8. Extra Virgin Olive Oil

Extra virgin olive oil, both European produced and certified organic US produced, is a high quality processed food product. Extra virgin olive oil is high quality oil that is within the reach of most cooks for everyday use in salads and cooking. As a monounsaturated oil, it is a "good fat" that is stable during heating.[258] This means that it is not reactive (does not mix with oxygen) and does not release free radicals or leach toxic debris into food during cooking. At its best, extra virgin olive oil is first pressed oil that is mechanically pressed from top quality olives (they are ripe and fresh) according to strictly applied procedures that keep acidity from exceeding 1%. The best extra virgin olive oil, as a result, retains rich, naturally-occurring nutritional content. At its worst, extra virgin olive oil (EVOO) is variable. It has a lengthy history of adulteration – and the possible extent of contemporary fraud in the olive oil industry is something about which consumers should be mindful.[259] Selection of certified organic or European produced extra virgin olive oil helps ensure the quality of a product.

- The fat product ghee substitutes for extra virgin olive oil in all Part II recipes except for Chapter Six salads.

Freshness consideration: Once an extra virgin olive container is opened, oil quality deteriorates with storage. It can become rancid, which spoils it. As a result,

- refrigerate most extra virgin olive oil, keeping only a small amount at room temperature for everyday use.
- purchase a relatively small amount of oil at a time.
- keep oil tightly covered to protect it from air.
- select bulk form extra virgin olive oil only from businesses with high product turnover.
- learn to identify the odor and taste of rancid oil.
- always check any extra virgin olive oil product for rancidity upon opening. Return newly opened containers to stores to exchange it for fresh oil.
- discard used oil that becomes rancid during storage.

---

258 Ibid., 132.
259 Helpful readings in this regard are Tom Mueller's 2007 article, "Slippery Business: The Trade in Adulterated Olive Oil" (*The New Yorker*: August 13, 2007) and his book *Extra Virginity: The Sublime and Scandalous World of Olive Oil* (New York: W.W. Norton, 2011). For a brief overview, see Dwight Garner's review of Mueller's book, "Olive Oil's Growers, Chemists, Cooks and Crooks" (*The New York Times*: December 7, 2011).

Nutrition-enhancing considerations:

- An important human health-promoting function of extra virgin olive oil is helping humans absorb the valuable fat-soluble nutrients and phytonutrients contained by raw leafy salad greens and other vegetables. Research shows that extra virgin olive oil does the best job of any oil of making these valuable nutritional components more absorbable during human digestion.[260] In contrast, vegetable oils impair vitamin absorption.[261]
- Packaging of oil in a green-tinted glass container protects the oil from light, which is destructive of oil quality. Oil packaged in tin containers is also protected from light.
- Select unfiltered oil when it is an option. Filtering removes valuable human health supporting components.[262] Because unfiltered oil retains greater nutritional content than filtered oil, it also has lower acidity. Natural food stores are most likely sources of unfiltered products.
- Select extra virgin olive oil products pressed by small presses that do not produce heat. These types of oil are genuinely cold-pressed extra virgin olive oil and have the highest nutritional quality.
- As each tablespoon of oil contains 120 calories, it is important to always measure oil content to avoid excessive oil content in recipes.

9. Coconut Oil

Certified organic expeller pressed coconut oil is a high quality processed food product. Non-hydrogenated coconut oil is a "good fat" that can handle the heat involved in processing or cooking.[263] A traditional fat that primarily contains saturated fat, coconut oil is not reactive during heating. Because of its natural saturated construction, coconut oil resists heat-related damage called oxidation that releases free radicals or other toxic debris into foods being cooked. Unlike polyunsaturated oil, saturated fats have no room for oxygen to squeeze in and even relatively high heat cannot force the tough molecules of saturated fat to let in oxygen or force distortions of the fat structure. Coconut oil, as a result, is stable during heating.

Nutrition-enhancing considerations:

- Coconut oil joins peanut oil, macadamia nut oil, extra virgin olive oil, and any artisanally-produced unrefined oil as stable oils. They contrast sharply with pure vegetable oils, non-butter spreads (including margarine), and what are called trans fat-free spreads, which are modern industrially created fats that are highly unnatural due to the extensive processing they are subjected to during refining. As a result, they are unstable oils that are reactive during heating and are highly dangerous to human health.[264]

---

260 Robinson, *Eating on the Wild Side*, 37.
261 Shanahan, *Deep Nutrition*, 132.
262 Robinson, *Eating on the Wild Side*, 37. Filtering removes half of the beneficial bionutrients of extra virgin olive oil, including a compound called squalene. One of the ways this compound aids human health is protecting skin from UV damage.
263 Shanahan, *Deep Nutrition*, 132. Shanahan explains that coconut is a natural fat, and that nature doesn't make bad fats. It is factories that do.
264 Ibid., 121-143.

PART 2

- Palm oil has essentially the same "good fat" characteristics as coconut oil, but *Cooked Alive!* is not recommending it as a fat selection because of the link between the industrial production of this oil and devastating loss of orangutan and other world forest habitats.

10. Canned Products with Concentrated Phytonutrient Content

Certified organic canned products with concentrated phytonutrient content are high quality processed food products. Though the extended cooking involved in canning is highly destructive of particular heat-sensitive nutrients (such as vitamin C and folate) and heat-sensitive phytonutrients (such as glucosinolates contained by cabbage family vegetables), canning does not harm some phytonutrient content. Canning even makes some phytonutrients more potent by transforming them into a more active form or into a form more easily absorbed (made more bioavailable) by humans.[265] Canning, in other words, converts foods containing particular phytonutrients into super food form. A variety of these canned food products are commonly marketed in certified organic form. These food products include, for example,

- **artichokes.** Antioxidant-rich canned artichoke hearts fit easily into Chapter Six salads, Chapter Eight soups and stews, and Chapter Twelve pizza toppings.
- **beans (mature).** Canning converts beans into super antioxidant-rich foods.[266] Canned beans are also rich sources of fiber (both soluble and insoluble). They are super convenient products as well. While canned beans are not as flavorful as home-cooked beans can be, canned beans are a convenient product. They are easy to keep on hand for inclusion in a wide variety of dishes, such as Chapter Eight tomato sauce-flavored stews and all Chapter Seven stir-fried dishes.
- **beets.** Canned beets have more antioxidant value than fresh cooked beets. Canned beets fit attractively into Chapter Six salads, Chapter Eight tomato-based stews, and Chapter Seven stir-fried dishes.
- **blueberries.** Modern research technology shows the phytonutrient content of canned blueberries is greater than that of fresh berries. Canning rearranges the structure of the blueberry phytonutrients in a manner that makes them more absorbable by humans. Canned blueberries, in turn, are perfect fruit sauce (Recipe #219) and Chapter Eleven dessert ingredients. They can be directly added to Chapter Thirteen pancakes (Recipe #215) and Chapter Eight muffins (Recipe #180).
- **yellow corn.** Carotene-rich canned yellow corn has greater carotene content than fresh yellow corn. Canned corn fits into Chapter Eight soups and stews and practically any Chapter Seven stir-fried dish.
- **sweet potatoes.** Diced beta-carotene-rich canned sweet potatoes easily mix into Chapter Seven stir-fried dishes, Chapter Eight soups and stews, and Chapter Nine curries. Mashed sweet potato fits into Chapter Thirteen pancakes (Recipe #218, where it substitutes for winter squash) and Chapter Eight muffins (Recipe #183).

---

265 Robinson, *Eating on the Wild Side*, 248.
266 Ibid, 187 and 193. Canned kidney beans and pinto beans ranked 1st and 2nd respectively in a 2011 listing of the 100 top ranked antioxidant-rich foods.

- **tomato paste**. Canning makes the lycopene content of tomatoes more absorbable for humans and, as a result, canned tomato products are the richest known sources of the human health-supporting phytonutrient lycopene.[267] Tomato paste, which is simply ripe tomatoes without any added salt or sugar, is the most concentrated form of canned tomato products. Thus, it is a very rich source of lycopene even when added in a small amount. As little as 1 T per serving contributes significant lycopene to a dish. Additionally, a small amount of tomato paste enhances the flavoring of such dishes as Chapter Eight tomato-based stews, Chapter Twelve pizza sauce, and Chapter Seven stir-fried dishes. Adding to its value, tomato paste is a super convenient product. Unlike other canned products, there is no packing liquid to drain from and separately utilize in order to avoid wasting valuable soluble content. Tomato paste is also widely marketed in reasonably priced certified organic form.

Freshness considerations for canned products:

- Observe "best by" dates included on containers.
- Select food products that are tightly sealed at purchase. Canned products should also not be bulging.

Nutrition-enhancing considerations:

- Utilize all packing juice. Using all packing liquid of products is crucial to retaining rich soluble content contained in the liquid. Utilizing packing juice is not so difficult for canned blueberries because packing liquid can be incorporated into the sauce. Adding any more than a small amount of weakly flavored packing liquid, however, easily dilutes dish flavoring. Therefore, only a small measured amount should be added and the rest collected for another use, freezing the broth in serving size amounts if the broth cannot be quickly used. Saving small jars with tight-fitting lids keeps useful liquid storage containers handy.
- Select canned products packaged in glass, which reliably does not contain chemicals that can be leached into canned food, but aseptic containers also work well for packaging canned products. The plastic lining of many canned products, however, commonly contains the chemical called bisphenol A, or BPA, which can be leached into the canned food. This chemical has been identified as an endocrine-disrupting chemical. By disrupting and interfering with human hormones, these chemicals cause a variety of serious human health problems, including obesity.[268]
- Select salt-free and otherwise unflavored products, which puts the cook in control of the amount of salt and flavoring added.
- Select water-packed as opposed to pickled artichokes and beets, which makes maximum conservation of soluble nutritional content possible. In pickled products, a significant amount (perhaps all) of the natural juice (and, hence, soluble nutritional content) is replaced by the pickling liquid.

---

267 Robinson, *Eating on the Wild Side*, 152-153. Lycopene protects tomatoes from UV rays, and lycopene obtained through eating tomatoes provides humans with this valuable protection.
268 Guthman, *Weighing In*, 107 and 109.

PART 2

11. Dry Frozen Blueberries

Certified organic dry frozen blueberries are a high quality processed food product. Research shows that the use of fast dry freezing methods which quickly deactivate enzymes that can destroy phytonutrients and vitamin C make frozen blueberries almost as nutritious as fresh berries.[269] Though freezing reduces firmness, dry frozen blueberries remain flavorful and highly useful dish ingredients. Available all year around, they are easy to keep on hand for quick inclusion in a variety of dishes. They, for example, convert into fruit sauce (Recipe #219) for use as a topping for Chapter Thirteen pancakes or for Chapter Eleven Mini Cheesecake Dessert (Recipe #207). They also fit directly into Chapter Thirteen pancakes (Recipe #215) and Chapter Eight muffins (Recipe #180).

Freshness considerations:

- Keep blueberries continually frozen. Thawing and re-freezing is destructive of nutritional content.
- Store frozen blueberries in freezer-quality plastic bags and press out as much air as is possible before sealing the bags.
- Do not store frozen blueberries for a long period. Use them within 3-4 months to retain the flavor and nutritional quality of the berries.

Nutrition-enhancing considerations:

- Speedy thawing of frozen blueberries is crucial for retaining nutritional quality. This means brief heating (for 25-30 seconds) of the berries in a microwave oven immediately after removing them from the freezer. An alternative method of quick thawing is to immediately add unthawed frozen berries to boiling liquid after removing them from the freezer. Letting them thaw at room temperature results in significant loss of phytonutrient content.

12. Natural Soy Sauce

Certified organic soy sauce is a high quality processed food product. The certified organic label ensures the soybeans used to make the product have been naturally fermented and are not genetically modified. This label also ensures the soy sauce is naturally flavored and colored.

Nutrition-enhancing considerations:

- Because the sodium content of soy sauce is very high (**1 t soy sauce contains 433 mg**

---

[269] Robinson, *Eating on the Wild Side*, 247.

sodium), it is important to use only the "few drops" called for in recipes, which means about ⅓ to ½ t soy sauce per serving.
- Also called shoyu, naturally fermented soy sauce should be made only from soy beans, wheat, and salt.
- Select a soy sauce product with a lid that releases soy sauce in drops. If a soy sauce product does not have such a dispensing lid, use some system of measuring soy sauce. For example, pour soy sauce into a dinner spoon, filling it about half full, before sprinkling it over a serving.
- If a restraint approach fails, either substitute fresh squeezed lemon juice as an accompaniment in place of soy sauce or omit soy sauce.

Reference #6

Maximizing the Attractiveness of Whole Food Ingredients Commonly Used in Part II Recipes

Reference #6 makes flavor-enhancing suggestions for maximizing the attractiveness of key intact whole food ingredients that are commonly used in Part II recipes. Covering whole foods other than vegetables and fruits (which are covered in Reference #1) and presenting ingredients in alphabetical order, Reference #6 covers the following whole food ingredients: 1) **dried fruit,** 2) **dried herbs and spices,** 3) **fresh herbs and spices,** 4) **legumes,** 5) **nuts,** 6) **protein (beef, poultry, and eggs),** 7) **brown rice,** and 8) **yogurt.**

1. Dried Fruit

Maximize the attractiveness of dried fruit in dishes.

In selecting dried fruit,

- select certified organic raisins. Organic raisins stand out as an organic product that is both more flavorful and free of pesticides and other artificial chemical content in comparison to industrially produced raisins. Industrially produced grapes are routinely picked before they are ripe. Because grapes do not ripen further after being harvested, commercially produced grapes never develop top flavor.
- select dried fruit that has somewhat tangy flavoring. For example, select dried pineapple, sweetened tart cherries or cranberries, and apricots. Sulphured California apricots add both attractive color and tartness to dishes.
- select dried fruit that adds color, such as Turkish apricots.
- purchase dried fruit in whole, uncut form or in pieces as large as possible. For example, purchase pineapple rings rather than diced pineapple. Whole or large pieces of fruit best retain flavor.

In storing dried fruit,

- store dried fruit tightly closed to prevent unattractive drying and loss of flavor due to exposure to air.
- keep a small amount of dried fruit within reach for easy inclusion in dishes, but refrigerate most dried fruit, tightly covered, to best preserve its flavor.

In adding dried fruit to dishes,

- cut large dried fruit pieces into bite-size pieces for easy eating. For example, halve prunes and apricots lengthwise into thin strips and thinly slice the strips crosswise; cut pineapple rings into thin slices and halve the slices crosswise; halve dried cherries.
- do not cut large dried fruit pieces into very small pieces. The flavor of small pieces is lost in dishes.
- plump hard dried fruit before serving it in salads and stir-fried dishes.

    - To plump dried fruit, briefly stir-fry whole, uncut fruit in a small amount of fruit juice or water. Bring the juice or water to boiling (2 T per 2-4 T dried fruit) over medium-high heat in a small nonstick or stainless steel skillet. Add and stir-fry the dried fruit for 30 seconds. Remove the skillet from the heat and set it aside, covered, for 5-10 minutes (10 minutes for very hard dried fruit). Drain the fruit in a colander placed over a bowl for collecting the drained juice. Pat plumped fruit dry before adding it to a salad or stir-fried dish. Save and use drained juice in any dish that uses sweet juice, such as fruit sauce topping for pancakes or fruit desserts.

- add only a small amount of dried fruit to dishes. The concentrated flavor of the fruit easily becomes too strong. They easily make a dish taste too sweet and possibly make it too laxative as well.
- combine dried fruits to take advantage of different flavors and colors.
- do not overcook dried fruit, which undermines both flavor and texture. Add it near the end of cooking or just in time to become softened and heated through before serving.

2. Dried Herb and Spice Flavoring

Maximize the flavoring contribution of dried herbs and spices in dishes. Dried herbs and spices are invaluable flavoring ingredients. They enhance flavor without adding sugar, salt, or fat.

In selecting herb and spice products,

- select a curry powder product on the basis of experimenting with a variety of products to locate one with flavor that is most pleasing to you. Curry powder is a collection of as many as twenty ground spices, and both the flavor and heat of curry powder can vary greatly from brand to brand. Natural food stores often sell curry powder in bulk form,

which provides cooks the opportunity to purchase a small amount of curry powder for tasting purposes. As an introductory product, Spice Island Curry Powder is an example of a reliably tasty and mild curry powder that is also quite widely marketed in grocery stores.
- select chili powder on the basis of experimenting with a variety of products to select the most flavorful product.
- select bulk form dried spices and herbs marketed by natural food stores. The flavor of these herbs and spices tends to be reliably high because of high initial quality and because rapid turnover keeps supplies fresh. Purchasing bulk form herbs and spices also provides cooks an economical opportunity to try out new herbs and spices.

In storing dried spices and herbs,

- store dried spices and herbs tightly covered to protect them from air, which causes flavor to fade.
- check the lids of containers with shaker tops (tops with holes for sprinkling spices or herbs over foods) to ensure the lid fits snugly. Ground powder tends to build up and prevent tight closing.
- check the flavor of dried spices and herbs periodically and replace them if they are not noticeably aromatic.

In preparing dried spices and herbs,

- freshly grind whole seeds for the tastiest ground spices. Invest in an electric seed grinder or a mortar and pestle.
- accurately measure dried spice and herb amounts. Even slightly too much or too little flavoring can make a difference, unpleasantly overpowering other dish flavoring or leaving the dish bland. Use measuring spoons and never guess or approximate without practice.
- reduce herb amount if substituting ground herbs for herb leaves in a recipe. As the flavor of herb leaves is milder than that of ground, adding an equal amount of ground can easily be too strong.
- crush dried herb leaves between your palms to best release flavor.
- evenly disperse spice and herb flavoring in a dish. Add dried spices/herbs to stir-frying onions. The spice/herb flavoring adheres to the oil-coated onion pieces and becomes evenly mixed in a dish. The oil also holds and protects the herb or spice flavoring.
- cook dried herbs and spices (except for curry powder, which requires little heating) at least briefly (5 minutes) to mellow the flavor, but avoid extended cooking, which dissipates flavor.
- dry roast and grind whole cumin seeds for especially tasty ground cumin. To roast cumin, add seeds to a hot skillet that has been pre-heated at a medium heat setting. Heat the seeds for several minutes until they become aromatic, stirring them often. Remove the skillet from the heat and transfer the seeds to another container to cool. Once the seeds are completely cool, grind them with a mortar and pestle or in an electric coffee or seed grinder. Store the seeds in an air-tight container.

PART 2

- enhance the overall herb flavoring in a dish by adding dried herbs to individual vegetables (such as carrots, celery, and cauliflower) during stir-fry/steaming and to ground beef during stir-frying.
- enhance curry powder flavoring in a dish by adding ½ t each of ground cumin and coriander, ¼ t of either or both ground ginger and cinnamon, and/or ¼ t green cardamom, pods removed and seeds freshly crushed in a mortar and pestle. Add a touch of heat by including a small amount (1/8 t or to taste) of cayenne, ground red pepper, or red pepper flakes.

Maximize the nutritional quality of dried herbs and spices.

- Select certified organic dried herbs and spices to avoid hidden chemical content. Dried and herbs make nutritional contributions, and certified organic products also contain more potent phytonutrients and greater overall nutritional content.
- Select certified organic dried herbs and spices for assurance that herbs and spices have not been irradiated.

3. Fresh Herbs and Spices

Maximize the flavoring contribution of fresh herbs and cilantro in dishes. Adding a completely different dimension of flavor to a dish, fresh herbs and cilantro lift dish attractiveness and enhance cooking satisfaction for very little cost and effort.

When adding fresh herbs and cilantro to dishes,

- add only a very small amount of fresh herbs or cilantro. As the flavor of fresh herbs and cilantro can easily be too intense, begin cautiously by adding 1 t snipped per individual salad or dish serving. Add more only after verifying the acceptability of the herb or cilantro.
- begin with milder herbs, such as parsley and mint. Move slowly to more intensely flavored herbs and spices, such as basil, oregano, marjoram, rosemary, and cilantro.
- do not judge the acceptability of a particular kind of herb on the basis of one or even two samples. Because flavor varies considerably within herb families, experiment with different varieties of herbs to locate the most pleasing varieties of an herb family.
- add herbs and cilantro that have been rinsed and thoroughly dried. To dry the leaves after rinsing them in cool water, spread the leaves over a strip of paper towels or a terry cloth towel, top them with another layer of towels, roll the towels around the leaves, and gently squeeze the towels to dry the leaves. Alternatively, spin the leaves dry in a salad spinner.
- cut fresh herbs and cilantro into small, but not very fine, pieces. First separate the leaves from the stems before cutting, setting aside the stems. Either snip the leaves with kitchen scissors or roughly stack them and use a sharp knife to slice them crosswise into thin

pieces for serving. Separately snip the stems. Holding the stems together with one hand, use kitchen scissors to cut them into thin pieces and add them to the snipped leaves. For tough stems, set them aside and stir-fry them with onion that will be added to a stir fry, curry, or stew.
- cut and add herbs and cilantro to dishes only shortly before serving them in order to keep leaves firm.
- serve fresh herbs or cilantro raw as a topping to individual servings of hot dishes just prior to serving. The distinctive flavoring of fresh herbs and cilantro is quickly lost with heating.

In storing fresh herbs and cilantro,

- refrigerate uncleaned and uncut herbs or cilantro completely wrapped within a paper towel and within a sealed plastic bag.
- keep sprigs of fresh basil handy by standing them in a glass of water within easy reach.
- grow some fresh basil or other herbs on a window sill, patio, or deck.

4. Legumes

Maximize the attractiveness of legumes in dishes.

In selecting cooked legume products,

- select attractively soft legumes. Texture varies greatly among different brands of canned and other packaged cooked beans, with texture ranging from mushy to crisp. Check out a variety of alternative products. Legumes should not have even a hint of crispness; they should also not have a mushy texture.
- select unflavored (or flavored only with salt) legumes packaged in a small amount of broth within a vacuum-packed aseptic container as an especially convenient legume product. Such products keep legumes on hand for use in salads and stir-fried dishes in an amount that can be quickly used. Very importantly, cooks remain in control of added flavoring. Look for such products in natural food stores, the natural food section of regular grocery stores, and the natural food section of some department stores, such as Target.

In storing cooked legumes,

- remove beans from a can and refrigerate them in an air-tight container and in a glass container in particular to maintain fresh flavor and moistness. As legumes spoil quickly, use stored canned beans within 4 days after opening the can or container. Always check legumes – spoiled legumes have an offensive odor – stored for a longer time before using them.
- freeze cooked legumes to avoid spoilage and/or to keep them on hand for quick and easy inclusion in dishes.

- Freeze legumes with a small amount of broth, in a serving size amount, and within a quart size zippered plastic freezer bag, first squeezing as much air as possible from the bag.
- Alternatively, dry freeze well-drained (but not rinsed) legumes. Spread the beans in a rectangular casserole dish, freeze them, and when they are hard, add them to a sealable plastic freezer bag, pressing out as much air as possible before sealing the bag. Separately freeze bean broth. Thawing very quickly, dry frozen legumes are easy to add in any amount to dishes.

In adding cooked legumes to dishes,

- thoroughly drain and pat the legumes dry before adding them to salads and stir-fried dishes. Otherwise undrained legume broth easily makes these dishes unattractively soggy, discolors vegetable and fruit ingredients, and dilutes dish flavor.

  - **To drain legumes**, drain them in a colander placed over a bowl for collecting broth. For legumes packed in very thick broth, first swish the beans in ½ c water before draining them in a colander. Spread drained beans over paper towels for complete drying. Because legume broth contains rich soluble nutrients and soluble fiber content, collect any drained broth and use in another way. For example, freeze collected legume broth in an air-tight glass container for future inclusion in a dish that adds liquid, such as when cooking a grain or cooking a whole chicken or beef for stews.
  - **To pat drained legumes dry**, spread them over a layer of paper towels and wrap the towels around the legumes.

- add only a small amount of legumes to dishes. A small amount blends almost invisibly into the dish, which enhances its acceptability as a dish ingredient. A small amount also does not unbalance dish flavoring.
- home-cook legumes to significantly enhance both flavor and texture. Begin with lentils (Recipe #168), which are reliably tasty and relatively quick-cooking legumes.

5. Nuts

Maximize the attractiveness of nuts in dishes. Nuts are distinctively flavorful ingredients that contribute both attractive texture and rich nutritional content to dishes.

In selecting nuts,

- carefully avoid selection of rancid nuts. Learn to recognize the taste and odor of rancid nuts as well as other physical indicators (black or dark spots) of rancidity and routinely check nut products for rancidity. Rancidity effectively spoils nuts, undermining both the flavor and nutritional quality of nuts. Containing free radicals, rancid nut oil is toxic to humans.

- select raw intact nuts as the most nutritious and flavorful nuts. Raw fresh nuts are delicious without added salt or fat.
- select unbroken raw nuts packaged in air-tight containers. Avoid selection of nuts broken into small pieces or sliced. Contact with air reduces flavor. Because contact between air and nut flesh stimulates enzymes that cause rancidity, whole unbroken nuts are far less likely to become rancid than broken open nuts. In the case of peanuts, unbroken peanuts are also less likely to be contaminated with toxic aflatoxin, a potent carcinogen produced by molds that commonly grow on peanuts and that can cause liver cancer.
- select unshelled nuts as the freshest products. As the most protected from contact with air, unshelled nuts are least likely to be rancid. Invest in a good shelling tool in order to take advantage of this highest-quality nut product.
- select nuts with skins. For example, select almonds with skins. In addition to being a source of valuable fiber, the skin protects nut pulp from air, which is destructive of flavor and evaporates moisture.
- purchase in-season nuts as the freshest, tastiest nuts. For example, purchase pecans in the fall after they are harvested. This is also when nuts are least expensive. Refrigerated or frozen whole unbroken (and especially unshelled) nuts have extended storage capacity.
- locate a good source of reliably fresh nuts. For example, look for natural food stores that market unbroken nuts in bulk form. While bulk nuts are exposed to air, the quality of these nuts tends to be reliably high because of rapid turnover. Bulk nuts are somewhat less expensive than packaged, and consumers have the opportunity to personally check the nuts for rancidity before purchase. Farmers' markets are a reliable source of in-season nuts. Mail order businesses bring fresh nuts within the easy reach of every part of the United States.
- select certified organic nuts to reliably avoid chemically tainted and irradiated nuts.

In adding nuts to dishes,

- add a small amount of nuts to dishes. Aim for a handful or about ½ oz (which is about ⅛ c or 2 T) per 2-3 serving dish or individual salad. A ½ oz amount – around 20 whole almonds, 8-9 cashews, 9-10 pecan halves, 5-7 walnut halves, 25 pistachios, and 9-10 hazelnuts – is an amount that enhances both the flavor and nutritional quality of a dish without loading the dish with calories (½ oz nuts generally contributes from 75-100 calories). Because they are expensive food ingredients, adding them in small amounts also makes them economically feasible ingredients.
- mix two or more nut varieties to take advantage of the different flavors and nutritional contributions of nuts.
- break or chop nuts into fairly large pieces to maximize the flavor of nuts in dishes. The flavor of finely chopped nuts is largely lost.
- freshly toast nuts to enhance crispness and flavor.

    - To toast nuts, preheat a heavy-bottomed skillet at a medium heat setting until hot, 5-7 minutes. Add enough nuts to cover the skillet bottom in a single layer and cook the nuts, stirring them regularly, until they are aromatic and lightly browned, for 5-8 minutes. Keep watch throughout the cooking to avoid scorching, over-browning, or burning, which undermine both flavor and quality. Cool the nuts completely before refrigerating them in an air-tight container. Without cooling, condensation will form around the nuts and undermine crispness.

- add nuts to dishes as last ingredients to maintain a crisp texture.

In storing nuts,

- refrigerate nuts within an air-tight package to largely inactivate enzymes that can cause nuts to become rancid.
- freeze nuts that will be stored for an extended length of time. Freezing nuts within an air-tight container preserves freshness by completely inactivating enzymes.

Combine nuts and seeds in salads. Add, for example, ¼ **oz (or 1 T) sunflower, pumpkin,** or **sesame seeds** per individual salad. To maximize the valuable nutritional contribution and to secure the attractive flavor of seeds, select, store, and use seeds in exactly the same way as nuts. Two differences in using seeds and nuts are as follows.

- To make the valuable inner seed content absorbable during human digestion, break open the seed skin by crushing the seeds with a rolling pin or mortar and pestle.
- Toast seeds for a shorter time than nuts, around 3-4 minutes only.

6. Protein
(Meat, Poultry, and Egg)

Maximize the attractiveness of lean beef, chicken breast, and egg in dishes.

In selecting protein products,

- select very fresh products. Always carefully inspect the "sell by" dates on packages of fresh beef, chicken, and egg cartons and select those packages with the most distant dates.
- select vacuum-packed and quick frozen sliced beefsteak, chicken breast, and chicken tenders. The flesh of frozen products should have natural color. No whitening of flesh or ice should be visible.

In preparing protein,

- precisely apply the *juice-protective* techniques used for cooking beef and poultry that are used in *Cooked Alive!* recipes and summarized in Reference #6 (*Juice-Protective* Techniques for Preparing Animal Protein).

- cook a small amount of minced fresh ginger root with sliced beef and chicken and with ground beef.
- add dried herbs or spices to sliced and ground beef and sliced chicken during stir-frying. Add dried herbs and spices to egg.
- stir-fry sliced chicken in toasted sesame oil for added attractive flavor.

In storing protein,

- cover beef and poultry tightly to prevent drying after opening packing containers.
- constantly refrigerate protein up to preparation for serving.
- use raw beef and poultry within 2-3 days.
- freeze any raw beef or poultry that will not be cooked within two days.
- home-freeze beef and poultry in serving size amounts to keep it on hand for quick use in dishes. Freeze individual portions within quart size zippered freezer bags. Wrap individual pieces tightly with plastic wrap, add several wrapped pieces per quart-size freezer package, press out as much air as possible from the storage bag before sealing it, and immediately freeze the bag.
- quickly thaw small portions of frozen protein shortly before cooking. Place an unwrapped portion within a larger water-proof bag, add the bag to a bowl of cool water, and turn the protein quite frequently for even thawing.
- thaw large pieces of frozen protein (such as whole chickens and beef chuck roasts) overnight within the packing container in the refrigerator.

7. Brown Rice

Maximize the attractiveness of cooked brown rice in dishes.

In selecting brown rice,

- select raw brown rice. Partially precooked instant brown rice has inferior flavor and texture in comparison.
- always check raw brown rice for rancidity. Raw brown rice should have a neutral, not sharp, aroma. Sharp aroma indicates the germ oil has become rancid. Rancidity effectively spoils the flavor and quality of brown rice. Rancid rice is also somewhat toxic to humans.
- select medium or short grain raw brown rice. These varieties yield moist and flavorful cooked rice. Long grain brown rice, in comparison, has a drier texture and a bland flavor.
- select the tastiest varieties of short and medium brown rice. The flavor of different varieties varies quite significantly.
  - Select, for example, Golden Rose, which is a medium grain rice marketed by Lundberg that has outstanding flavor and texture.

- Select brown rice marketed in natural food stores, which is quite reliably high quality brown rice. Brown rice marketed in regular grocery stores, in contrast, is often very low quality rice. In particular, it can contain lots of debris and require cleaning before use, but it may have poor flavor as well, which surely acts as a barrier to its use.
- Select aromatic brown rice as an attractive variation. For example, select brown basmati rice or Wehani, which is related to basmati rice. Wehani has a sweet and nutty flavor, has a light reddish color, and splits like wild rice when cooked.

In cooking brown rice,

- completely soften brown rice. Completely soft brown rice is also the most flavorful rice. Cooked brown rice should not have even a hint of crispness. Match cooking techniques with the bran coating of brown rice to achieve the softest rice. Recipe #166 does this matching, which involves cooking brown rice in water and adding salt to the rice after it is soft.
- avoid overcooking brown rice. While cooking time is somewhat flexible depending on individual texture preferences, overcooking (cooking brown rice much more than 50 minutes) easily gives the rice a somewhat mushy texture and watery flavor.
- prepare extra brown rice whenever cooking rice to have cooked rice, which stores very well for up to four days and also freezes well, on hand for instant use in dishes.

In serving brown rice,

- use only a small amount of cooked brown rice in dishes. A small amount blends in and does not upset the flavor balance of the dish. To include more brown rice in a meal, serve brown rice as a separate dish.
- avoid drying out rice during re-heating. Recipe #166 (Brown Rice) details some re-heating techniques that reliably retain rice moistness.
- re-heat cooked brown rice in a nonstick skillet to minimize sticking and to quickly heat through the rice.

In storing *cooked* brown rice,

- refrigerate cooked brown rice to maintain the most attractive flavor. Refrigerated brown rice stores well for about 4 days. Brown rice is, however, perishable, as is indicated by a foul odor. Always check the flavor of brown rice that has been stored for more than 4 days.
- constantly cover cooked brown rice in an air-tight container to protect it from contact with air, which evaporates moisture and causes unattractive drying out of the bran content. Thoroughly moistened bran is essentially invisible. Being highly absorptive, bran holds moisture and enhances brown rice moistness. Dried out bran, however, becomes somewhat coarse and gives brown rice an unattractively dry texture, which invites the addition of butter or cheese for softening and moistening.
- freeze extra cooked brown rice or rice that cannot be eaten within several days to keep it on hand for quick inclusion in dishes. Freeze it in serving size amounts within

quart-size sealable plastic freezer bags. Push out as much air as possible from the bag before sealing it. To thaw frozen rice, thaw it overnight in the refrigerator. For quick thawing, double bag the rice to ensure no water leaks into the rice, add the rice to a bowl filled with enough cool water to cover the rice, and flip the rice occasionally to evenly thaw it.

In storing *raw* brown rice,

- refrigerate raw brown rice within an air-tight container to best protect its flavor. By deactivating enzymes, chilling and protecting rice from air combine to protect rice germ oil from becoming rancid.
- avoid freezing to maximize the protection of the germ oil.

Substitute other cooked whole grain (Recipe #167) or cooked wild rice (also Recipe #167) for, or combine either with, brown rice. The flavor-enhancing suggestions for selecting, storing, preparing, and serving wild rice and other whole grains are exactly the same as for brown rice. One nutrition-enhancing point is that in comparison to whole grains in general, which are acid-forming when consumed, germinated grains are not acidic.

8. Yogurt

Maximize the attractiveness of yogurt served with dishes. Plain yogurt mixes perfectly with all Chapter Seven stir-fried dishes, Chapter Eight soups and stews, and Chapter nine curries, adding pleasing flavor, attractive moistening, and nutritional boosting all at the same time.

In selecting yogurt,

- select the most pleasingly mellow yogurt. As different brands of yogurt vary considerably with respect to tartness, experiment with different brands to locate the most mellow yogurt. Examples of reliably mild products are Stonyfield Farms Organic Plain Yogurt (both low fat and cream on top products) and Brown Cow (Cream on Top) Plain Yogurt.
- select the freshest yogurt, which is also the mildest yogurt. As tartness increases with age, always check the expiration date and choose the container with the most distant expiration date.
- select low or full fat yogurt as the most flavorful yogurt. Full fat yogurt in particular has an attractively smooth texture. In comparison to either full or low fat yogurt, non-fat yogurt has a gritty texture.
- select non-homogenized or "cream on top" yogurt as the most delicious yogurt.
- home prepare yogurt to be in control of yogurt tartness and texture. In home preparation, cooks control flavor through monitoring yogurt-making time; they control texture through milk product selection. Cooks have a variety of yogurt makers and yogurt-making techniques from which to choose.

In storing yogurt,

- store yogurt refrigerated and tightly closed. Remove yogurt from the refrigerator just before serving and return it to the refrigerator immediately after serving.
- store yogurt for a short time, within a week after opening it, for best flavor. Use older yogurt to make yogurt cheese or use it in preparing a curry (any Chapter Nine recipe).

In serving yogurt,

- stir yogurt until creamy smooth, which significantly enhances its attractiveness. While separated liquid is itself a tasty drink – it is often sold as a separate drink in some countries, such as countries of South Asia and the Middle East – stirring re-incorporates liquid. Never discard the separated liquid, which contains valuable nutritional content.
- serve yogurt raw, rather than in cooked form, to best take advantage of its nutritional value (its active bacteria content) and its flavoring capacity.

Reference #7

Juice-Protective Techniques for Preparing Animal Protein

Applying *juice-protective* techniques in preparing animal protein achieves the same cooking results as with vegetables and fruits. With juice retained within animal protein, animal protein is reliably tasty and juicy; tender cuts of beef reliably remain tender. To apply *juice-protective* techniques in animal protein preparation, apply four general guidelines.

1. **Maintain the flavor of animal protein (meat, chicken, and eggs) during storage.**

    - Immediately refrigerate protein, tightly covered, after purchase.
    - Immediately freeze meat and poultry that will not be soon cooked.

        - Rinse and dry meat and poultry chunks before freezing.
        - Freeze protein in tightly wrapped but convenient-to-use form. Cut it into serving size amounts, wrap each individual piece, and freeze the individual pieces together within a high-quality freezer container or plastic bag.
        - Do not freeze protein for an extended period of time.
        - Thaw frozen protein just before cooking. While small pieces quickly thaw, thaw whole or large pieces of protein within its freezer packaging overnight in the refrigerator.

2. **Protect animal protein (meat, chicken, and eggs) from overcooking.** As with vegetables and fruits, overcooking breaks down cell structure, which allows the flavorful natural juices to spill from the protein and leaves the protein dry and tasteless. Part II recipes apply the following specific *juice-protective* preparation techniques to avoid overcooking animal protein ingredients.

   - Cook protein separately from other dish ingredients. Set protein aside after cooking and re-heat it quickly with other dish ingredients just prior to serving.
   - Cut meat and chicken into uniformly thin pieces for stir-frying. Uniform pieces cook evenly. Without even cutting, the thinnest slices cook through and spill juices before thicker pieces are cooked. Thin pieces cook through quickly before cell structure breaks down and releases juice.
   - Conduct a readiness test prior to adding meat or poultry to a skillet for stir-frying. A fully hot skillet ensures the protein immediately begins to cook and quickly cooks through before cell breakdown occurs. An overly heated skillet quickly causes protein to shrink and toughen.
   - Precisely time cooking by using a timer.
   - Immediately remove protein from a hot skillet once it is cooked through. When protein is cooked through (when most redness has been removed from sliced beefsteak and all redness removed from ground beef; when chicken is white to the center), transfer the protein to another container to stop the cooking. Rinse boiled eggs with cold water to stop cooking.

3. **Protect animal protein from leaching.** As with vegetables and fruits, liquid leaches juice from cut meat and poultry. As leached juice immediately begins to leach more juice from the protein, substantial loss of juice quickly occurs. Juice loss undermines the attractiveness of meat and poultry in general, but juice loss consequences for lean steak and chicken are especially severe. While application of *juice-protective* preparation techniques makes lean steak an acceptable substitute for fatty meat in dishes, juice loss destroys lean steak acceptability. Part II recipes apply the following specific *juice-protective* preparation techniques to protect protein from leaching.

   - Thoroughly coat meat/chicken pieces with oil after adding them to the skillet. Stir-frying should at first be vigorous for at least 30 seconds in order to quickly and thoroughly coat them with oil. Oil provides a protective coating that holds in protein juice.
   - When simmering chicken in a liquid, cook the chicken in whole or large chunk and un-skinned form.
   - After cooking, set meat and chicken aside in a manner that protects it from contact with any spilling juices. Slant the holding container so that any juice spills away from the meat/chicken or add the cooked meat/poultry to a colander placed over a bowl for collecting any spilled juice.
   - When a dish contains liquid ingredients, add meat and poultry just prior to serving.

4. **Protect animal protein from extended high temperature heating.** Extended high temperature heating causes protein to shrink and become tough, which undermines its attractiveness. Shrinking squeezes juices from the protein, which causes dryness. Toughness undermines the attractiveness of meat in general, but it makes lean protein an unacceptable dish ingredient. Part II recipes apply the following specific *juice-protective* techniques to protect protein from extended high temperature heating:

   - Completely avoid heating at a high temperature setting. Meat and poultry are stir-fried at a medium-high setting.
   - Limit heating at a medium-high setting. Stir-fry meat and poultry at medium-high for 1 minute only and reduce heat to medium. When uniformly thin slices of meat or protein are added to a pre-heated skillet, one minute of stir-frying at medium-high temperature is all that is needed to get cooking well underway. The temperature can then be safely reduced to medium without extending cooking time.
   - Exactly time medium-high heating using a timer.
   - Exactly time the boiling of eggs. Eggs boiled for exactly three minutes and then removed from a burner and set aside, covered, for seven minutes become cooked through while remaining very tender.

CHAPTER SIX

Salads

Raw food is alive food with active enzymes and fully intact heat-sensitive nutritional content that adds an important nutritional dimension to daily diets, and Chapter Six salads are raw foods dishes par excellence. All recipes include a variety of both raw vegetables and fruits along with a heap of raw greens or lettuce and a small amount of raw dried fruits and nuts. These ingredients are embellished with additional high quality ingredients. Cut fruit ingredients are drizzled with a bit of honey and salads are topped with a basic dressing composed of vinegar or fresh lemon juice and extra virgin olive oil, which make nutritional contributions, including enhancement of the human body's absorption of the valuable fat-soluble nutrients contained in the colorful greens, vegetables, and fruits in the salads. *Cooked Alive!* salads are, as a result, both highly attractive and nutritional treasures filled with diverse nutritional content. Significantly, there are no refined carbohydrates (such as bread croutons), no bacon, and, with the exception of one salad that uses mayonnaise, no commercially prepared salad dressings. There is, accordingly, no salt, chemical preservative, or artificial ingredient content. *Cooked Alive!* salads are wonderfully alive dishes that significantly boost the quality of everyday eating.

Chapter Six salads are distinctively organized.

- Most salads are 2-serving size. This serving size accommodates and encourages salad-making in the modern 2-person and often enough single person home.
- Salads are individually prepared. This suits the making of 2-person size salads, but the number of servings is also easily expanded according to need. All salads contain an equal amount and distribution of salad ingredients, and ingredients are easily adjusted to individual tastes. With salads mixed only just before being eaten, this method of assembling maximizes the retention of the flavor and texture of the individual salad ingredients.

Salad Recipe Preparation Notes

Salad Preparation Notes provide helpful information about Chapter Six salad preparation that cannot fit into the individual recipes. These notes cover a variety of subjects, including,

PART 2

- technical details relating to recipe preparation (Notes #1-5).
- cooking tool information (Note #6).
- preparation of vegetable and fruit variation suggestions made in recipes (Note #7).
- salad resource references (Notes #8 and 9).

1. **Greens and lettuce content is highly variable.** This applies both to the variety and amount used.

   - With respect to variety, any combination of lettuce and greens may be substituted for the pre-washed greens typically called for in Chapter Six salad recipes. Recipes routinely rely on pre-washed greens because of the enormous convenience and general high quality of these products. *Cooked Alive!* encourages cooks to experiment with other greens and lettuce by including helpful assistance in the selection, rinsing and drying, and storing of lettuce and greens in general. This information is presented in handy form in a reference attached to Chapter Six: Reference #8 (Clinching Salad Flavor: Expanded Preparation Support), Ingredient #4 (Greens and Lettuce).
   - With respect to the amount of greens and lettuce used in a salad, content can be as much as doubled. When the amount of greens or lettuce is increased, however, it is important to increase oil content proportionately.

2. **It is important to maintain recipe ingredient proportions for all salad ingredients except for greens and lettuce.** Maintenance of ingredient proportion ensures a salad has a pleasing balance of flavorings and textures.

3. **It is important to observe certain rules regarding use of raw onion in salads.**

   - It is of utmost importance to select top quality green onions (or scallions) and red onions for use in salads. This is a green onion that is physically intact and unbruised (as indicated by uniform firmness). A red onion should also have a tight-fitting and unbroken skin. A physically intact and unbruised onion retains sweet natural flavor when cut.
   - It is equally important to maintain top quality form during preparation and serving. Green and red onions should be chilled before being cut and should be immediately coated with oil after being cut to protect the cut pulp from air. These onions should also be cut shortly before serving to minimize the chance that flavor-altering enzymes are activated.
   - Omit adding onion to a recipe if top quality onion is not at hand.

4. **Pre-cut vegetable and fruit ingredients called for in recipes – such as ¼ bell pepper, ½ cucumber, and broccoli florets – need to be cut from washed and dried produce.**

5. **The small amount of either feta or extra sharp cheddar cheese that is commonly included in Chapter Six salads is a variable salad ingredient.**

- To convert salad to vegan vegetarian form, substitute non-dairy cheese for dairy cheese. Agave nectar or sugar can be substituted for honey.
- Feta and cheddar cheese content can also be omitted.

6. **Important information about the cooking tools used in Chapter Six salads is as follows:**

    - Recipes list all preparation tools used except for some basic working tools (such as paper and cloth towels, plastic wrap, and vegetable scrubbing tools) as well as regular (multiple use) cutting boards. As these tools are used routinely in recipes, they need to be kept handy.
    - The General Cooking Tools listing included in the Part II Introduction serves as a descriptive reference for all tools used in Chapter Six salads except for three tools that are specific to or mainly used in salads. These tools are described below.

        - **Food scale.** A small food scale, one that registers ounces up to 1 pound, is useful for accurately determining the cheese content of salads.
        - **Salad spinner.** This tool very efficiently dries salad greens and lettuce leaves, and small leaves in particular, for use in salads.
        - **Zesting tool.** This is a tool that efficiently removes thin strips of the outer skin of citrus fruit for use as flavoring in salads.

7. **Two Part I Chapters serve as references for preparing the vegetable and fruit variation suggestions made in Chapter Six salad recipes.** These chapters include, as follows,

    - Chapter Four (Raw Fruit Pure and Simple). The recipe number attached to a fruit variation suggestion identifies the Chapter Four reference recipe, which provides preparation details as well as selection and nutritional information for the fruit variation.
    - Chapter Five (Raw and Barely Cooked Vegetable Recipes). The recipe number attached to a vegetable variation identifies the Chapter Five reference recipe, which provides preparation details as well as basic selection and nutritional information about the vegetable variation.

8. *Cooked Alive!* **includes two references specifically focused on assisting cooks achieve salad-serving success through boosting the flavor of key individual salad ingredients.** These references include, as follows,

    - Reference #8 (Clinching Salad Flavor: Expanded Preparation Support). This reference makes flavor-enhancing suggestions for key salad ingredients, including **feta cheese, boiled eggs, raw fruit, greens and lettuce, honey, olives, extra virgin olive oil, raw and parboiled vegetables, raw seasoning vegetables,** and **balsamic vinegar.**
    - Reference #6 (Maximizing the Attractiveness of Commonly Used Whole Food Ingredients in Part II Recipes). This general reference makes flavor-enhancing suggestions for key whole food ingredients commonly used in Part II recipes. Ingredients relevant to Chapter Six salads include **dried fruit, dried herbs and spices, fresh herbs, legumes, nuts,** and **poultry.**

PART 2

9. **Cooks can significantly boost salad quality through the selection of top quality salad ingredients.** *Cooked Alive!* includes three references to aid cooks in making top quality choices when selecting three different kinds of ingredients for use in Part II recipes. These references are, as follows,

   - Reference #1: Selecting Top Quality Fresh Vegetables and Fruits. This reference defines top quality vegetables and fruits as those that are raw, physically intact, and naturally produced. Naturally produced produce includes certified organic and locally produced vegetables and fruits, which in addition to being grown with natural fertilizer, have not been genetically modified and have not had any synthetic (man-made) chemical treatment (processing) during production and marketing.
   - Reference #4 (Selecting Top Quality Whole Foods for Use in Part II Recipes). This reference defines top quality whole food products other than vegetables and fruits (which are covered in Reference #1) as food products that are raw, intact, and naturally produced. Naturally produced products include 1) certified organic and locally produced plant products and 2) certified organic and/or grass-fed and locally produced animal and poultry products. In addition to being produced using natural food, these are products that are not genetically modified and have not been treated (processed) with synthetic (man-made) chemicals during production or marketing. Reference #4 identifies top quality products that are commonly available to cooks. Those relevant to Chapter Six salads include **legumes, grains, eggs,** and **poultry**.
   - Reference #5 (Selecting High Quality Processed Food Products for Use in Part II Recipes). This reference identifies a variety of processed food ingredients that retain significant nutritional quality. Those ingredients relevant to Chapter Six salads include **cheese, raisins, extra virgin olive oil, balsamic vinegar,** and **canned products with concentrated phytonutrient content (artichokes, beans, and beets)**.

Fruit-Centered Salad Recipes

137. Nectarine, Grape, Cauliflower, and Greens Salad
(Master Recipe)
(2 servings)

Vegetables and Fruits with Coating Oil

1 medium chilled carrot
½ chilled medium Japanese cucumber
¼ red bell pepper
2 large cauliflower florets with stems
2 t extra virgin olive oil

1 chilled nectarine
10 each red & green seedless grapes
1½ c pre-washed baby greens
1½ c pre-washed baby spinach

Other Ingredients

4 pitted Kalamata olives
1 heaping T certified organic raisins
1 heaping T dried tart cherries

1 oz chunk feta cheese (two 1 in. squares to yield 2 T crumbled)
8 raw pecan or walnut halves

Salad Dressing

approx. 2 t honey
5 T extra virgin olive oil

1½ T balsamic vinegar
½ lemon

Preparation Tools

1 cutting board reserved for vegetables & fruits
1 chef's knife
1 vegetable shredder with a coarse setting
2 large individual salad bowls
1 5 in. serrated knife
1 set each measuring spoons & cups

1 small mixing bowl
1 rubber spatula
1 colander
1 pie plate
1 dinner spoon
1 hand citrus juicer

1. **Gather all preparation tools and ingredients except for greens.** Leave greens refrigerated until assembling the salads for serving.

2. **Prepare the raw vegetables.**

    - Rinse and thoroughly dry the **carrot**. Use a chef's knife to slice the tip from the carrot. Coarsely grate the carrot and evenly divide it between two salad bowls. Rinse out the grater.
    - Use a chef's knife to slice the end from the **cucumber** and halve it lengthwise. Place the halves cut side down on a cutting board, halve each lengthwise, and cut the cucumber strips crosswise into ⅓ in. thick pieces. Evenly divide the cucumber pieces between and evenly spread them over the two salad bowls.
    - Use a serrated knife to cut out the stem of the **bell pepper**. Remove the seeds (but not the membrane). Use the serrated knife to cut the pepper lengthwise into ¼ in. thick strips and cut each strip crosswise into ¼ in. cubes. Evenly divide the pepper between and evenly spread them over the two salad bowls.
    - Rinse the **cauliflower florets** under cool water, wrap the florets within paper towels or in a terry cloth towel, and gently squeeze the florets to dry them completely. Cut any stems from the floret and cut the stems crosswise into thin slices. Break the florets into small florets. Add 2 t extra virgin olive oil to a small mixing bowl. Add the florets and sliced stems to the bowl and thoroughly toss the cauliflower in the oil to coat all pieces. Use a rubber spatula to scrape the cauliflower and any oil into the two salad bowls over the other vegetables.

PART 2

3. **Prepare the fruit.**

   - Rinse and thoroughly dry the **nectarine**. Place the nectarine on its side and use a serrated knife to cut the nectarine lengthwise into ¼ in. thick slices, cutting through to the pit and rocking the nectarine while cutting to cut completely from end to end. Cut the slices from the pit, cut each slice crosswise into 3 equal pieces, and evenly divide the pieces between and evenly spread them over the salads.
   - Add the **grapes** to a colander, rinse them, place them in a pie plate lined with a double thickness of paper towels or a terry towel, wrap the towels around them, and gently roll the grapes within the towels to dry them. Pick through the grapes and replace any spoiled ones. Use a serrated knife to cut off any brown stem ends and to halve the grapes lengthwise. Evenly divide the grapes between and evenly spread them over the two salads.

4. **Add honey.** Drizzle (pour in a thin stream) about 1 dinner spoon filled with honey over each salad, rotating around the bowl and attempting to touch as many fruit pieces as possible.

5. **Prepare remaining ingredients**.

   - Use a serrated knife to quarter the olives.
   - Use a chef's knife to cut the dried tart cherries into 2-3 pieces.
   - Crumble the 2 oz feta cheese onto plastic wrap.
   - Break the 8 nuts into 2-3 pieces.
   - Squeeze the lemon juice. Remove any seeds but leave pulp.

6. **Assemble the salads for serving.**

   - Drizzle first 1 T oil, then ¾ T balsamic vinegar, and finally 1 T lemon juice over each salad.
   - Layering the ingredients, evenly divide the olives, dried fruit, feta cheese, and nuts between the salads.
   - Divide the greens between the salads and drizzle 1½ T olive oil over each pile of greens.
   - Serve the salads.

   VARIATIONS: Make ingredient substitutions. Substitute, for example,

   - 1 **ripe peach** (Recipe #92) for nectarine.
   - 2 **mandarin** or **clementine oranges** (Recipe #90) for nectarine.
   - 1 **ripe pear** (Recipe #93) for nectarine. Only a delicious pear, however, satisfactorily substitutes for nectarine.
   - 4 **large parboiled broccoli florets** (Recipe #131) for cauliflower.

   Add ingredients. Add, for example,

COOKED ALIVE!

- **½ c fresh pineapple** (Recipe #94); add for special occasions.
- **½ c diced avocado** (Recipe #76), also a special occasion ingredient.
- **1 plum** (Recipe #95), preparing it exactly like the nectarine.
- **¼ c fresh berries**, such as blueberries (Recipe #78) or organic strawberries (Recipe #98).
- **4 raw small** or **medium sugar snap peas** (Recipe #124), 2 peas per salad.

138. Mandarin Orange, Grape, Pomegranate, and Greens Salad
(2 servings)

Fruits and Vegetables

1 chilled medium carrot
½ chilled medium Japanese cucumber
½ c small sugar snap peas
¼ red and ⅛ yellow bell pepper
2 chilled mandarin oranges

10 each red & green seedless grapes
⅓ c pomegranate seeds (Recipe #96)
1½ c pre-washed spring greens mixture
1½ c pre-washed baby spinach

Other Ingredients

4 pitted Kalamata olives
8 raw pecan or walnut halves
1 T certified organic raisins

1 T dried tart cherries
1 oz chunk feta cheese (two 1 in. squares, to yield 2 T crumbled)

Salad Dressing

approx. 2 t honey
½ lemon

5 T extra virgin olive oil
1½ T balsamic vinegar

Preparation Tools

1 cutting board reserved for vegetables & fruits
1 each chef's and 5 in. serrated knife
1 vegetable shredder with a coarse setting
2 large individual salad bowls
1 colander

1 pie plate
1 dinner spoon
1 hand citrus juicer
1 set each measuring spoons & cups

1. **Gather all preparation tools and ingredients except for the greens.** Leave the greens refrigerated until assembling the salads for serving.

PART 2

2. **Prepare the raw vegetables.**

    - Scrub and thoroughly dry the **carrot**. Use a chef's knife to cut the end from the carrot. Coarsely grate the carrot and evenly divide it between the two salad bowls.
    - Rinse and dry the **cucumber**. Use a chef's knife to cut off the end and halve the cucumber lengthwise. Place the halves cut side down on a cutting board, halve each lengthwise, and cut the cucumber strips crosswise into ⅓ in. thick pieces. Evenly divide the pieces between and evenly spread them over the two salad bowls.
    - Add the **sugar snap peas** to a colander and rinse them under cool water. Pour the peas onto a double thickness of paper towels or a terry towel, wrap the towels around the peas, and gently roll the peas within the towels to dry them. Remove strings by cutting nearly through the protruding stem end of a pea (cutting from the outside toward the curved side), grasping the stem end between your thumb and the flat side of a paring knife blade, and pulling the string down the inside curve of a pea. Cut off the remaining tip from the peas and halve each pea. Evenly divide the sugar snap peas between and evenly spread them over the two salads.
    - Use a serrated knife to cut out the stem of each **bell pepper**. Remove the seeds but not the pulp. Cut the peppers lengthwise into ¼ in. thick strips and cut the strips crosswise into ¼ in. cubes. Evenly divide the peppers between and evenly spread them over the salads.

3. **Prepare the fruit.**

    - Rinse and dry each **mandarin orange**. Peel the oranges, halve each orange crosswise, gently press out any seeds from segments, and gently separate the segments. Evenly spread the half orange segments in the salad bowls, one orange per bowl.
    - Add the **grapes** to a colander, rinse them, add them to a pie plate lined with a double thickness of paper towels or a terry towel, wrap the towels around them, and gently roll the grapes within the towels to dry them. Pick through the grapes and replace any spoiled ones. Use a serrated knife to cut off any brown stem ends and to halve the grapes lengthwise. Evenly divide the grapes between and evenly spread them over the salads.
    - Divide the **pomegranate seeds** evenly between the salad bowls.

4. **Add honey.** Drizzle about 1 dinner spoon filled with honey over the fruit in each salad bowl, rotating around the bowl and attempting to touch as much fruit as possible.

5. **Prepare remaining ingredients.**

    - Use a serrated knife to quarter the 4 olives.
    - Break the 8 nuts into 2-3 pieces.
    - Use a chef's knife to halve 1 T dried tart cherries.
    - Coarsely crumble the feta cheese onto plastic wrap.
    - Squeeze the lemon. Remove the seeds but not pulp.

6. **Assemble the salads for serving.**

   - Evenly drizzle first 1 T olive oil, ¾ T balsamic vinegar, and 1 T lemon juice over each salad, rotating around the salads to cover as many pieces as possible.
   - Layering the ingredients, evenly divide the olives, nuts, dried fruit, and feta cheese between the salads.
   - Divide the greens between the salad bowls and drizzle 1½ T olive oil over each pile of greens.
   - Serve the salads.

   VARIATIONS: Vary the **mandarin orange preparation technique** for either difficult to peel or very seedy mandarin oranges, using a serrated knife to cut each orange lengthwise, cut out the pulpy center, cut each half into slices, and cut the flesh from the skin of each slice. See Recipe #90 for specific details.

   Make ingredient substitutions. Substitute, for example,

   - **4-6 raw asparagus tips** (Recipe #111) for sugar snap peas.
   - **4 medium parboiled broccoli florets** (Recipe #131) for, or combine them with, sugar snap peas.
   - **8 macadamia nuts** or **whole almonds**, for pecans or walnuts. Use a chef's knife to chop the nuts roughly.

   Add ingredients. Add, for example,

   - ⅓ **avocado** (Recipe #76), cut into ⅓ in. cubes. Add 1 t oil to a small mixing bowl and gently mix the avocado in the oil before adding it to each salad.
   - **1 ripe mango** (Recipe #87), cut into cubes.
   - **½ c fresh pineapple chunks** (Recipe #94).
   - **1 ripe guava** (Recipe #84), in particular a red guava.
   - **1 c diced ripe papaya** (Recipe #91). Home-ripen slightly green papaya to best ensure tastiness. If the papaya is very flavorful, it can substitute for mango. To boost flavor, drizzle

     - 1 t extra lemon juice and or balsamic vinegar directly onto the papaya pieces in each salad.

   - **1 kiwi** (Recipe #86), with fuzz rubbed off to be able to include the nutritious skin. Add kiwi as a very last ingredient just before adding the greens for serving. While kiwi adds striking green color and a touch of attractive tartness, which complements mango flavoring, kiwi enzymes can undermine other fruit ingredients if left in contact with other fruit for long.
   - **1 dollop hummus** (commercially prepared or fresh-prepared, Recipe #152) per salad, added as a topping just before adding the greens. Hummus is a pleasing addition.

139. Berry, Cantaloupe, Pineapple, and Greens Salad
(2 servings)

Fruits and Vegetables

4 large broccoli florets with 1-2 in stems
1 chilled medium carrot
½ chilled medium Japanese cucumber
¼ red bell pepper
⅛ green bell pepper
⅓ c fresh blueberries

4 medium strawberries
2 1-in. thick slices cantaloupe
½ c fresh pineapple chunks
    (Recipe #94)
1½ c pre-washed spring greens
1½ c pre-washed baby spinach

Other Ingredients

1 oz chunk feta cheese (two 1 in. squares
    to yield 2 T crumbled)
4 pitted Kalamata olives

1 T certified organic raisins
1 T dried tart cherries
8 raw pecan or walnut halves

Salad Dressing

approx. 2 t honey
½ lemon

5 T extra virgin olive oil
1½ T balsamic vinegar

Preparation Tools

1 medium (4 qt) saucepan
1 timer
1 colander
1 cutting board reserved for vegetables
    & fruits
1 each chef's & 5 in. serrated knife

1 hand vegetable shredder
2 large individual salad bowls
1 pie plate
1 dinner spoon
1 hand citrus juicer
1 set each measuring spoons & cups

---

1. **Gather all preparation tools and ingredients except for the greens.** Leave the greens refrigerated until assembling the salads for serving.

2. **Parboil the broccoli.**

    - Add enough water to cover the broccoli florets by several inches to a medium saucepan and heat the water to full boiling over high heat.
    - Drop the florets into the water and immediately start a timer for 1 minute.
    - At the timer, drain the broccoli florets into a colander and rinse them with cold water.
    - Spread the florets over a paper towel to dry and cool them.

3. **Prepare the raw vegetables.**

    - Scrub, thoroughly dry, and use a chef's knife to cut off the tip of the **carrot**. Coarsely grate the carrot. Evenly divide the carrot between the two salad bowls.
    - Use a chef's knife to cut off the stem end, halve the **cucumber** lengthwise, halve each half lengthwise, and cut the cucumber strips crosswise into ⅓ in. thick chunks. Evenly divide the cucumber between and evenly spread it over the two salads.
    - Use a serrated knife to cut out the stem of the **bell pepper**. Remove any seeds but not the membrane. Use the serrated knife to cut the peppers into ¼ in. thick slices and to cut each slice crosswise into ¼ in. cubes. Evenly divide the peppers between and evenly spread them over the two salads.

4. **Prepare the raw fruit.**

    - Add the **blueberries** to a colander and thoroughly rinse them with cool water. Pour the blueberries into a pie plate lined with a double thickness of paper towels or a terry towel. Pick through the berries, removing stems and replacing soft and broken open berries. Wrap the towels around the berries and gently roll the berries within the towels to dry them completely. Evenly divide the berries between and evenly spread them over the salads.
    - Use a serrated knife to cut off the **strawberry** hulls. Add the strawberries to a colander, rinse them with cool water, spread the strawberries over a double layer of paper towels or a terry towel, and wrap the towels around the berries to dry them. Halve each strawberry lengthwise, place the halves cut side down on a clean cutting board, and cut each lengthwise into 3 slices. Evenly divide the slices between and evenly spread them over the two salad bowls.
    - Place the **cantaloupe slices** cut side up on a cutting board. Carefully cutting to but not through the skin, use a serrated knife to cut each slice crosswise into ½ in. thick pieces. Cutting close to the skin but avoiding any green flesh and peel, slice the cantaloupe from the skins. Evenly divide the pieces between and evenly spread them over the two salad bowls.
    - Use a serrated knife to cut **pineapple chunks** into ¼ in. wide slices. Evenly divide the pineapple between the salad bowls, evenly spreading the pineapple over the two salads.

5. **Add honey.** Drizzle 1 small dinner spoon filled with honey over the fruit in each salad, rotating around a salad bowl to cover as many pieces as possible.

6. **Prepare remaining ingredients.**

    - Roughly crumble the feta cheese onto plastic wrap.
    - Use a serrated knife to quarter the olives.
    - Break each nut into 2-3 pieces.
    - Use a chef's knife to halve the dried tart cherries.
    - Squeeze the lemon. Remove the seeds but not the pulp.

- Halve each broccoli floret lengthwise, place the halves cut side down onto a cutting board, and cut each half into 3 equal slices.

7. **Assemble the salads for serving.**

    - Drizzle first 1 T oil, then ¾ T balsamic vinegar, and finally 1 T lemon juice over each salad.
    - Layering the ingredients, evenly divide the feta cheese, olives, nuts, and dried fruit between the salads.
    - Divide the greens between the salads, drizzle 1½ T oil over each pile of greens, and serve the salads immediately.

VARIATIONS: Make ingredient substitutions. Substitute, for example,

- **1 ripe mango** (Recipe #87), **1 nectarine** (Recipe #88), or **1 ripe pear** (Recipe #93) for cantaloupe.
- **raw broccoli florets** for parboiled.

Add vegetable or fruit ingredients. Add, for example,

- **½ c small sugar snap peas**, halved (Recipe #124 or #133).
- **4 raw asparagus tips** (Recipe #111).
- **¼ c coarsely grated green or red cabbage** (Recipe #115).
- **1 T alfalfa or other sprouts** as a topping to each salad.
- **2 fresh raspberries** to each salad. Rinse and dry the berries exactly like blueberries except for draining water from the raspberry centers.

Add protein ingredients. Add, for example,

- **1 dollop hummus** per salad, added as a topping before adding greens. Use either commercially prepared or fresh-prepared (Recipe #152).
- **1 T tahini dressing** per salad, added as a topping before adding greens. To prepare the tahini dressing, combine ⅛ c prepared sesame tahini (raw or toasted), ¼ t ground cumin, 1 T fresh lemon juice, 1 T orange juice, and ½ T extra virgin olive oil.
- **1-2 T cooked garbanzo beans (chickpeas)** to each salad. Drain the beans in a colander and pat them dry before adding them to the salad.
- **1 heaping T canned chunk light tuna**, packed in oil, to each salad. Use a dinner fork to break up canned tuna and stir in the packing liquid before adding the tuna to each salad just before adding the greens. Use either canned or vacuum-packed tuna, but use only freshly or very recently opened tuna to best ensure tuna tastiness. Add no more than 1 or 2 T tuna to keep tuna from overwhelming other flavors. Select chunk light tuna as the tuna with lowest mercury contamination.
- **1 boiled egg** (Recipe #151) per salad, sliced.

140. Apple, Orange, Apricot, and Spinach Salad
(2 servings)

Vegetables, Fruits, and Coating Oil

2 chilled green onions
2 t extra virgin olive oil
1 medium carrot
½ chilled medium Japanese cucumber
¼ red bell pepper

1 navel orange
1 chilled tasty apple (such as Fuji)
3 c loosely packed pre-washed baby spinach

Other Ingredients

2 T orange juice with pulp
4 dried California apricot halves
1 oz chunk feta cheese (two 1 in. squares to yield 2 T crumbled)
8 raw pecan or walnut halves

2 T orange juice
4 pitted Kalamata olives
1 T certified organic raisins
1 T dried tart cherries

Salad Dressing

approx. 2 t honey
½ lemon

5 T extra virgin olive oil
1½ T balsamic vinegar

Preparation Tools

1 set each measuring spoons & cups
1 small (8 in.) skillet with an opaque lid
1 plastic or plastic-coated stir-fry spatula
1 cutting board reserved for vegetables & fruits
1 each 5 in. serrated, chef's, & paring knife
2 large individual salad bowls
1 rubber spatula

1 hand vegetable shredder
1 medium mixing bowl
1 colander
1 dinner plate
1 dinner spoon
1 hand citrus juicer

---

1. **Gather all preparation tools and ingredients except for the greens.** Leave the greens refrigerated until assembling the salads for serving.

2. **Soften dry apricots.** Bring 2 T orange juice to boiling in a small skillet over high heat. Add and stir-fry the apricot halves for 10-15 seconds, remove the pan from the heat, and set it aside, covered. (Omit this step if the apricots are already attractively moist.)

3. **Prepare the vegetables.**

- Rinse and thoroughly dry the **green onions**. Use a 5 in. serrated knife to cut off the root end and to cut the white portion of each onion crosswise into ¼ in. thick slices. Holding the green tops together with one hand, use a chef's knife to chop the tops. Evenly divide the onion between the salad bowls, drizzle 1 t oil over the onion in each bowl, and use a rubber spatula to mix the pieces in the oil to coat them completely.
- Scrub, thoroughly dry, cut off the tip, and coarsely shred the **carrot**. Evenly divide the carrot between the two salad bowls.
- Rinse and dry the **cucumber**. Use a serrated knife to cut off the end, halve each half lengthwise, halve the halves lengthwise, and cut the cucumber strips crosswise into ⅓ in. thick chunks. Evenly divide the chunks between and evenly spread them over the salads.
- Use a serrated knife to cut out the stem of the **red bell pepper**. Remove the seeds but not the membrane. Use the serrated knife to cut the pepper lengthwise into ¼ in. thick slices and to cut the slices crosswise into ¼ in. cubes. Evenly divide the pepper between and evenly spread them over the two salad bowls.

4. **Prepare the fruit.**

    - Rinse and dry the **navel orange**. Use a serrated knife to slice it lengthwise and place the halves cut side up on a clean cutting board. Remove the pulpy center from each half by making a lengthwise wedge cut on either side of the center. Slice each half lengthwise into ⅓ in. wide slices. Cutting to, but not through, the skin, use a serrated knife to cut each slice crosswise into 3-4 equal pieces. Being careful to avoid including any skin while deliberately including some pith (the white spongy membrane coating the inside of the orange skin), slice the orange flesh from the skins. Evenly divide the orange pieces between the two salads.
    - Rinse and thoroughly dry the **apple**. Add 2 T orange juice to a medium mixing bowl. Use a chef's knife to halve the apple lengthwise. Place each half cut side down on the clean cutting board and use the chef's knife to cut each half lengthwise into 6 slices. Use a paring knife to remove the core and seeds from the slices and to cut each slice crosswise into 4-5 chunks. Add the chunks to and swish them in the orange juice to coat pieces as they are cut. Drain the apple pieces in a colander placed over a dinner plate to collect the juice, spread the apples over a double layer of paper towels, wrap the towel around the apple pieces, roll the pieces within the towels to dry them, and evenly divide the apple between and evenly spread them over the salad bowls. Save the collected juice for another use.

5. **Add honey.** Drizzle 1 small dinner spoonful of honey over the fruit in each salad, rotating around the salad bowl to cover as many pieces as possible.

6. **Prepare remaining ingredients.**

    - Drain the soaked **apricots** in a colander (saving the juice for another use).
    - Use a chef's knife to slice the apricots into thin strips and to cut the strips crosswise into thirds.

- Use the chef's knife to halve the **tart cherries**.
- Coarsely crumble the **feta cheese** onto plastic wrap.
- Break each **nut** into 3-4 pieces.
- Squeeze the **lemon**, removing the seeds but saving pulp.

7. **Assemble the salads for serving.**

    - Drizzle first 1 T oil, then ¾ T balsamic vinegar, and finally 1 T lemon juice over each salad.
    - Layering the ingredients, evenly divide the apricots, feta cheese, nuts, and dried fruit over each salad.
    - Evenly divide the spinach over the salads, drizzle 1½ T oil over each pile of spinach, and immediately serve the salads.

VARIATIONS: Make ingredient substitutions. Substitute, for example,

- **1 chilled pear** (Recipe #93) for apple, preparing it exactly like the apple. Alternatively, use ½ each pear and apple. Only a fully ripe and tasty pear equally substitutes for apple.
- **2 mandarin oranges** (Recipe #90) or **tangerines** (Recipe #99) for navel orange. Both orange varieties add tangy flavor and attractive orange color.
- **1 c pre-washed spring greens** or either **2 medium romaine lettuce hearts** or **red leaf lettuce leaves**, torn into bite-size pieces, for 1 c spinach.

Add ingredients. Add, for example,

- **2 small sugar snap peas** (Recipe #124), halved, per salad.
- **1-2 T cubes or small (½ in. or halved 1 in.) balls fresh mozzarella cheese**, patted dry if moist, per salad.
- **1/8 c whole raw almonds, hazelnuts,** or **other favorite nuts**, coarsely chopped, for pecans.

141. Spiced Lentil, Pineapple, and Greens Salad
(2 servings)

Vegetables and Fruit with Seasonings, Cooking Oil, and Coating Oil

½ chilled medium yellow onion, halved lengthwise
⅛ in. thick slice fresh ginger root
1 T extra virgin olive oil
½ t cumin seed

2 chilled green onions
2 t extra virgin olive oil
1 medium carrot
½ chilled medium Japanese cucumber
⅛ each red & green bell pepper

PART 2

½ t curry powder
¼ t ground cinnamon
⅛ t ground ginger
⅛ t ground cloves

½ c fresh pineapple chunks (½ in. thick; Recipe #94)
1½ c pre-washed baby greens
1½ c pre-washed baby spinach

Other Ingredients

½ c cooked lentils (Recipe #168) or canned/packaged
4 pitted Kalamata olives
9 raw pecan or walnut halves
1 T certified organic raisins

1 T dried tart cherries
4 dried apricots
1 oz chunk feta cheese (two 1 in. squares, to yield 2 T crumbled)

Salad Dressing

1½ t honey
2 T apple cider vinegar
1½ T concentrated frozen orange juice

½ t Dijon mustard
4 T extra virgin olive oil

Preparation Tools

1 10 in. or 12 in. nonstick skillet
1 each chef's & 5 in. serrated knife
1 set measuring spoons & cups
1 plastic or plastic-coated stir-fry spatula
1 timer
1 each medium & small mixing bowl
1 colander

1 dinner plate
2 large individual salad bowls
1 rubber spatula
1 hand vegetable shredder
1 dinner spoon
1 dinner fork or small whisk

---

1. **Gather all preparation tools and ingredients except for the greens.** Leave the greens refrigerated until assembling the salad for serving.

2. **Stir-fry the yellow onion and ginger root with spices.**

   - Heat a nonstick skillet at a medium setting.
   - Use a chef's knife to cut off the ends of the onion half. Peel the onion, place the onion cut side down on a cutting board, and dice it. Mince the ginger.
   - Increase the skillet heat to medium-high.
   - When a drop of water added to the skillet instantly dances and disappears, add 1 T oil, add and heat the cumin seed for 30 seconds, stir in the onion and ginger, evenly sprinkle the spices (½ t curry powder, ¼ t ground cinnamon, ¼ ground ginger, and ⅛ t cloves) over the onion and ginger root, and stir-fry the onion for about 30 seconds. Reduce the heat to medium and cook the mixture for 2 minutes,

stirring it occasionally and setting a timer.
- At the timer, remove the skillet from the heat.

3. **Prepare the lentils.**

    - Add the lentils to a medium mixing bowl, add 2 T water, swish the lentils in the water, and drain the lentils in a colander placed over a dinner plate for collecting the lentil broth.
    - Spread the lentils over a paper towel to dry them.
    - Mix the lentils into the cooked onion mixture.
    - Collect and save the lentil broth for another use.

4. **Prepare the raw vegetables except for the greens.**

    - Rinse and thoroughly dry the **green onions**. Use a serrated knife to cut off the stem end and to slice the white portion of each onion crosswise into ⅛ in. slices. Holding the green ends of *one* onion together with one hand, use a chef's knife to chop the green tops thinly. Add 1 t extra virgin olive oil to each of two salad bowls, evenly divide the onion between the bowls, and use a rubber spatula to thoroughly mix the onion into the oil.
    - Rinse, dry thoroughly, cut the end from, coarsely shred, and divide the **carrot** between the two salads. Rinse out the shredder.
    - Use a chef's knife to cut off the end, halve the **cucumber** lengthwise, split each half lengthwise, and cut the strips into ¼ in. thick chunks. Evenly divide the chunks between and evenly spread them over the two salad bowls.
    - Use a serrated knife to cut out the stem of each **bell pepper**. Remove seeds but not the membrane. Use the serrated knife to cut the peppers lengthwise into ¼ in. thick slices and to cut the slices into ¼ in. cubes. Evenly divide the cubes between and evenly spread them over the two salads.

5. **Prepare the pineapple.** Pat the chunks dry, if necessary. Use a serrated knife to halve the chunks and evenly divide the pineapple between and evenly spread them over the salads.

6. **Drizzle honey over the pineapple.** Drizzle 1 small dinner spoonful of honey over the pineapple in each salad, rotating around a salad bowl to cover as many pieces as possible.

7. **Prepare remaining ingredients.**

    - Use a serrated knife to quarter the olives.
    - Use a chef's knife to halve the tart cherries, cut the apricots into ¼ in. thick slices, and halve the apricot slices.
    - Roughly crumble the feta cheese onto plastic wrap.
    - Add the salad dressing ingredients (2 T apple cider vinegar, 1½ T concentrated frozen orange juice, ½ t Dijon mustard, and 1 T extra virgin olive oil) to a small mixing bowl and use a salad fork or small whisk to combine the ingredients.

8. **Assemble the salads for serving.**

    - Evenly spread the spiced lentils between the two salads.
    - Drizzle one half of the dressing over each salad and slightly toss the ingredients for mixing.
    - Evenly divide the olives, nuts, dried fruits, and feta cheese between the salads.
    - Top each salad with one half of the greens, drizzle 1 T oil over each pile of greens, and serve the salads.

    VARIATIONS: Make ingredient substitutions. Substitute, for example,

    - **4 medium red leaf lettuce leaves** for greens. Individually rinse the lettuce leaves, shake each one to remove clinging water, and spread the leaves over a layer of paper or cloth towels as they are rinsed. Add a top layer of towels and wrap the towels around the leaves to dry them. As a last preparation step, unroll the leaves and tear each into bite-size pieces.
    - **1½ T freshly squeezed lemon juice** (½ lemon) for 1 T apple cider vinegar in the dressing. Alternatively, combine 1 T lemon juice and 1 T apple cider vinegar.

    Add ingredients. Add, for example,

    - **⅓ c small cauliflower florets**. Add the florets with the green onions and mix the cauliflower with the onion to coat the pieces with oil.

142. Spiced Chicken, Fruit, and Greens Supreme Salad
(2 servings)

Vegetables and Fruits

1 medium carrot	½ c fresh pineapple chunks (Recipe #94)
¼ red bell pepper	8 each red & green seedless grapes
⅛ yellow bell pepper	and/or 2 mandarin oranges
6 small sugar snap peas	1½ c pre-washed baby spring greens
¼ c pomegranate seeds (Recipe #96)	1½ c pre-washed baby spinach

Other Ingredients

½ boneless, skinless chicken breast half or 2 chicken tenders (approx. 2 oz)	¼ t salt
	1 heaping T organic raisins
⅓ t curry powder	1 heaping T dried tart cherries
¼ t each ground ginger and cinnamon	8-10 raw pecan or walnut halves
½ t garlic powder	6 pitted Kalamata olives

⅛ in. thick slice fresh ginger root
1 T toasted sesame oil

1 oz chunk feta cheese (two 1 in. squares; to yield 2 T crumbled)

Salad Dressing

approx. 2 t honey
4 T extra virgin olive oil

2 T plus 2 t balsamic vinegar

Preparation Tools

1 medium (10 in.) nonstick skillet
1 cutting board reserved for raw chicken
1 each slicing, 5 in. serrated, & paring knife
1 set each measuring spoons & cups
1 cutting board reserved for vegetables & fruits
1 plastic or plastic-coated stir-fry spatula

1 timer
1 vegetable shredder with a coarse setting
2 large individual salad bowls
1 colander
1 pie plate
1 dinner spoon

---

1. **Gather all preparation tools and dish ingredients except for the greens.** Leave the greens refrigerated until just before serving the salads.

2. **Stir-fry the chicken.**

   - Heat a large nonstick skillet on a large burner at a medium setting.
   - Rinse and thoroughly dry the chicken with a paper towel. Working on a cutting board reserved for raw poultry and using a sharp slicing knife, cut the chicken breast lengthwise into ¼ in. thick slices, discarding any fat and white membrane. Cut the slices into ¼ in. wide strips, cut the strips crosswise into ⅓ in. lengths, and spread the pieces over plastic wrap.
   - Thoroughly wash your hands and the slicing knife with soap in order to avoid contaminating the salad with dangerous bacteria that can potentially be on raw chicken. Set aside the cutting board used for cutting the chicken, separating it from all dish ingredients until it can be thoroughly cleaned.
   - Evenly sprinkle the spices (⅓ t curry powder, ¼ t each ground cinnamon and ginger, and ½ t garlic powder) over the chicken and gently toss the pieces for even mixing.
   - Wash your hands and cutting knife with soap.
   - Use a serrated knife to finely mince a ⅛ in. thick slice of ginger root on a clean cutting board.
   - Increase the skillet heat to medium-high. When a drop of water instantly dances and disappears, add 1 T toasted sesame oil, mix the chicken and ginger into the oil, and use a spatula to stir-fry the chicken for 1 minute, setting a timer. At the timer reduce the heat to medium and continue cooking the chicken for another 2 minutes, turning the pieces often and setting a timer. At the timer remove the skillet from the heat, evenly sprinkle ¼ t salt over the chicken, and set the skillet aside for the

chicken to cool. If the salad will not be assembled quickly, refrigerate the chicken, covering it once it cools completely.

3. **Prepare the vegetables.**

   - Scrub, dry thoroughly, cut the tip from, coarsely grate, and evenly divide the **carrot** between the two salad bowls.
   - Use a serrated knife to cut out the stem from each **bell pepper**. Remove the seeds but not the membrane. Use the serrated knife to cut the peppers lengthwise into ¼ in. thick strips and to cut the strips crosswise into ¼ in. cubes. Evenly divide the peppers between and evenly spread them over the salads.
   - Rinse, drain in a colander, and spread the **sugar snap peas** over paper towels or a terry towel. Wrap the towels around the peas to dry them. Remove strings from the peas. To do so, use a paring knife to cut nearly through the protruding stem end of a pea (cutting from the outside towards the curved side), grasp the stem end between your thumb and the flat side of the paring knife blade, and pull the string down the inside curve of the pea. Halve the peas crosswise and divide the peas between the two salad bowls.

4. **Prepare the fruit.**

   - Divide the **pomegranate seeds** evenly between the salads.
   - Use a serrated knife to slice the **pineapple chunks** into ¼ in. thick slices and divide the slices between the two bowls.
   - For **grapes**, add the grapes to a colander and thoroughly rinse them with cold water. Add a double thickness of paper towels or a terry towel to a pie plate. Add the grapes, wrap the towels around the grapes, and roll the grapes around gently within the towels to dry them thoroughly. Pick through the grapes to remove any stems and replace soft or broken open grapes. Use a serrated knife to cut off any brown stem ends and to halve the grapes lengthwise. Evenly divide the grapes between and evenly spread them over the salads.
   - For **mandarin oranges**, rinse and dry the oranges. Use a serrated knife to halve each orange crosswise. Peel the orange halves, gently pry out any seeds, and gently separate the segments. Evenly divide the half segments between the two salads. When using mandarin orange with grapes, use one mandarin orange. When using mandarin orange without grapes, use one orange per salad.

5. **Add honey.** Pour 1 dinner spoonful of honey in a thin stream over each salad, rotating around the salad bowl and attempting to touch as many fruit ingredients as possible.

6. **Prepare remaining ingredients.**

   - Break each of 8-10 nuts into 2 or 3 pieces
   - Use a chef's knife to halve the 1 T tart cherries.
   - Use a serrated knife to quarter the 6 olives.
   - Roughly crumble the 1 oz feta cheese onto plastic wrap.

7. **Assemble the salads for serving.**

    - Evenly drizzle first 1 T olive oil and then 1 T balsamic vinegar over the raw vegetables and fruit in each salad.
    - Layering ingredients, evenly divide the nuts, dried fruit, olives, and feta cheese over each salad.
    - Evenly divide the spiced chicken between the salads and drizzle 1 t balsamic vinegar over the chicken in each bowl.
    - Add the greens, drizzle 1 T oil evenly over the greens of each salad, and serve the salads.

VARIATIONS: Make ingredient substitutions. Substitute, for example,

- **4 parboiled broccoli florets** (Recipe #131) for sugar snap peas.
- **4 raspberries** (Recipe #97) or **¼ c fresh cranberries** for pomegranate seeds. Stir-fry the cranberries in 2 T water for 1 minute (until they pop open), drain them thoroughly in a colander (saving the cooking water for another use), and sweeten them with 2 t sugar.
- **1 simmered chicken breast** or **2 chicken tenders** for stir-fried spiced chicken. Add 1 c canned chicken broth and ½ t salt to a medium saucepan with a lid, bring the broth to boiling over high heat, add the whole chicken breast or tenders, stir the chicken into the broth, return the water to boiling, reduce the heat to a setting that maintains gentle boiling, cover the chicken, and cook the breast/tenders for 10 minutes, setting a timer. At the timer, turn off the heat and let the chicken sit on the burner, uncovered, for another 10 minutes before draining the broth (saving it for another purpose) and cutting the chicken for use in the salad once it cools completely. Alternatively, use the unflavored breast from chicken cooked when preparing broth (Reference #10). Lightly sprinkle pieces with freshly cracked pepper to taste.

Add ingredients. Add, for example,

- **2-3 green onions**, divided between the two salads. Thinly slice the green tops and include them in the salads. Add the onion as the first vegetable to the salad bowls. Add 1 t extra virgin olive oil to each salad bowl, add the onion, and stir in the onion.
- **1 clementine** or **mandarin orange** (Recipe #90), ½ orange per salad.
- **1 chilled nectarine** (Recipe #88) or **2 sliced red plums** (Recipe #95), divided between the salads.
- **½ chilled tasty and somewhat tart apple** (Recipe #74), such as Fuji or a dark red apple, which adds color. Swish the apple in 2 T orange juice, as in Recipe #140. Pat the apple pieces dry before dividing them between the salads.
- **2 t snipped cilantro**, 1 t per salad. Rinse the cilantro under cool water, shake it to remove excess water, wrap it in a paper towel to dry, and snip it finely with kitchen scissors.

COMMENTS: A chicken tender is a muscle attached to the underside of the breast.

PART 2

143. Mandarin Orange and Red Leaf Lettuce Salad
(Traditional 4-Serving Salad)

Vegetables and Fruits with Coating Oil

1 bunch red leaf lettuce (approx. 10 leaves)
2 chilled green onions
2 t extra virgin olive oil
1 chilled and fully ripe avocado
1 t extra virgin olive oil

½ red bell pepper
1 chilled medium Japanese cucumber
10-12 small sugar snap peas
2 mandarin oranges

Other Ingredients

2 T dried tart cherries

16 raw pecan or walnut halves (or 8 each)

Dressing

2 T premium orange juice with pulp
1 T frozen orange juice concentrate, thawed
1½ T sugar
⅛ t salt

3 T red wine vinegar
4 T extra virgin olive oil
1 certified organic lemon

Preparation Tools

1 set measuring spoons
1 small jar with a tight-fitting lid
1 hand citrus juicer
1 zesting tool
1 each 5 in. serrated, chef's, & paring knife
1 small storage container with a lid

1 colander
1 large salad bowl (approx. 10 c size)
1 rubber spatula
1 vegetable peeler
1 small mixing bowl
1 set salad serving forks

---

1. Gather all preparation tools and ingredients.

2. **Prepare the dressing.**

   - Add the 2 T orange juice, 1 T frozen orange concentrate, 1½ T sugar, 3 T red wine vinegar, and 2 T extra virgin olive oil to a small jar and vigorously shake the jar to mix the ingredients.
   - Rinse and dry the lemon. Use a zesting tool to remove ½-1 t zest from the lemon. Slice the zest into small pieces and add it to the dressing.

- Use a serrated knife to halve the lemon crosswise, squeeze ½ of the lemon, remove any seeds from the juice, add the juice to the dressing, and set the dressing aside, covered.
- Refrigerate the remaining ½ lemon within an air-tight container and save it for another use.

3. **Prepare the lettuce leaves**.

    - Separate the leaves. Quickly rinse each leaf under cold running water, gently shake the leaf to remove excess water, and drain it in a colander.
    - Use a serrated knife to slice off any pulpy or dry stem ends.
    - Spread the leaves over paper towels, add a top layer of towels, and roll the towels in jelly-roll fashion around the leaves. Set them aside.

4. **Prepare the vegetables**.

    - Rinse and shake excess water from the **green onions**. Remove loose outer skin and use a serrated knife to cut off the roots and green tops. Spread the onions and green tops over a layer of paper or terry cloth towels, roll the towels around the onions, gently squeeze the onions to dry them, and unroll the onions. Use a serrated knife to cut the white portion crosswise into ⅛-¼ in. thick slices. Cover and refrigerate one half of the green tops. Holding the remaining green tops together with one hand, use a chef's knife to thinly chop the green tops. Add 2 t oil to a 4-serving salad serving bowl, add the onion plus green top, and use a rubber spatula to thoroughly mix the onion into the oil to coat the pieces completely. Wipe the cutting board clean.
    - Prepare the **avocado**.

        - Halve the avocado. Use a serrated knife to circle around the avocado, cutting through to the stone on both the front and back of the avocado. To separate the avocado into halves, grab hold of each half with one hand and twist the halves in opposite directions. Refrigerate the avocado half with the stone, first coating the exposed flesh with oil and tightly covering the storage container.
        - To peel the avocado half to be used in the salad, use the serrated knife to halve the avocado lengthwise. Use your fingers to loosen the edge of the skin at the top of each slice of avocado, grasp the loosened edge with your fingers, and gently pull the skin downward.
        - Cut each peeled avocado slice lengthwise into ⅓ in. wide slices, cut the slices crosswise into ⅓ in. lengths, and evenly spread the pieces over the bottom of the two salad bowls. Drizzle 1 t olive oil over the avocado in each bowl and use a rubber spatula to turn the pieces over and over to coat all sides with oil.

    - Use a serrated knife to cut out the stem of the **bell pepper**. Remove any seeds but not the white membrane. Use a serrated knife to cut the pepper lengthwise into ¼ in. wide slices and to cut the slices crosswise into ¼ in. cubes. Evenly spread the bell pepper over the avocado in the salads.

PART 2

- Rinse and thoroughly dry the **cucumber**. Use a chef's knife to cut off the ends, halve the cucumber lengthwise, halve each half lengthwise, and cut the cucumber strips crosswise into ⅓ in. thick chunks. Evenly divide the cucumber between and evenly spread it over the salads.
- Add the **sugar snap peas** to a colander and rinse them with cold water. Pour the peas onto a double thickness of paper towels or a terry towel and wrap the towels around the peas to dry them. Remove strings. Using a paring knife and cutting from the outside towards the curved side of a pea, cut nearly through the protruding stem end of a pea, grasp the stem end between your thumb and the flat side of the knife blade, and pull the string down the inside curve of a pea. Halve the peas crosswise and evenly spread them over the other vegetables in the salad bowl.

5. **Prepare the mandarin oranges**.

   - Rinse and dry the oranges.
   - Use a serrated knife to halve each mandarin orange crosswise.
   - Peel the orange halves, gently pry out any seeds, and gently separate the half segments.
   - Evenly divide the half segments over the salads, one orange per salad.

6. **Do final ingredient preparations**.

   - Use a chef's knife to halve the dried cherries and to coarsely chop the nuts.
   - Unroll the lettuce leaves and pat any wet areas dry. Tear the leaves into bite-size (easy-to-eat) pieces.

7. **Assemble the salad for serving**.

   - Evenly drizzle 1 T extra virgin olive oil over the vegetables and avocado in the salad bowl and use salad forks to gently mix in the oil.
   - Shake the salad dressing, drizzle ½ of the dressing over the vegetables and avocado, and toss the ingredients with salad forks to mix in the dressing.
   - Spread the dried fruit, nuts, and then the lettuce evenly over the salad.
   - Evenly drizzle 1 T oil over the lettuce and toss the leaves (not the ingredients below) to mix in the oil.
   - Re-shake the remaining salad dressing, drizzle it evenly over the salad, and toss all the salad ingredients together.
   - Immediately serve the salad.

   VARIATIONS: Make ingredient substitutions. Substitute, for example,

   - **2 clementine oranges** (Recipe #90) or **2 tangerines** (Recipe #99) for mandarins.
   - **8 butter lettuce** or **romaine heart leaves** for red leaf lettuce. Alternatively combine either variety with red leaf lettuce.
   - **¼ chilled small red onion or 2 shallots**, diced, for green onion.

- ¼ c **toasted whole almonds** or **other favorite nuts** for raw pecans or walnuts. To toast the nuts, heat a dry skillet at a medium heat setting until hot, add whole or halved nuts, and heat them, stirring them occasionally and being watchful to avoid burning, until the nuts are aromatic and lightly browned, about 5 minutes.

Add ingredients. Add, for example,

- ¼ c **pomegranate seeds** (Recipe #96).
- 1 c **small sugar snap** or **snow peas** (Recipe #124).
- ¼ **green, yellow, and/or orange bell pepper**, prepared exactly like the red bell pepper.

Vegetable-Centered Salad Recipes

144. Greek Salad
(2 servings)

Vegetables

1 chilled small or ½ medium Japanese cucumber
6-8 grape tomatoes

2 c loosely packed pre-washed spring or other baby greens

Other Ingredients

1 oz chunk feta cheese (two 1 in. squares, to yield 2 T crumbled)

6 pitted Kalamata olives

Dressing

½ lemon

3½ T extra virgin olive oil

Preparation Tools

1 hand citrus juicer
2 individual salad bowls

1 5 in. serrated knife
1 set each measuring spoons & cups

---

1. **Gather all preparation tools and ingredients except for the greens.** Leave the greens refrigerated until just before assembling the salads for serving.

2. **Prepare the lemon.** Squeeze the lemon. Remove any seeds but not the pulp.

3. **Prepare the vegetables.**

    - Rinse and dry the **cucumber**. Use a serrated knife to cut off the ends, halve the cucumber lengthwise, halve each half lengthwise, and cut the strips crosswise into ⅓ in. thick pieces. Evenly divide the cucumber between the two salads, evenly spreading the cucumber on the bowl bottoms.
    - Rinse and thoroughly dry the **grape tomatoes**. Use a serrated knife to halve the tomatoes lengthwise. Evenly divide the tomato slices between the salads.

4. **Prepare the olives and feta cheese.** Use a serrated knife to quarter the olives lengthwise. Divide the olives between the salads, evenly spreading them over the other ingredients. Roughly crumble and evenly divide the feta between the two salads.

5. **Assemble the salads for serving.** Drizzle first 1 T oil and then 1 T lemon juice over each salad. Add 1 c greens to each salad, drizzle ¾ T oil over each pile of greens, and immediately serve the salads.

    VARIATIONS: Add **a sprinkling of salt and freshly cracked black pepper** (a few shakes of salt, a few turns of a pepper mill) to both the tomatoes and cucumber.

    COMMENTS: Lemon juice content is somewhat variable to taste. If the feta cheese is not tangy and flavorful, slightly increase the lemon juice, adding another 1 t lemon juice per salad.

    Select full-fat feta cheese, such as Valbreso sheep feta, as a special treat.

145. Everyday Vegetable Salad
(Master Recipe)
(2 servings)

Vegetables with Coating Oil

2 chilled green onions
2 t extra virgin olive oil
3 large cauliflower florets with stems (to yield approx. ⅓–½ c small florets)
2 t extra virgin olive oil
1 medium (6 in.) carrot

½ medium Japanese cucumber
¼ each red & green bell pepper
6 grape tomatoes
1½ c pre-washed spring greens
1½ c pre-washed baby spinach

Other Ingredients

1 oz chunk extra sharp cheddar cheese (to yield 2 rounded T diced cheese)

4 pitted Kalamata olives
⅛ c raw whole almonds

Dressing

approx. 2 t honey
½ lemon

2 T balsamic vinegar
4 T extra virgin olive oil

Preparation Tools

1 set each measuring spoons & cups
2 large individual salad bowls
1 cutting board reserved for vegetables & fruits
1 each 5 in. serrated & chef's knife

1 rubber spatula
1 vegetable shredder
1 dinner spoon
1 hand citrus juicer

---

1. **Gather all preparation tools and ingredients except for the greens.** Leave the greens refrigerated until assembling the salads for serving.

2. **Prepare the vegetables.**

   - Rinse and shake excess water from the **green onion**. Remove loose outer skin and use a serrated knife to cut off the roots and green tops of each onion. Spread the onions and green tops over a strip of paper or terry cloth towels, roll the towels around the onions, gently squeeze the onions to dry them, and unroll the onions. Use a serrated knife to cut the white portion of each onion crosswise into ⅛-¼ in. thick slices. Holding the green tops together with one hand, use a chef's knife to chop the tops of *one* green onion into thin slices. Add 1 t oil to each salad bowl, evenly divide the onion pieces between the bowls, and use a rubber spatula to coat all onion pieces with oil. Wipe the cutting board clean.
   - Rinse the **cauliflower florets**, spread them over a double thickness of paper towels or a terry towel, wrap the towels around them, and firmly squeeze them to dry them completely. Slice off and cut stems crosswise into thin (¼ in. thick) pieces. Break the florets into small florets. Evenly divide the florets and stem pieces between the salad bowls. Drizzle 1 t oil over the cauliflower in each bowl and use a rubber spatula to toss the florets and onion to thoroughly coat the cauliflower pieces with oil.
   - Scrub and thoroughly dry the **carrot**. Cut off the tip, coarsely grate, and evenly divide the carrot between the two salads. Rinse the shredder.
   - Rinse and dry the **cucumber**. Use a serrated knife to cut off the end, halve the cucumber lengthwise, halve each half lengthwise into two strips, and cut the strips crosswise into ⅓ in. thick pieces. Evenly divide the cucumber between and evenly spread it over the salads.
   - Use a serrated knife to cut out the stem of the **bell pepper**. Remove the seeds but not the white membrane. Use the serrated knife to cut each pepper lengthwise into ¼ in. thick slices and to cut the slices crosswise into ¼ in. thick pieces. Evenly divide the pepper between and evenly spread it over the salads.

- Rinse and thoroughly dry the **grape tomatoes**. Use a serrated knife to halve each tomato lengthwise. Divide the tomatoes between the salads.

3. **Add honey**. Drizzle about 1 dinner spoon filled with honey over each salad, rotating around the bowl and touching as many vegetable and avocado pieces as possible.

4. **Prepare remaining ingredients.**

   - Use a serrated knife to quarter each olive.
   - Use a chef's knife to cut the cheddar cheese into ¼ in. thick slices, cut the slices into ¼ in. thick strips, and cut the strips crosswise into ¼ in. cubes.
   - Use a chef's knife to roughly chop the almonds.
   - Squeeze the lemon. Remove seeds from the juice but not pulp.

5. **Assemble the salad for serving.**

   - Evenly drizzle 1 T extra virgin olive oil, 1 T balsamic vinegar, and then 1 T lemon juice over each salad.
   - Evenly divide the olives, cheddar cheese, and nuts over the salads.
   - Top each salad with 1½ c of each type of greens, drizzle 1 T olive oil over each pile of greens, and immediately serve the salads.

   VARIATIONS: Make ingredient substitutions. Substitute, for example,

   - **non-dairy cheese** for dairy cheese to convert the salad to vegan vegetarian form.
   - **agave nectar** or **sugar** for honey.
   - **½ c raw red or green cabbage** (Recipe #115), coarsely shredded, for cauliflower.
   - **4 medium red leaf lettuce leaves** or **medium romaine hearts**, rinsed and dried and torn into bite-size pieces, for spring greens.

   Add vegetable ingredients. Add, for example,

   - **¼ yellow bell pepper**, diced.
   - **2 T diced cooked beets** per salad. Use fresh cooked beets (boiled whole, Recipe #59), canned, or refrigerated vacuum-packed cooked beets.
   - **4 raw medium broccoli florets** (Recipe #114) or **4 parboiled broccoli florets** (Recipe #131). Halve the florets lengthwise, place the florets cut side down on a cutting board, and cut each half into 2-3 slices (into easy-to-eat size pieces).
   - **2 small fresh radishes** (Recipe #126) to each salad.

   Add protein ingredients. Add, for example,

   - **1 heaping T chunk-light tuna packed in oil** per salad. Use a dinner fork to break up the tuna and mix the packing oil into it. Increase the balsamic vinegar content to 1¼ T per salad and deliberately pour ¼ T over the tuna in each salad. Select tuna packed

in extra virgin olive oil as a top quality tuna product.
- **½-1 boiled egg** (Recipe #151) per salad.
- **2 T canned garbanzo beans**, well drained, per salad.
- **1 heaping T hummus** per salad, added as a topping before adding the greens. Use freshly prepared (Recipe #152) or commercially prepared hummus.

146. Guest Vegetable Salad
(2 servings)

Vegetables and Avocado with Coating Oil

2 chilled green onions
2 t extra virgin olive oil
2 large cauliflower florets with stems
1 fully ripe avocado, chilled
2 t extra virgin olive oil
1 medium carrot
6 asparagus spears
½ medium Japanese cucumber

¼ red bell pepper
⅛ each yellow & green bell pepper
6 grape tomatoes
4 small fresh radishes
2 c pre-washed spring or other baby greens
2 handfuls pre-washed arugula
2 c pre-washed baby spinach

Other Ingredients

4 pitted large green or Kalamata olives
¼ c raw whole almonds (or pecan halves, walnut halves, pistachios, hazelnuts, or nut mixture)
8 small (½ in.) fresh mozzarella cheese balls

1 oz chunk extra sharp cheddar cheese or full-fat feta cheese, such as Valbreso sheep feta (to yield 2 T crumbled)

Dressing

½ lemon
approx. 2 t honey

5 T extra virgin olive oil
2 T balsamic vinegar

Preparation Tools

1 cutting board reserved for vegetables & fruits
1 each 5 in. serrated & chef's knife
1 set each measuring spoons & cups
2 large individual salad bowls
1 rubber spatula

1 vegetable peeler
1 vegetable shredder
1 dinner spoon
1 hand citrus juicer

PART 2

1. **Gather all preparation tools and ingredients except for the greens.** Leave the greens and spinach refrigerated until assembling the salads for serving.

2. **Prepare the vegetables and avocado.**

    - Rinse and shake excess water from the **green onions**. Remove loose outer skin and use a serrated knife to cut off the green tops. Spread the onions and tops over a strip of paper towels or cloth towel, roll the towel around the onions, gently squeeze the onions to dry them, and unroll the onions. Use a serrated knife to cut off the root end from each onion and to thinly slice the white ends crosswise. Use a chef's knife to chop the green tops of *one* green onion crosswise into thin pieces. Add 1 t oil to each salad bowl, evenly divide the onions between the bowls, and use a rubber spatula to mix the onion pieces into the oil. Wipe the cutting board clean.
    - Rinse the **cauliflower florets**, spread them over a double thickness of paper towels or terry towels, wrap the towels around them, and firmly squeeze them to dry them completely. Use a serrated knife to cut off and slice stems crosswise into thin pieces. Break the florets into small florets. Evenly divide the florets and stem pieces between the salad bowls and use a rubber spatula to toss the cauliflower with the onion to coat the florets with oil.
    - Prepare the **avocado**.

        - Halve the avocado. Use a serrated knife to circle around the avocado, cutting through to the stone on both the front and back of the avocado. To separate the avocado into halves, grab hold of each half with one hand and twist the halves in opposite directions. Refrigerate the avocado half with the stone, first coating the exposed flesh with oil and tightly covering the storage container.
        - To peel the avocado half to be used in the salad, use the serrated knife to halve the avocado lengthwise. Use your fingers to loosen the edge of the skin at the top of each slice of avocado, grasp the loosened edge with your fingers, and gently pull the skin downward.
        - Cut each peeled avocado slice lengthwise into ⅓ in. wide slices, cut the slices crosswise into ⅓ in. lengths, and evenly spread the pieces over the bottom of the two salad bowls. Drizzle (pour in a thin stream) 1 t olive oil over the avocado in each bowl and use a rubber spatula to turn the pieces over and over to coat all sides with oil.

    - Scrub and dry the **carrot**. Cut off the tip, coarsely shred, and evenly divide the carrot between the two salads. Rinse out the shredder.
    - Prepare the **asparagus**. While holding a spear with one hand, bend the tip end with your other hand until the tip breaks off from the spear, which should yield about a 3 in. tip; repeat for each spear. Cover and refrigerate the remaining spears for another use. Break the tips into 1 in. pieces and evenly divide the tips between the salads.
    - Use a serrated knife to cut off the end of the **cucumber**, halve it lengthwise, halve each half lengthwise, and cut the strips crosswise into ⅓ in. thick pieces. Evenly divide the cucumber between the bowls.

- Use a serrated knife to cut out the stem of each **bell pepper**. Remove seeds but not the white membrane. Use the serrated knife to cut each pepper lengthwise into ¼ in. thick slices and to cut the slices crosswise into ¼ in. thick pieces. Evenly divide the peppers between and evenly spread them over the salads.
- Rinse and thoroughly dry the **grape tomatoes**. Use a serrated knife to halve each tomato lengthwise. Divide the tomatoes between the salads.
- Rinse and dry the **radishes**. Use a serrated knife to cut off the ends, cut each radish lengthwise into 3-4 equal slices, and evenly divide the slices between the salads. For larger radishes, cut the radishes into ⅛ in. thick slices and halve the slices lengthwise.

3. **Add honey to each salad.** Drizzle approx. 1 small dinner spoonful of honey over each salad, rotating around the salad bowl and attempting to touch as many ingredients as possible.

4. **Prepare the remaining ingredients.**

   - Squeeze the lemon. Remove seeds but leave pulp.
   - Use a serrated knife to quarter the olives.
   - Break pecan or walnut halves into 2-3 pieces. Use a chef's knife to coarsely chop other whole nuts.
   - Use a chef's knife to cut the cheddar cheese into ¼ in. thick slices, cut the slices into ¼ in. thick strips, and cut the strips crosswise into ¼ in. cubes. Halve mozzarella balls (cut larger balls into ½ in. cubes). If using feta cheese, crumble it onto plastic wrap.

5. **Assemble the salad for serving.**

   - Evenly drizzle 1 T extra virgin olive oil and then 1 T each lemon juice and balsamic vinegar over each salad.
   - Layering ingredients, evenly divide the olives, nuts, and cheeses between the salads.
   - Top each salad with 1 c each greens and spinach and 1 handful of arugula. Drizzle 1½ T olive oil over each pile of greens and immediately serve the salads.

VARIATIONS: Make ingredients substitutions. Substitute, for example,

- **non-dairy cheese** for dairy cheese to convert the salad into vegan vegetarian form.
- **agave nectar** or sugar for honey.
- **4 parboiled broccoli florets** (Recipe #131), sliced, or **4 boiled whole brussels sprouts** (Recipe #61), halved or quartered, for asparagus tips.
- **¼ chilled red onion**, halved lengthwise, diced or sliced, (Recipe #34) for green onions.

Add ingredients. Add, for example,

- **6 sugar snap peas** (Recipe #124), halved, or **¼ c freshly shelled raw green peas**.

- **1 small (2 in. diameter) beets**, diced. Use either boiled whole with skins (Recipe #59), canned, or vacuum-packed and refrigerated cooked beets, thoroughly patted dry.
- **⅓ c fresh pineapple chunks**, ½ in. thick, sliced (Recipe #94)

COMMENTS: Serving success is far more about using tasty and attractive vegetables (having a mix of flavors, colors, and textures) than about having lots of different kinds of vegetables. Mixing one or two somewhat distinctive vegetables with several ordinary but tasty vegetables is enough to make a special salad for guests.

147. Three Bean Vegetable Salad
(2-3 servings)

Vegetables with Seasonings and Coating Oil

10 slender green beans
¼ t salt
⅓ of a 12 oz package of frozen edamame pods (to yield approx. ⅓ c shelled edamame)
½ chilled medium yellow onion, halved lengthwise
⅛ in. thick quarter-size slice of fresh ginger root
1 T extra virgin olive oil
½ t each dried sweet basil & oregano leaves
¼ head green cabbage (to yield ½ c shredded)

1 medium carrot
1 small or ½ medium Japanese cucumber
¼ red bell pepper
⅛ each yellow & green bell pepper
6 grape tomatoes
2 chilled green onions
2 t extra virgin olive oil
2 c pre-washed spring or other baby greens
2 c pre-washed baby spinach

Other Ingredients

⅓ c cooked red kidney beans
4 pitted green olives

2-3 T raw whole almonds
1 oz chunk extra sharp cheddar cheese

Dressing

approx. 2 t honey
½ lemon

2 T balsamic vinegar
5 T extra virgin olive oil

Preparation Tools

1 medium saucepan
1 wooden spoon
1 timer
1 colander

1 each 5 in. serrated & chef's knife
1 plastic or plastic-coated stir-fry spatula
2 small mixing bowls
1 dinner plate

1 slotted spoon
1 medium mixing bowl
1 set each measuring spoons & cups
1 medium or large skillet
1 cutting board reserved for vegetables

1 vegetable shredder
2-3 large individual salad bowls
1 dinner spoon
1 hand citrus juicer
1 pair kitchen scissors

1. **Gather all preparation tools and ingredients except for the greens.** Leave the greens refrigerated until assembling the salads for serving.

2. **Boil the green beans whole.**

    - Add enough water to cover the beans by several inches to a medium saucepan and bring the water to full boiling over high heat.
    - Add the beans to a colander and rinse them with cool water but do not trim them.
    - When the water comes to full boiling, slowly add the whole beans to the boiling water, use a wooden spoon to push the beans down into the water, stir the beans until they become bright green, reduce the heat slightly but retain rapid boiling, partially cover the pan, and boil the beans for 7 minutes, setting a timer.
    - At the timer, use a slotted spoon to remove the beans from the boiling water into a colander, leaving the saucepan on the hot burner but lowering the heat to medium.
    - Quickly rinse the beans with cold water and spread them over a double thickness of paper towels or a terry cloth towel to dry them.
    - Add the beans to a medium mixing bowl, sprinkle ¼ t salt over them, toss the beans to mix in the salt, and refrigerate the beans for fast cooling.

3. **Boil the edamame pods.**

    - Add more water, if necessary, as is needed to cover the pods by three inches and return the water in the saucepan to full boiling over high heat.
    - Add the frozen pods, use a wooden spoon to stir them into the water, reduce the heat slightly but retain rapid boiling, partially cover the pan, and boil the pods for 5 minutes, setting a timer.
    - At the timer, drain the pods in a colander, rinse them with cold water, spread them over the double thickness of paper towels or a terry towel used for drying the green beans, and add the pods to the beans cooling in the refrigerator.

4. **Cook the yellow onion and ginger root with the dried herbs.**

    - Heat a medium or large skillet on a large burner at a medium setting.
    - Place the ½ onion cut side down on a cutting board and use a chef's knife to cut off the ends. Peel the onion, again place it cut side down on a cutting board, and dice it. While holding the onion together with one hand, thinly slice the onion first lengthwise and then crosswise.

PART 2

- Use the chef's knife to cut the ginger root into thin strips and to cut the strips crosswise into small pieces.
- Increase the skillet heat to medium-high. When a drop of water added to the skillet instantly dances and disappears, add 1 T oil, add the onion and ginger, crush ½ t each dried basil and oregano leaves between your palms over the onion and ginger, stir-fry the onion mixture for about 30 seconds, reduce the heat to medium, and cook the onion mixture for 2 minutes, stirring it occasionally and setting a timer.
- At the timer, remove the skillet from the heat and set the onion aside.

5. **Prepare the kidney beans.**

    - Add the beans to a small mixing bowl.
    - Add 2 T water, swish the beans in the water, and drain the beans in a colander placed over a dinner plate for collecting the bean broth. Spread the beans over a double thickness of paper towels and wrap the towels around the beans to dry them. Mix the beans with the cooked onion. Refrigerate the collected broth for another use.

6. **Prepare the vegetables.**

    - Scrub and thoroughly dry the **carrot**. Slice the tip from, coarsely shred, and evenly divide the carrot between 2-3 salad bowls.
    - Rinse and thoroughly dry a head of **cabbage**. Coarsely shred enough cabbage to yield ½ c cabbage. Immediately tightly cover the head of cabbage with plastic wrap and refrigerate it. Evenly divide the shredded cabbage between the salads. Rinse out the grater.
    - Rinse, dry, and slice the end from the half **cucumber**. Use a serrated knife to halve it lengthwise and to halve each half lengthwise. Cut the strips crosswise into ⅓ in. thick pieces and evenly divide the pieces between the salads.
    - Use a serrated knife to cut out the stem of each **bell pepper**. Remove the seeds but not the white membrane. Use a serrated knife to cut the peppers lengthwise into ¼ in. thick slices and to cut the slices crosswise into ¼ in. thick pieces. Evenly divide the pepper between the salads.
    - Add the **grape tomatoes** to a colander, rinse them with cool water, and dry them with paper towels or a terry towel. Use a serrated knife to halve each lengthwise and divide the tomatoes between the salads.
    - Add 2 t oil to a small mixing bowl. Rinse and shake excess liquid from the **green onions**. Remove loose outer skin and use a serrated knife to cut off the green tops and root end from the onions. Spread the onions and tops over a length of paper or cloth towels, roll the towels around the onions, gently squeeze the onions to dry them, and unroll the onions. Use a serrated knife to slice the white onion flesh crosswise into ⅛-¼ in. thick slices. Holding the green tops of *one* onion together with one hand, use a chef's knife to thinly chop the greens. Add the onion to the small bowl with the oil and use a rubber spatula to thoroughly coat the onion pieces with oil. Evenly divide the onion between the salads. Use the rubber spatula to scrape any oil remaining in the small bowl into the salad bowls. Wipe the cutting board clean.

7. **Add honey.** Drizzle 1 small dinner spoon filled with honey over the ingredients in each bowl, rotating around each bowl to touch as many vegetables as possible.

8. **Prepare remaining ingredients and cooked beans.**

    - Squeeze the ½ lemon. Remove any seeds but leave pulp.
    - Use a serrated knife to quarter the 4 olives.
    - Use a chef's knife to chop ¼ c nuts coarsely and to dice the 1 oz cheese.
    - Use kitchen scissors to snip off the ends and to cut each green bean into three pieces.
    - Remove the edamame beans from the pods.

9. **Assemble the salads for serving.**

    - Layering the ingredients, evenly divide the onion and kidney bean mixture and both the green and edamame beans over each salad.
    - Drizzle first 1 T olive oil and then 1 T each lemon juice and balsamic vinegar over each salad, rotating around the salads to coat as many pieces as possible.
    - Evenly divide the olives, nuts, and cheese between the salad bowls.
    - Top each salad with 1 c each spring greens and baby spinach and drizzle 1½ T olive oil over each pile of greens.
    - Immediately serve the salads.

    VARIATIONS: Make ingredient substitutions. Substitute, for example,

    - **non-dairy cheese** for cheddar cheese to convert the salad to vegan vegetarian form.
    - **agave nectar** or **sugar** for honey.
    - **4 Brussels sprouts**, halved, or **red cabbage** for green cabbage. Cook the sprouts in the water used for the green beans. Add more water, if necessary, to cover the sprouts completely. Boil the untrimmed sprouts for 3 minutes only before draining them in a colander and rinsing them with cold water.
    - **4 raw medium cauliflower florets** (Recipe #107), broken into very small florets with stems sliced, for cabbage. Mix the florets in 1 t oil before adding them to the salads.

    Add ingredients. Add, for example,

    - **2 T cooked beets**, patted dry and diced. Add fresh cooked with skins (Recipes # 59), canned (plain or pickled), or refrigerated vacuum-packed.
    - **2 T artichoke hearts**, plain canned, drained and patted dry, sliced and cut into small pieces, 1 T per salad.
    - **2 small handfuls mung bean** or **alfalfa sprouts**, rinsed and thoroughly dried in a salad spinner or with paper towels, one handful per salad.
    - **1 t finely snipped fresh basil** or **oregano leaves**, ½ t per salad.

PART 2

148. Corn and Black Bean Salad
(2-3 servings)

Vegetables with Seasonings, Cooking Water, and Cooking and Coating Oil

2 ears yellow corn
2 T water
¼ t salt
½ medium chilled yellow onion, sliced lengthwise
⅛ in. thick slice of ginger root
1 T extra virgin olive oil
½ t cumin seed
2 chilled green onions

2 t extra virgin olive oil
2 large cauliflower florets with stems
1 medium carrot
1 small or ½ medium Japanese cucumber
⅛ each red, yellow, & green bell pepper
6 grape tomatoes
1½ c pre-washed spring or other baby greens
1½ c pre-washed baby spinach

Other Ingredients

½ c cooked black beans
4 pitted large green olives

1 oz chunk extra sharp cheddar cheese
10 raw whole almonds

Dressing

approx. 2 t honey
½ lemon

4 T extra virgin olive oil
1½ T balsamic vinegar

Preparation Tools

1 medium (10 in.) skillet
1 pie plate
1 each chef's & 5 in. serrated knife
1 set each measuring spoons & cups
1 plastic or plastic-coated stir-fry spatula
1 colander
1 dinner plate
1 medium mixing bowl

1 timer
1 rubber spatula
1 small mixing bowl
2-3 large individual salad bowls
1 vegetable shredder
1 dinner spoon
1 hand citrus juicer

---

1. **Gather all preparation tools and ingredients except for the greens.** Refrigerate the greens until just before serving the salad.

2. **Stir-fry the corn in water.**

   - Heat a medium sized skillet on medium heat.
   - Remove the husks and silk from the corn. Stand each ear upright in a pie plate and

399

use a chef's knife to slice off the kernels, cutting close to the cob to include the corn germ.
- Add 2 T water to the skillet and bring it to boiling over high heat. Add the corn kernels, stir them into the water, and when the water returns to boiling, stir-fry the corn for 1 minute (just until heated through, until it slightly darkens in color).
- Remove the skillet from the heat and use a rubber spatula to scrape the corn into a colander placed over a dinner plate to collect any cooking water.
- Transfer the corn to a medium mixing bowl, evenly sprinkle ¼ t salt over the corn, mix in the salt, and set the corn aside to cool.
- Collect and save the cooking liquid for another use.
- Wipe the skillet clean.

3. **Stir-fry the yellow onion and ginger.**

- Heat the medium skillet at a medium setting.
- Place the ½ onion cut side down on a cutting board and use a chef's knife to cut off the ends. Peel the onion.
- Dice the onion. Placing it cut side down on a cutting board and while holding it together with one hand, slice it first lengthwise and then crosswise into ¼ in. thick slices, cutting the onion into roughly uniform ¼ in. cubes.
- Use the chef's knife to slice the ginger root into thin strips and to cut the strips crosswise into small pieces.
- Increase the skillet heat to medium-high, and when a drop of water added to the skillet instantly dances and disappears, add 1 T oil, add and heat ½ t cumin seed for 30 seconds, add the onion and ginger, and stir-fry the mixture for about 30 seconds.
- Reduce the heat to medium and cook the onion mixture for 2 minutes, stirring it occasionally and setting a timer.
- At the timer, remove the skillet from the burner and turn off the burner.

4. **Prepare the black beans.**

- Add ½ c beans to a small mixing bowl, add 2 T water, swish the beans in the water, and drain them in the colander placed over a dinner plate. Collect and save the bean broth for another use.
- Spread the beans over a paper towel to dry them.
- Add the beans to the cooked yellow onion mixture in the skillet and use a rubber spatula to combine the ingredients thoroughly.

5. **Prepare the vegetables.**

- Rinse and shake excess water from the **green onions**. Remove loose outer skin and slice the green tops and roots from the onions. Spread the onions and tops over a strip of paper towels or a terry cloth towel, roll the towels around the onions, gently squeeze the onions to dry them, and unroll the onions. Use a serrated knife to slice the white flesh crosswise into ⅛ in. thick slices. Holding the green tops of *one* green onion together with one hand, use a chef's knife to chop the tops crosswise into thin (⅛ in. thick) slices. Add 1 t oil to each of the 2 salad bowls or ½ t oil to 3 salad bowls, divide the green onion between the bowls, and use a rubber spatula to thoroughly toss the onion in the oil. Wipe the cutting board and cutting knives clean.

- Rinse the **cauliflower florets**, wrap them within paper towels or a terry cloth towel, and firmly squeeze them to dry them. Cut off the stems and cut the stems crosswise into ¼ in. thick slices. Break the florets into small florets. Evenly divide the cauliflower between the salad bowls and toss the pieces with the onion to coat them with oil.
- Scrub and dry the **carrot**. Cut off the tip, coarsely shred, and evenly divide the carrot between the 2 salads. Rinse out the grater.
- Rinse, dry, and slice the stem end from the **cucumber**. Use a chef's knife to halve it lengthwise and halve each half lengthwise. Cut the strips crosswise into ⅓ in. thick pieces and evenly divide the pieces between the bowls.
- Use a serrated knife to cut out the stem of each **bell pepper**. Remove the seeds but not the white membrane. Keeping the peppers separate, use a serrated knife to cut each bell pepper lengthwise into ¼ in. thick slices and to cut the slices crosswise into uniformly small pieces. Evenly divide each pepper variety between the bowls.
- Rinse and thoroughly dry the **grape tomatoes**. Use a serrated knife to halve each tomato lengthwise. Divide the halves between the salads.

6. **Add honey to each salad.** Drizzle 1 small dinner spoon filled with honey over the vegetables in each salad, rotating around the bowl to cover the greatest number of vegetables.

7. **Prepare remaining salad ingredients.**

    - Squeeze the ½ lemon. Remove seeds but save pulp.
    - Use a serrated knife to quarter the 4 olives lengthwise.
    - Use a chef's knife to chop the 10 nuts coarsely and to dice the 1 oz cheese, first cutting the chunk into ¼ in.thick strips and cutting the strips crosswise into ¼ in. cubes.
    - Remove the 3 c greens from the refrigerator.

8. **Assemble the salads for serving.**

    - Evenly divide the onion and black bean mixture and the corn between the salad bowls and slightly toss the mixtures.
    - Evenly drizzle first 1 T extra virgin olive oil and then 1 T each lemon juice and balsamic vinegar over each salad, rotating around the salads.
    - Evenly divide the olives, nuts, and cheese between the salad bowls.
    - Evenly divide the greens between the salad bowls, drizzle 1 T olive oil over each pile of greens, and immediately serve the salads.

VARIATIONS: Make ingredient substitutions. Substitute, for example,

- **soy** or **other non-dairy cheese** for cheddar cheese to convert the salad into vegan vegetarian form.
- **agave nectar** or **sugar** for honey.
- **2 c certified organic dry frozen whole kernel yellow corn** for fresh corn.

Add ingredients. Add, for example,

- **½ ripe avocado** (Recipe #76), cut into small chunks.
- **1 T pimento**, chopped, added as a topping to each salad.
- **2 t cilantro leaves**, thinly sliced, 1 t added as topping to each salad.
- **4-6 chilled garlic cloves** (Recipe #31), minced and cooked with the onion.
- **½ jalapeño pepper** or **¼ mild green chili pepper** (Recipe #36), diced.
- **½ raw small kohlrabi** (Recipe #121) or **½ young and tender turnip** (Recipe #128), diced.
- **2 stalks organic celery** (Recipe #118), diced.
- **⅓ c cooked quinoa** (Recipe #167), mixed into the black beans and onion mixture.
- **½ t garlic powder, ½ t ground cumin, pinch of cayenne** or **red pepper flakes**, and/or **½ t mild curry powder**, added to the onion during cooking.

149. Tabbouleh
(Traditional 4-Serving Salad)

Vegetables with Coating Oil and Fresh Herbs

4 chilled green onions
2 t extra virgin olive oil
⅛ each red, yellow, & green bell pepper
8-10 grape tomatoes
1 medium Japanese cucumber

8 sprigs fresh mint (to yield approx. 2 T sliced)
1 bunch fresh Italian (flat-leaf) parsley (to yield approx. 1 c loosely packed, chopped)
1 handful chives, sliced (opt)

Other Ingredients

½ c medium cracked whole wheat
1½ c water
½ t dried mint leaves

¼ t salt
⅛ c each raw pecan halves and whole raw almonds

Dressing

½ lemon
1½ T apple cider vinegar
1 t packed dark brown sugar

¼ t salt
4 T extra virgin olive oil

PART 2

Preparation Tools

1 medium heavy-bottomed saucepan
   with an opaque lid
1 set each measuring spoons & cups
1 timer
1 rubber spatula
1 medium mixing bowl
1 hand citrus juicer

1 cutting board reserved for vegetables
1 each 5 in. serrated & chef's knife
1 small mixing bowl
1 dinner fork or small whisk
2 wooden spoons or salad spoon & fork
1 large (10 c) serving bowl
1 colander

---

1. **Gather all preparation tools and ingredients.**

2. **Cook the cracked wheat.** Begin this cooking at least 30 minutes before serving.

   - Add ½ c cracked wheat, ½ t dried mint, and 1½ c water to a medium saucepan and bring the water to full boiling over high heat. Immediately lower the heat to a low setting, cover the pan, and set a timer for 25 minutes.
   - Check the saucepan after 5 minutes to make sure that the cooking water is gently boiling and adjust the temperature as may be needed, either reducing or increasing it slightly.
   - Check the saucepan again after 20 minutes to ensure that the cooking water has not been completely absorbed and that the cracked wheat is not sticking to the pan bottom. If the grain appears dry, add 2-4 T hot water.
   - At the timer, make a taste check. If the cracked wheat is soft (without any crispness), remove it from the heat. If the cracked wheat is not soft, turn off the heat, re-cover the saucepan, and leave the saucepan on the burner for 5 minutes, setting a timer.
   - Once the grain is soft, evenly sprinkle ¼ t salt over it and use a rubber spatula to mix in the salt and to scrape the grain into a medium mixing bowl. Set the grain aside to cool somewhat.

3. **Prepare the dressing.**

   - Squeeze the ½ lemon. Remove seeds but save any pulp in the juice.
   - Add 1½ T lemon juice, 1½ T apple cider vinegar, 1 t brown sugar, ¼ t salt, and 2 T extra virgin olive oil to a small mixing bowl and use a dinner fork or small whisk to mix the ingredients together.

4. **Mix ½ of the dressing into the cracked wheat.** Use two wooden spoons to toss the cracked wheat after adding the dressing. Refrigerate the cracked wheat, uncovered. Cover the grain if the salad will not quickly be assembled for serving.

5. **Prepare the vegetables while the cracked wheat chills.**

   - Rinse and shake excess water from the **green onions**. Remove any loose outer skin from the onions and use a serrated knife to cut off the roots and green tops. Spread the onions and green tops over a strip of paper towels or a terry towel, roll the towel around the onions, gently squeeze the onions to dry them, and unroll the onions. Working on a cutting board reserved for vegetables and fruits, use a serrated knife to cut the white portion of the onions crosswise into thin (⅛ in. thick) slices. Holding the green tops of *two* green onions together with one hand, use a chef's knife to chop the tops crosswise into thin slices. Add the green onions to a large serving bowl, drizzle 2 t extra virgin olive oil over them, and toss the onions to thoroughly coat pieces with oil. Wipe the cutting board and cutting knives clean.

- Use a serrated knife to cut out the stem of each **bell pepper**. Remove the seeds but not the white membrane. Keeping the different peppers separate, use a serrated knife to cut each pepper lengthwise into ¼ in. thick slices and to slice the strips crosswise into ¼ in. thick cubes. Evenly spread the peppers over the onion in the serving bowl.
- Rinse and dry the **grape tomatoes**. Use a serrated knife to halve each tomato lengthwise. Evenly spread the tomatoes over the bell pepper.
- Rinse and dry the **cucumber**. Use a chef's knife to cut off the ends, split the cucumber lengthwise, and split each half lengthwise. Use a serrated knife to slice each cucumber strip crosswise into ¼ in. thick slices. Evenly spread the cucumber over the grape tomatoes.
- Rinse the **parsley, mint, and chives** under cool water, shake them as they are rinsed to remove excess water, and drain them in a colander. Keeping the individual greens separate, spread the greens over a strip of paper towels or cloth towel, add a top layer, gently press the top layer into the greens, roll the greens in the towels, gently squeeze the greens to dry them, unroll the leaves, and add them to a cutting board. The fresh herbs can also be dried in a salad spinner.

    - Keeping the different greens separate, gently strip the **parsley leaves** from the stems, setting the stems aside. Roughly holding the parsley leaves together with one hand, use a serrated knife to finely slice the parsley. Holding the stems together with one hand, thinly slice the stems crosswise.
    - Prepare the **mint leaves** and the **chives** in exactly the same way as the parsley.
    - Mix the parsley, mint, and chives together on the cutting board.

6. **Prepare the nuts.** Use a chef's knife to chop the nuts coarsely.

7. **Assemble the salad.**

    - Drizzle 1 T extra virgin olive oil over the vegetables in the serving bowl, use two wooden spoons or a salad serving fork and spoon to toss the vegetables. Add the remaining dressing and again toss the vegetables to mix in the dressing.
    - Remove the cracked wheat from the refrigerator, use a dinner fork to evenly break up chunks into small (but not tiny, approx. ⅛ in. wide) pieces, add the grain to the vegetables, and gently toss the cracked wheat and vegetables together.
    - Make a taste check and add touches (1-2 t) more lemon and vinegar to taste. Make another taste check before adding more.

- Evenly spread the nuts and parsley, mint, and chives mixture over the cracked wheat and vegetable mixture.
- Drizzle 1 T extra virgin olive oil over the fresh herbs. Use two wooden spoons to first mix the oil into the fresh herbs and then to mix the herbs and nuts into the cracked wheat/vegetable mixture.

VARIATIONS: Make ingredient substitutions. Substitute, for example,

- **medium cracked whole bulgur** for whole cracked wheat. Cook and prepare the bulgur in the same way as cracked wheat except for shortening the cooking time by 10 minutes. Always check bulgur for rancidity.
- ½ **chilled red** or **yellow bulb onion**, halved lengthwise and diced (Recipe #34), for green onion.

Add ingredients. Add, for example,

- ¾ **c cooked quinoa** (Recipe #167, Variations). Increase dressing content slightly, adding ½ T each lemon juice and vinegar, ½ t brown sugar, a touch of salt, and ½ T extra virgin olive oil.
- ¾ **c cooked garbanzo beans**, well drained. Increase dressing content in the same way as for quinoa.
- **2-3 sprigs cilantro**, sliced like the parsley, adding it as a topping when serving the dish.

COMMENTS: Always check both the cracked wheat and nuts for rancidity. Both should have a neutral scent.

150. Broccoli, Sugar Snap Pea, and Grape Salad
(Traditional 4-Serving Salad)

Vegetables and Fruits with Seasonings and Coating Oil

1 chilled relatively large stalk broccoli or 1½ small stalks	2 chilled green onions
	2 t extra virgin olive oil
¼ t salt	1 c red seedless grapes
2 c chilled small sugar peas	1 c green seedless grapes
⅛ t salt	approx. 1 t honey

Other Ingredients

¼ c raw whole cashews, whole almonds, or pecan halves	1 heaping T dried tart cherries
	1 heaping T certified organic raisins

Dressing

2 t apple cider or rice vinegar
2 t balsamic vinegar
2 t honey or sugar

⅓ c avocado or certified organic canola oil mayonnaise (see comments below)

Preparation Tools

1 set each measuring spoons & cups
1 small mixing bowl
2 rubber spatulas
1 large (10-12 c), deep saucepan
1 each 5 in. serrated & chef's knife
1 wooden spoon
1 timer
1 long-handled large slotted spoon

1 colander
2 dinner plates
1 cutting board reserved for vegetables & fruits
1 large (10 c) serving bowl
1 pie plate
1 dinner spoon

---

1. **Gather all preparation tools and ingredients.**

2. **Prepare the dressing.**

   - Add 1½ t each apple cider and balsamic vinegar and 2 t honey to a small mixing bowl and use a rubber spatula to combine the ingredients roughly.
   - Add ⅓ c mayonnaise and stir the mixture until creamy smooth.

3. **Parboil the broccoli.**

   - Add enough water to cover the broccoli florets by several inches to a deep large saucepan and heat water over high heat.
   - Rinse the broccoli stalk in cool water, shake off excess clinging water, wrap the stalk in paper or cloth towels, and firmly squeeze the florets to dry them.
   - Turn the stalk on its side and use a serrated knife to slice off the florets, cutting stems off at the stalk. Separate the leaves. Set the stalk aside for another use such as peeling it for use as a raw snack.
   - Sort the florets into small/medium and large florets. When the water boils, drop the florets and leaves into the water, adding larger florets first, smaller florets second, and leaves last and adding the florets slowly enough to avoid stopping the boiling. Immediately use a wooden spoon to stir the florets into the water, and once all the florets are mixed into the water, begin timing the cooking. Boil the florets for exactly 1 minute.
   - At the timer, use a slotted spoon to transfer the florets and leaves into a colander and immediately rinse the broccoli with cold water.
   - Reduce the water heat to a medium setting.

- Transfer the broccoli to a dinner plate lined with a double thickness of paper towels or a terry towel.
- Wrap the paper towels around the broccoli florets and leaves, gently squeeze the florets to dry them, unwrap them, evenly sprinkle ¼ t salt evenly over them, and refrigerate them on the towels.

4. **Parboil the sugar snap peas.**

    - Add more water to the saucepan, if necessary, to cover the peas completely.
    - Return the water to full boiling, add the peas without stopping boiling, use a wooden spoon to stir in the peas, and boil them for exactly 1 minute, using a timer.
    - At the timer, drain the peas in a colander and rinse them with cold water.
    - Spread the peas on a dinner plate lined with a double thickness of paper towels or a terry towel.
    - Wrap the paper towels around the peas, gently squeeze the peas to dry them, unwrap the peas, evenly sprinkle ⅛ t salt over them, and refrigerate the peas on the towels.

5. **Prepare the green onions and grapes.**

    - Rinse and shake excess water from the **green onions**. Remove any loose outer skin from the onions and use a serrated knife to cut off the green tops and roots of each onion. Spread the onions and green tops over a strip of paper towels or a terry towel, roll the onions in the towels, gently squeeze the onions to dry them, and unroll the onions. Working on a cutting board reserved for vegetables and fruits, use a serrated knife to cut the white flesh of each onion crosswise into ¼ in. thick slices. Holding the green tops of *one* green onion together with one hand, use a chef's knife to chop the green tops crosswise into thin slices. Evenly spread the onion over the bottom of a large serving bowl, immediately drizzle 2 t oil over the onion and green tops, and use a clean rubber spatula to toss the onion to coat all pieces with oil. Wipe the cutting board and cutting knife clean.
    - Add the **grapes** to a colander and thoroughly rinse them with cold water. Add the grapes to a pie plate lined with a double thickness of paper towels or a terry cloth towel and spread the grapes over the towels. Pick over the grapes, discarding stems and replacing spoiled, soft, and broken open grapes. Wrap the paper towels around the grapes and gently press and roll the grapes around within the towels to dry them. Use a serrated knife to slice off any brown stem ends and to halve the grapes lengthwise. Spread the grapes evenly over the onion in the serving bowl.

6. **Add honey.** Drizzle a dinner spoon filled with honey over the grapes while rotating around the salad bowl, attempting to touch as many grape halves as possible.

7. **Make final ingredient preparations.**

    - Use a chef's knife to chop nuts coarsely and to halve 1 T dried cherries.
    - Use a serrated knife to slice off the broccoli floret stems and to cut the stems crosswise into ¼ in. thick slices. Halve the broccoli florets lengthwise, place each half cut side

down on a cutting board, and cut the halves lengthwise into ¼ in. thick chunks. Halve large leaves.
- Use the serrated knife to slice off the tips and to halve the sugar snap peas.

8. **Assemble the salad for serving.**

    - Evenly spread the broccoli and sugar snap peas over the onion and grapes in the salad bowl.
    - Spread the dried fruit evenly over the vegetables.
    - Use a rubber spatula to scrape the remaining dressing onto the salad and to thoroughly mix in the dressing.
    - Make a taste check and add a touch (1-2 t) more balsamic vinegar for tartness and ½ t honey for sweetening, drizzling the flavoring evenly over the salad before mixing it into the salad.
    - Evenly spread the nuts over the salad, roughly mix in the nuts, and serve the salad.

VARIATIONS: Make ingredient substitutions. Substitute, for example,

- **raw broccoli** and **raw small sugar snap peas** for parboiled broccoli and peas.
- **3 large raw cauliflower florets** (Recipe #117), broken into small florets, for ½ stalk broccoli. Drizzle the raw cauliflower florets with 1 t oil and toss the florets in the oil before mixing it into the salad.
- **white balsamic, white wine, rice vinegar,** or **apple cider vinegar** for regular balsamic vinegar to avoid coloring the dressing.
- **home-prepared mayonnaise** for commercially prepared mayonnaise using the recipe included the comments below.

COMMENTS: Avocado oil is a form of monounsaturated oil, the same "good fat" that is found in extra virgin olive oil. It aids in the absorption of fat soluble phytonutrients and nutrients contained in salad vegetables. In addition to being tasty, avocado mayonnaise is, as a result, especially high quality oil.

Homemade mayonnaise made from certified organic canola oil is also very tasty mayonnaise, especially in comparison to commercially made canola oil-based mayonnaise. To prepare canola oil mayonnaise,

- combine 5 T apple cider vinegar (unpasteurized vinegar in particular), 1 T sugar, 2 egg yolks, and ¾ t salt in a blender and blend the ingredients together for several seconds to mix the ingredients together.
- add approx. 1 c certified organic canola oil, slowly pouring it in a very thin stream during the blending. Continue pouring oil until the mayonnaise thickens enough to fill the blender center (about 40-60 seconds).
- use a thin-bladed rubber spatula to scrape the mayonnaise from the blender into a glass container with a tight-fitting lid.
- refrigerate the mayonnaise. It maintains top flavor for a week or so.

PART 2

Salad Accompaniments

151. Boiled Eggs
(4 servings)

Ingredients

4 large eggs

Cooking Tools

1 medium saucepan with a lid   1 timer

1. **Cook the eggs.**

   - Add the eggs to the saucepan and add enough cool water to cover them completely.
   - Bring the water to boiling over high heat.
   - Once the water begins to boil (the moment the water begins to bubble slowly), set a timer for 3 minutes, reduce the heat slightly, and boil the eggs uncovered.
   - At the timer, remove the saucepan from the burner and cover the pan.

2. **Set the eggs aside for 7 minutes, setting a timer.** At the timer, drain the eggs, rinse them with cold water, and set them aside covered in cool water to cool. For fast cooling, add ice cubes to the water.

   COMMENTS: It is important to add the eggs to cool, not already boiling, water to avoid breaking the shells. Because cooking time varies depending on altitude, cooking time may need to be adjusted somewhat. If the egg centers remain quite moist with 3 minutes of cooking, increase the cooking time by 30 seconds. Eggs should be pleasingly moist and tender. A green- coated and chalky yolk indicates overcooking.

   To select the most nutritious and tastiest eggs, select pastured eggs. See Reference #4 (Selecting Top Quality Whole Food Ingredients for Use in Part II Recipes), Ingredient #4, for selection details.

409

152. Hummus
(4 servings; approx. 1 cup)

Vegetables with Seasonings and Cooking Oil

1 chilled small onion
4 chilled garlic cloves
1 T extra virgin olive oil

1 t chili powder
1 t ground cumin
½ t garlic powder

Garbanzo Beans

1 15-oz can garbanzo beans

Dressing

½-1 lemon
1½ T Tamari or other natural soy sauce

¼ c tahini (either raw or toasted)

Preparation Tools

1 medium nonstick skillet
1 chef's knife
1 set each measuring spoons & cups
1 plastic or plastic-coated stir-fry spatula
1 timer
1 colander
1 dinner plate

1 rubber spatula
1 blender
1 narrow-bladed rubber spatula
1 hand citrus juicer
1 small mixing bowl
2-4 c glass storage container with a lid

---

1. **Gather all preparation tools and ingredients.**

2. **Stir-fry the onion and garlic with the spices.**

   - Heat the skillet at a medium setting.
   - Use a chef's knife to slice the ends from the onion and garlic. Peel and dice the onion; peel and mince the garlic.
   - Increase the skillet heat to medium-high.
   - When a drop of water added to the skillet instantly dances and disappears, add 1 T oil, add the onion, and stir-fry it for 30 seconds. Add the garlic, evenly sprinkle the spices (1 t chili powder, 1 t ground cumin, and ½ t garlic powder) over the onion and garlic, stir-fry the mixture about another 30 seconds, reduce the heat to medium, and cook the mixture for 2 more minutes, stirring it occasionally and setting a timer.
   - At the timer, remove the skillet from the heat.

3. **Blend the garbanzo beans.**

    - Drain the beans in a colander placed over a dinner plate for collecting the bean broth.
    - Measure 1 c beans, refrigerating the remaining beans, tightly covered, for another use. Use a rubber spatula to scrape the bean broth into a 1 c size measuring cup.
    - Blend ⅓ c beans and 2 T bean broth at a time, blending the beans for a few seconds, turning off the blender, and repeating this pulsing until the beans are finely blended.
    - Use a narrow-bladed rubber spatula to scrape the beans from the blender into the warm spiced onion mixture in the skillet.
    - Blend two more batches of beans, adding each batch to the skillet as they are blended.
    - Use a rubber spatula to thoroughly stir the blended beans into the warm spiced onion mixture in the skillet.
    - Immediately add some water to the blender to ease cleaning.

4. **Prepare the dressing.**

    - Halve the lemon crosswise and squeeze the juice from one half. Remove any seeds but leave pulp in the juice.
    - Add the ¼ c tahini, 1½ T Tamari sauce, and the squeezed lemon juice to a small mixing bowl and use a rubber spatula to combine the ingredients thoroughly.

5. **Assemble the hummus.**

    - Add the dressing to the spiced beans in the skillet and combine the ingredients thoroughly.
    - Check the flavoring. Add touches (1-2 t at a time) more lemon juice to taste, squeezing more juice as may be needed. Add touches of bean broth as may be needed to achieve a creamy, but not runny, consistency.
    - Use a rubber spatula to scrape the hummus into a 2-4 c glass storage bowl with a tight-fitting lid.
    - Refrigerate the hummus between servings. Use it within 3-4 days or freeze it in serving size amounts.

Reference #8

Clinching Salad Flavor: Expanded Preparation Support

Reference #8 makes suggestions for maximizing the flavor and attractiveness, and sometimes the nutritional quality, of key individual salad ingredients. Considering ingredients in alphabetical order, Reference #8 covers 1) **feta cheese,** 2) **boiled eggs,** 3) **raw fruit,** 4) **greens and lettuce,** 5) **honey,** 6) **olives,** 7) **extra virgin olive oil,** 8) **raw and parboiled vegetables,** 9) **raw seasoning vegetables,** and 10) **balsamic vinegar.**

Flavor-Enhancing Suggestions

1. Feta Cheese

Maximize the attractiveness of feta cheese in salads. The flavor and texture of different feta cheese products varies considerably, and feta cheese flavor changes during storage, becoming more assertive and less attractive with age. Selecting and handling feta cheese, as a result, requires some care.

- Select the freshest feta cheese, which has the mildest flavor. Check the "sell by" dates on labels and purchase feta with distant "sell by" dates. Use feta fairly quickly after opening it. Always check the flavor of opened feta cheese that has been home refrigerated for some time before adding it to a salad.
- Purchase feta cheese in block form and crumble it just prior to serving. Bulk cheese is more flavorful and crumbles more easily and evenly than pre-crumbled feta cheese.
- Experiment with feta products to select the most pleasing product. Feta flavor varies according to the type of milk used, with feta made from sheep, goat, or cows having distinctive flavors. Feta flavor and texture also varies depending on the fat content of the milk used. Feta made from full or reduced fat milk is tastiest and has the smoothest, creamiest texture. Feta cheese made from skim milk is coarse in comparison.
- Refrigerate a feta cheese container tightly covered within an air-tight zippered bag to best protect it from air, which undermines freshness.
- Measure feta cheese content. Observe the 1 T per serving recipe direction to ensure feta blends pleasingly into a salad. Increase this amount only on the basis of experience with using a feta cheese product.

Substitute goat cheese for feta cheese. Like feta cheese, goat cheese (also called chèvre) adds distinctively tangy flavoring to a salad. Also like feta cheese, goat cheese flavor can be too assertive and detract from salad attractiveness. Apply the same selection, storage, and serving size rules for goat cheese as for feta cheese.

Substitute a small amount (approx. 1 T per individual salad) of other tasty cheese for, or combine it with, feta cheese. Substitute or add, for example,

- extra sharp cheddar cheese, diced. This tasty aged cheddar cheese blends especially nicely in salads. Tillamook Extra Sharp Vintage White Cheddar is an outstanding example of this cheese. While including extra sharp cheddar cheese in freshly and coarsely shredded form is satisfactory, cheese cut into ¼ in. cubes is more flavorful.
- fresh mozzarella cheese. While itself bland in flavor, fresh mozzarella cheese blends deliciously in salads flavored with oil and vinegar dressing. Fresh mozzarella cheese is also alkaline while an aged cheese, in contrast, is acid-producing when consumed. To include fresh mozzarella, use whole or halved small (½ in.) balls, 3-4 balls per individual salad. Cut larger balls or chunks into easy-to-eat ⅓ in. cubes and add 3-4 cubes per individual salad.
- bleu or Roquefort cheese, crumbled.
- Swiss cheese, cut into ¼ in. cubes.

2. Boiled Eggs

Be particular about egg selection.

- Select eggs from pastured hens. See Reference #4 (Selecting Whole Food Ingredient and Other High Quality Ingredients for Part II Recipes), Ingredient #4, for selection details.
- Select fresh eggs. Check the expiration dates on cartons. Eggs should feel heavy and not float when added to the water for boiling. The white of a raw egg should be thick and cling to the yolk rather than spread out and have a runny consistency.

Minimally boil eggs. Extended boiling undermines the texture of the yolk of boiled eggs, giving it an unattractively dry, chalky, and somewhat toughened texture. Boiling eggs exactly as directed in Recipe #151, in contrast, yields perfectly cooked through, moist, and tender egg yolk.

3. Raw Fruit

Maximize the attractiveness of raw fruit in salads.

- Include at least one juicy fruit, one tangy fruit (such as pineapple, nectarine, tangerine, or mandarin orange), and at least one intensely colored fruit, which, in addition to providing attractive color, contributes rich phytonutrient content.
- Select fully ripe fruit, which has peak flavor. Home-ripen green fruit that can be ripened before serving it. This fruit includes apple, apricot, avocado, guava, kiwi, mango, nectarine, peach, pear, plum, and tomato.

- Select in-season fruit, which is most likely to be fully ripe fruit. This is especially important for oranges and other fruits that do not ripen after being picked (grapes, berries, cherries, pineapple, and pomegranate), which to meet off-season demand, are often picked early. In-season fruit also has not been stored for an extended period, which reduces both flavor and nutritional quality.
- Cut fruit into pieces that are both relatively large and easy-to-eat. Large pieces of fruit are more flavorful and hold juice better than small pieces. Use a very sharp knife to cut fruit in order to minimize juice spilling. In the case of very juicy fruits, do any cutting only shortly before serving.
- Swish cut fruit that easily browns in a citrus wash (2 T orange juice and 1 T water) to delay browning.
- Include novel fruit. Add, for example, ripe figs when they are in season, guava (Recipe #84), and different varieties of grapes.
- Include a small amount of distinctively attractive fruit, such as avocado (Recipe #76), which is also distinctively nutritious,[270] mandarin orange (Recipe #90), and fresh sweet cherries (Recipe #81).
- Do not include particular fruits, including watermelon (which is too juicy), banana (which browns too quickly), and grapefruit (which can become bitter).
- Add kiwi (Recipe #86) as a very last ingredient shortly before serving. Kiwi adds brilliant color and attractive tart flavor, but it can be harmful to other fruit ingredients if mixed with them for any length of time.
- When drizzling honey or agave nectar over fruit in salads, touch as many fruit pieces as possible, but always add only touches of sweetening. While a touch of honey attractively enhances the sweetness of fruit and mellows vinegar tartness, honey also easily overwhelms natural fruit flavor.

4. Greens and Lettuce

Maximize the attractiveness of greens (leafy green vegetables) in salads.

- Serve very fresh greens, which are the tastiest greens with the greatest phytonutrient content.
- Select young greens as the most tender and mild tasting greens. They are also more nutritious than larger, more mature leaves. Select **microgreens**, the youngest of all greens, as super nutritious greens.
- Select greens with reddish/purple coloring, such as **baby Swiss chard** and **baby beet greens**, which are both distinctively colorful and nutritious.
- Add a handful of distinctively flavored greens, such as **arugula** and **watercress**, which

---

270 Robinson, *Eating on the Wild Side*, 206. Avocados are among the few plants that retain most of the nutritional content of their ancestors. In addition to having rich phytonutrient (antioxidant) content, they are a good source of natural vitamin E, which is typically low in most American diets. Avocados are also a good source of folacin, potassium, and magnesium. They are standout sources of soluble fiber and monounsaturated fat, the same human health-promoting monounsaturated fat as contained by extra virgin olive oil.

also happen to be exceptionally nutritious.
- Always check commercially pre-washed greens for spoiled leaves, which will spoil salad attractiveness. Spreading the greens over a large surface eases sorting through leaves.
- Thoroughly rinse un-washed greens to remove all grit. Even a touch of grittiness can spoil salad attractiveness.
- Dry greens before adding them to a salad. Drying is important for two reasons. First, clinging water prevents oil from clinging to cut or torn leaves. Without an oil coating, clinging water quickly leaches juice from the leaves, undermining the flavor and texture of the greens. Second, clinging water and spilled juice dilute vinegar flavor.
- Tear all greens except for baby greens into bite-size pieces, first detaching firm stems from leaves. Separately slice stems crosswise into very thin pieces before adding them to a salad. As small and easy to eat pieces, stems mix discreetly into salads. The flavor of somewhat assertive greens, such as arugula, is also softened when such greens are torn into small pieces and mixed with other salad ingredients.

Maximize the attractiveness of lettuce in salads.

- Select the most colorful lettuce varieties, which are both attractive and highly nutritious lettuce varieties. For example,

    - select **looseleaf lettuce**. Because the leaves of this lettuce are loose, not tightly packed together, they are uniformly dark green, which means they contain rich phytonutrient content and, as a result, are especially nutritious. Select **red leaf lettuce** in particular. The reddish/purple tint of its leaves enhances its attractiveness, and because this tint is the highest ranking color of the phytonutrient color hierarchy, leaves have super concentrated phytonutrient content. At the same time that red leaf lettuce is tender it is also hearty and stores well.
    - select **romaine lettuce**. This lettuce has both outstanding flavor and crispness, and the outer dark green leaves have concentrated phytonutrient content. Also of importance, romaine lettuce leaves are hearty and store well.

- Tear lettuce into easy-to-eat pieces. When the leaves are re-refrigerated in an air-tight container, this is a salad-making task that can be done well ahead of serving.
- Minimize direct contact between lettuce and vinegar. As with greens, either coat pieces of lettuce thoroughly with oil before mixing lettuce with vinegar **or** add lettuce to a salad after vinegar has been added and as a very last ingredient just prior to serving.

Store prepared raw salad greens (including parsley and cilantro) and lettuce leaves to keep them on hand for quick and easy inclusion in salads.

- Rinse the leaves. Detach the leaves of bunched greens (such as spinach) and lettuce (such as loose leaf and romaine lettuce) from stems and add them to a sink or large bowl containing enough water to cover the greens. Swish each leaf in the water. For previously unwashed leaves, rub your thumb over both sides, especially in the case of curly or bumpy leaves, and swish the leaves once more. Shake most clinging water from

leaves as they are rinsed and set them aside, stacking them together.
- Dry the leaves. Spin dry small sturdy leaves (such as baby kale and beet greens) in a salad spinner. Spread more fragile greens (such as spinach), larger greens (such as chard and varieties of kale), and large lettuce leaves over a strip of paper towels or a large terry cloth towel, top the leaves with another layer of towel, gently press the towels over the leaves, roll the leaves in the towels, and unroll the leaves. Use a towel to pat remaining wet areas dry.
- Refrigerate the leaves. Stack the leaves into small piles. Loosely wrap a paper towel around each pile of leaves and refrigerate the leaves until they are thoroughly cooled. Once they are chilled, place the leaves into gallon-sized sealable plastic bags, first wrapping each bunch within a paper towel. Press out as much air as possible from each bag before sealing the bag. Greens and lettuce stored in this manner retain freshness for at least several days and up to a week.

5. Honey

Soften thick or crystallized honey for easy pouring. Pouring honey in a very thin stream, or drizzling, is an efficient way of spreading a small amount of honey over fruit pieces in salads. Thick honey, however, cannot be drizzled. Thick honey instead falls in clumps or in a heavy stream and easily over-sweetens a salad.

- **To soften honey,** scrape honey into a heat-proof glass container (such as a Pyrex glass measuring cup), add a trivet or metal jar lid to the bottom of a small but deep saucepan, add hot water to the saucepan (enough to mainly cover the sides of the honey container), set the honey container on the trivet or jar lid, and slowly heat the water over low heat until the honey becomes clear and fluid. Placing a trivet or jar lid under the honey container protects the glass container from direct contact with the hot saucepan, which can cause it to break.

Substitute other sweetening for honey but do not omit sweetening in recipes. In addition to providing attractive sweetening, honey or other sweetening mellows vinegar tanginess. If honey or agave nectar is not available, sprinkle a small amount (1 t per salad) of granulated sugar, sprinkling it evenly over fruit pieces. If agave nectar is substituted for honey, select USDA-certified organic products because excessive pesticide residues have reportedly sometimes been found in products imported from Mexico.[271]

---

[271] *Eating Well* (March/April, 2009): 38.

PART 2

6. Olives

Maximize the attractiveness of Kalamata olives in salads. Sometimes spelled calamata, Kalamata olives are richly flavored brine-cured black olives that add distinctive and interesting flavor in salads. As with other products, the flavor of different products varies, flavor fades or changes during extended storage, and texture changes (becomes unattractively soft) during extended storage.

- Select shiny, dark (not tinted purple), firm, and plump Kalamata olives.
- Avoid very salty Kalamata olive products.
- Cut olives into easy-to-eat size. For the most concentrated olive flavor in salads, halve olives. Quartering best disperses olive flavoring in a salad. Quartering also mellows olive flavor.
- Pit olives before adding them to salads. Pitting is important for avoiding the potential threat of pits to teeth. To pit an olive, place it on its side and gently press down on the olive with the flat side of a large knife blade until the olive splits (or collapses slightly). Alternatively, use a knife to cut the pulp from the pit. Place an olive on its side and slice it lengthwise, rotating around the olive until all flesh is removed. Kitchen shops also market easy to use olive pitting tools.
- Freeze olives to keep them on hand. When access to olives is limited, freezing provides a means of keeping them available. It effectively retains flavor and satisfactorily retains texture. To freeze olives, freeze the olives in some brine or packing oil within an air-tight freezer container. Freeze them in small amounts to maximize the time the olives retain top flavor and texture when they are thawed and used.

Substitute other olives, except for flavorless canned black olives, for Kalamata olives. There are many interesting varieties of olives from which to choose. There are olives that come from different countries – for example, Lebanese, Greek, Jordanian, and Spanish olives – and from California. Olives are green or black, packed in brine or oil, large or small, and variously stuffed (such as with nuts or garlic) or flavored with chilies. While such a selection is not always easily available, locating a source of varied olives is well worth the effort. Stores that sell olives in bulk form often provide tasting samples.

7. Extra Virgin Olive Oil

Maximize the attractiveness of extra virgin olive oil in salads.

- The flavor of different extra virgin olive oil products varies. Flavor differences can be due to the ripeness of the olives used, with the flavor of green olives and color (greenish color) being somewhat more bitter than oil pressed from ripe olives. Degree of processing also affects flavor, with first-pressed oil quite reliably being more flavorful than oil pressed 2 or more times, which can also be somewhat thinned. Try out a variety of oil products to select a first-pressed product with a rich flavor that has the most personally pleasing flavor. Use less flavorful varieties for cooking purposes.

- Use fresh extra virgin olive oil. Because flavor degrades during storage, purchase an amount of oil that can be used relatively quickly after it is opened. Alternatively, or at the same time, refrigerate the opened container, storing only a small amount of oil at room temperature for everyday use. As refrigeration causes the oil to harden, allow time for it return to liquid form when replenishing the oil stored at room temperature.
- Maintain at least a 2 parts oil to 1 part vinegar ratio as a reliably pleasing flavor balance. Keep a tablespoon measure handy for accurately measuring oil and vinegar content.
- As lemon juice is not as tart as vinegar, use at least a 1½ part lemon juice to 1 part extra virgin olive oil ratio when mixing them for use as a salad dressing. Best of all, combine both lemon juice and vinegar with extra virgin olive oil, using 1 part each lemon juice and vinegar per 2 parts oil.
- Never reduce oil content to reduce the calorie content of a salad. Oil mellows vinegar flavor, which is important to salad tastiness.
- Always check extra virgin olive oil for rancidity, which effectively spoils it. Store it tightly covered to protect the oil from air.
- Purchase extra virgin olive oil packaged in a green-tinted container, which is protective of the nutritional quality of the oil. Store extra virgin olive oil in a dark place protected from sunlight.

8. Raw and Parboiled Vegetables

Maximize the attractiveness of raw and parboiled vegetables in salads.

- Never include flavorless token vegetables, such as most industrially produced tomatoes.
- Maintain basic salad ingredient proportions. If vegetable content is increased, also increase vinegar and oil content proportionately to ensure the dressing is not diluted. To reduce vegetable content, decrease vinegar and oil content proportionately to keep vinegar flavor from being too strong. Add small amounts of all vegetables. Never increase the amount of any one vegetable no matter how tasty the vegetable happens to be.
- Add distinctively tasty, colorful, or crunchy vegetables to recipes. For example, add **radish** (Recipe #118), selecting small, young, and tender radishes that are sweet or only slightly hot. Add shredded young **beet**, which adds striking color, attractive sweetness, and nutritional value. Add diced **young turnip** (Recipe #122). While not colorful, raw tender turnip adds zesty flavor and crunchiness.
- Add novel vegetables, such as **kohlrabi, fennel**, and **sprouts**. Sprouts come in a wide variety of flavors, and in addition to adding different flavor, they add exceptional nutrition boosting.
- Coat cut or broken off pieces of highly absorptive raw vegetables with oil before adding them to a salad. Without an oil coating, cut pieces of these vegetables – such as **cabbage, cauliflower, celery**, and **mushrooms** – soak up a significant amount of vinegar or lemon juice and unexpectedly dilute dressing flavor.

- Parboil particular vegetables. Parboiling (brief boiling of untrimmed whole or large pieces of vegetables) attractively softens and improves the flavor of **broccoli** (Recipe #131), **green beans** (Recipe #130), and **zucchini** or **yellow summer squash** (Recipe #134).

9. Raw Seasoning Vegetables

Maximize the attractiveness of onion included in salads. Enzyme content makes raw onions (except for sweet onions, which do not contain flavor-altering enzymes) highly vulnerable to unpleasant flavor alteration, but application of simple enzyme-managing techniques convert raw onion into a reliably attractive salad ingredient. The following techniques apply to all onions except for sweet onions:

- Select any variety of onion that is in good physical condition. This is a uniformly firm onion with tight-fitting and completely unbroken skin. Do not select a strong smelling onion (which indicates that enzymes have already altered the onion flavor). Avoid using onion that has a spoiled area, which likely undermines onion flavor throughout.
- Chill onions prior to cutting. Pre-chilling is necessary because it deactivates enzymes, and this deactivation is crucial to the retention of the natural sweetness of onions. Without pre-chilling, air immediately activates flavor-altering enzymes during cutting.
- Cut and add cut onion to a salad shortly before serving a salad to maximize the time enzymes remain inactivated.
- Cleanly cut onions with a sharp knife. Never coarsely chop or cut an onion with a dull knife because this cutting bruises onion pulp. Bruising quickly activates both flavor- and color-altering enzymes, essentially overcoming protection provided by pre-chilling.
- Immediately coat cut onion with oil. An oil coating effectively protects cut pulp from contact with air.

Do not add raw garlic to salads. Garlic enzyme content makes the flavor of raw garlic very unstable. To best secure attractive garlic flavor, briefly stir-fry it, which deactivates enzymes and yields reliably mild tasting garlic. Recipe #31 provides basic garlic cooking details

10. Balsamic Vinegar

Maximize the attractiveness of balsamic vinegar in salads.

- Select aged balsamic vinegar products as the most reliably mellow products. While aged products can also be expensive, reasonably priced tasty aged balsamic vinegar products are also available.
- Mellow the tartness of balsamic vinegar by mixing it with less tart ingredients. In particular, mix balsamic vinegar with fresh lemon juice, using a 1 part lemon juice to 1

part balsamic vinegar ratio. Alternatively, mix balsamic vinegar with mild varieties of vinegar, such as rice wine vinegar. As sweetening also mellows vinegar tartness, slightly increase the honey content of a salad or substitute pomegranate molasses for one half the vinegar content.

- Precisely measure balsamic vinegar content and keep a one tablespoon measuring spoon handy to support routine measuring. Vinegar is a key flavoring ingredient in salads, but there is little room for error in the amount used. Too much vinegar easily causes a salad to be unpleasantly tart and sharp; too little leaves a salad unattractively bland. If family tastes are variable or if guests are present, reduce the recipe amount slightly and serve extra balsamic vinegar for individuals to add it to taste.
- Maintain at least a 2 part oil to 1 part vinegar ratio.
- Add vinegar to salads just prior to serving to maximize the attractiveness of vegetable and fruit ingredients and the vinegar. Adding vinegar just prior to serving minimizes the chance that vinegar will leach juice from and undermine the flavor and texture of cut vegetable and fruit ingredients. Leached out juice then dilutes vinegar flavor and undermines its flavor.
- Coat cut or broken off pieces of highly absorptive raw vegetables with oil before adding them to a salad. Without an oil coating, cut pieces of these vegetables – such as cabbage, cauliflower, celery, and mushrooms – soak up a significant amount of vinegar and unexpectedly dilute dressing flavor.

Substitute only equally tasty flavoring for balsamic vinegar. Substitute, for example,

- raspberry and sherry vinegar.
- flavored balsamic vinegar, such as huckleberry balsamic vinegar.
- pomegranate molasses for (or combine it with) balsamic vinegar.
- dressing made from milder flavored vinegar (such as apple cider vinegar and red and white wine vinegar) combined with a small amount of such standard dressing ingredients as prepared mustard, crushed garlic, frozen concentrated fruit juice, and sugar. For example, substitute a dressing composed of ½ lemon (approx. 2 T freshly squeezed), 1½ T red wine vinegar, 1 t packed dark brown sugar, ⅛ t salt, and 2 T extra virgin olive oil, with an additional 2 T extra virgin olive oil drizzled over greens or lettuce used in the salad.

CHAPTER SEVEN

Stir-Fried Dish Recipes

Stir-Fried Dish Description

IF THERE IS one kind of dish that *Cooked Alive!* would urge cooks to adopt as a routine meal-time choice, it would be stir-fried dishes. It is not just that stir-frying and stir-fry/steaming are appealing methods of quickly and efficiently preparing vegetables. Of far more importance, these cooking methods are nearly perfect ways to preserve vegetable attractiveness. As detailed in the Chapter One introduction, stir-frying and stir-fry/steaming are highly effective *juice-protective* preparation methods that protect the distinctive flavor, vivid natural color, attractive texture, and vast nutritional virtues of vegetables and fruits. Vegetables and fruits reliably emerge from the skillet in outstandingly attractive and nutritious form. As central ingredients in Chapter Seven stir-fried dishes, vegetables and fruits, in turn, transform overall dish quality, inject liveliness, and give dishes genuine health-sustaining capacity.

Because stir-frying and stir-fry/steaming permit a cook to assemble any number of vegetables to suit his/her taste, time, and purse, stir-fried dishes have enormous elasticity. Not only is there little limit on the kind of vegetables included, there is also great flexibility with respect to the ingredients that can be combined within them. Dried fruit, nuts, brown rice, legumes, beef, eggs, and chicken, to name a few, combine attractively, further enhancing both stir-fried dish flavoring and nutritional quality. Dish elasticity is so amenable to innovation and variation that cooks (be they vegan, vegetarian, or omnivore) can rely on stir-fried dishes practically every day. It is almost impossible to get bored with them. Once cooks get stir-frying and stir-fry/steaming techniques right, they liberate themselves to a considerable extent from the chore of deciding what to cook. Utterly reliable, stir-fried dishes stand by as ever satisfying mealtime choices.

Chapter Seven recipes follow a master recipe approach. This approach supports maximum exposure to different varieties of vegetables while easing recipe preparation. Recipes share, with minor variation, a common reliably attractive flavoring base (curry spice-flavored seasoning vegetables, carrots, bell pepper, dried fruits, and nuts), common accompaniments (unflavored yogurt and soy sauce), and a small amount of brown rice. All recipes contain a variety of vegetables and often fruit, and vegetable content varies widely from recipe to recipe. Protein content of recipes varies as well, and recipes are grouped according to type of protein in the following manner:

- Traditional Main Dishes, which include a small amount of beefsteak, chicken, or eggs.
- Traditional Vegetarian Main Dishes, which include legumes.
- Traditional Pilaf Recipes, which are side dishes that mix a host of vegetables with some variety of whole grain or wild rice.

Stir-Fried Dish Preparation Notes

Preparation Notes provide helpful recipe preparation instruction and information about Chapter Seven stir-fried dish recipes that cannot fit into the individual recipes. They cover a variety of subjects, including,

- technical details relating to recipe preparation (Notes #1-9), with information provided in Note #1 being of particular importance.
- cooking tool information (Note #10).
- information about preparing vegetable and fruit variation suggestions made in recipes (Note #11).
- recipe resource references (Notes #12-13).

1. **Vegetable stir-fry/steaming technique requires adjustment for gas burners.** The stir-fry/steaming technique used for preparing vegetables in Chapter Seven stir-fried dish recipes matches electric burners, which do not immediately cool when burner heat is reduced after one minute of stir-frying. Because the temperature does not quickly drop, the cooking of vegetables also reliably does not immediately stop. Instead, cooking slows slowly and vegetables continue to cook and reliably cook through in the recipe directed time. **Because gas burners *do* immediately respond to heat changes**, the reduction of heat to low after stir-frying is so abrupt that cooking quickly slows too much and can even stop completely. As a result, vegetables easily will not be tender after the recipe-directed cooking time. To adjust stir-fry/steaming technique when using a gas burner,

   - add 1 T hot water as a recipe directs after one minute of stir-frying, but reduce the heat to **medium low** rather than low. Cover the skillet and heat the vegetable on medium low for 30 seconds before reducing the heat to low and setting the timer for the directed steaming time.

2. **In stir-fry/steaming, hot water added for steaming a vegetable should immediately sizzle moderately and audibly.** This is an important clue for ensuring vegetables are tender in the recipe-specified cooking time. If the water sizzles wildly, the water will likely evaporate and the vegetable may scorch during steaming. An additional 1 T hot water needs to be added. If the water added for steaming does not sizzle at all, the vegetable is most likely not sufficiently hot and will not cook to tenderness in the recipe-directed cooking time. The skillet temperature should then be increased and not reduced until the steaming water is sizzling around vegetable pieces.

3. **To reduce stir-fried dish preparation time,**

PART 2

- reduce vegetable content. To reduce vegetable content without undermining dish flavor,

    - retain seasoning vegetables, which include onions, ginger root, and bell peppers.
    - retain carrots because they are a key flavoring and coloring vegetable.
    - add herbs to vegetables during cooking to make up for the flavoring loss involved in reduced vegetable content.
    - substitute vegetables with short cooking times and/or with the least preparation time. Include, for example, dry frozen peas (Recipe #71) or sugar snap peas (Recipe #16) and fresh or dry frozen whole kernel yellow corn (Recipe #65) as primary vegetables. Use pre-washed spinach and pre-washed baby greens as greens. Without any rinsing, drying, and vein/stem chopping required, these greens need only to be cut and cooked, and stir-frying takes only one minute.

- prepare at least some vegetables ahead. Any vegetable can be prepared well ahead of serving. To retain flavor and color, it is important that the vegetables be covered once they are cool, be refrigerated in a manner that keeps them dry and not in contact with spilled juice, and be protected from drying air.

4. **To easily and efficiently dice the ½ medium onion and mince the ⅛ in. thick slice of ginger root routinely included in stir-fried dishes,**

    - place the onion cut side down on a cutting board and use a chef's knife to slice off the tips. Peel the skin, again place the onion half cut side down on a cutting board and, while holding the onion together with one hand, use a chef's knife to cut the onion lengthwise into thin slices (⅛-¼ in.). Turn the onion sideways and, again while holding the onion together with one hand, repeat the slicing.
    - use a chef's or serrated knife to cut the ginger into thin slices. While holding the slices together with one hand, turn the ginger sideways and repeat the slicing.

5. **It is of utmost importance to use top quality onion.** This is necessary for onion to play its key flavoring ingredient role in stir-fried dishes. A top quality onion is uniformly firm and tightly covered with unbroken skin. The onion should not have any visible green coloring. Onions should also be chilled before being cut in order to inactivate enzymes that will negatively alter onion flavor when onion pulp is exposed to air during cutting.

6. **Already cut vegetable ingredients used in Chapter Seven recipes should always be cut from rinsed and dried vegetables.** Examples of such vegetable ingredients include ¼ or ⅓ bell pepper, ⅛ in. thick piece of fresh ginger root, and ½ cabbage.

7. *Cooked Alive!* **deliberately and exceptionally details recipe instruction in order to maximize preparation success.** *Cooked Alive!* promises that this detailing works. Cooks do reliably achieve serving success. *Cooked Alive!* also assures them that as they gain experience with the stir-fried recipes, they will master the techniques and will find that preparation speeds up significantly. With cooked brown rice on hand, most Chapter

Seven stir-fried recipes can be prepared in as little as 30 minutes. Cooking time becomes primarily a matter of the number of vegetables included.

8. **Brown rice content is variable in Chapter Seven recipes.**

   - Wild rice and other whole grains can be substituted for brown rice in recipes. *Cooked Alive!* includes the cooking details for wild rice, hulled barley, wheat berries, and quinoa (Recipe #167) to ease this substitution.
   - Cooked brown rice can also be omitted from recipes when it is not on hand. However, the nutritional contributions that brown rice and other whole grains or wild rice make to a dish make it worth the trouble of keeping whole grains on hand. They are a source of fiber-rich and energy-sustaining complex carbohydrate as well as of a host of natural nutrients, including vitamin E, which is a rare nutrient in the common diet of most consumers. Furthermore, serving brown rice, wild rice, or another whole grain in a stir-fried dish is a sure way to serve these whole food products successfully. The rich vegetable base of a stir-fried dish attractively moistens and flavors a whole grain or wild rice, reliably assuring its acceptance as a dish ingredient.

9. **To substitute extra lean ground beef for beefsteak in Traditional Main Dish recipes (Recipes #140-143)**, cook ⅓ lb extra lean ground beef with 1 finely minced ⅛ in. thick slice of fresh ginger root in the same way as sliced beef, with the same spice or herb flavoring, and the same amount of extra virgin olive oil. After adding the ground beef to the heated skillet, use a stir-fry spatula to break it up into small (but not fine) pieces and stir-fry the meat for 30 seconds at medium-high heat. Reduce the heat to a medium setting and cook the beef about 5 minutes until no red coloring remains, stirring occasionally.

10. **Listed below is important cooking tool information relating to Chapter Seven stir-fried dish recipes.**

    - Each Chapter Seven recipe lists all key cooking tools used, listing them in order of use, but recipes do not list some basic wiping, cleaning, wrapping, and working tools. These tools include paper and cloth towels, vegetable scrubbing tools, plastic wrap, and general cutting boards. These tools are used routinely in recipes and need to be kept handy.
    - The Part II Introduction listing of cooking tools serves as a descriptive reference for all tools used in Chapter Seven recipes except for two tools that are relatively specific to Chapter Seven recipes. These tools include, as follows:

        - **1 trivet.** This is a useful tool to have on hand when cooking brown rice, other whole grains, and wild rice on an electric burner that does not have a true low heat setting.
        - **1 flame tamer.** This is a useful tool to have on hand for preparing brown rice, other whole grains, and wild rice on a gas burner in case the burner does not reduce to a true low heat setting.

PART 2

11. **Chapter One (Stir-Fried and Stir-Fry/Steamed Vegetable Recipes) serves as a reference for preparing the vegetable variation suggestions made in Chapter Seven recipes.** The recipe number attached to a vegetable variation identifies the Chapter One reference recipe, which provides basic preparation details as well as selection and nutritional information for the vegetable variation.

12. **Cooks can significantly boost the nutritional quality of Chapter Seven dishes through selection of the highest quality dish ingredients.** *Cooked Alive!* includes three references to aid cooks in selecting high quality ingredients. These references are as follows:

    - Reference #1 (Selecting Top Quality Fresh Whole Vegetables and Fruits) details the nutritional significance of selecting vegetables and fruits that are both naturally intact and naturally produced. Naturally produced products include both certified organic and locally produced vegetables and fruits.
    - Reference #4 (Selecting Top Quality Whole Food Ingredients for Use in Part II Recipes) details the nutritional significance of selecting naturally intact and naturally produced whole foods other than vegetables and fruits. Reference #4 makes specific product selection recommendations. Whole food products covered that are relevant to Chapter Seven stir-fried dishes are **beef, poultry, eggs, legumes,** and **brown rice**.
    - Reference #5 (Selecting High Quality Processed Ingredients for Use in Part II Recipes) identifies food products that have undergone some physical processing but that retain significant nutritional quality. Products relevant to Chapter Seven stir-fried recipes include **canned beans, canned whole kernel yellow corn, extra virgin olive oil, raisins, cracked whole wheat,** and **yogurt**. Products relevant to Chapter Seven accompaniments (muffins and corn bread) include **dry frozen blueberries, whole corn flour, dairy products (milk),** and **whole wheat flour**.

13. **Determined to bolster successful inclusion of whole foods in Chapter Seven dishes,** *Cooked Alive!* includes Reference #6 (Maximizing the Attractiveness of Whole Food Ingredients Commonly Used in Part II Recipes). Whole foods covered in this reference that are relevant to Chapter Seven recipes include **dried fruit, herbs and spices (dried and fresh), legumes, nuts, protein (beef, poultry, and eggs), brown rice,** and **yogurt**.

Traditional Main Dish Recipes

153. Broccoli, Carrot, and Beefsteak Stir Fry
Master Recipe
(2-3 servings)

Vegetables with Seasonings and Cooking Oil and Water

1 chilled stalk broccoli
2 medium carrots
1 T extra virgin olive oil
1 T hot water
¼ t salt
¼ each red & yellow bell pepper

½ T extra virgin olive oil
½ chilled medium yellow onion, halved lengthwise
⅛ in. thick sliced fresh ginger root
1 T extra virgin olive oil
½ t cumin seed

Other Ingredients

¼ lb sirloin tip or other lean & tender beefsteak, ½ in. thick
½–1 t curry powder
½ t garlic powder
⅛ in. thick slice fresh ginger root
1 T extra virgin olive oil

1 heaping T certified organic raisins
1 heaping T dried tart cherries
8–10 raw pecan or walnut halves or
10 raw whole almonds
1 c cooked brown rice (Recipe #166)

Accompaniments

½ c plain yogurt

approx. 1½ t natural soy sauce or ½ lemon

Cooking Tools

1 large heavy-bottomed skillet with an opaque lid
1 electric tea kettle
1 cutting board for vegetables
1 each 5 in. serrated, slicing, & chef's knife
1 set each measuring spoons & cups
1 plastic or plastic-coated stir-fry spatula
1 timer

1 rubber or other heat-resistant spatula
1 colander
1 dinner plate
1 cutting board for raw meat
1 medium mixing bowl
1 hand citrus juicer (if using lemon)

---

1. Gather all cooking tools and ingredients.

2. **Stir-fry/steam the broccoli and carrots.**

    - Heat a large skillet on a large burner at a medium setting. Heat water in an electric tea kettle for steaming.
    - Quickly rinse the broccoli in cool water, shake it to remove clinging water, wrap it within a paper or terry towel, and firmly squeeze the stalk to dry it.
    - Working on a cutting board reserved for vegetables and fruits, use a serrated knife to cut the florets from the stalk (leaving the stems as long as possible by cutting them off at the stalk), and halve the florets lengthwise. Place each floret half cut side down and halve it lengthwise. Save any leaves, halving large ones.
    - Scrub, dry thoroughly, and cut the ends from the carrots. Use a chef's knife to halve each carrot lengthwise and to cut the carrot halves crosswise into ⅛ in. thick slices.
    - Increase the skillet heat to medium-high.
    - When a drop of water added to the skillet instantly dances and disappears, add 1 T oil, add the broccoli and carrot, and stir-fry them for 1 minute, setting a timer. Stir-frying should at first be vigorous but can slow to "flip often" pace by the end of the minute.
    - Add 1 T hot water, reduce the heat to low, cover the skillet, and steam the vegetables for 4 minutes, setting a timer. For larger carrots (greater than 1 in. thick at stem end), increase steaming time to 5 minutes.
    - At the timer, remove the skillet from the heat, evenly sprinkle ¼ t salt over the vegetables, and use a rubber spatula to scrape the vegetables and any cooking juice into a colander placed over a dinner plate to catch any cooking liquid.
    - Wipe the skillet clean.

3. **Stir-fry the bell peppers.**

    - Heat the skillet at medium.
    - Use a serrated knife to cut out the stem of each pepper. Remove any seeds but not the white membrane. Use the serrated knife to cut each pepper lengthwise into ¼ in. wide strips and to cut the strips crosswise into ¼ in. cubes.
    - Increase the skillet heat to medium-high, and when a drop of water added to the skillet instantly dances and disappears, add ½ T oil, add the peppers, and stir-fry them for about 30 seconds.
    - Reduce the heat to medium and cook the peppers for two minutes, stirring occasionally and setting a timer.
    - At the timer, use a rubber spatula to scrape the peppers and any cooking juice into the colander.
    - Wipe the skillet clean.

4. **Stir-fry the beefsteak.**

    - Quickly rinse the meat with cold water and thoroughly pat it dry with a paper towel.
    - Working on a cutting board reserved for raw meat preparation, use a slicing knife to trim fat from and to cut the meat across the grain into ⅛ in. thick slices. Cut the

slices into ½ in. lengths and spread the meat over plastic wrap.
- Evenly sprinkle the ½-1 t curry and ½ t garlic powders over the meat and toss the pieces for even mixing.
- Wash your hands and knife.
- Use a serrated knife to mince a ⅛ in. thick slice of ginger root on a clean cutting board.
- Increase the skillet heat to medium-high.
- When a drop of water added to the skillet instantly dances and disappears, add 1 T oil, mix in the ginger and then the meat, and stir-fry the meat until it remains only slightly pink, about 1 minute. Remove the skillet from the heat, evenly sprinkle ¼ t salt over the meat, and use a rubber spatula to scrape it into a medium mixing bowl. Slant the container to drain any juice away from the meat.
- Wipe the skillet clean.

5. **Prepare remaining ingredients**.

- Use a chef's knife to halve 1 T tart cherries and to chop the nuts coarsely.
- Stir the yogurt creamy smooth before measuring ½ cup.
- Squeeze lemon juice if using lemon juice as an accompaniment.

6. **Assemble the dish for serving**.

- Heat the skillet at a medium setting.
- Use a chef's knife to slice the ends from the onion. Peel the onion, place it cut side down on a cutting board and dice it. Mince the ginger.
- Increase the skillet heat to medium-high, and when a drop of water added to the skillet instantly dances and disappears, add 1 T oil, add and heat ½ t cumin seed for 30 seconds, add the onion and ginger, and stir-fry the mixture for about 30 seconds.
- Reduce the heat to medium and heat the mixture for 2 minutes, stirring occasionally and setting a timer.
- At the timer, mix 1 T raisins and the dried cherries into the onion mixture.
- Spread the rice in the skillet, evenly sprinkle ¼ t salt over the rice, add any collected vegetable cooking juice, and heat the ingredients for 1 minute, stirring occasionally.
- Increase the heat to medium-high.
- Add and heat the meat, stirring it often until it is hot, 1-2 minutes.
- Add the cooked vegetables and nuts and heat them for approx. 2 minutes until they are hot, stirring often.

7. **Serve the dish**. Immediately serve individual portions topped with a few drops of soy sauce (or about ½ t fresh squeezed lemon juice) and with 3-4 T yogurt alongside.

VARIATIONS: Make ingredient substitutions. Substitute, for example,

- **8 Brussels sprouts,** boiled whole (Recipe #61), for broccoli.

- 2 medium turnips (Recipe #22), **parsnips** (Recipe #14), **kohlrabi** (Recipe #12), **rutabagas** (Recipe #19), or **parsnips** (Recipe #14) for broccoli.
- 2 c red or green cabbage (Recipe #6) for broccoli. To successfully substitute for broccoli, it is very important that the cabbage be very fresh. Cabbage that is fresh and either certified organic or locally produced cabbage is typically far more flavorful than commercially produced cabbage. Steam red cabbage for 5 minutes.
- ½ t dried marjoram leaves or ½ t each dried sweet basil and oregano leaves, first crushing them between your palms, for the spices added to the beef and onion.

Add ingredients. Add, for example,

- ½ c fresh pineapple chunks, cut into ⅓ in. thick slices (Recipe #94), which is a delicious addition.
- ¼ c pomegranate seeds (Recipe #96), which adds color in addition to tastiness.
- 2 ears yellow corn or 1 c dry frozen yellow corn, stir-fried in water (Recipe #70).
- ½ medium fresh beet, diced (Recipe #2, stir-fry/steamed; Recipe #59, boiled whole; or Recipe #39, roasted whole) or ¼ c canned or vacuum-packed (refrigerated) beets, diced.
- ⅓-½ lb greens, any variety (Recipes #23-30).
- 3-4 chilled cloves garlic (Recipe #31), cooked with the onion.

COMMENTS: Set aside the broccoli stalk and peel it for use as a tasty raw snack. Alternatively, peel and cut the stalk crosswise into ⅛ in. thick slices and cook it with the broccoli and carrots.

154. Cabbage, Kale, and Beefsteak Stir Fry
(2-3 servings)

Vegetables with Seasonings and Cooking Oil and Water

¼ wedge chilled medium head red or green cabbage (to yield 2 c sliced; see comments below)
2 medium carrots
1 T extra virgin olive oil
1 T hot water
⅓ t salt
¼ red bell pepper
⅛ each green & yellow bell pepper
½ T extra virgin olive oil
3 large kale leaves (to yield approx. 3 c sliced)

1 T extra virgin olive oil
1 T hot water
¼ t salt
½ lb uniformly small sugar snap peas
2 T water
¼ t salt
½ c chilled medium yellow onion, halved lengthwise
⅛ in. thick slice fresh ginger root
1 T extra virgin olive oil
½ t cumin seed

Other Ingredients

¼ lb sirloin tip or other lean & tender beefsteak, ½ in. thick
½ t garlic powder
½-1 t curry powder
1 T extra virgin olive oil
¼ t salt

1 heaping T certified organic raisins
1 heaping T dried tart cherries
8-10 raw pecan or walnut halves or 10 raw whole almonds
1 c cooked brown rice (Recipe #166)

Accompaniments

½ c plain yogurt

approx. 1½ t natural soy sauce or ½ lemon

Cooking Tools

1 large heavy-bottomed skillet with a tight-fitting & opaque lid
1 electric tea kettle
1 each chef's & slicing knife
1 each 5 in. & 7 in. serrated knife
1 cutting board for vegetables & fruits
1 set each measuring spoons & cups
1 plastic or plastic-coated stir fry spatula

1 timer
1 rubber or other heat-resistant spatula
1 colander
1 dinner plate
1 cutting board for raw meat
1 medium mixing bowl
1 hand citrus juicer (if using lemon)

---

1. **Gather all cooking tools and dish ingredients.**

2. **Stir-fry/steam the cabbage and carrot.**

   - Heat a large skillet on a large burner at a medium setting. Heat an electric kettle for steaming water.
   - Place the ¼ cabbage wedge cut side down on a cutting board reserved for vegetables and fruits. Use a chef's knife to slice off ½-1 inches of the tip of the wedge, which removes a portion of the thick central core, setting it aside. Use the chef's knife to slice the cabbage wedge lengthwise into ⅓ in. thick slices. Cut the slices into thirds. Pick through the sliced cabbage to separate very thick pieces. Use the chef's knife to chop thick pieces, including the wedge tip, into thin (⅛ in. thick) pieces so all cabbage pieces cook uniformly.
   - Scrub and thoroughly dry the carrots. Use a chef's knife to slice off the stem end and tip of each carrot, split each carrot lengthwise, and cut the carrot halves crosswise into even ⅛ in. thick slices.
   - Increase the skillet heat to medium-high.
   - When a drop of water added to the skillet instantly dances and disappears, add 1 T oil, add the cabbage and carrots, and stir-fry them for 1 minute, setting a timer.

PART 2

Stir-frying should at first be vigorous to quickly and thoroughly coat pieces with oil but can slow to "flip often" pace midway through the minute.
- Add 1 T hot water, cover the skillet, reduce the heat to low, and steam the cabbage and carrots for 4 minutes, setting a timer.
- At the timer, remove the skillet from the heat, evenly sprinkle ⅓ t salt over the vegetables, and use a rubber spatula to scrape them into a colander placed over a dinner plate for collecting any spilled juice.
- Wipe the skillet clean.

3. **Stir-fry the bell pepper.**

   - Heat the skillet at a medium setting.
   - Use a 5 in. serrated knife to cut out the stem of the pepper. Remove any seeds but not the white membrane from the peppers. Use the serrated knife to cut the pepper lengthwise into ¼ in. wide strips and to cut the strips crosswise into ¼ in. cubes.
   - Increase the skillet heat to medium-high, and when a drop of water added to the skillet instantly dances and disappears, add ½ T oil, add the pepper, and stir-fry it for about 30 seconds.
   - Reduce the heat to medium and cook the pepper for 2 minutes, stirring occasionally and setting a timer.
   - At the timer, use a rubber spatula to scrape the pepper and any cooking juice into the colander with the other vegetables.
   - Wipe the skillet clean.

4. **Stir-fry/steam the kale.**

   - Heat the skillet at a medium setting. Heat an electric tea kettle to ready steaming water.
   - For unwashed kale, add the leaves to a sink or large bowl filled with enough cold water to cover the leaves completely. Swish each leaf in the water, rub your thumb over both sides, re-swish the leaf in the water, shake off clinging water, and place it in a colander. When all leaves are rinsed, spread them in a single layer over a strip of paper towels or a terry cloth towel. Pat flat leaves dry. Add a top layer of towels to curly leaves, roll the leaves in the towels, and gently squeeze the leaves to dry them thoroughly. Unroll the leaves and pat dry any wet spots.
   - Working on a large cutting board, use a 5 in. serrated knife to cut out the central vein of each leaf. Cutting close to the vein, cut the leaves from either side of the vein, setting the veins with attached stems aside as they are removed.
   - Stack the leaves, facing leaves in the same direction. Holding the leaves together with one hand and using a 7 in. serrated knife, cut the leaves into approx. ⅓ in. thick pieces, cutting lengthwise and crosswise through the leaves.
   - Holding the veins/stems together with one hand and keeping them separate from the leaves, use a chef's knife to finely chop the veins/stems.
   - Increase the skillet heat to medium-high.
   - When a drop of water added to the skillet instantly dances and disappears, add 1 T

oil, add the chopped veins/stems, and cook them, stirring them frequently for about 30 seconds.

- Add the kale leaves and stir-fry them for 1 minute, setting a timer. This stir-frying should remain vigorous in order to thoroughly coat the pieces of kale with oil and to heat all pieces through.
- At the timer, add 1 T hot water, reduce the heat to low, cover the skillet, and steam the kale for 4 minutes, setting a timer.
- At the timer, remove the skillet from the heat, evenly sprinkle ¼ t salt over the kale, and scrape the kale and any cooking juice onto the other vegetables.
- Wipe the skillet clean.

5. **Stir-fry the sugar snap peas in water.**

- Heat a medium skillet at a medium setting.
- Rinse the pea pods with cool water, spread them over paper towels, wrap the towels around them, and gently squeeze the pods to dry them thoroughly.
- Add 2 T water to the skillet, increase the heat to high, and bring the water to boiling.
- Add the pea pods and, when the water returns to a boil, stir-fry them for 1 minute, setting a timer.
- Reduce the heat to medium and continue heating the pea pods for another minute, stirring them occasionally and setting a timer.
- Remove the skillet from the heat, evenly sprinkle ¼ t salt over the pea pods, and use a rubber spatula to scrape them and any cooking juice onto the kale.
- Wipe the skillet clean.

6. **Stir-fry the beefsteak.**

- Quickly rinse the beefsteak with cold water and thoroughly pat it dry with a paper towel.
- Working on a cutting board reserved for raw meat, use a slicing knife to trim off fat and cut the meat across the grain into ⅛ in. wide slices. Cut the slices into ½ in. lengths and spread the meat over plastic wrap. Evenly sprinkle ½-1 t curry powder and ½ t garlic powder over the meat and toss the meat for even mixing. Wash your hands and knife.
- Working on a clean cutting board, mince the ginger root.
- Increase the skillet heat to medium-high.
- When a drop of water added to the skillet instantly dances and disappears, add 1 T oil, add the meat and ginger, and stir-fry the meat until it is slightly pink, about 1 minute.
- Remove the skillet from the heat, evenly sprinkle ¼ t salt over the meat, and scrape it into a medium mixing bowl, slanting the bowl to drain any juice away from the meat.
- Wipe the skillet clean.

7. **Prepare remaining ingredients.**

- Use a chef's knife to halve the tart cherries and to chop the nuts coarsely.
- Stir the yogurt creamy smooth before measuring ½ cup.
- Cut off the tips and halve each sugar snap pea crosswise.
- Squeeze the lemon if using lemon juice as an accompaniment.

8. **Assemble the dish for serving.**

   - Heat the skillet at a medium setting.
   - Use a chef's knife to slice the ends from the onion. Peel the onion, place it cut side down on a cutting board, and use the chef's knife to dice it. Mince the ginger.
   - Increase the skillet heat to medium-high.
   - When a drop of water added to the skillet instantly dances and disappears, add 1 T oil, add ½ t cumin seed, and cook the seeds for 30 seconds, stirring them occasionally.
   - Add the onion and ginger and stir fry them for about 30 seconds. Reduce the heat to medium and cook the onion/ginger mixture for 2 minutes, stirring it occasionally and setting a timer.
   - Mix in 1 heaping T raisins and the dried cherries.
   - Spread the rice in the skillet, evenly sprinkle ¼ t salt over it, add any collected vegetable cooking juice, and mix in the rice.
   - Increase the skillet heat to medium-high, add the meat, and heat the rice and meat until hot, one or two minutes. Add and heat the cooked vegetables and nuts for approx. 2 minutes until all ingredients are hot, stirring often.

9. **Serve the dish.** Immediately serve individual portions topped with a few drops of soy sauce (or approx. ½ t fresh squeezed lemon juice) and with 3-4 T yogurt alongside.

   VARIATIONS: Make ingredient substitutions. Substitute, for example,

   - **8 Brussels sprouts**, boiled whole (Recipe 61), **½ lb bok choy** (Recipe #3), or **⅓ head cauliflower** (Recipe #8) for cabbage. Evenly sprinkle ½ t curry powder over the cauliflower while it stir-fries.
   - **3 large chard leaves** (Recipe #24), **8 medium beet greens** (Recipe #23), **3 medium collards** (Recipe #25) or **½ lb spinach** (Recipe #28 or #29) for kale.
   - **2 c dry frozen green peas** (Recipe #71) for sugar snap peas.

   Add ingredients. Add, for example,

   - **1 leek** (Recipe #34) or **2 green onions** (Recipe #34), including the green tops.
   - **2 ears corn** or **1½ c dry frozen yellow whole kernel corn**, stir-fried in water (Recipe #65).
   - **½ beet**, diced; boiled whole (Recipe #59), canned, or vacuum-packed.
   - **4-6 chilled cloves garlic** (Recipe #34).
   - **1 turnip** (Recipe #22) or **2 parsnips** (Recipe #14).
   - **½ c fresh pineapple chunks**, cut into ⅓ in. thick slices (Recipe #94). Pineapple is a delicious addition.

- ¼ c **pomegranate seeds** (Recipe #96), which adds color in addition to tastiness, or add pomegranate with pineapple.
- ¼ c **cranberries**. Stir-fry the cranberries in 3 T orange juice for 1 minute, simmered another minute, and mixed with 2 t sugar. Cranberries add lovely color and tart flavor.
- ½ c **drained cooked black beans** or **red kidney beans**. Add them with the brown rice and heat them through before adding the cooked vegetables for serving.

COMMENTS: To cut a ¼ wedge of cabbage, halve a head of cabbage lengthwise. Place one half cut side down on a cutting surface and halve it lengthwise. Immediately tightly cover the unused ¾ cabbage head (in two pieces) with plastic wrap and refrigerate it.

For the most reliably tasty cabbage, select very fresh and either certified organic or locally grown cabbage. For the most nutritious cabbage, select red cabbage.

155. Sweet Potato, Broccoli, Pineapple, and Beefsteak Stir Fry
(3 servings)

Vegetables and Pineapple with Seasonings and Cooking Oil and Water

2 chilled medium sweet potatoes
1 T extra virgin olive oil
1 T hot water
¼ t salt
1 chilled stalk broccoli
1 T extra virgin olive oil
1 T hot water
¼ t salt

⅓ red bell pepper
½ c fresh pineapple chunks (Recipe #94)
½ chilled medium yellow onion, halved lengthwise
1 T extra virgin olive oil
⅛ in. thick slice fresh ginger root
½ t cumin seed

Other Ingredients

¼ lb sirloin tip or other tender & lean beefsteak, ½ in. thick
½-1 t curry powder
½ t garlic powder
⅛ in. thick slice of fresh ginger root
1 T extra virgin olive oil

1 heaping T certified organic raisins
1 heaping T dried tart cherries
8-10 raw pecan or walnut halves or raw whole almonds
1 c cooked brown rice (Recipe #166)

Accompaniments

½ c plain yogurt

approx. 1½ t natural soy sauce or ½ lemon

PART 2

Cooking Tools

2 large heavy-bottomed skillets, both with
    a tight-fitting & opaque lid
1 electric tea kettle
1 cutting board for vegetables & fruits
1 each chef's, 5 in. serrated, & slicing knife
1 set each measuring spoons & cups
1 plastic or plastic-coated stir-fry spatula

1 timer
1 rubber or other heat-resistant spatula
1 colander
1 dinner plate
1 cutting board reserved for raw meat
1 medium mixing bowl
1 hand citrus juicer (if using lemon)

---

1. **Gather all cooking tools and dish ingredients.**

2. **Stir-fry/steam the sweet potato.**

    - Heat a large skillet on a large back burner at a medium setting. Heat an electric tea kettle to prepare hot water for steaming.
    - Scrub and thoroughly dry the sweet potatoes. Use a chef's knife to slice off the ends and any blemished skin. Stand each potato upright on a flattened end cut the potatoes lengthwise into ¼ in. thick slices. Stacking two slices together, cut the slices lengthwise into ¼ in. thick strips. Cut the strips crosswise to make ¼ in. cubes.
    - Increase the skillet heat to medium high. When a drop of water added to the skillet instantly dances and disappears, add 1 T oil, add the sweet potato, and stir-fry it for 1 minute, setting a timer. Stir-frying should at first be vigorous but can slow to "flip often" pace midway through the minute.
    - At the timer, reduce the heat to medium (oil should sizzle gently around potato pieces) and heat the potato for 1 minute, stirring it occasionally and setting a timer.
    - At the timer, add 1 T hot water, reduce the heat to a low setting, tightly cover the skillet, and steam the potato for 10 minutes, setting a timer.
    - At the timer, turn off the heat, uncover the potato, and evenly sprinkle ¼ t salt over the potato.
    - Re-cover the skillet and set the potato aside.

3. **Stir-fry/steam the broccoli while the sweet potatoes cook.**

    - Heat another large skillet on a large burner at a medium setting. Heat an electric tea kettle for steaming water.
    - Rinse the broccoli stalk in cool water, shake it to remove excess clinging water, wrap it in paper towels or a terry cloth towel, and firmly squeeze the stalk to dry it thoroughly.
    - Use a 5 in. serrated knife to cut the florets from the stalk, leaving the stems as long as possible (cutting them off at the stalk) and saving leaves.

- Halve the florets lengthwise, place the halves cut side down on a cutting board, and use a serrated knife to halve them. Cut large halves into ¼ in. thick slices. Cut any large leaves into 2-3 pieces.
- Increase the skillet heat to medium-high. When a drop of water added to the skillet instantly dances and disappears, add 1 T oil, add the broccoli, and stir-fry it for 1 minute, setting a timer. Stir-frying should at first be vigorous but can slow to "flip often" pace by the end of the minute.
- At the timer, add 1 T hot water, reduce the heat to low, tightly cover the skillet, and steam the broccoli for 4 minutes, setting a timer.
- At the timer, remove the skillet from the heat, evenly sprinkle ¼ t salt over the broccoli, and use a rubber spatula to scrape the broccoli and any cooking juice into a colander placed over a dinner plate. Wipe the skillet clean.

4. **Stir-fry the red pepper**.

    - Heat the skillet at medium.
    - Use a 5 in. serrated knife to cut out the stem of the pepper. Remove any seeds but not the white membrane. Use the serrated knife to cut the pepper lengthwise into ¼ in. wide strips and to cut the slices crosswise into ¼ in. cubes.
    - Increase the skillet heat to medium-high. When a drop of water added to the skillet instantly dances and disappears, add ½ T oil, add the pepper, and stir-fry it for about 30 seconds.
    - Reduce the heat to medium and cook the pepper for 2 minutes, stirring it occasionally and setting a timer.
    - At the timer, use a rubber spatula to scrape the pepper and any cooking juice into the colander with the broccoli.

5. **Prepare the pineapple**. Use a serrated knife to cut the chunks into ¼ in. slices; halve the slices crosswise.

6. **Stir-fry the meat**.

    - Quickly rinse the beefsteak with cold water, pat it dry with a paper towel, and, working on a cutting board reserved for raw meat, use a slicing knife to trim off fat and to cut the meat across the grain into ⅛ in. wide slices. Cut the slices into ½ in. lengths and spread the meat over plastic wrap.
    - Evenly sprinkle ½-1 t curry powder and ½ t garlic powder over the meat and toss the meat for even mixing.
    - Wash your hands and the knife with soap.
    - Use a serrated knife to mince the ginger root on a clean cutting board.
    - Increase the skillet heat to medium-high. When a drop of water added to the skillet instantly dances and disappears, add 1 T oil, add and mix in the meat and ginger root, and cook the meat about 1 minute until it remains only slightly pink, turning it over frequently.
    - Remove the skillet from the heat, evenly sprinkle ¼ t salt over the meat, and scrape

it and any cooking juice into a medium mixing bowl, slanting the bowl to drain juice away from the meat.
- Wipe the skillet clean.

7. **Prepare remaining ingredients.**

- Use a chef's knife to halve the tart cherries and to chop the nuts coarsely.
- Stir the yogurt creamy smooth before measuring ½ cup.
- Squeeze fresh lemon juice if using lemon as an accompaniment.

8. **Assemble the dish for serving.**

- Heat the skillet at a medium setting.
- Use a chef's knife to slice the ends from the onion. Peel the onion, place it cut side down on a cutting board, and dice it. Mince the ginger root.
- Increase the skillet heat to medium-high, and when a drop of water added to the skillet instantly dances and disappears, add 1 T oil, add ½ t cumin seed, and heat the cumin seed for 30 seconds, stirring it occasionally.
- Add the onion and ginger and stir-fry the mixture for 30 seconds. Reduce the heat to medium and cook the mixture for 2 minutes, stirring occasionally and setting a timer.
- At the timer, mix 1 heaping T each raisins and dried cherries and the nuts into the onion mixture, spread the rice over the skillet, evenly sprinkle ¼ t salt over the rice, mix the salt into the rice, add any collected vegetable cooking juice, and add the sweet potato to the skillet.
- Increase the heat to medium-high. Add the meat and any meat juice and heat the ingredients for 2 minutes, stirring frequently and setting a timer.
- At the timer, add the cooked vegetables held in the colander and heat the ingredients for 2 minutes until the vegetables are hot, stirring frequently.
- Immediately serve the dish with individual portions topped with a few drops of soy sauce (or approx. ½ t fresh squeezed lemon juice) and with 3-4 T yogurt alongside.

VARIATIONS: Make ingredient substitutions. Substitute, for example,

- ¼ c **pomegranate seeds** (Recipe #96) or ¼ c **fresh cranberries** for pineapple. For cranberries, stir-fry rinsed cranberries in 2 T orange juice at high heat for 1 minute, or until the berries break open (adding more juice, if necessary). Remove the skillet from the burner and mix in 2 t sugar.
- 8 **Brussels sprouts**, boiled whole (Recipe #61) for broccoli.
- 2 c diced **butternut squash** for sweet potato. Use either stir-fried/steamed squash (Recipe #21), baked squash (Recipe #51; using the flesh from the long thin end), or frozen cubed squash.
- ½ t **dried herb leaves** for spices added to the beef and onion. For example, use marjoram, sweet basil, or oregano leaves, first crushing the leaves between your palms.

Add ingredients. Add, for example,

- **2 medium carrots** (Recipe #7).
- **1 leek** or **2 green onions** (Recipe #34), including the green tops.
- **3 large kale leaves** (Recipe #26), **3 large leaves chard** (Recipe #24), **½ lb spinach** (Recipe #28 or 29), or **4-5 c other sliced raw greens**.
- **2 ears corn** or **1½ c dry frozen whole kernel yellow corn**, stir-fried in water (Recipe #65).
- **2 c small sugar snap or snow peas** or **1½ c dry frozen greens**, stir-fried in water (Recipe #71).
- **½ beet**, boiled whole (Recipe #59) or canned, diced.
- **1 medium turnip** (Recipe #22) or **2 parsnips** (Recipe #14).
- **½ lb bok choy** (Recipe #3).
- **1 mild green chili pepper** or **1-2 jalapeño peppers**, stir-fried (Recipe #36).
- **4-6 chilled garlic cloves** (Recipe #31).
- **2-3 dried apricots**. Cut the apricots into ¼ in. thick strips; halve the strips.
- **3 T stirred canned coconut milk**. To enhance coconut flavoring, mix ½-1 T dried coconut powder into the coconut milk and/or add 2-3 T dried unsweetened shredded coconut (softened by soaking it in 2 T boiling water in a small, covered skillet as a first recipe step).

156. Zucchini, Chard, Corn, and Beefsteak Stir Fry
(Herb and Tomato Flavoring)
(2-3 servings)

Vegetables with Seasonings and Cooking Oil and Water

2 small zucchini
1 T extra virgin olive oil
½ t each dried sweet basil & oregano leaves
¼ t salt
2 medium carrots
1 T extra virgin olive oil
½ T hot water
¼ t salt
2 ears yellow corn
2 T water

¼ t salt
¼ each red & green bell pepper
½ T extra virgin olive oil
3 large chard leaves
1 T extra virgin olive oil
1 T hot water
¼ t salt
½ chilled medium yellow onion, halved lengthwise
⅛ in. thick slice fresh ginger root

Other Ingredients

¼ lb sirloin tip or other lean & tender beefsteak, ½ in. thick
½ t curry powder

1 heaping T dried tart cherries
8-10 raw pecan or walnut halves or raw whole almonds

PART 2

½ t garlic powder
1 T extra virgin olive oil
¼ t salt
⅛ in. thick slice fresh ginger root
1 heaping T certified organic raisins

1 c cooked brown rice (Recipe #166) &
    ¼ t salt
2 T tomato juice
3 T tomato paste

Accompaniments

½ c plain yogurt

Cooking Tools

1 large heavy-bottomed skillet with a
    tight-fitting & opaque lid
1 cutting board reserved for vegetables
1 each chef's and slicing knife
1 each 5 in. & 7 in. serrated knife
1 set each measuring spoons & cups
1 plastic or plastic-coated stir-fry spatula
1 timer

1 rubber or other heat-resistant spatula
1 colander
1 dinner plate
1 electric tea kettle
1 pie plate
1 large cutting board (approx. 16 x 24 in.)
1 cutting board reserved for raw meat
1 medium mixing bowl

---

1. **Gather all cooking tools and dish ingredients.**

2. **Stir-fry/steam the zucchini.**

   - Heat a large skillet on a large burner at a medium setting.
   - Rinse and dry the zucchini.
   - Working on a cutting board reserved for vegetables, use a chef's knife to cut off the tips, stand the zucchini upright and cut it lengthwise into ¼ in. wide slices, and cut the slices lengthwise into ¼ in. wide strips. Holding several the strips together with one hand, slice them crosswise into ¼ in. cubes.
   - Increase the skillet heat to medium-high. When a drop of water instantly dances and disappears, add 1 T oil, add the zucchini, evenly sprinkle ½ t each dried basil and oregano leaves (first crushing them between your palms) over the zucchini, and stir-fry the zucchini for 1 minute, setting a timer. This stir-frying should at first be vigorous but can slow to "flip often" pace midway through the minute.
   - At the timer, reduce the heat to low, cover the skillet, and steam the zucchini for 4 minutes, setting a timer. (The zucchini steams in its own juices.)
   - At the timer, remove the skillet from the heat, evenly sprinkle ¼ t salt over the zucchini, and use a rubber spatula to scrape it and any cooking juice into a colander placed over a dinner plate.
   - Wipe the skillet clean.

3. **Stir-fry/steam the carrots.**

    - Heat the skillet at a medium setting. Heat an electric tea kettle to prepare water for steaming.
    - Scrub and thoroughly dry the carrots. Use a chef's knife to cut off the ends, halve lengthwise, and cut the carrots crosswise into ⅛ in. thick slices.
    - Increase the skillet heat to medium-high. When a drop of water added to the skillet instantly dances and disappears, add 1 T oil, add the carrot, and stir-fry it for 1 minute, setting a timer. Stir-frying should at first be vigorous but can slow to "flip often" pace.
    - At the timer, add ½ T hot water, reduce the heat to low, cover the skillet, and steam the carrots for 4 minutes, setting a timer.
    - At the timer, remove the skillet from the heat, evenly sprinkle ¼ t salt over the carrots, and use a rubber spatula to scrape them and any cooking juice into the colander along with the zucchini.
    - Wipe the skillet clean.

4. **Stir-fry the corn.**

    - Heat the skillet at a medium setting.
    - Remove the husks and corn silk from the ears. Stand each ear upright in a pie plate and use a chef's knife to slice off the kernels, cutting close to the cob to include the corn germ.
    - Bring 2 T water to boiling over high heat in the skillet, thoroughly mix the corn into the water, and once the water returns to boiling, stir-fry the corn for approx. 1 minute, just until it is hot and its color darkens slightly.
    - Remove the skillet from the heat, evenly sprinkle ¼ t salt over the corn, and use a rubber spatula to scrape the corn and any cooking liquid into the colander with the zucchini and carrots.
    - Wipe the skillet clean.

5. **Stir-fry the bell peppers.**

    - Heat the skillet at a medium setting.
    - Use a 5 in. serrated knife to cut out the stem of each pepper. Remove any seeds but not the white membrane. Use the 5 in. serrated knife to cut the peppers lengthwise into ¼ in. wide strips and to cut the strips crosswise into ¼ in. cubes.
    - Increase the skillet heat to medium-high, and when a drop of water added to the skillet instantly dances and disappears, add ½ T oil, add the peppers, and stir-fry them for about 30 seconds.
    - Reduce the heat to medium and cook the peppers for two minutes, stirring occasionally and setting a timer.
    - At the timer, remove the skillet from the burner and use a rubber spatula to scrape the peppers and any cooking juice onto the other cooked vegetables.
    - Wipe the skillet clean.

6. **Stir-fry/steam the chard.**

    - Heat the skillet at medium. Heat an electric tea kettle to ready hot water for steaming.
    - For unwashed chard, add the leaves to a sink or large bowl filled with enough cold water to cover them completely. Swish each leaf in the water, rub your thumb over both sides of each leaf or rub each leaf between your hands, re-swish the leaf in the water, shake off clinging water, and place it in a colander.
    - When all leaves are rinsed, spread them in a single layer over a strip of paper towels or a terry cloth towel. Add a top layer of towels, roll the leaves in the towels, and gently squeeze the leaves to dry them thoroughly. Unroll the leaves and pat dry any wet spots.
    - Slice off the bottom tip of each stem. Use a 5 in. serrated knife to cut out the thick vein running through the center of each leaf, cutting close to each side of the vein. Set the veins with attached stem aside.
    - Working on a large cutting board, stack the leaves, forming two or three stacks, and facing leaves in the same way. Holding the leaves in place with one hand, use a 7 in. serrated knife to slice the leaves into small (⅓ in. thick) pieces, cutting first lengthwise and then crosswise through the leaves. Keep the leaves and vein/stems separate.
    - Holding the veins/stems together with one hand, use a chef's knife to chop them thinly.
    - Increase the skillet heat to medium-high. When a drop of water added to the skillet instantly dances and disappears, add 1 T oil, add the vein/stems, and cook them for about 30 seconds, stirring them occasionally.
    - Add the chard leaves and stir-fry them constantly for 1 minute until the leaves wilt slightly.
    - Add 1 T hot water, cover the skillet, reduce the heat setting to low, and steam the chard for 4 minutes, setting a timer.
    - At the timer, remove the skillet from the heat, evenly sprinkle ¼ t salt over the chard, and use a rubber spatula to scrape it and any juice into the colander with the other vegetables.
    - Wipe the skillet clean.

7. **Stir-fry the beefsteak.**

    - Heat the skillet at a medium setting.
    - Quickly rinse the beefsteak with cold water and thoroughly pat it dry with paper towels. Working on a cutting board reserved for raw meat, trim fat from and cut the steak across the grain into thin (⅛ in. wide) slices. Cut the slices into ½ in. lengths and spread the meat over plastic wrap.
    - Evenly sprinkle ½ t each dried basil and oregano leaves (first crushing the leaves between your palms) and ½ t garlic powder over the meat and toss the meat for even mixing.
    - Wash your hands and knife with soap.

- Peel and mince the ginger root on a clean cutting board.
- Increase the skillet heat to medium-high, and when a drop of water added to the skillet instantly dances and disappears, add 1 T oil, add the meat and ginger, and stir-fry the meat for approx. 1 minute, turning it over and over until it is only slightly pink.
- Remove the skillet from the heat, evenly sprinkle ¼ t salt over the meat, and scrape it into a medium mixing bowl, slanting the bowl to drain juice away from the meat and covering the meat to keep it warm.
- Wipe the skillet clean.

8. **Prepare remaining ingredients.**

- Use a chef's knife to halve the 1 T tart cherries and to chop the 8-10 nuts coarsely.
- Stir the yogurt creamy smooth before measuring ½ cup.
- Measure 3 T tomato paste; open a tomato juice container.

9. **Assemble the dish for serving.**

- Heat the skillet at a medium setting.
- Use a chef's knife to slice the ends from the onion. Peel the onion, place it cut side down on a cutting board, and dice it. Mince the ginger.
- Increase the skillet heat to medium-high, and when a drop of water added to the skillet instantly dances and disappears, add 1 T oil, add the onion and ginger, evenly sprinkle ½ t each dried basil and oregano leaves (first crushing them between your palms) over the onion, and stir-fry the mixture for about 30 seconds. Reduce the heat to medium and cook the onion mixture for 2 minutes, stirring it occasionally and setting a timer.
- At the timer, mix 1 heaping T raisins, the dried cherries, and the nuts into the onion mixture. Add and mix in 2 T tomato juice and 3 T tomato paste. Spread ½ c cooked rice over the skillet, evenly sprinkle ¼ t salt over the rice, add any collected vegetable cooking juice, and mix the rice into the other ingredients.
- Increase the skillet heat to medium-high, add the meat, and heat the meat for approx. 1 minute, until it is hot, stirring often.
- Add the cooked vegetables and heat the the dish for approx. 2 minutes until all ingredients are very hot, stirring often.
- Immediately serve individual portions with 3-4 T yogurt alongside each serving.

VARIATIONS: Make ingredient substitutions. Substitute, for example,

- **2 small (4 in. long) crookneck yellow squash** or **5-6 in. long straightneck yellow summer squash** for zucchini, cooking it in exactly the same way. Remove the long neck of crookneck squash, slice it crosswise into ¼ in. thick slices, and cook it with the rest of the yellow squash.
- **4-6 medium kale leaves** (Recipe #26) or **6-8 medium beet greens** (Recipe #23) for chard.

- 1-2 c **organic dry frozen yellow whole kernel corn**, stir-fried in water (Recipe #65), for fresh corn.
- 1 T **dried tomato** for tart cherries. As a first recipe step add 2-3 dried tomatoes to a small heat proof container with a lid, add 3 T boiling water, and set the container aside, covered. Use a chef's knife to dice the tomato into ⅛ in. cubes in Step #8.
- ½ t **dried marjoram leaves** for sweet basil and oregano leaves, first crushing them between your palms, wherever basil and oregano are used in the recipe.
- ½ t **curry powder** for dried sweet basil and oregano leaves wherever basil and oregano are used in the recipe. Cook **1 t cumin seed** with the onion, cooking it for 30 seconds before adding the onion.

Add ingredients. Add, for example,

- 5-6 **grape tomatoes**, stir-fried (Recipe #37). Add the cooked tomatoes as a very last ingredient when assembling the dish for serving, after all other ingredients are hot.
- 2 **green onions** or **1 leek** (Recipe #34), including the green tops.
- ⅛ **yellow bell pepper**, prepared like and cooked with the other bell pepper.
- ½ **globe eggplant** or **one 6 in. long and ½ in. thick Japanese eggplant** (Recipe #11).
- 1 **medium turnip** (Recipe #22) or ½ **medium rutabaga** (Recipe #19).
- 1 **green chili** or **1-2 jalapeño peppers** (Recipe #36), cooking them with the bell pepper. Add chili peppers after the bell peppers have stir-fried for 30 seconds and stir-fry the combined peppers for 30 seconds before reducing the heat to medium and cooking the peppers another 2 minutes.
- 4-6 **garlic cloves** (Recipe #31), either cooking them separately or with the onion.
- 1 c **organic dry frozen green peas** (Recipe #71), stir-fried in water.

157. Brussels Sprouts, Kale, Pineapple, and Chicken Stir Fry
(2-3 servings)

Vegetables with Seasonings and Cooking Oil and Water

8 small or medium Brussels sprouts
¼ t salt
2 medium carrots
1 T extra virgin olive oil
½ T hot water
¼ t salt
⅓ red bell pepper
1 t extra virgin olive oil
3 large kale leaves

1 T extra virgin olive oil
1 T hot water
¼ t salt
½ c fresh pineapple chunks (Recipe #94)
½ chilled medium yellow onion, halved lengthwise
⅛ in. thick slice fresh ginger root
1 T toasted sesame oil
½ t cumin seeds

Other Ingredients

½ chicken breast or 2-3 oz chicken tenders
½-1 t curry powder
¼ t ground ginger
½ t ground cinnamon
½ t garlic powder
⅛ in. thick slice fresh ginger root

1 T toasted sesame oil
1 heaping T certified organic raisins
1 heaping T dried tart cherries
8-10 raw pecan or walnut halves or raw whole almonds
1 c cooked brown rice (Recipe #166)

Accompaniments

½ c plain yogurt

1-1½ t natural soy sauce or ½ lemon

Cooking Tools

1 medium saucepan
1 timer
1 colander
1 medium bowl
1 large heavy-bottomed skillet with a tight-fitting & opaque lid
1 electric tea kettle
1 large cutting board (approx. 16 x 24 in.)
1 each chef's & slicing knife

1 each 5 in. & 7 in. serrated knife
1 set each measuring spoons & cups
1 plastic or plastic-coated stir-fry spatula
1 timer
1 rubber or other heat-resistant spatula
1 dinner plate
1 cutting board for raw chicken
1 hand citrus juicer if using lemon juice

---

1. **Gather all cooking tools and dish ingredients.**

2. **Boil the Brussels sprouts whole.**

   - Add enough water to cover the sprouts by several inches to a medium saucepan and heat the water to boiling over high heat.
   - Rinse the sprouts and remove any limp outer leaves but do not trim the sprouts in any other way.
   - When the water reaches full boiling, add the Brussels sprouts, adding them slowly so that the boiling does not slow. Immediately set the timer for 3 minutes and, at the timer, immediately drain the sprouts into a colander and rinse them with cold water.
   - Transfer the sprouts to a medium bowl lined with a paper towel and evenly sprinkle ¼ t salt over them.

3. **Stir-fry/steam the carrots.**

   - Heat a large skillet at a medium setting. Heat an electric tea kettle to ready steaming

water.
- Scrub, dry thoroughly, and use a chef's knife to cut off the ends, halve lengthwise, and cut the carrots crosswise into ⅛ in. thick slices.
- Increase the skillet heat to medium-high. When a drop of water instantly dances and disappears, add 1 T oil, add the carrots, and stir-fry them for 1 minute, setting a timer. Stir-frying should at first be vigorous but can slow to "flip often" pace.
- At the timer, add ½ T hot water, reduce the heat to low, cover the pan, and steam the carrot for 4 minutes, setting a timer.
- At the timer, remove the pan from the heat, evenly sprinkle ¼ t salt over the carrots, and use a rubber spatula to scrape them and any cooking juice into a colander with the Brussels sprouts.
- Wipe the skillet clean.

4. **Stir-fry the bell pepper.**

   - Heat the skillet at medium.
   - Use a 5 in. serrated knife to cut out the stem of the pepper. Remove any seeds but not the membrane. Use the serrated knife to cut the pepper lengthwise into ¼ in. wide strips and to cut the strips crosswise into ¼ in. cubes.
   - Increase the skillet heat to medium-high. When a drop of water added to the skillet instantly dances and disappears, add 1 t oil, add the pepper, and stir-fry it for about 30 seconds. Reduce the heat to medium and cook the pepper, stirring it occasionally for 2 minutes, setting a timer.
   - At the timer, remove the skillet from the heat and use a rubber spatula to scrape the pepper and any juice onto the other cooked vegetables.
   - Wipe the skillet clean.

5. **Stir-fry/steam the kale.**

   - For unwashed kale, add the leaves to a sink or large bowl filled with enough cold water to cover them completely. Swish each leaf in the water, rub your thumb over both sides, re-swish the leaf in the water, shake off clinging water, and place it in a colander. When all leaves are rinsed, spread them in a single layer over a strip of paper or terry cloth towels. Pat flat leaves dry. Add a top layer of towels to curly leaves, roll the leaves in the towels, and gently squeeze the leaves to dry them thoroughly. Unroll the leaves and pat dry any wet spots.
   - Heat the skillet at a medium setting. Heat an electric kettle to ready steaming water.
   - Using a 5 in. serrated knife and cutting close to the stem, cut the leaves from either side of the central vein of each leaf. Set the veins with attached stems aside.
   - Working on a large cutting board, roughly stack the leaves, forming several piles and facing leaves in the same direction. While roughly holding the leaves together with one hand, use a 7 in. serrated knife to cut the leaves into approx. ⅓ in. thick pieces, slicing lengthwise and crosswise through the leaves.
   - Holding the veins/stems together with one hand and keeping them separate from the kale leaves, use a chef's knife to thinly chop them.

- Increase the skillet heat to medium-high, and when a drop of water added to the skillet instantly dances and disappears, add 1 T oil, add the stems, and cook them for about 30 seconds, stirring them occasionally. Add the kale leaves and stir-fry them for 1 minute, constantly flipping them and setting a timer.
- At the timer, add 1 T hot water, reduce the heat to low, cover the skillet, and steam the kale for 4 minutes, setting a timer.
- At the timer, remove the skillet from the heat, evenly sprinkle ¼ t salt over the kale, and use a rubber spatula to scrape the kale and any cooking juice into the colander with the other cooked vegetables.
- Wipe the skillet clean.

6. **Prepare the pineapple.** Cut the chunks into ⅓ in. thick slices. Add the chunks to the colander with the cooked vegetables.

7. **Stir-fry the chicken.**

    - Heat the large skillet at low heat on a medium burner.
    - Quickly rinse the chicken under cool, running water and pat it dry with a paper towel.
    - Working on a cutting board reserved for preparing raw meat, use a slicing knife to cut the chicken into ¼ in. wide strips, discarding any white membrane and fat. Slice the strips into ½ in. lengths and spread the chicken over plastic wrap.
    - Evenly sprinkle the spices (½-1 t curry, ¼ t ginger powder, ½ t ground cinnamon, and ½ t garlic powder) over the chicken and toss the pieces for even mixing.
    - Wash your hands and knife with soap.
    - Using the clean vegetable cutting board, mince a ⅛ in. thick slice of ginger root.
    - Increase the skillet heat to medium-high. When a drop of water added to the skillet instantly dances and disappears, add 1 T toasted sesame oil, add the chicken and ginger root, and stir-fry them for 1 minute, setting a timer. Stir-frying should at first be vigorous but can slow to "flip often" pace.
    - At the timer, reduce the heat to medium (oil should sizzle gently around pieces of chicken) and cook the chicken for 2 minutes, stirring it occasionally and setting a timer.
    - At the timer, remove the skillet from the heat, evenly sprinkle ¼ t salt over the chicken, and scrape the chicken alongside the cooked vegetables in the colander.
    - Wipe the skillet clean.

8. **Prepare remaining ingredients.**

    - Use a chef's knife to halve the 1 T tart cherries and to chop the 8-10 nuts coarsely.
    - Stir the yogurt creamy smooth before measuring ½ cup.
    - Slice any tough tips from the stems of the Brussels sprouts and halve each sprout lengthwise.
    - Juice the lemon if using lemon juice as an accompaniment.

PART 2

9. **Assemble the dish for serving.**
    - Heat the skillet at a medium setting.
    - Use a chef's knife to slice the ends from the ½ yellow onion. Peel the onion, place it cut side down on a cutting board, and dice the onion. Mince the ginger.
    - Increase the skillet heat to medium high. When a drop of water added to the skillet instantly dances and disappears, add 1 T toasted sesame oil, mix in and heat the cumin seed for 30 seconds, add the onion and ginger, and stir-fry the mixture for about 30 seconds.
    - Reduce the heat to medium and cook the onion mixture for 2 minutes, stirring it occasionally and setting a timer.
    - At the timer, mix 1 heaping T raisins, the dried cherries, and the nuts into the onion mixture. Spread the rice in the skillet, evenly sprinkle ¼ t salt over it, and add any collected vegetable cooking juice.
    - Increase the skillet heat to medium-high and mix in and heat the chicken for about 1 minute, until the chicken is hot. Add the cooked vegetables and pineapple and heat the ingredients for approx. 2 minutes until they are heated through, stirring them frequently.
    - Immediately serve the dish with individual portions topped with a few drops of soy sauce (or approx. ½ t fresh lemon juice) and with 3-4 T yogurt alongside.

VARIATIONS: Make ingredient substitutions. Substitute, for example,

- **¼ c pomegranate seeds** (Recipe #96) or **¼ c cranberries** for pineapple. For cranberries, stir-fry rinsed berries in 3 T orange juice over high heat in a small skillet for 1 minute, remove the skillet from the heat, and mix in 2 t sugar.
- **1 chilled apple** for pineapple. Halve an unpeeled apple lengthwise. Place each half apple cut side down on a cutting board, cut lengthwise into 5 or 6 slices, and cut out the pulpy center and seeds from each slice. Cut each slice into ⅓ in. thick pieces. Stir fry/steam the apple exactly like the carrots except for evenly sprinkling ¼ t cinnamon over the apple during stir-frying.
- **½ lb pre-washed spinach** (Recipe #28) for kale.
- **⅓ lb collards** (Recipe #25) or **other greens** (Recipes #23-30) for kale.
- **1 stalk broccoli** (Recipe #4) for Brussels sprouts.

Add ingredients. Add, for example,

- **2 green onions** or **1 leek** (Recipe #34), including the green tops.
- **1-2 c sugar snap peas** or **snow peas** or **dry frozen organic green peas**, stir-fried in water (Recipe #71).
- **1½ c dry frozen certified organic whole kernel yellow corn** or **2 ears fresh corn**, stir-fried in water (Recipe #65).
- **2 jalapeño peppers** or **1 mild green chili** (Recipe #36).
- **4-6 garlic cloves** (Recipe #31).
- **1 sweet potato** (Recipe #18), diced. Alternatively use baked sweet potato (Recipe #51) or 2 c canned or frozen sweet potato, diced.

- **4-5 asparagus stalks** (Recipe #1).
- **4 dried apricots**, halved, halves cut into thin strips, strips halved.
- **3 T stirred canned coconut milk.** Add the coconut milk with the rice when assembling the dish (Step #8). To enhance coconut flavoring, mix **½-1 T dried coconut powder** into the coconut milk and/or add **2-3 T dried unsweetened shredded coconut,** first softening it by soaking it in 2 T boiling water in a small skillet as a first recipe step. Cover the coconut and let it sit during dish preparation and add it with the cooked vegetables for serving.

158. Red Potato, Pepper, and Egg Stir Fry
(2-3 servings)

Vegetables with Seasoning and Cooking Oil and Water

2 medium red or Yukon Gold potatoes
1 T extra virgin olive oil
½ t each dried sweet basil & oregano leaves
1 T hot water
⅓ t salt
⅓ red bell pepper
¼ green bell pepper

½ T extra virgin olive oil
½ chilled medium yellow onion, halved lengthwise
2 ⅛-in. thick slices fresh ginger root
1 T extra virgin olive oil
½ t each dried sweet basil & oregano leaves

Other Ingredients

3 large eggs
¼ t salt
½ t garlic powder
1 t each dried sweet basil & oregano leaves
8-10 raw pecan or walnut halves

3 t butter, divided into 1 t portions
approx. ⅛ t freshly cracked black pepper
1 c cooked brown rice (Recipe #166)
¼ t salt

Accompaniments

½ c plain yogurt

1-1½ t natural soy sauce or approx. ½ lemon

Cooking Tools

2 large skillets, each with a tight-fitting & opaque lid
1 electric tea kettle
1 cutting board reserved for vegetables
1 each chef's and 5 in. serrated knife

1 medium heavy-bottomed, in top quality condition, nonstick skillet
1 rubber or other heat-resistant spatula
2 medium mixing bowls
1 dinner fork or small whisk

PART 2

1 set each measuring spoons & cups
1 plastic or plastic-coated stir-fry spatula
1 timer

1 pepper mill
1 dinner plate
1 large rounded skillet lid or pie plate

---

1. **Gather all cooking tools and dish ingredients.**

2. **Stir-fry/steam the potato.**

    - Heat a large skillet on a large back burner at a medium setting. Heat an electric tea kettle to ready steaming water.
    - Scrub and thoroughly dry the potatoes with paper towels or a cloth towel.
    - Working on a cutting board reserved for vegetables, use a chef's knife to cut off the tips from each potato. Stand each potato upright on a flattened end and cut it lengthwise into ¼ in. wide slices. Stacking two slices together, cut the slices into ¼ in. wide strips. Holding several strips together, cut them crosswise into ¼ in. cubes.
    - Increase the skillet heat to medium-high. When a drop of water added to the skillet instantly dances and disappears, add 1 T oil, add the potatoes, evenly sprinkle ½ t each dried basil and oregano leaves over them (first crushing the herbs between your palms), and stir-fry the potatoes for 1 minute, setting a timer. This stir-frying should at first be vigorous but can slow to "flip often" pace midway through the minute.
    - At the timer, reduce the heat to medium (a level that keeps oil sizzling gently around potato pieces) and heat the potatoes for 1 minute, flipping pieces occasionally and setting a timer.
    - At the timer, add 1 T hot water, reduce the heat to low, cover the skillet, and steam the potato for 10 minutes, setting a timer.
    - At the timer, turn off the heat, uncover the skillet, evenly sprinkle ⅓ t salt over the potato, partially cover the skillet, and set it aside.

3. **Stir-fry the bell peppers while the potatoes cook.**

    - Heat a large skillet on a large burner at a medium setting on a front burner.
    - Use a 5 in. serrated knife to cut out the stem end of the peppers. Remove the seeds but not the white membrane. Use the serrated knife to cut the peppers lengthwise into ¼ in. wide strips and to cut the strips crosswise into ¼ in. cubes,
    - Increase the skillet heat to medium-high. When a drop of water added to the skillet instantly dances and disappears, add ½ T oil, add the peppers, and stir-fry them for about 30 seconds.
    - Reduce the heat to medium and heat the peppers for 2 minutes, stirring the peppers occasionally and setting a timer.
    - At the timer, use a rubber spatula to scrape the peppers and any cooking juice into a medium mixing bowl.
    - Wipe the skillet clean.

4. **Cook the eggs.**

    - Heat a medium nonstick skillet at a medium setting.
    - Add 3 eggs, ¼ t salt, and ½ t garlic powder to a medium mixing bowl and use a dinner fork or whisk to lightly beat the eggs.
    - Add ½ t each dried basil and oregano leaves to a small sheet of plastic wrap, first crushing them between your palms. Mix the herbs together and divide the herbs into three equal portions.
    - Place three 1 t portions of butter and a pepper mill within easy reach.
    - Increase the skillet heat to a high medium setting. When a drop of butter added to the skillet butter quickly begins to sizzle gently, add 1 t butter, use a rubber spatula to spread the butter evenly over the skillet bottom, and immediately pour ⅓ of the egg mixture into the center of the skillet. Quickly spread one pile of herbs over the egg. While rotating around the egg, use a rubber spatula to push edges of the egg inward while lifting and rocking the skillet back and forth to pour uncooked top egg directly onto the hot skillet where it can cook firmly. When the egg top is no longer runny (but still remains moist and shiny), flip the egg, cook it for 10 seconds, transfer it to a dinner plate, grind a sprinkling of cracked pepper over it, and cover it with a rounded pan lid or inverted pie plate to keep it warm. Wipe the skillet clean.
    - Cook the remaining two ⅓ egg portions in exactly the same way, stacking and covering the egg rounds as they are cooked. Wipe the skillet clean after each egg portion is cooked.

5. **Prepare remaining ingredients.**

    - Stir the yogurt creamy smooth before measuring ½ cup.
    - Use a chef's knife to chop the nuts coarsely.
    - Cut the egg rounds into ¼ in. thick strips, cut the strips into ⅓ in. lengths, and recover the egg.

6. **Assemble the dish for serving.**

    - Heat a large skillet at a medium setting.
    - Place the ½ onion cut side down on a cutting board and use a chef's knife to slice off the ends. Peel off the skin, again place the onion cut side down on the cutting board, and use the chef's knife to dice the onion. Mince the ginger root.
    - Increase the skillet heat to medium-high. When a drop of water added to the skillet instantly dances and disappears, add 1 T oil, add the onion and ginger, evenly sprinkle ½ t each dried basil and oregano leaves (first crushing them between your palms) over the onion, and stir-fry the onion mixture for about 30 seconds. Reduce the heat to medium and cook the onion and ginger for 2 minutes, stirring the mixture occasionally and setting a timer.
    - At the timer, spread the rice over the onion mixture in the skillet and evenly sprinkle ¼ t salt over the rice.

- Increase the skillet heat to medium-high, add the cooked potatoes, and heat the ingredients for approx. 2 minutes until the potatoes are very hot, stirring often and setting a timer.
- At the timer, mix in the nuts, bell pepper, and egg and heat the mixture for about 2 minutes until the egg is hot, stirring often.
- Immediately serve individual portions topped with a sprinkling of soy sauce (or approx. ½ t fresh squeezed lemon juice) and with 3-4 T yogurt alongside.

VARIATIONS: Make ingredient substitutions. Substitute, for example,

- **½ t dried Italian herb mixture, thyme leaves, marjoram leaves,** or **dill weed** for the garlic powder and dried basil and oregano leaves added to the potatoes, eggs, and onion.
- **2 baked potatoes,** freshly baked or leftover potato (Recipe #46), diced, or **6-8 boiled whole small red new potatoes** (Recipe #72), quartered, for stir-fry/steamed potatoes.

Add ingredients. Add, for example,

- **6 c loosely packed pre-washed baby greens,** stir-fried like spinach (Recipe #28).
- **1 c Brussels sprouts,** halved (boiled whole, Recipe #61) or **1 stalk broccoli** (Recipe #4).
- **1½ c small okra** (Recipe #13).
- **1-2 jalapeño peppers** or **1 mild green chili** (Recipe #36), cooked with the bell pepper.
- **4-6 cloves garlic,** either cooked separately (Recipe #31) or with the onion, adding it after the onion cooks for 1 minute.
- **1½ c small sugar snap peas** or **1½ c dry frozen organic green peas** (Recipe #71).
- **1½ c dry frozen organic whole kernel yellow corn** (Recipe #65).
- **2 stalks organic celery** (Recipe #9).
- **1 handful of parsley or chives,** finely chopped, added with the dried herbs to each egg portion during cooking.
- **1 T dried tart cherries,** cut into thirds.
- **¼ c pomegranate seeds** (Recipe #96).
- **¼ c cranberries,** stir-fried in 2 T orange juice over high heat for 1 minute; 2 t sugar mixed in.
- **4 oz fresh grass-fed ground sausage.** Heat a medium skillet at a medium-high setting on a back burner while cooking the potatoes. When the skillet is hot (a drop of water instantly dances and disappears), add and spread 1 t oil over the skillet bottom, add the ground sausage, and use a stir-fry spatula to break the meat into ⅓ in. thick chunks. Add dried herbs (⅓ t each dried sweet basil and oregano leaves, crushed) over the sausage. Stir-fry the sausage for about 30 seconds. Reduce the heat to a low medium (a level where oil sizzles gently around the meat pieces) and cook the sausage, turning the pieces occasionally, for 5 minutes, setting a timer. At the timer, remove the skillet from the burner, mix in ¼ t salt, and set the skillet aside, slanting it to allow any fat to drain from the sausage. Drain fat from the sausage before combining the sausage with other ingredients for serving.

COMMENTS: Selecting eggs from pasture-raised hens significantly upgrades the nutritional quality of this dish.

159. Sweet Potato, Sugar Snap Peas, and Egg Stir Fry
(2-3 servings)

Vegetables with Seasonings and Cooking Oil and Water

2 chilled medium sweet potatoes
1 T extra virgin olive oil
½ t curry powder
½ t garlic powder
1 T hot water
¼ t salt
1½ c uniformly small sugar snap peas
2 T water
¼ t salt
¼ each red & green bell pepper

½ T extra virgin olive oil
3 large chard leaves
1 T extra virgin olive oil
1 T hot water
¼ t salt
½ medium yellow onion, halved lengthwise
2 ⅛-in. thick slices fresh ginger root
1 T extra virgin olive oil
1 t cumin seed
½ t curry powder

Other Ingredients

3 large eggs
½ t garlic powder
1 t curry powder
¼ t salt
approx. ⅛ t freshly cracked black pepper

3 t butter, divided into 1 t portions
1 heaping T certified organic raisins
1 heaping T dried tart cherries
8-10 raw pecan or walnut halves
1 c cooked brown rice (Recipe #166)

Accompaniments

½ c plain yogurt

1-1½ t natural soy sauce or approx.
        ½ lemon

Cooking Tools

2 large heavy-bottomed skillets, each with
    a tight-fitting & opaque lid
1 electric tea kettle
1 large cutting board
1 each chef's and 7 in. serrated knife
1 set each measuring spoons & cups
1 plastic or plastic-coated stir-fry spatula
1 timer
1 medium heavy-bottomed and in top
    condition medium nonstick skillet

1 rubber or other heat-resistant spatula
1 colander
2 dinner plates
1 medium mixing bowl
1 dinner fork or small whisk
1 pepper mill
1 large domed skillet lid, pie plate,
    or aluminum foil
1 pair kitchen scissors
1 hand citrus juicer if using lemon

1. **Gather all cooking tools and dish ingredients.**

PART 2

2. **Stir-fry/steam the sweet potato.**

    - Heat a large skillet on a large back burner on medium. Heat an electric tea kettle to ready steaming water.
    - Scrub, dry, and slice tips and any blemished area from the potatoes.
    - Stand each potato upright on a flattened end and use a chef's knife to cut each lengthwise into ¼ in. wide slices. Stacking two slices together, cut the slices into ¼ in. wide strips. Holding several strips together, cut the strips crosswise into ¼ in. cubes.
    - Increase the skillet heat to medium-high. When a drop of water added to the skillet instantly dances and disappears, add 1 T oil, add the sweet potato, sprinkle ½ t each curry and garlic powder over the sweet potato, and stir-fry the potato mixture for 1 minute, setting a timer. This stir-frying should at first be vigorous but can slow to "flip often" pace midway through the minute.
    - At the timer, reduce the heat to medium and cook the potatoes for 1 minute, flipping pieces occasionally and setting a timer.
    - At the timer, add 1 T hot water, reduce the heat to low, cover the skillet, and steam the potato for 10 minutes, setting a timer.
    - At the timer, turn off the heat, uncover the skillet, evenly sprinkle ¼ t salt over the potatoes, partially cover the skillet, and set the skillet aside.

3. **Stir-fry the sugar snap peas while the sweet potato cooks.**

    - Rinse the peas with cool water.
    - Add 2 T water to a large skillet on a large burner and bring the water to boiling over high heat. Add 1½ c peas and stir-fry them for 1 minute, setting a timer.
    - At the timer, remove the skillet from the heat, evenly sprinkle ¼ t salt over the peas, and use a rubber spatula to scrape them into one side of a colander placed over a dinner plate.
    - Wipe the skillet clean.

4. **Stir-fry/steam the chard.**

    - Heat the large skillet on a large burner at medium.
    - Rinse each leaf in cool water, shake off excess clinging water, and spread the leaves
    - over an attached strip of paper towels or a terry cloth towel. Add a top layer of paper or terry towels and roll the towels around the chard. Gently squeeze the leaves and unroll the towels.
    - Use a chef's knife to slice off the bottom tip of each stem. Cut out the thick vein running through the center of each leaf, cutting close to each side of the vein. Set the veins with attached stem aside.
    - Working on a large cutting board, stack the leaves, forming two or three stacks and facing leaves in the same direction. Holding the leaves roughly in place with one hand, use a 7 in. serrated knife to cut the leaves into ⅓ in. thick pieces, cutting first

lengthwise and then crosswise through the leaves.
- Holding the veins/stems together with one hand and keeping them separate from the chard leaves, use a chef's knife to chop them thinly.
- Increase the skillet heat to medium-high. When a drop of water added to the skillet instantly dances and disappears, add 1 T oil, add the stems, and cook them for about 30 seconds, stirring them occasionally.
- Add the chard leaves and stir-fry them for 1 minute, setting a timer. This stir-frying should be vigorous throughout. The greens should just begin to wilt slightly.
- At the timer, add 1 T hot water, reduce the heat to low, cover the skillet, and steam the chard for 4 minutes, setting a timer.
- Remove the skillet from the burner, evenly sprinkle ¼ t salt over the chard, and use a rubber spatula to scrape it into the colander alongside the sugar snap peas.
- Wipe the skillet clean.

5. **Stir-fry the bell pepper.**

- Heat the large skillet on a large burner at a medium setting.
- Use a 5 in. serrated knife to cut out the stem end of the bell peppers. Remove any seeds but not the white membrane. Use the serrated knife to cut the pepper lengthwise into ¼ in. wide strips and to cut the strips crosswise into ¼ in. cubes.
- Increase the skillet heat to medium-high. When a drop of water added to the skillet instantly dances and disappears, add ½ T oil, add the pepper, and stir-fry it constantly for about 30 seconds. Reduce the heat to medium and cook the pepper for 2 minutes, stirring it occasionally and setting a timer.
- At the timer, use a rubber spatula to scrape the pepper and any cooking juice into one side of the colander with the sugar snap peas.
- Wipe the skillet clean.

6. **Cook the eggs.**

- Heat a medium nonstick skillet at a medium setting.
- Add the eggs and salt to a small mixing bowl. Evenly sprinkle ½ t garlic powder and 1 t curry powder over the eggs. Use a dinner fork or whisk to mix the ingredients together.
- Place three 1 t pieces of butter and a pepper mill within easy reach.
- Increase the skillet heat to high medium. When a drop of butter added to the skillet quickly begins to sizzle gently, add 1 t butter and use a spatula to spread the butter evenly over the skillet bottom as it melts.
- Pour ⅓ of the egg mixture into the center of the skillet. Rotating around the egg, use a rubber spatula to push the edges of the egg inward while lifting and rocking the skillet back and forth to pour uncooked top egg directly onto the hot skillet where it can cook firmly.
- When the egg top is no longer runny but remains moist and shiny, flip the egg, cook it 10 seconds, transfer it to a dinner plate, grind a sprinkling of cracked pepper over it, and cover it with a rounded pan lid, inverted pie plate, or aluminum foil to keep

PART 2

it warm.
- Wipe the skillet clean.
- Cook the remaining two ⅓ egg portions in exactly the same way, stacking and covering the egg rounds as they are cooked. Wipe the skillet clean after each egg portion is cooked.

7. **Prepare remaining ingredients.**

   - Use a chef's knife to halve 1 T tart cherries and to chop 8-10 nuts roughly.
   - Stir the yogurt creamy smooth before measuring ½ cup.
   - Use kitchen scissors to snip off the tips and to halve the sugar snap peas.
   - Cut the egg rounds into ¼ in. thick strips, cut the strips into ⅓ in. lengths, evenly grind approx. ⅛ t black pepper over the eggs, and re-cover them.

8. **Assemble the dish for serving.**

   - Heat a large skillet on a large burner at a medium setting.
   - Place the ½ onion cut side down on a cutting board and use a chef's knife to slice off the ends. Peel the onion. Again place the onion cut side down on the cutting board and use the chef's knife to dice the onion. Mince the ginger.
   - Increase the skillet heat to medium-high. When a drop of water added to the skillet instantly dances and disappears, add 1 T oil, add and heat 1 t cumin seed for 30 seconds, and add the onion and ginger. Evenly sprinkle ½ t curry powder over the onion and stir-fry the mixture for about 30 seconds.
   - Reduce the heat to medium and cook the onion mixture for 2 minutes, stirring it occasionally and setting a timer.
   - At the timer, mix 1 heaping T raisins and the dried cherries into the onion mixture, spread ½ c rice over the onion mixture, and evenly sprinkle ¼ t salt over the rice.
   - Increase the skillet heat to medium-high, mix in the cooked potatoes, and heat the mixture for approx. 2 minutes until the sweet potatoes and rice are hot, stirring often and setting a timer.
   - Mix in the egg, chard, bell pepper, and nuts.
   - Reduce the heat to medium and heat the mixture approx. 1½ minute to heat the eggs and vegetables until they are hot, frequently stirring the ingredients.
   - Immediately serve the dish with individual portions topped with a few drops of soy sauce or approx. ½ t fresh squeezed lemon juice and with 3-4 T yogurt alongside.

VARIATIONS: Make ingredient substitutions. Substitute, for example,

- **4 c diced baked butternut squash** (Recipe #51) for stir-fried/steamed sweet potato.

  - Use the firm flesh from the long thin end of baked squash. Slice the squash lengthwise into ¼ in. thick strips. Slice off the skin and cut the strips crosswise into ¼ in. thick pieces.
- **2 snow peas** or **1½ c green peas** (either fresh or dry frozen, Recipe #71) for sugar

snap peas.
- **6 c pre-washed medium spinach** (Recipe #28), **3 large leaves of kale** (Recipe #26), **6-8 medium beet greens** (Recipe #23), or **any other greens** (Recipes #23-30) for baby greens.
- **¼ c pomegranate seeds** or **¼ c cranberries** for, or combine either with, dried tart cherries. Stir-fry cranberries in 3 T orange juice over high heat for 1 minute, reduce the heat to low, cover the skillet, and steam the cranberries for 2 minutes. Mix in 2 t sugar.
- **½ t each dried sweet basil and oregano leaves, marjoram leaves,** or **Italian herb mixture** for curry spices added to the sweet potato, eggs, and the onion.

Add ingredients. Add, for example,

- **½ c fresh pineapple chunks** (Recipe #94), cut into ¼ in. thick slices.
- **4 pitted Kalamata or green olives**, quartered.
- **1 stalk broccoli** (Recipe #4), **6 Brussels sprouts** (Recipe #5 or #61), **¼ lb bok choy** (Recipe #3) or **¼ lb asparagus** (Recipe #1).
- **2 green onions** or **1 leek** (Recipe #34), including the green tops.
- **4-6 chilled garlic cloves** (Recipe #31), cooked with the yellow onion.
- **1 turnip** (Recipe #22) or **parsnip** (Recipe #14).
- **2 stalks organic celery** (Recipe #9).
- **1 T finely snipped parsley** or **1 t finely sliced chives**, added to each egg round before flipping it.

Vegetarian Stir-Fry Dishes – Traditional Vegetarian or Vegan

160. Broccoli, Pineapple, and Black Bean Stir Fry
(Master Recipe)
(2-3 servings)

Vegetables and Fruit with Seasonings and Cooking Oil and Water

1 chilled stalk broccoli
2 medium carrots
1 T extra virgin olive oil
1 T hot water
⅓ t salt
⅓ red bell pepper
½ T extra virgin olive oil
2 chilled green onions

½ c fresh pineapple chunks (Recipe #94)
½ chilled medium yellow onion, halved lengthwise
2 ⅛-in. thick slices fresh ginger root
1 T extra virgin olive oil
1 t cumin seed
1 t curry powder
½ t garlic powder

PART 2

½ T extra virgin olive oil

¼ t ground ginger

Other Ingredients

½ c cooked brown rice (Recipe #166)
¼ t salt
½ c cooked black beans with broth
1 heaping T certified organic raisins

1 heaping T dried tart cherries
8-10 raw pecan or walnut halves or
   raw whole almonds

Accompaniments

½ c plain yogurt (dairy or soy)

1-1½ t natural soy sauce or ½ lemon

Cooking Tools

1 large heavy-bottomed skillet with a
   tight-fitting and opaque lid
1 electric kettle
1 each 5 in. serrated and chef's knife
1 cutting board
1 set each measuring spoons & cups

1 plastic or plastic-coated stir-fry spatula
1 timer
1 rubber or other heat-resistant spatula
2 colanders
2 dinner plates
1 hand citrus juicer if using lemon

---

1. **Gather all cooking tools and ingredients.**

2. **Stir-fry/steam the broccoli and carrot.**

   - Heat a large skillet on a large burner at a medium setting. Heat an electric tea kettle to ready water for steaming.
   - Rinse the broccoli with cool water, wrap the stalk in paper towels or a terry cloth towel, and firmly squeeze it to dry it thoroughly.
   - Use a 5 in. serrated knife to slice off the florets, leaving long stems (cutting the stems off at the stalk). Cut off and set aside leaves.
   - Halve each floret lengthwise, place the halves cut side down on a cutting board, and halve each one lengthwise. Cut large halves into ¼ in. thick slices. Halve large leaves.
   - Scrub, dry, and cut off the ends of the carrots. Use a chef's knife to halve each carrot lengthwise and to cut the halves crosswise into ⅛ in. thick slices.
   - Increase the skillet heat to medium-high. When a drop of water added to the skillet instantly dances and disappears, add 1 T oil, add the broccoli and carrot, and stir-fry them for 1 minute, setting a timer. Stir-frying should at first be vigorous but can slow to "flip often" pace midway through the minute.
   - At the timer, add 1 T hot water, reduce the heat to low, cover the skillet, and steam the vegetables for 4 minutes, setting a timer. Steam large broccoli florets with thick stems for 5 minutes.
   - At the timer, remove the skillet from the heat, evenly sprinkle ⅓ t salt over the

vegetables, and use a rubber spatula to scrape them and any cooking juice into a colander placed over a dinner plate.
- Wipe the skillet clean.

3. **Stir-fry the bell pepper.**

    - Heat the skillet at a medium setting.
    - Use a 5 in. serrated knife to cut out the stem of the bell pepper. Remove any seeds but not the white membrane. Use the serrated knife to cut the bell pepper lengthwise into ¼ in. thick strips and to cut the strips crosswise into ¼ in. cubes.
    - Increase the skillet heat to medium-high. When a drop of water added to the skillet instantly dances and disappears, add ½ T oil, add the bell pepper, and vigorously stir-fry it for about 30 seconds. Reduce the heat to medium and cook the pepper for 2 minutes, stirring it occasionally and setting a timer.
    - At the timer, scrape the pepper and any cooking juice into the colander with the cooked carrots and broccoli.
    - Wipe the skillet clean.

4. **Prepare the green onions.**

    - Heat the skillet at a medium setting.
    - Rinse, shake off excess liquid, remove any loose outer skin, and use a serrated knife to slice off the roots and green tops. Spread the onions and tops over a paper or terry cloth towel, top the onion with add another towel, roll the onions in the towels, and gently squeeze the towel to dry the onion thoroughly. Unroll the towel.
    - Cut the white portion of each onion crosswise into ¼ in. thick slices. Holding the green tops together with one hand, use a chef's knife to thinly chop the tops.
    - Increase the skillet heat to medium-high. When a drop of water added to the skillet instantly dances and disappears, add ½ T oil, add the tops, and cook them for about 30 seconds, stirring them occasionally. Add the onion and vigorously stir-fry it for 30 seconds. Reduce the heat to medium and cook the onion for 1 minute, stirring it occasionally and setting a timer.
    - At the timer, remove the skillet from the heat and scrape the onion into the colander over the cooked vegetables.
    - Wipe the skillet clean.

5. **Prepare the pineapple.** Cut the pineapple chunks into ⅓ in. thick slices and add the chunks to the colander with the cooked vegetables.

6. **Prepare remaining ingredients.**

    - Use a chef's knife to halve 1 T tart cherries and the 8-10 nuts.
    - Stir yogurt creamy smooth before measuring ½ cup.
    - Drain ½ c canned beans in a second colander placed over a dinner plate, collecting any broth for another use.
    - Squeeze the lemon if using lemon as an accompaniment.

7. **Assemble the dish for serving.**

   - Heat the skillet at a medium setting.
   - Place the ½ onion cut side down on a cutting board and use a chef's knife to cut off the ends. Peel the onion. Again place the onion cut side down on the cutting board and use the chef's knife to dice the onion. Mince the ginger.
   - Increase the skillet heat to medium-high. When a drop of water added to the skillet instantly dances and disappears, add 1 T oil, add and heat 1 t cumin seed for 30 seconds, stirring it occasionally. Add the onion and ginger root, evenly sprinkle the spices (1 t curry powder, ½ t garlic powder, and ¼ t ground ginger) over the onion/ginger, and stir-fry the mixture for 30 seconds. Reduce the heat to medium and cook the onion mixture for 2 minutes, stirring it occasionally and setting a timer.
   - At the timer, mix 1 heaping T raisins, the dried tart cherries, and the nuts into the onion mixture. Spread ½ c rice over the mixture, evenly sprinkle ⅛ t salt over the rice, mix in the rice, add any collected vegetable cooking juice, and mix in the black beans.
   - Increase the skillet heat to medium-high. Heat the ingredients 2-3 minutes until all ingredients are hot, stirring often.
   - Mix in and heat the cooked vegetables and pineapple for 2-3 minutes until hot, stirring often.
   - Immediately serve the dish with individual portions topped with a few drops of soy sauce (or approx. ½ t fresh squeezed lemon juice) and with 3-4 T yogurt alongside.

VARIATIONS: Make ingredient substitutions. Substitute, for example,

- **1 t each dried sweet basil and oregano leaves** or **1 t dried marjoram leaves** for spice flavoring. Crush the leaves over the stir-frying onion/ginger. For more intense herb flavoring, crush the herbs over the stir-frying carrots and broccoli.
- **½ c cooked lentils** (Recipe #168 or canned), **canned garbanzo beans,** or **canned red kidney beans** for black beans.
- **¼ medium head of green** or **red cabbage** (Recipe #6), **8 Brussels sprouts** (Recipe #61, boiled whole), or **½ lb bok choy** (Recipe #3) for broccoli.
- **1 leek** (Recipe #34) for green onion.

Add ingredients. Add, for example,

- **1 mild green chili pepper** or **1 jalapeño** (Recipe #36), diced, cooking it with the bell pepper.
- **4-6 chilled cloves garlic** (Recipe #31).
- **2 ears yellow corn** or **1½ c dry frozen whole kernel corn,** stir-fried in water (Recipe #70).
- **1 beet,** boiled whole (Recipe #59), canned, or vacuum packed, diced.
- **6-8 c pre-washed spinach** (Recipe #28).
- **1 medium sweet potato** (Recipe #18, Recipe #47, or canned) or **baked butternut**

squash (Recipe #51).
- **1 turnip** (Recipe #22), cooked with the broccoli and carrot; cooking oil and steaming water increased to 1½ T.
- **2 c okra** (Recipe #13). Okra adds attractive color and juiciness.
- **¼ c stirred canned coconut milk**, adding it after adding the rice and beans. For more intense coconut flavor, mix **1 T powdered coconut** into the coconut milk or add **¼ c unsweetened dried shredded coconut**. To use dried coconut, soak it as a first recipe step to soften it. Combine ¼ c boiling water and the dried coconut in a small heat-proof container with a lid and set the coconut aside, covered, while preparing other ingredients. Add the soaked coconut when assembling the dish for serving.

COMMENTS: To keep the black beans from coloring and fading the bright color of the broccoli and carrot, drain the black beans thoroughly. When canned broth is especially thick, swish the beans in a small amount of water (¼ c), drain them in a colander, collect the drained bean broth for another use, and use paper towels to pat the beans dry.

161. Sweet Potato, Kale, Corn, and Kidney Bean Stir Fry
(2-3 servings)

Vegetables with Seasonings and Cooking Oil and Water

2 chilled medium sweet potatoes
1 T extra virgin olive oil
½ t curry powder
½ t garlic powder
1 T hot water
¼ t salt
4 large kale leaves
    (to yield 2 c sliced)
1 T extra virgin olive oil
1 T hot water
¼ t salt
2 medium ears yellow corn
2 T water

¼ t salt
¼ each red & green bell pepper
1 mild green chili or 1-2 jalapeño peppers
¾ T extra virgin olive oil
½ chilled medium yellow onion,
    halved lengthwise
2 ⅛-in thick slices fresh ginger root
1 T extra virgin olive oil
1 t cumin seed
1 t curry powder
⅓ t ground cinnamon
⅓ t ground ginger

Other Ingredients

1 heaping T dried tart cherries
1 heaping T certified organic raisins
10 raw pecan or walnut halves or almonds

½ c cooked brown rice (Recipe #166)
½ c cooked kidney beans

Accompaniments

PART 2

½ c plain yogurt   1-1½ t natural soy sauce or ½ lemon

Cooking Tools

2 large heavy-bottomed skillets, both with   1 plastic or plastic-coated stir-fry spatula
   a tight-fitting & opaque lid   1 timer
1 electric tea kettle   1 rubber or other heat-resistant spatula
1 large cutting board (approx. 16 x 24 in.)   2 colanders
1 chef's knife   2 dinner pates
1 each 7 in. & 5 in. serrated knife   1 pie plate
1 set each measuring spoons & cups   1 hand citrus juicer if using lemon

---

1. **Gather all cooking tools and ingredients.**

2. **Stir-fry/steam the sweet potato.**

    - Heat a large skillet on a large burner at a medium setting. Heat an electric tea kettle to ready water for steaming.
    - Use a chef's knife to slice off the ends and any blemished skin from the potatoes. Stand each potato upright on a fattened end and use the chef's knife to cut each lengthwise into ¼ in. wide slices. Stacking two slices together, cut the slices into ¼ in. thick strips. Holding several strips together, cut them crosswise into ¼ in. cubes.
    - Increase the skillet heat to medium high. When a drop of water added to the skillet instantly dances and disappears, add 1 T oil, add the sweet potato, evenly sprinkle ½ t each curry and garlic powder over the potato, and stir-fry the potato for 1 minute, setting a timer. Stir-frying should at first be vigorous but can slow to "flip often" pace midway through the minute.
    - At the timer, reduce the heat to medium and cook the potato for 1 minute, stirring occasionally and setting a timer.
    - At the timer, add 1 T hot water, reduce the heat to low, cover the skillet, and steam the potato for 10 minutes, setting a timer.
    - At the timer, turn off the heat, open the skillet, evenly sprinkle ⅓ t salt over the potatoes, and set the skillet aside with the lid closed.

3. **Stir-fry/steam the kale while the sweet potato cooks.**

    - Heat another large skillet on a large front burner at a medium setting. Heat an electric tea kettle to prepare steaming water.
    - Rinse each kale leaf in cool water, shake off excess clinging water, and spread the leaves over an attached sheet of paper towels or a terry cloth towel. For flat kale, use paper towels to pat the leaves dry. For kale with curly leaves, add a top layer of paper or terry cloth towels and roll the towels around the kale. Gently squeeze the leaves

- and unroll the paper towels.
- Add the leaves to a large cutting board. Cutting close to the central vein running through each leaf, use a serrated knife to cut the leaves from either side of the vein. Set the veins and attached stems aside. Stack the leaves, forming two or more stacks and facing the leaves in the same direction. Using a 7 in. serrated knife and, holding a stack together with one hand, cut each pile of leaves into approx. ⅓ in. thick pieces, slicing lengthwise and crosswise through the leaves.
- Keeping the veins/stems separate from the leaves and, holding the veins/stems together with one hand, use a chef's knife to thinly chop them.
- Increase the skillet heat to medium-high. When a drop of water added to the skillet instantly dances and disappears, add 1 T oil, add the stems, and cook them for about 30 seconds, stirring them frequently. Add the kale leaves and constantly stir-fry the leaves for 1 minute until they wilt slightly, setting a timer.
- At the timer, add 1 T of hot water, cover the skillet, reduce the heat to low, and steam the kale for 4 minutes, setting a timer.
- At the timer, remove the skillet from the heat, evenly sprinkle ¼ t salt over the kale, and use a rubber spatula to scrape it and any cooking juice into a colander placed over a dinner plate for collecting any spilled juice.
- Wipe the skillet clean.

4. **Stir-fry the corn.**

- Heat the skillet at a medium setting.
- Remove the husks and corn silk from the ears. Stand each ear upright in a pie plate and use a chef's knife to slice off the kernels, cutting close to the cob to include corn germ.
- Add 2 T water to the skillet and increase the heat to high. When the water boils, mix in the corn. Once the water again boils, stir-fry the corn for 1 minute, just until it is hot and its color darkens slightly and before the cooking water evaporates.
- Remove the skillet from the heat, evenly sprinkle ¼ t salt over the corn, and use a rubber spatula to scrape it and any cooking liquid into the colander with the kale.
- Wipe the skillet clean.

5. **Stir-fry the bell and chili peppers.**

- Heat the skillet at a medium setting.
- Use a 5 in. serrated knife to cut out the stem end of the bell peppers. Remove the seeds but not the white membrane. Use the serrated knife to cut the peppers lengthwise into ¼ in. wide strips and while holding the strips together with one hand, to cut the strips crosswise into ¼ in. cubes.
- Keeping the chili pepper(s) separate, cut out the stem end, seeds, and membrane from the chili pepper(s). Slice each chili lengthwise into ⅛ in. thick strips and cut the strips crosswise into ⅛ in. cubes. Add the cubes to a piece of plastic wrap. Immediately wash your hands and wash and dry the cutting board and cutting knife.
- Increase the skillet heat setting to medium-high, and when a drop of water added

PART 2

to the skillet instantly dances and disappears, add ¾ T oil, add the bell peppers, and stir-fry them for about 30 seconds.
- Add the chili pepper, stir-fry the mixture for 30 seconds, reduce the heat to medium, and cook the peppers for 2 minutes, stirring them occasionally and setting a timer.
- At the timer, use a rubber spatula to scrape the peppers and any cooking juice into the colander with the other cooked vegetables.
- Wipe the skillet clean.

6. **Prepare remaining ingredients.**

   - Use a chef's knife to halve 1 T tart cherries and the 10 nuts. Coarsely chop almonds.
   - Stir the yogurt creamy smooth before measuring ½ cup.
   - Drain ½ c kidney beans in a second colander placed over a dinner plate. Collect and save the broth for another use.

7. **Assemble the dish for serving.**

   - Heat a clean large skillet on a large burner at a medium setting.
   - Use a chef's knife to slice the ends from the onion. Peel the onion, place it cut side down on a cutting board, and dice it. Mince the ginger.
   - Increase the skillet heat to medium-high. When a drop of water added to the skillet instantly dances and disappears, add 1 T oil, add 1 t cumin seed, and heat it for about 30 seconds, stirring it occasionally. Add the onion and ginger, evenly sprinkle the spices (1 t curry powder, ½ t ground cumin, and ⅓ t each ground cinnamon and ginger) over the onion and ginger, and vigorously stir-fry the mixture for 30 seconds. Reduce the heat to medium and cook the onion mixture for 2 minutes, stirring it occasionally and setting a timer.
   - At the timer, mix the dried cherries, raisins, and nuts into the onion mixture, spread ½ c rice over the onion mixture, and evenly sprinkle ⅛ t salt over the rice, mix in the salt, and add any collected vegetable cooking juice.
   - Add and mix in the sweet potatoes and kidney beans.
   - Increase the skillet heat to medium-high and heat the ingredients for approx. 2 minutes until all ingredients are hot, stirring them often.
   - Add the cooked vegetables in the colander and continue heating the ingredients for approx. 2 minutes until again all ingredients are hot, stirring often.
   - Serve the dish immediately with individual portions topped with a few drops of soy sauce or approx. ½ t fresh squeezed lemon juice and with 3-4 T yogurt alongside.

VARIATIONS: Make ingredient substitutions. Substitute, for example,

- **1½ c dry frozen whole kernel yellow corn** (Recipe #65) for fresh corn.
- **½ lb pre-washed baby greens** (mixtures that include sturdy greens, such as beet greens and kale, cooking them like spinach), **beet greens** (Recipe #23) or **collards** (Recipe #25) for kale. Using pre-washed greens greatly reduces preparation time.
- **2 c diced canned sweet potato** for stir-fry/steamed sweet potato, which reduces

preparation time.

- **½ c black beans** for kidney beans.
- **⅛ t cayenne powder** or **red pepper flakes** for fresh chili pepper. Either of these ingredients can also be added with fresh chili pepper to intensify heat.
- **1 t dried basil leaves** and **½-1 t dried oregano leaves** or **marjoram leaves** for spice flavoring, crushed over both the stir-frying sweet potato and the onion/ginger.

Add ingredients. Add, for example,

- **coconut flavoring**. See Variations in Recipe #160 (Broccoli, Pineapple, and Black Beans) for details.
- **4-6 chilled garlic cloves** (Recipe #31).
- **2 medium carrots** (Recipe #7).
- **8 Brussels sprouts** (Recipe #61), boiled whole and halved.
- **1 medium turnip** (Recipe #22).
- **1½ c small okra**, stir-fried whole in water (Recipe #68) or stir-fry/steamed (Recipe #13).
- **1 small zucchini** or yellow straightneck squash; **2 small yellow crookneck squash** (Recipe #20), with ½ t curry powder sprinkled over the squash during stir-frying.
- **1 t snipped fresh mint** or **1 t snipped cilantro**, added as a topping to servings.
- **4 dried apricots**, halved, and halves sliced thinly; added with the other dried fruit.
- **¼ c fresh pineapple chunks** (Recipe #94), cut into ⅓ in. thick slices, added with the cooked vegetables when heating the dish for serving.
- **¼ c pomegranate seeds** (Recipe #96) or **cranberries**, added with the cooked vegetables when heating the dish for serving. To prepare cranberries, stir-fry them in 2 T orange juice heated to boiling for 1 minute, cook them another minute at medium heat, remove the cranberries from the heat, and mix in 2 t sugar.

COMMENTS: Drain the kidney beans thoroughly to keep the sweet potato and corn brightly colored. If the broth is especially thick, mix the beans with 2-4 T water before adding the beans to the colander. Collect the broth for another use.

162. Cauliflower, Brussels Sprouts, and Garbanzo Bean Stir Fry
(Herb and Tomato Flavoring)
(2-3 servings)

Vegetables with Seasonings and Cooking Oil and Water

4 large (approx. 2 in. thick) cauliflower florets
1 T extra virgin olive oil
½ t each dried sweet basil & oregano leaves
1 T hot water

½ T extra virgin olive oil
1½ c dry frozen green peas, unthawed
2 T water
¼ t salt

PART 2

¼ t salt
8 chilled small/medium Brussels sprouts
¼ t salt
2 medium carrots
1 T extra virgin olive oil
½ t each dried sweet basil & oregano leaves
½ T hot water
¼ t salt
⅓ red bell pepper

4 grape tomatoes
½ T extra virgin olive oil
½ chilled medium yellow onion, halved lengthwise
2 ⅛-in. thick slices ginger root
1 T extra virgin olive oil
½ t each dried sweet basil & oregano leaves
½ t garlic powder

Other Ingredients

1 heaping T certified organic raisins
10 whole raw almonds
2 T tomato juice
3 T tomato paste

½ c cooked brown rice (Recipe #166)
⅛ t salt
½ c cooked garbanzo beans

Accompaniment

½ c plain yogurt

Cooking Tools

1 large heavy-bottomed skillet with a tight-fitting & opaque lid
1 electric tea kettle
1 each chef's & 5 in. serrated knife
1 cutting board
1 set each measuring spoons & cups

1 plastic or plastic-coated stir-fry spatula
1 timer
1 rubber or other heat-resistant spatula
2 colanders
2 dinner plates
1 medium saucepan

1. **Gather all cooking tools and ingredients.**

2. **Stir-fry/steam the cauliflower.**

   - Heat a large skillet on a large burner at a medium setting. Heat an electric tea kettle to ready steaming water.
   - Rinse the cauliflower florets and use paper towels or a terry cloth towel to dry them. Use a chef's knife to slice off stems, setting them aside.
   - Break the florets into small, ½ in. thick florets, attempting to keep the florets even-sized for even cooking. Cut stems crosswise into thin (⅛ in. thick) slices.
   - Increase the skillet heat to medium-high. When a drop of water added to the skillet instantly dances and disappears, add 1 T oil, add the cauliflower florets and stems, crush the ½ t each dried basil and oregano leaves evenly over the cauliflower, and stir-fry the cauliflower for 1 minute, setting a timer. Stir-frying should at first be

vigorous but can slow to "flip often" pace midway through the minute.
- At the timer, add 1 T hot water, cover the skillet, reduce the heat to low, and steam the cauliflower for 4 minutes, setting a timer.
- At the timer, remove the skillet from the heat, evenly sprinkle ¼ t salt over the cauliflower, and use a rubber spatula to scrape it and any juice into a colander placed over a dinner plate for collecting any cooking juice.
- Wipe the skillet clean.

3. **Boil the Brussels sprouts whole.**

- Add enough water to cover the sprouts completely by several inches to a medium saucepan.
- Heat the water to boiling over high heat.
- Rinse the sprouts and remove any very loose outside leaves, but do not trim them in any way.
- Add the sprouts to the water without slowing the boiling. Immediately set a timer for 3 minutes.
- At the timer, immediately drain the sprouts into an empty colander and rinse them with cold water to stop the cooking.
- Bunch the sprouts together on a layer of paper towels and wrap the towels around the sprouts to dry them.
- Evenly sprinkle ¼ t salt over the sprouts and pour the sprouts onto the cauliflower.

4. **Stir-fry/steam the carrots.**

- Heat the large skillet at a medium setting. Begin heating an electric tea kettle to ready steaming water.
- Scrub and dry the carrots. Use a chef's knife to cut off the ends, halve lengthwise, and cut the carrots crosswise into ⅛ in. thick slices.
- Increase the skillet heat to medium-high. When a drop of water added to the skillet instantly dances and disappears, add 1 T oil, add the carrots, and stir-fry them for 1 minute, setting a timer. Stir-frying should at first be vigorous but can slow to "flip often" pace midway through the minute.
- At the timer, add ½ T hot water, cover the skillet, reduce the heat to low, and steam the carrots for 4 minutes, setting a timer.
- At the timer, remove the skillet from the heat, evenly sprinkle ¼ t salt over the carrots, and use a rubber spatula to scrape them and any cooking juice into the colander with the other cooked vegetables.
- Wipe the skillet clean.

5. **Stir-fry the red bell pepper.**

- Heat the skillet at a medium setting.
- Use a 5 in. serrated knife to cut out the stem of the pepper. Remove the seeds but not the white membrane. Use the serrated knife to cut the pepper lengthwise into ¼ in.

PART 2

- wide strips and to cut the strips crosswise into ¼ in. cubes.
- Increase the skillet heat to medium-high. When a drop of water added to the skillet instantly dances and disappears, add ½ T oil, add the pepper, and vigorously stir-fry it for about 30 seconds.
- Reduce the heat to medium and cook the pepper for 2 minutes, stirring it occasionally and setting a timer.
- At the timer, use a rubber spatula to scrape the pepper and any juice into the colander with the other cooked vegetables.

6. **Stir-fry the green peas in water.**

- Break up any clumps of frozen peas while the peas remain in the store package.
- Add 2 T water to the skillet, bring the water to boiling over high heat, add the peas, and, once the water returns to a boil, stir-fry them for 1 minute, setting a timer.
- At the timer, immediately remove the skillet from the heat, evenly sprinkle ¼ t salt over the peas, and use a rubber spatula to scrape the peas and any cooking water into the colander over the other cooked vegetables.
- Wipe the skillet clean.

7. **Stir-fry the tomatoes.**

- Heat the skillet at a medium setting.
- Rinse, thoroughly dry, and use a 5 in. serrated knife to halve the grape tomatoes lengthwise.
- Increase the skillet heat to medium-high. When a drop of water added to the skillet instantly dances and disappears, add ½ T oil, add the tomatoes, and stir-fry them for 1 minute, gently flipping them often and setting a timer.
- At the timer, remove the skillet from the heat and use a rubber spatula to scrape the tomatoes into one side of the colander holding the other cooked vegetables.
- Wipe the skillet clean.

8. **Prepare remaining ingredients.**

- Use the chef's knife to chop the 10 nuts coarsely.
- Stir the yogurt creamy smooth before measuring ½ cup.
- Halve the Brussels sprouts lengthwise.
- Drain the ½ c garbanzo beans in the colander used for the draining the Brussels sprouts after they were boiled whole. Place a dinner plate under the colander to collect bean broth. Collect and use the bean broth for another use.
- Open the tomato paste and tomato juice containers. Measure 3 T tomato paste.

9. **Assemble the dish for serving.**

- Heat the skillet at a medium setting.
- Place the ½ onion cut side down on a cutting board and use a chef's knife to cut off

the ends. Peel the onion. Again place the onion cut side down on the cutting board and use the chef's knife to dice the onion. Mince the ginger.
- Increase the skillet heat to medium-high. When a drop of water added to the skillet instantly dances and disappears, add 1 T oil, add the onion and ginger, evenly sprinkle the herbs (½ t each dried basil and oregano leaves, first crushing the leaves between your palms) and ½ t garlic powder over the onion/ginger, and vigorously stir-fry the mixture for about 30 seconds.
- Reduce the heat to medium and cook the onion mixture for 2 minutes, stirring it occasionally and setting a timer.
- At the timer, mix 1 heaping T raisins and the nuts into the onion mixture, add any collected vegetable cooking juice, add and mix in 2 T tomato juice and 3 T tomato paste, spread ½ c rice over the onion mixture, evenly sprinkle ⅛ t salt over the rice, and mix in the garbanzo beans.
- Increase the skillet heat to medium-high. Heat the ingredients for approx. 2 minutes until all ingredients are hot, stirring often.
- Add the cooked vegetables in the colander except for the tomato. Heat the ingredients for approx. 2 minutes until again all ingredients are hot, stirring often.
- Add the tomatoes and continue the heating another 30 seconds, gently stirring in the tomatoes.
- Immediately serve individual servings topped with 3-4 T yogurt alongside.

VARIATIONS: Make ingredient substitutions. Substitute, for example,

- ⅛ c **raw pecan halves** or **other favorite nuts** for almonds.
- 2 c **cabbage** (Recipe #6), **bok choy** (Recipe #3), or **turnip** (Recipe #22) for cauliflower.
- 1 stalk **broccoli** (Recipe #4) for Brussels sprouts.
- 1½ c **sugar snap** or **snow green peas** (Recipe #71) for dry frozen green peas.
- 4 **pitted prunes**, halved and each half thinly sliced crosswise, for raisins.
- ½ c **lentils** (Recipe #155), **black beans**, or **red kidney beans** for garbanzo beans.
- **spice flavoring** for herb flavoring. Omit the herbs and add ½ t **curry powder** to the cauliflower during stir-frying. Add **1 t each cumin seed**, ½ t **ground cumin**, and ½ t **garlic powder** to the stir-frying onion. Omit the tomato juice and paste. Substitute ½ c pineapple chunks for grape tomato. Add coconut flavoring as an option (see Variations, Recipe #160).

Add ingredients. Add, for example,

- 1½ c **dry frozen yellow corn** (Recipe #65, stir-fried in water).
- 4-8 **garlic cloves** (Recipe #31).
- 1 **green chili** or 1-2 **jalapeño peppers** (Recipe #36), stir-fried with the bell pepper, adding the chili/peppers after the bell pepper has stir-fried for 30 seconds.
- 4 c **sliced greens**, any variety, including simplest **pre-washed spinach** (Recipe #28) or **pre-washed baby greens** (a mixture that includes sturdy kale and beet greens).
- 2 c **diced zucchini** or **yellow summer squash** (Recipe #20), with ½ t each dried sweet basil and oregano leaves (crushed) added during stir-frying.

PART 2

- **1 c diced cooked beet**, boiled whole (Recipe #59) or canned, drained.
- **1 t snipped cilantro**, added as a topping to each serving.
- **2 T thick canned coconut milk**. Thoroughly stir canned coconut before measuring. Add the coconut with the tomato juice and paste.
- **2 T dried tomatoes**. As a first recipe preparation step, combine 2-3 dried tomatoes and ¼ c boiling water in a heat-proof container and set it aside, covered, while preparing other dish ingredients. Prepare them in Step #8: drain any unabsorbed water and substitute it for an equal amount of tomato juice. Use a chef's knife to cut the dried tomatoes into ¼ in. thick strips. Add the tomato when assembling the dish, adding them with the raisins. Alternatively, use dried tomatoes packed in oil, cutting them in the same manner.

163. Okra, Eggplant, Corn, Spinach, and Lentil Stir Fry
(Herb and Tomato Flavoring)
(2-3 servings)

Vegetables with Seasonings and Cooking Oil and Water

½ lb small okra
1 T extra virgin olive oil
¼ t salt
½ chilled medium globe eggplant or 1
    medium (10 in. long) Japanese eggplant
1 T extra virgin olive oil
½ t each dried sweet basil & oregano leaves
1 T hot water
¼ t salt
2 ears yellow corn
2 T water
¼ t salt
¼ each red and green pepper

½ T extra virgin olive oil
10 grape tomatoes
½ T extra virgin olive oil
½ lb pre-washed spinach
1 T extra virgin olive oil
¼ t salt
½ chilled medium yellow onion,
    halved lengthwise
2 ⅛-in. thick slices ginger root
1 T extra virgin olive oil
1 t each dried sweet basil & oregano leaves
½ t garlic powder

Other Ingredients

10 raw whole almonds
1 heaping T certified organic raisins
2 T tomato juice
3 T tomato paste

½ c cooked brown rice (Recipe #166)
⅛ t salt
½ c cooked lentils (canned or fresh,
    Recipe #168)

Accompaniment

½ c plain yogurt (dairy or soy)

Cooking Tools

1 large heavy-bottomed skillet with a tight-fitting & opaque lid	1 timer
	1 rubber or other heat-resistant spatula
1 each 5 in. & 7 in. serrated knife	2 colanders
1 chef's knife	2 dinner plates
1 set each measuring spoons & cups	1 electric tea kettle
1 plastic or plastic-coated stir-fry spatula	1 pie plate
1 timer	1 large cutting board (approx. 16 x 24 in.)

◆

1. **Gather all cooking tools and ingredients.**

2. **Stir-fry/steam the okra.**

    - Heat a large skillet on a large burner at a medium setting.
    - Rinse and thoroughly dry the okra. Use a 5 in. serrated knife to cut off the tips and stem ends from the okra and to cut the okra crosswise into ¼ in. wide slices, discarding any okra with woody pulp.
    - Increase the skillet heat to medium-high. When a drop of water added to the skillet instantly dances and disappears, add 1 T oil, add the okra, and stir-fry it for 1 minute, setting a timer. Stir-frying should at first be vigorous but can slow to "flip often" pace midway through the minute.
    - At the timer, reduce the heat to low, cover the skillet, and steam the okra in its own juice for 4 minutes, setting a timer.
    - At the timer, remove the skillet from the heat, evenly sprinkle ¼ t salt over the okra, and use a rubber spatula to scrape the okra and any cooking juice into a colander placed over a dinner plate.
    - Wipe the skillet clean.

3. **Stir-fry/steam the eggplant.**

    - Heat the skillet at a medium setting. Heat an electric tea kettle to ready water for steaming.
    - Rinse and dry the eggplant. Use a chef's knife to slice the end(s) from the eggplant. Stand the eggplant upright on a flattened end and cut the eggplant lengthwise into ¼ in. wide slices. Stacking 2 slices together, cut the slices lengthwise into ¼ in. wide strips. Holding several strips together at a time, evenly dice the strips into ¼ in. cubes.
    - Increase the skillet heat to medium-high. When a drop of water added to the skillet instantly dances and disappears, add 1 T oil, add the eggplant, evenly sprinkle the dried herbs over the eggplant (first crushing them between your palms), and stir-fry the eggplant for 1 minute, setting a timer. Stir-frying should at first be vigorous but can slow to "flip often" pace midway through the minute.
    - At the timer, add 1 T hot water, cover the skillet, reduce the heat setting to low, and steam the eggplant for 4 minutes, setting a timer.

- At the timer, remove the skillet from the heat, evenly sprinkle ¼ t salt over the eggplant, and use a rubber spatula to scrape it and any cooking juice into the colander with the okra.

4. **Stir-fry the corn**.

    - Heat the skillet at a medium setting.
    - Remove the husks and corn silk from the ears. Stand each ear upright in a pie plate and use a chef's knife to slice off the kernels, cutting close to the cob to include corn germ.
    - Add 2 T water to the skillet and bring it to boiling over high heat. Mix in the corn kernels and when the water returns to a boil, stir-fry the corn for 1 minute, turning kernels over and over until the color darkens slightly and the corn is heated through.
    - Remove the skillet from the heat, evenly sprinkle ¼ t salt over the corn, and scrape the corn and any cooking juice into the colander with the other cooked vegetables.
    - Wipe the skillet clean.

5. **Stir-fry the bell peppers**.

    - Heat the skillet at a medium setting.
    - Use a 5 in. serrated knife to cut out the stem of each pepper. Remove the seeds but not the membrane. Use the serrated knife to cut the peppers lengthwise into ¼ in. thick slices and to cut the slices crosswise into ¼ in. cubes.
    - Increase the skillet heat to medium-high. When a drop of water added to the skillet instantly dances and disappears, add ½ T oil, add the peppers, vigorously stir-fry them for 30 seconds, reduce the heat setting to medium, and cook the peppers for 2 minutes, stirring them occasionally and setting a timer.
    - At the timer, use a rubber spatula to scrape the peppers and any cooking juice into the colander with the other cooked vegetables.
    - Wipe the skillet clean.

6. **Stir-fry the spinach**.

    - Heat the skillet at a medium setting.
    - Form the spinach into a pile on a large cutting board. While roughly holding the leaves together with one hand, use a 7 in. serrated knife to slice the leaves into approx. ⅓ in. thick pieces, cutting through the leaves lengthwise and crosswise.
    - Increase the skillet heat setting to medium-high and when a drop of water added to the skillet instantly dances and disappears, add 1 T oil, add the spinach, and stir-fry it constantly for 1 minute until all leaves become uniformly darkened in color and are slightly wilted.
    - Immediately remove the skillet from the heat, evenly sprinkle ¼ t salt over the spinach, and use a rubber spatula to scrape it and any cooking juice into one side of the colander holding the other cooked vegetables.
    - Wipe the skillet clean.

7. **Stir-fry the grape tomatoes.**

    - Heat the skillet at a medium setting.
    - Rinse, thoroughly dry, and use a 5 in. serrated knife to quarter the tomatoes lengthwise.
    - Increase the skillet heat to medium-high, and when a drop of water added to the skillet instantly dances and disappears, add 1 t oil, add the tomatoes, and gently stir-fry them for one minute, setting a timer.
    - At the timer, use a rubber spatula to scrape them into one side of the colander with the spinach.
    - Wipe the skillet clean.

8. **Prepare remaining ingredients.**

    - Stir the yogurt creamy smooth before measuring ½ cup.
    - Use a chef's knife to chop the 10 nuts coarsely.
    - Drain the ½ c lentils in a second colander placed over a dinner plate. Collect and save the broth for another use.
    - Open the tomato paste and juice containers. Measure 3 T tomato paste.

9. **Assemble the dish for serving.**

    - Heat the skillet at a medium setting.
    - Place the ½ onion cut side down on a cutting board and use a chef's knife to cut off the ends. Peel the onion. Return the onion cut side down to the cutting board and use the chef's knife to dice the onion. Mince the ginger root.
    - Increase the skillet heat to medium-high, and when a drop of water added to the skillet instantly dances and disappears, add 1 T oil to the skillet, add the onion and ginger, evenly sprinkle the 1 t each dried basil and oregano leaves (first crushing them between your palms) and ½ t garlic powder over them, and stir-fry the mixture for 30 seconds. Reduce the heat to medium and cook the onion mixture for 2 minutes, stirring it occasionally and setting a timer.
    - At the timer, mix 1 heaping T raisins and the nuts into the onion mixture, add and thoroughly mix in the 2 T tomato juice and 3 T tomato paste, add ½ c rice, evenly sprinkle ⅛ t salt over the rice, add any collected cooking juice, and mix in the lentils.
    - Increase the skillet heat to medium-high and heat the mixture for approx. 2 minutes until all ingredients are hot, stirring often.
    - Add and heat the cooked vegetables (except for the tomatoes and spinach) for approx. 2 minutes until again all ingredients are hot, stirring often.
    - Gently mix in the tomatoes and the spinach and continue heating the dish another minute until the tomatoes and spinach are hot, stirring occasionally.
    - Immediately serve the dish with individual portions topped with 3-4 T yogurt alongside.

    VARIATIONS: Make ingredient substitutions. Substitute, for example,

- ½ **larger, more mature okra** for small okra. Extend steaming time to 4 minutes or boil the okra whole (Recipe #68).
- ½ **lb pre-washed baby greens** (a mixture that includes sturdy beet greens and kale; cooked exactly like pre-washed spinach), **chard** (Recipe #24), **beet greens** (Recipe #23), **kale** (Recipe #26), **un-washed spinach** (Recipe #29), or **collards** (Recipe #25) for pre-washed spinach.
- 2 **c dry frozen whole kernel yellow corn** for fresh corn.
- 2-3 **dried tomatoes** for grape tomatoes. See Variations, Recipe #162, for preparation details.
- ½ **c black beans, garbanzo beans,** or **red kidney beans** for lentils.
- ½ **c canned lentils** for fresh prepared. If the lentil broth is very thick, mix the lentils with ¼ c water before draining it (Step #8).

Add ingredients. Add, for example,

- 1 **medium zucchini** or **yellow straightneck summer squash**; 2 **small yellow crookneck summer squash** (Recipe #20), crushing ½ t each dried sweet basil & oregano leaves over the squash during stir-frying.
- 2 **medium carrots** (Recipe #7).
- 4-6 **chilled garlic cloves** (Recipe #31).
- 2 **T diced dried tomatoes**. See Recipe #162, Variations (Ingredient Additions), for preparation details.
- 2-3 **T stirred canned coconut milk**. Add it with the tomato juice and paste. To enhance the coconut flavor, add ¼ c unsweetened dried shredded coconut and/or 1 T coconut powder (see Variations in Recipe #160 for preparation details).

COMMENTS: Home-prepared lentils can be cooked ahead and refrigerated or frozen in individual serving size amounts to be kept on hand for use in dishes.

Traditional Pilaf – Vegetables with Whole Grains or Wild Rice

164. Vegetables and Cracked Wheat Pilaf
(4 servings)

Vegetables with Seasoning and Cooking Oil and Water

2 stalks organic celery
¾ T extra virgin olive oil
½ t dried sage leaves
2 medium carrots
1 medium turnip

½ T extra virgin olive oil
8 c loosely packed pre-washed spinach
1 T extra virgin olive oil
1½ c dry frozen yellow whole kernel corn, unthawed

COOKED ALIVE!

1 T extra virgin olive oil
½ t dried sage leaves
1 T hot water
⅓ t salt
¼ red bell pepper
⅛ each green & yellow bell pepper
½ t dried sage leaves

2 T water
¼ t salt
½ chilled medium yellow onion, halved lengthwise
⅛ in. thick slice fresh ginger root
1 T extra virgin olive oil

Other Ingredients

½ c medium cracked whole wheat
1½ c water
¼ t salt

8-10 raw pecan or walnut halves or whole almonds
1 heaping T certified organic raisins
1 heaping T dried tart cherries

Accompaniments

½ c plain yogurt, dairy or soy

½ lemon

Cooking Tools

1 heavy-bottomed medium saucepan with a tight-fitting & opaque lid
1 set measuring cups & spoons
1 timer
1 large heavy-bottomed skillet with a tight-fitting & opaque lid
1 chef's knife
1 each 5 in. & 7 in. serrated knife

1 plastic or plastic-coated stir-fry spatula
1 rubber or other heat-resistant spatula
1 colander
1 dinner plate
1 electric tea kettle
1 large (approx. 16 x 24 in.) cutting board
1 hand citrus juicer
1 dinner fork

---

1. **Gather all cooking tools and ingredients.**

2. **Cook the cracked wheat.**

   - Add the cracked wheat and 1½ c cool water to a saucepan and bring the water to boiling over high heat. Reduce the heat to low, cover the saucepan, and set a timer for 25 minutes.
   - Check the cracked wheat after 10 minutes to ensure the water is neither boiling too high or too low. If the boiling is too high, add a trivet for an electric burner or a heat tamer for a gas burner. Increase the heat slightly if there is no boiling at all.
   - Check the cracked wheat again after approx. 20 minutes to ensure that the cooking water has not been completely absorbed and that the grain is not sticking to the pan bottom. If the grain appears very dry, add 2-4 T hot water.

PART 2

- At the timer, make a taste test to check that the grain is completely softened. If even a trace of crispness remains, continue the cooking for 5 more minutes, adding another touch (2-4 T) more hot water if the cooking water has been absorbed. When the grain is attractively soft, remove it from the burner.
- Evenly sprinkle ¼ t salt over the cracked wheat, toss the wheat to mix in the salt, and set it aside in the saucepan, covered. When cooking the grain well ahead of serving, refrigerate the cracked wheat in a covered container.

3. **Stir-fry/steam the celery.**

   - Heat a large skillet on a large burner at a medium setting.
   - Rinse and dry the celery stalks.
   - Use a chef's knife to cut off the stem ends and leafy tops of the stalks, saving the stems and leafy tops for another use (such as for making chicken broth). Halve each stalk lengthwise, halve each half lengthwise (omit this halving for very thin stalks), and cut the stalks crosswise into ¼ in. thick slices.
   - Increase the skillet heat to medium-high, and when a drop of water added to the skillet instantly dances and disappears, add ¾ T oil, add the celery, evenly sprinkle ½ t dried sage leaves (first crushing them between your palms) over the celery, and stir-fry the celery for 1 minute, setting a timer. Stir-frying should at first be vigorous but can slow to "flip often" pace midway through the minute.
   - At the timer, cover the skillet, reduce the heat to low, and steam the celery in its own juice for 4 minutes, setting a timer.
   - At the timer, use a rubber spatula to scrape the celery and any cooking juice into a colander placed over a dinner plate.
   - Wipe the skillet clean.

4. **Stir-fry/steam the carrot and turnip.**

   - Heat the skillet at a medium setting. Heat an electric tea kettle to ready hot water for steaming.
   - Scrub and dry the carrot. Use a chef's knife to cut off the ends and to halve the carrots lengthwise. Place the halves cut side down on a cutting board and use the chef's knife to cut them crosswise into ⅛ in. thick slices.
   - Scrub and dry the turnip. Use a chef's knife to cut off the ends of the turnip. Standing the turnip upright on a flattened end, slice the turnip lengthwise into ¼ in. thick slices. Stacking two slices together and holding the slices together with one hand, cut the slices lengthwise into ¼ in. thick strips. Holding several strips together at a time, cut the strips crosswise into ¼ in. cubes.
   - Increase the skillet heat to medium-high, and when a drop of water added to the skillet instantly dances and disappears, add 1 T oil, add the carrots and turnip, evenly sprinkle ½ t dried sage leaves (first crushing the leaves between your palms) over them, and stir-fry the mixture for 1 minute, setting a timer. Stir-frying should at first be vigorous but can slow to "flip often" pace.
   - At the timer, add 1 T hot water, cover the skillet, reduce the heat setting to low, and

steam the carrots and turnip for 4 minutes, setting a timer.
- At the timer, evenly sprinkle ⅓ t salt over the vegetables and use a rubber spatula to scrape them and any cooking juice into the colander with the celery.
- Wipe the skillet clean.

5. **Stir-fry the bell peppers.**

   - Heat the skillet at a medium setting.
   - Use a 5 in. serrated knife to cut out the stem of the peppers. Remove the seeds but not the white membrane. Use the serrated knife to cut each bell pepper lengthwise into ¼ in. wide strips and to cut the strips crosswise into ¼ in. cubes.
   - Increase the skillet heat to medium-high, and when a drop of water added to the skillet instantly dances and disappears, add ½ T oil, add the peppers, and vigorously stir-fry the pepper for about 30 seconds.
   - Reduce the heat to medium and continue to cook the peppers for 2 minutes, stirring them occasionally and setting a timer.
   - At the timer, scrape the peppers and any cooking juice onto the other vegetables in the colander.
   - Wipe the skillet clean.

6. **Stir-fry the spinach.**

   - Heat the skillet at a medium setting.
   - Roughly bunch the spinach together on a large cutting board and, holding it together with one hand, use a 7 in. serrated knife to cut the spinach into approx. ⅓ in. wide pieces, cutting lengthwise and crosswise through the leaves.
   - Increase the skillet heat to medium-high, and when a drop of water added to the skillet instantly dances and disappears, add 1 T oil, add the spinach, and stir-fry it constantly until it uniformly darkens in color and slightly wilts, approx. 1 minute only.
   - Immediately remove the spinach from the heat, evenly sprinkle ¼ t salt over it, and use a rubber spatula to scrape the spinach and any cooking juice into one side of the colander holding the other cooked vegetables.

7. **Stir-fry the corn.**

   - Break apart any clumps of the unthawed frozen corn before removing it from the store package.
   - Add 2 T water to the skillet and heat it to full boiling over high heat. Mix the corn thoroughly into the water and once the water again boils, stir-fry the corn constantly for 1 minute, just until the corn is heated through and darkens in color slightly.
   - Remove the skillet from the heat, evenly sprinkle ¼ t salt over the corn, and use a rubber spatula to scrape the corn and any cooking liquid onto the other cooked vegetables.
   - Wipe the skillet clean.

8. **Prepare remaining ingredients.**

    - Use a chef's knife to halve the 1 T tart cherries and pecans or walnuts. Coarsely chop almonds.
    - Gently toss the cracked wheat with a dinner fork to evenly break it up into small pieces.
    - Stir the yogurt creamy smooth before measuring ½ cup.
    - Squeeze the ½ lemon.

9. **Assemble the dish for serving.**

    - Heat the skillet at a medium setting.
    - Place the ½ onion cut side down on a cutting board and use a chef's knife to slice off the ends. Peel the onion. Again place the onion cut side down on the cutting board and use the chef's knife to dice the onion, cutting it first lengthwise into ¼ in. thick slices and then crosswise into ¼ in. slices. Mince the ginger root.
    - Increase the skillet heat to medium-high, and when a drop of water added to the skillet instantly dances and disappears, add 1 T oil, add the onion and ginger, evenly sprinkle ½ t dried thyme leaves (first crushing it between your palms) over the onion mixture, and vigorously stir-fry the mixture for 30 seconds. Reduce the heat to medium and cook the onion mixture for 2 minutes, stirring it occasionally and setting a timer.
    - At the timer, mix the raisins, dried cherries, and nuts into the onion mixture. Spread the cracked wheat over and thoroughly mix it into the onion mixture.
    - Increase the skillet heat to medium-high and heat the onion mixture for 2 minutes to heat through the cracked wheat, stirring the mixture often.
    - Mix in the cooked vegetables (except for the spinach) and heat the combined ingredients for approx. 2 minutes until all ingredients are hot, stirring the mixture often. Add and mix in the spinach and heat the mixture another minute, stirring often.
    - Immediately serve the dish with individual servings topped with approx. ½ t fresh squeezed lemon juice and with 2-3 T yogurt alongside.

VARIATIONS: Make ingredient substitutions. Substitute, for example,

- **¾ medium whole bulgur** for cracked wheat. Reduce the water content to 1¼ cup. After cooking the bulgur for 10 minutes, add 1 c chicken or vegetable broth, return the liquid to boiling, re-cover the pan, reduce the heat setting to low, and set a timer for 10 minutes. At the timer, make a taste check and stop the cooking only if the bulgur is completely tender. It is not, continue the cooking, re-setting the timer for 5 minutes after each taste check. When purchasing bulgur, make sure that is in fact whole grain and that it is not rancid.
- **½ c hulled barley** (Recipe #167) or **½ c quinoa** (Recipe#167) for cracked wheat, or combine them with cracked wheat.
- **8 Brussels sprouts** (boiled whole, Recipe #61) for turnip or combine them.

- ½ lb pre-washed baby greens, 3-4 large leaves of kale (Recipe #26), **beet greens from 1 bunch of beets** (Recipe #23), or 3-4 medium collard leaves (Recipe #25) for spinach.
- 2 ears fresh yellow corn (Recipe #10) for dry frozen corn.
- 1½ c dry frozen green peas (Recipe #71) for turnip.

Add ingredients. Add, for example,

- **4 large cauliflower florets** (Recipe #8), broken into small florets and stir-fried with ½ t dried sage or thyme leaves.
- **1 medium zucchini** or **2 small yellow crookneck squash** (Recipe #20), with ½ t dried sage or thyme leaves added during stir-frying.
- **2 green onions** (Recipe #34), including the tops.
- **4 chilled garlic cloves** (Recipe #31).
- **2 c small okra** (Recipe #13).
- **1 10 in. Japanese eggplant, 2 small Japanese eggplants,** or **½ medium globe eggplant** (Recipe #11), cooked with ½ t dried sage leaves.
- **1½ c sugar snap** or **snow peas** or **1½ c dry frozen green peas**, stir-fried in water (Recipe #71).
- **¼ c pomegranate seeds** (Recipe #96) or **cranberries**. Stir-fry ¼ c cranberries in 2 T orange juice over high heat for 1 minute in a small skillet, reduce the heat to low, cover the pan, and steam the cranberries for 2 minutes. Mix in 2 t sugar.
- **4-6 sprigs fresh parsley**. Rinse and dry the parsley. Remove leaves from the stems. Use kitchen scissors to snip the leaves into small pieces. Separately finely snip or chop the stems. Add the leaves and stems as a topping to the dish as it is assembled for serving.
- **1-2 T finely sliced chives**, adding it as a topping.
- **½ c thinly sliced fresh pineapple** (Recipe #94).

COMMENTS: Three important points about preparing and using cracked wheat are 1) always check a cracked wheat product for rancidity, 2) prepare more cracked wheat than will be used in a recipe to have extra grain on hand for use in other dishes (such as stir-fried dishes, soups, or stews), and 3) freeze extra cracked wheat in an air-tight container and in serving size amounts to keep it on hand for quick use in dishes.

165. Guest Vegetable and Wild Rice Pilaf
(4 servings)

Vegetables and Fruit with Seasonings and Cooking Oil and Water

3 stalks organic celery
1 T extra virgin olive oil

¼ t salt
8-10 small Brussels sprouts

PART 2

½ t dried sage leaves
2 medium carrots
1 T extra virgin olive oil
½ t dried thyme leaves
½ T hot water
¼ t salt
½ red bell pepper
½ T extra virgin olive oil
3 large kale leaves
1 T extra virgin olive oil
1 T hot water

¼ t salt
2 c uniformly small sugar snap peas
2 T water
¼ t salt
½ c fresh pineapple chunks (Recipe #94)
½ chilled medium yellow onion, halved lengthwise
⅛ in. thick slice ginger root
1 T extra virgin olive oil
½–¾ t dried thyme leaves

Other Ingredients

¾ c wild rice
2 c water
¼ t salt
1 heaping T dried tart cherries

1 heaping T certified organic raisins
10 raw pecan or walnuts halves
10 raw almonds

Accompaniments

½ c plain yogurt, dairy or soy

½ lemon

Cooking Tools

2 medium heavy-bottomed saucepans, one with a tight-fitting & opaque lid
1 set measuring cups and spoons
1 timer
1 large heavy-bottomed skillet with an opaque lid
1 chef's knife
1 each 5 in. & 7 in. serrated knife

1 plastic or plastic-coated stir-fry spatula
1 rubber or other heat-resistant spatula
2 colanders
1 dinner plate
1 electric tea kettle
1 large cutting board (approx. 16 x 24 in.)
1 slotted spoon
1 hand citrus juicer

---

1. **Gather all cooking tools and ingredients.**

2. **Cook the wild rice.**

    - Add the wild rice and 2 c cool water to a saucepan and bring the water to boiling over high heat. Reduce the heat to medium and continue the boiling for 2 minutes. Cover the saucepan, reduce the heat to the lowest heat setting, and set a timer for 50 minutes.
    - Check the boiling level after several minutes. If the water continues to boil rapidly,

place a trivet under the saucepan on an electric burner or a flame tamer for a gas burner. If the boiling has completely stopped, increase the heat enough to bring the water to boiling and then reduce the heat to a point that is slightly higher than before.
- At the timer, make a taste check and continue the cooking, making a taste check every 5 minutes, as may be necessary until the wild rice is attractively soft. When the rice *is* attractively soft, remove the rice from the burner, evenly sprinkle ¼ t salt over it, toss the rice to mix in the salt, and set the rice aside, covered. When the wild rice is prepared well ahead of serving, refrigerate the rice in a tightly covered container.

3. **Stir-fry/steam the celery once the wild rice begins to cook.**

   - Heat a large skillet on a larger burner at a medium setting.
   - Rinse and dry the celery stalks. Use a chef's knife to cut off the leafy top and stem end of each stalk, setting the leaves aside for another use. Use the chef's knife to halve the stalks lengthwise and to cut the stalks crosswise into ¼ in. thick slices.
   - Increase the skillet heat to medium-high, and when a drop of water added to the skillet instantly dances and disappears, add 1 T oil, add the celery, evenly sprinkle the ½ t dried sage leaves (first crushing the leaves between your palms) over the celery, and stir-fry it for 1 minute, setting a timer. Stir-frying should at first be vigorous but can slow to "flip often" pace midway through the minute.
   - At the timer, cover the skillet, reduce the heat to low, and steam the celery in its own juice for 4 minutes, setting a timer.
   - At the timer, use a rubber spatula to scrape the celery and any cooking juice into a colander placed over a dinner plate for collecting any spilled juice.
   - Wipe the skillet clean.

4. **Stir-fry/steam the carrots.**

   - Heat the skillet at a medium setting. Heat an electric tea kettle to ready water for steaming.
   - Scrub and dry the carrots. Use a chef's knife to slice off the ends, halve the carrots lengthwise, and to cut the halves crosswise into ⅛ in. thick slices.
   - Increase the skillet heat to medium-high, and when a drop of water added to the skillet instantly dances and disappears, add 1 T oil, add the carrots, evenly sprinkle ½ t dried thyme leaves (first crushing them between your palms) over the carrots, and stir-fry them for 1 minute, setting a timer. Stir-frying should at first be vigorous but can slow to "flip often" pace midway through the minute.
   - At the timer, add ½ T hot water, cover the skillet, reduce the heat setting to low, and steam the carrot for 4 minutes, setting a timer.
   - At the timer, use a rubber spatula to scrape the carrot and any cooking juice into the colander with the celery.
   - Wipe the skillet clean.

5. **Stir-fry the bell pepper.**

PART 2

- Heat the skillet at a medium setting.
- Use a 5 in. serrated knife to cut out the stem of the pepper. Remove the seeds but not the white membrane. Use the serrated knife to cut the bell pepper lengthwise into ¼ in. wide strips and to cut the strips crosswise into ¼ in. cubes.
- Increase the skillet heat to medium-high, and when a drop of water added to the skillet instantly dances and disappears, add ½ T oil, add the bell pepper, and vigorously stir-fry the pepper for 30 seconds.
- Reduce the heat to medium and cook the pepper for 2 minutes, stirring it occasionally and setting a timer.
- At the timer, scrape the pepper and any cooking juice onto the other vegetables in the colander.
- Wipe the skillet clean.

6. **Stir-fry/steam the kale**.

    - Heat the skillet at a medium setting. Heat an electric tea kettle to ready water for steaming.
    - Rinse each leaf in cool water, shake off excess clinging water, and spread the leaves over a layer of attached paper towels or a terry towel. For flat leaves, pat the leaves dry with a paper towel. For curly leaves, add a top layer of paper towels or a terry towel and roll the leaves in the towels. Gently squeeze the leaves, unroll the towels, and add the leaves to a large cutting board.
    - Cutting close to the central vein running through each leaf, use a 5 in. serrated knife to cut the leaves from either side of the vein.
    - Holding the veins with attached stems together with one hand and keeping them separate from the leaves, use a chef's knife to finely chop them.
    - Stack the leaves, facing the leaves in the same direction. Holding the leaves together with one hand, use a 7 in. serrated knife to cut the leaves into approx. ⅓ in. pieces, cutting lengthwise and crosswise through the leaves.
    - Increase the skillet heat to medium-high, and when a drop of water added to the skillet instantly dances and disappears, add 1 T oil, add the chopped kale veins and stems and cook them for about 30 seconds, stirring occasionally.
    - Add the kale leaves and constantly stir-fry them for 1 minute, setting a timer.
    - At the timer, add 1 T hot water, cover the skillet, turn the heat setting to low, and cook the kale for 4 minutes, setting a timer.
    - At the timer, remove the skillet from the heat, evenly sprinkle ¼ t salt over the kale, and use a rubber spatula to scrape the kale and any cooking juice into the colander with the other cooked vegetables.
    - Wipe the skillet clean.

7. **Boil the Brussels sprouts whole.**

    - Add enough water to cover the Brussels sprouts by several inches to a saucepan and bring the water to boiling over high heat.
    - Add the Brussels sprouts to the boiling water without slowing the boiling and

immediately set a timer for 3 minutes.
- At the timer, use a slotted spoon to quickly remove the sprouts from the water into a second colander (not the one holding the other cooked vegetables) and rinse immediately with cold water to stop the cooking.
- Leave the saucepan with the boiling water on the burner but reduce the heat to medium.
- Pour the sprouts onto a double layer of paper towels or cloth towel and wrap the towels around the sprouts to dry them.
- Evenly sprinkle ¼ t salt over the sprouts.

8. **Boil the sugar snap peas whole.**

   - Rinse the peas.
   - Add more water to the saucepan as may be necessary to cover the peas by several inches and heat the water over high heat to boiling.
   - Add the peas without slowing the boiling and immediately set a timer for 1 minute (2 minutes for larger sugar snap peas).
   - At the timer, drain the peas into the colander used for the Brussels sprouts and immediately rinse the peas with cold water to stop the cooking.
   - Turn the burner off.
   - Pour the peas onto a double layer of paper towels or a cloth towel and wrap the towels around the peas to dry them.
   - Evenly sprinkle ¼ t salt over the peas.

9. **Prepare remaining ingredients.**

   - Use a 5 in. serrated knife to cut ½ c pineapple chunks into ¼ in. slices and add the slices to the cooked vegetables in the colander.
   - Use a chef's knife to halve the 1 T tart cherries and the pecan or walnut halves. Coarsely chop the almonds.
   - Slice the tips from the sugar snap peas, halve them crosswise, and add them to the colander with the other cooked vegetables.
   - Use a serrated knife to halve the Brussels sprouts lengthwise and add them to the other cooked vegetables.
   - Stir the yogurt creamy smooth before measuring ½ cup.
   - Squeeze the ½ lemon and remove any seeds.

10. **Assemble the dish for serving.**

    - Heat the large skillet on a large burner at a medium setting.
    - Place the ½ onion cut side down on a cutting board and use a chef's knife to cut off the ends. Peel the onion. Return the onion cut side down to the cutting board and use the chef's knife to dice the onion and mince the ginger root.
    - Increase the skillet heat to medium-high, and when a drop of water added to the skillet instantly dances and disappears, add 1 T oil, add the onion and ginger,

evenly crush ½-¾ t thyme leaves (first crushing them between your palms) over the onion, and vigorously stir-fry the onion/ginger mixture for about 30 seconds.
- Reduce the skillet heat to medium and cook the onion/ginger mixture for 1 minute, stirring occasionally and setting a timer.
- At the timer, mix the dried tart cherries, raisins, and nuts into the onion mixture. Spread the wild rice over and mix it into the onion mixture.
- Increase the skillet heat to medium-high and heat the mixture for approx. 2-3 minutes or until the rice is hot, stirring the mixture often.
- Add the cooked vegetables and pineapple and heat the mixture another 2 minutes until all the ingredients are hot, stirring often.
- Immediately serve the dish with individual servings topped with approx. ½ t lemon juice and with 2-3 T yogurt alongside.

VARIATIONS: Make ingredient substitutions. Substitute, for example,

- **1 stalk broccoli** (Recipe #4) for Brussels sprouts.
- **1½ c dry frozen green peas** (Recipe #71) for sugar snap peas.
- **8 c pre-washed spinach** (Recipe #28), **pre-washed baby greens** (a mixture that includes sturdy greens such as beet greens and kale, cooked exactly like spinach), or **any other greens** (Recipes #23-30) for kale.
- **¼ c pomegranate seeds** (Recipe #96) or **¼ c cranberries** for pineapple. Alternatively, combine either of these fruits with pineapple. Stir-fry rinsed cranberries in 2 T orange juice over high heat for 1 minute, reduce the heat to low, cover the skillet, steam them for 2 minutes, remove them from the heat, and mix in 2 t sugar.
- **1½ c pre-cooked wild rice** in place of raw wild rice.
- **½ c cooked brown rice** (Recipe #166) for ½ c cooked wild rice.

Add ingredients. Add, for example,

- **2-4 green onions** (Recipe #34) or **1 leek** (Recipe #34), including the green tops.
- **4 chilled garlic cloves** (Recipe #31).
- **⅛ each green** and **yellow bell pepper**. Cook it with the red bell pepper.
- **¼ c sliced parsley** or **2 T thinly sliced chives**, added as a topping when assembling the dish.
- **1 green chili** or **2 jalapeño peppers** (Recipe #36). Cook it with the bell pepper.
- **1 medium zucchini** or **yellow straightneck summer** squash; **2 small yellow crookneck squash** (Recipe #20). Crush ½ t dried thyme or sage leaves over the summer squash during stir-frying.
- **1½ c dry frozen whole kernel yellow corn** (Recipe #65).
- **1 medium turnip** (Recipe #22), **2 parsnips** (Recipe #14), or **1 medium rutabaga** (Recipe #19).
- **1½ c small okra** (Recipe #13).

COOKED ALIVE!

Whole Grain and Lentil Recipes

166. Brown Rice
(approx. 4 c)

Ingredients

1½ c medium or short grain brown rice
3 c cool water

½ t salt

Cooking Tools

1 2-qt enamel coated cast iron pot with a lid or 1 heavy-bottomed 2 qt saucepan (non-stick or stainless steel) with a tight-fitting & opaque lid
1 set measuring cups & spoons

1 timer
1 dinner fork
1 rubber or other heat-resistant spatula
1 quart-size air-tight storage container (glass in particular)

---

1. **Cook the brown rice.**

   - Add 1½ c rice and 3 c cool water to a saucepan and bring the water to full boiling over high heat.
   - Reduce the heat to medium and boil the rice for 2 minutes, timing this boiling.
   - At the timer, reduce the heat to a setting that maintains a very low level of boiling, tightly cover the pan with a lid, and set a timer for 50 minutes.
   - After several minutes, quickly check the cooking temperature of the rice. If the cooking water is bubbling rapidly, reduce the heat setting. If the water continues to boil rapidly, place a trivet under the saucepan on an electric stove and a flame tamer on a gas stove. If the water is very still, increase the heat to medium-high and, once the water again boils, lower the heat setting to one that is slightly above the first setting used. Re-set the timer for 45 minutes.
   - At the timer, make a taste check. A sample of cooked rice kernels should be very soft without any sign of crispness or grittiness. If the sample is not completely soft, re-cover the rice and continue the cooking for 5 minutes before again checking the rice.
   - Once the rice is satisfactorily soft, remove the saucepan from the burner.
   - For rice to be served immediately, sprinkle ½ t salt over the rice and toss the rice with a dinner fork to evenly mix in the salt.
   - For rice to be stored, add salt (¼ t per 1 c rice) when serving the rice.

2. **Refrigerate rice that will not be served immediately.**

   - Cool cooked rice slightly before storing it. Set hot cooked rice aside partially

uncovered for 5 or so minutes to allow it to cool somewhat, setting a timer in order to avoid drying.
- Use a rubber spatula to transfer the rice from the saucepan to a storage container with a tight-fitting and opaque lid. Immediately refrigerate the rice.

3. **Serve the rice within 5 days or freeze it.**

    - Keep cooked brown rice refrigerated constantly. Quickly refrigerate any leftover rice.
    - Freeze the brown rice in serving-size amounts within an air-tight container. A quart-size sealable plastic freezer bag (or gallon size for larger amounts) is an ideal freezing container. Press as much air from the bag as is possible before sealing the bag.

4. **Re-heat cooked brown rice using any one of three heating methods.**

    - **Steaming.** Heat water (1 T water per 1 c cooked brown rice) to boiling over medium-high heat in a 10 in. nonstick skillet with a tight-fitting and opaque lid. Add 1-4 c cooked rice, use a stir-fry spatula to break up any clumps and to spread the rice evenly in the skillet, evenly sprinkle salt (⅛ t per cup rice) over the rice, reduce the heat to low, cover the skillet, and heat the rice for 5 minutes, setting a timer. Remove the skillet from the heat at the timer and serve the rice immediately.
    - **Microwave oven heating.** Immediately before serving rice add it to a microwave oven- safe serving bowl, toss the rice to break up clumps, evenly sprinkle salt (⅛ t per 1 c rice) over the rice, toss the rice to mix in the salt, evenly drizzle water over the rice (1 T water per 1 c rice), cover the bowl with plastic wrap or add a microwave top, and heat the rice on high until hot, about 50 seconds per 2 c rice.
    - **Mixing with stir-fried onions.** Use at least ¼ medium chilled yellow onion per 1 c cooked rice. Preheat a skillet at medium heat. Remove the ends from the onion. Peel the onion and use a chef's knife to dice the onion. Increase the skillet heat to medium-high, add extra virgin olive oil (½ T for ¼ onion; 1 T per ½ onion), add and mix in the onion, stir-fry it constantly for 30 seconds, reduce the heat to medium, and cook the onion for 2 minutes, stirring it frequently and setting a timer. At the timer, spread the rice in the skillet, breaking up any clumps. Sprinkle salt evenly over the rice (using ⅛ t per ½ c rice) and thoroughly mix the rice into the onion. Heat the rice and onion mixture for 2 minutes or until the rice is hot, stirring it occasionally . Serve the rice immediately.

COMMENTS: Brown rice should be attractively soft, but it should also not be overcooked. In addition to being soft, kernels should also glisten. Overcooking dulls rice coloring, makes rice somewhat mushy, and reduces tastiness.

In selecting brown rice,

- select medium and short grain brown rice as especially flavorful varieties. More absorptive than long varieties of brown rice, these products are especially moist

when cooked. While long grain rice fluffs up nicely and is less chewy than medium and short grain rice, it is bland and dry in comparison.
- The Lundberg medium grain product called Golden Rose is an especially tasty brown rice selection that is widely marketed in natural food stores.
- Reference #6 (Maximizing the Attractiveness of Whole Food Ingredients Commonly Used in Part II Recipes), Ingredient #7, provides detailed selection, storage, and cooking techniques for reliably preparing attractive cooked brown rice.

167. Wild Rice
Hulled Barley, Wheat Berries, and Quinoa
(approx. 1½ c)

Ingredients

1 c wild rice
3½ c cool water

½ t salt

Cooking Tools

1 2-qt enamel-coated cast iron pot with lid or
   1 heavy-bottomed medium (2 qt) saucepan (nonstick or stainless steel) with a tight-fitting & opaque lid

1 set each measuring cups & spoons
1 timer
1 rubber or other heat-resistant spatula
1 quart-size air-tight storage container
   (glass in particular)

---

1. **Cook the wild rice.**

    - Add 1 c wild rice and 3½ c cool water to the saucepan and bring the water to full boiling over high heat.
    - Reduce the heat to medium and boil the wild rice for 2 minutes, timing this boiling.
    - At the timer, reduce the heat to a setting that maintains a very low level of boiling, tightly cover the pan, and set a timer for 55 minutes.
    - Check the cooking temperature of the wild rice after several minutes. If the cooking water continues to boil rapidly, reduce the heat. If lowering the setting does not stop rapid boiling, place a trivet under an electric burner or a flame tamer under a gas burner. Re-set the timer for 55 minutes once the heating temperature is reset.
    - At the timer, make a taste check. A sample of cooked wild rice kernels should be very soft without any sign of crispness or grittiness. If the sample is not completely soft, continue the cooking for 5 minutes at a time, making a taste check every 5 minutes until the rice is satisfactorily soft.
    - Once the wild rice is soft, remove it from the burner.

PART 2

- For wild rice to be served immediately, sprinkle ½ t salt evenly over the rice and use a dinner fork to toss the rice to mix in the salt. Leave the lid ajar for several minutes to stop the cooking (timing this uncovering to avoid drying of the rice) and set the rice aside tightly covered to keep it hot for serving.
- For wild rice to be stored, omit adding the salt. Leave the lid ajar for 5 or so minutes to allow the rice to cool somewhat, use a rubber spatula to transfer the rice from the saucepan into a storage container with a tight-fitting lid, and refrigerate the rice.
- Add salt to stored rice when serving. Add ¼ t per 1 c wild rice.

2. **Serve the rice within 5 days or freeze it.**

    - Package rice in an air-tight freezer quality zippered plastic bag, pressing out as much air as possible before sealing the bag.
    - Package rice for freezing in serving size amounts. For example, package it in quart size sealable plastic freezer bags.

3. **Re-heat wild rice or any whole grain in the same manner as brown rice (Recipe #166).**

VARIATIONS: Substitute **whole grains** (hulled barley, wheat berries, and quinoa) for wild rice. Substitute, for example,

- **hulled barley.** Soak the barley. Either soak it overnight or for at least 8 hours in a measured amount of cooking water or bring the barley to full boiling in its cooking water (1 c barley to 3 c water), remove it from the heat, and set it aside, covered, for 1 hour before either resuming cooking or cooling and refrigerating the grain for later cooking. To cook hulled barley, bring the soaked barley in its soaking water to full boiling, reduce the heat to low, and cook the barley for ¾ to 1 hour or until the barley is completely soft. Without soaking, cook the barley for 1¼-1½ hours or until completely soft. One cup barley yields approx. 3½ cooked barley.
- **wheat berries.** Soak the berries. Either soak them overnight or for at least 8 hours in a measured amount of cooking water or bring them to a full boiling in cooking water (3 c water per 1 c grain), remove the berries from the burner, and set them aside, covered, for 1 hour before either resuming cooking or cooling and refrigerating the berries for later cooking. To cook wheat berries, cook soaked wheat berries for 1¼-1½ hours or until completely soft. Cook unsoaked berries for 2 hours or until completely soft. One cup wheat berries yields about three cups cooked grain.
- **quinoa.** Pronounced keen-WHA, quinoa does not need to be soaked, but it may need to be rinsed in order to remove some bitterness according to product directions. Cook 1 c quinoa with 2 c water for approx. 15 minutes or until the grain is completely soft. One cup quinoa yields about 2½ c cooked grain.

COMMENTS: Soak whole grains for the softest grain.

168. Lentils
(1½ c)

Ingredients

1 c lentils (green or brown) ½ t salt
2¼ c water

Cooking Tools

1 2-qt enamel-coated cast iron pot or 1
   2-qt heavy-bottomed saucepan (nonstick
   or stainless steel) with a tight-fitting &
   opaque lid
1 timer

1 set each measuring cups & spoons
2 cup air-tight storage container
   (preferably glass)
1 small jar with a tight-fitting lid

---

1. **Gather all cooking tools and ingredients.**

2. **Soak the lentils.**

    - Add 1 c lentils to a medium saucepan, sort through the lentils to remove any stones, add 2¼ c water, bring the water to full boiling over high heat, remove the pan from the heat, and set it aside, covered, for one hour, setting a timer.
    - At the timer, either cook the lentils or refrigerate the lentils, covered.

3. **Begin cooking the lentils 20 minutes before adding them to a dish for serving.**

    - Return the cooking water to boiling over high heat, reduce the heat to a level that maintains very gentle boiling, cover the lentils, and set a timer for 15 minutes.
    - After several minutes, quickly check the cooking temperature of the lentils. If the cooking water is bubbling rapidly, reduce the heat setting. If the water continues to boil rapidly, place a trivet under the saucepan on an electric stove and a flame tamer on a gas stove. Rapid boiling can cause unexpected evaporation of the cooking water.
    - At the timer, taste the lentils and remove the pan from the heat if they are completely soft. They should not have any hint of crispness but they should also hold shape and not be mushy. If they are not completely soft, continue the cooking for another 5 minutes, setting a timer, before making another taste test.
    - Stop the cooking when the lentils are completely soft. Remove the pan from the stove, drain any unabsorbed broth into a small jar, evenly sprinkle ½ t salt over the lentils, and mix in the salt. Save any broth for another use.

4. **Store extra lentils.**

- Refrigerate lentils. Transfer lentils that will not be immediately served to an air-tight storage container and a glass container in particular. Refrigerate the lentils. Refrigerate the broth as well, also preferably in glass.
- Store the lentils for up to 4 days.
- Freeze lentils and lentil broth that will not be used within four days.

  - Freeze cooked lentils in serving-size amounts in an air-tight container with a small amount of lentil broth. For example, freeze a serving size amount of lentils in a quart size sealable plastic freezer bag, squeezing as much air as is possible from the bag before sealing it.
  - Dry freeze lentils. Spread drained lentils onto a pie plate or other shallow container that fits into a refrigerator freezer, freeze them until they are solid, and transfer them to an air-tight plastic freezer bag, squeezing out as much air as possible before sealing the bag. Separately freeze lentil broth in a small freezer-proof jar with a tight-fitting lid.

COMMENTS: Avoid selection of lentils that contain a large number of broken seeds because the lentils will not cook evenly. Broken open lentils cook more quickly than intact ones and, as a result, become overcooked. Overcooked lentils become unattractively mushy.

While soaking the lentils adds a preparation step, soaked lentils are most reliably soft and become soft in the shortest cooking time.

CHAPTER EIGHT

Soups and Stews

Soup and Stew Description

COOKED ALIVE! soups and stews are not soups and stews as typically presented. The vegetable content of these stews and soups distinguishes them. *Cooked Alive!* soups and stews, and stews in particular, reach the dinner table as robust concoctions of tasty and alluring vegetables and, very importantly, do so with minimal reliance on salt or fat.

The key to the attractiveness of vegetables in *Cooked Alive!* soups and stews is twofold: use of *juice-protective* techniques for preparing vegetables and use of *juice-protective* methods of serving soups and stews.

- Vegetables are protected from overcooking and direct contact with liquid throughout preparation. To do so, they are individually stir-fried or stir-fry/steamed just to tenderness, removed from heat, set aside and kept dry until serving, added to hot soup or stew only just prior to serving, and quickly heated through. Retaining the attractive flavor and texture of vegetables, in turn, protects them from pureeing, which destroys both the distinctive flavor and insoluble fiber content of vegetables.
- Recipes (all but one) serve vegetables in either a milk sauce or tomato sauce. These sauces serve as a highly attractive flavoring base. Both sauces enhance and protect vegetable flavoring up to the point a soup or stew is served. They hold vegetable flavoring during storage as well.

Milk sauce serves as an outstanding flavoring base in Chapter Eight soups (Recipes #169-172) for a number of reasons. Milk sauce, for example,

- is very quick and simple to prepare. A nonstick skillet makes quick heating of milk possible with minimal threat of scorching. Soups, as a result, are any day dishes that cooks can quickly assemble.
- is especially well matched to cabbage family vegetables, such as broccoli, cauliflower, turnips, kale, and collards. Milk heightens the color and natural sweetness of these vegetables. Very importantly, milk also neutralizes plant acids that spill from plant cells during cooking. This neutralization prevents the plant acids from mixing with

and breaking down flavor-altering sulfur compounds contained by cabbage family vegetables.[272] Milk sauce, as a result, converts cabbage family vegetables into reliably tasty and easy-to-use ingredients.

- heightens and holds the natural color and sweet flavor of a variety of other vegetables during both serving and storage, including onions, green peas (including dried split green peas as used in Recipe #179: Curried Split Pea and Chicken Stew), yellow vegetables (such as corn), winter squash, and potatoes.
- enhances and welcomes dark green leafy vegetables, which is of particular importance. These less familiar but highly nutritious vegetables are readily acceptable ingredients in milk sauce-based soups.
- welcomes a variety of hearty ingredients, such as whole grains and legumes, which can be successfully included to enhance the energy-carrying capacity of a soup.
- mixes attractively with fruit-flavored 100% whole wheat muffins (Recipes #180-184), which are both delicious and quick and simple-to-prepare soup accompaniments.

Herb-flavored tomato sauce also serves as an outstanding flavoring base in Chapter Eight stews (Recipes #173-179). Tomato sauce, for example,

- is itself completely quick and simple to prepare. Main ingredients are commercially prepared tomato products (tomato juice and tomato paste), canned broth, quick-cooking herb-flavored onions and ginger root, fresh lemon juice, and a touch of brown sugar. This sauce is simmered for five minutes only before being combined with already cooked vegetables and other prepared stew ingredients for serving. Sauce can be prepared well ahead of assembling a stew for serving.
- serves as a highly attractive flavoring base for almost all vegetables. This includes highly nutritious dark green leafy vegetables.
- readily welcomes a variety of other whole food ingredients, including beef or chicken, whole grains, and/or legumes that convert a stew into a hearty one-pot meal. Yielding 6-8 servings, a Chapter Eight stew satisfies a crowd or covers several meals.
- mixes attractively with a variety of accompaniments, including simple ones like plain yogurt and shredded cheese, 100% whole wheat muffins (Recipes #180-184) and 100% whole corn bread (Recipe #185), and special occasion Whole Rye Bread (Recipe #186).

One Chapter Eight stew recipe, Recipe #178 (Old Fashioned Chicken Stew), does not rely on sauce for flavoring. A somewhat different combination of flavoring ingredients – herb-seasoned onions, herb-seasoned vegetables, other vegetables, concentrated chicken broth, and chicken – underlies the rich broth flavor of this special stew.

Soup and Stew Recipe Preparation Notes

Soup and Stew Recipe Preparation Notes provide helpful instruction and information for cooks that cannot fit into individual recipes. These Preparation Notes present several types of information, including information about,

---

[272] Adelle Davis, "Keep the Flavor and Nutritive Value in Your Vegetables," *Let's Cook It Right* (New York: New American Library, Inc., 1970): 351-352.

- technical details relating to recipe preparation (Notes #1-9), with #1 being of particular importance.
- preparation of vegetable variation suggestions made in recipes (Note #10).
- recipe resource references (Notes #11-12).
- cooking tool information (Notes #13-14).

1. **Adjust vegetable stir-fry/steaming technique for gas burners.** The stir-fry/steaming technique used for preparing vegetables in Chapter Eight soup and stew recipes matches electric burners, which do not immediately cool when burner heat is reduced. Cooking of vegetables, as a result, slows slowly and vegetables continue to cook when heat is reduced after one minute of stir-frying. **Because gas burners *do* immediately respond to heat changes**, it is necessary to alter stir-fry/steaming technique. On a gas burner, the reduction of heat to low is so abrupt that cooking can stop completely, and vegetables, as a result, will not be tender at the recipe-directed cooking time. Therefore, when using a gas burner, adjust stir-fry/steaming technique in the following manner.

    - After one minute of stir-frying, add 1 T hot water as directed by recipes but reduce the heat to **medium**-low. Cover the skillet and heat a vegetable on medium-low for 30 seconds before reducing the heat to low and steaming the vegetable according to the recipe directed cooking time.

2. **In stir-fry/steaming of vegetables, it is important that hot water added for steaming should immediately sizzle and form steam.** This is a most important clue. It reliably ensures a vegetable will be tender in the recipe specified cooking time. If the water sizzles wildly, the water will likely evaporate and the vegetable may scorch during steaming. An additional 1 T hot water then needs to be added before covering the skillet for steaming. If the water added for steaming does not sizzle at all, the vegetable is not sufficiently hot to begin cooking and will not cook to tenderness in the recipe directed cooking time. The skillet temperature should then again be increased to medium-high and the skillet reheated until the steaming water boils before reducing the temperature and covering the skillet for steaming.

3. **To speed up stew preparation time,**

    - prepare all or part of the vegetable content ahead and refrigerate the cooked vegetables, tightly covered once they have cooled. The vegetables can be prepared hours or even a day ahead provided the vegetables remain dry and protected from air during refrigeration.
    - reduce vegetable content. To reduce vegetable content without undermining stew flavor,

        - retain seasoning vegetables, which include onions, ginger root, and bell peppers.
        - retain carrots because they are a key flavoring and coloring vegetable.
        - add herbs to all vegetables during cooking.
        - substitute vegetables with the shortest cooking times and/or least preparation

time for longer cooking vegetables. Substitute, for example, dry frozen green peas (Recipe #71) and dry frozen whole kernel yellow corn (Recipe #65) as primary vegetables. These vegetables significantly enhance both the color and sweetness of stews in general and prepare literally within minutes when stir-fried in water.
- substitute pre-washed spinach or pre-washed baby greens for un-washed greens. Without any rinsing, drying, and vein/stem trimming required, pre-washed spinach and baby greens need only to be cut and cooked, and this cooking (stir-frying) takes only one minute.

4. **To easily and efficiently dice the ½ medium bulb onion and mince the ⅛ in. thick slice of ginger root routinely called for in soup and stew recipes**,

- slice off the tips and peel the skin from the onion. Place the half onion cut side down on a cutting board and use a chef's knife to cut the onion lengthwise into thin slices (⅛-¼ in. wide) while holding the onion together with one hand. Turn the onion sideways and, again holding the onion together with one hand, repeat the slicing.
- use a chef's or serrated knife to cut the ginger into thin slices. While again holding the slices together with one hand and cutting diagonally away from your fingers to best protect them during this fine cutting, cut the ginger slices crosswise into uniformly small pieces.

5. **To convert Chapter Eight soups and stews into vegan vegetarian form**,

- substitute non-dairy for dairy milk products and extra virgin olive oil for butter in **soups** (Recipes #169-172). It should be noted that while non-dairy milk flavor is fully satisfactory, non-dairy milk does not have the same vegetable color-enhancing, flavor-sweetening, and flavor-holding capacity as dairy milk.
- substitute non-dairy for dairy cheese and yogurt in **vegetable stew** (Recipe #174, Extravagantly Vegetable Chili).
- omit ground beef in **stews**. Substitute vegetable for beef or poultry broth, substitute non-dairy for dairy cheese and yogurt, and both expand seasoning vegetable content and add herb or spice flavoring to vegetables during stir-frying to compensate for loss of beef flavoring.

6. **To substitute extra lean ground beef for chuck roast in Recipe #175 (Old Fashioned Beef Stew)**, cook 1 lb extra lean ground beef with 2 finely minced ⅛ in. thick slices of fresh ginger root. Pre-heat the skillet at medium-high heat, add when a drop of water added to the skillet instantly dances and disappears, add ½ T extra virgin olive oil, add the ground meat and ginger, use a stir-fry spatula to break up the ground beef into small (but not fine) pieces, evenly sprinkle ½ t ground curry powder or 1 t dried herb leaves (first crushing the leaves between your palms) over the meat, and stir-fry the meat for 30 seconds at medium-high heat. Reduce the heat to medium and cook the beef for approx. 1 minute until no red coloring remains, flipping pieces often. Remove the meat from the heat. Evenly sprinkle ½ t salt over the meat. Toss the meat to mix in the salt.

7. **To substitute chuck roast for ground beef in other stew recipes containing beef,** substitute either a 2-3 lb chuck or other variety of beef roast (such as shoulder roast) for ground beef in any of the stews containing beef. Prepare other varieties of beef roast in exactly the same way as chuck roast.

8. **To re-heat leftover portions of Chapter Eight soups,**

    - add ½-1 c milk to a nonstick skillet, add and thoroughly mix the soup into the milk, and heat the soup over medium-high heat, stirring it often with a rubber or other heat- resistant spatula until the soup nears boiling.
    - reduce the heat to medium and continue the heating for 3-4 more minutes until the soup is very hot, stirring often.

9. **Brown rice can be omitted in Chapter Eight soups and stews.** Should cooked brown rice not be on hand, it can be left out of recipes. However, brown rice makes important nutritional contributions that make it worth the effort to have it on hand or to prepare it fresh. Brown rice is a nutrient-dense whole food that makes valuable nutritional contributions, including vitamin E contained in the rice germ and high quality bran, which enhance the nutritional diversity of a dish. Brown rice contributes complex carbohydrates that add to the energy carrying capacity of the soup or stew. Preparing fresh brown rice is easy to do when preparing recipes including other longer-cooking ingredients, such as Recipe #175 (Old Fashioned Beef Stew) and Recipe #178 (Old Fashioned Chicken Stew).

10. **Chapter One (Stir-Fried and Stir-Fry/Steamed Vegetable Recipes) serves as a reference for preparing the vegetable variation suggestions made in Chapter Eight soup and stew recipes.** The recipe number attached to a vegetable variation suggestion identifies the Chapter One reference recipe, which provides preparation details as well as basic selection and nutritional information about the vegetable.

11. **Fully committed to assisting cooks achieve serving success,** *Cooked Alive!* **includes three references focused on securing the attractive flavor of key individual soup and stew ingredients.**

    - Reference #9 (Clinching Soup and Stew Flavor: Expanded Preparation Support) makes flavor securing suggestions for key soup and stew flavoring ingredients. These ingredients include **cheese, milk sauce, tomato sauce,** and **seasoning vegetables**.
    - Reference #6 (Maximizing the Attractiveness of Whole Food Ingredients Commonly Used in Part II Recipes) makes flavor-securing suggestions for key whole foods other than vegetables and fruits. Whole food ingredients covered that are relevant to Chapter Eight soup and/or stew recipes are **dried** and **fresh herb flavoring, legumes, beef** and **poultry, nuts, brown rice,** and **yogurt**.
    - Reference #10 (Fresh Chicken Broth Recipe) provides a simple recipe for home preparing poultry broth. Vastly more flavorful than commercially prepared canned broth, fresh home-prepared broth can be substituted for canned broth in Chapter Eight stews.

PART 2

12. **Cooks can substantially (even dramatically) boost the nutritional quality of Chapter Eight soup and stew recipes through selection of the highest quality dish ingredients.** *Cooked Alive!* includes three references to serve as resources for assisting cooks in making high quality individual ingredient selections.

    - Reference #1 (Selecting Top Quality Fresh Whole Vegetables and Fruits) identifies top quality vegetable products, which are products that are raw, physically intact, and naturally produced. Natural production means vegetables have been produced using natural fertilizer, have not been genetically modified, and have not undergone any synthetic (man-made) chemical treatment (processing) during production or marketing. They are certified organic and locally produced, but not industrially produced, vegetables.
    - Reference #4 (Selecting Top Quality Whole Food Ingredients for Use in Part II Recipes) identifies whole food ingredients (other than vegetables and fruits) that are raw, physically intact, and naturally produced. Natural production means products of plants, animals, and poultry that have been produced on a natural diet, have not been genetically modified, and have not undergone synthetic (man-made) chemical tampering (processing) during production and marketing. Specific whole food products covered in Reference #4 that are relevant to Chapter Eight soup and stew recipes are **protein (beef, poultry, and eggs)**, **nuts**, **brown rice**, and **lentils**.
    - Reference #5 (Selecting High Quality Processed Ingredients for Use in Part II Recipes) identifies specific products of different types of food that have undergone physical processing but that retain significant nutritional quality. Processed foods covered in Reference #5 that are relevant to Chapter Eight soups and stews are **ground beef, canned beans, canned whole kernel yellow corn, dairy products (cheese, milk, and butter), extra virgin olive oil,** and **tomato paste**. Processed foods covered that are relevant to Chapter Eight bread accompaniments include **raisins, whole wheat flour** and **whole corn flour**.

13. **Important cooking tool information relating to Chapter Eight soup and stew recipes is as follows:**

    - Recipes list all key cooking tools used, listing them in order of use, but they do not list some basic wiping, cleaning, wrapping, and working tools, including paper and cloth towels, vegetable scrubbing tools, plastic wrap, and general cutting boards. These tools are used routinely in recipes and, as a result, need to be kept handy.
    - The General Cooking Tools list contained in the Part II Introduction serves as a descriptive reference for all the kitchen tools used in Chapter Eight recipes except for those tools that are either specific to Chapter Eight recipes or not used commonly in Part II recipes. These tools include:

        - **Can opener.** This tool is needed for opening tomato products packed in cans.
        - **Cheese grater.** This can be a vegetable shredder. Both should have a fine and coarse setting.
        - **Garlic mincing tool.** Any variety of tool that speeds the preparation of garlic is

a very useful tool for use in Chapter Eight stew recipes. This tool encourages use of minced garlic, and minced garlic makes a distinctive flavoring contribution to stews. Without this tool, minced garlic is easily left out of dishes or used in minimal amounts. A top quality mincing tool is one with stainless steel blades.

- **Dutch oven with a tight-fitting and opaque lid.** This 8 cup pot serves two uses. First, it is large enough to hold and cook a chuck roast or whole chicken. Second, it is large enough for assembling a multi-ingredient vegetable stew. Any large pot with a tight-fitting and opaque lid substitutes.
- **Food scale.** A food scale with a 1 lb measuring capacity makes it possible for a cook to accurately measure cheese content. Without this tool, gauging cheese content and, hence, its calorie content, is very difficult.
- **Large ladle or scoop.** This tool eases the serving of stew.
- **Spatula, thin bladed.** This spatula should have a firm but pliable blade for easy removal of tomato paste from thin cans and small jars.
- **1 large soup or stew serving spoon.** This is a spoon large enough to efficiently serve soup or stew from a skillet or soup pan.
- **Trivet or flame tamer.** A trivet is a useful tool to have on hand when preparing brown rice on an electric burner that does not have a true low heat. A flame tamer is useful for preparing brown rice on a gas burner that does not reduce to a low temperature. Placed between the saucepan and burner, both reduce the heat level of a burner to a reliably low level.

14. Baking tools needed for preparing Chapter Eight bread accompaniment recipes include, as follows,

- **1 very large mixing bowl** (16 c minimum). This large bowl is needed for preparing rye yeast bread.
- **1 oven glove, padded.** One glove is essential for moving hot bread pans in and out of an oven; using two gloves provides extra protection.
- **1 loaf pan, 5 x 9 in.** The heavier the metal of the pan, the greater the protection from over-browning provided. A nonstick surface greatly eases bread removal and loaf pan clean-up.
- **1 nonstick muffin pan, 12 tins, 1¼ in. deep.** The heavier the metal of the muffin pan, the greater the protection from over-browning and burning provided. While not absolutely essential, a nonstick muffin pan greatly simplifies the removal of muffins from tins and tin cleanup, which are important helps.
- **1 potato masher with metal grid head.** This tool cuts banana, winter squash, and sweet potato into small even chunks that add flavor and texture to muffins. Mashing, in contrast, causes loss of distinctive fruit or vegetable flavor. Smoothly mashed banana also easily becomes too moist, which over-moistens batter and leaves muffins unattractively soggy. The grid squares of the masher should measure approximately ⅓ x ⅓ in. A non-slip grip on a potato masher is a useful feature. A long-handled dish brush is an efficient cleaning tool.
- **1 large baking sheet (9 x 13 in.).** Needed for baking rye bread rounds, a heavy-bottomed sheet best protects bread from over-browning or burning.

PART 2

- **1 wooden spoon with a big head.** Using a big-headed spoon (approx. 2½ in. wide) reduces the number of strokes needed to mix dry and wet ingredients when making muffins. Minimum stirring, in turn, minimizes the development of the gluten content of whole wheat flour, which is necessary for achieving light-textured muffins. Additionally, a big-headed spoon efficiently accomplishes the beating of yeast breads.
- **1 wire rack, large metal cooling (approx. 12 x 18 in.).** Because air freely circulates around muffins and other breads placed on a rack for cooling, steam does not condense on the bread bottom and cause it to become soggy.
- **1 zesting tool.** This simple tool greatly simplifies adding flavor-enhancing citrus zest (the outer colored portion of the skin) to muffins.

Chunky Vegetable Soup – Milk Sauce Base Recipes

169. Broccoli, Pepper, and Potato Soup
(2-3 servings)

Vegetables with Seasoning, Cooking Oil, and Steaming Water

1 stalk chilled broccoli
1 T extra virgin olive oil
1 T hot water
¼ t salt
2 medium red potatoes
1 T extra virgin olive oil

½ t dried sweet basil leaves
½ t dried oregano leaves
1 T hot water
⅓ t salt
½ red bell pepper, halved lengthwise
½ T extra virgin olive oil

Milk Sauce Ingredients

½ chilled medium yellow onion, halved lengthwise
2 ⅛-in thick slices of fresh ginger root
1 T extra virgin olive oil
½ t dried sweet basil leaves
½ t dried oregano leaves
⅓ t garlic powder
1½ T butter

1½ T whole wheat flour
¼ t salt
3 c milk (1%, 2% or full fat)
1 T packed dark brown sugar
½-1 c milk
10 raw pecan or walnut halves or raw whole almonds

Accompaniments

3 oz natural aged extra sharp cheddar cheese (to yield approx. ⅔ c shredded cheese)

½ c plain yogurt

Cooking Tools

1 large skillet with a tight-fitting & opaque lid	1 timer
1 each 5 in. serrated & chef's knife	1 rubber or other heat-resistant spatula
1 set each measuring spoons & cups	1 colander
1 large nonstick skillet with a tight-fitting & opaque lid	1 dinner plate
	1 cheese grater
1 electric tea pot	1 large soup serving spoon
1 plastic or plastic-coated stir-fry spatula	2-3 large soup bowls

---

1. **Gather all ingredients and cooking utensils.**

2. **Stir-fry/steam the broccoli.**

    - Heat a large skillet on a large burner at a medium setting. Heat an electric tea kettle to prepare hot water for steaming.
    - Rinse the broccoli stalk with cool water, briskly shake it to remove clinging water, wrap it in paper towels or a terry cloth towel, and firmly squeeze the stalk to dry it thoroughly.
    - Place the broccoli stalk on its side and use a serrated knife to slice the florets from the stalks, leaving the stems as long as possible (cutting them off at the stalk). Slice off and set aside any leaves. Slice off and discard the very bottom tip of each stalk. Halve each floret and attached stem lengthwise, place the halves cut side down, and halve them lengthwise. Cut large halved florets lengthwise into ⅛ in. thick slices.
    - Increase the skillet heat to medium-high.
    - When a drop of water added to the skillet instantly dances and disappears, add 1 T oil, add the sliced broccoli florets and any leaves, and stir-fry them for 1 minute, setting a timer. Stir-frying should at first be vigorous but can slow to "flip often" pace midway through the minute.
    - At the timer, add 1 T hot water, immediately cover the pan, reduce the heat to low, and steam the broccoli for 4 minutes, setting a timer.
    - At the timer, remove the skillet from the heat, evenly sprinkle ¼ t salt over the broccoli, and use a rubber spatula to scrape it and any cooking juice into a colander placed over a dinner plate for collecting any cooking juice.
    - Wipe the skillet clean.

3. **Stir-fry/steam the potatoes.**

    - Return the skillet to the stove and heat it at a medium setting on a large back burner. Heat an electric tea kettle to prepare hot water for steaming.
    - Scrub, dry, and slice off the tips and any eyes on the potatoes. Stand each potato upright on a flattened end and use a chef's knife to cut each potato lengthwise into ¼ in. thick slices, cut the slices lengthwise into ¼ in. thick strips, and cut the strips

PART 2

crosswise into ¼ in. cubes.
- Increase the skillet heat to medium-high, and when a drop of water added to the skillet instantly dances and disappears, add 1 T oil, add the potatoes, evenly sprinkle ½ t each dried basil and oregano leaves (first crushing them between your palms) over the potatoes, and stir-fry them for 1 minute, setting a timer. Stir-frying should at first be vigorous but can slow to "flip often" pace midway through the minute.
- At the timer, reduce the heat to medium and heat the potatoes for 1 minute, stirring them occasionally and setting a timer.
- At the timer, add 1 T hot water, reduce the heat to low, cover the pan, and steam the potato for 10 minutes, setting a timer.
- At the timer, turn off the heat, uncover the skillet, and evenly sprinkle ⅓ t salt over the potatoes. Set the skillet aside, covered.

4. **Stir-fry the bell pepper.**

- Heat a large nonstick skillet on a large burner at a medium setting.
- Use a 5 in. serrated knife to cut out the stem of the bell pepper. Remove the seeds but not the membrane. Use the serrated knife to cut cut the pepper lengthwise into ¼ in. thick strips and to cut the strips crosswise into ¼ in. cubes.
- Increase the skillet heat to medium-high.
- When a drop of water added to the skillet instantly dances and disappears, add ½ T oil, add the pepper, and vigorously stir-fry it for about 30 seconds. Reduce the skillet heat to a medium setting and cook the pepper for 2 minutes, stirring it occasionally and setting a timer.
- At the timer, use a rubber spatula to scrape the pepper and any cooking juice into the colander with the broccoli.
- Wipe the skillet clean.

5. **Prepare the milk sauce.**

- Return the large nonstick skillet to the stove and heat it at a medium setting.
- Place the ½ onion cut side down on a cutting board and use a chef's knife to slice off the ends. Peel the onion. Return the onion cut side down to the cutting board and use the chef's knife to dice it. Mince the ginger.
- Increase the skillet heat to medium-high, and when a drop of water instantly dances and disappears, add 1 T oil, add the onion and ginger, evenly sprinkle ½ t each dried basil and oregano leaves (first crushing the leaves between your palms) and ½ t garlic powder over them, and vigorously stir-fry the mixture for about 30 seconds.
- Reduce the heat to medium and cook the onion mixture for 2 minutes, stirring it occasionally and setting a timer.
- At the timer, add and melt 1½ T butter, evenly sprinkle 1½ T flour and ¼ t salt over the onion mixture, mix the ingredients together, and cook the mixture for about 30 seconds, stirring occasionally.
- Increase the skillet heat to medium-high.
- Slowly pour in 3 c milk, at first using a rubber spatula to rapidly stir the mixture to

- blend the flour mixture and milk.
- Heat the milk sauce until the milk starts to boil, stirring the milk frequently with a rubber spatula and regularly scraping the skillet bottom with the spatula to prevent sticking.
- When the milk begins to boil, reduce the heat to a high medium setting and heat the milk until the mixture thickens and becomes smooth, stirring it quite often to prevent sticking.
- When the sauce thickens, reduce the heat to low, mix in 1 T packed dark brown sugar, and partially cover the skillet. Remove the skillet from the heat, cover it, and set it aside if not assembling the soup immediately.

6. **Assemble the soup for serving.**

   - Heat the milk sauce at a medium setting.
   - Make final soup-making preparations. Stir the yogurt creamy smooth before measuring ½ cup. Coarsely grate the cheese and evenly divide it between two or three soup bowls. Use a chef's knife to halve pecans and walnuts and to coarsely chop almonds. Divide the nuts between the bowls. Add ½-1 c milk to thin the sauce to taste.
   - Increase the skillet heat to medium-high and bring the sauce to near boiling. Stir in the cooked vegetables and any collected cooking juice. Heat the soup until it reaches near boiling, stirring regularly.
   - Reduce the heat to medium and continue heating the soup for 3-4 minutes or until all ingredients are hot, stirring the soup occasionally.

7. **Serve the soup.** Pour the soup over the cheese in the soup bowls and top each serving with at least 2 dollops of yogurt.

   VARIATIONS: Make ingredient substitutions. Substitute, for example,

   - **baked potatoes** (Recipe #46) for stir-fry/steamed potatoes. Cut the unpeeled potatoes into ½ in. thick chunks.
   - **6-8 new small red potatoes** or **other tasty small potatoes** for medium potatoes. Boil the potatoes whole (Recipe #72). Either halve or quarter each potato for serving.
   - **2 c dry frozen yellow corn kernels** (Recipe #65), unthawed, for potatoes.
   - **3 c soy milk** or **other non-dairy liquid** for dairy milk, **soy yogurt** for dairy yogurt, and **soy cheese** for cheddar cheese to convert the soup to vegan vegetarian form.

   Add ingredients. Add, for example,

   - ⅛ **c thinly sliced chives.**
   - **2-3 stalks celery** (Recipe #9).
   - **1-2 dry frozen whole kernel yellow corn** (Recipe #65), unthawed.
   - **1 chilled medium turnip** (Recipe #22). Alternatively, add diced dry roasted turnip (Recipe #53). Use larger chunks of turnip for the most flavorful turnip.

PART 2

170. Corn, Pepper, and Potato Soup
(2-3 servings)

Vegetables with Seasonings, Cooking Oil, and Cooking Water

2 medium red potatoes
1 T extra virgin olive oil
1 t dried dill weed
1 T water
¼ t salt
2 ears yellow corn
2 T water

¼ t salt
½ red bell pepper, halved lengthwise
½ T extra virgin olive oil
½ lb pre-washed spinach
1 T extra virgin olive oil
¼ t salt

Milk Sauce Ingredients

½ chilled medium onion, halved lengthwise
2 ⅛-in. thick slices of fresh ginger root
1 T extra virgin olive oil
½ t dried dill weed
½ t garlic powder
1½ T butter
1½ T whole wheat flour

¼ t salt
3 c milk (1%, 2%, or full fat)
1 T packed dark brown sugar
½-1 c milk
½-1 c mil
10 raw pecan or walnut halves or ⅛ c raw whole almonds

Accompaniments

3 oz extra sharp cheddar cheese
(to yield approx. ⅔ c shredded cheese)

½ c plain yogurt

Cooking Tools

1 large skillet with a tight-fitting & opaque lid
1 electric tea kettle
1 each chef's & 7 in. serrated knife
1 large cutting board (16 x 24 in.)
1 set each measuring spoons & cups
1 plastic or plastic-coated stir-fry spatula
1 timer

1 large nonstick skillet with a tight-fitting & opaque lid
1 pie plate
1 rubber or other heat-resistant spatula
1 colander with dinner plate
1 cheese grater
2-3 large soup bowls
1 large soup serving spoon

---

1. Gather all dish ingredients and cooking tools.

2. **Stir-fry/steam the potatoes.**

    - Heat a large skillet on a medium setting on a large back burner. Begin heating an electric tea kettle to prepare hot water for steaming.
    - Scrub and thoroughly dry the potatoes.
    - Use a chef's knife to cut off the ends and cut out any potato eyes.
    - Stand each potato upright on a flattened end on a cutting board and use the chef's knife to cut each lengthwise into ¼ in. thick slices. Stacking 2 slices together, cut the slices into ¼ in. thick strips. Holding the strips together with one hand, slice them into ¼ in. cubes.
    - Increase the skillet heat to medium high and when a drop of water added to the skillet immediately dances and disappears, add 1 T oil, add the potatoes, evenly sprinkle 1 t dill weed (first crushing it between your palms) over the potatoes, and stir-fry the potatoes for 1 minute, setting a timer. Stir-frying should at first be vigorous but can slow to "flip often" pace midway through the minute.
    - At the timer, reduce the heat to medium and heat the potatoes for 1 minute, stirring them occasionally and setting a timer.
    - At the timer, add 1 T hot water, cover the skillet, reduce the heat to low, and steam the potato for 10 minutes, setting a timer.
    - At the timer, turn off the heat, uncover the potatoes, evenly sprinkle ⅓ t salt over them, and set them aside in the skillet, covered.

3. **Stir-fry the corn.**

    - Heat a large nonstick skillet at medium on a large front burner.
    - Remove the husks and corn silk from 2 ears of corn.
    - Stand each ear upright in a pie plate and use a chef's knife to slice the kernels from the cob, cutting close to the cob to include the corn germ.
    - Add 2 T water to the skillet and heat the water to boiling at high heat. Mix in the corn, evenly sprinkle ½ t dill weed over it (first crushing the dill between your palms) and when the water returns to a boil, stir-fry the corn for one minute, just until the kernels darken somewhat and are heated through.
    - Remove the skillet from the burner, evenly sprinkle ¼ t salt over the corn, and use a rubber spatula to scrape it and any cooking water into a colander placed over a bowl.
    - Wipe the skillet clean.

4. **Stir-fry the bell pepper.**

    - Heat the large nonstick skillet on a large burner at a medium setting.
    - Use a 5 in. serrated knife to cut out the stem of the pepper. Remove any seeds but not the membrane. Use the serrated knife to cut the pepper lengthwise into ¼ in. strips and to cut the strips crosswise into ¼ in. cubes.
    - Increase the heat to medium-high. When a drop of water added to the skillet

instantly dances and disappears, add ½ T oil, add the red pepper and vigorously stir-fry it for about 30 seconds. Reduce the heat to medium and cook the pepper for 2 minutes, stirring it occasionally and setting a timer.
- At the timer, use a rubber spatula to scrape the pepper and any cooking juice into the colander with the corn.
- Wipe the skillet clean.

5. **Stir-fry the spinach.**

    - Heat the large nonstick skillet at a medium setting.
    - Bunch the spinach together on a large cutting board. Using one hand to keep the spinach leaves roughly bunched together, use a 7 in. serrated knife to slice the leaves into ⅓ in. thick pieces, cutting through the leaves first lengthwise and then crosswise.
    - Increase the skillet heat to medium-high. When a drop of water added to the skillet instantly dances and disappears, add 1 T oil, add the spinach, and stir-fry it for about 1 minute only, flipping pieces over and over until the color of the spinach uniformly darkens and the leaves become slightly wilted.
    - Remove the skillet from the heat, evenly sprinkle ¼ t salt over the spinach, and scrape the spinach and any cooking juice into the colander.
    - Wipe the skillet clean.

6. **Prepare the milk sauce.**

    - Heat the large nonstick skillet at medium.
    - Place the ½ onion cut side down on a cutting board and use a chef's knife to slice the ends from the onion. Peel the onion. Again place the onion cut side down on the cutting board and use the chef's knife to dice the onion. Mince the ginger.
    - Increase the skillet heat to medium-high, and when a drop of water added to the skillet instantly dances and disappears, add 1 T oil, add the onion and ginger, evenly sprinkle ½ t dill weed (first crushing it between your palms) and ½ t garlic powder over the onion mixture, and vigorously stir-fry the mixture for about 30 seconds.
    - Reduce the heat to medium and cook the onion mixture for 2 minutes, stirring it occasionally and setting a timer.
    - At the timer, add and melt 1½ T butter, mix the butter into the onion mixture, evenly sprinkle the flour and salt over the onion mixture, mix in the flour, and cook the mixture for about 30 seconds, stirring it frequently.
    - Increase the heat to medium-high.
    - Slowly pour in 3 c milk, at first stirring rapidly with a rubber spatula to blend the flour and milk. Heat the sauce until it boils (several minutes), stirring frequently and often scraping the skillet bottom to prevent sticking.
    - When the sauce starts to boil, reduce the heat to a high medium setting and heat the milk until the mixture thickens and becomes smooth, stirring it quite often to prevent sticking.
    - When the sauce has thickened, reduce the heat to low, mix in 1 T packed brown

sugar, and partially cover the skillet. Remove the skillet from the heat and set it aside, covered, if the soup will not soon be assembled for serving.

7. **Assemble the soup for serving.**

   - Make final soup-making preparations. Coarsely grate the cheese and divide the cheese between the soup bowls. Stir the yogurt creamy smooth before measuring ½ cup. Use a chef's knife to halve pecan or walnut halves and to coarsely chop almonds. Divide the nuts between serving bowls. Add ½-1 c more milk to thin the sauce to taste.
   - Increase the skillet heat to medium-high and bring the sauce to near boiling, often stirring across the bottom.
   - Mix in the cooked vegetables and any cooking liquid and heat the soup to near boiling, stirring it often.
   - Reduce the heat to medium and heat the soup for another 3-4 minutes until all ingredients are hot, stirring often.

8. **Serve the soup.** Top individual servings with 2-3 heaping dollops of yogurt.

   VARIATIONS: Make ingredient substitutions. Substitute, for example,

   - **3-4 medium leaves kale** (Recipe #26) or **3-4 c loosely packed sturdy baby greens**, a mixture that includes baby kale and beet greens, for spinach.
   - **8-10 small new red potatoes**, boiled whole (Recipe #72), for medium potatoes.
   - **2-3 baked red potatoes** (Recipe #46) for stir-fry/steamed potatoes. Cut the potato into thick slices or chunks for serving. Chunks of roasted potato are especially tasty soup ingredients.
   - **1 medium sweet potato** (Recipe #18) for 1 medium potato.
   - **½ t dried marjoram leaves** or **½ t each dried sweet basil & oregano leaves** for dill weed.
   - **3 c soy milk** or **other non-dairy liquid** for dairy milk, **soy yogurt** for dairy yogurt, and **soy cheese** for cheddar cheese to convert the soup to vegan vegetarian form.

   Add ingredients. Add, for example,

   - **1 leek** (Recipe #34).
   - **6-8 chilled garlic cloves**, diced and stir-fried (Recipe #31).
   - **2 c dry frozen green peas (unthawed)** or **2 c sugar snap or snow peas** (Recipe #71).
   - **1 chilled medium turnip**, stir-fried/steamed (Recipe #22). Alternatively, add dry roasted turnip (Recipe #53), cut into quite large chunks. Chunks are especially flavorful.
   - **2 stalks organic celery**, stir-fried/steamed (Recipe #25).
   - **2 T dry sherry** to the soup just prior to serving.

PART 2

171. Kale and Sweet Potato Soup
(2-3 servings)

Vegetables with Seasonings, Cooking Oil, and Steaming Water

4-6 medium kale leaves (to yield 2 c sliced)
1 T extra virgin olive oil
½ t dried sweet basil leaves
1 T hot water
¼ t salt
1 medium to large sweet potato

1 T extra virgin olive oil
½ t dried basil leaves
1 T water
¼ t salt
½ red bell pepper, halved lengthwise
½ T extra virgin olive oil

Milk Sauce Ingredients

½ chilled medium onion, halved lengthwise
2 ⅛-in thick slices of fresh ginger root
1 T extra virgin olive oil
1 t dried sweet basil leaves
½ t garlic powder
1½ T butter

1½ T whole wheat flour
¼ t salt
3 c milk (1%, 2%, or full fat)
1 T packed dark brown sugar
½-1 c milk
10 pecan or walnut halves or ⅛ c almonds

Accompaniments

3 oz extra sharp cheddar cheese
    (to yield approx. ⅔ c coarsely shredded cheese)

½ c plain yogurt

Cooking Tools

1 large skillet with a tight-fitting & opaque lid
1 electric tea kettle
1 each 5 & 7 in. serrated knife
1 chef's knife
1 large cutting board
1 set each measuring spoons & cups
1 plastic or plastic-coated stir-fry spatula
1 timer

1 large nonstick skillet with a tight-
    fitting & opaque lid
1 rubber or other heat-resistant spatula
1 colander with dinner plate
1 cheese grater
2-3 large soup bowls
1 large soup serving spoon

---

1. **Gather all dish ingredients and cooking tools.**

2. **Stir-fry/steam the kale.**

- Heat a large skillet at a medium setting on a large burner. Heat an electric tea kettle to prepare hot water for steaming.
- Rinse each leaf in cool water, shake off excess clinging water, and spread the leaves over a strip of paper towels or terry cloth towels. For flat kale, use paper towels to pat the leaves dry. For kale with curly leaves, add a top layer of paper or terry cloth towels and roll the towels around the kale. Gently squeeze the leaves and unroll the paper towels.
- Add the leaves to a large cutting board. Cutting close to the central vein running through each leaf, use a 5 in. serrated knife to cut the leaves from either side of the vein. Set the veins with attached stems aside.
- Stack the leaves, forming two or more stacks and facing leaves in the same direction. Using a 7 in. serrated knife and holding the stack together with one hand, slice the leaves into approx. ⅓ in. thick pieces, cutting through the leaves lengthwise and crosswise.
- Slice the bottom tip from each vein with attached stem. Keeping the veins/stems separate from the leaves and holding the veins/stems together with one hand, use a chef's knife to thinly chop them.
- Increase the skillet heat to medium-high. When a drop of water added to the skillet instantly dances and disappears, add 1 T oil, add the veins/stems and cook them for about 30 seconds, stirring frequently. Add the kale leaves and constantly stir-fry them for 1 minute, setting a timer.
- At the timer, add 1 T of hot water, cover the skillet, reduce the heat to low, and steam the kale for 4 minutes, setting a timer.
- At the timer, remove the skillet from the heat, evenly sprinkle ¼ t salt over the kale, and use a rubber spatula to scrape it and any cooking juice into a colander placed over a dinner plate for collecting any juice.
- Wipe the skillet clean.

3. **Stir-fry/steam the sweet potato.**

- Return the large skillet to the stove and heat it at medium on a large back burner. Begin heating an electric tea kettle to prepare hot water for steaming.
- Scrub and thoroughly dry the potato. Use a chef's knife to cut off the ends and any blemishes on the sweet potato.
- Stand the potato upright on a flattened end and use the chef's knife to cut it lengthwise into ¼ in. thick slices. Stacking 2 slices together, cut the slices into ¼ in. thick strips. Holding several strips together at a time, cut the strips crosswise into ¼ in. cubes.
- Increase the skillet heat to medium-high, and when a drop of water added to the skillet immediately dances and disappears, add 1 T oil, add the sweet potato, evenly sprinkle ½ t dried basil (first crushing it between your palms) over the potato, and stir-fry it for 1 minute, setting a timer. Stir-frying should at first be vigorous but can slow to "flip often" pace midway through the minute.
- At the timer, reduce the heat to medium and heat the sweet potato for 1 minute,

PART 2

stirring it occasionally and setting a timer.
- At the timer, add 1 T hot water, cover the skillet, reduce the heat to low, and steam the sweet potato for 10 minutes, setting a timer.
- At the timer, turn off the heat, uncover the sweet potato, evenly sprinkle ¼ t salt over it, and set the skillet aside, covered.

4. **Stir-fry the bell pepper.**

   - Heat a large nonstick skillet at a medium setting.
   - Use a 5 in. serrated knife to cut out the stem of the pepper. Remove any seeds but not the white membrane. Use the serrated knife to cut the pepper lengthwise into ¼ in. strips and to cut the strips crosswise into ¼ in. cubes.
   - Increase the skillet heat to medium-high, and when a drop of water added to the skillet instantly dances and disappears, add ½ T oil, add the pepper, and vigorously stir-fry it for about 30 seconds.
   - Reduce the skillet heat to medium and cook the pepper for 2 minutes, stirring it occasionally and setting a timer.
   - At the timer, use a rubber spatula to scrape the pepper and any cooking juice into the colander with the kale.
   - Wipe the skillet clean.

5. **Prepare the milk sauce.**

   - Return the large nonstick skillet to the stove and heat it at a medium setting.
   - Place the ½ onion cut side down on a cutting board and use a chef's knife to cut off the onion tips. Peel the onion. Again place the onion cut side down on the cutting board and use the chef's knife to dice the onion. Mince the ginger root.
   - Increase the skillet heat to medium-high, and when a drop of water added to the skillet instantly dances and disappears, add 1 T oil, add the onion and ginger, evenly sprinkle 1 t dried basil (first crushing it between your palms) over the onion/ginger, and stir-fry the mixture for 1 minute, setting a timer. Stir-frying should at first be vigorous but can slow to "flip often" pace.
   - At the timer, reduce the heat to medium and cook the onion mixture for 2 minutes, stirring it occasionally and setting a timer.
   - At the timer, add and melt 1½ T butter, mix the butter into the onion mixture, sprinkle the 1½ T flour and ¼ t salt over the onion mixture, mix in the flour, and cook the mixture for about 30 seconds, stirring it occasionally.
   - Increase the skillet heat to medium-high.
   - Using a rubber spatula for stirring, slowly pour in 3 c milk, at first stirring quickly and constantly to blend the flour and milk. Heat the sauce for several minutes until it begins to boil, stirring frequently.
   - Reduce the skillet heat slightly to a high medium setting and heat the sauce until it thickens somewhat and becomes smooth, stirring often and regularly scraping the skillet bottom to prevent sticking.
   - Reduce the skillet heat to low and mix in 1 T brown sugar. Remove the skillet

from the heat, cover the skillet, and set it aside if not soon assembling the soup for serving.

6. **Assemble the soup for serving.**

   - Make final soup-making preparations. Grate the cheese and divide it between the soup bowls. Stir the yogurt creamy smooth before measuring ½ cup. Use a chef's knife to halve pecan or walnut halves and to chop almonds coarsely. Divide the nuts between the serving bowls. Add ½ to 1 c milk to thin the sauce to taste.
   - Increase the skillet heat to medium-high and bring the sauce to near boiling, often stirring and scraping across the skillet bottom to prevent sticking.
   - Stir in the cooked vegetables and any collected cooking juice and heat the soup to near boiling, stirring frequently. Reduce the heat to medium and heat the soup for another 2-3 minutes until all ingredients are hot, stirring the soup often.

7. **Serve the soup.** Pour the hot soup over the cheese in the individual bowls and top each serving with 2-3 dollops of yogurt.

VARIATIONS: Make ingredient substitutions. Substitute, for example,

- **1 leek** (Recipe #34) for onion.
- **1 medium baked sweet potato** (Recipe #47) for stir-fry/steamed sweet potato.
- **1 baked medium red potato** or **other tasty potato** (Recipe #46) for stir-fry/steamed sweet potato. Cut the unpeeled potatoes into thick slices (halved) or chunks for serving. Chunks of potatoes are especially tasty soup ingredients.
- **6-8 small red potatoes** (Recipe #72), boiled whole, for stir-fry/steamed sweet potato.
- **3-4 green onions** (Recipe #34), including green tops, for onion.
- **½ lb pre-washed spinach** (Recipe #28) for kale.
- **½ t dried marjoram leaves** or **½ t each dried sweet basil and oregano leaves** for dried basil.
- **3 c soy milk** or **other non-dairy liquid** for dairy milk and **soy yogurt** for dairy yogurt to convert the soup to vegan vegetarian form.

Add ingredients. Add, for example,

- **1 baked medium red** or **other tasty potato,** fresh baked (Recipe #46). Cut the potato into thick slices or chunks for serving. Potato is an especially tasty soup ingredient.
- **1 medium zucchini** or **2 small yellow summer squash** (Recipe #20).
- **⅛-¼ yellow bell pepper,** sliced lengthwise, cooked with the red bell pepper.
- **1 mild green chili** or **1-2 jalapeño peppers** (Recipe #36).
- **2 c dry frozen whole kernel yellow corn** (Recipe #65).
- **1-2 c dry frozen green peas** (Recipe #71) or **sugar snap peas** (Recipe #71).
- **1½ c Brussels sprouts** (Recipe #5 or Recipe #61), quartered.
- **4 medium garlic cloves** (Recipe #31).
- **2 T diced canned pimento,** with 2-4 T packing juice added to the soup.

PART 2

172. Butternut Squash Soup
(2-3 servings)

Vegetables and Apple with Seasonings, Cooking Oil, Butter, and Cooking Water

1 small or ½ medium butternut squash, halved lengthwise
approx. ½ t softened butter
¼ t salt
¼ each red & green bell pepper, sliced lengthwise
½ T extra virgin olive oil
2 medium carrots
1 T extra virgin olive oil
½ t curry powder
½ T hot water
¼ t salt
1 tart chilled apple
1 T extra virgin olive oil
⅓ t ground cinnamon
¼ t ground ginger
1 T hot water
2 c dry frozen yellow corn, unthawed
2 T water
¼ t salt

Milk Sauce Ingredients

½ chilled medium onion, halved lengthwise
2 ⅛-in .thick slices of fresh ginger root
1 T extra virgin olive oil
½ t cumin seed
½ -1 t curry powder
1½ T butter
1½ T whole wheat flour
¼ t salt
3 c milk (1%, 2%, or full fat)
1 T packed dark brown sugar
½-1 c milk
10 raw pecan or walnut halves or
⅛ c almonds
1 c cooked brown rice (Recipe #166), opt
⅛ t salt

Accompaniments

3 oz extra sharp cheddar cheese (approx. ⅔ c shredded cheese)
½ c plain yogurt

Cooking Tools

1 firm-bladed 9 in. slicing knife
1 large (9 x 13 in.) rectangular baking dish
1 timer
1 plastic or plastic-coated stir-fry spatula
1 large dinner spoon
1 medium mixing bowl
1 each 5 in. serrated, chef's, & paring knife
1 large nonstick skillet with a tight-fitting & opaque lid
1 set each measuring spoons & cups
1 rubber or other heat-resistant spatula
1 colander
1 dinner plate
1 electric tea kettle
1 cheese grater
2-3 large soup bowls
1 large soup serving spoon
1 dinner fork

1. **Bake the butternut squash.** One hour before serving, pre-heat an oven to 430 degrees (pre-heating takes ca 6 minutes).

    - When using a small butternut squash, stand the squash upright and use a 9 in. slicing knife to halve the squash lengthwise. Leave the seeds and stringy membrane in the squash halves.
    - Lightly butter the surface of the baking dish where the squash will be placed.
    - Add the squash cut side down to the buttered surface, center the dish on the middle oven rack of the fully pre-heated oven, and set a timer for 15 minutes.
    - At the timer, reduce the oven heat to 400 degrees and reset the timer for 15 minutes. At the timer, check the squash. If the rounded top sinks slightly and the sides feel soft when gently squeezed, remove the squash from the oven. If the squash remains fully hard, continue the baking another 10 minutes before checking again for readiness. Once the top and sides of the squash feel soft and before juice begins to spill, remove the baking dish from the oven.
    - Use a stir-fry spatula to flip the squash. Use a large dinner spoon to scrape out the seeds and membrane from the center of the squash, either discarding them or collecting the seeds and preparing them for use as a nutritious snack (see Comments in Recipe #21, Winter Squash, for details). Evenly sprinkle ¼ t salt over the scraped out squash.
    - Use the large dinner spoon to scrape out all very soft flesh, placing it in a medium mixing bowl.
    - Use a 5 in. serrated knife to slice any firm flesh into ⅓ in. thick slices. Slice the skin from the slices and cut the slices crosswise into ⅓ in. thick cubes. Set the soft and cubed squash aside, covered.

2. **Gather all dish ingredients and cooking tools.**

3. **Stir-fry the bell peppers.**

    - Heat a large nonstick skillet on a large burner at a medium setting.
    - Use a 5 in. serrated knife to cut out the stem of the peppers. Remove any seeds but not the white membrane. Use the serrated knife to cut the peppers lengthwise into ¼ in. thick slices and to cut the slices crosswise into ¼ in. cubes.
    - Increase the skillet heat to medium-high, and when a drop of water added to the skillet instantly dances and disappears, add ½ T oil, add the bell peppers, and vigorously stir-fry the peppers for about 30 seconds.
    - Reduce the heat to medium and cook the peppers for 2 minutes, stirring them occasionally and setting a timer.
    - At the timer, use a rubber spatula to scrape the peppers and any cooking juice into one side of a colander placed over a dinner plate.
    - Wipe the skillet clean.

4. **Stir-fry/steam the carrots.**

    - Heat the nonstick skillet at a medium setting. Begin heating an electric tea kettle to prepare hot water for steaming.
    - Scrub and thoroughly dry the carrots. Use a chef's knife to cut off the tips, halve the carrots lengthwise, and cut the carrot halves crosswise into ⅛ in. thick slices.
    - Increase the skillet heat to medium-high. When a drop of water added to the skillet instantly dances and disappears, add 1 T oil, add the carrots, evenly sprinkle ½ t curry powder over the carrot, and stir-fry the carrot for 1 minute, setting a timer. Stir-frying should at first be vigorous but can slow to "flip often" pace midway through the minute.
    - At the timer, add ½ T hot water, cover the skillet, reduce the heat to low, and steam the carrots for 4 minutes, setting a timer.
    - At the timer, remove the skillet from the heat, evenly sprinkle ¼ t salt over the carrots, and scrape the carrots and any cooking juice into the colander with the bell pepper.
    - Wipe the skillet clean.

5. **Stir-fry/steam the apple.**

    - Heat the nonstick skillet at a medium setting. Begin heating an electric tea kettle to prepare hot water for steaming.
    - Rinse and thoroughly dry the apple. Use a chef's knife to halve the apple lengthwise. Place the halves cut side down on a clean cutting board and cut each half lengthwise into 4-5 slices. Use a paring knife to cut the seeds and pulpy center from each slice and to cut each slice crosswise into 4-5 pieces.
    - Increase the skillet heat to medium-high. When a drop of water added to the skillet instantly dances and disappears, add 1 T oil, add the apple, evenly sprinkle ⅓ t cinnamon and ¼ t ginger powder over the apple, and stir-fry the apple for 1 minute, setting a timer. Stir-frying should at first be vigorous but can slow to "flip often" pace midway through the minute.
    - At the timer, add 1 T hot water, cover the skillet, reduce the heat to low, and steam the apple for 4 minutes, setting a timer.
    - At the timer, remove the skillet from the heat and scrape the apple and any cooking juice into the colander with the cooked vegetables.
    - Wipe the skillet clean.

6. **Stir-fry the corn.**

    - Break up any frozen clumps while the corn remains in its freezer package.
    - Bring 2 T water to boiling over high heat in the large nonstick skillet. Add the corn and when the water again boils, stir-fry the corn for 1 minute, just until the kernels are hot and the color slightly darkens.
    - Remove the skillet from the heat, evenly sprinkle ¼ t salt over the corn, and use a

rubber spatula to scrape the corn and any cooking juice into the colander.
- Wipe the skillet clean.

7. **Prepare the milk sauce.**

    - Heat the nonstick skillet at a medium setting.
    - Place ½ onion cut side down on a cutting board and use a chef's knife to cut off the ends. Peel the onion. Return the onion cut side down to the cutting board and use the chef's knife to dice the onion. Mince the ginger root.
    - Increase the skillet heat to medium-high, and when a drop of water added to the skillet instantly dances and disappears, add 1 T oil, add ½ t cumin seed, and heat the cumin for 30 seconds, stirring occasionally.
    - Add the onion and ginger, evenly sprinkle the ½-1 t curry powder over the onion mixture, and vigorously stir-fry the onion mixture for about 30 seconds.
    - Reduce the heat to medium and cook the onion mixture for 2 minutes, stirring it occasionally and setting a timer.
    - At the timer, add and melt 1½ T butter, mix the butter into the onion mixture, evenly sprinkle 1½ T flour and ¼ t salt over the onion, stir the flour thoroughly into the onion, and cook the mixture for approx. 30 seconds, stirring it occasionally.
    - Increase the burner heat to medium-high.
    - Using a rubber spatula for stirring, slowly pour in 3 c milk, at first stirring rapidly and constantly to blend the flour and milk. Heat the milk for several minutes until it beings to boil, stirring frequently.
    - Reduce the heat slightly to a high medium setting and heat the sauce until it thickens and becomes smooth, stirring often and regularly scraping the skillet bottom to prevent sticking.
    - Reduce the heat to low and mix in 1 T packed brown sugar. Remove the skillet from the heat, cover it, and set it aside if not soon assembling the soup for serving.

8. **Assemble the soup for serving.**

    - Heat the milk sauce at a medium setting.
    - Make final soup-making preparations. Use a chef's knife to halve pecans or walnuts or to coarsely chop almonds. Divide the nuts between the soup bowls. Grate the cheddar cheese and divide it between the soup bowls. Stir the yogurt creamy smooth before measuring ½ cup. Break up any clumps of rice and sprinkle ⅛ t salt over the rice. Use a dinner fork to mash any clumps of the soft squash. Add ½-1 c milk to thin the sauce to taste.
    - Increase the skillet heat to medium-high and heat the milk sauce to near boiling.
    - Add the rice, mashed squash, cubed squash, cooked vegetables and apple in the colander, and any collected vegetable cooking liquid.
    - Heat the soup to near boiling, stirring frequently with a rubber spatula.
    - Reduce the heat to medium and heat the soup another two minutes until all ingredients are hot, stirring the soup occasionally.

9. **Serve the soup.** Top individual servings with 1-2 generous dollops of yogurt.

VARIATIONS: Make ingredient substitutions. Substitute, for example,
- **3 c soy milk** or **other non-dairy liquid** for dairy milk, **soy yogurt** for dairy yogurt, and **soy cheese** for cheddar cheese to convert the soup to vegan vegetarian form.
- **10 hazelnuts** for pecans, walnuts, or almonds or use a combination of nuts.
- **2 c stir-fry/steamed butternut squash** (Recipe #21) for baked, omitting mashed squash.
- **3 ears fresh yellow corn** (Recipe #65) for frozen corn.
- **½ t dried sage leaves** for curry spices. Add ½ t sage to the carrots, apple, and onion during stir-frying.

Add ingredients. Add, for example,

- **1 medium red potato** or **other tasty potato** (Recipe #17 or leftover baked). Potato is an especially tasty addition.
- **1 medium turnip** (Recipe #22) or **2 parsnips** (Recipe #14). Evenly sprinkle ½ t curry powder over either vegetable during stir-frying.
- **1 small zucchini** (Recipe #20). Add ½ t curry powder to the zucchini during stir-frying.
- **½ lb pre-washed spinach leaves** (Recipe #28), **1 bunch unwashed spinach** (Recipe #29), or **3 or 4 medium kale leaves** (Recipe #26). Mix the greens into the soup or serve them as a topping on individual servings.
- **1 mild green chili** or **2 jalapeño peppers** (Recipe #35).
- **¼ t each ground cinnamon** and **ground ginger** to the onion during stir-frying.
- **2 T raisins**, added to the milk sauce with the brown sugar (Step #4).
- **½-1 c butternut squash skin broth.** Slice the butternut skin into thick slices, halve the slices crosswise, add the skin to a medium saucepan with a lid, add 1½ c water or canned vegetable broth and ¼ t salt, bring the liquid to boiling, reduce the heat to a level that maintains gentle boiling, cover the pan, and cook the skin for approx. 45 minutes before thoroughly draining the broth in a colander placed over a bowl. The membrane from the center of the squash can be included as well. The broth can also be used in other dishes.

Stews – Tomato Sauce Base Recipes

173. Chili con Carne
(4 large servings)

Vegetables with Seasonings, Cooking Oil, and Cooking Water

4 medium carrots
1 T extra virgin olive oil
1 T hot water
¼ t salt
2 ears yellow corn (or 2 c dry frozen)

2 T water
¼ t salt
1/3 each red and green bell pepper,
    sliced lengthwise
¾ T extra virgin olive oil

Beef with Seasonings and Cooking Oil

1 lb extra lean ground beef (7-10% fat)
2 ⅛-in. thick slices ginger root
2 t extra virgin olive oil
½ t curry powder

1 t chili powder
½ t garlic powder
1 t dried oregano leaves
⅓ t salt

Tomato Sauce Ingredients

½ chilled medium onion, halved lengthwise
2 ⅛-in. thick slices fresh ginger root
1 t cumin seeds
½ t curry powder
1 t chili powder
½ t dried oregano leaves
1 c canned beef or chicken broth

6 T tomato paste (1 6-oz can)
1 c tomato juice
¼ t salt
½-1 lemon
1½ T packed dark brown sugar
½ c tomato juice or beef broth

Beans and Brown Rice

15 oz can or 1½ c cooked red kidney beans
    with bean broth
4 c cooked brown rice (Recipe #166)

3 T water
⅓ t salt

Accompaniments

4 oz chunk aged extra sharp cheddar cheese
    (to yield approx. 1 c shredded)

¾ c plain yogurt

Cooking Tools

1 medium nonstick skillet with a tight-fitting
    & opaque lid
1 medium mixing bowl
1 rubber or other heat-resistant spatula
1 each chef's & 5 in. serrated knife
1 set each measuring spoons & cups
1 plastic or plastic-coated stir-fry spatula
1 timer
1 large skillet with a tight-fitting & opaque lid
1 electric tea kettle

1 colander
1 dinner plate
1 pie plate
1 can opener & 1 thin-bladed rubber
    spatula
1 hand citrus juicer
1 cheese grater
2-4 large soup bowls
1 large stew serving spoon

PART 2

1. **Gather all ingredients and cooking tools.**

2. **Cook the ground beef.**

    - Heat a medium nonstick skillet at a medium setting on a back burner.
    - Use a chef's knife to mince the ginger root.
    - Increase the skillet heat to medium-high, and when the skillet is hot (a drop of water instantly dances and disappears), add and spread 2 t oil over the skillet bottom, add the ginger and ground beef, and use a spatula to break the meat into ½ in. thick chunks.
    - Evenly sprinkle ½ t curry powder, 1 t chili powder, ½ t garlic powder, and ½ t dried oregano leaves (first crushing the leaves between your palms) over the meat. Vigorously stir-fry the meat for about 30 seconds, flipping it over and over.
    - Reduce the heat to medium (a level that keeps oil sizzling gently around the meat pieces) and cook the meat for 5 minutes, turning the pieces occasionally and setting a timer.
    - At the timer, remove the skillet from the burner, evenly sprinkle ⅓ t salt over the meat, mix in the salt, and use a rubber spatula to scrape the meat into a mixing bowl.
    - Wipe the skillet clean.

3. **Stir-fry/steam the carrots as the meat cooks.**

    - Heat a large skillet on a large burner at a medium setting. Heat an electric tea kettle to prepare hot water for steaming.
    - Scrub and dry the carrots.
    - Use a chef's knife to cut off the tips, halve the carrots lengthwise, and cut the carrot halves crosswise into uniformly thin (⅛ in. thick) slices.
    - Increase the skillet heat to medium-high. When a drop of water instantly dances and disappears, add 1 T oil to the skillet, add the carrots, and stir-fry them for 1 minute, setting a timer. Stir-frying should at first be vigorous but can slow to a "flip often" pace.
    - At the timer, add 1 T hot water, cover the skillet, reduce the heat to low, and steam the carrots for 4 minutes, setting a timer.
    - At the timer, remove the skillet from the heat, evenly sprinkle ¼ t salt over the carrots, and use a rubber spatula to scrape the carrots and any cooking juice into a colander placed over a dinner plate for collecting any cooking juice.
    - Wipe the skillet clean.

4. **Stir-fry the corn.**

    - Heat the large skillet at a medium setting.
    - Remove the husks and corn silk from the ears. Rubbing the ears under running water helps remove silk, but then dry the ears.

- Stand each ear upright in a pie plate and use a chef's knife to slice off the kernels, cutting close to the cob to include the corn germ.
- Bring 2 T water to boiling over high heat in the skillet. Add the kernels, mix them into the water, and when the water again boils, stir-fry the kernels for 1 minute until they are hot and the color slightly darkens.
- Remove the skillet from the heat, evenly sprinkle ¼ t salt over the corn, and scrape the corn and any cooking juice into the colander with the carrots.
- Wipe the skillet clean.

5. **Stir-fry the bell peppers.**

    - Heat the large skillet at a medium setting.
    - Use a 5 in. serrated knife to cut out the stem of the peppers. Remove any seeds but not the white membrane. Use the serrated knife to cut the peppers lengthwise into ¼ in. strips and to cut the strips crosswise into ¼ in. cubes.
    - Increase the skillet heat to medium-high, and when a drop of water added to the skillet instantly dances and disappears, add ¾ T oil, add the peppers, and vigorously stir-fry them for about 30 seconds.
    - Reduce the heat to medium and cook the peppers for 2 minutes, stirring them occasionally and setting a timer.
    - At the timer, use a rubber spatula to scrape the peppers and any cooking juice into the colander with the other vegetables.
    - Wipe the skillet clean.

6. **Prepare the tomato sauce**.

    - Heat the large skillet at a medium setting.
    - Open the tomato paste, tomato juice, and broth containers. Use a thin-bladed rubber spatula to easily scrape tomato paste from a 6 oz can.
    - Place ½ onion cut side down on a cutting board and use a chef's knife to cut off the tips. Peel the onion. Again place the onion cut side down on the cutting board and use the chef's knife to dice the onion. Mince the ginger root.
    - Increase the skillet heat to medium-high, and when a drop of water added to the skillet instantly dances and disappears, add 1 T oil, add 1 t cumin seed, and heat it for about 30 seconds, stirring it occasionally.
    - Add the onion and ginger root, evenly sprinkle ½ t curry powder, 1 t chili powder, and 1 t oregano (first crushing it between your palms) over the onion. Stir-fry the onion mixture for 1 minute, setting a timer. Stir-frying should at first be vigorous but can slow to "flip often" pace midway through the minute.
    - At the timer, reduce the heat to medium and cook the onion mixture for 2 minutes, stirring it occasionally and setting a timer.
    - At the timer, add and thoroughly mix in the 1 c broth, 6 T tomato paste, 1 c tomato juice, and ¼ t salt.
    - Increase the heat to medium-high, and when the mixture boils, reduce the heat to medium, partially cover the skillet, and cook the mixture for 5 minutes, stirring it

PART 2

   occasionally and setting a timer.
   - While the sauce cooks, squeeze ½ lemon and measure 1½ T packed brown sugar.
   - At the timer, mix the lemon juice and brown sugar into the tomato sauce. Turn off the heat, cover the skillet, and set the chili aside if it will not immediately be assembled for serving.

7. **Assemble the chili for serving.**

   - Heat the tomato sauce at medium heat.
   - Heat the brown rice. Bring 3 T water to boiling over medium-high heat in the nonstick skillet used for cooking the meat, mix in 4 c brown rice, break up any rice clumps, evenly sprinkle ⅓ t salt over the rice, stir in the salt, reduce the heat to a low setting, tightly cover the skillet, and slowly heat the rice while assembling the chili. Stir the rice at least once during this heating and add another 1 T hot water to prevent sticking as may be needed.
   - Make final preparations. Grate the cheese. Stir the yogurt creamy smooth before measuring ¾ cup. Open the canned beans.
   - Check the sauce flavoring, cautiously adding touches (1-2 t) of more lemon juice for tartness, 1-2 t sugar for mellowing the tomato flavor, or 1-2 T tomato paste for a more intense tomato flavor. Add ½ c tomato juice or broth for thinning the sauce to taste.
   - Increase the heat to medium-high, bring the sauce to near boiling, add the meat, 1½ c beans (including the broth), any collected vegetable cooking juice, and heat the sauce to boiling.
   - Add the cooked vegetables and again heat the sauce to boiling.
   - Reduce the heat to medium and heat the chili for 3-5 minutes until all ingredients are hot, stirring it regularly.

8. **Serve the chili.** Assembling one soup bowl at a time, add ½-1 c hot brown rice, top the brown rice with 2-4 T cheddar cheese, add chili to taste, and top the chili serving with 1 or 2 generous dollops of yogurt.

   VARIATIONS: Make ingredient substitutions. Substitute, for example,

   - **2 large carrots** for 4 medium carrots.
   - **2 oz (½ c grated) Parmesan cheese** for extra sharp cheddar cheese.
   - **1 c fresh poultry broth** (Reference #10) for beef broth.
   - **2 c dry frozen whole kernel corn,** unthawed, for fresh corn, cooked exactly the same.
   - **strained tomatoes,** such as the Italian product Pomi Strained Tomatoes, for tomato juice used in the tomato sauce.

   Add ingredients. Add, for example,

   - **⅓ yellow bell pepper**, cooked with the other bell pepper.
   - **8 c pre-washed spinach** (Recipe #28). Either mix the spinach into the stew when

assembling the dish for serving or quickly reheat the spinach and add ¼ c spinach as a topping on each chili serving. Pre-washed spinach can be prepared in a few minutes.

- **6-7 medium beet greens** (Recipe #23), which are especially tasty. Serving beet greens in tomato sauce eliminates the problem of beets coloring a broth.
- **3-4 medium kale leaves** (Recipe #26), **2-3 medium collard leaves** (Recipe #25), **1 or 2 bunches unwashed spinach leaves** (Recipe #19), **6-8 young turnip greens** (Recipe #30), or **6-7 medium mustard greens** (Recipe #27).
- **1 mild green chili** or **2 jalapeño peppers** (Recipe #36). Chili pepper adds authentic and distinctive flavor.
- **⅛ t cayenne** or **ground hot pepper,** or to taste.
- **8-10 medium chilled garlic cloves** (Recipe #31). Top individual servings of chili with ½ t cooked garlic. Garlic converts chili into a special dish.
- **1 fresh ripe tomato** (Recipe #37) or **4-6 grape tomatoes** (Recipe #37), stir-fried and added as a very last ingredient before serving.
- **½-1 c canned diced tomatoes** with ½ c tomato juice.

174. Extravagantly Vegetable Chili
(4 servings)

Vegetables with Seasonings, Cooking Oil, and Cooking Water

½ red bell pepper
1 mild green chili pepper or 2 jalapeños
¾ T extra virgin olive oil
2 c dry frozen yellow corn, unthawed
2 T water
¼ t salt
4 medium carrots
1 T extra virgin olive oil
½ t curry powder
½ t dried oregano leaves
1 T hot water

¼ t salt
4-5 medium kale leaves
1 T extra virgin olive oil
1 T hot water
¼ t salt
1 small (6 in. long, 1½ in. thick) zucchini
1 T extra virgin olive oil
½ t curry powder
½ t dried oregano leaves
¼ t salt

Tomato Sauce Ingredients

½ chilled medium onion, split lengthwise
2 ⅛-in. thick slices fresh ginger root
1 t cumin seeds
1 t curry powder
1 t chili powder

1 c vegetable broth
6 T tomato paste (6 oz can)
1 c tomato juice
¼ t salt
½-1 lemon

½ t ground cumin
1 t dried oregano leaves

1½ T packed dark brown sugar
½ c tomato juice or vegetable broth

Beans and Brown Rice

1½ c canned red kidney beans or pinto beans with bean broth
4 c cooked brown rice (Recipe #166)

3 T water
¼ t salt

Accompaniments

2 oz chunk of Parmesan cheese (to yield approx. ½ c finely shredded)

¾ c plain yogurt

Cooking Tools

1 large skillet with a tight-fitting & opaque lid
1 each 5 in. & 7 in. serrated knife
1 chef's knife
1 set each measuring spoons & cups
1 plastic or plastic-coated stir-fry spatula
1 timer
1 rubber or other heat-resistant spatula
1 colander with 1 dinner plate
1 electric tea kettle

1 large cutting board (16 x 24 in.)
1 can opener & 1 thin-bladed rubber spatula
1 medium nonstick skillet with a tight-fitting & opaque lid
1 hand citrus juicer
1 cheese grater
2-4 large soup bowls
1 large stew serving spoon

---

1. **Gather all ingredients and cooking tools.**

2. **Stir-fry the bell and chili pepper(s).**

    - Heat a large skillet on a large burner at a medium setting.
    - Use a 5 in. serrated knife to cut out the stem of the bell pepper. Remove any seeds but not the white membrane. Use the 5 in. serrated knife to cut the pepper lengthwise into ¼ in. thick strips and to cut the slices crosswise into ¼ in. cubes.
    - Rinse and thoroughly dry the chili pepper(s). Keeping the chili and bell pepper separate, prepare the chili pepper in exactly the same way as the bell pepper except for removing all membrane and dicing the chili pepper into ⅛ in. cubes. Add the chili pepper to a piece of plastic wrap and immediately wash your hands, knife, and cutting board with water.
    - Increase the skillet heat to medium-high, and when a drop of water added to the skillet instantly dances and disappears, add ¾ T oil, add the bell pepper, and vigorously stir-fry it for about 30 seconds.
    - Add the chili pepper and continue the vigorous stir-frying for about 30 seconds.
    - Reduce the heat to medium and cook the peppers for 2 minutes, stirring them

occasionally and setting a timer.

- At the timer, use a rubber spatula to scrape the bell and chili pepper and any cooking juice into one side of a colander placed over a dinner plate.
- Wipe the skillet clean.

3. **Stir-fry the corn.**

   - Break apart any clumps of corn before removing the corn from the store package.
   - Bring 2 T water to boiling over high heat in the large skillet. Add the corn and, once the water returns to a boil, stir-fry the corn for 1 minute, just until the kernels are hot and the color slightly darkens.
   - Remove the skillet from the heat, evenly sprinkle ¼ t salt over the corn, and scrape the corn and any cooking juice alongside the peppers in the colander.
   - Wipe the skillet clean.

4. **Stir-fry/steam the carrots.**

   - Heat the large skillet on a large burner at a medium setting. Heat an electric tea kettle to prepare hot water for steaming.
   - Scrub and dry the carrots. Use a chef's knife to cut off the tips, split the carrots lengthwise, and cut the carrot halves crosswise into uniformly thin (⅛ in. thick) slices.
   - Increase the skillet heat to medium-high and when a drop of water added to the skillet instantly dances and disappears, add 1 T oil, add the carrots, evenly sprinkle the ½ t curry powder and ½ t oregano leaves (first crushing them between your palms) over the carrots, and stir-fry them for 1 minute, setting a timer. Stir-frying should at first be vigorous but can slow to "flip often" pace midway through the minute.
   - At the timer, add 1 T hot water, reduce the heat to low, cover the skillet, and steam the carrots for 4 minutes, setting a timer.
   - At the timer, remove the skillet from the heat, evenly sprinkle ¼ t salt over the carrots, and use a rubber spatula to scrape the carrots and any cooking juice into the colander alongside the corn.
   - Wipe the skillet clean.

5. **Stir-fry/steam the kale.**

   - Heat the large skillet on a large burner at a medium setting. Begin heating an electric tea kettle to prepare hot water for steaming.
   - Rinse each kale leaf, shake off excess clinging water, and spread it on a strip of paper towels or a terry cloth towel. Pat flat leaves dry. For curly leaves, add a top layer of paper towels, roll the kale in the paper towels, gently squeeze the roll to dry the kale, and roll open the leaves.
   - Working on a large cutting board and using a 5 in. serrated knife, slice the leaves from either side of the vein running through the center of each leaf. Keep the veins

PART 2

with attached stems separate from the leaves.
- Holding the veins/stems together with one hand, use a chef's knife to thinly chop them.
- Form the leaves into one or more stacks, facing leaves in the same direction. While holding a pile of stacked leaves together with one hand, use a 7 in. serrated knife to cut leaves into approx. ⅓ in. thick pieces, cutting lengthwise and crosswise through the leaves.
- Increase the skillet heat to medium-high. When a drop of water added to the skillet instantly dances and disappears, add 1 T oil, add the kale veins/stems, and cook them for 30 seconds, stirring them often.
- Add the kale greens and constantly stir-fry them for 1 minute, setting a timer.
- At the timer, add 1 T hot water, cover the skillet, reduce the heat to low, and steam the kale for 4 minutes, setting a timer.
- At the timer, remove the skillet from the heat, evenly sprinkle ¼ t salt over the kale, and use a rubber spatula to scrape it into the colander onto the carrots.
- Wipe the skillet clean.

6. **Stir-fry/steam the zucchini.**

- Heat the large skillet at a medium setting.
- Rinse and dry the zucchini. Use a chef's knife to cut off the tips of the zucchini. Stand the zucchini upright on the flattened bottom and use the chef's knife to cut the zucchini lengthwise into ¼ in. wide slices. Stacking two slices at a time, cut the slices lengthwise into ¼ in. wide strips. Holding the strips together with one hand, slice them crosswise into ¼ in. cubes.
- Increase the skillet heat to medium-high. When a drop of water instantly dances and disappears, add 1 T oil, add the zucchini, evenly sprinkle the ½ t curry powder and ½ t oregano leaves (first crushing the leaves between your palms) over the zucchini, and stir-fry it for 1 minute, setting a timer. Stir-frying should at first be vigorous but can slow to "flip often" pace midway through the minute.
- At the timer, reduce the heat to low, cover the skillet, and steam the zucchini in its own juices for 4 minutes, setting a timer.
- At the timer, remove the skillet from the heat, evenly sprinkle ¼ t salt over the zucchini, and use a rubber spatula to scrape it and any cooking juice into the colander with the other vegetables.
- Wipe the skillet clean.

7. **Prepare the tomato sauce.**

- Heat the skillet at a medium setting. Open the tomato paste, tomato juice, and broth containers. Use a thin-bladed rubber spatula to easily scrape tomato paste from a 6 oz can.
- Place ½ onion cut side down on a cutting board and use a chef's knife to cut off its ends. Peel the onion. Again place the onion cut side down on the cutting board and use the chef's knife to dice the onion. Mince the ginger.

- Increase the skillet heat to medium-high, and when a drop of water added to the skillet instantly dances and disappears, add 1 T oil, add 1 t cumin seed, and cook it for 30 seconds, stirring it often.
- Add the onion and ginger, evenly sprinkle the spices (1 t curry powder, 1 t chili powder, ½ t ground cumin, and ½ t garlic power) and 1 t oregano (first crushing it between your palms) evenly over the onion, and stir-fry the onion mixture for 1 minute, setting a timer.
- Stir-frying should at first be vigorous but can slow to "flip often" pace midway through the minute.
- At the timer, reduce the heat to medium and cook the onion mixture for 2 minutes, stirring it occasionally and setting a timer.
- At the timer, add and thoroughly mix in the broth, tomato juice, tomato paste, and ¼ t salt. When the mixture nearly boils, reduce the heat to low or a level that maintains very gentle boiling, cover the skillet (leaving the lid slightly ajar), and cook the mixture for 5 minutes, stirring it occasionally and setting a timer.
- While the sauce cooks, squeeze the half lemon and measure 1½ T packed brown sugar.
- At the timer, mix in the measured lemon juice and brown sugar. Remove the skillet from the burner, cover it, and set it aside if the chili will not be soon assembled.

8. **Assemble the chili for serving**.

   - Heat the tomato sauce on medium.
   - Heat the brown rice. Add 3 T water to a medium nonstick skillet, bring the water to boiling over medium-high heat, add and mix in 4 c rice, use a rubber spatula to break up any clumps, immediately reduce the heat to low, evenly sprinkle ¼ t salt over the rice, mix in the salt, tightly cover the skillet, and slowly heat the rice, stirring it occasionally to prevent sticking, while assembling the chili for serving.
   - Prepare remaining ingredients. Grate the cheese. Stir the yogurt creamy smooth before measuring ¾ cup. Open the canned beans.
   - Check the sauce flavoring, adding touches (1-2 t) more lemon juice for tartness, sugar for sweetening, or tomato paste for more concentrated tomato flavor. Add ½ c tomato juice or vegetable broth for thinning to taste.
   - Increase the skillet heat to medium-high.
   - Add the kidney beans and bean broth to the sauce and heat the sauce to near boiling.
   - Mix in the cooked vegetables and any collected vegetable cooking liquid and heat the chili until the sauce is near boiling, stirring frequently.
   - Reduce the skillet heat to medium and heat the sauce for 3-4 more minutes until all ingredients are hot.

9. **Serve the chili**. Add ½-1 c hot brown rice per soup bowl, top the rice in each bowl with 1-2 T grated Parmesan cheese, add chili to taste, top each serving with 2 generous dollops of yogurt, and serve the chili.

   VARIATIONS: Make ingredient and serving pan substitutions. Substitute, for example,

- **non-dairy cheese** for Parmesan cheese to convert the stew into vegan vegetarian form. Alternatively, omit cheese and use only non-dairy yogurt as an accompaniment.
- **½ lb Brussels sprouts**, boiled whole (Recipe #61), for zucchini.
- **½ lb pre-washed spinach** (Recipe #28), **1 bunch unwashed spinach** (Recipe #29), **3-4 leaves chard** (Recipe #24), or **5-6 beet greens** (Recipe #23) for kale.
- **3 ears of yellow corn** (Recipe #65) for dry frozen corn.
- **⅛ t cayenne** or **ground hot pepper**, or to taste, for fresh chili pepper.
- **strained tomatoes,** such as the unflavored Italian product Pomi Strained Tomatoes, for tomato juice used in the tomato sauce.
- **1 Dutch oven** for a large skillet for serving the chili.

Add ingredients. Add, for example,

- **2-3 stalks organic celery** (Recipe #9) with ½ t dried oregano leaves crushed over any of these vegetables during stir-frying.
- **2 chilled medium turnips** (Recipe #22) with ½ t dried oregano leaves crushed over any of these vegetables during stir-frying.
- **1 medium sweet potato** (Recipe #18), diced, or **2 c diced butternut squash** (Recipe #21), stir-fried/steamed.
- **8-10 medium garlic cloves** (Recipe #31), added as a topping to individual servings.

175. Old Fashioned Beef Stew
(6-8 servings)

Beef with Seasonings and Cooking Liquid

2-3 lb beef chuck roast
1½ c canned beef or chicken broth
¾ t salt
4 1-in. thick chunks of fresh ginger root
3-4 whole, peeled garlic cloves
¼ t freshly cracked black peppercorns

Vegetables with Seasoning, Cooking Oil, and Cooking Water

4 medium carrots
1 T extra virgin olive oil
½ t dried oregano
1 t dried sweet basil leaves
1 T hot water
¼ t salt
½ red bell pepper or ¼ each red & green
½ T extra virgin olive oil
3 medium ears yellow corn
2 T water
¼ t salt
2 c dry frozen green peas, unthawed
2 T water
¼ t salt

Tomato Sauce Ingredients

½ chilled medium onion, split lengthwise
2 ⅛-in thick slices fresh ginger root
1 T extra virgin olive oil
1 t dried sweet basil leaves
1 t dried oregano leaves
1 c canned beef broth

6 T tomato paste (6 oz can)
1 c tomato juice
¼ t salt
½-1 lemon
1½ T packed dark brown
½ c tomato juice or canned beef broth

Brown Rice and Beans

1 c cooked brown rice (Recipe #166)

1 c canned kidney or pinto beans with up to ½ c bean broth

Accompaniments

4 oz chunk extra sharp cheddar cheese (to yield 1 c finely shredded)

¾-1 c plain yogurt

Cooking Tools

6 qt Dutch oven or soup pot with a tight-fitting & opaque lid
1 can opener
1 set each measuring spoons & cups
1 each 5 in. serrated & chef's knife
1 plastic or plastic-coated stir-fry spatula
1 timer
1 colander
1 large mixing bowl
1 quart-size Pyrex measuring cup or other heat-resistant container
1 dinner plate

1 large skillet with a tight-fitting & opaque lid
1 electric tea kettle
1 rubber or other heat-resistant spatula
1 pie plate
1 thin-bladed rubber spatula
1 hand citrus juicer
1 cheese grater
1 pepper mill
2-6 large soup bowls
1 large stew serving spoon

---

1. **Cook the beef roast several hours ahead (as much as a day) of preparing the stew.** Gather together the beef ingredients and the first seven cooking tools listed.

   - Rinse the chuck roast and add the roast, 1½ c broth, and ¾ t salt to a Dutch oven or soup pot.
   - Use a serrated knife to cut 4 1-in. slices of ginger root and to slice off the ends of 3-4 garlic cloves. Peel the garlic cloves and add the garlic cloves and ginger root to the Dutch oven or soup pot.
   - Bring the broth to boiling over high heat. Immediately reduce the heat to a level that maintains gentle boiling, slide a stir-fry spatula under the meat to ensure that it is not sticking to the bottom of the pan, cover the pot, and set a timer for 2¼

hours.
- After five minutes, check the meat to ensure it is gently, not rapidly boiling, lowering the temperature if necessary.
- Check the meat for readiness at the timer. Make a taste test to determine tenderness. A sharp knife should easily pierce each portion; the meat should hold together and not be dry and stringy. Drain tender meat into a colander placed in a large bowl for collecting the broth.
- Pour the broth into a quart-size glass measuring cup and refrigerate the broth so that fat gathers at the surface.
- Immediately place the meat within a sealable plastic freezer bag or other air-tight container to protect it from drying and refrigerate the meat.
- Clean the Dutch oven or add soaking water for easy later cleaning in order to use it for serving the stew.
- Clean the colander for use with cooking vegetable ingredients.

2. **Gather all other ingredients and cooking tools.**

3. **Stir-fry/steam the carrots.**

    - Heat a large skillet on a large burner at a medium setting. Begin heating an electric tea kettle to prepare hot water for steaming.
    - Scrub, dry thoroughly, and use a chef's knife to cut off the ends, halve the carrots lengthwise, and cut the carrot halves crosswise into ⅛ in. thick slices.
    - Increase the skillet heat to medium-high. When a drop of water added to the skillet instantly dances and disappears, add 1 T oil, add the carrots, evenly sprinkle ½ t dried oregano and 1 t basil leaves (first crushing the leaves between your palms) over the carrots, and stir-fry the carrots for 1 minute, setting a timer. Stir-frying should first be vigorous but can slow to "flip often" pace midway through the minute.
    - At the timer, add 1 T hot water, cover the skillet, reduce the heat to low, and steam the carrots for 4 minutes, setting a timer.
    - At the timer, remove the skillet from the heat, evenly sprinkle ¼ t salt over the carrots, and use a rubber spatula to scrape the carrots and any cooking juice into a colander placed over a dinner plate.
    - Wipe the skillet clean.

4. **Stir-fry the red bell pepper.**

    - Heat the large skillet at a medium setting.
    - Use a serrated knife to cut out the stem of the pepper. Remove any seeds but not the white membrane. Use the serrated knife to cut the pepper lengthwise into ¼ in. strips and to cut the strips crosswise into ¼ in. cubes.
    - Increase the skillet heat to medium-high, and when a drop of water added to the skillet instantly dances and disappears, add ½ T oil, add the pepper, and vigorously stir-fry it for about 30 seconds. Reduce the heat to medium and cook the pepper for 2 minutes, stirring it occasionally and setting a timer.

- At the timer, use a rubber spatula to scrape the pepper and any cooking juice into the colander with the carrot.
- Wipe the skillet clean.

5. **Stir-fry the corn.**

    - Heat the skillet at a medium setting.
    - Remove the husks and corn silk from the ears. Rubbing the ears under running water helps remove silk, but then dry the ears.
    - Stand an ear of corn upright in a pie plate and use a chef's knife to slice off its kernels, cutting close to the cob to include the corn germ.
    - Bring 2 T water to boiling over high heat in the skillet, add the kernels, and when the water returns to boiling, stir-fry the corn for 1 minute, just until the kernels are heated through and the color slightly darkens.
    - Remove the skillet from the heat, evenly sprinkle ¼ t salt over the corn, and scrape the corn and any cooking juice onto the other vegetables in the colander.
    - Wipe the skillet clean.

6. **Stir-fry the green peas.**

    - Heat the skillet at a medium setting.
    - Break up any clumps of frozen peas before opening the peas.
    - Bring 2 T water to boiling over high heat in the skillet. Add the unthawed green peas, and when the water returns to boiling, stir-fry them for 1 minute, just until they are hot.
    - Remove the skillet from the heat, evenly sprinkle ¼ t salt over the peas, and scrape the peas and any cooking juice onto the corn in the colander.
    - Wipe the skillet clean.

7. **Prepare the tomato sauce.**

    - Heat the skillet at a medium setting. Open tomato juice and paste and canned broth containers. Use a thin-bladed rubber spatula to easily scrape tomato paste from a 6 oz can.
    - Place ½ onion cut side down on a cutting board and use a chef's knife to cut off its tips. Peel the onion. Return the onion cut side down to the cutting board and use the chef's knife to dice the onion. Mince the ginger.
    - Increase the skillet temperature to medium-high, and when a drop of water added to the skillet instantly dances and disappears, add 1 T oil, add the onion and ginger, evenly sprinkle 1 t each dried basil and oregano leaves (first crushing the leaves between your palms) over the onion, and stir-fry the mixture for 1 minute setting a timer. Stir-frying should at first be vigorous but can slow to "flip often" pace midway through the minute.
    - At the timer, reduce the heat to medium and cook the onion mixture for 2 minutes, stirring it occasionally and setting a timer.
    - At the timer, mix in the 1 c broth, 6 oz tomato paste, 1 c tomato juice, and ¼ t salt.

- Increase the skillet heat setting to medium-high and heat the sauce to boiling, stirring occasionally.
- When the liquids begin to boil, reduce the heat to low, mainly cover the skillet, and cook the sauce for 5 minutes, stirring it occasionally and setting a timer.
- While the sauce cooks, squeeze the ½ lemon and measure 1½ T packed dark brown sugar.
- At the timer, remove the skillet from the heat, mix in the lemon juice and brown sugar, and scrape the sauce into the Dutch oven used for cooking the meat.

8. **Assemble the stew for serving.**

- Begin heating the tomato sauce in the Dutch oven at medium.
- Prepare the beef roast meat and fresh meat broth. Use a sharp slicing knife to cut the meat into serving size pieces. Remove chunks of fat, cut the meat into ⅓ in. thick slices, cut the slices into ⅓ in. thick strips, and cut the strips into ⅓ in. cubes. Cut a total of 3-4 cups meat and tightly cover and refrigerate extra meat.
- Crack black peppercorns over the cut meat to taste.
- Skim fat from the broth when it hardens during refrigeration and add the broth to the tomato sauce in the Dutch oven.
- Make final soup preparations. Coarsely grate the cheddar cheese and add 2 T grated cheese to each serving bowl. Stir the yogurt creamy smooth before measuring 1 cup. Check the flavoring of the sauce and cautiously add touches (1-2 t) more lemon juice for tartness, brown sugar for sweetening, tomato paste for more concentrated tomato flavor, or salt to taste. If the sauce remains very thick, add ½ c tomato juice or canned broth.
- Increase the skillet heat to medium-high and bring the tomato sauce to boiling.
- Break up any rice clumps and add the rice to the sauce. Add the canned beans with bean broth, add the meat, and bring the sauce to boiling.
- Add the cooked vegetables and any vegetable cooking liquid and return the stew to near boiling, stirring often.
- Reduce the heat to medium and heat the stew no more than five minutes until all ingredients are hot, stirring often.
- Immediately serve the stew. Serve individual servings poured over the cheese and topped with two heaping dollops of yogurt (or to taste).

VARIATIONS: Make ingredient substitutions. Substitute, for example,

- **2 c dry frozen yellow whole kernel corn,** unthawed, for fresh ears, cooked exactly the same.
- **1 c other whole grain** (Recipe #167) for brown rice.
- **Parmesan cheese** for cheddar cheese, 1 T per serving as a topping.
- **1 c other cooked beans** for kidney or pinto beans.
- **strained tomatoes,** such as the unflavored Italian product Pomi Strained Tomatoes, for tomato juice used in the tomato sauce.
- **1-1½ lb lean and tender beefsteak,** ½ in. thick, for chuck roast. Cut the meat across

the grain into ⅓ in. thick strips and cut the strips crosswise into ⅓ in. cubes, removing fat. Stir-fry the meat with two minced ⅛ in. thick slices of ginger root until most raw red coloring is removed from the cubes. Crush ¾ t each oregano and sweet basil leaves and evenly sprinkle 1 t garlic powder over the meat during cooking. Evenly sprinkle ½ t salt over the cooked meat. Substitute canned/packaged beef or chicken broth, fresh poultry broth (Reference #10), or reconstituted broth for fresh beef broth.

Add ingredients. Add, for example,

- **3-4 large cauliflower florets** (Recipe #8), cauliflower broken into ½ in. florets, or **2 c sliced green or red cabbage** (Recipe #6). Crush ½ t each dried oregano and sweet basil leaves over the cauliflower or cabbage during stir-frying.
- **1-2 medium turnips** (Recipe #22), **1-2 c Brussels sprouts** (Recipe #5 or #61), or **2 c diced rutabaga** (Recipe #19) with ½ t each crushed dried basil and oregano leaves added during stir-frying.
- **2 stalks organic celery** (Recipe #9) with ½ t each dried basil and oregano leaves added during stir-frying.
- **2-3 c string beans**, boiled whole (Recipe #56). Evenly sprinkle ¼ t salt over the beans after boiling. When assembling the stew, use kitchen scissors to snip tips from and to cut the beans into thirds.
- **½ lb spinach** (Recipe #28 or 29), **chard** (Recipe #24), **kale** (Recipe #26), or **beet greens** (Recipe #23). Add greens as a last ingredient when assembling the stew for serving. Alternatively, separately and quickly reheat the greens and serve them as a topping on individual servings.
- **8-10 garlic cloves** (Recipe #31) with garlic added as a topping to individual servings.
- **1 c thick whole wheat noodles, Italian pasta shells, or fresh or frozen fresh thick noodles,** cooked separately until tender in salted water according to package directions.

176. Lentil Stew
(4 large servings)

Vegetables with Seasonings, Cooking Oil, and Cooking Water

2 medium red potatoes
1 T extra virgin olive oil
1 t dried oregano leaves
1 T hot water
⅓ t salt
4 medium carrots
1 T extra virgin olive oil

3 ears yellow corn
2 T water
¼ t salt
3-4 medium kale leaves
1 T extra virgin olive oil
2 T water
¼ t salt

½ t curry powder
1 T hot water
¼ t salt

¼ each red and green bell pepper,
    sliced lengthwise
½ T extra virgin olive oil

Tomato Sauce Ingredients

½ chilled medium onion, halved lengthwise
2 ⅛-in. thick slices fresh ginger root
1 t cumin seeds
1 t curry powder
½ t ground cumin
1 t dried oregano leaves
1 c beef broth

6 T tomato paste (6 oz can)
1 c tomato juice
¼ t salt
½ lemon (to yield 2 T lemon juice)
1½ T packed dark brown sugar
½ c tomato juice or beef broth

Ground Beef with Seasonings and Cooking Oil

1 lb extra lean ground beef
2 ⅛-in. thick slices fresh ginger root
2 t extra virgin olive oil
1 t curry powder

1 t garlic powder
½ t dried oregano leaves
½ t ground cumin
⅓ t salt

Lentils and Brown Rice

½ c dry lentils (brown or green)
1¼ c water

⅓ t salt
1½ c cooked brown rice (Recipe #166)

Accompaniment

¾-1 c plain yogurt

Cooking Tools

1 set each measuring cups & spoons
2 qt heavy-bottomed saucepan
    with a tight-fitting & opaque lid
1 timer
1 heat proof measuring cup or small bowl
1 medium skillet with a lid
1 large skillet with a tight-fitting
    & opaque lid
1 electric tea kettle
1 chef's knife
1 each 5 in. & 7 in. serrated knife
1 plastic or plastic-coasted stir-fry spatula

1 rubber or other heat-resistant spatula
1 medium mixing bowl
1 colander
1 dinner plate
1 large cutting board (approx. 16 x 24 in.)
1 pie plate
1 can opener & 1 thin-bladed rubber
    spatula
1 hand citrus juicer
1-6 large soup bowls
1 large stew serving spoon

1. **Soak the lentils.** One hour, several hours, or a day before beginning dish preparations, add ½ c lentils to a medium saucepan, carefully look through the lentils to remove any stones, add 1¼ c cool water, bring the water to full boiling over high heat, remove the pan from the heat, and set it aside, covered. If soaking the lentils well ahead of stew preparation, cover and refrigerate the lentils in the soaking water after 1 hour.

2. **Gather all ingredients and cooking tools.**

3. **Cook the lentils.**

   - Bring the lentils to boiling in the soaking water, reduce the heat to a level that maintains very gentle boiling, cover the lentils, and set a timer for 25 minutes.
   - Check the lentils after five minutes to ensure the lentils are slowly boiling, reducing the heat if necessary.
   - At the timer, taste the lentils and remove the pan from the heat if they are completely soft without any hint of crispness.
   - If the lentils are not completely soft, continue the cooking. Check the lentil texture every five minutes until the texture is satisfactorily soft, setting a timer after each check to avoid overcooking.
   - Once the lentils are completely soft, remove the pan from the heat and roughly drain any unabsorbed liquid into a heat-proof measuring cup or small bowl.
   - Mix ⅓ t salt into the lentils and set them aside in the saucepan, covered.

4. **Cook the ground beef while the lentils cook.**

   - Heat a medium skillet at medium on a large back burner.
   - Use a 5 in. serrated knife to finely mince two ⅛ in. thick slices of ginger root.
   - Increase the skillet heat to medium-high, and when a drop of water added to the skillet instantly dances and disappears, spread 2 t oil over the skillet bottom, mix the ginger into the oil, add the beef, and use a stir-frying spatula to break up the meat into small (⅓ in. thick) chunks.
   - Reduce the heat to medium (oil should continue to sizzle gently around the meat chunks) and evenly sprinkle the 1 t curry powder, 1 t garlic powder, ½ t dried oregano leaves (first crushing them between your palms), and ½ t ground cumin over the meat.
   - Cook the meat for 5 minutes until no trace of raw red coloring remains, occasionally turning the meat and setting a timer.
   - At the timer, remove the skillet from the heat, evenly sprinkle ⅓ t salt over the meat, cover the skillet, and set the skillet aside, slanting it to drain any juice/fat away from the meat.

5. **Stir-fry/steam the potatoes.**

   - Heat a large skillet at a medium setting on a large back burner. Begin heating an

electric tea kettle to prepare hot water for steaming.
- Scrub and thoroughly dry the potatoes with paper towels or a terry cloth towel. Use a chef's knife to cut off the tips of each potato and to slice off any eyes. Stand each potato upright on a flattened end and cut it lengthwise into ¼ in. wide slices. Stacking two slices together, cut the slices lengthwise into ¼ in. wide strips. Holding several strips together, cut them crosswise into ¼ in. cubes.
- Increase the skillet heat to medium-high. When a drop of water added to the skillet instantly dances and disappears, add 1 T oil, add the potatoes, evenly sprinkle 1 t oregano leaves (first crushing them between your palms) over them, and stir-fry the potatoes for 1 minute, setting a timer. Stir-frying should at first be vigorous but can slow to "flip often" pace midway through the minute.
- At the timer, lower the heat to medium and heat the potatoes for 1 minute, stirring them occasionally and setting a timer.
- At the timer, add 1 T hot water, tightly cover the skillet, reduce the heat to low, and steam the potato for 10 minutes, setting a timer.
- At the timer, turn off the heat, uncover the potatoes, evenly sprinkle ⅓ t salt over the potatoes, and use a rubber spatula to scrape the potatoes and any cooking juice into a mixing bowl.
- Wipe the skillet clean.

6. **Stir-fry/steam the carrots.**

- Heat a second large skillet at a medium setting on a large front burner. Begin heating an electric tea kettle to prepare hot water for steaming.
- Scrub and thoroughly dry the 4 carrots. Use a chef's knife to cut off the ends, halve the carrots lengthwise, and cut the carrot halves crosswise into ⅛ in. thick slices.
- Increase the skillet heat to medium-high, and when a drop of water added to the skillet instantly dances and disappears, add 1 T oil, add the carrots, evenly sprinkle ½ t curry powder over them, and stir-fry the carrots for 1 minute, setting a timer.
- At the timer, add 1 T hot water to the carrots, cover the skillet, reduce the heat to low, and steam the carrots for 4 minutes, setting a timer.
- At the timer, remove the skillet from the heat, evenly sprinkle ⅓ t salt over the carrots, and use a rubber spatula to scrape them and any cooking juice into a colander placed over a dinner plate.
- Wipe the skillet clean.

7. **Stir-fry the corn.**

- Heat the skillet at a medium setting.
- Remove the husks and corn silk from the ears. Rubbing the ears under running water helps remove silk, but then dry the ears. Stand an ear upright in a pie plate and use a chef's knife to slice off the kernels, cutting close to the cob to include the corn germ.
- Bring 2 T water to boiling over high heat in the skillet. Add the kernels, mix them into the water, and when the water again boils, stir-fry the corn for 1 minute, just until the kernels are hot and darken in color slightly.

- Remove the skillet from the heat, evenly sprinkle ¼ t salt over the corn, and scrape the corn and any cooking liquid into the colander next to the carrots.
- Wipe the skillet clean.

8. **Stir-fry/steam the kale.**

    - Heat the large skillet at a medium setting. Begin heating an electric tea kettle to prepare water for steaming.
    - Rinse each kale leaf, shake off excess clinging water, and place it on a layer of paper towels. For flat leaves, pat the leaves dry with a paper or terry towel. For curly leaves, add a top layer of paper towels, roll the kale in the paper towels, gently squeeze the roll to dry the kale, and roll open the leaves.
    - Working on a large cutting board and using a 5 in. serrated knife, slice the leaves from either side of the central vein running through the center of each leaf. Keep the veins with attached stems separate from the leaves.
    - Holding the veins/stems together with one hand, use a chef's knife to thinly chop them.
    - Form the leaves into one or more stacks, facing leaves in the same direction. Holding a pile of stacked leaves together with one hand and using a 7 in. serrated knife, cut the kale leaves into approx. ⅓ in. thick slices, cutting first lengthwise and then crosswise through the leaves.
    - Increase the skillet heat to medium-high.
    - When a drop of water added to the skillet instantly dances and disappears, add 1 T oil, add the kale veins/stems, and cook them for 30 seconds, stirring often.
    - Add the kale greens and constantly stir-fry them for 1 minute, setting a timer.
    - At the timer, add 1 T hot water, cover the skillet, reduce the heat to low, and steam the kale for 4 minutes, setting a timer.
    - At the timer, remove the skillet from the heat, evenly sprinkle ¼ t salt over the kale, and use a rubber spatula to scrape it into the colander with the other vegetables.
    - Wipe the skillet clean.

9. **Stir-fry the bell peppers.**

    - Heat the large skillet on a large burner at medium.
    - Use a 5 in. serrated knife to cut out the stem of the peppers. Remove any seeds but not the membrane from the pepper. Use the serrated knife to cut the pepper lengthwise into ¼ in. strips and to cut the strips crosswise into ¼ in. cubes.
    - Increase the heat to medium-high, and when a drop of water added to the skillet instantly dances and disappears, add ½ T oil, add the peppers, and vigorously stir-fry them for about 30 seconds.
    - Reduce the heat to medium and cook the peppers for 2 minutes, stirring them occasionally and setting a timer.
    - At the timer, use a rubber spatula to scrape the pepper and any cooking juice into the colander with the other vegetables.
    - Wipe the skillet clean.

10. **Prepare the tomato sauce.**

    - Heat the large skillet on a large burner at a medium setting. Open the tomato juice, tomato paste, and broth containers. Use a thin-bladed rubber spatula to easily scrape tomato paste from a 6 oz can.
    - Place ½ onion cut side down on a cutting board and use a chef's knife to cut off its ends. Peel the onion. Again place the onion cut side down on the cutting board and use the chef's knife to dice the onion. Mince the ginger root.
    - Increase the skillet heat to medium-high, and when a drop of water added to the skillet instantly dances and disappears, add 1 T oil, mix in 1 t cumin seeds, heat it for about 30 seconds, add the onion and ginger, evenly sprinkle the spices (1 t curry powder, ½ t ground cumin, and ½ t garlic powder) and 1 t dried oregano leaves (first crushing them between your palms) over the onion and ginger, and stir-fry the mixture for 1 minute, setting a timer. Stir-frying should at first be vigorous but can slow to "flip often" pace midway through the minute.
    - At the timer, reduce the heat to medium and cook the mixture for 2 minutes, stirring occasionally and setting a timer.
    - At the timer, add and mix in the 1 c broth, 6 T tomato paste, 1 c tomato juice, and ¼ t salt.
    - Heat the mixture to near boiling, reduce the heat to a low-medium setting or a level that maintains slow boiling, partially cover the skillet, and cook the mixture for 5 minutes, stirring it occasionally and setting a timer.
    - Squeeze the ½ lemon and measure the 1½ T packed brown sugar while the sauce cooks.
    - At the timer, mix in the measured lemon juice and brown sugar. If the stew will not soon be assembled for serving, remove the skillet from the heat, cover it, and set it aside.

11. **Assemble the stew for serving.**

    - Heat the tomato sauce at a medium setting.
    - Stir the yogurt creamy smooth before measuring ¾ to 1 cup. Break up any rice clumps.
    - Check the flavoring of the sauce, adding touches (1-2 t) more lemon juice for tartness and brown sugar for sweetening. Add 1-2 T more tomato paste for more intense tomato flavoring, salt to taste, and ½ c tomato juice or broth for thinning to taste.
    - Increase the skillet heat to medium-high, and when the sauce boils, add the brown rice, lentils, and lentil broth. Heat the sauce to near boiling.
    - Add the ground beef, cooked vegetables, and any collected vegetable cooking water.
    - Heat the stew, stirring often, to near boiling, reduce the heat to medium, and heat the stew another 3-4 minutes until all ingredients are hot.

12. **Serve the stew.** Top individual servings with 2 or 3 dollops of yogurt.

    VARIATIONS: Make ingredient substitutions. Substitute, for example,

- **vegetable broth** for beef broth, omit the ground beef, and substitute **soya yogurt** or **other non-dairy cheese** for dairy yogurt to convert the stew into **vegan vegetarian form.**
- **6-8 beet greens** (Recipe #23), **3 medium collard leaves** (Recipe #40), **turnip greens** (Recipe #45), or **3 large chard leaves** (Recipe #24) for kale.
- **½ lb pre-washed spinach** (Recipe #28) or **½ lb pre-washed baby greens** (any variety) as the simplest and quickest substitution for kale.
- **2 c organic dry frozen whole kernel corn**, unthawed, for fresh corn, cooking it in the same way.
- **2 T finely grated extra sharp cheddar** or **freshly grated Parmesan cheese** per serving for yogurt.
- **strained tomatoes,** such as the unflavored Italian product Pomi Strained Tomatoes, for tomato juice.
- **fresh chicken broth** (Reference #10) for beef broth.

Add ingredients. Add, for example,

- **2 stalks organic celery** (Recipe #9) with ½ t dried oregano leaves crushed over the celery during stir-frying.
- **¼ medium head of cabbage**, green or red (Recipe #6).
- **¼ yellow bell pepper.** Increase the oil content to ¾ T and cook the bell peppers together.
- **1 c green or yellow snap/string beans**, boiled whole (Recipe #58). Add ¼ t salt to the beans after boiling. For serving, use kitchen scissors to snip off the ends and to cut the beans into thirds.
- **1½ c Brussels sprouts**, boiled whole (Recipe #61), halved or quartered.
- **8-10 chilled medium garlic cloves** (Recipe #31). Garlic retains its distinctive flavor when served as a topping on individual servings.

177. Minestrone Stew
(6 servings)

Vegetables with Seasonings, Cooking Oil, and Cooking Water

½ lb green beans
½ c water
¼ t salt
4 medium carrots
1 T extra virgin olive oil
½ t dried rosemary leaves

1 T hot water
¼ t salt
6-10 grape tomatoes
1 t extra virgin olive oil
½ red bell pepper, halved lengthwise
½ T extra virgin olive oil

Tomato Sauce Ingredients

½ chilled medium onion, halved lengthwise
2 ⅛-in. thick slices fresh ginger root
1 T extra virgin olive oil
1 t dried sage leaves
½ t dried rosemary leaves
1 c beef broth

6 T tomato paste (1 6-oz can)
1 c tomato juice
¼ t salt
½-1 lemon
1½ T packed dark brown sugar
½ c tomato juice or beef broth

Ground Beef with Seasonings and Cooking Oil

1 lb extra lean ground beef
2 ⅛-in. thick slices ginger root
½ t garlic powder
½ t dried sage leaves

½ t dried rosemary leaves
2 t extra virgin olive oil
⅓ t salt

Pasta, Brown Rice, and Beans

1 c whole wheat Italian pasta shells
¾ T salt
1½ c cooked brown rice (Recipe #166)

¼ t salt
1½ c (15 oz can) kidney beans
   with up to ½ c bean broth

Dish Accompaniment

3 oz chunk Parmesan cheese (to yield ¾ c fine grated, loosely packed)

Cooking Tools

1 large saucepan (3 qt) with a lid
1 set each measuring spoons & cups
1 long-handled wooden spoon
1 colander
1 medium skillet with a lid
1 each 5 in. serrated & chef's knife
1 plastic or plastic-coated stir-fry spatula
1 medium (2 qt) saucepan with a lid
1 timer
1 large skillet with a tight-fitting & opaque lid

1 pie plate
1 electric tea kettle
1 rubber or other heat-resistant spatula
1 can opener & 1 thin-bladed rubber
   spatula
1 hand citrus juicer
1 cheese grater
1 pair kitchen scissors
2-6 large soup bowls
1 large stew serving spoon

1. **Gather all ingredients and cooking tools.**

2. **Cook the pasta.**

   • Add enough water to cover the pasta completely by several inches to a large

saucepan.
- Bring the water to boiling over high heat, add ¾ T salt, add the pasta, stir it with a wooden spoon, and boil it, uncovered and stirring it occasionally to prevent sticking until it is tender but holds its shape (according to package directions; making tenderness checks often toward the end of the cooking time).
- Drain the pasta in a colander, return it to the pot, and set it aside, tightly covered.
- Wipe the colander clean.

3. **Cook the ground beef.**

    - Heat a medium skillet at a medium heat setting on a large back burner.
    - Use a 5 in. serrated knife to finely mince the ginger root.
    - Increase the skillet heat to medium-high, and when a drop of water added to the skillet instantly dances and disappears, spread 2 t oil over the skillet bottom, mix the ginger into the oil, add the ground beef, and use a stir-fry spatula to break up the meat into ½ in. thick (not fine) chunks.
    - Evenly sprinkle the ½ t garlic powder and ½ t each sage and rosemary leaves (first crushing the dried leaves between your palms) over the meat.
    - Cook the meat chunks, turning them over often, for one minute and reduce the heat to medium-low. Oil should continue to sizzle gently around meat pieces. Continue cooking the meat for 5 minutes until no trace of raw red remains, stirring it occasionally and setting a timer.
    - At the timer, remove the skillet from the heat, evenly sprinkle ⅓ t salt over the meat, cover the skillet, and set the meat aside.

4. **Boil the ½ lb green beans whole.**

    - Rinse the green beans but do not trim them in any way.
    - Bring ¼ c water to boiling over high heat in a medium saucepan, use a wooden spoon to thoroughly stir the beans into the boiling water, reduce the heat to low, cover the pan, and cook the beans for 7 minutes, setting a timer.
    - At the timer, immediately drain the beans into one side of a colander placed over a pie plate to collect the cooking water.
    - Evenly sprinkle ¼ t salt over the beans and push the beans into one side of the colander.

5. **Stir-fry/steam the carrots.**

    - Heat a large skillet at a medium setting. Begin heating an electric tea kettle to prepare hot water for steaming.
    - Scrub and thoroughly dry the carrots.
    - Use a chef's knife to cut off the ends, split the carrots lengthwise, and cut the carrot halves crosswise into ⅛ in. thick slices.
    - Increase the skillet heat to medium-high, and when a drop of water added to the skillet instantly dances and disappears, add 1 T oil, add the carrots, evenly sprinkle

½ t dried rosemary leaves (first crushing them between your palms) over the carrot, and stir-fry the carrots for 1 minute, setting a timer. Stir-frying should at first be vigorous but can slow to a "flip often" pace midway through the minute.

- At the timer, add 1 T hot water, cover the pan, reduce the heat to low, and steam the carrots for 4 minutes, using a timer.
- At the timer, remove the skillet from the stove, evenly sprinkle ¼ t salt over the carrots, and use a rubber spatula to scrape it and any cooking juice into the colander alongside the green beans.
- Wipe the skillet clean.

6. **Stir-fry the 6-10 grape tomatoes.**

   - Heat the large skillet at a medium setting.
   - Rinse and thoroughly dry the tomatoes and use a serrated knife to halve each lengthwise.
   - Increase the skillet heat to medium-high, and when a drop of water added to the skillet instantly dances and disappears, add 1 t oil, add the tomato, and gently stir-fry it for 1 minute, setting a timer.
   - At the timer, scrape the tomato and any cooking juice into the colander, but keep it to one side separate from the other vegetables.
   - Wipe the skillet clean.

7. **Stir-fry ½ red bell pepper.**

   - Heat the large skillet at a medium setting.
   - Use a 5 in. serrated knife to cut out the stem of the bell pepper. Remove any seeds but not the white membrane. Use the serrated knife to cut the pepper lengthwise into ¼ in. strips and to cut the strips crosswise into ¼ in. cubes.
   - Increase the heat to medium-high, and when a drop of water added to the skillet instantly dances and disappears, add ½ T oil, add the bell pepper, and vigorously stir-fry it for about 30 seconds.
   - Reduce the heat to medium and cook the pepper for 2 minutes, stirring it occasionally and setting a timer.
   - At the timer, use a rubber spatula to scrape the pepper and any cooking juice into the colander.
   - Wipe the skillet clean.

8. **Prepare a tomato sauce.**

   - Heat the large skillet at a medium setting.
   - Open the canned beef broth, tomato juice, and tomato paste containers. Use a thin-bladed rubber spatula to easily scrape tomato paste from a 6 oz can.
   - Place ½ onion cut side down on a cutting board and use a chef's knife to slice off its ends. Peel the onion. Again place the onion cut side down on the cutting board and use the chef's knife to dice the onion. Mince the ginger.

- Increase the skillet heat to medium-high, and when a drop of water added to the skillet instantly dances and disappears, add 1 T oil, add the onion and ginger, evenly sprinkle 1 t dried sage leaves and ½ t dried rosemary leaves (first crushing the leaves between your palms) over the onion, and stir-fry the mixture for 1 minute, setting a timer. Stir-frying should at first be vigorous but can slow to "flip often" pace midway through the minute.
- At the timer, reduce the heat to medium and cook the onion mixture for 2 minutes, stirring it occasionally and setting a timer.
- At the timer, add 1 c tomato juice, 6 T tomato paste, 1 c beef broth, and ¼ t salt. Increase the heat to medium-high to quickly bring the mixture to boiling, reduce the heat to medium low, mainly cover the skillet, and gently boil the mixture for 5 minutes, setting a timer.
- While the sauce cooks squeeze the ½ lemon and measure 1½ T packed dark brown sugar.
- At the timer, mix in the lemon juice and sugar.
- Reduce the heat to low. Move the skillet from the burner, cover it, and set it aside if the stew will not be immediately assembled.

9. **Assemble the stew for serving.**

    - Heat the sauce at a medium setting.
    - Finely grate the cheese. Open the canned beans. Break up any rice clumps.
    - Use kitchen scissors to snip off the tips of the green beans and to halve each bean.
    - Check the sauce flavoring, cautiously adding touches (1-2 t) of lemon juice for tartness and sugar for sweetening. Add 1-2 T tomato paste for more intense tomato flavoring. Add ½ c tomato juice or broth to thin the sauce.
    - Increase the skillet heat to medium-high. Add the brown rice, beans, and bean broth to the sauce and heat the stew to boiling.
    - Mix in the pasta, meat, cooked vegetables except for the tomatoes, and any collected vegetable cooking liquid.
    - Heat the stew to near boiling, stirring it often. When it boils, reduce the heat to medium and heat the stew 3-5 minutes, just until all ingredients are hot.
    - Mix in the tomatoes.

10. **Serve the stew.** Top individual servings topped with 1-2 T Parmesan cheese.

    VARIATIONS: Make ingredient substitutions. Substitute, for example,

    - **vegetable broth** for beef broth and omit the ground beef to convert the stew into **traditional vegetarian form.**
    - **vegetable broth** for beef broth and **non-dairy cheese** or **soy yogurt** for Parmesan cheese and omit the ground beef to convert the stew into **vegan vegetarian** form.
    - **¾ c plain yogurt**, stirred creamy smooth, for Parmesan cheese.
    - **1 c canned diced tomatoes**, including ¼ c packing juice, or **1 c strained tomatoes** (such as the unflavored Italian product Pomi Strained Tomatoes) for grape tomatoes.

- **1 c other high quality Italian pasta shells**, such as Barilla brand casarecce pasta, if whole wheat Italian pasta is not available.
- **1 c fresh poultry broth** (Reference #10) for canned beef broth.

Add ingredients. Add, for example,

- **2 c Brussels sprouts**, boiled whole (Recipe #61).
- **1 medium (6 in. long; 1½ in. thick) zucchini** or **2 small yellow summer squash** (Recipe #20) with ½ t dried sage or rosemary leaves crushed over the squash during stir-frying.
- **2 c cabbage** (Recipe # 6) or **cauliflower** (Recipe #8) with ½ t dried sage or rosemary leaves crushed over the vegetable during stir-frying.
- **¼ each green and yellow bell pepper**, cooking them with the red pepper and increasing the oil content to ¾ T oil.

Stew – Herbed Broth Base Recipe

178. Old Fashioned Chicken Stew
(6-8 servings)

Chicken with Cooking Ingredients

1 small whole chicken
2 ½-in. thick chunks fresh ginger root
4-6 whole peeled garlic cloves (opt)
top leaves from 1 bunch celery

1½ c (15 oz can) chicken broth
½ t salt
¼ t fresh cracked black peppercorns

Vegetables with Seasonings, Cooking Oil, and Cooking Water

4 medium carrots
1 T extra virgin olive oil
½ t each dried sage and thyme leaves
1 T hot water
¼ t salt
4 stalks organic celery
1 T extra virgin olive oil
½ t dried sage leaves

⅓ each red and green bell pepper
½ T extra virgin olive oil
½ lb pre-washed spinach
1 T extra virgin olive oil
¼ t salt
2 c dry frozen yellow corn, unthawed
2 T water
¼ t salt

Broth with Seasonings

½ medium chilled onion, halved lengthwise
2 ⅛-in. thick slices ginger root
1 T extra virgin olive oil

½-1 lemon
1½ T packed dark brown sugar
¼ t salt

1 t dried sage leaves
½ t dried thyme leaves
½ t garlic powder

½ c canned chicken broth
½-1 c plain yogurt (as topping)

Pasta and Brown Rice

1 c uncooked whole grain Italian pasta shells (thick pasta)

1½ c cooked brown rice (Recipe #166)

Cooking Tools

1 set each measuring spoons & cups
1 Dutch oven or soup pot with a tight-fitting & opaque lid
1 long-handled wooden spoon
1 timer
2 colanders
1 large mixing bowl
1 qt-size Pyrex measuring cup or heat-resistant jar or bowl
1 large (3 qt or 12 c) saucepan

1 large skillet with a tight-fitting & opaque lid
1 electric tea kettle
1 each chef's & 7 in. serrated knife
1 plastic or plastic-coated stir-fry spatula
1 rubber or other heat-resistant spatula
1 dinner plate
1 large (approx. 16 x 24 in.) cutting board
1 hand citrus juicer
1 soup ladle
2-6 large soup bowls

---

1. **Cook the chicken.**

   - Begin cooking the chicken 1½ hour ahead or as much as a day ahead of other stew preparation.
   - Open a 15 oz can of chicken broth. Use a 5 in. serrated knife to cut 2-3 ½-in. chunks of ginger root and to cut off the tips of 4-5 garlic cloves. Peel the garlic cloves.
   - Add the chicken broth, ginger root, garlic cloves, and ½ t salt to a Dutch oven.
   - Rinse both the chicken and celery top leaves under cool water and add them to the Dutch oven. Thoroughly wash your hands after handling the chicken and before handling any utensils.
   - Bring the broth to full boiling, use a long-handled wooden spoon to stir under the chicken to ensure it is not sticking to the pan bottom, reduce the heat to a level that maintains gentle boiling, and set a timer for 45 minutes for a small chicken or 60 minutes for a larger chicken.
   - At the timer, make a readiness check. The legs should move easily. If they do, drain the chicken in a colander placed within a large mixing bowl for collecting the broth.
   - Pour the broth into a quart size (4 cup) Pyrex measuring cup or other heat-resistant container and refrigerate it to harden fat that gathers on the surface of the broth, discarding the ginger root and garlic.
   - Allow the chicken to cool in the colander for handling. If the chicken will not be soon prepared for serving, place the chicken within a gallon size freezer bag to protect it from drying out and refrigerate the chicken.

PART 2

- Clean the cooking pot and the wooden spoon.

2. **Gather all ingredients and cooking tools.**
3. **Cook the pasta.**

    - Add approx. 6 c water to a large sauce pan (enough to cover the pasta by several inches).
    - Using a back burner, bring the water to boiling over high heat, add ¾ T salt, add the pasta, stir it with the long-handled wooden spoon to separate pieces, and boil the pasta uncovered, according to package directions until it is soft, timing the cooking. Stir the pasta occasionally to prevent sticking. Be watchful at first and reduce the heat setting somewhat as may be needed to prevent the pan from boiling over.
    - At the timer, make a taste check. If the pasta is attractively soft, drain the pasta in a clean colander. If is not soft, continue the cooking and make a taste check every 2-3 minutes until it is.
    - When the pasta is soft, drain it, immediately return it to the pot, and set it aside, tightly covered.

4. **Stir-fry/steam the carrots.**

    - Heat a large skillet on a large burner at a medium setting. Begin heating an electric tea kettle to have hot water for steaming.
    - Scrub and dry the 4 carrots. Use a chef's knife to cut off the ends, split the carrots lengthwise, and cut the carrot halves crosswise into ⅛ in. thick slices.
    - Increase the skillet heat to medium-high. When a drop of water added to the skillet instantly dances and disappears, add 1 T oil, add the carrot, evenly sprinkle ½ t dried sage and ½ t thyme leaves (first crushing them between your palms) over the carrot, and stir-fry the carrot for 1 minute, setting a timer. Stir-frying should at first be vigorous but can slow to "flip often" pace midway through the minute.
    - At the timer, add 1 T hot water, cover the skillet, reduce the heat to low, and steam the carrots for 4 minutes (until they are soft but retain bright orange color), setting a timer.
    - At the timer, remove the skillet from the burner, evenly sprinkle ¼ t salt over the carrot, and use a rubber spatula to scrape it and any cooking juice into a colander placed over a dinner plate.
    - Wipe the skillet clean.

5. **Stir-fry/steam the celery.**

    - Heat the skillet at a medium setting.
    - Rinse and dry the 4 stalks celery. Use a chef's knife to cut off the stalk ends and any leaves, saving the leaves for another use. Use the chef's knife to split the stalks lengthwise and to cut the stalk halves crosswise into ⅛ in. thick slices.
    - Increase the skillet heat to medium-high. When a drop of water added to the skillet instantly dances and disappears, add 1 T oil, add the celery, evenly sprinkle ½ t

dried sage leaves (first crushing them between your palms) over the celery, and stir-fry the celery for 1 minute, setting a timer. Stir-frying should at first be vigorous but can slow to "flip often" pace midway through the minute.

- At the timer, reduce the heat to low, cover the skillet, and steam the celery for 4 minutes in its own juice, using a timer.
- Remove the skillet from the burner and use a rubber spatula to scrape the celery and any cooking juice into the colander next to the carrots.
- Wipe the skillet clean.

6. **Stir-fry the spinach.**

    - Heat the skillet at a medium setting.
    - Bunch the spinach leaves together on a large cutting board.
    - Loosely holding the leaves together with one hand, use a 7 in. serrated knife to cut the spinach into approx. ⅓ in. thick pieces, cutting through the leaves first lengthwise and then crosswise.
    - Increase the skillet heat to medium-high, and when a drop of water added to the skillet instantly dances and disappears, add 1 T olive oil, add the spinach, and constantly stir-fry the spinach, turning it over and over, for 1 minute, just until it uniformly darkens and slightly wilts.
    - Remove the skillet from the heat, evenly sprinkle ¼ t salt over the spinach, and scrape it and any cooking juice into the colander alongside the carrots and celery.
    - Wipe the skillet clean.

7. **Stir-fry the corn.**

    - Break up any clumps before removing the frozen corn from its package.
    - Heat 2 T water to boiling over high heat in the skillet. Add and mix in the corn.
    - When the water again boils, stir-fry the corn for 1 minute, setting a timer.
    - Remove the skillet from the heat, evenly sprinkle ¼ t salt over the corn, and use a rubber spatula to scrape the corn and any cooking liquid over the carrots and celery in the colander.
    - Wipe the skillet clean.

8. **Stir-fry the bell peppers.**

    - Heat the skillet at a medium setting.
    - Use a 5 in. serrated knife to cut out the stem from the peppers. Remove any seeds but not the white membrane. Use the serrated knife to cut the peppers lengthwise into ¼ in. thick slices and to cut the slices crosswise into ¼ in. cubes.
    - Increase the skillet heat to medium-high, and when a drop of water added to the skillet instantly dances and disappears, add 1 T oil, add the peppers, and vigorously stir-fry them for 30 seconds.
    - Reduce the heat to medium and cook the peppers for 2 minutes, stirring them occasionally and setting a timer.

- At the timer, use a rubber spatula to scrape the peppers and any cooking juice into the colander next to the spinach.
- Wipe the skillet clean.

9. **Prepare the broth flavoring.**

    - Heat the skillet at a medium setting.
    - Place ½ onion cut side down on a cutting board and use a chef's knife to slice off its ends. Peel the onion. Again place the onion cut side down on a cutting board and use a chef's knife to dice the onion, cutting it first lengthwise and then crosswise into ¼ in. thick slices, holding the slices together with one hand as they are cut. Mince the ginger.
    - Increase the skillet heat to medium-high, and when a drop of water added to the skillet instantly dances and disappears, add 1 T oil, add the onion and ginger, evenly sprinkle the 1 t dried sage and ½ t thyme leaves (first crushing them between your palms) and ½ t garlic powder over the onion/ginger, and stir-fry the mixture for 1 minute, setting a timer. Stir-frying should at first be vigorous but can slow to "flip often" pace midway through the minute.
    - At the timer, reduce the heat to a medium setting and cook the mixture for 2 minutes, stirring it occasionally and setting a timer.
    - At the timer, remove the skillet from the heat and scrape the onion mixture into the Dutch oven.

10. **Assemble the stew for serving.**

    - Remove the chicken from the bones, discarding any fat and skin but saving the bones for later broth making. Set aside ½ of the chicken for another use (covering it tightly within a zippered plastic bag and refrigerating it). Use a 5 in. serrated knife to cut the remaining chicken into bite-size pieces and evenly sprinkle the pieces with approx. ¼ t black pepper (opt). If not immediately assembling the stew, cover the chicken.
    - Finish other ingredient preparations. Skim fat from the fresh chicken broth. Stir the yogurt creamy smooth before measuring 1 cup. Squeeze ½ lemon. Break up any clumps of rice. Open the canned chicken broth.
    - Add the fresh broth, ½ c canned chicken broth, lemon juice, 1½ T brown sugar, and ¼ t salt to the onion mixture in the Dutch oven.
    - Heat the Dutch oven at a medium setting. Check the flavoring of the broth, adding touches (1-2 t) more lemon juice for tartness and brown sugar for sweetening. For more liquid content, add ½ c canned poultry broth. It is important, however, to add broth cautiously to avoid diluting the soup broth flavor.
    - Increase the heat to medium-high and bring the broth mixture to near boiling.
    - Add the chicken and rice.
    - Return the broth to near boiling and add the pasta, cooked vegetables, except for the spinach, and any collected cooking juice.
    - Bring the broth to near boiling and reduce the heat to medium. Heat the stew another 2-3 minutes until all ingredients are hot, stirring often.

- Add the spinach and heat the stew another minute only.

11. **Serve the stew.**
    VARIATIONS: Make ingredient substitutions. Substitute, for example,

    - 1½ c **cooked brown rice** for pasta to make a total of 2½ c cooked brown rice added to the stew.
    - **4-6 medium kale leaves** (Recipe #26), **½ lb unwashed spinach** (Recipe #29), **8-10 beet green leaves** (Recipe #23), or **4-6 medium chard leaves** (Recipe #24) for spinach. Mix the greens into the soup or use them as a topping on individual servings.
    - **3 ears of yellow corn** (Recipe #10) for dry frozen whole kernel corn.
    - **fresh pasta**, either fresh or frozen, for dried. Select thick pasta in particular.

    Add ingredients. Add, for example,

    - ¼ **yellow bell pepper**, cooked with the other bell pepper.
    - **2 medium turnips** (Recipe #22).
    - **2 c Brussels sprouts** (Recipe #61, boiled whole), halved.
    - **8-10 garlic cloves** (Recipe #31), adding them with the other vegetables or topping individual servings with a portion of the garlic.
    - **2 c dry frozen green peas** (Recipe #71).

Stew – Broth and Milk Sauce Base Recipe

179. Curried Split Pea and Chicken Stew
(6-8 servings)

Split Peas and Brown Rice with Seasoning

¾ c dry green split peas
2½ c water
⅓ t salt

⅓ t salt
1 c cooked brown rice (Recipe #166)

Chicken with Seasonings and Cooking Oil

2 boneless, skinless chicken breast halves
    (approx. 4 oz)
1 t curry powder
½ t ground cinnamon
¼ t ground ginger

1 t garlic powder
⅛ in. thick slice of ginger root
1½ T toasted sesame oil
⅓ t salt

Vegetables with Seasonings, Cooking Oil, and Cooking Water

PART 2

4 medium carrots
1 T extra virgin olive oil
1 T hot water
¼ t salt
2 c organic dry frozen yellow corn, unthawed
2 T water
¼ t salt

2 c dry frozen organic green peas, unthawed
2 T water
¼ t salt
½ lb pre-washed spinach
1 T extra virgin olive oil
¼ t salt
½ red bell pepper, sliced lengthwise
¾ T extra virgin olive oil

Curried Milk Sauce Ingredients

½ medium chilled onion, halved lengthwise
2 ⅛-in. thick slices fresh ginger root
1 T extra virgin olive oil
1 t cumin seed
1 t curry powder
½ t garlic powder
¼ t ground ginger
½ t ground cumin

1 c canned poultry broth
¼ t salt
1 c milk (1%, 2% or full fat)
½ c regular canned coconut milk
½ c milk
½-1 lemon
1 T packed dark brown sugar
⅓ c plain yogurt

Accompaniment

1 c plain yogurt

Cooking Tools

1 medium (2 qt) heavy-bottomed saucepan with an opaque lid (an enamel-coated cast iron saucepan works especially well)
1 set each measuring cups & spoons
1 timer
1 large nonstick skillet with a tight-fitting & opaque lid
1 cutting board for raw chicken
1 each slicing, chef's, & 5 in. serrated knife
1 plastic or plastic-coated stir fry spatula
1 rubber or other heat-resistant spatula

1 colander
1 dinner plate
1 electric tea pot
1 large (approx. 16 x 24 in.) cutting board
1 7 in. serrated knife
1 can opener
1 hand citrus juicer
1 small mixing bowl
1 dinner spoon
1 large soup ladle
2-8 large soup bowls

---

1. **Gather all ingredients and cooking tools.**

2. **Prepare the split peas.**

- **Soak the split peas.** One hour ahead of preparing other ingredients or as much as a day ahead, pour the ¾ c dry peas into a medium saucepan and pick through them, discarding dark and broken kernels and looking for and removing any stones. Add 2½ c water, bring the water to boiling over high heat, remove the pan from the heat, cover it, and set it aside for 45 minutes, setting a timer.
- **Cook the split peas.** Return the cooking water to boiling on a back burner, reduce the heat to a level that maintains gentle boiling, cover the pan, and set a timer for 30 minutes. Check the split peas after 5 minutes to ensure the peas are gently, not rapidly, boiling. Check the water level near the end of the cooking time and add a touch more hot water (¼ to ⅓ c) as may be needed to prevent the peas from sticking to the bottom of the pan. At the timer, make a taste test to check softness. If the peas are not completely soft without any hint of crispness, continue the cooking, making a taste test every 5 minutes. When the peas are soft to the center but retain their shape, remove the pan from the heat, mix in ⅓ t salt, and set the peas aside in the pan, covered.

3. **Stir-fry the chicken.**

    - Heat a large nonstick skillet on a large front burner at a medium setting.
    - Quickly rinse the chicken under cool water and thoroughly dry it with paper towels.
    - Working on a cutting board reserved for raw meat, use a sharp slicing knife to cut the chicken into thin (¼ in. thick) strips, removing any white membrane and fat. Cut the strips into ½ in. lengths and add them to plastic wrap.
    - Evenly sprinkle 1 t curry, ½ t ground cinnamon, ¼ t ground ginger, and 1 t garlic powder over the chicken and toss the pieces for even coating.
    - Wash your hands before using a 5 in. serrated knife to mince a ⅛ in. thick slice of ginger root on a clean cutting board.
    - Increase the skillet heat to medium-high. When a drop of water added to the skillet instantly dances and disappears, add 1½ T toasted sesame oil, add and mix in the chicken and ginger root.
    - Vigorously stir-fry the chicken for 30 seconds, reduce the heat to medium, and continue the cooking for another 2 minutes until pieces are white to the center, stirring often and setting a timer.
    - At the timer, remove the skillet from the heat, evenly sprinkle ⅓ t salt over the chicken, and use a rubber spatula to scrape the chicken into one side of a colander placed over a dinner plate.
    - Wipe the skillet clean.

4. **Stir-fry/steam the carrots.**

    - Heat the nonstick skillet at a medium setting. Heat an electric tea kettle to prepare hot water for steaming.
    - Scrub and dry the 4 carrots. Use a chef's knife to cut off the ends, halve lengthwise, and cut the carrot halves crosswise into ⅛ in. thick slices.
    - Increase the skillet heat to medium-high. When a drop of water added to the skillet

instantly dances and disappears, add 1 T oil, add the carrots, and stir-fry it for 1 minute, setting a timer. Stir-frying should be vigorous but can slow to "flip often" pace midway through the minute.
- At the timer, add 1 T hot water, cover the skillet, reduce the heat to low, and steam the carrot for 4 minutes, setting a timer.
- At the timer, remove the skillet from the burner, evenly sprinkle ¼ t salt over the carrot, and use a rubber spatula to scrape it and any cooking juice into the colander next to the chicken.
- Wipe the skillet clean.

5. **Stir-fry the corn.**

- Break up any frozen clumps while the corn is in its package.
- Heat 2 T water to boiling over high heat in the nonstick skillet. Add the corn. Once the water returns to boiling, stir-fry the corn for 1 minute, using a timer, just until the corn is heated through.
- Remove the skillet from the heat, evenly sprinkle ¼ t salt over the corn, and use a rubber spatula to scrape the corn and any cooking water into the colander.
- Wipe the skillet clean.

6. **Stir-fry the bell pepper.**

- Heat the skillet at a medium setting.
- Use a 5 in. serrated knife to cut out the stem of the pepper. Remove any seeds but not the white membrane. Use the serrated knife to cut the pepper lengthwise into ¼ in. thick slices and to cut the slices crosswise into ¼ in. cubes.
- Increase the skillet heat to medium-high, and when a drop of water added to the skillet instantly dances and disappears, add ½ T oil, add the pepper, and vigorously stir-fry it for 30 seconds.
- Reduce the heat to medium and cook the pepper for 2 minutes, stirring it occasionally and setting a timer.
- At the timer, use a rubber spatula to scrape the pepper and any cooking juice into the colander with the carrots and corn.
- Wipe the skillet clean.

7. **Stir-fry the spinach.**

- Heat the nonstick skillet at medium.
- Bunch the spinach leaves together on a large cutting board.
- Holding the leaves loosely together with one hand, use a 7 in. serrated knife to slice the spinach into approx. ⅓ in. thick pieces, cutting through the leaves both lengthwise and crosswise.
- Increase the skillet heat to medium-high, and when a drop of water added to the skillet instantly dances and disappears, add 1 T oil, add the spinach, and constantly stir-fry the spinach for about 1 minute until it darkens in color and is evenly wilted, turning it over and over.

- Remove the skillet from the heat, evenly sprinkle ¼ t salt over the spinach, and scrape it and any cooking juice into the colander alongside the other vegetables.
- Wipe the skillet clean.

8. **Prepare the curried milk sauce.**

    - Heat the nonstick skillet at a medium setting.
    - Open the poultry broth and canned coconut milk. Use a dinner spoon to stir the coconut milk thoroughly before measuring ½ cup.
    - Place ½ onion cut side down on a cutting board and use a chef's knife to slice off its tips. Peel the onion, again place the onion cut side down on the cutting board, and use the chef's knife to dice the onion. Mince the ginger.
    - Increase the skillet heat to medium-high, and when a drop of water added to the skillet instantly dances and disappears, add 1 T oil, add and cook the cumin seeds for about 30 seconds, add the onion and ginger, evenly sprinkle the spices (1 t curry powder, ½ t garlic powder, ¼ t ginger powder, and ½ t ground cumin) over them, and stir-fry the onion mixture for 1 minute, setting a timer. Stir-frying should at first be vigorous but can slow to "flip often" pace midway through the minute.
    - At the timer, reduce the heat to medium and cook the onion mixture for 2 minutes, stirring it occasionally and setting a timer.
    - At the timer, add 1 c poultry broth and ¼ t salt to the onion mixture. Increase the heat to medium-high to quickly bring the broth to boiling, reduce the heat to low medium (a temperature that maintains gentle boiling), cover the skillet, and cook the mixture for 5 minutes, setting a timer.
    - At the timer, mix in 1 c milk and ½ c canned coconut milk. If not immediately assembling the stew, remove the skillet from the heat, cover it, and set it aside.

9. **Assemble the stew for serving.**

    - Heat the broth/milk sauce in the skillet at medium.
    - Finish ingredient preparations. Squeeze ½ lemon and add the lemon juice, 1 T packed dark brown sugar, and ⅓ c yogurt to a small bowl. Use a rubber spatula to thoroughly combine the ingredients. Stir yogurt creamy smooth before measuring 1 cup. Break up any rice clumps.
    - Scrape the lemon juice and yogurt mixture into the hot milk sauce while stirring quickly and constantly to avoid curdling the milk and yogurt.
    - Check the sauce flavoring, adding touches (1-2 t) more lemon juice for tartness and/or brown sugar for sweetening. If the sauce is too thick, add ½ c milk. Increase liquid cautiously in order to avoid diluting the soup flavor.
    - Increase the skillet heat to medium-high. Add the split peas, brown rice, and chicken and heat the stew to full boiling, stirring it frequently.
    - Add the cooked vegetables and any vegetable cooking liquid and again heat the stew to near boiling, reduce the heat to medium, and heat the stew 3-5 more minutes until all ingredients are hot, stirring often.

10. **Serve the stew.** Top individual servings with 1 or 2 generous dollops of yogurt.

PART 2

Reheat leftover stew in milk. Heat ½-1 c milk or a milk and broth mixture at a medium-high setting in a nonstick skillet until hot, add the soup, and heat the soup until it fully boils, stirring it frequently with a rubber spatula.

VARIATIONS: Make ingredient substitutions. Substitute, for example,

- **2-4 ears fresh yellow corn** (Recipes #10 or #65) for dry frozen corn.
- **¾ c yellow** for green split peas. Yellow peas have significantly greater phytonutrient content than green peas.
- **1 small whole chicken** for the chicken breasts (Reference #10). Substitute the fresh broth for, or combine it with, canned broth. Remove ½ of the chicken from the bones and cut it into bite-size pieces for serving. Evenly sprinkle the chicken with ¼ t salt. Immediately cover tightly and refrigerate the remaining chicken.
- **slow cooked split peas** for soaked and simmered split peas. Omit the soaking. Begin heating a slow cooker on high. Bring the peas to boiling in the cooking water on a large stove burner, boil them for 1 minute, add them to the slow cooker, reduce the cooker heat to low after 5 minutes, and cook the peas for 2 hours and 15 minutes or until pleasingly soft. Slow cooking yields especially soft peas.
- **un-soaked** for soaked split peas. When cooking the peas, begin checking for softness after 45 minutes. The split peas will be ready when assembling the soup for serving. Soaking, nevertheless, yields the softest texture.

Add ingredients. Add, for example,

- **2 medium red potatoes**, stir-fry/steamed (Recipe #17) or baked (Recipe #46), **6-8 small new red potatoes**, or **other small tasty potatoes**, boiled whole (Recipe #72), halved or quartered. Potatoes are especially tasty additions.
- **2 medium sweet potatoes** (Recipe #18) or **1 each medium red** and **sweet potato**.
- **1-2 medium turnips** (Recipe #22). For turnips with young turnip green tops, substitute **turnip greens** (Recipe #30) for spinach.
- **½ lb pre-washed baby greens, kale** (Recipe #26), **unwashed spinach** (Recipe #29), **beet greens** (Recipe #23), or **chard** (Recipe #24) for spinach.
- **2 stalks organic celery** (Recipe #9). Evenly sprinkle 1 t curry powder over the celery during stir-frying.
- **2 c butternut squash**, cubed (dry roasted, Recipe #52, or stir-fry/steamed, Recipe #21).
- **8-10 medium cloves garlic** (Recipe #31), topping individual servings with a portion of the garlic.

Bread Accompaniment Recipes

180. Blueberry Banana 100% Whole Wheat Muffins
(8 muffins)

Ingredients

1 T coconut oil, butter, or extra virgin olive oil
¾ c chilled medium ground whole wheat flour (flour with visible bits of bran)
2 T packed dark brown sugar
1 T white sugar
¾ t baking powder
⅛ t baking soda
⅓ t salt
¾ c fresh blueberries or dry frozen, unthawed
1 large egg
½ c milk
2 T premium orange juice with pulp
½ chilled medium banana

Baking Tools

1 small skillet
1 medium (6 c) mixing bowl
1 set each measuring cups & spoons
1 colander
1 pie plate
1 large (10 c) mixing bowl
1 dinner fork or small whisk
1 knife (any size)
1 potato masher with a metal grid head (⅓ in. cube size grid)
1 large-headed wooden spoon (approx. 2½ x 3½ in. head)
1 firm but pliable rubber spatula
12-tin nonstick muffin pan (1¼ in. deep tins), only 8 of 12 tins lightly buttered
1 timer
1 or 2 padded oven gloves
1 wire cooling rack
1 dinner knife

---

1. Preheat the oven to 375 degrees.

2. Gather together the baking tools and muffin ingredients.

3. **Melt 1 T coconut oil or butter.** If using either coconut oil or butter, add the coconut oil or butter to a small skillet and heat the skillet at a very low heat setting. Be watchful and, once the coconut oil or butter melts, remove the skillet from the burner and set it aside.

4. **Combine the dry ingredients.** Add ¾ c flour, 2 T packed brown sugar, 1 T white sugar, ¾ t baking powder, ⅛ t baking soda, and ⅓ t salt to a medium mixing bowl and thoroughly combine the ingredients.

PART 2

5. **Prepare the blueberries.**
   - Add ¾ c fresh berries to a colander and rinse them with cool water. Pour the berries into a pie plate lined with a double thickness of paper towels. Pick through the berries to remove any stems and to discard spoiled berries. Gently wrap the towel around the berries to dry them. Add the berries to the flour mixture and toss the berries to coat them with flour.
   - Break up frozen berries before tossing them with the flour mixture.

6. **Combine the wet ingredients.**

   - Add 1 egg, ½ c milk, and 2 T orange juice to a large mixing bowl and use a dinner fork or whisk to combine the ingredients.
   - Use a knife to cut ½ banana into 4-5 pieces, add the banana to the milk and egg, and use a potato masher to mash it roughly so that small banana chunks remain in the batter. To do this, push the potato masher through banana pieces once and use a knife blade to scrape the banana pieces from the masher into the batter.
   - If using coconut oil or butter, use a rubber spatula to scrape the melted oil or butter into the wet ingredients and roughly mix the melted oil or butter into the milk mixture. If using extra virgin olive oil, add the oil to the liquid ingredients and roughly mix in the oil.

7. **Mix the wet and dry ingredients together.**

   - Pour the flour mixture onto the milk mixture and use a wooden spoon to combine the ingredients roughly, stirring the batter only until the flour is barely moistened, about 15 strokes.
   - Use a rubber spatula to scrape batter clinging to the wooden spoon, the bowl sides, and the bowl bottom into the batter in the bowl.
   - Use the spatula to break open any remaining dry clumps of flour.

8. **Transfer the muffin batter to 8 tins for baking.** Use a rubber spatula to scrape the batter into tins, filling each tin approx. two-thirds full.

9. **Bake the muffins.**

   - Center the muffin pan on the middle oven rack
   - Set a timer for 19 minutes.
   - At the timer, make a readiness check. Wearing an oven glove, pull the muffin pan out from the oven far enough to touch a muffin top with the fingers of one hand. If it bounces back when touched lightly, immediately remove the muffin pan from the oven onto a cooling rack. If the muffin top does not bounce back, and instead is very moist, continue baking the muffins for 2 more minutes, setting a timer, before removing the muffin pan from the oven.
   - Allow the muffins to sit undisturbed for 2 minutes, setting a timer. If the muffins

stay in the tins much longer, steam will form and condense on the muffin bottom, which will make it unattractively soggy.

10. **Remove the muffins from the tins.**

    - Slide a dinner knife blade completely around a muffin to loosen it before slipping it onto a wire rack.
    - Should the bottom stick, let the muffin sit another few minutes before again attempting removal. It is important to avoid breaking open a muffin, which exposes it to drying air.

11. **Serve the muffins slightly or completely cooled.**

12. **Cover muffins that will not be quickly served.** Once the muffins are completely cool, store them within a sealed gallon-size plastic storage bag, first pressing out as much air as possible.

13. **Immediately freeze muffins that will not be used within a day.**

    - Tightly wrap completely cooled individual muffins in plastic wrap and freeze them within a sealed freezer-quality sealable plastic bag.
    - Use frozen muffins directly from the freezer, microwave heating unwrapped muffins for 20-30 seconds.

VARIATIONS: Double the recipe to make 12 large muffins. Divide the batter between 12 tins, filling the tins to the top to use all the batter. Large muffins are particularly suited for use as a breakfast bread or snacks.

Substitute large (2½ in.) chemical-free paper baking cups for buttering of individual muffin tins. This substitution greatly eases cleaning of the tins.

Add ingredients. Add, for example,

- **⅛-¼ c coarsely chopped pecan or walnut halves**, mixing the nuts into the flour mixture.
- **9 fresh or dry frozen raspberries**. Poke 2 halves or 1 whole berry into the batter of each muffin just prior to baking. Rinse and gently but thoroughly dry fresh berries (Recipe #97) before adding them to the muffin batter.
- **½ c ¼ in. thick slices fresh or dry frozen pineapple** (Recipe #94), each slice cut crosswise into three equal pieces. Toss the bits into the flour mixture before combining the dry and wet ingredients. Pineapple is an outstanding ingredient.
- **4 T fresh or dry frozen (unthawed) red currant berries** or **pomegranate seeds** (Recipe #96). Rinse and dry fresh currants; add currants or pomegranate seeds to the dry ingredients with the blueberries.

COMMENTS: The bran contained in medium whole wheat flour gives the flour a somewhat coarse texture and makes it absorptive. Finely ground flour, in comparison, is silky smooth. It is not absorptive and does not work in this recipe.

For easy cleaning, immediately use a dish brush to clean the potato masher after mashing the banana.

181. Banana Cranberry 100% Whole Wheat Muffins
(8 muffins)

Ingredients

1 T coconut oil, butter, or extra virgin olive oil
½ c fresh whole cranberries or dry frozen, unthawed cranberries
2 T premium orange juice with pulp
1 T packed dark brown sugar
¾ c chilled medium ground whole wheat flour (flour with visible bits of bran)
1 T packed dark brown sugar
½ T white sugar
¾ t baking powder
⅛ t baking soda
⅓ t salt
2 T sweetened dried cranberries or tart cherries
¼ c raw pecan halves
1 large egg
½ c milk
1-2 T premium orange juice with pulp
½ chilled medium or 1 small banana

Baking Tools

1 small skillet
1 colander
1 10 in. skillet
1 set each measuring spoons & cups
1 firm stir-fry spatula
1 dinner plate
1 small (2 c) mixing bowl
1 medium (6 c) mixing bowl
1 each chef's & 5 in. serrated knife
1 large (10 c) mixing bowl
1 dinner fork or whisk
1 potato masher with a metal grid head
1 large-headed wooden spoon
1 firm but pliable rubber spatula
12-tin nonstick muffin pan (1¼-in deep tins), only 8 of 12 tins lightly buttered
1 timer
1 or 2 padded oven gloves
1 wire cooling rack
1 dinner knife

1. **Preheat the oven to 375 degrees.**

2. **Gather together the baking tools and muffin ingredients.**

3. **Melt the coconut oil or butter.** When using either coconut oil or butter, add the coconut oil or butter to a small skillet and heat the skillet at a very low heat setting. Be watchful

and once the coconut oil or butter melts, remove the skillet from the heat and set it aside.

4. **Cook and sweeten the cranberries.**

    - Add ½ c cranberries to a colander and rinse them with cool water. Sort through the berries to remove stems and discard soft berries.
    - Bring 2 T orange juice to boiling over high heat in a small or medium skillet. Add the berries and cook them in stir-fry manner for about 1 minute until they pop open, turning them over and over and adding a touch more juice if the first juice evaporates.
    - Drain the berries in a colander placed over a dinner plate for collecting cooking juice.
    - Transfer the berries to a small bowl, sprinkle 1 T brown sugar over them, and lightly toss the berries and sugar.

5. **Combine the dry ingredients.**

    - Add the flour, sugars, baking powder, baking soda, and salt to a medium mixing bowl and thoroughly combine the ingredients.
    - Mix in the dried cranberries, breaking up any clumps.
    - Use a chef's knife to chop the ¼ c nuts coarsely. Add the nuts to the flour mixture.

6. **Add the cooked cranberries to the dry ingredients.** Gently toss the berries to coat them with flour.

7. **Combine the wet ingredients.**

    - Add the egg and ½ c milk to a large mixing bowl and use a dinner fork or whisk to combine the ingredients.
    - Measure the collected cranberry cooking juice and add more orange juice as needed to make 1 tablespoon juice.
    - Add the cranberry juice and 1 T orange juice to the milk/egg mixture.
    - Cut the banana into 4-5 slices and add the pieces to the wet ingredients. Use a potato masher to mash the banana roughly, leaving small chunks of banana in the batter. To do so, push the masher through the banana pieces once and use a knife blade to scrape the banana from the masher into the batter.
    - Use a rubber spatula to scrape 1 T melted coconut oil or butter into the liquid ingredients and to mix the oil or butter (or extra virgin olive oil) into the milk mixture.

8. **Combine the wet and dry ingredients.**

    - Pour the flour mixture onto the wet ingredients.
    - Use a wooden spoon to combine the ingredients, stirring the batter only as many strokes as needed to barely moisten the flour, approx. 15 strokes.

PART 2

- Use a rubber spatula to scrape batter clinging to the wooden spoon, bowl sides, and bowl bottom into the bowl and to break apart any remaining dry clumps of flour.

9. **Transfer the batter to muffin tins.** Use a rubber spatula to scrape the batter into eight muffin tins, filling each about two-thirds full.

10. **Bake the muffins.**

    - Center the muffin pan on the middle oven rack.
    - Set a timer for 19 minutes. At the timer, make a readiness check. Wearing an oven glove, pull the muffin pan out from the oven far enough to touch a muffin top with the fingers of one hand. The top should bounce back when touched lightly. If it does, immediately remove the muffin pan from the oven onto a cooling rack. If the muffin top does not bounce back and instead is moist, continue baking the muffins for 1-2 minutes, setting a timer, before removing the muffin pan from the oven.
    - Allow the muffins to sit undisturbed for 2 minutes, setting a timer. This timing is important. If the muffins remain in the tins for a much longer time, steam will form and make the muffin bottoms unattractively soggy.

11. **Remove the muffins from the tins.**

    - Slide a dinner knife blade completely around a muffin to loosen it from the tin and drop it onto a cooling rack.
    - Should a muffin bottom stick, let the muffin sit another 1-2 minutes before again attempting to remove it.

12. **Serve the muffins slightly or completely cooled.**

13. **Cover muffins that will not be quickly served.** Once the muffins are completely cool, store them within a sealed gallon-size plastic storage bag, first pressing out as much air as is possible.

14. **Freeze muffins that will not be used within 1 day.**

    - Tightly wrap individual muffins in plastic wrap and freeze them within a sealed freezer-quality gallon-size sealable plastic storage bag.
    - Use frozen muffins directly from the freezer. Microwave heat individual unwrapped muffins for 20-30 seconds.

    VARIATIONS: Expand or vary ingredients. For example,

    - **double the recipe** to make 12 large muffins. Divide the batter between 12 tins, filling the tins to the top to use all the batter. Large muffins serve especially well as breakfast breads and snacks.
    - add the **zest** of ¼ organic orange (one that has been rinsed and dried). Toss the zest with the dry ingredients (Step #4).
    - substitute **canned whole cranberries** for fresh cranberries. Drain the cranberries

and substitute 2 T packing juice for 2 T orange juice called for in the recipe. Do not sweeten canned cranberries.

Substitute large (2½ in.) chemical-free paper baking cups for buttering of individual muffin tins. This substitution greatly eases cleaning of the tins.

COMMENTS: The bran content of medium whole wheat flour gives the flour a somewhat coarse texture and makes it absorptive. Finely ground flour, in comparison, is silky smooth. It is not absorptive and does not work in this recipe.

For easy cleaning, immediately use a scrub brush to clean the potato masher after mashing the banana.

182. Pineapple Carrot 100% Whole Wheat Muffins
(8 muffins)

Ingredients

1 T coconut oil, butter, or extra virgin olive oil
¾ c chilled medium ground whole wheat flour (flour with visible bits of bran)
2½ T packed dark brown sugar
1 T white sugar
¾ t baking powder
⅛ t baking soda
⅓ t salt
¼ t ground cinnamon
⅛ t ground nutmeg

⅛ t ground ginger
2 T golden or dark organic raisins
2 T dried tart cherries or cranberries
¼ c pecan or walnut halves
½ c fresh pineapple chunks (½ in. thick) (Recipe #94)
1 medium carrot (½ c shredded)
1 large egg
½ c milk
2 T premium orange juice with pulp

Baking Tools

1 small skillet
1 medium (6 c) mixing bowl
1 set each measuring cups & spoons
1 each 5 in. serrated knife & chef's knife
1 hand vegetable shredder
1 large (10) c mixing bowl
1 dinner fork or small whisk
1 slicing knife

1 large-headed wooden spoon
1 rubber spatula
12-tin nonstick muffin pan (1¼ in. deep tins), only 8 of 12 tins lightly buttered
1 timer
1 or 2 padded oven gloves
1 wire cooling rack
1 dinner knife

1. **Preheat the oven to 375 degrees.**

PART 2

2. **Gather together the baking tools and muffin ingredients.**
3. **Melt the coconut oil or butter.** If using coconut oil or butter, add the coconut oil or butter to a small skillet and heat the skillet at a low setting. Be watchful and once the coconut oil or butter melts, remove the skillet from the heat and set it aside.

4. **Combine the dry ingredients and raisins.** Add the flour, sugars, baking powder, baking soda, salt, and spices to a small mixing bowl and thoroughly combine the ingredients. Mix in the raisins, breaking up any clumps.

5. **Prepare the dried cherries, nuts, pineapple, and carrot.**

    - Use a chef's knife to halve the dried cherries and to chop the nuts coarsely.
    - Mix the cherries and nuts into the flour mixture.
    - Use a serrated knife to cut the pineapple chunks lengthwise into ¼ in. wide strips; cut each strip crosswise into thirds. Pat juicy pineapple pieces dry with a paper towel.
    - Rinse, dry, slice off the stem end and tip, and coarsely shred the carrot. Measure ½ c carrot.
    - Add the pineapple and carrot to the dry ingredients and thoroughly toss the pieces to coat them with flour.

6. **Combine the wet ingredients.**

    - Add 1 egg, ½ c milk, and 2 T orange juice to a medium mixing bowl and use a dinner fork or whisk to combine the ingredients.
    - If using either coconut oil or butter, use a rubber spatula to scrape the melted coconut oil or butter into the liquid ingredients and to roughly mix in the oil or butter (or extra virgin olive oil).

7. **Mix the wet and dry ingredients together.**

    - Pour the flour mixture onto the egg mixture.
    - Use a wooden spoon to combine the ingredients, stirring only enough to moisten the flour, about 15 strokes.
    - Use a rubber spatula to scrape batter clinging to the wooden spoon, bowl sides, and bowl bottom into the mixing bowl and to break up any dry clumps of flour.

8. **Transfer the batter to the muffin tins.** Use a rubber spatula to scrape the batter into the muffin tins, filling each about two-thirds full.

9. **Bake the muffins.**

    - Center the muffin pan on the middle oven rack.
    - Set a timer for 19 minutes. At the timer, make a readiness check. Wearing an oven glove, pull the muffin pan out from the oven far enough to safely touch a muffin top

with the fingers of one hand. When touched, the top should bounce back. If it does, immediately remove the muffin pan from the oven onto a cooling rack. If the muffin top does not bounce back and instead is moist, continue baking the muffins for 1-2 minutes before removing the muffin pan from the oven, setting a timer.
- Let the muffins sit undisturbed for 2 minutes, setting a timer. Timing is important because steam that forms on the muffin bottoms quickly causes the bottoms to become unattractively soggy.

10. **Remove the muffins from the tins.**

    - Slide a dinner knife blade completely around a muffin to loosen it from a tin and drop the muffin onto a cooling rack.
    - Should the bottom stick, let the muffin sit another 1-2 minutes longer before again attempting removal. It is important to avoid breaking open the muffins, which exposes the muffins to drying air.

11. **Serve the muffins slightly or completely cooled.**

12. **Cover muffins that will not be quickly served.** Once the muffins are completely cool, store them within a sealed gallon-size sealable plastic storage bag, first pressing out as much air as is possible.

13. **Freeze muffins that will not be eaten within a day.**

    - Tightly wrap individual muffins in plastic wrap and freeze them within a freezer-quality sealable plastic storage bag.
    - Use frozen muffins directly from the freezer. Microwave heat individual unwrapped muffins for 20-30 seconds.

VARIATIONS: Expand the recipe or substitute ingredients.

- **Double the recipe** to make 12 large muffins; use only ⅓ t nutmeg. Divide the batter between 12 tins, filling the tins to the top to use all the batter. Large muffins serve especially well as breakfast bread or snacks.
- Substitute **canned pineapple chunks,** packed in their own juice, for fresh pineapple. Thoroughly drain the pineapple and substitute collected pineapple juice for the orange juice used in the recipe.

Add ingredients. Add, for example,

- ½ c **fresh** or **dry frozen (unthawed) blueberries.** Rinse and dry fresh blueberries. Add the blueberries to the dry ingredients with the pineapple and carrot.
- **2 T dried pineapple,** diced and added to the dry ingredients.
- **2-4 T red currant berries** or **pomegranate seeds** (Recipe #96), fresh or dry frozen.
- ½ c **coarsely shredded zucchini,** shredded like the carrot. Zucchini adds pretty

green flecks.
- **⅓ medium banana**, coarsely mashed in the milk/egg/orange juice mixture.

Substitute large (2½ in.) chemical-free paper baking cups for buttering of individual muffin tins. This substitution greatly eases cleaning of the tins.

COMMENTS: The bran content of medium ground whole wheat flour gives the flour a somewhat coarse texture and makes it absorptive. Finely ground flour, in comparison, is silky smooth. It is not absorptive and does not work in this recipe.

For easy cleaning, immediately use a scrub brush to clean the potato masher after mashing the banana.

183. Sweet Potato Pineapple 100% Whole Wheat Muffins
(8 muffins)

Ingredients

1 T coconut oil, butter, or extra virgin olive oil
¾ c chilled medium ground whole wheat flour
3 T packed dark brown sugar
¾ t baking powder
⅛ t baking soda
⅓ t salt
⅓ t ground cinnamon
¼ t ground nutmeg
¼ t ground ginger
¼ c certified organic raisins

¼ c pecan or walnut halves (opt)
½ c ¼-in. thick slices fresh or frozen pineapple (Recipe #94)
1 large egg
½ c milk
2 T premium orange juice with pulp
¾ baked medium sweet potato (Recipe #47; approx. 1 potato; to yield ½ c mashed)

Baking Tools

1 small skillet
1 medium (6 c) mixing bowl
1 set each measuring cups & spoons
1 each chef's & 5 in. serrated knife
1 large (10 c) mixing bowl
1 dinner fork or small whisk
1 potato masher with a metal grid head
1 small (2 c) mixing bowl

1 large-headed wooden spoon
1 rubber spatula
12-tin nonstick muffin pan (1¼ in. deep tins), only 8 of 12 lightly buttered
1 timer
1 or 2 padded oven gloves
1 wire cooling rack
1 dinner knife

1. **Preheat the oven to 375 degrees.**

2. **Gather together the baking tools and muffin ingredients.**

3. **Melt the coconut oil or butter.** When using either coconut oil or butter, add the coconut oil or butter to a small skillet and heat the skillet at a low setting. Be watchful and once the coconut oil or butter melts, remove the skillet from the heat and set it aside.

4. **Combine the dry ingredients.**

    - Add the flour, sugars, baking powder, baking soda, salt, and spices to a medium mixing bowl and thoroughly combine the ingredients.
    - Mix in the raisins, breaking up any raisin clumps.
    - Use a chef's knife to chop the nuts coarsely and mix the nuts into the flour mixture.

5. **Add the pineapple to the dry ingredients.**

    - Use a serrated knife to cut the pineapple slices crosswise into thirds.
    - Use a paper towel to pat very juicy pineapple pieces dry.
    - Add the pineapple to the flour mixture and toss the pineapple to coat pieces thoroughly.

6. **Combine the wet ingredients.**

    - Add an egg, ½ c milk, and 2 T orange juice to a large mixing bowl and use a dinner fork or whisk to combine the ingredients.
    - Peel and add the sweet potato to a small mixing bowl, use a potato masher to roughly mash it, measure ½ c potato, add the mashed sweet potato to the egg/milk mixture, and again use the potato masher to mix the potato with the other ingredients, making a largely smooth but slightly chunky mixture.
    - When using melted coconut oil or butter, use a rubber spatula to scrape the melted coconut oil or butter into the liquid ingredients. Use a rubber spatula to roughly mix in coconut oil, butter, or extra virgin olive oil into the milk mixture.

7. **Mix the wet and dry ingredients together.**

    - Pour the flour mixture onto the wet ingredients. Use a wooden spoon to combine the ingredients roughly, using around 15 strokes or just enough to barely wet the flour.
    - Use a rubber spatula to scrape batter clinging to the wooden spoon, bowl sides, and bowl bottom into the bowl and to break open any remaining dry clumps of flour.
    - Cut through the batter 2 times with the spatula to ensure all flour is moistened.

8. **Bake the muffins.**

    - Use a rubber spatula to scrape the batter into the muffin tins, filling each about two-thirds full.
    - Center the muffin pan on the middle oven rack.
    - Set a timer for 19 minutes. At the timer, make a readiness check. Wearing an oven glove, pull the muffin pan out from the oven far enough to safely touch a muffin top with the fingers of one hand. When touched, the top should bounce back. If it does, immediately remove the muffin pan from the oven onto a cooling rack. If the muffin top does not bounce back and instead is moist, continue baking the muffins for 1-2 minutes, setting a timer, before removing the muffin pan from the oven.
    - Allow the muffins to sit undisturbed for 2 minutes, setting a timer.

9. **Remove the muffins from the tins.**

    - Slide a dinner knife blade completely around the sides of a muffin to loosen it from the tin and slip the muffin onto a wire rack.
    - Should the bottom stick, let the muffin sit 1-2 minutes longer before again attempting removal. Avoid breaking open the muffins, which exposes a muffin to drying air.

10. **Serve the muffins slightly or completely cooled.**

11. **Cover muffins that will not be quickly served.** Once the muffins are completely cool, store them within a sealed gallon-size sealable plastic storage bag, first pressing out as much air as is possible.

12. **Freeze muffins that will not be eaten within a day.**

    - Tightly wrap individual muffins in plastic wrap and freeze them within an air-tight freezer-quality sealable plastic storage bag.
    - Use frozen muffins directly from the freezer. Microwave heat unwrapped muffins for 20-30 seconds.

VARIATIONS: Double the recipe to make 12 large muffins; use only ⅓ t nutmeg. Divide the batter between 12 tins, filling the tins to the top to use all the batter. Large muffins serve especially well as breakfast bread or snacks.

Make ingredient substitutions. Substitute, for example,

- ½ c mashed baked winter squash (Recipe #51 or #52) for ½ c mashed baked sweet potato. Increase brown sugar content to 4 T.
- ½ c canned pureed pumpkin or ¾ c canned sweet potato chunks for baked fresh sweet potato. Increase brown sugar content to 4 T.
- ¾ c stir-fry/steamed sweet potato for ¾ c baked sweet potato. Diced stir-fry/steamed sweet potato can be mashed with its nutritionally valuable skin.

Add ingredients. Add, for example,

- **⅓ c fresh or unthawed dry frozen blueberries**. Rinse and dry fresh berries (Recipe #78) and toss them with the flour mixture.
- **⅛ t ground cloves**, adding it to the flour mixture.
- **⅓ banana**, coarsely mashed (remains chunky) and added after the sweet potato has been mixed into the liquid ingredients.
- **2 T dried tart cherries** or **dried cranberries**, halved and mixed into the flour mixture.

Substitute large (2½ in.) chemical-free paper baking cups for buttering of individual muffin tins This substitution greatly eases cleaning of the tins.

COMMENTS: Medium ground whole wheat flour contains visible bits of bran. This bran content gives the flour a somewhat coarse texture and makes it absorptive. Finely ground flour, in comparison, is silky smooth. It is not absorptive and does not work in this recipe.

For easy cleaning, immediately use a scrub brush to clean the potato masher after mashing the banana.

184. Zucchini Applesauce 100% Whole Wheat Muffins
(8 muffins)

Ingredients

1 T coconut oil, butter, or extra virgin olive oil
¾ c chilled medium ground whole wheat flour (flour with visible bits of bran)
4 T packed dark brown sugar
⅓ t ground cinnamon
¼ t ground ginger
¾ t baking powder
⅛ t baking soda
⅓ t salt

½ medium zucchini (½ c shredded)
¼ c certified organic raisins
⅛ c tart dried cherries
¼ c coarsely chopped raw pecans or walnuts
1 large egg
½ c milk
2 T premium orange juice with pulp
½ c sweetened chunky applesauce

Baking Tools

1 small skillet
1 set each measuring cups & spoons
1 medium (6 c) mixing bowl
1 chef's knife
1 hand vegetable shredder

1 rubber spatula
12-tin nonstick muffin pan (1¼ in. deep tins), only 8 of 12 tins lightly buttered
1 timer
1 or 2 padded oven gloves

PART 2

1 large (10 c) mixing bowl
1 dinner fork or small whisk
1 large-headed wooden spoon

1 wire cooling rack
1 dinner knife

1. Preheat the oven to 375 degrees.

2. **Gather together the baking tools and muffin ingredients.**

3. **Melt 1 T coconut oil or butter.** Add the coconut oil or butter to a small skillet and heat the skillet at a low heat setting. Be watchful and once the coconut oil or butter melts, remove the skillet from the heat and set it aside.

4. **Combine the dry ingredients.** Add the flour, sugar, spices, baking powder, baking soda, and salt to a medium mixing bowl and combine the ingredients thoroughly.

5. **Add the zucchini to the flour mixture.**

    - Use a chef's knife to slice off the open tip of the ½ zucchini.
    - Coarsely shred the zucchini and measure ½ c, shredding more zucchini if necessary. Add the zucchini to the flour mixture and toss the flour mixture to coat the pieces thoroughly.

6. **Prepare and mix the dried fruit and nuts into the flour mixture.**

    - Mix the raisins into the flour mixture, breaking up any raisin clumps.
    - Use a chef's knife to halve each dried tart cherry and to chop the nuts coarsely.
    - Mix the cherries and nuts into the flour mixture, evenly distributing the pieces.

7. **Combine the wet ingredients.**

    - Add an egg, ½ c milk, and 2 T orange juice to a medium mixing bowl and use a dinner fork or whisk to combine the ingredients.
    - Add and mix in the ½ c applesauce, using a fork to slightly mash large chunks.
    - When using melted coconut oil or butter, use a rubber spatula to scrape the melted coconut oil or butter into the liquid ingredients. Quickly use the spatula to roughly mix in the oil or butter (or extra virgin olive oil).

8. **Combine the wet and dry ingredients.**

    - Pour the flour mixture onto the egg mixture.
    - Use a wooden spoon to roughly combine the ingredients, stirring the batter only enough to barely moisten the flour (approx. 15 strokes).
    - Use a rubber spatula to scrape batter from the wooden spoon, bowl sides, and bowl bottom into the bowl.
    - Use the spatula to break open any remaining clumps of flour.

9. **Assemble the muffins for baking.** Use the rubber spatula to scrape the batter into the muffin tins, filling each about two-thirds full.

10. **Bake the muffins.**

    - Center the muffin pan on the middle oven rack.
    - Set a timer for 19 minutes. At the timer, make a readiness check. Wearing an oven glove, pull the muffin pan out from the oven far enough to touch a muffin top. The top should bounce back when touched lightly. If it does, immediately remove the muffin pan from the oven onto a cooling rack. If the muffin top does not bounce back and instead is moist, continue baking the muffins for 1-2 minutes, setting a timer, before removing the muffin pan from the oven.
    - Allow the muffins to sit undisturbed for 2 minutes, setting a timer.

11. **Remove the muffins from the tins.**

    - Slide a dinner knife blade around each muffin to loosen it from a tin and slip it onto a wire rack for cooling.
    - Should a bottom stick, let the muffin sit another few minutes before again attempting removal.

12. **Serve the muffins slightly or completely cooled.**

13. **Cover muffins that will not be quickly served.** Once the muffins are completely cool, store them within a sealed gallon-size sealable plastic storage bag, first pressing out as much air as is possible.

14. **Freeze muffins that will not be eaten within a day.**

    - Tightly wrap individual muffins in plastic wrap and freeze them within an air-tight plastic freezer bag.
    - Use frozen muffins directly from the freezer, microwave heating unwrapped muffins for 20-30 seconds.

    VARIATIONS: Double the recipe to make 12 large muffins; use only ⅓ t nutmeg. Divide the batter between 12 tins, filling the tins to the top to use all the batter. Large muffins serve especially well as breakfast bread or snacks.

    Substitute **fresh applesauce** (Recipe #224) for commercially prepared.

    Add ingredients. Add, for example,

    - **½ chilled and unpeeled raw apple**, cut lengthwise into ¼ in. slices and slices cut crosswise into ¼ in. thick pieces. Mix the apple into the flour mixture with the

zucchini. Reduce applesauce content to ⅓ cup.
- **½ c pineapple chunks**, cut into ¼-in. thick slices, slices halved crosswise

Substitute large (2½ in.) chemical-free paper baking cups for buttering of individual muffin tins This substitution greatly eases cleaning of the tins.

COMMENTS: Medium ground whole wheat flour contains visible bits of bran. This bran content gives the flour a somewhat coarse texture and makes it absorptive. Finely ground flour, in comparison, is silky smooth. It is not absorptive and does not work in this recipe.

For easy cleaning, immediately use a scrub brush to clean the potato masher after mashing the banana.

185. 100% Whole Corn Bread
(4-5 servings)

Ingredients

1 T coconut oil, butter, or extra virgin olive oil
½ chilled medium onion, halved lengthwise
1 T extra virgin olive oil
3 T whole wheat flour
1 c medium ground whole corn flour
   (see comments below)
⅓ t salt

1½ T sugar
1 t baking powder
1 c milk
1 large egg
approx. 1¾ T softened butter for serving
approx. 1¾ T honey for serving

Baking Tools

1 small skillet
1 medium nonstick skillet
1 set each measuring spoons & cups
1 each chef's & 5 in. serrated knife
1 stir-fry spatula
1 rubber or other heat-resistant spatula
1 small (2-4 c) mixing bowl

1 medium (6-8 c) mixing bowl
1 large-headed wooden spoon
1 9 x 5-in. loaf pan, lightly buttered
1 timer
1 or 2 padded oven gloves
1 wire cooling rack

1. **Heat the oven at 375 degrees.**

2. **Gather together the baking tools and muffin ingredients.**

3. **Melt the coconut oil or butter.** Add the 1 T coconut oil or butter to a small skillet and heat the skillet on a small burner at a low heat setting. Be watchful and once the coconut oil or butter melts, remove the skillet from the heat and set it aside.

4. **Cook the onion.**

    - Heat the skillet on a large burner at a medium setting.
    - Use a chef's knife to cut the tips from the ½ onion. Peel and evenly dice the onion.
    - Increase the skillet heat to medium-high, and when a drop of water added to the skillet instantly dances and disappears, add 1 T oil, add and thoroughly mix in the onion, and stir-fry the onion for about 30 seconds.
    - Reduce the heat to medium and cook the onion, stirring often, another minute.
    - Set the skillet off the burner for the onion to cool.

5. **Combine the dry ingredients.** Add the 1 c corn flour, 3 T whole wheat flour, ⅓ t salt, 1½ T sugar, and 1 t baking powder to a small mixing bowl and thoroughly mix the ingredients together.

6. **Combine the wet ingredients.**

    - Add 1 c milk and 1 egg to a medium mixing bowl and use a dinner fork or whisk to mix the ingredients.
    - Add the cooked onion.
    - When using melted coconut oil or butter, use a rubber spatula to scrape the melted coconut oil or butter into the liquid ingredients and to quickly mix in the oil or butter before it hardens. For extra virgin olive oil, add the oil to the liquid ingredients and use a rubber spatula to roughly mix in the oil.

7. **Assemble the ingredients for baking.** Pour the dry ingredients onto the wet ingredients and use a wooden spoon to mix the batter until it is smooth.

8. **Bake the corn bread.**

    - Use a rubber spatula to scrape the batter into the loaf pan.
    - Center the pan on the middle oven rack.
    - Set a timer for 25 minutes. At the timer, make a readiness check. Wearing an oven glove, pull the loaf pan out from the oven far enough to safely touch the center of the corn bread top with the fingers of one hand. The top should bounce back when touched lightly. If it does, immediately remove the corn bread from the oven onto a cooling rack. If the corn bread top does not bounce back and instead is moist, continue baking the corn bread for 2-4 minutes, setting a timer, before making another readiness check.

9. **Serve the bread warm.**

PART 2

- Use a serrated knife to slice the bread just prior to serving,
- Use a stir-fry spatula to pick up and serve individual slices.
- Serve individual slices topped with butter (1 t per slice) and honey (approx. 1 t drizzled over each individual slice).

10. **Cover corn bread that will not be quickly served.** Cover it once it has completely cooled.

11. **Refrigerate leftover corn bread.**

- Tightly wrap the corn bread with plastic wrap.
- Reheat individual slices in a microwave oven for 10-15 seconds.

VARIATIONS: Make baking pan substitutions. Substitute, for example,

- **8 in. round cake pan** for a loaf pan.
- **8 in. cast iron skillet** for a loaf pan. A cast iron skillet gives the corn bread a crispy brown crust. Pre-heat the skillet in the oven before buttering it and adding the batter. Use a 10 in. skillet to double the recipe.

Add ingredients. Add, for example,

- **¼ each green and red bell pepper**, stir-fried (Recipe #35).
- **1 jalapeño or ½ mild green chili** (Recipe #36), cooked with the onion.
- **½ c yellow whole kernel corn**, fresh or dry frozen, mixed into the flour mixture.

COMMENTS: Medium ground whole corn flour has bits of corn bran in it, which give the flour a somewhat coarse texture and which identifies the flour as a source of high quality bran. Natural foods stores commonly market this corn flour product in both packaged and bulk form. Bob's Red Mill medium ground whole corn meal is a reliably high quality product that can be purchased in many grocery stores, in most natural food stores, and online. See Reference #5 (Selecting High Quality Processed Ingredients for Use in Part II Recipes), Ingredient #4 (whole corn flour), for other selection recommendations.

An important characteristic of whole corn flour is that it is alkaline. This characteristic distinguishes it from other flours, which in contrast are acid forming when consumed by humans, and makes it a perfect complement to tomato-sauce flavored stew.

186. 100% Whole Rye Bread
(2 8-in. rounds)

Bread Ingredients

1 c very warm water
1 T dry yeast

¼ c extra virgin olive oil
⅓ c blackstrap molasses

COOKED ALIVE!

1 t sugar
½ chilled medium onion, halved lengthwise
1 T extra virgin olive oil
1½ T caraway seeds
½ c milk
½ c water
¼ t salt
1 c milk
½ c medium ground whole wheat flour
1 c cold water

1 T salt
5 c room temperature whole wheat flour (medium ground), divided according to beating method used
2 c room temperature dark whole rye flour (medium ground, which contains visible bits of bran), such as Bob's Red Mill Stone Ground Dark Rye Flour
approx. 1½ T extra virgin olive oil

Baking Tools

1 very large mixing bowl (at least 16 c capacity)
1 set each measuring cups & spoons
1 large nonstick skillet
1 chef's knife
1 plastic or plastic-coated stir-fry spatula
1 timer
1 rubber or other heat-resistant spatula
1 medium mixing bowl
1 small mixing bowl
1 dinner fork or small whisk

1 large-headed wooden spoon, with or without 1 electric bread hook
1 large baking sheet (approx. 9 x 13 in.), lightly buttered or nonstick spray coated, or 2 10-in. quiche pans, lightly buttered
2 padded oven gloves
1 large wire cooling rack
1 7 in. serrated knife

---

1. **Warm the oven.** Set the oven at 200 degrees.

2. **Activate the yeast.** Add 1 c very warm but not hot water to a large mixing bowl and sprinkle (do not dump) 1 T yeast and 1 t sugar over it. Foam should almost immediately begin to develop on the surface of the water. If it does not foam, the yeast is not active. Discard the water and start over with fresh yeast.

3. **Cook the onion and caraway.**

    - Heat a large nonstick skillet on a large burner at a medium heat setting.
    - Use a chef's knife to slice the ends from ½ onion. Peel and evenly dice the onion.
    - Increase the skillet heat to medium-high, and when a drop of water added to the skillet instantly dances and disappears, add 1 T oil, mix in 1½ T caraway seeds, heat the seeds for 30 seconds, mix in the onion, stir-fry the mixture for 30 seconds, reduce the heat to medium, and cook the onion for another 2 minutes, stirring it occasionally and setting a timer.
    - At the timer, remove the skillet from the heat and use a rubber spatula to scrape the onion into a medium mixing bowl for cooling.

4. **Prepare a cooked flour mixture.**

    - Return the skillet to a large burner and heat it at a medium setting.
    - Add ½ c milk, ½ c water, and ¼ t salt to the skillet.
    - Add 1 c milk and ½ c whole wheat flour to a small mixing bowl. Use a dinner fork or whisk to mix in the flour.
    - Increase the skillet heat to medium-high, and while quickly and constantly stirring with a rubber spatula, pour the flour/milk mixture into the hot liquid in the skillet.
    - Cook the mixture about two minutes until the mixture is smooth and thickened, stirring constantly.
    - Immediately remove the skillet from the burner and pour the 1 c cold water over the hot cooked flour mixture.

5. **Prepare the dough for beating.**

    - Mix ¼ c oil, ⅓ c molasses, and 1 T salt into the *yeast mixture* that is in the large mixing bowl.
    - Add 2 c whole wheat flour to the *yeast mixture* and use a wooden spoon to mix in the flour.
    - Add 1 c whole wheat flour to the *cooked flour mixture* in the skillet and roughly mix in the flour.
    - Use a rubber spatula to scrape the *cooked flour mixture* onto the yeast mixture in the large mixing bowl.

6. **Beat the dough.**

    - **To use an electric bread hook:**

        - Pour the remaining 2 c whole wheat flour into the combined yeast and cooked flour mixtures in the mixing bowl. Use a wooden spoon to roughly mix in the whole wheat flour, stirring until the flour is moistened and holds together (no dry flour remains at the bottom of the bowl). Beat the dough for 2 minutes with the electric bread hook, setting a timer.
        - At the timer, use a wooden spoon to roughly mix in the cooked onion/caraway mixture and then the 2 c rye flour.
        - Use the bread hook to beat the dough another two minutes, setting a timer.

    - **To beat the dough by hand:**

        - Mix 1¼ c whole wheat flour into the yeast mixture. The aim is to make the batter as thick as possible in order to beat the maximum amount of flour. Therefore, if the batter seems sticky after adding 1¼ c flour, mix in another ¼ c flour. However, measure carefully as if the batter becomes too thick, it is difficult to beat.
        - Use a wooden spoon to beat the dough 300 strokes.

7. **Knead hand-beaten dough.**

    - Mix ½ c rye flour into the dough and use the wooden spoon to roughly mix the flour into the dough.
    - Pour another 1½ c rye flour onto a kneading surface. Spread the flour somewhat and use a rubber spatula to scrape the dough over the rye flour.
    - Flatten the dough somewhat and spread the cooked onion/caraway mixture evenly over the dough.
    - Slip a rubber spatula under an edge of the dough (oil the spatula if it sticks) and fold the dough edge up and over the top of the dough. Repeat this flipping, going all around the dough until all exposed dough is floured.
    - Lightly oil your hands and place a small of amount of flour nearby.
    - Knead the dough, cleaning and re-oiling your hands and adding touches more whole wheat flour to the kneading surface as is necessary to prevent sticking, until a hole pushed into the dough remains. Kneading will take around five minutes.

8. **Return the hand-beaten and kneaded dough to the very large mixing bowl.**

    - Clean, dry, and lightly oil the mixing bowl before adding the dough.
    - Drop the dough into the bowl, gently press the dough into the bowl, and then flip it. This step oils the top of the dough, protecting it from drying air during rising.
    - Tightly cover the bowl with plastic wrap. This is a crucial step that protects the dough from drying during rising.

9. **Turn off the oven and place the bread dough inside the warm oven for rising.**

    - Set a timer for 40 minutes.
    - At the timer's alert, check the dough. Remove the dough if it has risen to or about to the top of the bowl. If it has not, return it to the oven and check it often until it has risen to this extent. Adequate rising contributes to fine texture.

10. **Shape the dough for baking.**

    - Once the dough has risen, use a rubber spatula to scrape the dough from the mixing bowl onto a large oiled surface.
    - Lightly oil your hands and gently press down on the dough to break air bubbles and to shape it into a rectangle. Cut the dough into two equal halves. Shape each portion into a round by folding the edges under.
    - Place the rounds on a lightly buttered baking sheet or into two quiche pans. For rounds on a baking sheet, cover each round with a piece of oiled plastic wrap that is large enough to cover the round completely to protect the dough from drying but still loose enough to give the dough room to expand during rising. If one sheet of plastic wrap is not wide enough to cover a round, use two sheets. When using a quiche pan, loosely cover each round with a piece of oiled plastic wrap that is large enough to reach the sides of the quiche pans but do not attach the plastic wrap to the

sides of the baking pan. Once the rounds of dough are covered, set them aside in a warm place and let them rise for 15 minutes.

11. **Heat the oven to 400 degrees while the bread dough rises.**
12. **Bake the rounds.**

    - When the oven reaches 400 degrees and the bread dough has risen, carefully remove the plastic covering from the rounds, being careful to avoid tearing open the dough.
    - Center a baking pan on the middle oven rack. Place quiche dishes on either side of the middle oven rack.
    - Bake the bread for 10 minutes at 400 degrees.
    - Reduce the heat to 350 degrees and bake the bread another 30 minutes until the bread tops are lightly browned and sound somewhat hollow when lightly tapped.
    - Using padded oven gloves, remove the rounds from the oven and transfer them to a cooling rack.

13. **Wrap the bread for storage when it is completely cool.**

    - Store a whole uncut round within a sealed zippered bag, pressing out as much air as possible before sealing the bread.
    - Tightly wrap cut open bread with plastic wrap before storing the bread within a sealed plastic bag.

14. **Freeze bread that will not be used within two days.**

    - Slice the bread before freezing.
    - Tightly wrap the bread with plastic wrap and freeze the bread in a sealed gallon-size freezer bag, pressing out as much air as possible before sealing the bag.

15. **To thaw frozen bread.**

    - For individual slices, remove a slice from a frozen loaf immediately before serving and heat it for 10 seconds per side (15 seconds per side for thicker slices) in a microwave oven. Alternatively, briefly toast it in a bread toaster.
    - For a whole round, transfer the frozen wrapped bread to the refrigerator and thaw it overnight within its freezer wrapping. Alternatively, remove the loaf from its freezer wrapping and either defrost the bread at room temperature or in a toaster oven on the defrost setting.

VARIATIONS: Convert one loaf into dinner rolls. Lightly butter a 9 in. quiche dish. Cut one of the rounds into strips (approx. 1½ in. wide) and cut the strips into 1½ in. squares. Using oiled hands, fold the edges of each square under to form a round. Place the rounds loosely touching in the baking dish. Bake the round and the rolls at 400 degrees for 10 minutes. Reduce the heat to 350 degrees and bake the rolls for 15 minutes and the round for 35 minutes, removing them from the oven when the tops are lightly browned.

COMMENTS: Select and measure caraway seeds carefully because they can either have too little or too much flavor. For flavorful, pungent caraway seeds, use no more than 1½ T seeds per recipe. A greater amount overwhelms bread flavor. This amount of old seeds that have lost pungency, however, does not satisfactorily flavor the bread. When using older seeds, therefore, use 1¾-2 T seeds.

Always check both whole rye and whole wheat flour for rancidity. Natural food stores commonly carry high quality whole wheat and rye flour in bulk form, which allows cooks to check for rancidity at the time of purchase.

Reference #9

Clinching Soup and Stew Flavor: Expanded Preparation Support

Reference #9 makes flavor-enhancing suggestions and sometimes quality-enhancing suggestions for key flavoring ingredients used in Chapter Eight soups and stews. These ingredients include **cheese**, **milk sauce**, and **tomato sauce**.

1. Cheese

Maximize cheese tastiness. Cheese flavor can vary enormously among cheese varieties and among different brands of the same cheese. As cheese flavoring can also be easily lost during storage and cheese texture can be undermined by exposure to air and high heat, maximizing cheese attractiveness involves giving careful attention to both storage and heating, along with careful selection of cheese products.

- Select naturally aged extra sharp white cheddar as particularly tasty cheese. Tillamook Vintage White Extra Sharp Cheddar is an excellent example.
- Select the most flavorful Parmesan cheese to ensure an attractively tart flavor. Parmigiano Reggiano is a top product.
- Purchase cheese in chunk form. Chunk cheese is best protected from air, which undermines cheese flavor and unattractively dries cheese.
- Store cheese refrigerated, tightly wrapped within plastic wrap to retain flavor and to avoid drying. The plastic wrap should be tightly stretched over the surface to form an airtight barrier. In addition, the cheese should be stored within an air-tight plastic bag.
- Grate cheese just prior to serving it with a soup or stew. Coarsely grated cheese has more flavor than finely grated cheese.

- Do not heat a stew or soup after adding cheese. As high temperature heating damages natural cheese protein, toughening it and giving it a stringy texture, add cheese to already heated stew and only after the stew has been removed from heat. For example, 1) evenly spread cheese over the top of hot stew that has been removed from heat and cover the pot until the cheese melts, 2) add cheese as a topping to individual servings of hot stew or soup, or 3) pour hot stew/soup over cheese added to individual serving bowls.

Maximize the nutritional quality of cheese.

- Always measure cheese content. Use approx. ¼ c shredded cheese, which amounts to about 1 ounce per serving. While cheese adds pleasing flavor, it also adds significant calories (114 calories per ounce) and salt. Furthermore, cheese is an acid-producing ingredient when consumed, especially in the case of aged cheese. Relying on herb-flavored vegetables as primary flavoring ingredients, Chapter Eight soups and stews are tasty with minimal addition of cheese. To add more cheese converts Chapter Eight soups and stews into standard form and undermines the low-fat status of the recipes.
- Select cheese made from the milk of certified organically-raised dairy cows, and especially from dairy cows that have certified organic credentials and are also 100% pastured, which is top quality cheese. Reference #5 (Selecting High Quality Processed Ingredients for Use in Part II Recipes) details the nutritional reasons for selecting these naturally produced products, particularly greater nutritional value and lack of antibiotics, the absence of genetically modified ingredients (hormones injected into dairy cows to expand milk production and genetically modified grain), and the absence of pesticides, which are routinely sprayed on the grain fed to industrially managed dairy cows.
- Select natural cheese made from raw milk as special quality cheese.
- Select uncolored cheese. Orange cheese has been artificially colored to look like the especially high quality cheese made from pastured dairy cows.

2. Milk Sauce

Select the tastiest milk for use in milk sauce. Use 1%, 2%, and full fat, but not skim, milk. Using whole milk gives the soup a creamier texture, and research is showing it to be the superior nutritional selection.[273]

Select certified organic milk and, especially, certified organic milk that is also from 100% pastured dairy cattle. Reference #5 (Selecting High Quality Processed Ingredients for Use in Part II Recipes) details the nutritional reasons for selecting milk products made from naturally raised dairy

---

[273] "Myth: Full-Fat Milk Is Unhealthy," *Eating Well* (September/October, 2014): 52. There is growing evidence that full-fat milk is in fact the most nutritious form and is being connected with smaller waistlines and lower risk of obesity. It is not as yet clear why this is so, but possible suggested reasons include 1) that it causes greater satiety, which causes people to eat less, and 2) that full-fat milk also contains more conjugated linoleic acid (CLA) than reduced fat milk, and these fatty acids may affect the way insulin causes body fat to be stored.

cows, particularly greater nutritional value for humans and lack of antibiotics, genetically modified ingredients (hormones injected into dairy cows to expand milk production and genetically modified grain), and pesticides (from the grain diet), which are characteristics of all the milk of industrially produced dairy cows.

Maximize the flavor and use of seasoning vegetables in milk sauce. Expand the role of seasoning vegetables, which are top flavoring ingredients both with respect to flavor and nutritional quality.

- Increase onion amount to 1 full onion.
- Select a medium-sized bulb onion as the easiest to dice onion. Being able to easily dice encourages onion use.
- Expand onion variety (Recipe #34). Add some green onions, including the phytonutrient rich green tops, or leeks, also including the nutritious green tops. In addition to boosting nutritional value and flavor, the bright green color of the tops enhances the attractiveness of a soup or stew.
- Cut green onions and leeks crosswise into relatively thick, not very thin, slices to maximize the flavor contribution they make to a milk sauce-flavored soup.
- Include garlic (Recipe #31). Prepare garlic separately and use it as a topping on individual servings of a soup or stew to take best advantage of its distinctive flavor.
- Add chili peppers (Recipe #36) to milk sauce. Providing both attractive color and distinctive flavor, chili peppers are very attractive ingredients that can almost single-handedly lift soups into special occasion form.
- Expand bell pepper content. Bell pepper enhances milk sauce flavor in addition to providing attractive color and enhancing nutritional quality.
- Do not omit ginger root but also only very cautiously increase ginger root content. Ginger easily becomes an unpleasantly assertive dish ingredient. Note that some ginger products have a stronger flavor than others.

Make fullest use of dried herb flavoring in milk sauce.

- Use dried herb leaves as opposed to ground leaves, which will have a much stronger flavor. Alternatively, add only small amounts of ground herbs and increase the amount on the basis of tasting.
- Use flavorful dried herb leaves. The flavor of products varies and products also lose flavor during storage. When crushed, leaves should release an intense fragrance. Replace them when they do not. Store herbs in air-tight containers away from sun to retain freshness.
- Accurately measure spice and herb content. Use measuring spoons. Even slightly too much or too little flavoring can make a difference, unpleasantly overpowering other dish flavoring or leaving the dish bland.
- Evenly disperse dried spice/herb flavoring in dishes. Spread them over stir-frying onions. The spice/herb flavoring adheres to oil-coated onion pieces and becomes evenly mixed into a dish. The oil coating holds the herb flavoring.
- Release the flavor of dried herb leaves by crushing them between your palms when adding them to stir-frying onions.
- Experiment using different herbs. For example, substitute ½ t dried marjoram, thyme,

PART 2

or sage leaves for the basil and oregano leaves often used in Part II dishes.
- Select certified organic herbs. Herbs make both flavoring and nutritional contributions to dishes. In addition to having greater nutritional value, certified organic herbs do not contain pesticides and are reliably neither genetically modified and/or irradiated.

3. Tomato Sauce

Minimize the broth and liquid content of tomato sauce. Precisely observe the recipe-directed amount of canned broth or other liquid. Adding too much broth, even flavorful broth, unbalances recipe ingredients and, as a result, unattractively dilutes sauce flavoring.

- Do any thinning shortly before serving. It is far easier to thin a sauce than it is to fix diluted sauce flavor.
- Add additional canned broth or liquid only after a taste test.
- Add only a small amount of liquid at a time and make a taste test before adding any more.

Maximize the flavor of canned broth and other liquid used in making tomato sauce. Using tasty broth and liquid is an important key to stew success.

- Rely on herb- or spice-flavored stir-fried onions rather than boiled onion to flavor stew broth. Stir-fried onion, and especially onion in combination with ginger root and garlic, contributes incomparably more flavor than onion boiled in a broth. The boiling of onions and other seasoning vegetables in liquid largely wastes the valuable flavoring capacity of these vegetables.
- Add dried herbs or spices to the vegetable ingredients of stews as a means of enhancing the flavor of tomato sauce. In particular, add dried herbs to somewhat less flavorful vegetables, such as celery, cauliflower, and summer squash. These vegetables easily absorb herb and spice flavoring added during stir-frying and are enhanced by it.
- Use only flavorful liquid to thin a tomato sauce. Never add plain water. Add tomato juice, additional broth, bean broth, or vegetable cooking liquid.
- Precisely measure fresh lemon juice content. Lemon juice is a key flavoring ingredient. Adding too little lemon wastes the pleasing tartness it adds while adding too much easily makes broth flavor unattractively tart. It is important, therefore, to never add "extra" lemon juice to a broth without first tasting broth to determine its need. When there is extra lemon juice, place it in a small glass container and refrigerate it tightly covered to keep it on hand. Save small jars with lids for freezing juice that cannot be used within a few days. Freeze it in small amounts that can quickly be used once the juice is thawed.
- Add bouillon or other concentrated flavor cubes or powder to enhance the flavor of canned broth, especially vegetable broth. Choose organic products to avoid chemical flavorings and beware of high sodium content. Natural food stores commonly carry one or more varieties of flavoring products, including vegan products, using concentrated dried vegetable flavoring.
- Substitute fresh poultry broth for commercially prepared broth. Fresh poultry broth (Reference #10) has a far superior flavor to any canned or packaged product, and home preparation places a cook in control of salt content. Adding even a small amount of fresh

broth enhances stew flavor.
- Substitute fresh vegetable broth prepared from winter squash skin for part of the commercially prepared broth called for in a stew recipe. Gently boil chopped up skin from 1 certified organic or locally produced winter squash (and other collected vegetable parts, such as celery tops and green pea pods) in 1½ c water with ¼ t salt covered for 45 minutes. Drain the skins in a colander, collecting and storing the broth.
- Collect leftover meat or poultry bones to make a fresh gelatinous broth. Boil them (one small batch of bones) in 1½-2 c water and ½ t salt for 45 minutes. Any of this broth that cannot be immediately used can be frozen for later use. Save small jars with lids to use for freezing small amounts of such broth. Add 1 T vinegar to leach minerals from the bones into the broth.

Maximize the nutritional quality of commercially prepared broth. The quality of prepared broth products is highly variable.

- Select low sodium commercially-prepared broth products.
- Select canned broth from BPA (bisphenol A) free cans.[274] Alternatively, select broth from glass (best of all) or aseptic containers, which are coated paper containers. These containers do not contain chemicals that can be leached into the broth.
- Select certified organic poultry or beef broth and especially broth made from poultry or cattle that is both certified organic and grass-fed, which is top quality broth. Reference #4 (Selecting Top Quality Whole Food Ingredients for Part II Recipes) explains the nutritional significance of making these naturally produced product selections.

Maximize the flavor of tomato products.

- Select the tastiest tomato products for use in tomato sauce. Because the flavor of products varies significantly, experiment with different commercially prepared products (tomato paste, tomato juice, and diced canned tomatoes) to locate the tastiest products.
- Add tomato paste to enhance tomato sauce flavor, adding it 1 T at a time, followed by tasting.
- Substitute thick strained tomato, such as the unflavored Italian product Pomi Strained Tomato, for tomato juice.
- Add ½ c fresh diced tomato (Recipe #37) to enhance the tomato flavor of a stew, including the skin and seeds. To maximize tomato flavor, cook fresh tomatoes separately from other vegetables, set them aside, and add them to a stew just in time to be heated through before serving. Select grape tomatoes as especially tasty and sturdy tomatoes.

Maximize the nutritional quality of commercially prepared tomato products used in tomato sauce. Quality varies significantly between products.

- Select certified organic products.
- Select low sodium tomato products.

---

[274] BPA has been identified as an endocrine disrupting chemical, which is a chemical that negatively affects human hormones with lethal consequences, such as obesity, especially for a fetus.

PART 2

- Select products packaged in glass or aseptic (coated paper) containers or in BPA (bisphenol A) free cans. This is especially important because of the high acid content of tomatoes. This acidity results in the leaching out of BPA from the lining used in some metal containers. As noted above, BPA has been identified as an endocrine disrupting chemical in humans and especially in the case of a fetus.
- Quickly transfer any extra portion of a canned tomato product into a glass container and refrigerate it tightly covered. This storage maintains the freshness of the product, but glass also protects the tomato product from air-activated chemical reactions that can leave chemical residues in a tomato product stored in a can.

Make fullest use of seasoning vegetables in tomato sauce. Expand seasoning vegetable content. Maximize the flavoring contribution of individual seasoning vegetables.

- Increase onion amount to 1 full onion.
- Select medium-sized bulb onions as the easiest to dice onion. Being able to easily dice encourages onion use.
- Expand onion variety. Add some green onions, including the phytonutrient rich green tops, or leeks, also including the nutritious green tops. In addition to boosting nutritional value and flavor, the bright green color of tops enhances the attractiveness of a soup or stew.
- Cut green onions and leeks crosswise into relatively thick, not very thin, slices to maximize the flavor contribution they make to a tomato sauce-flavored stew.
- Include garlic (Recipe #31). Prepare garlic separately and use it as a topping on individual servings of a soup or stew to take best advantage of its distinctive flavor.
- Add chili peppers (Recipe #36) to tomato sauce. Providing both attractive color and distinctive flavor, chili peppers are very attractive ingredients that can almost single-handedly lift soups and stews into special occasion form.
- Maximize use of bell pepper. Even a small amount enhances dish flavor and dish color.
- Do not omit ginger root but keep the amount added low. Ginger flavor easily becomes too assertive.

Make fullest use of *dried* herb flavoring in tomato sauce.

- Rely on dried leaves as opposed to ground herbs, which have much more assertive flavor. Use ground herbs to increase herb flavor intensity, but use only a small amount and follow up an addition with a taste test before adding more.
- Use flavorful dried spices and herbs. When crushed, leaves and seeds should release an intense fragrance. They should be stored in air-tight containers away from sun to retain freshness.
- Accurately measure spice and herb content. Use measuring spoons. Even slightly too much or too little flavoring can make a difference, unpleasantly overpowering other dish flavoring or leaving the dish bland.
- Evenly disperse dried spice/herb flavoring in dishes. Spread them over stir-frying onions. The spice/herb flavoring adheres to oil-coated onion pieces and becomes evenly mixed into a dish. The oil coating holds the herb flavoring.

- Release the flavor of dried herb leaves by crushing them between your palms when adding them to stir-frying onions.
- Experiment with using different herbs, such as substituting marjoram, sage, rosemary, and thyme in place of the basil and oregano commonly included in Part II recipes.

Make fullest use of *fresh* herb and spice flavoring in tomato sauce. Fresh spices and herb leaves can provide a special flavor-lifting boost to dishes. See Ingredient #3, "Fresh Herbs & Spices," in Reference #6: Maximizing the Attractiveness of Whole Food Ingredients Commonly Used in Part II Recipes. This reference makes specific suggestions for selecting, storing, and preparing herbs and cilantro for use in dishes.

Select certified organic dried and fresh herb and spice products as the highest quality products for use in tomato sauce.

- The certified organic label ensures that both dried and fresh herb and spice products have been naturally produced, which means they have been produced without artificial fertilizer and have not been sprayed with pesticides during production.
- This label also ensures dried herbs and spices have not been irradiated. Commercially produced dried herbs and spices can be irradiated without this processing having to be indicated to consumers.

Reference #10

Preparing Fresh Chicken Broth

Broth Ingredients

1 small to medium (2-3 lb) lean fryer
1½ c canned/packaged poultry broth
¾ t salt

4-5 garlic cloves (or to taste)
3-4 1-in. thick pieces of fresh ginger root

Cooking Utensils

1 Dutch oven or soup pot with a tight-fitting & opaque lid
1 set each measuring cups & spoons
1 5 in. serrated knife
1 large stirring spoon
1 can opener for canned broth

1 timer
1 colander
1 large (10 c) mixing bowl
1 gallon-size sealable plastic storage bag
2 c glass storage container with lid
1 pepper mill

PART 2

———◆———

1. Gather together the cooking ingredients and cooking utensils.

2. **Prepare the chicken for cooking.**

   - Rinse the chicken inside and out under cool, running water. Remove and discard obvious fat. Add the chicken to the Dutch oven. Use soap to thoroughly wash your hands and the working area where the chicken was handled. Raw chicken can easily carry bacteria that can cause human illness.
   - Working on a cutting board and with a knife untouched by the raw chicken, use a serrated knife to slice off the tips of 4-5 garlic cloves and to slice 3-4 1-in. thick pieces of fresh ginger root. Peel the garlic cloves. Add the ginger root and garlic to the Dutch oven.
   - Open the broth container and add the broth and ¾ t salt to the Dutch oven.

3. **Cook the chicken.**

   - Bring the broth to boiling over high heat, reduce the heat to a level that maintains gentle boiling, use a large spoon to stir under the chicken to ensure that it is not sticking to the pan bottom, and cover the pan.
   - Set a timer for one hour and ten minutes.
   - Check the chicken after five or so minutes of cooking to ensure the water is gently, not rapidly, boiling and lower the heat as may be needed.
   - At the timer, check the chicken for readiness. If the legs move easily, remove the cooking pot from the stove and pour the chicken and broth into a colander placed over a large bowl for collecting the broth. If the legs do not easily move, continue the cooking, setting a timer and checking for readiness every 5 minutes. This careful checking ensures that the chicken is not overcooked and, as result, remains juicy and tender as opposed to being dry and stringy.

4. **Collect and refrigerate the broth.**

   - Pour the broth into a 2 c glass container and refrigerate it uncovered, discarding the garlic and ginger root.
   - Skim off and discard fat that hardens at the top of refrigerated broth. However, when the cooked chicken is pasture raised, in particular, and also certified organic, the fat can be collected and used as cooking fat.
   - Either use the broth within 3-4 days or immediately freeze it. Freeze the broth in serving size amounts.

5. **Prepare the cooked chicken.**

- To serve the chicken later, immediately place the whole chicken, cooled somewhat, within a gallon-size freezer storage bag, pressing out as much air as is possible, and refrigerate it.
- To immediately use the chicken in a dish, use ½ chicken per 4-6 serving dish, such as Recipe #178 (Old Fashioned Chicken Stew), Recipe #179 (Curried Split Pea and Chicken Stew), or Recipe #187 (Chicken Curry).

- Immediately refrigerate extra chicken in tightly covered and uncut form.
- Remove the chicken from the bones as soon as it is cool enough to handle, discarding the skin and collecting the bones. Use a slicing or 5 in. serrated knife to cut the chicken pieces into thin strips, and cut the strips into bite-size pieces.
- Add freshly cracked black pepper to taste.
- Add the chicken to a dish only shortly before serving. This step retains the juiciness and tenderness of the chicken.

6. **Save and re-cook chicken bones.**

    - Return collected bones to a cooking pot, add 1½-2 c water, ½ t salt, and 1 T apple cider vinegar (to leach minerals from the bones into the broth) and bring the bones to boiling over high heat. Reduce the heat to a level that maintains gentle boiling, cover the pot, and cook the bones for an hour, setting a timer.
    - Check the bones midway during cooking to ensure the cooking water is only gently boiling in order to avoid unexpected evaporation.
    - Drain the bones in a colander placed over a bowl.
    - Transfer the broth to a glass storage container and refrigerate it. Generally scrape off and discard fat that hardens on the surface of the broth, but the small amount of fat that collects in broth made from a lean pasture-raised chicken (certified organic or locally raised) can be collected and used as flavoring in a stew or curry.

VARIATIONS: Substitute 2-3 lbs lean chicken parts for 1 whole chicken.

COMMENTS: For top quality chicken, select a chicken that is both raised in accordance with certified organic standards and that is also 100% pastured. A locally raised chicken that is significantly pastured is also a top quality selection. Avoid use of an industrially raised chicken, which in comparison to naturally produced chicken has greater fat content, lower nutritional quality, and contains antibiotics and pesticides from the grain diet it is fed, as Reference #4 (Selecting Top Quality Whole Ingredients for Use In Part II Recipes) details.

CHAPTER NINE

Curries

Curry Dish Description

CURRIES CALL TO mind exotic India and the alluring variety of spices and taste-tempting dishes that have made Indian restaurants a favorite dining choice from one end of the globe to another. Chapter Nine recipes ease bringing these wonderful creations into everyday use. Recipes accomplish this through use of a simple-to-prepare and low fat curry sauce that is made from a variety of ready-made products (canned coconut milk, commercially prepared broth, plain yogurt, and curry spices), fresh lemon juice, and quick-cooking seasoning vegetables. Individual Chapter Nine curry recipes mix this basic curry sauce with different combinations of vegetables and typically some form of protein (which can be legumes). They also substitute brown rice for white rice. With spice-mellowing yogurt and fruity chutney served as dish accompaniments, Chapter Nine curries retain the authentic look and taste of traditional curry while also serving nutritional purposes.

Cooked Alive! curry recipes share the outstanding characteristics of curries. First and foremost, curry sauce is an amazing flavoring base. Curry sauce, for example,

- attractively integrates a wide spectrum of vegetables. Providing cooks nearly a 100% chance of serving success, curry sauce encourages cooks to experiment widely with vegetable content. Curries welcome, for example,

    - standard favorite vegetables, such as green peas and potatoes.
    - less familiar vegetables, such as okra, eggplant, and winter squash.
    - especially nutritious vegetables, such as green leafy vegetables, which are peerless vegetables in terms of adding both lovely color and nutritional richness to curries.

- welcomes nuts and both fresh and dried fruit, which richly enhance both the attractiveness and nutritional quality of curry dishes.
- combines attractively with a variety of protein ingredients, including beef, poultry, eggs, and legumes. Protein, in turn, converts dishes into main dish and full meal form.
- successfully integrates whole grain brown rice. With curry sauce moistening its absorptive bran content, brown rice mixes essentially unnoticed into a curry dish.

Brown rice, in turn, enhances the nutritional diversity of dishes and provides energy-carrying complex carbohydrates.
- holds the flavor of ingredients through refrigeration and freezing.

Second, curry dishes have boundless serving versatility. Curries easily adjust to cover a wide variety of eating occasions.

- Curries can be served in very basic form – reduced to seasoning vegetables and curry powder flavoring – to make most Chapter Nine curries practical dishes that provide interesting variety in everyday eating.
- Vegetable curries easily convert into vegan vegetarian form.
- All curries easily dress up into special occasion form. There is an enormous variety of simple ways for a cook to make this conversion. Cooks can, for example,
    - substitute aromatic brown rice for plain brown rice. This is a completely simple change as aromatic brown rice cooks exactly like regular brown rice.
    - expand vegetable content. Each recipe includes a variety of vegetable variation suggestions.
    - expand spice content. Reference #11 (Clinching Curry Flavor: Expanded Preparation Support, Ingredient #4) makes spice variation suggestions.
    - vary chutney. It is marketed in a variety of interesting flavors. It is also simple to home prepare (Recipes #194-196).
    - convert yogurt into a vegetable or fruit flavored salad (Raita, Recipe #192).
    - add a simple lentil dish (Spiced Dhal, Recipe #193), which enhances the South Asian character as well as appetite-satisfying capacity of a curry meal.
    - serve flat bread (chapatis) with a curry dish. Used in traditional South Asian style with pieces of the bread torn off and used as scoops for eating the curry dish, flat bread is an extra special addition. Cooks can purchase these chapatis in both ready-to-bake and pre-baked form. With a little practice, cooks can make their own super chapatis (Recipe #197).
    - serve whole wheat muffins (Recipes #180-183), which are also outstanding accompaniments.

Vegetable curries easily convert into vegan vegetarian form.

Curry Preparation Notes

Preparation Notes provide helpful instruction and information about Chapter Nine curries that cannot fit into the individual recipes. These Notes cover a variety of subjects, including:

- technical details relating to recipe preparation (Notes #1-4), with information provided in Note #1 being of particular importance.
- cooking tool information (Note #5).

- preparation of vegetable variation suggestions made in recipes (Note #6).
- securing the flavor of key curry dish ingredients (Note #7).
- expanding the nutritional quality of curries (Notes #8-9).

1. **Adjust vegetable stir-fry/steaming technique when using gas burners.** The stir-fry/steaming technique used for preparing vegetables in Chapter Nine curry recipes is matched with electric burners, which do not immediately cool when burner heat is reduced. Cooking of vegetables, as a result, slows slowly and vegetables continue to cook when heat is reduced after one minute of stir-frying. **Because gas burners *do* immediately respond to heat changes**, it is necessary to alter stir-fry/steaming technique. On a gas burner, the reduction of heat to low is so abrupt that cooking can stop completely. If it does, steam will not form and vegetables will not be tender at the recipe-directed cooking time. Therefore, when using a gas burner, adjust stir-fry/steaming technique as follows:

   - After one minute of stir-frying, add 1 T hot water as directed to do by the recipes but reduce the heat to **medium low**. Cover the skillet and heat the vegetable on medium low for 30 seconds before reducing the heat to low.

2. **Keep the liquid content of curries low.** Flavorful, thick liquid is essential to curry success. Too much liquid dilutes curry flavor and unattractively thins curry texture. It is much easier to thin a sauce that is a bit too thick shortly before serving than it is to re-flavor and thicken a diluted sauce.

   - Always use standard measuring cups to measure liquid content.
   - Avoid the temptation to add any leftover liquid to the curry dish, no matter how tasty the liquid. Add any additional liquid only when assembling a curry for serving and it is clear that added liquid will not unattractively thin the curry.

3. **Important information about the onion content of Chapter Nine curries is as follows:**

   - The routinely called for "½ chilled medium onion, halved lengthwise" is a yellow or other bulb onion. It is chilled to keep enzymes from quickly altering the onion flavor when the onion flesh becomes exposed to air during cutting. As a sweet onion does not contain the offending enzymes, it need not be chilled before cutting. Sweet onion, it should be noted, is also not as nutritious as yellow onion.
   - A medium size onion is one approx. 2¾ in. in diameter. Recipes specify its use because it is as an easy-to-dice size.
   - A simple way to dice the onion is to place the onion half cut side down on a cutting board and while holding the onion together with one hand, use a chef's knife to cut the onion lengthwise into ¼ in. thick slices. Turn the onion sideways and, while holding the onion together with one hand, repeat the slicing.
   - As onion serves as a key flavoring ingredient in recipes, it is of utmost important that top quality onion be selected. Onion should be intact with tight-fitting and unbroken skin; flesh should be uniformly firm, which indicates it is not bruised. The

flesh of very top quality onions is also uniformly white without green coloration.
- Onion should be immediately added to hot oil after being cut to deactivate enzymes that can quickly alter natural sweet onion flavor.

4. **Substitute fresh cooked for pre-cooked brown rice in recipes.** Recipes generally call for use of pre-cooked brown rice as a convenient dish preparation-reducing step. As cooked brown rice retains its flavor and moistness well during several days of storage, it can be usefully prepared ahead and kept on hand for near instant use in dishes. When cooked brown rice is not on hand, however, easily substitute raw brown rice as follows:

   - Start brown rice as the first recipe preparation step. If the brown rice is not fully cooked by the time the curry is prepared, the wait will be short.
   - Use Recipe #166. This recipe includes helpful brown rice product selection information and applies preparation steps matched to brown rice characteristics that yield reliably attractive cooking results.

5. **Important information about cooking tools is as follows:**

   - Individual Chapter Nine curry recipes list all basic cooking tools used in preparing curry dishes, but some general wiping, drying, scrubbing, and wrapping tools – paper and cloth towels, vegetable scrubbing tools, and plastic wrap – and regular cutting boards are not listed. As these tools are used routinely in recipes, they need to be kept handy.
   - The General Cooking Tools listing included in the Part II Introduction serves as a descriptive reference for all tools used in recipes except those specific to curries. Two tools specific to curries are as follows:
     - **Electric seed grinder.** This tool quickly and evenly grinds whole spices.
     - **Mortar and pestle.** This traditional tool works efficiently for hand grinding small amounts of whole spices.

6. **Chapter One (Stir-Fried and Stir-Fry/Steamed Vegetables Recipes) serves as a preparation reference for vegetable variation suggestions made in Chapter Nine curry recipes.** The recipe number attached to a vegetable variation suggestion identifies the Chapter One reference recipe, which provides preparation details as well as basic selection and nutritional information.

7. *Cooked Alive!* **includes two references focused on assisting cooks achieve curry-making success.** These references are as follows:

   - Reference #11 (Clinching Curry Flavor: Expanded Preparation Support), which is included in Chapter Nine, focuses on making flavor-enhancing suggestions for key individual flavoring ingredients routinely used in curry sauce. Ingredients covered include **canned broth, canned coconut milk, ground curry spices,** and **seasoning vegetables.**
   - Reference #6 (Maximizing the Attractiveness of Whole Food Ingredients Commonly

Used in Part II Recipes) makes flavor-enhancing suggestions for several other key individual curry ingredients, including **dried fruit, legumes, nuts, protein (beef, poultry, and eggs), brown rice,** and **yogurt.**

8. **Cooks significantly expand the nutritional quality of curry dishes through selection of naturally produced ingredients.** *Cooked Alive!* provides three references to assist cooks in making naturally produced curry ingredient selections.

   - Reference #1 (Selecting Top Quality Fresh Whole Vegetables and Fruits) details the nutritional significance of selecting vegetables and fruits that are both naturally intact and naturally produced. Naturally produced products include both certified organic and locally produced produce.
   - Reference #4 (Selecting Top Quality Whole Food Ingredients for Use in Part II Recipes) details the nutritional significance of selecting physically intact and naturally produced whole foods other than vegetables and fruits. Reference #4 makes specific product selection recommendations. Whole food products covered that are relevant to Chapter Nine curries are **beef, poultry, egg, legume, nuts,** and **brown rice.**
   - Reference #5 (Selecting High Quality Processed Ingredients for Use in Part II Recipes) identifies physically processed products that retain significant nutritional quality. Products relevant to Chapter Nine curries are **ground beef, dairy products,** and **ground whole grain.**

9. **Cooks importantly expand the nutritional quality of curry accompaniment dishes through selection of naturally produced ingredients.** Select, for example,

   - certified organic brown sugar and white sugar to avoid genetically modified and chemically tainted sugar. While these products are as highly processed as industrially produced sugar products, industrially produced sugar, both brown and white, is commonly (nearly always in the case of sugar beets) produced from genetically modified sugar cane or sugar beets that is also heavily sprayed with herbicides during production. Certified organic sugar products are also naturally produced while industrially produced sugars are produced by chemically dependent agricultural methods that are highly destructive of the environment.
   - grass-fed yogurt and milk as opposed to yogurt made from and the milk of industrially raised dairy cows, which are fed an unnatural grain diet that includes antibiotics. The grain fed to industrially raised dairy cows is also typically genetically modified and contains pesticides from heavy spraying during production. Industrially managed dairy cows are also injected with genetically modified hormones to increase milk production. The pesticides and antibiotics contained in the grain diet and the hormones, in turn, are passed into the food products made from the milk.
   - certified organic whole wheat flour for use in chapatis.
   - certified organic lentils.

Curry Recipes

187. Chicken Curry
(4 servings)

Chicken, Seasonings, and Cooking Oil

4 oz skinless, boneless chicken breast or chicken tenders
1 t curry powder
½ t ground ginger

½ t garlic powder
⅛ in. thick slice of ginger root
1 T toasted sesame or extra virgin olive oil
⅓ t salt

Vegetables, Fruit, and Cooking Oil

⅓ each red, yellow & green bell pepper, sliced lengthwise

1 T extra virgin olive oil
½ c fresh pineapple chunks (Recipe #94)

Curry Sauce Ingredients

1 chilled medium yellow onion
2 ⅛-in. wide slices fresh ginger root
1 T extra virgin olive oil
1 t cumin seed
2 t curry powder
½ t ground cinnamon
approx. 10 green cardamom pods
¼ t ground ginger
¼ t ground nutmeg
½ t chili powder
¾ c canned poultry broth

¼ t salt
2-3 T certified organic raisins
2 T dried tart cherries (approx. 12 cherries)
½ c canned regular coconut milk
1½ T packed dark brown sugar
⅓ c plain yogurt
½-¾ lemon (approx. 2-3 T lemon juice)
¼ c raw pecan or walnut halves or raw whole cashews or almonds
½ c canned poultry broth

Dish Accompaniments

4 c cooked brown rice (Recipe #166)
3 T water
⅓ t salt

¾ c plain yogurt, stirred creamy smooth
4 T mango chutney, commercially prepared (e.g. Major Grey) or fresh prepared (Recipe #196)

Cooking Tools

1 large skillet with a tight-fitting & opaque lid
1 cutting board reserved for raw poultry
1 each slicing, 5 in. serrated, & chef's knife

2 dinner plates
1 colander
1 can opener
1 mortar & pestle or electric spice grinder

PART 2

1 set each measuring spoons & cups
1 plastic or plastic-coated stir-fry spatula
1 timer
1 rubber or other heat-resistant spatula

1 medium nonstick skillet with a tight-fitting & opaque lid
1 hand citrus juicer
1 small mixing bowl

---

1. **Gather all dish ingredients and cooking tools.**

2. **Stir-fry the chicken.**

   - Heat a large skillet on a large burner at a medium setting.
   - Quickly rinse the chicken with cold water and pat it completely dry with paper towels.
   - Working on a cutting board reserved for raw meat, use a sharp slicing knife to cut the chicken into ¼ in. thick strips, discarding any fat and white membrane. Cut the strips into ½ in. lengths.
   - Use soap to wash your hands and slicing knife. Separate the cutting board used for the chicken.
   - Use a serrated knife to mince the ginger on a clean cutting board.
   - Increase the skillet heat to medium-high. When a drop of water added to the skillet instantly dances and disappears, add 1 T toasted sesame oil, mix the chicken and ginger into the oil, evenly sprinkle the ground spices (1 t curry powder, ½ t ground ginger, and ½ t garlic powder) over the chicken, and stir-fry the mixture for 1 minute, setting a timer.
   - At the timer, reduce the heat to medium and continue the cooking another 2 minutes, stirring the chicken often and setting a timer.
   - Remove the skillet from the heat, evenly sprinkle ⅓ t salt over the chicken, use a rubber spatula to scrape the chicken onto a dinner plate, and set it aside. If necessary, slant the plate so any juice spills away from the chicken.
   - Wipe the skillet clean.

3. **Prepare the bell peppers and pineapple.**

   - **Stir-fry the bell peppers.**

     - Heat the large skillet at a medium setting on a large burner.
     - Use a 5 in. serrated knife to cut out the stem end of each pepper. Remove the seeds but not the white membrane. Use the serrated knife to cut the peppers lengthwise into ¼ in. thick strips and to cut the strips crosswise into ¼ in. cubes.
     - Increase the skillet heat to medium-high, and when a drop of water added to the skillet instantly dances and disappears, add 1 T oil, add the peppers, and vigorously stir-fry them for about 30 seconds. Reduce the heat to medium and cook the peppers for 2 minutes, stirring them occasionally and setting a timer.

- At the timer, use a rubber spatula to scrape the pepper and any cooking juice into a colander placed over a dinner plate.
- Wipe the skillet clean.
- **Prepare the pineapple.** Use a serrated knife to cut the pineapple chunks lengthwise into ¼ in. wide slices. Add the pineapple to the colander with the bell pepper.

4. **Prepare the curry sauce.**

    - Heat the large skillet at a medium setting.
    - Open the canned broth and coconut milk containers.
    - Remove the cardamom seeds from the 10 pods and use a mortar and pestle or electric grinder to crush the seeds, crushing enough seeds to yield ½ t seeds.
    - Use a chef's knife to halve an onion lengthwise, place the halves cut side down on a cutting board, and cut off the ends of each half. Peel the halves. Again place the onion halves cut side down on the cutting board and use the chef's knife to dice the onion halves. Mince the ginger.
    - Increase the skillet heat to medium-high, and when a drop of water added to the skillet immediately dances and disappears, add 1 T oil, add and heat the cumin seed for 30 seconds, add the onion and ginger, evenly sprinkle the spices (2 t curry powder, ½ t each ground cinnamon and crushed cardamom, ¼ t each ground ginger and nutmeg, and ½ t chili powder) over the onion, and stir-fry the mixture for 1 minute, setting a timer. Stir-frying should at first be vigorous but can slow to "flip often" pace.
    - At the timer, reduce the heat to medium and cook the onion mixture for 2 minutes, stirring it occasionally and setting a timer.
    - At the timer, add ½ c chicken broth and ¼ t salt, bring the sauce to boiling, reduce the heat to medium, partially cover the skillet, and gently boil the curry sauce for 5 minutes, setting a timer.
    - As the sauce cooks, use a chef's knife to halve the 2 T dried tart cherries and ¼ c nuts. Thoroughly stir the coconut milk before measuring ½ c coconut. Measure 2 T raisins.
    - At the timer, reduce the skillet heat to low and mix in the dried fruits, nuts, and coconut milk.
    - If the curry will not be quickly assembled for serving, remove the skillet from the heat, cover the skillet, and set the curry sauce aside.

5. **Assemble the curry for serving.**

    - Heat the curry sauce at a medium setting.
    - Begin heating the rice. Bring 3 T water to boiling over medium-high heat in a medium nonstick skillet, mix in the brown rice, break up any clumps, evenly sprinkle ⅓ t salt over it, cover the skillet, reduce the heat to very low, and heat the rice while assembling other ingredients. Stir the rice periodically and add touches more water as may be needed to keep the rice from sticking.
    - Squeeze ½ lemon and add the juice to a small mixing bowl. Add ⅓ c yogurt and 1½ T packed brown sugar and thoroughly combine the ingredients.

PART 2

- Use a rubber spatula to slowly mix the yogurt mixture into the curry sauce, stirring quickly to avoid curdling the yogurt.
- Check the curry sauce flavoring, adding touches (1-2 t) of lemon juice for tartness and brown sugar for sweetness. If the sauce is too thick, cautiously add ¼-½ c poultry broth, stirring each addition in thoroughly before adding more. It is important to avoid making the curry sauce too thin.
- Stir yogurt creamy smooth before measuring ¾ c yogurt for use as an accompaniment.
- Increase the burner heat to medium-high and bring the curry sauce to near boiling, mix in the chicken, and return the sauce to near boiling, stirring the sauce often.
- Add the cooked vegetables, any collected cooking juice, and the pineapple. Heat the curry sauce until it comes close to boiling, stirring it frequently.
- Reduce the heat to medium and heat the curry another 2-3 minutes, just until all ingredients are hot.

6. **Serve the curry.** Serve each individual portion of the curry over 1 c hot rice with 1 T chutney and 2-4 dollops of yogurt alongside.

VARIATIONS: Make ingredient substitutions. Substitute, for example,

- **½ t commercially ground cardamom** for pods.
- **1 small cooked whole chicken** (Reference #10) for chicken breast or tenders. Add ½ of the cooked chicken in the curry, first removing skin and bones and cutting it into bite-size (approx. ⅓ in.) cubes before adding it to the curry. Substitute the fresh broth for canned poultry broth.
- **1 tasty apple** for pineapple or combine apple and pineapple. Prepare apple slices as in Recipe #74. Cut each apple slice crosswise into 4 equal chunks. Pre-heat a medium skillet to medium high; add 1 T extra virgin olive oil, add the apple, evenly sprinkle ⅓ t ground cinnamon over the apple, and stir-fry the apple for 1 minute, setting a timer. Stir-frying should at first be vigorous but can slow to "flip often" pace. Add 1 T hot water or orange juice, cover the skillet, reduce the heat to low, and steam the apple for 4 minutes.

Add ingredients. Add, for example,

- **1 mild green chili** or **2 jalapeño peppers** (Recipe #36).
- **2 c sugar snap peas** (Recipe #71) or **2 c dry frozen green peas** (Recipe #71), unthawed.
- **1 medium to large sweet potato** (Recipe #18).
- **8-12 medium garlic cloves** (Recipe #31).
- **⅛ t cayenne.**
- **½ lb pre-washed spinach** (Recipe #28) or any **other greens** presented in Recipes #23-30.
- **2 c bok choy** (Recipe #3).

COMMENTS: When using green cardamom pods, seeds should be black and have a pungent flavor. Light brown seeds have oxidized and are flavorless in comparison.

188. Meatball Curry
(4 servings)

Meatball Ingredients

½ c unseasoned Japanese panko (dried bread crumbs)
1½ t curry powder
1 t ground cumin powder
1 t garlic powder

1 t salt
1 lb extra lean ground beef
2 ⅛-in. thick slices ginger root
1 large egg
1 c beef or poultry broth

Vegetables with Seasoning and Cooking Oil

½ lb pre-washed spinach
1 T extra virgin olive oil
¼ t salt

¼ each red, green, & yellow bell pepper, sliced lengthwise
¾ T extra virgin olive oil

Curry Sauce Ingredients

½ chilled medium onion, halved lengthwise
2 ⅛-in. thick slices ginger root
1 T extra virgin olive oil
1 t cumin seed
2½ t curry powder
½ t ground cinnamon
½ t garlic powder
8 pods green cardamom (to yield approx. ½ t crushed)
1 c beef or poultry broth

¼ t salt
½ c canned coconut milk
1 heaping T dried tart cherries
2-4 T certified organic raisins
⅓ c plain yogurt
1½ T packed dark brown sugar
½ lemon
½ c broth
10-12 pecan halves
1 t garam masala spice mixture (opt)

Accompaniments

4 c cooked brown rice (Recipe #166)
2 T water
⅓ t salt

¾ c plain yogurt
4 T mango chutney, commercially prepared (e.g. Major Grey) or fresh prepared (Recipe #196)

Cooking Tools

1 set each measuring spoons & cups
1 can opener
1 large (10 c) mixing bowl

1 large (approx. 16 x 24 in.) cutting board
1 plastic or plastic-coated stir-fry spatula
1 rubber or other heat-resistant spatula

PART 2

2 large skillets, each with a tight-fitting
    & opaque lid
1 each 5 & 7 in. serrated knife
1 chef's knife
1 small mixing bowl
1 dinner fork or whisk
1 timer

1 colander
1 dinner plate
1 mortar & pestle or electric spice grinder
1 medium nonstick skillet with a tight-
    fitting & opaque lid
1 hand citrus juicer
1 small mixing bowl

1. **Gather all ingredients and cooking tools.**

2. **Prepare the meatballs.**

    - Heat a large skillet on a large burner at a low setting. Add 1 c canned beef broth to the skillet.
    - Thoroughly combine the ½ c panko, spices (1½ t curry powder, 1 t ground cumin, and 1 t garlic powder), and 1 t salt in a large mixing bowl.
    - Break up the meat into small (½ in. thick) chunks and spread it over the crumb mixture in the bowl.
    - Use a 5 in. serrated knife to mince the ginger and spread the ginger over the meat.
    - Use your hands to roughly mix the meat, ginger root, and panko and spice mixture together.
    - Add 1 egg to a small mixing bowl and use a dinner fork or whisk to mix the yolk and white.
    - Evenly pour the egg over the ground meat mixture. Combine the ingredients gently (using your hands works best), avoiding compacting the meat, which will toughen the texture of the meatballs. Gently press the meat into 1 in. balls. Keep the meatballs small for fast and even cooking.
    - Add the meatballs to the skillet as they are formed.
    - When all meatballs are added, increase the burner heat to medium-high.
    - Immediately use soap to thoroughly wash your hands. Immediately clean the mixing bowl with soap or separate it from other dishes until thoroughly cleaned with soap to avoid any possible contamination by bacteria that can be on raw ground meat.
    - When the broth boils, use a dinner fork to flip the balls.
    - Lower the heat to medium-low and cook the meatballs partly covered (do not tightly cover them, which will toughen the meat) for 20 minutes, setting a timer. Adjust the heat level as may be necessary to maintain gentle (not rapid) boiling. Turn the balls one or two times during this cooking.
    - At the timer, remove the pan from the heat, cover the skillet, and set it aside.

3. **Prepare the spinach and bell pepper as the meatballs cook.**

    - **Stir-fry the spinach.**

- Heat another large skillet on a large burner at a medium setting.
- Bunch the spinach leaves on a large cutting board. Holding the leaves loosely together with one hand, use a 7 in. serrated knife to slice the spinach into approx. ⅓ in. thick slices, cutting lengthwise and crosswise through the leaves.
- Increase the skillet heat to medium-high, and when a drop of water added to the skillet instantly dances and disappears, add 1 T oil, add the spinach, and stir-fry it about 1 minute until it is evenly darkened in color and slightly wilted, turning it over and over.
- Remove the skillet from the heat, evenly sprinkle ¼ t salt over the spinach, and use a rubber spatula to scrape it and any cooking juice into a colander placed over a dinner plate for collecting juice. Wipe the skillet clean.

- **Stir-fry the bell peppers.**

  - Heat the large skillet at a medium setting.
  - Use a 5 in. serrated knife to cut out the stem ends of each pepper. Remove the seeds but not the white membrane. Use the 5 in. serrated knife to cut each pepper lengthwise into ¼ in. thick slices and to cut the slices crosswise into ¼ in. cubes.
  - Increase the skillet heat to medium-high, and when a drop of water added to the skillet instantly dances and disappears, add ¾ T oil, add the peppers, and vigorously stir-fry them for about 30 seconds.
  - Reduce the heat to medium and cook the peppers for 2 minutes, stirring occasionally and setting a timer.
  - At the timer, use a rubber spatula to scrape the peppers and any cooking juice into the colander next to the spinach.
  - Wipe the skillet clean.

4. **Prepare the curry sauce.**

   - Remove the cardamom seeds from the pods and crush them using either a mortar and pestle or electric spice grinder. Measure ½ t cardamom, adding more seeds as necessary to make ½ teaspoon.
   - Heat a large skillet on a large burner at a medium setting.
   - Place ½ onion cut side down on a cutting board and use a chef's knife to cut off its ends. Peel the onion. Again place the onion cut side down on the cutting board and use the chef's knife to dice the onion. Mince the two slices of ginger root.
   - Increase the skillet heat to medium-high, and when a drop of water added to the skillet instantly dances and disappears, add 1 T oil, add and heat 1 t cumin seed for 30 seconds, add the onion and ginger, evenly sprinkle the spices (2½ t curry powder, ½ t ground cinnamon, ½ t garlic powder, and ½ t crushed or ground cardamom) over the onion mixture, and stir-fry the onion mixture for 1 minute, setting a timer. Stir-frying should at first be vigorous but can slow to "flip often" pace midway through the minute.
   - At the timer, lower the heat to medium and cook the onion mixture for 2 minutes, stirring it occasionally and setting a timer.

PART 2

- At the timer, stir in 1 c canned broth, bring the broth to boiling, reduce the heat to low, mix in ⅓ t salt, partially cover the skillet, and very gently boil the curry sauce for 5 minutes, setting a timer.
- While the curry sauce cooks, prepare remaining curry ingredients. Open the canned coconut, stir it thoroughly, and measure ½ cup. Use a chef's knife to halve the dried cherries and pecans.
- At the timer, uncover the skillet and mix the stirred canned coconut milk, 2 T raisins, and 1½ T dried cherries into the curry sauce.
- Use a rubber spatula to scrape the meatballs into the curry sauce. Thoroughly mix in the meatballs.
- If the curry will not be assembled soon, remove the skillet from the heat, cover it, and set it aside.

5. **Assemble the curry for serving.**

   - Heat the meatball curry sauce at a medium setting.
   - Begin heating the rice. Bring 3 T water to boiling over medium-high heat in a medium nonstick skillet. Add, break up, and mix the rice thoroughly in the water. Reduce the heat to a very low setting, evenly sprinkle ⅓ t salt over the rice, cover the rice, and slowly heat the rice while assembling the curry for serving. Stir the rice occasionally and add 1-2 T water as may be needed to keep the rice from sticking to the skillet.
   - Stir yogurt until creamy smooth before measuring ⅓ c for use in the sauce and 1 c yogurt for use as an accompaniment.
   - Squeeze the lemon. Add the juice, ⅓ c yogurt, and 1½ T packed brown sugar to a small mixing bowl and stir the mixture until smooth.
   - Use a rubber spatula to mix the yogurt mixture into the curry sauce, stirring quickly and constantly to prevent the yogurt from curdling.
   - Check the curry flavoring, adding touches (1-2 t) of lemon juice and sugar to taste. If the curry sauce is very thick, mix in ½ c broth.
   - Increase the skillet temperature to medium-high and heat the curry sauce until it begins to boil, stirring it often.
   - Reduce the heat to medium and heat the curry for several minutes uncovered until the meatballs are thoroughly heated through, stirring regularly.
   - Add and stir in the cooked vegetables, any collected vegetable cooking juice, and the nuts. Heat the curry sauce for another 2 minutes until all ingredients are hot, stirring regularly.

6. **Serve the curry.**

   - If including the 1 t garam masala spice mixture, evenly sprinkle the spice over the hot curry sauce and stir it into the sauce shortly before serving.
   - Serve individual portions of curry over 1 c hot rice with 2 heaping dollops of yogurt and 1 T chutney alongside.

   VARIATIONS: Make ingredient substitutions. Substitute, for example,

- ½ lb (approx. 4 large leaves) **kale** (Recipe #26), **chard** (Recipe #24), **un-washed spinach** (Recipe #29), or **pre-washed baby greens** for spinach.
- ½ lb **green beans** (boiled whole, Recipe #58) for spinach. When assembling the curry for serving, trim the ends from the beans, use kitchen scissors to cut the beans into thirds, and add them to the hot assembled meatball curry sauce shortly before serving.
- **raw walnut halves, whole almonds,** or **whole cashews** for pecan halves.

Add ingredients. Add, for example,

- **4 large cauliflower florets** (Recipe #8). Break the florets into small (½ in. wide) florets. Sprinkle ½ t curry powder over the cauliflower while it stir-fries.
- ⅓ c **sliced fresh pineapple** (Recipe #94), cut into ¼ x ½ in. slices.
- **1 mild green chili** or **2 jalapeño peppers** (Recipe #36). Chili pepper adds distinctive flavor and a touch of authentic heat.
- ⅛ t (or to taste) **cayenne** or **ground red pepper.**
- **4 dried apricots,** halved lengthwise; each apricot half cut into thin strips.
- **8-10 medium cloves garlic** (Recipe #31). To best retain its distinctive flavor, add garlic as a topping to individual servings.
- **1 medium sweet potato,** stir-fry/steamed (Recipe #18) or baked (Recipe # 47), diced.

Omit ingredients. Omit, for example,

- ½ lb **spinach**.
- ½ t **cardamom**. While this spice adds distinctive and traditional curry flavor to curries, it can be omitted without undermining dish attractiveness.

COMMENTS: This curry freezes well, but do not add bell pepper and spinach to curry sauce that will be frozen. Add freshly cooked vegetables when the curry has been thawed and re-heated for serving.

The pungency of curry spices depends on freshness and the quality of spice products. This is important to keep in mind when first using spice products, especially in the case of spice mixtures like curry powder and garam masala. The amount of very fresh spices should be reduced slightly and cautiously added to taste.

189. Egg Curry
(4 servings)

Eggs with Seasoning

4 large eggs	¼ t salt

PART 2

Vegetables with Seasonings, Cooking Oil, and Cooking Water

1 medium zucchini (approx. 6 in. long, 1½ in. thick)
1 T extra virgin olive oil
½ t curry powder
¼ t salt
⅓ c fresh pineapple (Recipe #94)

¼ each red, green, & yellow bell pepper
1 T extra virgin olive oil
2 c dry frozen green peas, unthawed
2 T water
¼ t salt

Curry Sauce Ingredients

½ chilled medium yellow onion, split lengthwise
2 ⅛-in. thick slices ginger
1 T extra virgin olive oil
1 t cumin seed
2½ t curry powder
⅓ t ground cinnamon
1 T butter
1½ T whole wheat flour
¼ t salt
1 c vegetable or poultry broth
1 c milk (1%, 2%, or full fat)

1½ T certified organic raisins
1 T dried tart cherries
½ c canned regular coconut milk
½ lemon
1½ T packed dark brown sugar
⅓ c unflavored yogurt
¼-½ c milk (1%, 2%, or full fat)
¼ c raw pecan or cashew halves or raw whole almonds
½ c milk or broth

Accompaniments

3 T water
4 c cooked brown rice (Recipe #166)
⅓ t salt
¾ c plain yogurt

4 T mango chutney, commercially prepared (e.g. Major Grey) or fresh prepared (Recipe #196)

Cooking Tools

1 medium (8 c) saucepan with a lid
1 timer
1 large nonstick skillet with a tight-fitting & opaque lid
1 each chef's & 5 in. serrated knife
1 set each measuring spoons & cups
1 plastic or plastic-coated stir-fry spatula
1 rubber or other heat-resistant spatula

1 colander
1 dinner plate
1can opener
1 dinner spoon
1 medium (10 in.) nonstick skillet with a tight-fitting & opaque lid
1 hand citrus juicer
1 small mixing bowl

---

1. Gather all ingredients and cooking tools.

2. **Boil the eggs.**

    - Add the eggs to a medium saucepan and cover the eggs completely with cold water.
    - Heat the eggs over high heat. When the water begins to boil (water bubbles appear around the eggs), set a timer for 3 minutes. Reduce the heat slightly once the water boils fully to avoid breaking the eggs.
    - At the timer, remove the pan from the heat, cover it, and set it aside for 7 minutes, setting a timer.
    - At the timer, immediately drain the cooking water and rinse the eggs with cold water. Set the eggs aside in cool water to cool. For quick cooling, add ice to the water.

3. **Stir-fry/steam the zucchini.**

    - Heat a large nonstick skillet at a medium setting on a large back burner.
    - Rinse and dry the zucchini.
    - Use a chef's knife to cut off the ends of the zucchini. Stand it upright on a flattened end and cut it lengthwise into ¼ in. thick slices. Stacking two slices and holding the slices together with one hand, cut the slices lengthwise into ¼ in. thick strips and cut the strips crosswise into ¼ in. cubes.
    - Increase the skillet heat to medium-high. When a drop of water added to the skillet instantly dances and disappears, add 1 T oil to the skillet, add the zucchini, evenly sprinkle the curry powder over the zucchini, and stir-fry it for 1 minute, setting a timer. Stir-frying should at first be vigorous but can slow to "flip often" pace midway through the minute.
    - At the timer, cover the skillet, reduce the heat to low, and steam the zucchini for 4 minutes, setting a timer.
    - At the timer, uncover the skillet, evenly sprinkle ¼ t salt over the zucchini, and use a rubber spatula to scrape it into a colander placed over a dinner plate.
    - Wipe the skillet clean.

4. **Stir-fry the bell peppers.**

    - Heat the skillet on a large burner at a medium setting.
    - Use a 5 in. serrated knife to cut out the stem ends of the bell peppers. Remove any seeds but not the white membrane. Use the serrated knife to cut the peppers lengthwise into ¼ in. thick strips and to cut the strips crosswise into ¼ in. cubes.
    - Increase the skillet heat to medium-high, and when a drop of water added to the skillet instantly disappears, add 1 T oil, add the peppers, and vigorously stir-fry them for about 30 seconds.
    - Reduce the heat to medium and cook the peppers for 2 minutes, stirring them occasionally and setting a timer.
    - At the timer, use a rubber spatula to scrape the pepper and any cooking juice into the colander with the zucchini.
    - Wipe the skillet clean.

PART 2

5. **Stir-fry the green peas.**

    - Heat the skillet at a medium setting.
    - Break up any frozen clumps while the peas remain in the package.
    - Add 2 T water to the skillet, bring the water to full boiling over high heat, add the peas, and stir-fry them for 1 minute, just until the pieces are heated through.
    - Remove the skillet from the burner, evenly sprinkle ¼ t over the peas, and use a rubber spatula to scrape them and any cooking juice into the colander next to the bell pepper.
    - Wipe the skillet clean.

6. **Prepare the curry sauce.**

    - Heat the large nonstick skillet at a medium setting. Open the broth and coconut milk containers.
    - Place ½ onion cut side down on a cutting board and use a chef's knife to cut off its ends. Peel the onion. Again place the onion cut side down on the cutting board and use the chef's knife to dice the onion. Mince the ginger root.
    - Increase the skillet to medium-high, and when a drop of water added to the skillet instantly dances and disappears, add 1 T oil, add 1 t cumin seed, cook it for 30 seconds, add the onion and ginger, evenly sprinkle the spices (2½ t curry powder and ⅓ t ground cinnamon) over the onion/ginger, and stir-fry the mixture for 1 minute, setting a timer. Stir-frying should at first be vigorous but can slow to "flip often" pace midway through the minute.
    - At the timer, reduce the heat to medium and heat the onion mixture for 2 minutes, stirring it occasionally and setting a timer.
    - At the timer, add and melt 1 T butter. Sprinkle 1½ T flour and ¼ t salt evenly over the onion mixture.
    - Mix the ingredients together and cook the mixture for about 30 seconds, stirring often.
    - Increase the heat to a medium-high setting.
    - Slowly, stirring quickly and constantly with a rubber spatula, mix in 1 c broth. Continue the stirring until the flour is mixed into the broth and stir in the 1 c milk.
    - Cook the sauce until it thickens and is smooth, stirring it frequently.
    - Reduce the heat to low or a level that maintains very gentle boiling, mainly cover the skillet, and cook the sauce for 5 minutes, stirring across the skillet bottom occasionally to prevent sticking and setting a timer.
    - While the sauce cooks, use a dinner spoon to stir the coconut thoroughly before measuring ½ cup. Use a chef's knife to halve the dried cherries.
    - At the timer, mix the coconut milk, cherries, and 1½ T raisins into the hot sauce.
    - If the curry will not be assembled within a short time, remove the skillet from the heat, cover it, and set it aside.

7. **Assemble the curry for serving.**

- Return the curry sauce to the burner and heat it at a medium setting.
- Heat the rice. Add 3 T water to a medium nonstick skillet and bring the water to boiling over high heat. Add the rice, break up any clumps, evenly sprinkle ⅓ t salt over it, cover the skillet, reduce the heat to low, and slowly heat the rice while assembling the curry. Stir the rice periodically throughout this heating and add a touch more water as may be needed to prevent sticking.
- Make final ingredient dish preparations.

   - Prepare the eggs. Peel the eggs, halve each lengthwise, cut each half lengthwise into three wedges, and evenly sprinkle ¼ t salt over the wedges.
   - Use a chef's knife to chop the nuts coarsely.
   - Stir the yogurt creamy smooth before measuring ⅓ c and 1 c yogurt.
   - Squeeze the ½ lemon. Using a rubber spatula, combine the lemon juice, 1½ T packed brown sugar, and ⅓ c yogurt in a small mixing bowl.

- Scrape part of the yogurt mixture into the curry sauce at a time, stirring the sauce quickly and constantly after each addition to avoid curdling the yogurt.
- Check the sauce flavoring, adding touches (1-2 t) more lemon juice for tartness or sugar for sweetening. If the sauce is too thick, add ¼-½ c milk for thinning.
- Increase the skillet heat to medium-high and heat the sauce to near boiling, stirring regularly.
- Distributing the vegetables evenly over the curry, add and mix in the zucchini, bell peppers, green peas, and any vegetable cooking liquid. Add the nuts.
- Heat the curry sauce approx. 2-3 minutes until it is near boiling, stirring often.
- Reduce the heat to medium and arrange the egg wedges over the curry sauce, white side up. Heat the curry 2-3 minutes to heat through the eggs.

8. **Serve the curry.** Serve individual portions of curry over 1 c hot brown rice with 2 heaping dollops of yogurt and 1 T chutney served alongside.

VARIATIONS: Make ingredient substitutions. Substitute, for example,

- **2 c diced tofu** for eggs, **soy** or **other non-dairy milk** for dairy milk, and **extra virgin olive oil** for butter to convert the curry into **vegan vegetarian form.**

   - **To prepare the tofu,** thoroughly drain and cut 8-10 oz extra firm tofu into ½ in. cubes. Thoroughly combine 1 t curry powder, ½ t ground cumin, ¼ t ground ginger, and ½ t garlic powder. Evenly sprinkle spices over the tofu and toss the cubes to mix the flavoring evenly. Pre-heat a medium or large skillet to medium-high, add 1 T extra virgin olive oil, add the tofu, stir-fry the tofu for about 30 seconds, reduce the heat to medium, and cook the tofu for another 2 minutes, stirring it regularly. Transfer the tofu to another container, cover it, and set it aside until assembling the curry for serving.

- **2 small (4-6 in.) yellow summer squash** for zucchini.

- **2 c small or medium sugar snap peas** for green peas. Sort the pods by size, selecting small or medium pods for cooking. Cook them like the green peas. Cut the peas crosswise into thirds when assembling the curry for serving (Step #6).

Add ingredients. Add, for example,

- ½ c fresh pineapple chunks (Recipe #94), chunks sliced into ¼ in. thick pieces.
- 2 c okra (Recipe #13).
- ½ lb pre-washed spinach (Recipe #28), pre-washed baby greens (a mixture that includes sturdy greens like kale and beet greens), or any variety of greens (Recipes #23-30). Greens blend perfectly.
- 1 medium sweet potato (Recipe #18, 1 baked sweet potato (Recipe #47), or 1 c canned sweet potato.
- ½-1 mild green chili or 1-2 jalapeño peppers (Recipe #36). Chili peppers add special and distinctive flavor. Cook the chilies with the bell peppers, adding the chilies after stir-frying the bell peppers for 30 seconds.
- ⅛ t cayenne powder, added to the stir-frying onion with the other spices.
- 1 t chopped cilantro added as a topping to each individual serving.

COMMENTS: To re-heat the curry, heat ½ c milk in a large nonstick skillet over medium-high heat until hot, mix in the curry, and heat the curry until it boils, stirring often.

To freeze this curry, double the curry sauce and set aside ½ of this curry sauce before adding the eggs and vegetables, which do not freeze well. Freeze the curry sauce in serving size amounts and add freshly cooked eggs and vegetables for serving.

190. Eggplant Curry
(4 servings)

Beef with Seasonings and Cooking Oil

½ lb extra lean ground beef
⅛ in. thick slice ginger root
1 t curry powder
¼ t ginger powder

½ t garlic powder
2 t extra virgin olive oil
¼ t salt

Vegetables with Seasonings, Cooking Oil, and Cooking Water

1 chilled small or ½ medium globe eggplant
    or 2 medium Japanese eggplants
    (to yield approx. 2 c diced)

1 T extra virgin olive oil
1 T hot water
¼ t salt

COOKED ALIVE!

1 T extra virgin olive oil
½ t curry powder
1 T hot water
¼ t salt
4 medium carrots

¼ each red, yellow, & green bell pepper
¾ T extra virgin olive oil
½ lb pre-washed spinach
1 T extra virgin olive oil
¼ t salt

Curry Sauce Ingredients

½ chilled medium onion, halved lengthwise
2 ⅛-in. thick slices of ginger root
1 T extra virgin olive oil
2½ t curry powder
½ t ground cinnamon
⅓ t ginger powder
6-8 green cardamom pods
½ t garlic powder
1 c beef broth

¼ t salt
½ c regular canned coconut milk
2 T certified organic raisins
1 T dried tart cherries
⅓ c unflavored yogurt
½-¾ lemon
1½ T packed dark brown sugar
¼ c pecan, walnut, or cashew halves
½ c broth

Dish Accompaniments

3 T water
4 c cooked brown rice (Recipe #66)
⅓ t salt
¾ c unflavored yogurt

4 T mango chutney, commercially prepared (e.g., Major Grey) or fresh prepared (Recipe #166)

Cooking Tools

1 each medium nonstick and 1 large skillet with a tight-fitting & opaque lid
1 5 in. serrated knife
1 each set measuring spoons & cups
1 plastic or plastic-coated stir-fry spatula
1 timer
1 rubber or other heat-resistant spatula
1 each small & medium mixing bowl
1 electric tea kettle
1 each chef's & 7 in. serrated knife

1 colander
1 dinner plate
1 large (approx. 16 x 24 in.) cutting board
1 mortar & pestle or electric spice grinder
1 can opener
1 dinner spoon
1 medium (10 in.) nonstick skillet with a tight-fitting & opaque lid
1 hand citrus juicer

---

1. **Gather all ingredients and cooking tools.**

2. **Cook the ground beef.**

    - Heat a medium nonstick skillet on a large back burner at a medium setting.

- Use a 5 in. serrated knife to mince the ginger root.
- Increase the skillet heat to medium-high. When a drop of water added to the skillet instantly dances and disappears, add and spread 2 t oil over the skillet bottom. Add the ground beef and ginger root and use a stir-fry spatula to break the ground meat into small (⅓ in. thick) chunks. Thoroughly wash your hands with soap if you have any direct contact with the ground meat to avoid being contaminated by any bacteria that may be on the meat.
- Evenly sprinkle the spices (1 t curry powder, ¼ t ginger, and ½ t garlic powder) over the meat, mix the spices into the meat, and stir-fry the meat for about 30 seconds.
- Reduce the heat to medium and cook the meat approx. 5 minutes until all traces of raw red coloring disappears, flipping pieces regularly and setting a timer.
- At the timer, or when the meat is cooked through remove the skillet from the heat, evenly sprinkle ¼ t salt over the meat.
- Use a rubber spatula to scrape the meat into a small bowl. Slant the bowl as may be needed to drain any juice away from the meat.
- Wipe the skillet clean.

3. **Stir-fry/steam the eggplant.**

   - While the meat cooks, heat a large skillet on a large front burner at a medium setting. Heat an electric tea kettle to prepare hot water for steaming.
   - Rinse and dry the eggplant.
   - Use a chef's knife to slice the ends from the eggplant. Stand the eggplant upright on a flattened end and cut it lengthwise into ¼ in. thick slices. Stacking two slices together and holding the slices together with one hand, cut the slices lengthwise into ¼ in. wide strips. Cut the strips crosswise into ¼ in. cubes.
   - Increase the skillet heat to medium-high. When a drop of water added to the skillet instantly dances and disappears, add 1 T oil, add the eggplant, evenly sprinkle ½ t curry powder over the eggplant, and stir-fry the eggplant for 1 minute, setting a timer. Stir-frying should at first be vigorous but can slow to "flip often" pace midway through the minute.
   - At the timer, add 1 T hot water, cover the skillet, reduce the heat to low, and steam the eggplant for 4 minutes, setting a timer.
   - At the timer, remove the skillet from the heat, evenly sprinkle ¼ t salt over the eggplant, and use a rubber spatula to scrape the eggplant and any cooking juice into a colander placed over a dinner plate for collecting juice.
   - Wipe the skillet clean.

4. **Stir-fry/steam the 4 carrots.**

   - Heat the large skillet at a medium setting. Heat the electric tea kettle to prepare hot water for steaming.
   - Scrub and dry the carrots.
   - Use a chef's knife to cut off the ends, split the carrots lengthwise, and cut the carrots halves crosswise into ⅛ in. thick slices.

- Increase the skillet heat to medium-high. When a drop of water added to the skillet instantly dances and disappears, add 1 T oil, add the carrots, and stir-fry them for 1 minute, setting a timer. Stir-frying should at first be vigorous but can slow to "flip often" pace midway through the minute.
- At the timer, add 1 T hot water, cover the skillet, reduce the heat to low, and steam the carrots for 4 minutes, setting a timer.
- At the timer, remove the skillet from the burner, evenly sprinkle ¼ t salt over the carrots, and use a rubber spatula to scrape it and any cooking juice into the colander with the eggplant.
- Wipe the skillet clean.

5. **Stir-fry the bell peppers.**

    - Heat the skillet at a medium setting.
    - Use a 5 in. serrated knife to cut out the stem end from each pepper. Remove any seeds but not the white membrane. Use the serrated knife to cut the peppers lengthwise into ¼ in. thick strips and to cut the strips crosswise into ¼ in. cubes.
    - Increase the skillet heat to medium-high, add ¾ T oil, add the peppers, and vigorously stir-fry them for 30 seconds.
    - Reduce the heat to medium and cook the peppers for 2 minutes, stirring them occasionally and setting a timer.
    - At the timer, use a rubber spatula to scrape the peppers and any cooking juice into the colander alongside the other cooked vegetables.
    - Wipe the skillet clean.

6. **Stir-fry the spinach.**

    - Heat the large skillet at a medium setting.
    - Working on a large cutting board, loosely stack or bunch the spinach leaves.
    - Holding the leaves loosely together with one hand, use a 7 in. serrated knife to slice the spinach into approx. ⅓ in. thick pieces, cutting lengthwise and crosswise through the leaves.
    - Increase the skillet heat to medium high, and when a drop of water added to the skillet instantly dances and disappears, add 1 T oil, add the spinach, and constantly stir-fry it about 1 minute until it is evenly darkened in color and slightly wilted, turning the leaves over and over.
    - Remove the skillet from the heat, evenly sprinkle ¼ t salt over the spinach, and use a rubber spatula to scrape it and any cooking juice into the colander alongside, but separate from, the other vegetables.
    - Wipe the skillet clean.

7. **Prepare the curry sauce.**

    - Remove the cardamom seeds from the pods and either crush the seeds using a mortar and pestle or grind them using an electric spice grinder. Measure ½ t cardamom.

PART 2

- Open the broth and measure 1 cup.
- Heat the large skillet at a medium setting.
- Place ½ onion cut side down on a cutting board and use a chef's knife to cut off its tips. Peel the onion. Return the onion cut side down to the cutting board and use the chef's knife to dice the onion. Mince the ginger root.
- Increase the skillet heat to medium-high, and when a drop of water added to the skillet instantly dances and disappears, add 1 T oil, add and heat the 1 t cumin seed for 30 seconds, add the onion and ginger, evenly sprinkle the spices (2½ t curry, ½ t ground cinnamon, ⅓ t ginger powder, and ½ t crushed cardamom) and ½ t garlic powder over the onion and ginger, and stir-fry the mixture for 1 minute, setting a timer. Stir-frying should at first be vigorous but can slow to "flip often" pace midway through the minute.
- At the timer, reduce the heat to medium and cook the mixture for 2 minutes, stirring the onion mixture occasionally and setting a timer.
- At the timer, mix in 1 c broth and ¼ t salt, bring the broth to boiling, reduce the heat setting to one that maintains gentle boiling, mainly cover the skillet, and cook the sauce for 5 minutes, stirring the sauce occasionally and setting a timer.
- While the sauce cooks, ready remaining curry sauce ingredients. Open the coconut milk container and use a dinner spoon to thoroughly mix the coconut before measuring ½ c coconut milk. Use a chef's knife to halve 1 T dried tart cherries.
- At the timer, add the coconut milk, 2 T raisins, and dried cherries to the curry sauce.
- If the curry will not be assembled soon, remove the skillet from the heat, cover it, and set it aside.

8. **Assemble the curry for serving.**

    - Heat the curry sauce at a medium heat setting.
    - Begin heating the rice. Bring 3 T water to boiling over medium-high heat in a medium nonstick skillet, mix in the 4 c brown rice, break up any clumps of rice, evenly sprinkle ⅓ t salt over the rice, mix in the salt, reduce the heat to a very low setting, cover the rice, and heat it while assembling the dish for serving. Stir the rice occasionally during this heating and add a touch more water as may be needed to keep the rice from sticking to the skillet.
    - Do final ingredient preparations.

        - Use a chef's knife to chop the nuts coarsely.
        - Stir yogurt until creamy smooth before measuring ⅓ c and ¾ c yogurt.
        - Squeeze the ½ lemon and add the lemon juice, ⅓ c yogurt, 1½ T packed dark brown sugar to a small bowl. Mix the ingredients together until smooth.

    - Scrape the yogurt/lemon/brown sugar mixture into the curry sauce in parts, stirring quickly and constantly after each addition to keep the yogurt from curdling.
    - Check the curry sauce flavoring, adding touches (1-2 t) of lemon juice for tartness and brown sugar for sweetening. If the curry is too thick, add ½ c broth to thin it.

- Increase the skillet heat to medium-high and add the meat, cooked vegetables except for the spinach, nuts, and any collected vegetable cooking liquid.
- Heat the curry sauce to near boiling, stirring frequently.
- Stir in the spinach and heat the sauce another 2 minutes, stirring the sauce often.

9. **Serve the curry.** Serve individual portions of curry over 1 c hot brown rice with 2 dollops of yogurt and 1 T chutney served alongside.

VARIATIONS: Make ingredient substitutions. Substitute, for example,

- **vegetable broth** for beef broth and omit the beef to convert the curry to **traditional vegetarian form**.
- **vegetable broth** for beef broth and **soy yogurt** for dairy yogurt and omit the beef to convert the dish to **vegan vegetarian form**,
- **½ lb kale** (Recipe #26), **beet greens** (Recipe #23), **chard** (Recipe 24), or **unwashed spinach** (Recipe # 29) for pre-washed spinach.
- **2 c dry frozen green peas** (Recipe #71) for spinach.
- **½ lb lean beefsteak**, cut into small pieces, for ground beef. Cook it in the same way except that beefsteak can remain somewhat pink in color. Cut the beefsteak on a cutting board reserved for raw meat and either immediately clean the board with soap or set it aside separate from other utensils and ingredients until later cleaning. Wash your hands and the cutting knife with soap after adding the meat to the skillet for stir-frying.
- **1 T toasted sesame oil** for extra virgin olive oil for cooking the eggplant and the onion and ginger root in the curry sauce.

Add ingredients. Add, for example,

- **2 c small or medium okra** (Recipe #13).
- **2 c dry frozen green peas** (Recipe #71), unthawed.
- **1 t garam masala**, sprinkled over and mixed into the curry while heating the curry for serving.
- **1 T powdered coconut milk**, using a dinner fork or whisk to mix it into the canned coconut milk to enhance its coconut flavor.

191. Vegetable Curry
(4 servings)

Vegetables with Seasonings, Cooking Oil, and Cooking Water

2 medium red potatoes
1 T extra virgin olive oil

1 T extra virgin olive oil
½ t curry powder

PART 2

1 t curry powder
1 T hot water
⅓ t salt
4 medium carrots
1 T extra virgin olive oil
½ t curry powder
1 T hot water
¼ t salt
6 large cauliflower florets with 1-2-in stems

⅓ t ground cinnamon
1 T hot water
¼ t salt
⅓ each red & green bell pepper, sliced lengthwise
½ T extra virgin olive oil
2 c small sugar snap peas
2 T water
¼ t salt

Curry Sauce Ingredients

½ chilled medium onion, halved lengthwise
2 ⅛-in thick slices ginger root
1 T extra virgin olive oil
1 t cumin seeds
2½ t curry powder
⅓ t ground cinnamon
¼ t ground ginger
1 T butter
1½ T whole wheat flour
¼ t salt

1 c vegetable broth
1 c milk (1%, 2%, or full fat)
1½ T certified organic raisins
1 T dried tart cherries
½ c canned regular coconut milk
½ lemon
1-1½ T packed dark brown sugar
⅓ c plain yogurt
¼ c raw pecan, walnut, or cashew halves
½-1 c milk or vegetable broth

Accompaniments

3 T water
4 c cooked brown rice (Recipe #166)
⅓ t salt
¾ c plain yogurt

1 T mango chutney, commercially prepared (e.g. Major Grey's) or fresh prepared (Recipe #196)

Cooking Tools

1 each regular and nonstick large skillets, each with a tight-fitting & opaque lid
1 electric tea kettle
1 each chef's & 5 in. serrated knife
1 set each measuring spoons & cups
1 plastic or plastic-coated stir-fry spatula
1 timer
1 rubber or other heat-resistant spatula

2 colanders
2 dinner plates
1 medium nonstick skillet with a tight-fitting & opaque lid
1 hand citrus juicer
1 small mixing bowl
1 pair kitchen scissors

---

1. **Gather all ingredients and cooking tools.**

2. **Stir-fry/steam the potatoes.**

   - Heat a large skillet at a medium setting. Heat an electric tea kettle to prepare hot water for steaming.
   - Scrub and dry the potatoes. Use a chef's knife to cut off the tips and any eyes from each potato. Stand each potato upright on a flattened end and use a chef's knife to cut each potato lengthwise into ¼ in. thick slices, cut the slices lengthwise into ¼ in. thick strips, and cut the strips crosswise into ¼ in. cubes.
   - Increase the skillet heat to medium-high, and when a drop of water added to the skillet instantly dances and disappears, add 1 T oil, add the diced potatoes, evenly sprinkle 1 t curry powder over the potatoes, and stir-fry them for 1 minute, setting a timer. Stir-frying should at first be vigorous but can slow to "flip often" pace midway through the minute.
   - At the timer, reduce the heat to medium and cook the potatoes for 1 minute, stirring them occasionally and setting a timer.
   - At the timer, add 1 T hot water, reduce the heat to medium low, cover the pan, and steam the potato for 10 minutes, setting a timer.
   - At the timer, turn off the heat, uncover the potatoes, evenly sprinkle ⅓ t salt over them, re-cover the skillet, and set it aside.

3. **Stir-fry/steam the 4 carrots.**

   - Heat a large nonstick skillet at a medium setting. Heat an electric tea kettle to prepare hot water for steaming.
   - Scrub and dry the carrots. Use a chef's knife to cut off the ends, halve the carrots lengthwise, and cut the carrot halves crosswise into ⅛ in. thick slices.
   - Increase the skillet heat to medium-high. When a drop of water added to the skillet instantly dances and disappears, add 1 T oil, add the carrot, evenly sprinkle ½ t curry powder over it, and stir-fry the carrot for 1 minute, setting a timer. Stir-frying should at first be vigorous but can slow to "flip often" pace midway through the minute.
   - At the timer, add 1 T hot water, cover the skillet, reduce the heat to low, and steam the carrot for 4 minutes, setting a timer.
   - At the timer, remove the skillet from the burner, evenly sprinkle ¼ t salt over the carrot, and use a rubber spatula to scrape it and any cooking juice into a colander placed over a dinner plate.
   - Wipe the skillet clean.

4. **Stir-fry/steam the 6 cauliflower florets.**

   - Heat the large nonstick skillet at a medium setting. Heat an electric tea kettle to heat water for steaming.
   - Rinse and pat dry the cauliflower florets. Use a 5 in. serrated knife to cut the stems from the florets and to cut them crosswise into ¼ in. thick slices.
   - Break the florets into small (approx. ½ in. wide) florets.

PART 2

- Increase the skillet heat to medium-high. When a drop of water added to the skillet instantly dances and disappears, add 1 T oil, add cauliflower florets and stems, evenly sprinkle ½ t curry powder and ⅓ t ground cinnamon over the cauliflower, and stir-fry the cauliflower for 1 minute. Stir-frying should at first be vigorous but can slow to "flip often" pace midway through the minute.
- At the timer, add 1 T hot water, cover the skillet, reduce the heat to low, and steam the cauliflower for 4 minutes, setting a timer.
- At the timer, remove the skillet from the heat, evenly sprinkle ¼ t salt over the cauliflower, and use a rubber spatula to scrape it and any juice into the colander with the carrot.
- Wipe the skillet clean.

5. **Stir-fry the bell peppers.**

    - Heat the large nonstick skillet at a medium setting.
    - Use a 5 in. serrated knife to cut out the stem end of each pepper. Remove any seeds but not the white membrane. Use the serrated knife to slice each pepper lengthwise into ¼ in. thick strips and to cut the strips crosswise into ¼ in. cubes.
    - Increase the burner heat to medium-high, and when a drop of water added to the skillet instantly dances and disappears, add ¾ T oil, add the peppers, and vigorously stir-fry them for about 30 seconds.
    - Reduce the heat to medium and heat the peppers for 2 minutes, stirring occasionally and setting a timer.
    - At the timer, use a rubber spatula to scrape the peppers and any cooking juice into the colander with the other cooked vegetables.

6. **Stir-fry the sugar snap peas.**

    - Rinse the peas, shake off most clinging water, and drain them in a second colander.
    - Bring 2 T water to boiling over high heat in the large nonstick skillet, add the peas, and once the water again boils, stir-fry the peas for 1 minute, setting a timer.
    - At the timer, remove the skillet from the heat, evenly sprinkle ¼ t salt over the peas, add them to a second colander placed over a plate, and set them aside.
    - Wipe the skillet clean.

7. **Prepare the curry sauce.**

    - Heat the large nonstick skillet at a medium setting.
    - Open the vegetable broth container and measure 1 cup broth.
    - Place ½ onion cut side down on a cutting board and use a chef's knife to cut off its tips. Peel the onion. Return the onion cut side down on the cutting board and use the chef's knife to dice the onion. Mince the ginger root.
    - Increase the skillet heat to medium-high, and when a drop of water added to the skillet instantly dances and disappears, add 1 T oil, add and heat the 1 t cumin seed for 30 seconds, add the onion and ginger, evenly sprinkle the spices (2½ t curry

powder, ⅓ t ground cinnamon, and ¼ t ground ginger) over the onion and ginger, and stir-fry the mixture for 1 minute, setting a timer. Stir-frying should at first be vigorous but can slow to "flip often" pace midway through the minute.
- At the timer, reduce the heat to medium and cook the onion mixture for 2 minutes, stirring it occasionally and setting a timer.
- At the timer, add and melt 1 T butter. Sprinkle 1½ T flour and ¼ t salt evenly over the onion mixture. Mix the ingredients together and cook the mixture for about 30 seconds, stirring occasionally.
- Increase the heat to medium-high and slowly stir in 1 c vegetable broth while quickly and constantly stirring the mixture with a rubber spatula. Continue the stirring until the sauce is somewhat smooth and stir in 1 c milk.
- Bring the curry sauce to boiling, reduce the heat setting to one that maintains gentle boiling, mainly cover the skillet, and cook the sauce for 5 minutes, stirring the sauce occasionally and setting a timer.
- While the sauce cooks, prepare remaining ingredients. Use a dinner spoon to thoroughly stir the coconut milk before measuring ½ c coconut milk. Use a chef's knife to halve 1 T dried cherries. Measure 1½ T raisins.
- At the timer, mix the coconut milk, dried cherries, and raisins into the hot curry sauce.
- If the curry will not be assembled soon, cover the skillet, remove it from the heat, and set it aside.

8. **Assemble the curry for serving.**

    - Heat the curry sauce at a medium setting.
    - Re-heat the cooked brown rice. Bring 3 T water to boiling over medium-high heat in a medium nonstick skillet, add and break up the 4 c brown rice, evenly sprinkle ⅓ t salt over the rice, cover the skillet, reduce the heat to low, and slowly heat the rice while assembling the curry. Stir the rice periodically during this heating and add touches of water as may be needed to prevent sticking.
    - Make final curry ingredient preparations.

        - Use kitchen scissors to snip the tips from the sugar snap peas and to halve them. Add the peas to the other cooked vegetables.
        - Stir the yogurt creamy smooth and measure ⅓ c and ¾ c yogurt.
        - Squeeze ½ lemon and add the lemon juice, 1½ T packed dark brown sugar, and ⅓ c yogurt to a small mixing bowl. Stir the ingredients together.
        - Use a chef's knife to chop the nuts coarsely.

    - Scrape the lemon juice/brown sugar/yogurt mixture into the hot curry sauce in parts, quickly stirring each addition to prevent the yogurt from curdling.
    - Check the curry sauce flavoring, adding touches (1-2 t) more lemon juice and/or brown sugar to taste. If the sauce is too thick, add ½-1 c milk or vegetable broth.
    - Increase the skillet heat to medium-high and heat the curry sauce to near boiling, stirring it often with a rubber spatula.

- Add the potatoes, other cooked vegetables, and any collected vegetable cooking juice and again heat the sauce to near boiling, frequently stirring it and often rubbing the spatula across the skillet bottom to prevent sticking.
- When the sauce is near boiling, reduce the heat to medium and heat the curry sauce for 2-3 minutes until all ingredients are hot, stirring it often.

9. **Serve the curry.** Serve individual portions of curry over 1 c hot brown rice with 2 dollops of yogurt and 1 T chutney served alongside.

VARIATIONS: Make ingredient substitutions. Substitute, for example,

- **soy** or **other non-dairy milk** for dairy milk, **extra virgin olive oil** for butter, and **soy yogurt** for dairy yogurt to convert the curry to **vegan vegetarian form.**
- **2 c dry frozen green peas**, unthawed, for sugar snap peas, stir-fried in the same way.
- **1 medium sweet potato** for 1 red potato, stir-fry/steaming it with the remaining red potato. Alternatively, substitute **1 diced baked sweet potato** (Recipe #47) for 1 red potato.

Add ingredients. Add, for example,

- ½ lb small okra (Recipe #13).
- ½ c fresh pineapple chunks (Recipe #94), cut into ¼ x ½ in. pieces.
- ½ lb pre-washed spinach (Recipe #28), ½ lb baby greens (mixture that includes kale and beet greens, cooked like spinach), ½ lb kale (Recipe #26), or **any other greens** (Recipes #23-30).
- 1 medium zucchini or 2 small yellow summer squash (Recipe #20).
- 1 tasty apple. See Reference #11 (Clinching Curry Flavor: Expanded Preparation Support, Suggestion #3) for preparation details.
- 1 medium turnip (Recipe #22) or 2 medium parsnips (Recipe #14).
- ⅓ lb bok choy (Recipe #3).
- 1 mild green chili pepper or 1-2 jalapeño peppers (Recipe #36).
- 1/8 t cayenne.
- 1 t snipped cilantro, added as a topping on each individual serving.
- 1 T coconut powder. Use a dinner fork or whisk to mix the powder into the canned coconut milk to enhance its coconut flavor.
- ¼ c dried unsweetened shredded coconut. As a first curry preparation step, bring ¼ c water to boiling in a small skillet, mix in the coconut, remove the skillet from the heat, and set it aside covered. Mix the coconut into the curry when assembling it for serving.

Curry Accompaniment Recipes

192. Spiced Yogurt
(Raita)
(4 servings)

Ingredients

1 c plain yogurt
½ t ground cumin
¼ t chili powder
¼ t salt

½ chilled medium Japanese cucumber
   or 1 small or ½ medium regular
   cucumber
2-4 sprigs fresh mint (to yield 2 T
   minced), opt

Cooking Utensils

1 set each measuring cups & spoons
1 small (2 c) glass serving bowl
1 stirring spoon
1 each chef's & 5 in. serrated knife

1 cutting board for vegetables
1 vegetable peeler
1 vegetable shredder with a coarse setting

---

1. **Add the yogurt to a glass serving bowl.** Stir it until creamy smooth.

2. **Add the spice flavoring.**

    - Add and mix ½ t ground cumin, ¼ t chili powder, and ¼ t salt into the yogurt.
    - Refrigerate the yogurt for at least 30 minutes.

3. **Prepare fresh mint.**

    - Rinse the mint under cool water, shake it to remove excess liquid, and spread it over a layer of paper towels. Roll the paper towels around the mint to dry the leaves.
    - Remove the leaves from the stems, keeping the stems.
    - Use a serrated knife to slice the leaves into small pieces on a cutting board.
    - Holding the stems together with one hand, cut the stems crosswise into thin pieces.

4. **Prepare the cucumber shortly before serving.** Use a chef's knife to slice the ends from the cucumber. Peel commercially-produced cucumber. If it has large seeds, halve the cucumber lengthwise and scrape out the seeds. Coarsely grate the cucumber onto plastic wrap.

5. **Assemble the raita for serving.** Add the cucumber and mint to the cooled spiced yogurt and stir the ingredients to mix them.

VARIATION: Substitute ½ **c fresh pineapple** (Recipe #94), thinly sliced and drained, ½ **medium banana**, diced, and/or ½ **ripe mango**, diced, for cucumber.

COMMENTS: Adding the cucumber as a last ingredient shortly before serving prevents cucumber juice from unattractively diluting the dish flavor and thinning its consistency.

193. Spiced Lentils (Dhal)
(4 servings)

Ingredients

½ chilled medium onion, halved lengthwise
⅛ in. wide slice fresh ginger root
1 T extra virgin olive oil
½ t cumin seeds
½ t chili powder

½ t ground coriander
1½ c cooked lentils (Recipe #168) or canned
½ c lentil broth (or lentil broth and water to yield ½ c)

Cooking Utensils

1 medium nonstick skillet with a lid
1 chef's knife
1 set each measuring spoons & cups

1 plastic or plastic-coated stir-fry spatula
1 timer
1 rubber or other heat-resistant spatula

1. **Cook the onion.**

   - Heat a large nonstick skillet on a large burner at a medium setting.
   - Use a chef's knife to cut off the ends of the ½ onion. Peel the onion, place the onion cut side down on a cutting board, and use the chef's knife to dice the onion. Mince the ginger.
   - Increase the skillet heat to medium-high, and when a drop of water added to the skillet instantly dances and disappears, add 1 T oil, add and heat ½ t cumin seeds for 30 seconds, add and mix in the onion and ginger, evenly sprinkle ½ t each chili powder and ground coriander over the onion mixture, and stir-fry the mixture for about 30 seconds.
   - Reduce the heat to medium and cook the onion mixture for 2 minutes, setting a timer.

2. **Mellow the spices.**

   - At the timer, add ½ c lentil broth to the onion, bring the broth to boiling, reduce the heat to low or a level that maintains gentle boiling, mainly cover the skillet, and cook the mixture for 5 minutes, stirring it occasionally with a rubber spatula and setting a timer.

- At the timer, use a rubber spatula to stir the lentils into the onion mixture. For unsalted lentils, sprinkle ¼ t salt over the lentils. If not serving the dish immediately, remove the skillet from the burner, cover it, and set it aside.

3. **Serve the dish.**

    - Heat the lentils for 3-4 minutes at medium until hot, stirring occasionally, and scrape the lentils into a dish for serving.

VARIATIONS: Add spices. Add, for example, **½ t ground cumin**, **¼ t ground cinnamon**, and/or **2 green cardamom pods**, seeds removed from pods and crushed with a mortar and pestle.

Add **½ T butter**. Add the butter to the hot lentils shortly before serving, stirring it into the lentils once it melts.

194. Pineapple Chutney
(4 servings)

Ingredients

⅓ c red wine vinegar
⅓ c packed dark brown sugar
¾ t ground ginger
⅛ t salt
⅛ t ground cloves

¼ c golden raisins
1 c canned pineapple chunks packed in pineapple juice, drained
¼ c raw whole almonds

Cooking, Serving, and Storage Utensils

1 small or medium stainless steel or other nonreactive saucepan with a lid
1 set each measuring cups & spoons
1 can opener
1 rubber or other heat-resistant spatula

1 timer
1 chef's knife
2 c glass serving dish
2 c glass storage container with lid

1. **Combine all the ingredients except for the almonds in the saucepan.**

2. **Cook the ingredients.**

- Bring the vinegar to boiling over medium-high heat, reduce the heat to a setting that maintains gentle boiling, mainly cover the pan, and cook the mixture for 15 minutes, stirring it occasionally with a rubber spatula and setting a timer.
- Prepare the almonds while other ingredients cook. Use a chef's knife to thinly slice them.
- At the timer and when the chutney liquid is somewhat thickened, remove the pan from the stove.
- Mix in the almonds.

3. **Assemble the chutney for serving.**

- Scrape the chutney into a glass serving container.
- Serve the chutney at room temperature.

4. **Store the chutney refrigerated in an air-tight glass container.** Use the chutney within a week or so.

VARIATION: Make ingredient substitutions. Substitute, for example,

- **organic dark raisins** for golden.
- **fresh pineapple chunks** (Recipe #94) for canned.

195. Apple Chutney
(4 servings)

Ingredients

¼ c premium orange juice with pulp
2 chilled tart apples
½ organic lemon, halved lengthwise
½ in. long piece of ginger root
  (¾-1 in. thick)
¼ c apple cider vinegar
⅓ c packed dark brown sugar
¼ c golden raisins or certified organic dark

⅛ t salt
⅛ t ground nutmeg
½ t ground cinnamon
¼ t ground ginger
$1/16$-⅛ t ground cloves
⅛ t cayenne or ¼ t medium hot chili powder
¼ c raw whole almonds

Cooking, Serving, and Storing Utensils

1 set each measuring cups & spoons
1 medium (2 qt) stainless steel or other
  nonreactive saucepan with a lid
1 each chef's, paring, & 5 in. serrated knife

1 cutting board for vegetables & fruits
1 rubber or other heat-resistant spatula
2 c glass serving bowl
2 c glass storage container with lid

1. Heat ¼ c orange juice in the saucepan at medium.

2. **Prepare the apples.** Rinse and dry the apples. Use a chef's knife to halve the apples lengthwise. Place each half cut side down on a cutting board and slice each apple lengthwise into 5-6 slices. Use a paring knife to cut out any core and seeds from the slices and to cut the slices crosswise into ⅓ in. thick chunks. Add the apple chunks to the saucepan as they are cut.

3. **Prepare the lemon.** Remove any seeds from the lemon. Place the half cut side down on the cutting board, use a serrated knife to cut the lemon lengthwise into ¼ in. thick slices, and add the slices to the saucepan.

4. **Prepare the ginger root.** Use a serrated knife to cut the ginger root crosswise into ⅛ in. wide slices. Stacking several slices together and holding them together with one hand, cut them into thin strips. Holding several strips together at a time, mince the ginger strips. Add the ginger to the saucepan.

5. **Add the spices to the saucepan.**

    - Add ⅛ t ground nutmeg, ½ t ground cinnamon, ¼ t ground ginger, $1/16$-⅛ t ground cloves, and ⅛ t ground cayenne or ¼ t medium hot chili powder to the saucepan.

6. **Cook the chutney.**

    - Bring the liquid to full boiling over medium-high heat, reduce the heat to a level that maintains gentle boiling, mainly cover the pan, and cook the mixture for 15 minutes, using a rubber spatula to stir the mixture occasionally and setting a timer.
    - At the timer, check the apples and liquid content. Remove the saucepan from the heat when the apples are very soft and the liquid is somewhat reduced. If additional cooking is needed, set a timer for 5 minutes and remove the chutney from the stove at the timer.

7. **Prepare the almonds while the chutney cooks.** Use a chef's knife to thinly slice the almonds lengthwise. Set the almonds aside.

8. **Assemble the chutney for serving.**

    - Remove the lemon slices if desired, first squeezing out as much lemon juice as possible.
    - Add the almonds to the hot chutney.
    - Scrape the chutney into a 2 c glass serving bowl.
    - Cool the chutney to room temperature for serving.

PART 2

9. **Store leftover chutney refrigerated in an air-tight glass container.** Use the chutney within a week or so.

   VARIATIONS: Substitute **peaches** for apples to make **peach chutney**. Use **15 oz canned peaches**, packed in peach juice, drained. Select flavorful peach brands, such as Dole or Del Monte.

196. Mango Chutney
(4 servings)

Ingredients

¼ c premium orange juice
2 ripe mangoes
½ in. long piece of ginger root (¾-1 in. thick)
¼ c apple cider vinegar
⅓ c packed dark brown sugar
1 heaping T dried tart cherries
¼ c golden raisins or certified organic dark

¼ c raw whole almonds
⅛ t salt
⅛ t ground cinnamon
⅛ t ground cloves
¼ t ground ginger
¼ t ground nutmeg

Cooking, Serving, and Storing Utensils

1 set each measuring cups & spoons
1 medium stainless steel or other non-reactive saucepan with a lid
1 each 5 in. serrated & chef's knife
1 vegetable peeler

1 timer
1 rubber or other heat-resistant spatula
2 c glass serving bowl
2 c glass storage container with lid

---

1. **Heat the orange juice in a saucepan at a medium heat setting.**

2. **Prepare the mangoes.**

   - Rinse and dry the mangoes.
   - Use a serrated knife to slice off an end of each mango. Stand a mango upright on this flattened end and slice the fruit lengthwise from both fat sides of the pit, closely following its curve.
   - Place each slice flesh side up and, being careful not to cut through the skin, score the flesh at ½ in. intervals, cutting both lengthwise and crosswise.
   - Push each mango slice inside out so that the scored mango cubes protrude. Place the mango on a cutting board and holding the skin firmly with one hand and, cutting close to the skin, slice off the mango cubes. Place the cubes on plastic wrap.

- Peel the skin from the two thin sections of flesh remaining on the pit and cut this flesh from the pit, following the pit closely. Cut the strips crosswise into ½ in. thick cubes.
- Add the mango cubes to the saucepan.

3. **Prepare the ginger root and dried tart cherries.**

    - Use a serrated knife to cut the ginger root into ⅛ in. wide slices. Stacking several slices together and holding them together with one hand, cut them into thin strips. Holding several strips together at a time, mince the ginger strips. Add the ginger to the saucepan.
    - Use a chef's knife to halve the cherries. Add the cherries to the saucepan.

4. **Add the remaining ingredients except for the almonds to the saucepan.**

    - Add the ¼ c vinegar, ⅓ c brown sugar, and ¼ c raisins.
    - Add ⅛ t each salt, cinnamon, and cloves. Add ¼ t each ground ginger and nutmeg.

5. **Cook the ingredients.**

    - Bring the liquid to full boiling over medium-high heat, reduce the heat to a level that maintains gentle boiling, mainly cover the pan, and cook the mixture for 15 minutes or until the liquid is reduced by almost half, using a rubber spatula to stir the mixture occasionally. Set a timer for the first 15 minutes and for any additional cooking.
    - At the timer, remove the saucepan from the heat.

6. **Prepare the almonds while other ingredients cook.**

    - Use a chef's knife to thinly slice the almonds lengthwise.

7. **Assemble the chutney for serving.**

    - Mix the almonds into the hot chutney.
    - Scrape the chutney into a 2 c serving bowl.
    - Cool the chutney to room temperature before serving.

8. **Store leftover chutney refrigerated in an air-tight glass container.** Use the chutney within a week or so.

    VARIATIONS: Add ingredients. Add, for example,

    - ⅛-¼ **t red chili pepper flakes**, ⅛ **t cayenne**, or ¼ **t medium hot chili powder**.
    - ¼ **t ground cardamom or 3-4 cardamom pods**, seeds removed from the pods and crushed with a mortar with a pestle.

PART 2

- ¼ t **ground turmeric**, ¼ t **ground coriander**, and/or ¼ t **ground cumin**.
- 1 T **crystallized ginger**, chopped.
- 1 small stick **cinnamon**.
- 2 cloves **garlic**, peeled and minced (Recipe #31), or ½ **red onion**, minced (Recipe #34).

197. 100% Whole Wheat Flat Bread (Chapatis)

Ingredients

½ c water
¼ c milk
½ c medium ground whole wheat flour (see comments below)
½ c milk
¼ c water
¼ t salt

1¾ c chilled whole wheat flour (medium ground)
¾ t salt
1 T butter
approx. 1 T extra virgin olive oil
approx. ½ c whole wheat flour
approx. 2 T butter, softened

Cooking Tools

1 set each measuring spoons & cups
1 large nonstick skillet
1 medium bowl
1 dinner fork or whisk
1 rubber or other heat-resistant spatula
1 large mixing bowl
1 large-headed wooden spoon
1 large (approx. 16 x 24 in.) cutting board

1 rolling pin, lightly oiled
1 small mixing bowl
1 buttering knife or spatula
plastic wrap or wax paper
1 or 2 dry dish clothes
1 wire cooling rack
1 dome-shaped skillet lid
1 damp sponge or cloth

1. **Cook a small portion of the flour.**

   - Add ½ c water and ¼ c milk to a large nonstick skillet and heat the mixture at medium.
   - Add ½ c milk, ¼ c water, and ¼ t salt to a medium mixing bowl. Add ½ c flour and, using a fork or whisk, stir the mixture until it is smooth.
   - Increase the skillet heat to medium-high. Use a rubber spatula to scrape the flour mixture into the hot liquid, slowly adding the flour mixture. When the flour is added, stir the mixture quickly and constantly with the spatula so that lumps do not form. Continue the constant stirring until the mixture thickens, which should be within a minute or two. Remove the skillet from the burner and scrape the cooked flour into a large mixing bowl.

- Add 1 T butter to the hot cooked flour and stir the butter into the mixture once it melts.
- Add hot water to the skillet for easy cleaning.

2. **Add the remaining flour and salt to the cooked flour.**

   - **When using an electric mixer,** add all the flour (1¾ c) and ¾ t salt to the cooked flour mixture in the mixing bowl. Use a wooden spoon to combine the ingredients roughly, stirring the mixture until the flour sticks together. No dry flour should remain at the bottom of the bowl.
   - **When hand beating the dough,** add ¾ c flour and ¾ t salt to the cooked flour mixture in the mixing bowl. Use a wooden spoon to mix the ingredients together thoroughly.

3. **Beat the dough.**

   - **When using an electric mixer,** beat the dough for 2 minutes at a medium setting. Using an oiled spatula, scrape the dough onto a lightly oiled work surface. Form the dough into a ball. Wrap the dough in lightly oiled plastic wrap.
   - **When hand-beating the dough,** beat the dough 150 strokes with a wooden spoon. Pile the remaining 1 c flour on the work area, spread it slightly, and scrape the dough onto it. Use an oiled rubber spatula to press the dough into the flour. Starting at any point, slip the spatula under an edge of the dough and flip the edge up over the top of the dough. Rotating around the dough, continue the flipping until the top of the dough is covered with flour. With oiled hands, knead the flour into the dough. Continue the kneading until the dough is smooth and soft (a few minutes). If the dough remains very sticky, knead more flour into it, sprinkling 1 T flour over the dough at a time. Shape the dough into a ball. Wrap the dough in lightly oiled plastic wrap.

4. **Clean the nonstick skillet and heat it on a large burner at a medium setting.**

5. **Roll the dough into rounds.**

   - Lightly oil a rolling pin. Place a small bowl containing at least 1c flour, a small amount of softened butter and a buttering knife, and either plastic wrap or wax paper nearby.
   - Pile 1½ T flour on the work surface and spread it into an 8 in. circle. Flour your hands, pull off a walnut-sized piece of dough, roll the dough into a ball, and roll the ball in the flour, completely coating it. Press the ball into the flour, flattening it into a small circle. Pick up the round, add 1 T flour to re-flour the work surface, flip the round, and again press it into the flour. Repeat this turning and pressing, adding flour as needed, until the dough does not stick to the board when pressed onto it.
   - Rolling from the center to the edges and rotating around the dough, roll the dough into a ⅛ in. thick circle. Whenever the dough sticks during the rolling, gently lift the

dough and spread a touch more flour onto the work surface. Be careful to roll the dough evenly.
- Stack the rounds as they are prepared, placing plastic wrap or wax paper between them to avoid sticking and to keep them from drying.

6. **Bake the bread.**

   - Increase the skillet heat to medium-high. When a drop of water added to the skillet immediately jumps about and disappears, add a round of dough.
   - Cook the dough for 25 seconds, counting off the seconds. Flip the bread and let it cook until small brown spots appear on its underside. Again flip the bread and, using a dry cloth, quite firmly press down on the top of the bread, moving over the entire surface. The bread should puff up as it is pressed, which is a sign of success.
   - Once the bread is fully puffed, transfer it to a wire cooling rack. Spread a small amount of butter over the top and loosely cover the bread, using a dome-shaped skillet lid or a shallow bread basket turned upside down and covered with a towel.
   - Wipe the skillet clean with a damp towel or sponge and add another round of dough.

7. **Tightly cover and refrigerate leftover dough.** The dough keeps for up to a week and can be used directly from the refrigerator.

COMMENTS: Medium ground whole wheat flour has clearly visible pieces of bran in it, which gives the flour a somewhat coarse texture and make the flour absorptive. Fine ground flour does not work in this recipe.

Some helpful information for successfully preparing 100% whole wheat chapatis, which closely resemble the South Asian flat bread called roti, is as follows:

- Because flours differ somewhat, flour content cannot be exact. If the dough immediately seems very sticky during stirring or beating, cautiously mix in more flour, adding 1 or 2 T flour at a time. It is better to err on the side of moistness than to add too much flour, which is difficult to handle.
- Because trapped steam is what puffs open and cooks the inside of the flat bread, it is very important to protect the dough from tearing, which makes holes from which steam escapes. Carefully handle the dough during rolling and when transferring it to the skillet. Always keep the dough covered with plastic wrap to protect it from drying as dried dough easily cracks during cooking. Avoid burning, which creates holes in the bread.

Reference #11

Clinching Curry Flavor:
Expanded Preparation Support

Reference #11 focuses on securing the attractiveness of Chapter Nine curry recipes through careful selection and preparation of key individual flavoring ingredients used in curries. It makes flavor-enhancing and sometimes nutrition-enhancing suggestions for commonly used curry flavoring ingredients, which include **broth, canned coconut, curry powder, ground curry spices,** and **seasoning vegetables**. Reference #11 also provides flavor-enhancing suggestions for **fresh fruit** and **cilantro**, which are attractive flavoring ingredients that can be added to Chapter Nine curries. Ingredients are covered alphabetically.

1. Broth

Maximize the flavor of broth used in curry sauce. Tasty broth is a basic key to curry sauce flavor.

- Precisely observe the amount of canned broth called for in a curry recipe. Adding too much liquid unattractively dilutes curry sauce flavor. To thin a curry sauce, add only a small amount of additional liquid at a time and make a taste test before adding any more. Never add extra flavorful liquid, no matter how flavorful it is. Save and freeze such flavorful liquid for another use, collecting small jars with lids for this purpose.
- Use only flavorful liquid to thin curry sauce. Never add plain water. Add milk, bean broth, vegetable cooking liquid, canned vegetable packing liquid, or canned broth.
- Rely on spice-flavored stir-fried onions rather than boiled onion for enhancing broth flavor. Adding stir-fried onion to broth at serving time contributes incomparably more flavor than boiling onion in the broth. Cooking onion, ginger root, and garlic in a broth mainly wastes the flavor of these valuable flavoring ingredients.
- Add spice flavoring to individual vegetables during stir-frying. Cooking vegetables with spices is a simple and effective means of boosting overall curry flavor without adding salt or calories to a curry. Some vegetables in particular – cauliflower, potatoes, celery, carrots, and squash (summer and winter) – easily absorb and are enhanced by spice flavoring.
- Add bouillon or other concentrated flavor cubes to enhance the flavor of canned broth. These ingredients serve as an effective means of enhancing broth flavor. Choose organic flavoring products to avoid chemical flavorings. Natural food stores commonly carry one or more varieties of flavoring products, including vegan compatible products. When selecting these products, always be wary of high sodium content.
- Always measure fresh lemon juice content. Use a standard measuring spoon. Too much can make a broth unattractively sour and adding too little leaves a broth bland. When using an organic lemon, include a small amount of lemon zest (e.g., 1 t or to taste) to enhance broth flavor.

- Never omit lemon juice. Lemon juice makes an important flavoring contribution.
- Substitute fresh poultry broth (Reference #10) for commercially prepared poultry broth. Fresh poultry broth has incomparably superior flavor to any canned or packaged broth, and home preparation also places a cook in complete control of salt and other flavoring content. Nearly any amount of leftover bones/meat scraps cooked in a small amount of canned broth (1-1½ c) for 45 minutes yields a gelatinous broth that can be frozen for later use. Saving small jars with lids to use for freezing small amounts of broth eases storage. Freezing broth in small or serving size amounts also best ensures the use of frozen broth. Significantly enhance the nutritional quality of fresh poultry broth through use of grass-fed poultry.
- Select certified organic broth products to avoid chemical additives, such as MSG (monosodium glutamate), which is often not listed in broth product labels.

2. Cilantro

Cautiously experiment with adding fresh cilantro to curry sauce. Always test the acceptability of cilantro to family and friends before including it in a curry. Cilantro is a commonly used South Asian fresh spice that contributes a refreshingly pungent flavor to a curry. As raw, nutrient-rich green leaves, cilantro contributes a small but significant nutritional punch as well. Because of its highly assertive flavor, however, it not uniformly enjoyed. It is very important, therefore, to cautiously experiment with using cilantro.

Use cilantro as a topping on individual servings of curry.

- Use 1 t coarsely chopped leaves per serving. Increase content only on the basis of experience.
- To rinse and dry cilantro, rinse several sprigs in cool water, shake off excess clinging water, spread the leaves over a layer of paper towels or a terry cloth, add another layer of towels, roll the cilantro in the towels, and gently squeeze the towels. Alternatively, spin the leaves dry in a salad spinner.
- To cut cilantro, gently strip leaves from stems, bunch the leaves together on a cutting board, and use a sharp knife to slice the leaves into pieces, cutting lengthwise and crosswise though the pile. Collect the stems and include them when making stock.
- To keep fresh cilantro on hand, refrigerate it wrapped in a paper towel within a sealed plastic bag, pushing out as much air as possible before sealing the bag. Alternatively, refrigerate it in a small, wide-bottomed jar, standing it upright in a small amount of water within a plastic bag. Cilantro is also easy to grow in a garden or in a pot.

3. Canned Coconut Milk

Maximize the flavoring contribution of canned coconut milk in curry sauce. Coconut milk is an important flavoring ingredient in Chapter Nine curries. Careful selection of products, preparation, and storage techniques ensures coconut milk actually plays this role.

- Experiment with canned coconut milk products to locate the most flavorful product as flavor varies considerably among products.
- Do not select "light" canned coconut milk. While it may have fewer calories than regular coconut milk, its flavor is far inferior.
- Thoroughly stir canned coconut milk before measuring the amount called for by a recipe. Sometimes liquid separates, and this liquid alone has little coconut flavor.
- Retain coconut flavor during storage. Immediately refrigerate leftover coconut, tightly covered. Immediately transfer extra coconut milk to another container, and especially a glass container, for refrigeration. Freeze leftover coconut milk that will not be quickly used. Freeze it in serving size amounts for easy re-use, such as in small glass jars.
- Select the 7 oz can size as exactly matched to Chapter Nine curry size.
- Substitute commercially frozen coconut milk for canned. This especially flavorful form of coconut milk can be substituted for canned coconut milk in recipes.

Enhance canned coconut flavoring.

- Add powdered coconut to intensify coconut flavor. Add only a small amount (2 T per ½ c canned coconut milk) of coconut powder.
- Add shredded dried coconut. Soak the coconut in a very hot liquid (2 T water or milk per 1 T dried coconut for 10-15 minutes, covered) before mixing it with canned coconut milk.

4. Curry Powder

Experiment with curry powder products to select products with the most pleasing flavor. Curry powder is the key spice flavoring in Chapter Nine curries.

- Curry powder flavor is highly variable, with some products having a clearly different taste than others. This is because curry powder is a collection of as many as twenty ground spices. As both the particular spice content and the heat of the powder can vary greatly from brand to brand, experimentation is the best way of locating a combination that best suits an individual cook.
- Natural food stores may sell two or more varieties of curry powder in bulk form, which in addition to being economical provides a cook the opportunity to purchase a small amount of curry powder for tasting purposes.
- Spice Island Curry Powder is a reliably tasty and mild curry powder that is quite widely marketed in grocery stores.

Add other spices to curry powder for a more intense or varied flavor. Combine any or all of the following spices or spice mixtures with curry powder.

- Green cardamom. Cardamom is a highly aromatic spice which adds authentic South Asian flavoring to Chapter Nine curries. Use approx. 10 crushed seeds or ½ t ground cardamom per 4-serving curry. For crushed seeds, remove the seeds from 10 pods or enough to yield ½ t crushed seeds and crush the seeds with either a pestle and mortar or electric seed grinder for serving. Seeds removed from pods should be dark black as opposed to pale brown seeds, which have lost vitality and should be discarded.
- Cayenne. Cayenne provides authentic heat. Add it very cautiously, however, adding it a touch ($^{1}/_{16}$-⅛ t) at a time and tasting the results before adding more.
- Ground cumin and ground coriander. Add ½ t per 4-serving dish. Provided they are fresh, these spices attractively intensify the flavor of any curry. If these spices are not mellowed by at least five minutes of cooking, they can give a sharp, somewhat coarse edge to a curry sauce.
- Chili powder. Add 1 t per 4-serving dish. Chili powder is a spice mixture that is marketed with and without salt. Like cumin and coriander, chili powder should be mellowed by at least five minutes of cooking. It should also be accurately measured. If an excessive amount of chili powder is added or chili powder is not mellowed, it can give a sharp, somewhat coarse edge to a curry sauce. Chili powder products also vary in tastiness. Frontier Chili Powder is a reliably tasty product. Natural food stores market this spice mixture in bulk form, which is less expensive than purchasing it in a container and provides the opportunity to test spice flavor.
- Freshly roasted ground cumin seed. This spice has an especially appealing, rich flavor. To prepare it, roast cumin seed in a dry skillet pre-heated at medium, stirring the seeds frequently until they are lightly browned and aromatic. Cool them completely, finely grind them in a spice grinder or with a mortar and pestle, and store them in a tightly covered container. Use 1 t per 4-serving curry.
- Garam masala. This South Asian spice mixture means "warm spices" and is composed of cinnamon, cloves, nutmeg, and cardamom. As the flavor of this spice mixture quickly disperses, evenly sprinkle it over the curry shortly before serving. As with curry powders in general, the flavor of very fresh garam masala is far more pungent than older powder. It is important to judge the amount used by the strength of flavor.
- Ground ginger. Add ¼-½ t per 4-serving curry sauce. Ginger powder combines especially well with chicken curry. As it bears no resemblance to fresh ginger, ground ginger should not be substituted for fresh ginger.

Home-prepare a basic curry powder. Home mixing allows a cook to adjust the content of individual spices to taste as well as to secure the quality of the curry powder. Combine the following ground spices together and store the mixture in an air-tight container, particularly a glass container.

- 1 T commercial curry powder
- 1 T ground turmeric
- 2 t ground cumin
- 2 t ground ginger

- 2 t ground coriander
- 2 t ground fennel seed

Select the highest quality curry powder products.

- Be aware that curry powder products can include salt.
- Be aware that spices can be irradiated. Select certified organic products to reliably avoid selection of irradiated spices.

5. Single Curry Spices

Maximize the flavoring contribution of individual ground spices in curry sauce.

- Accurately measure ground spices. Use measuring spoons. Even slightly too much or too little flavoring can make a difference, unpleasantly overpowering other dish flavoring or leaving the dish bland.
- Cautiously expand recipe-directed spice content. Add only a very small amount at a time and taste the results before adding more.
- Evenly disperse spice flavoring in a curry sauce. Evenly spread spices over stir-frying onions. The spice flavoring adheres to oil-coated onion pieces and becomes evenly mixed into the curry sauce.
- Do not overcook spices. If not immediately serving an assembled curry, remove it from heat and set it aside, covered, after it has cooked for five minutes. Five minutes is sufficient to blend and mellow spices in Chapter Nine curries.
- Protect spice flavoring during storage. Store spices tightly covered to protect them from flavor-reducing air.
- Invest in a seed grinder and home grind whole spices. Freshly ground spices are by far the most flavorful spices.

Maximize the nutritional contribution of ground spices in curry sauce. Spices make nutritional contributions to dishes, contributing both nutrients and phytonutrients.

- Select fresh products to maximize the nutritional contribution of spices.
- Select certified organic products to reliably avoid selection of irradiated spice products. Irradiation is processing that is destructive of nutritional content.

6. Fresh Fruit

Take maximum advantage of fresh fruit flavoring. Fruit is a top flavoring ingredient in curries.

- Add apple.

    - To prepare apple, use a chef's knife to halve an apple lengthwise, place the halves cut side down on a clean cutting board, and slice each half lengthwise into 4-5 slices. Use a paring knife to remove seeds and the pulpy center from slices and to cut each slice crosswise into 4-5 chunks. Increase the skillet heat to medium-high. When a drop of water added to the skillet instantly dances and disappears, add 1 T oil, add and mix in the apple, evenly sprinkle ½ t ground cinnamon over the pieces, and stir-fry the apple for 1 minute. Add 1 T juice (or hot water), cover the skillet, reduce the heat to low, and steam the apple for 4 minutes until pieces are softened but still retain shape. Use a rubber spatula to scrape the apple and any cooking juice into a colander holding cooked vegetables. Wipe the skillet clean.

- Add tart fruit. For example, add ½ c fresh pineapple chunks (Recipe #94) or ½ c tart pitted cherries (Recipe #81).
- Cut fruit into small but not very small chunks to best retain fruit flavor.
- Cut fresh fruit cleanly with a sharp knife. Clean cutting minimizes juice spilling.
- Do not cook most fruit. To retain the best fruit flavor, serve it raw by adding it to yogurt (Spiced Yogurt, Recipe #192) served with a curry dish.

Take maximum advantage of the nutritional value of fresh fruit in curries.

- Select certified organic and locally grown fruit. Reference #1 (Selecting Top Quality Fresh Whole Vegetables and Fruits) details the nutritional significance of selecting these kinds of naturally produced fruit, including more potent phytonutrient content, greater overall nutritional value, and minimal pesticide content in comparison to industrially-produced fruit products.
- Do not overcook fruit, which is destructive of the nutritional content of fruit, notably of its vitamin C content.

7. Seasoning Vegetables

Take maximum advantage of the flavoring capacity of seasoning vegetable in curry sauce.

- Expand the onion content (Recipe #34) of curry sauce. Adding attractive moistening and flavoring as well as nutritional boosting, onion is an invaluable flavoring ingredient that can be increased significantly. Provided onion quality is good (the onion is uniformly firm with a tightly fitting and unbroken skin), onion content can easily be increased from ½ to 1½ bulb onion per curry recipes.

    - Add green onion (also called scallions), including most or all of the green leaves, or leeks, also including the green tops.

- Dice bulb onions and thickly slice green onions and leeks to best retain onion flavor. Recipe #34 details a simple dicing technique for bulb onion.

- Maintain the amount of ginger root called for in recipes. Ginger root flavor easily becomes unattractively assertive.
- Include garlic (Recipe #31). To best retain the distinctive and highly attractive flavoring of garlic, add it as a topping to individual servings.
- Routinely include bell pepper (Recipe #35). Bell pepper is an invaluable flavoring ingredient and adds attractive color as well.
- Add chili pepper (Recipe #36) to add special flavor and a touch of authentic South Asian "heat" to dishes.

Take maximum advantage of the nutritional contribution of seasoning vegetables.

- Select certified organic and locally grown seasoning vegetables. Reference #1 (Selecting Top Quality Fresh Whole Vegetables and Fruits) details the nutritional significance of selecting these kinds of naturally produced vegetables, including more potent phytonutrient content, greater overall nutritional value, and minimal pesticide content in comparison to industrially produced fruit products.
- Include garlic and allow minced garlic to sit exposed to air for 10 minutes before stir-frying. This exposure to air activates enzymes that bring about a chemical reaction that converts of garlic's alliin content into allicin, which then acts as a potent antioxidant when consumed by humans, providing protection from highly destructive oxidative stress.

CHAPTER TEN

Quiche

Quiche Description

A LONGTIME FAVORITE dish for special occasions, a quiche can just as well serve more every day and nutritional purposes. Boosting the amount of vegetables while reducing fat content and substituting a pat-in whole wheat and nut crust for refined flour crust, *Cooked Alive!* quiche does just this while retaining all the appeal of traditional quiche.

Quiche has outstanding serving pluses.

First and foremost, quiche provides a delicious flavoring base for a variety of vegetables that are notably nutritious but that have somewhat temperamental cooking characteristics. Heightening both color and natural sweetness, milk boosts the attractiveness and, hence, the serving success of these vegetables, which include:

- cabbage family vegetables, such as broccoli, bok choy, Brussels sprouts, cabbage, turnips, turnip greens, kale, and collards. Milk holds the natural sweet flavoring of these vegetables because it neutralizes plant acids that spill from plant cells during cooking. This neutralization prevents the acids from breaking down the sulfur compounds contained by all cabbage family vegetables. Sulfur compounds, as a result, do not alter the flavor of cabbage family vegetables and do not release an unpleasant sulfur odor during cooking.
- green leafy vegetables in general.
- asparagus.
- onions.

Quiche has excellent serving versatility. Quiche can, for example,

- be served alone as a one-pot meal. Its egg content provides high quality protein that gives quiche full-meal status.
- be easily dressed up into special occasion form by adding a salad and/or muffins (Recipes #180-184).

- be served hot or warm. Quiche, as a result, is a perfect buffet or carry-along dish, such as for pot luck affairs.

Quiche Preparation Notes

Preparation Notes provide helpful instruction and information about Chapter Ten quiche recipes that cannot fit into individual recipes. These Notes cover a variety of subjects, including:

- technical details for both securing successful recipe preparation (Notes #1-5), with Note #1 being of particular importance.
- preparation of vegetable variation suggestions made in recipes (Note #6).
- cooking tool information (Note #7).
- recipe resource references for expanding the nutritional quality of dishes (Notes #8-9).

1. **Adjust vegetable stir-fry/steaming technique when using gas burners.** The stir-fry/steaming technique routinely used for preparing vegetables in Chapter Ten quiche recipes matches electric burners, which do not immediately cool when burner heat is reduced. Cooking of vegetables, as a result, slows slowly and vegetables continue to cook when heat is reduced after one minute of stir-frying. **Because gas burners *do* immediately respond to heat changes**, it is necessary to alter stir-fry/steaming technique somewhat. On a gas burner, the reduction of heat to low is so abrupt that cooking can stop completely. Steam will then not form immediately and vegetables will not be tender at the recipe-directed cooking time. Therefore, when using a gas burner, adjust stir-fry/steaming technique as follows:

    - After one minute of stir-frying, add 1 T hot water as directed to do by the recipes but reduce the heat to **medium-low**. Cover the skillet and heat the vegetable at medium-low for 30 seconds before reducing the heat to low.

2. **To maximize crust attractiveness,**

    - minimize orange juice content. While well moistened flour is easy to pat into the quiche pan, too much liquid undermines crust tenderness. The baked crust will be unattractively tough and difficult to cut.

        - Add orange juice cautiously. When adding more orange juice than the recipe-directed amount, add it one tablespoon at a time.
        - Evenly spread juice over the flour mixture. Drizzle it over as much of the flour as possible rather than pouring it all in at one place.
        - Thoroughly stir added juice into the flour, repeatedly tossing the flour. Add more juice only if dry flour remains on the bottom of the mixing bowl.

    - avoid overspilling when pouring the milk/egg mixture into the quiche crust for baking. If the egg/milk filling gets close to the top of the crust,

        - stop the pouring, add the nutmeg, and place the quiche into the hot oven.

PART 2

- use a rubber spatula to scrape the remaining quiche mixture into a ½ c measuring cup and slowly pour this remaining liquid into the quiche after it is in the oven.

• avoid scorching of the crust edges. Be watchful and if the edges start to become brown, loosely cover the quiche with aluminum foil. Add the foil without pressing it down around the sides of the quiche and without touching the quiche top.

3. **To maximize the attractiveness of the quiche custard base,**

  • do not over-bake the custard. Bake the quiche just until the custard is firm. Extended cooking unattractively toughens and dries the texture and may scorch the vegetable content.
  • do not under-bake, which leaves the center of the quiche runny. To help protect against under-baking:

    - Thoroughly pre-heat the oven to ensure the quiche immediately begins to bake and, as a result, reliably bakes within the recipe-directed time.
    - Do not omit heating of a portion of the milk while assembling the quiche for baking. This heating speeds overall baking time.

  • always conduct a readiness test before ending baking. A knife blade or toothpick inserted into the center of the quiche should come out clean.

4. **To reheat quiche**, heat it uncovered in a pre-heated 350 degree conventional or toaster oven or within a mainly, but not completely, covered lightly buttered skillet pre-heated at a medium heat setting, checking for readiness after 15 minutes of heating.

5. **To minimize overall calorie content, it is important to control cheese content.** Cheese is an invaluable flavoring ingredient that makes nutritional contributions as well, but it is also a calorie-dense food, with 1 oz of cheese (for hard cheese this is about the size of two dice) contributing **114 calories**. As cheese does not come in conveniently measured ounce size, cooks must do this measuring.

  • A 4 oz piece of cheese is approximately a 2¾ in. x 2¾ in. square of cheese that is ½ in. thick.
  • A 4 oz amount of cheese is about 1½ c loosely packed shredded cheese.
  • The most accurate way to measure cheese is with a food scale.

6. **Chapter One (Stir-Fried and Stir-Fry/Steamed Vegetables) serves as a reference for preparing the vegetable variation suggestions made in Chapter Ten quiche recipes.**

  • The recipe number attached to a vegetable variation identifies the Chapter One reference recipe, which supplies preparation details and basic selection and nutritional details.

7. **Important information about quiche cooking tools is as follows:**

    - Recipes list all tools used in recipe preparation except for some basic working tools – plastic wrap, paper or cloth towels, and vegetable and skillet cleaning tools – and multi-purpose cutting boards. As these tools are used routinely in recipes, they need to be kept handy.
    - The General Cooking Tools list contained in the Part II Introduction serves as a descriptive reference for all Chapter Ten cooking tools except for tools specific to quiche. These tools are described as follows:

        - **1 blender.** A blender is needed for fine grinding of nuts to be used in the quiche crust. A seed grinder substitutes.
        - **1 quiche dish (either 9 or 10 inch size).** A high-sided 9 in. glass pie plate substitutes for an 9 in. quiche dish.
        - **1 food scale.** A scale that measures ounces for at least 1 pound ensures accurate measurement of cheese content.
        - **1 thin-bladed spatula.** This type spatula eases the removal of ground nuts from a blender.

8. **Cooks can significantly upgrade the nutritional quality of Chapter Ten quiche recipes by selecting the highest quality dish ingredients.** *Cooked Alive!* provides three references to assist cooks in selecting the highest quality dish ingredients.

    - Reference #1 (Selecting Top Quality Fresh Whole Vegetables and Fruits) identifies top quality vegetables, which are vegetables that are both naturally intact and naturally produced. Naturally produced vegetables include both certified organic and locally produced vegetables.
    - Reference #4 (Selecting Top Quality Whole Food Ingredients for Use in Part II Recipes) identifies commonly available top quality whole food products other than vegetables and fruits. These products are both naturally intact and naturally-produced products. Whole food products relevant to Chapter Ten quiche recipes are **eggs** and **nuts**.
    - Reference #5 (Selecting High Quality Processed Ingredients for Use in Part II Recipes) identifies naturally produced products that retain significant nutritional quality despite being physically processed. Products relevant to Chapter Ten quiche recipes are **dairy products (milk, cheese,** and **butter), extra virgin olive oil,** and **ground whole wheat.**

9. *Cooked Alive!* **includes a reference specifically focused on assisting cooks to successfully include whole foods other than vegetables and fruits in Part II dishes.** Whole foods covered in this reference – Reference #6 (Maximizing the Attractiveness of Whole Food Ingredients Commonly Used in Part II Recipes) – that are relevant to quiche recipes are **eggs** (Ingredient #6) and **nuts** (Ingredient #5).

PART 2

Quiche Recipes

198. Broccoli Quiche
(4 servings)

Pat-In 100% Whole Wheat and Ground Nut Crust

¼ c raw pecan or walnut halves
¾ c chilled medium ground whole wheat flour
¼ t salt

2½ T chilled butter
2-2½ T cold orange juice

Vegetables

2 chilled stalks broccoli
1 T extra virgin olive oil
1 T hot water
⅓ t salt
⅓ each red & green bell pepper

¾ T extra virgin olive oil
½ chilled medium onion, halved lengthwise
2 ⅛-in. thick slices ginger root
1 T extra virgin olive oil

Egg Custard Filling

1 c milk (not skim)
3 large eggs
⅓ t salt

¼ c milk
4 oz extra sharp cheddar cheese
¼ t ground nutmeg

Cooking Tools

1 blender
1 set each measuring cups & spoons
1 thin-bladed rubber spatula
1 medium (6 c) mixing bowl
1 each slicing, 5 in. serrated & chef's knife
1 dinner fork
9 in. quiche dish or high-sided glass pie plate, lightly buttered
1 timer
1 cooling rack

1 large nonstick skillet with a tight-fitting & opaque lid
1 electric tea kettle
1 cutting board reserved for vegetables
1 plastic or plastic-coated stir-fry spatula
1 rubber or other heat-resistant spatula
1 colander
1 dinner plate
1 cheese grater
1 dinner fork or whisk

---

1. Preheat the oven to 400 degrees.

2. Gather all cooking tools and ingredients.

3. **Prepare the pat-in crust.**

    - Finely grind the nuts in the blender, blending ⅛ c nuts at a time and using a thin-bladed rubber spatula to scrape out the ground nuts into a medium mixing bowl before adding more nut halves.
    - Add the flour and salt to the ground nuts in the mixing bowl and thoroughly combine the ingredients.
    - Use a sharp knife to dice the butter finely. Cut it into strips and cut the strips crosswise into small pieces. The more finely diced, the easier the mixing.
    - Add the diced butter to the flour mixture. Use your fingers to mash the butter into the flour, working quickly to avoid melting the butter. Continue mashing until the mixture resembles coarse crumbs.
    - Evenly drizzle 2 T juice over the flour mixture, circling around the flour. Use a dinner fork to toss the mixture over and over until the mixture appears crumbly. If dry flour remains at the bottom of the bowl, drizzle another ½ T juice over the flour and toss the mixture until all flour sticks together. It is very important for crust tenderness that the flour and nut mixture remain dry and crumbly and not be wet and sticky.
    - Spread the flour mixture evenly over the bottom of the quiche dish or pie plate, piling it higher next to the sides. Use your fingers to push flour up the sides and as close to the top as possible and to flatten the flour evenly over both the sides and pie plate bottom.
    - Center the crust on the middle oven rack and bake the crust for 8 minutes until the edges are lightly browned, setting a timer.
    - At the timer, remove the crust from the oven and place it on a cooling rack.
    - Reduce the oven heat to 350 degrees.
    - Wipe the mixing bowl clean.

4. **Stir-fry/steam the broccoli.**

    - Heat a large nonstick skillet at medium. Begin heating an electric tea kettle to prepare hot water for steaming.
    - Rinse and thoroughly dry the broccoli stalks, wrap each stalk within paper towels, and firmly squeeze each stalk to dry it.
    - Remove and save the leaves. Slice the florets from the stalks, cutting the stems off at the stalk.
    - Halve each floret lengthwise, place the halves cut side down on a cutting board, and use a 5 in. serrated knife to halve the floret halves lengthwise. Cut large broccoli florets into ¼ in. thick slices.
    - Halve large leaves. Either peel and cut each stalk crosswise into ⅛ in. thick slices, discarding the very tip of the stalk, or set both peeled stalks aside for use as a raw snack.
    - Increase the skillet heat to medium-high, and when a drop of water added to the skillet immediately dances and disappears, add 1 T oil, add any stalk slices, and cook them for 30 seconds, stirring frequently. Add the broccoli slices and stir-fry

PART 2

them for 1 minute, setting a timer. Stir-frying should at first be vigorous but can slow to "flip often" pace by the end of the minute.
- At the timer, add 1 T hot water, cover the skillet, reduce the heat to low, and steam the broccoli for 4 minutes, setting a timer.
- At the timer, remove the skillet from the heat, evenly sprinkle ⅓ t salt over the broccoli, and use a rubber spatula to scrape the broccoli and any cooking juice into a colander placed over a dinner plate.
- Wipe the skillet clean.

5. **Stir-fry the bell peppers.**

   - Heat the skillet at a medium setting.
   - Use a 5 in. serrated knife to cut out the stem end of each pepper. Remove any seeds but not the white membrane. Use the serrated knife to cut the peppers lengthwise into ¼ in. thick strips and to cut the strips crosswise into ¼ in. cubes.
   - Increase the skillet heat to medium-high, and when a drop of water added to the skillet immediately dances and disappears, add ¾ T oil, add the peppers, and vigorously stir-fry them for about 30 seconds.
   - Reduce the heat to medium and cook the peppers for 2 minutes, stirring them occasionally and setting a timer.
   - At the timer, use a rubber spatula to scrape the peppers and any cooking juice onto the colander with the broccoli.
   - Wipe the skillet clean.

6. **Stir-fry the onion and ginger.**

   - Heat the skillet at a medium setting.
   - Place ½ onion cut side down on a cutting board and use a chef's knife to cut off its ends. Peel the onion. Again place the onion cut side down on the cutting board and use the chef's knife to dice the onion. Mince the ginger root.
   - Increase the heat to medium-high, and when a drop of water added to the skillet instantly dances and disappears, add 1 T oil, add the onion and ginger, and vigorously stir-fry them for about 30 seconds.
   - Reduce the heat to medium and cook the onion mixture for 2 minutes, stirring it occasionally and setting a timer.
   - At the timer, use a rubber spatula to scrape the mixture onto a dinner plate separate from the other vegetables.

7. **Coarsely grate the cheese onto plastic wrap.**

8. **Assemble the quiche for baking.**

   - Add 1 c milk to the skillet and heat it at a medium setting.
   - Add 3 eggs to the medium mixing bowl used for mixing the crust and use a dinner fork or whisk to mix the yolks and whites.

- Mix ¼ c milk and ⅓ t salt into the eggs.
- When the milk in the skillet is hot, remove the skillet from the heat. While stirring quickly and constantly with a rubber spatula to avoid cooking and hardening the eggs, slowly pour the egg mixture into the hot milk.
- Evenly spread the onion and then the cheese over the crust.
- Mix together the broccoli and bell pepper and spread the mixture over the onion. Add any cooking juice to the milk mixture in the skillet.
- Pour the egg/milk mixture into the crust, being careful to not spill liquid over the top of the crust. Should the liquid get close to the top of the crust, stop the pouring and scrape any remaining liquid into a measuring cup.
- Evenly sprinkle the nutmeg over the quiche and place the quiche in the oven for baking, centering it on a middle oven rack. Pour any leftover liquid onto the quiche.

9. **Bake the quiche for 30 minutes, setting a timer.**

    - At the timer, make a readiness check to verify the custard has set. A knife inserted in the center of the quiche while it remains in the oven should come out clean. If the custard is not set, continue the baking and make readiness checks every 5 minutes until it is.
    - When the custard it set, remove the quiche from the oven onto a cooling rack.
    - For easiest cutting, cool the quiche 10 or so minutes.

10. **Serve the quiche when it is still hot or at least warm.**

    VARIATIONS: Make baking dish or ingredient substitutions. Substitute, for example,

    - **10 in. quiche dish** for 9 in. dish. Increase the total milk content to 1½ c (mixing ½ c with the eggs) and increase the cheese content to 5 oz (approx. 1¼ c shredded). To adjust crust ingredients, use 1 c flour, ½ c ground nuts, 3 T chilled butter, ⅓ t salt, and 2½-3 T juice.
    - **⅓ c nuts** for ¼ c nuts in the crust.
    - **whole almonds** for pecans, or use a combination of almonds and pecans in the crust.
    - **freshly grated nutmeg** for ground nutmeg added as a topping.

    Add ¼ c **coarsely chopped nuts to the quiche.** For example, add pecan or walnut halves or almonds. Spread the nuts over the onions when assembling the quiche for baking.

    COMMENTS: Medium whole wheat flour has clearly visible bits of bran, which give the flour a somewhat coarse texture. Fine ground flour, in comparison, is silky smooth. Finely ground bran is effectively destroyed bran. See Reference #5 (Selecting High Quality Processed Ingredients for Use in Part II Recipes), Ingredient #3, for information about selecting high quality whole wheat flour.

PART 2

199. Asparagus and Green Onion Quiche
(4 servings)

Pat-In 100% Whole Wheat and Ground Nut Crust

¼ c raw pecan or walnut halves
¾ c chilled medium ground whole wheat flour
¼ t salt

2½ T chilled butter
2-2½ T cold orange juice

Vegetables

1 lb fresh asparagus
1 T extra virgin olive oil
½ t dried dill weed
1½ T hot water
⅓ t salt
⅓-½ red bell pepper

½ T extra virgin olive oil
4 chilled green onions
2 ⅛-in. thick slices ginger root
1 T extra virgin olive oil
½ t dried dill weed

Egg Custard Filling

1 c milk (not skim)
3 large eggs
⅓ t salt

¼ c milk
4 oz extra sharp cheddar cheese
¼ c raw pecan or walnut halves

Cooking Tools

1 blender
1 set each measuring cups & spoons
1 thin-bladed spatula
1 medium (6 c) mixing bowl
1 each 5 in. serrated knife & chef's knife
1 dinner fork
9 in. quiche dish or high-sided glass
    pie plate, lightly buttered
1 timer
1 cooling rack

1 large nonstick skillet with a tight-
    fitting & opaque lid
1 electric tea kettle
1 cutting board reserved for vegetables
1 plastic(or plastic-coated stir-fry spatula
1 rubber or other heat-resistant spatula
1 colander
2 dinner plates
1 cheese grater with a coarse setting
1 dinner fork or whisk

---

1. **Preheat the oven to 400 degrees.**

2. **Gather all cooking tools and ingredients.**

3. **Prepare the crust.**

    - Finely grind the nuts in the blender, blending ⅛ c nuts at a time and using a

thin-bladed rubber spatula to scrape out the ground nuts into a medium mixing bowl before adding more nut halves.
- Add the flour and salt to the ground nuts in the mixing bowl and thoroughly combine the ingredients.
- Use a sharp knife to dice the butter finely. Cut it into strips and cut the strips crosswise into small pieces. The more finely diced, the easier the mixing.
- Add the diced butter to the flour mixture. Use your fingers to mash the butter into the flour, working quickly to avoid melting the butter. Continue mashing until the mixture resembles coarse crumbs.
- Evenly drizzle 2 T juice over the flour mixture (pour a very thin stream of juice around and around the flour). Use a dinner fork to toss the mixture over and over until the mixture appears crumbly. If dry flour remains at the bottom of the bowl, drizzle another ½ T juice over the flour and toss the mixture until all flour sticks together. It is very important for crust tenderness that the flour and nut mixture remain dry and crumbly and not be wet and sticky.
- Spread the flour mixture evenly over the bottom of the quiche dish or pie plate, piling it higher next to the sides. Use your fingers to push flour up the sides as close to the top as possible and to flatten the flour evenly over both the sides and quiche dish/pie plate bottom.
- Center the crust on the middle oven rack and bake the crust for 8 minutes until the edges are lightly browned, setting a timer.
- At the timer, remove the crust from the oven and place it on a cooling rack.
- Reduce the oven heat to 350 degrees.
- Wipe the mixing bowl clean.

4. **Stir-fry/steam the asparagus.**

- Heat a large nonstick skillet on a large burner at medium. Heat an electric tea kettle to prepare water for steaming.
- Rinse the asparagus, shake it to remove clinging water, spread it over a layer of paper towels or cloth towel, add a top layer of towels, wrap the spears in the towels, gently squeeze the spears to dry them, and unwrap the spears.
- Use a serrated knife to slice off the very bottom end of each spear.
- Snap the spears into pieces. Beginning at the tip end bend a spear until it naturally breaks off and break the spear into approx. 1 in. pieces. Continue the bending and breaking until the spear bends only.
- Use a serrated knife to cut off the portion of each spear that does not snap off. Use the knife to slice these thicker or tougher stalk ends into ⅛ in. thick pieces, keeping these pieces separate from the 1 in. long asparagus pieces. For especially tough spear bottoms, use a vegetable peeler to peel off the skin before slicing the spears.
- Increase the skillet heat to medium-high, and when a drop of water added to the skillet instantly dances and disappears, add 1 T oil, add the thinly sliced spear ends, stir-fry them for 30 seconds, add the remaining asparagus, and stir-fry it 1 minute, setting a timer. Stir-frying should at first be vigorous but can slow to "flip often" pace midway through the minute.

PART 2

- At the timer, add 1 T hot water, cover the skillet, reduce the heat to low, and steam the asparagus for 3 minutes, setting a timer.
- At the timer, remove the skillet from the heat, evenly sprinkle ⅓ t salt over the asparagus, and use a rubber spatula to scrape it and any cooking juice into a colander placed over a dinner plate.
- Wipe the skillet clean.

5. **Stir-fry/steam the red bell pepper.**

    - Heat the skillet at medium.
    - Use a 5 in. serrated knife to cut out the stem end of the pepper. Remove any seeds but not the white membrane. Use the serrated knife to cut the pepper lengthwise into ¼ in. thick strips and to cut the strips crosswise into ¼ in. cubes.
    - Increase the skillet heat to medium-high, and when a drop of water added to the skillet instantly dances and disappears, add ½ T oil, add the pepper, and vigorously stir-fry it for about 30 seconds.
    - Reduce the heat to medium and cook the pepper for 2 minutes, stirring it occasionally and setting a timer.
    - At the timer, use a rubber spatula to scrape the pepper and any cooking juice into the colander with the asparagus.
    - Wipe the skillet clean.

6. **Stir-fry the green onions and ginger.**

    - Heat the skillet at a medium setting.
    - Rinse, shake off clinging water, peel off loose skin from, and use a serrated knife to cut off the root ends and green tops of each onion. Spread the onions and tops over a strip of paper or cloth towels, top the onions with another layer of paper towels, and roll the onions in the paper towels to dry them.
    - Use the serrated knife to slice the white portions crosswise into ¼ in. thick slices. While holding the tops together with one hand, use a chef's knife to chop the green tops into thin slices.
    - Use the serrated knife to mince the ginger.
    - Increase the skillet heat to medium-high, and when a drop of water added to the skillet instantly dances and disappears, add 1 T oil, add the onions and ginger, evenly sprinkle the dill weed (first crushing it between your palms) over the onion, and vigorously stir-fry the mixture for about 30 seconds.
    - Reduce the heat to medium and cook the onion mixture for 2 minutes, stirring occasionally and setting a timer.
    - At the timer, remove the skillet from the stove and use a rubber spatula to scrape the onion mixture onto a dinner plate separate from the other vegetables.

7. **Coarsely grate the cheese onto plastic wrap.**

8. **Coarsely chop the nuts.** Use a chef's knife to chop the nuts.

9. **Assemble the quiche for baking.**

    - Add 1 c milk to the skillet and heat it at a medium setting.
    - Add 3 eggs to the medium mixing bowl and use a dinner fork or whisk to mix the yolks and whites. Mix ¼ c milk and ⅓ t salt into the eggs.
    - When the milk in the skillet is hot, remove the skillet from the heat. While stirring quickly and constantly with a rubber spatula to avoid cooking and hardening the eggs, slowly pour the egg mixture into the hot milk.
    - Evenly spread the onion, nuts, and cheese over the crust.
    - Mix together the asparagus and bell pepper and spread the mixture over the onion mixture. Add any collected vegetable juice to the egg/milk mixture.
    - Pour the egg/milk mixture into the crust, being careful to not spill liquid over the top of the crust. Should the liquid gets close to the top of the crust, stop the pouring. Pour the remaining liquid into a measuring cup.
    - Center the quiche on the middle rack of the oven for baking. Pour any remaining liquid onto the quiche.

10. **Bake the quiche for 30 minutes, setting a timer.**

    - At the timer, make a readiness check to verify that the custard has set. A knife inserted in the center of the quiche while it remains in the oven should come out clean. If the custard is not set, continue baking the quiche and make a readiness check every 5 minutes until it is set.
    - When the custard is set, remove the quiche from the oven onto a cooling rack.
    - For easiest cutting, cool the quiche 10 or so minutes.

11. **Serve the quiche when it is still hot or warm.**

    VARIATIONS: Make baking dish or ingredient substitutions. Substitute, for example,

    - **10 in. quiche dish** for 9 in. dish. Increase the total milk content to 1½ c (mixing ½ c with the eggs) and the cheese content to 1¼ cup. For preparing the crust use 1 c flour, ½ c ground nuts, 3 T chilled butter, ⅓ t salt, and 2½-3 T juice.
    - **⅓ c nuts** for ¼ c nuts in the crust.
    - **raw whole almonds** for pecan halves or a **combination of almonds and pecan halves** added to the quiche.
    - **½ yellow onion, sliced lengthwise,** for green onions.

    Add ingredients. Add, for example,

    - **¼ each green and yellow bell pepper,** cooking them with the red bell pepper. Increase oil content to ¾ cup.
    - **4-6 chilled garlic cloves** (Recipe #31).
    - **½-1 mild green chili** or **1-2 jalapeños** (Recipe #36).
    - **6-8 fresh mushrooms** (Recipe #33).

COMMENTS: Medium whole wheat flour has clearly visible bits of bran, which give the flour a somewhat coarse texture. Fine ground flour, in comparison, is silky smooth. Finely ground bran is effectively destroyed bran. See Reference #5 (Selecting High Quality Processed Ingredients for Use in Part II Recipes), Ingredient #3, for whole wheat flour selection information.

200. Cabbage and Red Pepper Quiche
(4 servings)

Pat-In 100% Whole Wheat and Ground Nut Crust

¼ c raw pecan or walnut halves
¾ c chilled medium ground whole wheat flour
¼ t salt

2½ T chilled butter
2-2½ T cold orange juice

Vegetables

½ medium head red or green cabbage (to yield approx. 4 c sliced)
1½ T extra virgin olive oil
1 t dried marjoram leaves
1½ T hot water
⅓ t salt

½ red bell pepper, sliced lengthwise
½ T extra virgin olive oil
½ chilled medium onion, halved lengthwise
2 ⅛-in. thick slices ginger root
½-1 t dried marjoram leaves
1 T extra virgin olive oil

Egg Custard Filling

1 c milk (whole or reduced fat)
3 large eggs
⅓ t salt

¼ c milk
4 oz extra sharp cheddar cheese
¼ c raw pecan or walnut halves

Cooking Tools

1 blender
1 set each measuring cups & spoons
1 thin-bladed spatula
1 medium (6 c) mixing bowl
1 each chef's & 5 in. serrated knife
1 dinner fork
9 in. quiche dish or high-sided glass pie plate, lightly buttered
1 timer
1 cooling rack

1 large nonstick skillet with a tight-fitting & opaque lid
1 electric tea kettle
1 cutting board reserved for vegetables
1 plastic or plastic-coated stir-fry spatula
1 rubber or other heat-resistant spatula
1 colander
2 dinner plates
1 cheese grater
1 dinner fork or whisk

COOKED ALIVE!

1. **Preheat the oven to 400 degrees.**

2. **Gather all cooking tools and ingredients.**

3. **Prepare the crust.**

    - Finely grind the nuts in the blender, blending ⅛ c nuts at a time and using a thin-bladed spatula to scrape out the ground nuts into a medium mixing bowl before adding more nut halves.
    - Add the flour and salt to the ground nuts in the mixing bowl and thoroughly combine the ingredients.
    - Use a sharp knife to dice the butter finely. Cut it into strips and cut the strips crosswise into small pieces. The more finely diced, the easier the mixing.
    - Add the diced butter to the flour mixture. Use your fingers to mash the butter into the flour, working quickly to avoid melting the butter. Continue mashing until the mixture resembles coarse crumbs.
    - Evenly drizzle 2 T juice over the flour mixture (pour a very thin stream of juice around and around the flour). Use a dinner fork to toss the mixture over and over until the mixture appears crumbly. If dry flour remains at the bottom of the bowl, drizzle another ½ T juice over the flour and toss the mixture until all flour sticks together. It is very important for crust tenderness that the flour and nut mixture remain dry and crumbly and not be wet and sticky.
    - Spread the flour mixture evenly over the bottom of the quiche dish or pie plate, piling it higher next to the sides. Use your fingers to push flour up the sides as close to the top as possible and to flatten the flour evenly over the sides and quiche dish/pie plate bottom.
    - Bake the crust for 8 minutes until the edges are lightly browned, setting a timer. At the timer, remove the crust from the oven and place it on a cooling rack.
    - Reduce the oven heat to 350 degrees.

4. 4. **Stir-fry/steam the cabbage.**

    - Heat a large nonstick skillet at medium. Begin heating an electric tea kettle to prepare water for steaming.
    - Place the cabbage half cut side down on a cutting board and use a chef's knife to halve it lengthwise to form two wedges.
    - Place each wedge on a cutting board and slice off the thickest portion of the stem end.
    - Use a chef's knife to cut the cabbage lengthwise into ⅓ in. wide slices. Cut the slices into ½ in. lengths. Go through the cabbage and finely chop any pieces with thick core to equalize the cooking time of pieces. Measure approx. 4 c cabbage.
    - Increase the skillet heat to medium-high, and when a drop of water added to the skillet instantly dances and disappears, add 1½ T oil, add the cabbage, evenly

PART 2

   sprinkle the dried marjoram leaves (first crushing them between your palms) over the cabbage, and stir-fry the cabbage for 1 minute, setting a timer.
   - At the timer, reduce the heat to medium (oil should continue to sizzle gently around cabbage pieces) and cook the cabbage for 1 minute, stirring it occasionally and setting a timer.
   - Add 1½ T hot water, cover the skillet, reduce the heat to low, and steam the cabbage, 4 minutes for green cabbage and 5 minutes for red cabbage, setting a timer.
   - At the timer, remove the skillet from the heat, sprinkle ⅓ t salt evenly over the cabbage, and use a rubber spatula to scrape the cabbage and any cooking juice into a colander placed over a dinner plate.
   - Wipe the skillet clean.

5. **Stir-fry the bell pepper.**

   - Heat the skillet at medium.
   - Use a 5 in. serrated knife to cut out the stem of the pepper. Remove any seeds but not the membrane. Use the serrated knife to cut the pepper lengthwise into ¼ in. thick strips and to cut the strips crosswise into ¼ in. cubes.
   - Increase the skillet heat to medium-high and when a drop of water added to the skillet instantly dances and disappears, add ½ T oil, add the pepper, and vigorously stir-fry it for about 30 seconds.
   - Reduce the heat to medium and cook the pepper for 2 minutes, stirring it occasionally and setting timer.
   - At the timer, use a rubber spatula to scrape the pepper and any cooking juice into the colander with the cabbage.
   - Wipe the skillet clean.

6. **Stir-fry the onion and ginger.**

   - Heat the skillet at a medium setting.
   - Place ½ onion cut side down on a cutting board and use a chef's knife to cut off its ends. Peel the onion. Again place the onion cut side down on the cutting board and use the chef's knife to dice the onion. Mince the ginger root.
   - Increase the heat to medium-high, and when a drop of water added to the skillet instantly dances and disappears, add 1 T oil, add the onion and ginger, evenly sprinkle the ½-1 t dried marjoram (first crushing it between your palms) over the onion/ginger, and vigorously stir-fry the mixture for about 30 seconds.
   - Reduce the heat to medium and cook the onion mixture for 2 minutes, stirring it occasionally and setting a timer.
   - At the timer, use a rubber spatula to scrape it onto a separate dinner plate separate from the other vegetables.

7. **Coarsely grate the cheese onto plastic wrap.**

8. **Chop the ¼ c nuts.** Use a chef's knife to coarsely chop the nuts.

9. **Assemble the quiche for baking.**

    - Add 1 c milk to the skillet and heat it at a medium setting.
    - Add 3 eggs to the medium mixing bowl and use a dinner fork or whisk to mix the yolks and whites. Mix ¼ c milk and ⅓ t salt into the eggs.
    - When the milk in the skillet is hot, remove the skillet from the heat. While stirring quickly and constantly with a rubber spatula to avoid cooking and hardening the eggs, slowly pour the egg mixture into the hot milk.
    - Evenly spread the onion, cheese, and nuts over the crust. Mix together the cabbage and bell pepper, including any cooking juice, and spread the vegetables over the onion mixture.
    - Pour the egg/milk mixture into the crust, being careful to add liquid only up to the top of the crust. Should the liquid gets close to the top of the crust, stop the pouring. Pour the remaining liquid into a measuring cup.
    - Center the quiche on a middle rack of the oven for baking. Pour any remaining liquid onto the quiche after it is in the oven.

10. **Bake the quiche for 30 minutes, setting a timer.**

    - At the timer, make a readiness check to verify that the custard has set. A knife inserted in the center should come out clean. If the knife is not clean, continue the baking for another 5 minutes and again make a readiness check.
    - When the custard is set, remove the quiche from the oven onto the cooling rack.
    - For easiest cutting, cool the quiche 10 or so minutes.

11. **Serve the quiche while it is still hot or at least warm.**

    VARIATIONS: Make ingredient or cooking dish substitutions. Substitute, for example,

    - **½-1 t each dried sweet basil and oregano leaves** for marjoram.
    - **10-12 Brussels sprouts** (boiled whole and halved, Recipe #61), halved, for cabbage.
    - **½ lb baby or mature bok choy** (Recipe #3) for cabbage.
    - **½ lb collard greens** (stir-fried/steamed, Recipe #25, or boiled whole, Recipe #64)) or any **other greens** (stir-fried/steamed, Recipes #23-30) for one half of the cabbage.
    - **whole raw almonds** or **raw walnut halves** for pecans in the crust.
    - **10 in. quiche dish**. For the quiche, increase the total milk content to 1½ c (mixing ½ c with the eggs), salt content to ½ c, and cheese content to 1¼ cup. For the crust, use 1 c flour, ⅓ c ground nuts, 3 T chilled butter, ⅓ t salt, and 2½-3 T juice.

    Add ingredients. Add, for example,

    - **6-8 mushrooms** (Recipe #33), sliced.
    - **6-8 chilled garlic cloves** (Recipe #31), minced.
    - **⅛ c Kalamata olives, quartered.** Evenly spread the olives over the vegetables before adding the milk/egg mixture.

COMMENTS: Medium whole wheat flour has clearly visible bits of bran, which give the flour a somewhat coarse texture. Even this small amount of bran makes a nutritional difference. Fine ground flour, in comparison, is silky smooth. Finely ground bran is effectively destroyed bran. See Reference #5 (Selecting High Quality Processed Ingredients for Use in Part II Recipes) for information about selecting whole wheat flour.

CHAPTER ELEVEN

Fruit Desserts

Fruit Dessert Description

CHAPTER ELEVEN FRUIT-BASED desserts are a variety of taste-tempting dishes that add both a pleasing and wholesome finish to a meal. These dual characteristics stand them a world apart from the typical modern dessert, which is all too commonly out of control – too big, too sugary, flavored with artificial ingredients, and including fruit as a mere decoration. Chapter Eleven desserts are decidedly different. Genuinely tasty fruit takes center stage, and it is combined with other high quality ingredients.

Fruit in Chapter Eleven desserts retains its vivid color, juiciness, and full flavor due to use of *juice-protective* preparation techniques. Recipes follow up this protective preparation with use of two serving methods that maintain natural fruit flavor through serving. These two serving methods are:

- serving fruit in a sauce, which protects juice that leaches from fruit as a result of cooking.
- serving fruit in dry form, which protects fruit juice from being leached from fruit during serving.

Chapter Eleven desserts also achieve high dish quality by routinely using less processed ingredients as opposed to highly processed and/or artificial ingredients. Recipes, for example, either use or recommend use of:

- pure extract as opposed to artificially flavored vanilla.
- unflavored and uncolored rather than artificially flavored and colored gelatin.
- butter rather than margarine.
- whole as opposed to white flour.
- certified organic flour and gelatin to avoid significant chemical tainting.
- dairy cream as opposed to artificial cream topping (Cool Whip).
- naturally flavored as opposed to artificially flavored ice cream.
- orange juice made from fresh squeezed or frozen orange juice concentrate as opposed to canned orange juice.
- orange juice with maximum pulp as opposed to pulp free.

PART 2

While desserts remain traditional desserts (they use fat and are similarly sweet), they do contain less fat and sugar than typical desserts and, outside of sugar, contain essentially no artificial chemical and highly processed food content. Family and friends can readily enjoy all Chapter Eleven fruit desserts both as traditional and wholesome dishes.

Fruit Dessert Preparation Notes

Preparation Notes provide helpful instruction and information about Chapter Eleven fruit desserts that cannot fit into individual recipes without over-cluttering them. These Notes cover a variety of subjects, including,

- details for maximizing the nutritional quality of ingredients used in recipes (Notes #1-2).
- information about preparing fruit variation suggestions made in recipes (Note #3).
- cooking tool information (Note #4).

1. **To significantly boost the nutritional quality of desserts, select naturally produced ingredients.** There is a great difference in the quality of naturally and industrially produced food products. *Cooked Alive!* includes three references to assist cooks in selecting naturally produced ingredients for use in Chapter Eleven fruit dessert recipes.

    - Reference #1 (Selecting Top Quality Fresh Whole Vegetables and Fruits) identifies and describes top quality fruit selections, which are fruits that are both naturally intact and naturally produced. Naturally produced fruit includes both certified organic and locally produced fruit. As fruits often used in Chapter Eleven dessert recipes, including apples, cherries, strawberries, grapes, and peaches, are among the most highly polluted of industrially produced fruit, the selection of naturally produced fruit is of particular significance.
    - Reference #4 (Selecting Top Quality Whole Food Ingredients for Use in Part II Recipes) identifies and describes whole food ingredients other than vegetables and fruits that are both naturally intact and naturally produced. Such products of relevance to Chapter Eleven desserts are certified organic and pastured eggs and certified organic nuts.
    - Reference #5 (Selecting High Quality Processed Ingredients for Use in Part II Recipes) identifies a variety of naturally produced food products that are physically processed but that retain significant nutritional quality. Products relevant to Chapter Eleven desserts include certified organic whole wheat flour, certified organic canned and dry frozen blueberries, certified organic and grass-fed dairy products (milk, butter, cream, sour cream, and cream cheese), and certified organic raisins.

2. **To boost the nutritional quality of highly processed ingredients in Chapter Eleven fruit desserts, select certified organic products.** While the nutritional content of these products is as depleted as industrially processed counterpart products, certified organic white sugar, brown sugar, and corn starch are naturally produced, which is an important difference. This means these ingredients are not genetically modified and are largely free of pesticide contamination. It means that sustainable agricultural production methods

have been used as opposed to chemically dependent methods that are highly destructive of the environment. Reference #4 (Selecting Top Quality Whole Food Ingredients for Use in Part II Recipes) details the significance of natural production.

3. **Chapter Four (Raw Fruit Pure and Simple) serves as a reference for preparing the fruit variation suggestions made in Chapter Eleven fruit dessert recipes.** The recipe number that is attached to the fruit variation identifies the Chapter Four reference recipe, which supplies basic preparation details as well as selection and nutritional information about the fruit.

4. **Important information about the cooking tools used in Chapter Eleven desserts is as follows:**

   - Recipes list all preparation tools used except for some basic wiping, drying, wrapping, and scrubbing tools – paper and cloth towels, plastic wrap, and vegetable scrubbing sponges and brushes – and regular size cutting boards. As these tools are routinely used in recipes, they need to be kept handy.
   - The General Cooking Tools list contained in the Part II Introduction serves as a descriptive reference for all Chapter Eleven cooking tools except for two tools that are specific to fruit desserts. These tools are:

     - **Zesting tool.** This tool efficiently removes thin strips of the outer skin of citrus fruit for use as flavoring in desserts.
     - **Apple corer.** A corer with an easy-to-grip handle is very useful. One that also releases the core is especially handy. Without this release handle, it is necessary to use an additional tool to push the core from the corer. A wooden spoon with a thin handle serves this purpose.

Fruit Dessert Recipes

201. Fruit Cup Dessert
(4 servings)

Fruit

10 fresh pineapple chunks (½ in. thick) (Recipe #94)
1 chilled nectarine
8 ripe strawberries (medium size)

10 each red & green seedless grapes
½ c blueberries
2 mandarin or clementine oranges
12 raspberries

PART 2

Other Ingredients

4 T frozen orange juice concentrate
3 t sugar

approx. 4 t honey (soft, easily spreadable)
⅓ c raw shelled pistachios

Preparation Tools and Serving Dishes

1 set each measuring spoons & cups
1 each 5 in. serrated, paring, & chef's knife
4 dessert bowls
1 small mixing bowl

1 cutting board for fruit
1 colander
1 pie plate
1 small dinner spoon

---

1. **Gather all ingredients and preparation tools.**

2. **Thaw the frozen orange juice concentrate.** Add it to a small bowl for thawing.

3. **Prepare the fruit.** Layer the fruit in the 4 dessert bowls.

   - Working on a clean cutting board, use a 5 in. serrated knife to halve the **pineapple chunks** lengthwise and evenly divide the pieces between 4 dessert bowls.
   - Rinse and dry the **nectarine** and use the serrated knife to cut it lengthwise into ⅓ in. thick slices. Cut the slices crosswise into 3 or 4 chunks. Evenly divide the chunks between the bowls.
   - Add the **strawberries** to a colander, use a 5 in. serrated knife to slice off the hulls, quickly rinse them under cool running water, and pour the berries onto a double layer of paper towels or a terry towel. Wrap the towels around the berries to dry them thoroughly. Use a serrated knife to halve each strawberry lengthwise. Place each half cut side down on a cutting board and cut it lengthwise into 3 slices. Divide the strawberry slices between the bowls, evenly spreading them over the nectarine. Evenly sprinkle ½ t sugar over the berries in each dessert bowl.
   - Add the **grapes** to the colander and rinse them with cool water. Pour the grapes into a pie plate lined with a double thickness of paper towels or a terry towel, wrap the towels around the grapes, and roll the grapes within the towels to dry them completely. Pick through the grapes, discarding stems and replacing spoiled or broken open grapes. Use a serrated knife to slice off any brown stem ends and to halve the grapes lengthwise, keeping red and green grapes separate. Evenly divide the grapes between the dessert bowls.
   - Add the **blueberries** to a colander and rinse them with cool water. Pour the berries into a pie plate lined with a double thickness of fresh paper towels or a terry cloth and wrap the towels around the berries to dry them completely. Pick through the berries to discard stems and to replace spoiled or broken open berries. Divide the berries between the dessert bowls.
   - Rinse and dry the **mandarin** or **clementine oranges**. Use a 5 in. serrated knife to

halve them crosswise. Peel the halves, use the point of a paring knife to pry out any seeds, gently separate the segments, and evenly divide the segments between the dessert bowls.
- Add the **raspberries** to a colander and rinse them with cool water. Spread the berries over a double thickness of paper towels. Loosely wrap the towels around the berries to dry them. Arrange the berries hole side down on the towels and evenly sprinkle 1 t sugar over them.

4. **Chop the nuts.** Use a chef's knife to chop the nuts coarsely.

5. **Assemble the desserts for serving.** Gently toss the fruit ingredients in each dessert bowl together. Add 3 raspberries per bowl. For each dessert, dip a dinner spoon into honey and drizzle the honey evenly over the fruit. Add 1 T thawed frozen orange juice concentrate per bowl. Top the fruit with nuts.

VARIATIONS: Make ingredient substitutions. Substitute, for example,

- ⅓ c **raw pecan halves, walnut halves, almonds,** or a **mixture of nuts** for pistachios.
- **4 cantaloupe** slices (½ in. thick; Recipe #80) for nectarine. Slice the cantaloupe flesh from the skins and cut each slice crosswise into 4-5 equal chunks.
- **1 peach** (Recipe #92) for nectarine.
- **2 c sweet cherries** (Recipe #81) for grapes and strawberries when cherries are
- in season. Pit and halve the cherries lengthwise.
- **2 tangerines** (Recipe #99) or **other tasty and brightly colored citrus fruit,** such as **tangelo** (Recipe #89), for mandarin or clementine oranges.

Add fruit ingredients, adding approx. ¼ t honey and 1 t concentrated orange juice for each added fruit. Add, for example,

- **1 mango** (Recipe #87).
- **8 blackberries** (Recipe #79).
- **1 sliced plum** (Recipe #95).
- **4 T pomegranate seeds** (Recipe #96).
- **1 kiwi** (Recipe #86). Kiwi adds striking color, but it should be added as a last ingredient only just prior to serving.

COMMENTS: To prepare the fruit several hours ahead of serving, cover and refrigerate the individual fruits. Always cut orange immediately before – or as close as possible to – serving. Cut nectarine shortly before serving to avoid browning.

202. Raspberry Sauce and Ice Cream Dessert
(4 servings)

Fruit

2 c dry frozen unsweetened raspberries, unthawed

½ lemon

Other Ingredients

2 T frozen orange juice concentrate
2 T frozen cranberry juice concentrate or frozen grape juice concentrate
2 t cornstarch

3 T orange juice with pulp
2 T sugar
1 qt premium vanilla ice cream or frozen yogurt (see comments below)

Preparation Tools and Serving Dishes

1 medium nonstick skillet
1 small mixing bowl
1 hand citrus squeezer
1 dinner fork or small whisk
1 plastic or plastic-coated stir-fry spatula

1 rubber or other heat-resistant spatula
1 small heat-resistant glass serving bowl
1 ice cream scoop
4 dessert goblets or bowls

1. **Gather all preparation tools and ingredients.**

2. **Heat a medium nonstick skillet on a low heat setting.** Add and melt the orange and cranberry frozen fruit concentrate. Be watchful and do not let the juice get hot; remove the skillet from the burner once the juice melts.

3. **Combine the orange and cranberry juice concentrates, cornstarch, and lemon.**

    - Add the melted concentrated juices (2 T each) and 2 t cornstarch to a small mixing bowl and use a dinner fork or whisk to combine the ingredients.
    - Squeeze the lemon and add it (including pulp) to the mixture.

4. **Cook the frozen raspberries.**

    - Add 3 T orange juice to the nonstick skillet, bring the juice to full boiling over near high heat in the skillet, mix the berries into the juice, and, once the juice again begins to boil, reduce the heat to medium-high and stir-fry the berries for about 1 minute until the berries are heated through, turning them over and over.
    - Reduce the skillet heat to medium and mix in the 2 T sugar.

5. **Add the cornstarch mixture to the cooked raspberries.**

    - Quickly re-stir the cornstarch mixture and slowly add it to the cooked raspberries, stirring quickly and constantly with a rubber spatula to prevent lumping.
    - Increase the skillet heat to medium-high.
    - Heat the raspberry sauce until it begins to boil, stirring often.
    - Once the sauce boils, immediately reduce the heat to medium and cook the sauce for a few minutes until it thickens and clears, stirring the sauce frequently and rubbing across the skillet bottom to prevent sticking.
    - Remove the skillet from the heat. Taste the sauce and add touches (1 t at a time) of lemon juice and sugar to taste.
    - Use a rubber spatula to scrape the sauce into a heat-resistant glass serving bowl.

6. **Serve the sauce warm over ice cream.** Add ice cream to 4 dessert goblets and add 2-3 dollops of raspberry topping.

7. **Refrigerate extra sauce, tightly covered.** Re-serve the sauce chilled or reheat it in a microwave oven for about 1 minute.

    VARIATIONS: Add **1 c fresh raspberries** (Recipe #97). Evenly sprinkle 1 t sugar over the rinsed and dried berries. Stir the berries into the sauce once the sauce has cooled thoroughly or serve them as a topping over the sauce.

    Make ingredient substitutions. Substitute, for example,

    - **1 c whole dry frozen strawberries** or **whole dry frozen blackberries** for 1 c frozen raspberries. Add unthawed strawberries to a small bowl and microwave heat them for 30 seconds. Use a chef's knife to halve them lengthwise. Place halved strawberries cut side down on the cutting board and halve them lengthwise.
    - **frozen cherry juice concentrate** for frozen cranberry juice concentrate. This juice varies the flavor somewhat and, like cranberry juice, gives the sauce deep red coloring. Include half frozen orange juice concentrate for tanginess.
    - **home-prepared fresh ice cream** for commercially prepared. Several different types of electric ice cream machines that quickly (in around 25 minutes) yield a small amount of ice cream are being marketed, such as by Cuisinart, Krups, and Donvier. One basic recipe that yields a small batch (6 c) of delicious ice cream is as follows:

        - Combine **1 c milk (whole or 2%; not skim)** and **1 c sugar** in a large mixing bowl and stir the mixture continuously with a rubber spatula until the sugar dissolves. Refrigerate the milk until it is chilled, at least 1 hour. This chilling of the 1 c milk and sugar is optional, but with this chilling the ice cream is reliably firm at the end of churning.
        - Mix in **1 c more milk (whole or 2%)**, **1 c heavy whipping cream**, and **2 t pure extract vanilla** and pour the mixture into the freezer of the ice cream machine for churning.

PART 2

- Churn the ice cream for 26 minutes. Scrape the ice cream into a storage container, tightly seal the container, and freeze the ice cream.

COMMENTS: The flavor of frozen fruit juice concentrate is variable depending on the brand of the product. Select Minute Maid frozen orange juice concentrate and Welch's frozen grape juice concentrate as especially tasty products.

203. Peaches and Cream Dessert
(2 servings)

Fruit and Flavoring

2 T frozen orange juice concentrate
2 chilled ripe peaches

2 t honey (easily spreadable, not thick)
4 T heavy whipping cream

Preparation Tools and Serving Dishes

1 set measuring spoons
2 dessert goblets or dessert bowls
1 dish scrubbing sponge with a rough side

1 dinner fork
1 dinner spoon
1 serrated knife

1. **Add 1 T orange juice concentrate to two dessert bowls.** Mash the concentrate with a dinner fork to speed thawing.

2. **Prepare the peaches.**

    - Rinse the peaches under cool running water. If the peaches are organic, use the rough side of a dish scrubbing sponge to gently rub off the fuzz on the skin and thoroughly dry each peach with a paper towel. If the peaches are not organic, peel the peaches after drying.
    - Use a serrated knife to cut out any spoiled spots and cut each peach lengthwise into ¼ in. thick slices, cutting to the pit. For non-free stone peaches, cut the slices from the pit.
    - Cut the slices crosswise into 3-4 chunks and add the chunks to a serving bowl as they are cut.
    - Gently stir the chunks into the orange juice concentrate to coat them completely.

3. **Assemble the peaches for serving.** Dip a dinner spoon into honey and evenly drizzle the honey over the peaches, one spoonful per peach. Top each bowl of peaches with 2 T heavy cream.

VARIATION: Make ingredient substitutions. Substitute, for example,

- **2 nectarines** (Recipe #88) for peaches.
- **2 c in-season sweet cherries** (Recipe #81) for peaches.
- **2 t certified organic agave syrup** or **sugar** for honey.

Add ingredients. Add, for example,

- **2 T chopped pistachios** or **pecan halves** per dessert, added as a topping.
- **½-1 c fresh blueberries** (Recipe #78).
- **1 t fresh squeezed lemon juice** to the frozen orange juice concentrate.

COMMENTS: In selecting peaches, select ripe peaches with flesh that gives slightly when gently squeezed, that feel heavy for their size, and that are aromatic. Because peaches are regularly included in lists of fruits with the greatest pesticide content, select certified organic peaches whenever they are an option.

In selecting cream, select certified organic cream and, in particular, select certified organic cream from grass-fed dairy cows.

204. Berry, Mandarin Orange, and Yogurt Dessert
(4 servings)

Fresh Fruit

1 c blueberries
8 raspberries
8 blackberries

1 t sugar
2 mandarin oranges

Other Ingredients

4 c plain, very fresh cream-on-the-top yogurt, stirred before being measured
4 t sugar
1½ T dried tart cherries

1½ T organic raisins
⅓ c raw pecan or walnut halves or almonds or a mixture of pecans and almonds
approx. 4 t honey (soft, easy to pour)

Preparation Tools and Serving Dishes

4 roomy goblets or dessert bowls (10 oz size)
1 set each measuring cups & spoons
1 large dinner spoon
1 each chef's, 5 in. serrated, & paring knife

1 cutting board
1 colander
1 pie plate
1 small dinner spoon

PART 2

1. **Gather all preparation tools and ingredients.**

2. **Add ¾-1 c yogurt to each dessert bowl.** Sprinkle 1 t sugar over the top of each serving of yogurt and use a dinner spoon to stir the sugar into the yogurt.

3. **Prepare the nuts and dried tart cherries.** Use a chef's knife to chop the nuts coarsely on a cutting board and to chop the dried cherries, chopping each into 2-3 smaller pieces. Mix the dried cherries and nuts together.

4. **Prepare the blueberries.** Add the blueberries to a colander and rinse them with cool water. Pour them into a pie plate lined with a double thickness of paper towels or a terry towel and wrap the towels around the berries to dry them completely. Pick through the berries to discard stems and to replace any mushy, soft, moldy, and broken open berries. Evenly divide the blueberries between the dessert bowls, centering them on the yogurt in each bowl.

5. **Prepare the blackberries** and **raspberries**. Add the berries to a colander, rinse them with cool water, and add them to the pie plate lined with a double thickness of paper towels. Gently wrap the paper towels around the berries to dry them completely. Pick through the berries and replace overripe, broken open, and moldy berries. Closely group the raspberries hole side down on the paper towel, evenly sprinkle 1 t sugar over them, and evenly divide the raspberries between the desserts, centering them with the blueberries. Use a serrated knife to halve each blackberry lengthwise and divide the blackberries between the dessert bowls, centering them cut side down with the raspberries.

6. **Prepare the mandarin oranges**.

    - Rinse and dry the oranges.
    - Use a serrated knife to halve the oranges crosswise.
    - Peel the halves, use the point of a paring knife to pry out any seeds, and gently separate the segments.
    - Evenly divide the segments between the dessert bowls, ½ orange per bowl.

7. **Assemble the desserts for serving.** For each dessert, dip a dinner teaspoon into honey and evenly drizzle most of the clinging honey over the fruit. Top each bowl with an equal portion of the dried fruit and nut mixture.

    VARIATIONS: Make ingredient substitutions. Substitute, for example,

    - **2 clementine oranges** (Recipe #90) or **tangerines** (Recipe #99) for mandarin oranges. Prepare tangerines exactly like mandarin oranges.
    - **2 c in-season sweet cherries** (Recipe #81), such as Rainier or Bing cherries, pitted and halved lengthwise, for berries.

- **2 ripe peaches** (Recipe #92) or **nectarines** (Recipe #88) for mandarin oranges.
- **2% fat plain yogurt** for cream-on-top yogurt.

Add ingredients. Add, for example,

- ½-1 c **fresh pineapple chunks** (Recipe #94), cut into ½ in. chunks.
- **banana** (Recipe #77), ⅓ medium banana cut into chunks per dessert. Add the banana as a first fruit ingredient and press the pieces down into the yogurt to help protect them from browning.
- ⅛ c **fruit topping** (Recipes #219-223) per dessert.
- 1-2 t **frozen orange juice concentrate**, thawed, or **other flavor of frozen juice concentrates**, such as Welch's grape, to the fruit in each dessert bowl before adding the honey.
- **sprinkling of the zest of an organic orange**, either to the yogurt or as a topping.

COMMENTS: To prepare the dessert well ahead of serving, prepare and separately cover and refrigerate the sweetened yogurt, nuts, and the individual fruits except for banana, if using, which is best cut shortly before serving. Assemble the desserts somewhat ahead of serving, adding the frozen fruit concentrate when serving the dish.

205. Baked Apples
(8 servings)

Fresh Fruit

8 chilled apples   ½ lemon

Other Ingredients

1½ c premium orange juice with pulp   16 raw pecan halves
½ c packed dark brown sugar   1 t ground cinnamon
2-4 T frozen orange juice concentrate   2 T chilled butter (opt)
¼ c packed dark brown sugar   ½ c heavy cream or half & half
3 T certified organic raisins

Cooking Tools

2½ qt rectangular baking dish with a lid or 10 in.   1 apple corer
   square shallow baking dish or non-stick   1 swivel vegetable peeler
   baking pan with an aluminum foil cover   1 or 2 padded oven gloves
1 set each measuring cups & spoons   1 large (9 x 13 in.) sided baking pan
1 hand lemon squeezer   1 timer
1 chef's knife

PART 2

1. **Gather all cooking tools and ingredients.**

2. **Preheat an oven to 375 degrees.**

3. **Prepare the cooking sauce.**

   - Add the 1½ c orange juice to the baking dish.
   - Squeeze the lemon and add the lemon juice to the baking dish.
   - Add ½ c packed dark brown sugar.
   - Heat the baking dish at a medium heat setting on a large stove burner while preparing the apples.

4. **Prepare the butter.** Use a chef's knife to cut the butter into 8 equal pieces.

5. **Prepare the apples.**

   - Rinse and dry each apple.
   - Level any apple that does not sit straight in the baking dish. This leveling eases the removal of the apple core. To level an apple, use a chef's knife to slice off a bit of the bottom of the apple.
   - Use an apple corer to remove the apple cores.
   - Use a swivel vegetable peeler to remove a thin strip of skin from around the hole made at the top of each apple. This step is optional.
   - Set each apple into the baking dish as it is prepared.

6. **Stuff the apples.** Layering ingredients, fill each apple with ½ T (approx. 10) raisins, ½ T packed brown sugar, 2 pecan halves (roughly broken), 1 piece of butter, and ⅛ t cinnamon powder.

7. **Bring the cooking sauce in the baking dish to near boiling.** Increase the heat slightly to bring about boiling.

8. **Bake the apples.**

   - Cover the baking dish and use baking gloves to transfer the dish to the center of a middle rack in the oven.
   - Place a baking pan directly below the dish to catch juice in case a spillover occurs.
   - Set a timer for 20 minutes. If the apples are completely softened (they begin to break apart and are very aromatic) at the timer, remove them from the oven. If they are not, continue the baking and check them every 5 minutes until they are.

9. **Serve the apples warm.** Add an apple to an individual serving bowl and top it with 2-3 T cooking juice and 2 T cream or half & half.

10. **Refrigerate leftover apples tightly covered.** For reheating, add an individual apple and a small amount (1-2 T) of baking juice to a small microwave safe serving bowl and heat the apple until hot, from 40-60 seconds. Add cream or half & half after the heating.

VARIATIONS: Make ingredient substitutions. Substitute, for example,

- **¾ c apple juice** (and fresh apple juice in particular) for ¾ c orange juice in the cooking sauce.
- **frozen apple juice concentrate** for frozen orange juice concentrate in the cooking sauce.

COMMENTS: In selecting apples, select slightly tart apples. Given the extremely high pesticide content of industrially produced apples, select certified organic or locally produced apples. See Recipe #74 for apple selection details.

In selecting an apple corer, select one with an easy to grip handle and one that releases the core. Otherwise, use a long thin tool such a wooden spoon with a narrow handle to push the apple cores from the corer.

206. Fruit Gelatin Dessert
(With Sweetened Whipped Cream Topping)
(6-8 servings)

Fresh Fruit

½ c fresh or frozen pineapple, ½ in. thick chunks
¼ c premium orange juice with pulp
1 c each red & green seedless grapes
6-8 medium strawberries
1 t sugar

1 c fresh blueberries
2 chilled nectarines
4 mandarin or clementine oranges
½ c raspberries
1 t sugar

Gelatin

1 c cold water
2 1-oz packages unflavored gelatin
⅓ c honey
⅓ c frozen orange juice concentrate

1½ c premium orange juice with pulp
1 c unsweetened pineapple or mango juice
   with pulp or add 1 c more orange juice

Whipped Cream

1 c heavy whipping cream
2 T sugar

1 t pure extract vanilla

PART 2

Cooking and Preparation Tools

1 set each measuring cups & spoons
2 medium stainless steel or nonstick skillets
1 small mixing bowl
1 timer
1 rubber or other heat-resistant spatula
1 stir-fry spatula
1 colander
1 dinner plate

3 medium (6 c) glass or stainless steel mixing bowls
1 cutting board reserved for fruit
1 each 5 in. serrated & paring knife
1 pie plate
1 large (16 c) glass serving bowl
1 electric or hand rotary mixer
2 c glass storage container with lid

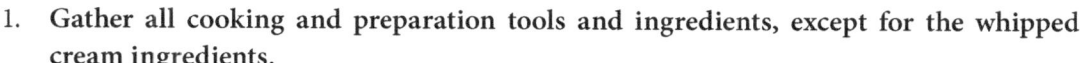

1. **Gather all cooking and preparation tools and ingredients, except for the whipped cream ingredients.**

2. **Soften the gelatin.** Add 1 c cold water to a medium skillet, sprinkle the gelatin over it, and let the gelatin soften for 5 minutes, setting a timer. At the timer, heat the gelatin over low heat until it dissolves completely, stirring it occasionally with a rubber spatula.

3. **Cook the pineapple while the gelatin softens.**

    - Add ¼ c orange juice to another medium skillet and heat the juice to full boiling over near high heat.
    - Mix in the pineapple, and when the juice returns to boiling, cook it in stir-fry manner for 1 minute until the pieces are heated through, turning the pieces over and over and setting a timer.
    - Immediately scrape the pineapple and any cooking juice into a colander placed over a bowl or a dinner plate for collecting the juice.
    - Add the pineapple to a small mixing bowl and refrigerate it for chilling.

4. **Prepare the gelatin.**

    - Add ⅓ c each honey and frozen orange juice concentrate to the warmed gelatin in the skillet. Use a rubber spatula to thoroughly mix in the honey and juice.
    - Add and mix in 1½ c orange juice, either 1 c pineapple or mango juice, and the collected pineapple cooking juice.
    - Remove the skillet from the heat and scrape the gelatin mixture into a medium glass mixing bowl.
    - Refrigerate the gelatin until it begins to thicken, about 30 minutes, setting a timer.
    - At the timer, begin checking for thickening. The gelatin is ready when it slightly holds together during gentle shaking. **It is very important that the gelatin not completely set before adding the fruit.** It then becomes impossible to mix in the fruit.

5. **Prepare the fruit while the gelatin thickens.** Check the gelatin periodically while preparing the fruit and begin adding fruit as it is cut should the gelatin begin to thicken.

- Add the **grapes** to a colander and rinse them with cool water. Add the grapes to a pie plate lined with a double thickness of paper towels or a terry towel. Pick through the grapes, removing any stems and replacing any spoiled or broken ones. Wrap the paper towels around the grapes and gently squeeze the grapes to dry them thoroughly. Working on a cutting board, use a serrated knife to cut off any brown stem ends and to halve each grape lengthwise. Add the grapes to a large (16 c) serving bowl, spreading them evenly over the bowl bottom.
- Add the **blueberries** to a colander and rinse them with cool water. Add a fresh double layer of paper towels or terry towel to the pie plate and add the blueberries. Pick through them, discarding stems and replacing overripe, spoiled, or broken berries. Wrap the towels around the berries to dry them thoroughly and spread them over the grapes.
- Add the **strawberries** to a colander, use a serrated knife to slice off the hulls, rinse the strawberries with cool water, and spread the strawberries in a pie plate lined with a dry double thickness of fresh paper towels. Pick through the strawberries and cut off any spoiled areas, white pulp, or rough tips. Wrap the towels around the berries and lightly squeeze them to dry them thoroughly. Halve each berry lengthwise, place the halves cut side down on a clean and dry cutting surface, and slice each lengthwise into equal 3 slices. Spread the slices over the blueberries and evenly sprinkle 1 t sugar over them.
- Rinse and dry the **nectarines**. Use a serrated knife to slice each nectarine lengthwise into ⅓ in. thick slices, cutting under the slices to remove from the pit as they are cut. Cut each slice crosswise into 3-4 equal chunks and evenly spread the chunks over the strawberries.
- Add the **raspberries** to the colander and rinse them with cool water. Spread the berries in a pie plate lined with paper towels, wrap the towels around the berries, and very lightly press the berries to dry them. Place the raspberries hole side down on the paper towel, bunch them together, and evenly sprinkle 1 t sugar over them. Add ½ to the other fruit and set ½ of the raspberries aside.
- Rinse and dry the **mandarin oranges** and use a serrated knife to halve each crosswise.
- Peel the halves, use a paring knife to pry out any seeds, gently separate the segments, and add the orange to the other fruit.
- Remove the **cooled pineapple** from the refrigerator, use a serrated knife to cut the chunks into ¼ in. wide slices, add the pineapple to the other fruit in the bowl, and gently toss the fruit pieces to distribute them evenly.

6. **Immediately assemble the gelatin when it begins to thicken.**

- Use a rubber spatula to scrape the slightly thickened gelatin over the fruit in the serving bowl. Gently stir the fruit into the gelatin.
- Evenly distribute the reserved raspberries over the top of the gelatin, pushing them slightly into the gelatin.
- Tightly cover the bowl with plastic wrap (which should not touch the gelatin) and refrigerate the gelatin.

PART 2

7. **Refrigerate the gelatin until it is firmly set, at least one hour.**

8. **Prepare sweetened whipped cream while the gelatin sets.**

   - Add 1 c heavy cream to a medium and deep mixing bowl and use an electric or hand rotary mixer to beat the whipping cream until it begins to thicken.
   - Add 2 T sugar and ½ t vanilla and beat the cream until it thickens fully. Be careful to avoid over-beating, which will cause the cream to separate.
   - Refrigerate the whipped cream in a small (2 cup) glass storage container, covered, until serving.

9. **Serve the gelatin in dessert bowls with individual portions topped with whipped cream.**

10. **Refrigerate extra gelatin, covered.** Use within 4-5 days. Refrigerate extra whipped cream, covered, and re-stir it for serving. Make additional whipped cream as may be needed.

    VARIATIONS: Make ingredient or serving container substitutions. Substitute, for example,

    - **2 clementine oranges** for mandarin oranges.
    - **1 navel orange** (Recipe #89), **2 tangerines** (Recipe #99), **2 tangelos** (Recipe #89), or any **other tasty orange** for mandarin oranges.
    - **1 peach** (Recipe #92) for nectarine.
    - **individual serving goblets/dessert bowls** for 1 large serving bowl. Alternatively, divide part of the fruit gelatin into individual serving bowls and thicken the remaining gelatin in a medium serving bowl. Fill individual goblets ½ full with fruit and pour gelatin over the fruit, enough to mix into and cover the fruit.

    Add ingredients. Add, for example,

    - **1 mango** (Recipe #87), cubed.
    - **2 sliced red or purple plums** (Recipe #95).
    - **½ c sweet cherries** (Recipe #81).
    - **½ c of ½ in. cubes of cantaloupe** (Recipe #80).
    - **½ c pomegranate seeds** (Recipe #96).
    - **¼-⅓ c raw pecan** or **walnut halves**, coarsely chopped.

    Do not add **raw kiwi, pineapple,** or **papaya**, which contain enzymes that will prevent jelling. Do not add **banana** due to browning. Include only **apple** or **pear** dipped in a citrus wash (1 T water, 2 T orange juice) and thoroughly drained in a colander.

    COMMENTS: This is an extra special gelatin dessert that is both lovely in appearance and flavor. It has outstanding keeping quality. It maintains the flavor, texture, and color of the fruit ingredients in top quality form for several days. Additionally, this gelatin contains no chemicals and minimal sweetening. Serving the gelatin in glass dessert goblets converts the dessert into special occasion form. Select fairly large goblets to leave plenty of room for both fruit and the whipped cream topping.

Select certified organic fruit products, heavy whipping cream, and unflavored gelatin to significantly reduce the pesticide content of fruit gelatin dessert.

207. Mini Cheesecake Dessert
(4 servings)
(8 Cheesecakes)

Fruit Sauce Topping Ingredients

½ c premium orange juice with pulp
2 t cornstarch
½ c premium orange juice with pulp
2 T frozen orange juice concentrate

½ lemon
2 T sugar
1 c dry frozen unsweetened blueberries, pitted sweet cherries, or raspberries

Crust Ingredients

2 T butter
½ c raw walnut or pecan halves
¼ t salt

½ c medium ground whole wheat flour
1-2 t cold orange juice

Cheesecake Filling Ingredients

1 large egg
3 oz cream cheese, softened

2 T sugar
½ t pure extract vanilla

Fruit Sauce Cooking Tools

1 set each measuring cups & spoons
1 medium nonstick skillet
1 small mixing bowl
1 dinner fork or small whisk

1 hand lemon squeezer
1 rubber or other heat-resistant spatula
1 heat-resistant medium storage bowl

Crust Baking Tools

1 set each measuring cups & spoons
1 small skillet
1 blender
1 thin-bladed spatula
1 medium mixing bowl
1 rubber spatula

1 dinner fork
12-tin (1 in. deep) nonstick muffin pan, with the sides and the bottoms of 8 tins lightly buttered or coated with nonstick spray

PART 2

Cheesecake Cooking Tools

1 medium mixing bowl
1 wooden spoon or hand electric beater
1 firm rubber spatula
1 timer

1 or 2 padded oven gloves
1 cooling rack
4 dessert plates

1. **Prepare the fruit sauce.** Gather together all fruit sauce ingredients and cooking tools except for the frozen berries. Leave the berries frozen until just before cooking them.

   - Add ½ c orange juice to a small skillet and heat the skillet at medium.
   - Add ½ c orange juice and 2 t cornstarch to a small mixing bowl and use a fork or whisk to mix in the cornstarch.
   - Squeeze the lemon and add 1 T lemon juice, 2 T frozen orange juice concentrate, and 2 T sugar to the juice in the skillet. Refrigerate any leftover lemon juice, covered, for another use.
   - Increase the skillet heat to medium-high and bring the juice to boiling.
   - Break up any clumps of frozen fruit while the fruits remains in its freezer package and add the frozen fruit to the boiling juice. When the juice returns to boiling, re-stir the cornstarch mixture and slowly pour it into the fruit juice mixture while stirring quickly and constantly with a rubber spatula to avoid lumping.
   - Once the cornstarch mixture is mixed in, reduce the heat to medium and cook the mixture for about two minutes until the sauce thickens and clears, stirring it frequently.
   - Remove the skillet from the heat, scrape the mixture into a heat-resistant bowl, and refrigerate it, uncovered. When preparing the mixture ahead, cover the mixture once it cools.

2. **Prepare the crusts.** Gather together all crust ingredients and preparation tools.

   - Melt 2 T butter in a small skillet on low-low heat.
   - Finely grind ½ c nuts in a blender, blending ⅛ c at a time and using a thin-bladed spatula to scrape the nuts from the blender into a medium mixing bowl as they are blended.
   - Mix ½ c flour and ¼ t salt into the ground nuts.
   - Using a rubber spatula to scrape the melted butter from the skillet, drizzle the butter evenly over the flour mixture. Use a dinner fork to mix in the butter, tossing the mixture continually and adding touches of juice 1 t at a time until the flour and nut mixture sticks together (no dry flour should remain at the bottom). For a tender crust, it is very important to avoid adding any more juice than is necessary to barely hold the flour mixture together.
   - Evenly divide the flour mixture between 8 muffin pan tins and use your fingers to gently and evenly press the mixture over the tin bottoms and halfway up the sides of each tin.

3. **Assemble and bake the cheesecakes.** Set the oven at 350 degrees. Gather all cheesecake ingredients and preparation tools.

- Add 1 egg and 3 oz cream cheese to a medium mixing bowl and use a wooden spoon or electric mixer to mix them together until smooth.
- Add and mix in 2 T sugar and ½ t vanilla.
- Use a rubber spatula to evenly scrape the filling into the crusts, being careful to avoid overfilling.
- Center the muffin pan on a middle oven rack and bake the cheesecakes for 10 minutes, setting a timer.
- At the timer, place the muffin pan on a cooling rack and allow the cheesecakes to cool completely before carefully removing them from the tins.

4. **Serve the mini cheesecakes.** Top each cheesecake with fruit topping and serve two cheesecakes per serving on dessert plates.

VARIATION: Make ingredient and baking pan substitutions. Substitute, for example,

- **a mixture of berries** in the fruit topping in place of either blueberries or raspberries. For example, use ½-¾ **c each dry frozen blueberries** and **sweet or sour cherries** (Recipe #81, adding 3 T sugar for sour cherries) or ½-¾ **c each dry frozen blueberries** and **raspberries**.
- **a nonstick muffin pan with 12 small, shallow tins** (½ in. deep; 2½ in. wide) or **two 6-tin small muffin pans** for a muffin pan with 12 1-in. deep tins. Kitchen stores market these small muffin pans.

Add ingredients. Add, for example,

- Add **½ t lemon extract** to the cheesecake batter.
- Add a **sour cream topping** to the cheesecakes. Mix together ¼ c sour cream and 1 t sugar and spread the mixture over the cheesecakes before adding the fruit sauce topping.

208. Individual Cherry Trifle Dessert
(4 servings)

Vanilla Pudding

1½ c milk (whole or 2%)
¼ c sugar
⅛ t salt
1 T cornstarch

¼ c milk (whole or 2%)
2 large egg yolks
¼ c milk (whole or 2%)
1 t pure vanilla extract

PART 2

Cherry Sauce Topping

¾ c premium orange juice with pulp
1½ T sugar
½ lemon
¼ c premium orange juice with pulp

2 t cornstarch
1 c dry frozen pitted unsweetened dark red tart or Bing cherries, unthawed

Whipped Sweet Cream Topping

¾ c heavy whipping cream
1½ T sugar

½ t pure vanilla extract

Fresh Fruit and Nut Toppings

½ c fresh pineapple chunks (½ in. thick) (Recipe #94)
16 fresh dark sweet cherries (Bing or Rainier cherries)

½ c fresh blueberries
⅓ c raw pistachios, pecan halves, or walnut halves

Vanilla Pudding Preparation Tools

1 large heavy-bottomed nonstick skillet
1 set each measuring cups & spoons
2 small mixing bowls
1 dinner fork or small whisk

1 rubber or other heat-resistant spatula
4 large (10 oz) clear dessert goblets or
4 large (10 oz) dessert bowls

Cherry Sauce Cooking Tools

1 set each measuring cups & spoons
1 large heavy-bottomed nonstick or other nonreactive skillet
1 hand lemon squeezer
1 small mixing bowl

1 dinner fork or small whisk
1 cutting board
1 chef's knife
1 rubber or other heat-resistant spatula
1 heat-resistant medium glass serving bowl

Whipped Cream Preparation Tools

1 set each measuring cups & spoons
1 small, deep mixing bowl

1 electric or hand rotary beater

Fresh Fruit and Nut Topping Preparation Tools

1 set measuring cups
1 each serrated & chef's knife
3 small glass mixing bowls
1 colander

1 pie plate
1 cherry pitting tool
1 cutting board

1. **Prepare the vanilla pudding.**

    - Gather all the pudding ingredients and cooking tools.
    - Add 1½ c milk, ¼ c sugar, and ⅛ t salt to a large nonstick skillet and heat the mixture at a medium setting.
    - Add 1 T cornstarch and ¼ c milk to a small mixing bowl and use a dinner fork or whisk to mix in the cornstarch.
    - In another small bowl, use the same dinner fork or whisk to mix 2 egg yolks and ¼ c milk together.
    - Increase the skillet heat to a high medium. When the milk is very hot (a slight scum will appear on its surface), re-stir the cornstarch and milk mixture and slowly pour it into the hot milk, stirring quickly and constantly with a rubber spatula to keep the cornstarch from lumping. Continue stirring, often scraping over the bottom of the skillet to prevent sticking, until the pudding thickens, clears, and begins to boil.
    - Remove the skillet from the heat.
    - Mix in the egg yolk and milk mixture. First pour ½ c of the hot pudding into the egg and milk mixture while stirring quickly and constantly with a rubber spatula. Then slowly pour all of the egg and milk mixture into the hot pudding, again stirring quickly and constantly to keep the egg yolks from hardening.
    - Stir in the vanilla.
    - Scrape the pudding into a heat resistant medium bowl and allow the pudding to cool somewhat, 5-10 minutes.
    - Divide the pudding between four dessert bowls, filling each goblet or bowl no more than ⅓ full. If extra pudding remains, either add it to a small bowl or assemble more goblets or bowls.
    - Cover each dessert glass with plastic wrap and refrigerate the puddings.
    - Immediately add hot water to and clean the nonstick skillet.

2. **Prepare the cherry topping.**

    - Gather the cooking tools and ingredients except for the frozen cherries, which should be kept frozen until just before being cooked.
    - Add ¾ c orange juice and 1½ T sugar to the cleaned large nonstick skillet and heat the mixture at medium.
    - Squeeze the ½ lemon and add 1 T lemon juice to the skillet. Refrigerate remaining lemon juice, covered, for another use.
    - Add 2 t cornstarch and ¼ c orange juice to a small mixing bowl and use a dinner fork or whisk to mix in the ingredients.
    - Remove the cherries from the freezer, break apart any clumps of cherries while they remain in the freezer package, empty the cherries onto a cutting board, allow the cherries to sit about 1 minute (no more; do not allow them to thaw) to soften slightly, and then use a chef's knife to halve the cherries.

PART 2

- Increase the skillet heat to medium-high and bring the juice to full boiling. Add and stir in the cherries and return the juice to boiling.
- Re-stir the cornstarch mixture and slowly pour it into the boiling juice while stirring quickly and constantly with a rubber spatula.
- Reduce the heat to medium and cook the mixture for a few minutes until it boils, clears, and thickens, stirring frequently.
- Remove the skillet from the heat, scrape the topping into a heat resistant medium bowl, and refrigerate the bowl, uncovered. For quick cooling, place the topping in the freezer for 10 minutes, setting a timer, before refrigerating it.

3. **Prepare the whipped cream.**

   - Gather the dish ingredients and preparation tools.
   - Add ¾ c cream to a small, deep bowl and use an electric or rotary hand beater to beat the cream until it begins to thicken.
   - Add 1½ T sugar and ½ t pure vanilla extract and continue beating the cream until it fully thickens, being careful to avoid over-beating, which will cause the cream to separate.
   - Cover and refrigerate the whipped cream.

4. **Prepare the fresh fruit and nuts.**

   - Gather the needed preparation tools.
   - Use a serrated knife to slice the **pineapple chunks** lengthwise into thirds and set them aside in a small bowl.
   - Place the **cherries** in a colander, rinse them under cool running water, and add them to a pie plate lined with a double thickness of paper towels or a terry towel. Pick through the cherries to remove any stems and to replace any spoiled or broken berries. Wrap the paper towels around the berries to dry them completely. Use a pitting tool to remove the pits, use a serrated knife to halve the berries lengthwise, add the cherries to a small glass bowl, and refrigerate them.
   - Place the **blueberries** in a colander, rinse them under cool running water, and spread them in the pie plate lined with a double thickness of paper towels or a terry towel. Sort through the berries, removing stems and replacing spoiled berries. Wrap the paper towels around the berries to dry them completely. Add the berries to a small bowl and refrigerate them.
   - Use a chef's knife to roughly chop the **nuts** on a cutting board.

5. **Assemble the trifles for serving.**

   - Remove the 4 puddings from the refrigerator and uncover them.
   - Spread a layer of cooled sauce over each pudding.
   - Spread a layer of whipped cream over the sauce in each dessert.
   - Combine the fruits and spread a layer of fruit over the whipped cream in each dessert.

- Top the fruit in each dessert with a small handful (approx. 1 T) of nuts.
- Top each dessert with a dollop of whipped cream.

VARIATIONS: Make ingredient substitutions. Substitute, for example,

- **16 raspberries** (Recipe #97) for cherries when cherries are out of season.
- **dry frozen raspberries** for frozen cherries in the sauce.

Add ingredients. Add, for example,

- **8 blackberries** (Recipe #78). Rinse and dry the berries. Use a serrated knife to halve each lengthwise. When spreading the fruit over the whipped cream, place the blackberries cut side down.

COMMENTS: To prepare this dessert well ahead of serving, prepare the pudding, divide it between the dessert bowls, and refrigerate the bowls, tightly covered with plastic wrap. Prepare, cool, cover, and refrigerate the fruit topping. Prepare, cover, and separately refrigerate the blueberries, pineapple, and nuts. Prepare the cherries and whipped cream topping quite close to serving time.

209. Fruit-Topped Vanilla Pudding Dessert
(4 servings)

Vanilla Pudding

1½ c milk (whole or 2%)
¼ c T sugar
⅛ t salt
1 T cornstarch

¼ c milk (whole or 2%)
2 large egg yolks
½ c milk (whole or 2%)
1 t pure vanilla extract

Fruit and Nut Topping

½ c fresh pineapple chunks (½ in. thick; Recipe #94)
½ c blueberries
8 blackberries

8-12 raspberries
8 strawberries
⅓ c raw pecan or walnut halves
approx. 4 t honey (easy to pour, not thick)

Whipped Cream Topping

1 c heavy whipping cream
2 T sugar

½ t pure vanilla extract

Vanilla Pudding Cooking Tools

1 set each measuring cups & spoons
1 large heavy-bottomed nonstick skillet
2 small mixing bowls
1 dinner fork or small whisk

1 rubber or other heat-resistant spatula
1 medium heat-resistant mixing bowl
4 large dessert serving bowls (10 oz)

Fruit and Nut Topping Preparation Tools

1 set measuring cups
1 cutting board reserved for fruit
1 each 5 in. serrated & chef's knife
1 medium mixing bowl

1 colander
1 pie plate
1 dinner spoon

Whipped Cream Topping Preparation Tools

1 set each measuring cups & spoons
1 small, deep mixing bowl

1 hand electric or hand rotary beater

---

1. **Prepare the pudding.**

   - Gather together the pudding ingredients and cooking tools.
   - Add 1½ c milk, ¼ c sugar, and ⅛ t salt to a large nonstick skillet and heat the mixture at a medium setting.
   - Add 1 T cornstarch and ¼ c milk to a small mixing bowl and use a dinner fork or whisk to mix in the cornstarch.
   - In another small bowl, use a dinner fork or whisk to mix 2 egg yolks and ½ c milk together.
   - Increase the skillet heat to a high medium. When the milk becomes very hot (a slight scum appears on its surface), re-stir the cornstarch mixture and add it to the milk mixture while stirring quickly and constantly with a rubber spatula to keep the cornstarch from lumping. Continue constant stirring, often scraping over the bottom of the skillet to prevent sticking, until the pudding thickens, clears, and boils.
   - Remove the skillet from the heat.
   - Carefully combine the egg yolk and milk mixture and hot thickened milk mixture (the pudding). First pour ½ c of the hot pudding into the egg and milk mixture while stirring quickly and constantly and then stir all of the egg and milk mixture into the hot pudding, again stirring quickly and constantly to keep the egg yolks from hardening.
   - Add and mix in the vanilla.
   - Use a rubber spatula to scrape the pudding into a heat-resistant medium mixing bowl and set it aside for 5-10 minutes for some cooling.

- Divide the pudding between the four dessert bowls, filling the bowls around ⅔ full. If extra pudding remains, either add it to a small bowl or assemble more bowls. Cover each dessert bowl with plastic wrap and refrigerate the puddings.

2. **Prepare the fruit and nuts while the pudding cools.**

    - Gather together the fruits, nuts, and needed preparation tools.
    - Use a serrated knife to halve the **8 pineapple chunks** lengthwise and add the pineapple to a medium mixing bowl.
    - Add the **½ c blueberries** and **8 blackberries** to a colander, quickly rinse them under cold running water, spread them over a double thickness of paper towels or a terry cloth towel in a pie plate, and pick through them, discarding stems and replacing spoiled and broken berries. Wrap the paper towels around the berries and gently roll the berries around within the towels to dry them thoroughly. Add the blueberries to the pineapple. Pick out and set the blackberries aside on the paper towel used for drying.
    - Add the **8-12 raspberries** to the colander, quickly rinse them under cold running water, spread them over a double thickness of paper towels or a terry towel, and pick through them, removing and replacing spoiled, broken, or moldy berries. Wrap the paper towels around the berries and gently roll the berries around within the towels to dry them thoroughly. Place the berries open end down on the towel to drain thoroughly.
    - Add the **8 strawberries** to the colander and rinse them under cool running water. Use a serrated knife to slice off the hulls and re-rinse the strawberries. Spread the strawberries over a double thickness of paper towels or terry towel. Wrap the paper towels around the berries to dry them completely. Use a serrated knife to remove any blemishes, white stem ends, or rough tips. Halve each strawberry lengthwise, place the halves cut side down on a cutting board, and cut each half lengthwise into 3 equal slices. Spread the strawberry slices over the blueberries.
    - Use a chef's knife to chop the **⅓ c nuts** roughly. Set the nuts aside.

3. **Prepare the whipped cream.**

    - Gather the ingredients and preparation tools.
    - Add 1 c cream to a small, deep mixing bowl and use an electric or rotary hand beater to beat the cream until it begins to thicken.
    - Add 2 T sugar and ½ t pure vanilla extract and continue beating the cream until it fully thickens, being careful to avoid over-beating, which will cause the cream to separate.
    - Cover the whipped cream bowl with plastic wrap and refrigerate it.

4. **Assemble the desserts for serving.**

    - Remove the puddings from the refrigerator and uncover them.
    - Combine the fruits (except for the blackberries), gently mix them together, and evenly divide the fruit mixture between the 4 bowls of pudding.

- Use a serrated knife to halve the blackberries lengthwise and equally divide the blackberry halves between the dessert bowls, placing the halves cut side down.
- Dip a dinner spoon into honey and drizzle the honey over the fruit, attempting to touch all pieces, one teaspoon per dessert.
- Evenly divide the nuts between the desserts.

5. **Serve the puddings topped with whipped cream.**

    VARIATIONS: Substitute **1 c dark red Bing** or **Rainier cherries** (Recipe #81) for blackberries and raspberries when cherries are in season.

    Add ingredients. Add, for example,

    - 1 **peach** (Recipe #92), **nectarine** (Recipe #88), or **mango** (Recipe #87), sliced and cut into chunks.
    - 1 **clementine orange** (Recipe #90), **mandarin orange** (Recipe #90), or 1 **tangerine** (Recipe #99).
    - 1 **medium chilled banana** (Recipe #77), dipped in a citrus wash (2 T orange juice and 1 T water) and patted dry. Add banana only shortly before serving.

    COMMENTS: To prepare these desserts well ahead of serving, prepare and separately refrigerate, tightly covered, the dessert bowls of pudding and the individual fruits. Do not cut the blackberries (or an orange, nectarine, or peach if these fruits are included) or prepare the whipped cream topping until quite shortly before serving.

CHAPTER TWELVE

100% Whole Wheat Pizza

Pizza Description

CHAPTER TWELVE PIZZA recipes make tasty roasted vegetables central ingredients, heaping them – bell peppers, onion, and mushroom in particular, but also such varied vegetables as greens, eggplant, zucchini, and garlic – on to create veggie pizza extraordinaire. Roasted vegetables in combination with a variety of nutrition-enhancing ingredient changes – notably the substitution of herb-flavored extra lean ground beef for pepperoni and fatty sausage, natural for processed cheese, and whole wheat for white flour in the crust – transform Chapter Twelve pizza. It is both enormously wholesome and highly pleasing despite its low fat content. It is pizza that cooks can proudly and successfully serve. It is also a dish that is easily within the reach of any interested home cook. Given the variety of vegetables and ingredients that can be added as toppings, *Cooked Alive!* pizza ideally suits the creative cook as well.

Pizza Preparation Notes

Preparation Notes provide helpful general instruction and information about Chapter Twelve pizza recipes that cannot fit into the individual recipes. They cover a variety of subjects, including:

- cooking tool information (Note #1).
- preparation of vegetable variation suggestions (Note #2).
- boosting pizza making success (Note #3).
- boosting the nutritional quality of Chapter Twelve pizzas (Note #4).

1. **Important information about cooking tools is as follows:**

- Chapter Twelve pizza recipes list all key cooking tools used in recipe preparation, listing them in order of use, but recipes do not list some basic working tools – including paper and cloth towels, vegetable scrubbing tools, plastic wrap, and multi-purpose cutting boards – that are also routinely used and need to be kept handy.

PART 2

- The general cooking tool list included in the Part II Introduction supplies a full description for all tools used in Chapter Twelve recipes except for those tools that are specific to Chapter Twelve pizza recipes, which are described as follows:

    - **Baking dish, large rectangular.** This dish is for roasting vegetables. It should be around 10 x 13 in. in size. As staining during roasting seemingly inevitably occurs, an inexpensive oven-proof baking dish, such as a clear Pyrex dish, is a practical selection.
    - **Bread board, large.** A bread board that is around 14 x 20 in. in size is ideal. It provides space for comfortably mixing flour into dough and for kneading dough without flour spilling. Having some type of gripping legs that keep the board in place during mixing and kneading is a very useful feature. An alternative is to place non-sliding material, such as a towel or pad (as is used with rugs), under the board.
    - **Food scale.** This scale, which should register at least 1 pound in ounces, is an important tool for accurately measuring cheese content.
    - **2 padded oven gloves.** Having a glove for each hand is essential for safely handling a hot pizza stone or pan.
    - **Spoon, wooden with a large head (approx. 2½ x 4½ in. size).** This tool provides efficient beating of pizza dough, which is highly important for bran-rich whole wheat flour (bran somewhat interferes with gluten development and beating overcomes this interference). A rounded handle provides a comfortable grip. A non-slip grip is a convenient feature.
    - **Pizza stone, 13 in. diameter size.** A stone reliably yields a crispy pizza crust. Pizza can be served from the stone, which keeps pizza warm during serving. Handles on a pizza stone are highly useful. A heavy-bottomed metal 13 in. round pan can be substituted. When a pan is substituted, a cooling rack and a wide spatula with a firm handle become additional necessary equipment.

2. **Chapter Two (Roasted Vegetable Recipes) serves as a reference for preparing the vegetable variation suggestions made in Chapter Twelve pizza recipes.** The recipe number attached to each suggested vegetable variation identifies the Chapter Two reference recipe.

3. **Reference #12 (Clinching Pizza Serving Success: Expanded Preparation Support)** walks cooks through the five key pizza-making steps, which include 1) dough rising, 2) beating of dough, 3) shaping of dough, 4) baking of the crust, and 5) the adding of toppings.

4. **Cooks can substantially boost the nutritional quality of pizza through careful selection of individual pizza ingredients.** Because each individual pizza ingredient is marketed in a variety of forms and there is tremendous difference in nutritional quality among alternative products, *Cooked Alive!* provides two product selection references to aid cooks in selecting the highest quality ingredients. These references are as follows:

    - Reference #1 (Selecting Top Quality Fresh Whole Vegetables and Fruits) identifies

top quality vegetables as those that are both naturally whole and naturally produced. Raw, whole, certified organic and locally produced vegetables meet these criteria.
- Reference #5 (Selecting High Quality Processed Ingredients for Use in Part II Recipes) identifies naturally produced products that have undergone some physical processing but that retain significant nutritional quality. Products covered that are relevant to Chapter Twelve pizza recipes include:

  - whole wheat flour (Ingredient #3).
  - cheese (Dairy Products, Ingredient #2).
  - ground beef (Ingredient #1).
  - extra virgin olive oil (Ingredient #8).
  - certified organic tomato paste (Canned Products, Ingredient #9).

Pizza Recipes

210. 100% Whole Wheat Pizza Crust
(13 in. round; 4 servings)

Ingredients

1 c warm water
2 t dry yeast
1 T sugar
¾ t salt
1 T extra virgin olive oil

1⅓-1¾ c room temperature medium ground whole wheat hard flour (see comments for a flour description)
approx. 1 T extra virgin olive oil

Cooking Tools

1 set each measuring cups & spoons
1 large (10 c) mixing bowl
1 large-headed wooden spoon
1 firm rubber spatula

1 large (16 x 24 in.) cutting board
13 in. pizza stone, lightly buttered
2 padded oven gloves

---

1. **Preheat the oven at 450 degrees.** Place one oven rack on the lowest position.

2. **Activate the yeast.** Add the 1 c very warm water (but not hot water) to a large mixing bowl and sprinkle the 2 t yeast over it. Add 1 T sugar. Let the yeast sit for a minute or two until it begins to foam, which verifies that it is active.

3. **Prepare the dough.**

PART 2

- Add ¾ t salt and 1 T oil to the yeast mixture.
- Add 1⅓ c flour to the yeast mixture and use a wooden spoon to combine the ingredients.
- If the dough remains quite thin, add up to ¼ c flour. Mix in ⅛ c flour at a time and assess the dough stiffness before adding more flour. It is important that the dough not be too thick. Thick dough is difficult to spread onto the pizza stone.
- Beat the dough 150 strokes with a wooden spoon.
- Add and stir in 2 or 3 T more flour until the dough becomes stiff and difficult to stir.
- Add 2 T flour to a kneading surface, slightly spread the flour, use a rubber spatula to scrape the dough onto the flour, and slightly press the dough into the flour.
- Rotating around the dough, slide the spatula under an edge of the dough and flip the floured bottom dough up and over onto the top of the dough. Continue this flipping until the top is completely floured.
- Lightly oil your hands and knead the dough until a hole pushed into the dough with a finger remains, adding touches of flour to the kneading surface and re-oiling your hands as may be needed to keep the dough from sticking. This kneading will take only a few minutes.
- Shape the dough into a ball.

4. **Spread the dough onto the buttered baking stone.** Add the dough to the center of the stone, lightly oil your hands, and evenly press the dough over the baking stone, pressing from the center outward to the edges, and using your palms and fingers, not just your finger tips. Re-oil your hands as needed to prevent sticking and be careful to spread the dough evenly (not leaving thin spots), except on the edges, which should be left somewhat thicker than the center area.

5. **Cover and set the dough aside to rise.**

   - Lightly oil one side of a strip of plastic wrap that is long and wide enough to loosely cover the dough completely. If one strip of plastic wrap is not large enough, prepare two strips.
   - Loosely place the sheet(s) oiled side down over the dough, covering all exposed dough while allowing room for the yeast to expand.
   - Set the dough aside to rise in a warm area until it has doubled in thickness (for at least 15 minutes and ideally 30 minutes).
   - When the dough has doubled, gently press down on the plastic wrap to break large bubbles. If, however, the dough has risen for so long that very large bubbles have formed, firmly press the dough down to break the bubbles and allow the dough to re-rise for another 10-15 minutes before baking.
   - Carefully peel off the plastic wrap covering to avoid breaking open bubbles.

6. **Bake the dough.**

   - Place the stone on the lowest rack of the hot oven.
   - Bake the dough for 8 minutes, setting a timer. Bake the crust just until the bottom

and edges are slightly browned, being watchful to avoid over-browning. To check the bottom, use a stir-fry spatula to lift an edge of the crust.
- When the dough is slightly browned, wear 1 or 2 padded oven gloves to remove the stone from the oven to a heat-resistant surface such as a cutting board.
- Assemble the pizza immediately.

VARIATIONS: Assemble the pizza later. To assemble the pizza shortly (within 15 minutes) after the crust has baked, set the crust aside on the stone after removing it from the oven, uncovered. To assemble the crust later than 15 minutes after baking it, remove the crust onto a cooling rack and cover it tightly once it has cooled completely.

Freeze the baked crust. Tightly wrap the completely cooled crust in plastic wrap and freeze it enclosed in an extra large and air-tight freezer quality plastic bag. Thaw the crust in one of the following ways:

- unwrap the crust and allow it to thaw on a cooling rack.
- defrost the crust, unwrapped, overnight in a refrigerator.
- use the crust directly from the freezer. Add it to a pizza stone preheated in a 450 degree oven for 5 minutes, heat the crust for 4-5 minutes in the 450 degree oven, remove the pizza stone from the oven, and add the pizza toppings to the crust for final baking.

Vary crust size. For example,

- form the dough into **mini-rounds**. Divide the dough into 3 or 4 equal pieces and spread each piece into a round shape, leaving edges somewhat thicker. For completely baked rounds, bake the rounds for approx. 5 minutes or just until lightly browned. For crusts to be assembled into small pizzas, bake the rounds for 4 minutes.
- form the dough into **2-serving size**. Cut the dough into two equal parts. Shape one part for immediate baking (baking it for 6-7 minutes, just until edges are barely browned) and either freeze the remaining dough, first covering it tightly, or first bake and then freeze the remaining dough.

Vary the baking pan used. For example,

- substitute a **heavy-bottomed pizza pan** for pizza stone. Use either a 12 in. round or rectangular (approx. 9 x 13 in.) pan. To prevent the crust bottom from becoming soggy, immediately transfer a baked pizza crust to a cooling rack after removing it from the oven. Transfer a baked assembled pizza to a cutting board for cutting.
- substitute a **heavy-bottomed nonstick pizza pan** for a pizza stone. Using a baking pan with a nonstick surface greatly eases removal of a pizza crust from a pan.

COMMENTS: Medium ground hard winter wheat flour is also called bread flour. It contains visible bits of bran, which give the flour a somewhat coarse texture and which make the flour absorptive. Silky smooth fine ground whole wheat flour does not work in this recipe without reduction in liquid content and flour quality.

PART 2

211. Basic Roasted Pepper and Cheese Pizza
(13 in. pizza; 4 servings)

Pizza Dough

1 unbaked 100% Whole Wheat Pizza Crust dough (Recipe #210), shaped on a lightly buttered 13 in. pizza stone

Vegetables with Seasoning

¾ each green & red bell pepper or ½ each red, green, & yellow bell pepper
1 chilled medium onion

2 T extra virgin olive oil
½ t dried sweet basil leaves
½ t dried oregano leaves

Tomato Sauce

½ chilled medium onion, halved lengthwise
⅛ in. wide slice ginger root
1 T extra virgin olive oil
½ t dried sweet basil leaves

½ t dried oregano leaves
⅓ c tomato paste (½ of a 6 oz can tomato paste)
½ c tomato juice

Toppings

8 pitted Kalamata olives (optional)
3 oz extra sharp cheddar cheese

3 oz mozzarella cheese or another 2 oz extra sharp cheddar cheese

Cooking Tools

1 set each measuring cups & spoons
1 cutting board reserved for vegetables
1 each 5 in. serrated & chef's knife
1 large (10 c or 2½ qt) mixing bowl
1 large (approx. 23 x 9 in.) rectangular baking dish
1 rubber or other heat-resistant spatula

1 timer
2 padded oven gloves
1 can opener
1 thin-bladed rubber spatula
1 large nonstick or stainless steel skillet
1 plastic or plastic-coated stir-fry spatula
1 cheese grater

---

1. **Set the pizza dough aside to rise.** Lightly oil one side of a strip of plastic wrap large enough to loosely cover the dough completely. If one strip does not cover the dough, prepare two strips. Loosely spread the sheet(s) oiled side down over the dough, completely covering all exposed dough but allowing it space for rising. Set the dough aside in a warm place to rise for 15-30 minutes until it has doubled in height.

2. **Gather all cooking tools and ingredients.**

3. **Roast the vegetables.**

    - Preheat the oven to **430 degrees**. Move one oven rack to the lowest position, leaving the middle rack in place.
    - Add 2 T oil to a large mixing bowl.
    - Prepare the **bell peppers**. Use a 5 in. serrated knife to cut out the stem of each pepper. Remove any seeds but not the white membrane. Use the serrated knife to slice each pepper lengthwise into ½ in. thick strips and to cut the strips crosswise into thirds. Add the pepper pieces to the mixing bowl and use a rubber spatula to swish them in the oil to coat all pieces thoroughly.
    - Prepare the **onion**. Use a chef's knife to halve an onion lengthwise. Place each half cut side down on a cutting board and use the chef's knife to cut off the ends. Peel the onion. Place the onion halves cut side down onto a cutting board, cut each lengthwise into 5 thick slices, add the slices to the mixing bowl, break the slices apart, and thoroughly mix the onion pieces into the oil.
    - Evenly sprinkle ½ **t each dried basil and oregano leaves** over the vegetables, first crushing the herbs between your palms. Use a rubber spatula to thoroughly mix the vegetables and herbs together, to scrape the vegetables into a large rectangular baking pan, and to evenly spread the vegetables in a single layer in the baking dish.
    - Center the baking dish on the middle rack of the pre-heated oven.
    - Roast the pepper and onion for **8 minutes**, setting a timer. At the timer, use padded oven gloves to remove the vegetables from the oven, stir them, return them to the oven, and set a timer for **8 minutes.**
    - At the timer, remove the roasted vegetables from the oven onto a heat-resistant surface.
    - Immediately increase the oven temperature to **450 degrees**.

4. **Prepare the tomato sauce while the vegetables roast**.

    - Heat a large skillet on a large burner at a medium setting. Open and measure the tomato paste and tomato juice. Use a thin-bladed rubber spatula to easily remove tomato paste from a 6 oz can or other small container.
    - Place ½ onion cut side down on a cutting board and use a chef's knife to cut off its ends. Peel the onion. Again place the onion cut side down on the cutting board and use the chef's knife to dice it. Mince the ginger root.
    - Increase the skillet heat to medium-high, and when a drop of water added to the skillet instantly dances and disappears, add 1 T oil, add the onion and ginger, evenly sprinkle ½ t each dried sweet basil and oregano leaves (first crushing them between your palms) over the onion, and use a stir-fry spatula to vigorously stir-fry the onion mixture for about 30 seconds.
    - Reduce the heat to medium and cook the onion mixture for another 2 minutes, stirring it occasionally and setting a timer.
    - At the timer, add and thoroughly mix in the ⅓ c tomato paste and ½ c tomato juice.

PART 2

- Remove the skillet from the heat and set it aside.

5. **Bake the pizza dough once the vegetables are roasted and the oven reaches 450 degrees.**

    - Gently press down on the plastic wrap covering the dough to break large bubbles and carefully remove the plastic wrap to avoid tearing the dough.
    - Place the pizza stone on the bottom oven rack.
    - Bake the pizza dough for **8 minutes**, just until the crust edges and bottom become lightly browned. Set a timer and be watchful to avoid over-browning. To check the crust bottom at the timer, use a stir-fry spatula to quickly lift an edge for viewing while the crust remains in the oven.
    - When the crust is lightly brown, wear two padded oven gloves to remove the pizza stone to a heat-resistant surface.

6. **Prepare the cheese and olives during the 8 minutes the pizza dough bakes.** Coarsely grate the cheese. Use a serrated knife to halve the Kalamata olives lengthwise.

7. **Immediately assemble the pizza after removing the baked crust from the oven.**

    - Use a rubber spatula to spread the tomato sauce (leaving the edges uncovered) and then the roasted vegetables evenly over the crust.
    - Return the pizza stone to the bottom oven rack and bake the pizza for **5 minutes** until the exposed crust is lightly browned, setting a timer. Be watchful to avoid over-browning, which spoils the flavor and texture of the crust.
    - At the timer, either immediately remove the pizza from the oven or add 1 more timed minute of baking if the crust needs more browning. Turn off the oven heat after removing the pizza.
    - Add and evenly spread the olives and cheese over the pizza top, return the pizza stone to a middle oven rack, and heat the pizza for 2-3 minutes to melt the cheese.
    - Serve the pizza directly from the pizza stone.

VARIATIONS: Make ingredient substitutions. Substitute, for example,

- **unflavored strained tomatoes** for tomato juice, such as the Italian product Pomi Strained Tomatoes.

Expand roasted vegetable content. Add, for example,

- **5-6 medium mushrooms** (Recipe #43). Mix the mushroom slices into the other vegetables after they have roasted for 8 minutes. Increase the herb content added to the vegetables from ½ t each dried basil and oregano leaves to 1 t each. Using the same bowl that was used for mixing the other vegetables, toss the mushrooms with ½-1 T oil in order to coat them before mixing them with the other vegetables midway through the roasting.

- **1 small (6 in. long; 1½ in. thick) zucchini** (Recipe #50). Increase the herb content added to the vegetables from ½ t each dried basil and oregano leaves to 1 t each. Sprinkle ¼ t salt over the vegetables after roasting.
- **1 medium chilled (6-8 in. long) Japanese eggplant** or **½ medium chilled globe eggplant** (Recipe #42). Increase the herb content added to the vegetables to 1 t each dried basil and oregano leaves; increase the oil added to the mixing bowl to 3 T oil. Evenly sprinkle ¼ t salt over the vegetables after roasting.

Add other toppings. Add, for example,

- **½ lb greens**, any variety (Recipes #23-30). Stir-fry or stir-fry/steam them rather than roasting them with the other vegetables and add them as a topping to the pizza, adding them with the cheese.
- **½ lb extra lean ground beef** cooked with ½ t minced ginger root, ½ t each dried sweet basil and oregano leaves, and ½ t garlic powder. Prepare the ground meat exactly as in Recipe #212 (Roasted Pepper, Zucchini, Eggplant, and Ground Beef). Spread the ground beef over the tomato sauce when assembling the pizza for baking. Completely drain any fat before adding the cooked meat to the crust, which can make the crust soggy.
- **1 t fennel** or **anise seed**. Stir-fry the seeds with the onion when preparing the sauce (Step #4), adding and cooking the seeds for 30 seconds in the oil before adding the onion.
- **6-8 green olives**, pitted; halved or sliced.
- **½ c fresh pineapple chunks** (Recipe #94), cut into ⅓ in. thick slices.

212. Roasted Pepper, Zucchini, Eggplant, and Ground Beef Pizza
(13 in. pizza; 4 servings)

Pizza Dough

1 unbaked 100% Whole Wheat Pizza Crust dough (Recipe #210), shaped on a lightly buttered 13 in. pizza stone

Vegetables with Seasoning

3 T extra virgin olive oil
1 chilled medium onion
¾ each green & red bell pepper or ½ each green, red, & yellow
1 chilled medium (6-8 in. long) Japanese eggplant or ½ small globe eggplant
1 small (approx. 6 in. long, 1½ in. thick) zucchini
6 mushrooms
1½ t dried sweet basil leaves
1½ t dried oregano leaves
⅓ t salt

PART 2

Ground Beef

⅛ in. thick slice of ginger root
2 t extra virgin olive oil
¾ lb extra lean ground beef

½ t garlic powder
½ t each dried basil & oregano leaves
⅓ t salt

Tomato Sauce Topping

½ chilled medium onion, halved lengthwise
⅛ in. wide slice ginger root
1 T extra virgin olive oil
½ t dried sweet basil leaves

½ t dried oregano leaves
⅓ c tomato paste (½ of a 6 oz can of tomato paste)
½ c tomato juice

Toppings

8 pitted Kalamata olives (opt)
3 oz extra sharp cheddar cheese

3 oz mozzarella cheese or another 2 oz extra sharp cheddar cheese

Cooking Tools

1 set each measuring spoons & cups
1 each 5 in serrated & chef's knife
1 large (10 c or 2½ qt) mixing bowl
1 rubber spatula
1 medium mixing bowl
1 large (9 x 13 in.) rectangular baking dish

2 padded oven gloves
1 can opener
1 thin-bladed rubber spatula
2 skillets (either medium or large)
2 plastic or plastic-coated stir-fry spatulas
1 cheese grater

---

1. **Set the pizza dough aside to rise.** Lightly oil one side of a strip of plastic wrap large enough to loosely cover the dough completely. If one strip does not cover the dough, prepare another strip. Loosely spread the sheet(s) oiled side down over the dough, completely covering the dough and allowing space for it to rise. Set the dough aside in a warm place to rise for at least 15 minutes and ideally until it has doubled in height, at least 15 minutes and ideally about 30 minutes.

2. **Gather all cooking tools and ingredients.**

3. **Prepare the vegetables for roasting.**

   - Preheat the oven to **430 degrees**. Move the bottom oven rack to the lowest position, leaving the middle rack in position.
   - Add 2½ T oil to a large mixing bowl.
   - Prepare the **bell peppers**. Use a 5 in. serrated knife to cut out the stem of each pepper. Remove any seeds but not the white membrane. Use the serrated knife to cut each

- pepper lengthwise into ½ in. thick strips and to cut the strips crosswise into thirds. Add the pepper pieces to the mixing bowl and use a rubber spatula to swish them in the oil to coat all pieces thoroughly.
- Prepare the **onion**. Use a chef's knife to halve an onion lengthwise. Place the halves cut side down on a cutting board and use a chef's knife to cut off the ends. Peel the onion. Again place the onion halves cut side down onto a cutting board and use the chef's knife to cut each lengthwise into 5 thick slices, add the slices to the mixing bowl, break them apart, and thoroughly mix the onion pieces into the oil.
- Rinse and dry the **eggplant**. Use a chef's knife to cut off the ends of the eggplant. Stand the eggplant upright on one flattened end and slice it lengthwise into ⅓ in. thick slices. Cut the slices lengthwise into ⅓ in. thick strips and cut the strips crosswise into ⅓ in. cubes. Make a taste check to ensure that the eggplant is not bitter. Replace bitter eggplant or omit it completely. Add the eggplant to the mixing bowl and thoroughly mix it into the oil.
- Rinse and thoroughly dry the **zucchini**. Use a chef's knife to slice the ends from the zucchini. Stand it upright on one flattened end, slice it lengthwise into ½ in. thick slices. Cut the slices lengthwise into ½ in. thick strips, cut the strips crosswise into ½ in cubes, add the zucchini to the mixing bowl, and mix the cubes into the oil.
- Quickly rinse the **mushrooms** under cool running water, dry them thoroughly with a paper towel, and cut each mushroom lengthwise into 3 equal slices. Add the slices to a separate medium mixing bowl, add ½ T oil, toss the mushroom slices thoroughly to coat them, and set them aside.
- Evenly sprinkle 1½ t each dried basil and oregano leaves over the vegetables in the large mixing bowl, first crushing the herbs between your palms.
- Use a rubber spatula to thoroughly mix the vegetables and herbs together, to scrape the vegetables into a large baking dish, and to spread the vegetables evenly in a single layer in the baking dish.

4. **Roast the vegetables.**

    - Center the baking dish on the middle rack of the pre-heated oven.
    - Roast the vegetables for **8 minutes**, setting a timer. At the timer, use padded oven gloves to remove the vegetables from the oven. Stir the vegetables.
    - Mix in the mushrooms, return the baking dish to the oven, and roast the vegetables another **8 minutes**, again setting a timer.
    - At the timer, remove the roasted vegetables from the oven onto a heat-resistant surface.
    - Evenly sprinkle ⅓ t salt over the vegetables.
    - Immediately increase the oven temperature to **450 degrees**.

5. **Cook the ground beef while the vegetables roast in the oven.**

    - Heat a medium skillet on a back burner at a medium setting.
    - Use a serrated knife to mince a ⅛ in. thick slice of ginger root.
    - Increase the heat to medium-high, and when a drop of water added to the skillet

instantly dances and disappears, add 2 t oil, mix in the ginger root, add the ground beef, use a stir-fry spatula to break the meat into ½ in. thick chunks, evenly sprinkle ½ t garlic powder and ½ t each dried basil and oregano leaves, first crushing them between your palms, over the meat, and stir-fry the meat for about 30 seconds, turning it over and over.

- Reduce the heat to a low medium setting and cook the meat 5 minutes until it is cooked through (it has no red coloring), stirring it occasionally and setting a timer.
- At the timer, remove the skillet from the heat, drain off any fat, and evenly sprinkle ¼ t salt over the meat.

6. **Prepare the tomato sauce while the vegetables roast in the oven.**

- Heat a medium or large skillet at a medium setting. Measure ⅓ c tomato paste and ½ c tomato juice. Use a thin-bladed rubber spatula to easily remove tomato paste from a 6 oz can.
- Place ½ onion cut side down on a cutting board and use a chef's knife to cut off its ends. Peel the onion. Again place the onion cut side down on the cutting board and use the chef's knife to dice the onion. Mince the ginger root.
- Increase the skillet heat to medium-high, and when a drop of water added to the skillet instantly dances and disappears, add 1 T oil, add the onion and ginger, evenly sprinkle ½ t each dried basil and oregano leaves (first crushing them between your palms) over the onion, and vigorously stir-fry the onion mixture for about 30 seconds.
- Reduce the heat to medium and cook the onion mixture for 2 minutes, stirring it occasionally and setting a timer.
- At the timer, add and thoroughly mix in the ⅓ c tomato paste and ½ c tomato juice.
- Remove the skillet from the heat and set it aside.

7. **Bake the pizza dough for 8 minutes at 450 degrees.**

- When the pizza dough has risen, gently press down on the plastic wrap covering the dough to break large bubbles and carefully remove the plastic wrap to avoid tearing the dough.
- Place the pizza stone on the bottom oven rack.
- Bake the pizza dough for **8 minutes** until the crust edges and crust bottom become lightly browned, setting a timer.
- At the timer, check for browning. For example, turn on the oven light or use a stir-fry spatula to lift an edge of the crust. It is important that the crust edges and bottom be only slightly browned.
- Once the crust is slightly browned, wear padded oven gloves and remove the pizza stone to a heat-resistant surface.

8. **Prepare the cheeses and olives while the pizza dough bakes for 8 minutes.** Coarsely grate the cheeses. Use a serrated knife to halve the olives.

9. **Immediately assemble the pizza once the crust is baked.**

- Use a rubber spatula to spread the tomato sauce, leaving the edges uncovered.
- Add and evenly spread the roasted vegetables and meat over the tomato sauce.
- Return the pizza stone to the bottom oven rack and bake the pizza for **5 minutes** or until the exposed crust and crust bottom are medium but not over-browned, setting a timer. Over-browning undermines the flavor and texture of the crust.
- Remove the pizza from the oven. Turn off the oven heat.
- Add and evenly spread the olives and cheese over the pizza top, return the pizza stone to a middle oven rack, heat the pizza for 2-3 minutes to melt the cheese, and remove the pizza from the oven.
- Turn off the oven.

10. **Serve the pizza directly from the pizza stone.** Use a serrated knife to cut the pizza into serving size pieces and use a stir-fry spatula to remove individual slices.

VARIATIONS: Make ingredient substitutions. Substitute, for example,

- **unflavored strained tomato**, such as the Italian product Pomi Strained Tomatoes, for tomato juice.
- **green pitted olives** for Kalamata olives, or combine them.
- **extra lean fresh pork sausage** for ground beef. Alternatively, use a **half beef** and **half pork mixture**. Cook ground pork exactly like beef.

Expand the roasted vegetable content. Add, for example,

- **2-3 very small (2-3 in. long, not counting the neck) yellow crookneck squash** (Recipe #50) or 1 small yellow straightneck summer squash (Recipe #50). Add ½ t more of each dried basil and oregano leaves to the vegetables. Increase the amount of oil used for coating the vegetables to 3⅓ T and increase salt content to ½ t.
- **8-10 chilled medium garlic cloves**, peeled and halved lengthwise. Mix ½-1 T oil into the mushrooms and mix the mushrooms into the other roasted vegetables after the vegetables have roasted for 8 minutes.

Add additional toppings with the roasted vegetables and meat. Add, for example,

- **8-10 garlic cloves, stir-fried** (Recipe #31). Using a garlic mincing tool makes this delicious topping an option.
- **½ lb greens** (Recipes #23-30).
- **8-10 raw grape tomatoes**, rinsed, dried, and halved lengthwise.
- **½ c chunks canned or fresh pineapple** (Recipe #94), cut into ¼ in. thick slices and patted dry if juicy.

213. Roasted Pepper, Spinach, and Pineapple Pizza
(13 in. pizza; 4 servings)

Pizza Dough

1 unbaked 100% Whole Wheat Pizza Crust dough (Recipe #210), shaped on a lightly buttered 13 in. pizza stone

Vegetables and Pineapple with Seasonings

2 T extra virgin olive oil
1 chilled medium onion
¾-1 green & red bell pepper or
    ½ each red, green, & yellow
8-10 chilled medium garlic cloves
1 t dried sweet basil leaves
1 t dried oregano leaves

5-6 mushrooms
1 T extra virgin olive oil
1 c fresh pineapple chunks (½ in. thick; Recipe #94)
½ lb pre-washed spinach
1 T extra virgin olive oil
¼ t salt

Ground Beef

¾ lb extra lean ground beef
⅛ in. thick slice fresh ginger root
2 t extra virgin olive oil
½ t dried sweet basil leaves

½ t garlic powder
½ t each dried basil & oregano leaves
⅓ t salt

Tomato Sauce

½ chilled medium onion, halved lengthwise
⅛ in. wide slice ginger root
1 T extra virgin olive oil
½ t dried sweet basil leaves

½ t dried oregano leaves
⅓ c tomato paste (½ of 6 oz can tomato paste)
½ c tomato juice

Toppings

8-10 pitted Kalamata olives (optional)
3 oz extra sharp cheddar cheese
1 oz Parmesan cheese (opt)

3 oz mozzarella cheese or another 2 oz extra sharp cheddar cheese

Cooking Tools

1 set each measuring spoons & cups
1 large (10 c or 2 ½ qt) mixing bowl
1 each 5 and 7 in. serrated & chef's knife
1-2 rubber or other heat-resistant spatulas
2 medium mixing bowls
1 timer

1-2 stir-fry spatulas
2 large skillets
1 thin-bladed rubber spatula
1 large (approx. 16 x 24 in.) cutting board
1 large (approx. 9 x 13 in.) rectangular baking dish

1 colander
2 padded oven gloves
1 medium skillet

1 dinner plate
1 cheese grater with a coarse setting

---

1. **Set the pizza dough aside for rising.** Lightly oil one side of a strip of plastic wrap large enough to loosely cover the dough completely. If one strip does not cover the dough, prepare another one. Loosely place the strip(s) oiled side down over the dough, allowing space for the dough to rise. Place the dough aside in a warm area to rise for at least 15 minutes and ideally for about 30 minutes.

2. **Gather all cooking tools and ingredients.**

3. **Prepare the vegetables for roasting.**

   - Preheat the oven to **430 degrees**. Move the bottom oven rack to the lowest position, leaving the middle rack in position.
   - Add 2 T oil to a large (approx. 9 x 13 in.) mixing bowl.
   - Prepare the **bell peppers**. Use a 5 in. serrated knife to cut out the stem of each bell pepper. Remove any seeds but not the white membrane. Use the serrated knife to cut each pepper lengthwise into ½ in. thick strips and to cut the strips crosswise into ½ in. cubes. Add the pepper pieces to the mixing bowl and use a rubber spatula to swish them in the oil to coat all pieces thoroughly.
   - Prepare the **onion**. Use a chef's knife to halve an onion lengthwise. Place each half cut side down on a cutting board and use a chef's knife to slice off the ends. Peel the onion. Place the onion halves cut side down onto the cutting board, cut each lengthwise into 5 thick slices, break the slice apart, add them to the mixing bowl, and use a rubber spatula to thoroughly mix the onion pieces into the oil.
   - Use a serrated knife to cut the ends from **8-10 garlic cloves**. Peel the cloves, halve the cloves lengthwise, add them to the mixing bowl with the onion and peppers, and use a rubber spatula to mix in the garlic pieces and thoroughly coat all pieces with oil.
   - Evenly sprinkle 1 t each dried basil and oregano leaves over the vegetables in the large mixing bowl, first crushing the herbs between your palms. Use a rubber spatula to thoroughly mix the vegetables and herbs together.
   - Quickly rinse the **5-6 mushrooms** under cool running water, dry them thoroughly with a paper towel, and cut each mushroom lengthwise into 3 equal slices. Add the slices to a separate medium mixing bowl, drizzle 1 T oil over the mushrooms, and use a rubber spatula to toss the mushroom slices thoroughly to coat them.
   - Use a rubber spatula to scrape the vegetables in the large mixing bowl into a large baking dish and to evenly spread the vegetables in a single layer over the bottom of the baking dish.

4. **Roast the vegetables.**

PART 2

- Center the baking dish on the middle rack of the pre-heated oven.
- Roast the vegetables for **8 minutes**, setting a timer. Use padded oven gloves to remove the vegetables from the oven and use a rubber spatula to stir them.
- Mix in the mushrooms, return the baking dish to the oven, and roast the vegetables another **8 minutes**, again setting a timer.
- At the timer, remove the roasted vegetables from the oven onto a heat-resistant surface.
- Immediately increase the oven temperature to **450 degrees**.

5. **Cook the ground beef while the vegetables roast in the oven.**

    - Heat a medium skillet on a back burner at a medium setting.
    - Use a 5 in. serrated knife to mince a ⅛ in. thick slice of ginger root.
    - Increase the heat to medium-high, and when a drop of water added to the skillet instantly dances and disappears, add 2 t oil, mix in the ginger root, add the ground beef, use a stir-frying spatula to break up the meat into ½ in. thick chunks, evenly sprinkle ½ t garlic powder and ½ t each dried basil and oregano leaves (first crushing them between your palms) over the meat, and vigorously stir-fry the meat for about 30 seconds.
    - Reduce the heat to a low medium setting and cook the meat 5 minutes or until it is cooked through (no red coloring remains), stirring the meat occasionally and setting a timer.
    - At the timer, remove the skillet from the heat, drain off any fat, and evenly sprinkle ¼ t salt over the meat. Set the skillet aside.

6. **Prepare the tomato sauce while the vegetables roast in the oven.**

    - Heat a large skillet at a medium setting. Measure ⅓ c tomato paste and ½ c tomato juice. Use a thin-bladed rubber spatula to easily scrape tomato paste from a 6 oz can of tomato paste.
    - Place ½ onion cut side down on a cutting board and use a chef's knife to cut off its ends. Peel the onion. Again place the onion cut side down on the cutting board and use the chef's knife to dice the onion. Mince the ginger root.
    - Increase the skillet heat to medium-high, and when a drop of water added to the skillet instantly dances and disappears, add 1 T oil, add the onion and ginger, evenly sprinkle ½ t each dried basil and oregano leaves (first crushing them between your palms) over the onion, and vigorously stir-fry the onion mixture for about 30 seconds.
    - Reduce the heat to medium and cook the onion mixture for 2 minutes, stirring it occasionally and setting a timer.
    - At the timer, add and thoroughly mix in the ⅓ c tomato paste and ½ c tomato juice. Remove the skillet from the heat and use a rubber spatula to scrape the tomato sauce into a medium mixing bowl.
    - Clean the skillet.

7. **Stir-fry the spinach while the other vegetables roast.**

- Heat the skillet on a large burner at medium.
- Form the spinach leaves into a large pile on a large cutting board. While holding leaves roughly together with one hand, use a 7 in. serrated knife to slice the spinach into ½ in. thick pieces, slicing through the leaves lengthwise and crosswise.
- Increase the skillet heat to medium-high, and when a drop of water added to the skillet instantly dances and disappears, add 1 T oil, add the spinach, and use a stir-fry spatula to continually stir-fry it for 1 minute or until the leaves are uniformly wilted and darkened, but before juice begins to spill.
- Remove the skillet from the heat, evenly sprinkle ¼ t salt over the spinach, and use a rubber spatula to scrape spinach into a colander placed over a dinner plate to collect any spilling juice.

8. **Bake the pizza dough once the vegetables are roasted and the oven temperature reaches 450 degrees.**

    - Gently press down on the plastic wrap covering the dough to break large bubbles and carefully remove the plastic wrap to avoid tearing the dough.
    - Center the pizza stone on the bottom oven rack.
    - Bake the pizza dough for **8 minutes** until the crust edges and crust bottom become slightly browned, setting a timer.
    - At the timer, check the crust for slight browning. For example, turn on the oven light for viewing or open the oven and quickly use a stir-fry spatula to lift a crust edge to examine the crust for slight browning.
    - Once the crust is slightly browned, wear padded oven gloves and remove the pizza stone to a heat-resistant surface.

9. **Prepare the cheeses, olives, and pineapple while the pizza dough bakes.** Coarsely grate the cheeses. Use a serrated knife to halve the olives and to cut the pineapple chunks into ¼ in. thick slices.

10. **Immediately assemble the pizza when the crust is removed from the oven.**

    - Scrape any spinach cooking juice into the tomato sauce.
    - Use a rubber spatula to spread the tomato sauce evenly over the crust, leaving the edges uncovered.
    - Use a rubber spatula to scrape the roasted vegetables and meat evenly over the crust.
    - Return the pizza stone to the bottom oven rack and bake the pizza for **5 minutes** until the exposed crust is lightly browned, setting a timer.
    - At the timer, remove the pizza from the oven.
    - Add and evenly spread the pineapple, spinach, olives, and cheese over the pizza top.
    - Return the pizza stone to a middle oven rack, heat the pizza for **2-3 minutes** until the cheese melts, and immediately remove the pizza from the oven.
    - Turn off the oven.

11. **Serve the pizza directly from the pizza stone.** Use a serrated knife to cut the pizza into serving size pieces and use a spatula to remove individual slices.

VARIATIONS: Make ingredient substitutions. Substitute, for example,

- **unflavored strained canned tomato**, such as the Italian product Pomi Strained Tomatoes, for tomato juice.
- **fresh extra lean ground sausage** or **a ½ beef and ½ pork mixture** for ground beef. Cook and season ground pork exactly like the ground beef.
- **other greens** (Recipes #23-30) for pre-washed spinach.
- **stir-fried rather than roasted garlic**. Serve stir-fried garlic (Recipe #31) as a topping, which shows up the distinctive and especially appealing flavor of garlic. Use a garlic-mincing tool to speed garlic preparation. Prepare garlic ahead of other ingredients.

Expand roasted vegetable content, adding 2 t oil and ½ t each dried basil and oregano leaves per vegetable and sprinkling ¼ t salt per vegetable after roasting. Add, for example,

- 8-10 Brussels sprouts (Recipe #40).
- 1 small (6 in. long, 1½ in. wide) zucchini or yellow straightneck or 2 small yellow crookneck summer squash (Recipe #50).
- 1 Italian eggplant or ½ medium globe eggplant (Recipe #42).
- 5-6 large cauliflower florets (Recipe #41).

Reference #12

Clinching Pizza Attractiveness: Expanded Preparation Support

To assist cooks in successfully preparing Chapter Twelve pizza recipes, Reference #12 walks cooks though five key pizza crust preparation steps – dough rising, beating dough, shaping dough, baking crust, and adding toppings. Reference #12 also identifies some specific nutrition-boosting pizza ingredient product selections.

1. Dough Rising

Measure, test, and maintain the vitality of yeast.

Observe the recipe-directed type of yeast and yeast amount. Use dry active yeast granules and measure 2 t granules. Adding too little yeast slows rising while adding too much causes very fast and excessive rising, which results in large bubbles that easily break and collapse. Small bubbles also yield a finer, more attractive crust texture than larger bubbles.

- Sprinkle yeast evenly over the warm water to speed its activation. Do not dump it in a pile into the water.

- Always test yeast. Let it sit in warm water for a minute. If it is alive and vigorous, it should begin to foam by the end of the minute.
- Once opening a yeast package, and when purchasing bulk yeast, tightly cover and refrigerate the yeast to keep it alive and vigorous.

Once the dough has been beaten (step #2), keep dough warm during rising. While this location does not have to be very warm, it should not be a cool or drafty area.

Break open large bubbles and let dough rise again. If dough over-rises and develops large bubbles, break the bubbles by evenly pushing down on the plastic wrap covering and let the dough rise again. Though this adds to preparation time, the dough will rise quickly and this double rising actually results in crust with an extra fine texture.

2. Beating Dough

Maximize beating effectiveness. Effective beating reliably develops gluten (or protein), and maximum gluten development is the key step that makes it possible for *Cooked Alive!*'s crust to be both bran rich *and* have a reliably light and tender texture. Beating overcomes bran interference with gluten development. With beating, gluten becomes sticky and elastic, and sticky and elastic dough, in turn, effectively holds bubbles formed by active yeast as they release carbon dioxide. Small bubbles make dough rise and give baked pizza crust an attractively light texture.

Standard whole wheat flour pizza crust recipes solve the problem of bran interference with gluten development by using finely ground flour, which only minimally interferes with gluten development. Standard whole wheat flour pizza crust recipes also commonly mix finely ground whole wheat flour with completely bran-free white flour. While both of these methods effectively avoid bran interference, they also degrade or eliminate bran content, which *Cooked Alive!* does not accept. In sharp contrast to standard whole wheat pizza crust recipes, its pizza crust overcomes bran interference with use of a variety of simple techniques that maximize beating effectiveness. Chapter Twelve pizza recipes, for example,

- use hand as opposed to electric bread hook beating. Hand and electric bread hook beating can be combined, but most beating needs to be done by hand.
- count beating strokes (150).
- use a big-headed, firm wooden spoon for beating. This tool provides more efficient beating than a smaller-headed wooden spoon.
- keep dough moist for easy and thorough hand beating. Strictly observe recipe-directed amounts when adding flour to dough before beating and only very cautiously add more flour. If the batter remains very sticky after the called for amount of flour has been added, add a small portion of flour at a time and mix each addition in to determine stickiness (checking that it remains moist enough for easy beating) before adding more flour. The aim is to beat as much flour as is possible but to keep beating easy to ensure thorough beating.

- use room temperature or warm flour. Because warm gluten develops more easily than chilled gluten, remove flour from a refrigerator well ahead of preparation time to allow it to reach room temperature.
- work with a small amount of dough at a time. Because it is far easier to hand beat a small amount of whole wheat dough, it is best to prepare two separate batters when more than doubling the pizza crust recipe.

3. Shaping Dough

Keep dough flexible for shaping. Cautiously add flour to dough during kneading. It is important for the dough to be soft and pliable for easy spreading onto the pizza stone. When dough remains somewhat sticky after kneading in the called for amount of flour, cautiously add more flour, adding only 1-2 T at a time to the kneading surface, just enough to remove stickiness and make dough dry enough to handle. As kneading progresses, lightly re-oil your hands to keep dough from sticking to them rather than adding more flour. As kneading progresses, also scrape the kneading surface clean, lightly oil the kneading surface, and knead the dough on the oiled surface as a way to remove stickiness without adding more flour.

Butter the pizza stone completely. Buttering eases the spreading of the dough over the stone. Butter also prevents sticking better than oil. Crust will likely stick on an unbuttered surface.

Protect dough from tearing.

- Cover pizza dough completely with lightly oiled plastic wrap during rising to protect the dough from drying air. Dry dough loses elasticity and easily breaks. If dough breaks, air escapes and bubbles collapse. Areas of dough with collapsed bubbles remain flat during baking; this area of a baked crust will have unattractive texture.
- Carefully remove plastic wrap to avoid tearing the dough.

4. Baking Crust

Prevent over-browning of the pizza crust during baking. Over-browning undermines both the texture and flavor of the crust. The goal is to achieve slight browning of the crust top edges and the crust bottom during the initial baking and to add only slightly darker browning during the baking of the fully assembled crust.

- Completely preheat an oven before adding the crust for baking. In a pre-heated oven the crust immediately begins to bake and is reliably ready in the recipe-directed time. Without thorough preheating, the crust will require extended baking. Because the needed time is uncertain, over-browning easily occurs.

- Make visual checks to assess browning. Because the temperature of different ovens can vary, visual checks provide important backup information, at least when first trying out an oven. After only 7 minutes of baking and while leaving the pizza crust in the oven and protecting your hands with padded gloves, use a stir-fry spatula to lift an edge to see whether the bottom is also slightly browned. If slight browning has already occurred, immediately remove the crust.

Protect pizza crust from becoming soggy after baking. Sogginess irreparably undermines pizza crust attractiveness.

- Immediately transfer pizza baked on a metal pan to a cooling rack after removing it from the oven. If left on the baking pan, steam will quickly condense on the crust bottom and cause it to become soggy.
- Never tightly cover warm pizza crust (assembled or non-assembled). Covering will cause steam to condense on the crust edges and bottom, which will make the crust unattractively soggy. Thoroughly cool pizza before covering it for storage.

5. Adding Toppings

Protect pizza crust from toppings that can cause a crust to become soggy.

- Add relatively dry tomato sauce. If it is juicy, add more tomato paste to thicken it.
- Do not add fatty ground beef. If ground beef is oily, thoroughly drain the fat before adding it to the crust. Use a paper towel to pat dry very oily cooked ground beef.
- Add only halved raw grape tomatoes with other toppings when assembling a pizza for baking. Briefly stir-fry other tomatoes (Recipe #37) and add any juice collected from this cooking to the tomato sauce topping. Then add the cooked tomatoes as a last ingredient with the cheese.

Cut vegetables with different cooking times in a way that supports even cooking. The aim should be to have the vegetables roast to tenderness in the same amount of time.

- Cut somewhat faster cooking vegetables (such as onions, bell peppers, zucchini, yellow summer squash, and mushrooms) into relatively large chunk form. Large chunks hold juice well and, as a result, color and flavor. Large chunks are also less likely to overcook before the end of the recipe-directed roasting time.
- Cut longer cooking vegetables, such as eggplant, into somewhat small or thin pieces.

Adjust the recipe to expand or vary vegetable content.

- Increase herb and oil amount slightly per added vegetable.
- Add a bit of salt (a few shakes) for all added vegetables except for seasoning vegetables

(onion, garlic, mushroom, tomato, bell pepper, and chili pepper).
- If cauliflower is added, separately oil the cauliflower before combining it with other vegetables for roasting. Cauliflower is highly absorptive. It can easily absorb most of the oil intended for other vegetables.
- Do not overcrowd the vegetable roasting pan, which can result in the undercooking of vegetables. Use two roasting pans, if necessary, to maintain a thin layer of vegetables.

Maintain the juiciness of the ground beef topping.

- Do not break ground beef into small pieces. Chunk size ground beef retains the most flavor and juice.
- Never cook ground meat at a high temperature. High temperature heating quickly causes meat protein to shrink, which forces out flavorful juice. Shrinking also results in toughening.
- Do not brown ground beef. Quickly heat through ground beef at the start of cooking but then cook it slowly. Add it to a pre-heated skillet and cook it at a medium-high temperature for a very short time only, just enough to heat it through, and then immediately reduce the heating temperature to medium or a temperature that keeps oil gently sizzling around the edges of meat chunks.
- Immediately remove meat from heat once it is cooked through. Do not heat it again until adding it to a dish being heated for serving.
- Add salt after the ground beef is fully cooked. As salt draws juices from the meat, adding salt reduces the juiciness of meat.

Thoroughly cook ground meat. Cook ground beef just until all raw red/pink coloring is removed. Because ground meat is highly vulnerable to bacterial contamination, thorough cooking is necessary to protect the cook and those being served from bacterial infections, some of which can be serious. To avoid potential contamination, it is also important for cooks to use soap for washing their hands after handling raw meat and for cleaning any cooking utensils coming into contact with raw ground beef.

Select flavorful cheese. Cheese is a key pizza flavoring ingredient. Selecting flavorful cheese makes it possible to somewhat reduce the amount of cheese, especially when cheese is combined with flavorful vegetables. Reducing cheese content in this manner, in turn, reduces the number of calories without undermining serving success. Select, for example,

- chunk form cheese. Freshly grated chunk cheese is the most flavorful cheese. Selecting cheese in chunk form also provides a wider selection of flavorful cheese. Chunk cheese must be stored tightly wrapped and refrigerated to maintain good flavor and texture.
- naturally aged cheese as opposed to processed cheese.

Select top quality cheese. Select, for example,

- cheese made from the milk of naturally raised dairy cows. Examples of such products are certified organic and locally produced cheese products. These cheese products are significantly different from cheese made from the milk of industrially raised dairy cows. In comparison to industrially produced cheese, naturally produced cheese will have higher overall nutritional value in addition to being free of antibiotics, genetically modified (GM) hormones, genetically modified natural and artificial flavors,[275] and pesticides. Reference #4 (Selecting Top Quality Whole Food Ingredients for Part I Recipes) explains these important differences between naturally and industrially produced cheese products.

- cheese made from dairy cows that are both certified organic and 100% grass-fed, which stands above all other cheese products as high quality cheese. Only cheese that is also made from raw milk has higher quality.
- European produced cheese. European cheese products made from the milk of 100% pastured dairy cows and especially cheese made from the raw milk of 100% pastured dairy cows are top quality cheese products.

Minimize high temperature heating of cheese. Add natural cheese as the very last ingredient at the end of baking in order to avoid shrinking and hardening of the cheese. Heat it only until it is completely melted, which takes a few minutes only.

Measure cheese added to pizza. A highly appealing ingredient, cheese is just too easy to add. Measuring cheese provides a means for keeping on top of the amount added and, as a result, of the calories added. Specific measuring prevents cheese from adding significant "hidden" calories and from converting *Cooked Alive!* pizza into standard high fat form. The combination of cheese and tasty roasted vegetables provides sufficient compensating juiciness and flavoring to make modest addition of cheese fully acceptable.

- Acquire a kitchen scale to measure cheese content accurately.
- Mark blocks of cheese off in ounces before slicing or grating.

Select top quality commercially prepared tomato products. Select, for example,

- certified organic tomato products.
- certified organic single ingredient tomato products as opposed to mixed ingredient products, such as tomato sauce.
- tomato paste as the primary tomato flavoring ingredient. Reference #5 (Selecting High Quality Processed Ingredients for Use in Part II Recipes), Ingredient #10, explains why tomato paste is an ingredient with outstanding nutritional value.
- low salt products.
- products marketed in glass containers in particular but also aseptic (coated paper) containers, which do not leach chemicals into the acidic tomato products.
- canned tomatoes marketed in BPA (bisphenol A)-free cans.

---

275 Barry Estabrook & Anne Treadwell, "Where the GMOs Are," *Eating Well* (July/August 2015): 84-85.

CHAPTER THIRTEEN

100% Whole Wheat Pancakes

Pancake Description

THE *COOKED ALIVE!* pancake is perfect breakfast fare. Made from a variety of nourishing ingredients – including eggs, milk, bran-rich whole wheat flour, banana, nuts, and topped with a tangy fruit sauce – and with minimal sugar and fat content, it is genuinely wholesome. Reliably tasty and attractive, appetite satisfying, and providing energy to carry those served through a full morning of activity, Chapter Thirteen pancakes stand a world apart from the typical anemic white flour pancake smothered in sweet syrup.

Cooked Alive! pancakes are completely within the reach of cooks in general. They are as simple and quick to prepare as white flour – or mixed white and whole wheat – counterpart pancakes. Relying on preparation techniques carefully adapted to whole flour characteristics, Chapter Thirteen recipes yield pancakes that are just as tender and moist, too. *Cooked Alive!* basic pancakes are a winning dish that cooks can successfully prepare over and over without their families and friends ever tiring of them. They also serve as special guest fare.

Pancake Preparation Notes

Preparation Notes provide helpful general preparation instruction for and information about Chapter Thirteen pancake recipes that cannot fit into the individual recipes. They cover a variety of types of information, including,

- miscellaneous pancake information (Notes #1-5).
- boosting serving success information (Note #6).
- boosting nutrition-quality information (Note #7).
- cooking tool information (Note #8).

1. **To expand the number of pancake servings**, double or triple the recipe to make 4-6 servings. For ease of preparation and most satisfactory baking results, however, prepare two equal batches for making 8-12 servings.

2. **To convert Chapter Thirteen pancakes into vegan vegetarian form**, substitute non-dairy for dairy milk, omit the butter and egg, and increase the orange juice content to ¼ cup to make up for the loss of egg liquid. Serving the pancakes with fruit sauce satisfactorily substitutes for the butter topping. While texture is somewhat negatively affected, omitting the egg works satisfactorily enough.

3. **Leftover pancakes make tasty snacks.** Tightly covered once cooled, leftover pancakes, and especially those with a fruit filling, are pleasing and appetite-satisfying snacks. Especially because they do not need any added enhancement (butter or topping), they are nourishing snacks as well. Leftover pancakes, however, should be eaten on the day they were baked or frozen for later use.

4. **To carry along pancake-making packets for outdoor camping**, mix all dry ingredients including non-instant dried milk or buttermilk powder (2 T per 2-serving batch) and the chopped nuts in a zippered plastic bag. Separately pack an egg and fruit sauce or maple syrup in spill- and break-proof containers. Fresh milk can also be separately carried. Non-dairy milk can be substituted and an egg can be quite satisfactorily omitted from the batter provided the banana or other moistening ingredient is included.

5. **Do not omit butter or oil from pancake batter as a way to reduce calories.** This fat is an important ingredient for giving pancakes a tender and moist texture. Also do not substitute any vegetable oil for either extra virgin olive oil or coconut oil. Vegetable oils are unstable oils when heated.

6. **Chapter Thirteen includes a preparation reference specifically focused on aiding cooks in achieving pancake serving success.** Including helpful preparation suggestions too detailed to fit into recipes, Reference #13 (Clinching Pancake Attractiveness: Expanded Preparation Support) covers five key pancake preparation steps. These steps include selecting mixing batter, cooking pancakes, flipping pancakes, serving pancakes, and preparing a fruit topping.

7. **Cooks can substantially boost the nutritional quality of Chapter Thirteen pancakes through the selection of high quality pancake ingredients.** *Cooked Alive!* provides three references that assist cooks in making high quality ingredient selections:

    - Reference #1 (Selecting Top Quality Fresh Vegetables and Fruits) and Reference #4 (Selecting Top Quality Whole Food Ingredients for Use in Part II Recipes) identify specific whole food ingredients.
    - Reference #5 (Selecting High Quality Processed Ingredients for Use in Part II Recipes). Reference #5 identifies a variety of high quality processed food products. Products covered that are relevant to pancakes include:

        - dairy products (milk and butter) (Ingredient #2).
        - whole wheat flour (Ingredient #3).
        - coconut oil (Ingredient #9).

- extra virgin olive oil (Ingredient # 8).
- canned and dry frozen blueberries (Ingredient #10).

8. **Important information about cooking tools is as follows:**

    - Chapter Thirteen pancake and fruit topping recipes list all key cooking tools used in recipes, listing them in order of use, but do not list some basic working tools. These tools – paper and cloth towels, plastic wrap, vegetable and fruit scrubbing tools, and multi-purpose cutting boards – are routinely used in recipes and need to be kept handy.
    - The general cooking tool list presented in the Part II Introduction serves as a descriptive reference for most tools used in pancake recipes, but it does not include two tools that are either specific to pancakes or that are used only in a few Part II chapters. These tools are described as follows:

        - **1 griddle, stove top or electric.** A griddle provides extra space for cooking several pancakes at a time and for easy flipping of pancakes. A nonstick surface greatly eases both flipping and cleanup. An electric nonstick griddle significantly reduces pre-heating time, but a stove top griddle best retains an even baking temperature.
        - **1 potato masher with a metal grid mashing head.** This tool cuts banana into small chunks that provide attractive banana flavor in pancakes. It works the same for baked sweet potato and winter squash. A masher with a looped wire, in contrast, mashes banana finely rather than coarsely. Finely mashed banana lacks flavor and easily makes batter too moist. A stainless steel grid head cuts more easily and cleanly than a plastic grid head. A dish washing brush with a long handle serves as an efficient cleaning tool.

Pancake Recipes

214. Basic 100% Whole Wheat Pancakes
(Pancake Master Recipe)
(2 servings; 1 7-in. pancake per serving)

Pancakes

½ c chilled medium ground whole wheat flour (see comments for a description)
½ t baking powder
1/16 t baking soda
2 t sugar

½ c milk (whole or fat reduced, not skim)
2 T premium orange juice with pulp
½ chilled medium banana (3-4 in. long)
1 T coconut oil or extra virgin olive oil
2 t butter, divided in half

COOKED ALIVE!

¼ t salt
1 large egg

¼ c raw whole almonds or ⅛ each raw almonds and raw pecan or walnut halves

Topping

⅔ c fruit sauce (Recipes #219-224)

2 t chilled butter

Cooking Tools

2 large heavy-bottomed skillets or 1 electric griddle
1 small skillet
1 set each measuring cups & spoons
2 medium mixing bowls
1 cutting board
1 each chef's & slicing knife
1 dinner fork or small whisk

1 potato masher with a metal grid-style head
2 rubber spatulas
1 large-headed (2½ in. wide) wooden spoon
1 timer
1 wide (approx. 4 in.) plastic or plastic-coated stir-fry spatula
1 dish washing brush

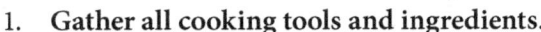

1. **Gather all cooking tools and ingredients.**

2. **Heat two skillets on two large burners or an electric griddle at a medium setting.** If using coconut oil, add 1 T coconut oil to a small skillet and heat the oil on a small burner at a low heat setting. Be watchful and remove the skillet from the heat once the oil melts.

3. **Combine the dry ingredients.** Add the ½ c flour, ½ t baking powder, ¹⁄₁₆ t baking soda, 2 t sugar, and ¼ t salt to a medium mixing bowl. Combine the ingredients thoroughly.

4. **Chop the nuts and dice 2 t topping butter.** Working on a cutting board, use a chef's knife to chop the nuts coarsely and to dice the butter. Divide the butter into two equal piles.

5. **Combine the wet ingredients and banana.**

   - Add the egg, ½ c milk, and 2 T orange juice to a medium mixing bowl. Use a fork or whisk to mix the egg yolk into the milk mixture.
   - Peel and cut the banana into 3-4 slices, add the slices to the egg mixture, and use a potato masher to cut the banana into small chunks. Push the masher through the banana pieces once or twice if a chunky mix is preferred, more if a creamier texture is wanted. Use the dull side of the slicing knife to scrape the banana chunks from the masher into the mixing bowl. Immediately rinse the masher with water and clean the masher using a dish brush.
   - Add and stir in 1 T oil. If using coconut oil, use a rubber spatula to scrape the melted oil into the milk mixture and quickly stir the oil into the other ingredients.

PART 2

6. **Combine the dry and wet mixtures.**

    - Pour the dry ingredients onto the wet mixture and use a wooden spoon to combine the ingredients, stirring the batter just until the flour is fully moistened (about 15 strokes).
    - Use a rubber spatula to finish the mixing. Scrape batter from the spoon and bowl sides, scrape the bowl bottom to mix in any dry flour, and break up any lumps of flour.

7. **Bake the pancakes.**

    - Increase the skillet heat slightly to a high medium setting.
    - When a bit of butter added to the skillet instantly sizzles moderately, add 1 t butter to each skillet and use a rubber spatula to spread the butter over the skillet bottoms. Alternatively, quickly rub the open end of a wrapped stick of butter over the bottom of each skillet.
    - Immediately divide the batter between the skillets, forming two or three pancakes, and set a timer for 4 minutes.
    - Evenly divide the nuts over the batter.

8. **Flip and add butter to the pancakes.**

    - At the timer, check pancake readiness for flipping. When readiness is indicated – bubbles are appearing in the batter, an edge lifts without the pancake breaking, and a lifted edge shows the bottom is lightly browned – use a stir-fry spatula to flip each pancake.
    - Evenly spread 1 t diced butter over each pancake.
    - Lower the heat skillet slightly (back to medium).
    - Be watchful to prevent scorching.

9. **Serve the pancakes when they are cooked through.** When the centers bounce back when lightly touched and the bottoms are lightly browned, which will be approximately 3 minutes after flipping, remove the pancakes from the skillet onto a dinner plate for immediate serving or onto a wire cooling rack for somewhat delayed serving. Do not stack the pancakes or temporarily place them on a platter, which will cause the pancake bottoms to become unattractively soggy.

10. **Serve each pancake topped with ⅓ c fruit sauce.**

    VARIATIONS: Vary the number of pancake servings. For example,

    - make **three servings**, making three 5 in. pancakes instead of two 7 in. pancakes.
    - make **1 pancake**. Halve all ingredients except for the egg and orange juice. Use 1 egg and only ½ T orange juice.

Make ingredient substitutions. Substitute, for example,

- **maple syrup** for fruit sauce, 2-3 T per pancake. As a less processed product, Grade B maple syrup is more flavorful than Grade A syrup.
- **1 baked apple (Recipe #205), heated, per pancake for fruit sauce.**
- **1 T butter** for extra virgin olive oil or coconut oil. Melt the butter in a small skillet over low heat, being careful to avoid browning.
- **⅓ c room temperature salted mashed potato** or **thick cooked oatmeal** for ½ medium banana in the recipe.
- **2 T buttermilk powder** for milk. Thoroughly mix the buttermilk powder into the flour mixture, substitute water for milk, and increase baking soda content to ¼ t per ½ c flour.
- **non-dairy** (any variety) for dairy milk to convert the pancakes to **vegan vegetarian form**. Omit the egg and increase the orange juice content to ¼ c to make up for the reduced liquid content.

Add ingredients. Add, for example,

- **½ banana** (Recipe #77), sliced, **¼ mango** (Recipe #87), diced, **¼ pear** (Recipe #93), diced, or **a combination of banana, mango,** and **pear**, added as a pancake topping along with either fruit sauce or maple syrup.
- **½ c sweet cherries** (Recipe #81), halved and added as a topping with fruit sauce or maple syrup.
- **1-2 T diced fruit per pancake**, spread over the batter along with the nuts after adding the batter to the skillets for baking. For example, use **apple** (Recipe #74), **pear** (Recipe #93), **plum** (Recipe #95), or **pineapple** (Recipe #94).
- **½ c coarsely shredded zucchini** or **yellow summer squash** (Recipe #127), mixed into the flour mixture when assembling the pancake batter.
- **1 t dried tart cherries**, sliced into several pieces, per pancake, spread over the batter of a baking pancake.
- **1-2 T freshly ground flax seeds**, added to the flour mixture.

COMMENTS: Medium ground whole wheat flour is high-protein hard winter wheat bread flour that has clearly visible bits of bran. The bran gives the flour a somewhat coarse texture. The bran content makes this flour absorptive. See Reference #5 (Selecting High Quality Processed Ingredients for Use in Part II Recipes), Ingredient #3, for a description of the highest quality medium whole wheat flour.

215. 100% Whole Wheat Blueberry and Nectarine Pancakes
(2 servings; 1 7-in. pancake per serving)

Fruit

½ c fresh blueberries

½ chilled nectarine

Pancakes

½ c chilled medium ground whole wheat flour (see Comments for a description)
½ t baking powder
1/16 t baking soda
2 t sugar
¼ t salt
1 large egg

½ c milk (whole or fat reduced; not skim)
2 T premium orange juice with pulp
½ chilled medium banana (3-4 in. long)
1 T coconut oil or extra virgin olive oil
2 t butter, divided in half
⅛ c each raw whole almonds and raw pecan or walnut halves

Toppings

⅔ c fruit sauce (Recipes #219-224) or 4 T maple syrup

2 t chilled butter

Cooking Tools

2 large heavy-bottomed skillets or 1 electric griddle
1 small skillet
1 colander
1 pie plate
1 cutting board
1 each 5 in. serrated & chef's knife
1 small bowl

2 medium mixing bowls
1 dinner fork or small whisk
1 potato masher with grid-style head
1 dish washing brush
1 large-headed wooden spoon
2 rubber spatulas
2 plastic or plastic-coated stir-fry spatulas
2 dinner plates or 1 cooling rack

---

1. Gather all cooking tools and ingredients.

2. **Heat two large skillets on two large burners or 1 electric griddle at a medium setting.** If using coconut oil, add 1 T coconut oil to a small skillet and melt the oil at a low setting. Be watchful and set the skillet aside once the oil melts.

3. **Prepare the blueberries, nectarine, ¼ c nuts, and 2 t butter.**

   - Add fresh **blueberries** to a colander and rinse them with cool water. Pour the berries into a pie plate lined with a double thickness of paper towels or a terry cloth towel.

- Pick through the berries to remove stems and replace spoiled berries. Wrap the towels around the berries to dry them completely and set the berries aside in the pie plate.
- Rinse and dry the **nectarine**. Working on a clean cutting board, use a serrated knife to slice the nectarine lengthwise into ¼ in. thick slices. Cut the slices crosswise into ¼ in. wide cubes. Add the nectarines to a small bowl and refrigerate them.
- Use a chef's knife to chop the **nuts** coarsely.
- Use the chef's knife to dice 2 t **butter**.

4. **Combine the dry ingredients.** Add the ½ c flour, ½ t baking powder, $\frac{1}{16}$ t baking soda, 2 t sugar, and ¼ t salt to a medium mixing bowl. Combine the ingredients thoroughly.

5. **Combine the wet ingredients and banana.**

   - Add the egg, ½ c milk, and 2 T orange juice to another medium mixing bowl. Use a fork or whisk to mix the egg yolk into the milk mixture.
   - Peel and cut the banana into 3-4 slices, add the slices to the egg mixture, and use a potato masher to cut the banana into small chunks. Push the masher through the banana pieces once or twice if a chunky mix is preferred, more times if a creamier mix is desired. Use the dull side of the serrated knife to scrape the banana bits from the masher into the mixing bowl. Immediately rinse the masher with water and clean the brush using a dish brush.
   - Add and stir in 1 T oil. If using coconut oil, use a rubber spatula to scrape the melted oil into the liquid ingredients and to quickly mix in the oil before it hardens

6. **Combine the wet and dry ingredients.**

   - Pour the dry ingredients onto the wet mixture and use a wooden spoon to combine the ingredients, stirring the batter just until the flour is fully moistened (about 15 strokes).
   - Use a rubber spatula to finish the mixing. Scrape batter from the spoon and bowl sides, scrape the bowl bottom to mix in any dry flour, and break up any lumps of flour.

7. **Bake the pancakes.**

   - Increase the skillet heat slightly to a high medium setting.
   - When a bit of butter added to the skillet instantly sizzles moderately, add 1 t butter to each skillet and use a rubber spatula to spread the butter over the skillet bottoms. Alternatively, quickly rub the open end of a wrapped stick of butter over the bottom of each skillet.
   - Immediately divide the batter between the skillets and set a timer for 4 minutes.
   - Evenly divide the nuts, blueberries, and nectarine over the pancakes.

8. **Flip and add butter to each pancake.**

PART 2

- Check for readiness at the timer's alert. When readiness is indicated – bubbles should start to appear in the batter, an edge lifts with a spatula without the pancake breaking, and a lifted edge shows the bottom is lightly browned – use a stir-fry spatula to flip each pancake.
- Evenly spread 1 t diced butter over each pancake.
- Lower the heat skillet slightly (back to medium). Be watchful to prevent scorching.

9. **Serve the pancakes when they are cooked through.** When the centers bounce back when lightly touched and the bottoms are lightly browned, remove the pancakes from the skillet onto a plate for immediate serving or onto a wire cooling rack for somewhat delayed serving. Do not stack the pancakes or place them on a platter, which will cause the pancake bottoms to become unattractively soggy.

10. **Serve each pancake topped with ⅓ c fruit sauce or 2 T maple syrup.**

    VARIATIONS: Vary the number of pancake servings.

    - Make **three 5 in. pancakes** instead of two 7 in. pancakes.
    - Make **1 pancake**. Halve all ingredients except for the egg and orange juice. Use 1 egg and ½ T orange juice only.

    Make ingredient substitutions. Substitute, for example,

    - **1 T melted butter** for extra virgin olive or coconut oil. Melt the butter in a small skillet over low heat, being careful to avoid browning. Use a rubber spatula to scrape the butter into the wet ingredients immediately before combining the wet and dry ingredients (before it hardens).
    - **4 chunks fresh pineapple** (Recipe #94), cut into ¼ in. thick slices, for nectarine. Alternatively, combine pineapple and nectarine.
    - **1 ripe red or purple plum** (Recipe #95), sliced thinly, for nectarine.
    - **honey** for maple syrup. If the honey is thick and does not easily pour, warm it in a small skillet or microwave heat it before serving.

    Add ingredients. Add, for example,

    - **6 raspberries** (Recipe #97), halved lengthwise, either dividing them over the pancake batter with the nectarine and blueberries or serving them as a topping with either sauce or syrup.

    COMMENTS: Medium ground whole wheat flour is high-protein hard winter wheat bread flour that has clearly visible bits of bran, which gives the flour a slightly coarse texture. The bran gives the flour a somewhat coarse texture. The bran content makes this flour absorptive. See Reference #5 (Selecting High Quality Processed Ingredients for Use in Part II Recipes), Ingredient #3, for a description of the highest quality medium whole wheat flour.

COOKED ALIVE!

216. 100% Whole Wheat Zucchini Pancakes
(2 servings; 1 7-in. pancake per serving)

Fruit and Zucchini

½ c fresh blueberries

⅓ c ½ in. pineapple chunks (Recipe #94)

½ medium (6 in.) zucchini (to yield approx. ½ c shredded)

Pancakes

½ c chilled medium ground whole wheat flour (see Comments for a description)

½ t baking powder

1/16 t baking soda

¼ t ground cinnamon

1 t sugar

¼ t salt

1 large egg

½ c milk (whole or reduced fat)

2 T premium orange juice with pulp

½ chilled medium banana (3-4 in. half)

1 T coconut oil or extra virgin olive oil

¼ c raw pecan or walnut halves or ⅛ c each whole raw almonds and either pecan or walnut halves

2 t butter, divided into equal parts

Toppings

⅔ c fruit sauce (Recipes #219-224) or 4 T maple syrup

2 t chilled butter, diced

Cooking Tools

2 large heavy-bottomed skillets or a electric griddle

1 each measuring cups & spoons

1 colander

1 pie plate

1 cutting board

1 each serrated & chef's knife

1 vegetable shredder with a coarse setting

2 medium (6 c) mixing bowls

1 dinner fork or small whisk

1 potato masher with grid head

1 dish washing brush

1 large-headed wooden spoon

2 rubber spatulas

2 plastic or plastic-coated stir-fry spatulas

2 dinner plates or 1 cooling rack

---

1. **Gather all cooking tools and ingredients.**

2. **Heat two skillets on two large burners or an electric griddle at a medium setting.** If using coconut oil, heat 1 T coconut oil in a small skillet on a small burner at a low heat setting. Be watchful and remove the skillet from the heat once the oil melts.

PART 2

3. **Prepare the blueberries, pineapple, zucchini, nuts, and 2 t diced butter.**

   - Add ½ c **blueberries** to a colander and rinse them with cool water. Pour them into a pie plate lined with a double thickness of paper towels or a terry cloth towel. Pick through the berries to remove stems and replace spoiled berries. Wrap the towels around the berries to dry them completely. Set the berries aside in the pie plate.
   - Working on a clean cutting board, use a serrated knife to slice the ⅓ c **pineapple chunks** lengthwise into ¼ in. thick slices; halve the slices crosswise. Add the pineapple to the pie plate with the blueberries and mix the fruits together.
   - Use the serrated knife to slice off the stem end of ½ **zucchini**. Coarsely grate the zucchini and measure ½ c zucchini (this can be slightly more or less than ½ cup).
   - Use a chef's knife to chop the ¼ c **nuts** coarsely.
   - Use the chef's knife to dice 2 t **butter** into small (¼ in.) cubes. Make two equal piles of butter.

4. **Combine the dry ingredients.** Add the ½ c flour, ½ t baking powder, ¹⁄₁₆ t baking soda, ¼ t ground cinnamon, 2 t sugar, and ¼ t salt to a medium mixing bowl. Combine the ingredients thoroughly.

5. **Mix the zucchini into the dry ingredients.**

6. **Combine the wet ingredients and banana.**

   - Add the egg, ½ c milk, and 2 T orange juice to another medium mixing bowl. Use a fork or whisk to mix the egg yolk into the milk mixture.
   - Peel and cut the ½ banana into 3-4 slices, add the slices to the egg mixture, and use a potato masher to cut the banana into small chunks. Push the masher through the banana pieces once or twice for a chunky mix and more for a creamier mix. Use the dull side of a knife to scrape the banana chunks from the masher into the mixing bowl. Immediately rinse the masher with water and use a dish washing brush to clean it.
   - Add and stir in 1 T oil. If using coconut oil, use a rubber spatula to scrape the melted oil from the skillet into the milk mixture and to roughly mix in the oil.

7. **Combine the wet and dry ingredients.**

   - Pour the dry ingredients onto the wet mixture and use a wooden spoon to combine the ingredients, stirring the batter just until the flour is moistened (about 15 strokes).
   - Use a rubber spatula to finish the mixing. Scrape batter from the spoon and bowl sides, scrape the bowl bottom to mix in any dry flour, and break up open any lumps of flour.

8. **Bake the pancakes.**

   - Increase the skillet heat slightly to a high medium setting.

- When a bit of butter added to the skillet instantly sizzles moderately, add 1 t butter to each skillet and use a spatula to spread the butter over the skillet bottoms. Alternatively, quickly rub the open end of a wrapped stick of butter over the bottom of each skillet.
- Immediately divide the batter between the skillets and set a timer for 4 minutes.
- Evenly divide the nuts, blueberries, and pineapple over the batter of each pancake.

9. **Flip and add butter to each pancake.**

   - At the timer, check for readiness. When readiness is indicated –
   - bubbles start to appear in the batter, an edge lifts without the pancake breaking, and a lifted edge shows the bottom is lightly browned – use a stir-fry spatula to flip each pancake.
   - Evenly spread 1 t diced butter over each pancake.
   - Lower the heat to medium. Be watchful to prevent scorching (over-browning), which undermines pancake flavor.

10. **Serve the pancakes when they are cooked through.** When the centers bounce back when lightly touched and the bottoms are lightly browned, remove the pancakes from the skillet onto a plate for immediate serving or onto a wire cooling rack for somewhat delayed serving. Do not stack the pancakes or temporarily place them on a platter, which will cause the pancake bottoms to become unattractively soggy.

11. **Serve each pancake topped with ⅓ c fruit sauce or 2 T maple syrup.**

    VARIATIONS: Vary the number of servings.

    - Make **three 5 in. pancakes** rather than two 7 in. pancakes.
    - Make **1 pancake**. Halve all ingredients except for egg and orange juice. Use 1 egg and only ½ T orange juice.

    Make ingredient substitutions. Substitute, for example,

    - **1 T butter** for extra virgin olive oil. Melt the butter in a small skillet over low heat, being careful to avoid scorching, and use a rubber spatula to scrape the butter into the liquid ingredients immediately before combining the wet and dry ingredients.
    - **½ c coarsely grated unpeeled carrot** for zucchini.
    - **⅓ diced apple** (Recipe #74) for pineapple.
    - **1 baked apple** (Recipe #205), heated, per pancake for fruit topping.

    Add ingredients. Add, for example,

    - **4 raspberries** and/or **2 blackberries**, halved lengthwise, either added to the batter with the nectarine and blueberries or served raw as a topping with a fruit sauce or maple syrup.

- **2 T red currant berries** or **2 T pomegranate seeds** (fresh or dry frozen, unthawed) per pancake, either baked in the pancakes or added raw as a topping.
- **⅛ t ground nutmeg**, mixed into the flour mixture.
- **½ medium banana**, sliced, per serving, added as a topping.
- **⅓ c fresh pineapple**, sliced, or **⅓ pear**, diced, per pancake. Add the fruit as a topping along with either fruit sauce or maple syrup.

COMMENTS: Medium ground whole wheat flour is high-protein hard winter wheat bread flour that has clearly visible bits of bran. The bran gives the flour a somewhat coarse texture. The bran content makes this flour absorptive. See Reference #5 (Selecting High Quality Processed Ingredients for Use in Part II Recipes), Ingredient #3, for a description of the highest quality medium whole wheat flour.

217. 100% Whole Wheat Applesauce Pancakes
(2 servings; 1 7-in. pancake per serving)

Fruit

½ c fresh blueberries
⅓ c fresh or dry frozen pineapple chunks, ½ in. thick (Recipe #94)

⅓ c thick & chunky sweetened applesauce

Pancakes

½ c chilled medium ground whole wheat flour (see Comments for a description)
½ t baking powder
1/16 t baking soda
2 t sugar
¼ t ground cinnamon
¼ t salt

1 large egg
½ c milk (whole or reduced fat)
2 T premium orange juice with pulp
1 T extra virgin olive oil or coconut oil
2 t butter, divided in half
⅛ c each raw whole almonds and either raw pecan or walnut halves

Topping

⅔ c fruit sauce (Recipes #219-224) or 4 T maple syrup

2 t chilled butter

Cooking Tools

2 large heavy-bottomed skillets or 1 electric griddle
1 small skillet

2 medium mixing bowls
1 dinner fork or small whisk
1 potato masher with a metal grid-style head

1 set each measuring spoons & cups	1 dish washing brush
1 colander	1 large-headed wooden spoon
1 pie plate	2 rubber spatulas
1 cutting board reserved for fruit & vegetables	2 plastic or plastic-coated stir-fry spatulas
1 each 5 in. serrated & chef's knife	2 dinner plates or 1 cooling rack

---

1. **Gather all cooking tools and ingredients.**

2. **Heat two skillets on two large burners or an electric griddle at a medium setting.** If using coconut oil, add 1 T coconut oil to a small skillet and melt the oil at a low-low setting. Be watchful and, once the oil melts, set the skillet off the burner.

3. **Prepare the fruit, nuts, and topping butter.**

    - Add ½ c **blueberries** to a colander, rinse them with cool water, and pour the berries into a pie plate lined with a double thickness of paper towels or a terry cloth towel. Pick through the berries to remove stems and replace spoiled berries. Wrap the towels around the berries to dry them completely. Set the berries aside in the pie plate.
    - Working on a clean cutting board, use a serrated knife to slice ⅓ c **pineapple chunks** into ¼ in. thick slices and halve the slices crosswise.
    - Use a chef's knife to chop the **nuts** coarsely.
    - Use the chef's knife to dice 2 t **butter**. Make two equal piles of butter.

4. **Combine the dry ingredients.** Add the ½ c flour, ½ t baking powder, ¹⁄₁₆ t baking soda, 2 t sugar, ¼ t cinnamon, and ¼ t salt in a medium mixing bowl. Combine the ingredients thoroughly. Add and toss the blueberries and pineapple thoroughly.

5. **Combine the wet ingredients.**

    - Add the egg, ½ c milk, and 2 T orange juice to another medium mixing bowl. Use a fork or whisk to mix the egg yolk into the milk mixture.
    - Add the applesauce. Use a dinner fork to coarsely mash any large chunks.
    - Add and stir in 1 T oil. If using coconut oil, use a rubber spatula to scrape the melted oil from the skillet into the milk mixture and to quickly mix in the oil before it hardens.

6. **Combine the wet and dry ingredients.**

    - Pour the dry ingredients onto the wet mixture and use a wooden spoon to combine the ingredients, stirring the batter just until the flour is fully moistened (about 15 strokes).
    - Use a rubber spatula to finish the mixing. Scrape batter from the spoon and bowl sides, scrape the bowl bottom to mix in any dry flour, and break up any lumps of flour.

PART 2

7. **Bake the pancakes.**

   - Increase the skillet heat slightly to a high medium setting.
   - When a bit of butter added to the skillet instantly sizzles moderately, add 1 t butter to each skillet and use a spatula to spread the butter over the skillet bottoms. Alternatively, quickly rub the open end of a wrapped stick of butter over the bottom of each skillet.
   - Immediately evenly divide the batter between the skillets and set a timer for 4 minutes.
   - Evenly divide the nuts, blueberries, and pineapple over the batter of the baking pancakes.

8. **Flip and add butter to each pancake.**

   - At the timer, check for readiness. When readiness is indicated – bubbles start to appear in the batter, an edge lifts without the pancake breaking, and a lifted edge shows the bottom is lightly browned – use a stir-fry spatula to flip each pancake.
   - Evenly spread 1 t diced butter over each pancake.
   - Lower the heat skillet to medium. Be watchful to prevent scorching, which undermines pancake flavor.

9. **Serve the pancakes when they are cooked through.** When the centers bounce back when lightly touched and the bottoms are lightly browned (approximately 3 minutes after flipping), remove the pancakes from the skillet onto a plate for immediate serving or onto a wire cooling rack for somewhat delayed serving. Do not stack the pancakes or place them on a platter, which will cause the pancake bottoms to become unattractively soggy.

10. **Serve each pancake topped with ⅓ c fruit sauce or 2 T maple syrup.**

    VARIATIONS: Vary the number of servings.

    - Make **3 5-in. pancakes** rather than 2 7-in. pancakes.
    - Make **1 pancake**. Halve all ingredients except for egg and orange juice. Use 1 egg and ½ T orange juice.

    Make ingredient substitutions. Substitute, for example,

    - **1 T butter** for extra virgin olive oil or coconut oil. Melt the butter in a small skillet over low heat, being careful to not brown it. Use a rubber spatula to scrape the butter into the batter just before combining the wet and dry ingredients (before the butter hardens).
    - **⅓ c home-prepared prepared applesauce** (Recipe #224) for commercially prepared.

    Add ingredients. Add, for example,

    - **2 raspberries, 2 blackberries, 2 T red currant berries, or 2 T pomegranate seeds** to each pancake.

- ½ **banana**, sliced, per pancake, added as a topping with either fruit sauce or maple syrup.
- ⅓ **chilled raw apple**, diced (Recipe #74), mixed into the flour mixture.
- **1 baked apple (Recipe #205), heated, per pancake as a topping.**
- ¼ t **ground nutmeg**, mixed into the flour mixture.
- 2 T **certified organic raisins** mixed into the flour mixture.
- 1 heaping T **dried tart cherries**, coarsely chopped and mixed into the flour mixture.

COMMENTS: Medium ground whole wheat flour is high-protein hard winter wheat bread flour with clearly visible bits of bran, which gives the flour a slightly coarse texture. See Reference #5 (Selecting High Quality Processed Ingredients for Use in Part II Recipes), Ingredient #3, for a description of the highest quality medium whole wheat flour as Ingredient #3.

218. 100% Whole Wheat Winter Squash Pancakes
(2 servings; 8 in. pancake per serving)

Fruit and Squash

½ c fresh blueberries
½ chilled apple, halved lengthwise

½ c mashed baked butternut squash (Recipe #52)

Pancakes

½ c chilled medium ground whole wheat flour (see Comments for a description)
½ t baking powder
1/16 t baking soda
2 t sugar
¼ t salt
¼ t ground cinnamon
⅓-½ c milk (whole or reduced fat)

2 T premium orange juice with pulp
1 large egg
1 T extra virgin olive oil or coconut oil
¼ c raw pecan or walnut halves (or ⅛ c each whole almonds and pecan or walnut halves)
2 t butter, divided in half

Topping

⅔ c fruit sauce (Recipes #219-224) or 4 T maple syrup

2 t chilled butter

Cooking Tools

2 large heavy-bottomed skillets or 1 electric griddle

1 each chef's, paring, & slicing knife
2 medium mixing bowls

PART 2

1 small skillet
1 set each measuring cups & spoons
1 colander
1 pie plate
1 cutting board reserved for fruit

1 dinner fork or small whisk
1 large-headed wooden spoon
2 rubber spatulas
2 plastic or plastic-coated spatulas
2 dinner plates or 1 wire cooling rack

1. **Gather all cooking tools and ingredients.**

2. **Heat two skillets on two large burners or an electric griddle at a medium setting.** If using coconut oil, add 1 T coconut oil to a small skillet and melt the oil at a low heat setting. Be watchful and, once the oil melts, remove the skillet from the heat.

3. **Prepare the fruit, nuts, and topping butter.**

    - Add ½ c **blueberries** to a colander, rinse them with cool water, and pour the berries into a pie plate lined with a double thickness of paper towels or a terry cloth towel. Pick through the berries to remove stems and replace spoiled berries. Wrap the towels around the berries to dry them completely. Set the berries aside in the pie plate.
    - Place ½ **apple** cut side down on a clean cutting board and use a chef's knife to slice the apple lengthwise into ¼ in. thick slices. Use a paring knife to cut out the pulpy center and seeds. Cut the slices crosswise into ¼ in. cubes.
    - Use the chef's knife to chop ¼ **c nuts** coarsely.
    - Use the chef's knife to dice **2 t butter**. Make two equal piles of butter.

4. **Combine the dry ingredients.** Add the ½ c flour, ½ t baking powder, ¹⁄₁₆ t baking soda, 2 t sugar, ¼ t salt, and ¼ t cinnamon to a medium mixing bowl. Combine the ingredients thoroughly. Add and toss the blueberries and diced apple thoroughly.

5. **Combine the wet ingredients.**

    - Add the egg, milk (⅓ c if the squash is very moist otherwise ½ c), and 2 orange T juice to another medium mixing bowl. Use a fork or whisk to mix the egg yolk into the milk mixture.
    - Add and mix in the mashed squash.
    - Add and stir in 1 T oil. If using coconut oil, use a rubber spatula to scrape the melted oil from the skillet into the milk mixture and to roughly mix in the oil.

6. **Combine the wet and dry ingredients.**

    - Pour the dry ingredients onto the wet mixture and use a wooden spoon to combine the ingredients, stirring the batter just until the flour is fully moistened (about 15 strokes).

- Use a rubber spatula to finish the mixing. Scrape batter from the spoon and bowl sides, scrape the bowl bottom to mix in any dry flour, and break up any lumps of flour.

7. **Bake the pancakes.**

    - Increase the skillet heat slightly to a high medium setting.
    - When a bit of butter added to the skillet instantly sizzles moderately, add 1 t butter to each skillet and use a spatula to spread the butter over the skillet bottoms. Avoid browning the butter. Alternatively, quickly rub the open end of a wrapped stick of butter over the bottom of each skillet.
    - Immediately evenly divide the batter between the skillets and set a timer for 4 minutes.
    - Evenly divide the nuts, blueberries, and apple over the batter of the two baking pancakes.

8. **Flip and add butter to each pancake.**

    - Check for readiness at the timer. When readiness is indicated – bubbles start to appear in the batter, an edge lifts with a spatula without breaking the pancake, and a lifted edge shows the bottom is lightly browned – use a stir-fry spatula to flip each pancake.
    - Evenly spread 1 t diced butter over each pancake.
    - Lower the heat skillet to medium; be watchful to prevent scorching.

9. **Serve the pancakes when they are cooked through.** When the centers bounce back when lightly touched and the bottoms are lightly browned (approximately 3 minutes after flipping), remove the pancakes from the skillet onto a plate for immediate serving or onto a wire cooling rack for somewhat delayed serving. Do not stack the pancakes or place them on a platter, which will cause the pancake bottoms to become unattractively soggy.

10. **Serve each pancake topped with ⅓ c fruit sauce or 2 T maple syrup.**

    VARIATIONS: Vary the number of servings.

    - Make **3 6-in. pancakes** rather than 2 8-in. pancakes.
    - Make **1 pancake.** Halve all ingredients except for egg and orange juice. Use 1 egg and ½ T orange juice.

    Make ingredient substitutions. Substitute, for example,

    - **1 T butter** for extra virgin olive oil. Melt the butter in a small skillet over low heat. Use a rubber spatula to scrape the melted butter into the batter immediately before combining the wet and dry ingredients (before the butter hardens).

PART 2

- **½ pear**, diced, for apple, preparing it in exactly the same way.
- **¼ c fresh pineapple chunks, ½ in. thick** (Recipe #94), diced, for apple.
- **½ c mashed canned** or **dry frozen butternut squash** for fresh baked.
- **½ c mashed sweet potato**, either fresh baked (Recipe #47) or canned, for winter squash.
- **½ c canned pumpkin puree** for butternut squash. Increase the sugar content to 1 T and reduce the milk content to ⅓ cup.
- **1 baked apple** (Recipe #205), heated, per pancake for fruit sauce.

Add ingredients. Add, for example,

- **2 fresh or dry frozen raspberries** or **blackberries**, halved lengthwise, per pancake, added as a topping with either a fruit sauce or maple syrup.
- **⅓ c cooked brown rice** (Recipe #166), spreading it on the batter with the fruit, which enhances the appetite-satisfying and energy-supplying capacity of pancakes.
- **ground spices**, such as ⅛ t ground nutmeg and/or ⅛ t ground ginger. Add ¹⁄₁₆ t (or slightly more to taste) each ground allspice and cloves.

COMMENTS: Medium ground whole wheat flour is protein-rich hard winter wheat flour that has clearly visible bits of bran, which gives the flour a slightly coarse texture. See Reference #5 (Selecting High Quality Processed Ingredients for Use in Part II Recipes), Ingredient #3, for a description of the highest quality medium whole wheat flour.

219. Blueberry Sauce
(Fruit Sauce Master Recipe)
(2½ c; approx. 7 servings)

Sauce

1 c premium orange juice with pulp
2 T frozen orange juice concentrate
2 T sugar
2 c fresh or unthawed dry frozen blueberries

½ c premium orange juice with pulp
2 T cornstarch
½ lemon

Cooking Tools

1 set each measuring cups & spoons
1 medium or large nonstick skillet
1 colander
1 pie plate
1 small mixing bowl
1 dinner fork or small whisk

1 hand citrus juicer
1 rubber or other heat-resistant spatula
1 timer
1 medium (6 c) heat-resistant glass storage bowl with a lid

1. **Gather all cooking tools and ingredients.** Do not, however, remove frozen berries from the freezer until just prior to cooking.

2. **Begin heating 1 c orange juice in a nonstick skillet at a medium setting.** Add 2 T frozen orange juice concentrate and 2 T sugar.

3. **Prepare fresh blueberries.** Rinse the blueberries in a colander under cool water and spread them in a pie plate lined with a double layer of paper towels or a terry towel. Pick through the berries and remove stems and replace any spoiled berries. Wrap the towels around the berries and gently roll the berries within the towels to dry them thoroughly.

4. **Prepare the cornstarch mixture.** Add ½ c orange juice and 2 T cornstarch to a small mixing bowl and use a dinner fork or whisk to mix the cornstarch into the juice.

5. **Prepare the lemon.** Squeeze the lemon, remove any seeds but save pulp, measure 1½ T juice, and add it to the orange juice mixture in the skillet. Refrigerate any remaining juice within a small glass container with a tight-fitting lid.

6. **Cook the sauce.**

    - For frozen blueberries, remove frozen berries from the freezer and break apart any clumps while they are still in the freezer package.
    - Increase the skillet heat to high. When the juice boils, add the blueberries. Return the juice to boiling, reduce the heat to medium high, and briefly continue boiling the berries (about 30 seconds).
    - Re-stir the cornstarch mixture and slowly pour it into the skillet while quickly and constantly stirring the juice with a rubber spatula to prevent lumps from forming. Continue stirring the sauce until the sauce boils, often scraping the skillet bottom to prevent sticking.
    - Reduce the heat to medium, or to a level that maintains gentle boiling, and cook the sauce for 2 minutes until the sauce thickens and clears, stirring it often and setting a timer.
    - At the timer, remove the sauce from the heat and use a rubber spatula to scrape it into a heat-resistant glass storage bowl.
    - Add hot water to the skillet for easy cleaning.

7. **Serve the sauce hot or cold.** Refrigerate the sauce tightly covered in a glass storage container. Use within 5-6 days for best flavor.

    VARIATIONS: Make ingredient substitutions. Substitute, for example,

    - **a mixture of orange and mango juice** or **pineapple juice** for orange juice.
    - **other juice** (such as **grape, cranberry** or **apple**) for ½ c orange juice. Grape and cranberry help give rich color to the sauce.

- **2 c canned blueberries** (packed in light syrup) for dry frozen blueberries. Substitute the packing juice of canned berries for an equal amount of orange juice. Add only 1 T sugar. Increase lemon juice content to 2 T. While canned blueberries lack flavor and texture in comparison with fresh or dry frozen berries, they actually have greater phytonutrient value than fresh-picked fruit.

Add ingredients. Add, for example,

- **1 or 2 T Welch's frozen grape juice concentrate.** This concentrate enhances both the flavor and purple color of the sauce.
- **½ c dry frozen raspberries, currants,** or **tart cherries.** Add 1 T more sugar to the sauce. These berries add an attractive touch of color and tartness in addition to making a nutritional contribution.
- **½ c fresh pineapple chunks** (½ in. cubes), halved (Recipe #94).
- **1 t lemon zest**, particularly when using dry frozen or canned berries. Use organic lemon. Adjust zest amount to taste.

COMMENTS: Select cornstarch that is not genetically modified and does not contain aluminum, such as Rumford non-GMO cornstarch. Natural food stores and natural food sections of regular grocery stores commonly carry other non-GMO brands of cornstarch. Natural food stores also market certified organic sugar, which is reliably non-GMO. In contrast, industrially produced sugar is often genetically modified.

220. Raspberry Sauce
(2½ c; approx. 7 servings)

Sauce

1 c premium orange juice with pulp	2 T cornstarch
2 T frozen orange juice concentrate	½ lemon
2 T sugar	2 c unthawed dry frozen unsweetened raspberries
½ c premium orange juice with pulp	

Cooking Tools

1 set each measuring cups & spoons	1 hand citrus juicer
1 medium or large nonstick skillet	1 rubber or other heat-resistant spatula
1 small mixing bowl	1 medium heat-resistant glass storage bowl with a tight-fitting lid
1 dinner fork or small whisk	

1. **Gather all cooking tools and ingredients.** Do not, however, remove frozen berries from the freezer until just prior to cooking.

2. **Heat 1 c orange juice.** Add the juice to a nonstick skillet and heat it at medium. Add 2 T frozen orange juice concentrate and 2 T sugar.

3. **Prepare the cornstarch mixture.** Add ½ c orange juice and 2 T cornstarch to a small mixing bowl and use a dinner fork or whisk to mix the cornstarch into the juice.

4. **Prepare the lemon.** Squeeze the lemon, remove any seeds but save pulp, measure 1½ T juice, and add it to the orange juice mixture in the skillet. Refrigerate any remaining juice within a small glass container with a tight-fitting lid.

5. **Cook the sauce.**

    - Remove frozen raspberries from the freezer and break apart any clumps while they are still in the freezer package.
    - Increase the skillet heat to high. When the juice boils, add the raspberries. Return the juice to boiling, reduce the heat to medium high, and briefly continue boiling the berries (about 30 seconds).
    - Re-stir the cornstarch mixture and slowly pour it into the skillet while quickly and constantly stirring the juice with a rubber spatula to prevent lumps from forming. Continue stirring the sauce until the sauce boils, often scraping the skillet bottom to prevent sticking.
    - Reduce the heat to medium, or to a level that maintains gentle boiling, and cook the sauce for two minutes or until the sauce thickens and clears, stirring it often and setting a timer.
    - At the timer, remove the sauce from the heat and scrape it into a heat-resistant glass storage bowl.
    - Add hot water to the skillet for easy cleaning.

6. **Serve the sauce hot or cold.** Refrigerate the sauce tightly covered in a glass storage container. Use within 5-6 days for best flavor.

    VARIATIONS: Make ingredient substitutions. Substitute, for example,

    - **10 oz package Birds Eye Raspberries Frozen in Syrup,** light not heavy syrup, for dry frozen raspberries. Reduce the orange juice content to1 c (heating ½ c in the skillet and mixing ½ c with the cornstarch). Thaw the berries enough to be able to break the berries into small clumps before cooking. Reduce the sugar content, adding only 1 T sugar. Increase lemon juice content to 2 T.
    - **2 c fresh strawberries** (Recipe #98) or **2 c dry frozen strawberries,** unthawed, for raspberries to convert the sauce to **strawberry sauce.** Halve whole berries lengthwise, place the halves cut side down on a clean cutting board, and cut each half lengthwise into 3 equal slices.

- **1 c fresh or dry frozen strawberries**, sliced and sprinkled with 1 t sugar, for 1 c raspberries.

Add ingredients. Add, for example,

- **1-2 T Welch's frozen grape juice concentrate**.
- **1 c fresh raspberries,** added to the cooked sauce once it cools. Raw raspberries enhance the flavor, texture, and nutritional value of a fruit sauce.
- **1 c blueberries**, fresh or dry frozen (unthawed), cooked with the raspberries.
- **1 c canned blueberries**, substituting ½ canned blueberry juice for ½ c orange juice.
- **½ c fresh** or **dry frozen blackberries**. Add ½ T more sugar to the sauce. Cook fresh blackberries with the raspberries or leave them raw and add them to the sauce once it fully cools.
- **1 t lemon zest**. Use only zest of organic or locally produced lemons. Zest amount is adjustable to taste.

COMMENTS: Select cornstarch that is not genetically modified, such as Rumford non-GMO cornstarch. Natural food stores and natural food sections of regular grocery stores commonly carry other non-GMO brands of cornstarch. Natural food stores likely market certified organic sugar, which is reliably non-GMO. In contrast, industrially produced white sugar is commonly genetically modified.

221. Cherry Sauce
(2½ c; 6-7 servings)

Sauce

1 c premium orange juice with pulp
2 T frozen orange juice concentrate
2 T sugar (2½-3 T for tart cherries)
½ c premium orange juice with pulp

2 T cornstarch
½ lemon
2 c unthawed dry frozen unsweetened cherries (sweet or tart cherries)

Cooking Tools

1 set each measuring cups & spoons
1 medium or large nonstick skillet
1 small mixing bowl
1 dinner fork or small whisk
1 hand citrus juicer
1 cutting board reserved for fruit & vegetables

1 chef's knife
1 rubber or other heat-resistant spatula
1 timer
1 medium heat-resistant glass storage bowl with a tight-fitting lid

1. **Gather all cooking tools and ingredients.** Do not, however, remove frozen cherries from the freezer until just prior to cooking.

2. **Heat 1 c orange juice.** Add the orange juice to a nonstick skillet and heat it at medium. Add 2 T frozen orange juice concentrate and 2 T sugar (2½ T for tart cherries).

3. **Prepare the cornstarch mixture.** Add ½ c orange juice and 2 T cornstarch to a small mixing bowl and use a dinner fork or whisk to mix the cornstarch into the juice.

4. **Prepare the lemon.** Squeeze the lemon, remove any seeds but save pulp, measure 1½ T juice, and add the juice to the orange juice mixture heating in the skillet. Refrigerate any remaining juice within a small glass container with a tight-fitting lid.

5. **Cook the sauce.**

    - Remove frozen cherries from the freezer and break apart any clumps while they are still in the freezer package. Spread the cherries on a cutting board and use a chef's knife to halve them. If they do not at first easily slice, wait 30-60 seconds to allow slight thawing and try again. Do not let the cherries fully thaw.
    - Increase the skillet heat to high. When the juice boils, add the cherries. Return the juice to boiling, reduce the heat to medium high, and briefly continue boiling the cherries (about 30 seconds).
    - Re-stir the cornstarch mixture and slowly pour it into the skillet while quickly and constantly stirring the juice with a rubber spatula to prevent lumps from forming. Continue stirring the sauce until the sauce boils, often scraping the skillet bottom to prevent sticking.
    - Reduce the heat to medium, or to a level that maintains gentle boiling, and cook the sauce for two minutes or until the sauce thickens and clears, stirring it often and setting a timer.
    - At the timer, remove the sauce from the heat and scrape it into a heat-resistant glass storage bowl.
    - Add hot water to the skillet for easy cleaning.

6. **Serve the sauce hot or cold.** Refrigerate the sauce tightly covered in a glass storage container. Use within 5-6 days for best flavor.

    VARIATIONS: Make ingredient substitutions. Substitute, for example,

    - **fresh sweet** or **tart cherries** (Recipe #81) for frozen cherries.
    - **½ cranberry juice** (made from frozen juice concentrate) or **½ c grape juice** for ½ c orange juice in order to give the sauce a deeper red color.
    - **2 T frozen cherry** or **cranberry juice concentrate** for frozen orange juice concentrate. Both add attractive flavor and enhance the red color of the sauce.
    - **canned cherries** for dry frozen. Substitute ½ canning liquid for ½ c orange juice. Add only 1 T sugar.

Add ingredients. Add, for example,

- **1-2 T frozen cranberry, cherry,** or **grape juice concentrate,** which adds flavor and enhances the red coloring.
- **1 c raw sweet cherries,** pitted and halved lengthwise, to the thoroughly cooled cooked cherry sauce.
- **1 t lemon zest,** especially when using dry frozen or canned cherries. Use only zest of certified organic or locally produced lemons. Zest amount is adjustable to taste.

COMMENTS: Select cornstarch that is not genetically modified, such as Rumford non-GMO cornstarch. Natural food stores and natural food sections of regular grocery stores commonly carry other non-GMO brands of cornstarch. Natural food stores also market certified organic sugar, which is reliably non-GMO. In contrast, industrially produced white sugar is commonly genetically modified.

222. Peach Sauce
(2½ c; 6-7 servings)

Sauce

1 c premium orange juice with pulp
2 T frozen orange juice concentrate
2 T sugar
½ c premium orange juice with pulp
2 T cornstarch

½ lemon, certified organic if using zest
    1 t lemon zest (opt)
2 c unthawed dry frozen unsweetened
    sliced peaches

Cooking Tools

1 set each measuring cups & spoons
1 medium or large nonstick skillet
1 small mixing bowl
1 dinner fork or small whisk
1 hand citrus juicer

1 chef's knife
1 cutting board reserved for fruit
1 rubber or other heat-resistant rubber
    spatula
1 medium heat-resistant glass storage bowl
    with a tight-fitting lid

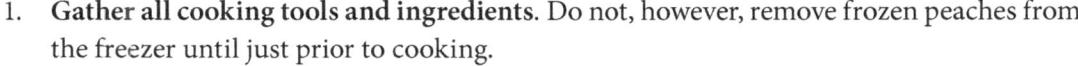

1. **Gather all cooking tools and ingredients.** Do not, however, remove frozen peaches from the freezer until just prior to cooking.

2. **Heat 1 c orange juice.** Add the orange juice to a nonstick skillet and heat the skillet at medium. Add 2 T frozen orange juice concentrate and 2 T sugar (2½ T for tart cherries).

3. **Prepare the cornstarch mixture.** Add ½ c orange juice and 2 T cornstarch to a small mixing bowl and use a dinner fork or whisk to mix the cornstarch into the juice.

4. **Prepare the lemon.** Squeeze the lemon, remove any seeds but save pulp, measure 1½ T juice, and add the juice to the orange juice mixture in the skillet. Refrigerate any remaining lemon juice.

5. **Cook the sauce.**

    - Remove frozen peaches from the freezer, break apart any clumps while they are still in the freezer package, spread the peaches on a cutting board, and use a chef's knife to cut each slice crosswise into 3-4 pieces. If they do not at first easily slice, wait 30-60 seconds to allow slight thawing and try again. Do not let the peaches fully thaw.
    - Increase the skillet heat to high. When the juice boils, add the peaches. Return the juice to boiling, reduce the heat to medium high, and briefly continue boiling the peaches (about 30 seconds).
    - Re-stir the cornstarch mixture and slowly pour it into the skillet while quickly and constantly stirring the juice with a rubber spatula to prevent lumps from forming. Continue stirring the sauce until it boils, often scraping the skillet bottom to prevent sticking.
    - Reduce the heat to medium, or to a level that maintains gentle boiling, and cook the sauce for two minutes or until it thickens and clears, stirring it often and setting a timer.
    - At the timer, remove the sauce from the heat and scrape it into a heat-resistant glass storage bowl.
    - Add hot water to the skillet for easy cleaning.

6. **Serve the sauce hot or cold.** Refrigerate the sauce tightly covered in a glass storage container. Use within 5-6 days for best flavor.

    VARIATIONS: Make ingredient substitutions. Substitute, for example,

    - **1 c blueberries**, fresh (Recipe #78), **dry frozen blueberries** (unthawed), or **canned blueberries** (including ½ c canned blueberry liquid) for 1 c peaches to make **peach blueberry sauce**.
    - **4 fresh peaches** (Recipe #92), sliced, for dry frozen peaches.
    - **2 c canned peaches**, packed in peach juice, for frozen peaches. Substitute ½ c peach packing juice for ½ c orange juice.
    - **4 fresh nectarines** (Recipe #88), sliced, for peaches. Nectarines are exactly the same as peaches except for the fuzziness of peach skin.

    Add ingredients. Add, for example,

    - **1-2 T frozen apple juice concentrate**.

- **1 t lemon zest**. Use only zest of certified organic or locally produced lemons. Zest amount is adjustable to taste.

COMMENTS: When selecting fresh peaches, select white-fleshed peaches, which have greater phytonutrient content than orange peaches. Because of the high pesticide content of commercially-produced peaches, select certified organic or locally grown peaches.

Select cornstarch that is not genetically modified, such as Rumford non-GMO cornstarch. Natural food stores and natural food sections of regular grocery stores commonly carry other non-GMO brands of cornstarch. Natural food stores also market certified organic sugar, which is reliably non-GMO. In contrast, industrially produced white sugar is commonly genetically modified (GM).

223. Strawberry Rhubarb Sauce
(2½ c; 6-7 servings)

Sauce

½ c premium orange juice with pulp
½ c cranberry or cherry juice
2 T frozen cranberry or cherry juice concentrate
2 T frozen orange juice concentrate
3-4 T sugar
½ c premium orange juice with pulp

2 T cornstarch
½ lemon
4 stalks fresh rhubarb (enough to yield ½ c)
2 c unthawed dry frozen unsweetened strawberries

Cooking Tools

1 medium or large nonstick skillet
1 small mixing bowl
1 dinner fork or small whisk
1 hand juicer
1 cutting board reserved for fruits & vegetables

1 chef's knife
1 rubber or other heat-resistant spatula
1 timer
1 medium heat-resistant glass storage bowl with a tight-fitting lid

1. **Gather all cooking tools and ingredients.** Do not, however, remove frozen strawberries from the freezer until just prior to cooking.

2. **Heat ½ c orange juice and ½ c cranberry or cherry juice.** Add the juices to a nonstick skillet and heat the skillet at medium. Add 2 T each frozen orange, cranberry, or cherry juice concentrate and 4 T sugar to a skillet.

3. **Prepare the cornstarch mixture.** Add ½ c orange juice and 2 T cornstarch to a small mixing bowl and use a dinner fork or whisk to mix the cornstarch into the juice.

4. **Prepare the lemon.** Squeeze the lemon. Remove any seeds but save pulp. Measure 1½ T juice and add it to the cornstarch mixture. Refrigerate any remaining juice within a small glass container with a tight-fitting lid.

5. **Prepare the rhubarb.** Working on a cutting board, use a chef's knife to slice the tips from the stalks and to halve the stalks lengthwise (except for very thin stalks). Cut the stalks crosswise into uniform ⅓ in. thick slices.

6. **Cook the sauce.**

    - Remove frozen strawberries from the freezer, break apart any clumps while they are still in the freezer package, spread the strawberries on a cutting board, and use a chef's knife to halve each berry lengthwise. If the strawberries do not at first easily slice, wait 30-60 seconds to allow slight thawing and try again. Do not, however, let the strawberries fully thaw.
    - Place each strawberry half cut side down on the cutting board and cut it lengthwise into 3 slices.
    - Increase the skillet heat to high. When the juice boils, add the strawberries and rhubarb. Return the juice to boiling, reduce the heat to medium-high, and briefly continue boiling the strawberries and rhubarb (about 30 seconds), stirring occasionally with a rubber spatula.
    - Re-stir the cornstarch mixture and slowly pour it into the skillet while quickly and constantly stirring the juice with a rubber spatula to prevent lumps from forming. Continue stirring the sauce until it boils, often scraping the skillet bottom to prevent sticking.
    - Reduce the heat to medium, or to a level that maintains gentle boiling, and cook the sauce for two minutes or until it thickens and clears, stirring it often and setting a timer.
    - At the timer, immediately remove the sauce from the heat and scrape it into a heat-resistant glass storage bowl.
    - Add hot water to the skillet for easy cleaning.

7. **Serve the sauce hot or cold.** Refrigerate the sauce tightly covered in the glass storage container. Use within 5-6 days for best flavor.

    VARIATIONS: Make ingredient substitutions. Substitute, for example,

    - **2 c fresh strawberries** (Recipe #98) for dry frozen.
    - **10 oz package Birds Eye Strawberries Frozen in Syrup**, light rather than heavy syrup, for dry frozen or fresh strawberries. Reduce the sugar content to 1 tablespoon. Reduce orange content by ½ cup.
    - **dry frozen rhubarb**, unthawed, for fresh rhubarb.

Add ingredients. Add, for example,

- **1-2 T frozen Welch's grape** or **cranberry juice concentrate.**
- **1 t orange or lemon zest,** removed from certified organic orange or lemon.

COMMENTS: Select cornstarch that is not genetically modified, such as Rumford non-GMO cornstarch. Natural food stores and natural food sections of regular grocery stores commonly carry other non-GMO brands of cornstarch. Natural food stores also market certified organic sugar, which is reliably non-GMO. In contrast, industrially produced white sugar is commonly genetically modified (GM).

Given the high pesticide content of industrial produced strawberries, select certified organic or locally produced berries.

224. Applesauce
(4 servings)

Sauce

1 c premium orange juice with pulp
¼ c frozen orange juice concentrate
½ lemon
⅓ c premium orange juice with pulp

6 tasty chilled apples
½ c packed dark brown sugar
½ t ground cinnamon

Cooking Tools

1 set each measuring cups & spoons
1 large nonstick, stainless steel, or other non-reactive skillet with an opaque lid
1 hand citrus juicer
1 large (10 c) mixing bowl
1 each chef's & paring knife

1 cutting board
1 timer
1 rubber or other heat-resistant spatula
1 small mixing bowl
1 large (10 c) glass storage/serving bowl with a lid

1. **Gather all cooking utensils and applesauce ingredients.**

2. **Heat 1 c juice and ¼ c frozen orange juice concentrate.** Add the juice and concentrate to a large skillet and heat the skillet at medium.

3. **Prepare the lemon.** Squeeze the lemon, remove seeds but save pulp, and add the juice to a large mixing bowl.

4. **Prepare the apples for cooking.**

   - Add ⅓ c orange juice to the large mixing bowl holding the lemon juice.
   - Use a chef's knife to halve each apple lengthwise.
   - Place each half cut side down on a clean cutting board and use the chef's knife to cut them lengthwise into uniform ½ in. thick slices.
   - Use a paring knife to remove the core and seeds from the slices and to cut each slice crosswise into 3-4 even-sized chunks.
   - As each half is cut into chunks, add the chunks to the juice in the bowl and swish them in the juice to coat pieces thoroughly.

5. **Cook the apple.**

   - Increase the burner heat of the skillet to high, bring the juice to boiling, add the apple chunks and the juice in the bowl, return the juice to full boiling, reduce the heat to a low medium setting (a setting that maintains gentle boiling), cover the skillet when the boiling slows, and gently boil the apples for 4 minutes, setting a timer.
   - At the timer, check the apples for readiness. Remove the skillet from the heat if the apples are broken down and very soft (a knife easily pierces the center of a chunk). If the apples are not uniformly soft, continue the cooking and recheck for complete softening every 3-4 minutes.
   - Remove the skillet from the heat once the apples are uniformly soft.

6. **Prepare the applesauce for serving.**

   - Add flavoring. Add the brown sugar to a small bowl, evenly sprinkle the cinnamon over the brown sugar, and thoroughly mix the cinnamon into the sugar. Evenly spread all of the sugar over the hot apples and use a rubber spatula to mix in the sugar.
   - Check the flavoring, adding touches of lemon juice for tartness and sugar for sweetening.
   - Check the texture. Slightly mash the apples with a dinner fork or potato masher with a metal grid head to provide a smoother texture.
   - Use a rubber spatula to scrape the hot applesauce into a large (2 qt) heat-resistant glass serving bowl with a lid.

7. **Serve the applesauce warm or chilled.** Allow the applesauce to cool somewhat before either serving it warm or refrigerating it for chilling.

8. **Refrigerate leftover applesauce, tightly covered.** Freeze applesauce that will not be used within several days. Freeze it in serving size amounts in freezer-tolerant glass containers, tightly covered.

   VARIATIONS: Make ingredient substitutions. Substitute, for example,

   - **½ c apple juice** for ½ c orange juice as the cooking liquid.

PART 2

- **certified organic brown sugar** for conventionally produced dark brown sugar to reliably avoid genetically modified brown sugar.

Add ingredients. Add, for example,

- **1-2 T frozen apple juice concentrate**.
- **⅛ c certified organic raisins**. Add the raisins to the cooking apples near the end of cooking.
- **⅛-¼ c raw nuts** coarsely chopped. Add, for example, chopped whole almonds or pecan or walnut halves. Add the nuts after the apples are finished cooking, just after mixing in the sugar.
- **1 t lemon zest**, or to taste. Use a certified organic lemon.

COMMENTS: To select especially nutritious apples, refer to Comments in the basic raw apple recipe (Recipe #74).

Select certified organic ground cinnamon to ensure that it has not been irradiated.

Select certified organic apples to significantly reduce pesticide content and select certified organic brown sugar to significantly reduce pesticide content and avoid genetically modified ingredients.

Reference #13

Clinching Pancake Attractiveness and Quality: Expanded Preparation Support

To assist cooks in both achieving successful pancake baking results and in maximizing the nutritional quality of pancakes, Reference #13 provides helpful explanatory comments for five key pancake preparation steps – mixing batter, cooking pancakes, flipping pancakes, serving pancakes, and preparing fruit sauce topping.

1. Mixing Batter

Select reliably effective baking powder. As the leavening ingredient in pancakes, baking powder plays a key role in pancake preparation success. If it fails, pancakes will also fail. They will not rise and will have an unattractively heavy texture. To ensure baking powder effectively leavens pancakes,

- select fresh baking powder. Baking powder is perishable. It completely loses its leavening capacity over time. When purchasing baking powder, therefore, always check the

expiration date printed somewhere on the container. Recheck this expiration date from time to time during use. Immediately suspect baking powder if pancakes do not satisfactorily rise or do not rise using the recipe-directed amount.
- select double acting baking powder.

Accurately measure baking powder and baking soda content.

- Use a standard measuring spoon and smooth off the top when measuring baking power. While baking powder plays the important role of causing pancakes to rise, it also adds sodium. Maintain a ½ t baking powder per ½ c flour ratio (or ¼ t baking powder and ¼ c flour for a 1 pancake serving). Increase baking powder content slightly only if pancakes fail to rise satisfactorily when using fresh baking powder.
- Baking soda is included in Chapter Twelve pancake recipes to help keep fruit in pancakes from becoming sour during cooking. Baking soda contributes to rising as well. It is important to keep baking soda content low, however, because it also plays destructive roles. Baking soda, for example,

  - contains sodium.
  - is destructive of B vitamins contained in whole grain flour.
  - can negatively affect dish flavor.
  - neutralizes hydrochloric acid contained in the human stomach. Because hydrochloric acid plays a crucial digestive role, any more than a very small amount of baking soda interferes with digestion.

Maintain liquid/flour proportions. It is important to measure liquid and flour content accurately using standard measuring cups. Too much liquid or too little flour complicates flipping and undermines texture.

- Very moist pancakes are difficult to flip without breaking. They are also difficult to cook through before the pancake bottom becomes unattractively over-browned. If, however, a pancake is not cooked through, its center remains uncooked and unattractively soggy. To avoid adding too much liquid to pancake batter,

  - do not finely mash banana, which converts it into a liquid.
  - add dry fruit chunks to batter, not shredded fruit, which releases juice.
  - do not add juicy apple sauce or juicy squash. Drain juice and use it as part of the orange juice content called for in the recipe.
  - do not increase or decrease egg content without adjusting liquid content, counting 1 egg as equal to ¼ c liquid.

Too much flour or too little liquid results in an unattractively dry pancake texture, one that invites the addition of butter.

Do not develop the gluten content of flour. While gluten (or protein content) enhances the nutritional quality of flour, it also easily undermines pancake texture. This is because when gluten bits are developed, they become sticky and clump together, which gives pancakes an unattractively heavy and dense texture. Using a variety of simple **gluten-managing techniques**, however, easily prevents flour gluten from negatively affecting pancake texture. To reliably achieve pancakes with a light and tender texture:

- minimally stir flour. Minimal stirring is the main key to avoiding gluten development. To aid minimal stirring,

    - count stirring strokes as opposed to stirring until flour is thoroughly moistened.
    - finish mixing with a rubber spatula. A rubber spatula efficiently integrates batter clinging to the sides and bottom of the mixing bowl without mixing.

- use chilled flour. Chilling slows gluten development.
- thoroughly premix all wet and dry ingredients before combining them. This premixing minimizes stirring when liquid is added.
- use a wooden spoon with a relatively big head for mixing. This important tool provides efficient stirring. Flour becomes mixed with liquid ingredients with the least possible number of strokes.
- work with a small amount of batter at a time. It is easiest to combine wet and dry ingredients with minimal stirring in a small batch of batter. As a result, for the most reliably tender pancakes, double (and perhaps triple) recipes, but prepare separate batches for more servings.

2. Cooking Pancakes

Heat a large skillet on a large burner. This is important for efficient and even cooking of pancakes.

Use a heavy-bottomed skillet. This cooking equipment is crucially important to successful pancake cooking. A heavy-bottomed skillet, for example,

- protects pancake bottoms from over-browning during cooking.
- minimizes the amount of butter needed to be added to the skillet to prevent sticking and over-browning.

Thoroughly preheat the skillet or griddle. The importance of thorough preheating to cooking success cannot be overemphasized. When pancakes are preheated, pancakes reliably 1) do not stick to the skillet/griddle, 2) cook to the center in a reasonable time, and 3) become attractively browned but not over-browned. To ensure full preheating,

- begin heating a dry skillet or griddle at a low temperature as a first preparation step.
- always make the recipe-directed readiness test to verify full pre-heating before adding butter and batter for baking. A bit of butter added to a hot skillet should immediately

begin to sizzle gently. It should not immediately turn brown, which indicates the skillet is too hot. Browned butter needs to be cleaned from a skillet.

Add butter, ghee, or coconut oil to a pre-heated skillet just prior to adding pancake batter.

- Butter better prevents sticking than extra virgin olive oil, but butter is also more vulnerable to high temperature heating. It can easily brown, which undermines its quality, flavor, and color. If butter immediately browns, the butter needs to be removed, the heating temperature reduced, and fresh butter added.
- Coconut oil substitutes perfectly for butter and adds especially attractive flavor to the pancakes.
- Never substitute a pure vegetable oil product for either butter, coconut oil, or extra virgin olive oil. Pure vegetable oil is a highly processed and, as a result, unnatural oil that is also highly reactive when heated. This means it reacts with oxygen during heating, and this chemical reaction produces free radicals, which are then consumed by those served the pancakes. Pure vegetable oil also leaves toxic residues in pancakes during cooking.

Monitor skillet or griddle temperature throughout pancake baking. Sometimes burners become hotter during cooking. Always be watchful to avoid over-browning before the center is cooked.

Never increase skillet heat to speed pancake cooking. This does not work. A pancake will become excessively browned before the center cooks through, leaving the pancake center unattractively raw.

Do not overload pancakes with juicy fruit or vegetables. Juicy fruit or vegetables can make it difficult to cook the pancake through to the center. Either over-browning or an unattractively soggy center results.

3. Flipping Pancakes

Accurately measure liquid content. If too much liquid is added, flipping pancakes without breaking them is difficult. Use measuring cups and resist any temptation to add extra or leftover liquid.

Add only dry fruit to pancake batter.

- Add berries with skins or small chunks of firm fruit.
- Do not add finely mashed, shredded, coarsely chopped, or very juicy fruit. Fine mashing effectively converts fruits into another liquid ingredient. Shredded, chopped, and juicy fruit easily releases significant juice into the batter. Extra liquid, in turn, causes the batter to break apart during flipping.

Do not overload pancakes with fruit. No matter how tasty the fruit, overloading can easily leave a batter too moist for successful flipping and cause extended cooking as well.

- Do not add more than ½ banana per 2-serving batter.
- Add only a small amount of fruit – 1-2 T per pancake – to batter.
- Add juicy fruit as a topping rather than including it within a pancake. An unlimited amount of fruit works as a topping.

Completely butter the space where pancake batter will be added to a skillet or griddle. Buttering prevents sticking, which, in turn, both eases flipping of pancakes and avoids scorching of pancake bottoms.

- Use a nonstick surface skillet to minimize the amount of butter needed to prevent sticking.
- Partially butter skillet sides if there is any possibility that the batter will touch the sides. Batter touching an unbuttered side may stick and cause the pancake to tear during flipping.
- As an easy way of adding butter and adding minimal butter, use the open end of a stick of wrapped butter.

Make relatively small pancakes. Large pancakes easily break during flipping.

Use a wide spatula with a sharp edge and a firm handle for flipping pancakes. A spatula with these features greatly eases flipping.

Conduct readiness tests before flipping pancakes.

- Lightly press the center of a pancake. The center should bounce back.
- The pancake should hold together when the spatula is slipped under and lifts an edge slightly. If the pancake is not ready, batter on either side of the spatula will run onto the skillet.

4. Serving Pancakes

Add a raw fruit topping to individual pancakes. Banana, berries, and any other variety of diced tasty fruit are perfect pancake toppings. Combined with either fruit sauce or maple syrup, fruit adds attractive juiciness, color, flavor, and nutritional enhancement while reducing the need or temptation to add more sauce or very sweet syrup to pancakes.

Use the tastiest butter. Butter flavoring varies enormously between products. To select the tastiest butter,

- select fresh butter. It is very important that butter not be rancid, which undermines its flavor and makes it somewhat toxic for humans as well. It is important to keep butter refrigerated, tightly covered, to maintain top flavor and to protect it from becoming rancid.

- select domestically produced butter made from the milk of certified organically raised dairy cows that are also 100% grass-fed. This is very reliably tasty as well as highly nutritious butter.
- European butter made from the milk of 100% pastured dairy cows. Such European butter has outstanding – incomparable – flavor. Examples of products include Lurpac and Kerrygold.

Top pancakes with a measured amount of butter *before* serving them. Added as a final preparation step once the pancake is flipped, the butter reliably melts. When the cook adds butter, those served are less tempted to add their own (and potentially excessive amounts of) butter. Butter, as a result, is both a pleasing *and* nutrition-enhancing dish ingredient.

Serve pancakes with a measured amount of the tastiest maple syrup.

- Serve syrup in a small container rather than in a large container. This is a means of limiting the use of sweetening.
- Select grade B maple syrup, which is first pressed syrup and, hence, both the least processed and most flavorful syrup. Natural food stores commonly market grade B maple syrup in economical bulk form.

5. Preparing Fruit Sauce Topping

Select top quality ingredients. Select, for example,

- non-genetically modified (non-GMO verified) cornstarch and white sugar. These products are commonly made from genetically modified crops.[276] Because genetically modified status does not have to be indicated, the only reliable way to avoid GMOs is to select products labeled certified organic or non-GMO. In the case of cornstarch, another alternative is to choose another thickener, such as arrowroot flour. Arrowroot is in fact a less processed form of thickener. Cornstarch happens to be used instead in recipes because of its easy availability and reliable thickening in comparison. Reference #4 (Selecting Top Quality Ingredients for Use in Part II Recipes) explains the nutritionally and agriculturally destructive reasons for avoiding selection of GMO products.
- premium orange juice with maximum pulp. Premium orange juice is juice made from freshly squeezed oranges or from frozen orange juice concentrate rather than canned orange juice.
- dry frozen fruit as opposed to fruit frozen in sugar-flavored sauce.

Always include a measured amount of fresh lemon juice. Adding attractive tanginess and flavor to a sauce, lemon juice is a key flavoring ingredient. Because lemon juice easily overwhelms juice flavor,

---

276 Estabrook & Treadwell, "Where the GMOs Are," 84-85.

making a sauce too sour and making additional sugar necessary, it is important to not casually add lemon juice.

- Use a standard measuring tablespoon.
- Keep small glass containers with tight-fitting lids handy for easy storage of any freshly squeezed lemon juice that may be left over after measuring the recipe-directed juice content for a sauce.
- Freeze fresh extra frozen lemon juice or the juice of lemons that will otherwise spoil in small amounts to keep it on hand.

Measure cornstarch accurately. Though the amount can be slightly increased to make a thicker sauce (the measuring spoon can be somewhat rounded), too much cornstarch can negatively affect sauce flavor.

Add cornstarch after fruit boils in juice. This timing is important for both successful thickening and attractive coloring. The techniques used in Chapter Thirteen recipes – add the berries to boiling juice, return the fruit juice to boiling, and boil the berries for a short time (30 seconds) before mixing in the cornstarch mixture – ensure berries pop open and start to release some juice before cornstarch is added. Berry juice, as a result, will reliably color the sauce, and spilled juice will become thickened. Without boiling the berries for a brief period before adding the cornstarch, less juice spills from berries to color the sauce and juice that spills after the cornstarch is added does not become thickened. The sauce, as a result, may remain anemic in color and thinner than desirable.

Add unthawed dry frozen fruit to boiling juice. Adding frozen fruit in this way quickly destroys harmful fruit enzymes that otherwise are destructive of some of the nutritional content of fruit, including phytonutrients. If frozen fruit is instead allowed to thaw at room temperature and/or is slowly heated by being added to cool or lukewarm juice, fruit enzymes become activated and the destruction of fruit nutritional content occurs.

Do not overcook fruit. Minimal cooking maintains the attractive texture of fruits. Fruits hold enough juice to retain an attractively firm and juicy texture. While particular berries (blueberries and raspberries) are notable exceptions to this rule (with these berries extended cooking actually significantly enhances the nutritional value of the phytonutrients they contribute to humans), fruits in general are harmed by extended cooking. This cooking is destructive of valuable heat-sensitive nutrients, phytonutrients, and fiber. In the case of heat-sensitive prebiotic fibers, cooking shortens the length of the fibers. As a result, the fibers cannot survive the long journey through the human intestinal tract. They do not reach the large intestine where they serve as food for beneficial microbes.

INDEX

A

Acid/alkaline (pH) balance, human
    acid or acid-forming foods 18
Agribusiness corporation. *See also* food production, industrial
    a driver of processed food dependence 9-10
        begins food processing process 9
        no inherent interest in nutritional quality 9
            produces food as a commodity 8, 43, 325
            expanded production and lowest cost serve as top production goals 8, 43
        blocks contrary research 11
Aflatoxins 334
Alkaline minerals. *See* acid-alkaline (pH) balance
Allicin 161-162
Alliin 161-162
Allium 171
Allport, Susan 2, 6*n*, 13*n*
    impact of processing on omega-3 fatty acids 26*n*
    nutritional role of omega-3 essential fatty acids 23*n*, 24*n*
        omega-3/omega-6 fatty acids imbalance 26*n*
Antibiotics
    impact of routine use of antibiotics, both direct and indirect, in industrial agriculture 327-328
    residues of glyphosate, a patented antibiotic, in both animal and plant food products 327
        source of residues
            feeding of glyphosate-laden GM Roundup Ready grain to livestock and poultry 327
            spraying of glyphosate containing Roundup on plant crops during production 9-10
    residues of pharmaceutical antibiotics in animal food products 327, 585
impact on human health
    destruction of beneficial bacteria in human gut 47, 327
        direct connection between healthy gut and human health *20n*, *20-22*, 99, 341
    development of antibiotic resistant super bugs 327-328
    super bugs carried to market on animal and egg products 327-328, 328*n*
    super bugs threaten the effectiveness of antibiotics used for treating infections in humans 328
Antioxidants
    protective role in human health 19, 71-72
    sources of antioxidants
        phytonutrients. *See also* phytonutrients

        anthocyanins 19
        betalain 73
        gluosinolates 73-74
    vegetables and fruits as primary source of phytonutrients 19
    vulnerabilities of phytonutrients during preparation 72
        stir-frying and stir-fry/steaming as cooking methods protective of phytonutrients 66
Apple
    dish recipes
        Apple and Warmed Brie 284-285
        Apple Chutney 613-615
        Apple, Orange, Apricot, and Spinach Salad 376-378
        Applesauce 721-723
        Baked Apples 654-656
        Butternut Squash Soup 509-513
        100% Whole Wheat Applesauce Pancakes 705-708
        100% Whole Wheat Zucchini Applesauce Muffins 562-565
    juice-protective preparation
        baked 654-656
        raw 216-217
        stir-fry/steamed 511, 589, 625
    nutritional profile 217
    selection 217-218
    storage 54, 59, 220
Apricot, dried
    dish recipe
        Fruit and Havarti Kebabs 288-289
    plumping 376
Apricot, fresh
    dish recipes
        Apple, Orange, Apricot, and Spinach Salad 376-378
        Creamy Apricot Dip 279-281
    juice-protective preparation 219
    nutritional profile 219
    selection 219-220
    storage 220
    as stone fruit 54, 251
Artichoke
    juice-protective preparation
        boiled whole 201-202, 204
    nutritional profile 204
    selection
        canned as source of concentrated phytonutrient content 347
        non-pickled 348

Asparagus
    dish recipes
        Asparagus and Green Onion Quiche 635–639
    juice-protective preparation
        boiled whole 201–202, 205
        dry roasted whole spears 188–189, 191
        parboiled 296–298, 308
        raw 295–296, 298
        stir-fry/steamed 76
        stir-fried whole in water 202–203, 205
    nutritional profile 77
    selection 77
    storage 78
Avocado
    dish recipes
        Guest Vegetable Salad 392–395
        Mandarin Orange and Red Leaf Lettuce 385–388
    juice-protective preparation 220–221
        peeling technique 221
    nutritional profile 222
    selection 222
    storage 59 (cut), 222–223

B

Banana
    dish recipes
        Banana Cranberry 100% Whole Wheat Muffins 553–556
        Berries and Yogurt Snack 291–293
        Blueberry Banana 100% Whole Wheat Muffins 550–552
        Orange and Yogurt Snack 290–291
        Peanut or Almond Butter Spread 281–282
        Basic 100% Whole Wheat Pancakes 695–698
    juice-protective preparation 223
    nutritional profile 224
    selection 224–225
    storage 54, 59 (cut), 225
Barley, hulled. *See* whole grain, intact
Basil, sweet. *See* herbs and spices, dried and fresh
Beans, green and yellow wax
    dish recipes
        Minestrone Stew 534–539
        Three Bean Vegetable Salad 395–398
    juice-protective preparation
        boiled whole 201–202, 206
        parboiled 296–298, 309
        raw 295–296, 298
    nutritional profile 206
    selection 206–207
    storage 207
Beef, grass-fed
    form of natural production 325
    nutritional value for humans in comparison with grain-fed beef 325–335
    products marketed 334–335
    selection 338–339
    serving
        maximizing serving attractiveness 320, 357–358
            maximizing acceptability of lean meat 318–319
Beef, ground 338–339
    dish recipes
        Chili con Carne 513–518
        Eggplant Curry 599–604
        Lentil Stew 528–534
        Meatball Curry 590–594
        Minestrone Stew 534–539
        Roasted Pepper, Spinach, and Pineapple Pizza 683–687
        Roasted Pepper, Zucchini, Eggplant, and Ground Beef Pizza 678–682
    juice-protective preparation 424, 691
    selection
        grass-fed 338. *See also* beef, grass-fed products marketed
    storage 339
Beefsteak
    dish recipes
        Broccoli, Carrot, and Beefsteak Stir Fry 426–429
        Cabbage, Kale, and Beefsteak Stir Fry 429–434
        Sweet Potato, Broccoli, Pineapple, and Beefsteak Stir Fry 434–438
        Zucchini, Chard, Corn, and Beefsteak Stir Fry 438–443
    juice-protective preparation 361–363
    selection
        grass-fed 357. *See also* beef, grass-fed products marketed
    serving
        maximizing attractiveness of lean meat 357–358
            utilizing vegetable and fruit flavoring 318–319
        substituting ground beef 424
    storage 335
Beet
    juice-protective preparation
        boiled whole 201–202, 207
        dry roasted whole 189–191
        raw 80, 418
        stir-fry/steamed 78–79
    nutritional profile 73, 79
    selection
        canned as source of concentrated phytonutrients 347, 348
        raw 80
    storage 80
Beet greens
    cooking characteristics
        matched to milk sauce 491
        matched to tomato sauce 491
        oxalate content 153
        vulnerabilities 69
    juice-protective preparation
        stir-fry/steamed 135–136
    nutritional profile 137. *See also* 73
    selection 137
    storage 138
Beta-carotene/vitamin A. *See* phytonutrients, carotenoid
Black beans. *See also* legumes
    dish recipes
        Broccoli, Pineapple, and Black Bean Stir Fry 456–460
        Corn and Black Bean Salad 399–402
Blackberries
    dish recipes
        Berry, Mandarin Orange, and Yogurt Dessert 652–654
        Fruit Topped Vanilla Pudding Dessert 666–669
    juice-protective preparation 227
    nutritional profile 227–228
    selection 228
    storage 228

INDEX

Blueberries, fresh
   dish recipes
      100% Whole Wheat Blueberry and Nectarine
         Pancakes 699–701
      Berries and Yogurt Snack 291–293
      Berry, Mandarin Orange, and Yogurt Dessert
         652–654
      Blueberry Sauce 711–713
   juice-protective preparation 225
   nutritional profile 226
   selection 226
   storage 226
Blueberries, processed
   canned as source of concentrated phytonutrients 347,
      348
   dry frozen 62, 63, 349
      quick thawing 349
Boiling whole procedures for vegetables 201–203
   boiling whole covered with water 201–202
   stir-fried in water 202–203
Bok Choy
   juice-protective preparation
      raw 299
         stir-fried 80–81
   nutritional profile 81–82. See also 68–69, 73–74, 75
   selection 82
   storage 82
Bowls, mixing 320
BPA (bisphenol A)
   chemical in lining of some canned goods identified as
      endocrine disruptive in humans 348, 576–577,
      576n, 692
Bread, home prepared
   baking tools 496–497
   bread recipes
      100% Whole Corn Bread 565–567
      100% Whole Rye Bread 567–572
      100% Whole Wheat Flat Bread Rounds (Chapatis)
         617–619
      100% Whole Wheat Pizza Crust 672–674
Broccoli
   dish recipes
      Broccoli, Carrot, and Beefsteak Stir Fry 426–429
      Broccoli, Pepper, and Potato Soup 497–500
      Broccoli, Pineapple, and Black Bean Stir Fry 456–460
      Broccoli Quiche 631–634
      Broccoli, Sugar Snap Pea, and Grape Salad 405–408
      Sweet Potato, Broccoli, Pineapple, and Beefsteak Stir
         Fry 434–438
   juice-protective preparation
      boiled whole florets 201–202, 207
      parboiled 296–298, 309
      raw 295–296, 299
      stir-fry/steamed 82–84
   nutritional profile 84. See also 68–69, 73–74, 75
   selection 85
   storage 85
Broth, commercially prepared
   enhancing flavor 575–576, 620–621
   selection 576
Broth, fresh
   chicken 578–580
Brown rice. *See* rice, brown
Brussels sprouts
   dish recipes
      Brussels Sprouts, Kale, Pineapple, and Chicken Stir
         Fry 443–448
      Cauliflower, Brussels Sprouts, and Garbanzo Bean Stir
         Fry 464–469
   juice-protective preparation
      boiled whole 201–202, 208
      dry roasted 188–189, 191
      stir-fry/steamed 86–87
   nutritional profile 87. See also 68–69, 73–74, 75
   selection 88
   storage 88
      pre-rinsed and dried 60
Bulgur, medium cracked 343, 405, 477
Butter. *See also* dairy products, pasture-raised
   selection 412–413, 727, 728
      grass-fed or European 326–328, 339
Butter beans, fresh
   juice-protective preparation
      boiled whole 201–202, 205

C

Cabbage
   dish recipes
      Cabbage and Red Pepper Quiche 639–643
      Cabbage, Kale, and Beefsteak Stir Fry 429–434
   juice-protective preparation
      raw 295–296, 300, 418
      stir-fry/steamed 88–89
   nutritional profile 90. See also 68–69, 73–74, 75
   selection 90–91
   storage 91
Cabbage family vegetables
   cooking characteristics 68–69, 75
      matched with milk sauce 490–491
         Broccoli Quiche 631–634
         Broccoli, Pepper and Potato Soup 497–500
         Cabbage and Red Pepper Quiche 639–643
         Kale and Sweet Potato Soup 505–508
   nutritional benefits
      glucosinolate phytonutrient content 73–74
      human intestinal health support 68–69
CAFOs (concentrated animal feeding operations)
   form of industrial animal/poultry production
      livestock produced as a commodity 8, 43, 325
         CAFOs make expanded production at lowest cost
            top production priorities 8, 43
         nutritional value of food products is sidelined 8
   destructive nutritional impact of commodity production
      of animals and poultry
      feeding of unnatural food to livestock 326
         alteration of nutritional composition of food
            products 46
         reduction of nutritional value of animal food
            products 326
         contrast in the nutritional content grass- and
            grain-fed livestock 326
         animal food products of CAFOs carry super bugs
            328, 328n
         animal food products of CAFOs carry genetically
            modified (GM) derivatives 329
         animal food products of CAFOs carry pharmaceutical
            residues
            GM bovine growth hormone 329
            antibiotics and other drug residues 327–328
         animal food products routinely carry pesticide

residues from routine feeding of glyphosate-laden grain to CAFO livestock 327
impact on human health. *See* antibiotics, impact on human health, and glyphosate, impact on human health
California Avocado Commission 221
Cantaloupe
  dish recipes
    Berry, Cantaloupe, Pineapple, and Greens Salad 373–375
  juice-protective preparation 228–229
  nutritional profile 230
  selection 230–231
  storage 231
Capsaicin 178
Carbohydrate. *See* whole grain, intact, and legumes
Carrot
  dish recipes
    Broccoli, Carrot, and Beefsteak Stir Fry 426–429
    Pineapple Carrot 100% Whole Wheat Muffins 556–559
  juice-protective preparation
    boiled whole 201–202, 208
    raw 295–296, 300
    stir-fry/steamed 91–92
  nutritional profile 93
  selection 93–94
  storage 94
Cauliflower
  dish recipes
    Cauliflower, Brussels Sprouts, and Garbanzo Bean Stir Fry 464–469
    Nectarine, Grape, Cauliflower, and Greens Salad 367–370
  juice-protective preparation
    boiled whole florets 201–202, 207
    dry roasted florets 188–189, 192
    parboiled 296–298, 309–310
    raw 295–296, 301, 418
    stir-fry/steamed 94–96
  nutritional profile 96. *See also* 68–69, 73–74, 75
  selection 96–97
  storage 97
  pre-rinsing and drying 60
Celery
  dish recipes
    Old Fashioned Chicken Stew 539–544
    Guest Vegetable and Wild Rice Pilaf 478–483
    Vegetables and Cracked Wheat Pilaf 473–478
  juice-protective preparation
    raw 285–296, 301, 418
    stir-fry/steamed 97–99
  nutritional profile 99
    source of heat sensitive prebiotic fiber cellulose 73
  selection 99
  storage 100
Certified organic
  form of natural production 42–44, 325
    comparison of natural and industrial production 42–50, 324–332
      United States Department of Agriculture (USDA) verified standards 9, 42–43, 51
  selection 50–51
    biodynamic 50–51, 333
    loopholes
      fertilizer variation 51
      post-harvest physical processing 9
      seed quality variation 51
Chard
  dish recipes
    Sweet Potato, Sugar Snap Peas, and Egg Stir Fry 452–456
    Zucchini, Chard, Corn, and Beefsteak Stir Fry 438–443
  juice-protective preparation
    boiled whole 201–202, 208–209
    stir-fry/steamed 138–139
  nutritional profile 140
    cooking characteristics
      matched to milk sauce 491
      matched to tomato sauce 491
      oxalate content 153
      vulnerabilities 69
  serving
    matched to milk sauce 491
  selection 140–141
  storage 141
Cheese
  dish recipes
    Apple and Warmed Brie 284–285
    Basic Roasted Pepper and Cheese Pizza 675–678
    Creamy Apricot Dip 279–281
    Fruit and Havarti Cheese Kebabs 288–289
    Grape Tomato and Mozzarella Cheese Kebabs 289
    Herbed Onion and Garlic Dip 311–313
    Mini Cheesecake Dessert 660–662
    Raw Fruit Pita Pizza 285–287
    Raw Vegetable Pita Pizza 313–315
  nutritional profile
    calorie content per ounce 573, 629
    grass-fed 339–340, 573, 691–692
    to avoid pesticides, GMO hormones and flavoring (both artificial and natural) 692
  preparation
    grating 572
    heating 572–573, 692
    measuring 573, 692
  selection 691–692
    cheddar 413, 572, 573, 691–692
    feta 365, 412–413
      Valbreso as special treat 389
    goat cheese
      substitute for feta
    mozzarella 413
    parmesan 572
      Parmigiano Reggiano 572
    Roquefort or bleu 413
    Swiss 413
  storage 572
Cherries, fresh sweet and tart
  dish recipes
    Cherry Sauce 715–717
    Individual Cherry Trifle Dessert 662–666
  juice-protective preparation 231
  nutritional profile 232
  selection 232
  storage 232
Chicken
  dish recipes
    Brussels Sprouts, Kale, Pineapple, and Chicken Stir Fry 443–448
    Chicken Curry 586–589

INDEX

Spiced Chicken, Fruit, and Greens Supreme Salad 381–384
Curried Split Pea and Chicken Stew 544–549
Old Fashioned Chicken Stew 539–544
juice-protective preparation
general techniques 361–363
simmered, breast 384
simmered, whole 578–580
stir-fried 382–383
selection 337. *See also* chicken, pastured
Chicken broth
preparation
enhancing flavor of canned 575
enhancing nutritional quality of canned 576
fresh prepared 576, 578–580, 621
selection
canned/commercially prepared 621
canned/pastured and certified organic 621
Chicken, pastured 325–332, 337
form of natural production 325
nutritional comparison with grain-fed 326, 329
Chilling injury, stone fruits 54, 215
Chutney, home prepared. *See* curry accompaniments
Cilantro. *See* herbs and spices, fresh
Cinnamon. *See* herbs and spices, dried
Citrus wash 59, 63, 669
Clementine orange. *See* orange, clementine and mandarin
Coconut milk, canned 622
enhancing coconut flavor 448, 460
Coconut oil. *See* oil, coconut
Collards
juice-protective preparation
boiled whole 201–202, 209
stir-fry/steamed 141–142
nutritional profile 143. *See also* 68–69, 73–74, 75
selection 144
storage 144
Commodity, food defined as. *See* food production, industrial; food marketing corporations; and processed food
Concentrated Animal Feeding Operations. *See* CAFOs
Condensaton, prevention of
fruits and vegetables during refrigeration 61
muffins 497, 551
pancakes 697
Conjugated linoleic acid 326, 326n, 340, 573
Cooking tools, description
Part I: Introduction 34–35
Part II: Introduction 320–322
recipe preparation notes of individual chapters
breads 496–497
curries 584
desserts 646
pancakes 695
quiche 630
salads 366
soups and stews 495–496
stir-fried and stir-fry/steamed, individual vegetables 69–71
stir-fried dishes 424
Corn, fresh whole kernel
dish recipes
Corn and Black Bean Salad 399–402
Corn, Pepper, and Potato Soup 500–504
Okra, Eggplant, Corn, Spinach, and Lentil Stir Fry 469–472

Sweet Potato, Kale, Corn, and Kidney Bean Stir Fry 460–464
Zucchini, Chard, Corn, and Beefsteak Stir Fry 438–442
juice-protective preparation
stir-fried in oil 100–101
stir-fried in water 202–203, 209
nutritional profile 101
selection 101–102
storage 102
Corn, processed whole kernel
canned yellow corn as source of concentrated phytonutrients 347, 348
dry frozen 62
Corn flour, whole
dish recipe
100% Whole Corn Bread 565–567
nutritional profile 342
alkalinity status 342
selection 341–342
certified organic 34
storage 342
Cracked wheat. *See* wheat, whole cracked
Cranberry, stir-fried in juice 437, 451, 464, 554
Cucumber
dish recipe
Spiced Yogurt 610–611
juice-protective preparation
raw 295–296, 302
nutritional profile 302
selection 302–303
substituting another variety for Japanese 301–302
certified organic or locally produced 303
storage 59 (cut), 303
Curries
dish description 581
curry sauce versatility 625–626
vegetable and fruit compatibility 624–625
dish recipes
Chicken Curry 586–589
Egg Curry 594–599
Eggplant Curry 599–604
Meatball Curry 590–594
Vegetable Curry 604–610
preparation support
Curry Preparation Notes 582–585
cooking tools 584
Clinching Curry Flavor 620–626
Curry accompaniments
Apple Chutney 613–615
Mango Chutney 615–617
Pineapple Chutney 612–613
Spiced Lentils (Dhal) 611–612
Spiced Yogurt (Raita) 610–611
100% Whole Wheat Flat Bread Rounds (Chapatis) 617–619
Curry powder
enhancing/varying flavor 623
recipe, home-assembled 623–624
selection 622, 624
Curry spices
mortar and pestle 584
preparation 624
selection 594
certified organic 624
storage 624

D

Dairy products, pasture raised. *See also* butter, cheese and milk
   form of natural production 324–325
      comparison of nutritional quality with grain-fed dairy products 326–328
   selection
      grass-fed and certified organic 326, 328
      products marketed 339–340
Davis, Adelle 2
   juice-protective preparation of vegetables 31*n*
   milk sauce and sulfur compounds 491
   nutritional waste 14*n*, 183
Dead foods 1, 5, 14, 47, 214
Degreening of citrus fruits 214–215. *See also* specific citrus fruits
   form of post-harvest chemical processing. *See* food processing
   ethylene gas 73
Desserts. *See* fruit desserts
Dips
   Herbed Onion and Garlic Dip 311
Dirty Dozen. *See* Environmental Working Group
Dressing, salad
   apple cider vinegar 379, 420
   balsamic vinegar 419–420
   mayonnaise, homemade 408
   red wine 385–420
   tahini 375, 411
Dry roasting procedures for vegetables 188–190
Dutch oven description 496

E

Edamame pods (fresh soybeans)
   dish recipe
      Three Bean Vegetable Salad 395–398
   juice-protective preparation
      boiled whole 210
   nutritional profile 210
Egg
   dish recipes
      Asparagus and Green Onion Quiche 635–639
      Broccoli Quiche 631–634
      Cabbage and Red Pepper Quiche 639–643
      Egg Curry 594–599
      Red Potato, Pepper, and Egg Stir Fry 448–451
      Sweet Potato, Sugar Snap Peas, and Egg Stir Fry 452–456
   juice-protective preparation
      boiled 363, 409, 413
      stir-fried 450
   selection 336–337. *See also* egg, pasture-raised
      eggs of hens with a diet supplemented with flax or aquatic grass 337
   storage 361
Egg, pasture-raised
   form of natural production
   nutritional profile
      comparison of nutritional quality with eggs of industrial-raised hens 25, 325–333
   selection 335–337, 413
      products marketed 336
Eggplant
   dish recipes
      Eggplant Curry 599–604
      Okra, Eggplant, Corn, Spinach, and Lentil Stir Fry 469–473
      Roasted Pepper, Zucchini, Eggplant, and Ground Beef Pizza 678–683
   juice-protective preparation
      dry roasted/cubed 188–189, 192
      stir-fry/steamed 102–103
   nutritional profile 103–104
   selection 104
   storage 59 (cut), 104–105
Environmental Working Group 73
   Clean Fifteen list (least contaminated with pesticides) 73
      asparagus 77
      cauliflower 97
      corn 101–102
      eggplant 104
      peas, dry frozen 113
      sweet potato 123
   Dirty Dozen list (most contaminated with pesticides) 73, 183
      bell pepper 176
      celery 99
      cherries 231
      collards 144
      kale 148
      potato 119
      spinach 154, 156
      strawberries 271
      tomatoes 181
Enzymes, plant 8, 32, 38
   activation during preparation 55, 295
   deactivation during preparation 53, 294, 295, 296, 349, 365, 419, 423, 724
   fruits with distinctive enzymes
      kiwi 242
      papaya 254
      pineapple 262
   link to ripening process 53, 55
Ethylene gas 55, 73, 300
   industrial use in food processing
      degreening of produce 73, 214–215
   vegetables and fruits that naturally emit
      apple 55, 218
      banana 55, 225
      cantaloupe 231
      plum 55, 265
      potato 55, 119–120
      scallions 55
   vegetables and fruits sensitive to
      carrot 55, 94
      kale 56
      kiwi 243
      papaya 255
      watermelon 278–279

F

Farmers' markets 51–52, 334
Fennel bulb
   juice-protective preparation
      raw 295–296, 303
   nutritional profile 303

selection 303–304, 418
storage 304
Fiber, vegetable and fruit
  forms of fiber
    insoluble 22
      cellulose 13, 20, 73
      sources 20n
    soluble 20–22
      fructans 14, 21, 73, 268
      sources 20
    resistant starch dietary fiber 22
  preparation vulnerability
    heat sensitivity 14, 73, 729
      discarding of plant parts by cooks
        peeling off skin 13
        discarding of pulp and stems 13
      pureeing 14, 213
      water solubility 14, 22
  role in brain health 20
  role in human intestinal health 20n, 341
    sustaining/feeding of beneficial microflora
      prebiotic fiber 13, 14, 20–22, 73
Flour, corn. *See* corn flour, whole
Flour, wheat. *See* wheat flour, whole
Folate. *See* micronutrients, heat sensitivity
Food marketing corporations
  key driver of processed food dependence 8–9
    blocking/discrediting of contrary research 11, 12–13, 48n
    lack of inherent interest in nutritional quality 7–11
      apply industrial model of food production 8
        treat food as a commodity 8
        commodity production allows endless processing of food. *See* processed food
        alteration of food from natural form undermines nutritional value of food 324
      dependent on salt, sugar, and fat for marketing success 8
      supported by reigning food ideology of Nutritionism 14n
  political power 10–11, 12n, 50, 332
Food production, industrial
  key driver of processed food dependence
    form of agricultural and livestock production that produces food as a commodity 8, 43, 325
      expanded production and lowest cost serve as top production priorities 8
      nutritional value of food products gets sidelined 8
    far-reaching destructive impact of commodity production
      impact on animal/poultry health 327, 328, 329–330
      impact on environmental health 45, 48–49, 330–332
        creation of super weeds 49, 331
        creation of dead zones in bodies of water 48
        destruction of microbial life in soil 49
        wildlife destruction 331
      impact on nutritional quality of industrial food products
        presence of antibiotic residues and other drugs in food products 327, 585. *See also* glyphosate
        presence of unnatural genetically modified (GM) derivatives in food products 44n, 47–48. *See also* genetically modified (GM) foods
        presence of toxic pesticides in food products 327. *See also* pesticides and glyphosate
        reduction of nutritional value of food products 9, 46, 326, 326n
        alteration of food from its natural form undermines its human health supporting capacity 9, 45, 46n, 324
        reduction of phytonutrient content in food 46n
        reduction of soil quality reduces the nutritional diversity of foods 9, 45
      impact on plant health 9, 43-45
        destructive of soil 49
      political and economic power of agrichemical and agribusiness corporations to retain commodity production 12–13, 48, 332, 332n
        discrediting of opposing views 11, 48n
      resulting impact on human health 6–15, 42–48, 326–328
        development of antibiotic resistant super bugs 325, 328, 328n
      role of United States government in promoting/maintaining commodity food production
        active participant in industrial food production 11, 48
        active supporter of industrial animal production research 330
        infiltration of government regulatory agencies by corporations 10
Food production, natural
  natural food production defined 42, 43, 324
    natural food production is an essential indicator of whole food quality 43–47, 324–325
    natural food production is intricately linked to the nutritional value of food products 43
    natural production maintains the natural form of foods, which matches human nutritional needs 43, 45, 324, 326
    foods have a diversity of nutrients in combinations required by humans 45
    natural production is essentially connected to human health 8, 43
    natural production is directly linked to the quality of animal food products
      nutritional quality of grass- and grain-fed livestock contrasted 326
  natural production methods
    certified organic farming 19, 325–332
    local farming methods that essentially practice organic farming principles 51
      sources of locally produced produce 51–53
    pasturing of animals and poultry. *See* beef, grass-fed, and chicken, pastured
  natural production contrasted with industrial production 42–48, 324–332
Food supplements 15, 16n, 71
Free radicals
  antioxidants as protectors against 19n, 72
    vegetables and fruits as invaluable source of antioxidants for humans 19, 72
  description of free radicals 71–72
  link to extensive refining of oils 72, 344n
    stripping away of vitamin E content and other antioxidants 27n, 310
  link to oil rancidity 333, 340, 344, 355–356
  threat to human health
    destructive of omega-3 essential fatty acids 3, 25, 27n
    deadly impact on brain 27n
  vegetable oil as source. *See also* oil, vegetable
    heating 27n, 344

releases free radicals and other toxic substances. *See*
    oil, vegetable link to extensive refining of oils
    72, 344n
  unstable (reacts with oxygen) 27n
Fruit, cooked
  juice-protective stir-fried or stir-fry/steamed
    apple 511, 589, 625
    cranberry 451, 464, 554
    pineapple 262
  juice-protective sauce
    See pancake, fruit toppings
    See fruit desserts
      Raspberry sauce and Ice Cream Dessert 649–651
      Mini Cheesecake Dessert 660–662
      Individual Cherry Trifle Dessert 662–666
Fruit, dried
  dish recipes
    Apple, Orange, Apricot, and Spinach Salad 375–376
    Creamy apricot dip 279–281
  preparation
    apricots 376
    plumping 351
    raisins. *See* raisins
  serving
    maximizing attractiveness in dishes 350, 351
Fruit, processed
  canned
    blueberries 347
    enhancing nutrition 348
    freshness 348
  dry frozen
    blueberries 349
    in sauces 729
    technique 62–63
Fruit, raw whole
  definition of whole food 36–37
  dish recipes
    desserts. See fruit desserts
    salads. See fruit-centered salads
    snacks. See fruit snacks
  juice-protective preparation
    recipes, individual fruits
      Chapter Four: Raw Fruit Pure and Simple Recipes #74–101
    home-ripening 39
      fruits that home-ripen 39
      fruits that do not ripen after harvesting 39
  nutritional profile
    fiber 20–22, 73–74
    micronutrients 17–18
    omega-3 essential fatty acids 23–26
    phytonutrients 18–19
  selection, general guidelines
    Reference #1: Selecting Top Quality Fresh Whole Vegetables and Fruits 36–53
  storage, general guidelines
    Reference #2: Key Home Storage Guidelines for Conserving Vegetable and Fruit Quality 53–64
Fruit desserts
  fruit dessert description 644–645
  dish recipes
    desserts
      Baked Apples 654–656
      Berry, Mandarin Orange, and Yogurt Dessert 652–654
      Fruit Cup Dessert 646–648
      Fruit Gelatin Dessert 656–659
      Fruit-Topped Vanilla Pudding Dessert 666–668
      Individual Cherry Trifle Dessert 662–666
      Mini Cheesecake Dessert 660–662
      Peaches and Cream Dessert 651–652
      Raspberry Sauce and Ice Cream Dessert 649–651
  preparation support
    Fruit Dessert Preparation Notes 645–646
Fruit sauce. *See* pancakes, fruit sauce toppings
Fruit snacks
  dish recipes
    Apple and Warmed Brie 283–284
    Berries and Yogurt Snack 291–293
    Creamy Apricot Dip 279–281
    Fruit and Havarti Cheese Kebabs 288–289
    Grape Tomato and Mozzarella Kebabs 289
    Lettuce Fruit Cups 283–284
    Peanut or Almond Butter Spread 281–282
    Orange and Yogurt Snack 290–291
    Raw Fruit Pita Pizza 285–287
Fungi, mycorrhizal
  destructive impact of pesticides 49
  role in plant health 45
  role in soil health 3, 45–46

G

Garbanzo beans. *See also* legumes
  dish recipes
    Cauliflower, Brussels Sprouts and Garbanzo Bean Stir Fry, Herb and Tomato Flavoring 464–469
    Hummus 410–411
Garlic
  dish recipes
    Herbed Onion and Garlic Dip 311
  juice-protective preparation
    mincing technique 160
    mincing tool 495–496
    stir-fried 160–161
  nutritional profile 161–162, 626
  selection
    hard and softneck 162–163
  serving
    as topping 574
    raw 419
  storage 54, 163
Gastrointestinal (G.I.) tract, human 73
  gastrointestinal health, supporting roles
    beneficial microflora 21, 22, 101
    glusocinolate phytonutrients. *See* cabbage family vegetables
    vegetable and fruit fiber 20–22, 341
      prebiotic fiber 22
  gastrointestinal health, destructive factors
    glyphosate residues contained in industrial food products 10, 47, 337
    pharmaceutical antibiotic residues contained in industrial animal products 327
  link between G.I. and brain health 20
Gelatin
  dish recipe
    Fruit Gelatin Dessert 656–659
  selection 644
Genetically modified (GM) foods

INDEX

impact of GM derivatives in widely consumed food products on human health
  unnaturalness for humas 44, 44*n*, 47–48
  nutritional differences 48
impact on seed security 44
political power of agribusiness corporations in promoting GM foods 48*n*
  discredit contrary research 48
  conduct public relation efforts 48
  federal government allows them to police themselves 48
source of GM derivatives in food products
  Roundup-ready commodity crops 10*n*, 327, 329, 342

Ghee as cooking oil 345

Ginger root
  juice-protective preparation
    mincing 164
    stir-fried 164
  nutritional profile 164–165
  selection 165
  storage 165

Gluten, wheat
  gluten intolerance in humans 10, 341
  role in bread-making
    developed 497, 688–689 (pizza)
    not developed 724–725 (pancakes)

Glycemic index (GI) 74

Glyphosate 327–328
  negative human health impact of residues in food
    as an antibiotic disrupts beneficial bacteria 47, 327
    chelates (binds) minerals in human gut 10, 47
    chelates (binds) minerals in soil, which reduces the nutritional content of plant foods 10*n*
    disrupts endocrine system of humans 47
    linked with wide array of health problems 10*n*, 47*n*
    probable human carcinogen 10*n*, 47, 327, 341, 342
  source of glyphosate residues in animal food products
    feeding of grain grown from GM Roundup Ready seeds to livestock by industrial animal producers 327
  source of glyphosate residues in plant food products
    near universal use of GM Roundup Ready seeds for growing crops converted into innumerable food products (corn, soybeans, sugar cane, and sugar beets) 10*n*, 327, 585
    widespread agricultural practice of spraying glyphosate on wheat, which is converted into innumerable food products 342
    widespread spraying on vegetables and fruits during production 46–47, 327
    widespread use of glyphosate-laden CAFO manure as fertilizer on crops made into livestock feed or made directly into human food products 328, 331
  lack of government regulation of glyphosate residues in food products 10
    citizens serve as guinea pigs 10*n*

Grapefruit
  juice-protective preparation 232–234
  nutritional profile 234
  selection
    avoiding degreened fruit 214–215
  storage 235

Grapes, red and green
  dish recipes
    Fruit and Havarti Kebabs 288–289
    Lettuce Fruit Cups 283–284
    Mandarin Orange, Grape, Pomegranate, and Greens Salad 370–372
    Nectarine, Grape, Cauliflower, and Greens Salad 367–370
    Raw Fruit Pita Pizza 285–287
  juice-protective preparation 235–236
  nutritional profile 234
  selection 237
    gibbing 237
  storage 237

Grass-fed beef. *See* beef, grass-fed

Green leafy vegetables, dark. *See* vegetables, dark green leafy

Green onion *See also* onion
  dish recipes
    Asparagus and Green Onion Quiche 635–639

Greens, salad
  dish recipes
    see salads, fruit-centered
    see salads, vegetable-centered
  maximizing serving attractiveness 414–415
  preparation 364–366
    tearing 415
    washing and drying 60, 415–416
  selection 414, 415
    microgreens 414
    pre-washed baby spinach leaves 60, 153–154
  storage 54
    rinsed, dried, and wrapped in paper towels for quick use 415–416

Guava
  juice-protective preparation 238
  nutritional profile 238
  selection 238–239
  storage 239

Guthman, Julie 3–4
  link between industrial agriculture and processed food dependence 4, 15*n*
  link between industrial food production and obesity 348
  organic food movement 3

H

Herbs and spices, dried
  preparation 57
    herbs 352, 574
    spices 352, 574
      cumin seed, roasted 352, 623
      curry powder
        enhanced 353, 623
        home-prepared 623–624
  selection
    certified organic 353, 574, 578, 624
    herbs 352, 574
    spices
      curry powder 351–352, 622
      curry spices 623–624
  serving
    maximizing flavor in dishes 352–353
      herbs 577–578
      spices 624
    maximizing quality 353, 624
  storage 352

Herbs and spices, fresh
  preparation
    cilantro 353–354, 621
    parsley 353–354
  selection 578
  serving
    maximizing flavor contribution
      cilantro 353–354, 621
      parsley 353–354
  storage 354
Homogenization 339
  non-homogenized products marketed
    milk 339
    yogurt 360
Honey 416
  softening 416
  substituting another sweetener
    agave nectar 416
    sugar 416
Honeydew melon
  juice-protective preparation 239–240
  nutritional profile 240–241
  selection 240–241
  storage 241
Human gut. *See* gastrointestinal (G.I.) tract, human
Hummus
  preparation 410–411

I

Ice cream, home prepared 650–651
Industrial farming. *See* food production, industrial
Irradiate. *See* processed food, post-harvest physical processing

J

Juice, orange
  selection 644
    orange juice concentrate 651
    orange juice, premium 728
Juice-protective cooking methods, vegetables
  boiling whole
    description 199–200
    basic procedure
      boiling whole covered with water 201–202
      stir-fried in water 202–203
    recipes #54–73 204–212
  dry roasting
    description 187
    basic procedure, firm fleshed
      sliced or diced 188–189
      whole or halved 189–190
    basic procedure, soft fleshed 188–189
    recipes #38–53 191–198
  parboiling (barely cooking)
    description 294
    basic parboiling procedure 296–298
    recipes #129–134 308–310
  stir-frying
    description 65–66
    summary of techniques 182–186
      cooking tools 69–71
      principles underlying 182
  stir-fry/steaming
    description 65–66
    summary of techniques 182–186
      cooking tools 69–71
      principles underlying 182
    stir-frying and stir-fry/steaming recipes #1–37 75–179
Juice-protective preparation techniques, animal protein 361–363
Juice-protective preparation, vegetables and fruits
  underlying juice protection conservation strategy 31–32
  benefits
    conversion of vegetables and fruits into magical flavoring ingredients 27
    conversion of vegetables and fruits into nutritional goldmines 27–28, 29
Juice-protective serving methods, vegetables and fruits 317–318
Juice-protective serving and preparation techniques combined
  accomplishments possible
    transformation of dish quality 27–28, 317–320
      ingredient substitutions made possible 318–319
        whole foods become acceptable dish ingredients 318
      ingredient reductions made possible 319–320
    ending of processed food dependence
      removal of processed ingredients from everyday eating 12n, 318, 319
    health-building capacity of everyday eating stupendously increased 320
    consumer acceptability of traditional dishes retained 28, 318–319
    consumers take control of their health 29
Juice-protective stir-frying and *juice-protective* stir-fry/steaming steps summarized 182–186
  underlying principles 182–184

K

Kalamata olives. *See* Olives
Kale
  dish recipes
    Brussels Sprouts, Kale, Pineapple, and Chicken Stir Fry 443–448
    Cabbage, Kale, and Beefsteak Stir Fry 429–434
    Kale and Sweet Potato Soup 505–508
    Sweet Potato, Kale, Corn, and Kidney Bean Stir Fry 460–463
  juice-protective preparation
    boiled whole 201–202, 210
    stir-fry/steamed 145–146
  nutritional profile 146–147. *See also* 68–69, 73–74, 75
  selection 147–148
  storage 148
Kettle, electric tea 70
Kidney beans. *See also* legumes
  dish recipes
    Chili con Carne 513–518
    Extravagantly Vegetable Chili 518–523
    Minestrone Stew 534–539
    Old Fashioned Beef Stew 523–528
    Sweet Potato, Kale, Corn, and Kidney Bean Stir Fry 460–464

INDEX

nutritional profile
    kidney beans are a top-ranked antioxidant-rich food 347n
Kiwi
    juice-protective preparation 241
    nutritional profile 242
        distinctive enzyme content 242
    selection 242–243
    storage 243
Knife
    chef's 34
    serrated 34
Kohlrabi
    juice-protective preparation
        raw 304
        stir-fry/steamed 105–106
    nutritional profile 106. *See also* 68–69, 73–74, 75
    selection 106–107
    storage 107

L

Leek. *See* onion
Legumes 354–355. *See also* black beans, garbanzo beans, kidney beans, lentils, and split peas
    nutritional profile
        acid-forming status 17–18
        digestibility 18
            role played by micronutrients in human digestion of legumes 18
            juice-protected vegetables and fruits as sources of micronutrients 18, 320
    nutritional contribution 28, 347
    preparation
        maximizing attractiveness in dishes 355
        mixing with vegetables and fruits 28, 318
    selection 354
        canned as a source of concentrated phytonutrient content 347, 348
        certified organic 332
        selection of BPA-free cans 348
    storage 354–355
Lemon juice, use as a flavoring ingredient 575
Lentils. *See also* legumes
    dish recipes
        Lentil Stew 528–534
        Okra, Eggplant, Corn, Spinach, and Lentil Stir Fry 469–473
        Spiced Lentil, Pineapple, and Greens Salad 378–381
        Spiced Lentils (Dhal) 611–612
    selection 489
        certified organic 332, 585
    serving
        maximizing attractiveness in dishes 355
        mixing with vegetables and fruits to enhance serving attractiveness 28, 318
    storage 488–489
Lettuce
    dish recipes
        Lettuce Fruit Cups 283–284
        Mandarin Orange and Red Leaf Lettuce Salad 385–388
    preparation 414–415
        rinsing and drying of bunched 60, 381, 415
        spinning dry 416
    selection
        looseleaf, green and red 415
        romaine 415
    serving
        maximizing attractiveness in salads 415
        varying amount used in recipes 365
    storage
        rolled in paper towels 57–58, 60, 415–416
Locally produced food 50, 51. *See also* food production, natural products marketed
    beef 335
    eggs 336
    poultry 337
    plant products 50, 51–53, 334
    selection
        freshness considerations 334
        nutritional considerations 336–337
        verification of natural production 52
    sources of locally produced foods 51–52

M

Macronutrients 18, 28, 341
    vegetables and fruits as critical to body's processing and utilization of macronutrients 18, 28
Mandarin orange. *See* orange, clementine and mandarin
Mango
    dish recipes
        Mango Chutney 615–617
    juice-protective preparation 243–244
    nutritional profile 244–245
    selection 245
    storage 245
Master Recipe 30, 421
    master recipes
        curries: Chicken Curry 586–589
        muffins: 100% Whole Wheat Blueberry Banana 550–553
        pancakes: Basic 100% Whole Wheat Pancakes 695–699
        pizza: Roasted Pepper and Cheese Pizza 675–678
        quiche: Broccoli 631–634
        salads: Nectarine, Grape, Cauliflower, and Greens 367–370
        soups: Broccoli, Pepper, and Potato 497–500
        stews: Chili Con Carne 513–518
        stir-fried dish: Broccoli, Carrot, and Beefsteak 426–429
        stir-fried dish, vegetarian: Broccoli, Pineapple, and Black Bean Stir Fry 456–460
Mateljan, George 2, 221n
    nutritional value of vegetables and fruits 17n, 87n, 90n, 103n, 118n, 122n, 137n, 140n, 143n, 147n, 150n, 153n, 159n, 174n, 181n, 206n
    impact of freezing on fruit and vegetable nutritional quality 227n
    omega-3 essential fatty acids 171n
    oxalates 153n
    phytonutrients 19n, 74n, 213n
        phytonutrient content, comparison of naturally and industrially produced produce 19n, 268n, 326n
Microbiome (also microflora and microbacteria). *See also* gastrointestinal (G.I.) tract, human
    link of beneficial microflora to human intestinal health

20n, 20-22, 99, 341
    production of short chain fatty acids (SCFAs) 21, 22, 101
    link to brain health and function 20n
    role of vegetable and fruit fiber in microbiome health 21
        prebiotic 14, 20-22
            fiber preparation vulnerabilities 22
            compatibility of juice-protective stir-frying and stir-fry/steaming with fiber protection 65
    role of whole grains in microbiome health 341
Micronutrients
    protective roles played in human health
        anti-inflammation: vitamins E and K and mineral magnesium 150
        antioxidant: vitamins C, E and A and minerals magnesium, zinc, copper, iron, and selenium 72
        balancing
            alkaline minerals 17-18
                potassium 17
        control of free radicals
            linked to body's natural defenses 72
            digestion/utilization of macronutrients 18, 28
    vegetables and fruits as primary sources 17
    vulnerability during food preparation
        fat solubility
            compatibility of stir-frying and stir-fry/steaming with absorption of fat soluble nutrients 66
            inability of the body to absorb fat soluble nutrients without fat 66, 150
        sensitivity to heat 72-73
            folate and other B vitamins 294
            vitamin C 68, 69
        sensitivity to air and light
            B2 (riboflavin) 70
            vitamin C 32, 75, 294
        water solubility 14
Microorganisms. *See also* mycorrhizal fungi
    bacteria 20-22, 47, 48, 49, 328
    fungi 45, 48-49
    link to healthy and nutritious plants 13-14, 37, 45, 48
    link to healthy soil 3, 45
    link to human intestinal health. *See* gastrointestinal (G.I.) tract, human; destructive factors 45, 47, 49
Microwave heating 555, 558, 561
    quick thawing of frozen fruit 349
Milk, grass-fed. *See also* dairy products, pasture-raised
    nutritional quality of milk from grass-fed and grain-fed cows compared 573
        milk of grass-fed cows contributes omega-3 essential fatty acids 25
    selection of products
        full fat 573
        non-homogenized 339
        grass-fed and certified organic as top quality selection 326, 328, 339-340, 573
Milk sauce. *See also* soups and stews, milk sauce base, and quiche, milk sauce base
    description 490-491, 573-574
    matched to cabbage family vegetables, asparagus, onions 627
    preparation 573-574
    subsituting non-dairy for dairy milk 493, 500
Moss, Michael 319n
    role of food and agribusiness corporations in processed food dependence 2, 6n, 7n, 8, 10, 11n
    treatment of animals in industrial agriculture 11n, 330n
    U.S. government as participant in industrial food production/marketing of food 11n
Muffins, 100% whole wheat
    baking tools 496-497
    recipes
        Banana Cranberry Muffins 553-556
        Blueberry Banana Muffins 550-553
        Pineapple Carrot Muffins 556-559
        Sweet Potato Pineapple Muffins 559-562
        Zucchini Applesauce Muffins 562-565
Mushroom
    juice-protective preparation
        dry roasted 188-189, 193
        raw 295-296, 304-305, 418
        stir-fried 165-166
    nutritional profile 166-167
    selection 167-168
    storage 168
Mustard greens
    juice-protective preparation
        stir-fry/steamed 149-150
    nutritional profile 150-151. *See also* 68-69, 73-74, 75
    selection 151
    storage 151

N

Natural food production. *See* food production, natural
Natural food stores 52, 263, 334
Nectarine
    dish recipes
        Nectarine, Grape, Cauliflower, and Greens Salad 367-370
        100% Whole Wheat Blueberry and Nectarine Pancakes 699-701
    juice-protective preparation 245-246
    nutritional profile 246-247
    selection 247
    storage 248
        as stone fruit 54, 215
Nut oil. *See* oil, nut
Nutrients. *See* Micronutrients
Nutritional Term Guide 71-75
Nutritionism 11n, 13n, 14n
Nuts and Seeds (including peanuts)
    dish recipes
        Peanut or Almond Butter Spread 281-283
    nutritional benefits
        almond 333-334
        pecan 333
        pistachio 334
        walnut 333
    preparation 356-357
    selection
        certified organic 332, 356
        intact form 333, 334, 356
        rancidity 333-334, 355-356
        selecting a variety of nuts 333-334
    serving
        maximizing attractiveness in dishes 356
        mixing nuts and seeds 357
        toasting 357
    storage 33, 357

INDEX

O

Obesity 573n
   link to chemicals/pesticides 19, 348, 576
   link to omega-3 essential fatty acid deficiency 23
   link to processed food dependence 3, 6–7, 23
      link to sugar 6, 7, 10
Oil, avocado 408
Oil, coconut
   nutritional profile 346–347
      nonreactive when heated 346
      mostly saturated fat 346
   selection
      certified organic 346
Oil, nut
   selection
      expeller pressed 344–345
      macadamia 344
      peanut 345
      rancidity 344
      unrefined 344
   storage 344
Oil, olive, extra virgin
   nutritional profile as "good fat"
      balanced omega-3/omega-6 fatty acid ratio 27
      enhances absorption of fat soluble nutrients and phytonutrients contained in leafy greens 27, 66, 346
      monounsaturated
         nonreactive when heated 27, 66n, 346
            stable and does not mix with oxygen and release free radicals 66n, 345
            heating does not cause the oil to contain toxic ingredienets and trans fat 66n
      low acidity 345
   selection of products 346, 412, 417–418
      certified organic or European produced 345
      unfiltered 346
   serving
      120 calories per tablespoon 346
   substitution of other oil or fat
      coconut oil 346–347
      ghee 345
      nut oil 344–345
      peanut oil 345–346
   storage 345–346
Oil, vegetable 19
   dangerously unhealthy oil for humans
      extensively refined 25–26, 319n, 344, 344n, 346
         acidic 319n
         nutritionally stripped of antioxidants 27n, 319n
         unnatural fat for humans 344, 726
      impairs vitamin absorption by humans 346
      unstable when heated
         reacts with oxygen (reactive) 27n, 319n, 726
         releases free radicals 24, 27n, 72, 319n, 333, 344, 726
            destructive impact on heart and brain 3, 27n
            destructive impact on omega-3 essential fatty acids 27n
         releases toxic ingredients and trans fats 27n, 66, 726
Okra
   dish recipe
      Okra, Eggplant, Corn, Spinach, and Lentil Stir Fry 469–473

juice-protective preparation
   boiled whole 201–202, 210
   stir fried in water 202–203, 211
   stir fry/steamed 107–108
nutritional profile 108
selection 109
storage 109
Olive oil, extra virgin. *See* oil, olive, extra virgin
Olives
   black olives 417
   green olives 417
   Kalamata olives 417
Omega-3 essential fatty acids
   description 23
   link to human health
      alpha linolenic acid (ALA) 2, 16, 23, 326
         good vegetable and fruit sources of 24
      docosahexacnoic acid (DHA) 23, 24
         health problems linked to deficiency 23, 24
      eicosapentacnoic acid (EPA) 24
         health problems linked to deficiency 24
   perishability 25–27
   sources
      food products of grass-eating animals and poultry 25
      vegetables and fruits 24–25
   causes of deficiency in diet
      over-consumption of omega-6 fatty acid rich foods, which crowd out omega-3 fattay acids
         food products made from grain-fed industrial livestock and poultry 25
         pure vegetable oils of all kinds 26
         margarine 25
      over-consumption of saturated fat 26
      under-consumption of vegetables and fruits 16
      use of wasteful vegetable and fruit preparation methods 13–14
Omega-3/omega-6 fatty acid imbalance
   impact of unnatural balance on human health 25–26
      crowding out of omega-3 essential fatty acids in diet 27
   link of imbalance to industrial agriculture
      massive number of CAFOs (concentrated animal feeding operations) feeding livestock omega-6 fatty acid rich grain 327
      massive production of omega-6 fatty acid rich animal products (meat, egg, and dairy product) 25
   link with corporate food processing 25
      massive conversion of grains into omega-6 fatty rich pure vegetable oils 25
      refining out of omega-3 fatty acids from pure vegetable oil products 25–26
   link to government dietary guidelines
      consumers urged to use vegetable oil as "good fat" for heart health 26, 26n
      saturated fat condemned as cause of heart disease 26
   oils with natural balance
      extra virgin olive oil 27
   oils with unnatural balance
      all pure vegetable oils 25, 26
      peanut oil 325
Omega-6 fatty acids 13, 25–26, 326
Onion
   dish recipes
      Asparagus and Green Onion Quiche 635–639

Herbed Onion and Garlic Dip 311–313
juice-protective preparation
    diced 423, 493, 574, 583
    roasted 188–189, 193
    stir-fried 168–171
nutritional profile 171–172
selection
    chives 173
    green/scallions 173
    leeks 173
    red onion 173
    shallot 173
    yellow 173
storage 173–174. *See also* 53–54
    cut bulb onion 59
    pre-washed/dried green onion 60

Orange
  dish recipes
    Apple, Orange, Apricot, and Spinach Salad 376–378
    Orange and Yogurt Snack 290–291
  juice-protective preparation 248–249
  nutritional profile 249
  selection 249–250
    avoiding degreened 214–215
  storage 253. *See also* 54

Orange, clementine and mandarin
  dish recipes
    Berry, Mandarin Orange, and Yogurt Dessert 652–654
    Mandarin Orange and Red Leaf Lettuce Salad 385–388
    Mandarin Orange, Grape, Pomegranate, and Greens Salad 370–372
    Orange and Yogurt Snack 290–291
  juice-protective preparation 251–252
  nutritional profile 252
  selection 252
    avoiding degreened 214–215
  storage 253. *See also* 54

Oregano, dried leaves. *See* herbs and spices, dried
Organic, certified. *See* certified organic
Organic farming. *See* food production, natural
Oxalates
  impact on calcium content of dark green leafy vegetables
    beet greens/chard 137
    spinach 153n
Oxidative stress. *See* free radicals
Oxygen
  impact on produce during refrigeration 55–56
  impact on produce with high respiration rate 57

P

Pancakes, 100% whole wheat
  description 693
  dish recipes
    Basic 100% Whole Wheat Pancakes 695–699
    Applesauce Pancakes 705–708
    Blueberry and Nectarine Pancakes 699–701
    Winter Squash Pancakes 708–711
    Zucchini Pancakes 702–705
  preparation support
    Pancake Preparation Notes 693–695
      cooking tools 695

Clinching Pancake Attractiveness and Quality, pancake-making steps 723–728
Pancakes, fruit sauce toppings
  dish recipes
    Applesauce 721–723
    Blueberry Sauce 711–713
    Cherry Sauce 715–717
    Peach Sauce 717–719
    Raspberry Sauce 713–715
    Strawberry Rhubarb Sauce 719–721
  sauce preparation support 728

Papaya
  juice-protective preparation 253–254
  nutritional profile 254
    distinctive enzyme content 254
  selection 254–255
  storage 255

Parboiling procedure for vegetables 296–297
Parsley, Italian, flat leaf. *See also* herbs and spices, fresh
  dish recipe
    Tabbouleh 402–405
  preparation
    rinsing/drying/storing 415–416

Parsnip
  juice-protective preparation
    stir-fry/steamed 109–111
  nutritional profile 110. *See also* 68–69, 73–74, 75
  selection 110–111
  storage 111

Pattypan squash. *See* summer squash

Peach
  dish recipes
    Peaches and Cream Dessert 651–652
    Peach Sauce 717–719
  juice-protective preparation 255–256
  nutritional profile 256
  selection 256–257
  storage 257
  as stone fruit 54, 215

Peanut butter
  dish recipe
    Peanut or Almond Butter Spread 281–282
  selection 282–283

Peanuts. *See* nuts and seeds

Pear
  dish recipes
    Creamy Apricot Dip 279–281
    Peanut or Almond Butter Spread 281–282
  juice-protective preparation 258–259
  nutritional profile 259
  selection 259–260
  storage 260

Peas, green
  juice-protective preparation
    raw 295–296, 305
    stir-fried in water 202–203, 211–212
    stir-fry/steamed in oil 111–112
  nutritional profile 112–113
  selection 113
  storage 113

Peas, Sugar Snap and Snow
  dish recipes
    Broccoli, Sugar Snap Pea, and Grape Salad 405–408
    Raw Vegetable Pita Pizza 312–315
    Sweet Potato, Sugar Snap Peas, and Egg Stir Fry 452–456

INDEX

juice-protective preparation
    boiled whole 201–202, 211
    parboiled 296–298, 310
    raw 295–296, 305–306
    stir-fried in oil 114–115
    stir-fried in water 202–203, 211
nutritional profile 115
selection 115–116, 306
storage 116
Pecan. *See* nuts and seeds
Pepper, bell
  dish recipes
    pizza
      Basic Roasted Pepper and Cheese Pizza 675–678
      Roasted Pepper, Spinach, and Pineapple Pizza 683–687
      Roasted Pepper, Zucchini, Eggplant, and Ground Beef Pizza 678–682
    quiche
      Cabbage and Red Pepper Quiche 639–643
    soups
      Broccoli, Pepper, and Potato Soup 497–500
      Corn, Pepper, and Potato Soup 501–504
    stir-fried dish
      Red Potato, Pepper, and Egg Stir Fry 448–451
  juice-protective preparation
    dry roasted/sliced 188–189, 193–194
    raw 295–296, 306
    stir-fried 174–175
  nutritional profile 175–176
  selection 176
  storage 177
  cut 59
Pepper, chili
  dish recipes
    Extravagantly Vegetable Chili 518–523
    Sweet Potato, Kale, Corn, and Kidney Bean Stir Fry 460–464
  juice-protective preparation
    stir-fried 177–178
  nutritional profile 178
  selection 179
  storage 179
Pesticides, use in industrial agriculture 9–10
  impact on human health 9–10, 10*n*, 46–47. *See also* glyphosphate
    pesticide residues in human food
      fruits and vegetables 46–47
        exceptional tainting
          potatoes 46
          strawberries 46*n*
      animal and poultry products 585
    pesticide residues other than glyphosphate in human food products
      chlorpyrifos on vegetables and fruits 29*n*
    impact of pesticides on wildlife 331
    lack of government oversight and regulation 29*n*
    source of pesticide residues in human foods
      use of CAFO manure as fertilizer 328, 331
      heavy spraying of the herbicide Roundup on crops (corn, wheat, soybeans, sunflowers, sugar cane, and sugar beets) converted into innumerable food products 10*n*, 327
      feeding of CAFO livestock grain grown from glyphosate-laden grain 327
      spraying of the herbicide Roundup on vegetables and fruits during production 9–10. *See also* Environmental Working Group, yearly listing of most contaminated produce 73
      spraying of insecticides onto crops converted into foods 327
    treating of vegetables and fruits after harvest 47
Phytonutrients
  link to human health 18–19, 74
    protective capacity of phytonutrients for plants is transferred to humans 4
    health protections provided
      anti-inflammatory 19, 71
      antioxidant 19, 71–72
      anthocyanin 19, 71
      detoxification 19, 73
    phytonutrient families
      betalain 73
      carotenoid 71
      glucosinalate 71, 73–74
        cabbage family 50, 68-69. *See also* cabbage family vegetables
  preparation techniques
    protective role of stir-frying and stir-fry/steaming cooking methods 66
    preparation/storage vulnerabilities 72
      air and light sensitivity 72
        plant respiration 75
      fat solubility 68, 150
      heat sensitivity 68–69, 73, 74
      water solubility 73, 74
  selection techniques 39-41, 74
    color groupings 41–42
      most nutritious colors 41
    color hierarchy 41, 74
  vegetables and fruits as primary sources 16, 19
Pilaf
  dish recipes
    Guest Vegetable and Wild Rice Pilaf 478–483
    Vegetables and Cracked Wheat Pilaf 473–478
Pineapple
  dish recipes
    curries
      Pineapple Chutney 612–613
    muffins
      100% Whole Wheat Pineapple Carrot 556–559
      100% Whole Wheat Sweet Potato Pineapple 559–562
    pizza
      Roasted Pepper, Spinach, and Pineapple 683–687
    salads
      Berry, Cantaloupe, Pineapple, and Greens 373–375
      Spiced Chicken, Fruit, and Greens Supreme 381–384
      Spiced Lentil, Pineapple, and Greens 378–381
    snack
      Raw Fruit Pita Pizza 285–287
      Raw Vegetable Pita Pizza 312–315
    stir fry
      Broccoli, Pineapple, and Black Bean 456–460
      Brussels Sprouts, Kale, Pineapple, and Chicken 443–444
      Sweet Potato, Broccoli, Pineapple, and Beefsteak 434–438
  juice-protective preparation 260–262
    raw 260–262
    stir-fried 262

　　　　nutritional profile 262
　　　　　　distinctive enzyme content 262
　　　　selection 262–263
　　　　storage 263
　　　　　　dry freezing 26, 62–64
　Pizza
　　　　dish description 670
　　　　dish recipes
　　　　　　100% Whole Wheat Pizza Crust 672–674
　　　　　　Basic Roasted Pepper and Cheese Pizza 675–678
　　　　　　Raw Vegetable Pita Pizza 313–315
　　　　　　Roasted Pepper, Spinach, and Pineapple Pizza 683–687
　　　　　　Roasted Pepper, Zucchini, Eggplant, and Ground Beef Pizza 678–682
　　　　preparation support
　　　　　　Clinching Pizza Attractiveness
　　　　　　　　ground beef topping 691
　　　　　　　　pizza-making steps 687–690
　　　　　　Pizza Preparation Notes 670–672
　　　　　　　　cooking tools 671
　Plum
　　　　juice-protective preparation 263–264
　　　　nutritional profile 264
　　　　selection 264
　　　　storage 265
　Pollan, Michael 2
　　　　link of food production/marketing corporations to processed food dependence 8, 15*n*
　　　　nutritional value of vegetables and fruits 16*n*, 17*n*, 46*n*
　　　　Nutritionism 11*n*, 13*n*, 14*n*
　　　　omega-3/omega-6 fatty acids imbalance 26*n*
　　　　phytonutrient content, comparison of naturally and industrially produced produce 19*n*, 226*n*
　　　　political power of food and agribusiness corporations 50*n*, 332*n*
　Pomegranate seeds
　　　　dish recipes
　　　　　　Mandarin Orange, Grape, Pomegranate, and Greens Salad 370–372
　　　　juice-protective preparation 265–266
　　　　nutritional profile 266
　　　　selection 266–267
　　　　storage 267
　Potassium. *See* micronutrients, alkaline and balancing mineral
　Potato
　　　　dish recipes
　　　　　　Broccoli, Pepper, and Potato Soup 497–500
　　　　　　Corn, Pepper, and Potato Soup 501–504
　　　　　　Red Potato, Pepper, and Egg Stir-Fry 448–451
　　　　juice-protective preparation
　　　　　　boiled whole 201–202, 212
　　　　　　dry roasted, fries 188–189, 195
　　　　　　dry roasted, whole 189–190, 194
　　　　　　stir-fry/steamed 116–117
　　　　nutritional profile 118–119
　　　　selection 118
　　　　storage 54, 119
　Potato, sweet
　　　　dish recipes
　　　　　　muffins
　　　　　　　　100% Whole Wheat Sweet Potato Pineapple 559–562
　　　　　　soup
　　　　　　　　Kale and Sweet Potato 505–508

　　　　　　stir fry
　　　　　　　　Sweet Potato, Broccoli, Pineapple, and Beefsteak 434–438
　　　　　　　　Sweet Potato, Kale, Corn, and Kidney Bean 460–464
　　　　　　　　Sweet Potato, Sugar Snap Peas, and Egg 452–456
　　　　juice-protective preparation
　　　　　　boiled whole 201–202, 212
　　　　　　dry roasted, fries 188–189, 195
　　　　　　dry roasted, whole 189–190, 194–195
　　　　　　stir-fry/steamed 120–121
　　　　nutritional profile 121–122
　　　　selection 122–123
　　　　　　canned as source of concentrated phytonutrient content 347
　　　　storage 54, 123
　Poultry, pastured. *See* chicken, pastured
　Prebiotic. *See* fiber, vegetable and fruit
　Preparation Notes
　　　　Chapter One (stir-fried and stir-fried/steamed vegetables) 67–71
　　　　Chapter Four (raw fruit) 214–215
　　　　Chapter Six (salads) 364–367
　　　　Chapter Seven (stir-fried dishes) 422–425
　　　　Chapter Eight (soups and stews) 491–496
　　　　Chapter Nine (curries) 582–585
　　　　Chapter Ten (quiche) 628–630
　　　　Chapter Eleven (fruit deserts) 645–646
　　　　Chapter Twelve (pizza) 670–672
　　　　Chapter Thirteen (pancakes) 693
　Processed food 6
　　　　definition
　　　　　　food commercially produced as a commodity 8, 43
　　　　　　　　food altered from natural form in pursuit of industrial production goals 8, 43, 325
　　　　　　　　nutritional quality of food gets sidelined 8
　　　　impact of food processing on human health 46–47, 48
　　　　　　chemical tainting of foods 10, 46–47
　　　　　　disconnects food from human nutritional needs 43
　　　　　　reduction and alteration of the nutritional composition of foods 45, 46–47
　　　　　　tainting of foods with genetically modified (GM) derivatives 47–48
　　　　types of commercial processing
　　　　　　post-harvest chemical processing of foods
　　　　　　　　addition of chemical additives 6–9
　　　　　　post-harvest physical processing
　　　　　　　　addition of flavoring (salt, sugar, and fat) 6–9
　　　　　　　　irradiation 154, 313, 325, 356
　　　　　　　　refining 13–15, 344*n*
　　　　　　pre-harvest chemical processing 6
　　　　　　　　feeding chemically tainted grain to livestock 327
　　　　　　　　giving pharmaceutical drugs and antibiotics to livestock and poultry 327–328
　　　　　　　　spraying crops with pesticides 9–10, 46, 47, 49
　　　　　　pre-harvest physical processing
　　　　　　　　feeding of unnatural food 45, 48–49
　　　　　　　　　　artificial fertilizer to plants 9
　　　　　　　　　　genetically modified (GM) grain to livestock 329
　　　　　　　　　　grain to livestock and poultry 329
　　　　　　　　use of genetically modified drugs
　　　　　　　　　　bovine growth hormone 329
　　　　　　　　use of GM seeds for plant crops 327
　　　　role of U.S. government 7
　　　　　　active participant 11, 48, 332*n*
　　　　　　infiltration of Big Ag and Big Food into governmental

INDEX

regulatory agencies 10-11
Processed food dependence 6-7
   breaking free with vegetables and fruits 5, 16
   Cooked Alive! strategy 6, 27-28, 317-320
   powerful forces underlying 6-16, 332
      lack of effective opposition 15, 15*n*
      tenacious grip 6, 50
   negative impact on human health 6-7
Protein, animal
   juice-protective preparation
      Reference #7: *Juice-Protective* Techniques for
         Preparing Animal Protein 361-363
   nutritional profile
      acid-forming when consumed 18
      link to vegetables and fruits as source of alkaline
         minerals 17-18
   selection
      grass-fed as naturally produced top quality meat. *See*
         beef, grass-fed
      pastured chicken as naturally produced top quality
         poultry. *See* chicken, pastured
      pastured eggs as naturally produced top quality eggs.
         See eggs, pastured
   serving
      removing commercially processed and cured meat
         from diet 12*n*, 319
      using vegetables and fruits to replace processed and
         cured meat 318-319
Protein, plant. *See* legumes

Q

Quiche
   dish description 627-628. *See also* milk sauce
      compatible vegetables 627
   dish recipes
      Asparagus and Green Onion Quiche 635-639
      Broccoli Quiche 631-634
      Cabbage and Red Pepper Quiche 639-643
   preparation support
      Quiche Recipe Preparation Notes 628-630
         cooking tools 630
         maximizing crust attractiveness 629
Quinoa. *See also* whole grain, intact
   preparation 486-487

R

Radish, regular and Daikon
   juice-protective preparation 306-307
      raw 295-296, 306-307
   selection 307
   serving 418
Raisins
   nutritional profile 343-344
   preparation
      plumping 351
   selection 412-413
      certified organic 343
      raisin varieties 344
      substituting other dried fruit 344
Rancidity 333, 340, 341, 342, 244, 345, 347, 348, 355-356,
   357, 360, 404, 418

Raspberries
   dish recipes
      Berries and Yogurt Snack 291-293
      Fruit Gelatin Dessert 656-660
      Raspberry Sauce 713-715
      Raspberry Sauce and Ice Cream 649-651
   juice-protective preparation
      raw 62-63
      stir-fried in juice 649
   nutritional profile 268
      fructan fiber (prebiotic) content 268
   selection 268-269
   storage 269
      dry freezing 62-63, 269
Reactive oil. *See* oil, vegetable
References
   Reference #1
      Selecting Top Quality Fresh Whole Vegetables and
         Fruits 36-53
   Reference #2
      Key Home Storage Guidelines for Conserving
         Vegetable and Fruit Quality 53-64
   Reference #3
      Summarizing Stir-Frying and Stir-Fry/Steaming
         Techniques 182-186
   Reference #4
      Selecting Top Quality Whole Food Ingredients for Use
         in Part II Recipes 324-337
   Reference #5
      Selecting High Quality Processed Ingredients for Use
         in Part II Recipes 338-350
   Reference #6
      Maximizing the Attractiveness of Whole Food
         Ingredients Commonly Used in Part II Recipes
         350-361
   Reference #7
      Juice-Protective Techniques for Preparing Animal
         Protein 361-363
   Reference #8
      Clinching Salad Flavor:
         Expanded Preparation Support 412-420
   Reference #9
      Clinching Soup and Stew Flavor:
         Expanded Preparation Support 572-578
   Reference #10
      Preparing Fresh Chicken Broth 578-580
   Reference #11
      Clinching Curry Flavor: Expanded Preparation
         Support 620-626
   Reference #12
      Clinching Pizza Attractiveness:
         Expanded Preparation Support 687-692
   Reference #13
      Clinching Pancake Attractiveness and Quality:
         Expanded Preparation Support 723-729
Respiration rate of plants 74-75
   link to flavor and nutritional loss in vegetables 62, 74-75
   slowing the rate of respiration
      protection from air 55, 56-58
         Robinson's vented storage bag method 57, 75
      refrigeration 57
      storage time 62
Rice, brown. *See also* whole grain, intact
   dish recipes
      curries. *See* recipes #187-191

stews. See recipes #173–177
stir-fried dishes. See recipes #153–179
preparation 484–486. See also 359
selection 358–359, 485–486
   checking for rancidity 358
serving
   maximizing attractiveness in dishes 358–359
   re-heating 485
   substituting other whole grains 360, 424
storage
   cooked 359, 485
   frozen 359–360, 485
   raw 360

Rice, wild
   dish recipe
      Guest Vegetable and Wild Rice Pilaf 478–483
   preparation 486–487

Roberts, Paul 3
   agribusiness control of information 48n
   Monsanto seed monopoly 44n

Robinson, Jo 2, 33, 57
   commercial processing of vegetables and fruits 47n, 163n, 343n
   controlling the ripening process 53
   nutritional impact of commodity production of food 46
   nutritional value of extra virgin olive oil 346n
   nutritional value of vegetables and fruits 13n, 46n, 118n, 146n, 167n, 173n, 228n, 232n, 238n, 263n, 268n, 414n
      Robinson as source of nutritional information 51
   nutritional comparison of naturally and industrially produced livestock and poultry 326n
   nutritional wasting 94n
   pesticide content of industrially produced vegetables and fruits 46n, 49n, 101n, 156n, 218n, 232n, 257n, 271n, 343n
   phytonutrient content 19n, 41n, 72n, 79n, 91n, 101n, 113n, 156n, 172n, 173n, 217n, 218n, 219n, 222n, 226n, 249n, 263n, 278n, 348n
   phytonutrient content, comparison of naturally and industrially produced produce 46n, 257n
   plant respiration 37n, 55n, 75n
   storage of vegetables and fruits (including frozen) 53, 57, 57n, 62n, 63n, 85n, 88n, 113n, 215n, 237n, 275n, 278n, 349n

Robinson's vented storage bag method 57

Romaine lettuce. See also lettuce
   dish recipe
      Lettuce Fruit Cups 283–284

Rutabaga
   juice-protective preparation
      dry roasted/fries 188–189, 195–196
      stir-fry/steamed 123–125
   nutritional profile 125. See also 68–69, 73–74, 75
   selection 125
   storage 125

Rye bread. See bread, home prepared

S

Salads, fruit-centered
   dish description 364
   dish recipes
      Apple, Orange, Apricot, and Spinach 376–378
      Berry, Cantaloupe, Pineapple, and Greens 373–375
      Mandarin Orange, Grape, Pomegranate, and Greens 370–372
      Mandarin Orange and Red Leaf Lettuce 385–388
      Nectarine, Grape, Cauliflower, and Greens 367–370
      Spiced Chicken, Fruit, and Greens Supreme 381–384
      Spiced Lentil, Pineapple, and Greens 378–381
   preparation support
      Clinching Salad Flavor 413–420
         cheese 412–413
         fruit 413–414
         greens and lettuce 414–416
      Salad Recipe Preparation Notes 364–367
      preparation tools 366

Salads, vegetable-centered
   dish description 364
   dish recipes
      Broccoli, Sugar Snap Pea, and Grape Salad 405–408
      Corn and Black Bean Salad 399–402
      Everyday Vegetable Salad 389–392
      Greek Salad 388–389
      Guest Vegetable Salad 392–395
      Tabbouleh 402–405
      Three Bean Vegetable Salad 395–398
   preparation support
      Clinching Salad Flavor 413–414
         raw and parboiled vegetables 418–419
         raw seasoning vegetables 419–420
         raw onion 365
      Salad Recipe Preparation Notes 364–367
      preparation tools 366

Saturated fat 26, 318
   role in human health
      acidifying 318
      heart disease
         falsly demonized as cause of hardening of arteries and heart disease 13, 26
         redeemed as cause of hardening of arteries and heart disease 7, 13, 26
      link to omega-3 essential fatty acids 26
      link to consumption of vegetables and fruits
         as source of micronutrients for healthy management of saturated fat 318n
         to avoid crowding out omega-3 essential fatty acids 318
   use as cooking oil
      coconut oil as source 346
      nonreactive when heated 346

Saucepans description 321

Sausage, pork
   preparation 451
   substitution for ground beef 319, 670

Scallion. See onion

Seasoning vegetables. See vegetables, seasoning

Seeds. See nuts and seeds (including peanuts)

Shanahan, Catherine, Ph.D. 3
   extra virgin olive oil as "good fat" 66n, 136n, 345n
   other "good fats" 344n, 346n
   free radical description 19n, 27n
   health threat to humans of trans fat 11n
   impact of commercial processing on oil quality 341n
   vegetable oil as "bad fat" 27n, 66n, 72n, 136n, 344n, 346n

Short chain fatty acids (SCFAs). See microbiome

"Sitting duck" health category 29

Skillet descriptions

INDEX

large 321
medium 322
nonstick 68, 70
stir-frying 65
stir-fry/steaming 65
Snacks, raw fruit
    Apple and Warmed Brie 284–285
    Berries and Yogurt Snack 291–293
    Creamy Apricot Dip 279–281
    Fruit and Havarti Cheese Kebabs 288–289
    Grape Tomato and Mozzarella Kebabs 289
    Lettuce Fruit Cups 283–284
    Orange and Yogurt Snack 290–291
    Peanut or Almond Butter Spread 281–282
    Raw Fruit Pita Pizza 285–287
Snacks, raw vegetable
    Herbed Onion and Garlic Dip 311–313
    Raw Vegetable Pita Pizza 313–314
Soil. *See also* fungi, mycorrhizal, and microorganisms, link to healthy soil
    link of naturally fertilized soil to nutritional value of food 44, 45, 333
    organic matter
        link to healthy soil 44–45
Soups and stews, milk sauce base
    description of milk sauce
        milk sauce versatility 490–491
            compatible vegetables 491
    dish recipes
        Broccoli, Pepper, and Potato Soup 497–500
        Butternut Squash Soup 508–513
        Corn, Pepper, and Potato Soup 500–504
        Curried Split Pea and Chicken Stew 544–549
        Kale and Sweet Potato Soup 504–508
    preparation support
        Clinching Soup and Stew Flavor 572–574
            conversion to vegan form 493–500
            milk sauce preparation 572–573
            selection of soup ingredients 572–573
        Soup and Stew Preparation Notes 490–495
            cooking tools 495–496
    serving
        re-heating of soup 494
Soy sauce, natural
    selection 350
    serving
        sodium per teaspoon (433mg) 349
Spinach, pre-washed
    dish recipe
        Apple, Orange, Apricot, and Spinach Salad 376–378
    juice-protective preparation
        stir-fried 152
    nutritional profile 156. *See also* 73
        cooking characteristics
            matched to milk sauce 491
            matched to tomato sauce 491
            oxalate content 153
            vulnerabilities 69
    selection 153–154
    storage 154
Spinach, un-washed/bunched
    juice-protective preparation
        stir-fried 155–156
    nutritional profile 156. *See also* spinach, pre-washed, cooking characteristics

selection 156
storage
    rinsing and drying 154
Split peas. *See also* legumes
    dish recipes
        Curried Split Pea and Chicken Stew 544–549
Sprouts 418
Squash, summer (zucchini and yellow)
    dish recipes
        100% Whole Wheat Zucchini Applesauce Muffins 562–565
        100% Whole Wheat Zucchini Pancakes 702–705
        Roasted Pepper, Zucchini, Eggplant, and Ground Beef Pizza 678–682
        Zucchini, Chard, Corn, and Beefsteak Stir Fry 438–443
    juice-protective preparation
        boiled whole 201–202, 212
        dry roasted/sliced 188–189, 196
        parboiled 296–298, 310
        raw 295–296, 307
        stir-fry/steamed 126–127
    nutritional profile 127–128
    selection 128
Squash, winter
    dish recipes
        100% Whole Wheat Winter Squash Pancakes 708–711
        Butternut Squash Soup 509–513
    juice-protective preparation
        dry roasted/cubed 188–189, 197
        dry roasted/halved 189–190, 196–197
        stir-fry/steamed 129–131
    nutritional profile 131
    selection 131–132
    serving
        preparing broth from squash skins 131
        preparing seeds as a snack 130–131
    storage 132
Stew, herbed broth-based
    stew description 491
    dish recipe
        Old Fashioned Chicken Stew 539–544
    preparation support
        Clinching Soup and Stew Flavor 572–578
            broth 576
            herbs 577
            seasoning vegetables 577–578
        Soup and Stew Recipe Preparation Notes 491–496
            additional cooking tools 495–496
Stew, tomato sauce base
    stew description
        tomato sauce versatility and simplicity 491
        vegetable compatibility 491
            green leafy vegetables 491
        whole food compatibility 491
    dish recipes
        Chili Con Carne 513–518
        Extravagantly Vegetable Chili 518–523
        Lentil Stew 528–534
        Minestrone Stew 534–539
        Old Fashioned Beef Stew 523–528
    preparation support
        Clinching Soup and Stew Flavor 572–578
            broth 575–576

    cheese 572–573
    Soup and Stew Recipe Preparation Notes 491–497
        cooking tools 495–496
        conversion to vegan form 493
        speeding preparation 492
Stir fry, traditional main dish (vegetables with beefsteak, chicken, or egg)
    dish description 65–66, 421
    dish recipes
        Broccoli, Carrot, and Beefsteak Stir Fry 426–429
        Brussels Sprouts, Kale, Pineapple, and Chicken Stir Fry 443–448
        Cabbage, Kale, and Beefsteak Stir Fry 429–434
        Red Potato, Pepper, and Egg Stir Fry 448–451
        Sweet Potato, Broccoli, Pineapple, and Beefsteak Stir Fry 434–438
        Sweet Potato, Sugar Snap Pea, and Egg Stir Fry 452–456
        Zucchini, Chard, Corn, and Beefsteak Stir Fry, Herb and Tomato Flavoring 438–443
    preparation support
        Reference #3: Summarizing Stir-Frying and Stir-Fry/Steaming Techniques 182–186
        Stir-fried Dish Preparation Notes 422–425
            additional cooking tools 424
            substituting ground beef for beefsteak 424
Stir fry, traditional pilaf (vegetables with whole grain or wild rice)
    dish description 65–66
    dish recipes
        Vegetables and Whole Cracked Wheat Pilaf 473–478
        Guest Vegetable and Wild Rice Pilaf 478–483
    preparation support
        Reference #3: Summarizing Stir-Frying and Stir-Fry/Steaming Techniques 182–186
        Stir-Fried Dish Preparation Notes 422–425
            additional cooking tools 424
Stir fry, traditional vegetarian or vegan main dish (vegetables with legumes)
    dish description 421
    dish recipes
        Broccoli, Pineapple, and Black Bean Stir Fry, Master Recipe 456–460
        Cauliflower, Brussels Sprouts, and Garbanzo Bean Stir Fry, Herb and Tomato Flavoring 464–469
        Okra, Eggplant, Corn, Spinach, and Lentil Stir Fry 469–473
        Sweet Potato, Kale, Corn, and Kidney Bean Stir Fry 460–464
    preparation support
        Reference #3: Summarizing Stir-Frying and Stir-Fry/Steaming Techniques 182–186
        Stir-Fried Dish Preparation Notes 422–425
            additional cooking tools 424
Stir frying. *See juice-protective* cooking methods
Stir fry/steaming. *See juice-protective* cooking methods
Strawberries
    dish recipes
        Berries and Yogurt Snack 291–292
        Creamy Apricot Dip 279–281
        Raw Fruit Pita Pizza 285–287
        Strawberry Rhubarb Sauce 719–721
    juice-protective preparation 269–270
    nutritional profile 270
    selection 270–271
    storage 54, 271
Sugar, refined
    dependence of commercial food processors on sugar for marketing success 6–8, 10, 12
    determination of commercial food processors to exploit sugar for marketing success
        bliss point 7
    impact on human health 12
        acid-forming when consumed 17–18
        carrier of glyphosate residues 585
        carrier of genetically modified (GM) derivatives 585
        linked to obesity 6–7, 10
        linked to heart disease 7, 12
            sugar industry covered up a study linking sugar to heart disease 12
    selection, white and brown
        certified organic 585
Sulfur compounds 68, 75, 491
Super bugs. *See* food production, industrial
Super weeds. *See* food production, industrial
Swartz, Judith 3
    soil health 45*n*
Sweet potato. *See* potato, sweet
Swiss chard. *See* chard

T

Tabbouleh 402–405
Tangerine
    juice-protective preparation 271–272
    nutritional profile 272–273
    selection 273
        avoiding degreened 273. *See also* 214–215
    storage 273
        as citrus fruit 54
Tofu
    dish recipe
        Egg Curry 594–599, vegan variation 598
    preparation 598
Tomato, dried
    preparation 469
Tomato, fresh
    dish recipes
        Cauliflower, Brussels Sprouts, and Garbanzo Bean Stir Fry 464–469
        Greek Salad 388–389
        Minestrone Stew 534–539
        Okra, Eggplant, Corn, Spinach, and Lentil Stir Fry 469–473
        Raw Vegetable Pita Pizza 313–315
    juice-protective preparation
        grape tomato, raw 273–274
        stir-fried 179–180
    nutritional profile
        grape 274–275
        regular 180–181
    selection
        grape 275
        regular 181
    storage
        grape 54, 275–276
        regular 54, 181
Tomato, processed products
    selection

INDEX

certified organic 692
packaged in glass 348, 692
tomato paste as source of concentrated phytonutrient (lycopene) 348
Tomato sauce. *See* stew, tomato sauce base
Traditional dishes. *See* stir fry, traditional main dish, traditional pilaf, and traditional vegetarian or vegan
Trans fat
    health threat to humans 7n, 10–11, 27n, 346
        food processing/agribusiness corporations blocked/obstructed information about the threat of trans fat to human health 11
    margarine as source 10–11, 26
    vegetable oil as source 66
        produces trans fat when oxidized during heating 27n
Trivet 496
Tuna 375, 391
Turnip
    juice-protective preparation
        dry roasted/ fries or diced 188–189, 198
        raw 295–296, 308
        stir-fry/steamed 133–134
    nutritional profile 134. *See also* 68–69, 73–74, 75
    selection 134
    serving 418
    storage 134–135
Turnip greens
    juice-protective preparation
        stir-fry/steamed 158
    nutritional profile 158–159. *See also* 68–69, 73–74, 75
    selection 159
    storage 159–160

V

Vasey, Christopher 3
    alkaline foods 333, 333n
    foods that are acid-forming when consumed by humans 318n, 339n
    role of minerals in neutralizing acid 18n
    vegetables as source of alkaline minerals 17n
    vegetables as source of micronutrients needed for complete digestion of macronutrients (legumes and grains in particular) 18
Vegan vegetarian
    conversion of recipes to vegan form
        curries 582
        pancakes 694
        salads 366
        soups and stews 493
Vegan or traditional vegetarian main dish recipes
    curry
        Egg Curry 594–599
        Eggplant Curry (ground beef omitted) 599–604
        Vegetable Curry 604–609
    pancake: all recipes, recipes #214–218
    pizza
        Basic Roasted Pepper and Cheese Pizza 675–678
    quiche: all quiche recipes, recipes #198–200 (traditional vegetarian only)
    soup: all soups, recipes #169–172
    stew
        Extravagantly Vegetable Chili 518–523

stir fry
    Broccoli, Pineapple, and Black Bean 456–460
    Cauliflower, Brussels Sprouts, and Garbanzo Bean, Herb and Tomato Flavoring 464–469
    Okra, Eggplant, Corn, Spinach, and Lentil Herb and Tomato Flavoring 469–473
    Red Potato, Pepper, and Egg 452–456
    Sweet Potato, Kale, Corn, and Kidney Bean 460–464
    Sweet Potato, Sugar Snap Pea, and Egg 452–456
Vegetable oil. *See* oil, vegetable
Vegetable snacks
    dish recipes
        Herbed Onion and Garlic Dip 311–312
        Raw Vegetable Pita Pizza 313–315
Vegetables, dark green leafy, stir-fried or stir-fry/steamed recipes
    recipe description 66
        shared preparation traits
            beet greens, chard, spinach 69
            cabbage family greens (collards, kale, mustard greens, and turnip greens) 68–69
    preparation support
        Reference #3: Summarizing Stir-Frying and Stir-Fry/Steaming Techniques 182–186
        Stir-frying and Stir-fry/Steaming Preparation Notes 67–71
            cooking tools 69–71
    selection, general guidelines
        Reference #1: Selecting Top Quality Fresh Whole Vegetables and Fruits 36–53
    stir-fried or stir-fry/steamed recipes
        beet greens 135
        chard 138
        collards 141
        kale 145
        mustard greens 148
        spinach (pre-washed) 152
        spinach (un-washed/bunched) 154
        turnip greens 157
    storage, general guidelines
        Reference #2: Key Home Storage Guidelines for Conserving Vegetable and Fruit Quality 53–64
    storage
        rinsed/dried/refrigerated wrapped in paper towels for quick preparation 58
Vegetables, general (commonly used), stir-fried or stir-fry/steamed recipes
    recipe description 66
    preparation support
        Stir-frying and Stir-fry/Steaming Preparation Notes 67–71
        Reference #3: Summarizing Stir-Frying and Stir-Fry/Steaming Techniques 182–186
    stir-fried or stir-fry/steamed recipes
        Chapter One, Recipes #1–22
    selection, general guidelines
        Reference #1: Selecting Top Quality Fresh Whole Vegetables and Fruits 36–53
    storage, general guidelines
        Reference #2: Key Home Storage Guidelines for Conserving Vegetable and Fruit Quality 53–64
Vegetables, raw whole
    description of natural wholeness 36, 42

dish recipes
    salads. *See* salads, vegetable-centered
    snacks. *See* snacks, raw vegetable
juice-protective preparation
    Chapter Five: Raw or Barely Cooked Vegetable Recipes #111–128
nutritional profile
    nutritional value for humans 16–26
        fiber 20–22, 73–74
        micronutrients 17–18
        omega-3 essential fatty acids 23–26
        phytonutrients 18–19, 39–41, 71–74
selection, general guidelines
    Reference #1: Selecting Top Quality Fresh Whole Vegetables and Fruits 36–53
    certified organic 42–43, 50–51
    locally produced 50, 51–53
serving
    garlic 419
    onion 419
storage, general guidelines
    Reference #2: Key Home Storage Guidelines for Conserving Vegetable and Fruit Quality 53–64
Vegetables, seasoning, stir-fried
    recipe description 66
    stir-fried recipes
        garlic 160
        ginger root 163
        mushroom 165
        onion 168
        pepper, bell 174
        pepper, chili 177
        tomato 179
    selection, general guidelines 36–53
        Reference #1: Selecting Top Quality Fresh Whole Vegetables and Fruits 36–53
    serving
        maximizing serving attractiveness 625–626
    storage, general guidelines
        Reference #2: Key Home Storage Guidelines for Conserving Vegetable and Fruit Quality 53–64
Vegetarian, traditional main dish recipes. *See* vegan or traditional vegetarian main dish recipes
Vinegar, apple cider 311
    dish recipe
        Herbed Onion and Garlic Dip 311–312
    dressing recipes. *See* dressing, salad
Vinegar, balsamic
    selection 419–420
    serving
        maximizing attractiveness in salads 419
        substituting other vinegars 420
Vitamin E. *See* micronutrients, anti-inflamatory role

W

Walnuts. *See* nuts and seeds
Watermelon
    juice-protective preparation 276–277
    nutritional profile 277–278
    selection 278
    storage 54, 278–279
Weeds, super. *See* pesticides and food production, industrial

Wheat, whole cracked 342–343
    dish recipe
        Vegetables and Whole Cracked Wheat Pilaf 473–478
    selection
        certified organic 342
        checking for rancidity 342
    storage 342
Wheat flour, whole
    bread recipes
        100% Whole Rye Bread 567–572
        100% Whole Wheat Flat Bread Rounds 617–619
        100% whole wheat muffins recipes #180–184, 550–565
        100% whole wheat pancakes recipes #214–218, 695–711
        100% Whole Wheat Pizza Crust 672–675
        crust, Mini Cheesecake Dessert 662–666
        quiche crust, recipes #198–200, 631–643
    nutritional profile 341
        bran 341
        gluten 341
            gluten intolerance in humans 341
    preparation
        gluten development
            pizza crust 688–689
        gluten non-development
            muffins (minimal stirring) 551
            pancakes 724–725
    selection
        certified organic 340–341
        checking for rancidity 340
        fresh ground 340
        hard flour 341
        medium grind 341, 552
Whole corn flour. *See* corn flour, whole
Whole foods
    definition 36–42, 324
    essential characteristics 36, 324
        natural food production as an essential indicator of whole food quality 324, 325–332
    link to human health 36–37
        intricate matching with human nutritional needs 43, 326
Whole grain, ground. *See* corn flour, whole and wheat flour, whole
Whole grain, intact
    dish recipes
        Guest Vegetable and Wild Rice Pilaf 478–483
        Tabbouleh 402–405
        Vegetables and Cracked Wheat Pilaf 473–478
    nutritional profile 424
        whole grain as a whole food 332. *See also* whole foods
        acid-forming status 17, 18
        digestibility 18
            link to vegetables and fruits as source of needed micronutrients 18, 319–320
    preparation
        brown rice 484–486. *See also* brown rice
        hulled barley 487
        quinoa 487
        whole wheat berries 487
        wild rice 486–487
    selection
        certified organic 332–334
        checking for rancidity 333

INDEX

serving
    maximizing attractiveness in dishes 318, 358–360
    mixing with *juice-protected* vegetables and fruits to enhance serving attractiveness 28
storage 333, 360
Whole grain, ground. *See* corn flour, whole, and wheat flour, whole
Wild rice
    dish recipe
        Guest Vegetable and Wild Rice Pilaf 478–483
    preparation 486–487

Y

Yellow squash. *See* squash, summer
Yogurt, plain
    dish recipes
        curry accompaniment
            Spiced Yogurt (Raita) 610–611
        dessert
            Berry, Mandarin Orange, and Yogurt Dessert 652–654
    snacks
        Berries and Yogurt Snack 291–292
        Creamy Apricot Dip 279–281
        Orange and Yogurt Snack 290–291
    preparation
        fresh yogurt cheese 281
    selection 360
        freshest 360
        full fat 339–340, 585
        grass-fed 339–340, 585
            100% grass-fed and certified organic 339
        non-homogenized 339, 360
    serving
        maximizing serving attractiveness 360–361
    storage 361

Z

Zesting tool 215
Zucchini. *See* squash, summer

ABOUT THE AUTHOR

BORN IN 1944, Nancy Wirsing grew up in rural South Dakota. In 1968, she earned an MA degree from the Graduate School of International Studies at the University of Denver, where she met her husband. Together they began a life centered around the study of international politics. Right from the beginning of this life, she had a special interest in whole food cooking as a means for maintaining health and vitality. This meant cooking with raw foods that retain all naturally occurring parts as opposed to processed foods that have been refined or otherwise altered from natural form. Fully committed to whole foods, she devoted much of her time to experimenting with them. As she sought to expand the variety of dishes she was preparing for her three growing sons, she found a dearth of practical help and recipes for cooks interested in converting traditional dishes into whole food form. She decided to write her own cookbook, one consciously designed as a guide for successful conversion to whole food cooking. She has been passionately committed to this project ever since. Before culminating in the publication of *Cooked Alive!*, it evolved considerably, changing with Nancy's different life experiences. Years spent in South Asia and the Middle East played a notable role. They opened Nancy's eyes to the dazzling diversity of cuisine to be found around the world and exhibited the inevitably close connection between the way people eat and the health problems they suffer. But nothing impacted her cookbook's development more than the experience of living on the small ranch in South Dakota that she inherited from her parents. There she began vegetable gardening, which immeasurably expanded her knowledge of vegetables and fruits, propelling them into "top gun" ingredients in her recipes and central actors in her whole food cooking approach. There she became a regular vendor at a local farmers market, enabling close observation of what her customers knew about vegetables and fruits. What she discovered was a gigantic void in practical knowledge about vegetable and fruit preparation as well as about the importance of these foods to human health. Of no less importance, country living placed her in direct and daily contact with the industrial agricultural domain in which modern food processing starts. This prompted some final important additions to *Cooked Alive!*. It became clear that unnatural treatment of plants and animals during production – such as chemical spraying and the use of genetically modified seeds and artificial fertilizer in the case of plants and use of antibiotics, hormones, and grain in the case of livestock – is as much a form of destructive processing as alterations made to food after harvesting. Accordingly, she expanded her definition of a whole food. Being raw and physically intact was not enough. To qualify as a whole food, a food must also have been naturally produced from the start. And with this change, Nancy was satisfied that *Cooked Alive!* was ready for publication.

www.ingramcontent.com/pod-product-compliance
Lightning Source LLC
Chambersburg PA
CBHW081341080526
44588CB00016B/2344